Troubleshooting, Maintaining, and Repairing Personal Computers
A Technician's Guide

Stephen J. Bigelow

TAB Books
Imprint of McGraw-Hill

New York   San Francisco   Washington, D.C.   Auckland   Bogotá
Caracas   Lisbon   London   Madrid   Mexico City   Milan
Montreal   New Delhi   San Juan   Singapore
Sydney   Tokyo   Toronto

McGraw-Hill

A Division of The **McGraw·Hill** *Companies*

©1996 by **The McGraw-Hill Companies, Inc**.
Published by TAB Books an imprint of McGraw-Hill.

pbk   7 8 9 DOC/DOC 9 0 0 9 8 7
hc   **10 11 12 13 14 15 DOC/DOC 9 0 0 9 8 7**

Library of Congress Cataloging-in-Publication Data
Bigelow, Stephen J.
     Troubleshooting, maintaining, and repairing personal computers : a
technician's guide / by Stephen J. Bigelow
       p.   cm.
   Includes bibliographical references and index.
   ISBN 0-07-912098-9 (H).   ISBN 0-07-912099-7 (P)
   1. Microcomputers—Maintenance and repair.   I. Title.
TK7887.B553   1995
621.39'16—dc20   95-22071
                                          CIP

Acquisitions editor: Roland S. Phelps
Editorial team: B.J. Peterson, Book Editor
                  Andrew Yoder, Supervising Editor
                  Joanne M. Slike, Executive Editor
                  Joann Woy, Indexer
Production team: Katherine G. Brown, Director
                   Toya B. Warner, Computer Artist
                   Janice Stottlemyer, Computer Artist
                   Lisa M. Mellott, Desktop Operator
                   Linda L. King, Proofreading
                   Nancy K. Mickley, Proofreading
Design team: Jaclyn J. Boone, Designer   EL1
                 Katherine Lukaszewicz, Associate Designer   9120997

Dedication

This book is dedicated to my wonderful wife, Kathleen.
Without her loving support and understanding,
this book would still have been possible, but it would not
nearly have been worth the effort.

Contents

SECTION 3   System maintenance and support

Acknowledgments

There is no way that a contemporary technical book can be developed without the cooperation and support of industry. I express my most sincere gratitude to the following individuals and organizations that helped to make this book a reality.

May Adachi, Division Coordinator, Teac America, Inc.

Elizabeth Berglund, Director of Marketing Communication, CTIA

Tiffini Bloniarz, Marketing Manager, Quatech

Nick Blozan, Product Manager, Mountain Network Solutions

Carol Cassara, Director, Corporate Communications, Maxtor Corporation

Elizabeth Dessuge, VP Marketing and Sales, Accurite Technologies Inc.

Katherin Dockerill, Director, US Public Relations, Cyrix Corporation

Gregg Elmore, Advertising Manager, B+K Precision

David Feinstein, President, Innoventions, Inc.

Paula Fisher, Graphic Design, NEC Technologies, Inc.

Wendy Foster, MARCOM Specialist, Iomega Corporation

Kim Gallagher, Contracts Administration Manager, Hayes Microcomputer Products, Inc.

Penny Giever, Intel Corporation

Michelle Gjerde, Public Relations Specialist, Gateway 2000

John M. Grathwol, Sr. Writer, Best Power Technology, Inc.

Jennifer Hennigan, Advertising Coordinator, AMP, Inc.

Amanda Higgins, Public Relations, Logitech, Inc.

Janice Jacobson, Marketing Manager, PC Power & Cooling, Inc.

Bill James, Executive Account Manager, Olson Computer & Metal Products

Kathi Lebow, MarketSmart, Inc. (for Tadrian Battery)

Randy Leninger, Media Relations, Improve Technologies

Debbie Long, Account Executive, S&S Public Relations (for Multi-Tech Systems, Inc.)

Angela Miller and Warren White, Landmark Research International, Inc.

Lisa-Jo Mitchell, Sales and Marketing Manager, Vista Microsystems

Vivienne Oestergaard, Marketing Assistant, Future Domain Corp.

Lori Parent, Director of Marketing, Curtis Manufacturing Co., Inc.

Marilyn E. Ponzio, Marketing Communications Coordinator, Cherry Electrical Products

Traci Renner, Account Executive, Maples & Associates (for Toshiba America Information Systems)

Linda Rohrbough

Barbara Rowland, Manager, Technical Communications, Quantum Corporation

Barbara Rubin, Director of Member Services, ISCET/NESDA

Helen Sands, President, Sandcastle Advertising (for IERC)

Irene Santoyo, Marketing Services, QLogic Corporation

Stephanie Shore, Media Liason, Micro 2000

Michele Spring, Account Coordinator, Copithorne & Bellows (for Hewlett-Packard Co.)

Mary Pay Strouse, Marketing Communications Assistant, NTI

Daniel Taylor, Plastic Systems, Inc.

Jeffery A. Tatum, VP and General Council, Chips and Technologies, Inc.

Ron Trumbla, Media Relations Representative, Tandy Corporation

Tracey Ward, AMI

Amy Weaver, Marketing, Hauppauge Computer Works, Inc.

Kirsten Wisdom, PR Manager, Hewlett-Packard Co.

Dan Zemaitis, Marketing Manager, Suncom Technologies

James Zimmerman, President, Windsor Technologies, Inc.

I also want to extend very special thanks to the hard-working authors whose software is features on the companion disks:

Alex Alexander, Marketing Director, Ultra-X, Inc.

George Campbell, President, OsoSoft

Robert Falbo, Author, TheRef™

Maurice Fuller, Marketing Director, Parallel Technologies, Inc.

Robert Hurt, President, Data Depot, Inc.

John Jerrim, President, Computer Telecom Systems, Inc.

Thomas Mosteller, Author (CMOSRAM2.ZIP)

John Vias, President, Vias and Associates

Last, but certainly not least, I want to thank my Acquisitions Editor, Roland S. Phelps, my Executive Editor, Joanne Slike, and the entire staff at TAB/McGraw-Hill for their endless patience and consideration during the development of this book.

Disclaimer and cautions

Personal risk and limits of liability

It is important that you read and understand the following information. Please read it carefully!

The repair of personal computers and their peripherals involves some amount of personal risk. Use *extreme* caution when working with ac (alternating current) and high-voltage power sources. Every reasonable effort has been made to identify and reduce areas of personal risk. You are instructed to read this book carefully before attempting the procedures discussed. If you are uncomfortable following the procedures that are outlined in this book, do *not* attempt them—refer your service to qualified service personnel.

Neither the author, the publisher, nor anyone directly or indirectly connected with the publication of this book and accompanying computer software shall make any warranty either expressed or implied, with regard to this material, including, but not limited to, the implied warranties of quality, merchantability, and fitness for any particular purpose. Further, neither the author, publisher, nor anyone directly or indirectly connected with the publication of this book and computer software shall be liable for errors or omissions contained herein, or for incidental or consequential damages, injuries, or financial or material losses resulting from the use, or inability to use, the material and software contained herein. This material and software is provided as-is, and the reader bears all responsibilities and risks connected with its use.

Virus warning

Although the software associated with this book was thoroughly checked for viruses before publication, you are strongly advised to inspect all new software, including this book's companion software, for the presence of computer viruses before executing the software. Antivirus software can be obtained through commercial and shareware sources. Neither the author, publisher, nor anyone directly or indirectly connected with this book assume any liability whatsoever for incidental or consequential damages, financial loss, or material loss, resulting from the occurrence of computer viruses on your system or network. You use this software at your own risk.

Vendor warning

The products, materials, equipment, manufacturers, service providers, and distributors listed and presented in this book are shown for reference purposes only. Their mention and use in this book shall not be construed as an endorsement of any individual or organization, nor the quality of their products or services, nor their performance or business integrity. The author, publisher, and anyone directly or indirectly associated with the production of this book expressly disclaim all liability whatsoever for any financial or material losses or incidental or consequential damages that might occur from contacting or doing business with any such organization or individual.

Preface

It used to be that when a PC failed, it wound up sitting on a test bench surrounded by a battalion of test equipment. An experienced technician would be hovering over the PC—logic probe or test leads in hand. Technicians relied on their knowledge of electronics and microprocessor operations to track the problem to a faulty IC (integrated circuit) or passive component which could then be replaced with relatively simple soldering tools. There were few add-on devices or peripherals to worry about, and only 1Mb of memory or so to work with. The few expansion devices that did exist were often plagued by compatibility problems and proprietary interfaces.

Well, times certainly have changed. Today's PC is largely a collection of inexpensive subassemblies—many of which are now manufactured in the Pacific Rim—and assembled in high volumes at factories around the world. The diverse array of peripherals that are now available (tape drives, PC cards, CD-ROMs, pointing devices, and so on) enjoy a remarkable level of hardware compatibility using well-established interface schemes (SCSI, IDE, ISA, or VLB). The labor cost involved in a component-level repair today is usually more expensive than the cost of a replacement assembly. There is little doubt that the day of component-level PC repair is over.

However, PCs still fail—in ways that continue to exhaust even the most patient mind. When you realize that there are now well over 100 million PCs in operation (and growing at 10 to 12% annually), you see that effective troubleshooting requires more than simply an arbitrary swapping of boards and drives. Now, more than ever, efficient and cost-effective troubleshooting requires an understanding of PC hardware and operating systems, along with a keen knowledge of symptoms and diagnostics. Setting up, optimizing, and upgrading a PC are three other important areas that demand the attention of today's technician.

This book is intended for the modern computer enthusiast and technician. It is not designed to explain computer theory—there are already plenty of theory books available. Instead, this book is designed to be a hands-on desktop (or workbench) reference for PC repair, maintenance, and upgrading. This book concentrates on the symptoms and problem areas that occur in every area of the modern PC, as well as proper diagnosis of problems. Resources and glossaries to consider are included on the companion disk, which makes the book ideal for classroom or home study.

The book is divided into three sections. Section 1 is the technician's primer. The first 13 chapters provide novice readers with the technical foundation to address PC service issues. If you're new to repair, these chapters take you inside the PC and its peripherals, show you the diagnostic tools that are currently in the marketplace, explains how to set up a first-rate workspace, and guides you through some important preservice checkout procedures. Section 2 addresses system data and troubleshooting. These 42 chapters are really the heart of the book, which brings PC problems and troubleshooting into focus with an unprecedented array of documented, well-explained service procedures. The chapters are arranged alphabetically for easy reference. You'll find help with everything from batteries to virus symptoms and countermeasures. Section 3 handles system maintenance and support to aid today's technician in mastering the many upgrade procedures that are so vital to PC users. The 18 chapters in Section 3 brings you real-world, hands-on considerations, procedures, and troubleshooting guidance for everything from adding a CD-ROM to upgrading a system BIOS. Again, the topics are alphabetized to make reference easier. Don't miss the nine appendices, which are designed for busy technicians. Not only will you find handy resource and reference information, but you will also find a variety of useful forms that you can photocopy, information on the accompanying software, details to help you use *TechNet* BBS, and more. I believe that this is the first PC book to provide such highly integrated, hands-on, troubleshooting resources.

This book and its companion disk are meant to be a lifeline and a resource to help you repair your PC, keep it running, and get the most out of it. You'll find almost 400 PC problems fully detailed and explained. There are references to hundreds more POST and diagnostic codes to help you identify even the most obscure problems. But the support you'll find here goes far beyond these book pages. You'll find a set of power tools—shareware and freeware diagnostics and utilities designed to help you identify even the peskiest PC problems. This book is one of the only PC hardware books to bundle diagnostic software with the text. In addition to these tools, you can access additional shareware through TechNet BBS (Dynamic Learning Systems premier, bulletin board service for computer technicians and enthusiasts). TechNet is approved by the Association of Shareware Professionals (ASP).

Many readers also complain that PC books suffer from a limited life span. All too often, a book is dated as soon as it gets on bookstore shelves. You can avoid this kind of technical obsolescence by subscribing to our #1 newsletter: *The PC Toolbox*™. With it, you will stay informed of the latest hands-on service articles and optimization techniques, and you'll find the answers to your PC questions. As a subscriber to *The PC Toolbox*™, you get extended time and privileges on TechNet BBS, which includes full access to the ASP's shareware CD-ROM—more than 640Mb of shareware that is updated monthly. Even if you don't fix computers for a living, a subscription can save you hundreds of dollars in shop costs. You can find the ad and order form for *The PC Toolbox*™ at the back of this book.

There are even more cost savings. At the back of this book, you'll find a coupon for a full $50 off premier PC diagnostic software: PC-Technician by Windsor Technologies. In addition, Micro 2000 has extended a 25% discount off their troubleshooting products MicroScope and POST Probe. There is no coupon for the Micro 2000 discount—just mention this book.

Worried about keeping yourself employable? Go for the Dynamic Learning Systems Technician's Certificate. As the purchaser of this book, you can take the electronic DLS Technician's Examination included with the DLS shareware disk. Readers who pass receive a certificate showing their mastery of the material in this book. But the certificate is not just for framing—readers who successfully complete the examination are eligible for a $100 discount on NRI courses. The DLS Technician's Certificate not only demonstrates your technical competence, but saves you money as well.

Finally, I am interested in your success. I've taken every possible measure to ensure a thorough and comprehensive book. Your comments, suggestions, and questions about this book are welcome at any time, as well as any troubleshooting experiences that you might wish to share. Feel free to write to me directly, or contact me through e-mail at:

Dynamic Learning Systems
Attn: Stephen J. Bigelow
P.O. Box 805
Marlboro, MA 01752 USA
Fax: 508-898-9995
CompuServe: 73652,3205
Internet: sbigelow@cerfnet.com
Worldwide Web: http://www.dlspubs.com/home.htm

1
SECTION

The technician's primer

1
CHAPTER

The technician's job

If you have followed the PC industry at all over the last 10 or 15 years, you are well aware of the many profound changes that have shaped (and continue to shape) today's personal computer. The explosive growth in PC sales and use has resulted in substantial problems for technicians, as well as substantial opportunities for those who are enterprising enough to take advantage of them. This chapter is intended to be a general overview of the PC service industry for technicians and PC enthusiasts. It also is designed to provide some educational and business guidelines for anyone interested in starting and developing their own part-time PC service or consulting business.

The ever-changing PC

The success of personal computers is unparalleled in human history. Computers had been around for decades, but the humble PC established something that no other computer had before—a standard that other manufacturers could use to add their own devices to the computer. IBM's use of an *open architecture* unleashed an age of automation, information processing and management, and entertainment that could hardly have been dreamed of by the PC's original designers. As PCs enter their fifth generation, there is no end to this growth in sight.

Consider the hard drive. In 1984, a 10 or 20Mb hard drive was considered to be state-of-the-art PC storage. In 1994, most well-equipped systems offered drives with 500Mb or more (even notebook PCs). Memory (once limited to 1Mb and considered a hideously expensive add-on) is now in high demand. A well-equipped system now comes with 16Mb of RAM, and many systems can be upgraded to 32Mb. The CPU also has enjoyed radical improvements. The Intel 8086 used in early IBM/PCs and XTs has given way to the i286, i386, i486, and now the Pentium. Motherboard chipsets have reduced the hundreds of discrete ICs needed to only a small handful. Every other expansion board and drive developed for the PC also has benefited from specialized chipsets and highly integrated electronics. This list of PC improvements can easily go on and on, but the reality is easy enough to see—a new generation of PC is appearing every 18 to 24 months.

The way PCs are designed and manufactured also has changed dramatically in the last decade. IBM (once the sole and dominant force in the PC industry) has given way to a host of *clone* manufacturers. As clone manufacturers vie for the best prices and discounts, more and more of the PC has been "farmed out" to other specialty manufacturers. For example, one manufacturer designs and manufactures the motherboard, another designs and manufactures the hard drive, another designs and manufactures the hard drive controller, another designs and manufactures the video adapter, another designs and manufactures the monitor, and so on. Today, virtually none of the PC makers you purchase from actually design or manufacture the elements that go into their PCs.

This trend toward *SAL* (subassembly level) manufacturing has had both positive and negative effects on the PC industry. First, the intense competition between the manufacturers of various assemblies has been a driving factor behind the rapid drop in PC prices and the development of better, faster devices—clearly a positive impact for every PC buyer. It is highly unlikely that you would be able to buy 500Mb and larger hard drives today if only one or two companies in the world made them. The same holds true for every other device used in the PC (motherboards, video boards, drive controllers, etc.).

Challenges of today's PC repair

SAL manufacturing, however, has forced PC technicians to rethink the fundamental approaches they use in their business. Successful component-level troubleshooting relies on the ready availability of replacement parts and technical information such as schematics and block diagrams. Because virtually all PC assembly manufacturers are in competition with one another, their schematics and detailed service data has become *proprietary* to prevent it from falling into the hands of competitors. As a result, current service information has virtually disappeared from PC service shops around the world. The little real data that remains available is often quite pricey, and even then is often only available for older devices.

The situation is no better for component parts. In the early days of PCs, manufacturers used discrete logic components that were readily available from almost any electronics store. As the demand for speed and performance increased, manufacturers incorporated specialized chipsets and *ASIC*s (application-specific integrated circuits) into their designs. Such specialized components were much more expensive than their discrete counterparts, and no longer available "off the shelf." In fact, because the actual assembly process for most PC products is performed in Mexico, Asia, or the Pacific Rim, few manufacturers in the United States even have the physical components to sell in the first place. Why would a video board maker in Santa Clara have the parts for their board being built in Bejing? As a result, the manufacturer can sell you a replacement board, but not the individual parts.

This broad lack of data and parts is further complicated by the demands of *SMP* (surface-mount technology). Traditional (or *through-hole*) printed-circuit assembly uses components with metal leads that protrude through the circuit board where they are then soldered. Surface-mount assembly uses smaller parts (with metal tabs instead of long leads). Smaller parts allow more components to be placed on the same area of printed circuit board, or the existing circuit board can be made smaller.

Because there are now no leads to protrude through the circuit board, components can be soldered to both sides of the board, increasing component density even more. Desoldering surface-mounted components (especially ICs) is almost impossible without specially designed desoldering tools with precisely designed heated tips, an unwelcome expense even for the most profitable repair shops.

A technician's changing role

In spite of the lack of data, scarcity of parts, and demands of SMT, it has been the simple economics of PC service that have really changed the industry. Today's overhead for professional technicians can easily exceed $40.00 per hour in wages, benefits, and burden. Most shops can no longer justify several hours of a technician's time in order to diagnose a problem to the component level. Even if service data and parts were available, the troubleshooting and replacement time can often be just as expensive (if not more so) as simply replacing the defective subassembly outright. Consider the following case study.

A case study

Assume you run a one-person PC service shop. It's an active business and you have several new PCs coming in each day. You already have several PCs on the bench waiting to be serviced with a variety of problems. Suppose you charge your customers $40.00 per hour for your labor (one hour minimum) plus parts (which you mark up by 20%).

Scenario 1—a component-level PC repair

You are a talented technician and not afraid of a challenge, so you open a computer and go to work. In 1.5 hours, using a variety of test equipment and schematics you bought from a reverse-engineering company, you manage to isolate the problem to a specific component on the VGA video adapter board. You spend another 0.5 hour tracking down and ordering the replacement part (assuming you can find it). The IC is a graphics controller chip that you can buy for $5 in low quantities. When the part arrives two weeks later, you spend 1.0 hour installing the new part and testing the board. Your talent shows through once again and the PC is working just fine now. You place the PC back on the shelf to run for a while. Altogether, you spent 3.0 hours repairing the PC. When the customer comes in (two weeks later) to get the PC, you hand the customer the following bill:

Labor	3.0 hours @ $40.00/hour	$120.00	
Labor total			$120.00
Parts ICxyz	1 @ $5.00	$5.00	
Parts subtotal		$5.00	
Parts markup	$5.00 × 0.2	$1.00	
Parts total			$6.00
(You might need to add sales tax for parts)			
Labor and parts total			$126.00

Even though the customer complains that a brand-new SVGA board costs nearly the same, the customer pays the bill and leaves with the PC. After three hours of your time, you only managed to repair one computer. At that rate, you'll only manage to repair two or three PCs a day. You'll keep the shop open, but only just.

Scenario 2—a subassembly-level PC repair

Use a subassembly level approach for repair of the same system with the faulty VGA board. Given that there is no display, you immediately check the monitor and its connection. You test the monitor on your bench reference PC and it works fine, you then suspect the video board, so you try a known-good video board in the PC. *Voilà*—the video system is restored. You order a new SVGA board for $85.00 (because it costs as much as a new VGA board) from your favorite supplier who has them in stock (or buy a new one from your local superstore on the way home that night). In total, you spend about 15 minutes on the diagnosis. You install the new board when it arrives, check the system for viruses, then run a full system diagnostic and print out the results. This takes roughly another 15 minutes. In total, you spend 0.5 hour on the repair. When your customer comes in to pick up the machine, you hand them the following bill:

Labor	1.0 hour @ $40.00/hour	$40.00 (the minimum charge)
Labor total		$40.00

Parts	SVGA board 1 @ $85.00	$85.00		
Parts subtotal			$85.00	
Parts markup	$85.00 × 0.2		$17.00	
Parts total				$102.00
(You might need to add sales tax for parts)				

Labor and parts total	$142.00

Your customer complains about the price a bit—it's a bit more than they were hoping to pay, but they're satisfied with the upgraded video board. They also like the diagnostic report and clean bill of health from your virus checker (very professional). You can quote a really good price on an SVGA monitor too whenever they're ready to upgrade. Some problems will certainly take over 30 minutes to find and resolve, but you can get to a lot more machines in the course of a day. A fast turnaround keeps your customers happy, and the higher repair volume adds more to your bottom line.

This case study shown is just one of many examples where efficient SAL troubleshooting can be very cost-effective for you without raising prices for your customer to any great degree. Some readers might argue with the choice of examples, but the principles are sound. This is not to say that SAL troubleshooting is easy or foolproof. You will certainly encounter your share of confusing and exasperating problems—the tremendous variety of PCs and their configurations virtually guarantees it. The trick here is understanding and diagnosing the symptoms. You must be able to identify the faulty subassembly to a very high degree of confidence before choosing to order the replacement part(s).

Changing relationships between customers and technicians

Technical purists have predicted doom and gloom for the PC service industry. In truth, profit margins are often quite slim, and the difference between red ink and black will depend on your knowledge of the computer, your diagnostic skills, your resourcefulness, and the volume of your workload. However, purists have failed to take into account the changing attitudes of today's PC owners. For many PC owners and users around the world, the computer has become much more than an interesting novelty. They are an indispensable part of our everyday lives. In many ways, the personal computer has attained the status and importance of the automobile. And like an automobile, a faulty PC can interrupt lives, disrupt schedules, prevent you from getting jobs done, and generally make your life miserable.

Just as many have developed relationships with auto mechanics (whether they are friends, relatives, or small local shops), PC owners are serious about finding and keeping good technicians who are quick, inexpensive (relatively speaking), and knowledgeable. It is for this reason that more "garage" PC shops grow by word-of-mouth than by most other forms of advertisement combined. The technician who takes the time to work with and tutor a customer is especially prized.

A technician's credentials

Do not confuse *education* and *credentials*. *Education* is a means of expanding your knowledge and skills. It can be accomplished through hands-on practice and informal personal study (such as reading this book), as well as more formalized classroom work in many of the fine PC courses offered through local adult-education programs and training companies around the United States, Canada, and the world. On the other hand, *credentials* are used to classify and document your education. Because most customers and employers are hardly equipped to gauge your knowledge, a recognized certification is used instead as a general measure. If you have the certification, you should know what you're talking about, right?

Well, there has been an ongoing debate over the value and effectiveness of professional credentials. You have all heard at least one horror story about the "certified professional" who could barely turn the PC on, let alone repair it. Some readers might take this to mean that it is not important to have the piece of paper showing certification. However, most employers and customers look for certifications—in some cases, you might not even be considered for a job or contract unless you have established credentials. As a general rule, certification of some type is a good idea, and you should consider at least one or two recognized certifications. The thing to keep in mind here is that a certification must be backed up by a good education. The following sections outline a number of certifications.

CET certification

The venerable *CET* (Certified Electronics Technician) exam was developed by *ISCET* (International Society of Certified Electronics Technicians) in 1965 (Fig. 1-1). The intent of the exam is to certify the theoretical electronic knowledge and technical proficiency of technicians. Although the certification is 30 years old, the test and

1-1
Official logo of the International
Society of Certified Electronics
Technicians (ISCET).

its implementation has been upgraded numerous times to include current consumer electronics equipment.

There are two levels of certification. The *Associate-Level* CET exam is intended for a technician or electronics student with under four years of experience and is designed to test your knowledge of basic electronics, math, dc and ac (direct current and alternating current) circuits, transistors, and troubleshooting. A score of 75% or better is required to pass, and the certification is good for four years. The *Journeyman-Level* CET exam starts with the Associate-Level test, but then adds one or more areas of concentration such as communications, computers, medical, or video (there are actually nine concentrations). You also must have four or more years of experience or education to take the Journeyman-Level exam. CET certification isrelatively inexpensive. Associate-Level testing is about $25.00 (including one Journeyman-Level option). Additional Journeyman-Level options each cost about $25.00. Contact information for the ISCET is provided on the companion disk.

A+ Certification

With the explosive growth in computer service needs, The *CompTIA* (Computing Technology Industry Association, formerly known as ABCD: The Microcomputer Industry Association) sponsored and worked with industry to develop the A+ Certification for Computer Service Technicians (Fig. 1-2). What makes A+ Certification different from other credentials is the strong support that it has received from the computer industry. More than 37 corporations, some of the largest PC makers in the world, have backed A+ Certification as a requirement for their service staff, as well as the technical staff of other companies that they do business with.

The Computing Technology Industry Association

1-2
Official logo of the A+
Certification Program. A+ is a
program of the Computing
Technology Industry Association.

The test itself focuses on configuring, installing, diagnosing, repairing, and maintaining computers. Although this book is devoted to the IBM-compatible PC, the A+ exam is not vendor specific, so a wide range of hardware and software is covered. Unlike the CET exam, an A+ exam can be taken by anyone interested in the test. There are no educational or experience prerequisites. Although the CompTIA is responsible for developing the test, it is implemented nationwide (and in most Canadian provinces) by Drake Training and Technologies, Inc. The test is given on computers that will actually compile your scores and grade the test before you leave the test room. Some readers might consider the A+ certification a bit pricey at $165.00 (U.S.), but few can argue that it's a small price for your professional development. Contact data for CompTIA and Drake is provided on the companion disk.

DLS Technician's Certificate

Certification can be a real chore for anyone just starting out in PC service. Many current certification options available to newcomers demand a diverse array of hardware knowledge that might take you years to accumulate. The *Dynamic Learning Systems Technician's Certificate* is designed to verify your knowledge of IBM-compatible PC testing, diagnosis, setup, and optimization. Anyone can take the test that is included in Appendix I. This is a serious and comprehensive test. There are 120 questions involving every technical topic covered in the book. However, there are no time limits, so you can work on the test at your own pace in the comfort and privacy of your own home. NRI (a division of McGraw-Hill) recognizes the DLS Technician's Certificate, and provides a $100.00 discount toward any home study course they offer should you decide to further your education even more.

Microsoft certifications

There also are a large number of certifications available for operating systems and network management if those are areas where you plan to specialize. Most notable among these certifications is the *MCP* (Microsoft Certified Professional) program. To become an MCP, you will need to take at least two courses: Introduction to MS-DOS and Microcomputer Hardware, and MS-Windows 3.1 Operating System Administration. MCP recognition might be most beneficial for anyone looking to configure and set up new PCs. The prices and scheduling for these courses varies depending on location, so contact Microsoft Inside Sales for detailed information. Keep in mind that Microsoft has plans in the works to release their next version of Windows known tentatively as Chicago (also known as *Windows 95*). Once this new version is released, you should probably wait to pursue MCP training until the courses are revised and tested.

A business of your own

These are uncertain times. As the United States economy continues to integrate into the global economy, employers all over are seriously re-evaluating their staffing and the overall direction of their companies. It is an unfortunate fact of modern life that lifetime employment, secure pensions, and even the promise of eventual retirement are things of the past. Many people who share this concern for their financial welfare are looking to supplement their income through a sideline or part-time, home-based business. This part of the chapter is intended for those readers who have considered putting together their own "garage" business in PC repair or consulting. If you are a reader looking to repair your own PC, then feel free to skip this part of the chapter. You can always refer to it later.

Philosophers and cynics will say "the Devil's in the details." This is probably the single most important concept of starting your own business effort. It's not terribly difficult to start a business, especially a home-based business, but it requires a bit of patience and persistence. By starting small and working from your cellar, garage, or spare bedroom, you avoid the overhead of office rental (usually a storefront that can be very expensive) and other utilities such as additional electricity, gas, water, and so on. Under some circumstances, you also might be able to take advantage of tax benefits. Another advantage of home-based businesses is that you can hone your skills, get the feel of running a business, and build a client base with an absolute minimum of financial risk.

Before you go too far, you should be aware that this part of the chapter is intended to provide you with some general guidelines and considerations to keep in mind when starting your own business. Much of this information has been gleaned from interviews with home-based PC business owners. This is by no means an all-inclusive tutorial nor is it intended to offer legal, accounting, or financial advice. Because the rules, limitations, and liabilities of starting and running a small-business will vary from state to state and country to country around the world, you are strongly urged to consult with an attorney and accountant very early in your planning.

A question of experience

The rule here is "do what you do well." Customers look for experience in a technician, so one of your early priorities when contemplating a small-business venture is to match your services with your skills. For example, you would not want to offer services as a network consultant if you've never touched a *LAN* (local-area network) card before—well, you get the idea. For those of you who feel that you have very little PC service experience, there are certainly ways to get experience.

Practice is the best teacher, so one of the simplest methods of developing experience is to tinker. Yes, get some broken PCs and repair them. Chances are pretty good that you have a friend or relative with a broken PC. Yard sales and flea markets are excellent sources for broken PCs. You also should check local want ads for giveaways or liquidations. The growing trend toward PC auctions is another potential source for broken or disabled units. You should be able to pick up broken PCs for some small token fee. When working on a PC, keep excellent notes of what you find and what you do.

So what do you do when the PC is finally fixed? Well, if the PC belongs to someone else, giving it back is usually good for customer relations. If the PC is yours, you can keep it as a test bed for other boards and peripherals that you encounter. You also might consider selling it. Even if you get back the money you put into it, the experience is much more valuable for a novice. Even giving it away to a school, church, friend, or colleague can start word-of-mouth referrals.

Income and taxes

There is nothing you can do to escape the reality of taxes. The income you receive in hourly fees and parts markup is fully taxable at the federal level. If your state has a state income tax, you will be liable for state income tax as well. If you sell parts, you also might be required to collect and forward sales tax if your state has a state sales tax. Consult with your accountant; do it now! Your accountant can best advise you as to your tax liabilities and what kind of records you should keep. As a general rule, you should keep excellent records including all receipts of purchased parts and equipment, as well as receipts of all bank deposits from business. Your record keeping need not be fancy, but it must be accurate and complete.

Knowing what to charge

Hourly fees for PC service vary radically (anywhere from $20.00 to $70.00 per hour). As you might expect, this great disparity is due to a lot of factors. Geographic location plays a big part in pricing, because busy urban centers can usually command higher fees than slow, rural areas. Your own experience affects pricing; only the very confident or very foolish try for top dollar when they are just starting out. Overhead is another factor in hourly pricing. You will have to charge more to support a storefront shop and additional utilities than you would when operating out of your home. The best way to gauge an appropriate hourly fee is to do a little detective work and call around to various local shops. Most reputable shops will not hesitate to quote an hourly fee over the phone.

It also is typical to apply a markup for parts and materials used in the PC. Because you will be repairing PCs at the subassembly level, most parts are available through any number of computer superstores or mail order organizations around the world. This availability limits the amount of markup that you can reasonably charge. After all, a customer is not going to pay you $300.00 for a video board if it is $150.00 at the nearest PC store. As a rule, markups between 10 and 30% are justifiable. Higher markups might be appropriate for old or difficult-to-find parts. At a 20% markup, if the part costs you $100.00 to buy, you would charge your customer ($100.00 + [$100.00 × 0.2]) or $120.00.

When you need help

Don't be afraid to ask for help. As computers and peripherals become more complex, you might need help. The ability to ask questions, check with manufacturers, and consult with other professionals can get you through difficult problems that might otherwise be impossible to resolve. Fortunately, there are more resources available than you might realize. On-line resources include such services as CompuServe, America On Line, and other services shown on the companion disk. On CompuServe, for example, many PC manufacturers maintain on-line forums that put you in touch with technical support personnel. There also are PC hardware, operating system, and consultant's forums where you can reach other professionals.

There also are a great many BBS facilities operating around the country. Tech-Net BBS is one such facility. Typical PC manufacturers also maintain their own BBSs. Don't forget your local user groups. Making contacts and sharing information at monthly or semi-weekly meetings can provide you with volumes of useful tips and tricks. Finally, keep a close eye on current technical literature like *The PC Toolbox*™ to keep you informed of trends and techniques in PC service.

Just say "No" (Thank You)

There is no rule that says you have to take on every task sent your way. When you are faced with a problem PC that you know you are not equipped to repair, you are often best advised to politely and tactfully direct your customer elsewhere. Give the headaches to your competitors. This might be a disappointment to your customers, but it is far less painful than dealing with their frustration as you struggle to get their system running.

Making the business "real"

Eventually, your persistence and hard work will start to pay off as referrals and repeat customers vie for your time. Many small PC businesses, even established businesses, report that work is often cyclic. There are periods of relative calm followed by a fury of activity. As you become busier, you might give some thought to re-investing a portion of your income to grow your fledgling venture. The following sections outline some ideas to help your business take shape.

Choosing a name

If you have been using a business name at all up to now, chances are that you have been using your own name or initials (*Ed's PC Service* or *E.H.D. Computers*). There's nothing wrong with this, but now that your business is growing, you might want to consider a name that is catchier and more memorable (such as *The PC Depot*). You can even get geographic (*The Boston Computer Clinic*). However, the name also should invoke a positive, hopeful image (would you leave your valuable computer at *The PC Pit* or *the Busted Board*?) A clever, memorable name can stay in a person's mind very effectively.

Setting up your bank account

It certainly is possible for you to operate your small business out of your personal checking account. Eventually, however, you will want to separate the business money from your personal money. It might seem like this is just extra work for you, but a separate checking account for your business actually makes things easier by allowing you to keep your business income and expenses separate from your personal income and expenses. Once you have an established business and business name, you can easily open a *DBA* (doing business as) checking account with your local bank. Keep in mind that some banks do not accommodate DBA accounts very well at all. If your banker gives you a problem with opening a DBA account, feel free to shop around at other banks. Of course, you can open a full-fledged business checking account, but the costs and fees associated with a full business account are often too high for a small business. Once you establish the account, you can get checks printed with your business name and mailing address. You will really need a full-fledged business account if you should choose to incorporate.

Equipping for business

At this point, you need to be accessible to your customers. The standard for today's small business is a telephone, fax machine, and answering machine. This combination provides a clean, professional image for your business. Integrated telephone/fax/answering machines are readily available at your local consumer electronics store (their prices are dropping every day). You will probably want your local telephone company to install at least one new phone line exclusively for your business. It would probably be cheaper to have the wiring for two or three lines installed at the same time (but only activate the lines as you need them).

Polishing the image

Now that you are well along in the establishment of your business, you might consider polishing your image with a set of stationery. Business cards, letterhead, envelopes, and mailing labels are a great place to start. Prices are very competitive, and any local printer can do the job for you if you want to shop around. There also are many national printing houses that specialize in customized stationery. Because you are working on PCs, you also might consider adhesive labels to place on the units that you repair. You don't have to spend a lot of money for stationery, but even the blandest stationery gives your venture a certain amount of validity and confidence.

Inventory blues

In order to run an efficient business, pay very close attention to your inventory. As a general rule, you should keep as little inventory as possible; don't let your workspace become a warehouse. Given the tremendous diversity of PC boards and peripherals that are available, and the speed at which new products are being added, it is almost impossible to anticipate what parts you will need. Because virtually all PC parts can be purchased from local superstores or mail-order organizations, it makes little sense to stock more than one or two of any major item (such as video boards, hard drives, controllers, sound boards, and so on). In fact, you would probably use such stock to help you diagnose problems; then order the real replacement parts as needed.

As the venture grows

If all goes well, you will gradually see an increase in your business volume. Before you know it, you will be an experienced PC technician, and you might ultimately choose to leave your "day job" in order to pursue PC service as a full-time venture. If you reach this point, you are to be congratulated; few get this far. However, there are growing pains for all businesses, and there are additional factors to consider as your business reaches full-time status.

Incorporation versus proprietorship

Incorporation offers several advantages over a *sole proprietorship*. First, a corporation exists as its own legal entity. This makes it very convenient if you should choose to sell the business at any point in the future. Incorporation protects your personal assets in the event that your business is sued for any reason. However, incorporation also carries additional overhead. The process of incorporation carries a price tag (about $1000.00 for a corporation in the United States) and requires you to file annual corporate paperwork. Your business might be subject to additional corporate taxes. You also will need to upgrade your accounting practices and bank accounts to meet the corporate standards for your state. Ultimately, anyone can incorporate, but you should seek the counsel of an attorney skilled in small-business law to weigh the advantages and disadvantages of incorporation in your state or province.

Getting a Federal ID#

A Federal ID# in small-business development generally ties in to income and taxes. In many cases, your own social security number can be used with your existing checking account to operate your business. As your business grows, you might want to hire people to assist you. Before you hire people, you should obtain a Federal ID# (also referred to as an *Employer ID#* or *EIN*). To get the proper forms for EIN application, you should contact your local Internal Revenue Service facility. Taxation rules vary dramatically outside of the United States, so a local accountant can typically advise you on procedures for your own country or province.

Liability concepts

Few words carry the terror and worry as *liability*. Loosely defined, *liability* is indebtedness or responsibility to another person. Liability takes many forms, but general liability and business (malpractice) liability are two aspects of business that you should understand. Essentially, when a person enters your business to drop off or pick up their system, you are liable for their safety and well-being. This concept is often referred to as *general liability*. You also are liable for the PC while it is in your care. If you cause damage to the PC or otherwise render it unable to perform the functions it performed before it was brought to you, there is liability involved there as well. This liability is usually considered *malpractice or professional liability*. An attorney can best advise you as to your precise liabilities depending on the services you offer.

There are several things you can do to protect yourself from liability. First, acquire the proper insurance for your business. Local insurance agents can usually offer packages that cover general liability, as well as professional liability and equipment insurance. Insurance is expensive, but then so is a lawsuit. Of course, the very best ways to prevent a lawsuit is to keep one from happening in the first place. Good business conduct is hardly bulletproof, but it is cheap and easy protection. Making a good-faith effort to try and do the right thing for a customer can avoid a lot of problems before they escalate to the courtroom. A strong disclaimer also is highly advisable. Ask your customer to sign a work order and disclaimer before accepting the system for repair. Such a work order should disclaim such things as:

- Your ability to repair the unit at all
- Your responsibility for any and all data on the system's hard drive(s)
- Your responsibility for the unit while it is in your care
- Your responsibility for the unit's performance after the repair is complete
- The work order also should include provisions where the customer expressly agrees to pay for parts and labor at your current rates

You can probably think of other provisions and disclaimers for your work order. Your attorney can help you prepare the proper wording.

Merchant accounts

One of the hallmarks of a "real" business is the *merchant account*. The ability to accept MasterCard and VISA lends an amazing amount of validity to a business. Before opening a merchant account, you should have several years of successful business activity behind you, as well as a business (DBA or otherwise) checking account. To investigate a merchant account, contact your local full-service bank and ask to speak with a merchant representative. They can give you the information and pricing you need to get started. Keep in mind that a bank will charge anywhere from 2% to 5% (or more) of each transaction (plus an additional $0.15 to $0.30 or more per transaction) to process your credit purchases. You also should keep in mind that fees vary from bank to bank, and you will be required to lease a terminal (one of those "swipe boxes") or purchase a PC software package so that you can process the day's transactions. Neither option is cheap. Terminals can run more than $30.00 per month, and the proprietary software can cost more than $1000.00. Feel free to shop around from bank to bank. If you cannot find an accommodating bank, they can probably refer you to one of the nationwide credit processing services that specialize in setting up merchant accounts for small businesses. Although a credit service might be more accommodating than a bank, you will typically pay more in processing fees, terminal rental, or software licensing. Ultimately, a merchant account is a nice (but expensive) business step that should be reserved for when your business becomes well established.

2
CHAPTER

Computer math and conversions

The personal computer, for all its current speed and processing power, is still essentially a programmable number processor that is able to transfer and manipulate millions of numbers every second. However, the form that numbers take inside the PC is quite different than the form of numbers you learned in school. By understanding how numbers are represented and processed, you can better understand how PCs work. The purpose of this chapter is to explain the various number systems used in computers, show how each system relates to our familiar decimal system, and demonstrate how to perform basic math and translations between various number systems.

Before you begin this chapter, you should know that this material is not vital for the successful maintenance and repair of modern personal computers. If you are using this book to help you resolve a particular difficulty, you can skip directly to that chapter; refer to this material later as you need it. On the other hand, mastering various number systems now can take much of the mystery and guesswork out of PC specifications or technical data.

Binary concepts

The first number system that you should understand is the *binary* system. This system is at the core of all digital electronics and PC design. Once you understand binary numbering, it is a simple matter to convert to other number systems. Binary is a base-2 number system. That is, only two characters (or digits) are used. The term *bit* comes from the contraction of *binary digit*. The digits themselves are irrelevant—any two characters could have been used—but it just so happens that the characters 0 and 1 were adopted. It is vital for you to realize that because you are working in a different number system, the characters 0 and 1 are not the same as the 0 and 1 in the decimal system. This will become clearer as you see the applications of binary numbers. To fully appreciate the importance of binary numbers in the computer, you must understand how bits and logic correspond.

Bits and logic levels

Digital logic operates in terms of on and off conditions (also known as true and false or high and low respectively). Because digital logic works in only two conditions, and there are only two digits in the binary system, binary expressions have become synonymous with logic circuits. This relationship is where the physical world of digital electronics meets the logical world of the computer. The myriad of signals that traverse a computer's buses and control lines can be represented with binary levels. Traditionally, a signal level of 2.4 to 4.9 Vdc (volts direct current) in a logic circuit represents a binary 1 (a high or true condition), and a signal level of 0.0 to 0.8 Vdc represents a binary 0 (a low or false state). In logic design circles, this is known as *active-high logic*. You also must be aware that true and false nomenclature can be reversed for some logic circuitry. For example, it is not uncommon for some circuitry to use a binary 1 to represent a false condition instead of true, and a binary 0 to represent a true condition instead of false. This logic is known as *active-low logic*. It might sound confusing at first, but circuit designers are only reversing logic conventions rather than logic operations.

Bits, bytes, and words

When reading a binary number such as 1001010_2 (the $_2$ indicates a base 2 or binary number), the digit on the left is the *most-significant digit* (MSD), and the digit on the right is the *least-significant digit* (LSD). Counting in binary applies exactly the same principles as counting in decimal. The only thing to keep in mind is that instead of carrying when the digit exceeds 9, you carry when the digit exceeds 1. Table 2-1 shows a typical counting process. Also note that binary numbers are read differently than decimal numbers. For example, the binary number 1011_2 is read "one zero one one," not "one thousand and eleven." This misinterpretation is common among PC novices.

Table 2-1. A typical binary progression

Decimal equivalent	MSD			LSD
0				0
1				1
2			1	0
3			1	1
4		1	0	0
5		1	0	1
6		1	1	0
7		1	1	1
8	1	0	0	0
9	1	0	0	1
10	1	0	1	0
11	1	0	1	1
12	1	1	0	0
and so on . . .				

A binary number can have any number of digits, but it will usually be a multiple of two (such as 8, 16, or 32 bits). Eight bits are known as a *byte*. Although there are no formal terms for larger numbers of bits, you can refer to multiple bytes (or larger collections of bits) as a *word*. For example, you might have heard the phrases "16-bit word" or "32-bit word." Generally speaking, when bits are collected into bytes and words, they are being used to represent memory locations (on the PC's *address bus*) or data and instructions (via the PC's *data bus*). When a bit is represented alone (such as an *IRQ* or interrupt line), it is said to be *discrete*.

Binary to decimal conversion

Converting a binary number to its decimal equivalent is a simple matter. It merely requires you to add up the place value of each 1, then add those values together. Table 2-2 illustrates the conversion. The least significant digit is 2^0 (1), 2^1 (2), 2^2 (4), 2^3 (8), 2^4 (16), 2^5 (32), 2^6 (64), and 2^7 (128). For larger numbers, simply add powers of two. Suppose you wish to convert the binary number 10110010_2. The least significant digit is the 0 at the far right. Starting at the top of the chart, place each digit (least to most significant) into the chart as in Table 2-2. Wherever a 1 appears, add the value of that place to the total. As you see, there is a 1 in the 128ths, 32nds, 16ths, and 2s places. As a result, the binary number 10110010_2 is equivalent to the decimal number 178. A second example shows you how to convert the binary word 11101110_2. As you see, there are 1s in the 2nds, 4ths, 8ths, 32nds, 64ths, and 128ths places. Altogether, the decimal equivalent is 238.

Table 2-2. Converting a binary number to a decimal number

		Weight	Binary word #1	Binary word #2
LSD	2^0	1	0	0
	2^1	2	1 = 2	1 = 2
	2^2	4	0	1 = 4
	2^3	8	0	1 = 8
	2^4	16	1 = 16	0
	2^5	32	1 = 32	1 = 32
	2^6	64	0	1 = 64
MSD	2^7	128	1 = 128	1 = 128
		Total	178	238

If you deal with number systems at all, it is important that you become proficient in binary to decimal conversions. As shown in this chapter, octal and hexadecimal numbers can be converted quite quickly to binary and then from binary to decimal with this technique.

Decimal to binary conversion

Although converting a binary number to decimal is not difficult, converting a decimal number into its binary equivalent is a bit more complicated. The conversion involves repeatedly dividing the decimal number by 2, and using the remainder from each division to form the binary sequence. Table 2-3 illustrates this process using the number 179. For example, 2 divides into 179 evenly 89 times, with 1 remaining. Because this 1 is the remainder of the first division, it represents the least significant digit (LSD). The resulting 89 is then used for the next subsequent division, being divided by 2 evenly 44 times and leaving a remainder of 1 (our next bit). The 44 is used for the next division and so on. The division process stops when 2 can no longer divide into a number evenly. For the example in Table 2-3, 2 cannot divide evenly into 1, so the answer is 0, and the remainder of 1 is carried out as the most significant digit (MSD). Thus, 179 translates to 10110011_2 in binary. Because the conversion from binary to decimal is so simple, it is an easy matter for you to check your work.

Table 2-3. Converting a decimal number to a binary number

179/2 = 89	remainder = 1	(LSD)
89/2 = 44	remainder = 1	
44/2 = 22	remainder = 0	
22/2 = 11	remainder = 0	
11/2 = 5	remainder = 1	
5/2 = 2	remainder = 1	
2/2 = 1	remainder = 0	
2/1 = 0	remainder = 1	(MSD)
179 = 10110011_2		

Although the conversion from decimal to binary numbers is not difficult, it does require some attention to detail. An error anywhere in your division can lead to erroneous results—not just for that bit, but for all subsequent (and more significant) bits. Just imagine what would have happened to the example in Table 2-3 if an error in the first division had yielded 88 instead of 89.

Binary addition

Once you are proficient at translating numbers from decimal to binary and back, you can give some attention to binary math. Understanding how a computer adds and subtracts binary numbers lends a real appreciation for the processes that a computer must go through. Novice readers often think that binary math is some sort of advanced theory—it is not. The concepts of binary addition are exactly the same as those of decimal addition. Binary simply works with two characters instead of ten. Table 2-4 shows you some simple examples of binary addition.

Table 2-4. An example of binary addition

```
  1           (carry)      1         1  1              (carry)
  1  1  0     (6)          1  1  0  0  1  1  0  0      (204)
+ 1  1  0     (6)        + 0  1  0  0  1  1  1  1      (79)
--------------          --------------------------
1 1  0  0     (12)        1  0  0  0  1  1  0  1  1    (283)
```

The first example adds 110_2 and 110_2. Just as with decimal addition, you should start with the LSDs at the right. In the right-most column, $0 + 0 = 0$. The resulting 0 drops into the LSD location in the answer. In the middle column, you see $1 + 1$, which is equal to 10. Because there is no binary equivalent for 2, you must carry the 1 into the next higher place. As a result, the 1 carries into the left-most column, and the 0 drops down into the answer. The left-most column now presents a problem because you are adding three 1s. Well, $1 + 1 = 10$, so $10 + 1 = 11$. The entire 11 drops down into the answer. If you convert the answer back to decimal, you will see that $6 + 6 = 12$.

The second example adds 11001100_2 and 01001111_2. Even though there are many more digits in this second example, the process and rules used to solve the problem are exactly the same as those used for the first example. Once you have an answer, you can convert it back to decimal and check your answer.

Binary subtraction

The process of subtraction is a bit more complex for computers. By their nature, computers cannot subtract using the rules of mathematics that you are familiar with. Instead of subtracting one number from another, classical subtraction of binary numbers is accomplished by adding the *2's complement* of a number to another number. Before you go any further, you must understand what a 2's complement is. The ordinary complement of a number is simply its opposite. For example, the complement of 1010_2 is 0101_2. This also is known as the *1's complement* of a number. To form a 2's complement number, simply add 1 to the 1's complement number. As another example, the complement of 10010100_2 is 01101011_2, and the 2's complement would be 01101100_2. By adding a 2's complement number to another number, the answer would be the same as if a subtraction occurred.

Table 2-5 demonstrates how this is accomplished. Suppose you wish to subtract 101_2 from 1111_2. By their inherent design, computers cannot perform subtraction. However, computers are very adept at inverting and adding. So, instead of adding circuitry to perform subtraction, the computer converts the number to be subtracted into a 2's complement equivalent, then adds it to the other number. For the example in Table 2-5, the 2's complement of 0101_2 is 1011_2. By adding this number to 1111_2, the result is 11010_2. However, any carry is ignored here, which leaves 1010_2.

Table 2-5. An example of binary subtraction

		1 1 1	
1 1 1 1 (15)	equivalent to:	1 1 1 1 (15)	
− 0 1 0 1 (5)		+ 1 0 1 1 (2's complement of 5)	
1 0 1 0 (10)		₊1 0 1 0 (the leading 1 is ignored)	
	or	1 0 1 0 (10)	

		1	
1 0 1 1 0 1 (45)	is equivalent to:	1 0 1 1 0 1 (45)	
− 0 0 1 1 1 1 (15)		+ 1 1 0 0 0 1 (2's comp of 15)	
1 1 1 1 0 (30)		₊0 1 1 1 1 0 (leading 1 ignored)	
	or	1 1 1 1 0 (30)	

The second example might help to clarify the process even further. Table 2-5 shows a binary 15 being subtracted from a binary 45. The binary 15 is converted to its 2's complement equivalent and added to the binary 45. The leading 1 generated in the addition is ignored, leaving you with a binary 30 (11110_2).

Binary-coded decimal (BCD)

Before you leave this section on binary concepts, you should understand the idea of *binary-coded decimal* (BCD). Simply speaking, BCD is the process of expressing decimal integers using their four-digit binary equivalents. For example, the decimal number 23 would be expressed as 0010 0011 in BCD (as opposed to the conventional binary expression of 10111_2). As another example, the decimal number 1499 would be shown 0001 0100 1001 1001 in BCD. In most cases, BCD has limited utility in computers today. It is generally employed as a method to quickly and easily convert real-life situations (such as thumbwheel switch settings) into digital information. You might, however, find references to BCD in various pieces of technical literature.

Hexadecimal concepts

As you saw in the last section, binary numbers correspond very closely to the digital signals at work in a computer. Unfortunately, dealing with long strings of 1s and 0s is not very convenient, especially when trying to express large numbers of memory addresses or significant quantities of data. Early computer designers realized that it would be necessary to denote binary information in a much more concise way. The *hexadecimal* numbering system is the result of that need. Hexadecimal (or hex) refers to a system with 16 characters (as opposed to the two characters used in binary or the 10 characters used in decimal). You will often see hexadecimal numbers marked with an h or $_{16}$. The convenience and ease of translation between binary and hex numbers have made hex the preferred means of expressing digital information in computer literature (that is, memory maps, port addresses, and so on). The hexadecimal system uses 16 characters: 0 through 9, as well as A through F to represent the quantities 10 through 15 respectively.

Binary to hexadecimal

The conversion from binary to hexadecimal numbers is exceptionally easy. Because a hexadecimal character can represent 16 discrete levels, one hex character is equivalent to four binary digits. For example, the binary number 1000_2 equals 8h, the binary number 1010_2 equals the hex number Ah, and the binary number 1111_2 equals Fh. This concept also can be extended to much larger binary numbers. To convert larger binary numbers, simply separate the binary digits into groups of four and translate each group. The number 1010110011110100_2 can be translated to A (1010), C (1100), F (1111), and 4 (0100), or ACF4h. If there are not enough binary characters to make complete sets of 4 bits, add 0(s) to the left of the MSD to make a complete set. For example, the binary word 11000_2 only contains five characters, so add three leading 0s (i.e. 00011000_2), then break the word into hex groups such as 1 (0001) and 8 (1000). The word 11000_2 equals 18h.

Hexadecimal to binary

The conversion process is just as easy when converting hex numbers to their binary equivalents. Because each hex digit equates to four bits, it is a simple matter to assemble a complete binary word from any number of hex bits. For example, the hex number FFh equals 11111111_2. The number A6D3h would be 1010011011010011_2, and so on. This rule extends to hexadecimal words of any length.

Hexadecimal to decimal

If you were able to convert binary numbers into their decimal equivalents, you will find the conversion from hexadecimal to decimal almost as easy. Like binary to decimal conversions, the translation from hex to decimal involves placing each hex character into a weighted position as shown in Table 2-6. Instead of each weighted position being a power of 2, each hexadecimal weight is a power of 16. Insert the hexadecimal digits into their weighted positions, then multiply the weight times the value of each position. The sum of each result will be the decimal equivalent. For the first example of Table 2-6, insert the word 43D5h into the chart (where 4h is the MSD and 5h is the LSD). The 5h is in the 1s position, so 5×1 is 5. The Dh (13) is in the 16ths position, so 13×16 is 208. The 3h is in the 256ths position, so 3×256 is 768. Finally, the 4h is in the 4096ths position, so 4×4096 is 16384. Altogether, the answer is (5 + 208 + 768 + 16384) 17365.

Table 2-6. Converting a hexadecimal number to a decimal number

	Weight		Hex word #1	Hex word #2
LSD	16^0	1	5 = 5	F = 15
	16^1	16	D = 208	F = 240
	16^2	256	3 = 768	F = 3840
	16^3	4096	4 = 16384	F = 61440
MSD	16^4	65536	...	...
	Total		43D5h = 17365	FFFFh = 65535

A second example is illustrated in Table 2-6 using the word FFFFh. Using the procedure outlined above, you can insert each character into the weighted table. The MSD is on the left, and the LSD is on the right. Because the value of Fh is 15, you can say that the decimal equivalent of FFFFh is ($15 \times 1 + 15 \times 16 + 15 \times 256 + 15 \times 4096$) 15 + 240 + 3840 + 61440, or 65535.

Decimal to hexadecimal

When converting a decimal number to its hexadecimal equivalent, you will be employing the same tactic as you did to convert decimal numbers to binary—repetitive division. Instead of dividing a decimal number by two, however, you will be dividing by 16. Table 2-7 shows how this works. To convert 34261 to its hexadecimal equivalent, divide it by 16. This leaves 2141 with a remainder of 5. The 5 becomes the LSD for your conversion. You then divide 2141 by 16, yielding 133 with a remainder of 13 (or D in hex). When 133 is divided by 16, it leaves 8 with a remainder of 5, and because 8 cannot be divided by 16 evenly, the 8 becomes the MSD. Thus, the hexadecimal equivalent of 34261 is 85D5h.

Table 2-7. Converting decimal numbers to hexadecimal numbers

34261/16 = 2141	remainder = 5	(LSD)
2141/16 = 133	remainder = D	(13)
133/16 = 8	remainder = 5	
8/16 = 0	remainder = 8	(MSD)
34261 = 85D5h		
2450/16 = 153	remainder = 2	(LSD)
153/16 = 9	remainder = 9	
9/16 = 0	remainder = 9	(MSD)
2450 = 992h		

Another example of this conversion is illustrated in Table 2-7. To convert the decimal number 2450 to hex, it is divided by 16 three times. The first division yields 153 with a remainder of 2 (the LSD). When 153 is divided by 16, it leaves 9 with a remainder of 9. In the third iteration, 9 cannot be divided by 16 evenly, so the remainder is 9. As a result, 992h is the equivalent of 2450.

Octal concepts

At about the same time that hexadecimal notation appeared in computer circles, a third number system appeared known as *octal*. Generally speaking, octal serves the same purpose as hex by providing a more efficient and convenient means of expressing long, cumbersome binary numbers. Unlike the binary (base 2) or hexadecimal system (base 16), the octal system uses a base of 8, and you will usually see octal numbers denoted with an $_8$. You might wonder why anyone even bothered to develop the octal system at all—why not just use decimal? Well, as you will see in the following sections, a base of 8 makes it extremely easy to convert to or from binary. Because the octal system works in base 8, there are 8 characters: 0 through 7. The octal number system is no longer prominent in computer circles; the large numbers, address ranges, and data words used in today's computers are expressed much more effectively in hex, but you should still understand the nature and conversions involved with the octal system in the event that you encounter octal notation in any technical literature.

Binary to octal

The use of eight characters in the octal system was hardly an accidental or arbitrary choice. Eight characters can be represented by exactly three binary digits (0 through 7 are represented by 000_2 to 111_2). As a result, you can convert a binary number to its octal equivalent simply by separating the binary string into groups of three bits, then converting each three-bit sequence to its corresponding octal character. For example, the binary number 101110000_2 could be broken down into 5 (101), 6 (110), and 0 (000), so 101110000_2 equals 5608. If there are not enough binary characters to make complete sets of 3 bits, add 0(s) to the left of the MSD to make a complete set. For example, the binary word 11000_2 only contains five characters, so add a leading 0 (that is, 011000_2), then break the word into octal groups such as 3 (011) and 0 (000). The word 11000_2 equals 308.

Octal to binary

The process of converting an octal number back to its binary equivalent is just as easy. Because each octal character represents exactly three bits, it is a simple matter to translate each character. For example, the octal number 32438 can be broken down into 011 (3), 010 (2), 100 (4), and 011 (3), which yields the binary number 11010100011_2 (we can disregard the leading 0 used then the first octal 3 was converted).

Octal to hexadecimal

Although there is no direct conversion from octal to hexadecimal, it is still possible to make the conversion by first translating the octal number to binary, then translating the binary number to octal. Even though there is an interim step in the conversion, the translations should go very quickly. Suppose you need to convert the octal number 64418 to hex. Start by converting the number to binary, which should yield 110, 100, 100, and 001 (or 110100100001_2). Now, separate the bits into groups of four. You will find three groups 1101 (Dh), 0010 (2h), and 0001 (1h), which is D21h. Thus, 64418 equals D21h. If you wish to check your work, convert both the octal and hex numbers to decimal—the decimal equivalents should match.

Hexadecimal to octal

The conversion from hex to octal is exactly opposite that of the octal to hex conversion. There is no direct translation between the two systems, but it is a simple matter to convert a hexadecimal number to binary first, then convert the binary number to octal. To illustrate this concept, reverse the example shown in the last section. Suppose the hexadecimal number D21h must be converted to octal. Begin by translating the hex number to binary. D21h breaks down into 1101 (D), 0010 (2), and 0001 (1) (which is 110100100001_2). Now that the binary equivalent is established, convert it to octal by separating the binary bits into groups of three. The word 110100100001_2 breaks down into 110 (6), 100 (4), 100 (4), and 001 (1) yielding 64418. As you see, this is the same answer you started with in the last section.

Octal to decimal

When converting binary and hexadecimal numbers to decimal, each digit was placed into its corresponding position on a weighted chart. For binary, each weight was a power of 2. For hexadecimal, each weight was a power of 16. To convert an octal number to decimal, each octal digit is weighted to the power of 8 as shown in Table 2-8. For example, suppose you need to convert the octal number 372_8 to its decimal equivalent. Place each digit of the octal number into its weighted position (starting with the LSD), then multiply each digit by its weighted value. When you add up each result, the total is the decimal equivalent. As Table 2-8 shows, 372_8 corresponds to decimal 250. Table 2-8 illustrates a slightly more complicated example with the octal number 3707_8. Place each digit into its weighted position and multiply the octal value by its weight. When each result is totaled, 3707_8 corresponds to decimal 1991. When you must convert octal numbers with more than five digits, simply expand the weight chart in Table 2-8 by powers of 8 (that is, 85, 86, 87, 88, and so on).

Table 2-8. Converting an octal number to a decimal number

	Weight		Octal word #1	Octal word #2
LSD	8^0	1	2 = 2	7 = 7
	8^1	8	7 = 56	0 = 0
	8^2	64	3 = 192	7 = 448
	8^3	512	...	3 = 1536
MSD	8^4	4096	...	...
		Total	$372_8 = 250$	$3707_8 = 1991$

Decimal to octal

The conversion from decimal to an octal equivalent follows much the same concepts as decimal conversion to binary or hex; repeatedly divide the decimal number by the number system base. To convert a decimal number to octal, the decimal number must be divided repeatedly by 8 as illustrated in Table 2-9. Suppose the decimal number 250 must be translated to octal. Divide 250 by 8, this yields 31 with a remainder of 2 (this is the octal LSD). The 31 is divided by 8 next, which results in 3 with a remainder of 7. Finally, the three cannot be divided by 8 evenly, so the 3 becomes a remainder (and MSD). Thus, the decimal number 250 equals 372_8. You can tackle much larger numbers just as easily.

Table 2-9. Converting a decimal number to an octal number

250/8 = 31	remainder = 2	(LSD).
31/8 = 3	remainder = 7	
3/8 = 0	remainder = 3	(MSD)
250 = 372_8		

3
CHAPTER

Mastering parts,
schematics, and diagrams

The personal computer and its peripherals are built from hundreds of individual component parts. For our purposes, components range from simple mechanical parts and linkages to microprocessors and other complex ICs. When various physical and electronic components are combined, they form a *subassembly*. As subassemblies are interconnected, a *system* (or completed assembly) is formed. Although this book is designed to focus on subassembly level diagnosis and repair, it is important for technicians (and computer enthusiasts in general) to identify parts on sight and understand what tasks each component is responsible for.

This chapter is a tutorial intended to familiarize novices with the functions and schematic symbols used for typical mechanical, electromechanical, and electronic components found in the PC and its peripherals (such as printers, modems, and drives). You also will read about current component packaging and marking conventions, along with the popular connector approaches. If you have already studied components in depth, you can feel free to skip this chapter, but refer to it later for reference.

Mechanical components

Computer enthusiasts might argue that a discussion of mechanical parts has no place in a modern PC book. Although it is true that the core logic of a PC (that is, its motherboard and expansion boards) is entirely solid state, mechanical parts play a vital role in peripheral devices such as printers and drives. This part of the chapter looks at some of the essential mechanical elements that you might encounter.

To deal with mechanical problems effectively, you must have an understanding of how mechanical parts fail in the PC. There are two factors that will influence the performance of mechanical parts: friction, and foreign objects. *Friction* is a natural part of every mechanical system, and it exists wherever two or more physical surfaces are in contact. Friction has two effects on mechanical parts. First, friction produces wear (which will eventually damage the parts). Second, friction makes a system inefficient—more power is needed to overcome friction. Fortunately, most of today's mechanical parts are made from light, low-friction materials such as plastics. However, physical damage from abuse or accident, the accumulation of dirt and dust, and the accidental introduction of foreign objects can still pose a serious threat to PC mechanical systems.

Bushings and bearings

It is important to reduce wear between key load-bearing surfaces such as rollers and their support structures. Without reducing wear, metal-on-metal surfaces would simply grind away at one another. This would send metal shards into other mechanical assemblies (or an exposed circuit board), and ruin any mechanical alignment. There are three classical means of reducing wear between metal surfaces: lubrication, bushings, and bearings. Lubrication is simple and inexpensive, but it must be replaced frequently, and lubricants attract the dust and debris that can bog down delicate mechanical assemblies. With the exception of a few printers, very little lubrication is used in PC mechanisms.

Bushings are essentially throw-away wear surfaces that are inserted between two metal or hard plastic wearing surfaces. A bushing is made of softer materials than the parts it is separating, so any friction generated by moving parts will wear out the bushing before making contact themselves. When a bushing wears out, it can often be replaced with a new one. Bushings are much less expensive and easier to replace than major mechanical parts such as slides or frames. With the light parts and low-friction materials in use today, bushing materials are quite reliable, and can generally last throughout the entire working life of an assembly.

Probably the most effective devices for reducing friction between metal parts are *bearings*. Bearings consist of a hard metal case with steel balls or rollers packed inside. Because each steel ball contacts a load-bearing surface at only one point, friction (and wear) is substantially lower than for bushings. Unfortunately, bearing assemblies are often much more expensive than bushings. As a result, bearings are used to handle only the heaviest loads, or in places that would be too difficult to change bushings. Most printers and other peripheral assemblies avoid the expense of bearings in favor of inexpensive bushings.

Gears

Gear arrangements, such as the one shown in Fig. 3-1, are used to perform several important tasks. Their most common application is to transfer *mechanical force* from one rotating shaft to another. The simplest arrangement uses two gears in tandem. The gear that provides turning force is known as the *primary gear*, and the gear that turns as a result is known as the *secondary gear*. When two gears are used, the direction of secondary rotation is opposite that of the primary shaft. If primary and secondary directions must be the same, a third gear can be added between the primary and secondary gears. It is possible to change the orientation of applied force by using angled (or *beveled*) gears. By varying the angles of both gears, force can be

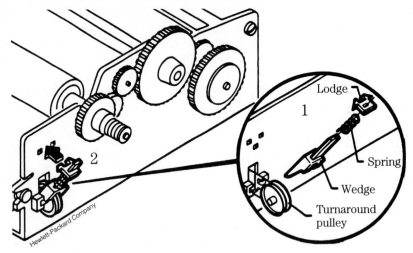

3-1 A typical printer gear arrangement.

directed just about anywhere around an assembly. It also is possible to run several secondary gears from a single primary (or drive) gear in order to distribute force to multiple locations simultaneously—a critical attribute for laser printer operation.

Not only can gears transfer force, they also can alter speed and amount of force that is applied at the secondary shaft. Figure 3-2 illustrates the effects of simple gear ratios. A *gear ratio* is usually expressed as the size ratio of the primary gear to that of the secondary gear. For a *high* ratio, the primary gear is larger than the secondary gear. As a result, the secondary gear will turn faster, but with less mechanical force (or *torque*). The effect is just the opposite for a *low* ratio. A small primary will turn a larger secondary slower, but with more force. Finally, an equal ratio causes a primary and secondary gear to turn at the same speed and force.

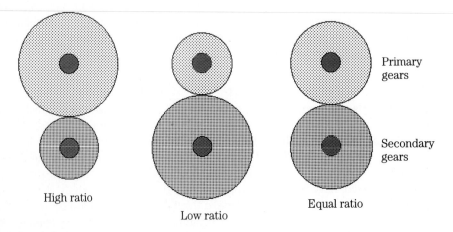

3-2 The effects of gear ratios.

Pulleys and rollers

Like gears, *pulley* assemblies are used to transfer force from one point to another. Instead of direct contact, however, pulleys are joined together by a *drive linkage* usually composed of a belt, wire, or chain (much the same way as a belt in your automobile). A basic pulley set found in an older floppy drive is illustrated in Fig. 3-3. A motor turns a drive pulley that is connected to a secondary pulley (in this case it is the disk spindle) through a drive belt under tension. As the drive pulley turns, force is transferred to the secondary through the linkage, so the secondary pulley also turns. Notice that both pulleys turn in the same direction. In laser printers, a pulley-belt configuration is sometimes used as a conveyor to carry charged paper evenly to the fusing rollers.

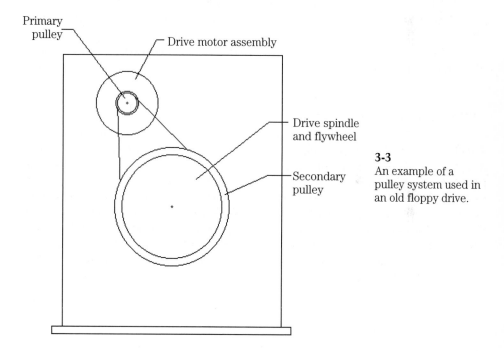

Primary
pulley

Drive motor assembly

Drive spindle
and flywheel

Secondary
pulley

3-3
An example of a
pulley system used in
an old floppy drive.

Pulleys and drive linkages will vary depending on their particular application. Low-force applications can use narrow pulleys (little more than a wheel with a groove in it) connected with a wire linkage. Wire is not very rugged, and its contact surface area with both pulleys is relatively small. Therefore, wire can slide when it stretches under tension, or if load becomes excessive. Belts and their pulleys are wider, so there is much more surface contact around each pulley. Belts are usually stronger than wire, so there is less tendency to stretch under tension. This makes belt-driven pulleys better suited for heavier loads. Pulleys can be replaced by sprocket wheels and a chain linkage. Because each chain link meshes with the sprocket wheels, any chance of slipping is eliminated. Chains are almost immune to stretching under tension, so chain drives are used to handle the largest and heaviest loads such as large dot matrix impact print heads.

Rollers are really a focal point of most printer operations. In a laser printer, rollers not only serve to grab a sheet of paper from the paper tray, but rollers position (or *register*) the paper prior to printing. The Image Formation System uses several rollers to distribute toner and transfer the image to paper. By passing the paper through a set of heated rollers, the transferred image is fused to paper. You can see where damaged, old, or dirty rollers might have an adverse effect not only on paper handling, but on overall image quality. For dot matrix and ink jet printers, rollers keep paper straight, and absorb impact from the dot matrix print head.

Electromechanical components

The PC supports a host of electromechanical parts. The term *electromechanical* indicates that the component converts mechanical force into electrical action, or converts electrical force into mechanical action. This concept will become clearer as you read the sections that follow. As with strictly mechanical parts, many electromechanical components are relegated to peripheral devices (such as printers and modems) or drives.

Switches

Simply speaking, a *switch* is used to manually connect or disconnect electrical signals. As Fig. 3-4 illustrates, a switch is little more than a set of electrical contacts with a wiper between the points. When the wiper is closed, contact is made, and the switch is on. When the wiper is open, contact is broken, and the switch is off. Switches can take a variety of forms depending on the circuit where they are needed, but PCs typically use an ac power switch to turn the system on and off. Many motherboards and most expansion boards also use switches in the form of *DIP* (*d*ual *i*n-line *p*ackage) switches. DIP switches are ideal for selecting system resources such as interrupts (IRQs), DMA channels, and I/O address ranges.

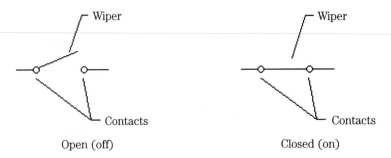

3-4 Typical switch contact positions and nomenclature.

Fuses

A *fuse* is designed to protect a circuit (primarily a power supply) from drawing excessive current due to an internal circuit fault, or failure in the load (the circuit being powered or driven). If left unprotected, a short circuit or circuit failure could easily draw enough current to present a fire hazard. Essentially, a fuse is just a length of thin wire suspended between two metal ends (Fig. 3-5). The type and gauge of wire used in the fuse dictates how much current that will pass safely. When current exceeds that limit, the wire will burn out and open the circuit. This cuts off the flow of current entirely—thus, the circuit is protected. Although fuses take a variety of physical forms (some fuses look like small resistors or surface-mount components), every fuse works the same way.

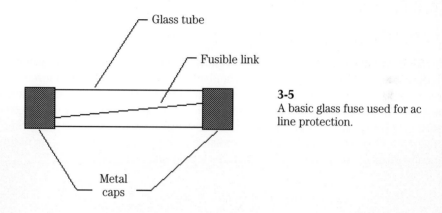

3-5
A basic glass fuse used for ac line protection.

Relays

A *relay* is simply a mechanical switch that is actuated with the electromagnetic force generated by an energized coil. A typical relay diagram is shown in Fig. 3-6. The switch (or *contact set*) can be normally-open (NO) or normally-closed (NC) while the coil is de-energized. When activated, the coil's magnetic field will cause normally-open contacts to close, or normally-closed contacts to open. Contacts are held in their actuated positions as long as the coil is energized. If the coil is turned off, contacts will return to their normally open or closed states. Keep in mind that a coil can drive more than one set of contacts.

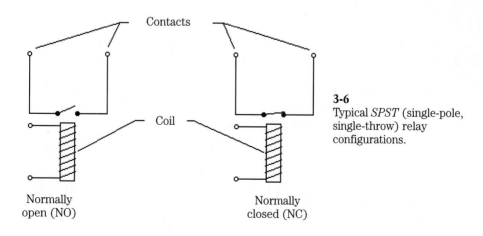

3-6
Typical *SPST* (single-pole, single-throw) relay configurations.

Relays are not always easy to recognize on sight. Most relays used in electronic circuits are housed in small, rectangular containers of metal or plastic. Low-power relays can be fabricated into oversized IC-style packages and soldered right into a PC board just like any other integrated circuit. Unless the relay's internal diagram is printed on its outer case, you will need a printer schematic or manufacturer's data for the relay to determine the proper input and output functions of each relay pin. Relays are commonly used in modems to connect or disconnect the telephone line.

Solenoids

A *solenoid* converts electromagnetic force directly into motion as illustrated in Fig. 3-7. Unlike ordinary electromagnets (such as those in relays) whose cores remain fixed within a coil, a solenoid core is allowed to float back and forth without restriction. When energized, the magnetic field generated by a coil exerts a force on its core (called a *plunger*) that pushes it out from its rest position. If left unrestrained, a plunger would simply shoot out if its coil and fall away. Plungers are usually tethered by a spring or some other sort of mechanical return assembly. That way, a plunger will only extend to some known distance when the coil is fired, then automatically return to its rest position when the coil is off.

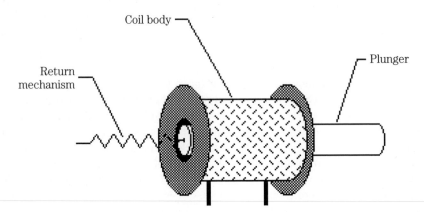

3-7 A typical solenoid assembly.

Solenoids are commonly used as clutches in laser printer paper handling systems. Remember that the motor providing mechanical force in the printer is constantly running while a page is being printed. However, the paper grab and registration rollers need only turn briefly during the printing cycle. Solenoid *clutches* are used to engage and disengage the motor force as needed. Solenoids also form the basis for dot matrix print heads where each individual print wire is driven by a small solenoid.

Motors

Motors are an absolutely essential part of printers and drives manufactured today (Fig. 3-8). Motors spin platters and disks, operate mechanical transport systems, and move print heads. You will see much more on motors throughout this book, but

Drive motor

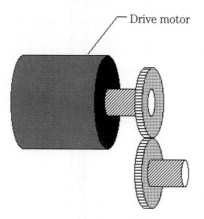

3-8
A motor driving a series of gears.

for now, you should concentrate on the motor itself. All motors convert electrical energy into rotating mechanical force. In turn, that force can be distributed with mechanical parts to turn a roller or move a belt. An *induction* motor performs this task by mounting a series of powerful electromagnets (coils) around a permanent magnet core. The core (known as a *rotor*) is little more than a shaft that is free to rotate as its poles encounter electromagnetic forces. Each coil (also called a *phase* or *phase winding*) is built into the motor's stationary frame (or *stator*).

By powering each phase in its proper order, the rotor can be made to turn with some amount of force. The amount of angular force generated by a motor is known as *torque*. Induction motors generally require two ac signals separated by a 90° phase difference. These sinusoidal driving signals vary the strength of each phase evenly to cause a smooth rotation. Induction motors are rarely used in today's commercial computer assemblies because they do not lend themselves easily to the precise positioning requirements that most printers demand. Instead, a close cousin of the induction motor is used. This motor is called a *dc servo* motor.

The dc servos are powered by bipolar dc signals rather than by sinusoidal ac. Like the induction motor, a dc servo is turned by bipolar driver signals in rapid succession. Although dc servos are not very precise for positioning, they are able to hold a constant speed very accurately. This characteristic makes dc servos ideal for driving the scanner mirrors in laser printers, or drive spindles—both of which must rotate at a precise rate.

A popular variation of the dc servo motor is called a *stepping motor*. Physically, a stepping motor (or *stepper*) is very similar to a dc servo, but the rotor/stator arrangement is much more intricate. Like dc servos, stepper motors are driven by a series of square wave pulses separated by a phase difference. The sudden shift in drive signals coupled with the intricate mechanical arrangement causes the rotor to jump (or *step*) in certain angular increments, not a smooth, continuous rotation. Once the rotor has reached its next step, it will hold its position as long as driver signals maintain their conditions. If driver signals hold steady, the motor could remain stationary indefinitely. A typical stepping motor can achieve 1.8° per step. This means a motor must make (360/1.8) 200 individual steps to complete a single rotation. However, gear ratios can be used to break down motor movement into much finer divisions.

Stepping motors are ideal for precise positioning in systems such as printers. Because the motor moves in known angular steps, it can be rotated to any position simply by applying the appropriate series of driver pulses. For example, suppose your motor had to rotate 180 degrees. If each step equals 1.8°, you need only send a series of (180/1.8) 100 pulses to turn the rotor exactly that amount. Logic circuits in the printer generate each pulse, then driver circuits amplify those pulses into the high-power signals that actually operate the motor.

Electronic components

Even if you never plan to troubleshoot a PC or peripheral, you should have an understanding of the various electronic components that are being used. Most circuits contain both active and passive components working together. *Passive* components include resistors, capacitors, and inductors. They are called passive because their only purpose is to store or dissipate a circuit's energy. *Active* components make up a broader group of semiconductor-based parts such as diodes, transistors, and all types of integrated circuits. They are referred to as active because each component uses a circuit's energy to perform a specific set of functions—they all do something. It might be as simple as a rectifier, or as complex as a microprocessor, but active parts are the key elements in modern electronic circuits. This part of the chapter shows you each general type of component, their basic principles, how to read their markings, and how they fail. Keep in mind that this information is intended simply as an overview.

Resistors

All resistors ever made serve a single purpose—to dissipate power in a controlled fashion. Resistors appear in just about every circuit, but they are used for such things as voltage division, current limiting, and so on. Resistors dissipate power by presenting a resistance to the flow of current. Wasted energy is then shed by the resistor as heat. In logic circuits, so little energy is wasted by resistors that virtually no temperature increase is detectable. In high-energy circuits, such as power supplies, resistors can shed substantial amounts of heat. The basic unit of resistance is the *ohm*, but you will see resistance also presented as kilohms (kohms or thousands of ohms) or megohms (Mohms or millions of ohms). The symbol for resistance is the Greek symbol omega (Ω). The schematic symbols for a resistor are shown in Fig. 3-9.

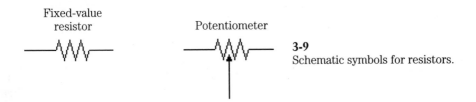

Fixed-value resistor

Potentiometer

3-9
Schematic symbols for resistors.

Carbon-film resistors have largely replaced the older carbon-composition resistors in most circuits requiring through-hole resistors. Instead of carbon filling, a very precise layer of carbon film is applied to a thin ceramic tube. The thickness of this coating affects the amount of resistance—thicker coatings yield lower levels of resistance, and vice versa. Metal leads are attached by caps at both ends, and the entire finished assembly is dipped in epoxy or ceramic. Carbon-film resistors are generally more accurate than carbon-composition resistors because a film can be deposited very precisely during manufacture.

As with carbon-film resistors, *surface-mount* resistors are formed by depositing a layer of carbon film onto a thin ceramic substrate. Metal tabs are attached at both ends of the wafer. Surface-mount resistors are soldered directly on the top or bottom sides of a printed circuit board instead of using leads to penetrate the PC board. Surface-mount resistors are incredibly small devices (only a few square millimeters in area), yet they offer very tight tolerances. They are used almost exclusively in computers and printers.

Adjustable resistors, known as *potentiometers* or *rheostats*, are usually used to adjust contrast, volume, and intensity. A typical potentiometer consists of a movable metal wiper resting on a layer of resistive film. Figure 3-9 illustrates a schematic diagram for a potentiometer. Although the total resistance of the film, end-to-end, will remain unchanged, resistance between either end and the wiper blade will vary as the wiper is moved. There are two typical types of adjustable resistor: knob type, where the wiper is turned clockwise or counterclockwise using a rotating metal shaft, or slide-type, where the wiper is moved back and forth in a straight line.

As long as the power being dissipated by a resistor is below its rating, a resistor should hold its value and perform indefinitely. However, when a resistor is forced to exceed its power rating, it cannot shed heat fast enough to maintain a stable temperature. Ultimately, the resistor will overheat and burn out. In all cases, a burned-out resistor forms an open circuit. A faulty resistor might appear slightly discolored, or it might appear burned and cracked. It really depends on the severity and duration of its overheating. Extreme overheating can burn a printed circuit board, and possibly damage the printed copper traces.

Failures among potentiometers usually take the form of intermittent connections between the wiper blade and resistive film. Remember that film slowly wears away as the wiper moves back and forth across it. Over time, enough film might wear away that the wiper might not make good contact at certain points. This can result in all types of erratic or intermittent operation. With PCs, it is rarely necessary to continually make adjustments once optimum levels are found, so it is unlikely for adjustable resistors to wear out. However, dust and debris might collect and cause intermittent operation when adjustment is needed. Try cleaning an intermittent potentiometer with a high-quality electronic contact cleaner.

Reading resistors

Every resistor is marked with its proper value. Marking allows resistors to be identified on sight and compared versus schematics or part layout drawings. You should know how to identify their value without having to rely on test equipment. There are three ways to mark a resistor: explicit marking, color coding, and numerical marking. It is important to decipher all three types of marks because many circuits use resistors with a mix of marking schemes. Explicit marking is just as the name implies—the actual value of the part is written right onto the part. Large, ceramic power resistors often use explicit marking. Their long, rectangular bodies are usually large enough to hold clearly printed characters.

Color coding has long been a popular marking scheme for carbon film resistors that are simply too small to hold explicit markings. The twelve colors used in color coding are shown in Table 3-1. The first ten colors (black through white) are used as *value* and *multiplier* colors. Silver and gold colors serve as *tolerance* indicators. The color code approach uses a series of colored bands. Band number 1 is always located closest to the edge of the resistor. Bands one and two are the value bands, and band three is the multiplier. A fourth band (if present) will be silver or gold to indicate the resistor's tolerance. On rare occasions, you might encounter a fifth band that indicates the reliability of a resistor (and is used only for military/aerospace-grade resistors).

Table 3-1. The standard resistor color code

Color	1st band	2nd band	Multiplier	Tolerance
Black	0	0	1	
Brown	1	1	10	
Red	2	2	100	
Orange	3	3	1,000	
Yellow	4	4	10,000	
Green	5	5	100,000	
Blue	6	6	1,000,000	
Violet	7	7	10,000,000	
Gray	8	8	100,000,000	
White	9	9	—	
(none)				±20%
Silver				±10%
Gold				±5%

For example, suppose a resistor offered a color sequence of brown, black, and red. You can see from Table 3-1 that brown = 1, black = 0, and red = 100 (because the red band occupies the multiplier position). The sequence would be read as [band 1] [band 2] × [band 3]: 1 0 × 100, or 1000 Ω (1 kΩ). If the first three color bands of a re-sistor read red, red, orange, the resistor would be read as 22 × 1000, or 22,000 Ω (22 kΩ), and so on.

When a fourth band is found, it shows the resistor tolerance. A gold band repre-sents an excellent tolerance of ±5% of rated value. A silver band represents a fair tol-erance of ±10%, and no tolerance band indicates a poor tolerance of ±20%. When a faulty resistor must be replaced, it should be replaced with a resistor of equal or smaller tolerance whenever possible.

Color coded resistors are rapidly being replaced by *SM* (surface-mount) resis-tors. Surface-mount resistors are far too small for clear color coding. Instead, a three-digit numerical code is used (even though you might need a small magnifying glass to see it). Each digit corresponds to the first three bands of the color code. The first two numbers are value digits, and the third number is the multiplier. The multi-plier digit indicates how many places to the right that the value's decimal place must be shifted. For example, a numerical code of 102 denotes a value of 10 with 2 zeros added on to make the number 1000 (1 kΩ). A marking of 331 would be read as 330 Ω, and so on.

Capacitors

Capacitors are simply energy storage devices. They store energy in the form of an electrical charge. By themselves, capacitors have little practical use, but the capacitor principle has important applications when combined with other components in filters, resonant or timing circuits, and power supplies. Capacitance is measured in *farads* (F). In actual practice, a farad is a very large amount of capacitance, so most normal capacitors measure in the microfarad (μF or millionths of a farad) and picofarad (pF or millionths of a millionth of a farad) range. In principle, a capacitor is little more than two conductive plates separated by an insulator (called a *dielectric*). The amount of capacitance provided by this type of assembly depends on the area of each plate, their distance apart, and the dielectric material that separates them. Even larger values of capacitance can be created by rolling up a plate/dielectric assembly and housing it in a cylinder.

There are generally two types of capacitors that you should be familiar with. These can be categorized as *fixed* or *electrolytic*. Figure 3-10 shows the schematic symbols for both capacitor types. Fixed capacitors are nonpolarized devices—they can be inserted into a circuit regardless of their lead orientation. Many fixed capacitors are assembled as small wafers or disks. Each conductive plate is typically aluminum foil. Common dielectrics include paper, mica, and various ceramic materials. The complete assembly is then coated in a hard plastic, epoxy, or ceramic housing to keep out humidity. Larger capacitors can be assembled into large, hermetically sealed canisters. Fixed capacitors also are designed in surface-mount form.

Fixed-value capacitor

Electrolytic capacitor

3-10
Schematic symbols for capacitors.

Electrolytic capacitors are polarized components—they must be inserted into a circuit in the proper orientation with respect to the applied signal voltage. Tantalum capacitors are often found in a dipped (or *teardrop*) shape, or as small canisters. Aluminum electrolytic capacitors are usually used in general-purpose applications where polarized devices are needed. The difference between fixed and electrolytic capacitors is primarily in their materials, but the principles and purpose of capacitance remain the same.

Like resistors, most capacitors tend to be rugged and reliable devices. Because they only store energy (not dissipate it), it is virtually impossible to burn them out. Capacitors can be damaged or destroyed by exceeding their *WV* (working-voltage) rating, or by reversing the orientation of a polarized device. Damage can occur if a failure elsewhere in a circuit causes excessive energy to be applied across a capacitor, or if you should install a new electrolytic capacitor incorrectly.

Reading capacitors

Like resistors, all capacitors carry markings that identify their value. Once you understand the markings, you will be able to determine capacitor values on sight. Capacitors are typically marked in two ways: explicit marking and numerical codes. Explicit marking is used with capacitors that are physically large enough to carry their printed value. Large ceramic disk, mylar, and electrolytic capacitors have plenty of surface area to hold readable markings. Note that all polarized capacitors, regardless of size, *must* show which of their two leads are positive or negative. Be certain to pay close attention to polarizer markings whenever you are testing or replacing capacitors.

Small, nonpolarized capacitors and many sizes of surface-mount capacitors now make use of numerical coding schemes. The pattern of numerical markings is easy to follow because it is very similar to the marking technique used with numerically coded resistors. A series of three numbers is used—the first two numbers are the value digits, and the third number is the multiplier digit (how many zeros are added to the value digits).

Almost all capacitor numerical markings are based on picofarad measurements. Thus, the capacitor marked 150 would be read as a value of 15 with no zeros added (or 15 pF). A marking of 151 would then be 15 with one 0 added (or 150 pF). The marking 152 would be 15 with two 0s added (or 1500 pF), and so on. A marking of 224 would be 22 with four 0s (or 220,000 pF). As you see, the decimal place is always shifted to the right. Although this marking system is based on picofarads, every value can be expressed as microfarads (µF) simply by dividing the pF value by 1 million. For example, a 15-pF capacitor could be called a [15 pF / 1,000,000 pF/µF] 0.000015-µF capacitor. Of course, there is no advantage in marking such a small capacitor in the µF range when 15 pF is such a convenient value, but the conversion is a simple one. The 15,000-pF capacitor also could be shown as [15,000 pF / 1,000,000 pF/µF] 0.015 µF. Capacitors with large picofarad values are often expressed more effectively as microfarads. To confirm your estimates, you can measure the capacitor with a capacitance meter.

Inductors

The inductor also is an energy-storage device. But unlike capacitors, inductors store energy in the form of a magnetic field. Before the introduction of integrated circuits, inductors served a key role with capacitors in the formation of filters and resonant (tuned) circuits. Although advances in solid-state electronics have rendered inductors virtually obsolete in traditional applications, they remain invaluable for high-energy circuits such as power supplies. Inductors also are used in transformers, motors, and relays. Inductance is measured in *henrys* (H), but smaller inductors can be found in the *millihenry* (mH) or *microhenry* (µH) range. The schematic symbols for various inductors are shown in Fig. 3-11.

Transformers

A transformer is actually a combination of inductors all working in tandem. As Fig. 3-11 illustrates, it is composed of three important elements: a *primary* (or in-

Standard inductor

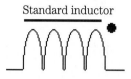

Transformer

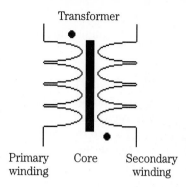

Primary   Core   Secondary
winding   winding

3-11 Schematic symbols for inductive devices.

put) winding, a *secondary* (or output) winding, and a *core* structure of some type. Transformers are used to alter (or transform) ac voltage and current levels in a circuit, as well as to isolate one circuit from another. An ac signal is applied to the primary winding. Because the magnitude of this input signal is constantly changing, the magnetic field it generates will constantly fluctuate as well. When this fluctuating field intersects the secondary coil, another ac signal is created (or *induces*) across it. This principle is known as *magnetic coupling*. Any secondary ac signal will duplicate the original signal. Primary and secondary windings are often wound around the same core structure that provides a common structure and efficient magnetic coupling from primary to secondary.

The actual amount of voltage and current induced on a secondary coil depends on the ratio of the number of primary windings versus the number of secondary windings. This relationship is known as the *turns ratio*. If the secondary coil contains more windings than the primary coil, then the voltage induced across the secondary coil will be greater than the primary voltage. For example, if the transformer has 1000 primary windings and 2000 secondary windings, the turns ratio is 1000/2000 (1/2). With 10 Vac applied to the primary, the secondary will output roughly 10/(1/2), or 20 Vac (volts alternating current). Such an arrangement is known as a *step-up* transformer. If the situation were reversed where the primary coil had 2000 windings with 1000 windings in the secondary, the turns ratio would then be 2000/1000 (2/1). If 30 Vac were now applied to the primary, the secondary output would be 30/(2/1), or 15 Vac. This is known as a *step-down* transformer.

Current also is stepped in a transformer, but opposite to the proportion of voltage steps. If voltage is stepped down by the factor of a turns ratio, current is stepped up by the same factor. This relationship ensures that power out of a transformer is about equal to the power into the transformer.

Because inductors are energy-storage devices, they should not dissipate any power by themselves. However, the wire resistance in each coil, combined with natural magnetic losses in the core, does allow some power to be lost as heat. Heat buildup is the leading cause of inductor failure. Long-term exposure to heat can eventually break down the tough enamel insulating each winding and cause a short circuit. Short circuits lower the coil's overall resistance that draws even more cur-

123154

rent. Breakdown accelerates until the coil is destroyed. You will encounter transformers most frequently in power supplies and modem circuits.

Diodes

The classic diode is a two-terminal semiconductor device that allows current to
flow in one direction (or polarity) only, but not in the other. This one-way property
is known as *rectification*. As explained elsewhere in the book, rectification is absolutely essential to the basic operation of every power supply. As Fig. 3-12 shows,
diodes have two terminals: an *anode* and a *cathode*. When a positive potential is applied to the anode, the diode is *forward-biased*, and it will conduct with only a small
voltage drop across itself (usually 0.6 Vdc). If a positive potential is applied to the
cathode, the diode is *reverse-biased*, and it will not conduct at all.

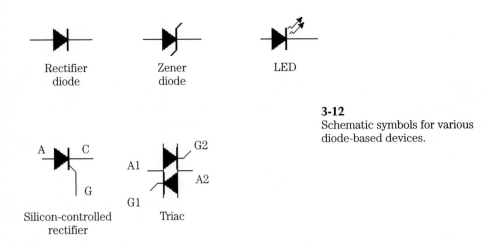

Rectifier
diode

Zener
diode

LED

3-12
Schematic symbols for various
diode-based devices.

A   C

G

Silicon-controlled
rectifier

A1

G1

G2

A2

Triac

Although rectifier diodes are not meant to be operated in the reverse-biased
condition, the *zener* diode is a special species designed exclusively for reverse biasing. Figure 3-12 illustrates a common zener diode symbol. When applied voltage is
below the zener's *breakdown* voltage (typical zener diodes operate at 5, 6, 9, 12, 15,
or 24 Vdc), voltage across the zener diode will equal the applied voltage, and no current will flow in the diode. As applied voltage exceeds the zener's breakdown voltage, current begins to flow through the diode and voltage across the zener remains
clamped at the zener's level (i.e., 5, 6, 9, 12 Vdc, etc.). Any additional applied voltage
is then dropped across an adjacent current limiting resistor. As long as applied voltage exceeds the zener's breakdown voltage, zener voltage will remain constant. This
"zener" action makes zener diodes perfect as simple regulators, and is the basis for
most methods of linear voltage regulation.

Keep in mind that it is impossible to differentiate between rectifier and zener
diodes by their outward appearance—both types of diodes appear identical in every
way. The only way you will be able to tell the two types of diodes apart is to look up
the particular device in a cross-reference manual, look at the part's representation in
a schematic, or look at the device's silk screening on the PC board. Rectifier-type

diodes are typically labeled with a D prefix (D32, D27, D3, etc.), but zener diodes often use Z or ZD prefixes (i.e., ZD5, ZD201, etc.). Similarly, it is impossible to discern a faulty diode simply by looking at it, unless the diode has been destroyed by some kind of sudden, severe overload. In most cases, you must use test instruments to confirm a diode's condition. It is more likely that you will diagnose the problem to a board or drive, then replace the offending subassembly.

Light-emitting diodes

In all semiconductor devices, electrons must bridge a semiconductor junction during operation. By modifying the construction of a junction and encapsulating it inside a diffuse plastic housing, electrons moving across a junction will liberate photons of visible (or infrared) light. This is the basic principle behind *LEDs* (light-emitting diodes). An LED is shown in Fig. 3-12. Notice that an LED is little more than a diode—the wavy arrows indicate that light is moving away from the device. Altering the chemical composition of an LED's materials will alter the wavelength of emitted light (that is, yellow, orange, red, green, blue, infrared, etc.). Like ordinary diodes, LEDs are intended to be forward biased, but LED voltage drops are higher (0.8 to 3.5 Vdc), and LEDs often require 10 to 35 mA (milliamperes) of current to generate the optimum amount of light.

Silicon-controlled rectifiers

An *SCR* (silicon-controlled rectifier) is shown in Fig. 3-12. Notice that SCRs are three-terminal devices. In addition to an *anode* and a *cathode*, a *gate* terminal is added to control the SCR. An ordinary diode turns on whenever it is forward biased. An SCR also must be forward biased, as well as *triggered* by applying a positive voltage (or trigger signal) to the gate. Once triggered, an SCR will continue to conduct as long as current is flowing through the SCR. Removing the gate voltage will *not* stop the SCR from conducting once it has started. If current stops after the gate voltage is removed, the SCR will have to be retriggered.

Triacs

A triac behaves very much like an SCR, but a triac can be triggered to conduct current in either direction through the device instead of only one direction as in the SCR. Figure 3-12 illustrates the schematic symbol for a typical triac. Notice that a triac is given two anodes (A1 and A2) because it can conduct in both directions. A triac will conduct once triggered by a voltage applied to its gate lead. The trigger voltage *must* be the same polarity as the voltage across the triac. For example, if there is a positive voltage from A1 to A2, the trigger voltage must be positive. If there is a negative voltage from A1 to A2, the trigger voltage must be negative. Once triggered, a triac conducts until current stops flowing. After current stops, the triac must be retriggered before it will conduct again.

Diode markings

All diodes carry two very important markings as shown in Fig. 3-13: the part number and the cathode marking. The *cathode marking* indicates the cathode (or

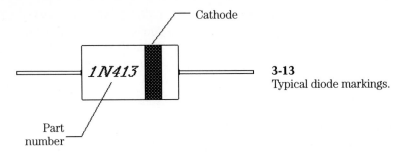

3-13
Typical diode markings.

negative) diode lead. Because diodes are polarized devices, it is critical that you know which lead is which. Otherwise, an incorrectly replaced diode will almost certainly cause a circuit malfunction. Unlike passive components, diode part numbers contain no tangible information on a diode's performance specifications or limits. Instead, the part number is an index or reference number that allows you to look up the particular specification in a manufacturer's or cross-reference data book. Standard diode part numbers begin with the prefix 1N, followed by anywhere from one to four digits. The 1N prefix is used by the *JEDEC* (Joint Electron Devices Engineering Council) in the United States to denote devices with one semiconductor junction (diodes). Standard Japanese diode part numbers begin with the prefix 1SS, where SS means *small signal*. You will probably encounter diodes with many unique and arcane markings. Fortunately, there are many clues to guide you along. Your first clue will be the white (or gray) cathode band—at least you can identify the part as a diode. The second identifier will be the silk screen lettering on the PC board. Diodes are usually assigned D or ZD numbering prefixes to denote a rectifier-type or zener diode.

Bipolar transistors

A transistor is a three-terminal semiconductor device whose output signal is directly controlled by its input signal. With passive components, a transistor can be configured to perform either amplification or switching tasks. Unfortunately, there is just not enough room in this book to discuss the theory and characteristics of transistors, but it is important that you know the most important concepts of transistors, and understand their various uses. There are two major transistor families shown in Fig. 3-14: bipolar and *FET* (field-effect transistor). *Bipolar* transistors are common, inexpensive, general-purpose devices that can be made to handle amplification and switching tasks with equal ease. The three leads of a bipolar transistor are the base, emitter, and collector. In most applications, the *base* serves as the transistor's input— that is where the input signal is applied. The *emitter* is typically tied to ground (usually through one or more values of resistance), and the *collector* provides the output signal. The transistor also can be configured such that the input signal supplied to the collector with the base grounded, and the output appearing on the emitter.

There are two species of bipolar transistor: NPN and PNP. For an NPN transistor, base and collector voltages must be positive (with respect to the emitter). As base voltage increases, the transistor is turned on and current begins to flow from collector to emitter. As base voltage increases further, the transistor continues to turn on and allow more current into the collector until the transistor finally satu-

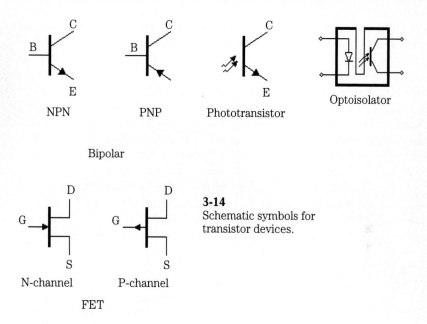

NPN

PNP

Phototransistor

Optoisolator

Bipolar

N-channel

P-channel

FET

3-14
Schematic symbols for transistor devices.

rates. A *saturated* transistor cannot be turned on any further. A PNP transistor requires negative base and collector voltages (with respect to the emitter) in order to cause the transistor to turn on and conduct current. As base voltage becomes more negative, the transistor turns on harder until it saturates. By far, NPN transistors are more commonly used in small electronics.

Phototransistors

Phototransistors are a unique variation of bipolar transistors. Instead of an electrical signal being used to control the transistor, photons of light provide the base signal. Notice the new schematic symbol for a phototransistor. The wavy lines indicate that light is entering at the base. Light enters the phototransistor through a clear quartz or plastic window on the transistor's body. Light that strikes the transistor's base liberates electrons that become base current. The more light that enters the phototransistor, the more base current that is produced, and vice versa. Because of their high sensitivity, phototransistors are most often found in switching circuits that detect the absence or presence of light.

Although phototransistors can detect light from a wide variety of sources, it is normal to use an LED to supply a known, constant light source. When a phototransistor and LED are matched together in this way, an *optocoupler* (or *optoisolator*). Optocouplers are often used in printers to detect the presence or absence of paper, or to detect whether the printer's enclosures are closed completely. Optocouplers also can be found in disk drives to detect the presence of diskettes.

Field-effect transistors

Field-effect transistors (FETs) are constructed in a radically different fashion from bipolar transistors. Although FETs make use of the same basic materials and can operate as either amplifiers or switches, they require biasing components of much higher value to set the proper operating conditions. FETs are either n-channel or p-channel devices as shown in Fig. 3-14. The difference in transistor types depends on the materials used to construct the particular FET. An FET has three terminals: a source, a gate, and a drain. These leads correspond to the emitter, base, and collector of a bipolar transistor. The gate is typically used for the input or control signal. The source is normally tied to ground (sometimes through one or more values of resistance), and the drain supplies the output signal.

When no voltage is applied to an FET's gate, current flows freely from drain to source. Any necessary current limiting must be provided by inserting a resistor in series into the drain or source circuit. By adjusting the control voltage at the gate, current flow in the drain and source can be controlled. For an n-channel FET, control voltage must be a negative voltage. As gate voltage is made more negative, channel current is restricted further until it is cut off entirely. For a p-channel FET, a positive control voltage is needed. Higher positive gate voltage restricts channel current further until the channel is cut off.

A variation of the FET is the *MOSFET* (metal-oxide semiconductor FET). The MOSFET is not illustrated in Fig. 3-14. It is unlikely that you will ever encounter discrete MOSFET devices in your smallcomputer, but most sophisticated digital integrated circuits make extensive use of MOSFETs. One of the few undesirable characteristics of FETs and MOSFETs is their sensitivity to damage by *ESD* (electrostatic discharge). You can learn about ESD in Chapter 7.

Transistor markings

As shown in Fig. 3-15, a transistor's part number is merely an index or reference number that allows you to look up the part's equivalent components or specifications in a data book or cross-reference manual. The number itself contains no useful information about the part's actual performance characteristics or limits. Classical bipolar transistor part numbers begin with the prefix 2N, followed by up to five digits. The 2N prefix is used by JEDEC in the United States to denote devices with two semiconductor junctions. Japanese transistor part numbers begin with any of four prefixes: 2SA (high-frequency PNP transistor), 2SB (low-frequency PNP transistor), 2SC (high-frequency NPN transistor), and 2SD (low-frequency NPN transistor). JEDEC uses the prefix 3N to denote FETs or Junction FETs (JFETs). The prefixes 2SJ (p-channel JFET), 2SK (n-channel JFET), and 3SK (n- or p-channel MOSFETs) have been used in Japan. As with diodes, transistors rarely show any outward signs of failure unless they have melted or shattered from an extreme overload. You generally must use test equipment to identify faulty transistors. Testing can be accomplished by measuring the device while the circuit is running, or removing the device from the circuit and measuring its characteristics out of circuit. It is more likely that you will diagnose the failure to a particular board or drive, then replace the offending subassembly.

Integrated circuits

Integrated circuits (ICs) are by far the most diverse and powerful group of electronic components that you will ever deal with. They have rapidly become the fun-

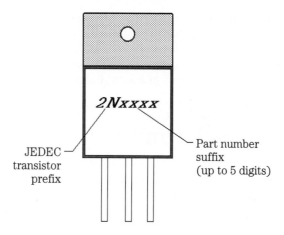

JEDEC
transistor
prefix

Part number
suffix
(up to 5 digits)

3-15 JEDEC transistor markings.

damental building blocks of modern electronic circuits. Amplifiers, memories, microprocessors, digital logic arrays, oscillators, timers, regulators, and a myriad of other complex functions can all be manufactured as ICs. Circuits that only a decade ago would have required an entire PC board are now being fabricated on a single IC. Although you can often estimate the complexity (and importance) of an integrated circuit from the number of pins that it has, it is virtually impossible to predict precisely what an IC does just by looking at it. You will need a schematic of the circuit or manufacturer's data of a particular IC in order to fully determine what the IC does.

Every integrated circuit is composed largely of microscopic transistors, diodes, capacitors, and resistors that are fabricated onto an IC die. Many capacitors and inductors cannot be fabricated on ICs, so conventional parts can be attached to an IC through one or more external leads. Your PC and its peripherals are predominantly digital systems. That is, most of the ICs are designed to work with binary signals. The microprocessor, memory, and most of the controller ICs are digital logic components. Other ICs, however, are intended to work with analog signal levels. Serial communication ICs, drives, and video and sound boards use some amount of analog circuitry.

The vast majority of logic components used in today's small computers contain so very many logic gates that it would simply be impossible to show them all on a schematic diagram. Current microprocessors, gate arrays, and application-specific ICs (ASICs) can each contain thousands of gates. To simplify schematics and drawings, most highly integrated ICs are shown only as generic logic blocks that are interconnected to one another.

Every logic IC requires a power source in order to operate. At least one positive voltage source (V_{cc}) must be applied to the IC. The IC also must be grounded with respect to the source voltage. An ICs ground pin is usually labeled Vss or GND. Since the days of the first logic IC's, supply voltage has been a standard of +5 Vdc. Using a +5-Vdc source, logic 1 outputs are interpreted as +2.4 Vdc or higher, and logic 0 outputs are considered to be +0.4 Vdc or lower. The transistor circuitry within each logic gate accepts inputs at these levels. If +5 Vdc is not supplied to the IC, it will function erratically (if at all). If more than +6 Vdc is forced into the IC, excess power dissipation will destroy the IC. It is exceptionally rare for any type of IC to show outward signs of failure, so it is very important for you to carefully diagnose possible causes of failure before committing to the replacement of a subassembly.

Component packaging

Now that you have seen a cross-section of component parts and the symbols associated with them, you should understand how the various components are packaged. This part of the chapter outlines some of the more conventional packaging techniques used for electronic PC components, and offers a number of insights on surface-mount components.

Conventional packaging

The term *conventional* usually refers to through-hole components—those components with metal leads that will protrude through a PCB. Conventional packaging is usually referred to as axial or radial. An *axial* component offers leads protruding from either end of the part, and a *radial* component provides all leads protruding from the same end. Passive components are typically dipped or coated with a layer of hard epoxy or resin. In some cases, a layer of plastic is used. Coating a part helps to hold it together, and prevents damage during storage, shipping, and handling. Coatings also help to prevent humidity from altering the component's value over time.

Diode packaging takes on several different forms (Fig. 3-16) depending on the diode's intended job, and the amount of current that must be carried. For small-signal diodes, clear glass is the preferred packaging material. When the diode must carry larger amounts of current, plastic and ceramic are usually used.

Transistors are available in a wide variety of case styles and sizes depending on the amount of power that must be handled. Figure 3-17 illustrates a selection of five popular case styles. Low-power, general-purpose devices are often packaged in the small, plastic TO-92 cases. The TO-18 metal case also is used for low-power devices, but the TO-18 shown houses a phototransistor—note the quartz window on the case top that allows light to enter the device. For regular transistor applications, the TO-18 *top-hat* case is all metal. Medium-power transistors use the larger plastic TO-128 or TO-220 cases. The TO-128 uses a thin metal heatsink molded into the top of the device. TO-220 cases use a large metal mounting flange/heatsink located directly behind the plastic case. The flange provides mechanical strength, as well as a secure thermal path for an external heatsink. An all-metal TO-3 case is used for high-power transistors. Two mounting holes are provided to bolt the device to a chassis or external heatsink. As a general rule, case size is proportional to the power capacity of the transistor.

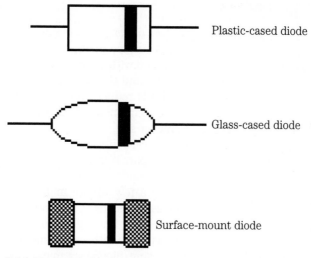

Plastic-cased diode

Glass-cased diode

Surface-mount diode

3-16 Typical diode case styles.

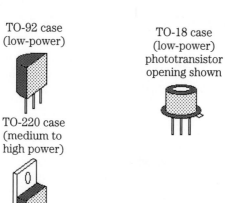

TO-92 case
(low-power)

TO-18 case
(low-power)
phototransistor
opening shown

TO-220 case
(medium to
high power)

3-17
Typical transistor case styles.

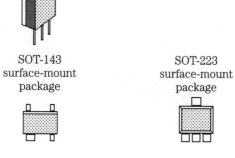

SOT-143
surface-mount
package

SOT-223
surface-mount
package

SMT packaging

The push to place ever-greater numbers of components into ever-smaller spaces has been a driving factor in the adoption of surface-mount technology (SMT) for PC assembly. Because most of the bulk associated with classical active and passive components has been due to their metal leads (and the associated package needed to support those leads), eliminating metal leads reduces the size, weight, and cost of most parts. The vast majority of electronic components dissipate very little power in a PC, so SMT parts can be made even smaller still.

Two-terminal passive components (i.e., resistors and capacitors) are usually referred to as *chip components*. That is, the part is implemented on a small ceramic chip capped with a minute metal electrode bonded at each end. Such chip parts are quite small, and rarely require more than a few square millimeters of PCB area. Other more particular components, such as LEDs, fuses, and inductors, also are fabricated on chips. SMT diodes are similarly sized, but slightly different in packaging. Diodes are often thicker parts coated with plastic with a small metal stub protruding from each end. As with conventional packaging, diodes are marked with a light band to indicate the cathode terminal. SMT transistors get just a bit more involved because three terminals are needed. Figure 3-17 illustrates two popular SMT transistors known as *small-outline transistors* (or SOTs). The typical SOT is encased in plastic with three or more tabs protruding from the case.

IC packaging

Integrated circuits are manufactured in a staggering array of package styles that can be divided into two categories: inserted and surface-mounted. Figure 3-18 shows a selection of both types. *Inserted* IC packages are just as the name implies—the IC package is designed to be inserted into a through-hole PC board or socket. Classical insertion package styles included the *DIP* (dual in-line package), *SIP* (sin-

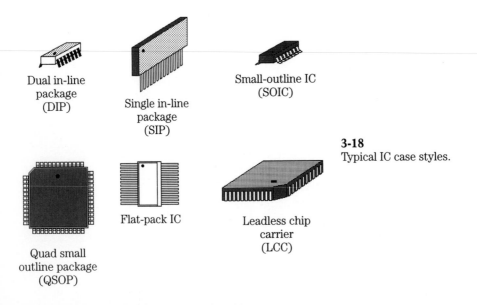

Dual in-line
package
(DIP)

Single in-line
package
(SIP)

Small-outline IC
(SOIC)

3-18
Typical IC case styles.

Quad small
outline package
(QSOP)

Flat-pack IC

Leadless chip
carrier
(LCC)

gle in-line package), and *ZIP* (zig-zag in-line package). However, the *PGa* (pin grid array) has become a very popular insertion package for microprocessors.

Surface-mount ICs have proliferated to take advantage of high pin density and small IC case size. The *QFP* (quad flat pack), *PLCC* (plastic leaded chip carrier), and *SOP* (small outline package) are three of the most popular SMT packages—you can find these on just about any motherboard. Where extra high density is required, the *TSOP* (thin small-outline package) can be used. Where high-density ICs might have to be occasionally updated or replaced, the *LCC* (leadless chip carrier) can be inserted into a socket, and removed with a specialized extraction tool.

4

Reading logic
and timing diagrams

Successful computer operation relies on a complex interaction of logic signals. Each signal is precisely timed so that control, address, and data information are available to desired components at the appropriate points in time. Today's PCs measure their timing in microseconds (μs or millionths of a second) or nanoseconds (ns or billionths of a second). As you might suspect, there is very little room for timing errors—a fault of even a few nanoseconds can result in system problems. As a technician, you do not have to work out the critical timing that a PC needs (the designers have already done that). However, your understanding of timing parameters can help you to make sense of the PC's intricate (often confusing) operations. You also will need the skills to interpret logic and PC architecture diagrams. This chapter shows you how to follow the flow of signals throughout the PC's architecture.

Logic and logic signals

The lineage of modern digital logic can be traced back to 1854. George Boole developed a new way of thinking called *symbolic logic*. Symbolic logic used symbols instead of words in order to reach logical conclusions. You might know this symbolic logic today as *Boolean logic* or *Boolean algebra*. Perhaps the most intriguing and far-reaching aspect of Boolean logic is that every input and output condition can be expressed only as true or false (yes or no) states. Although Boole's concepts had little practical application during the nineteenth century, they would form the basis for electronic logic devices less than a century later.

With the advent of electron tubes, it was possible to construct circuits that would automatically solve Boole's addition (OR operation) and multiplication (AND operation) relationships. Because these logic circuits only dealt with two conditions (on or off, 1 or 0), they were dubbed *binary* (base 2) logic circuits. When vacuum tubes gave way to semiconductor components such as transistors and diodes, additional logic functions appeared that took their roots in Boole's concepts: NAND, NOR, inverters, buffers, XOR, and XNOR. It was not long before each logic function was implemented using fairly standard electronic circuitry, and each logic circuit was called a *gate*. The suite of functions also was known as *digital logic* because one of the very first applications of logic was to solve mathematical computations. For the purposes of this book, the terms Boolean logic, binary logic, and digital logic are all identical and can be used interchangeably. When discrete electronic circuits were finally fabricated as integrated circuits, the *gate* term stuck and remains in use today.

Logic signals and levels

For an electronic circuit to deal with binary logic, there must be a clear, direct relationship between logic states and electrical signal levels. This is a critical relationship because circuits perform their operations based upon the voltage signals at each logic input. A binary TRUE or ON condition usually indicates the presence of some minimum signal voltage, and a binary FALSE or OFF condition indicates a low or nonexistent signal voltage. This type of operation is generally known as conventional or *active-high* logic. In some cases, however, the convention is reversed such that an ON state is represented by the *absence* of a signal voltage, and the OFF state is shown by the *presence* of a signal voltage. This is known as *active-low* logic. Active-low logic signals are generally represented with a solid bar over the signal label or some other identifying mark. For the purposes of this book, all active-low signals will be identified with a minus sign (–) preceding the signal name (that is, –low01 would be an active-low signal).

An example of active-high versus active-low logic is illustrated in Fig. 4-1. The label "Error" is an active-high signal. When a logic 1 signal voltage is present, the condition is true. When a logic 0 voltage is present, the condition is false. If the label

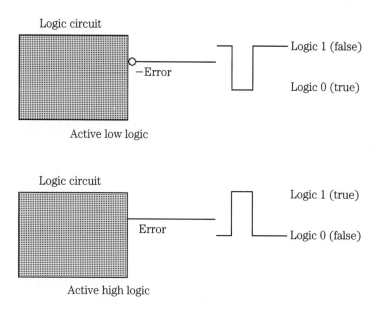

4-1 Active-high versus active-low logic.

were marked "–Error," an active-low logic signal would be indicated. In that case, a logic 1 voltage would indicate a false or off condition, and a logic 0 voltage would indicate a true or on condition. Some schematics and detailed block diagrams also might represent active-low signal lines using small circles (or *bubbles*) at the circuit's output.

Classic gates

To understand logic signals and conventions, the next step is to review the operations of basic logic gates (sometimes known as *glue logic*). There are eight basic gates as illustrated by the schematic symbols of Fig. 4-2: AND, OR, NAND, NOR, buffer, inverter (sometimes called a NOT gate), XOR, and XNOR. Except for the buffer and inverter, each gate is shown with two inputs. In actual practice, those gates can have 10 or more inputs.

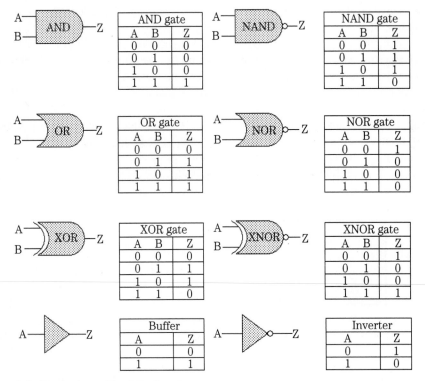

4-2 Comparison of basic logic gates.

The purpose of a gate is to produce a logical output based on its logical inputs. Each gate has its own unique decision-making process that can be expressed in tabular form. These tables are known as *truth tables*. A truth table defines the gate's output for every possible input combination, and all logic ICs (no matter how complex) can be defined by such a table. The gates in Fig. 4-2 are shown with their corresponding truth tables.

Consider the AND gate in Fig. 4-2. An AND gate will only produce a logic 1 output when both of its inputs (A and B) are logic 1. If either of the inputs are logic 0, the AND gate output also will be logic 0. The NAND (an inverted AND or NOT-AND) gate works in just the opposite fashion. The output of a NAND gate is logic 1 if either or both of its inputs are logic 0. Only when both inputs are logic 1 will the NAND gate produce a logic 0. An OR gate operates differently, and will generate a logic 1 when either or both of the inputs are logic 1. When both of the inputs are logic 0, the output will fall to logic 0. The NOR (an inverted OR or NOT-OR) gate behaves just the opposite of an OR gate. The NOR gate produces a logic 1 only when both inputs are in the logic 0 state. If either or both of the inputs are logic 1, the NOR gate produces a logic 0 output. A buffer simply acts as an amplifier gate, so its output will always follow its input. An inverter reverses the input, so a logic 1 input will result in a logic 0 output, and a logic 0 input will cause a logic 1 output.

The XOR (exclusive OR) gate is a variation on the OR gate. When the inputs are both logic 0 or logic 1, the XOR gate produces a logic 0 output. If either (but not both) of the gate's inputs are logic 1, the XOR gate produces a logic 1. The XNOR (exclusive NOR) gate works in the reverse. When the inputs are both logic 1 or logic 0, the XNOR gate produces a logic 1 output. If either (but not both) of the gate's inputs are logic 1, the XNOR gate produces a logic 0.

ASICs

As logic circuits became more and more involved, it was obvious that discrete logic ICs would be totally inadequate to handle complex circuits. You can see this by looking at any old PC motherboard. The sheer number of discrete ICs demanded a great deal of board space (or *real estate*) and power. PC designers sought new ways to reduce the number of logic components by implementing complete logic circuits on the same IC rather than interconnecting discrete ICs. Unfortunately, once generic logic functions are incorporated into a single IC, the logic is no longer generic—the resulting IC is *application-specific*. The use of *ASIC*s (application-specific ICs) is now mandatory in PCs (and all other consumer electronics devices). For the purposes of this book, any IC that performs a single specific function can be referred to as an ASIC (keyboard controllers, video signal generators, programmable interrupt controllers, clock signal generators, and so on). The broad use of ASICs has lead to development of PC chipsets—several related ASICs designed to be used as a set. In fact, PC chipsets have become so powerful and commonplace that glue logic is rarely used at all in current systems.

Standard and low-voltage logic

No matter how complex digital ICs might be, they are still electronic devices. There is a direct relationship between logic levels and voltage levels. Standard logic is based on *TTL* (transistor-transistor logic) components operating with a +5.0-Vdc power supply. As shown in Fig. 4-3, any input signal (V_{ih}) over +2.0 Vdc is considered to be a logic 1, and any input signal (V_{il}) under +0.8 Vdc is interpreted as a logic 0. The range between +0.8 and +2.0 Vdc is typically a region of ambiguity—the gate might interpret the signal as either a 1 or 0. Also notice that the output levels pro-

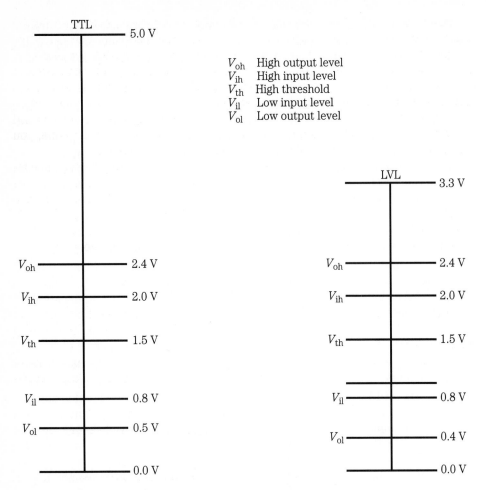

V_{oh} High output level
V_{ih} High input level
V_{th} High threshold
V_{il} Low input level
V_{ol} Low output level

4-3 Comparison of standard versus low-voltage logic levels.

vided by the gate are not the same as the input levels. A gate will produce an output of +2.4 Vdc or higher (V_{oh}) for a logic 1, and +0.5 Vdc or lower (V_{ol}) for a logic 0. This is done on purpose to ensure that a gate's output will drive the input of subsequent gates properly. Although true TTL components have long since been replaced by devices based on CMOS and its variations (that is, HMOS, NMOS, PMOS, and so on), PC circuitry continues to be based on TTL signal levels.

These signal voltages have remained virtually unchanged since the introduction of TTL in the late 1960s, and would probably continue to dominate the logic market if it were not for the explosive growth of portable computers. Even PCs with the most efficient MOS devices make significant demands on available battery power. Although it is the backlight and drives that consume most of a portable PC's power, reducing motherboard and expansion circuit power requirements has become an important priority for PC designers. One of the key elements of reducing power lies in reducing the voltage level required.

To accomplish this feat, many logic devices are systematically being re-designed to accommodate a supply voltage of +3.3 Vdc rather than +5.0 Vdc. Such *LVL* (low-voltage logic) is rapidly becoming standard in sub-notebook and palmtop computers. Even desktop systems are slowly beginning to incorporate low-voltage elements into their design. Figure 4-3 compares the logic signal levels of LVL with those of standard TTL. You will notice that the levels are exactly the same. This was done intentionally to ensure that LVL and TTL components will work together when combined in the same circuit. When examining LVL with a logic probe or oscilloscope, you should not be able to tell the difference between LVL and TTL levels.

When discussing logic circuits, there is often a third state that you should be familiar with. A *high-impedance* state (sometimes referred to as *high-Z* or *tri-state*) is typically used in order to effectively disconnect the component from its signal line or bus without having to physically disconnect the device. This feature is particularly useful when several devices must use the same signal line(s), and you will find that data and address buses make extensive use of high-impedance logic devices.

Interpreting signals and timing

Up to now, you have reviewed logic states, gates, and signal level conventions. This part of the chapter shows you how signals are arranged and expressed. In many cases, you will see that interrelated signals are expressed graphically. Oscilloscope traces, logic analyzer displays, and even specification sheets express signal timing characteristics graphically. The three signal states (1, 0, and high impedance) are illustrated graphically in Fig. 4-4.

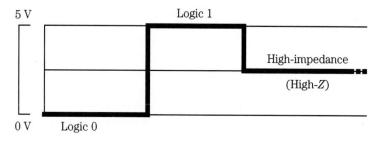

4-4 Comparison of TTL signal levels.

The concept of time

When interpreting timing diagrams, the question of time and timing relationships becomes very important. Although humans measure time in terms of hours and seconds, computers work in much smaller terms. A millisecond (ms or one thousandth of a second) is a relatively long time for a computer. A microsecond (μs) is one millionth of a second, and a nanosecond (ns) is one billionth of a second. As you look at timing signals, time is expressed along the horizontal axis as shown in Fig. 4-5.

Figure 4-5 shows a waveform divided into four distinct areas labeled T_1, T_2, T_3, and T_4. Area T_1 measures the time required for a signal to move from a logic 0 to a valid

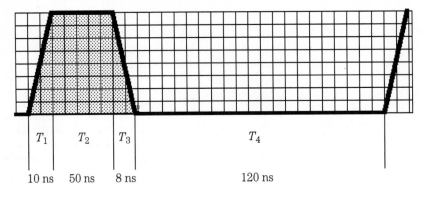

T_1 T_2 T_3 T_4

10 ns   50 ns   8 ns   120 ns

4-5 An example of waveform timing.

logic 1—this is known as *rise time*. Note that this line is slanted rather than a straight vertical line. All signals take some finite amount of time to change state—signals cannot change instantly. If you observe relatively slow signals, the rise time is so small compared to the overall signal that the rise appears vertical. When looking at fast signals, however, the rise time becomes obvious. This is typically a very small amount of time (usually measured in nanoseconds). Because computer operations usually occur on the order of a few microseconds, signal transition times must be considered.

The time T_2 represents the amount of time that the signal is in the logic 1 state. Area T_3 shows the time required for a signal to move from a logic 1 to a valid logic 0—this is known as *fall time*. As with rise time, a signal's fall time is not instantaneous. Although the transition back to logic 0 might appear as a straight vertical line in slow signals, fall time will usually become obvious when observing fast signals. Fall time is generally measured in nanoseconds. Note that fall time does not always equal rise time. Time T_4 represents the amount of time that the signal is in the logic 0 state.

The sum of all four time periods ($T_1 + T_2 + T_3 + T_4$) equals the period (or one *cycle*) of the signal. You can determine *frequency* by taking the reciprocal of the period. For the example of Fig. 4-5, one full cycle of the signal is 170 ns. The reciprocal of 170 ns is ($\frac{1}{170} \times 10^{-9}$) 5.88 MHz (megahertz). If the period were 17 ns, the frequency would be ($\frac{1}{17} \times 10^{-9}$) 58.8 MHz, and so on.

Groups of related signals can be expressed as shown in Fig. 4-6. Data and address bus groups tend to use this type of notation. There are generally four conditions to understand. The signals start off in the high-impedance state. When the buffer or other controlling element enables the signal outputs, there is a brief period of time where the data becomes valid. After the data reaches its stable condition, valid data is available to the rest of the system. Eventually, the data lines will have to return to their high-impedance states, so data will become invalid, then return to a high-impedance state.

Reading the diagram

You can now see a typical timing diagram in action. Figure 4-7 illustrates the timing for a simple ROM (read-only memory) read cycle. Note that there are four key el-

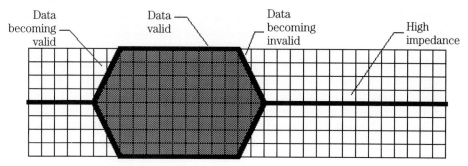

Data becoming valid — Data valid — Data becoming invalid — High impedance

4-6 An example of group signaling.

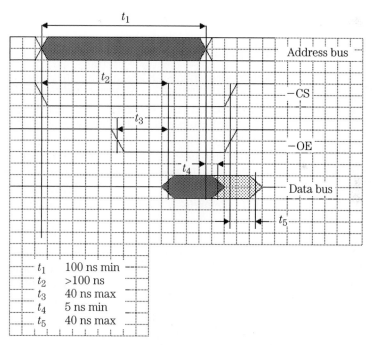

t_1	100 ns min
t_2	>100 ns
t_3	40 ns max
t_4	5 ns min
t_5	40 ns max

4-7 Interpreting a typical ROM read cycle.

ements involved: the memory address, the –Chip Select (–CS) line, the –Output Enable (–OE) line, and the data out of the ROM. Before a ROM can provide data, the
address signals must become valid first, along with the –Chip Select signal. An address specifies the particular memory location to be read, and the –Chip Select line
specifies the particular IC to be activated at that address. Once the address and
–Chip Select is valid, the ROM's –Output Enable line must be activated. After those
three items are in place, data at the selected address will become valid on the ROM's
output, and will remain valid for some amount of time after the –Output Enable and
–Chip Select lines have been deactivated. Note that the –Chip Select and –Output
Enable signals are active-low signals, so they are true in the logic 0 state.

There are strict timing relationships associated with each signal—especially when the entire process just described above takes only a little over 100 ns. For the example of Fig. 4-7, address signals must be valid for at least 100 ns (t_1), and the –Chip Select line must be valid for *no more than* 100 ns (t_2). Similarly, the –Output Enable signal (t_3) must become valid no more than 40 ns before data is to become available. Finally, data is available at the ROM output. Once valid data is available, the address can change or become invalid. Data will remain valid for at least 5 ns (t_4) after the address changes. Also, data will remain valid for no more than 40 ns (t_5) after the –CS or –OE lines are deactivated. Either an address change or enable line shutdown will return the data output to its high-impedance state.

There is little doubt that reading complex timing diagrams is a challenging pursuit that takes effort and practice to master. However, a well-prepared timing diagram can reveal volumes about the operation of a component, system, or bus.

Interpreting architectural diagrams

One of the essential elements to understanding a computer is understanding how each component is interconnected. There are typically two documents that define how any circuit is interconnected: the schematic and the block diagram. *Schematics* offer precise and specific information detailing exactly where every signal and component is connected. However, schematics are often difficult to obtain, and are often so unwieldy that the time needed to fully understand each connection far outstrips any reasonable repair time. Because you are often more concerned with subassembly level repair, it is more beneficial to review the system at a level of abstraction that is removed from a schematic—this is known as the *block diagram* (or architectural diagram).

Figure 4-8 presents the block diagram for a Tandy 1500 HD IBM-compatible AT notebook computer. Although this diagram might appear daunting at first glance, a little bit of study can reveal substantial information about the design and interconnection of key components. In spite of how complex Fig. 4-8 might appear, you will see that there are only three types of symbols: blocks, thin lines, and thick lines. Each symbol has a definite meaning.

A *block* represents a component or a group of components. You might note the DA70108-10 CPU represented as a block, and system ROM and RAM (random-access memory) are presented as groups of blocks. A thin arrowed line is used to represent a single signal line (i.e., an enable line or a single address or data line). Thin lines are often used to denote signals of particular importance or noteworthiness. However, the majority of a PC block diagram is composed of thick arrowed lines. Whenever you see a thick line, you can be certain that a group of signals (a bus) is being represented. Figure 4-8 illustrates three buses at work in the PC: the control bus, the address bus, and the data bus. By following each of these three buses around the diagram, you can see how these signals are distributed and shared throughout the PC. You can even see where the three buses are distributed to the motherboard's expansion slots.

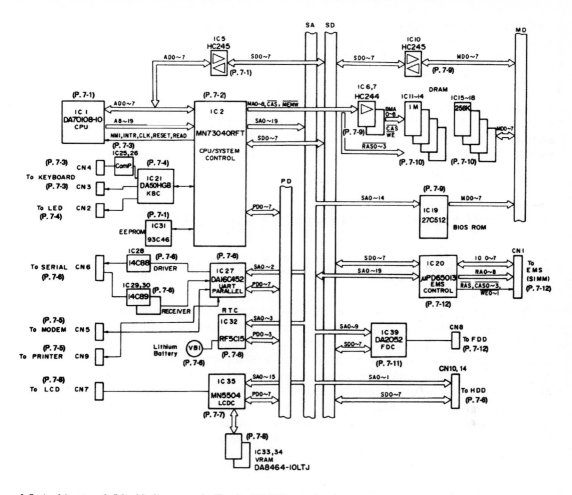

4-8 Architectural (block) diagram of a Tandy 1500HD notebook computer. Tandy Corporation

The flow of signals is determined by the direction of arrows. For example, the system RAM data buffer connects to the data bus over a bidirectional pathway (both ends of the line have an arrow), so data can flow to or from the data bus. However, the control signals that operate that same system RAM are received from the control bus only (only one end of the line has an arrow), so no signals are returned to the control bus.

5
CHAPTER

General-purpose diagnostic tools

The first step in every repair is *diagnosis*—the process of identifying a fault to a high degree of certainty. After all, you cannot fix a problem unless you know where the problem is originating from. So many new technicians fall into the rut of part swapping without really understanding the diagnostic process, or the diagnostic tools at their disposal. As a result, the technician winds up guessing rather than making an informed decision. Through sheer repetition, very experienced technicians tend to have a high probability of success without diagnostics, but new technicians can learn a great deal from diagnostic tools. This chapter is intended to show you a selection of general diagnostic hardware and illustrate some of the test procedures each tool can perform.

Multimeters

Multimeters (Fig. 5-1) are by far the handiest and most versatile pieces of test equipment that you will ever use. If your toolbox does not contain a good-quality multimeter already, now would be a good time to consider purchasing one. Even the most basic digital multimeters are capable of measuring resistance, ac and dc voltage, and ac and dc current. For under $150, you can buy a digital multimeter that includes handy features like a capacitance checker, a frequency meter, an extended current measuring range, a continuity buzzer, and even a diode and transistor checker. These are features that will aid you not only in computer and peripheral repairs, but in many other types of electronic repairs as well. Digital multimeters are easier to read, more tolerant of operator error, and more precise then their analog predecessors.

Meter setup

For most multimeters, there are only three considerations during setup and use. First, turn the meter on. Unlike analog multimeters, digital multimeters require power to operate liquid crystal or LED displays. Make sure that you turn meter

B+K Precision

5-1
A B+K Precision
Model 2707 multimeter.

power off again when you are done with your testing. Power awareness will help you conserve battery life. Second, your meter must be set to its desired function or mode. The function might be frequency, voltage, capacitance, resistance, etc., depending on the particular physical parameter that you wish to measure.

Finally, you must select the meter *range* for its selected function. Ideally, you should choose the range that is nearest to (but higher than) the level you expect to measure. For example, suppose you are measuring a 9-Vdc transistor battery. You would set your meter to the dc voltage function, then set your range as close to (but greater than) 9 Vdc as possible. If your voltage ranges are 0.2 Vdc, 2 Vdc, 20 Vdc, and 200 Vdc, selecting the 20-Vdc range is the best choice.

If you are unsure about just which range to use, start by choosing the highest possible range. Once you actually take some measurements and get a better idea of the actual reading, you can then adjust the meter range "on the fly" to achieve a more precise reading. If your reading exceeds the meter's current range, an over-range warning will be displayed until you increase the meter's range above the measured value. Some digital multimeters are capable of automatically selecting the appropriate range setting once a signal is applied.

Checking test leads

It is usually a good idea to check the integrity of your test leads from time to time. Because test leads undergo a serious amount of tugging and general abuse, you should be able to confirm that the probes are working as expected. There are few experiences more frustrating than to invest time and money replacing assemblies that your meter suggested were faulty, only to discover that meter leads had an internal fault.

To check your probes, set your meter to the *resistance* function, then select the lowest scale (that is, 0.1 Ω). You will see an overrange condition—this is to be expected when setting up for resistance measurements. Check to be sure that both test probes are inserted into the meter properly, then touch the probe tips together. The resistance reading should drop to about 0 Ω to indicate that your meter probes are intact. If you do not see roughly 0 Ω, check your probes carefully. After you have proven out your test probes, return the multimeter to its original function and range so that you can continue testing.

You might see other terms related to multimeter testing: static and dynamic. *Static* tests are usually made on components (either in or out of a circuit) with power removed. Resistance, capacitance, and semiconductor junction tests are all static tests. *Dynamic* tests typically examine circuit conditions, so power must be applied to the circuit, and all components must be in place. Voltage, current, and frequency are the most common dynamic tests.

Measuring voltage

Every signal in your PC has a certain amount of voltage associated with it. By measuring signal voltages with a multimeter (or other test instrument), you can usually make a determination as to whether or not the signal is correct. Supply voltages that provide power to your circuits also can be measured to ensure that components are receiving enough energy to operate. Voltage tests are the most fundamental (and the most important) dynamic tests in electronic troubleshooting.

Multimeters can measure both dc voltages (marked DCV or Vdc) and ac voltages (marked ACV or Vac) directly. Remember that **all** voltage measurements are taken **in parallel** with the desired circuit or component. **Never** interrupt a circuit and attempt to measure voltage in series with other components. Any such reading would be meaningless, and your circuit will probably not even function.

Follow your setup guidelines and configure your meter to measure ac or dc voltage as required, then select the proper range for the voltages you will be measuring. If you are unsure just what range to use, always start with the largest possible range. An autoranging multimeter will set its own range once a signal is applied. Place your test leads across (**in parallel with**) the circuit or part under test (or PUT) as shown in Fig. 5-2, then read voltage directly from the meter's digital display. Voltage readings of dc are polarity sensitive, so if you read +5 Vdc and reverse the test leads, you will see a reading of –5 Vdc. Voltage readings of ac are not polarity sensitive.

Measuring current

Most general-purpose multimeters allow you to measure ac current (marked ACA or Iac) and dc current (marked DCA or Idc) in an operating circuit, although there are typically fewer ranges to choose from. As with voltage measurements, current is a dynamic test, so the circuit or component being tested must be under power. However, current *must* be measured *in series* with a circuit or component.

Unfortunately, inserting a meter in series is not always a simple task. In many cases, you must interrupt a circuit at the point you wish to measure, then connect your test leads across the break. Although it might be quite easy to interrupt a circuit, remember that you also must put the circuit back together, so use care when choosing a point to break. *Never* attempt to measure current in parallel across a component or circuit. Current meters, by their very nature, exhibit a very low resistance across their test leads (often below 0.1 Ω). Placing a current meter in parallel can cause a short circuit across a component that can damage the component, the circuit under test, or the meter itself.

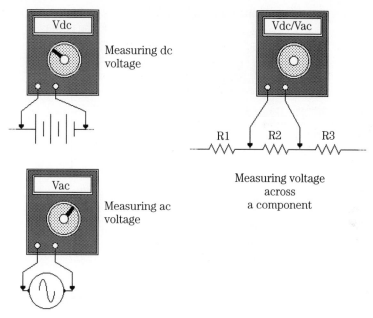

5-2 Measuring voltage.

Set your multimeter to the desired function (DCA or ACA) and select the appropriate range. If you are unsure about the proper range, set the meter to its largest possible range. It is usually necessary to plug your positive test lead into a current input jack on the multimeter. Unless your multimeter is protected by an internal fuse (many meters are protected), its internal current measurement circuits can be damaged by excessive current. Make sure that your meter can handle the maximum amount of current you are expecting.

Turn off all power to a circuit before inserting a current meter. Deactivation prevents any unpredictable or undesirable circuit operation when you actually interrupt the circuit. If you wish to measure power supply current feeding a circuit such as in Fig. 5-3, break the power supply line at any convenient point, insert the meter carefully, then re-apply power. Read current directly from the meter display. This procedure also can be used for taking current measurements within a circuit.

Measuring resistance

Resistance (ohms) is the most common static measurement that your multimeter is capable of. This is a handy function, not only for checking resistors themselves, but for checking other resistive elements like wires, solenoids, motors, connectors, and some basic semiconductor components. Resistance is a static test, so all power to the component or circuit must be removed. It is usually necessary to remove at least one component lead from the circuit to prevent interconnections with other components from causing false readings.

Ordinary resistors, coils, and wires can be checked simply by switching to a resistance function (often marked OHMS, or with the Greek symbol omega, Ω) and se-

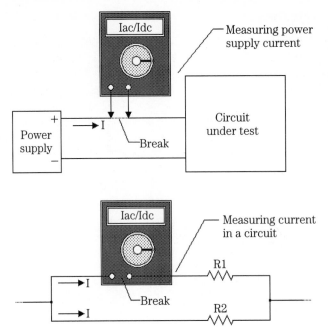

5-3 Measuring current.

lecting the appropriate range. Auto-ranging multimeters will select the proper range after the meter's test leads are connected. Many multimeters can reliably measure resistance up to about 20 MΩ. Place your test leads *in parallel* across the component as shown in Fig. 5-4 and read resistance directly from the meter display. If resistance exceeds the selected range, the display will indicate an overrange (or infinite resistance) connection.

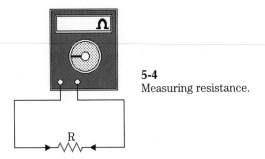

5-4
Measuring resistance.

Continuity checks are made to ensure a reliable, low-resistance connection between two points. For example, you could check the continuity of a cable between two connectors to ensure that both ends are connected properly. Set your multimeter to a low resistance scale, then place your test leads across both points to measure. Ideally, good continuity should be about 0 Ω. Continuity tests also can be taken to show that a short circuit has not occurred between two points.

Measuring capacitors

There are two methods of checking a capacitor using your multimeter: by *exact measurement* and by a *quality check*. The exact measurement test determines the actual value of a capacitor. If the reading is close enough to the value marked on the capacitor, you know the device to be good. If not, you know the device is faulty and should be replaced. Exact measurement requires your multimeter to be equipped with a built-in capacitance checker. If your meter does not have a built-in capacitance checker, you can measure a capacitor directly on any other type of specialized component checker such as the B&K Precision Model 390 Test Bench shown in Fig. 5-5. You also could use your multimeter to perform a simple quality check of a suspect capacitor.

5-5
A B+K Precision Model 391
parts tester.

Capacitor checkers, whether built into your multimeter or part of a stand-alone component checker, are extremely simple to use. Turn off all circuit power. Set the function to measure capacitors, select the range of capacitance to be measured, then place your test probes in parallel across the capacitor to be measured. You should remove at least one of the capacitor's leads from the circuit being tested in order to prevent the interconnections of other components from adversely affecting the capacitance reading. In some cases, it might be easier to remove the suspect part entirely before measuring it. Some meters provide test slots that let you insert the component directly into the meter face. Once in place, you can read the capacitor value directly from the meter display.

If your multimeter is not equipped with an internal capacitor checker, you could still use the resistance ranges of your ohmmeter to approximate a capacitor's quality. This type of check provides a quick-and-dirty judgment of whether the capacitor is good or bad. The principle behind this type of check is simple: all ohmmeter ranges use an internal battery to supply current to the component under test. When that current is applied to a working capacitor as shown in Fig. 5-6, it will cause the capacitor to charge. Charge accumulates as the ohmmeter is left connected. When first connected, the uncharged capacitor draws a healthy amount of current—this reads as low resistance. As the capacitor charges, its rate of charge slows down and less and less current is drawn as time goes on—this results in a gradually increasing resistance level. Ideally,

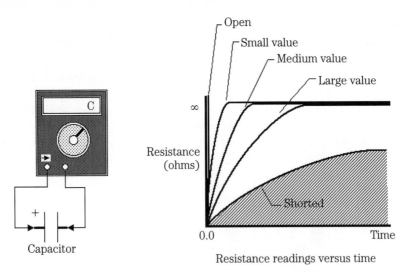

5-6 Making capacitor quality checks using a multimeter.

a fully charged capacitor stops drawing current—this results in an over-range or infinite resistance display. When a capacitor behaves in this way, it is probably good.

Understand that you are not actually measuring resistance or capacitance here, but only the profile of a capacitor's charging characteristic. If the capacitor is extremely small (in the picofarad range), or is open-circuited, it will not accept any substantial charge, so the multimeter will read infinity almost immediately. If a capacitor is partially (or totally) short circuited, it will not hold a charge, so you might read 0 Ω, or resistance might climb to some value below infinity and remain there. In either case, the capacitor is probably defective. If you doubt your readings, check several other capacitors of the same value and compare readings. Be sure to make this test on a moderate to high resistance scale. A low resistance scale might over-range too quickly to achieve a clear reading.

Diode checks

Many multimeters provide a special diode resistance scale used to check the static resistance of common diode junctions. Because working diodes only conduct current in one direction, the diode check lets you determine whether a diode is open or short circuited. Remember that diode checking is a static test, so all power must be removed from the part under test. Before making measurements, be certain that at least one of the diode's leads have been removed from the circuit. Isolating the diode prevents interconnections with other circuit components from causing false readings.

Select the diode option from your multimeter resistance functions. You generally do not have to bother with a range setting while in the diode mode. Connect your test leads *in parallel* across the diode in the forward-bias direction as shown in Fig. 5-7A. A working silicon diode should exhibit a static resistance between about 450 and 700 Ω that will read directly on the meter display. Reverse the orientation of your test probes to reverse bias the diode. Because a working diode will not conduct at all in the reverse direction, you should read infinite resistance.

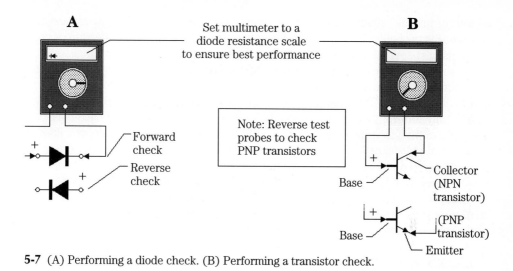

5-7 (A) Performing a diode check. (B) Performing a transistor check.

A short-circuited diode will exhibit a very low resistance in the forward and re-verse-biased directions. This indicates a shorted semiconductor junction. An open-circuited diode will exhibit very high resistance (usually infinity) in both its forward and reverse-biased directions. A diode that is opened or shorted must be replaced. If you feel unsure how to interpret your measurements, test several other comparable diodes and compare readings.

Transistor checks

Transistors are slightly more sophisticated semiconductor devices that can be tested using a transistor checking function on your multimeter or component checker. Transistor junctions also can be checked using a multimeter diode function. The following procedures show you both methods of transistor checking.

Some multimeters feature a built-in transistor checker that measures a bipolar transistor's gain (called *beta*, β, or h_{fe}) directly. By comparing measured gain to the gain value specified in manufacturer's data (or measurements taken from other identical parts), you can easily determine whether the transistor is operating properly. Multimeters with a transistor checker generally offer a test fixture right on the meter face. The fixture consists of two, three-hole sockets: one socket for NPN devices and another hole for PNP devices. If your meter offers a transistor checker, insert the transistor into the test fixture on the meter's face.

Because all bipolar transistors are three-terminal devices (emitter, base, collector), they must be inserted into the meter in their proper lead orientation before you can achieve a correct reading. Manufacturer's data sheets for a transistor will identify each lead and tell you the approximate gain reading that you should expect to see. Once the transistor is inserted appropriately in its correct socket, you can read gain directly from the meter's display.

Set the meter to its transistor checker function. You should not have to worry about selecting a range when checking transistors. Insert the transistor into its test fixture. An unusually low reading (or zero) suggests a short-circuited transistor, and a high (or infinite) reading indicates an open-circuited transistor. In either case, the transistor is probably defective and should be replaced. If you are uncertain of your readings, test several other identical transistors and compare your readings.

If your particular multimeter or parts tester only offers a diode checker, you can approximate the transistor's condition by measuring its semiconductor junctions individually. Figure 5-7B illustrates the transistor junction test method. Although structurally different from conventional diodes, the base-emitter and base-collector junctions of bipolar transistors behave just like diodes. As a general rule, you should remove the transistor from its circuit to prevent false readings caused by other interconnected components. Junction testing also is handy for all varieties of surface-mount transistors that will not fit into conventional multimeter test sockets.

Set your multimeter to its diode resistance function. If your suspect transistor is NPN type (manufacturer's data or a corresponding schematic symbol will tell you), place your *positive* test lead at the transistor's base and place your *negative* test lead on the transistor's emitter. This test lead arrangement should forward-bias the transistor's base-emitter junction and result in a normal amount of diode resistance (450 to 700 Ω). Reverse your test leads across the base-emitter junction. The junction should now be reverse-biased showing infinite resistance. Repeat this entire procedure for the base-collector junction.

If your suspect transistor is the PNP type, the placement of your test leads will have to be reversed from the procedure described in the previous paragraph. In other words, a junction that is forward-biased in an NPN transistor will be reverse-biased in a PNP device. To forward bias the base-emitter junction of a PNP transistor, place your positive test lead on the emitter and your negative test lead on the base. The same concept holds true for the base-collector junction.

Once both junctions are checked, measure the diode resistance from collector to emitter. You should read infinite resistance in both test lead orientations. Although there should be no connection from collector to emitter while the transistor is unpowered, a short-circuit can sometimes develop during a failure. If any of your junctions read an unusually high (or infinite) resistance in both directions, the junction is probably open-circuited. An unusually low resistance (or 0 Ω) in either direction suggests that the junction is short-circuited. Any resistance below infinity between the collector and emitter suggests a damaged transistor. In any case, the transistor should be replaced.

Logic probes

The problem with multimeters is that they do not relate very well to the fast-changing signals found in digital logic circuits. A multimeter can certainly measure whether a logic voltage is on or off, but if that logic signal changes quickly (that is, a clock or bus signal), a dc voltmeter will only show the average signal. A logic probe is little more than an extremely simple voltage sensor, but it can precisely and conveniently detect digital logic levels, clock signals, and digital pulses. Some logic probes can operate at speeds greater than 50 MHz.

Logic probes are rather simple-looking devices as shown in Fig. 5-8. Indeed, logic probes are perhaps the simplest and least expensive test instruments that you will ever use, but they provide valuable and reliable information when you are troubleshooting digital logic circuitry. Logic probes are usually powered from the circuit under test, and they must be connected to the common (ground) of the circuit being tested to ensure a proper reference level. Attach the probe's power lead to any *logic* supply voltage source in the circuit. This is usually +5.0 Vdc, but logic probes are typically capable of working from a wide range of supply voltages (typically +4 to +18 Vdc).

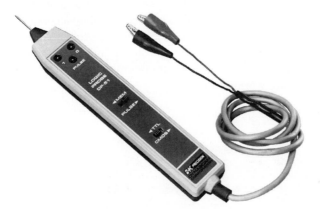

5-8
A B+K Precision Model DP-51
logic probe. B+K Precision

Reading the logic probe

Logic probes use a series of LED indicators to display the measured condition: a logic HIGH (or 1), a logic LOW (or 0), or a pulse (or clock) signal. Many models offer a switch that allows the probe to operate with two common logic families (TTL or CMOS). You might sometimes find TTL and CMOS devices mixed in the same circuit, but one family of logic devices will usually dominate.

In order to use a logic probe, touch its metal tip to the desired IC or component lead. Be certain that the point you wish to measure is, in fact, a logic point—high-voltage signals can damage your logic probe. The logic state is interpreted by a few simple gates within the probe, then displayed on the appropriate LED (or combination of LEDs). Table 5-1 illustrates the LED sequences for one particular type of logic probe. By comparing the probe's measurements to the information contained in an IC service chart or schematic diagram, you can determine whether or not the signal (or suspect IC) is behaving properly.

Table 5-1. Typical logic probe display patterns

Input signal	Hi LED	Low LED	Pulse LED
Logic "1" (TTL or CMOS)	On	Off	Off
Logic "0" (TTL or CMOS)	Off	On	Off
Bad logic level or open circuit	Off	Off	Off
Square wave (<200 kHz)	On	On	Blink
Square wave (>200 kHz)	On/Off	On/Off	Blink
Narrow "high" pulse	Off	On/Off	Blink
Narrow "low" pulse	On/Off	Off	Blink

Oscilloscopes

When it comes to reading signals, oscilloscopes offer a tremendous advantage over multimeters and logic probes. Instead of reading signals in terms of numbers or lighted indicators, an oscilloscope will show voltage versus time on a graphical display. Not only can you observe ac and dc voltages, but oscilloscopes enable you to watch any other unusual signals occur in real time. When used correctly, an oscilloscope allows you to witness signals and events occurring in terms of microseconds or less. If you have used an oscilloscope (or seen one used), then you probably know just how useful they can be. Oscilloscopes, such as the one shown in Fig. 5-9, might appear somewhat overwhelming at first, but many of their operations work the same way regardless of what model you are working with.

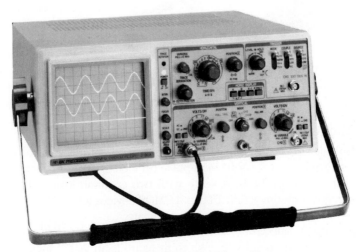

5-9 A B+K Precision Model 2190A 100-MHz oscilloscope. B+K Precision

Oscilloscope start-up procedure

Before you begin taking measurements, a clear, stable trace must be obtained (if not already visible). If a trace is not already visible, make sure that any CRT screen storage modes are turned off and that trace intensity is turned up to at least 50%. Set *trace triggering* to its automatic mode and adjust the horizontal and vertical offset controls to the center of their ranges. Be sure to select an internal trigger source from the channel your probe is plugged in to, then adjust the trigger level until a stable trace is displayed. Vary your vertical offset if necessary to center the trace in the CRT.

If a trace is not yet visible, use the *beam finder* to reveal the beam's location. A beam finder simply compresses the vertical and horizontal ranges to force a trace onto the display. This gives you a rough idea of the trace's relative position. Once you are able to finally move the trace into position, adjust your focus and intensity controls to obtain a crisp, sharp trace. Keep intensity at a moderately low level to improve display accuracy and preserve the *CRT* (cathode-ray tube) phosphors.

Your oscilloscope should be calibrated to its probe before use. A typical oscilloscope probe is shown in Fig. 5-10. Calibration is a quick and straightforward operation that requires only a low-amplitude, low-frequency square wave. Many models have a built-in calibration signal generator (usually a 1-kHz, 300-mV square wave with a duty cycle of 50%). Attach your probe to the desired input jack, then place the probe tip across the calibration signal. Adjust your horizontal (TIME/DIV) and vertical (VOLTS/DIV) controls so that one or two complete cycles are clearly shown on the CRT.

5-10
A B+K Precision Model PR-46
10:1 oscilloscope probe. B+K Precision

Observe the visual characteristics of the test signal as shown in Fig. 5-11. If the square wave's corners are rounded, there might not be enough probe capacitance (sometimes denoted with the label "Cprobe"). Spiked square wave corners suggest too much capacitance in the probe. Either way, the scope and probe are not matched properly. You must adjust the probe capacitance to establish a good electrical match—otherwise, signal distortion will result during your measurements. Slowly adjust the variable capacitance of your probe until the corners shown on the calibration signal are as square as possible. If you are not able to achieve a clean square wave, try a different probe.

Voltage measurements

The first step in any voltage measurement is to set your normal trace (called the *baseline*) where you want it. Normally, the baseline is placed along the center of the graticule during start-up, but it can be placed anywhere along the CRT so long as the trace is visible. To establish a baseline, switch your input coupling control to its ground position. Grounding the input disconnects any existing input signal and ensures a zero reading. Adjust the vertical offset control to shift the baseline wherever you want the zero reading to be (usually in the display center). If you have no particular preference, simply center the trace in the CRT.

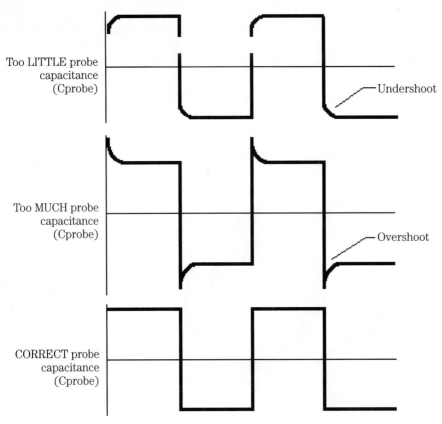

Too LITTLE probe capacitance (Cprobe)

Undershoot

Too MUCH probe capacitance (Cprobe)

Overshoot

CORRECT probe capacitance (Cprobe)

5-11 Oscilloscope calibration waveforms.

To measure dc, set your input coupling switch to its DC position, then adjust the VOLTS/DIV control to provide the desired amount of sensitivity. If you are unsure just which sensitivity is appropriate, start with a very low sensitivity (a large VOLTS/DIV setting), then carefully increase sensitivity (reduce the VOLTS/DIV setting) after your input signal is connected. This procedure prevents a trace from simply jumping off the screen when an unknown signal is first applied. If your signal does happen to leave the visible portion of the display, you could reduce the sensitivity (increase the VOLTS/DIV setting) to make the trace visible again.

For example, suppose you were measuring a +5-Vdc power supply output. If VOLTS/DIV is set to 5 VOLTS/DIV, each major vertical division of the CRT display represents 5 Vdc, so your +5-Vdc signal should appear 1 full division above the baseline (5 VOLTS/DIV × 1 DIV = 5 Vdc) as shown in Fig. 5-12. At a VOLTS/DIV setting of 2 VOLTS/DIV, the same +5 Vdc signal would now appear 2.5 divisions above your baseline (2 VOLTS/DIV × 2.5 DIV = 5 Vdc). If your input signal were a negative voltage, the trace would appear below the baseline, but it would be read the same way.

Alternating-current signals also can be read directly from the oscilloscope. Switch your input coupling control to its ac position, then set a baseline just as you would for dc measurements. If you are unsure about how to set the vertical

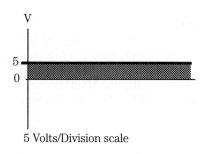 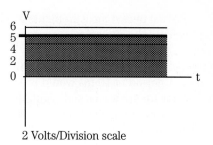

5 Volts/Division scale   2 Volts/Division scale

5-12 Measuring dc voltages with an oscilloscope.

sensitivity, start with a low sensitivity (a large VOLTS/DIV setting), then slowly increase the sensitivity (reduce the VOLTS/DIV setting) once your input signal is connected. Keep in mind that ac voltage measurements on an oscilloscope will not match ac voltage readings on a multimeter. An oscilloscope displays instantaneous peak values for a waveform, and ac voltmeters measure in terms of *rms* (root mean square) values. To convert a peak voltage reading to rms, divide the peak reading by 1.414. Another limitation of multimeters is that they can only measure sinusoidal ac signals. Square, triangle, or other unusual waveforms will be interpreted as an average value by a multimeter.

When actually measuring an ac signal, it might be necessary to adjust the oscilloscope's trigger level control to obtain a stable (still) trace. Signal voltages can be measured directly from the display. For example, the sinusoidal waveform of Fig. 5-13 varies from –10 to +10 V. If oscilloscope sensitivity were set to 5 VOLTS/DIV, signal peaks would occur two divisions above and two divisions below the baseline. Because the oscilloscope provides peak measurements, an ac voltmeter would show the signal as peak/1.414 [10/1.414] or 7.07 V_{rms}.

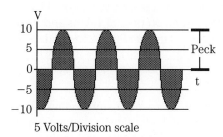 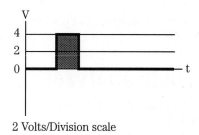

5 Volts/Division scale   2 Volts/Division scale

5-13 Measuring ac voltages with an oscilloscope.

Time and frequency measurements

An oscilloscope is an ideal tool for measuring critical parameters such as pulse width, duty cycle, and frequency. It is the horizontal sensitivity control (TIME/DIV) that comes into play with time and frequency measurements. Before making any measurements, you must first obtain a clear baseline as you would for voltage measurements. When a baseline is established and a signal is finally connected, adjust the TIME/DIV control to display one or two complete signal cycles.

Typical period measurements are illustrated in Fig. 5-14. With VOLTS/DIV set to 5.0 ms/DIV, the sinusoidal waveform shown repeats every two divisions. This represents a period of [5mS/DIV × 2 DIV] 10 ms. As you saw in the previous chapter, frequency is simply the reciprocal of time, so it can be calculated by inverting the time value. A period of 10 ms would represent a frequency of [1/10 ms] 100 Hz. This also works for square waves and regularly repeating nonsinusoidal waveforms. The square wave shown in Fig. 5-14 repeats every four divisions. At a TIME/DIV setting of 1mS/DIV, its period would be 4.0 ms. This corresponds to a frequency of [1/4 mS] 250 Hz.

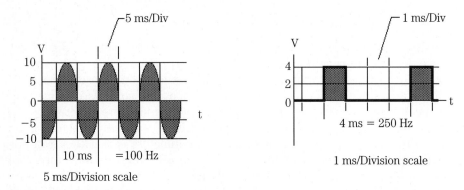

5-14 Measuring time and frequency with an oscilloscope.

Instead of measuring the entire period of a pulse cycle, you also can read the time between any two points of interest. For the square wave of Fig. 5-14, you could read the pulse width to be 1.0 ms. You also could read the low portion of the cycle as a duration of 3.0 ms (added together for a total signal period of 4.0 ms). A signal's *duty cycle* is simply the ratio of a signal on time to its total period expressed as a percentage. For example, a square wave that is on for 2.0 ms and off for 2.0 ms would have a duty cycle of [2 ms / (2 ms + 2 ms) × 100%] 50%. For an on time of 1.0 ms and an off time of 3.0 ms, its duty cycle would be [1 ms / (1 ms + 3 ms) × 100%] 25%, and so on.

Logic analyzer

As useful and flexible as an oscilloscope can be, there are many circumstances when it would be very helpful to evaluate a selection of digital signals simultaneously so that logic signals can be compared in terms of state (1s and 0s) and timing relationships. A logic analyzer is a powerful analytical tool that can represent digital information in terms of waveform timing, *ACSII* (American Standard Code for Information Interchange) characters, or binary and hexadecimal patterns. Many logic analyzers can record their readings on a printer, or record to a floppy disk or solid-state memory card for further evaluation. Although most logic analyzers are sophisticated stand-alone pieces of test equipment, there are a growing number of PC-based analyzers that can be run through an ordinary desktop computer. PC-based analyzers often lack the bells and whistles found in stand-alone units, but are well suited for basic, budget-conscious repair shops. Logic analyzers are extremely effective at studying computer bus operations, so you can locate problems in core logic.

Because of the setup complexity and operating variations between logic analyzers, it is impossible to describe them adequately in only a few book pages—manufacturer's guides and owner's manuals will tell you everything that you need to know. For the moment, you should realize that a logic analyzer is an important (but expensive) troubleshooting tool that can speed your repairs of microprocessor-based systems such as computers or computer peripherals.

High-voltage probes

Although multimeters and oscilloscopes are handy for measuring potentials up to several hundred volts, they are totally inappropriate instruments for measuring high voltage at the CRT anode of a monitor. Under normal operation, anode voltage can be anywhere from 15 to 30 kV (kilovolts) or more depending on the size and vintage of the individual monitor. A high-voltage probe is a specially designed test instrument that can safely and effectively measure anode voltages. The B+K Precision Model HV-44 shown in Fig. 5-15 can handle up to 40 kV. Because excessive high voltage can present an X-radiation danger, it is important that you check the anode voltage as the very first step in every monitor repair. If you do not have a high-voltage probe, it is a worthwhile investment.

5-15 A B+K Precision Model HV-44 high-voltage probe.

Using a high-voltage probe is every bit as easy as using a multimeter. Connect the probe's ground clip to power supply ground, then gently slip the probe tip beneath the rubber anode cover until you reach the anode's metal conductors. Take your high-voltage reading directly from the meter. The B&K HV-44 provides you with two interchangeable metal probe tips.

High-voltage probe safety

Even though high-voltage probes are designed to operate safely at very high voltages, remember these important safety considerations. First, inspect the high-voltage probe very carefully before using it. Its insulating properties can be compromised if there are any chips or cracks in the plastic housing. The probe surface also must be completely clean and dry. Make sure that the metal probe tip is inserted properly and completely, but do not use hand tools to tighten the tip—scratches in the tip can act as discharge points for high voltage. Use only one hand to hold the probe and keep your other hand behind your back or in a pocket. Serious shocks can still occur if the probe's insulation should breach while you are holding onto a ground conductor with the other hand. Finally, commercial high-voltage probes are designed for measuring positive voltages. Connecting a negative or alternating voltage can damage the probe.

CRT testers/restorer

In spite of their size and complexity, CRTs are basically nothing more than big vacuum tubes. Like all vacuum tubes, CRTs gradually degrade over time and eventually fail. Degrading CRTs can reduce picture quality, brightness, and sharpness. When supply voltages and electrical signal levels measure properly during a monitor repair, the CRT becomes suspect. You can simply replace the CRT when troubleshooting symptomatically. When you have to deal with a large volume of monitors (especially older monitors), it is often worth investing in a full-featured CRT tester/restorer. The B&K Precision Model 480 (Fig. 5-16) is one such piece of test equipment.

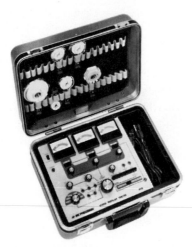

5-16
A B+K Precision Model 480 video.
B+K Precision

The Model 480 is designed for use with most monochrome and color CRTs. In actual use, the 480 tests for emission, leakage, tracking, life, and focus. These five tests provide a comprehensive picture of the CRT's overall condition. *Emission* tests the CRT's electron gun(s) to see that each one can produce adequate brightness on the picture tube. *Leakage* tests check the CRT's cathode(s) for partial short circuits. Because cathodes provide the source for an electron beam, leakage can reduce the brightness of an image or result in too little of a primary color. A *life expectancy* test is performed when the results of an emission test show marginal results. *Tracking* checks that each of the three electron guns in a color CRT exhibit roughly equal performance as their excitation signals vary. If the guns do not perform equally, variations in monitor power might cause color fluctuations in the screen image. The *focus* test checks the integrity of a CRT's focus grid(s).

The Model 480 also can perform a limited amount of CRT rejuvenation by clearing shorts, cleaning and balancing electron guns, and rejuvenating cathodes. Although rejuvenation will not make a CRT as good as new, it can restore a monitor's operation for a while longer and save the customer the expense of a new CRT installation. Electron gun assemblies are extremely small and tightly packaged devices. Over time, coating materials can become loose and short with adjacent elements. The *remove shorts* feature uses a high energy discharge from a capacitor to zap any shorts that might be causing excessive leakage. The *rejuvenate cathode* function can be used after a low or marginal emission test. Rejuvenation restores a cathode's operation by applying a large positive voltage between the cathode and the controlling grid.

Monitor testers/analyzers

Because you often judge the performance of monitors based on what you see on the screen, image quality can easily become a subjective matter. Monitor testers provide a class of test equipment that allows you to test and align the monitor using standard visual patterns. Some testers also incorporate meter functions that allow you to actually perform circuit measurements while the equipment is connected.

The Network Technologies MONTEST AD24 (Fig. 5-17) is one such monitor tester. The AD24 is designed to offer four major test patterns at eight horizontal scanning frequencies ranging from 15.7 to 35.0 kHz. The AD24 supports VGA, MAC II, MCA, CGA, EGA, PGA, Hewlett-Packard, MicroVax, and Apollo monitors. Both TTL and analog video signals are provided. A *cross hatch* (or Xhatch) pattern is used to test convergence and focus. The *raster* pattern tests color purity. An array of *color bars* tests color balance between various colors as well as overall screen intensity settings. A *window* pattern helps discern the condition of a monitor's high-voltage system. NTI offers several different models of MONTEST monitor testers. At about the price of a good oscilloscope, NTI's line of testers is a handy addition to the professional test bench.

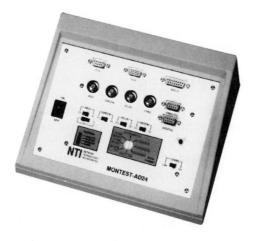

5-17
A Montest AD24 monitor tester.
Montest A5D3, Montest AD16, and Montest AD24 are the manufactured products of Network Technologies, Inc. 1275 Danner Drive, Aurora, OH 44202 Tel: 216-562-7070 or 800-742-8324

6
CHAPTER

PC-specific
diagnostic tools

Diagnostics play an important role in PC service. True, many PC faults can be predicted based upon a system's symptoms, but the ability of diagnostics to identify and define a specific fault can take the guesswork out of many repairs, preventing an error or misinterpretation of a symptom can save you precious repair time and reduce the cost of the repair for your customer. This chapter examines the attributes and features of many of the commercial PC diagnostic software available, as well as a selection of PC hardware tools. This chapter is certainly not intended to be an all-inclusive review of available products, but it does represent a broad cross-section.

Before you read on, you also should understand that the information provided in this chapter is not intended to be an endorsement or recommendation of any particular product or manufacturer—few diagnostics are significantly better or worse than any other. Instead, this chapter is intended to emphasize the strengths and advantages of each product. As a technician, it is up to you to match each product against your own diagnostic needs before making any purchase decisions.

Test and alignment packages

One of the compelling advantages of digital circuitry is its absolute nature—a bad bit (even a series of bad bits) can be detected from a massive stream of data and corrected with great accuracy. Although the personal computer and its peripherals are almost entirely digital systems, there are two major areas that continue to rely on analog circuitry and mechanical fixturing: drives and monitors. Analog circuits are hardly absolute. Mechanical wear and signal variations in the physical world can easily result in problems such as drive read/write errors or monitor image distortion. In actual practice, floppy drives are the only drive type to tolerate physical alignment (hard drives are sealed devices, and CD-ROM drives are far too delicate). Image problems also can be evaluated and adjusted. The following tools illustrate several alignment products.

AlignIt (Landmark Research International, Inc.)

Landmark's AlignIt is a simple, low-end test/alignment product designed more for the end-user than busy technicians. Although it is menu driven and easy to use, the AlignIt display is extremely spartan; test results are illustrated as rudimentary black-and-white bar graphs. The update times for many of the tests appear quite slow. In spite of the questionable display, AlignIt boasts an accuracy of ±0.3 mil and a repeatability of 0.3% using a specially formatted SpiralTrack™ disk. Eleven tests cover all of the major floppy drive parameters: (1) head alignment, (2) read and write testing, (3) head linearity, (4) head hysteresis, (5) file access, (6) write-protect detection, (7) track 0 detection, (8) disk clamping and centering, (9) spindle speed, (10) interference, and (11) head wear.

AlignIt supports 360K, 1.2Mb, 720K, and 1.44Mb floppy drives, and no specialized hardware is needed. Test reports can be printed. In addition to the alignment product, the AlignIt package also comes with prelubricated 5¼- and 3½-inch cleaning disks that are rated for 300 uses. This is a product for cost-conscious PC enthusiasts who occasionally test and tweak floppy drives.

DriveProbe (Accurite Technologies Inc.)

Of all the floppy testing and alignment products in the marketplace, Accurite's DriveProbe is probably the most precise software-based package available. Accurite actually manufactures many of the reference disks used by other floppy alignment packages, so they are well-versed in the techniques of accurate drive testing. Their High-Resolution Diagnostic (HRD™) disk allows testing with accuracy of 50 µ", more than enough for confident drive alignment. The menu-driven software provides test information in the form of black-and-white bar graphs and tables. Although this is still rather plain, the displays are updated continuously that supports real-time adjustment of the drive. DriveProbe provides the six key tests that are essential to proper drive operation: (1) spindle speed, (2) disk clamping and alignment, (3) radial head alignment, (4) azimuth head alignment, (5) index to data timing, and (6) positioner hysteresis. DriveProbe also offers a series of data patterns that can be used to test the drive's ability to read and write data without errors.

DriveProbe supports 360K, 1.2Mb, 720K, and 1.44Mb floppy drives, and no specialized hardware is needed. Test reports can be printed. Unlike other floppy alignment products, DriveProbe does not provide cleaning diskettes. DriveProbe is a product for professionals—if you're a technician, or have a large number of floppy drives to deal with, this is a worthwhile investment.

FloppyTune (Data Depot, Inc.)

At its core, Data Depot's FloppyTune is a carbon copy of Landmark's AlignIt; it performs the same 11 tests: (1) head alignment, (2) read and write testing, (3) head linearity, (4) head hysteresis, (5) file access, (6) write-protect detection, (7) track 0 detection, (8) disk clamping and centering, (9) spindle speed, (10) interference, and (11) head wear. FloppyTune uses the same SpiralTrack™ disk as AlignIt, and subsequently offers the same ±0.3 mil of accuracy. Even the menu and data displays are remarkably similar. The real strength of FloppyTune is its manual that is probably the most thorough and complete of any floppy alignment product. Not only does the manual describe how to use the product, it also discusses remedial action, and provides some unique reference notes that are hard to find elsewhere.

FloppyTune supports 360K, 1.2Mb, 720K, and 1.44Mb floppy drives, and no specialized hardware is needed. Test reports can be printed. In addition to the alignment product, the FloppyTune package also comes with prelubricated 5¼- and 3½-inch Marauder cleaning disks.

System inspection utilities

System inspection utilities allow you to peek inside a PC without removing the cover. An inspection program will typically present you with a series of hardware parameters (that is, the drives, expansion boards and adapters, main chipsets, and hardware resources available) as well as the system's software parameters (that is, DOS version, hooks, drivers loaded, and so on). A system inspection utility is generally not regarded as a diagnostic, although they might be marketed as such. The advantage of an inspection program is that a technician can rapidly and accurately know what is detected in the system before starting the work. Prospective system buyers can get a clear picture of a system's configuration before making a purchase. Several inspection packages are detailed in this section.

CheckIt Pro: Advanced System Information Utility (TouchStone Software)

SysInfo is one half of the two-part CheckIt Pro package from TouchStone Software. The DOS utility provides over 50 screens of charts, tables, and graphic representations to illustrate the hardware and software configuration of a system. Technicians who see a large number of systems coming across their workbench will find this to be a very helpful tool—especially information on IRQ and I/O port utilization—but the CPU, expansion bus, memory, drive, video, network, and modem data offer a first-class picture of the current system. A built-in CMOS save and restore function allows the system CMOS contents to be saved as a file, then restored if the CMOS IC or its battery ever fail. SysInfo also benchmarks the CPU, drive subsystem, and video sub-system that allows you to compare the current system against other PCs. Quick and easy to use, SysInfo goes a long way toward filling the PC information gap for busy technicians.

Computer Consultant (Micro2000)

Computers today are commodity items; many are sold with a great deal of hype, where the specifications thrown at you without any real frame of reference. When you couple this with the dreadful lack of expertise shown by many computer sales people, it isn't hard to see how buying a PC is often a headache that leads to rapid disappointment. Micro 2000 has developed their Computer Consultant as a carry-along advisor that can be used to check the system's configuration and performance before making a purchasing decision. The Computer Consultant makes no attempt to portray itself as a diagnostic. On the contrary, it is packaged and marketed strictly as an end-user tool. The 3½- and 5¼-inch disks come packaged in a nifty binder, along with a pad where you can write down the specifications revealed by the software.

The idea is that you haul this along when you go computer shopping and tell the sales person to take a hike. Plug the disk into the drive, and boot the system. Computer Consultant boots automatically without DOS or Windows to clutter things up, then identifies a range of system capabilities: (1) PC model and manufacturer, (2) BIOS manufacturer, (3) expansion bus type, (4) resident operating system, (5) available drives, (6) hard drive model and parameters, (7) video type and manufacturer, (8) monitor type, (9) available serial and parallel ports, (10) keyboard type, and (11) network adapter. Real-time testing shows you true processor speed, memory access speed, video speed, and hard drive speed. This package fills a vital niche for end users by showing PC capabilities without forcing the user to wade through screen after screen of technical information.

Microsoft Diagnostic (MSD) (Microsoft Corp.)

It's not often that Microsoft gives something away, but MSD is one of those utilities that have been bundled with DOS and Windows for several years now. MSD is clearly a lightweight utility when compared to most of the commercial and shareware products that are available, but it can provide you with a surprising amount of information about the way a system is configured. MSD will tell you what IRQ lines and I/O ports are in use, and will reveal a variety of memory address problems. MSD also offers system information such as CPU type, BIOS data, video, network, ports (serial and parallel), DOS, and version. You can find which device drivers are loaded (very handy when configuring an upgrade). MSD does a great job of revealing drives, including CD-ROM drives. If you need a quick system rundown, and you're hesitant to go out and buy a product off-the-shelf, give MSD a try. It lacks any bells and whistles, but it is generally regarded as quite accurate.

PC Tools (Central Point)

PC Tools by Central Point represents a collection of powerful tools that are assembled into a single toolkit. Available in both DOS and Windows versions, PC Tools brings some significant resources to the average PC (you will see several references to PC Tools throughout this chapter). One of the more frequently used features is the System Consultant. For the most part, the System Consultant provides the standard system configuration data including video, drives, ports, BIOS, CPU, and so on. DOS parameters allow you to view the DOS version, environment, startup files, memory map, and so on. Under Windows, you can view .INI files, and review Windows resources. Although the System Consultant is not a particular strength of PC Tools, it is a handy feature that augments the antivirus and drive management control that PC Tools is known for.

WhatCOM (Data Depot, Inc.)

One of the most difficult configurations in a PC is the modem (more specifically, the serial ports). Determining what COM ports are available, and how to configure the modem to work with those ports can often be a nightmare, even for experienced technicians. WhatCOM by Data Depot automatically tests for the presence of COM ports and looks for attached modems or other serial devices. It then provides advice on how to install new serial ports and modems, and allows you to test the devices to see that they are working. It can even test most modems that are not Hayes-compatible. WhatCOM is not a generic inspection utility, but it does provide a guide that fills an important need for technicians and PC users alike.

DOS diagnostics

DOS diagnostics are the backbone of PC troubleshooting. Good diagnostics tend to be small, utility-oriented products that require an absolute minimum operating system (DOS or self-loading) and system resources. Diagnostics not only detect a system configuration and resources, but test those resources to ensure proper operation. The following products represent a cross-section of popular diagnostics.

AMIDiag (American Megatrends)

AMIDiag by American Megatrends has a long-standing history of aggressive and thorough testing. Version 4.5 continues that tradition. AMIDiag is designed to test 6 areas of the PC: (1) the system board, (2) the memory, (3) the hard disk, (4) the floppy disk, (5) the keyboard, and (6) the video system. Although this might not seem terribly versatile at first glance, these are the key areas of all PCs, and the testing routines themselves are considered to be remarkably comprehensive. Of particular note are the memory tests—few diagnostics test the BIOS, cache, and memory paging and interleave—in addition to system RAM testing. Floppy drive testing includes a check of the disk Change Line signal. Change Line faults cause the phantom directory problem that can wreak havoc with files when changing floppy disks. AMIDiag provides some of the best keyboard and controller testing available.

AMIDiag 4.5 tests EISA and PCI operations. By selecting the appropriate test, AMIDiag will proceed to examine the corresponding EISA or PCI devices in the system. This proves to be a powerful asset for newer motherboards. AMIDiag also provides a test for SoundBlaster and compatible sound cards. There are two other areas where AMIDiag 4.5 is effective: it can detect SCSI devices in the system (provided that ASPI drivers are loaded), as well as PCMCIA devices (card and socket services driv-ers must be loaded). As an added bonus, AMIDiag can be set to run in continuous loops for system testing and "burn-in."

All in all, AMIDiag is a good package that provides technicians with a variety of powerful tools rarely found together in the same product. Although SCSI and PCMCIA support are still a bit light, AMI is clearly moving in the right direction.

CheckIt Pro: Advanced Diagnostic Software (TouchStone Software)

Tests & Tools is the second half of TouchStone Software's CheckIt Pro package. Where SysInfo emphasized the detection of PC hardware and utilization, Tests & Tools focuses on diagnosing problem areas in the PC. System board tests include the

CPU, MCP, RTC, IRQ controllers, and DMA controllers. Memory tests check conventional, upper, EMS, XMS, and video memory areas. Drive tests include the typical hard and floppy drives, as well as DOS data structures. It is interesting to note that the floppy testing uses the same SpiralDisk_ technology used by AlignIt and Floppy-Tune, but the spiral disk is not included with the package. Video test routines allow you to inspect both the video adapter and monitor. Serial and parallel port tests check the system's communication ability. Tests & Tools also provides a series of basic printer checks to make sure your printer is working properly with the system. In addition, the package provides checking for over 2000 virus signatures.

Although Tests & Tools covers a lot of basic ground, it lacks some of the more advanced features that technicians have come to need such as CD-ROM, network board, SCSI adapter, and sound board tests. The floppy spiral disk also is noticeably absent. Ultimately, Tests & Tools (and CheckIt Pro in general) is a fair beginner's package that offers a bit of everything for the PC enthusiast. But professionals might find themselves disappointed.

MicroScope (Micro2000)

Like so many other diagnostic products, MicroScope by Micro2000 is split between a system information gatherer, and a system tester. In its system information mode, MicroScope offers a complete breakdown of the system's configuration—processing components, BIOS, drives, ports, memory, CMOS settings, and video adapter information are all presented. An interesting plus is MicroScope's active ROM search that details the check for other ROMs in the system, and attempts to identify each one. MicroScope also details a listing of IRQs, I/O port assignments, and memory vectors. As a system diagnostic, MicroScope tests the major system areas including the system board, memory, floppy drive, hard drive, ports, keyboard, and video system.

Although MicroScope sounds run-of-the-mill, there are some important features that are vital to technicians that are found almost nowhere else. First, MicroScope allows virtually unlimited access to a hard drive's partition tables, including the ability to write and edit master boot records and partitions. Although errors and viruses can damage these areas resulting in an unusable drive, the ability to edit these areas makes MicroScope an unusually powerful drive tool. The range and variety of floppy and hard drive tests are unparalleled by other diagnostics. Floppy and fixed disk editor utilities allow data to be changed on a drive at the byte level in either ASCII or hexadecimal. MicroScope offers a master boot sector rebuilding tool and a floppy head cleaning function. Finally, MicroScope supports the low-level format of IDE drives, as well as a low-level format of SCSI drives using the SCSI adapter BIOS. Ultimately, MicroScope is one of the most versatile and powerful drive diagnostics available, well worth the high price tag if you specialize in drive recovery.

PC Clinic SB (Data Depot, Inc.)

The PC Clinic is a self-booting (SB) product from Data Depot that does not require DOS or Windows in order to run. There are three major areas to PC Clinic: system configuration data, system diagnostics, and benchmarks. When used to test the system's configuration, PC Clinic behaves much like the inspection utilities covered in the previous section. It provides a detailed report on the system type, BIOS date,

BIOS maker, CPU MCP, keyboard, expansion bus, video system, memory fixed and floppy disks, and ports. It also presents a breakdown of CMOS information, shows IRQ, DMA, and I/O use, and provides a detailed device driver memory map. This makes PC Clinic useful when examining a system before a repair or upgrade.

PC Clinic then offers a suite of diagnostics to test the motherboard circuits, memory, floppy drives, hard drives, serial ports, parallel ports, video system, and keyboard. To evaluate a system against other standard systems, PC Clinic offers a series of benchmark tests. Benchmarks and diagnostic timing measurements are typically regarded as more accurate without the software interrupts called under DOS. What PC Clinic lacks are advanced features such as SCSI adapter testing and CD-ROM evaluation. Aside from those limitations, PC Clinic is a versatile midrange evaluator/test package that will come in handy for just about any do-it-yourselfer, and many technicians.

PC Technician (Windsor Technologies)

Of all the products in this chapter, the PC Technician by Windsor Technologies (Fig. 6-1) is the most pure and professional self-booting diagnostic. On the surface, PC Technician checks all of the areas covered by other diagnostics: the motherboard, memory, drives, and ports. When you look deeper, though, you find a comprehensive set of features that are very well-balanced for day-to-day PC troubleshooting. Testing is divided into two levels: certification and diagnostics. The certification level puts the overall PC through its paces by testing the system board, MCP, memory (conventional, upper, extended, and expanded), floppy drives, hard drives, COM ports, and LPT ports.

6-1
The PC Technician from Windsor Technologies. Windsor Technologies, Inc.

When errors are detected, the diagnostic level can be applied to isolate the problem area. Diagnostics cover the keyboard, video system, parallel port, floppy drives, hard drives, serial ports, and memory. Keyboard testing supports five different styles of keyboard. Video system testing supports not only standard monitor alignment patterns, but video adapter operations also. Parallel interface testing works through a loopback plug to isolate problems in data lines or handshake signals. Serial interface testing also uses a loopback plug to examine port operations. PC Technician can perform a variety of testing on ST506/412, ESDI, IDE, and SCSI drives with equal ease, and it can low-level format both IDE and SCSI drives. In addition to SCSI drive support, PC Technician also tests SCSI tape drives. Although SCSI CD-ROMs are not yet covered, future revisions might support it and other SCSI devices. PC Technician offers a wide array of memory testing features (including cache memory), and even provides guidance finding bad memory modules. Serious technicians should consider adding the PC Technician to their toolbox.

QAPlus and QAPlus/FE (DiagSoft)

QAPlus by DiagSoft has proven to be one of the smoothest crosses between a system information product and a system diagnostic. In general, QAPlus runs a system information routine that reports the hardware that is installed and running. What makes the package so handy is that in addition to a complete breakdown of standard hardware (that is, the CPU, MCP, memory, video system, and so on), it includes devices such as game ports, the mouse, a sound board, a CD-ROM, and a scanner. Disk performance and system performance routines provide a benchmark comparison of the system against a standard. Interactive testing allows real-time testing of a mouse, joystick, serial port, speaker, and keyboard, as well as helping to track down bad RAM locations. Although QAPlus is marketed as a diagnostic, the style and layout of the program indicate a strong emphasis on production line testing, even its CMOS editor and utilities such as QAClean (for cleaning floppy drives), Hard Disk Prep (to low-level format MFM drives, and Hard Disk Park (to park R/W heads) suggest that the PC is ready to ship out the door any moment. The lack of fundamental support for drives other than MFM is a serious shortcoming. If you're building PCs in volume, QAPlus is a good choice for, well, Quality Assurance. If you're faced with a faulty PC, however, you might want to consider a more powerful tool like QAPlus/FE.

DiagSoft's QAPlus/FE contains all of the basic system information and reporting infrastructure found in QAPlus, but /FE takes the QAPlus line several steps further by adding MIDI port testing, and a CMOS editor that can save to or recall from diskette. /FE also brings a variety of new hard drive tests (including a test series dedicated to SCSI devices), but IDE support is still rather weak. With a high-resolution diskette (available separately), /FE can support floppy drive alignment. /FE brings in a myriad of new serial and parallel port tests, video tests, and system board tests (including EISA bus tests). A set of CD-ROM tests round out the improvements. The big criticism of the manuals for both products is that there is only a handful of information on interpreting the results and correlating fault warnings to corrective action.

QuickTech Pro (UltraX, Inc.)

QuickTech Pro is a popular offering from UltraX. A limited system information option allows you to review the basic system configuration, along with a CPU analysis, system interrupt assignments, and a system memory map. Each major subsystem of the PC is covered by a comprehensive suite of tests. Memory testing covers the customary base RAM and extended/expanded RAM areas, but you also have access to system video RAM, VESA video RAM, cache RAM, and CMOS RAM. Floppy drive testing offers traditional tests, along with a floppy controller test and a cleaning function. Hard drive tests also are largely familiar, but a hard drive controller test can be quite handy. QuickTech Pro also provides low-level IDE formatting. Video tests concentrate on the adapter itself, so monitor alignment is not supported. Keyboards, serial ports, and parallel ports are all tested using loopback plugs. QuickTech Pro offers a suite of benchmarks (CPU, video, and hard drive) that allow system performance measurements. A burn-in feature allows tests to be selected and run repetitively. QuickTech Pro is a package on par with some other general-purpose diagnostics, but the lack of advanced testing is a definite disadvantage.

Service Diagnostics (Landmark Research)

Over the years, Landmark's Service Diagnostics has endured and evolved as a good, general-purpose diagnostic tool, although it tends to lag a bit behind current technology. The test routines are familiar: CPU, motherboard, keyboard, serial port, parallel port, video adapter, floppy disk, and hard disk. Loopback plugs are provided to support the port tests. There are three attributes to Service Diagnostics that make it particularly useful. First, the package offers monitor alignment patterns. If you work with monitors at all, these patterns can be quite useful. A printer test allows various printers to be exersized actively. Third, a digital diagnostic disk (DDD) is included with the package for a floppy alignment test routine. Another interesting factor to consider is the extensive explanations of each test provided in the documentation, handy if you want a better perspective on the diagnostic's operation. If you find yourself working on a large number of older systems, Service Diagnostics will probably fill the bill, but its price tag is a bit high compared to other diagnostics that are kept more current.

An additional module to Service Diagnostics is the ROM POST that is installed in place of the system BIOS. ROM POST boots the system with a unique series of tests that can help to isolate the system failure when it occurs before the video system is initialized. ROM POST is not a regular part of Service Diagnostics, and must be purchased separately.

The Troubleshooter (AllMicro)

The Troubleshooter by AllMicro is a self-booting diagnostic. Like so many other diagnostics, The Troubleshooter can provide comprehensive system information including CPU type and speed, BIOS data, DOS data and device drivers, interrupt vectors, memory configuration, mouse status, drives, and video information. But it goes further to identify sound cards. Video support includes SVGA and VESA support. Drive identification includes CD-ROM drives. A CMOS editor rounds out the system information capabilities.

The Troubleshooter also provides a comprehensive suite of PC testing. Thorough motherboard testing checks the CPU, MCP, DMA and IRQ controllers, CMOS RAM and RTC operation, timers, and keyboard controller. Memory checking offers a selection of tests that can isolate problems in conventional, upper, expanded, or extended memory (up to 99Mb). External cache memory also can be checked. Floppy and hard drive testing includes a suite of examinations, as well as drive controller diagnostics. Serial and parallel ports are tested using loopback plugs. Video testing not only handles the video adapter and video memory (up to 4Mb of VESA memory), but test patterns are provided for monitor alignment. Keyboard and mouse tests check the typical input devices. The Troubleshooter's multimedia tests check AdLib and SoundBlaster compatible boards, as well as CD-ROM drive performance. As an added advantage, The Troubleshooter supports IDE low-level formatting, as well as system burn-in testing. Although The Troubleshooter lacks SCSI and ESDI support, is a worthwhile addition to any technician's toolbox.

Drive enhancement, data recovery, and backup

Data is one of the most vital elements of a PC; in many cases, the data is more valuable than the PC itself. The ability to fix hard drives and back up data quickly and efficiently has become an important part of every business day. Data recovery from hard drives and floppy disks also has matured into a useful and reliable technology suitable for technicians and end users. The products below form a special troubleshooting category.

Disk manager (Ontrack Computer Systems)

The Disk Manager from Ontrack Computer Systems is perhaps the most known and respected product available for new drive initialization, partitioning, and preparation for use. One of the factors that make Disk Manager so attractive is its support of IDE and SCSI drive preparation. Disk Manager software overcomes the DOS 528Mb limitation, so IDE drives larger then 528Mb can be installed as a single bootable partition. It also overcomes the traditional 1024-cylinder physical BIOS limit to gain full capacity from a hard drive of virtually any size. You can use drives whose parameters do not match any BIOS entry. Diagnostics are provided that check the drive and controller. Secondary controller support allows you to use up to four IDE or ESDI drives on the same PC. When combined with other features, the Disk Manager is an important tool for technicians involved in high-end drive replacement and upgrades.

DrivePro (MicroHouse)

DrivePro by MicroHouse is probably the most versatile and powerful hard drive troubleshooting package available today. Not only is DrivePro capable of performing diagnostics on MFM, IDE, ESDI, and SCSI drives, but it offers a first-aid kit for faulty drives. With DrivePro, you can create or rebuild partition tables and master boot records. A general-purpose drive boot fixer will attempt to reconstruct any areas of the drive that are preventing it from booting. If CMOS settings have been lost, Drive-Pro can retrieve the parameters that the drive was partitioned with. A super sector editor allows you to adjust data on a byte level. Finally, DrivePro offers an IDE low-level formatter. The manual itself offers a wealth of definitions and troubleshooting information. Combined with its relatively low price, DrivePro is a worthy addition to your toolbox.

PC Tools (Central Point)

Among the many features included with PC Tools, its disk features, especially the disk defragmenter, are well recognized. Defragmentation is important to maintain the drive at optimum performance. If you have PC Tools or have considered purchasing it, you will find its features to be quite worthwhile for regular drive maintenance.

Rescue Professional (AllMicro)

In these days where the data contained on a drive is often more valuable than the entire PC, it is little wonder that the ability to recover that data is a vital part of hard drive troubleshooting. Rescue Professional by AllMicro seeks to provide an easy-to-use tool that is capable of recovering files that have been lost as a result of media damage, bad boot records, bad FATs, bad directory tables, scratches, and so on. Using Rescue Professional is often as simple as indicating the file you need recovered, then specifying where the recovered file must be sent. Even entire subdirectories can be recovered. Rescue Professional uses its own operating system, so it is able to bypass many of the limitations imposed by DOS. It is compatible with MFM/RLL, IDE, ESDI, and SCSI drives, including drives compressed with Stacker, DoubleSpace, and Superstor. Of all the drive tools now available, Rescue Professional is uniquely capable of recovering precious files.

SpinRite (Gibson Research)

SpinRite by Gibson Research is regarded as a foremost drive repair and data recovery tool that is compatible with MFM/RLL, IDE, ESDI, and SCSI drive architectures. SpinRite reads and recovers most (if not all) data from hard drives and floppy drives that are otherwise completely unrecoverable. It can optimize and reset sector interleaves, perform surface checks for media defects and move questionable data to safer areas, mark out defective media, and verify drive characteristics and setup information. SpinRite also can handle most low-level format operations. Although the SpinRite manual is quite colorful, it lacks the depth of coverage and explanations that would make it more of a resource. As a recovery tool, however, it is well worth considering.

PC diagnostic instruments

Software products alone are not always enough to support your troubleshooting effort. Whether you repair other computers or only your own, you should be aware of some hardware tools that are available. The next section shows you a selection of general-purpose tools that range from inexpensive commodities to high-end PC diagnostic packages.

Drive Probe: Advanced Edition (Accurite Technologies)

For service installations that deal with a high volume of floppy drive problems or specialize in floppy drive repairs, the DriveProbe Advanced Edition by Accurite

Technologies provides a hardware-based diagnostic solution of unparalleled accuracy. Using a high-resolution diskette and a Universal Floppy Controller board, you can turn a PC into a floppy drive test station that can handle 360K, 1.2Mb, 720K, 1.44Mb, and 2.88Mb drives, as well as 800Kb and 1.4Mb Macintosh drives, and most typical floppy duplicator drives. Nine major tests are provided: (1) spindle speed, (2) disk centering and clamping, (3) radial head alignment, (4) azimuth head alignment, (5) index to data timing, (6) positioner hysteresis, (7) read/write testing, (8) window margin, and (9) asymmetry. Utility functions also allow testing drive sensors such as write protect, drive ready, and change line. Floppy drive specialists will find this to be the "Swiss army knife" of drive testing and alignment.

KickStart Card (Landmark Research International)

When a serious failure disables a PC, software diagnostics might not load properly, so they will not help you. However, virtually all PCs generate I/O POST codes as the BIOS executes each step of its initialization. As tests are started (or completed), BIOS sends a one-byte hexadecimal code to an I/O port (usually PORT 80h). A POST board, such as the KickStart card from Landmark (Fig. 6-2), checks port 80h and displays the hexadecimal codes as a series of LEDs. By comparing the last LED sequence to be completed against the BIOS code list, you can tell where the PC stopped initializing, that is likely where it failed. The KickStart card plugs into any ISA slot. Four power LEDs light to indicate the presence of +5, –5, +12, and –12 V from the power supply. If any of these voltages are missing, it could indicate a fault in the power supply.

6-2
The KickStart 1 board.

Unfortunately, the KickStart board is not without its drawbacks. First, novices will have a difficult time converting the eight green code LEDs into a hexadecimal equivalent; all other POST-compatible hardware in this section display the code directly on seven-segment LEDs. The board only checks codes at 80h and 280h. Although these are the most common addresses, it is not compatible with all systems that use unusual addresses. The tiny manual only provides POST codes for five types of BIOS. Fortunately, you can use Chapter 28 as your POST code reference, but as a self-standing product, it is seriously lagging behind competitive products.

MicroPost (Data Depot, Inc.)

Measuring only about 38 × 935 mm (1.5 × 3.68 inches), the MicroPOST card by Data Depot is truly a "micro" tool, yet it provides many current features such as seven-segment displays, four power LEDs, and a DIP switch that allows you to select the I/O POST port for almost any PC. In addition, the decimal points on each 7-segment display shows +5 V and Reset signal status. The small manual is packed with POST code tables for many current BIOS versions, so translating the hexadecimal display into an error message is quick and easy. When you need a POST card with maximum versatility and minimum space, the MicroPOST board is an ideal choice.

PC PowerCheck (Data Depot, Inc.)

Power problems due to faulty or overloaded supplies can wreak havoc on a PC. The PC PowerCheck from Data Depot serves as a plug-in test and measurement tool that inspects the four key system voltages (+5, –5, +12, –12 V) and reports on any over voltage, under voltage, noise, and transient (spike) conditions. All four monitoring circuits are independent, preventing a error in one supply from causing false readings in the other displays. In addition, PC PowerCheck monitors the system Reset signal that can be triggered falsely from low supply voltages. A "trap mode" is available that allows brief power faults to be kept on the display after they occur, so you can install PC PowerCheck and walk away from the system, then check the board later to see is any anomalies have occurred. PC PowerCheck is a handy and practical tool that relieves the guesswork often encountered when measuring voltages with an ordinary voltmeter. A small and easily portable device, PC PowerCheck deserves a spot on any technician's workbench.

PocketPOST (Data Depot)

Critically disabled PCs often demand the use of POST cards in order to read the POST codes written to I/O port 80h (or other ports) by the system BIOS. PocketPOST by Data Depot provides the ability to read these codes, along with a range of other features that are difficult to find with other products. First, PocketPOST can be set to read POST codes at many different I/O addresses, so it is compatible with virtually every IBM AT compatible system. It provides four LEDs to verify the presence of power (+5, –5, +12, and –12 V). The key signals that are normally present on an ISA bus can be displayed on the PocketPOST; absent signals are often a direct clue to the problem. Finally, a plug-in logic probe allows you to check bus and IC signals as needed for hands-on component-level work. For PS/2 systems, a MicroChannel adapter is available separately. The accompanying manual provides setup instructions, logic probe instructions, and POST codes for dozens of BIOS versions. The Pocket-POST card has proven itself a remarkable and versatile tool that is relatively low-priced for the features it provides. Its 68.8 × 935 mm (2.71 × 3.68 inches) form factor makes the PocketPOST extremely portable—a valued addition for PC technicians.

PostProbe (Micro2000)

The PostProbe by Micro2000 is the second half of the troubleshooting set formed with MicroScope. Dual 7-segment displays show the hexadecimal POST code from one of several popular I/O addresses. A series of 8 LEDs illustrates the continuous behavior of major ISA bus signals (that is, I/OR, I/OW, MR/W, ALE, Reset, and so on). An additional four LEDs show the status of each power supply output. The PostProbe is equipped with a logic probe to support signal testing and component-level troubleshooting. The PostProbe manual contains a wide variety of POST code indexes, as well as pinouts for a selection of popular motherboard ICs, which allows direct component-level examination of the appropriate components. A PS/2 adapter is included with the PostProbe kit. Although PostProbe is a bit pricey for what it does, it is a proven and reliable troubleshooting tool.

Racer II (UltraX, Inc.)

The Real-time AT/XT Computer Equipment Repair (RACER) II is a plug-in diagnostic board that allows technicians to troubleshoot and isolate component-level failures in a PC. Where most diagnostic tools rely on software, RACER II uses a combination of hardware and BIOS-replacement firmware that allows the system to be tested without DOS or other operating systems; only the CPU, power supply, and system buses must be functioning. If a working video system is available, RACER II initializes the video system immediately and displays test progress right on the monitor. More than 25 tests are available for the AT. If any part of the system fails a test, a list of potential faults is displayed. When multiple tests fail, you can compare the common fault probabilities to find the most probable failure. For extended testing, the RACER II can be set to run continuously to handle burn-in testing. If the RACER II BIOS is not used, you can run the card in "POST mode" where the original BIOS POST codes can be reviewed. A series of LEDs keeps check of the power supply outputs (+5, –5, +12, and –12). The RACER II is an exciting and up-to-date tool for PC technicians. If you do a lot of component-level work, the RACER II is well worth considering.

SIMCHECK (Innoventions, Inc.)

Innoventions manufactures an entire line of RAM testing instruments as part of their SIMCHECK line. Both dynamic RAM (Fig. 6-3) and static RAM (Fig. 6-4) devices can be thoroughly tested and stressed. Different devices can be handled simply by replacing plug-in modules. Timing and performance information is displayed

6-3
The basic SIMCHECK unit. Innoventions, Inc.

6-4
The SIMCHECK Static RAM
Tester add-on. Innoventions, Inc.

on a two-line LCD. SIMCHECK systems can be essential and very cost effective if you deal with system RAM troubleshooting and upgrading.

The Discovery Card (AllMicro)

One of the problems with system inspection and diagnostic software is that there is no guarantee that it will successfully detect all of the IRQs or DMA channels in use. When resource conflicts occur, a diagnostic that does not report resources with 100% accuracy can actually cost you precious time and effort. The Discovery Card from AllMicro is an ISA expansion tool that can trap and indicate eight DMA and 16 IRQ channels with absolute confidence. The active channels are displayed by a bank of illuminated LEDs. The Discovery Card is a powerful asset for anyone responsible for upgrading PCs and resolving resource conflicts. Simply plug the card into an available 16-bit expansion slot before an upgrade, note the available resources, then remove the Discovery Card and set your new device to use the available IRQs or DMA channels. This can be particularly handy if a hardware conflict is preventing a PC from booting.

V-ATE (Vista Microsystems, Inc.)

The V-ATE system designed and manufactured by Vista Microsystems, really represents the ultimate in system motherboard testing (Fig. 6-5). By installing a PC-based test board into a motherboard, a V-ATE setup can perform thorough hardware-level testing of the motherboard. Bus signals, power signals, ROM, CPU, RAM, MCP, RTC, DMA, IRQ, and keyboard controller are all tested completely. Because the motherboard is designed to be tested alone, V-ATE is an ideal choice for high-volume or depot motherboard repair operations. Motherboard BIOS testing also is supported, and the V-ATE manual contains an index of codes from dozens of BIOS manufacters. A comprehensive index of V-ATE test results allows you to focus immediately on the failure area. For top-of-the-line testing, Vista's V-ATE gives professional technicians a true advantage.

Vista Microsystems, Inc.

6-5
A view of the Vista Microsystems
V-ATE unit in action.

7
CHAPTER

A safe and
functional workspace

A successful repair depends upon your ability to recognize and diagnose problems, but knowledge and diagnostics alone are often not enough. A technician needs a reliable work area that has the hand tools, supplies, and conditions to facilitate a repair. The work area also must provide safety for you, as well as for the equipment you are working on. If you are planning to set up and equip a workspace (or revamp the workspace you already have), this chapter is intended to provide you with a set of useful guidelines. It is important for you to keep in mind that these are only guidelines—how you choose to implement these ideas will depend on your business objectives, personal space limitations, and budget.

The workspace

Make no mistake, a PC can be repaired just about anywhere. The computer certainly has no preference, and many a broken PC has laid open on the family dining room table at one time or another. However, the choice of location will have a dramatic impact on your ability to concentrate and work through a problem. This becomes especially important when you move beyond your own PC to start fixing other systems as a sideline. A quality workspace also portrays a serious, positive image of you to your customers. If you already rent a storefront or other facility, you might wish to skip the following sections.

Choosing the spot

Your workspace should be in an area that is quiet, and away from the distractions of common family areas. In home environments, a spare bedroom, cellar area, or finished garage are the three popular choices. A spare bedroom is often the most popular location because it is a well-defined private space that is typically clean and dry, and can be heated or cooled (depending on the season and your geographic location) at least as well as the rest of your home. On the down side, power outlets are often few and far between, and there might be no phone line(s) available. Although it is a relatively simple matter to run more power and phone lines, it is an extra expense to consider while weighing other options. Choose a room on the ground floor if possible—carrying equipment up and down flights of stairs can be hazardous for you and your customer's equipment. Also consider that this is your home. If you or your spouse are uncomfortable with the idea of relative strangers walking through your home to drop off or pick up equipment, you might want to consider other options.

The cellar is a popular second choice, but the environment can be a bit more difficult to manage. Cellar space is usually plentiful and easy to partition. Because most homes locate their circuit breakers and telephone junctions in the cellar, power and phone lines can be run to the workspace with a minimum of difficulty. You will probably have to have ample lighting installed to accommodate the new workspace. Cellars that tend to flood during a rain storm or spring thaw should be avoided. Also, cellars tend to become cool and damp during summer months. A strong dehumidifier can help curtail dampness. If you do not receive enough heat during winter months, an electric area heater (not a space heater) can be added.

The garage is the least-attractive workspace alternative because they are often the most insecure and environmentally unstable parts of a residence. A garage is notorious for inadequate insulation and drafty doors. This means that the garage is usually hot in the summer and cold in the winter. Power and lighting are totally inadequate for bench work, and only the rare few homeowners ever thought to include a phone jack in their garage. In order to use a garage for your workspace, you would have to commit the space exclusively as a workshop. Disable and seal the garage doors (cars will have to be parked outside), add ample all-weather insulation, power, lighting, telephone lines, baseboard electric heating (for the winter months), and an air-conditioner space (for the summer months). In other words, you will have to turn your garage into a clean, finished space before using it as your shop. Although finishing a garage usually carries the greatest setup expense, the separate entrance and relative isolation from the rest of your residence can yield a lot of advantages. More than one major corporation was born in a garage.

The workbench

Once you have an appropriate workspace, you will undoubtedly populate the space with furnishings. A good-sized bookshelf, locking file cabinet, and one or two locking storage cabinets are good to start with. These items will support your reference material, customer files and information, and supplies or spare parts. But you also will need a workbench—the main work area where repairs will actually be performed. The size and shape of the work surface itself is up to your own personal taste and discretion. A used metal or wood desk will work just fine, but bigger is definitely better. An elevated work surface (such as an industrial workbench) is preferred. Make sure to find a chair or stool that fits comfortably with the work surface.

Protecting yourself and your customer

Now that you have a secure place to work, you should familiarize yourself with a variety of the hazards involved in PC and peripheral repair. Not only are there risks of injury to yourself from the equipment, but you also risk damaging the equipment by electrostatic discharge through careless handling or storage. This section of the chapter illustrates many of the key safety considerations that all technicians should understand.

Please read this entire section carefully! One of the most important aspects of all computer service is safety for yourself and those working and living around you, so it is important that you read and understand the following safety information. **If you are uncomfortable working around such hazards or do not understand the implications of these warnings, do NOT attempt to repair the equipment—refer the service to someone else.**

Alternating-current electricity hazards

No matter how harmless a PC or peripheral device might appear, always remember that potential shock hazards can exist. Although the vast majority of PC components operate from dc voltages produced by the computer's power supply, the supply itself is powered by ac line voltage. When an ac-powered circuitry is disassembled, there can be several locations where live ac voltage is exposed and easily accessible. Electronic equipment operates from 120 Vac at 60 Hz. Many European countries use 240 Vac at 50 Hz. When this kind of voltage potential establishes a path through your body, it can cause a flow of current that might be large enough to stop your heart. Because it only takes about 100 mA to trigger a cardiac arrest, and a typical power supply fuse is rated for 1 or 2 A, fuses and circuit breakers will *not* protect you.

It is your skin's resistance that limits the flow of current through the body. Ohm's law states that for any voltage, current flow increases as resistance drops (and vice versa). Dry skin exhibits a high resistance of several hundred thousand ohms, but moist, cut, or wet skin can drop to only several hundred ohms. This means that even comparatively low voltages can produce a shock if your skin resistance is low enough. Take the following steps to protect yourself from injury:

- **Keep the device under repair unplugged** (not just turned off) as much as possible during disassembly and repair. When you must perform a service procedure that requires power to be applied, plug the supply into an isolation transformer (Fig. 7-1) just long enough to perform your procedure, then unplug it again. This makes the repair safer for you, as well as for anyone else that might happen along.
- Whenever you must work on a power supply, try to wear rubber gloves. These will insulate your hands just like insulation on a wire. You might think that rubber gloves are inconvenient and uncomfortable, but they are far better than the inconvenience and discomfort of an electric shock. Make it a point to wear a long-sleeved shirt with sleeves rolled down and buttoned—this will insulate your forearms.
- If rubber gloves are absolutely out of the question for one reason or another, remove all metal jewelry and work with one hand behind your back. The metals in your jewelry are excellent conductors. Should your ring or watchband hook onto a live ac line, it can conduct current directly to your skin. By keeping one hand behind your back, you cannot grasp both ends of a live ac line to complete a strong current path through your heart.

B+K Precision

7-1
A B+K Precision TR-110 isolation transformer.

- Work dry! *Do not* work with wet hands or clothing. Do not work in wet or damp environments. Make sure that any nearby fire extinguishing equipment is suitable for electrical fires.
- Treat electricity with tremendous respect. Whenever electronic circuitry is exposed (especially power supply circuitry), a shock hazard *does* exist. Remember that it is the flow of current through your body, not the voltage potential, that can injure you. Insulate yourself as much as possible from any exposed wiring.
- If you are uncomfortable with the idea of working on a power supply assembly, you can replace the assembly outright. This avoids exposing the live circuitry.

High voltages

The high anode voltages available in a monitor also present a serious shock hazard. Most monitors can produce voltages easily exceeding 15,000 V. Fortunately, high-voltage power supplies are not designed to source significant current, but serious burns can be delivered with ease. Not only is there a great risk of injury, but normal test probes (such as multimeter test leads) only provide insulation to about 600 V. Testing high voltages with standard test leads could electrocute you right through the lead's insulation! **Be sure to use specially designed high-voltage probes (as shown in chapter 5) when measuring CRT anode voltages.**

Even after the monitor is turned off and unplugged, the CRT bell (its large, flat face) can retain a significant charge, so you must discharge the CRT anode before working on the monitor. You also will need to discharge the monitor after each time it is powered up and tested on your workbench. Make sure the monitor is turned off. Use a screwdriver as shown in chapter 10 (Fig. 10-5). Attach a large alligator clip from the screwdriver to the monitor's metal frame. Slide the screwdriver blade gently under the anode insulator and contact the metal anode clip. This effectively shorts any potential on the CRT to ground. You will hear mild crackling sounds as the CRT is discharged. Be very careful to avoid twisting the screwdriver inside the CRT—it is still a fragile glass assembly. Short the CRT for several seconds to ensure a full discharge.

X radiation

When an electron moving at high speed strikes a phosphor particle, a number of X-ray particles are liberated. The CRT face is basically a big X-ray emitter. Since the early days of TV when X rays were discovered from TV picture tubes, ordinary lead was added to the CRT glass. Monitors' CRTs also use leaded glass to contain X-ray particles. Leaded glass is quite effective at containing X rays so long as the high-voltage level at the anode is not too high. If high-voltage becomes too high, X-ray generation increases and ultimately penetrates the lead shielding in the CRT. Because long-term exposure to X radiation has been linked to cancer and other health problems, it is important for you to check and correct excessive high-voltage conditions in computer monitors. This helps to ensure your safety, as well as the long-term safety of the monitor user(s). The following points will help you deal with X-ray dangers:

- X rays are *always* generated in CRT operation, but leaded glass used in CRTs will contain X rays as long as the high-voltage level at the anode is within its specified limits. If high voltage becomes excessive, X rays might penetrate the leaded glass. One of your first routine checks when a monitor is opened for service should be to check the high-voltage level with a calibrated high-voltage probe. If high voltage exceeds the monitor specifications, adjust the high voltage or troubleshoot the high-voltage circuit. Under *no* circumstances should the monitor be returned to service with excessive high voltage.

- If you do discover that high voltage is excessive, do not operate the monitor any longer than absolutely necessary while troubleshooting the cause of the excessive high voltage.

- Larger CRTs using high voltages in excess of 25 kV (where the chances of excessive high voltage are much greater) often use a set of supplemental radiation shields bolted around the CRT bell and neck. *Do not* test or operate the monitor with these supplemental shields removed—especially if you are aware that high voltage is excessive.

- If the CRT must be replaced during the course of your repair, replace the CRT with ONLY an *exact* replacement part. A different part might not offer enough lead in the glass. There also might be variations in the phosphors' quality and characteristics that will affect the ultimate quality of the display. Similarly, if you replace components in the high-voltage circuit, be sure to use only *exact* replacement parts. This ensures that the high-voltage circuit will behave as expected.

Carrying the CRT

Ultimately, the CRT is still a glass tube. It can crack and shatter like any other large glass vessel. When replacing the CRT, there are some common-sense things to keep in mind. First, wear gloves and goggles when carrying a CRT (especially a large CRT). *Never* under any circumstances should you lift, suspend, or carry the CRT by its thin neck. Instead, hold the CRT with its face to your chest and grasp it around the width of its bell. When setting the CRT down, *do not* rest it on the neck. Rest the

CRT face-down on a thick, soft, cushion such as plush towels or foam padding. A soft resting place prevents the CRT screen from being scratched. Also make sure that the resting place is untravelled and very stable such as a table top. Leaving the CRT on a chair or the floor can result in accidental injury (and irreparable damage to the CRT). Also remember that CRTs are typically heavy items (especially large CRTs). When lifting CRTs, be sure to lift from the knees in order to reduce the stress on your back—it's tough to repair a monitor while you're in traction.

Static electricity

As with any type of electronic troubleshooting activity, there is always a risk of further damage being caused to equipment accidentally during the repair process. With sophisticated computer electronics, that damage hazard comes in the form of electrostatic discharge (or ESD) that can destroy sensitive electronic parts. If you have ever walked across a carpeted floor on a cold, dry winter day, you have probably experienced the effects of ESD firsthand while reaching for a metal object (such as a door knob). Under the right conditions, your body can accumulate static charge potentials that exceed 20,000 V!

When you provide a conductive path for electrons to flow, that built-up charge rushes away from your body at the point closest to the metal object. The result is often a brief, stinging shock. Such a jolt can be startling and annoying, but it is generally harmless to people. Semiconductor devices, on the other hand, are highly susceptible to real physical damage from ESD when you handle or replace circuit boards and subassemblies. This section introduces you to static electricity and shows you how to prevent ESD damage during your repairs.

When two dissimilar materials are rubbed together (such as a carpet and the soles of your shoes), the force of friction causes electrons to move from one material to another. The excess (or lack) or electrons cause a charge of equal but opposite polarities to develop on each material. Because electrons are not flowing, there is no current, so the charge is said to be static. However, the charge does exhibit a voltage potential. As materials continue to rub together, their charge increases—sometimes to potentials of thousands of volts.

In a human, static charges are often developed by normal, everyday activities such as combing your hair. Friction between the comb and your hair causes opposing charges to develop. Sliding across a vinyl car seat, pulling a sweater on or off, or taking clothes out of a dryer are just some of the ways static charges can develop in the body—it is virtually impossible to avoid. ESD is more pronounced in winter months because dry (low humidity) air allows a greater accumulation of charge. In the summer, humidity in the air tends to bleed away (or short circuit) most accumulated charges before they reach shock levels that you can physically feel. Regardless of the season, though, ESD is always present to some degree, and always a danger to sensitive electronics.

Device damage

ESD poses a *serious* threat to most advanced ICs. ICs can easily be destroyed by static discharge levels of just a few hundred volts—well below your body's ability to even feel a static discharge. Static discharge at sufficient levels can damage bipolar transistors, transistor-transistor logic (TTL) gates, emitter-coupled logic (ECL) gates, operational amplifiers (op-amps), silicon-controlled rectifiers (SCRs), and junction field-effect transistors (JFETs), but certainly the most susceptible components to ESD are those ICs fabricated using variations of metal-oxide semiconductor (MOS) technology (that is, CMOS, HMOS, NMOS, and so on).

The MOS family of devices has become the cornerstone of high-performance ICs such as memories, high-speed logic and microprocessors, and other advanced components that can be found in today's PCs. Typical MOS ICs can easily fit over 500,000 transistors onto a single IC die. Every part of these transistors must be made continually smaller to keep pace with the constant demand for ever-higher levels of IC complexity. As each part of the transistor shrinks, however, their inherent resistance to static discharge drops, and their susceptibility to ESD damage escalates.

A typical MOS transistor breakdown is shown in Fig. 7-2. Notice the areas of positive and negative semiconductor material that forms its three terminals: (1) source, (2) gate, and (3) drain. The gate is isolated from the other parts of the transistor by a thin film of silicon dioxide (sometimes called the *oxide layer*). Unfortunately, this layer is extremely thin. High voltages, like those voltages from electrostatic discharges, can easily overload the oxide layer—this results in a puncture through the gate. Once this happens, the transistor (and therefore the entire IC) is permanently

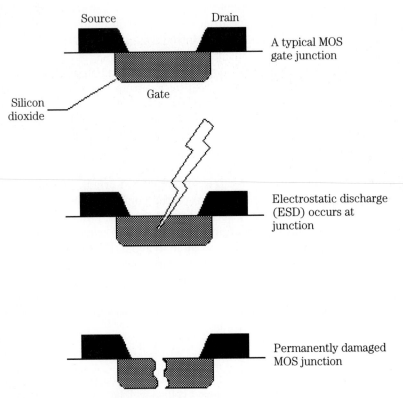

7-2 An example of MOS breakdown.

defective and must be replaced. Because you are primarily dealing with subassemblies, the entire subassembly would then have to be replaced.

Controlling static electricity

Never underestimate the importance of static control during your repairs. Without realizing it, you could destroy a new IC or circuit board before you even have the chance to install it—and you would never even know that static damage has occurred. All it takes is the careless touch of a charged hand or a loose piece of clothing. Take the necessary steps to ensure the safe handling and replacement of your sensitive (and expensive) electronics.

One way to control static is to keep charges away from boards and ICs to begin with. This is often accomplished as part of a device's packaging and shipping container. ICs are typically packed in a specially made conductive foam (Fig. 7-3). Carbon granules are compounded right into the polyethylene foam to achieve conductivity (about 3000 Ω per centimeter). Foam support helps to resist IC lead bending, absorb vibrations, and keeps every lead of the IC at the same potential (known as *equipotential bonding*). Conductive foam is reusable, so you can insert ICs for safekeeping, then remove them as needed. You can purchase conductive foam from just about any electronics retail store.

Plastic Systems

7-3 Antistatic foam used for holding ICs and PC boards safely.

Circuit boards are normally held in conductive plastic bags that dissipate static charges before damage can occur. Antistatic bags (Fig. 7-4) are made up of different material layers—each material exhibiting different amounts of conductivity. The bag acts as a *Faraday cage* for the device it contains. Electrons from an ESD will dissipate along a bag's surface layers instead of passing through the bag

Plastic Systems

7-4 An antistatic bag used for holding and storing PC boards.

wall to its contents. Antistatic bags also are available through many electronics retail stores.

Whenever you work with ICs, expansion boards, or sensitive electronic assemblies, it is important to dissipate charges that might have accumulated on your body. A conductive fabric wrist strap that is soundly connected to an earth ground will slowly bleed away any charges from your body. Avoid grabbing hold of a ground directly. Although this will discharge you, it can result in a nasty jolt if you have picked up a large electrostatic charge.

Even the action of wiping a plastic cabinet or video monitor can produce a large electrostatic buildup. Antistatic chemical agents added to lint-free cleaning wipes (Fig. 7-5) allow cleaning to be performed without the fear of excessive ESD accumulation. Wipes are typically pretreated and sealed in small pouches for convenience. Larger areas can be treated with antistatic chemical agents such as the spray in Fig. 7-6.

Work surfaces also must be as static-free as possible. This is very important! When circuit boards or chassis are removed from their systems and brought to your workbench, use an antistatic mat (such as the one in Fig. 7-7) to protect your delicate electronics. The antistatic mat is essentially a conductive layer that is unrolled onto desks or benches, and it connects to earth ground rather like an ordinary wrist strap. A well-grounded antistatic mat is a vital addition to your workbench.

As PC circuitry becomes ever more intricate, static sensitivity will continue to be a critical aspect of all service activity. Remember to make careful use of your static controls. Keep ICs and circuit boards in their antistatic containers at all times. *Never* place parts onto or into synthetic materials (such as nonconductive plastic cabinets or fabric coverings) that could hold a charge. Handle static sensitive parts carefully.

Plastic Systems

7-5
Antistatic wipes.

Plastic Systems

7-6
Antistatic spray.

Avoid touching IC pins if at all possible—even when using static controls. Be sure to use a conductive wrist strap and mat connected to a reliable earth ground.

Tools and materials

If you don't have a well-stocked toolbox yet, now is the time to consider the things you need. Before you begin a repair, gather a set of small hand tools and some inexpensive materials. It might seem rather trivial at this moment, but *never* under-

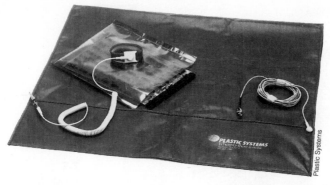

Plastic Systems

7-7 An antistatic mat for workspace protection of parts and tools.

estimate the value of having the proper tools—they can often make or break your repair efforts.

Hand tools

Hand tools are basically used to disassemble and reassemble your housings, enclosures, mounting brackets, and expansion card rail guides. It is not necessary to stock top-quality tools, but your tools should be of the proper size and shape to do the job. Because many of today's computers and peripheral devices are extremely small and tightly packaged assemblies, you should select tools that are small and thin wherever possible. Many electronics stores offer a number of prefabricated tool kits that carry a selection of properly sized hand tools (such as the ones shown in Figs. 7-8 and 7-9). Of course, you can assemble your own toolkit from scratch.

7-8
A mobile PC toolkit. Curtis, a division of
Rolodex, Secaucus, NJ 07094

Screwdrivers should be the first items on your list. Computer assemblies are generally held together with small or medium-sized Phillips-type screws. Once you are able to remove the outer housings, you will probably find that most other internal parts also are held in place with Phillips screws. Consider obtaining one or two small Phillips screwdrivers, as well as one medium-sized version. You will almost

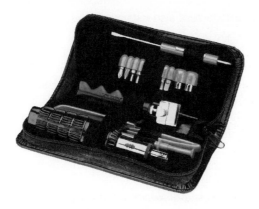

7-9
A small installer's toolkit. Curtis,
a division of Rolodex, Secaucus, NJ 07094

never need a large screwdriver. Each screwdriver should be about 10.16 centimeters (4 inches) to 15.24 centimeters (6 inches) long with a wide handle for a good grip. Jewelers screwdrivers are recommended for very fine or delicate assemblies. Round out your selection of screwdrivers by adding one small and one medium regular (flat blade) screwdriver. You won't use them as often as Phillips screwdrivers, but regular screwdrivers will come in handy.

There are three specialized types of screw heads that you should be aware of. Allen screws use a hex (six-sided) hole instead of a regular or Phillips-type blade. Torx and spline screws use specially-shaped holes that only accept the corresponding size and shape of driver. It is a good idea to keep a set of small hex keys on hand, but you will rarely find specialized screw heads. Torx and spline screws are almost never encountered in PCs.

Wrenches are used to hold hex-shaped bolt heads or nuts. There are not many instances where you need to remove nuts and bolts, but an inexpensive set of small electronics-grade open-ended wrenches is recommended. If you prefer, a small adjustable wrench can be used instead.

Needle-nose pliers are valued additions to your toolbox. Not as bulk- and awkward as ordinary mechanic's pliers, needle-nose pliers can be used to grip or bend both mechanical and electronic parts. Needle-nose pliers also can serve as heatsinks during desoldering or soldering operations. Obtain a short nose and long nose set of needle-nose pliers. Short-nose pliers make great heatsinks, and can grasp parts securely. Long-nose pliers are excellent for picking up and grasping parts lost in the tight confines of a computer or peripheral. All sets of needle-nose pliers should be small, good-quality electronics-grade tools with well-insulated handles.

Diagonal cutters also are an important part of your tool collection. Cutters are used to cut wire and component leads. You really only need one good set of cutters, but the cutters should be small, good-quality electronics-grade tools. Cutters should have a low profile and a small cutting head to fit in tight spaces. Also make sure that the cutter's handles are well-insulated. Never use cutters to cut plastic, metal, or PC board material.

Add a pair of tweezers to your tool kit. The tweezers should be small, long, and made from anti-static plastic material. Metal tweezers should be avoided wherever possible to prevent accidental short circuits (as well as a shock hazard) if they come into contact with operating circuitry. Metal tweezers also can conduct potentially damaging static charges into sensitive ICs.

Soldering tools

You need a good-quality, general-purpose soldering iron to repair your small-computer's circuitry. A low-wattage iron of 15 to 20 W (watts) with a fine tip is usually best. You can obtain a decent soldering iron from any local electronics store. Most soldering irons are powered directly from ac, and these are just fine for general touch-ups and simple wiring repairs. However, you should consider a dc powered or gas-fueled iron for desoldering delicate, static-sensitive ICs. No matter what iron you buy, try to ensure that it is recommended as "static-safe."

The iron *absolutely must* have its own metal stand! *Never, under any circumstances, allow a soldering iron to rest on a counter or table top unattended.* The potential for nasty burns or fire is simply too great. Also be certain to use protective eye wear such as goggles or safety glasses whenever soldering. Even a small speck of molten solder launched into the eye by a taut wire or lead can cause permanent damage. Keep a wet sponge handy to periodically wipe the iron's tip. Invest in a roll of good-quality electronics-grade rosin-core solder. If you do a great deal of soldering, you should consider adding a multi-purpose fire extinguisher to your workspace. The extinguisher should be suitable for electrical fires.

Desoldering tools are necessary to remove faulty components and wires. Once the solder joint is heated with the soldering iron, a desoldering tool can remove the molten solder to free the joint. A solder vacuum uses a small, spring-loaded plunger mounted in a narrow cylinder. When triggered, the plunger recoils and generates a vacuum that draws up any molten solder in the vicinity. Solder wick is little more than a fine copper braid. By heating the braid against a solder joint, molten solder wicks up into the braid through capillary action. Such conventional desoldering tools are most effective on through-hole components. Surface-mounted components also can be desoldered with conventional desoldering tools, but there are more efficient techniques for desoldering surface-mount parts. Specially shaped desoldering tips can ease surface-mount desoldering by heating all of the component's leads simultaneously.

Software tools

No PC tool kit is complete without a selection of software. Chapter 6 outlines a wide range of system inspection and diagnostic software. No matter what diagnostic products you decide to invest in, you should always make it a point to include 5¼- and 3½-inch bootable disks. After all, a diagnostic won't do you any good if you can't get the system started. You can include general-purpose CONFIG.SYS and AUTO-EXEC.BAT files for system configuration. Make sure to add any startup files needed by CONFIG.SYS or AUTOEXEC.BAT (that is, HIMEM.SYS or EMM386.EXE) to your bootable disk(s). To adjust system startup files and Windows .INI files, the bootable disks should contain a simple ASCII text editor such as DOSEDIT.

You also should add disk support files to your bootable disks such as FDISK, FORMAT, SYS, DEBUG, and CHKDSK. Because CMOS battery failures are very common, you will need to restore the system's setup. Most i386 and i486 systems require a particular SETUP utility to alter the memory or disk configuration. SETUP gets a bit sticky because each utility is a bit different. If a customer is planning to bring in their system for you to work on, be sure to ask them to include their SETUP disk.

CD-ROMs offer another wrinkle. The MS-DOS driver MSCDEX added in the AU-TOEXEC.BAT file is relatively generic and can easily be included on your bootable disk(s). However, each CD-ROM requires a low-level driver (used in the CONFIG .SYS file), and each manufacturer requires their own driver. If you will be working on the CD-ROM drive, you will need to obtain the proper low-level driver from either your customer or the drive manufacturer's forum on CompuServe. PC makers also place updated drivers in their own forums.

Miscellany

A hand-held, battery-powered vacuum cleaner will be helpful in your routine maintenance operations. Periodically removing dust and debris from your keyboard can prevent intermittent key operation. You also should brush or vacuum any dust that might be accumulating in your computer's vent holes, fan grills, and fan blades. Clear air paths help to keep computers and peripherals running cooler. Be sure to include a flashlight. An average-sized, inexpensive flashlight is more than adequate.

Most computer systems now use surface-mount ICs and components, so you rarely have need of IC inserters and extractors. The exceptions to this rule are for PLCCs (plastic leaded chip carriers) and PGAs (pin grid arrays). Once a PLCC or PGA has been inserted into its socket, there is virtually no way to remove it without the use of a specialized extraction tool. The extractor tool's tips either grasp the PGA ICs edges directly, or are inserted into slots at either set of opposing corners on a PLCC socket. Squeeze the extractor gently to push the tips under the IC, then wiggle the IC to pull it free. Once an IC is free, be certain to keep it on an antistatic mat or on a piece of antistatic foam.

Your tool kit should always have a supply of antistatic materials to help prevent accidental damage to your expensive electronics. An antistatic wrist strap connects your body to ground in order to remove any static charge buildup from your body. Whenever working with PC boards and ICs, use antistatic foam to hold ICs and antistatic bags to hold PC boards. Avoid styrofoam and other plastics that hold static charges. You also might like to invest in an antistatic mat. A mat rolls out onto a desk or workbench and connects to ground much like a wrist strap. An antistatic mat will allow you to place delicate PC boards and chassis on your workbench while you work with them.

Keep an assortment of solid and stranded hookup wire in your toolbox. Wire should be between 18 to 24 *AWG* (American Wire Gauge)—preferably above 20 AWG. Heat shrink tubing is another handy material for your repairs. Tubing can be cut to length as needed, then positioned and shrunk to insulate wire splices and long component leads. You might wish to buy a specialized heat gun to shrink the tubing, but an ordinary blow drier for hair will usually work just as well. When heating tubing, be certain to direct hot air **away** from ICs and PC boards.

8
CHAPTER

Inside today's desktop and tower

In order to troubleshoot a PC effectively, the technician must be familiar with the general mechanical and physical aspects of the PC. They must be able to disassemble the unit quickly (without causing damage to the case or internal assemblies in the process), then accurately identify each subassembly, expansion board, and connector. Once a diagnosis and repair has been completed, the technician must be able to reassemble the PC and its enclosures (again without damaging assemblies or enclosures). This chapter is designed to provide you with a guided tour of the typical desktop (Fig. 8-1) and tower PC, point out the various operating subassemblies, and offer a series of assembly guidelines.

Under the hood

Figure 8-2 shows an exposed view of a desktop PC. Although it might look crowded at first glance, you will see that there are actually only a handful of subassemblies to deal with. With a little practice, identifying various assemblies should become almost automatic. An average tower system is shown in Fig. 8-3. With few exceptions, desktop and tower PCs incorporate seven key items: (1) the enclosure, (2) the power supply, (3) the motherboard, (4) a floppy disk drive, (5) a hard disk drive, (6) a video adapter, and (7) a drive controller. The following sections detail each item.

Enclosure

The *enclosure* is the most obvious and least glamorous element of a PC. Yet, the enclosure serves some very important functions. First, the enclosure (such as the Olson Baby AT case of Fig. 8-4) forms the mechanical foundation (or *chassis*) of every PC. Every other subassembly is bolted securely to this chassis. Second, the chassis is electrically grounded through the power supply. Grounding prevents the buildup

Computer cases designed and manufactured by Olson Metal Products, Seguin, TX

8-1 A selection of PC enclosures.

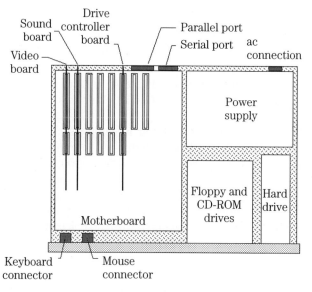

8-2
Layout of a typical desktop PC.

or discharge of static electricity from damaging other subassemblies. If you do not have an antistatic wrist strap, you can discharge yourself on the PC's metal chassis as long as the power supply is plugged in. Because you are strongly urged to protect yourself by unplugging the power supply ac, do not rely on the chassis to discharge

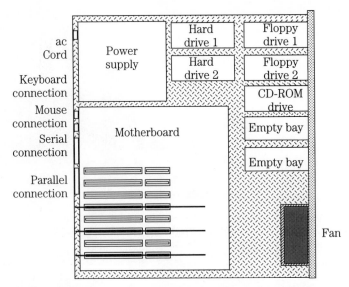

8-3 Layout of a typical tower PC.

you. If a fault should occur in the power supply that causes ac to reach the enclosure, grounding will prevent injury (and probably pop the supply fuse).

The enclosure also limits the PC's expansion capacity. Average-size desktop enclosures typically offer room for motherboards with six to eight expansion slots, and provide space for three or four drives—two drives mounted in front slots (or *external* drive bays), and one or two drives mounted inside the PC (in *internal* drive bays). An average-size enclosure such as this allows a fair amount of space to expand the system as your customer's needs change. Unfortunately, the push toward smaller PCs has led to the use of smaller, more confined enclosures. Small (or *low-profile*) enclosures (such as the Olson Slimline Chassis in Fig. 8-5) restrict the size of the motherboard that results in fewer expansion slots (usually four to six), and allows room for only one to three drives.

The great advantage to tower enclosures is their larger physical size. Towers usually offer four or five external drive bays, as well as three or four internal bays. To accommodate such expandability, a large power supply (250 to 300 W) is often included. Tower cases also can fit larger motherboards that tend to support a greater number of expansion slots. The higher power demands of a tower system result in greater heat generation. Towers compensate for heat by providing one or more internal fans to force air into the enclosure. If a second internal fan is included, it generally works in conjunction with the first fan to exhaust heated air.

Power supply

The *power supply* is the silver box that is usually located in the rear right quarter of the enclosure. Alternating current enters the supply through the ac line cord connected at the rear of the enclosure. A supply then produces a series of dc outputs that connect to the motherboard and drives. The importance of a power supply is

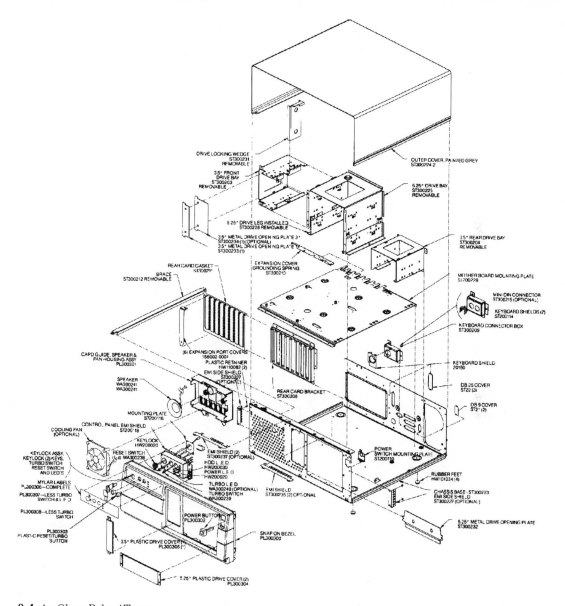

8-4 An Olson Baby AT case. Computer cases designed and manufactured by Olson Metal Products, Seguin, TX

easy enough to understand, but its implications for system integrity and expandability might not be as obvious.

Power supplies sustain a great deal of electrical stress in normal everyday operation. The conversion of ac into dc results in substantial heat (which is why so many power supplies are equipped with a cooling fan). Surges, spikes, and other anomalies that plague ac power distribution also find their way into PC power supplies where damage can occur. The quality of a power supply's components and design dictate

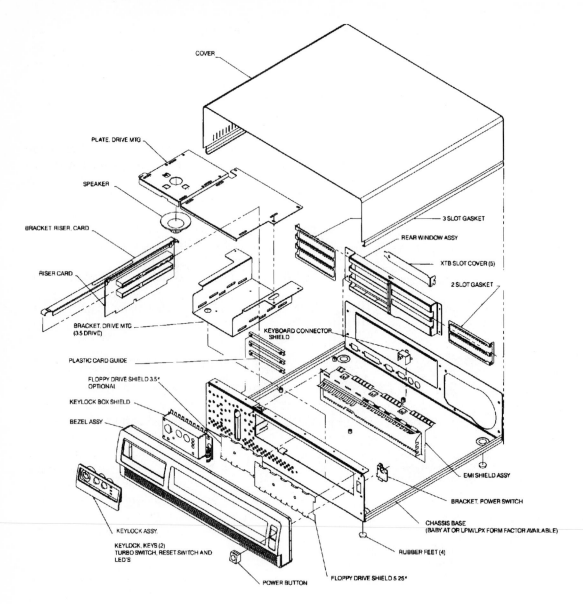

COVER

PLATE, DRIVE MTG

SPEAKER

BRACKET RISER, CARD

RISER CARD

BRACKET, DRIVE MTG
(3.5 DRIVE)

PLASTIC CARD GUIDE

FLOPPY DRIVE SHIELD 3.5"
OPTIONAL

KEYLOCK BOX SHIELD

BEZEL ASSY

KEYLOCK ASSY.

KEYLOCK, KEYS (2)
TURBO SWITCH, RESET SWITCH AND
LED'S

POWER BUTTON

KEYBOARD CONNECTOR
SHIELD

FLOPPY DRIVE SHIELD 5.25"

3 SLOT GASKET

REAR WINDOW ASSY

XTB SLOT COVER (5)

2 SLOT GASKET

EMI SHIELD ASSY

BRACKET, POWER SWITCH

CHASSIS BASE
(BABY AT OR LPM/LPX FORM FACTOR AVAILABLE)

RUBBER FEET (4)

8-5 An Olson Slimline chassis. Computer cases designed and manufactured by Olson Metal Products, Seguin, TX

how long it will last in operation. A quality supply will resist power problems and tolerate the rigors of normal operation, but a substandard supply can fail spontaneously after only a few months of operation. When replacing or upgrading a power supply, be sure to choose a reliable model.

Power supplies also limit a system's expandability. Every element used in the PC requires a certain amount of power (watts). The supply must be capable of producing enough power to adequately meet the system's demand. An under-powered supply (especially in low-profile systems) or a supply overloaded by excessive expansion might not be able to support the power needs of the system. Inadequate power results in very strange system behavior such as unpredictable system lockups, random memory faults, or disk access problems. When replacing a power supply, be certain that the new supply can provide at least as much power as the supply being replaced. When upgrading a supply, choose a supply that offers at least 50 W more than the original supply.

Motherboard

The *motherboard* (also known as the *main board, system board, backplane board*, or *planar board*) holds the majority of a computer's processing power. As a minimum, a motherboard contains the system CPU, co-processor, clock/timing circuits, RAM, BIOS ROM, serial port(s), parallel port, and expansion slots. Each portion of the motherboard is tied together with interconnecting logic circuitry. Some advanced motherboards also include circuitry to handle drive and video interfaces. You can identify the motherboard easily as shown in Fig. 8-2 or Fig. 8-3; it is the single large printed circuit board located just off of the enclosure's base.

As you might expect, it is the motherboard more than any other element of the PC that defines the limitations of a computer. The CPU (central processing unit) is responsible for processing each instruction needed by the computer (whether the instruction is for BIOS, the operating system, or an application). The speed and performance of the CPU limit the PC's processing power. For example, a PC with an i486 CPU runs Windows much better than a PC with an i386 CPU. Even when CPUs are the same, clock speed (measured in MHz) affects performance. For example, a PC with an i486/66-MHz CPU will run faster than a PC with an i486/25-MHz CPU.

The BIOS ROM contained on the motherboard also limits the system's capabilities—although such limits are not as drastic or obvious as CPU performance. BIOS is a set of small programs recorded onto ROM ICs that allow the operating system (such as MS-DOS or Windows) to interact with memory and the various drives and devices in the system. Although the BIOS versions produced today are generally quite uniform, older BIOS ICs might not support some of the new features we now expect from computers. For example, many systems using i286-based motherboards do not support the format process for 3½-inch 1.44Mb floppy disk drives directly as newer systems do. As another example, older systems might not support CD-ROMs. Overcoming BIOS incompatibilities is often a matter of upgrading the BIOS IC(s), or upgrading the motherboard entirely.

Each motherboard offers a number of expansion slots. The number of expansion slots limits the number of features and devices that can be added to the system. Internal modems, scanner boards, video boards, drive controller boards, sound boards, network cards, and SCSI controllers are only some of the devices competing for expansion space in your PC. The fewer slots that are available, the less a system can be expanded. The type of expansion slots also influences expandability. Classic motherboard designs offer a mix of 8-bit XT and 16-bit ISA slots. Today's motherboards have added one or two slots to accommodate new expansion technologies such as the VL bus for high-performance video boards (a second VL slot might be available for high-performance IDE adapters). Instead of the VL bus, a motherboard might incorporate one or two PCI slots for high-performance video or drive controller boards. The remainder of available expansion slots will generally be 16-bit ISA slots.

Drives

The modern PC would be entirely useless without long-term, high-volume storage, as well as the ability to transfer files between PCs. *Drives* represent a variety of devices used for storing or retrieving relatively large amounts of information. Floppy disk drives (FDDs), hard disk drives (HDDs), and CD-ROM drives are the three most popular drive types for desktop and tower PCs, although floptical drives and tape drives are occasionally used. Figure 8-6 shows the standard profile for each drive.

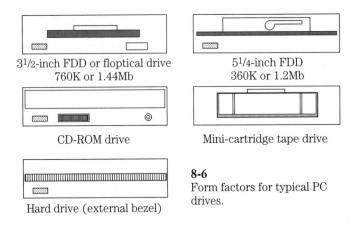

3¹/₂-inch FDD or floptical drive
760K or 1.44Mb

5¹/₄-inch FDD
360K or 1.2Mb

CD-ROM drive

Mini-cartridge tape drive

Hard drive (external bezel)

8-6
Form factors for typical PC drives.

Drives are typically located in the front right quarter of the desktop enclosure. Each drive is secured into an available drive bay within the enclosure. There are two types of drive bays that you should be familiar with: internal and external. The external drive bay allows a drive to be mounted facing the outside world. Floppy, CD-ROM, and tape drives rely on the availability of external drive bays. After all, what good is the drive if you can't insert or remove the media? On the other hand, hard disk drives use nonremovable media. This means the drive can be mounted in an internal (or nonaccessible) bay. A typical desktop PC offers two external and two internal bays. The external bays usually hold a 3½-inch FDD and a CD-ROM. The internal drive bay(s) are typically reserved for one or two hard drives. Larger desktop cases might offer additional external bays. Tower cases can easily support a full range of external drives mounted along the upper front of the enclosure. A tower's internal drive bays can handle another three or four hard drives.

Expansion boards

Although many PCs today incorporate video and FDD/HDD controller circuitry directly on the motherboard, those circuits can often be disabled when expansion boards are used. In fact, many such "integrated" controllers are eventually disabled so that video and drive systems can be upgraded with more advanced expansion boards. In most cases, you should expect to find at least a video board plugged into an expansion slot. The video board will often be accompanied by an FDD/HDD controller board. Of course, there will probably be additional boards in the system as well. This part of the chapter is intended to help you identify each category of expansion board on sight.

Video boards

Video adapter circuits (whether implemented on the motherboard or on an expansion board) are designed to convert raw graphic data traveling over the system bus into pixel data that can be displayed by a monitor. Without the monitor attached, however, the video adapter can only be identified through its video port connector. Figure 8-7 compares the four major generations of video adapters: MDA, CGA, EGA, and VGA. The illustrations shown in Fig. 8-7 are typical examples—some video board designs might not follow these layouts exactly. Chapter 52 describes video adapter standards and service in more detail.

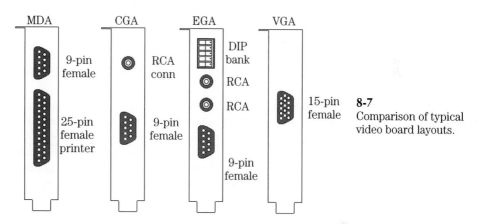

8-7 Comparison of typical video board layouts.

The *Monochrome Display Adapter* (MDA) is the oldest video adapter board, and few are still in service. MDA boards are noted for their use of a 25-pin parallel port included with the 9-pin video connector. You might find MDA boards used in IBM PC/XTs or compatible systems. The *Color Graphics Adapter* (CGA) is roughly the same vintage as MDA, and is the first graphics adapter to introduce color to PC displays. A CGA board can often be identified by a round RCA-type feature connector located just above a 9-pin video connector. Like the MDA boards, CGA is long-since obsolete, and many of the older systems that used CGA boards have been scrapped, or have been upgraded to later video systems. The *Enhanced Graphics Adapter* (EGA) offers more colors and higher display resolution than CGA. You can identify an EGA board by its small bank of DIP switches located above two RCA-type feature connectors and a 9-pin video connector.

The *Video Graphics Array* (VGA) board marked a departure from previous video systems. VGA abandoned logic-level video signals (on/off signaling) in favor of analog video levels. Thus, primary colors could be mixed together to provide many more color combinations than ever before—up to 262,144 possible colors for ordinary VGA. You can easily identify a VGA connector as a 15-pin high-density connector (15 pins stuffed into a 9-pin shell).

Drive boards

Once you open a PC and peek inside, drive boards are a dead giveaway. You will find a ribbon cable leading from the drive to its corresponding controller board. The type of controller depends on what drive(s) are attached to it. For example, if a controller board is attached to both a hard drive and one or two floppy drives, the adapter board would be an FDD/HDD controller. If the controller is attached to a CD-ROM, the adapter would be a CD-ROM controller board. You get the idea.

Typically, there are no external connectors available from ordinary drive controller boards. However, this trend is changing as advances in electronics allow more circuitry to be packed onto an expansion board. For example, it is common for multimedia upgrade kits to include a CD-ROM and sound board. When you install the kit, you find that the CD-ROM controller cable plugs into a connector on the sound board—in this case, the sound board doubles as the CD-ROM controller. Similarly, do not be surprised to find that the controller cables from your floppy and hard drives connect directly to the motherboard.

SCSI adapters

The *Small-Computer System Interface* (SCSI) offers impressive expandability by allowing SCSI-compatible devices (SCSI hard drives, SCSI CD-ROMs, SCSI tape drives, SCSI scanners, and so on) to all be connected together over the same daisy-chained cable. There are several ways to detect the presence of a SCSI adapter. First, you will see a screen message generated by the SCSI adapter BIOS when the PC initializes. You also can detect the presence of a SCSI adapter by identifying the interconnecting cables. Internally, SCSI cables are 50-pin ribbon cables—be careful not to confuse them for 40-pin IDE cables. Because many SCSI adapters can handle both internal and external devices, the adapter will have an external 50-pin D-type connector available. Chapter 48 covers SCSI concepts and troubleshooting in more detail.

Ports and modems

Communication is accomplished through one of several ports. Traditionally, parallel ports allow the PC to drive printers, but a new class of peripherals is available to operate through a parallel port (that is, parallel port tape drives, hard drives, and CD-ROM drives). Such devices are particularly handy when they must be moved between several machines. A parallel port is implemented as a 25-pin (female) connector (Fig. 8-8). Although older PCs included parallel ports as part of the MDA video board (Fig. 8-7) or as a stand-alone expansion board, virtually all current PCs incorporate at least one parallel port directly on the motherboard.

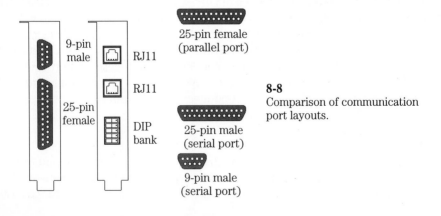

9-pin male

RJ11

RJ11

25-pin female

DIP bank

25-pin female (parallel port)

25-pin male (serial port)

9-pin male (serial port)

8-8
Comparison of communication port layouts.

The ability of a PC to communicate with peripheral devices or other computers has become a vital element of modern computing, and serial communication has evolved substantially over the last decade. As a result, you will likely find one or two serial ports located on the PC as shown in Fig. 8-8. Older PCs typically implement a single serial (or *RS-232*) port as a 25-pin D-type (male) connector. Do not confuse this with 25-pin D-type female connectors that are used for parallel ports. Because most serial communication can be accomplished with far fewer than 25 pins, some PC manufacturers replaced the 25-pin D-type male connector with a 9-pin D-type male connector. Newer systems offer two 9-pin D-type male serial ports directly on the motherboard. When implemented on a stand-alone expansion board, you will often find a 9-pin D-type male serial port combined with a 25-pin D-type female parallel port.

To communicate over a telephone line, serial signals must be translated into tones that can be carried within the frequency bandwidth of an ordinary voice telephone line. Returning signals also must be decoded into serial signals. The device that performs this PC-telephone line interface is called a *modem*. External modems are stand-alone devices that attach to an available serial port. Internal modems, however, are quite popular, and combine the circuitry for a serial port and modem on a single expansion board. You can usually identify an internal modem board by its two RJ11 (phone jack) connectors. One jack is for the telephone line itself, and the second connector is a feed-through that can be connected to any standard telephone.

Sound boards

The acceptance of sound boards in everyday PCs has been simply staggering. What started as a novel means of moving beyond the limitations of PC speakers has quickly evolved into a low-cost, CD-quality stereo sound system. Even business applications are embracing sound cards for simple speech recognition tasks. Sound cards have become an essential part of every PC used for educational, game, and multimedia applications. Fortunately, sound boards are relatively easy to recognize as shown in Fig. 8-9.

The giveaway here is the volume-control knob. Sound cards are the only devices that currently require such manual adjustments. Three miniature jacks also are included. The *Line Input* jack allows prerecorded sound (that is, output from tape player, CD player, or synthesizer) to be digitized and recorded by the sound board. The *Microphone Input* supports recording from an ordinary 600 microphone. The *Stereo Output* is the main output for the board where digitized voice and music files are reproduced. An output can drive amplified speakers or an interim stereo amplifier deck. Keep in mind that your particular sound board might have slightly different features. You also will note that the sound board shown in Fig. 8-9 offers a 15-pin D-type female connector. This feature connector is designed to serve double-duty as either a joystick port or a MIDI interface. Chapter 50 covers sound board concepts and troubleshooting in detail.

Joystick adapters

The use of PC games and simulators often requires the use of an analog joystick. Joysticks are connected to one of two 15-pin D-type female connectors on the joystick adapter (also called the *gameport*). Figure 8-10 shows the typical layout for a joystick adapter. Because two connectors are usually included, an adapter can sup-

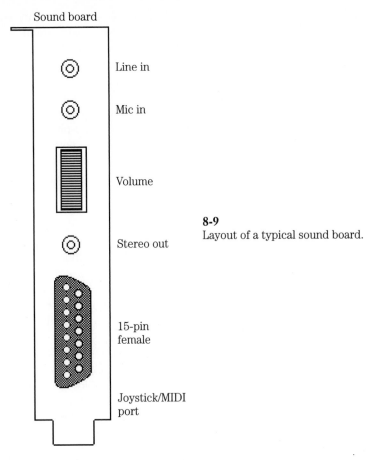

Sound board

Line in

Mic in

Volume

8-9
Layout of a typical sound board.

Stereo out

15-pin
female

Joystick/MIDI
port

port two analog joysticks. Another hallmark of a joystick adapter is its small size—typically an 8-bit (or *half-slot*) board. Chapter 30 outlines joystick and gameport installation and troubleshooting.

Notes for disassembly and reassembly

All too often, the mechanics of PC repair—taking the system apart and putting it back together again—are overlooked or treated as an afterthought. As you saw in the first part of this chapter, PC assemblies are not terribly complicated, but a careless or rushed approach to the repair can do more harm than good. Lost parts and collateral damage to the system are certain ways to lose a customer (and perhaps open yourself to legal recourse). The following section outlines a set of considerations that can help ensure a speedy, top-quality repair effort.

The value of data

It is a fact of modern computing that the data contained on a customer's hard drive(s) is usually more valuable than the PC hardware itself. If your customer is an

Gameport

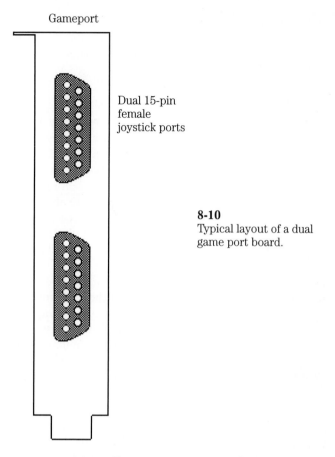

Dual 15-pin
female
joystick ports

8-10
Typical layout of a dual
game port board.

entrepreneur or corporate client, you can expect that the system contains valuable accounting, technical, reference, design, or operations information that is vital to their business. As a consequence, you should make it a priority to protect yourself from any potential liability issues connected with your customer's data. Even if the drives are causing the problem, a customer might hold you responsible if you are unable to restore or recover their precious information. Start a consistent regimen of written and oral precautions. Such precautions should include (but are not limited to):

- Always advise your customers to back up their systems regularly. Before the customer brings in their system, advise them to perform a complete backup of their drives if possible.
- When a customer delivers a system for repair, be sure that they sign a work order. Work orders should expressly give you authority and permission to work on the customer's system, outline such things as your hourly rate, labor minimums for evaluation and service, and show all applicable disclaimers. Your work order should include a strong disclaimer expressly relieving you of any and all liability for the contents of any magnetic media (such as hard drives) in the system. If you attempt data recovery, the disclaimer should

also disclaim any warranty or guarantee of results—that way, you're not liable if you are unable to recover vital files. Because liability issues vary from state to state and country to country, a local attorney can advise you on specific wording.

Opening the system

Most desktop and tower systems use a metal chassis covered by a painted metal cover or shroud that is secured with a series of screws. There are often nine screws—two on either side of the enclosure, and five at the rear of the chassis. Although this pattern covers many of the desktop PCs in service, you are likely to encounter a number of variations. You might find that instead of bolting screws in from the sides, the screws might be bolted in from the bottom. There also might be more or fewer screws in the rear of the chassis. Only on very rare occasions will you find screws used to secure the enclosure at its front—the molded plastic housing found on most desktop PCs does not accommodate screws without spoiling the finished "look."

Tower cases are a bit different. The metal shroud also uses about nine screws— all secured from the rear. The bottom and front edges of the enclosure are typically bent inward to interlock with the chassis when seated properly. This approach allows the entire enclosure to fit securely along the whole chassis while using only a minimum of screws. Enclosures that do not interlock, however, might require screws along the bottom and front edges. As a general rule, PC enclosure manufacturers tend to minimize the use of visible screws in order to enhance a seamless appearance—this is why most screws are relegated to the back chassis.

There are three factors to keep in mind when removing screws and other mounting hardware. First, be extremely careful not to mark or gouge the painted metal enclosure. Customers are rightfully possessive of their PC investment, and putting a scratch or dent in an enclosure is tantamount to dinging their new car (a careless reputation is very bad for business). Be equally careful of the enclosure after removing and setting it aside. Second, store the screws in a safe, organized place. The old "egg carton" trick might seem cliché, but it really does work. Of course, you are free to use plastic bags or organizer boxes as well—the idea here is to keep screws and other hardware off the work surface (unless you enjoy picking them up off the floor). Third, take note of each screw as you remove it, and keep groups of screws separated. This allows you put the right screws back into the corresponding locations. Because most enclosures use screws of equal size and length, this is rarely an issue at this phase of disassembly. But as you dismantle other subassemblies for upgrade or repair, keeping track of hardware becomes an important concern.

Use care when sliding the enclosure away. Metal inserts or reinforcements welded to the cover can easily catch on ribbon cables or other wiring. This can result in damage to the cable, and damage to whatever the cable is attached to. The rule is simple: force nothing! If you encounter any resistance at all, stop and search for the obstruction carefully—it's faster to clear an obstruction than to replace a damaged cable.

Closing the system

After your repair or upgrade is complete, you will need to close the system. Before sliding the enclosure back into place, however, make it a point to check the PC carefully. Make sure that every subassembly is installed and secured into place with the proper screws and hardware—leftover parts are unacceptable. A little care in organizing and sorting hardware during disassembly really pays off here. Remember to re-attach power and signal cables as required. Each cable must be installed properly and completely (in its correct orientation). Take time to route each signal cable with care and avoid jamming them into the system haphazardly. Careless cable runs stand a good chance of being caught and damaged by the enclosure during reassembly, or the next time the system needs to be disassembled. Properly routed cables also reduce the chance of signal problems (such as noise or crosstalk) that can result in unstable long-term operation. Also check the installation of any auxiliary cables such as CD-ROM sound cables, the speaker cable, and the keylock cable.

Once the system components are reassembled securely, you can apply power to the PC and run final diagnostics to test the system. When the system checks properly, you can slide the enclosure into place (being careful not to damage any cables or wiring) and secure the enclosure with its full complement of screws.

9
CHAPTER

Inside today's notebook

Computer users have long dreamed of shedding the bonds of their desk and wall outlet to take their computing tasks "on the road." PC manufacturers have been eager to respond, and the heavy, bulky, "portable" computers of years past have been replaced by a new generation of notebook and sub-notebook systems. Today's notebook computer (Fig. 9-1) offers levels of speed, performance, and storage capacity that rival almost any desktop system, and they do so in packages that are small, light, and energy efficient. Unfortunately, compressing so much utility into such a small volume results in very specialized and complex assemblies. This chapter of the book takes you inside a typical notebook PC to illustrate its major assemblies. You also will learn some disassembly and reassembly guidelines, along with a selection of security tips.

9-1
A Tandy 4800HD notebook
computer. Tandy Corporation

Inside the notebook

In spite of its small appearance, a notebook computer is an astoundingly complex assembly as you see in the exploded diagram of Fig. 9-2. Each subassembly must be fit together very carefully in order to make best use of the limited available space. This concentration of devices makes notebook disassembly and reassembly particularly difficult—there is literally no room for error here. Fortunately, most full-featured notebook and sub-notebook PCs are quite similar in the subassemblies used (and the relative location where each device is located). You can expect to find seven key items: (1) the enclosure, (2) the power source, (3) the motherboard, (4) a floppy disk drive, (5) a hard disk drive, (6) a display, and (7) a keyboard. Notice that unlike desktop and tower PCs, notebooks incorporate a display and keyboard.

Enclosure

The typical notebook enclosure is fabricated out of injection-molded plastic components (which you can see in Fig. 9-2). The lower base enclosure (marked K45 in the lower left of the diagram) serves as the chassis for the entire PC—just about all other subassemblies are attached to the base in one way or another. Once the motherboard, floppy drive, hard drive, and keyboard are assembled onto the base, the upper base enclosure (marked K37 in the upper right of the diagram) can be seated over the base and secured into place. The battery pack (marked K34) plugs into the motherboard and seats into the remaining opening at the rear of the upper enclosure. This essentially completes the lower half of the overall enclosure.

The rear display enclosure (marked K22) serves as the chassis for the upper half of the enclosure. It is this component that provides support for the display system. The backlight, display panel, and backlight power converter are mounted to the rear display enclosure, then covered with the front display enclosure (marked K1 in the middle left of the diagram) that virtually completes the upper half of the overall enclosure. The completed display system is then plugged into the motherboard and mated with the finished lower enclosure. When the upper and lower halves of the enclosure are mated together, the display panel swings down and interlocks with the lower enclosure. This classic enclosure scheme is known as a *clamshell* design. When the display is closed, the rear display enclosure not only protects the display, but the keyboard as well.

Normally, notebook and subnotebook PCs are not designed with expandability in mind; that is the price users pay for the smallest, lightest package. The only add-ons that most notebook systems are designed to tolerate are a modem and a memory expansion module. In both cases, the enclosure will reserve space expressly for the add-on. The net result of this trend is that small-computer add-ons tend to be expensive, manufacturer-specific products. With the broad introduction of PCMCIA ports into new notebook and subnotebook designs, however, manufacturer-specific add-ons are slowly giving way to generic add-on cards (memory cards, modem cards,

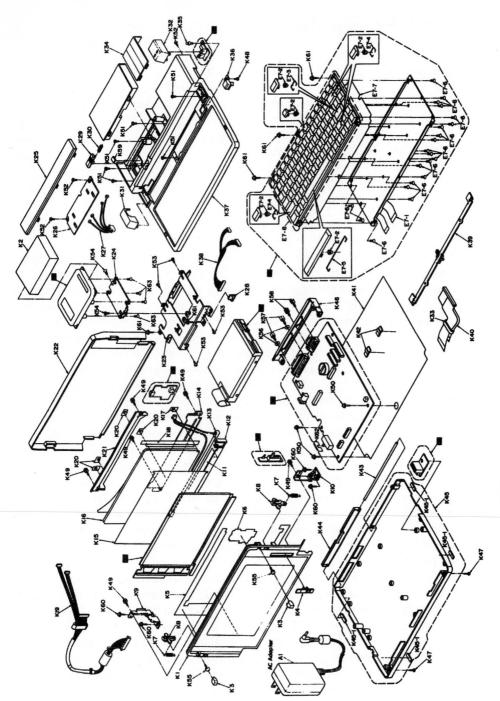

9-2 An exploded view of a Tandy 1500HD computer. Tandy Corporation

LAN cards, hard drive cards, and so on). Now that PCMCIA standards are stable and well recognized, even more add-ons will become available in the future.

Power source

Early laptop and notebook computers were small, but not truly mobile. These vintage systems required too much power to rely on an internal battery pack. To achieve true mobility, the PC would have to work from an internal rechargeable battery. By the late 1980s, portable PC designs improved (requiring substantially less power) and better batteries became available, so it became feasible to incorporate internal batteries that could be charged quickly from an external ac/dc power pack. This was the point where portable computing really took off. Figure 9-2 shows both of these elements. The ac adapter (marked A1) plugs into an available ac outlet and provides a level of dc (usually 12 to 24 V) directly to a power regulating circuit on the motherboard. While external power is available, the battery pack (marked K34) will charge and remain charged. When external power is absent, the system will run from battery power. In most cases, you will not find power supplies built into a notebook PC—there simply is not enough room in the system. Only older laptop and portable PCs will incorporate full supplies.

A notebook computer also will use a small power converter circuit to power the display backlight. *LCD*s (liquid-crystal displays) cannot be seen in indoor or low-light environments without the use of a light source located behind the display. In the diagram of Fig. 9-2, backlighting is provided by a fluorescent tube (marked K13). A fluorescent tube requires several hundred volts ac in order to light properly. A circuit called an ac inverter (marked E2) is used to chop dc into a low-current ac signal that drives the fluorescent tube. Note that the ac inverter is usually located in the display assembly. Chapter 33 covers displays and backlighting in detail. Chapter 47 details the operation and troubleshooting of high-voltage supply circuits.

Motherboard

The notebook motherboard (marked E1 in Fig. 9-2) contains virtually all of the processing and controller circuitry needed by a small computer. Not only will you find the CPU, co-processor, clock/timing circuits, RAM, and BIOS ROM, but the motherboard also must carry a serial port, parallel port, video control circuits and memory, drive controller circuits, and power regulation/battery-charging circuits. In effect, the notebook motherboard is a complete single-board computer. As shown in Fig. 9-3, there also are no expansion slots. With the exception of a modem and a bit of extra memory, most notebook PCs cannot be expanded beyond their original scope. Because portable PCs are advancing so rapidly, it is unlikely that you will even be able to find an upgraded motherboard to enhance the system. When you detect a fault on a notebook motherboard, your best bet is usually to exchange the motherboard outright with an exact replacement obtained from the manufacturer or their distributor(s).

Drives

Notebook computers typically offer two drives. An externally-mounted floppy disk drive (marked E8 in the middle of Fig. 9-2) is located in the right front quarter

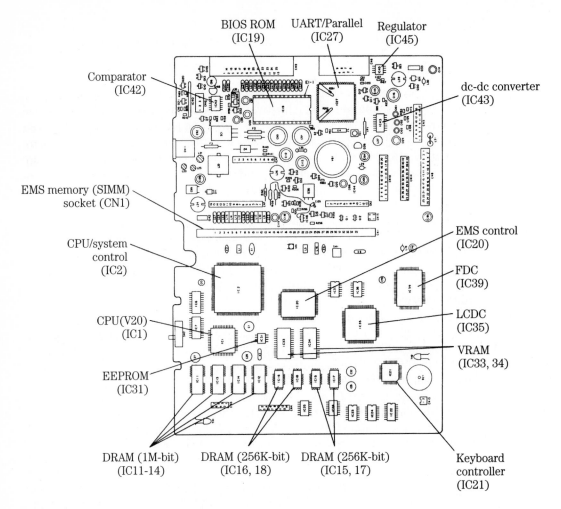

9-3 The motherboard for a Tandy 1500HD computer. Tandy Corporation

of the lower enclosure, and an internal hard disk drive (marked E9) is bolted in the rear left quarter of the lower enclosure—under and behind the keyboard. As you might expect, there are several variations to this theme. Some subnotebook systems abandon the built-in floppy drive that is then sold as a separate module. Unfortunately, carrying around a separate floppy drive limits the portability of the subnotebook. Instead of a floppy drive, you might find one or more PCMCIA slots designed to accommodate memory cards used to transfer data back and forth between the subnotebook and a desktop host machine. Hard drives are rarely overlooked in notebook and subnotebook PCs.

Given the small size of a notebook computer, there are no free drive bays as there are in most desktop and tower systems. Replacing or upgrading the drives must be accomplished with an exact physical replacement. For example, it is not difficult to upgrade a notebook's 120Mb hard drive with a 300Mb model—as long as the 300Mb drive has precisely the same form factor and mounting holes as the drive it is replacing.

Display

Unlike desktop and tower PCs that rely on stand-alone monitors, all notebook and subnotebook systems are equipped with a built-in display. Although the display is obvious to spot on sight, you should be familiar with some of their variations. There are generally two types of display systems that you will encounter: liquid crystal and plasma. Older laptop and notebook PCs often used *plasma* displays. You can identify a plasma display by its bright monochrome red-orange image. However, plasma displays tend to use a great deal of power, so virtually all portable systems today have abandoned plasma displays in favor of liquid crystal displays (LCDs). Liquid crystal displays also are easily identified: they produce either gray scale or full-color images. Figure 9-2 shows an LCD panel (marked E6).

In spite of its simple appearance, an LCD panel actually contains all of the circuitry needed to drive each picture element (or *pixel*). An LCD providing a resolution of 640 pixels wide and 480 pixels high will require enough circuitry to drive (640 × 480) 307,200 pixels. It is this large concentration of circuitry that makes an LCD panel one of the most delicate and expensive parts of a small computer. Chapter 33 covers LCD technology and troubleshooting in detail.

Keyboard

Notebook and subnotebook computers contain built-in keyboards. You can see the entire keyboard subassembly (marked as E7) in Fig. 9-2. The actual keyboard unit itself is marked as E7-8. Fortunately keyboards are obvious enough to spot on sight.

Connectors and ports

Normally, ports allow the PC to communicate with other devices. There are three major port connectors accessible from the rear panel of a notebook or subnotebook PC: a serial port, a parallel port, and an auxiliary video port. Figure 9-4 shows each of these connectors. The parallel port is identified as a 25-pin D-type female connector. Parallel ports are traditionally used to drive printers, but current ports are bidirectional, and can be used to support peripheral devices such as parallel port CD-ROMs, sound devices, joystick adapters, tape drives, and so on.

25-pin male   9-pin male   15-pin female
(serial)   (serial)   (VGA video)

25-pin female   RJ11   PS/2
(parallel)   (modem)   (mouse)

9-4 Comparison of typical notebook connectors.

You also can expect to find at least one serial port available. Older portable systems implement the serial port as a 25-pin D-type male connector. Do not confuse this with the parallel port connector. Because most serial communication can be accomplished with far fewer than 25 pins, newer computer designs implement the serial port as a 9-pin D-type male connector. Serial ports also can operate printers, but are more popular for communication between two or more PCs.

There are three other types of ports that you should be familiar with, although not all notebook or subnotebook PCs will have them. First is the auxiliary video port. The current video standard for PCs is the *VGA* (video graphics array). VGA typically supports 16 colors at 640 × 480 resolution, and 256 colors at 320 × 200 resolution. The video controller circuits in small computers support this color just fine, but many inexpensive small computers employ gray-scale displays. To take full advantage of the color potential, an auxiliary 15-pin D-type female VGA port is added to the motherboard. This allows a color monitor to be attached to the notebook. Earlier notebooks (prior to the wide acceptance of VGA) do not support auxiliary video outputs.

Second, widespread use of the mouse and trackball require an available port to connect the pointing device. Traditionally, the serial port has been used to support pointing devices, but with the growing popularity of external modems (which require a serial port), a dedicated mouse port is being added to newer systems. As you see in Fig. 9-4, the mouse port is often a dedicated PS/2 style connector. Third, you can tell when an internal modem is installed by the presence of an RJ11 telephone line connector. It is interesting to note that if an internal modem and dedicated mouse port are available, the serial port will probably remain unused.

Notes for disassembly and reassembly

Unfortunately, one of the greatest causes of collateral damage to a notebook or subnotebook computer is not static discharge, but technician error. Small-computer assemblies are almost diabolical in their intricacy, so excessive force applied to the wrong place at the wrong time can easily do more harm than good. In the best of circumstances, you will mar or scratch the plastic enclosures. In the worst of circumstances, you will rip out a cable or fracture a printed circuit board. As you might expect, the process of disassembly for a notebook or subnotebook PC is much more involved than for a desktop or tower system. This part of the chapter explains some basic tricks of disassembly and reassembly for small computers.

Note: The following discussions reflect current assemblies used on a variety of small computers. Your own notebook or subnotebook PC is probably similar, but is not necessarily the same. You should interpret the following material as a general guide rather than product-specific procedures.

The value of data

Although you might have seen this section in Chapter 8, it is worth repeating here. It is a fact of modern computing that the data contained on a customer's hard drive is usually more valuable than the PC hardware itself. If your customer is an entrepreneur or corporate client, you can expect that the system contains valuable accounting, technical, reference, design, or operations information that is vital to their business. As a consequence, you should make it a priority to protect yourself from any potential liability issues connected with your customer's data. Even if a drive is causing the problem, a customer might hold you responsible if you are unable to restore or recover their precious information. Start a consistent regimen of written and oral precautions. Such precautions should include (but are not limited to):

- Always advise your customers to back up their systems regularly. Before the customers bring in their system, advise them to perform a complete backup of their drive if possible.
- When a customer delivers a system for repair, be sure that they sign a work order. Work orders should expressly give you authority and permission to work on the customer's system, outline such things as your hourly rate, labor minimums for evaluation and service, and show all applicable disclaimers. Your work order should include a strong disclaimer expressly relieving you of any and all liability for the contents of any magnetic media (such as hard drives) in the system. If you attempt data recovery, the disclaimer also should disclaim any warranty or guarantee of results—that way, you're not liable if you are unable to recover vital files. Because liability issues vary from state to state and country to country, a local attorney can advise you on specific wording.

Opening the system

Computer manufacturers use two clever tricks to hide screws in order to achieve a smooth, seamless enclosure. First, many screws are hidden under slide-in or snap-in panels. Second, enclosures use pieces that snap together. Snap-fit pieces look great and provide even support, but taking the enclosure apart might be a nightmare unless you know where each snap point is located and how to disengage them. Once you are aware of these two factors, you will not be surprised when every visible screw has been removed—and the enclosures still won't part. When working with a notebook or subnotebook enclosure, remember the golden rule of disassembly: *force nothing!* Before beginning a disassembly, be sure to remove any expansion devices such as memory add-ons or PCMCIA cards that might interfere with the disassembly.

Base enclosure

Start your disassembly by closing the PC and placing it on a very soft cushion such as plush towels or foam. Remember that small computers use plastic enclosures, and plastic is highly prone to marks and scratches. The first step is to decouple the lower base enclosure from the upper base enclosure. Place the PC with its bottom up. You will likely find a series of six or eight small screws (several around the edges with one or two somewhere in the middle). Be sure to look under stickers, rubber feet, and snap-in panels for any hidden screws. When removing screws, be extremely cautious of their lengths and locations. Where desktop and tower systems use screws of the same length, small computers often do not. Sort each screw and diagram their locations if necessary.

Hold the entire PC carefully (so nothing falls apart in your hands) and place it bottom-down. Open the display panel and look for any screws that might be holding the base enclosures together. They will rarely be obvious. Check under hidden panels just behind the keyboard. Also check in the area of the display hinges. At this point, the upper base enclosure should be free. If not, the keyboard should be free, and the remaining screws that hold the upper base enclosure will probably be located under the keyboard. Remember to document your screw lengths and locations carefully. You can likely remove the upper base enclosure and entire display. If the enclosures still refuse to part, check for plastic snaps or latches. However, the base enclosure rarely relies on plastic latches. Gently ease the upper base enclosure off the lower base enclosure—remember that there will be display and power wiring connected to the motherboard. If you must disconnect any such cabling to free the upper enclosure and display, make careful note of the connector's position and orientation. Make a reference mark with an indelible marker if necessary.

Working the base enclosure

Now that the upper base enclosure and display have been moved aside, you should see the system's floppy drive, hard drive, motherboard, and battery compartment all bolted to the lower base enclosure. If the keyboard has not yet been freed, there will probably be several screws holding the keyboard in place. At this stage of disassembly, you can probably access the drives, motherboard, battery compartment (and keyboard if necessary) to replace the defective subassembly.

Display enclosure

The display enclosure contains three items: the display panel itself, the backlight assembly, and an ac inverter to drive the backlight. When any of these three subassemblies must be replaced, you can usually remove the front display enclosure without disassembling the base enclosure at all. In fact, you can even replace the plastic housings without touching the base enclosures. The only time you might ever need to break down the entire PC at the same time is when replacing fatigued or damaged wiring between the display and motherboard.

The front and rear display enclosures are usually held together with four screws as shown in Fig. 9-5—two in the upper corners and one in each of the hinges. It is important to realize that most displays hide these screws. The upper screws are usually hidden by small rubber plugs in either corner. If you gently pry out these plugs, you should find the screws. The lower screws are hidden by adhesive squares. Gently pry away these adhesive squares (but be very careful not to lose them). Once you remove the four screws, the front and rear display enclosures are interlocked by a series of plastic latches around the entire enclosure seam. You must gently disengage each latch without marking or breaking the enclosure.

Use wide, thin tools such as medium-sized regular screwdrivers. Insert the wide blade into the seam and use it as a lever to gently try to pull the rear display enclosure up. Remember—*force nothing!* If there is a latch, you will see it. Never rock or rotate the blade! Otherwise, the blade will leave permanent scars in the plastic. If you can free the latch, move onto the next adjacent latch. Free each latch in a clockwise or counterclockwise direction. The bottom latches are the most difficult because there is little room to work, but if you save those until last, there should be enough space between the enclosures where you can clearly see each remaining

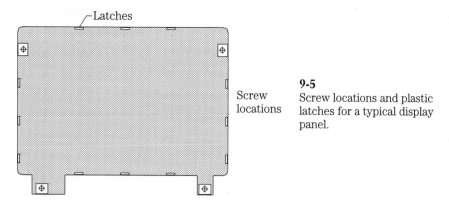

Screw
locations

9-5
Screw locations and plastic
latches for a typical display
panel.

latch. When the front display enclosure is free, put it aside in a safe place. You can then replace the display panel, backlight, or ac inverter as required.

Once again, be extremely careful not to mark or gouge the molded plastic enclosures. Customers are rightfully possessive of their PC investment, and putting a scratch or crack in an enclosure is tantamount to dinging their new car (a careless reputation is very bad for business). Be equally careful of the enclosure after removing and setting it aside. Second, store all screws in a safe, organized place. The old egg-carton trick might seem like a cliché, but it really does work. Of course, you are free to use plastic bags or organizer boxes as well—the idea here is to keep screws and other hardware off the work surface (unless you enjoy picking them up off the floor). Third, take note of each screw as you remove it, and keep groups of screws separated. This allows you put the right screws back into the corresponding locations. small computers regularly mix screws of varying lengths to accommodate their tight spaces.

Closing the system

After your repair or upgrade is complete, you will need to close the system. Before securing the enclosures back into place, however, make it a point to check the PC carefully. Make sure that every subassembly is installed and secured into place with the proper screws and hardware—leftover parts are unacceptable. A little care in organizing and sorting hardware during disassembly really pays off here. Remember to reattach power and signal cables as required. Each cable must be installed properly and completely (in its correct orientation). Take time to route each signal cable with care and avoid jamming them into the system haphazardly. Remember that there is virtually no extra room to work with, and careless cable runs stand a good chance of being caught and compressed by the enclosure during reassembly that can lead to damage or premature failure. Properly routed cables also reduce the chance of signal problems (such as noise or crosstalk) that can result in unstable long-term operation.

Seat the enclosures into place but do not secure them yet. Apply power to the PC and run a set of diagnostics to test the system. If diagnostics still register a fault, you will be spared the time and aggravation of having to disassemble the enclosures again. When the system checks properly, remove all power from the PC and re-assemble the enclosures securely. Restore power once again and run final diagnostics to check the system.

Notebook security

The great advantage to notebook and subnotebook computers is their easy portability. Unfortunately, that same portability makes small computers an easy target for PC thieves. As small computers have proliferated in homes and businesses around the world, so has their theft. Not only does theft result in a loss of physical hardware, but the loss of productivity and the loss of vital information as well. This part of the chapter shows you some ways to protect notebook and subnotebook PCs from becoming a statistic.

Insuring the hardware

One of the most tried-and-true methods of protecting valuable property (although certainly not the cheapest) is to insure it. If you own a PC for your home, ordinary homeowner's or renter's insurance can usually be arranged to cover the property. You should check with your current insurance broker to arrange the specific coverage (and determine the limitations of coverage). Be very cautious and inquisitive when arranging insurance for a portable computer. Some insurance policies might only cover the PC if it is stolen from a certain location (such as your home). Because portable PCs also might be stolen from your home, office, automobile, airplane luggage, and so on, make sure that any insurance covers the PC wherever it might be. When arranging insurance, also be sure to protect the replacement value of the PC rather than its book or depreciated value. For example, the i486/25 notebook you buy today for $2000.00 (US) might only be valued at $500.00 (US) in two years. If you only receive the value of the property, it is very unlikely that you will be able to purchase a comparable system for that amount.

Inscriptions and visible warnings

Another strategy is to inscribe the PC with traceable identification markings. Thieves rarely steal for themselves. In most cases, stolen property is sold to others looking for a bargain. However, most thieves look for clean property—items that cannot be traced back to the original owner. An effective means of deterring crime is to mark your property in a way that can be easily traced back to you. No thief wants to be caught with marked property—especially when marked property is more difficult to unload.

Although the idea of inscription is a good one, most people are not sure just what to inscribe. After all, phone numbers and addresses change—even then, you don't want thieves to know your phone number or address. Under most circumstances, you can inscribe three pieces of information: your name, your company's name (if appropriate), and the serial number of the unit. Although a serial number is usually included on an adhesive label, a label can be removed, an inscribed number cannot. You also should note the model and serial number on a piece of paper and include it with your purchase documentation for the PC. If the unit is stolen, law authorities can trace the PC by its serial number.

Lock and key

One of the most reliable ways to prevent a theft is to keep the PC under lock and key whenever you must leave it unattended for any period of time. Thieves look for a quick grab. Locking the system in your car, desk, or filing cabinet keeps the PC hidden and provides a line of defense against any thief who has the inclination to search for goodies. As a general rule, avoid tether systems that require you to use adhesive mounts and tie your PC to a desk or wall with plastic or metal wire. Adhesives are rarely strong enough to withstand a determined tug, and the connecting cable can usually be defeated with a pair of heavy diagonal cutters.

Securing the software

Data has value—in some cases, lots of value. Hardware can be replaced fairly easily, but more than one company has gone under after losing valuable computerized records. The best protection of your data can be accomplished with a full backup to tape or diskette. Back up *now*, and back up regularly. Keep your backups in an area that is physically separate from your hardware—perhaps a locked cabinet or fire-proof safe. Even if a thief manages to make off with your PC, you can restore a good-quality backup to an alternate PC and continue operating virtually without interruption.

But what about the information on the stolen PC? Even though a regimen of backups can preserve your data, thieves still have access to your sensitive or valuable information. In many cases, the thief has little interest in data, but rendering the hard drive useless to a thief is often important for your piece of mind. Try a hard drive locking utility such as *The Guardian*, which is included on the companion disk. When installed, The Guardian shows an initialization screen showing that the PC is protected. It then asks for a password. After three inaccurate passwords, The Guardian locks the hard drive by scrambling the hard drive's directory. Only the proper password will unlock the disk again. If you want extra security, you can use The Guardian to lock your drive manually (before you power down the system for the evening). Of course, a bootable floppy disk can be used to circumvent the password request, but if the hard drive is already locked, your data is relatively safe from prying eyes. Even disk reconstruction programs cannot return the drive to its pre-locked state.

10
CHAPTER

Inside today's monitors

The ability to display images and information has evolved right along with CPUs, memory, hard drive space, and all of the other computer attributes that we associate with PC performance. Although the essential principles of a monitor have remained virtually unchanged, the small, drab monochrome displays of just a decade ago have been almost entirely replaced by flicker-free, high-resolution monitors capable of producing photo-realistic color images (Fig. 10-1). Today's monitor is more than just an output device—it has become a window into the complex virtual world created by computers. This chapter shows you what is inside the typical color monitor, and provides some guidelines for monitor disassembly and reassembly.

10-1 A Gateway 2000 4DX2-66 system with a CrystalScan monitor.

Monitor assembly

As shown in Fig. 10-2, a typical computer monitor is not very complicated. Compared to notebook computers and low-profile desktop systems, the monitor assembly is spacious. This is not an accident—monitors require substantial amounts of

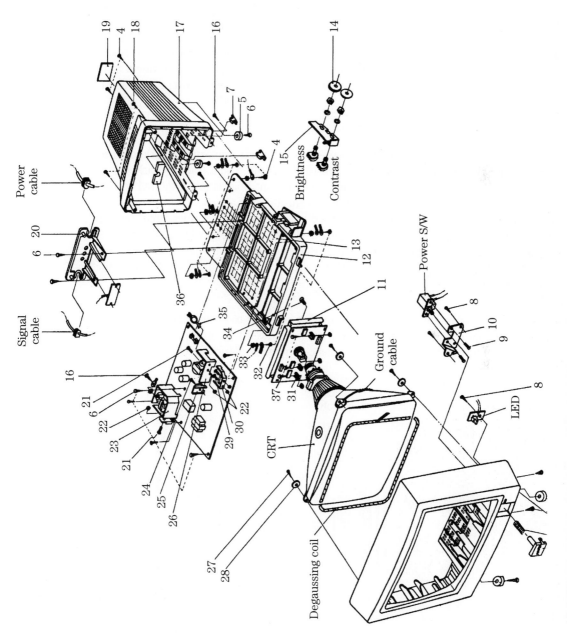

10-2 Exploded diagram of a Tandy VGM220 monitor. Tandy Corporation

energy for operation. Much of this energy is dissipated as heat. Extra space prevents a buildup of heat from damaging the monitor's circuitry, and heat is allowed to escape through ventilation slots in the enclosure. Another reason for ample enclosure space is to ensure ample high-voltage insulation. Some monitors generate up to 30 kV during normal operation, and normal plastic wire insulation is hardly sufficient to ensure safety. High-voltage insulation and plenty of unobstructed space keeps high-voltage from arcing to other circuits. The typical monitor can be broken down into five sections: (1) the enclosure, (2) the CRT, (3) a CRT drive board, (4) a raster drive board, and (5) a power supply.

Enclosure

Monitor enclosures are built as two pieces, The front enclosure (marked 3) is used to mount the CRT and degaussing coil. This is bolted to a frame (marked 12) that forms the base of the monitor. Once other circuit boards are attached to the frame, the rear enclosure (marked 17) forms a shroud over almost all of the monitor. In most cases, the rear enclosure can be freed by removing four screws (marked 18) as shown in Fig. 10-2. A few monitor enclosures are held together by plastic latches in addition to screws. If the rear enclosure does not slide away easily, suspect the presence of snap-in latches, or extra screws installed into the frame from the bottom.

CRT

Although color monitors rely on extra video circuitry to process color signals, it is the design and construction of the CRT itself (marked CRT in Fig. 10-2) that really makes color monitors possible. The basic principles of a color CRT (Fig. 10-3)

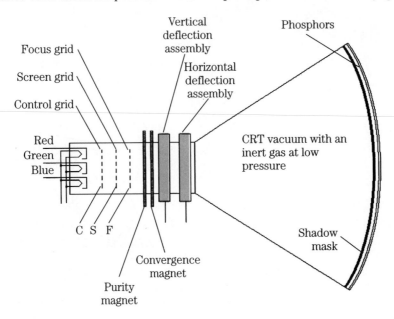

10-3 Diagram of a typical color CRT assembly.

are very similar to a monochrome monitor—electrons "boil" off the cathode and are accelerated toward the phosphor-coated front screen by a high positive potential. Color CRTs use three cathodes and video control grids—one for each of the three primary colors. Control (brightness), screen, and focus grids serve the same purpose as they do in monochrome CRTs. The control grid regulates the overall brightness of the electron beams, the screen grid begins accelerating the electron beams toward the front screen, and the focus grid narrows the beams. Once the electron beams are focused, vertical and horizontal deflection coils (or deflection yokes) apply magnetic force to direct the beams around the screen.

You will notice a shadow mask added to the color CRT. A shadow mask is a thin plate of metal that contains thousands of microscopic perforations—one perforation for each screen pixel. The mask is placed in close proximity to the phosphor face. There also is a substantial difference in the screen phosphors. Where a monochrome CRT uses a homogeneous layer of phosphor across the entire face, a color CRT uses phosphor *triads* as shown in Fig. 10-4 (the distance between the shadow mask and phosphor screen is shown greatly exaggerated). Red, green, and blue phosphor dots are arranged in sets such that the red, green, and blue electron beams will strike the corresponding phosphor. In actual operation, the color dots are so close together that each triad appears as a single point (or pixel). A *degaussing coil* (shown in Fig. 10-2) mounted in front of the CRT works to keep the shadow mask demagnetized.

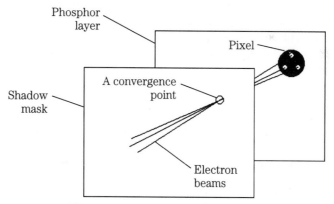

*Sizes and distances are NOT shown to scale

10-4 The relationship of a shadow mask and color phosphors.

Color CRTs also must be more precise in how the three electron beams are directed around the screen. Because there are now three phosphors instead of just one, it is critical that each electron beam strike only its corresponding phosphor color—not adjoining phosphors. This is known as *color purity*. A purity magnet added to the CRT yoke helps to adjust fine beam positioning. By using a shadow mask, the electron beams are only allowed to reach the phosphors where there are holes in the mask. Also realize that each of the three electron beams must converge at each hole in the shadow mask. A convergence magnet added to the CRT yoke adjusts beam convergence in the display center (known as static convergence), while a convergence coil driven by the raster circuitry optimizes beam convergence at the edges of the display (known as dynamic convergence). It is this delicate balance of purity and convergence adjustments, as well as the presence of a shadow mask, that give today's color monitors such rich, precise color.

CRT drive board

The CRT drive board (marked 31 in Fig. 10-2) attaches directly to the CRT pins through a circular connector. Control (brightness), screen, and focus grid voltages are applied to the CRT through this board. The CRT drive board also contains the red, green, and blue video amplifiers and drivers. Because more CRT drive circuitry is needed for a color monitor than a monochrome monitor, the CRT drive board for a color monitor is usually much larger than that of a monochrome monitor. Once the monitor is unplugged and discharged, make sure that this board is attached evenly and securely to the CRT. It is the CRT drive circuit that regulates the strength of each electron beam by adjusting signal strength on the corresponding video control grid in the CRT. The CRT drive circuit must convert a small video signal (usually no more than 0.7 V) into a signal large enough to drive the CRT (typically around 50 V). For color monitors with three analog video lines, three separate video drive circuits are required. Problems can strike the CRT drive circuits in a number of ways, but there are clues to help guide your way. If the display should disappear, but the raster remains (*raster* is that dim haze you see by turning up the monitor's brightness), the video signal might have failed at the video adapter board in your PC. If there is suddenly not enough (or far too much) red, green, or blue in the displayed image, the corresponding DAC (digital-to-analog converter) on the video adapter might have failed, or the corresponding CRT drive circuit in the monitor might have broken down. Try a known-good monitor. If the correct image appears, you know the video adapter is producing the desired output, and the original monitor is probably defective. If no display appears on a known-good monitor, suspect the video adapter board in your PC. If the screen is black, suffers from fixed brightness (with or without video input), or loses focus, one or more grids in the CRT might have shorted and failed. Refer to Chapter 38 for detailed instructions on monitor troubleshooting.

Raster drive board

The main raster board contains the vertical raster, horizontal raster, and high-voltage circuits that actually drive the CRT and direct the electron beam(s) around the screen. Depending on the design of your particular monitor, the raster board might contain part or all of the power supply circuit as well. Just about all monitors mount the raster board directly to the frame horizontally below the CRT neck. This assembly can be difficult to remove because it is obstructed by the CRT neck and yoke, as well as the interconnecting wiring that connects to the power supply, front panel controls, and flyback transformer.

The vertical drive circuit is used to operate the vertical deflection yoke. This is accomplished with a vertical sweep oscillator, which is little more than a free-running oscillator set to run at either 60 or 70/72 Hz (depending on the design of the particular monitor). When the oscillator is triggered, it produces a sawtooth wave—the start of the sawtooth wave corresponds to the top of the screen, while the end of the sawtooth wave corresponds to the bottom of the screen. When the sawtooth cycle is complete, there is a blank period for blanking and retrace. One vertical sweep will be accomplished in less than $\frac{1}{60}$ of a second (or $\frac{1}{70}$ or $\frac{1}{72}$ of a second depending on the monitor).

Trouble with the vertical drive circuit usually strikes the vertical output driver circuit. If part of the driver should fail, either the upper or lower half of the image will disappear. If the entire driver should fail, the screen image will compress to a straight horizontal line in the center of the screen (there would be no vertical deflection—only horizontal deflection). Another problem is vertical oversweep that elongates the picture to the extent where it "wraps back" on itself in the lower portion of the screen. The area where the vertical image oversweeps will appear with a whitish haze and is typically the fault of the vertical oscillator circuit.

The horizontal drive circuit is the second part of the color monitor's raster circuit, and it is designed to operate the horizontal deflection yoke. This is accomplished with a horizontal oscillator, which is little more than a free-running oscillator set to run at a frequency between 15 kHz and 48 kHz. A CGA monitor will typically use a horizontal sweep frequency of about 15.75 kHz. The actual oscillator might be based on a transistor, but is usually designed around an integrated circuit that is more stable at the higher frequencies that are needed. When a horizontal synchronization trigger pulse is received from the video adapter board, the oscillator is forced to fire. When the oscillator is triggered, it produces a square wave. The start of the square wave corresponds to the left side of the screen. When the cycle is complete, there is a blank period for blanking and retrace. At an operating frequency of 31.5 kHz, one horizontal sweep will be accomplished in about 31.7 μs.

Trouble with the horizontal drive circuit usually strikes the horizontal output drive circuit because that is the circuit that sustains the greatest stress in the monitor. If the drive circuit should fail, the entire image will disappear because high-voltage generation also will be affected. Unfortunately, a fault in the horizontal oscillator also will result in an image loss because high-voltage generation depends on a satisfactory horizontal pulse. If the horizontal oscillator or amplifier fails, high-voltage fails as well, and the image becomes too faint to see—this makes troubleshooting horizontal problems a bit more difficult than troubleshooting vertical problems.

The high-voltage system is actually part of the horizontal drive circuit. A monitor's power supply generates relatively low voltages (usually not much higher than 140 V). This means that the high positive potential needed to excite the CRT's anode is *not* developed in the power supply. Instead, the 15 to 30 kV needed to power a CRT anode is generated from the horizontal output. The amplified, high-frequency pulse signal generated by the horizontal driver circuit is provided to the primary winding of a device known as the *FBT* (flyback transformer). It is the FBT that produces the high voltage.

Power supply

The power supply is typically a hand-sized assembly that converts ac into several dc voltage levels (usually +135, +20, +12, +6.3, and +87 Vdc) that will be needed by other monitor circuits. The ac itself might be filtered and fused by a separate small assembly. If there is no stand-alone power supply board in your particular monitor, the supply is probably incorporated into the raster board. As you saw earlier, the only voltage that is not produced in the power supply is the high-voltage source. A stand-alone power supply is typically mounted vertically to the frame. The metal frame not only provides a rigid mounting platform, but it serves as a chassis common, and helps to contain RF signals generated by the monitor.

Notes on monitor disassembly and reassembly

Warning: The computer monitor operates with exposed voltages that are potentially lethal! **This makes monitors unusually dangerous in the hands of novice or inexperienced troubleshooters. Make sure that the monitor is *unplugged* and allowed several minutes to discharge before reaching into the assembly. Do not operate the monitor without its X-ray and RF shields in place (if applicable). It also is advisable to work with a second person nearby.**

The process of monitor disassembly is remarkably straightforward. In most cases, only the rear enclosure must be removed to expose the entire inner workings of the monitor. The rear enclosure itself is typically held in place with only four screws (there might be additional screws inserted at the bottom). On some occasions, you also might encounter a number of plastic latches, but this is rare. After removing the rear enclosure, you will see the bell and neck of the CRT, the CRT drive board, the raster board, and the power supply (if a separate supply is used).

Take note of any metal shrouds or coverings that are included with the monitor assembly. Metal shielding serves two very important purposes. First, the oscillators and amplifiers in a monitor produce *RF* (radio frequency) signals that have the potential to interfere with radio and TV reception. The presence of metal shields or screens helps to attenuate any such interference, so always make it a point to replace shields securely before testing or operating the monitor. Second, large CRTs (larger than 17 inches) use very high voltages (25 kV or more) at the anode. With such high potentials, X radiation becomes a serious concern. CRTs with lower anode voltages can usually contain X rays with lead in the CRT glass. Metal shields are added to the larger CRTs as supplemental shielding in order to stop X rays from escaping the monitor enclosure. When X-ray shielding is removed, it is vital that it be replaced before the monitor is tested and returned to service. X-ray shields will usually be clearly marked when you remove the monitor's rear cover.

Discharging the CRT

Before removing any wiring or boards from the monitor, it is important to be sure that the CRT is fully discharged. Even though unplugging the monitor will prevent ac and high-voltage electrocution, there might still be enough high-voltage charge stored in the CRT to provide a fair kick to the careless. Make sure the monitor is turned off and allow several minutes for the ac supply to discharge. Use a regular-blade screwdriver with a heavy-duty alligator clip attached between the screwdriver shaft and the metal chassis. Gently insert the screwdriver blade under the high-voltage anode cap as shown in Fig. 10-5. You will probably hear a mild crackle as the CRT is grounded. Do not rotate the screwdriver or force it in the CRT—remember that the CRT is still a glass assembly, and excessive force can damage it easily. Once the crackle stops, remove the screwdriver and unplug the monitor's ac cord. The assembly should now be safe to work on.

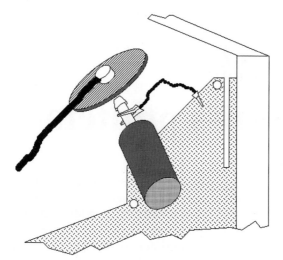

10-5 Discharging an unpowered CRT before servicing.

Removing subassemblies

Removing boards is often a simple matter. The CRT drive board is simply plugged into the CRT through a circular connector. Rock the video board back and forth gently to pull it away from the CRT. The raster board is typically mounted to the frame with several screws. After the screws are removed, the raster board should be free. When removing any board, be sure to make a careful note of each connector's location and orientation. A CRT is held in place with a metal bracket bolted to the front enclosure. Unfortunately, replacing the CRT usually means removing the video and raster boards along with the frame. If you must place the monitor (or front enclosure alone) face down onto a work surface, be sure to use a layer of soft towels or foam to prevent scratches to the front enclosure or CRT.

Replacing subassemblies

The most important rule to remember when exchanging a board or CRT is to use an exact replacement part. Monitors are precisely timed, high-energy systems, so "close" doesn't count. An improper replacement assembly might cause the monitor to malfunction, or it might work only for a limited amount of time. When reassembling a monitor, be extremely careful of the wiring interconnecting each board and the CRT. Be sure that all wiring and connectors are installed properly and completely. Loose connectors can cause erratic or intermittent operation. Pay close attention to wire paths—do not allow wiring to be pinched under boards or against the metal chassis. Finally, make it a point to re-install any RF or X-ray shielding that might have been removed during the repair.

11
CHAPTER

Inside today's printers

Printers, once a high-priced commodity reserved only for businesses and other institutions, have rapidly become indispensable tools in homes and offices around the world (Fig. 11-1). Printers produce business letters or newsletters, address the mail, plot complex drawings, generate long listings of information, and perform many other boring, redundant jobs. The sheer variety of printer sizes, shapes, technologies, and features simply stagger the imagination. Yet in spite of this diversity, every printer ever made performs the same function—to translate a computer's output to paper as an intricate series of dots. This chapter is intended to take you inside of contemporary printers using impact, ink jet, and electrostatic printing technologies.

11-1
A Tandy LP800 laser printer.
Tandy Corporation

Carriage-type printers

All printers form an image by placing dots onto a page surface, but carriage-type printers use a discrete print head that is carried left-to-right and right-to-left across a page surface. Once the print head completes a pass, the page advances slightly, and the print head completes another pass. This repetitive cycle continues until the document is completed. It is the print head itself that defines the technology being employed. Impact, ink jet, and thermal transfer printing technologies each make use of carriage-type platforms that are very similar to each other—only the head and head driving circuitry are noticeably different. For the purposes of this book, only impact and ink jet printers will be considered. Thermal transfer printers are devoted to small, point-of-sale printers, and are rarely used in current PC full-page printers. Figure 11-2 shows a typical carriage-type printer. There are five key sections to the assembly: (1) the enclosure, (2) the printer logic board, (3) the paper transport system, (4) the carriage transport system, and (5) the print head. Each element is examined in detail.

Enclosure

The carriage-type printer enclosure is essentially a two-piece plastic assembly. The base enclosure (marked 17 in Fig. 11-2) forms the chassis—electronic and mechanical assemblies are fixed to the base enclosure. As a result, the base enclosure tends to be relatively heavy gauge plastic. The upper enclosure (marked 2) fits directly over the base. The two pieces are held together with little more than four screws inserted from the underside (items marked 22). You might notice that the top enclosure has an open face. When the printer is assembled, an open front gives a technician easy access to the print head and carriage area. A face enclosure (marked 6) snaps into place to provide a cosmetic finish. The paper guide (marked 1) acts as a paper separation pawl. Paper entering the printer enters through a space underneath the guide, and paper exiting the printer exits over the guide. Finally, a small smoked plastic shroud (marked 7) fits into the face enclosure and extends out to cover part of the carriage area. This supplemental covering helps to keep dust and debris out of the carriage area.

Printer logic board

The logic board is the heart and mind of a carriage-type printer. You might find a large board (or several different boards) in older printers, but current printer designs are able to carry the printer's power supply and logic on a single small printed circuit board. The power supply can easily be included on the logic board because only a few, low-current, dc voltages are needed by the printer. The logic portion communicates with the host computer (the parallel port) and stores received characters, then translates each character into dot sequences while driving the carriage and paper advance. The board itself (marked 13 in Fig. 11-2) is actually mounted to a metal subchassis (marked 15). A power switch (marked 16) fits into the metal structure and plugs into the logic board. The entire subassembly then simply snaps into waiting plastic tabs on the base enclosure. A small control panel (marked 4) plugs into the logic board through a thin control panel.

Paper transport

Paper has to be moved through the printer. The paper transport system is the mechanical subassembly responsible for handling paper movements. There are two ways to carry paper through a printer: friction feed and traction feed. The friction

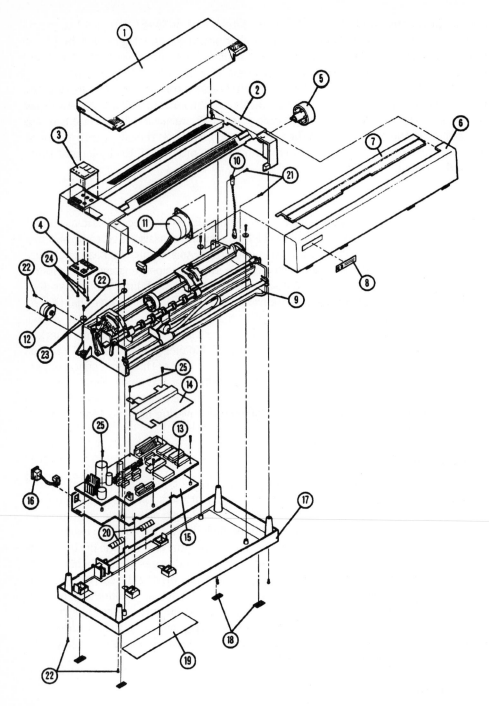

11-2 An exploded diagram of an HP QuietJet printer. Hewlett-Packard Company

feed system is shown in Fig. 11-3. A sheet of paper is inserted between the platen and one or two pressure rollers that are then placed in compression. As the platen advances, pressure between the platen and roller will force the paper through. Because this technique relies on friction, coated or low-friction papers might not work properly. Smooth and even paper feed also relies on even compression between the platen and pressure roller(s). If there is any misalignment, paper will tend to pull (or walk) to the left or right. Friction feed systems do not accommodate continuous forms very well.

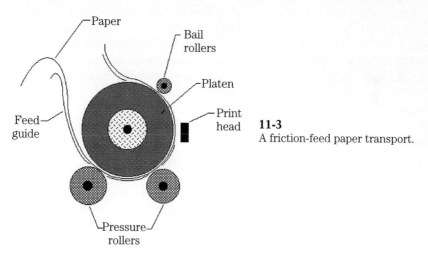

11-3
A friction-feed paper transport.

The tractor-feed system is shown in Fig. 11-4. Continuous-form paper is inserted around the platen, and the sprocket holes in either side of the paper are inserted into corresponding points on the printer's sprocket wheels. Because there is no pressure to force paper through, this approach relies on hard contact between the paper holes and sprocket wheels. As the platen advances, the sprocket wheels also advance and pull the paper through evenly. There is no tendency for the paper to walk, so tractor feed is ideal for long documents or large quantities of forms.

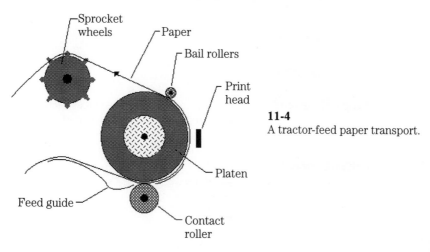

11-4
A tractor-feed paper transport.

The paper transport for Fig. 11-2 is a tractor-feed mechanism that is integrated into the paper/head transport assembly (marked 9 in Fig. 11-2). A platen index motor (marked 11) mounts to the rear right side of the mechanical assembly, and a gear arrangement between the motor and platen provides the drive force. A platen knob (marked 5) passes through a hole in the upper enclosure and fits into the platen. This allows you to rotate the platen by hand.

Carriage transport

The print head has to be carried back and forth across the page surface, so the platen/head transport assembly (marked 9) also contains the carriage transport mechanism. A carriage motor (marked 12 in Fig. 11-2) rotates and draws a pulley attached to the print head cradle. For example, when the motor rotates clockwise, the print head slides to the right along a smooth track. When the motor rotates counterclockwise, the print head slides to the left. The entire platen/head transport assembly seats into the printer's base enclosure where it is bolted into place.

Print head

The print head is an electro-mechanical device that actually transcribes dots onto the page surface. As mentioned elsewhere in this chapter, this book is concerned with two carriage-type print heads: impact and ink jet. A basic impact print head is shown in Fig. 11-5. Essentially, the impact print head is little more than a collection of independent solenoids. Typical impact heads have 9 or 24 solenoids, and each solenoid can be fired independently. When an electrical pulse is sent to a solenoid, a hard, small print wire shoots out and impresses itself on the page through an inked ribbon. As the pulse passes, the print wire retracts into the solenoid to be fired again. Because a relatively large amount of energy is required to operate solenoids, impact heads generate a large amount of heat. Impact heads will typically have a metal case and heatsink fins to help dissipate the heat. Never touch an impact print head until it has had ample time to cool.

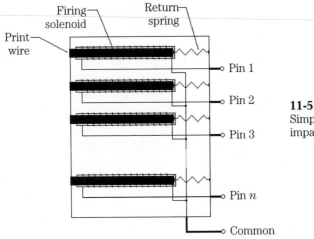

11-5
Simplified cross-section of an impact print head.

An ink-jet print head does not require an inked ribbon. Instead, the head carries its own ink supply in a rubber *bladder* as shown in Fig. 11-6. Ink flows to the tip of each nozzle where it is retained by capillary action. Each ink tube is fitted with a small piezoelectric crystal. When an electrical pulse is applied to the corresponding crystal, the crystal suddenly contracts—this ejects a droplet of ink from the nozzle. As the pulse passes, the crystal relaxes and creates a vacuum that draws more ink from the bladder. When the bladder is exhausted, the entire print head is easily replaced. The replacement process is often as simple as unsnapping and removing the spent cartridge, then snapping in a fresh one.

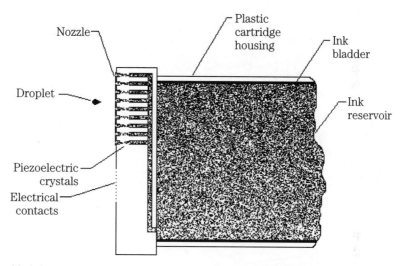

11-6 Simplified cross-section of an ink-jet print head.

An alternate carriage printer

The classic problem with carriage-type printers such as the type dissected in Fig. 11-2 is that, although it is capable of single-sheet operation, each sheet has to be inserted and aligned manually before the page can be printed—a frustrating and labor-intensive operation. Because many ink-jet printer designs are well suited to high-quality graphic output, printer makers such as Hewlett-Packard developed a carriage-type printer expressly designed to handle single sheets automatically. Figure 11-7 shows the HP DeskJet assembly. As with ordinary carriage-type printers, the alternate carriage design features five prominent elements: (1) the enclosure, (2) the printer circuits, (3) the paper transport system, (4) the carriage transport system, and (5) the print head.

Enclosure

The enclosure offers some substantial differences over the classic design. The base enclosure (marked 20 in Fig. 11-7) serves as the printer's chassis. The upper enclosure (marked 5) is molded as a single piece that snaps into place over the base

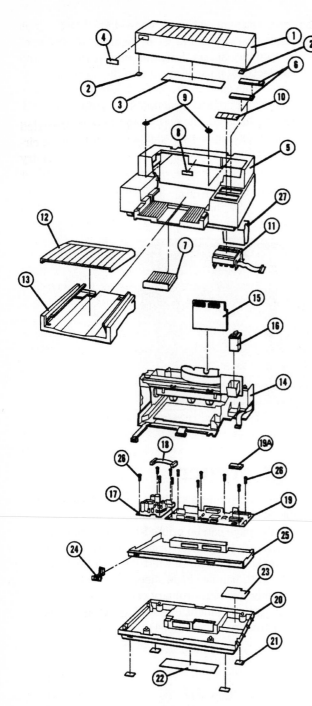

11-7
An exploded diagram of an
HP DeskJet printer. Hewlett-
Packard Company

enclosure. A stack of single-sheet paper loads into the front deck of the upper enclosure and is held in place with a paper retainer (marked 7). Notice that the upper
enclosure is largely open at the top. This provides a technician with easy access to
the ink cartridge and carriage assembly. The top enclosure (marked 1) inserts into

hinges on the upper enclosure that allows the top enclosure to swing up or down as needed. When the printer is assembled, the paper output tray (marked 13) receives the sheets ejected from the paper transport. The smoked tray cover (marked 12) sits over the paper output tray and completes the cosmetic image.

Printer circuits

The printer in Fig. 11-2 showed only a single printed circuit board that carried the power supply, printer logic, communication circuits, and print head driving circuits. Although the printer in Fig. 11-7 is no more complex, it breaks the circuitry into three separate assemblies: the logic board, the power supply, and the driver board. The logic board (marked 19 in Fig. 11-7) handles all communication between the printer and host computer, and translates stored printer characters into control signals for the paper/head transport assembly and print head driver board. A power supply (marked 17) sits adjacent to the logic board. Both the power supply and logic board are mounted to a metal subchassis (marked 25). A power switch fits into a subchassis hole and connects to the power supply. The entire subassembly then sits into the base enclosure. It is interesting to note that the subchassis is not bolted or snapped into the base enclosure. The print head driver board (marked 15) slides into an available slot in the paper/head transport assembly and connects to the print head cradle. An ink-jet cartridge (marked 16) snaps into the cradle. The only other electronic element is the control panel (marked 11) that plugs into the logic board and sits in place beneath the top enclosure.

Paper transport

Single sheets of paper are fed into the printer using a technique very similar to that shown in Fig. 11-8. A small stack of paper fits into the printer. When a new sheet is needed, a paper take-up roller turns once. One rotation will grab the next subsequent page and drag it to the feed roller, which in turn pulls the page in an arc past a fixed platen. As the ink-jet print head travels back and forth across the page, the feed roller advances the paper. Once the page is finished, it drops into the paper out-

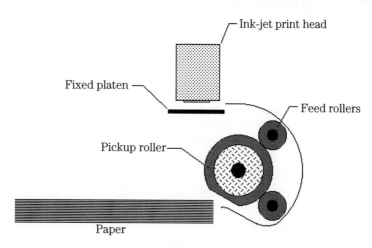

11-8 Simplified diagram of a typical ink-jet paper transport.

put tray. The paper pickup and advance motor is built into the paper/head transport assembly (marked 14 in Fig. 11-7).

Carriage transport

Of course, the print head must be carried back and forth across the page surface—this is the task of the carriage transport. It works just like the carriage transport covered in the last section. A motor drives a pulley attached to the print head cradle. As the motor turns in one direction, the print head carriage moves in one direction along a fixed track. When the carriage motor reverses, the print head carriage reverses its direction. The carriage transport system is incorporated into the paper/head transport assembly (marked 14 in Fig. 11-7).

Print head

The print head used in Fig. 11-7 is an ink-jet cartridge (marked 16). Replaceable cartridges use the same operating principles as the ink-jet head shown in Fig. 11-6. You can see a close-up of a contemporary print head in Fig. 11-9.

11-9
A replaceable ink-jet print head
and reservoir. Hewlett-Packard Company

Page-type printers

All printers form their images as a series of dots that are transferred to a page surface. Where carriage-type printers operate by passing a print head across the paper, page-type printers develop the entire page image that is transferred to a page all at once. Page printers are typically based on *EP* (electro-photographic) technology. As shown in Fig. 11-10, the EP system is one of the most complex and intricate printing systems available—it also is capable of unsurpassed printing quality and consistency at resolutions up to 600 *DPI* (dots per inch). To appreciate the differences between carriage and page printing, you should understand the basics of page printer operation.

Image-formation system

In a carriage-type printer, a print head produces the image, and it is easy to see the point at which an image appears on the page. On the other hand, an EP printer requires a variety of assemblies needed to produce a permanent image—in fact, most of the printer is used to make the image (referred to as the image formation

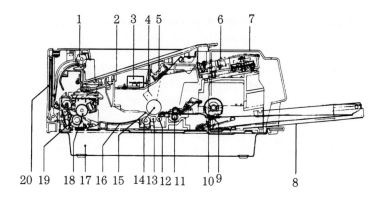

1. Delivery assembly
2. Face-down tray
3. Erase lamp assembly
4. Primary corona
5. Beam-to-drum mirror
6. Laser/scanning assembly
7. Main body covers
8. Paper tray
9. Separation pad
10. Feed roller assembly
11. Registration rollers
12. Transfer corona roller
13. Transfer corona assembly
14. Photosensitive EP drum
15. EP drum protective shield
16. Feed guide assembly
17. Lower main body
18. Upper fusing roller
19. Lower pressure roller
20. Face-up output tray (closed)

11-10 Cross-sectional diagram of an HP LaserJet-type printer. Hewlett-Packard Company

system or IFS). Electro-photographic printing starts with a stack of paper in a paper tray (marked 8 in Fig. 11-10). When a printing cycle begins, a single sheet of paper is grabbed by a feed roller (marked 10) and separation pad (marked 9), and is passed to a set of registration rollers (marked 11) that hold the paper sheet in place until the image is ready to be transferred.

EP image formation starts and ends with a photosensitive drum (marked 14) that receives electrical charges across its surface that correspond to the individual dots of the image being formed. A rotating EP drum is erased by exposing it to light from an erase lamp (marked 3). As the drum continues to rotate, a primary corona (marked 4) places a uniform charge along the drum's surface. To form the image, the drum must be discharged at the points where dots are to appear. This is accomplished by means of a writing mechanism. In a laser printer, a laser beam is produced and scanned across the drum surface using a laser/scanning assembly (marked 6). The beam is reflected off a beam-to-drum mirror (marked 5) and down to the drum surface. As the beam scans, it is turned on and off corresponding to the presence or absence of each dot. One pass is equal to one complete row of pixels across the page. For a printer working at 300 DPI, one pass is $\frac{1}{300}$ of an inch. As the drum continues to rotate, areas of the drum discharged by the laser light pick up toner that is attracted to the drum.

At this point, the drum has a developed image, which can now be transferred to paper. The registration rollers that had been holding the paper now start the page moving. A transfer roller (marked 12) grabs the page and passes it over a transfer corona (marked 13). The transfer corona places a high charge on the paper that attracts toner off of the drum and onto the page surface. Excess toner is gently removed from the drum that is cleaned by the erase lamp assembly in preparation for another pass. The drum continues to rotate as the page moves by, and the image is continuously transferred to paper. The charged paper is discharged by a static eliminator comb, and it moves to the fusing assembly. Toner is still in its powder form, so it must be melted and pressed into the paper. The fusing assembly uses a heated upper fusing roller (marked 18) and a lower pressure roller (marked 19) to accomplish fusing. After that, the completed page is passed in an upward clockwise arc where it is ejected into the paper output tray.

Enclosure

As shown in Fig. 11-10, an EP printer is hardly a trivial assembly. A great deal of mechanical precision is packed into a relatively small package. Fortunately, EP printer design has evolved to a point where almost all of the critical devices are fabricated into subassemblies that can easily be replaced on the workbench. Figure 11-11 shows a completed view of a Hewlett-Packard LaserJet III showing the location of each housing screw. Unlike carriage-type enclosures that tend to divide into upper and lower halves, page printer enclosures are a combination of several different upper and lower pieces. You also will note the portion of the upper housing that is swung open—this allows easy access for the user in order to clean the paper path and replace expendable elements such as the EP cartridge.

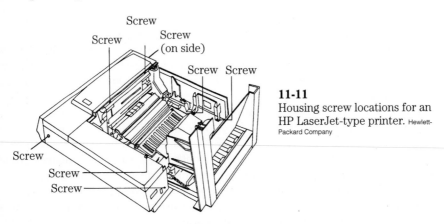

11-11
Housing screw locations for an HP LaserJet-type printer. Hewlett-Packard Company

Once the upper housings and EP cartridge are removed as shown in Fig. 11-12, you can see many of the major assemblies quite clearly. The erase lamp array and beam-to-drum mirror are located in the access cover itself. Looking down into the main body of the printer, you can see the fusing assembly, plastic feed guide, transfer corona, registration rollers, laser/scanning assembly, and power supplies are all easily visible. Upon closer inspection, you also will note many of the gears and mechanical linkages that interconnect all of the printer's major assemblies. The pickup assembly is not visible in Fig. 11-12 because it is being obscured by other assemblies. Removing the lower enclosure exposes the printer's main circuitry.

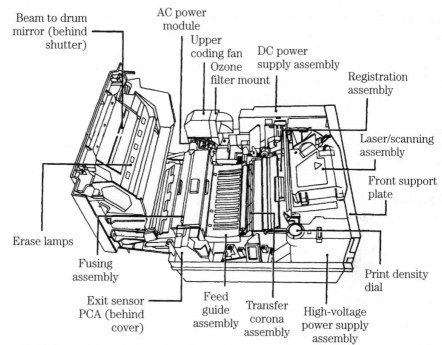

11-12 Upper internal view of an HP LaserJet-type printer. Hewlett-Packard Company

Printer circuits

When the printer is placed upside-down and the bottom enclosures are removed, the printer's main logic and driver circuitry is exposed as shown in Fig. 11-13. Ultimately, EP circuitry performs the same essential jobs as carriage-type circuitry: communication with the host PC, processing host data into dots and storing that information in memory, running the printer's mechanisms to process each page properly, and responding to a variety of sensory feedback to prevent dangerous printer conditions. The dc controller board performs most of the logic and printer control functions, although the interface/formatter board handles communication, control

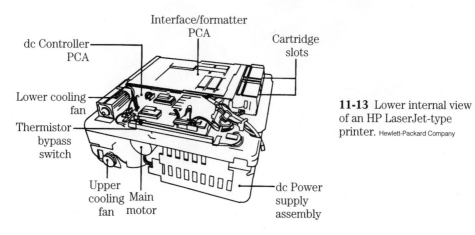

11-13 Lower internal view of an HP LaserJet-type printer. Hewlett-Packard Company

panel operation, and expansion cartridges. It is important to note here that not all EP printers include so much circuitry. Low-end EP printers might use only one board. You also might note that there are several other small printed circuit boards in the printer. Some of these boards are clutch boards that use solenoids to start and stop various printer mechanics such as the pickup and registration roller assemblies. A control panel board is typically located under the upper front enclosure.

Power supplies

A typical EP printer uses three power supplies: an ac supply, a dc supply, and a high-voltage supply. You can see each supply pointed out in Fig. 11-12. The ac supply is little more than a transformer that provides one or more ac levels to drive the fusing heater lamps. The dc supply is the printer's main supply that powers the logic, sensors, and main dc motor. Because powerful static charge is vital to the EP printer, a high-voltage power supply is used to drive the coronas. Generally speaking, it is advisable to replace failed power supplies outright—especially the high-voltage supply.

EP cartridge

With so many mechanical operations needed in an EP printer, it does not take long for key components (such as the EP drum and coronas) to wear out. Even the various gears and linkages are subject to significant wear. The most substantial design evolution for EP printers was incorporating several key components into a single, easily replaceable assembly such as the ones in Fig. 11-14. It is important for you to remember that not all EP cartridges carry the same components—larger, more expensive EP cartridges tend to pack more components. Simple cartridges only carry toner, and leave the EP "engine" as a separate mechanical subassembly. More sophisticated EP cartridges include toner, a fresh EP drum, a new primary corona, and perhaps even more.

11-14 Various EP cartridge assemblies for HP printers.

Writing mechanisms

The writing mechanism is the device that exposes a latent image onto the charged EP drum. Beams of light that strike the drum cause those points on the drum to discharge. Those discharged points then attract toner to the drum surface—areas of the drum that were not exposed by the writing mechanism remain charged, and will refuse toner. Thus, areas with and without toner develop on the drum. Typically, two well-established technologies are available for exposing the drum: laser scanning, and LED bars.

Laser scanning is the classical exposure method—thus the term *laser printer*. A laser beam is shot into a rotating hexagonal mirror. As the mirror rotates, the angle of the reflected beam is constantly changing. In this way, the beam is swept across the drum continuously (and always in the same direction). By turning the laser on and off in synchronization with each scan, dots can be aligned between scans with extreme precision. Original laser printers used a separate helium-neon gas laser and spinning mirror assembly. Today, a diode laser and small motor/mirror assembly are combined in the same prefabricated subassembly. Laser scanning can achieve resolutions of 600 DPI. Unfortunately, laser printers tend to be heavy, and sensitive to physical abuse.

LED bars represent a fairly new development in EP printing that is smaller, lighter, and generally more rugged than a laser/scanning assembly. Instead of tracing a modulated laser beam, a row of microscopic light-emitting diodes (LEDs) are fabricated into a single line that is positioned in close proximity to the drum. At 300 DPI, an LED bar uses 2550 LEDs to cover an 8.5-inch width of paper. The ultimate resolution of an LED bar is limited only by the IC technology used to fabricate it. However, the LED bar is a subassembly unto itself—if one LED should fail, the entire print bar would have to be replaced. For the purposes of this book, you will see EP printers using LED print bars referred to as *LED printers*.

Notes on disassembly and reassembly

Shock warning: Be sure to unplug the printer and allow ample time for the power supply (or supplies) to discharge before attempting to open the enclosure. High-voltage supplies are especially dangerous, and can result in a nasty shock if not allowed to discharge.

Burn warning: Impact print heads can become extremely hot during long printing sessions. Allow plenty of time for the print head to cool before attempting to remove or replace the impact head. Fusing assemblies in EP printers also reach over 200°F during normal operation. Even when opening the EP printer for routine maintenance, allow ample time for the fuser to cool before reaching inside.

The disassembly and reassembly of printers is not terribly difficult, but it often requires a bit of finesse to overcome the variety of plastic latches and screws that hold the units together. Carriage-type printers are fairly straightforward in their use of enclosures and internal assemblies. Be careful to note the location of each screw, because virtually all printers (carriage and page) tend to mix and match screw lengths to accommodate tight space limitations (especially with the internal assemblies). As with any electro-mechanical disassembly, be very careful to denote the location and orientation of each connector as you remove it. Make a reference mark with an indelible marker if necessary. When working with mechanical assemblies, try to replace at the subassembly level wherever possible. Printer mechanics are relatively precise configurations—if critical tensions or dimensions should change during a repair, the mechanism might never work satisfactorily for your customer. Page printer mechanical assemblies are unusually unforgiving. When electronic assemblies must be removed or replaced, be sure to follow good static precautions to prevent accidental damage to the board(s).

When reassembling a printer, pay close attention to the way each subassembly fits together. As with notebook PCs, printer manufacturers try to make every cubic centimeter count. If assemblies are not seated and secured properly, the printer will probably not work right. This consideration is especially important for all types of EP printers. Be careful to route cables and connectors properly. A loose or improperly seated cable can wreak havoc with the printer. Pinched or sliced cables also can impair the printer. Reassemble the printer, but do not install the upper enclosure(s). Run a diagnostic to check the printer thoroughly. If a problem remains, leaving the upper housing off will make another disassembly that much easier. If the printer checks properly, secure the upper housing(s) and run the diagnostics again as a final test before returning the printer to service.

12
CHAPTER

Operating systems and the boot process

As a technician, it is vital for you to understand the relationship between PC hardware and software. In the early days of computers, hardware was typically the center of attention. Because early software was written for a specific computer, and early computers were very limited in their storage and processing capacity, software often arrived as an afterthought (to this day, you still see software development lagging behind hardware advances). With the introduction of personal computers in the mid 1970s, designers realized that a wide selection of software would be needed to make PCs attractive. Instead of writing software specifically for particular machines, a uniform environment would be needed to manage system resources and launch applications. In this way, applications would be portable between systems whose hardware resources would otherwise be incompatible. This uniform environment became known as the *operating system* (or *OS*). When IBM designed the PC, they chose to license a simple operating system from a fledgling company called Microsoft, and the rest is history.

Although this book is dedicated to dealing with PC hardware (because it is the hardware that "breaks"), you must realize that the operating system has a profound effect on PC resources, and how those resources are allocated to individual software applications. This is especially true of the more sophisticated operating systems such as Windows and OS/2. Every good technician is sensitive to the fact that problems with an OS will result in problems with PC performance. This chapter explains the relationship between PC hardware and software, then walks you through a typical PC boot process.

The PC hierarchy

Before you dig into the operating system itself, you should understand the complex (and often frustrating) relationship between computer hardware and software.

This relationship is often expressed as a *hierarchy* shown in the diagram of Fig. 12-1. Each layer in the hierarchy serves a very specific function in PC operation. There are four levels to this hierarchy: (1) the hardware, (2) the BIOS, (3) the OS, and (4) the application(s).

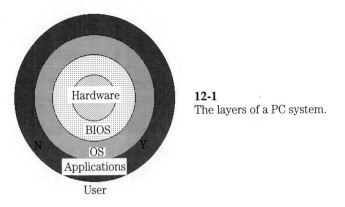

12-1
The layers of a PC system.

Hardware

As you might expect, *hardware* forms the core of a PC hierarchy—there is no computer without the hardware. The hardware includes all of the circuits, drives, expansion boards, power supplies, peripheral devices, and their interconnecting wiring or cables. The hardware extends not only to the PC itself, but to monitors, keyboards, pointing devices, printers, and so on. By sending bytes of information to various ports or addresses in memory, it is possible to manipulate almost anything attached to the system CPU. Unfortunately, controlling PC hardware is a difficult process that requires an intimate knowledge of a PC's electronic architecture. How is it that Microsoft can sell an operating system that works on an i286-based AT, as well as a new Pentium-based system? Because each PC manufacturer designs their circuitry (especially motherboard circuitry) differently, it is virtually impossible to create a "universal" operating system without some sort of interface between the one standard OS and the myriad variations of hardware. This interface is accomplished by the *BIOS* (basic input/output system).

BIOS

Simply put, a BIOS is a set of small programs (or *services*) that are designed to operate each major PC subsystem (such as, video, disk, keyboard, and so on). Each of these *BIOS Services* is invoked by a set of standard calls—originally developed by IBM—that are made from the operating system. When the operating system requests a standard BIOS service, the particular BIOS program will perform the appropriate function tailored to the particular hardware. Thus, each PC design requires its own BIOS. Using this methodology, BIOS acts as a glue that allows diverse (and older) hardware to operate with a single uniform OS. In addition to services, the BIOS runs a *POST* (power-on self-test) program each time the PC is initialized. POST checks the major subsystems before attempting to load an operating system.

Because BIOS is specific to each PC design, BIOS resides on the motherboard in the form of a read-only memory (ROM) IC, although newer systems employ electrically-erasable ROMs that allow the BIOS to be updated without having to replace the BIOS ROM IC. You may see BIOS referred to as *firmware* rather than software because it is software permanently recorded on an IC. As you might imagine, the efficiency and accuracy of BIOS code will have a profound impact on the overall operation of a PC—better BIOS routines will result in superior system performance, while clumsy, inefficient BIOS routines can easily bog a system down. *Bugs* (software errors) in BIOS can have very serious consequences for the system (such as lost files and system lockups).

Operating system

The operating system serves two very important functions in the modern PC. First, an OS interacts with, and provides an extension to the BIOS. This extension provides applications with a rich selection of high-level file handling and disk control functions. It is this large number of disk-related functions, which added the term *disk* to *operating system* (that is, disk operating system or DOS). When an application needs to perform disk access or file handling, it is the DOS layer that performs most of the work. By providing access to a library of frequently used functions through DOS, application programs can be written without the need to incorporate the code for such complex functions into each application itself. In actual operation, the OS and BIOS work closely together to give an application easy access to system resources.

Second, an OS forms an environment (or *shell*) through which applications can be executed, and provides a user interface allowing you and your customers to interact with the PC. MS-DOS uses a keyboard-driven, command-line interface signified by the command-line prompt (such as C:>_) that you have become so familiar with. The Windows OS provides a *GUI* (graphical user interface) relying on symbols and icons that are selected with a mouse or other pointing device.

Applications

Ultimately, the aim of a computer is to execute applications (such as games, word processors, spreadsheets, and so on). An OS loads and executes the application. As the application requires system resources during run-time, it will make an appropriate call to DOS or BIOS, which in turn will access the needed function and return any needed information to the calling application. The actual dynamics of such an exchange is more complex than described here, but you get the general idea. Now that you have seen an overview of the typical PC hierarchy and understand how each layer interacts with one another, it is time to take a closer look at the OS layer itself.

Details of MS-DOS

As you learned in the last section, the operating system provides I/O resources to application programs, as well as an environment that can be used to execute programs or interact with the operating system. To accomplish these two tasks, MS-DOS uses only three files: IO.SYS, MSDOS.SYS, and COMMAND.COM. Note that the myriad of other files shipped with MS-DOS are technically not part of the operating system itself, but are instead a library of utilities intended to help you optimize and maintain the system. The following sections examine each of the three core MS-DOS files in more detail. Keep in mind that loading and running an operating system relies on system disk and memory operations that are detailed elsewhere in the book.

IO.SYS

The IO.SYS file provides many of the low-level routines (or *drivers*) that interact with BIOS. Some versions of IO.SYS are customized by *OEM* (original equipment manufacturers) to supplement the particular BIOS for their system. However, OS customization is rare today because it leads to system incompatibilities. In addition to low-level drivers, IO.SYS contains a system initialization routine. The entire contents of the file (except for the system initialization routine) is kept in low memory throughout system operation. IO.SYS is a file assigned with a hidden-file attribute, so you will not see the file when searching a bootable disk with an ordinary DIR command. Although Microsoft uses the filename IO.SYS, other OS makers might use a different name. For example, the corresponding file name in IBM's PC-DOS is IBM-BIO.COM.

In order for a disk (floppy or hard disk) to be *bootable* under MS-DOS 3.x or 4.x, IO.SYS must be the first file in the disk directory, and it must occupy at least the first available cluster on the disk (usually cluster 2). This is the disk's *OS volume boot sector*. Of course, subsequent clusters containing IO.SYS can be placed anywhere in the disk just like any other ordinary file. MS-DOS 5.x and later eliminate this requirement and allow IO.SYS to be placed in any root directory location anywhere on the disk. When disk access begins during the boot process, the bootable drive's boot sector is read that loads IO.SYS into memory and gives it control of the system. Once IO.SYS is running, the boot process can continue, as you can learn in this chapter. If this file is missing or corrupt, you will see some type of boot failure message, or the system might lock up.

MSDOS.SYS

This is the core of MS-DOS. The MSDOS.SYS file is listed second in the boot disk's directory, and is the second file to be loaded during the boot process. It contains the routines that handle OS disk and file access. Like IO.SYS, the MSDOS.SYS file is loaded into low memory where it resides throughout the system's operation. If the file is missing or corrupt, you will see some kind of boot failure message, or the system might lock up.

COMMAND.COM

The COMMAND.COM file serves as the MS-DOS shell and command processor. This is the program that you are interacting with at the command-line prompt. COMMAND.COM is the third file loaded when a PC boots, and it is stored in low memory along with IO.SYS and MSDOS.SYS. The number of commands that you have available depend on the version of MS-DOS in use. MS-DOS uses two types of commands in normal operation: resident and transient.

Resident commands are procedures that are coded directly into COMMAND .COM. As a result, resident commands execute almost immediately when called from the command line. CLS and DIR are two typical resident commands. *Transient* commands represent a broader and more powerful group of commands. However, transient commands are not loaded with COMMAND.COM. Instead, the commands are available as small .COM or .EXE utility files in the DOS directory (such as DE-BUG and EMM386). Transient commands must be loaded from the disk and executed each time they are needed. By pulling out complex commands as separate utilities, the size of COMMAND.COM can be kept very small. A table of commands for MS-DOS 6.x are given in Table 12-1.

Table 12-1. A list of MS-DOS commands

Resident commands	Transient commands	
CD or CHDIR	APPEND	FORMAT
CHCP	ASSIGN	GRAFTABL
CLS	ATTRIB	GRAPHICS
COPY	BACKUP	JOIN
CTTY	BASIC	KEYB
DATE	BASICA	LABEL
DEL or ERASE	CHCP	MEM
DIR	CHKDSK	MIRROR
EXIT	COMMAND	MODE
EXPAND	COMP	NLSFUNC
LOADHIGH or LH	DEBUG	PRINT
MD or MKDIR	DISKCOMP	RECOVER
PATH	DISKCOPY	REPLACE
PROMPT	DOSKEY	RESTORE
RD or RENAME	DOSSHELL	SETVER
SET	EDIT	SHARE
TIME	EDLIN	SORT
TYPE	EMM386	SUBST
VER	EXE2BIN	SYS
VERIFY	FASTOPEN	TREE
VOL	FC	UNDELETE
	FDISK	UNFORMAT
	FIND	XCOPY

Recognizing and dealing with OS problems

Because the operating system is an integral part of the PC, any problems with using or upgrading the OS can adversely affect system operation. Software does not fail like hardware—once software is loaded and running, it will not eventually break down from heat or physical stress. Unfortunately, software is hardly perfect. Upgrading from one OS to another can upset the system's operation, and bugs in the operating system can result in unforeseen operation that might totally destroy a system's reliability.

Virtually all versions of operating systems have bugs in them—especially in early releases. In most cases, such bugs are found in the transient commands that are run from the command line rather than in the three core files (IO.SYS, MSDOS.SYS, and COMMAND.COM). Even the latest version of MD-DOS (6.22) has endured several incarnations since its initial release as 6.0. As a technician, you should be sensitive to the version of DOS being used by your customer. Whenever the customer complains of trouble using a DOS utility (such as BACKUP or EMM386), one of your first steps should be to ensure that the version in use is appropriate. If it has been updated, you should try the new release. Remember that a software fault can manifest itself as a hardware problem. Check with the OS maker to find their newest releases and fixes. Microsoft maintains a download service bulletin board for this purpose. Check in regularly to find error reports and upgrades.

Another concern for technicians is dealing with old versions of an OS. Remember that part of the task of an OS is to manage system resources (i.e., disk space, memory, and so on). New OS versions such as MS-DOS 5.0 and later, do a much better job of disk and memory management than MS-DOS 4.x and earlier. Should you recommend an upgrade to your customer? As a general rule, any MS-DOS version older than 5.0 is worth upgrading to MS-DOS 6.22 or later—especially if your customer is planning to keep or upgrade the PC. If the MS-DOS version is 5.0 or later, the only good reason to upgrade would be to take advantage of advanced utilities such as MemMaker or DoubleSpace that have been refined and included with MS-DOS 6.22.

The boot process

Computer initialization is a process—not an event. From the moment power is applied until the system sits idle at the command-line prompt, the PC *boot* process is a sequence of predictable steps that verify the system and prepare it for operation. By understanding each step in system initialization, you can develop a real appreciation for the way that hardware and software relate to one another—you also stand a much better chance of identifying and resolving problems when a system fails to boot properly. This part of the chapter provides a step-by-step review of a typical PC boot process.

Applying power

PC initialization starts when you turn the system on. When all output voltages from the power supply are valid, the supply generates a *PG* (power good) logic signal. It can take up to 500 ms for the supply to generate a PG signal. When the motherboard timer IC receives the PG signal, the timer stops sending a *Reset* signal to the CPU. At this point, the CPU starts processing.

The bootstrap

The very first operation performed by a CPU is to fetch an instruction from address FFFF:0000h. Because this address is almost at the end of available ROM space, the instruction is almost always a jump command (JMP) followed by the actual BIOS ROM starting address. By making all CPUs start at the same point, the BIOS ROM can then send program control anywhere in the particular ROM (and each ROM is usually different). This initial search of address FFFF:0000h and the subsequent redirection of the CPU is traditionally referred to as the *bootstrap*, in which the PC "pulls itself up by its bootstraps" or gets itself going. Today, the term is shortened to *boot*, and has broadened its meaning to include the entire initialization process.

Core tests

The core tests are part of the overall power-on self-test (POST) sequence that is the most important use of a system BIOS during initialization. As you might expect, allowing the system to initialize and run with flaws in the motherboard, memory, or drive systems can have catastrophic consequences for files in memory or on disk. To ensure system integrity, a fundamental self-test routine checks the major motherboard components, and identifies the presence of any other specialized BIOS ICs in the system (that is, drive controller BIOS, video BIOS, SCSI BIOS, and so on).

BIOS starts with a test of the motherboard hardware such as the CPU, math co-processor, timer ICs, *DMA* (direct memory access) controllers, and interrupt (IRQ) controllers. If an error is detected in this early phase of testing, a series of beeps (or *beep codes*) are produced. By knowing the BIOS manufacturer and the beep code, you can determine the nature of the problem. Chapter 15 deals with BIOS and beep codes in more detail. Beep codes are used because the video system has not been initialized.

Next, BIOS looks for the presence of a video ROM between memory locations C000:0000h through C780:000h. In just about all systems, the search will reveal a video BIOS ROM on a video adapter board plugged into an available expansion slot. If a video BIOS is found, its contents are evaluated with a *checksum* test. If the test is successful, control is transferred to the video BIOS that loads and initializes the video adapter. When initialization is complete, you will see a cursor on the screen, and control returns to the system BIOS. When no external video adapter BIOS is located, the system BIOS will provide an initialization routine for the motherboard's video adapter, and a cursor also will appear. Once the video system initializes, you are likely to see a bit of text on the display identifying the system or video BIOS ROM maker and revision level. If the checksum test fails, you will see an error message such as: *C000 ROM Error* or *Video ROM Error*. Initialization will usually halt right there.

Now that the video system is ready, system BIOS will scan memory from C800: 0000h through DF80:0000h in 2K increments to search for any other ROMs that might be on other adapter cards in the system. If other ROMs are found, their contents are tested and run. As each supplemental ROM is executed, they will show manufacturer and revision ID information. When a ROM fails the checksum test, you will see an error message such as: *XXXX ROM Error*. The *XXXX* indicates the segment address where the faulty ROM was detected. When a faulty ROM is detected, system initialization will usually halt.

POST

BIOS then checks the memory location at 0000:0472h. This address contains a flag that determines whether the initialization is a cold start (power first applied) or a warm start (reset button). A value of 1234h at this address indicates a warm start, in which case the (POST) routine is skipped. If any other value is found at that location, a cold start is interpreted, and the full POST routine will be executed.

The full POST checks many of the other higher-level functions on the motherboard, memory, keyboard, video adapter, floppy drive, math co-processor, printer port, serial port, hard drive, and other subsystems. There are dozens of tests performed by the POST. When an error is encountered, you will see an error message on the display (and system initialization will halt). Keep in mind that POST codes and their meanings will vary slightly between BIOS manufacturers. If the POST completes successfully, the system will respond with a single beep from the speaker. Chapter 28 covers I/O port POST codes, and Chapter 44 discusses each diagnostic POST code and their associated meanings.

Finding the OS

The system now needs to load an operating system (usually MS-DOS or PC-DOS). The first step here is to search for a *DOS volume boot sector* on the A: drive. If there is no disk in the drive, you will see the drive light illuminate briefly, and then BIOS will search the next drive. If there is a disk in drive A:, BIOS will load sector 1 (head 0 cylinder 0) from the disk's DOS volume boot sector into memory starting at 0000:7C00h. If the first nine words of the sector contain the same data pattern, you will see an error message similar to: *Diskette boot record error*. Other error messages can occur if the system files are not the first two files in the disk's directory, if the boot sector is corrupt, or if a problem was encountered in loading the file(s). Otherwise, the first program in the directory (IO.SYS) will begin to load, followed by MSDOS.SYS. If the OS cannot load from drive A:, the system will search the B: drive for a diskette.

If the OS cannot be loaded from any floppy drive, the system will search the first fixed drive (hard drive). Hard drives are a bit more involved than floppy disks. BIOS loads sector 1 (head 0 cylinder 0) from the hard drive's *master partition* into memory starting at 0000:7C00h, and the last two bytes of the sector are checked. If the final two bytes of the master partition boot sector are NOT 55h and AAh respectively, the boot sector is invalid, and you will see an error message similar to: "No boot device available" and system initialization will halt. Otherwise, the disk will search for any extended partitions. Once any extended partitions have been identified, the drive's original boot sector will search for a flag marking a partition as bootable. If none of the partitions are bootable (or if more than one partition is marked bootable), a disk error message will be displayed such as: *Invalid partition table*.

When an active bootable partition is found in the master partition boot sector, the DOS volume boot sector from the bootable partition is loaded into memory and tested. If the DOS volume boot sector cannot be read, you will see an error message similar to: *Error loading operating system*. When the DOS volume boot sector does load, the last two bytes are tested for a signature of 55h and AAh respectively. If these signature bytes are missing, you will see an error message such as: *Missing operating system*. Under either error condition, system initialization will halt.

After the signature bytes are identified, the DOS volume boot sector (now in memory) is executed as if it were a program. This "program" checks the root directory to ensure that IO.SYS and MSDOS.SYS are available. In older MS-DOS versions, IO.SYS and MSDOS.SYS have to be the first two directory entries. If the DOS volume boot sector was created with MS-DOS 3.3 or earlier and the two startup files are not the first two files in the directory, the system will produce an error code such as: *Non-System disk or disk error*. If the boot sector is corrupt, you might see a message like: *Disk boot failure*.

Loading the OS

If there are no problems detected in the disk's DOS volume boot sector, IO.SYS is loaded and executed. IO.SYS contains extensions to BIOS that start low-level device drivers for such things as the keyboard, printer, and block devices. Remember that IO.SYS also contains initialization code that is only needed during system startup. A copy of this initialization code is placed at the top of conventional memory that takes over initialization. The next step is to load MSDOS.SYS that is loaded such that it overlaps the part of IO.SYS containing the initialization code. MSDOS .SYS (the MS-DOS kernel) is then executed to initialize base device drivers, detect system status, reset the disk system, initialize devices such as the printer and serial port, and set up system default parameters. The MS-DOS essentials are now loaded, and control returns to the IO.SYS initialization code in memory.

Establishing the environment

If a CONFIG.SYS file is present, it is opened and read four times. The first pass reads and executes all statements except DEVICE, INSTALL, and SHELL. The second pass reads and executes each DEVICE (or DEVICEHIGH) statement in the order in which they appear. The third pass reads and executes any INSTALL statements. The fourth pass reads and executes any SHELL statement to load the command processor. If no SHELL statement is present, the COMMAND.COM processor is loaded. When COMMAND.COM is loaded, it overwrites the initialization code left over from IO.SYS (which is no longer needed).

When an AUTOEXEC.BAT file is present, COMMAND.COM (which now has control of the system) will load and execute the batch file. After batch file processing is complete, the familiar DOS prompt will appear. If there is no AUTOEXEC.BAT in the root directory, COMMAND.COM will request the current DATE and TIME, then show the DOS prompt. You can now launch applications, or use any available OS commands. AUTOEXEC.BAT also can call a shell (such as Windows) or start an application.

13
CHAPTER

The preservice checkout

As a PC technician, you must understand a basic rule of business—time is money. Whether you are the boss, or work for someone else, the ability to identify and isolate a fault quickly and decisively is a critical element to your success. It requires a keen eye, some common sense, and a little bit of intuition. It also requires an understanding of the troubleshooting process, and a reliable plan of action. You see, even though the number of PC configurations and setups are virtually unlimited, the methodology used to approach each repair is always about the same. This chapter is intended to illustrate the concepts of basic troubleshooting, and show you how to apply a battery of cause-and-effect relationships that will help you narrow the problem down *before* you even take a screwdriver to the enclosure. By applying a consistent technique, you can shave precious time from every repair.

The universal troubleshooting process

Regardless of how complex your particular computer or peripheral device might be, a dependable troubleshooting procedure can be broken down into four basic steps as illustrated in Fig. 13-1: (1) define your symptoms, (2) identify and isolate the potential source (or location) of your problem, (3) replace the suspected subassembly, and (4) retest the unit thoroughly to be sure that you have solved the problem. If you have not solved the problem, start again from step 1. This is a universal procedure that you can apply to any troubleshooting, not just for computer equipment.

Define your symptoms

When a PC breaks down, the cause might be as simple as a loose wire or connector, or as complicated as an IC or subassembly failure. Before you open your tool box, you must have a firm understanding of *all* the symptoms. Think about the symptoms carefully. Is the disk or tape inserted properly? Is the power or activity LED lit? Does this problem occur only when the computer is tapped or moved? By recogniz-

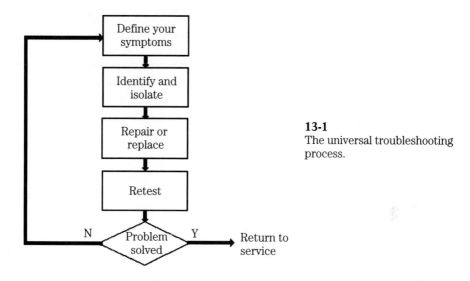

13-1
The universal troubleshooting process.

ing and understanding your symptoms, it can be much easier to trace a problem to the appropriate assembly or component. Take the time to write down as many symptoms as you can. This note taking might seem tedious now, but once you have begun your repair, a written record of symptoms and circumstances will help to keep you focused on the task at hand. It also will help to jog your memory if you must explain the symptoms to someone else at a later date. As a professional troubleshooter, you must often log problems or otherwise document your activities anyway.

Identify and isolate

Before you try to isolate a problem within a piece of computer hardware, you must first be sure that it is the equipment itself that is causing the problem. In many circumstances, this will be fairly obvious, but there might be situations that appear ambiguous (there is no power, no DOS prompt, and so on). Always remember that a PC works because of an intimate mingling of hardware and software. A faulty or improperly configured piece of software can cause confusing system errors.

When you are confident that the failure lies in your system's hardware, you can begin to identify possible problem areas. Because this book is designed to deal with subassembly troubleshooting, start your diagnostics there. The troubleshooting procedures throughout this book will guide you through the major sections of today's popular PC components and peripherals, and aid you in deciding which subassembly might be at fault. When you have identified a potential problem area, you can begin the actual repair process and swap the suspect subassembly.

Replace

Because computers and their peripherals are designed as collections of subassemblies, it is almost always easier to replace a subassembly outright rather than attempt to troubleshoot the subassembly to its component level. Even if you had the time, documentation, and test equipment to isolate a defective component, many

complex parts are proprietary, so it is highly unlikely that you would be able to obtain replacement components without a significant hassle. The labor and frustration
factor involved in such an endeavor is often just as expensive as replacing the entire
subassembly to begin with anyway. On the other hand, manufacturers and their distributors often stock a selection of subassemblies and supplies. Keep in mind that
you might need to know the manufacturer's part number for the subassembly in order to obtain a new one.

During a repair, you might reach a roadblock that requires you to leave your
equipment for a day or two (maybe longer). This generally happens after an order
has been placed for new parts, and you are waiting for those parts to come in. Make
it a point to reassemble your system as much as possible before leaving it. Gather any
loose parts in plastic bags, seal them shut, and mark them clearly. If you are working
with electronic circuitry, make sure to use good-quality antistatic boxes or bags for
storage. Partial reassembly (combined with careful notes) will help you remember
how the unit goes together later on.

Retest

When a repair is finally complete, the system must be reassembled carefully before testing it. All guards, housings, cables, and shields must be restored before final
testing. If symptoms persist, you will have to re-evaluate the symptoms and narrow
the problem to another part of the equipment. If normal operation is restored (or
greatly improved), test the computer's various functions. When you can verify that
your symptoms have stopped during actual operation, the equipment can be returned to service. As a general rule, it is wise to let the system run for at least 24
hours in order to ensure that the replacement subassembly will not fail prematurely.
This is known as letting the system *burn-in*.

Do not be discouraged if the equipment still malfunctions. Perhaps you missed a
jumper setting or DIP switch, or maybe software settings and device drivers need to
be updated to accommodate the replacement subassembly. If you get stuck, simply
walk away, clear your head, and start again by defining your current symptoms.
Never continue with a repair if you are tired or frustrated—tomorrow is another day.
Even the most experienced troubleshooters get overwhelmed from time to time. You
also should realize that there might be more than one bad assembly to deal with. Remember that a PC is just a collection of assemblies, and each assembly is a collection
of parts. Normally, everything works together, but when one assembly fails, it might
cause one or more interconnected assemblies to fail as well.

Viruses and computer service

Few developments in the personal computer field have caused more concern
and alarm then the computer *virus*. Although viruses do not damage computer
hardware, they can irrevocably destroy vital data, disable your PC (or network), and
propagate to other systems through networks, disk swapping, and on-line services.
Even though virus infiltration is generally rare, good PC technicians will always protect themselves (and their customers) by checking the system for viruses before and
after using their diagnostic disks on the PC. A careful process of virus isolation can

detect viruses on the customer's system before any hardware-level work is done. Isolation also prevents your diagnostic disks from becoming infected—and subsequently transferring the virus to other systems (for which you would be liable). This section of the chapter outlines a virus screening procedure for PCs. Chapter 54 discusses the symptoms and countermeasures for viruses in more detail.

Computer viruses explained

There have been many attempts to define a computer virus, and most definitions have a great deal of technical merit. For the purposes of this book, however, consider a virus to be some length of computer code (a program or program fragment) that performs one or more—often destructive—functions, and replicates itself wherever possible to other disks and systems. Because viruses generally want to escape detection, they often hide by copying themselves as hidden, system, or read-only files. However, this only prevents casual detection. More elaborate viruses affect the boot sector code on floppy and hard disks, or attach themselves to other executable programs. Each time the infected program is executed, the virus has a chance to wreak havoc. Still other viruses infect the partition table. Most viruses exhibit a code sequence that can be detected. Many virus scanners work by checking the contents of memory and disk files for such virus "signatures." As viruses become more complex, however, viruses are using encryption techniques to escape detection.

Just as a biological virus is an unwanted (and sometimes deadly) organism in a body, "viral" code in software can lead to a slow, agonizing death for your customer's data. In actual practice, few viruses immediately crash a system (with notable exceptions such as the much-publicized Michelangelo virus). Most viruses make only small changes each time they are executed and creating a chronic problem. This slow manifestation gives viruses a chance to replicate—infecting backups and floppy disks that are swapped to infect other systems.

The telltale signs

Viruses are especially dangerous because you are rarely made aware of their presence until it is too late and the damage is already done. However, there are a number of behaviors that might suggest the presence of a virus in your system. Once again, remember that one of the best protections against viruses (or other drive failures) is to maintain regular backups. None of these symptoms alone guarantee the presence of a virus—there are other reasons why such symptoms can occur. When symptoms do surface, it is always worth running an antivirus checker just to be safe.

The following symptoms are typical of virus activity:

- The hard drive is running out of disk space for no apparent reason. Some viruses multiply by attaching copies of themselves to .EXE and .COM files—often multiple times. This increases the file size and consumes more disk space. If left unchecked, files can grow until the disk runs short of space. However, disk space also can be gobbled up by many *CAD* (computer-aided design), graphics, and multimedia applications such as video capture systems. Be aware of what kind of applications are on the disk.
- You notice that various .EXE and .COM programs have increased in size for no reason. This is a classic indicator of a virus at work. Unfortunately, few

rational people make it a habit to keep track of file sizes, but dates can be a giveaway. For example, if most of the files in a subdirectory are dated six months ago when the package was installed, but the main .EXE file is dated yesterday, it's time to run that virus checker.

- You notice substantial hard drive activity but were not expecting it. It is hardly unusual to see the drive indicator LED register activity when programs are loaded and run. In disk-intensive systems such as Windows, you should expect to see extensive drive operation. However, you should not expect to see disk activity when the system is idle. If the drive runs for no apparent reason—especially under MS-DOS—run the virus checker.

- System performance slowed down noticeably. This symptom is usually coupled with low drive space, and is usually the result of a filled and fragmented disk such as those found in systems that deal with CAD and multimedia applications. Run the virus checker first. If no virus is detected, try eliminating any files you don't need; then defragment the drive completely.

- Files have been lost or corrupted for no apparent reason, or there are an unusual number of access problems. Under ordinary circumstances, files should not be lost or corrupted on a hard drive. Even though bad sectors will crop up on extremely rare occasions, you should expect the drive to run properly. Virus infiltration can interrupt the flow of data to and from the drives and result in file errors. Such errors might occur randomly, or they might be quite consistent. You might see error messages such as *Error in .EXE file*. Regular errors might even simulate a drive failure. Try running a virus checker before running a diagnostic.

- The system locks up frequently or without explanation. Faulty applications and corrupted files can freeze a system. Memory and motherboard problems also can result in system lockups. Although viruses rarely manifest themselves in this fashion, it is possible that random or consistent system lockups might suggest a virus (or virus damage to files).

- There are unexplained problems with system memory or memory allocation. Although there might be one or more memory defects, it is quite common for viruses to exist in memory where other files can be infected. In some cases, this can affect the amount of free memory available to other applications. You might see error messages such as: *Program too big to fit in memory*. If you are having trouble with free memory or memory allocation, run a virus checker that performs a thorough memory check. If the system checks clear of viruses, you can run diagnostics to check the memory.

Antivirus software

In the race between good and evil, evil usually has the head start. As a result, antivirus detection and elimination packages are constantly trying to keep up with new viruses and their variations (in addition to dealing with more than 1300 virus strains that have already been identified). This leads to an important conclusion about antivirus software—they all become obsolete eventually. Even though first-class shareware and commercial packages can be quite comprehensive, they must all be updated frequently. Some of the most notable antivirus products are found in PC Tools, Norton Anti-Virus, and shareware antivirus tools from McAfee and Associates. If you already own MS-DOS 6.0 or later, you already own Microsoft Anti-Virus (MSAV).

Another important factor in antivirus programs is their inability to successfully remove all viruses from executable (.EXE) files. Files with a .COM extension are simply reflections of memory, but .EXE files contain header information that is easily damaged by a virus (and are subsequently unrecoverable). It is always worth trying to eliminate the virus—if the .EXE header is damaged, you've lost nothing in the attempt, and you can reload the damaged .EXE file from a backup or its original distribution disk if necessary. Remember that there is no better protection against viruses and other hardware faults than keeping regular backups. It is better to restore an infected backup and clean it, than to forgo backups entirely.

Sterilizing your shop

Sterilization starts by assuming that all machines coming in for service are infected with a virus. You should assume the possibility of an infection even if the complaint is something innocent (such as a keyboard acting up). This section of the chapter shows you how to create an *MBD* (master boot disk) that will be known virus-free, then use that MBD to create virus-free *UWD* (user work disks) that will be used to boot and check the systems brought in for service. Guard your MBDs set by placing them somewhere outside of your shop. That way they won't be infected accidentally. Immediately write-protect your MBDs. Also, be ready to discard your work disks frequently. Replacing a 50-cent work disk is much cheaper than having to scan and clean every disk in your shop! If possible, write-protect work disks, too. If the antivirus software, DOS and the DISKCOPY program can all fit, you should use double-density disks rather than high-density disks. Double-density disks can be used in high-density drives (but not vice versa).

Creating antivirus check disks is a simple procedure. **Before starting, make sure that the licensing for your antivirus software allows the creation of multiple work disks**. Start with a box of 10 disks or so, then format each disk as a system disk using the latest version of DOS (MS-DOS or PC-DOS) on a thoroughly virus-checked PC. Start with one disk and copy the following DOS files from the DOS directory: MEM, SYS, and FORMAT. Next, switch to the drive containing antivirus files, and copy the active files to the floppy. For example, if you are using MSAV, copy MSAV.EXE, MSAV.INI, and MSAV.HLP to the floppy disk. Finally, create an AUTOEXEC.BAT file to run the antivirus program when the system is booted from the floppy. Write-protect the disk and set it aside as the Master Boot Disk. Then, use the DOS DISKCOPY command to duplicate the MBD to the other formatted disks. These other disks will be your work disks. Write protect each work disk and set them aside. If you need additional instruction to create master or work disks, Chapter 54 describes the procedure in detail.

Virus isolation in action

As each machine comes into your shop for service, assume it has been infected. Before you take a screwdriver to it or even insert a diagnostic disk of your own, set it up on the bench and boot one of your antivirus work disks on it. Once the bootable floppy starts, the antivirus software (such as MSAV) will scan the drives and memory for viruses. If a virus is found, MSAV will automatically attempt to clean it. Remember that although viruses can be removed from .EXE files, the file itself might not be recoverable. Once a virus has been found and you have cleaned it off the system, *throw the work disk away!* That disk has been run in an infected system and is now possibly infected itself. It is not worth trying to save the 50 cents that the disk costs. By reusing a work disk, there is a risk of reinfecting other machines or your other shop disks. When you run out of work disks, simply go get the master and make another batch. Remember, never use a master in the shop.

Remember that an infected machine might have more than one type of virus on it! For example, just because you found and cleaned the Stoned virus doesn't mean a system can't also have the Michelangelo virus on it! Use a second work disk to scan the system again. Continue using fresh work disks to scan and clean the system until the system tests clean. Keep your antivirus software up-to-date so you don't miss new viruses or variants of old viruses. Shareware products (such as McAfee's SCAN and CLEAN) are updated more frequently than MSAV, and so are more likely to find the newest viruses.

Routine, preservice virus scanning makes good sense. First, it will save time by detecting virus-related problems right away. You won't waste time disassembling cabinets and troubleshooting hardware. Second, eliminating viruses are much easier than reformatting or replacing the hard drive (a devastating choice if your customer has no current backup). Reformatting a hard drive on a system with a virus might not solve the problem and result in a callback. On the other hand, *not* wiping out your customer's entire drive is a sure way to make a friend. Third, preservice virus checking is quick—the computer is on the bench anyway. Sticking in a disk and turning on the computer is all the labor required.

Initial bench testing

Now that the PC is on your workbench, you are faced with the thankless task of isolating the problem area. Because every PC is set up and configured a bit differently, the same problems might manifest themselves differently from machine to machine. This is the true challenge (and fun) of PC service—no two systems are exactly alike, so you will need to perform some quick detective work to narrow down the problems. This part of the chapter explains a series of guidelines that can help you make more informed troubleshooting decisions. The actual amount of time needed to follow most of these guidelines is under five minutes.

A spontaneous failure

One of the keys to understanding a PC problem is to know the circumstances under which the fault occurred. For the purposes of this book, problems can occur either spontaneously, or after an upgrade or expansion. A *spontaneous* failure generally occurs suddenly and without human intervention. For example, the system was working fine when you turned it off last night, but failed when you turned it on this morning. Perhaps the system went down with the power during a lightning storm, but now that power is restored, the system refuses to operate. As you might imagine, the customer can be an important resource for this kind of information. Once you determine the fault to be spontaneous, the following steps can help you identify system initialization problems:

1. Is the power LED on when the power switch is pressed? No PC is going to work without power. Check that the PC is plugged in securely to a working ac outlet, and see that the power LED is illuminated when the power switch is turned on. If the power LED stays out, check the power supply fuse (usually located next to the ac cord). Some supplies also incorporate a 120/240-V switch near the ac cord. Make sure the switch is set to the appropriate voltage setting.

2. Is there no screen, beep, or disk activity after about 30 seconds? If the power LED is lit—but there is no system activity (disk spinup)—the power supply might still be defective. You will have to open the system and check that each power connector is installed correctly on the motherboard and in each drive. If problems persist, the supply might be defective. Refer to the chapters on power supply service for detailed procedures. When system activity starts, the supply is likely intact.

3. Do you hear a series of beeps (while the monitor remains dark)? If there is sufficient power to the motherboards and drives, the system should follow its BIOS ROM bootstrap and start the normal initialization process. Part of initialization involves checking the motherboard circuitry. When a problem is detected before the video system is initialized, a series of beeps are generated through the PC speaker. By understanding the beep code, you can identify the fault and correct it. Keep in mind that beep codes will vary between BIOS manufacturers. If you do not hear a beep code (but the monitor remains dark), you might need to open the PC and boot the system with a POST board installed. A POST board displays the two-digit hexadecimal code corresponding to each test. The last test to be completed (before the initialization stops) indicates the fault location. Beep codes are explained in Chapter 15, and Chapter 28 presents a comprehensive review of POST codes. If you hear only a single beep and do not yet see a screen image, check that monitor is on and attached to the video board correctly.

4. Do you see an error code screen message? When you see a cursor and screen messages, you know that the PC has booted successfully to the point where the video system was initialized. At this point, the PC begins to test memory and other high-level systems (such as drives and controllers). When an error is detected after video initialization, an error code will usually be displayed along with a text message that gives some indication of the problem. Refer to Chapter 44 to find an index of diagnostic codes and notes on how to handle each one.

5. Does the system boot from its hard drive? After the POST has been completed (and assuming no problems are found), the PC will attempt to load its operating system—first from a floppy drive, then from the first hard drive. If you watch the system, you should see the floppy drive LED and hard disk LED illuminate in that order. If the hard drive contains a bootable

DOS partition, and is formatted as a bootable drive, it should load MS-DOS (or PC-DOS). When loading is complete, you will see the DOS command-line prompt. If there is trouble with the drive's DOS partition, its DOS volume boot sector, or the DOS files themselves, you will see an error message to that effect. When a hard drive error is generated, the drive or its controller circuit also might be at fault. Try booting the system from a floppy containing virus checking software, and ensure that the system is free of viruses before continuing.

6. Does the system boot from a floppy disk? *Warning: Do not attempt to boot a customer's machine from your own floppy or diagnostic disks unless you use an antivirus work disk first. Under no circumstances should you try to boot your own test bench systems with disks provided by a customer.* In order to run diagnostics to test the system further, it will be necessary to access a bootable drive. If the hard drive is disabled for any reason, your only real alternative is to boot from a floppy drive. Use your antivirus boot disk. This will load DOS and virus-check the system at the same time. Once the virus check is complete (the system checks clean or all viruses have been eliminated), you can then use diagnostic disks to check the system in detail. Keep in mind that a few diagnostics are self-booting—that is, they do not need MS-DOS to run. Do *not* use a self-booting diagnostic without virus-checking the PC first.

After an upgrade

Just about every PC owner will perform some sort of upgrade to their system from time to time. Upgrading typically involves adding hardware and software to the system, and this is a ripe opportunity for conflicts to interrupt normal PC operation. Fortunately, when problems occur after an upgrade, it is usually the fault of the upgrade rather than an actual hardware failure. Reversing the upgrade will typically clear the problem. This section explains some of the things you should look for when suspecting an upgrade problem. Be sure to confer with your customer to find what equipment has been added or removed. If a customer is bringing the system to you for upgrade or correction, make it a point to have complete documentation for the upgrade handy.

1. Does the system fail to boot, freeze during the boot process, or freeze during operation for no apparent reason? This is the classic sign of a hardware conflict. A PC is designed with a limited number of resources (memory, I/O addresses, interrupt (IRQ) lines, DMA channels, and so on). For the PC to function properly, each device added to the system must use its own unique resources. For example, no two devices can use the same IRQ, DMA, or I/O resources. When such an overlap of resources occurs, the PC can easily malfunction and freeze. Unfortunately, it is virtually impossible to predict when the malfunction will occur, so a conflict can manifest itself early (any time during the boot process), or later on (after DOS is loaded) while an application is running.

Resolving a conflict is not difficult, but it requires patience and attention to detail. Examine the upgrade and its adapter board and check the IRQ, DMA, and I/O address settings of other boards in the system. Make sure that the upgrade hardware is set to use resources that are *not* in use by other devices already in the system. For example, some motherboards offer built-in video controller circuits. Before another video adapter can be added to the system, the motherboard video adapter must be disabled— usually with a single motherboard jumper. Some sophisticated adapter boards (especially high-end video adapters and video capture boards) require the use of extra memory space. If memory exclusions are needed, be sure that the appropriate entries are made in CONFIG.SYS and AUTOEXEC.BAT files. If memory exclusions are not followed, multiple devices might attempt to use the same memory space and result in a conflict.

2. Does the system fail to recognize its upgrade device? Even if the hardware is installed in a system correctly, the PC might not recognize the upgrade device(s) without the proper software loaded. A great example of this is the CD-ROM drive. It is a simple matter to install the drive and its adapter board, but the PC will not even recognize the drive unless the low-level CD-ROM device driver is added to CONFIG.SYS and the MS-DOS CD-ROM driver (MSCDEX) is included in AUTOEXEC.BAT. If the PC is running in a stable fashion, but it does not recognize the expansion hardware, make sure that you have loaded all required software correctly.

   If you are mixing and matching existing subassemblies from new and old systems, make sure that each device is fully compatible with the PC. Incompatibilities between vintages and manufacturers can lead to operational problems. For example, adding a 3½-inch floppy drive to an i286 AT system can result in problems because the older BIOS could not format 3½-inch high-density (1.44Mb) floppy disks. A DOS utility (such as DRIVER.SYS) is needed to correct this deficiency.

   It also is possible that the upgrade device might simply be defective or installed incorrectly. Open the system and double-check your installation. Pay particular attention to any cables, connectors, or jumpers. When you confirm that the hardware and software installation is correct, suspect a hardware defect. Try the upgrade in your test system if possible. If the problem persists when you attempt the upgrade on another PC, one or more elements of the upgrade hardware are probably defective. Return it to the vendor for a prompt refund or replacement. If the upgrade works on another system, the original system might be incompatible with the upgrade, or you might have missed a jumper or DIP switch setting on the motherboard.

3. Do one or more applications fail to function as expected after an upgrade? This is not uncommon among video adapter and sound board upgrades. Often, applications are configured to work with various sets of hardware. When that hardware is altered, the particular application(s) might no longer run properly (this is especially true under Windows). The best way to address this problem is to check and change the hardware configuration for each affected application. Most DOS applications come with a setup utility. You can adjust most Windows configurations under the Control Panel icon.

The spare parts dilemma

Once a problem is isolated, technicians face another problem: the availability of spare parts. Novice technicians often ask what kinds and quantity of spare parts they should keep on hand. The best answer to give here is simply: none at all. The reason for this answer is best explained by the two realities of PC service:

1. Parts are always changing. After only 15 years or so, the PC is in its fifth CPU generation. As a result, a new generation matures every 24 to 36 months (although the newer generations have been arriving in 18 to 24 months). Even the newer products such as CD-ROM drives have proliferated in different speeds and versions (1×, 2×, 3×, and even 4× speeds). Once production stops for a drive or board, stock rarely remains for very long. You see, even if you know what the problem is, the chances of your locating an exact replacement part are often quite slim if the part is over two years old. Note the word *exact*—this is the key word in PC repair. This is the reason why so many repairs involve an upgrade. For example, why replace a failed EGA board with another EGA board when you can install an SVGA board (which is typically EGA compatible) for the same price. Choosing the "right" parts to stock is like hitting a moving target, so don't bother.

2. Inventory costs money. Financial considerations also play a big role in choosing parts. For computer enthusiasts or novice technicians just tinkering in their spare time, the expense and space demands required for inventory are simply out of the question. Even for more serious businesses, inventory can burden the bottom line.

A better strategy

Unless you are in the business of selling replacement parts and upgrade components yourself, don't waste your money and space stocking parts that are going to be obsolete in less than 24 months. Rather than worry about stocking parts yourself, work to develop your contacts with computer parts stores and superstores that specialize in parts and subassemblies—let them stock the parts for you. Because parts stores generally have an inside line with distributors and manufacturers, parts that they do not stock can often be ordered for you. Even many reputable mail-order firms can provide parts in under 48 hours with today's delivery services.

2
SECTION

System data and troubleshooting

14
CHAPTER

Batteries

Of all the elements in a PC, few are as overlooked and ignored as the battery. Batteries (Fig. 14-1) play an important role in all PCs by maintaining the system's configuration data while main ac power is turned off (just imagine how inconvenient it would be to reenter the entire system setup in CMOS before being able to use the system each time). For portable systems such as notebook and subnotebook PCs, battery packs also provide working power for the entire system. This chapter outlines the technologies and operating characteristics of today's battery families, and illustrates a selection of battery-related problems that can plague a PC.

14-1
A set of Tadrian batteries.

A battery primer

The battery is perhaps the most common and dependable source of power ever developed. It is an electrochemical device that uses two dissimilar metals (called *electrodes*) that are immersed or encapsulated in a chemical catalyst (or *electrolyte*). The chemical reaction that takes place in a cell causes a voltage differential to be developed across its electrodes. When a battery is attached to a circuit, the battery provides current. The more current required by a load, the faster a chemical reaction will occur. As the chemical reaction continues, electrodes are consumed. Eventually, the battery will wear out. It is important to realize that a battery and a cell are not necessarily the same. A *cell* is the basic element of a battery; however, a battery might be made up of several individual cells.

For some batteries, the chemical reaction is irreversible. When the battery is dead, it must be discarded. These are known as nonrechargeable (or *primary*) cells. However, some types of batteries can be recharged. By applying energy to the battery from an external source, the expended chemical reaction can be almost entirely reversed. Such rechargeable batteries are referred to as *secondary* cells. Secondary cells are used to supply main power for most small computers.

Battery ratings

Batteries carry two important ratings: cell voltage and ampere-hours (Ah). *Cell voltage* refers to the cell's working voltage. Most everyday cells operate around +1.5 Vdc, but can range from +1.2 to +3.0 Vdc depending on the particular battery chemistry in use. The *ampere-hour* rating is a bit more involved, but it reflects the energy storage capacity of a battery. A large Ah rating suggests a high-capacity battery and vice versa.

As an example, suppose your battery is rated for 2 Ah. Ideally, you should be able to draw 2 A from the battery for 1 hour before it is exhausted. However, you also should be able to draw 1 A (ampere) for 2 hours, 0.5 A for 4 hours, 0.1 A for 20 hours, and so on. Keep in mind that the ampere-hour relationship is not always precisely linear. Higher current loads can shorten battery life to less than that expected by the ampere-hour rating, and small loads can allow slightly more battery life than expected. Regardless of the ampere-hour rating, all batteries have an upper current limit; attempting to draw excess current can destroy the battery. Physically large batteries can usually supply more current (and last longer) than smaller batteries. Another way to express a battery's energy capacity is in watt-hours per kilogram (Wh/kg) or watt-hours per pound (Wh/lb). For example, a 1-kg battery rated at 60 Wh could provide 60 W of power for 1 hour, 30 W of power for 2 hours, 10 W of power for 6 hours, etc.

Charging

In its simplest sense, *charging* is the replacement of electrical energy to batteries whose stored energy has been discharged. By applying an electrical current to a discharged battery over a given period of time, it is possible to cause a chemical recombination at the battery's electrodes that will restore the cell's spent potential. Essentially, you must backfeed the battery at a known, controlled rate. Keep in mind that recharging only works for secondary cells such as nickel-cadmium or nickel metal-hydride batteries. Attempting to recharge a primary battery will quickly destroy it.

Before you dive into an overview of charging circuits and troubleshooting, you must understand the concept of C. The term C designates the normal current capacity of a battery (in amperes). In most circumstances, the value of C is the ampere-hour current level. For example, a battery rated for 1300 mAh (1.30 Ah) would be considered to have a C value of 1.30 A. A battery rated for 700 mAh (0.70 Ah) would have a C of 0.70 A. Charging rates are based upon fractions or multiples of C.

To charge a battery, you must apply a voltage across the cell that will cause the appropriate amount of charging current to flow back into the battery. Ideally, the battery should be charged at a rate of 0.1 C. For batteries with a C of 500 mA (0.5 A), 0.1 C would be 50 mA (0.05 A). At 0.1 C, the battery could be left connected in the charger indefinitely without damage. Low-current charge rates such as 0.1 C are sometimes referred to as a *slow charge*. Slow charging produces the least physical or thermal stress within a battery, and ensures the maximum possible number of charge/discharge cycles.

Many types of secondary batteries can be charged well above the 0.1 C rate. The *quick charge* approach uses current levels of 0.3 C (three times the rate of a slow charge) to recharge the cell in four to six hours. For a battery with a C of 600 mA (0.60 A), the 0.1 C charging rate would be 60 mA (0.06 A), but the quick charge rate would be 180 mA (0.18 A). However, the quick charging process runs the risk of *overcharging* a battery. Once a battery is fully recharged, additional current at or above the quick charge rate causes temperature and pressure buildups within the cell. In extreme cases, a severely overcharged cell might rupture and be destroyed. When quick charging, the 0.3 C charging rate should be used only long enough to restore the bulk of a cell's energy. The rate should be reduced to 0.1 C (or less) for continuous operation.

New NiCd and NiMH batteries allow for an even faster charge of 1 hour. The *1-hour charge* uses a rate of 1.5 C, which is 1.5 times the amount of current that the cell is intended to provide. A battery with a C of 1400 mA (1.40 A) would use a one-hour charge rate of 2100 mA (2.10 A). Remember that only specially designed secondary cells can be safely charged in one hour or less. With one-hour charging, current control and timing become critical issues. The battery charging current MUST be reduced as soon as the cell approaches its full charge, or catastrophic battery failure will almost certainly result. Rapid charging causes substantial temperature and pressure increases that eventually take their toll on a cell's working life. You should expect the working life of any cell to be curtailed when it is regularly operated in a one-hour charge mode.

The *constant-current charger* is designed to automatically compensate for changes in battery terminal voltage in order to maintain charging current at a constant level. Constant-current charging is very efficient, but it is not adjustable. If the charger were set to deliver substantial charging currents, the battery pack could charge quickly, but the pack could eventually be damaged by overcharging. The charger could be set to a lower level for safe charging (perhaps 0.1 C), but the low charging rate means very long charge times for a battery pack (10 hours or more). Such limitations make constant-current chargers ill-suited for use in small computers. Instead, constant-current chargers are typically used in stand-alone battery pack charging units.

A more effective approach for portable computers is a *variable-current* (constant-voltage) scheme. When a battery is deeply discharged and its terminal voltage is low, there will be a substantial difference between the power supply source and battery voltage level. This difference results in a sizable current flow through R1 to the battery. Charging usually starts out around the 0.5 C to 0.3 C rate for fast charge operation. As the battery takes on a charge, its terminal voltage increases. Higher battery voltage reduces the difference between the supply and battery; current flow into the battery decreases. When the battery pack reaches full charge, there is almost no voltage difference across R1, so only a small amount of current trickles into the battery. Current flow can reach levels as low as 0.05 C.

Backup batteries

When IBM released its PC/AT in the early 1980s, one of the many design changes over the older PC/XT was the elimination of DIP switches used for system configuration. Instead of discrete physical switches, PC designers chose to set system parameters using bit sequences stored in small areas of static RAM (or CMOS RAM). With static RAM, however, contents are lost as soon as power is removed. Fortunately, CMOS RAM requires exceptionally little power to operate, so designers included a battery in the memory circuit that would back up the RAM contents when system power was turned off. This battery became known as the *CMOS backup battery*.

In actual practice, CMOS RAM does not distinguish where it receives power from. However, there are some battery characteristics that are desirable for CMOS RAM backup applications. First, the battery should have a long shelf life—that is, they should not lose energy sitting idle. Also, the battery should be able to produce a stable, constant voltage at low currents throughout its working life. One of the best primary battery technologies for these characteristics is the lithium cell.

Lithium batteries

Lithium/manganese-dioxide (Li/MnO_2 or *lithium*) batteries use a layer of lithium as the anode, a specially formulated manganese-dioxide alloy as the cathode, and a conductive organic electrolyte. Depending on the overall size and shape of the cell, a lithium battery can supply +3.0 Vdc at up to 330 Wh/kg of energy density. Lithium cells also offer a five-year shelf life with almost no loss of power. Although their energy density is quite high, lithium cells offer only low ampere-hour ratings between 70 mAh (0.70 Ah) and 1300 mAh (1.30 Ah). Limited Ah ratings allow lithium cells to maintain an almost constant output voltage over a long working life.

The classic type of lithium *coin cell* design is shown in Fig. 14-2. The typical coin cell is designed in two halves with a lithium anode at the top, and a manganese-dioxide cathode layer on the bottom. Both halves are separated by a thin membrane containing a conductive electrolyte. The finished electrochemical assembly is then packaged into a small metal can. The lid forms the negative electrode, and the side walls and bottom of the coin form the positive electrode. The lid is physically isolated from the rest of the metal can by a thin insulating grommet—thus, the coin cell is not sealed. A grommet keeps moisture and contaminants out, yet will allow any pressure buildup to escape the battery.

Backup battery replacement

All battery life has a finite limit. Eventually, all backup batteries will discharge to the point where they can no longer sustain the system. When the battery finally does

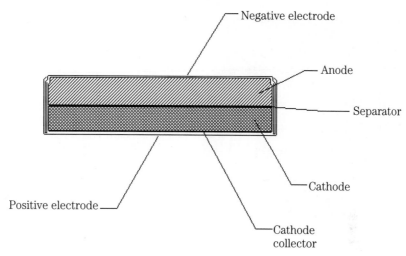

Negative electrode

Anode

Separator

Cathode

Positive electrode

Cathode collector

14-2 Cross-section of a lithium coin cell.

fail, CMOS information is lost. The next time you attempt to turn the PC on, the system will generate an error code or message indicating that the system configuration does not match the CMOS setup information. The loss of a CMOS setup suddenly leaves a system disabled until new (and correct) CMOS information is entered. This presents a serious problem for most PC users, because few users bother to back up or record their CMOS setup. As you might imagine, it then becomes an exercise in frustration to load the setup routine and reconstruct the system setup from scratch.

Fortunately, there are two things you can do to avoid this problem. First, make it a point to replace the backup battery every 2 years (no more than 3 years). If you change the backup battery for a customer, note the battery part number and replacement date on a sticker, then place the sticker inside the PC enclosure. You also might note the next replacement date on your customer's bill. Second, back up the system CMOS entries before replacing the battery. You can note the entries on paper (using the form included in the appendix of this book) and tape the page inside the enclosure, or you can use a shareware utility to back up CMOS contents as a disk file. CMOS backup as a disk file is quick and easy, and the file can be restored in a matter of seconds. A backup utility is especially handy when there is no SETUP disk available for the system being worked on. Make it a point to keep the backup current as system parameters change. Otherwise, you would be restoring information that is no longer valid.

The actual process of backup battery replacement is simply a matter or removing the old battery and inserting a new one. Because the battery is often located prominently on the motherboard (Fig. 14-3), it is possible to replace a backup battery with system power applied (this lets the system maintain its CMOS settings). However, working inside a hot system is against the safety protocols that we have established for this book, so be sure to record the CMOS settings on floppy disk or paper first, then power down and unplug the PC before opening it. Replace the battery, then restart the PC and reload the CMOS settings from disk or paper. Replacing the backup battery in a notebook or subnotebook PC is sometimes easier because the

14-3
A coin cell mounted to a C&T
motherboard. Copyright © Chips and
Technologies, Inc. 1995. Reprinted with permission of
copyright owner. All rights reserved.

battery is usually accessible from a small panel on the bottom enclosure (you do not
have to disassemble the notebook enclosures to replace the battery). Even with easy
access, you should make it a point to remove power before replacing the battery.

Troubleshooting backup battery problems

Lithium CMOS backup batteries are typically rugged and reliable devices whose
greatest weakness is simply old age. Because lithium cells are the primary type, they
cannot be recharged, so they MUST be replaced. Under most circumstances, there
are three symptoms that account for the majority of backup battery problems.

Symptom 1. The system configuration is lost intermittently A lithium
battery generally produces a very stable output voltage until the very end of its operating life. When the battery finally dies, it tends to be a permanent event. When a
system loses its setup configuration without warning, but seems to hold the configuration once it is restored, a loose or intermittent connection is suggested. Turn the
PC off and unplug it. Check the battery and make sure it is inserted correctly and
completely in its holder. A coin cell should fit snugly. If the cell is loose, gently
tighten the holder's prongs to hold the cell more securely. Make sure to remove any
corrosion or debris that might be interfering with the contacts. High-quality electrical contact cleaner on a moistened swab is particularly effective at cleaning contacts.
When the battery is attached by a short cable, see that the cable is not broken or
frayed, and make sure it is inserted properly into its receptacle. If problems persist,
replace the battery.

Symptom 2. The backup battery is going dead frequently This is a rare
and perplexing problem that is often difficult to detect because it might only manifest itself several times a year. Ideally, a lithium coin cell should last for several years
(perhaps three years or more). A lithium battery pack can last five years or more.
When a system loses its setup more than once a year due to battery failures, it is very
likely that an error in the motherboard design is draining the backup batteries faster

than normal. Unfortunately, the only way to really be sure is to replace the motherboard with a different or updated version. Before suggesting this option to your customer, you might wish to contact technical support for the original motherboard manufacturer and find out if similar cases have been reported—and if so, find if there is a fix or correction that will rectify the problem.

Symptom 3. You see a 161 error or message indicating that the system battery is dead Depending on the particular system you are working with, there also might be a message indicating that the CMOS setup does not match the system configuration. In either case, the backup battery has probably failed, and should be replaced. Remember to turn off the system before replacing the battery. Once the backup battery is replaced, restart the system. You will likely receive a message that the CMOS setup does not match the system configuration. Restore the configuration from paper notes or a file backup. The system should now function normally.

Source batteries

Besides providing power to back up the system's configuration, notebook and subnotebook computers rely on batteries for main power when operating away from ac. Such power is typically provided from a battery pack installed from the bottom or side of the computer. The requirements for battery packs are ever more stringent—packs have to provide as much power for as long as possible, yet be as light and small as possible. Further, today's battery packs must be quickly rechargeable, and offer a long working life. The two battery technologies best suited to these requirements are Nickel-Cadmium and Nickel Metal-Hydride.

Nickel-cadmium batteries

The nickel-cadmium (NiCd) battery is one of the most cost-effective power sources in mass-production today. Large NiCd battery packs are widely used in small computers (primarily laptops and notebooks) as a main power source. Because NiCd cells can be manufactured in almost limitless shapes and sizes, they are ideal for systems requiring unusual battery configurations. Although NiCd batteries initially cost more than primary batteries, they can be recharged often—usually recovering their initial cost many times over.

Nickel-cadmium batteries are secondary (rechargeable) devices using an anode of nickel hydroxide and a cathode consisting of a specially formulated cadmium compound. The electrolyte is made of potassium hydroxide. NiCd cells can supply up to +1.2 Vdc each with ampere hour ratings from 500 mAh (0.50 Ah) to 2300 mAh (2.30 Ah). Energy densities in NiCd cells can approach 50 Wh/kg (23 Wh/lb). Respectable ampere-hour ratings allow NiCd cells to supply sizable amounts of current, but their inherently low energy density means that NiCds must be recharged fairly often.

A standard NiCd cell is shown in Fig. 14-4. Both the positive and negative electrodes are long, sintered strips that are isolated by a thin, porous separator material. This long assembly is then wrapped tightly around a core and inserted into a casing of solid steel. Any pressure accumulated in the battery during normal operation can be released through the cell's safety vent.

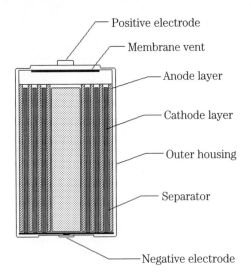

Positive electrode

Membrane vent

Anode layer

Cathode layer

14-4
Cross-section of a NiCd battery.

Outer housing

Separator

Negative electrode

The NiCd *memory effect* is a unique phenomenon that is not entirely understood. In operation, a NiCd battery can develop a "memory" that serves to limit either the capacity or terminal voltage of a cell. As you might expect, either limit can result in problems with the battery. *Voltage memory* is generally caused by prolonged charging over a period of weeks and months. High ambient temperatures and high charging currents can accelerate this condition. In effect, the battery is charged for so long, or at such a high rate or temperature, that the efficiency of the electrochemical reaction is impaired. As a result, the battery suffers from low terminal voltage.

The *memory capacity* problem is probably more widely recognized, and is usually expressed as the loss of a NiCd's ability to deliver its full power capacity. The generally accepted cause of capacity problems is the result of frequent partial battery discharge, followed by a full recharge. Over several such cycles, the battery "learns" that only a portion of its capacity is used. This renders the battery unable to deliver a full discharge when needed. Although the chemical reason for memory capacity is not fully understood, it is believed to be caused by oxidation reactions that temporarily coat the electrodes with nonreactive chemical compounds. Fortunately, the memory effect is usually temporary, and can usually be cleared by forcing the battery through several full discharge/recharge cycles. Generally speaking, if you are in the habit of using your notebook or laptop PC until you receive low-battery warnings, you will probably not have to worry about NiCd memory problems. It is interesting to note that the newer nickel metal-hydride batteries do not seem to suffer from memory problems.

NiCd cells also have a very limited charged life when sitting idle. Although alkaline and lithium cells can hold close to their original charge for years, NiCds will lose approximately 25 to 35% of their remaining charge each month. After several months of inactivity, a NiCd battery pack will need to be recharged before use. As a general rule, you should fully recharge any new or rarely used NiCd battery or battery pack prior to use.

Nickel metal-hydride batteries

Nickel metal-hydride (*NiMH*) batteries are a fairly new type of rechargeable battery designed to offer substantially greater energy density than NiCd cells for small-computer applications. Since their introduction in 1990, NiMH cells have already undergone some substantial improvements and cost reductions to make NiMH cells more competitive with the established NiCd battery family.

NiMH batteries are remarkably similar in construction and operating principles to NiCds. A positive electrode of nickel-hydroxide remains the same as that used in NiCds, but the negative electrode replaces cadmium with a metal-hydroxide alloy. When combined with a uniquely formulated electrolyte, NiMH cells are rated to provide at least 40% more capacity than similarly sized NiCd cells. NiMH batteries can provide +1.2 Vdc with discharge ratings from 800 mAh (0.80 Ah) to more than 2400 mAh (2.40 Ah) at continuous discharge currents of 9 A or more. Energy densities can exceed 80 Wh/kg (38.1 Wh/lb). Such specifications suggest widespread future use of NiMH battery packs.

The general construction of a cylindrical NiMH cell is illustrated in Fig. 14-5. You might notice the similarities between NiMH and NiCd construction. The positive and negative electrodes are formed in long strips. A porous separator membrane is sandwiched between each electrode. The entire assembly is wrapped around a core, then inserted into a nickel-plated steel case. A venting mechanism virtually identical to NiCd devices is used to bleed off any pressure buildup within the cell.

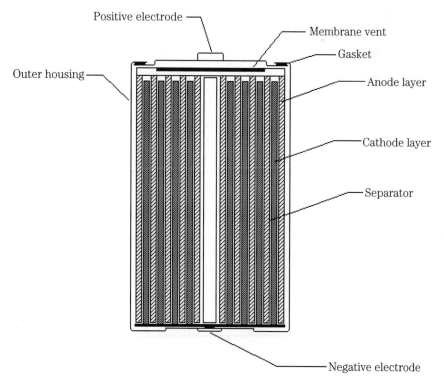

14-5 Cross-section of a NiMH battery.

Recognizing rechargeable battery failures

Rechargeable batteries can and do fail eventually. The process of discharge and recharge generates physical stress in the battery that will eventually wear it out. As a rule of thumb, a NiCd battery will last from about three to five years (through 500 to 1500 complete charge cycles). However, proper charging in a cool environment can extend battery life much further (up to as much as 10,000 complete charge cycles have been reported). Over the life of a rechargeable cell, microscopic "whiskers" of conductive compounds develop between the electrodes. Ultimately, these deposits work to short-circuit the cell. Although "zapping" techniques have been developed using brief surges of current to remove these deposits, such techniques are very risky because the battery stands a good chance of exploding. Another failure mode is the premature loss of liquid electrolyte during high-current or high-temperature charging. Improperly designed quick-charge chargers can drive a battery so hard that electrolyte starts to corrode the battery's pressure relief vent. If the vent is damaged or frozen in the open position, electrolyte will continue to evaporate.

Conserving battery power

Battery life is affected by the current drawn by a mobile computer—greater current draw results in shorter battery life, and vice versa. A large portion of battery troubleshooting is to ensure that your system setup is adequate. The following steps should help you to optimize battery life. First, use the lowest screen brightness that you are comfortable with by adjusting the display's brightness and contrast control(s). Backlights gobble up substantial amounts of power, so set a short time-out interval for the backlight (one or two minutes is often a good selection). Light characters and images on a dark background generally consumes less power than dark characters or images on a light background. Try setting your screen mode to a light-on-dark configuration.

The hard disk drive is another major power user—not only by spinning, but during spinup as well. Select a moderate time-out interval for the hard drive (not so long where it spins forever, and not so short where it is constantly starting). Otherwise, you will waste more power constantly spinning up the drive than you save by turning it off. Also, constant starting and stopping can reduce the life expectancy of the drive. RAM consumes much less power than hard drives, so try setting up a disk cache or RAM disk to reduce the number of disk accesses. This allows the hard drive to shut down fairly quickly and not require access for a relatively long period of time.

Finally, microprocessor speed can be a serious drain on battery power. If your small computer allows you to select processor speed, use the slowest speed possible for all but the most demanding applications. Most word processors and conventional DOS utility software runs just fine with slower processor speeds.

Troubleshooting source battery problems

When discussing batteries as main power sources, not only are the batteries or battery pack involved, but a whole host of other circuitry is included as well (such as battery charging, battery protection, and power management circuits). As a result, you should understand that problems running or charging the battery might be originating outside of the battery compartment. Because batteries power notebook and subnotebook systems, trouble might be on the motherboard (where most charging and power management functions are located).

Symptom 1. The battery pack does not charge In this type of situation, the computer might run fine from the ac-powered supply, and the system might very well run from its on-board battery when the ac-powered supply is removed. However, the battery pack does not appear to charge when the ac supply is connected and running. Without a charge, the battery will eventually go dead. Remember that some computers will not recharge their battery packs while the system is on—the computer must be turned off with the ac supply connected in order for the battery pack to charge. Refer to the User's Manual for your particular system to review the correct charging protocol.

Your clue to the charging situation comes from the computer's battery status indicator. Most notebook/laptop systems incorporate a multicolor LED to show battery information. For example, the LED might be red when the small computer is operating from its internal battery. A yellow color might appear when the ac-powered supply is connected to indicate the battery is charging. The LED might turn green when the battery is fully charged. If the battery status indicator fails to show a charging color when the ac-powered supply is being used, that is often a good sign of trouble. The user's manual for your particular computer will cover its charging indicators.

Check the battery pack with all computer power off. Make sure that the battery pack is inserted properly and completely into its compartment. Also check any cabling and connectors that attach the battery pack to the charging circuit. Loose or corroded connectors, as well as faulty cable wiring, can prevent energy from the ac-powered supply from reaching the battery. Re-seat any loose connectors and reattach any loose wiring that you might find.

After you are confident of your connections, you should trace charging voltage from the ac-powered supply to the battery terminals. If charging voltage does not reach the battery, the battery can never charge. Set your multimeter to measure dc voltage (probably in the 10- to 20-Vdc range) and measure the voltage across your battery pack. You should read some voltage below the pack's rated voltage because the battery pack is somewhat discharged. Now, connect the computer's ac-powered supply and measure voltage across your battery pack again. If charging voltage is available to the battery, your voltage reading should climb above the battery pack's rated voltage. If charging still does not seem to take place, try replacing the battery pack that might be worn out or damaged. If charging voltage is not available to your battery pack, the charging circuit is probably faulty. Replace the charging circuit. Because the charging circuit is typically located on the motherboard, it might be necessary to replace the entire motherboard assembly.

Symptom 2. The system does not run on battery power, but runs properly from main power This symptom usually suggests that your computer runs fine whenever the ac-powered supply is being used, but the system will not run from battery power alone. The system might or might not initialize depending on the extent of the problem. Before you disassemble the computer or attempt any sort of repair, make sure that you have a fully charged battery pack in the system. Remove the battery pack and measure the voltage across its terminals. You should read approximately the battery voltage marked on the pack. A measurably lower voltage might indicate that the battery is not fully charged. Try a different battery pack, or try to let the battery pack recharge. The charging process might take several hours on older systems, but newer small-computer battery systems can charge in an hour or so. If the discharged battery pack does not seem to charge, refer to Symptom 1.

When you have a fully-charged battery, check to be sure that it is inserted completely and connected properly. Inspect any wiring and connectors that attach the battery pack to its load circuit. Faulty wiring or loose connectors can cut off the battery pack entirely. At this point, it is safe to assume that battery power is not reaching the load circuit(s). In this event, the battery charging/protection circuit might be defective and should be replaced. If the circuit is incorporated into the motherboard, the motherboard should be replaced.

Symptom 3. The system suffers from a short battery life Today's small computers are designed to squeeze up to 6 hours of operation (or more) from every charge. Most systems get at least 2 hours from a charge. Short battery life can present a perplexing problem—especially if you do a great deal of computing on the road. All other computer functions are assumed to be normal.

Begin your investigation by inspecting the battery pack itself. Check for any damaged batteries. Make sure the battery pack is inserted properly into the computer, and see that its connections and wiring are intact. Try replacing the battery pack. Keep in mind that rechargeable batteries do not last forever—typical NiCd packs are usually good for about 1500 cycles. Fast-charge battery packs are subject to the greatest abuse and can suffer the shortest life spans. It is possible that one or more cells in the battery pack might have failed. The battery pack also might have developed a "memory" problem. Try several cycles of completely discharging and recharging the pack. If the problem remains, replace the battery pack.

The computer's configuration itself can largely determine the amount of running time that is available from each charge. The CPU, an *EL* (electroluminescent) backlight, a spinning hard drive, floppy drive access: each of these items consume substantial amounts of power. Many small computers are designed to shut down each major power consumer after some preset period of disuse. For example, an LCD screen might shut off if there is no keyboard activity after two minutes, or the hard drive might stop spinning after three minutes if there is no hard drive access, and so on. Even reducing CPU clock speed during periods of inactivity will reduce power consumption. The computer's BIOS keeps track of elapsed time for each device, then initiates the appropriate shutdown sequence. The amount of time required before shutdown can usually be adjusted through setup routines in the computer.

Symptom 4. The battery pack becomes extremely hot during charging As you learned in this chapter, energy must be applied to a battery from an external source in order to restore battery charge. When a battery receives significant charging current (during or after the charging process), its temperature will begin to rise. Temperature rise continues as long as current is applied. If high charging current continues unabated, battery temperature might climb high enough to actually damage the cells. Even under the best circumstances, prolonged high-temperature conditions can shorten the working life of a battery pack. Today's high-current charging circuits must be carefully controlled to ensure a full, rapid battery charge, but prevent excessive temperature rise and damage.

Battery packs or compartments are fitted with a *thermistor* (a temperature-sensitive resistor). When the battery pack is fully charged, the thermistor responds to the subsequent temperature increase and signals charging circuitry to reduce or stop its charging current. In this way, temperature is used to detect when full charge had been reached. It is normal for most battery packs to become a bit warm during the charging process—especially packs that use fast-charge currents. However, the cell(s) should not give off an obnoxious odor or become too hot to touch. Hot batteries are likely to be damaged. In many cases, the thermistor (or thermistor's signal conditioning circuitry) has failed and is no longer shutting down charge current. Try another battery pack. If the new pack also becomes very hot, the fault is in the charging circuit that should be replaced. If the new pack remains cooler, the fault is probably in the original battery pack.

Symptom 5. The computer quits without producing a low-battery warning Computers are rarely subtle in regard to low-power warnings. Once a battery pack falls below a certain voltage threshold, the computer initiates a series of unmistakable audible (and sometimes visual) queues that tell you there are only minutes of power remaining. Such a warning affords you a last-minute opportunity to save your work and switch over to ac power if possible. If you choose to ignore a low-power warning, the system will soon reach a minimum working level and crash on its own—whether you like it or not.

Small computers measure their battery voltage levels constantly. A custom IC on the motherboard is typically given the task of watching over battery voltage. When voltage falls below a fixed preset level, the detector IC produces a logic alarm signal. The alarm, in turn, drives an interrupt to the CPU, or passes the signal to a power management IC that then deals with the CPU or system controller. Once the alarm condition reaches the CPU, the computer typically initiates a series of tones, or flashes a *power* LED (or sometimes both).

Most PCs produce at least one beep during initialization in order to test the internal speaker. If you do not hear this beep, the speaker or its driving circuit might be damaged. Try replacing the speaker, then try replacing the motherboard. When an audible beep is heard during initialization, there is probably a fault in the computer's battery detection or power management circuits. Try replacing the motherboard.

15

BIOS and beep codes

Although every personal computer uses the same essential subassemblies, each sub-assembly is designed a bit differently. This is especially true of the processing components contained on a motherboard. Unfortunately, variations in hardware make it difficult to use a single standard operating system. Instead of tailoring the operating system (and applications) to specific computers, a *BIOS* (basic input/output system) is added on ROM ICs to provide an interface between the raw PC hardware and the operating system—BIOS gives an OS access to a standard set of functions. As a result, every system uses a slightly different BIOS, but each BIOS contains the same set of functions. It is the BIOS that makes today's IBM-compatible PCs possible. This chapter explains the internal workings of a typical BIOS, and shows you how to interpret and troubleshoot various beep code sequences.

Of course, BIOS is not limited solely to the motherboard (although system BIOS ROMs carry enough routines to run the system in a very basic fashion). But, what happens when a new video card is developed that the system BIOS does not know how to work with, or an advanced drive controller board becomes available? A common practice in computer design is to include a BIOS ROM for major subsystems such as video and drive control. One of the early steps of system initialization is to check for the presence of other valid BIOS ROMs located in upper memory (between 640 and 1024K). When another BIOS is located, it also is tested and used by the PC. In general, a PC might be fitted with up to five or more BIOS ROMs:

- System (motherboard) BIOS
- Video BIOS
- Drive controller BIOS
- Network adapter board BIOS
- SCSI adapter BIOS

A look inside motherboard BIOS

The typical BIOS ROM occupies 128K of space in the system's *UMA* (upper-memory area) from E0000h to FFFFFh (within the PC's first MB of memory). Contrary to popular belief, BIOS is not a single program, but an arsenal of individual programs—most quite small. In general, BIOS contains three sections as shown in Fig. 15-1: (1) the POST, (2) the SETUP, and (3) the System Routines. The particular section of BIOS code that is executed depends on the computer's state and its activities at any given moment.

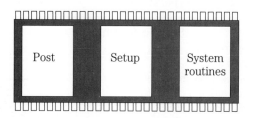

Post   Setup   System routines

15-1
Inside a typical BIOS ROM.

POST

Although many novice technicians are aware that POST checks the system, few are aware that POST actually manages the entire system startup. The power-on self-test handles virtually all of the initialization activities for a PC. POST performs a low-level diagnostic and reliability test of the main processing components (including ROM programs and system RAM). It tests and initializes the CPU and other main processing ICs, checks the 64 bytes of CMOS system configuration data, and sets up an index of interrupt vectors for the CPU (from 0000h to 02FFh). POST then sets up a BIOS Stack Area (from 0300h to 03FFh), and loads the BIOS Data Area (BDA) in low memory (0400h to 04FFh), detects any optional equipment in the system, and proceeds to boot the operating system.

SETUP

In order for BIOS to operate correctly, it must be aware of the system configuration parameters (that is, the amount of memory that is available, whether or not math coprocessor is available, the number of hard drives and floppy drives installed, and so on). In addition to basic CMOS settings, many new systems offer advanced settings that configure characteristics such as RAM and ROM wait states and memory relocation. System parameters are held in CMOS RAM, and are accessible on newer i486 and Pentium-based systems through a BIOS setup routine. Older i286- and i386-based systems used a setup utility included on floppy disk.

System routines

The system routines (also referred to as *BIOS Services*) are a set of individual functions that form the layer between hardware and the operating system. Services are called through the use of interrupts. An *interrupt* essentially causes the CPU to stop whatever it was working on and sends program control to another address in memory that usually starts a subroutine designed specifically to deal with the particular interrupt. When the interrupt handling routine is complete, the CPU's original state is restored, and control is returned to where the PC left off before the interrupt occurred. There are a wide range of interrupts that can attract the attention of a CPU, and interrupts can be produced from three major sources: (1) the CPU itself, (2) a hardware condition, and (3) a software condition. Table 15-1 lists 56 standard interrupts found in a typical BIOS. Keep in mind that the BIOS used in your particular system might offer more or fewer functions depending on its vintage.

Table 15-1. BIOS service summary

INT code	Type	Service description
00h	Processor	Divide by zero
01h	Processor	Single step
02h	Processor	Non-maskable interrupt (NMI)
03h	Processor	Breakpoint
04h	Processor	Arithmetic overflow
05h	Software	Print screen
06h	Processor	Invalid op-code
07h	Processor	Co-processor not available
08h	Hardware	System timer service routine
09h	Hardware	Keyboard device service routine
0Ah	Hardware	Cascade from 2nd programmable interrupt controller
0Bh	Hardware	Serial port service (COM2)
0Ch	Hardware	Serial port service (COM1)
0Dh	Hardware	Parallel printer service (LPT2)
0Eh	Hardware	Floppy disk drive service
0Fh	Hardware	Parallel printer service (LPT1)
10h	Software	Video service routine
11h	Software	Equipment list service routine
12h	Software	Memory size service routine
13h	Software	Hard disk drive service
14h	Software	Serial communication service routines
15h	Software	System services support routines
16h	Software	Keyboard support service routines
17h	Software	Parallel printer support services
18h	Software	Load and run ROM BASIC
19h	Software	DOS loading routine
1Ah	Software	Real-time clock service routines
1Bh	Software	<CTRL><BREAK> service routine
1Ch	Software	User timer service routines
1Dh	Software	Video control parameter table
1Eh	Software	Floppy disk parameter table
1Fh	Software	Video graphics character table
20h–3Fh	Software	DOS interrupt points
40h	Software	Floppy disk revector routine
41h	Software	Hard disk drive C: parameter table
42h	Software	EGA default video driver
43h	Software	Video graphic characters
44h	Software	Novell NetWare API
45h	Software	. . . not used . . .
46h	Software	Hard disk drive D: parameter table

Table 15-1. Continued

INT code	Type	Service description
47h–49h	Software	. . . not used . . .
4Ah	Software	User alarm
4Bh–63h	Software	. . . not used . . .
64h	Software	Novell NetWare IPX
65h–66h	Software	. . . not used . . .
67h	Software	EMS support routines
68h–6Fh	Software	. . . not used . . .
70h	Hardware	Real-time clock
71h	Hardware	Redirect interrupt cascade
72h–74h	Hardware	Reserved . . . do not use . . .
75h	Hardware	Math co-processor exception
76h	Hardware	Hard disk support
77h	Hardware	Suspend request
78h–79h	Software	. . . not used . . .
7Ah	Software	Novell NewWare API
78h–BFh	Software	. . . not used . . .

Interrupts produced by the CPU itself (known as *processor interrupts*) are often the result of an unusual, unexpected, or erroneous program result. For example, if a program tries to divide a number by zero, the CPU will generate INT 00h that causes a *Divide by zero* error message. There are five processor interrupts (00h to 04h).

The hardware interrupts are generated when a device is in need of the CPU's attention to perform a certain task. Hardware interrupts are invoked by asserting a logic level on a physical interrupt request (IRQ) line. The CPU suspends its activities and executes the interrupt handling routine. When the interrupt handler is finished, the CPU resumes normal operation. For example, each time a keyboard key is pressed, the keyboard buffer asserts a logic line corresponding to INT 09h (IRQ 1). This invokes a keyboard handling routine. PC/AT-compatible systems typically provide 16 hardware interrupts (IRQ 0 to IRQ 15) that correspond to INT 08h to 0Fh and 70h to 77h respectively.

Software interrupts are generated when a hardware device must be checked or manipulated by the PC. The print screen function is a prime example of a software interrupt. When the Print Screen button is pressed on the keyboard, an INT 05h is generated. The interrupt routine dumps the contents of its video character buffer to the printer port.

BIOS shortcomings and compatibility issues

Device drivers

As you might expect, no BIOS can possibly address every piece of hardware in the PC marketplace, or keep pace with the rapid advances of those devices that a

BIOS does support. As a result, PC designers have devised a way to augment BIOS through the use of *device drivers*. CD-ROMs are an excellent example. There are a number of CD-ROM designs in use today—each CD-ROM and their corresponding adapter board use their own (often proprietary) circuitry to operate the drive and interface it to the PC bus. Neither the CD-ROM application, DOS, or BIOS are capable of identifying the drive or interface. To get around this, a low-level device driver is loaded into conventional memory from disk once the PC initializes. The low-level device driver translates a set of standard DOS calls into the instructions necessary to operate the adapter and drive. An extension of DOS (MSCDEX for MS-DOS-based systems) also is loaded into memory after the low-level driver. The DOS extension works seamlessly with MSDOS.SYS to provide applications with a standard set of software interrupt CD-ROM services. Generally speaking, device drivers all serve to supplement BIOS. Video, SCSI, and network adapters all make use of device drivers at some level.

Improving BIOS performance

Another problem with BIOS ICs is their inherently slow speed. BIOS is typically burned onto read-only memory devices (ROMs) or *EEPROM*s (electrically erasable programmable ROMs). These devices are necessary because BIOS data must be maintained even when power is removed. Unfortunately, permanent storage ICs such as these have hideously slow access times (150 ns to 200 ns) when compared to the fast DRAM used in today's PCs (60 ns to 80 ns). When you consider that the services stored in a BIOS ROM are used almost continuously, it is easy to see that each delay is additive. The net result is an overall reduction in PC performance.

In order to overcome this limitation, it would be necessary to accelerate the access time of BIOS ROM. However, this is not too likely given the current state of semiconductor technology, so PC designers do the next best thing—*ROM shadowing*. The process of "shadowing" basically copies ROM contents from the BIOS IC into available RAM in the upper memory area. Once the copy is complete, the system will work from the copy rather than the original. This allows BIOS routines to take advantage of faster memory. Not only system BIOS, but ALL BIOS can be shadowed. Video BIOS is particularly popular for shadowing. ROM shadowing can typically be turned on or off through the CMOS setup routine.

Direct control

In the race to wring every last clock-tick of performance from a PC, even the most elegant BIOS is simply too slow for high-performance applications. If the application could work with PC hardware directly, system performance (especially disk and video subsystems) could be substantially improved. Writing directly to hardware is hardly new. Pre-IBM PCs relied on direct application control. The use of BIOS was included by IBM to ensure that variations in PC hardware would still remain compatible with operating system and application software. As it turns out, today's PC hardware is remarkably standardized (often more so than the BIOS). With this broad base of relatively standard PCs, software developers are reviving the direct control approach and ignoring the use of BIOS services in favor of routines written into the application.

BIOS bugs

As with all software-based products, BIOS code is subject to accidental errors or omissions (*software bugs*). When BIOS ICs are manufactured, they are made by the thousands and purchased by motherboard manufacturers who incorporate the ICs into their motherboards. If a bug is present in the BIOS, the system will typically lock up or crash unexpectedly, or during a certain operation. Because the same BIOS might be used in several motherboards, the bug might not manifest itself in all cases. As one example, some users of AMI BIOS (dated 04/09/90 or earlier) reported problems with the keyboard controller when running Windows or OS/2. As you can imagine, BIOS bugs are particularly frustrating. If an application contains a bug, you can turn the application off. Unfortunately, you cannot turn the BIOS off, so the only way to correct a bug in BIOS is to update the BIOS (or replace the entire motherboard).

When investigating a customer complaint for a PC, you might wish to check with the BIOS manufacturer (through technical support, fax-back service, or CompuServe forum) and find if there have been any problems with the BIOS when used in the particular motherboard (for example, a Phoenix BIOS in an Intel motherboard). If your symptoms match other symptoms that have been reported, a quick BIOS upgrade might save the day for your customer.

Troubleshooting the beep codes

One of the key purposes of any POST is to detect fatal errors—any system fault that would prevent the PC from completing its boot process, or processing properly once the boot process is complete. Unfortunately, detecting a fault is hardly useful unless the fault can be conveyed to a technician. Thus, POST diagnostics generate a unique code that corresponds to the detected fault. Text messages are certainly the most common and preferred means of conveying errors; however, the video system is not tested and initialized (the display remains blank) until after the core processing components have been checked. So what happens if a fault is detected before the video system is initialized? Errors are indicated with a series of beeps (called *beep codes*).

Because each BIOS is a bit different, the accuracy, precision, and quality of error detection and reporting varies from BIOS to BIOS. Although most POST routines today follow a remarkably similar pattern, the reporting style can vary greatly. Some routines (such as AMI) generate a continuous string of beeps, and other routines (such as Phoenix) create short beep sequences. This part of the chapter is intended to help you understand the actions of major POST procedures and interpret beep codes produced by AMI and Phoenix BIOS ROMs.

AMI

American Megatrends is renowned for their BIOS, PC diagnostics, and motherboards. AMI BIOS performs a fairly comprehensive suite of 24 steps in order to check and initialize the PC. The general AMI BIOS POST procedure is listed below, and Table 15-2 explains the AMI beep codes. Just about all faults listed below can be corrected by replacing the motherboard.

Table 15-2. AMI beep codes

Beeps	Error message
1s	*System RAM Refresh Failure.* The programmable Interrupt timer (PIT) or programmable interrupt controller (PIC) has probably failed. Replace the motherboard.
2s	*Memory Parity Error.* A parity error has been detected in the first 64KB of RAM. The RAM IC is probably defective. Replace the memory or motherboard.
3s	*Base 64Kb Memory Failure.* A memory failure has been detected in the first 64Kb of RAM. The RAM IC is probably defective. Replace the memory or motherboard.
4s	*System Timer Failure.* The system clock/timer IC has failed.
5s	*CPU Failure.* The system CPU has failed. Try replacing the CPU or motherboard.
6s	*Gate A20 Failure.* The keyboard controller IC has failed, so Gate A20 is no longer available to switch the CPU into protected mode. Replace the keyboard controller or motherboard.
7s	*Exception Error.* The CPU has generated an exception error due to a fault in the CPU or some combination of motherboard conditions. Try replacing the motherboard.
8s	*Video Memory Read/Write Error.* The system video adapter is missing or defective. Try replacing the video adapter.
9s	*ROM Checksum Error.* The contents of the system BIOS ROM does not match the expected checksum value. The BIOS ROM is probably defective and should be replaced.
10s	*CMOS Shutdown Register Read/Write Error.* The shutdown register for the CMOS memory has failed. Try replacing the RTC/CMOS IC.
1l-3s	*Memory Test Failure.* A fault has been detected in memory over 64Kb. Replace the memory or the motherboard.
1l-8s	*Display Test Failure.* The display adapter is missing or defective. Replace the video adapter board. If the video adapter is on the motherboard, try replacing the motherboard.

Legend: *l*=long *s*=short

1. *Disable the NMI*   BIOS disables the nonmaskable interrupt line to the CPU. A failure here suggests a problem with the CMOS RAM IC or its associated circuitry.
2. *Power-On Delay*   The system resets the soft and hard reset bits. A fault here indicates a problem with the keyboard controller IC or system clock generator IC.
3. *Initialize Chipsets*   BIOS initializes any particular motherboard chipsets (such as Chips & Technologies chipsets) that might be present in the system. A problem here might be caused by the BIOS, the clock generator IC, or the chipset(s).
4. *Reset Determination*   The system reads the reset bits in the keyboard controller to determine whether a hard or soft reset (cold or warm boot) is required. A failure here might be caused by the BIOS or keyboard controller IC.
5. *BIOS ROM Checksum*   The system performs a checksum test of ROM contents and adds a factory preset value that should make the total equal to 00h. If this total does not equal 00h, the BIOS ROM is defective.

6. *Keyboard Test* The system tests the keyboard controller. A fault here is likely the keyboard controller IC.

7. *CMOS Shutdown Check* BIOS tests the shutdown byte in CMOS RAM, calculates the CMOS checksum, and updates the CMOS diagnostic byte. The system then initializes a small CMOS area in conventional memory and updates the date and time. A problem here is likely in the RTC/CMOS IC, or the CMOS backup battery.

8. *Controller Disable* BIOS now disables the DMA and IRQ controller ICs before proceeding. A fault at this point suggests trouble in the respective controller.

9. *Disable Video* BIOS disables the video controller IC. If this procedure fails, the trouble is probably in the video adapter board.

10. *Detect Memory* The system proceeds to check the amount of memory available. BIOS measures system memory in 64K blocks. A problem here might be in the memory IC(s).

11. *PIT Test* BIOS tests the programmable interrupt timer vital for memory refresh. A problem with the PIT test might reflect a fault in the PIT IC or in the RTC IC.

12. *Check Memory Refresh* BIOS now uses the PIT to try refreshing memory. A failure indicates a problem with the PIT IC.

13. *Check Low Address Lines* The system checks the first 16 address lines controlling the first 64K of RAM. A problem with this test typically means a fault in an address line.

14. *Check Low 64K RAM* The system now checks the first 64K of system RAM. This is vital because this area must hold information that is critical for system initialization. A problem here is usually the result of a bad RAM IC.

15. *Initialize Support ICs* BIOS proceeds to initialize the programmable interrupt timer (PIT), the programmable interrupt controller (PIC), and the direct memory access (DMA) ICs. A fault here would be located in one of those locations.

16. *Load INT Vector Table* BIOS loads the system's interrupt vector table into the first 2K of system RAM.

17. *Check the Keyboard Controller* BIOS reads the keyboard controller buffer at I/O port 60h. A problem here indicates a fault in the keyboard controller IC.

18. *Video Tests* The system checks for the type of video adapter in use, then tests and initializes the video memory and adapter. A problem with this test typically indicates a fault with the video memory or adapter respectively. After a successful video test, the video system will be operational.

19. *Load the BDA* The system now loads the *BDA* (BIOS data area) into conventional memory.

20. *Test Protected-Mode Memory* BIOS checks all memory below 1MB. A problem here is typically the fault of one or more RAM ICs, the keyboard controller IC, or a bad data line.

21. *Check DMA Registers* BIOS performs a register-level check of the DMA controller(s) using binary test patterns. A problem here is often due to a failure of the DMA IC(s).

22. *Check the Keyboard*   The system performs a final check of the keyboard interface. An error at this point is usually the fault of the keyboard.
23. *Perform High-Level Tests*   This step involves a whole suite of tests that check such high-level devices as the floppy and hard disks, serial adapters, parallel adapters, mouse adapter, and so on. The number and complexity of these tests vary with the BIOS version. When an error occurs, a corresponding text message will be displayed. If the system hardware does not match the setup shown in the CMOS setup, a corresponding error code will be displayed.
24. *Load the OS*   At this point, BIOS triggers INT 19h that is the routine that loads an operating system. An error here generally results in an error message such as *Non-system disk*.

Phoenix Technologies

Phoenix Technologies is one of the premier BIOS manufacturers for IBM-compatible PCs. Although a typical Phoenix BIOS performs essentially the same steps as an AMI BIOS, Phoenix beep code sequences are highly detailed as shown in Table 15-3. Just about every fault listed below can be corrected by replacing the motherboard. By listening for the unique pattern of beeps (rather than just the number of beeps) you can readily locate the fault. The reason why Phoenix BIOS is so popular is its level of proliferation—Phoenix licenses their BIOS to OEMs, so you might find many variations of Phoenix products in the PC marketplace.

Table 15-3. Phoenix beep codes for ISA/MCA/EISA POST

Beeps	Error message
1-1-2	*CPU Register Test Failure.* The CPU has likely failed. Replace the CPU.
Low 1-1-2	*System Board Select Failure.* The motherboard is suffering from an indeterminate fault. Try replacing the motherboard.
1-1-3	*CMOS Read/Write Failure.* The RTC/CMOS IC has probably failed. Try replacing the RTC/CMOS IC.
Low 1-1-3	*Extended CMOS RAM Failure.* The extended portion of the RTC/CMOS IC has failed. Try replacing the RTC/CMOS IC.
1-1-4	*BIOS ROM Checksum Error.* The BIOS ROM has probably failed.
1-2-1	*Programmable Interval Timer (PIT) Failure.* The PIT has probably failed.
1-2-2	*DMA Initialization Failure.* The DMA controller has probably failed.
1-2-3	*DMA Page Register Read/Write Failure.* The DMA controller has probably failed.
1-3-1	*RAM Refresh Failure.* The refresh controller has failed.
1-3-2	*64Kb RAM Test Disabled.* The test of the first 64Kb of system RAM could not begin. Try replacing the motherboard.
1-3-3	*First 64Kb RAM IC or Data Line Failure.* The first RAM IC has failed.
1-3-4	*First 64Kb Odd/Even Logic Failure.* The first RAM control logic has failed.
1-4-1	*Address Line Failure 64Kb of RAM.*
1-4-2	*Parity Failure First 64Kb of RAM.* The first RAM IC has failed.
1-4-3	*EISA Failsafe Timer Test Fault.* Replace the motherboard.
1-4-4	*EISA NMI Port 462 Test Failure.* Replace the motherboard.

Table 15-3. Continued

Beeps	Error message
2-1-1	*Bit 0 First 64Kb RAM Failure.* This data bit in the first RAM IC has failed.
2-1-2	*Bit 1 First 64Kb RAM Failure.*
2-1-3	*Bit 2 First 64Kb RAM Failure.*
2-1-4	*Bit 3 First 64Kb RAM Failure.*
2-2-1	*Bit 4 First 64Kb RAM Failure.*
2-2-2	*Bit 5 First 64Kb RAM Failure.*
2-2-3	*Bit 6 First 64Kb RAM Failure.*
2-2-4	*Bit 7 First 64Kb RAM Failure.*
2-3-1	*Bit 8 First 64Kb RAM Failure.*
2-3-2	*Bit 9 First 64Kb RAM Failure.*
2-3-3	*Bit 10 First 64Kb RAM Failure.*
2-3-4	*Bit 11 First 64Kb RAM Failure.*
2-4-1	*Bit 12 First 64Kb RAM Failure.*
2-4-2	*Bit 13 First 64Kb RAM Failure.*
2-4-3	*Bit 14 First 64Kb RAM Failure.*
2-4-4	*Bit 15 First 64Kb RAM Failure.*
3-1-1	*Slave DMA Register Failure.* The DMA controller has probably failed.
3-1-2	*Master DMA Register Failure.* The DMA controller has probably failed.
3-1-3	*Master Interrupt Mask Register Failure.* The interrupt controller has probably failed.
3-1-4	*Slave Interrupt Mask Register Failure.* The interrupt controller has probably failed.
3-2-2	*Interrupt Vector Loading Error.* BIOS is unable to load the interrupt vectors into low RAM. Replace the motherboard.
3-2-3	. . . reserved . . .
3-2-4	*Keyboard Controller Test Failure.* The keyboard controller has failed.
3-3-1	*CMOS RAM Power Bad.* Try replacing the CMOS backup battery. Try replacing the RTC/CMOS IC. Replace the motherboard.
3-3-2	*CMOS Configuration Error.* The CMOS configuration has failed. Restore the configuration. Replace the CMOS backup battery. Replace the RTC/CMOS IC. Replace the motherboard.
3-3-3	. . . reserved . . .
3-3-4	*Video Memory Test Failed.* There is a problem with the video memory. Replace video memory or replace the video adapter board.
3-4-1	*Video Initialization Test Failure.* There is a problem with the video system. Replace the video adapter.
4-2-1	*Timer Tick Failure.* The system timer IC has failed.
4-2-2	*Shutdown Test Failure.* The CMOS IC has failed.
4-2-3	*Gate A20 Failure.* The keyboard controller has probably failed.
4-2-4	*Unexpected Interrupt in Protected Mode.* There is a problem with the CPU.
4-3-1	*RAM Test Address Failure.* System RAM addressing circuitry has failed.
4-3-3	*Interval Timer Channel 2 Failure.* The system timer IC has probably failed.
4-3-4	*Time of Day Clock Failure.* The RTC/CMOS IC has failed.
4-4-1	*Serial Port Test Failure.* A fault has developed in the serial port circuit.
4-4-2	*Parallel Port Test Failure.* A fault has developed in the parallel port circuit.
4-4-3	*Math Co-processor Failure.* Try replacing the math co-processor.

1. *Check the CPU* The registers and control lines of the CPU are checked. Any problems will usually be the result of a faulty CPU or clock IC.
2. *Test CMOS RAM* The CMOS IC is tested. A fault is usually due to a failure of the RTC/CMOS IC.
3. *BIOS ROM Checksum* A checksum is performed on the BIOS ROM. If the calculated checksum does not match the factory-set value, an error is generated. A checksum problem is typically the result of a faulty BIOS ROM. Try replacing the BIOS ROM.
4. *Test Chipsets* The system checks any chipsets (such as Chips & Technologies) for proper operation with the BIOS. A problem here is typically due to a fault in the chipset. Replace the motherboard.
5. *Test PIT* The programmable interrupt controller (PIT) is tested to ensure that all interrupt requests are handled properly. A problem here indicates that the PIT IC is defective.
6. *Test DMA* The direct memory access (DMA) controller is tested next. A fault at this point is typically caused by the CPU, the DMA IC, or an address line problem.
7. *Test Base 64K Memory* BIOS checks the lowest 64K of system RAM. A problem here is due to a fault in memory, or an address line problem.
8. *Check Serial and Parallel Ports* The system checks the presence of serial and parallel port hardware, and I/O data areas are assigned for any devices found.
9. *Test PIC* The programmable interrupt controller (PIC) is tested to see that proper interrupt levels can be generated. A problem here is typically due to a fault in the PIC IC.
10. *Check Keyboard Controller* The keyboard controller IC is tested for proper operation. When a problem occurs, the keyboard controller is likely defective.
11. *Verify CMOS Data* Data within the CMOS is checked for validity. If the extended area returns a failure, CMOS data has probably been set up incorrectly. However, continuous failures typically represent a faulty RTC/CMOS IC.
12. *Verify Video System* Video RAM is tested, then the video controller is located, tested, and initialized. A fault is usually the result of a defective video controller. If the controller is located on an expansion board, try replacing the video board.
13. *Test RTC* The *RTC* (real-time clock) is tested next, and each frequency output is verified. A problem here is usually due to a fault in the RTC, PIT, or system crystal.
14. *Test CPU in Protected Mode* The CPU is switched to protected mode and returned to POST at the point indicated in CMOS RAM offset 0Fh. When this step fails, the CPU, keyboard controller IC, CMOS IC, or address line(s) might be at fault.
15. *Verify PIC 2* Counter #2 is tested on the PIC IC. If this test fails, the PIC IC is likely defective.
16. *Check NMI* The NMI is checked to be sure it is active. A problem here often indicates trouble with the CMOS IC, but also could reflect problems in the BIOS ROM, PIC IC, or CPU.

17. *Check the Keyboard* The keyboard buffer and controller are checked.
18. *Check the Mouse* BIOS initializes the mouse (if present) through the keyboard controller. A fault is usually caused in the mouse adapter circuit.
19. *Check system RAM* All remaining system RAM is tested in 64K blocks. Trouble usually means a defective memory IC.
20. *Test Disk Controller* Fixed and floppy disk controllers are checked using standard BIOS calls. Problems here are usually the result of defective controllers or faulty drives. If the controllers are installed on expansion boards, you can try replacing the respective expansion board.
21. *Set Shadow RAM Areas* The system looks at CMOS to find that ROM(s) will be shadowed into RAM. Problems here are often due to a faulty adapter ROM, or problems in RAM.
22. *Check Extended ROMs* BIOS looks for signatures of 55AAh in memory that indicate the presence of additional ROMs. The system then performs a checksum test on each ROM. A problem with this step generally indicates trouble with the extended ROM or related adapter circuitry.
23. *Test Cache Controller* The external cache controller IC is tested. A problem is usually due to a fault in the cache controller IC itself, or a defect in cache memory.
24. *Test CPU Cache* The internal cache present on some i486 CPUs is tested. A problem here is almost always due to a CPU fault.
25. *Check Hardware Adapters* BIOS proceeds to check the high-level subsystems such as the video system, floppy disk, hard disk, I/O adapters, serial ports, and parallel ports. Problems usually reflect a fault with the respective adapter, or an invalid CMOS setup.
26. *Load the OS* At this point, BIOS triggers INT 19h, which is the routine that loads an operating system. An error here generally results in an error message such as *Non-system disk*.

Other beep codes

AMI and Phoenix are by no means the only two BIOS manufacturers that use beep codes during their POST process. AST, Compaq, Mylex, IBM, and Quadtel also incorporate beep code sequences to represent fatal errors. For your reference, Tables 15-4 through 15-8 include the beep codes for each of these other manufacturers.

Table 15-4. AST beep codes

Beeps	Error message
1s	*CPU Register Test Failure.* The CPU has failed. Try replacing the CPU or replace the motherboard.
2s	*Keyboard Controller Buffer Failure.* The keyboard controller IC has failed.
3s	*Keyboard Controller Reset Failure.* The keyboard controller IC or its associated circuitry has failed.
4s	*Keyboard Communication Failure.* The keyboard controller IC or its associated circuitry has failed. Try replacing the keyboard assembly. Try replacing the motherboard.
5s	*Keyboard Input Port Failure.* The keyboard controller IC has failed.

Table 15-4. Continued

Beeps	Error message
6s	*System Board Chipset Initialization Failure.* The chipset(s) used on the motherboard cannot be initialized. Either an element of the chipset(s) or the motherboard has failed.
9s	*BIOS ROM Checksum Error.* The BIOS ROM has failed. Try replacing the BIOS ROM or replace the motherboard.
10s	*System Timer Test Failure.* The master system clock IC has failed.
11s	*ASIC Register Test Failure.* Motherboard circuitry has failed. Replace the motherboard.
12s	*CMOS RAM Shutdown Register Failure.* The RTC/CMOS IC has failed. Try replacing the RTC/CMOS IC or replace the motherboard.
1l	*DMA Controller 0 Failure.* The DMA controller IC for channel 0 has failed.
1l-1s	*DMA Controller 1 Failure.* The DMA controller IC for channel 1 has failed.
1l-2s	*Video Vertical Retrace Failure.* The video adapter has failed. Replace the video adapter board.
1l-3s	*Video Memory Test Failure.* A fault has occurred in video memory. Replace the video adapter.
1l-4s	*Video Adapter Test Failure.* The video adapter has failed. Replace the video adapter board.
1l-5s	*64Kb Base Memory Failure.* A failure has occurred in the low 64Kb of system RAM. Replace memory or replace the motherboard.
1l-6s	*Unable to Load Interrupt Vectors.* BIOS was unable to load interrupt vectors into low memory. Replace the motherboard.
1l-7s	*Unable to Initialize Video System.* There is a defect in the video system. Replace the video adapter board. Replace the motherboard.
1l-8s	*Video Memory Failure.* There is a defect in video memory. Replace the video adapter or replace the motherboard.

Table 15-5. Compaq beep codes

Beeps	Error message
1s	*No Error.* No error has been detected.
1l-1s	*BIOS ROM Checksum Error.* The BIOS ROM has failed. Replace the BIOS ROM.
2s	*General Error.* A fault has occurred on the motherboard, memory, disk, or CMOS configuration. Replace the motherboard.
1l-2s	*Video Adapter Error.* The video system has failed. Replace the video adapter.

Legend: *l*=long   *s*=short

Table 15-6. Mylex beep codes

Beeps	Error message
1	*Start of Test.* No error has yet been detected. If no other errors are encountered, the PC should work satisfactorily.
2	*Video Adapter Error.* A video adapter problem has been detected. Try replacing the video adapter.
3	*Keyboard Controller Error.* Replace the keyboard controller IC or replace the motherboard.

Table 15-6. Continued

Beeps	Error message
4	*Keyboard Error.* The keyboard is not responding properly. Try replacing the keyboard.
5	*PIC 0 Error.* Programmable Interrupt Controller 1 has failed. In some systems, this may be expressed as PIC 1. Replace PIC 0 or replace the motherboard.
6	*PIC 1 Error.* Programmable Interrupt Controller 1 has failed. In some systems, this may be expressed as PIC 2. Replace PIC 1 or replace the motherboard.
7	*DMA Page Register Error.* The DMA controller has failed. Replace the DMA controller or replace the motherboard.
8	*RAM Refresh Error.* The RAM refresh circuit has failed. Replace the motherboard.
9	*RAM Data Error.* One or more RAM ICs has failed. Replace the RAM or replace the motherboard.
10	*RAM Parity Error.* One or more RAM ICs has failed. Replace the RAM or replace the motherboard.
11	*DMA Controller 0 Error.* DMA controller 0 has failed. In some systems, this may be expressed as DMA controller 1. Replace the DMA controller or replace the motherboard.
12	*CMOS RAM Error.* The RTC/CMOS IC has failed. Replace the RTC/CMOS IC or replace the motherboard.
13	*DMA Controller 1 Error.* DMA controller 1 has failed. In some systems, this may be expressed as DMA controller 2. Replace the DMA controller or replace the motherboard.
14	*CMOS RAM Battery Error.* Replace the CMOS backup battery.
15	*CMOS RAM Checksum Error.* Replace the RTC/CMOS IC.
16	*BIOS ROM Checksum Error.* Replace the BIOS ROM IC.

Table 15-7. IBM beep codes

Beeps	Error message
1s	*Start of Test.* No error has yet been detected.
2s	*Initialization Error.* A problem has occurred initializing the motherboard.
1l-1s	*System Board Error.* A fault has been detected on the motherboard. Replace the motherboard.
1l-2s	*Video Adapter Error.* Replace the video adapter board.
1l-3s	*EGA/VGA Adapter Error.* Replace the video adapter board.
3l	*Keyboard Adapter Error.* Replace the keyboard adapter IC or replace the motherboard.
999s	*Power Supply Error.* Replace the power supply.

Legend: *l*=long *s*=short

Table 15-8. Quadtel beep codes

Beeps	Error message
1s	*Start of Test.* No error has been detected.
2s	*CMOS IC Error.* Replace the CMOS battery. Replace the RTC/CMOS IC. Replace the motherboard.
1l–2s	*Video Controller Error.* Replace the video controller board.
1l>2s	*Peripheral Controller Error.* Replace the motherboard.

Legend: *l*=long *s*=short

16
CHAPTER

CD-ROM drives
and adapters

The *compact disc* (or CD) first appeared in the commercial marketplace in early 1982. Sony and Philips developed the CD as a joint venture and envisioned it as a reliable, high-quality replacement for aging phonograph technology. With the introduction of the audio CD, designers demonstrated that huge amounts of information can be stored simply and very inexpensively on common, nonmagnetic media. Unlike previous recording media, the CD recorded data in *digital* form through the use of physical *pits* and *lands* in the disc. The digital approach allowed excellent stereo sound quality, but also attracted the attention of PC designers who saw CDs as a natural for all types of computer information (text, graphics, programs, video clips, audio files, and so on). This chapter explains the technologies and troubleshooting techniques for CD-ROM drives and their adapter boards (Fig. 16-1).

The argument for computer CDs (dubbed *CD-ROM* for *compact disc—read-only memory*) was compelling: a CD-ROM disk can hold over 650 million characters, which is roughly analogous to over 1500 high-density floppy diskettes, or more than 200,000 pages of printed text. By including compression to reduce file sizes, this capacity can be extended significantly. Such capacities support the development and distribution of massive databases and complex programs on inexpensive plastic discs no more than 12 cm in diameter. By 1985, the first CD-ROM drives and applications had become available for the PC. By the mid 1990s, CD-ROMs are virtually standard equipment in all new PCs.

The similarities between audio CDs and CD-ROM discs are startling—in fact, most CD-ROM drives can actually play audio CDs (so long as the PC is running a program that will interpret the audio data). However, a PC needs additional information to handle programs and other computerized data. Unlike audio CDs, CD-ROM discs include a header (called a *volume table of contents* or *VTOC*) that describes the nature and location of all data on the disc. Multiple layers of error-correction codes are added to the data, and error-correcting circuitry is added to

Diamond Multimedia Systems, Inc.

16-1 A Diamond Multimedia CD-ROM drive.

the CD-ROM drive to ensure that there are no errors introduced as programs and data are read from the disc—your ear won't notice a few dropped bits on an audio disc, but a single bad program bit can crash your PC. The structure of data and the use of error-correction techniques is clearly defined through a set of comprehensive standards (or *Books*).

Understanding the media

CDs are mass produced by stamping the pattern of pits and lands onto a molded polycarbonate disc. It is this stamping process (much like the stamping used to produce records) that places the data on the disc. But the disc is not yet readable—there are finish steps that must be performed to transform a clear plastic into viable, data-carrying media. The clear polycarbonate disk is given a silvered (reflective) coating so that it will reflect laser light. Silvering coats all parts of the disk side (pits and lands) equally. After silvering, the disk is coated with a tough, scratch-resistant lacquer that seals the disk from the elements (especially oxygen that will oxidize and ruin the reflective coating). Finally, a label can be silk-screened onto the finished disk before it is tested and packaged. Figure 16-2 shows each of these layers in a cross-sectional diagram.

CD data

CDs are not segregated into concentric tracks and sectors as magnetic media is. Instead, CDs are recorded as a single, continuous spiral track running from the spindle to the lead-out area. Figure 16-3 shows the spiral pattern recorded on a CD. The

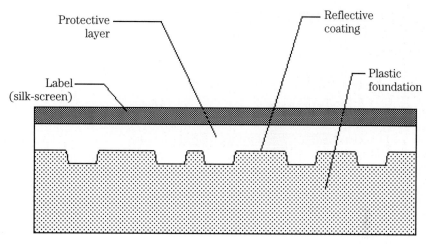

16-2 A cross-sectional view of pits and lands.

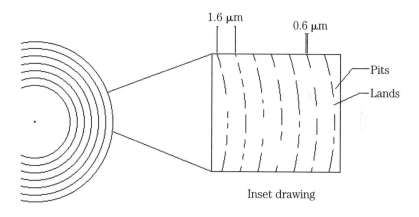

16-3 Pits and lands spaced along a CD's spiral track.

inset shows the relationship between the pits and lands. Each pit is about 0.12 μm (micrometers) deep and 0.6 μm wide. Pits and lands might range from 0.9 μm to 3.3 μm long. There are approximately 1.6 μm between each iteration of the spiral. Given these microscopic dimensions, a CD-ROM disc offers about 16,000 *tpi* (tracks per inch)—much more than floppy disks or hard disks.

During playback, CDs use a highly focused laser beam and laser detector to sense the presence or absence of pits. Figure 16-4 shows the reading behavior. The laser/detector pair is mounted on a carriage that follows the spiral track across the CD. A laser is directed at the underside of the CD where it penetrates more than 1 mm of clear plastic before shining on the reflective surface. When laser light strikes a land, the light is reflected toward the detector that, in turn, produces a very strong output signal. As laser light strikes a pit, the light is slightly out of focus. As a result, most of the incoming laser energy is scattered away in all directions, so very little

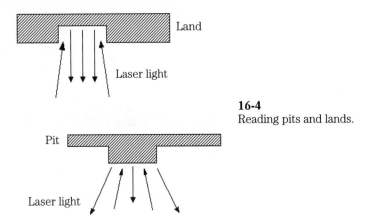

16-4
Reading pits and lands.

output signal is generated by the detector. As with floppy and hard drives, it is the transition from pit to land (and back again) that corresponds to binary levels, not the presence or absence of a pit or land. The analog light signal returned by the detector must be converted to logic levels and decoded. A process known as *EFM* (eight-to-fourteen modulation) is very common with CD-ROMs.

EFM and CD storage

A complex decoding process is necessary to convert the arcane sequence of pits and lands into meaningful binary information. The technique of *eight-to-fourteen modulation* (EFM) is used with CD-ROMs. For hard disk drives, techniques such as *2,7 RLL encoding* can be used to place a large number of bits into a limited number of flux transitions. The same is true for CDs using EFM. User data, error correction information, address information, and synchronization patterns are all contained in a bit stream represented by pits and lands.

Magnetic media encodes bits as flux transitions—not the discrete orientation of any magnetic area. The same concept holds true with CD-ROMs, where binary 1s and 0s do not correspond to pits or lands. A binary 1 is represented wherever a transition (pit-to-land or land-to-pit) occurs. The length of a pit or land represents the number of binary 0s. Figure 16-5 shows this concept. The eight-to-fourteen encoding technique equates each byte (eight bits) with a fourteen-bit sequence (called a *symbol*) where each binary 1 must be separated by at least two binary 0s. Table 16-1 shows part of the eight-to-fourteen conversion. Three bits are added to merge each 14-bit symbol together.

0010000000000100100001001000001000010010001000010001000100001001001000

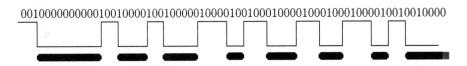

16-5 An example of EFM encoding.

**Table 16-1. A sample of eight-to-fourteen
modulation codes**

Number	Binary pattern	EFM pattern
0	00000000	01001000100000
1	00000001	10000100000000
2	00000010	10010000100000
3	00000011	10001000100000
4	00000100	01000100000000
5	00000101	00000100010000
6	00000110	00010000100000
7	00000111	00100100000000
8	00001000	01001001000000
9	00001001	10000001000000
10	00001010	10010001000000

A CD-ROM *frame* is composed of 24 synchronization bits, 14 control bits, 24 of the 14-bit data symbols you saw previously, and eight complete 14-bit error-correction (EC) symbols. Keep in mind that each symbol is separated by an additional three merge bits, bringing the total number of bits in the frame to 588. Thus, 24 bytes of data are represented by 588 bits on a CD-ROM expressed as a number of pits and lands. There are 98 frames in a data *block*, so each block carries [98 × 24] 2048 bytes (2352 with error correction, synchronization, and address bytes). The basic CD-ROM can deliver 153.6 kilobytes of data (75 blocks) per second to its host controller.

Remember that the CD-ROM disc is recorded as one continuous spiral track running around the disk, so ordinary sector and track ID information that we associate with magnetic disks does not apply very well. Instead, information is divided in terms of 0 to 59 minutes, and 0 to 59 seconds recorded at the beginning of each block. A CD-ROM (like an audio CD) can hold up to 79 minutes of data. However, many CD-ROMs tend to limit this to 60 minutes because the last 14 minutes of data are encoded in the outer 5 millimeters of disk space that is the most difficult to manufacture and keep clean in everyday use. There are 270,000 blocks of data in 60 minutes. At 2048 data bytes per block, the disk's capacity is 552,950,000 bytes (553 megabytes). If all 79 minutes are used, 681,984,000 bytes (681 megabytes) will be available in 333,000 blocks. Most CD-ROMs run between 553 and 650 megabytes in normal production.

CD-ROM standards and characteristics

Like so many other PC peripheral devices, the early CD-ROM faced a serious problem of industry standardization. Just recording the data to a CD is not enough—the data must be recorded in a way that any CD-ROM drive can read. Standards for CD-ROM data and formats were developed by consortiums of influential PC manufacturers and interested CD-ROM publishers. Ultimately, this kind of industry-wide cooperation has made the CD-ROM one of the most uniform and standardized peripherals in the PC market. There are a number of CD-ROM standards that you should understand.

High Sierra

In 1984 (before the general release of CD-ROM), the PC industry realized that there must be a standard method of reading a disc's VTOC—otherwise, the CD-ROM market would become extremely fragmented as various (incompatible) standards vied for acceptance. PC manufacturers, prospective CD publishers, and software developers met at the High Sierra Hotel in Lake Tahoe, California, to begin developing just such a uniform standard. By 1986, the CD-ROM standard file format (dubbed the High Sierra format) was accepted and approved. High Sierra remained the standard for several years, but has since been replaced by ISO 9660.

ISO 9660

High Sierra was certainly a workable format, but it was primarily a domestic US development. When placed before the *ISO* (International Standards Organization), High Sierra was tweaked and refined to meet international needs. After international review, High Sierra was absorbed (with only few changes) into the *ISO 9660* standard. Although many technicians refer to High Sierra and ISO 9660 interchangeably, you should understand that the two standards are not the same. For the purposes of this book, ISO 9660 is the current CD-ROM file format.

By adhering to ISO 9660, CD-ROM drive makers can write software drivers (and use MSCDEX under MS-DOS) to enable a PC to read the CD's VTOC. ISO 9660 also allows a CD-ROM disc to be accessed by any computer system and CD-ROM drive that follows the standard. Of course, just because a disc is recognized does not mean that it can be used. For example, an ISO 9660-compliant Mac can access an ISO 9660 MPC disc, but the files on the disc cannot be used by the Mac.

The "Books"

When Philips and Sony defined the proprietary standards that became CD audio and CD-ROM, the documents were bound in different colored covers. By tradition, each color now represents a different level of standardization. *Red Book* (also known as *Compact Disc Digital Audio Standard: CEI IEC 908*) defines the media, recording and mastering process, and the player design for CD audio. When you listen to your favorite audio CD, you are enjoying the benefits of the Red Book standard. CDs conforming to Red Book standards will usually have the words "digital audio" printed below the disc logo. Today, Red Book audio can be combined with programs and other PC data on the same disc.

The *Yellow Book* standard (ISO 10149:1989) makes CD-ROM possible by defining the additional error correction data needed on the disc, and detection hardware and firmware needed in the drive. When a disc conforms to Yellow Book, it will usually be marked "data storage" beneath the disc logo. Mode 1 Yellow Book is the typical operating mode that supports computer data. Mode 2 Yellow Book (also known as the *XA format*) supports compressed audio data and video/picture data.

The *Orange Book* (also known as *Recordable Compact Disc Standard*) serves to extend the basic Red and Yellow Book standards by providing specifications for recordable products such as (Part 1) *magneto-optical* (MO) and (Part 2) *write-once CDs* (CD-R). The *Green Book* standard defines an array of supplemental standards for data recording, and provides an outline for a specific computer system that supports CD-I (compact disc-interactive). *Blue Book* is the standard for laser discs and their players. For the purposes of this book, we will not be concerned with Orange, Green, or Blue Book standards.

The multispin drive

The Red Book standard defines CD audio as a stream of data that flows from the player mechanism to the amplifier (or other audio manipulation circuit) at a rate of 150K/s. This data rate was chosen to take music off the disc for truest reproduction. When the Yellow Book was developed to address CD-ROMs, this basic data rate was carried over. Designers soon learned that data can be transferred much faster than Red Book audio information, so the *multispin* (or *multispeed*) drive was developed to work with Red Book audio at the normal 150K/s rate, but run faster for Yellow Book data in order to multiply the data throughput.

The most common multispin drives available today are 2× drives. By running at 2× the normal data transfer speed, data throughput can be doubled from 150K/s to 300K/s. If Red Book audio is encountered, the drive speed drops back to 150K/s. Increased data transfer rates make a real difference in CD-ROM performance—especially for data-intensive applications such as audio/visual clips. CD-ROM drives with 4× transfer speed (600K/s) are now commonly available, and their falling cost makes them competitive with 2× CD-ROMs. New 6× drives (900K/s) are expensive devices, but as their prices plummet, the jump from 600K/s to 900K/s might be enough of a performance boost to justify upgrading the well-established 2× or 4× drives.

The MPC

One of the most fundamental problems of writing software for PCs is the tremendous variability in the possible hardware and software configurations of individual machines. The selection of CPUs, DOS versions, available memory, graphics resolutions, drive space, and other peripherals make the idea of a " standard" PC virtually impossible. Most software developers in the PC market use a base (or minimal) PC configuration to ensure that a product will run properly in a minimal machine. CD-ROM multimedia products have intensified these performance issues. Microsoft assembled some of the largest PC manufacturers to create the *MPC* (Multimedia Personal Computer) standard. By adhering to the MPC specification, software developers and consumers can anticipate the minimal capacity needed to run multimedia products. The accepted MPC specification is Level 2, but Level 3 has recently been approved. Appendix A shows the MPC standards.

Effects of CD-ROM caching

The limiting factor of a CD-ROM is its data transfer rate. Even at 600K/s or so, it takes a fairly substantial amount of time to load programs and files into memory—this causes system delays during CD-ROM access. If the PC could predict the data needed from a CD and load that data into RAM or virtual memory (the hard drive) during background operations, the effective performance of a CD-ROM drive can be enhanced dramatically. CD-ROM caching utilities provide a look-ahead ability that enables CD-ROMs continue transferring information in anticipation of use.

However, CD-ROM caching is a mixed blessing. The utilities required for caching must reside in conventional memory (or loaded into upper memory). In systems that are already strained by the CD-ROM drivers and other device drivers that have become so commonplace on PC platforms, adding a cache might prohibit some large DOS programs from running. Keep this in mind when evaluating CD-ROM caches for yourself or your customers. Several cache products are listed in the companion disk.

CD-ROM drive construction

Now that you have an understanding of CD-ROM media and standards, you can review a CD-ROM drive in some detail. CD-ROM drives are impressive pieces of engineering. The drive must be able to accept standard-sized disks from a variety of sources (each disk can contain an assortment of unknown surface imperfections). The drive must then spin the disk at a *CLV* (constant linear velocity)—that is, the disk speed varies inversely with the tracking radius. As tracking approaches the disk edge, disk speed slows, and vice versa. Keep in mind that CLV is different than the *CAV* (constant angular velocity) method used by floppy and hard drives that move the media at a constant speed. The purpose of CLV is to ensure that CD-ROM data is read at a constant rate. A drive must be able to follow the spiral data path on a spinning CD-ROM accurate to within less than 1μm along the disk's radius. The drive electronics must be able to detect and correct any unforeseen data errors in real-time, operate reliably over a long working life, and be available for a low price that computer users have come to expect.

CD-ROM mechanics

You can begin to appreciate how a CD drive achieves its features by reviewing the exploded diagram of Fig. 16-6. At the center of the drive is a cast aluminum or rigid stainless steel frame assembly. As with other drives, the frame is the single primary structure for mounting the drive's mechanical and electronic components. The front bezel, lid, volume control, and eject button attach to the frame, providing the drive with its clean cosmetic appearance, and offering a fixed reference slot for CD insertion and removal. Keep in mind that many drives use a sliding tray, so the front bezel (and the way it is attached) will not be the same for every drive.

The drive's electronics package has been split into several PC board assemblies: (1) the main PC board that handles drive control and interfacing, and (2) the headphone PC board that simply provides an audio amplifier and jack for headphones. The bulk of the drive's actual physical work, however, is performed by a main CD subassembly called a drive engine, often manufactured by only a few companies. As a result, many of the diverse CD-ROM drives on the market actually use identical "engines" to hold/eject, spin, and read the disk. This interchangeability is part of the genius of CD-ROM drives—a single subassembly performs 80% of the work. Sony, Philips, and Toshiba are the major manufacturers of CD-ROM engines, but other companies such as IBM and Ikka also are producing engines.

A typical drive engine is shown in Fig. 16-7. The upper view of the engine features a series of mechanisms that accept, clamp, and eject the disk. The foundation

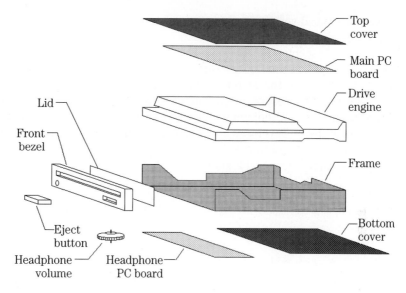

16-6 An exploded diagram of a typical CD-ROM.

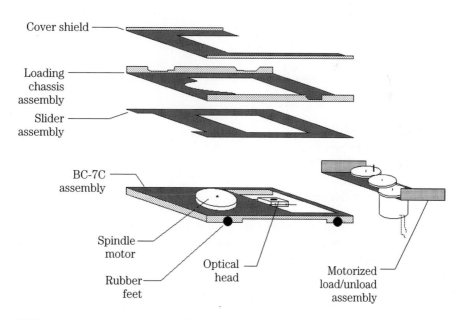

16-7 An exploded diagram of a CD drive engine.

of this engine is the BC-7C assembly. It acts as a subframe that everything else is mounted to. Notice that the subframe is shock mounted with four rubber feet to cushion the engine from minor bumps and ordinary handling. Even with such mounting, a CD-ROM drive is a delicate and fragile mechanism. The slider assembly, loading chassis assembly, and the cover shield provide the mechanical action needed to accept the disk and clamp it into place over the drive spindle, as well as free the disk and eject it on demand. A number of levers and oil dampers serve to provide a slow, smooth mechanical action when motion takes place. A motor/gear assembly drives the load/unload mechanics.

The serious work of spinning and reading a disk is handled under the engine as shown in Fig. 16-8. A spindle motor is mounted on the subframe and connected to a spindle motor PC board. A thrust retainer helps keep the spindle motor turning smoothly. The most critical part of the CD engine is the optical device containing the 780-nm (nanometer) 0.6-mW gallium aluminum arsenide (GaAlAs) laser diode and detector, along with the optical focus and tracking components. The optical device slides along two guide rails and shines through an exposed hole in the subframe. This combination of device mounting and guide rails is called a *sled*.

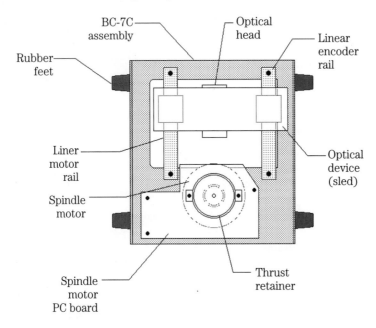

16-8 Underside view of a typical BC-7C assembly.

A sled must be made to follow the spiral data track along the disk. Although floppy disks (using clearly defined concentric tracks) can easily make use of a stepping motor to position the head assembly, a CD drive ideally requires a linear motor to act much like the voice coil motor used to position hard drive R/W heads. By altering the signal driving a sled motor and constantly measuring and adjusting the sled's position, a sled can be made to track very smoothly along a disk—free from the sudden, jerky motion of stepping motors. Some CD drives still use stepping motors with an extremely fine-pitch lead screw to position the sled. The drive's main PC board is responsible for managing these operations.

CD-ROM electronics

The electronics package used in a typical CD-ROM drive is illustrated in Fig. 16-9. The electronics package can be divided into two major areas: the controller section

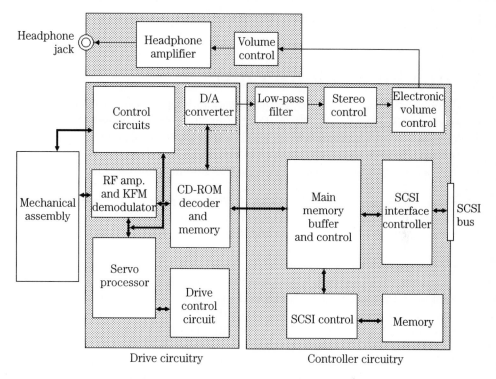

16-9 Electronics block diagram for a typical CD-ROM drive.

and the drive section. The controller section is dedicated to the peripheral inter-face—its connection to the adapter board. Much of the reason for a CD-ROM's elec-tronic sophistication can be traced to the controller section. Notice that the controller circuitry shown in Fig. 16-9 is dedicated to handling a SCSI interface. This allows the unit's intelligence to be located right in the drive itself. You need only con-nect the drive to a system-level interface board (a *SCSI adapter*) and set the drive's device number to establish a working system. For the many CD-ROMs that use pro-prietary interfaces, the controller area of the drive is often much simpler—its con-troller functions being off-loaded to the proprietary adapter board.

The drive section manages the CD-ROM's physical operations (that is, load/un-load, spin the disk, move the sled, and so on), as well as data decoding (EFM) and error correction. Drive circuitry converts an analog output from the laser diode into an EFM signal that is, in turn, decoded into binary data and *CIRC* (cross-interleaved Reed-Solomon code) information. A drive controller IC and servo processor IC are responsible for directing laser focus, tracking, sled motor control (and feedback), spindle motor control (and feedback), and loading/unloading motor control.

When it comes to CD drive electronics, you should treat the diagram of Fig. 16-9 more as a guideline than as an absolute. There are quite a few different iterations of drive electronics and interfaces. Although many manufacturers use SCSI interfaces, some systems use proprietary interfaces, a few use the IDE system-level interface, and several manufacturers implement subtle, nonstandard variations on the SCSI system. Obtain manufacturer's service data wherever possible for specific information on your particular drive.

Caring for a compact disc

A compact disc is a remarkably reliable long-term storage media (conservative expectations place the life estimates of a current CD at about 100 years). However, the longevity of a CD is affected by its storage and handling—a faulty CD can cause file and data errors that you might otherwise interpret as a defect in the drive itself. This part of the chapter looks at ways to protect and maintain the disc itself. First, some don'ts are in order:

- Don't bend the disc. Polycarbonate is a forgiving material, but you risk cracking or snapping (and thus ruining) the disc.
- Don't heat the disk. Remember, the disc is plastic. Leaving it by a heater or on the dashboard of your car will cause melting.
- Don't scratch the disc. Laser wavelengths have a tendency to look past minor scratches, but a major scratch can cause problems. Be especially careful of circular scratches (one that follows the spiral track). A circular scratch can easily wipe out entire segments of data that would be unrecoverable.
- Don't use chemicals on the disc—especially chemicals containing solvents such as ammonia, benzene, acetone, carbon tetrachloride, or chlorinated cleaning solvents. Such chemicals damage the plastic surface. Eventually, a buildup of excessive dust or fingerprints can interfere with the laser beam enough to cause disc errors. When this happens, the disc can be cleaned easily using a dry, soft, lint-free cloth. Hold the disc from its edges and wipe radially (from hub to edge). Do not wipe in a circular motion. For stubborn stains, moisten the cloth in a bit of fresh isopropyl alcohol (*do not use water*). Place the cleaned disc in a caddie or jewel case for transport and storage.

Understanding the software

Hardware alone is not enough to implement a CD-ROM drive. In an ideal world, BIOS and MS-DOS would provide the software support to handle the drive, but in practice, the variations between CD-ROM designs and interfaces make it impractical to provide low-level BIOS services. Manufacturers provide a hardware-specific device driver used to communicate with the CD-ROM adapter board. An MS-DOS extension (MSCDEX) provides file handling and logical drive letter support. This part of the chapter explains the operations and features of CD-ROM device drivers and MSCDEX.

Device drivers

A low-level device driver allows DOS to access the CD-ROM adapter properly at the register (hardware) level. Because most CD-ROM adapters are designed differently, they require different device drivers. If you change or upgrade the CD-ROM drive at any point, the device driver must be upgraded as well. A typical device driver uses a .SYS extension, and is initiated by adding its command line to the PC's CONFIG.SYS file such as: DEVICE=HITACHIA.SYS /D:MSCD000 /N:1 /P:300 (the DEVICE command can be replaced by the DEVICEHIGH command if you have available space in the *UMA* (upper memory area).

A CD-ROM device driver will typically have three command line switches associated with it. These parameters are needed to ensure that the driver installs properly. For the example command line shown above, the /D switch is the name used by the driver when it is installed in the system's device table. This name must be unique, and matched by the /D switch in the MSCDEX.EXE command line (covered later). The /N switch is the number of CD-ROM drives attached to the interface card. The default is 1 (which is typical for most general-purpose systems). Finally, the /P switch is the I/O port address the CD-ROM adapter card resides at. As you might expect, the port address should match the jumper settings on the adapter board. If there is no /P switch, the default is 0300h.

MSCDEX.EXE

MS-DOS was developed in a time when no one anticipated that large files would be accessible to a PC, and it is severely limited in the file sizes that it can handle. With the development of CD-ROMs, Microsoft created an extension to MS-DOS that allows software publishers to access 650Mb CDs in a standard fashion—the Microsoft CD-ROM Extensions (MSCDEX). As with most software, MSCDEX offers some vital features (and a few limitations), but it is required by a vast majority of CD-ROM products. Obtaining MSCDEX is not a problem—it is generally provided on the same disk containing the CD-ROM's low-level device driver. New versions of MSCDEX can be obtained from the Microsoft Download BBS, or from the Microsoft forum on CompuServe (GO MSL-1).

Loading and running MSCDEX

In actual operation, MSCDEX is loaded in the AUTOEXEC.BAT file. It should be loaded after any mouse driver, and loaded before any MENU, SHELL, DOSSHELL, or WIN line. It also should be loaded before any .BAT file is started. Keep in mind that if a .BAT file loads a network, MSCDEX must be included in the batch file after the network driver. Further, MSCDEX must be loaded after that network driver with the /S (share) switch in order to hook into the network driver chain. If you want to use the MS-DOS drive caching software (SmartDrive) to buffer the CD-ROM drive(s), load MSCDEX before SmartDrive. The MSCDEX /M (number of buffers) switch can be set to 0 when using SmartDrive. If you find that SmartDrive is interfering with MPC applications like Video for Windows, you can load SmartDrive before MSCDEX, and set the /M switch for at least 2. When loading MSCDEX, remember that the MSCDEX /D switch MUST match the /D label used in the low-level driver. Otherwise, MSCDEX will not load. If SETVER is loaded in the CONFIG.SYS file, be sure to use the latest version of MSCDEX.

MSCDEX switches

Although the vast majority of CD-ROM bundles includes installation routines that automate the installation process for the low-level driver and MSCDEX, you should understand the various command line switches that make MSCDEX operate. Understanding these switches can help you to overcome setup problems.

/D:xxxxxx Device Name—The label used by the low-level device driver when it loads. MSCDEX must match this label for the device driver and MSCDEX to work together. A typical label is MSCD000.

/M:x Buffers Allocated—The number of 2K buffers allocated to the CD-ROM drives. There are typically 8 buffers (16K) for a single drive, and 4 buffers for each additional drive. This number can be set to 1 or 2 of conventional memory space is at a premium.

/L:x Drive Letter—This is the optional drive letter for the CD-ROM. If this is not specified, the drive will be automatically assigned to the first available letter (usually D:). There must be a LASTDRIVE= entry in CONFIG.SYS to use a letter higher than the default letter. When choosing a letter for the LASTDRIVE entry, do not use Z—otherwise, network drives cannot install after MSCDEX.

/N Verbose Option—This switch forces MSCDEX to show memory usage statistics on the display each time the system boots.

/S Share Option—This switch is used with CD-ROM installations in network systems.

/K Kanji Option-Instructs MSCDEX to use Kanji (Japanese) file types on the CD if present.

/E Expanded Memory—Allows MSCDEX to use expanded memory for buffers. There must be an expanded memory driver running (for example, EMM386.EXE) with enough available space to use it.

Troubleshooting CD-ROM drives

CD-ROMs are delicate and unforgiving devices. Considering that their prices have plummeted over the last few months (and still continue to drop), there is little economic sense in attempting a lengthy repair. When an error occurs in the drive or in its adapter board, your best course is typically to replace the defective subassembly outright.

Symptom 1. The drive has trouble accepting or rejecting a CD This problem is typical of motorized CD-ROM drives where the disc is accepted into a slot, or placed in a motorized tray. Before performing any disassembly, check the assembly through the CD slot for any obvious obstructions. If there is nothing obvious, expose the assembly and check each linkage and motor drive gear very carefully. Carefully remove or free any obstruction. Be gentle when working around the load/unload assembly. Notice how it is shock mounted in four places.

Disconnect the geared dc motor assembly and try moving the load/unload mechanism by hand. If you feel any resistance or obstruction, you should track it down by eye and by feel. Replace any worn or damaged part of the mechanism, or replace the entire load/unload assembly. Also check the geared motor for any damage or obstruction. Broken or slipping gear teeth can interfere with the transfer of force from motor to mechanism. Replace any damaged gears or replace the entire geared assembly. You also can simply replace the CD-ROM drive mechanism outright.

Symptom 2. Read heads do not seek. An optical head is used to identify pits and lands along a CD-ROM, and to track the spiral data pattern as the head moves across the disk The optical head must move very slowly and smoothly to ensure accurate tracking. Head movement is accomplished using a linear stepping motor (or *linear actuator*) to shift the optical assembly in microscopic increments—head travel appears perfectly smooth to the unaided eye. When the optical head fails to seek, the easiest and fastest fix is simply to replace the CD-ROM mechanism. If you choose to explore further, try the procedure below.

Power down the computer, expose the CD-ROM, and begin your examination by observing the head carriage assembly. Check for any objects or foreign matter that might interfere with normal carriage movement. If the head carriage is free to move, measure the driving voltage across the linear actuator. If there is no voltage applied to the linear actuator at runtime, the motor's driver circuitry is probably defective (usually a driver or servo controller IC). Track down the defective component (if possible) or replace the drive's main PC board. If there is voltage across the motor at runtime but the motor does not move, the linear motor is probably defective. Linear actuator replacement requires drive disassembly to the chassis level, so such a procedure should only be attempted by a highly skilled and experienced individual. Careless replacement can result in a totally useless drive. It might be simpler to replace the entire drive.

Symptom 3. Disc cannot be read This type of problem might result in a DOS level *sector not found* or *drive not ready* error. Before you reach for your tools, however, check the CD itself to ensure that it is the right format, inserted properly, and physically clean. Cleanliness is very important to a CD. Although the laser will often "look past" any surface defects in a disc, the presence of dust or debris on a disc surface can produce serious tracking (and read) errors. Try a different disc to confirm the problem. If a new or different disc reads properly, the trouble might indeed be in (or on) the original disc itself. Not only the disc must be clean, but the head optics also must be clear. Gently dust or clean the head optics as suggested by your drive's particular manufacturer.

If read problems persist, check the physical interface cable between the drive and its adapter board. Be sure that the cable is connected correctly and completely. Many CD drives use SCSI interfaces, although most CD installations employ proprietary interfaces. If you are using multiple SCSI devices from the same controller card and other SCSI devices are operating properly, the SCSI controller board is probably intact. If other SCSI devices also are malfunctioning, try a new SCSI host controller board. At this point, either the drive's optical head or electronics are defective. Your best course here is to try replacing the drive. If problems persist on a drive with a proprietary interface, replace the adapter board.

Symptom 4. The disc does not turn. The disc must turn at a constant linear velocity that is directed and regulated by the spindle If the disc is not spinning during access, check to be sure that the disc is seated properly, and is not jammed or obstructed. Before beginning a repair, review your drive installation and setup carefully to ensure that the drive is properly configured for operation. If the drive's BUSY LED comes on when drive access is attempted (you also might see a corresponding DOS error message), the drive spindle system is probably defective.

If the computer does not recognize the CD drive (for example, *invalid drive specification*), there might be a setup or configuration problem (either the low-level device driver or MSCDEX might not have loaded properly). If your particular drive provides you with instructions for cleaning the optical head aperture, perform that cleaning operation and try the drive again. A fouled optical head can sometimes upset spindle operation. If operation does not improve, replace the CD-ROM drive mechanism.

Symptom 5. The optical head cannot focus its laser beam As you saw in this chapter, a CD-ROM drive must focus its laser beam to microscopic precision in order to properly read the pits and lands of a disk. To compensate for the minute fluctuations in disc flatness, the optical head mounts its objective lens into a small focusing mechanism that is little more than a miniature voice coil actuator—the lens does not have to move very much at all to maintain precise focus. If focus is out or not well maintained, the laser detector might produce erroneous signals. This might result in DOS drive error messages.

If random but consistent DOS errors appear, check the disc to be sure that it is optically clean—dust and fingerprints can result in serious access problems. Try another disc. If a new disc continues to perform badly, try cleaning the optical aperture with clean (photography-grade) air. When problems persist, the optical system is probably damaged or defective. Try replacing the CD-ROM drive mechanism outright.

Symptom 6. There is no audio being generated by the drive Many CD-ROM drives are capable of not only reading computer data, but reading and reproducing music and sounds under computer control. Audio CDs can often be played in available CD-ROM drives through headphones or speakers. Start your investigation by testing the headphones or speakers in another sound source such as a stereo. Once you have confirmed that the speakers or headphones are working reliably, check the drive's audio volume setting that is usually available through the front bezel. Set the volume to a good average place (perhaps mid-range). Make sure that the disk you are trying to play actually contains valid Red Book audio. Check any software required to operate the CD drive's audio output to be sure that it is installed and loaded as expected. CD-ROMs will not play audio CDs without an audio driver. Also check the line output that would drive amplified speakers or stereo inputs. If speakers work through the line output but headphones or speakers do not work through the front bezel connector, the volume control or output audio amplifier might be defective. If the headphone output continues to fail, replace the headphone PC board or replace the entire CD-ROM drive outright.

Symptom 7. Audio is not being played by the sound card Normally, the sound card will not play Red Book audio from a CD—that is usually fed directly to the CD's headphone or line output. However, audio can be channeled to the sound board for playback. Most CDs offer an audio connector that allows audio signals to be fed directly to the sound board. If this "audio cable" is missing or defective, Red Book audio will not play through the sound board. Check or replace the cable. If the cable is intact (and audio IS available from the CD-ROM headphone output), try replacing the sound board. If the cable is intact (and audio is not available from the CD-ROM headphone output), the audio amplifier circuit in the CD-ROM is probably defective—try replacing the CD-ROM drive.

Symptom 8. You see a "Wrong DOS version" error message when attempting to load MSCDEX You are running MS-DOS 4, 5, or 6 with a version of MSCDEX that does not support it. The solution is then to change to the correct version of MSCDEX. The version compatibility for MSCDEX is shown below:

_v1.01 14,913 bytes (No ISO9660 support—High Sierra support only)

_v2.00 18,307 bytes (High Sierra and ISO9660 support for DOS 3.1–3.3)

_v2.10 19,943 bytes (DOS 3.1–3.3 and 4.0—DOS 5.x support provided with SETVER)

_v2.20 25,413 bytes (same as above with Win 3.x support—changes in audio support)

_v2.21 25,431 bytes (DOS 3.1–5.0 support with enhanced control under Win 3.1)

_v2.22 25,377 bytes (DOS 3.1–6.0 & higher with Win 3.1 support)

_v2.23 25,361 bytes (DOS 3.1–6.2 and Win 3.1 support—supplied with MSDOS 6.2)

When using MS-DOS 5.x to 6.1, you will need to add the SETVER utility to CONFIG.SYS in order to use MSCDEX v2.10 or v2.20 properly (that is, DEVICE = C:\DOS\SETVER.EXE). SETVER is used to tell programs that they are running under a different version of DOS than DOS 5.0. This is important because MSCDEX (v2.10 and v2.20) refuses to work with DOS versions higher than 4.0. SETVER is used to fool MSCDEX into working with higher versions of DOS. In some versions of DOS 5.0 (such as Compaq DOS 5.0), you will need to add an entry to SETVER for MSCDEX (that is, SETVER MSCDEX.EXE 4.00). This entry modifies SETVER without changing the file size or date.

Symptom 9. You cannot access the CD-ROM drive letter You might see an error message such as *Invalid drive specification*. This is typically a problem with the CD-ROM drivers. The MS-DOS extension MSCDEX has probably not loaded. Switch to the DOS subdirectory and use the MEM /C function to check the loaded drivers and TSRs. If you see the low-level driver and MSCDEX displayed in the driver list, check the CD-ROM hardware. Make sure that the data cable between the drive and adapter board in inserted properly and completely. If problems persist, try replacing the adapter board. If you do *not* see the low-level driver and MSCDEX shown in the driver list, inspect your CONFIG.SYS and AUTOEXEC.BAT files. Check that the drivers are included in the startup files to begin with. Make sure that the label used in the /D switch is the same for both the low-level driver and MSCDEX. If the label is not the same, MSCDEX will not load. If you are using MS-DOS 5.0, be sure the SETVER utility is loaded. You also could try updating MSCEDX to v2.30.

Symptom 10. You see an error message when trying to load the low-level CD-ROM driver Check that you are using the proper low-level device driver for your CD-ROM drive. If you are swapping the drive or adapter board, you probably need to load a new driver. If the driver fails to load with original hardware, the adapter board might have failed. Check the signal cable running between the drive and adapter board. If the cable is crimped or scuffed, try replacing the cable. Next, try replacing the adapter board. If problems persist, try replacing the CD-ROM drive mechanism itself.

Symptom 11. You see an error message such as "Error: not ready reading from drive D:" Check that a suitable disc is inserted in the drive and that the drive is closed properly. Make sure that the low-level device driver and MSCDEX are loaded correctly. If the drivers do not load, there might be a problem with the adapter board or drive mechanism itself. Also check that the data cable between the drive and adapter is connected properly and completely. If problems persist, suspect a weakness in the PC power supply (especially if the system is heavily loaded or upgraded). Try a larger supply in the system.

Symptom 12. SmartDrive is not caching the CD-ROM properly The version of SmartDrive supplied with DOS 6.2 provides three forms of caching, although older forms of SmartDrive (such as the ones distributed with Windows 3.1, DOS 6.0 and 6.1) will not adequately cache CD-ROM drives. The BUFFERS statement also does not help caching. So if you are looking to SmartDrive for CD-ROM cache, you should be using the version distributed with DOS 6.2. You also should set BUFFERS=10,0 in the CONFIG.SYS file, and the SmartDrive command line should come after MSCDEX. When using SmartDrive, you can change the buffers setting in the MSCDEX command line (/M) to 0—this allows you to save 2K per buffer.

17
CHAPTER

CMOS

With the introduction of their PC/AT computer, IBM abandoned the configuration DIP switches that had been used for the PC/XT. Rather than limit the system's configuration options, IBM chose to store the system's setup parameters in a small, specialized RAM IC called the CMOS RAM (in actual practice, CMOS RAM is typically combined on the same IC with the real-time clock or *RTC*). In effect, the discrete switches of the XT were replaced with logical switches of each CMOS bit (after all, a bit can be high or low, just as a switch can be on or off). When an AT-type computer starts, its system attributes are read by the BIOS POST. BIOS then uses those attributes during normal system operation.

Many novice technicians erroneously consider BIOS and CMOS to be the same thing. Make no mistake—they are NOT. BIOS and CMOS ICs are entirely different devices located on the motherboard, but BIOS and CMOS are intimately related. The system will not function unless CMOS parameters are complete, correct, and copied successfully into memory. This chapter explains the CMOS setup in detail, and provides some guidelines for proper CMOS maintenance.

What CMOS does

In simplest terms, CMOS RAM is nothing more than 64 bytes of static RAM. For newer, more sophisticated PCs, CMOS RAM can add an extra 64 bytes (128 bytes total) to store advanced system parameters. For the purposes of this book, we will consider a 128-byte CMOS system. Because RAM is lost when system power is removed, a battery is added to the PC that continues to provide power to the CMOS RAM (and RTC). It is this CMOS battery backup that keeps the date, time, and system parameters intact until you turn the system on again. Of course, if the battery should fail, the system will lose its date, time, and all of its setup parameters. Many a tear has been shed trying to reconstruct lost system parameters by trial and error. You can learn about CMOS backup techniques elsewhere in this chapter.

The CMOS map

To truly appreciate the importance of CMOS RAM, you should understand the contents of a typical CMOS RAM IC as shown in Table 17-1. You will find that a standard 128 byte ISA-compatible CMOS is divided into four fairly distinct sections: (1) 16 bytes of real-time clock data [00h–0Fh], (2) 32 bytes of ISA configuration data [10h–2Fh], (3) 16 bytes of BIOS-specific configuration data [30h–3Fh], and (4) 64 bytes of extended CMOS data [40h–7Fh].

Table 17-1. A typical CMOS RAM map

Offset	Description
00h	*RTC Seconds.* Contains the seconds value of current time.
01h	*RTC Seconds Alarm.* Contains the seconds value for the RTC alarm.
02h	*RTC Minutes.* Contains the minutes value of current time.
03h	*RTC Minutes Alarm.* Contains the minutes value for the RTC alarm.
04h	*RTC Hours.* Contains the hours value of current time.
05h	*RTC Hours Alarm.* Contains the hours value for the RTC alarm.
06h	*RTC Day of Week.* Contains the current day of the week.
07h	*RTC Date Day.* Contains day value of current date.
08h	*RTC Date Month.* Contains month value of current date.
09h	*RTC Date Year.* Contains year value of current date.
0Ah	*Status Register A.* Various bits that define:

	Bit 7	Update progress flag
	Bit 6-4	Time base frequency setting
	Bit 3-0	Interrupt rate selection

0Bh	*Status Register B.* Various bits that define:

	Bit 7	Halt cycle to set clock
	Bit 6	Periodic interrupt disable/enable
	Bit 5	Alarm interrupt disable/enable
	Bit 4	Update ended interrupt disable/enable
	Bit 3	Square wave rate disable/enable
	Bit 2	Date and time format (BCD/binary)
	Bit 1	Hour mode (12/24)
	Bit 0	Daylight savings disable/enable

0Ch	*Status Register C.* Read-only flags indicating system status conditions.
0Dh	*Statuc Register D.* Valid CMOS RAM flag on bit 7 (battery condition flag).
0Eh	*Diagnostic Status Flags.* Various bits that define:

	Bit 7	RTC IC power invalid/valid
	Bit 6	CMOS RAM checksum invalid/valid
	Bit 5	CMOS RAM configuration mismatch/match
	Bit 4	CMOS RAM memory size mismatch/match
	Bit 3	Hard Disk C: initialization failed/passed
	Bit 2	Time status is invalid/valid
	Bit 1-0	reserved . . . should be 0

0Fh	*CMOS Shutdown Status.* Allows the CPU to reset after switching from protected to real mode addressing. The shutdown code is written here so that after reset, the CPU will know the reason for the reset.

Table 17-1. Continued

Offset	Description

Description

00h	Normal POST execution
01h	Chipset initialization for return to real mode
02h-03h	Internal BIOS use
04h	Jump to bootstrap code
05h	User-defined shutdown. Jump to pointer at 40:67h. Interrupt controller and math co-processor are initialized.
06h	Jump to pointer at 40:67h
07h	Return to INT 15 function 87h
08h	Return to POST memory test
09h	INT 18 function 87h block move shutdown request
0Ah	User-defined shutdown. Jump to pointer at 40:67h. Interrupt controller and math co-processor are not initialized.

10h *Floppy Drive Type.* Defines drives A: and B:

Bits 7-4	Drive A: type
0h	No drive
1h	360Kb drive
2h	1.2Mb drive
3h	730Kb drive
4h	1.44Mb drive
5h	2.88Mb drive
Bits 3-0	Drive B: type
0h	No drive
1h	360Kb drive
2h	1.2Mb drive
3h	730Kb drive
4h	1.44Mb drive
5h	2.88Mb drive

11h *System Configuration Settings.* Various bits that define:

Bit 7	Mouse support disable/enable
Bit 6	Memory test above 1MB disable/enable
Bit 5	Memory test tick sound disable/enable
Bit 4	Memory parity error check disable/enable
Bit 3	Setup utility trigger display disable/enable
Bit 2	Hard disk type 47 RAM area (0:300h or upper 1Kb of DOS area)
Bit 1	Wait for <F1> is any error message disable/enable
Bit 0	System Boot up with NumLock (off/on)

12h *Hard Disk Type ID.*

Bits 7-4	Hard disk drive C: type
0000h	No drive installed
0001h	Type 1
	.....
1110h	Type 14
1111h	Type 16-47 (defined later in 1Ah)
Bits 3-0	Hard disk drive D: type
0000h	No drive installed
0001h	Type 1
	.....

Table 17-1. Continued

Offset	Description

	1110h Type 14
	1111h Type 16-47 (defined later in 19h)
13h	*Typematic Parameters.*
	Bit 7 Typematic rate programming disabled/enabled
	Bits 6-5 Typematic rate delay
	Bits 4-2 Typematic rate
14h	*Equipment Parameters.* Lists a selection of equipment parameters.
	Bits 7-6 Number of floppy drives.
	00h No drives
	01h One drive
	10h Two drives
	Bits 5-4 Monitor type
	00h Not CGA or MDA
	01h 40×25 CGA
	10h 80×25 CGA
	11h MDA
	Bit 3 Display adapter installed/not-installed
	Bit 2 Keyboard installed/not-installed
	Bit 1 Math co-processor installed/absent
	Bit 0 Always set to 1
15h	*Base Memory* (in 1Kb increments) - least significant byte
16h	*Base Memory* (in 1Kb increments) - most significant byte
17h	*Extended Memory* (in 1Kb increments) - least significant byte
18h	*Extended Memory* (in 1Kb increments) - most significant byte
19h	*Hard Disk C: Type* (16-46)
	10h to 2Eh Type 16 to 46 respectively
1Ah	*Hard Disk D: Type* (16-46)
	10h to 2Eh Type 16 to 46 respectively
1Bh	*User-Defined Drive C: Number of Cylinders* - least significant byte
1Ch	*User-Defined Drive C: Number of Cylinders* - most significant byte
1Dh	*User-Defined Drive C: Number of Heads*
1Eh	*User-Defined Drive C: Write Precomp. Cylinder* - least significant byte
1Fh	*User-Defined Drive C: Write Precomp. Cylinder* - most significant byte
20h	*User-Defined Drive C: Control Byte*
21h	*User-Defined Drive C: Landing Zone* - least significant byte
22h	*User-Defined Drive C: Landing Zone* - most significant byte
23h	*User-Defined Drive C: Number of Sectors*
24h	*User-Defined Drive D: Number of Cylinders* - least significant byte
25h	*User-Defined Drive D: Number of Cylinders* - most significant byte
26h	*User-Defined Drive D: Number of Heads*
27h	*User-Defined Drive D: Write Precomp. Cylinder* - least significant byte
28h	*User-Defined Drive D: Write Precomp. Cylinder* - most significant byte
29h	*User-Defined Drive D: Control Byte*
2Ah	*User-Defined Drive D: Landing Zone* - least significant byte
2Bh	*User-Defined Drive D: Landing Zone* - most significant byte

Table 17-1. Continued

Offset	Description

Offset

2Ch — *User-Defined Drive D: Number of Sectors*

2Dh — *System Operational Flags.*

Bit 7 — Weitek processor present/absent

Bit 6 — Floppy drive seek at boot enable/disable

Bit 5 — System boot sequence (C: then A: / A; then C:)

Bit 4 — System boot CPU speed high/low

Bit 3 — External cache enable/disable

Bit 2 — Internal cache enable/disable

Bit 1 — Fast Gate A20 operation enable/disable

Bit 0 — Turbo switch function enable/disable

2Eh — *Standard CMOS Checksum* - most significant byte

2Fh — *Standard CMOS Checksum* - least significant byte

30h — *Extended Memory Found by BIOS* - least significant byte

31h — *Extended Memory Found by BIOS* - most significant byte

32h — *Century Byte.*   BCD value for century of current date.

33h — *Information Flags.*   Various bytes that define:

Bit 7 — BIOS Length (64Kb/128Kb)

Bits 6-1 — reserved . . . should be set to 0

Bit 0 — POST cache test passed/failed

34h — *BIOS and Shadow Option Flags.*

Bit 7 — Boot sector virus protection disabled/enabled

Bit 6 — Password checking option disabled/enabled

Bit 5 — Adapter ROM shadow C800h (16Kb) disabled/enabled

Bit 4 — Adapter ROM shadow CC00h (16Kb) disabled/enabled

Bit 3 — Adapter ROM shadow D000h (16Kb) disabled/enabled

Bit 2 — Adapter ROM shadow D400h (16Kb) disabled/enabled

Bit 1 — Adapter ROM shadow D800h (16Kb) disabled/enabled

Bit 0 — Adapter ROM shadow DC00h (16Kb) disabled/enabled

35h — *BIOS and Shadow Option Flags.*

Bit 7 — Adapter ROM shadow E000h (16Kb) disabled/enabled

Bit 6 — Adapter ROM shadow E400h (16Kb) disabled/enabled

Bit 5 — Adapter ROM shadow E800h (16Kb) disabled/enabled

Bit 4 — Adapter ROM shadow EC00h (16Kb) disabled/enabled

Bit 3 — System ROM shadow F000h (64Kb) disabled/enabled

Bit 2 — Video ROM shadow C000h (16Kb) disabled/enabled

Bit 1 — Video ROM shadow C400h (16Kb) disabled/enabled

Bit 0 — Numeric Processor Test disabled/enabled

36h — *Chipset-specific Information.*

37h — *Password Seed and Color Option.*   Variables used for password control.

Bits 7-4 — Password seed (do not change)

Bits 3-0 — Setup screen color palette

07h — White on black

70h — Black on white

17h — White on blue

20h — Black on green

Table 17-1. Continued

Offset		Description
	30h	Black on turquoise
	47h	White on red
	57h	White on magenta
	60h	Black on brown
38h-3Dh		*Encrypted Password* (do not change)
3Eh		*MSB of Extended CMOS Checksum*
3Fh		*LSB of Extended CMOS Checksum*

The setup routine

As you might expect, CMOS data does not simply materialize out of the ether— it must be entered manually (initially by the system manufacturer, and later by you or your customers) through a setup routine. Early AT-compatible PCs relied on a disk-based setup program. That is, you needed to boot the computer from a floppy disk containing the setup utility. The great danger with a setup disk is that the disk might fail and leave you without a setup disk. If you find yourself with a setup disk, be sure to make a backup copy of it as soon as possible. Later systems incorporate the setup utility onto the BIOS IC(s). When the setup routine is resident in the system, you can usually access the setup during system initialization by pressing one or more keys simultaneously (such as <DEL> or <CTRL>+<F1>). When a setup utility is available through BIOS, the screen display will typically tell you which key(s) to press. The main menu for an AMIBIOS Setup Program is shown in Fig. 17-1.

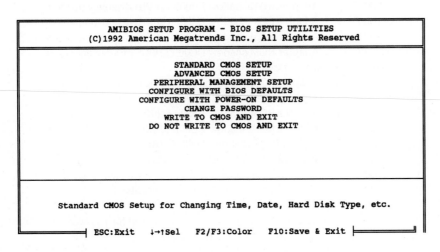

17-1 A CMOS setup main menu.

Understanding basic parameters

The standard CMOS Setup display for AMIBIOS is illustrated in Fig. 17-2. Standard CMOS setup is used to configure generic system parameters such as the date

```
┌─────────────────────────────────────────────────────────────────┐
│              AMIBIOS SETUP PROGRAM - STANDARD CMOS SETUP          │
│            (C)1992 American Megatrends Inc., All Rights Reserved  │
├─────────────────────────────────────────────────────────────────┤
│                                                                   │
│  Date (mn/date/year): Tue, Nov 22 1994        Base Memory : 640 KB│
│  Time (hour/min/sec): 15 : 00 : 45            Ext. Memory : 15360 KB│
│                                                                   │
│  Floppy Drive A:     : 1.44 MB, 3½"                               │
│  Floppy Drive B:     : 1.2  MB, 5¼"                               │
│                                     Cyln Head Sect Size           │
│  Drive C: Type       : USER TYPE 1  1023 16   63   504 MB         │
│  Drive D: Type       : AUTO-CONFIG  0    0    0    0 MB           │
│  Drive E: Type       : AUTO-CONFIG  0    0    0    0 MB           │
│  Drive F: Type       : AUTO-CONFIG  0    0    0    0 MB           │
│                                                                   │
│  Drive C: Timeout    :   5 Seconds                                │
│  Drive D: Timeout    :   5 Seconds                                │
│  Drive E: Timeout    :   5 Seconds                                │
│  Drive F: Timeout    :   5 Seconds                                │
│                                                                   │
│  Keyboard            : Installed                                  │
│                                                                   │
│        ESC:Exit ↓→↑Select F2/F3:Color PU/PD:Modify                │
└─────────────────────────────────────────────────────────────────┘
```

17-2 Basic CMOS setup parameters.

(month, day, and year) and time (hour, minute, and second). When entering hour values, be sure that you enter data in the right format. When working in 12-hour format, see that the proper AM/PM label is used. When working in 24-hour format, AM/PM labels are not needed, but see that you use 13-23 (instead of 1 to 11 PM). When daylight savings is available, you can compensate the time for daylight savings without having to reset the time.

CMOS setup supports two floppy drives (usually labeled A: and B:). Of course if either floppy drive is not installed, its entry should be set to *Not Installed*. Otherwise, the corresponding drive size should be entered (i.e., 360K, 1.2Mb, 760K, 1.44Mb, or 2.88Mb). Keep in mind that older versions of BIOS might not support 1.44 or 2.88Mb floppy drives.

Standard setup routines also allow for the selection of two hard drives (C: and D:). Figure 17-2 allows space for up to four drives. If a drive is not installed, the *Not Installed* label should be selected. Otherwise, you can select an appropriate drive type from a menu of available types. If your drive does not conform to any available type, you can enter the drive parameters as a user-definable type. User-definable drives require several detained designations: drive type (typically Type 47 or User Type 1), number of cylinders, number of heads, and sectors. Some setup displays include entries such as write precompensation (called write precomp. or WPcom) and the landing zone. Chapter 25 defines hard drive parameters in more detail. If your system is using SCSI drives, be sure to enter *Not Installed* type entry. For Fig. 17-2, a drive is disabled by entering *Auto-Config*. The drive time-out entries define how long after access is attempted that an error will be indicated if the drive does not respond. This allows support for slower drives.

Video options play an important role in the CMOS setup. Classical selections include monochrome, 40×25 CGA, 80×25 CGA, EGA/VGA, or not installed. The reason that such a broad range of EGA and VGA adapters seem grouped together and buried in a footnote is that EGA (and later) video adapters use their own BIOS ROM that occupies virtually the same range of addresses regardless of the adapter. The only time you would use *Not Installed* as a video option is if the system were being used as a network file server. Figure 17-2 does not show an entry for a video adapter because the use of EGA or higher is assumed. Older systems will almost always offer a video setup selection.

Finally, you often have the choice of specifying whether the keyboard is installed or not, but there will invariably be a keyboard available unless the system is a file server. Base memory and extended memory also can be defined in the standard setup screen.

Understanding advanced parameters

Beyond the basic setup elements of time, drives, memory, and video, many current CMOS setup utilities provide an array of advanced features as shown in Fig. 17-3. Advanced features typically include typematic settings, boot selections, cache and shadow controls, memory and cache optimizations, and a series of ISA bus switches. Although basic parameters are often easy to follow, advanced parameters require a bit of explanation. Keep in mind that the advanced setup parameters in Fig. 17-3 represent just one of the many setup routines available. The order and number of options might differ from system to system.

```
          AMIBIOS SETUP PROGRAM - ADVANCED CMOS SETUP
          (C)1992 American Megatrends Inc., All Rights Reserved

  Typematic Rate Programming : Disabled   ISA IRQ 10              : Used
  Typematic Rate Delay (msec): 500         ISA IRQ 11              : Used
  Typematic Rate (Chars/Sec) : 15
  Press <F1> Message Display : Enabled
  System Boot Up Num Lock    : On
  System Boot Up Sequence    : A:, C:
  System Boot Up CPU Speed   : High
  Cache Memory               : Enabled
  Network Password Checking  : Disabled
  ISA Linear Frame Buffer    : Disabled
  Set Linear Frame Address to: (N/A)
  Disable Shadow Memory Size : Disabled
  Disable Shadow Memory Base : D0000h
  Base Memory Size           : 640 KB
  IDE DMA Transfer Mode      : Type F
  IDE Multiple Sector Mode   : 64 S/B
  Enhanced ISA Timing        : Enabled
  ISA IRQ 9                  : Used

  ESC:Exit  ↓→↑Sel  (Ctrl)Pu/Pd:Modify  F1:Help  F2/F3:Color
  F5:Old Values  F6:BIOS Setup Defaults  F7:Power-On Defaults
```

17-3 Advanced CMOS setup parameters.

The term *typematic* refers to keyboard responses. The *Typematic Rate* function allows you to hold down a key and have the key repeat at a certain rate until you release the key. This is normally disabled because most programs (such as word processors) incorporate their own typematic function that does not need BIOS interaction. The *Typematic Rate Delay* is the amount of time after a key is pressed that the key will repeat. The *Typematic Rate* defines how many characters per second that will be produced once the repeat starts.

A series of boot controls follows the typematic entries. When the system first starts, it displays a message indicating how to access the built-in setup routine (older systems with disk-based setup utilities will not use this). The *Press <F1> to run Setup* message can be turned on or off through the *Press <F1> Message Display* switch. *System Boot Up Num Lock* defines whether the system boots with the keyboard Num Lock control on or off. The *System Boot Up Sequence* specifies the order in which drives are searched for a boot device. The classic approach is to search drive A: then C:, but you can change this order (for example, C: then A:, B: then C:, or C: then B:). *System Boot Up CPU Speed* details whether the system should be started at high or low CPU speed. The *Cache Memory* switch is used to enable or disable the external cache found in the PC. For PCs on a network, a password function can be enabled or disabled.

When using a video board through the ISA bus, a *linear frame buffer* might help to improve video system performance. You can specify a buffer size of 1Mb, 2Mb, or 4Mb. It is disabled here because the motherboard supports a VL bus fitted with a VL graphics board—the ISA bus does not have to support video. The *Set Linear Frame Address* selection is automatically configured when the linear frame buffer is enabled.

The next few entries outline memory configurations. The *Disable Shadow Memory Size* setting allows you shadow a 16K or 64K ROM area in RAM. The amount of memory available depends on the location you wish to shadow specified in the *Disable Shadow Memory Base* line. You can only use a 64K shadow when the base is set to C0000h or D0000h—otherwise, you can shadow a 16K area starting at addresses such as C4000h or CC000h. For example, Fig. 17-3 shows the Shadow Base at D0000h, so if the Shadow Memory Size were enabled, you could select 16K, 32K, 48K, or 64K. The *Base Memory Size* specifies the amount of conventional memory available in the system. You can enter 640K or 512K (but the default is 640K).

Timing and data transfer parameters are outlined last. The *IDE DMA Transfer Mode* allows you to choose three types of DMA transfers to the IDE drive—Standard, Type B, and Type F that is the fastest. Not all IDE hard drives support Type B or Type F transfers. A related entry is the *IDE Multiple Sector Mode* that allows the system to transfer multiple sectors of data in a burst (noted S/B or sectors/burst). Typical values are 1, 2, 4, 8, 16, 32, and 64 S/B. A value of 64 represents the absolute maximum burst size possible. Not all IDE drives will support such a large burst size. *Enhanced ISA Timing* will drive the ISA bus at 10 MHz rather than 8.33 MHz. This can cause problems with older ISA boards that might not work properly at that slightly higher speed. Finally, there are three ISA configuration switches: *ISA IRQ 9*, *ISA IRQ 10*, and *ISA IRQ 15*. These can be set to free or used. If there is an ISA board in the system that uses the respective interrupt, the corresponding switch should be set to used.

Other parameters

There are several other CMOS setup parameters that you should be familiar with. Although these do not appear in the setup examples of this chapter, you might well encounter them in other setup situations:

- *Extended Memory Test* When enabled, this feature will invoke the POST memory routines on the RAM above 1Mb (if present on the system). If disabled, the BIOS will only check the first 1Mb of RAM.
- *Memory Test Tick Sound* This option will enable (turn on) or disable (turn off) the "ticking" sound during the memory test.
- *Memory Parity Error Check* If the system board does not have parity RAM, the user might disable the memory parity error checking routines in the BIOS. However, virtually all RAM contains an extra bit for every 8 data

bits that is used to check parity. If you are not sure whether the memory in a system supports parity or not, check with the motherboard manufacturer.

- *Internal Cache Memory* This option will appear only on i486-based systems that use CPU's with an internal cache structure. With this option, a user can enable or disable the internal cache of the system's CPU.
- *External Cache Memory* This option appears only on i486 systems that can have a caching scheme external to the CPU. With this option, a user can specify whether the external cache is present or absent.
- *Fast Gate A20* This option uses the fast gate A20 line (supported in some chip sets) to access any memory above 1 Mb. Normally, all RAM access above 1 Mb is handled through the keyboard controller chip. Using this option will make the access faster than the normal method. This option is very useful in networking operating systems.
- *256K/384K Memory Relocation* In some systems, this option will allow the upper memory between 640K and 1Mb on the system board to be relocated and used as extended memory.

Backing up CMOS RAM

The selections in Figs. 17-2 and 17-3 are hardly intuitive—proper settings require an understanding of each CMOS variable, and a detailed knowledge of the individual system. Unfortunately, most end users are not familiar enough with the intricacies of their PC or the meaning of each setup variable to adequately reconstruct their CMOS setup should the backup battery ever fail. When the battery does fail (it will eventually), it might take an unprepared user hours to restore settings that can be entered in a matter of minutes. This is the real tragedy—with just a few minutes of advance planning, CMOS contents can be backed-up with complete safely. There are two methods of backing-up CMOS contents: hard copy backup, and file backup.

Hard copy backup is just as the name implies—CMOS contents are recorded on paper that is filed away or taped to the inside of the PC enclosure. The simplest method of hard copy backup is to connect the PC to a printer and capture a *Print Screen* of each data screen. This provides a fast, simple, and permanent record. On the other hand, it might take several minutes to restore the configuration. If there is no printer available, you can photocopy and complete the CMOS Setup form included in the Appendix.

File backup is a fairly new alternative that uses a small utility to copy CMOS contents to a data file (usually on floppy disk), then restore the file to CMOS addresses later. Shareware utilities such as CMOSRAM2.EXE are ideal for this kind of support. When saving a CMOS file, be sure to save it to a floppy disk because losing CMOS contents will often disable the hard drive. The advantage of a backup file is speed—CMOS contents can be restored in a matter of moments.

CMOS maintenance and troubleshooting

CMOS tends to be a very reliable element in most PCs, but it is not immune to eventual failure. There are two essential checks that POST makes on the RTC/CMOS

IC: a battery test and a checksum test. These tests are usually made before the video system is initialized, so errors will typically be indicated by a series of beeps (refer to Chapter 15) or I/O POST codes (refer to Chapter 28). When a battery failure is indicated, you can simply replace the battery as described below. If a CMOS checksum error is detected, you will often have to replace the CMOS IC outright. If you are unable to replace a defective CMOS IC, you will need to replace the entire motherboard.

CMOS maintenance

Ordinarily, the RTC/CMOS IC requires no maintenance. However, the backup battery will need to be replaced on a fairly regular basis (often every few years). Before replacing the battery (or battery pack), be sure that you have a valid CMOS backup—either on paper or floppy disk. Turn off system power, unplug the system, and remove the battery. This will cause the CMOS RAM IC to lose its contents. Discard the original battery and install the new one according to the system manufacturer's instructions. Secure the battery and restart the system. When the system boots, go directly to the CMOS setup routine and restore each setting. If you have CMOS information recorded in a file, boot the system from a floppy disk and use the CMOS backup/restore utility to restore the file. You should then be able to restart the system as if nothing had ever happened.

18
CHAPTER

Conflict troubleshooting

The incredible acceptance and popularity of the PC is largely caused by the use of an *open architecture*. An open architecture allows any manufacturer to develop new devices (video boards, modems, sound boards, and so on) that will work in conjunction with the PC. When a new expansion board is added to the PC, the board makes use of various system resources in order to obtain CPU time and transfer data across the expansion bus. Ultimately, each board that is added to the system requires unique resources. No two devices can use the same resources—otherwise, a *hardware conflict* will result. Low-level software, such as device drivers and *TSR*s (terminate-and-stay-resident programs) that uses system resources can also conflict with one another during normal operation. This chapter explains system resources, then shows you how to detect and correct conflicts in both hardware and software.

Understanding system resources

The key to understanding and eliminating conflicts is to understand the importance of each system resource that is available to you. PCs provide three types of resources: interrupts, DMA channels, and I/O areas. Do not underestimate the importance of these areas—conflicts can occur anywhere, and carry dire consequences for a system.

Interrupts

An *interrupt* is probably the most well-known and understood type of resource. Interrupts are used to demand attention from the CPU. This allows a device or subsystem to work in the background until a particular event occurs that requires system processing. Such an event may include receiving a character at the serial port, striking a key on the keyboard, or any number of other real-world situations. An interrupt is invoked by asserting a logic level on an *IRQ* (physical interrupt request) line. AT-compatible PCs provide 16 IRQ lines (noted IRQ 0 to IRQ 15). Table 18-1 illustrates the IRQ signals for XT and AT systems. These lines run from pins on the expansion bus connector or key ICs on the motherboard to *PIC*s (programmable interrupt controllers) on the motherboard. The output signals generated by a PIC triggers the CPU interrupt. Keep in mind that Table 18-1 covers *hardware interrupts* only. There are also a proliferation of processor and software-generated interrupts.

Table 18-1. XT and AT interrupt assignments

IBM PC/XT

IRQ	Function	Bus slot required
0	System Timer IC	No (motherboard)
1	Keyboard Controller IC	No (motherboard)
2	unused	No
3	Serial Port 2 (COM2)	Yes
4	Serial Port 1 (COM1)	Yes
5	Hard Disk Controller Board	Yes
6	Floppy Disk Controller Board	Yes
7	Parallel Port 1 (LPT1)	Yes

IBM PC/AT

IRQ	Function	Bus slot required
0	System Timer IC	No (motherboard)
1	Keyboard Controller IC	No (motherboard)
2	Second IRQ Controller IC	No (motherboard)
3	Serial Port 2 (COM2)	Yes (8 bit)
4	Serial Port 1 (COM1)	Yes (8 bit)
5	Parallel Port 2 (LPT2)	Yes (8 bit)
6	Floppy Disk Controller Board	Yes (8 bit)
7	Parallel Port 1 (LPT1)	Yes (8 bit)
8	Real-Time Clock (RTC)	No (motherboard)
9	unused (*redirected to IRQ 2*)	Yes (8 bit)
10	unused	Yes (16 bit)
11	unused	Yes (16 bit)
12	Motherboard Mouse Port	Yes (16 bit)
13	Math Co-processor	No (motherboard)
14	Hard Disk Controller Board	Yes (16 bit)
15	unused	Yes (16 bit)

The use of IRQ 2 in an AT system deserves a bit of explanation. An AT uses IRQ 2 right on the motherboard, which means the expansion bus pin for IRQ 2 is now empty. Instead of leaving this pin unused, IRQ 9 from the AT extended slot is wired to the pin previously occupied by IRQ 2. In other words, IRQ 9 is being *redirected* to IRQ 2. Any AT expansion device set to use IRQ 2 is actually using IRQ 9. Of course, the vector interrupt table is adjusted to compensate for this sleight of hand.

After an interrupt is triggered, an interrupt handling routine saves the current CPU register states to a small area of memory (called the *stack*), then directs the CPU to the *interrupt vector table*. The interrupt vector table is a list of program locations that correspond to each interrupt. When an interrupt occurs, the CPU will jump to the interrupt handler routine at the location specified in the interrupt vector table and execute the routine. In most cases, the interrupt handler is a device driver associated with the board generating the interrupt. For example, an IRQ from a network card will likely call a network device driver to operate the card. For a hard disk controller, an IRQ calls the BIOS ROM code that operates the drive. When the handling routine is finished, the CPU's original register contents are popped from the stack, and the CPU picks up from where it left off without interruption.

As a technician, it is not vital that you understand precisely how interrupts are initialized and enabled, but you should know the basic terminology. The term *assigned* simply means that a device is set to produce a particular IRQ signal. For example, a typical hard drive controller board is assigned to IRQ 14. Assignments are usually made with one or more jumpers or DIP switches. Next, interrupts can be selectively enabled or disabled under software control. An *enabled* interrupt is an interrupt where the PIC has been programmed to pass on an IRQ to the CPU. Just because an interrupt is enabled does not mean that there are any devices assigned to it. Finally, an *active* interrupt is a line where real IRQs are being generated. Note that active does not mean assigned or enabled.

Interrupts are an effective and reliable means of signaling the CPU, but the conventional ISA bus architecture—used in virtually all PCs—does not provide a means of determining which slot contains the board that called the interrupt. As a result, interrupts cannot be shared by multiple devices. In other words, no two devices can be actively generating interrupt requests on the same IRQ line at the same time. If more than one device is assigned to the same interrupt line, a hardware conflict can occur. In most circumstances, a conflict might prevent the newly installed board (or other previously installed boards) from working. In some cases, a hardware conflict can hang up the entire system.

The *MCA* (micro channel architecture) and *EISA* (extended ISA) buses overcome this IRQ sharing limitation, but MCA was never widely accepted in the PC industry because the slots are not backwardly compatible with the well-established base of ISA boards. EISA bus slots are backwardly compatible with ISA boards, but an ISA board in an EISA slot was still faced with the same IRQ limitations.

DMA channels

The CPU is very adept at moving data. It can transfer data between memory locations, I/O locations, or from memory to I/O and back with equal ease. However, PC designers realized that transferring large amounts of data (one word at a time) through the CPU is a hideous waste of CPU time. After all, the CPU really isn't processing anything during a data move, just shuttling data from one place to another. If there were a way to off-load such redundant tasks from the CPU, data could be moved faster than would be possible with CPU intervention. *DMA* (direct memory access) is technique designed to move large amounts of data from memory to an I/O location, or vice versa, without the direct intervention by the CPU. In theory, the DMA controller IC acts as a stand-alone data processor, leaving the CPU free.

A DMA transfer starts with a *DRQ* (DMA request) signal generated by the requesting device (such as the floppy disk controller board). If the channel has been previously enabled through software drivers or BIOS routines, the request will reach the corresponding DMA controller IC on the motherboard. The DMA controller will then send a *HOLD* request to the CPU, which responds with an *HLDA* (hold acknowledge) signal. When the DMA controller receives the HLDA signal, it instructs the bus controller to effectively disconnect the CPU from the expansion bus and allow the DMA controller IC to take control of the bus itself. The DMA controller sends a *DACK* (DMA acknowledge) signal to the requesting device, and the transfer process can begin. Up to 64K can be moved during a single DMA transfer. After the transfer is done, the DMA controller will reconnect the CPU and drop its HOLD request—the CPU then continues with whatever it was doing without interruption.

Table 18-2 illustrates the use of DMA channels for both XT and AT systems. There are twice as many DMA channels available in an AT than an XT, but you might wonder why the AT commits fewer channels. The issue is DMA performance. DMA was developed when CPUs ran at 4.77 MHz, and is artificially limited to 4-MHz operation. When CPUs began to work at 8 MHz and higher, CPU transfers (redundant as they are) actually became faster than a DMA channel. No current performance-conscious device would rely on DMA. As a result, the AT has many channels available, but only the floppy drive controller (which has always been limited in speed and throughput) continues to use DMA. In an AT system, DMA channel 4 serves as a cascade line linking DMA controller ICs. Of course, DMA channels are a resource, and there are many devices that do make use them (such as sound boards and network controller cards).

Table 18-2. XT and AT DMA assignments

	IBM PC/XT	
DMA	**Function**	**Bus slot required**
0	Dynamic RAM Refresh	No (motherboard)
1	unused	Yes (8 bit)
2	Floppy Disk Controller Board	Yes (8 bit)
3	Hard Disk Controller Board	Yes (8 bit)
	IBM PC/AT	
DMA	**Function**	**Bus slot required**
0	unused	Yes (16 bit)
1	unused	Yes (8 bit)
2	Floppy Disk Controller Board	Yes (8 bit)
3	unused	Yes (8 bit)
4	First DMA Controller IC	No (motherboard)
5	unused	Yes (16 bit)
6	unused	Yes (16 bit)
7	unused	Yes (16 bit)

As with interrupts, a DMA channel is selected by setting a physical jumper or DIP switch on the particular expansion board. When the board is installed in an expansion slot, the channel setting establishes a connection between the board and DMA controller IC. Often, accompanying software drivers must be DMA assignment so that the DMA controller can be manipulated properly. Also, DMA channels cannot be shared between two or more devices. Although DMA sharing is possible in theory, it is extremely difficult to implement in actual practice. If more than one device attempts to use the same DMA channel at the same time, a conflict will result.

I/O areas

Both XT and AT computers provide 1024 *I/O* (input/output) ports. An *I/O port* acts very much like a memory address, but it is not for storage. Instead, an I/O port provides the means for a PC to communicate directly with a device. This allows the PC to pass commands and data efficiently between the system and various expansion devices. Each device must be assigned to a unique address (or address range). Table 18-3 lists the typical I/O port assignments for 8-bit and 16-bit expansion devices.

Table 18-3. I/O port addresses

IBM PC/XT systems	
000h-00Fh	8237 DMA IC
020h-021h	8259 Programmable Interrupt Controller IC
040h-043h	8253 System Timer IC
060h-063h	8255 Programmable Peripheral Interface IC
080 h	POST Code Port
080h-083h	DMA Page Registers
0A0h	NMI Mask Register
0C0h-0CFh	reserved
0E0h-0EFh	reserved
200h-20Fh	Game Control Ports
201h	Game Card I/O Port
210h-217h	Expansion Unit I/O Ports
278h-27Fh	Parallel Port 2 (LPT2)
2B0h-2DFh	Alternate EGA Ports
2E1h	GPIB Port (Adapter 0)
2E2h-2E3h	Data Acquisition Ports (Adapter 0)
2F8h-2FFh	Serial Port 2 (COM2)
300h-31Fh	unassigned
320h-32Fh	Hard Disk Controller Ports
348h-357h	DCA 3278
360h-367h	Network Card Ports (low)
368h-36Fh	Network Card Ports (high)
378h-37Fh	Parallel Port 1 (LPT1)
380h-38Fh	SDLC (or Bisync 2) Ports
390h-393h	Cluster Ports (Adapter 0)
3A0h-3AFh	Bisync 1 Ports
3B0h-3BFh	MDA Ports
3C0h-3CFh	EGA Ports
3D0h-3DFh	CGA Ports

Table 18-3. Continued

3F0h-3F7h	Floppy Disk Controller Ports
3F8h-3FFh	Serial Port 1 (COM1)

IBM PC/AT systems

000h-00Fh	8237A-5 DMA Controller IC #1
020h-03Fh	8269A Programmable Interrupt Controller IC #1
040h-05Fh	8254-2 System Timer IC
060h	8042 Keyboard/Mouse Controller IC
061h	System Board I/O Port
064h	8042 Keyboard/Mouse Controller IC
070h-07Fh	RTC Port and NMI Mask Port
080h	POST Code Port
080h-09Fh	74LS612 DMA Page Registers
0A0h-0BFh	8237A-5 Programmable Interrupt Controller IC #2
0F0h	Clear Math Co-processor busy
0F1h	Reset Math Co-processor
0F8h-0FFh	Math Co-processor Ports
1F0h-1F8h	Hard Disk Controller Ports
200h-20Fh	Game Control Ports
238h-23Bh	Bus Mouse Adapter Ports
23Ch-23Fh	Alternate Bus Mouse Adapter Ports
278h-27Fh	Parallel Printer 2 (LPT2)
2B0h-2DFh	Alternate EGA Ports
2E0h-2E7h	GPIB (Adapter 0)
2E8h-2EFh	Serial Port 4 (COM4)
2F8h-2FFh	Serial Port 2 (COM2)
300h-31Fh	unassigned
360h-363h	Network Card Ports (low)
368h-36Bh	Network Card Ports (high)
378h-37Fh	Parallel Printer 1 (LPT1)
380h-38Fh	SDLC (Bisync 2) Ports
3A0h-3AFh	Bisync 1 Ports
3B0h-3BBh	Monochrome Display Adapter (MDA) Ports
3BCh-3BFh	Parallel Printer 3 (LPT3)
3C0h-3CFh	Enhanced Graphics Adapter (EGA) Ports
3D0h-3DFh	Color Graphics Adapter (CGA) Ports
3E8h-3EFh	Serial Port 3 (COM3)
3F0h-3F7h	Floppy Disk Controller Ports
3F8h-3FFh	Serial Port 1 (COM1)

I/O assignments are generally made by setting jumpers or DIP switches on the expansion device itself. As with other system resources, it is vitally important that no two devices use the same I/O port(s) at the same time. If one or more I/O addresses overlap, a hardware conflict will result. Commands meant for one device might be erroneously interpreted by another. Keep in mind that although many expansion devices can be set at a variety of addresses, some devices cannot.

Recognizing the signs of conflict

Fortunately, conflicts are almost always the result of a PC upgrade gone awry. Thus, a technician can be alerted to the possibility of a system conflict by applying the *Last Upgrade* rule. The rule consists of three parts:

1. A piece of hardware and/or software has been added to the system very recently.
2. The trouble occurred after a piece of hardware and/or software was added to the system.
3. The system was working fine before the hardware and/or software was added.

If all three of these common-sense factors are true, chances are very good that you are faced with a hardware or software conflict. Unlike most other types of PC problems that tend to be specific to the faulty subassembly, conflicts usually manifest themselves as much more general and perplexing problems. The following symptoms are typical of serious hardware or software conflicts:

- The system locks up during initialization.
- The system locks up during a particular application.
- The system locks up randomly or without warning regardless of the application.
- The system might not crash, but the device that was added might not function (even though it seems properly configured). Devices that were in the system previously might still work correctly.
- The system might not crash, but a device or application that was working previously no longer seems to function. The newly added device (and accompanying software) might or might not work properly.

What makes these problems so generic is that the severity and frequency of a fault, as well as the point at which the fault occurs, depends on such factors as the particular devices that are conflicting, the resource(s) that are conflicting among the devices (IRQs, DMAs, or I/O addresses), and the function being performed by the PC when the conflict manifests itself. Because every PC is equipped and configured a bit differently, it is virtually impossible to predict a conflict's symptoms more specifically.

Confirming and resolving conflicts

Recognizing the possibility of a conflict is one thing, proving and correcting it is another issue entirely. However, there are some very effective tactics at your disposal. The first rule of conflict resolution is *LIFO* (last in first out). The LIFO principle basically says that the fastest means of overcoming a conflict problem is to remove the hardware or software that resulted in the conflict. In other words, if you install board X and board Y ceases to function, board X is probably conflicting with the system, so removing board X should restore board Y to normal operation. The same concept holds true for software. If you add a new application to your system, then find that an existing application fails to work properly, the new application is likely at fault. Unfortunately, removing the offending element is not enough. You still have to install the new device or software in such a way that it will no longer conflict in the system.

Dealing with software conflicts

There are two types of software that can cause conflicts in a typical PC: TSRs and device drivers. *TSRs* (sometimes called *popup utilities*) load into memory, usually during initialization, and wait until a system event (such as a modem ring or a keyboard hot-key combination). There are no DOS or system rules that define how such utilities should be written. As a result, many tend to conflict with application programs (and even DOS itself). If you suspect that such a popup utility is causing the problem, find its reference in the AUTOEXEC.BAT file and disable it by placing the command REM in front of its command line (REM C:\UTILS\NEWMENU.EXE /A:360 /D:3). The REM command turns the line into a *REMark* that can easily be removed later if you choose to restore the line. Remember to reboot the computer so that your changes will take effect.

Device drivers present another potential problem. Most hardware upgrades require the addition of one or more device drivers. Such drivers are called from the CONFIG.SYS file during system initialization, and use a series of command line parameters to specify the system resources that are being used. This is often necessary to ensure that the driver operates its associated hardware properly. If the command line options used for the device driver do not match the hardware settings (or overlap the settings of another device driver) system problems can result. If you suspect that a device driver is causing the problem, find its reference in the CONFIG.SYS file and disable it by placing the command REM in front of its command line (for example, REM DEVICE = C:\DRIVERS\NEWDRIVE.SYS /A360 /I:5). The REM command turns the line into a REMark that can easily be removed later if you choose to restore the line. Remember that disabling the device driver in this fashion will prevent the associated hardware from working, but if the problem clears, you can work with the driver settings until the problem is resolved. Remember to reboot the computer so that your changes will take effect.

Finally, consider the possibility that the offending software has a bug. Try contacting the software manufacturer. There might be a fix or undocumented feature that you are unaware of. There might also be a patch or update that will solve the problem.

Dealing with hardware conflicts

A PC user recently added a CD-ROM and adapter board to their system. The installation went flawlessly using the defaults—a 10-minute job. Several days later when attempting to back up the system, the user noticed that the parallel port tape backup did not respond (although the printer that had been connected to the parallel port was working fine). The user tried booting the system from a clean bootable floppy disk (no CONFIG.SYS or AUTOEXEC.BAT files to eliminate the device drivers), but the problem remained. After a bit of consideration, the user powered down the system, removed the CD-ROM adapter board, and booted the system from a clean bootable floppy disk. Sure enough, the parallel port tape backup started working again.

244 Conflict troubleshooting

Stories such as this remind technicians that hardware conflicts are not always the monstrous, system-smashing mistakes that they are made out to be. In many cases, conflicts have subtle, noncatastrophic consequences. Because the CD-ROM was the last device to be added, it was the first to be removed. It took about five minutes to realize and remove the problem. However, removing the problem is only part of conflict troubleshooting—reinstalling the device without a conflict is the real challenge.

Ideally, the way to correct a conflict would be to alter the conflicting setting. That's dynamite in theory, but another thing in practice. The trick is that you need to know what resources are in use and which ones are free. Unfortunately, there are only two ways to find out. On one hand, you can track down the user manual for every board in the system, then inspect each board individually to find their settings, then work accordingly. This will work (assuming you have the documentation) but it is cumbersome and time-consuming. As an alternative, you can use a resource testing tool such as the Discovery Card by AllMicro, Inc. The Discovery Card plugs into a 16-bit ISA slot and uses a series of LEDs to display each IRQ and DMA channel in use. Any LED not illuminated is an available resource. It is then simply a matter of setting your expansion hardware to an IRQ and DMA channel that is not illuminated. Remember that you might have to alter the command line switches of any device drivers. The only resources not illustrated by the Discovery Card are I/O addresses, but because most I/O ports are reserved for particular functions (as you saw in Table 18-3), you can typically locate an unused I/O port with a minimum of effort.

Keep your notes

Once you have determined the IRQ, DMA, and I/O settings that are in use, a thorough technician will note each setting on paper, then tape the notes inside the system's enclosure. This extra step will greatly ease future expansion and troubleshooting. To make your note taking process even faster, you can photocopy and use the *System Setup Form* included in Appendix F of this book.

19
CHAPTER

CPUs and math coprocessors

The *central processing unit* (also called a CPU or microprocessor) has become one of the most important developments in integrated circuit technology (Fig. 19-1). Yet on the surface, a CPU is a rather boring device. In spite of its relative complexity, a typical CPU only performs three general functions: mathematical calculations, logical comparisons, and data manipulation—not a very big repertoire for a device carrying millions of transistors. When you look deeper, however, you realize that it is not the number of functions that makes a CPU so remarkable, but that each function is carried out as part of a *program* that the CPU reads and follows. By changing the program, the activities of a CPU could be completely rearranged without modifying the computer's circuitry.

19-1 The 33-MHz i386DX microprocessor provides 25 times the performance of the original PC, and the 25-MHz i486 microprocessor provides 50 times the original PC's performance.

Once the concept of a generic central processing function was born, designers realized that the same system could be used to solve an incredibly diverse array of problems (given the right set of instructions). This was the quantum leap that gave birth to the computer, and created the two domains that you know today as hardware and software. As you might have guessed, the idea of *central processing* is hardly new. The very earliest computers of the late 1940s and 1950s applied these concepts to simple programs stored on punched cards or paper tape. The mainframe and minicomputers of the 1960s and 1970s also followed the central processing concept. However, it was the integration of central processing functions onto a single IC (the *microprocessor*) in the mid-1970s that made the first *personal* computers possible—and spawned the explosive developments in CPU speed and performance you have seen ever since.

Although a CPU can handle mathematical calculations, the CPU itself was not (until recently) designed to handle floating-point math as an internal function. Of course, floating point math was possible through software emulation, but the performance of such an approach was unacceptable for math-intensive applications (such as CAD and scientific programs). In order to deal with floating point math, an *MCP* (math coprocessor) was developed to work in conjunction with the CPU. Although the classical MCP was implemented as a stand-alone device, newer generations of CPU incorporate the MCP's functions right into the CPU.

The CPU is closely related to the overall speed and performance of personal computers. As a technician, you should understand the essential specifications and characteristics of CPUs and MCPs. This chapter is intended to provide some insights into CPU evolution, and illustrate some of the problems that can manifest themselves in microprocessor operation.

The basic CPU

A generic microprocessor can be represented by a block diagram such as the one in Fig. 19-2. As you can see, there are several sets of signals (or *buses*) that you should be familiar with: the *data* bus, the *address* bus, and the *control* bus. It is these three buses that allow the CPU to communicate with the other elements of the PC and control its operations.

The buses

The *data bus* carries information to and from the CPU, and it is perhaps the most familiar yardstick of CPU performance. The number of wires in the bus represents the number of bits (or data volume) that can be carried at any point in time. Data lines are typically labeled with a *D* prefix (such as, D0, D1, D2, D_n, and so on). The size of a data bus is typically 8, 16, 32, or 64 bits. As you might expect, larger data buses are preferred because it allows more data to be transferred faster.

In order for the CPU to read or write data, it must be able to specify the precise I/O port or location in system memory. "Locations" are defined through the use of an *address bus*. The number of bits in the address bus represent the number of physical locations that the CPU can access. For example, a CPU with 20 address lines can address 2^{20} (1,048,576) bytes. A CPU with 24 address lines can address 2^{24} (16,777,216) bytes, etc. Address lines are generally represented with an *A* prefix (such as A0, A1, and A19).

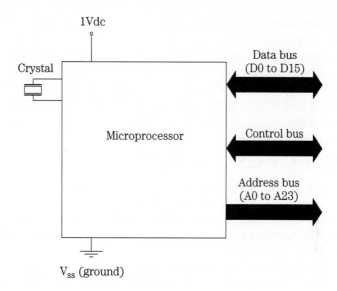

19-2 Diagram of a generic CPU.

Control signals are used to synchronize and coordinate the operation of a CPU with other devices in the computer. Although the number and use of each control signal varies a bit from generation to generation, most control signals fall into several categories:

- Reading or writing functions (to memory or I/O locations)
- Interrupt channels
- CPU test and reset
- Bus arbitration and control
- DMA control
- CPU status
- Parity checking
- Cache operation

Addressing modes

When you consider a microprocessor, you also must consider the means it uses to address its memory. As you can see in this chapter, the original Intel CPUs (such as the 8088 and 8086) used only 20 address lines (labeled A0 to A19). With 20 address lines, the CPU can access only 1Mb. Technically, this was not a problem, and DOS was written to work within this 1Mb of space. Unfortunately, when newer CPUs were designed to break the 1Mb memory barrier, DOS was stuck with this 1Mb limitation (although more sophisticated software such as DOS extenders and extended memory managers allow DOS programs to access memory areas above 1Mb).

To maintain backward compatibility with older CPUs, newer CPUs can operate in one of two modes. In the *real-mode*, a CPU behaves like an 8088/8086, and will only access up to 1Mb. DOS and DOS programs operate in the real-mode exclusively. Newer operating systems (such as Windows and OS/2) allow a CPU to use all of its address lines when accessing memory. This is known as *protected-mode* operation. Protected-mode operation not only supports much greater amounts of physical memory, but it also supports *virtual memory*. When a program calls for more memory than actually exists in a system, the CPU is able to swap code between memory and the hard drive. In effect, the hard drive can be used to simulate extra RAM. The software running on a CPU in protected-mode could be far more sophisticated than real-mode programs.

The Intel CPUs

There is little doubt that Intel Corporation has been a driving force behind the personal computer revolution. Each new generation of microprocessor represents not just mediocre improvements in processing speed, but technological leaps in execution efficiency, raw speed, data throughput, and design enhancements (such as internal cache). Of course, Intel is not the only CPU manufacturer in the PC market. *AMD* (Advanced Micro Devices), Cyrix, NEC, and IBM are other large manufacturers, but each of their PC microprocessors is fully Intel-compatible. Motorola is another premier CPU manufacturer, but their products are found in the Apple computer line—Intel and Motorola CPUs are not compatible. This part of the chapter provides a historical overview of Intel microprocessors, and compares their performance. A summary of Intel CPU specifications is shown in Table 19-1.

8086/8088 (1978/1979)

The 29,000-transistor 8086 marked the first 16-bit microprocessor—that is, there are 16 data bits available from the CPU itself. This immediately offered twice the data throughput of earlier 8-bit CPUs. Each of the 24 registers in the 8086/8088 is expanded to 16 bits rather than just 8. Twenty address lines allow direct access to 1,048,576 bytes (1Mb) of external system memory. Although 1Mb of RAM is considered almost negligible today, IC designers at the time never suspected that more than 1Mb would ever be needed. Both the 8086 and 8088 (as well as all subsequent Intel CPUs) can address 64K of I/O space (as opposed to RAM space). The 8086 was available for four clock speeds: 5 MHz, 6 MHz, 8 MHz, and 10 MHz. These clock speeds allowed the 8086 to process 0.33, 0.66, and 0.75 *MIPS* (millions of instructions per second) respectively. The 8088 was only available in 5-MHz and 8-MHz versions (for 0.33 and 0.75 MIPS respectively), but its rather unique multiplexing nature reduces its data bandwidth to only 2Mb/s.

For all intents and purposes, the 8088 is identical to the 8086. They are exactly the same microprocessor—with only one exception: the 8088 multiplexes (time-shares) 8 of the 16 address lines between the address bus and the data bus. If you look at a pinout of an 8088, you will see only 8 data lines available to the outside world (D8 to D15). During one part of a bus cycle, the lower 8 address lines serve as the lower 8 data bits (D0 to D7). During another part of the bus cycle, those 8 shared bits are used as the lower 8 bits of the address bus (A0 to A7). Both CPUs are designed to work with the 8087 MCP.

Table 19-1. A comparison of Intel microprocessors

Processor	Data	Addr	Internal data	Speeds (MHz)	Addressable memory	Virtual memory	MCP	OverDrive compatible
8086	16	20	16	5, 8, 10	1Mb	No	8087	No
8088	8	20	16	5, 8	1Mb	No	8087	No
80186	16	20	16	8, 10, 12	1Mb	No	8087	No
80188	8	20	16	8, 10	1Mb	No	8087	No
80286	16	24	16	8, 10, 12.5	16Mb	Yes	80287	No
80386DX	32	32	32	16, 20, 25, 33	4Gb	Yes	80387DX	No
80386SX	16	24	32	16, 20, 25, 33	16Mb	Yes	80387SX	No
80386SL	16	24	32	20, 25	32Mb	Yes	80387SL	No
80486DX	32	32	32	25, 33, 50	4Gb	Yes	On-Chip	Yes
80486SX	32	32	32	16, 20, 25, 33	4Gb	Yes	80487SX	Yes
80486SX-LP	32	32	32	16, 20, 25, 33	4Gb	Yes	80487SX	Yes
80486SL	32	32	32	16, 20, 25, 33	4Gb	Yes	80487SX	Yes
80486DX2	32	32	32	50, 66	4Gb	Yes	On-Chip	Yes
80486DX4	32	32	32	100, 132	4Gb	Yes	On-Chip	Yes
Pentium	64	32	32	60, 66, 90, 100, 120, 133	4Gb	Yes	On-Chip	Yes

80186 (1980)

The 16-bit 80186 was built on the x86 foundation to offer additional features such as an internal clock generator, system controller, interrupt controller, *DMA* (direct memory access) controller, and timer/counter circuitry right on the CPU itself. No Intel CPU before or since has offered so much integration in a single CPU. The x186 also was first to abandon 5-MHz clock speeds in favor of 8 MHz, 10 MHz, and 12.5 MHz. Aside from these advances, however, the x186 remained similar to the 8086/8088 with 24 registers and 20 address lines to access up to 1Mb of RAM. The x186 were used as CPUs in embedded applications and never saw service in personal computers. The limitations of the early x86 architecture in the PC demanded a much faster CPU capable of accessing far more than 1Mb of RAM.

80286 (1982)

The 24-register, 134,000-transistor 80286 CPU (first used in the IBM PC/AT and compatibles) offered some substantial advantages over older CPUs. Design advances allow the i286 to operate at 1.2 MIPS, 1.5 MIPS, and 2.66 MIPS (for 8, 10, and 12.5 MHz respectively). The i286 also breaks the 1Mb RAM barrier by offering 24 address lines instead of 20 that allow it to directly address 16Mb of RAM. In addition to 16Mb of directly accessible RAM, the i286 can handle up to 1Gb (gigabyte) of *virtual memory* that allows blocks of program code and data to be swapped between the i286's real memory (up to 16Mb) and a secondary (or *virtual*) storage location such as a hard disk. To maintain backward compatibility with the 8086/8088 that can only address 1Mb of RAM, the i286 can operate in real mode. One of the great failings of the i286 is that it can switch from real mode to protected mode, but it cannot switch back to real mode without a warm reboot of the system. The i286 uses a stand-alone math coprocessor, the 80287.

80386 (1985–1990)

The next major microprocessor released by Intel was the 275,000-transistor, 32-register, 80386DX CPU in 1985. With a full 32-bit data bus, data throughput is immediately double that of the 80286. The 16-, 20-, 25-, and 33-MHz versions allow data throughput up to 50Mb/s and processing power up to 11.4 MIPS at 33 MHz. A full 32-bit address bus allows direct access to an unprecedented 4Gb of RAM in addition to a staggering 64Tb (terabytes) of virtual memory capacity. The i386 was the first Intel CPU to enhance processing through the use of instruction *pipelining* (also known as *scalar* architecture) that allows the CPU to start working on a new instruction while waiting for the current instruction to finish. A new operating mode (called the *virtual real-mode*) enables the CPU to run several real-mode sessions simultaneously under operating systems such as Windows.

Intel took a small step backward in 1988 to produce the 80386SX CPU. The i386SX uses 24 address lines for 16Mb of addressable RAM and an external data bus of 16 bits instead of a full 32 bits from the DX. Correspondingly, the processing power for the i386SX is only 3.6 MIPS at 33 MHz. In spite of these compromises, this offered a significantly less expensive CPU that helped to propagate the i386 family into desktop and portable computers. Aside from changes to the address and bus width, the i386 architecture is virtually unchanged from that of the i386DX.

By 1990, Intel integrated the i386 into an 855,000-transistor, low-power version called the 80386SL. The i386SL incorporated an *ISA* (Industry Standard Architecture)-compatible chipset along with power management circuitry that optimized the i386 for use in mobile computers. The i386SL resembled the i386SX version in its 24 address lines and 16-bit external data bus.

Each member of the i386 family use stand-alone math coprocessors (80387DX, 80387SX, and 80387SL respectively). All versions of the 80386 can switch between real-mode and protected-mode as needed, so they will run the same software (and are backwardly compatible with) the 80286 and the 8086/8088.

80486 (1989–current)

The consistent push for higher speed and performance resulted in the development of Intel's 1.2 million-transistor, 29-register, 32-bit microprocessor called the 80486DX in 1989. The i486DX provides full 32-bit addressing for access to 4Gb of physical RAM and up to 64Tb (terabytes) of virtual memory. The i486DX offers twice the performance of the i386DX with 26.9 MIPS at 33 MHz. Two initial versions (25 MHz, 33 MHz) were available.

As with the i386 family, the i486 series uses pipelining to improve instruction execution, but the i486 series also adds 8KB of *cache memory* right on the IC. Cache saves memory access time by predicting the next instructions that will be needed by the CPU and loading them into the cache memory before the CPU actually needs them. If the needed instruction is indeed in cache, the CPU can access the information from cache without wasting time waiting for memory access. Another improvement of the i486DX is the inclusion of a *floating-point unit* (an MCP) in the CPU itself rather than requiring a separate coprocessor IC. This is not true of all members of the i486 family however. A third departure for the i486DX is that it is offered in 5- and 3-V versions. The 3-V version is intended for laptop, notebook, and other low-power mobile computing applications.

Finally, the i486DX is *upgradeable*. Up to 1989/1990, personal computers were limited by their CPU—when the CPU became obsolete, so did the computer (more specifically the *motherboard*). This traditionally forced the computer user to purchase new computers every few years in order to use current technology. The architecture of the i486 is intended to support CPU upgrades where a future CPU using a faster internal clock can be inserted into the existing system. Intel has dubbed this as *OverDrive* technology. Although OverDrive performance is not as high as a newer PC would be, it is much less expensive, and allows computer users to protect their computer investments for a longer period of time. It is vital to note that not all i486 versions are upgradeable, and the CPU socket on the motherboard itself must be designed specifically to accept an OverDrive CPU.

The i486DX was only the first in a long line of variations from Intel. In 1991, Intel released the 80486SX and the 80486DX/50. Both the i486SX and i486DX/50 offer 32-bit addressing, a 32-bit data path, and 8K of on-chip cache memory. The i486SX takes a small step backward from the i486DX by removing the math coprocessor and offering slower versions at 16, 20, 25, and 33 MHz. At 33 MHz, the i486SX is rated at 20.2 MIPS. Such design compromises reduced the cost and power dissipation of the i486SX that accelerated its acceptance into desktop and portable computers. The i486SX is upgradeable with an OverDrive CPU (if the computer's motherboard is designed to accept an OverDrive CPU), is compatible with an 80487 CPU/MCP, and the i486SX is available in 5- and 3-V versions. The i486DX/50 operates at a clock speed of 50 MHz where it performs at 41.1 MIPS. The i486DX/50 does integrate an on-board math coprocessor, but it is not OverDrive upgradeable, and it is not available in a 3-V version.

The first wave of OverDrive CPUs arrived in 1992 with the introduction of the 80486DX2/50 and the 80486DX2/66. The 2 along with the *DX* indicate that the IC is using an internal clock that is double the frequency of the system. The i486DX2/50 actually runs in a 25-MHz system, yet the CPU performs at 40.5 MIPS. The i486DX2/66 runs in a 33-MHz system, but it runs internally at 54.5 MIPS. The slower system speed allowed the CPU to work directly with existing PC motherboard designs. Both OverDrive CPUs offer on-board math coprocessors, and are themselves upgradeable to even faster OverDrive versions. The i486DX2/50 is available in 5-V and 3-V versions, but the i486DX2/66 is only available in the 5-V version.

In 1992, Intel produced a highly integrated, low-power version of the 80486 called the 80486SL. Its 32-bit data bus, 32-bit address bus, 8K of on-board cache, and integrated math coprocessor make it virtually identical to other i486 CPUs, but the SL uses 1.4 million transistors. The extra circuitry provides a low-power management capability that optimize the SL for mobile computers. The i486SL is available in 25- and 33-MHz versions, as well as 3- and 5-V designs. At 33 MHz, the i486SL operates at 26.9 MIPS.

Intel rounded out its x486 family in 1993 with the introduction of three other CPU models: the 80486DX2/40, the 80486SX/SL-enhanced, and the 80486DX/SL-enhanced. The i486DX2/40 is the third OverDrive CPU intended to run in 20-MHz PCs, while the CPU's internal clock runs at 40 MHz and performs at 21.1 MIPS. The i486SX/SL (26.9 MIPS at 33 MHz) and i486DX/SL (26.9 MIPS at 33 MHz) are identical to their original SX and DX versions, but the SL enhancement provides power management capability intended to support portable computers such as notebook and subnotebook computers.

It is important to note that all versions of the 80486 will run the same software, and are backwardly compatible with all CPUs back to the 8086/8088. As this chapter is being written, Intel is releasing its second wave of OverDrive CPUs called the 80486DX4. The 4 indicates that the CPU's internal clock speed is 4× the system speed. For example, a DX4 CPU in a 25-MHz PC will run at 100 MHz.

Pentium (1993–current)

By 1992, the i486 series had become well entrenched in everyday desktop computing, and Intel was already laying the groundwork for its next generation of CPU. Although most users expected Intel to continue with its traditional numbering scheme and dub its next CPU the 80586, legal conflicts regarding trademarking forced Intel to use a name that it could trademark and call its own. In 1993, the 3.21

million-transistor Pentium microprocessor (Fig. 19-3) was introduced to eager PC manufacturers. The Pentium retains the 32-bit address bus width of the i486 family. With 32 address bits, the Pentium can directly address 4Gb of RAM, and can access up to 64Tb of virtual memory. The 64-bit data bus width can handle twice the data throughput of the i486s. AT 60 MHz, the Pentium performs at 100 MIPS, and 66 MHz yields 111.6 MIPS (twice the processing power of the i486DX2/66). All versions of the Pentium include an on-board math coprocessor, and are intended to be compatible with future OverDrive designs.

19-3 A Pentium microprocessor.

The Pentium uses two 8K caches—one for instructions and another for data. A dual pipelining technique (known as *superscalar* architecture) allows the Pentium to actually work on more than one instruction per clock cycle. Another substantial improvement in the Pentium's design includes on-board power management features (similar to the i486SL line) allowing use in portable computers. For now, all Pentium versions work from 5 V; 3-V versions are likely to be available very soon. Finally, the Pentium is fully backward-compatible with all software written for the 8086/8088 and later CPUs. As of this writing, Intel has released 90-, 100-, 120-, and 133-MHz versions of the Pentium. Versions up to 200 MHz are on the drawing board.

CPU problems and troubleshooting

The term *microprocessor troubleshooting* is not the misnomer it once was. Early CPUs such as the 8088 carried only 29,000 transistors. When one of those transistors failed, it would usually result in a complete system failure—the PC would crash or freeze entirely. Further, the system would subsequently fail to boot at all. However, CPUs have become far more complex in the last 15 years or so, and new generations such as the Pentium are exceeding 3 million transistors. With so many more transistors, the probability of an immediate catastrophic fault is far less. Of course, any CPU fault is very serious, but there are now many cases where a system might boot, but crash when certain specific CPU functions are attempted (such as trying to execute protected-mode instructions). These kinds of errors might give the impression that a piece of software is corrupt, or that one or more expansion devices might be faulty. This part of the chapter looks at a selection of CPU failure modes, and offers some tactics to help resolve the problem.

Knowing the signs

Symptom 1. The system is completely dead (the system power LED lights properly) CPU faults are never subtle. When a CPU problem manifests itself, the system will invariably crash. Consequently, systems that do not boot (or freeze without warning during the boot process) stand an excellent chance of suffering from a CPU fault. The frustration with this kind of symptom is that the PC typically does not run long enough to execute its POST diagnostics, nor does the system boot to run any third-party DOS diagnostics. As a result, such "dead" systems require a bit of blind faith on the part of a technician.

Before considering a CPU replacement, you should use a multimeter and check the power supply outputs very carefully. Even though the power LED is lit, one or more outputs might be low or absent. Excessively low outputs can easily result in logic errors that will freeze the system. If this problem occurred after adding an upgrade, the supply might be overloaded—try removing the upgrade. If system operation returns, consider upgrading the supply. If an output is low or absent and there has been no upgrade (or the problem continues after removing the upgrade), try replacing the power supply.

Next, strip the system of its peripherals and expansion boards, then try the system again. If operation returns, one of the expansion devices is interrupting system operation. Re-install one device at a time and check the system. The last expansion device to be installed when the PC fails is the culprit. Replace the defective device. If the failure persists, try a new CPU.

Remember to shut down and unplug the PC before continuing. When removing the original CPU, be *extremely* careful to avoid bending any of the pins (you might want to re-install the CPU later). Use care when installing the new CPU as well—bent pins will almost always ruin the IC. If a new CPU fails to correct the problem, replace the motherboard outright.

Symptom 2. You receive a beep code or I/O POST code indicating a possible CPU fault When the POST starts, it will test each of the PC's key motherboard components (including the CPU). If a CPU fault is indicated during the POST, check each output from the system power supply. If one or more outputs is low or absent, there might be a problem in the supply. Try a new supply. If all supply outputs measure properly, try a new CPU. If a new CPU does not resolve the problem, replace the motherboard. Refer to Chapter 15 for beep codes, and Chapter 28 for I/O POST codes.

Symptom 3. The system boots with no problem, but crashes or freezes when certain applications are run It might seem as if the application might be corrupt, but try a diagnostic such as *AMIDIAG* from AMI or *The Troubleshooter* by AllMicro. Run repetitive tests on the CPU. Although the CPU might work in real-mode, diagnostics can detect errors running protected-mode instructions and perform thorough register checking. AMIDIAG stands out here because of the very specific error codes that are returned. Not only will it tell you if the CPU checks bad, but you also will know the specific reason why. When an error code is returned suggesting a CPU fault, try another CPU. If a CPU fault is not detected, expand the diagnostic to test other portions of the motherboard. If the entire system checks properly, you might indeed have a corrupt file in your application.

Heat problems

Heat is one of the greatest enemies of a CPU, especially the high-performance CPUs such as the i486 DX2 and DX4 OverDrive processors, as well as Pentiums. When a CPU becomes too hot, transistor operation becomes very unstable, and can easily fail. Although the transistors themselves are probably not permanently damaged, overheating will certainly shorten a CPU's life.

Symptom 1. The system boots with no problem, but crashes or freezes after several minutes of operation (regardless of the application being run) Also, you will probably note that no diagnostic indicates a CPU problem. If you shut the system off and wait several minutes, the system will probably boot fine and run for several more minutes before stopping again—this is typical of thermal failure. When the system halts, check the CPU for heat. *Use extreme caution when checking for heat—you can be easily burned.* An i486-series CPU might or might not be fitted with a heatsink. As a rule, i486 CPUs below 25 MHz are run without a heatsink, but i486 CPUs running at 33 MHz and higher do use a heatsink. DX2 and DX4 versions almost certainly use a heatsink. All Pentium processors require a heatsink.

If the CPU is not fitted with a heatsink, make sure that the system cooling fan is working, and that there is an unobstructed path over the CPU. If not, consider applying a heatsink with a generous helping of thermal compound. If the CPU is already fitted with a heatsink, make sure that there is an ample layer of thermal compound between the CPU case and heatsink base. In many cases, the compound is omitted. This ruins the transfer of heat, and allows the CPU to run much hotter. If you find that there is no thermal compound, allow the PC to cool, then add thermal compound between the CPU case and heatsink.

20
CHAPTER

Disk compression
troubleshooting

It is an amusing fact of PC life that you never seem to have enough storage space. No matter how large our hard drive is or how many hard drives might be in the system, just about all PC users find themselves removing files and applications at one time or another in order to make room for new software. Looking back, it is hard to imagine that 10Mb and 20Mb hard drives were once considered spacious—today, that much space would barely cover a single DOS game or application. For many years, overcoming storage limitations has meant replacing the hard drive. Given the rate at which hard drive technology is moving, a new drive generally doubles or triples a system's available space. Although new drive hardware is remarkably inexpensive (typically well under $1.00 per megabyte), the total bill for a 300Mb to 500Mb drive is a serious expense for PC owners.

Over the last few years, companies such as Stac and Microsoft have developed an alternative to hard drive swapping known as *disk compression*. Instead of an invasive procedure to upgrade and reconfigure a PC's hardware, a software utility reorganizes the drive using compression techniques that can allow a drive to safely store up to 100% or more than its rated capacity. For example, a properly compressed 100Mb hard drive would typically be able to offer 200Mb or more of effective storage space. Since the initial introduction of disk compression, its acceptance and popularity has soared, and compression is now quite commonplace on DOS and Windows platforms. As you can imagine, however, disk compression is not always flawless—the vast differences between PC designs and the software used on them virtually guarantee problems at some point. This chapter is intended to illustrate the factors that affect current disk compression, and show you the symptoms and solutions for a wide variety of compression problems.

Concepts of compression

In order to understand some of the problems associated with disk compression, it is important that you be familiar with the basic concepts of compression, and how those concepts are implemented on a typical drive. Disk compression generally achieves its goals through two means: superior disk space allocation, and an effective data compression algorithm.

Disk space allocation

The traditional DOS system of file allocation assigns disk space in terms of clusters (where a *cluster* can be 4, 8, 16, or more *sectors*—each sector is 512 bytes long). The larger a drive is, the more sectors are used in each cluster. For example, a 2Gb drive typically consumes 64 sectors in each cluster. When you consider it, each cluster commits (512 × 64) 32,768 bytes per cluster. Because the drive's file allocation table (FAT) works in terms of clusters, a file that only takes 20 bytes, or 1000 bytes, or 20K will still be given the entire cluster even though much less than the full cluster might be needed. This is phenomenally wasteful of disk space. Disk compression forms a barrier between the DOS file system and the drive. This *compression interface* simulates a FAT for the compressed drive, so the compressed drive also allocates space in terms of clusters, but a compressed cluster can have a variable number of sectors rather than a fixed number. That way, a file that only needs three sectors has three sectors assigned to the cluster. A file that needs 8 sectors has 8 sectors assigned to its cluster, and so on.

Data compression

Now that the DOS limitations of file allocation have been overcome, the data that is stored in each sector is compressed as it is written to disk, then decompressed as it is read from the disk into memory. This is known as *on-the-fly* compression. That way, the program that might ordinarily need 20 sectors on a disk can be compressed to only 10 sectors. You can start to see that this combination of cluster packing and compression offer some powerful tools for optimizing drive space.

In simplest terms, *data compression* works by locating repetitive data, and replacing the repetitive data with a short representative data fragment (called a *token*). For example, consider any ordinary sentence. In an uncompressed form, each text character would require 1 byte of disk space. On closer inspection, however, you can detect a surprising amount of repetition. In the last sentence alone, the letters *er* were used twice, the letters *on* are used three times, and the letters *tion* were used twice. You can probably find other repetitions as well. If each repetition were replaced by a 1-byte token, the overall volume of data can be reduced—sometimes significantly. The key to data compression is the ability to search sequences of data and replace repeated sequences with shorter tokens. The amount of compression then depends on the power of the search and replace algorithm. A more powerful algorithm might be able to search larger amounts of data for larger repeating sequences—replacing larger sequences results in better compression. Unfortunately, more powerful compression algorithms require larger commitments of CPU time, and this in turn slows down a disk's operations. Of course, any token must be shorter than the sequence it is replacing, otherwise there would be no point to compression in the first place. DoubleSpace looks at data in 8K blocks, so the chances of finding repetitive data sequences are much higher than that of a single sentence.

The importance of repeating data sequences raises an important question. What happens when a data sequence does not repeat? This is a very real and common possibility in everyday operation. If a data stream has few repeating elements, it cannot be compressed very well (if at all). For example, a graphic image (such as a screen shot) undergoes a certain amount of compression when the screen pixels are saved to a file. The .PCX file format uses an early form of compression called *run-length encoding* that finds and removes repeating pixels (a much faster and simpler process than looking for repeating pixel sequences). When a compression utility tries to compress that .PCX file, there might be little or no effect on the file because many of the repeating sections have already been replaced with tokens of their own. As a rule, remember that compression is only as good as the data it is compressing. Highly repetitive data will be compressed much better than data with few or no repetitions. Table 20-1 illustrates some typical compression ratios for various file types.

Table 20-1. Typical compression ratios

Executable programs	(.EXE and .COM files)	1.4:1
Word processor documents	(.DOC files)	2.8:1
Spreadsheet files	(.XLS files)	3.3:1
Raw graphic bitmaps	(.BMP files)	4.0:1
Conventional ASCII text	(.TXT or .BAT files)	2.0:1
Sound files	(.WAV files)	1.1:1
Already compressed files	(.ZIP files)	1.0:1 (no subsequent compression)

The compression system

At this point, you can see how compression is implemented on the system. Traditionally, DOS assigns a logical drive letter to each drive (such as drive C: for the first hard drive). When a compression system is installed on a PC, a portion of your drive is compressed into what is known as the *CVF* (compressed volume file). The CVF effectively becomes the compressed drive. It contains all compressed files, and it is treated by DOS as if it were a separate logical drive. The drive that holds the CVF (that is, your original C: drive) is known as the *host drive*. Because the vast majority of the drive will be compressed into the CVF, there will be little space left on the host drive. In actual practice, some files (such as the Windows permanent swap file) must be left uncompressed, so you will normally leave 6Mb to 10Mb uncompressed—the remainder of the drive can be compressed.

Figure 20-1 shows the process for a small 70Mb drive. Suppose your uncompressed drive C: contains 60Mb in files throughout various directories. On a 70Mb drive, this

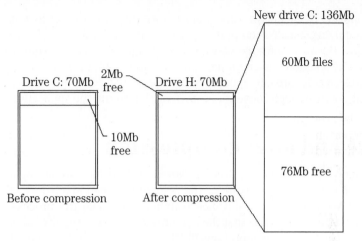

New drive C: 136Mb

60Mb files

Drive C: 70Mb   2Mb   Drive H: 70Mb
                  free

10Mb
free

76Mb free

Before compression   After compression

20-1 A hard disk drive before and after compression.

leaves only 10Mb free for your use. When a compression system is installed, the host drive is renamed to another drive letter (in this case, drive H:) and some small amount of space is kept aside as uncompressed space (for example, 2Mb). The remaining 68Mb of the 70Mb drive undergoes compression and becomes the CVF. Even though the CVF is physically located on the same hard drive, the CVF is assigned its own drive letter (in this case the CVF is "mounted as drive C:"). If you assume an average compression ratio of 2.0:1, the compressed drive C: now has (68Mb × 2.0) 136Mb available. Because the original drive C: had 60Mb in files, those same files are now available in compressed form. Instead of only 10Mb free, the compressed volume now has about 76Mb free. As far as DOS is concerned, any access to drive C: will affect the CVF. Any access to drive H: will affect the uncompressed area. The system boot drive is now drive H:.

If you list the directory for a host drive (using the /ah switch to include archive and hidden files), you will see the three DOS files: IO.SYS, MSDOS.SYS, and COMMAND.COM. If you use Windows, you also might find a fairly large file with a .PAR extension (such as 386SPART.PAR). This is the Windows permanent swap file. There also are several files that are critical for compression. For DoubleSpace, three files are needed. DBLSPACE.000 is the CVF file itself—the heart and soul of compression. Stacker uses the filename STACVOL.DSK. If you were to erase this file, your compressed drive C: would be gone. DBLSPACE.BIN is the DoubleSpace driver that allows DOS access to the CVF. DBLSPACE.INI is the DoubleSpace initialization file containing all of the information needed to configure DoubleSpace.

Factors that affect compression

As a technician, you should understand the factors that influence compression performance: (1) the extra space created, (2) the speed of compression/decompression, and (3) the amount of memory needed to support compression/decompression. Of course, the primary purpose of compression is to provide additional disk space, so that is the principal measure of compression performance. Because compression products add a layer of processing between DOS and the disk, reads and writes will take a bit longer. These delays work to slow down the system—hardly crippling—but it can be annoying. Finally, compression needs memory-resident software to handle compression. Because software consumes conventional memory (often more than 35K), this puts a serious strain on precious system resources. If possible, you should load compressor software into upper memory rather than conventional memory. If not, there might not be enough conventional memory left to run the applications you need.

Before and after compression

Whether you are installing a compression system for yourself or a customer, there are some steps and precautions that should be taken in advance of the actual installation. A few minutes of advance planning can make the process much less painful. First, you must realize that the compression process requires about 1 minute per Mb of space. If you are compressing 60Mb, the process will take about 60 minutes, so even though the process is automated, the system is going to be on your bench for a while. Do yourself a favor and start the installation in the morning. You also will need to decide in advance how you want to arrange the compressed and uncompressed drives on the system. Do you want a single compressed volume? Do you want two or more compressed volumes? How much uncompressed space is required? Hammer this out with your customer. Finally, backup, backup, backup! Don't even consider installing a compression system unless a complete system backup is performed.

Scan the disk

Compression problems can arise if the CVF tries to use sectors on the physical drive that are defective. If this occurs, you will not be able to access the file written in the damaged sector. To ensure that there are no undetected defects in the drive, run a disk scanning utility such as ScanDisk (included with MS-DOS 6.2) or use the scanning functions included with PC Tools or Norton Utilities. Any sectors that check bad will be marked in the FAT and avoided.

Defragment the disk and check free space

Fragmentation is a common and undesirable by-product of DOS file allocation. The clusters that are used to hold a file become scattered around a disk rather than positioned contiguously. When clusters become scattered, the drive has to work much harder to locate and reach each part of the file. Defragmentation rearranges the files on your disk so that the clusters associated with each file are contiguous. You should thoroughly defragment your disk prior to compression. Use DEFRAG (included with MS-DOS 6.0 and 6.2x) or a third-party defragmentation utility such as PC Tools or Norton Utilities. After compressing the disk, check that there is at least 1.5Mb of free space—some free work space is needed in order to perform the compression process.

Run CHKDSK or ScanDisk

It is important to detect any lost clusters or cross-linked files before installing a compression product. Use the DOS CHKDSK utility to find any disk errors. If lost clusters are reported, rerun CHKDSK with the /f (fix) switch to recover the lost clusters. Each lost cluster is recovered as a root directory file with a .CHK extension. You can then simply delete all .CHK files before continuing. If cross-linked files are indicated, note the names of those cross-linked files. Copy those files to new files and delete the originals—this should clear the cross-link conditions, but one or both of those files are now likely to be defective, so restore all cross-linked files from the system backup. If you have MS-DOS 6.2 available, you can use fix disk errors using ScanDisk instead of CHKDSK.

Check the memory

Keep in mind that a compression package will need to run a TSR or device driver to achieve on-the-fly operation. This compression utility should be loaded into the upper memory area (if possible). Otherwise, it will consume precious conventional memory that might prevent other memory-hungry DOS applications from running. Use the MEM function and look at the report for the "largest free upper memory block." If that number is larger than 45K, chances are good that you can load the utility into the UMA during system initialization. If there is little or no upper memory free, you will have to free sufficient memory by removing other drivers or TSRs, or seriously consider the impact of leaving the compression utility in conventional memory (this is highly undesirable).

Initiate compression

If everything looks good up to now, you can go ahead and begin installation of the compression product. Both DoubleSpace and Stacker can be started very simply, and the installation process for each is very automated. For specific installation and operation information, you should refer to the detailed instructions that accompany each product.

Creating a bootable disk

As discussed in Chapter 25, hard disks do fail for a variety of reasons. Now that your drive is compressed, you will need to create bootable disks that are "compression-aware." You could certainly boot the system from a conventional boot disk, but you would be unable to access your compressed drive(s). Fortunately, creating a compression-compatible boot disk is a simple matter.

For DoubleSpace
1. Format a blank floppy disk using the /s switch (for example, FORMAT /s). For DOS 6.0 and later, DBLSPACE.BIN will be copied along with IO.SYS, MSDOS.SYS, and COMMAND.COM.
2. Copy CONFIG.SYS to the floppy (for example, COPY CONFIG.SYS A:).
3. Copy AUTOEXEC.BAT to the floppy (COPY AUTOEXEC.BAT A:).
4. Copy needed files referenced by CONFIG.SYS and AUTOEXEC.BAT, such as HIMEM.SYS, EMM386.EXE, MOUSE.COM, MSCDEX.EXE, and so on. Check the startup files to find exactly what files are needed. You might have to edit CONFIG.SYS and AUTOEXEC.BAT to change the file paths to the floppy disk.
5. Copy other important DOS utilities such as FDISK.EXE, FORMAT.COM, CHKDSK.EXE, DBLSPACE.EXE, and MEM.EXE.

For Stacker

1. Format a blank floppy disk using the /s switch (FORMAT /s).
2. Copy CONFIG.SYS to the floppy (COPY CONFIG.SYS A:).
3. Copy AUTOEXEC.BAT to the floppy (COPY AUTOEXEC.BAT A:).
4. Copy needed files referenced by CONFIG.SYS and AUTOEXEC.BAT such as HIMEM.SYS, EMM386.EXE, MOUSE.COM, MSCDEX.EXE, and so on. Check the startup files to find exactly what files are needed. You might have to edit CONFIG.SYS and AUTOEXEC.BAT to change the file paths to the floppy disk.
5. Copy other important DOS utilities such as FDISK.EXE, FORMAT.COM, CHKDSK.EXE, STACKER.EXE, and MEM.EXE.

Test the boot disk and see that there are no errors during initialization. You also should have access to the compressed disks.

Troubleshooting compressed drives

Disk compression products are some of the most thoroughly tested and robust computer programs ever released. They have to be; programs that trash a customer's vital data don't last long in the marketplace. However, the bewildering assortment of PC setups and utilities now in service will result in incompatibilities or disk errors somewhere along the line. This part of the chapter takes you through a selection of symptoms and solutions for Stacker and DoubleSpace. Keep in mind that a complete system backup should be made (if possible) *before* attempting to deal with compression problems.

Stacker

Symptom 1. You see an error message indicating "Lost Sector Groups" You will typically see this error when running the Stacker CHECK utility. This is not nearly as ominous as it might sound—data has not yet been lost or corrupted. A lost sector group can occur on a Stacker drive when data is written to a cluster, but the cluster has not been allocated to a file. Once the operating system does allocate the cluster to a file, the error goes away. In most cases, CHECK will report a lost sector group when a file is extended and truncated without the operating system updating the FAT. For the most part, you can leave lost sector groups alone. If you want to clear any such groups, however, run SDEFRAG or select the Stacker Optimizer in the Stacker Toolbox. You can select Full Optimize, Quick Optimize, or Restack, and any of these choices will completely clear lost sector groups.

Symptom 2. You see the error message: "SIZE MISMATCH, EXISTING INSTALLATION" This kind of error can result if the STACKVOL.DSK file were corrupted or destroyed (either by a hardware disk fault or software error). When Stacker initializes, it verifies the STACVOL.DSK (the CVF) file *before* mounting a compressed drive. If the size of the STACVOL.DSK file is incorrect, Stacker pauses the normal startup of your computer with this message until the problem is corrected:

E: = C:STACVOL.DSK (Size mismatch) (Write protected)
Press any key to continue...

The solution for this type of fault is rather involved, and you will require the RE-PAIR.EXE utility included with your Stacker disks (or available from the Stac BBS). Note the compressed and uncompressed volume letters. For this example, the compressed volume is C:, and the host drive (containing STACVOL.DSK) is E:. Next, unmount the Stacker drive by typing STACKER -d where d is the compressed drive (C:). Run a disk repair utility such as CHKDSK or ScanDisk on the host drive (E:). As the disk utility runs, it will ask if you want to save lost chains as files—do not! *Remember, you should not save new files to the disk while this recovery procedure is in progress.* If the disk utility indicates that STACVOL is cross-linked with other files, delete the other files and run the disk utility again until the STACVOL file checks clean.

At this point, insert the floppy disk containing REPAIR.EXE and switch to the floppy drive (if REPAIR.EXE is in a floppy subdirectory, switch to that subdirectory as well). Run the REPAIR utility using the syntax: REPAIR /=U d:\STACVOL.XXX where d:\STACVOL.XXX is the uncompressed drive letter and STACVOL filename you determined in a previous step. For example:

```
REPAIR /=U E:\STACVOL.DSK<Enter>
```

You will see a series of messages as the REPAIR.EXE executes. If the repair process is successful, you will have to remove the REPAIR floppy and reboot the machine for changes to take effect. You should now have access to the compressed volume again.

Symptom 3. You see an error message such as "The drive is too fragmented" You might encounter this kind of message when attempting to upgrade Stacker from a previous version. Abort the upgrade procedure and use the Stacker Optimizer to defragment the drive. You can then rerun the upgrade installation.

If the upgrade process introduces additional fragmentation, the upgrade process might fail again. In that event, you can update the Stacker drive manually. Perform a quick optimization by typing: SDEFRAG /Q and continue with the procedure even if the drive reports fragmentation. After optimization, type STACKER and locate the line referring to the drive that failed to update. For example, you might see a line such as:

Drive C was drive C at boot time [D:\STACVOL.DSK = 115.3Mb]

Take note of the drive letter inside the brackets (for example, D:). Next, start the manual conversion:

```
HCONVERT drive:\STACVOL.DSK /C
```

where `drive:` is the host drive letter (for example, D:). Once the drive is updated, run the Stacker Optimizer again to take full advantage of Stacker 4.0 compression.

Symptom 4. The Stacker drive does not update or HCONVERT hangs up The upgrade to Stacker 4.0 should yield a noticeable gain in drive space over previous versions. If you do not notice an improvement, the update process might not have been successful. There might be situations where you do not receive warnings about excessive fragmentation, yet the disk might be too fragmented to sustain an update. The first step here is to determine if the drive has indeed been updated. Switch to the Stacker directory and type SYSINFO to find information concerning your system. Find the area detailing the system's physical drives—the second column of information is labeled "version." Stacker drives will have a version number listed in this column.

A version of 3.0 (or earlier) indicates that the Stacker drive has not been updated. A version of 5.0 indicates that the Stacker drive has been updated, but not recompressed to gain additional space. If this is the case, leave the system information screen and start the Stacker Toolbox. Select Optimize, then Full-MaxSpace. This should recompress the drive to provide additional space. A version of 5.01 indicates that the drive has been updated and recompressed.

When the disk has not been updated, switch to the Stacker directory and type STACKER. You will see a profile of your Stacker drive(s). For example:

Drive C was drive C at boot time [D:\STACVOL.DSK = 112.3Mb]

This shows drive C: is the Stacker drive and drive D: is the uncompressed drive. Run CHKDSK against the host drive. If errors are reported, run CHKDSK /f to correct the errors. Now, defragment the drive using SDEFRAG /Q *drive:* where *drive:* is the Stacker drive (for example, C:). Once the drive is defragmented, update the drive immediately (do not perform any other write operations). Unmount the Stacker drive by typing STACKER -*drive:* where *drive:* is the Stacker drive (C:). Next, type:

```
HCONVERT /C drive:\STACVOL.XXX<Enter>
```

where *drive:* is the host drive (D:) and *.XXX* is the STACVOL extension (.DSK). Remove any floppy disks and reboot the PC for changes to take effect. Finally, recompress the drive by entering the Stacker Toolbox, select Optimize, then select Full-MaxSpace.

Symptom 5. You see a "Setup Error #2002" message This error occurs when a floppy drive writes information to the Stacker installation disk improperly. This might be due to improper floppy drive alignment or floppy drive damage, but chances are that the vital Stacker files on the floppy disk(s) are already corrupted. This is why software manufacturers tell you to make a backup copy of the product, and install from the backup copy. By formatting and copying backup disks on your PC, you compensate for any mild alignment problems. It might not be a bad idea to clean the floppy drive heads. When alignment problems persist, replace the floppy drive. If you have not made a backup copy of your Stacker installation disks, call Stac Electronics for a new set of disks. When the new disks arrive, create a backup set and write-protect the master disks.

Symptom 6. After converting a DoubleSpace or SuperStor /DS drive to Stacker, there is no additional space detected In some cases, drive space will not increase after moving to Stacker 4.0—usually when you are near the DOS limit for a drive. DOS limits refer to the size of clusters on a drive. For example, a 512Mb drive uses 8K clusters, a 1Gb drive usually employs 16K clusters, and a 2Gb drive offers 32K clusters. However, the following techniques might draw additional space from a converted drive.

Start by recompressing the drive after Stacker is installed. Open the Stacker Toolbox, select Optimize, and select Full-MaxSpace. When the drive is recompressed, check the space available on the drive and write it down. Next, uncompress the drive and rerun Stacker Setup. This step allows Stacker to select the optimum cluster size for the drive. As an alternative to removing and re-installing Stacker, try to shrink—then grow—the Stacker drive size. This will not set a new cluster size, but might gain additional space. Keep in mind that you might not have much latitude to change the STACVOL file size if the compressed drive is quite full already.

Symptom 7. When using the Stacker CHECK utility, you see an error message indicating that the file allocation tables are not identical Normally, a hard drive maintains two copies of the file allocation table (FAT) in the event of just such an emergency. This is a potentially disastrous fault for your hard drive, and you must carefully choose which copy of the FAT to use when repairing the problem. After this initial warning, CHECK will run a second integrity check using the alternate copy of the FAT. After CHECK completes its second examination, you will be presented with three choices: (1) exit and try using the first FAT, (2) exit and try using the second FAT, or (3) copy the first FAT over the second FAT and let CHECK repair any errors. *Keep in mind that the FAT currently being tested is considered the first FAT.* The objective here is to make sure that the first (the currently tested) FAT is the error-free version. You can then copy that error-free FAT to the second FAT and repair the damage. Here is a procedure that will help you.

Select option 1. This will return you to DOS (if you started CHECK from DOS). If you started CHECK from the Stacker Toolbox in Windows, leave Windows and return to the DOS prompt. Run CHECK again, and pay close attention to whether the errors are reported running the first FAT or the second FAT. If the errors are on the first FAT, end CHECK using menu option 2 (exit and try using the second FAT). If the errors are on the second FAT, end CHECK using menu option 1 (exit and try using the first FAT). At the DOS command line, run CHECK /f to fix the disk. When presented with the menu options again, select option 3 (copy the first FAT over the second FAT and let CHECK repair the drive).

Symptom 8. You encounter SDEFRAG errors 109/110, 120, or 170 A media error has been detected on the disk during the defragmentation process. The 109/110 or 170 errors indicate that SDEFRAG is unable to read, write, or verify a physical cluster on the disk—often the result of a media problem. The 120 error indicates that SDEFRAG is unable to decompress a physical cluster. Either the media is damaged, or the cluster is corrupted. In either case, you are faced with a serious defect. If a physical disk flaw is crippling your Stacker drive, a disk repair utility can be used to detect and repair the fault. Physical disk utilities can be found in packages such as Norton Utilities, PC Tools, and SpinRite.

Start by locating a file attribute utility such as ATTRIB. Type STACKER and locate the drive reference line. It should look something like this:

```
Drive C was drive C at boot time [ E:\STACVOL.DSK =
173.5Mb]
```

The drive letter in brackets is the host drive. The drive outside of brackets is the compressed drive. Go to the DOS subdirectory on your uncompressed drive (or wherever ATTRIB is located). Next, reboot the system with a *clean* boot disk—*do not load any device drivers at all.* At the A: prompt, switch to the DOS subdirectory on the host drive and use ATTRIB to unhide STACVOL.DSK. A typical command is:

```
attrib -s -h -r drive:\STACVOL.* <Enter>
```

where *drive:* is the drive letter you are repairing (for example, E:). Now that STACVOL is readily available as an ordinary file, run the surface scan on the drive. Be sure to run the surface scan utility from a floppy drive. Use the most rigorous test pattern available, and allow the utility to repair any defective areas. Keep in mind that such a thorough scan might take up to several hours depending on the size and speed of the drive. After repairs are complete, remove the floppy disk and reboot the PC.

Now, run CHECK /f and allow it to perform a surface check. If CHECK detects any errors and asks you to delete damaged files, respond YES, and be sure to follow any on-screen instructions that CHECK provides. You are now ready to run SDE-FRAG again. If the error code(s) persist, you will need to invoke the special diagnostic mode in CHECK /f as shown in the following paragraph.

For this procedure, you will need to modify your floppy boot disk to disable all device drivers except for STACKER.COM and SWAP.COM. Use REM statements to remark-out all other device drivers in the CONFIG.SYS file as shown in Table 20-2. After you complete these modifications, reboot the computer and run CHECK /f. When asked to perform a surface scan test, answer YES. If CHECK detects errors and prompts you to delete damaged files, answer YES, and follow any further instructions provided by CHECK. After CHECK is complete, run SDEFRAG /r again. If SDEFRAG executes without errors, the system is fully optimized, and you can reboot the system from its original configuration files. Otherwise, switch the PC to a slower speed and try running SDEFRAG again.

**Table 20-2. Disabling
all device drivers except for
STACKER.COM and SWAP.COM**

```
REM device=c:\dos\himem.sys
REM device=c:\dos\emm386.exe noems
REM dos=high,umb
buffers=20
files=30
lastdrive=e
REM devicehigh=c:\mouse\mouse.sys /c1
REM devicehigh=c:\dos\smartdrv.sys 1024
devicehigh=c:\stacker\stacker.com
device=c:\stacker\sswap.com
```

Symptom 9. You encounter an SDEFRAG/OPTIMIZER error 101 This error indicates that your system does not have enough memory to run the SDE-FRAG utility. Increase the conventional memory available to your system (or reduce SDEFRAG's memory requirements). Typical memory requirements depend on cluster size:

4K clusters=503K SDEFRAG
8K clusters=534K SDEFRAG
16K clusters=560K SDEFRAG
32K clusters=642K SDEFRAG

To run SDEFRAG, you must increase the amount of conventional memory available, or reduce the memory requirement. If you have access to a memory management tool such as QEMM, 386MAX, NETROOM, or MemMaker, running such a manager will often increase the available conventional memory and allow SDEFRAG to run successfully. If you cannot use any of these tools, use a boot disk and edit its CONFIG.SYS or AUTOEXEC.BAT file to disable various device drivers and TSRs. This will leave more conventional memory space. Remember, do NOT disable your memory managers or Stacker command lines. If problems persist, try running SDEFRAG with its /buffer=# switch, where # is a value between 256 and 4096. Larger numbers save more memory.

SDEFRAG /buffer=3072=21K of conventional memory saved
SDEFRAG /buffer=2048=42K of conventional memory saved
SDEFRAG /buffer=256=78K of conventional memory saved

Some final notes. If you receive these error messages while trying to grow or shrink the Stacker drive, run the Optimizer as: SDEFRAG /buffer=*nnn* /GP where *nnn* is the memory number. If the errors occur when trying to change the *ECR* (expected compression ratio), run the Optimizer as: SDEFRAG /buffer=*nnn* /GL where *nnn* is the memory number.

Symptom 10: While running the Stacker CHECK utility, you see an error indicating "not enough disk space to save header" The header of a STACVOL file contains control information about how and where data is stored, and information relating to the data area in which all of the drive's compressed data is stored. A copy of the STACVOL header is saved every time CHECK is run. If the STACVOL header is damaged, it can be repaired by using the saved copy. CHECK runs automatically each time the system is started. If there is not enough space on the host drive to save the header, you will see an error message similar to: "not enough disk space to save header."

Start by determining the host drive letter. Type STACKER and find the information line similar to the one that follows:

```
Drive D was drive D at boot time [F:\STACVOL.DSK =
123.4Mb]
```

The drive letter within brackets (for example, F:) is the host drive, and the drive outside of the bracket (for example, D:) is the compressed drive. Also, take note of the STACVOL file extension. Next, find the space needed to store the STACVOL file by switching to the host drive. Take a directory of the drive and note the free space available. Type DIR /AH to display all hidden or archive files on the drive, then note the size of the STACVOL file. You should expect the header size to approximate the sizes shown in Table 20-3.

Table 20-3. Typical STACVOL header sizes

For a compressed drive of:	Expect a header size of about:
50Mb	94Kb
120Mb	108Kb
200Mb	171Kb
500Mb	207Kb
1000Mb	396Kb

Now that you know approximately the amount of space needed for the header, you can make extra uncompressed space available. Type SDEFRAG /GP, select the host drive, then select the *More Uncompressed Space Available* option. After the drive is defragmented, you will be allowed to enter the desired amount uncompressed space in kilobytes. Add 50K to the anticipated amount of space needed for a header and enter that value. Select the *Perform changes on Stacker drive* option, and restart the system to allow your changes to take effect. You should now have enough space to store the STACVOL header.

Symptom 11. The uncompress process fails. UNCOMP.EXE is used to uncompress a Stacker drive Before uncompressing the drive, SDEFRAG is invoked to defragment the drive. If UNCOMP fails, you will have to determine where the fault occurred, find the specific error message (if possible), and correct the error. First, find where the error occurred. When UNCOMP is running, "UNCOMP" is shown in a title bar at the top of the screen. When SDEFRAG is running, "Stacker Optimizer" is shown in the title bar. Note which title is shown when the error occurs. Next, denote any SDEFRAG error message. If the process fails without any error message (for example, the system freezes or drops back to DOS unexpectedly), note what was happening before the fault. Please read the following procedures carefully before proceeding.

For UNCOMP problems

If UNCOMP drops back to DOS without uncompressing the Stacker drive, download an updated UNCOMP tool: UNCMP4.EXE from the Stac BBS, America On-Line, or CompuServe. Place the file in a temporary subdirectory and run it. UNCMP4.EXE is a self-extracting file that will make other files available in your subdirectory. Copy the newly generated files UNCOMP2.EXE and SDEFRAG2.EXE to the STACKER subdirectory, then run UNCOMP again.

If UNCOMP hangs up while uncompressing files, you will probably have to reboot your system to get control. On reboot, you will likely see the error *Size Mismatch—Write Protected* (similar to Symptom 2). The Stacker drive is partially uncompressed, and is no longer the size indicated by the header. A write-protect function prevents any further damage. Try running UNCOMP again—in some cases, UNCOMP might start where it left off and begin uncompressing the drive normally. If problems continue, locate and unhide the STACVOL file, unfragment the drive, and run UNCOMP again. This can be accomplished by typing STACKER and noting the drive letter and file name in brackets (for example, *D:\STACVOL.DSK*). Use the DOS ATTRIB utility to unhide the STACVOL file (for example, ATTRIB -S -H -R D:\STACVOL.DSK). From a floppy disk, defragment the host drive (for example, D:) using a defragmenter such as Norton Speedisk or MS-DOS DEFRAG. Be sure to do a full optimization. Then, run UNCOMP from a floppy disk.

If UNCOMP still fails, check the available (uncompressed) space on the host drive. If there is sufficient uncompressed space to hold the remaining Stacker files, copy (or XCOPY) the files from the Stacker drive to the uncompressed drive, or floppy disks, then remove the Stacker drive using the REMOVDRV function. Note that REMOVDRV deletes all data on the Stacker drive, so make sure you recover any necessary files before deleting the Stacker drive. One way or another, you should be able to recover your vital files prior to deleting the Stacker drive.

If you see an error message indicating "Drive x: is not a Stacker Drive," type STACKER to find the drive descriptions (Stac calls this a *drive map*), and it appears similar to:

Drive C was drive C at boot time [D:\STACVOL.DSK=123.4Mb]

Remember that the drive letter within the brackets is the *host* drive, and the drive letter outside of the brackets is the *Stacker* drive. If you inadvertently tried to UNCOMP the host drive, the process certainly will not work.

If you see a message indicating that "The Stacker drive x: contains more data then will fit on the host drive. You must delete about nnn Kbytes before uncompressing," there is more data on the compressed drive than will fit on the physical drive when it is uncompressed. Your only real option here is to back up and delete enough files so that the remainder will fit on the drive when uncompressed. After you off-load or back up a sufficient number of files, run UNCOMP again.

If you see an error message such as "There is insufficient free space on the uncompressed drive x: to uncompress the drive. You must free up at least nnn Kbytes on the uncompressed drive, or about twice that amount on the Stacker drive, and re-run UNCOMP," there is not enough working space on the host drive to uncompress the Stacker drive. Try backing up and deleting the prescribed amount of space—that might clear the problem. Otherwise, type SDEFRAG /GP at the DOS prompt, and select the *More uncompressed Space Available* option. This will defragment the drive and ask how much space you wish to uncompress. Enter a number larger than the prescribed amount and allow the changes to be made. Restart the system and run UNCOMP.

If you see an error message such as "There are errors on the Stacker Drive. Please run CHKDSK or another disk repair utility before uncompressing," there are lost clusters or cross-linked files on the Stacker drive. Run CHKDSK to determine the nature of any errors. Run CHKDSK /f to fix lost clusters. You also might run disk repair utilities such as Norton Disk Doctor or PC Tools DiskFix. When the disk errors are corrected, try running UNCOMP again.

For SDEFRAG problems

If you see *SDEFRAG Error 101*, refer to Symptom 9. If you see *SDEFRAG Error 109/110, 120, or 170*, refer to Symptom 8. If you see an *SDEFRAG Error 157: Internal Error*, you might need updated files from the Stac BBS, America On-line, or CompuServe. Download UNCMP4.EXE into a temporary subdirectory and run it. It will self-extract into several new files. Copy the new files UNCOMP2.EXE and SDEFRAG2.EXE into the Stacker subdirectory, and run UNCOMP again.

Symptom 12. You see the error message "Not a Stacker STACVOL file—NOT MOUNTED" or "Invalid # reserved sectors—NOT MOUNTED" Each Stacker drive is a STACVOL file stored on the uncompressed drive. Each STACVOL file includes a header that contains information on how and where data is stored, and the actual compressed data. Either of the error messages listed above indicate that the STACVOL header is damaged or corrupt. Fortunately, a copy of the header is saved for each Stacker drive, and can be used to restore a damaged header. Each time the PC starts, CHECK /WP saves the header as STACSAVQ.nnn. When you start Windows or use the CHECK utility yourself, the header is saved as STACSAVE.nnn.

Start by determining which of these saved headers is newest. *Warning: Do not follow this procedure if you have just run SDEFRAG without running CHECK or restarting your PC.*

Start your PC (from a bootable floppy if necessary) and switch to the root directory of the uncompressed drive and type: DIR STACSAV*.* /AH to see the hidden header file(s). Note the save file with the latest date and time. Now, restore the header. Type DIR /AH to see a directory including all hidden files, and note the STACVOL extension (for example, .DSK). Use the ATTRIB function to unhide the STACVOL file. Type ATTRIB -S -H -R *drive:*\STACVOL.*xxx* where *drive:* is the drive letter containing STACVOL, and *.xxx* is the STACVOL extension. Insert a disk containing the REPAIR.EXE utility. If the newest backup header is a STACSAVE file, type REPAIR /F *drive:*\STACVOL.*xxx* where *drive:* is drive containing STACVOL, and *.xxx* is the proper STACVOL extension. If the newest backup header is a STACSAVQ file, type REPAIR /F *drive:*\STACVOL.*xxx* /Q where *drive:* is drive containing STACVOL, and *.xxx* is the proper STACVOL extension. Then, remove all disks from the system and restart the computer.

Symptom 13. You see an error message similar to "CHECK I/O Access Denied: Error 27" You have corrupt data in the drive's FAT. Such errors might be due to bad sectors on the physical drive itself, a faulty program or virus that overwrote the FAT, or a program that incorrectly uses EMS (expanded memory). You will have to determine which areas of the hard drive have been damaged, then correct the damaged areas. Boot the system from a clean floppy drive to disable all device drivers and unhide the STACVOL file using the ATTRIB function. Look at the CONFIG.SYS file. If you see a command line that appears similar to: DEVICE=C:\STACKER\STACKER.COM then Stacker does not preload. Otherwise, you have a preloading version of Stacker.

For preloading versions of Stacker, type STACKER and note the drive map (for example, *Drive C was drive C at boot time [D:\STACVOL.DSK = 123.4Mb]*). You need to know the drive letter and STACVOL extension in the brackets. Restart the PC and press F% when MS-DOS starts. When presented with a command line prompt, unhide the STACVOL file (for example, ATTRIB -S -H -R drive:\STACVOL .*xxx* where *drive:* is the drive letter containing STACVOL, and *.xxx* is the STACVOL extension). Change to the Stacker subdirectory and type STACKER -*drive:* where *drive:* is the letter of the compressed drive.

If Stacker does not preload, type STACKER and note the drive map (for example, *Drive C was drive C at boot time [D:\STACVOL.DSK = 123.4Mb]*). You need to know the drive letter and STACVOL extension in the brackets. Change to the DOS subdirectory and copy ATTRIB to an uncompressed directory. Clean-boot the system to disable all device drivers, switch to the host drive and subdirectory containing ATTRIB, then unhide the STACVOL file (for example, ATTRIB -S -H -R *drive:* \STACVOL.*xxx* where *drive:* is the drive letter containing STACVOL, and *.xxx* is the STACVOL extension).

Now that the disk and STACVOL file have been prepared, run a disk repair utility such as Norton Utilities, PC Tools DiskFix, or Gibson Research SpinRite to detect and correct damaged disk areas. *Be sure to run any such utility from a floppy disk.* Run a vigorous test (this might take a few hours), and allow the utility to fix any defective areas. When the test is complete, remove any floppy disks and restart the computer. Run CHECK /f to perform a Stacker check of the drive. When no errors are reported, the drive is fixed, and normal use can resume. If problems persist, there are three procedures that might allow you to access the damaged drive before having to start from scratch.

First, try removing write protection on the drive by typing CHECK /=W x: where *x:* is the compressed drive. *Warning: you must complete this entire procedure before resuming use of the drive.* Now, run CHECK /f again, and follow the instructions to repair the drive. When asked to perform a surface test, answer YES and delete any damaged files. When CHECK reports no more errors, the drive should be repaired.

If problems persist, the drive's FAT might be damaged, so try removing the /EMS parameter in the STACKER.INI file. Some programs that use EMS do so improperly, and this can damage a FAT. Further corruption can be prevented by disabling Stacker's use of EMS. Type ED /l and look for an entry similar to */EMS*. Delete the line and press CTRL+Z to save the file and exit. Then restart the system and run CHECK /f to finish the repairs.

If errors continue, there is one last card you can play—try restoring a backup copy of the STACVOL header. If the STACVOL header is error-free, restoring it to the STACVOL file might correct a FAT error. Unhide the STACVOL file as you saw earlier in this procedure. Insert a floppy disk containing **REPAIR.EXE**, switch to that drive, and type REPAIR /F *drive:*\STACVOL.*xxx* where *drive:* and *.xxx* are the drive and extension you used when unhiding STACVOL. Allow REPAIR to replace the STACVOL file header. Restart the system and run CHECK /f to see if the damage was repaired. If the problem persists, the FAT might be damaged beyond repair. You might have to repartition and reformat the drive, then re-install the compression package and restore the most recent system backup. (There is a backup, isn't there?)

DoubleSpace

Symptom 1. You see an "A CVF is damaged" error message when the system starts The *CVF* (compressed volume file) is a single file that contains all of the compressed drive's data that is accessed as a unique logical drive. In effect, the CVF is the compressed drive. The physical hard drive that contains the CVF is the host drive. Under most circumstances, the CVF occupies most of the host drive except for some area that should not be compressed (such as a Windows permanent swap file).

When DoubleSpace activates on system startup, it performs a check on the CVF's internal data structures that is equivalent of a DOS CHKDSK. If DoubleSpace detects an error such as lost allocation units or cross-linked files, the *CVF is damaged* error message appears. The way to correct this type of problem is to run a correction utility. DOS 6.2 offers the ScanDisk utility, but DOS 6.0 and earlier versions of DOS provide you with CHKDSK. Once the disk is corrected, DoubleSpace should work correctly.

Symptom 2. An application does not work once DoubleSpace is installed Most DOS and Windows applications should work just fine with DoubleSpace, but with the proliferation of complex software in the marketplace today, there might be some applications that are copy protected, or do not perform well from the compressed state. If such a situation occurs, try moving the application to the uncompressed host drive (or reinstalling it to the uncompressed drive outright). To fit your application into uncompressed space, you might have to resize the CVF to free additional space on the host drive. You can resize the CVF through the DBLSPACE control panel, or directly from the DOS command line. For example:

```
C:\> dblspace /size /reserve=3
```

will change the CVF size so that there are 3Mb free on the host drive.

It also might be that the application needs an unusually large amount of conventional memory. Because DBLSPACE.BIN needs about 33K of memory, try loading DBLSPACE.BIN into upper memory by changing the command line in CONFIG.SYS to:

```
devicehigh = c:\dos\dblspace.bin /move
```

Symptom 3. You see a DoubleGuard alert DoubleGuard is a DOS 6.2 utility that helps protect DoubleSpace from memory conflicts that otherwise might corrupt data on the CVF. If DoubleGuard detects a checksum error in the memory used by DoubleSpace, a rogue program or device driver has probably written in the DoubleSpace memory area. When an error is detected by DoubleGuard, the system simply halts before damage can occur (you'll have to reboot the computer to continue).

Boot the system clean (with no device drivers), then use ScanDisk or CHKDSK to deal with any potential errors on the hard disk. Re-activate one device driver at a time until you can re-create the error. When you find the offending device driver, you can keep it unloaded, or find a way to load it without conflict.

Symptom 4. Free space is exhausted on a compressed drive One of the problems with DoubleSpace is that it is difficult to know how much space there is available. Because different files compress differently, there is no way to be *absolutely* sure just how much space you have to work with. Available disk space must be "predicted" using a compression ratio that you set. By adjusting the predicted compression ratio, you can adjust the amount of reported free space. As a result, MS- DOS can "lie." If you seem to be running low on space, try changing the compression ratio from the DOS command line such as:

```
C:\> dblspace /ratio=2.5
```

Ideally, you want to set the compression ratio as close as possible to the actual compression ratio—this will yield the most accurate prediction of available space. If you are unable to change your drive's compression ratio, it might be time to defragment the drive. DoubleSpace has trouble making use of highly fragmented drives for file storage. If you are having trouble with drive space, try defragmenting the drive with DOS DEFRAG or another defragmentation utility.

If the drive really is out of space, you can increase the size of the CVF by taking space from the uncompressed host (if there is any more uncompressed space available). From the DOS command line, start DBLSPACE and use the Change Size function to alter the compressed volume size. You also can adjust the volume size directly from the command line. For example:

```
C:\> dblspace /size /reserve=1.5
```

This command will change the compressed drive size leaving 1.5Mb of uncompressed space on the host drive. If you need to free space on the host drive so that you can increase the size of the CVF, try deleting unneeded files from the uncompressed host drive.

Symptom 5. Free space is exhausted on the host drive Under normal use, there will be little free space reserved for the host drive anyway—the greatest space advantage with DoubleSpace will be realized when the maximum amount of host drive space is compressed. Only Windows swap files and incompressible applications will reside outside of the CVF. However, there will be occasions when it becomes necessary to place data on the uncompressed drive. Eventually, the host might run out of space. If the files listed in the host directory do not seem large enough to exhaust the space, there might be some hidden files on the host drive. Perform a DIR /AH to list all files including archive and hidden files. The easiest way to correct this problem is to resize the CVF to reserve more free space for the host drive. This can be done from the DBLSPACE control panel or directly from the DOS command line with a command such as:

```
C:\> dblspace /size /reserve=4
```

That would resize the CVF to keep 4Mb of uncompressed space on the host drive. Of course, there must be enough free space on the CVF to be freed to the host drive. If the CVF is very full, or is highly fragmented, it might not be possible to resize the CVF. See Symptom 7.

Symptom 6. Estimated compression ratio cannot be changed You might be setting the estimated compression ratio too high. Keep in mind that the amount of free space reported for the CVF is only an estimate based on the compression ratio that you set in DoubleSpace. If you make the estimated compression ratio larger, more free space is reported, and vice versa. However, DoubleSpace can only work with compressed drive sizes up to 512Mb. Consider the following example.

Assume you have a compressed drive with 300Mb of files and 100Mb of true (uncompressed) free space. A compression ratio of 2:1 would cause this 100Mb to be reported as 200Mb. The 200Mb estimated free space plus the 300Mb of used space results in total CVF drive space of (300Mb + 200Mb) 500Mb. If you try adjusting the estimated compression ratio to 2.5:1, that 100Mb of true free drive space would be reported as 250Mb. Because 300Mb and 250Mb add to more than 512Mb, an error will be produced. Keep the compression ratio down so that the total CVF drive space does not exceed 512Mb.

Symptom 7. Compressed drive size cannot be reduced DoubleSpace is extremely sensitive to file fragmentation because of the way in which disk space is assigned. As a result, it is important to defragment the CVF regularly in order to keep your compressed drive's performance at an optimum level. You can use DEFRAG or other defragmentation utilities to defragment the drive.

There also might be other factors that contribute to fragmentation warnings that prevent reducing the CVF size. A delete-tracking program such as MIRROR might be saving its MIRORSAV.FIL file at the end of the drive volume—this creates immediate fragmentation of the drive because the file skips all free space to the very end of the volume. The Norton Utilities delete-tracking program IMAGE creates the same problem by saving its IMAGE.IDX file at the end of the CVF. Thus, DoubleSpace cannot reduce the size of the CVF because the tracking file now occupies the highest sectors. Your best tactic here is to disable the delete-tracking utility in CONFIG.SYS or AUTOEXEC.BAT, change the tracking file's attributes with the DOS ATTRIB function, erase the tracking file, and defragment the drive.

(for files created by MIRROR) C:\> attrib mirorsav.fil -s -h -r

(for files created by IMAGE) C:\> attrib image.idx -s -h -r

You should then be able to resize the CVF without problems. It also might be impossible to reduce the size of your CVF because a FAT entry for the CVF indicates that an allocation unit is unreadable (including a "bad allocation unit") entry. The CVF can only be reduced to the point at which the bad entry occurs. If you suspect a problem with a bad cluster, it is possible to use a disk editor such as The Norton Utilities or *PC Tools* to change the FAT entry from bad (FFF7h) to unused (0h). Be sure to *use extreme caution* if you choose to use a disk editor. You can corrupt the entire disk by making erroneous changes to the FAT.

Symptom 8. DEFRAG fails to fully defragment the drive DoubleSpace reports that the drive is still fragmented even after performing a full defragmentation procedure. This type of symptom is another manifestation of hidden system delete-tracking files generated by utilities such as IMAGE or MIRROR. You can see the file by performing a DIR /AH. Because both utilities place hidden system files at the end of the drive volume, DEFRAG cannot move the file. You can delete the offending file,

(for files created by MIRROR) C:\> deltree mirorsav.fil

(for files created by IMAGE) C:\> deltree image.idx

Then disable the delete-tracking utility from your AUTOEXEC.BAT or CONFIG.SYS files. You also can change the attributes of the offending file that will allow DEFRAG to move the file appropriately during the defragmentation process.

(for files created by MIRROR) C:\> attrib mirorsav.fil -s -h -r

(for files created by IMAGE) C:\> attrib image.idx -s -h -r

Symptom 9. You see a "Swap File is Corrupt" error message when starting Windows Unless your PC is packed with more than 16Mb of RAM, Windows will need supplemental storage space to support the various applications that are loaded and run during normal operation. The hard drive is used to provide this supplemental space in the form of *virtual memory*—that is, an area of the hard drive is used to hold the contents of RAM. This virtual area is known as the *swap file*. Although you have the choice between a permanent and temporary swap file, most installations of Windows use a *PSF* (permanent swap file). Unfortunately, Windows does not support a compressed permanent swap file under DoubleSpace. If you compress your drive and include the Windows PSF, the swap file will be reported as corrupt when you try to start Windows. You will need to re-create a PSF on the host (uncompressed) drive.

Start the Control Panel from the Program Manager's Main group. Double-click on the 386 Enhanced icon to open the 386 Enhanced dialog box, then click on the Virtual Memory button to access the Virtual Memory dialog box. Click on the Change button. Choose an uncompressed drive (usually the host drive) by selecting the drive from the Drive pull-down list. Choose the Permanent file type from the Type pull-down list. Enter the desired size for the new PSF in the New Size box (Windows will suggest a default size based on the amount of memory and disk space available). You can select the default or enter a new value. Select OK to initiate the new PSF.

Symptom 10. You cannot access compressed drive(s) after booting from a system disk created by the Windows File Manager The DoubleSpace utility has not been copied to the floppy. The Windows File Manager allows you to create bootable floppy disks. However, Windows will not copy the vital DBLSPACE.BIN file to the floppy (although the FORMAT /s command under DOS 6.0 and 6.2 will). If you make a bootable disk from Windows, you will have to complete the process in DOS by copying the DBLSPACE.BIN file to the floppy manually using a command such as:
C:\> copy \dos\dblspace.bin a:\

21
CHAPTER

Dot-matrix printers

Dot-matrix printers (Fig. 21-1) represent some of the most well-established, reliable, and inexpensive printing technology available for PCs. By firing an array of solid wires against an inked ribbon, a myriad of text styles and graphics can be printed on a variety of paper weights and finishes (it even works for multipart forms). The low cost and long working life provided by dot-matrix printers have earned them a place as workhorses in modern homes and offices everywhere. This chapter shows you the inner workings of a typical *DMP* (dot-matrix printer) and shows you a series of fixes for each major subassembly.

21-1 A Tandy DMP 2104 printer.

A typical DMP is composed of five main areas as shown in the block diagram of Fig. 21-2: (1) the print head, (2) the paper transport, (3) the carriage transport, (4) the ribbon transport, and (5) the *ECU* (electronic control unit). This part of the chapter discusses the first four subassemblies in detail.

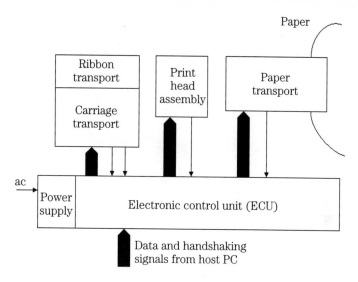

21-2 Block diagram of a dot-matrix printer.

The print head

Each dot is generated by an individual metal *print wire* driven through a solenoid as shown in Fig. 21-3. When an electrical pulse reaches the solenoid, it energizes the coil and produces a brief, intense magnetic field. This field "shoots" its print wire against the page. After the pulse passes, the solenoid's magnetic field collapses. A return spring pulls the wire back to a rest position. In actual practice, DMP solenoids and print wires are very small assemblies. A typical print wire might only travel about 0.5 mm. This distance is known as the *wire stroke*.

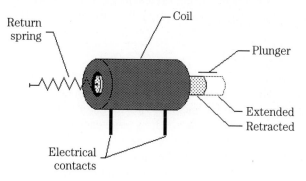

21-3 Action of a single DMP solenoid.

Not all DMP heads hold their print wire directly within the solenoid's coil. Although this approach might work just fine for smaller general-purpose heads, heavy-duty heads need larger coils that can be stacked vertically. Each solenoid is mounted offset from one another, then connected to their respective print wires using a mechanical linkage as shown in Fig. 21-4. Because of the additional mechanical components, heavy-duty print heads operate somewhat slower than direct-drive heads, and they usually do not last as long.

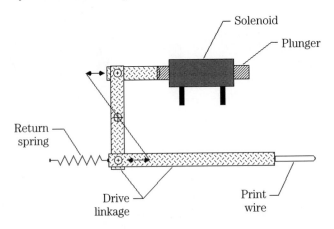

21-4 An offset DMP solenoid assembly.

Electrically, solenoids are not very efficient devices. Only 1% or 2% of the energy provided is actually converted to force. The remaining energy is wasted as heat. Heating can have severe effects that include print wire jamming, coil burnout, and even a potential burn hazard. Solenoids usually require anywhere from 12 to 24 Vdc at currents greater than 1.5 A, so the on-time for a typical solenoid must be kept very short (often below 1 ms) to prevent excessive heating. Metal heatsinks are often diecast into the head housing to dissipate excess heat as quickly as possible. Short pulses also allow extremely fast firing cycles. Most current DMP print heads can fire at greater than 300 Hz. Some models can be fired as fast as 600 Hz.

Print-head characteristics

DMP heads use an array of 7, 9, or 24 print wires arranged in vertical columns as shown in Fig. 21-5. There are three major mechanical specifications that you should be familiar with. *Wire diameter* specifies the diameter of each print wire (normally expressed in millimeters). This tells you how large each dot will be. The distance between the center of each dot is known as *wire pitch* (also expressed in millimeters). Finally, the height of each fully formed character is specified (in millimeters) as *CH* (character height). Wire diameter and pitch are much smaller for 24-pin heads than for nine- or seven-pin heads.

Not all wires can be used to form every character. For example, a 9-pin print head with a 2.5-mm CH can only use 7 wires to form most characters. Wires 8 and 9 could be used to form characters with *descenders*. The concept of *true descenders* is shown in Fig. 21-6. When all nine wires are used to form characters, there will be no room left for descenders, so characters can be printed with *false descenders*. Overall character size might appear larger when all nine wires are used, but many people find false descenders awkward to read.

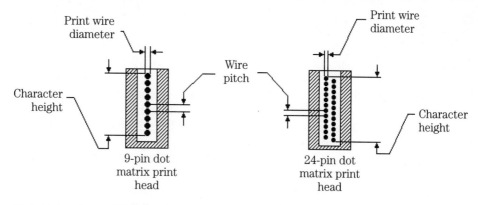

21-5 Comparison of DMP head arrangements.

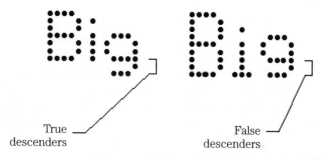

21-6 Comparison of true versus false descenders.

Early DMPs lacked the dot resolution and electronic sophistication to produce *letter-quality* print as typewriters could. Characters were printed uppercase in a 5-x-7 dot matrix. Such printing was clear and highly legible, but not visually pleasing. Advances in electronics and printer communication allowed both upper- and lower-case characters to be printed, and improvements in materials and construction techniques resulted in smaller, more reliable print heads. This made dot-matrix printing easier to look at, but still could not approach letter-quality. With the introduction and widespread acceptance of nine-pin print heads, enhanced features became possible.

The additional dots offered by a nine-pin head improved the appearance of each character even more, and provided enough detail to make several different font styles practical, but individual dots were still visible. *NLQ* (near-letter-quality) was finally accomplished through multipass printing of the same line. Paper position is shifted just a fraction, then a subsequent series of dots would fill in some of the spaces left by a previous pass. Two, three, and four passes might be required to form a line of NLQ characters (depending on the particular printer). A single pass per line became known as *draft mode.*

NLQ printing is limited by the printer's speed. The more passes needed to form a line of print, the more time is required. For example, suppose a single pass (draft) takes one second. If two passes are required for an NLQ line, print time would be twice as long (two seconds). If four passes are required, print time would be four times as long (four seconds). For long documents, this additional time can really add up. As a general rule, you can save a great deal of time (and your ribbon) by using the draft mode until you are ready to print the final version of your document.

It was not until the introduction of the 24-pin DMP print head that NLQ print could be accomplished in only one pass. Two vertical columns of 12 wires are offset from one another as in Fig. 21-5. As a 24-pin head moves across the page, the leading column places a first *pass* of dots. This forms a basic character image that is already superior to the 9-pin equivalent. Immediately after the leading column fires, the lagging column places a second pass of dots to fill in each character. In this way, two passes are made effectively at the same time.

Today, letter quality printing is relatively easy to achieve with DMPs. Because today's DMPs typically offer a selection of built-in high-quality fonts, letters appear much more complete and visually pleasing then older models. With graphics-mode drivers and operating systems such as Windows, virtually any TrueType font can be printed in any size or enhancement on an ordinary DMP.

Advantages and disadvantages of dot-matrix printing

To this day, DMP technology remains a cornerstone of commercial printing technology. They are flexible devices, capable of a wide variety of fonts and enhancements, as well as draft or NLQ performance and bit-mapped graphics. DMPs are reasonably fast, so they can achieve speeds easily exceeding 160 CPS. They are reliable devices. Heavy-duty print heads can last through more than 30 million characters. Smaller, general-purpose heads can last for more than 100 million characters. Impact printing is mandatory for printing multicopy forms. Finally, they require very little maintenance except for periodic routine cleaning.

However, impact printing is very noisy. The continuous drone of print wires striking paper can become quite annoying. Although DMP printers are now made with plastic coverings that baffle much of its noise, they do not quiet the printer completely. Limited dot resolution is another concern. You might not notice this for NLQ text, but you can see individual dots in draft or bit graphics modes. You can only achieve just so many dots per inch.

Another problem with dot-matrix printing is the eventual buildup of heat. The substantial current needed to fire a solenoid is mostly given up as heat. Under average use, the metal housing will dissipate heat quickly enough to prevent problems. Heavy use, however, can cause heat to build faster than it dissipates. This happens most often when printing bit-image graphics where many print wires can fire continuously. Heating can cause unusual friction and wear in print wires. In extreme cases, uneven thermal expansion of hot pins within the housing might cause them to jam or bend.

Troubleshooting print heads

The technique of dot-matrix printing is every bit as straightforward as character printing, but the actual formation of each letter, number, or symbol is a bit more involved. Data sent from a host computer is interpreted by the printer's main logic and converted to a series of vertical dot patterns. Motor commands start the carriage (and print head) moving across the platen. Simultaneously, printer circuits will send each dot pattern to the print head in series. Each dot pattern fires the corresponding print wires through an inked ribbon to leave a permanent mark on the page. This also is called *serial* or *moving-head* operation.

To successfully troubleshoot a dot-matrix print head, you should understand a bit about the electrical signals that drive it. Solenoids require a substantial amount of electrical energy very quickly in order to develop a magnetic field strong enough to move a print wire. Figure 21-7 shows a driver circuit similar to one used in ordinary DMP printers. A printer's ECU produces a narrow logic pulse that is sent along to a transistor driver. The transistor acts as a switch that turns the solenoid on and off. A driver voltage, usually higher than the logic supply voltage, provides the voltage and current required. One such driver circuit is required for every print wire. Heavy-duty solenoids might require even more power than a single-transistor driver can handle. The circuit shown in Fig. 21-8 uses the same logic input, but extra current is handled by two transistors configured as a *Darlington pair*. Each print wire requires its own driver circuit.

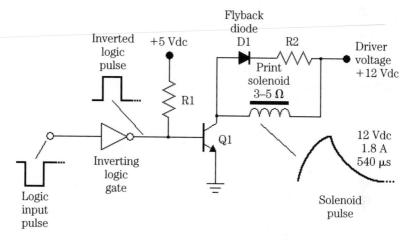

21-7 A single-transistor solenoid driver circuit.

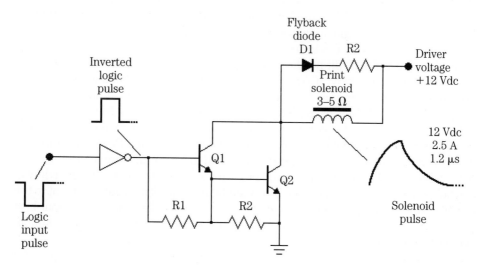

21-8 A dual-transistor solenoid driver circuit.

Symptom 1. The print quality is poor (dots appear faded or indistinct) All other operations appear normal. Begin by carefully examining the ribbon. It should be reasonably fresh and it should advance normally while the carriage moves back and forth. A ribbon that is not advancing properly (if at all) might be caught or jammed internally, so install a fresh ribbon and retest the printer. A fresh ribbon might improve image quality, but that will fade again quickly if the ribbon does not advance. If the ribbon still does not advance properly, the ribbon transport (part of the carriage transport) might be defective. You can inspect the transport assembly as discussed in this chapter, or replace the transport assembly outright.

Examine the print head spacing next. Most printers are designed with a small mechanical lever adjustment that can alter the distance between a print head and platen by several thousandths of an inch. This adjustment allows print intensity to be optimized for various paper thicknesses. If the print head is too far away from the platen for your current paper thickness, the resulting print might appear light or faded. If spacing is already close or nonadjustable, turn your attention to the print head itself.

Check each print wire in the head assembly. They should all be free to move, sliding in and out without restriction—except for mechanical tension from the return spring. Keep in mind that you will probably have to remove the print head from its carriage assembly. *Warning: Hot print heads are a burn hazard; allow plenty of time for the print head to cool before removing it.* Over an extended time, paper dust and ink forms a sticky glue that can work its way into each print wire. As this gunk dries, it can easily restrict a wire's movement or jam it all together. If you find a tremendous buildup of foreign matter, wipe off each wire as gently as possible. Use a stiff cotton swab dipped lightly in alcohol or light-duty household oil. *Do not use harsh chemical solvents!* Finally, wipe down the front face of the print head. Once all wires are moving freely again, replace the print head and retest the printer.

Remember that it is the print head driver circuitry that supplies energy necessary for print wire operation. There could be a loss of solenoid driving voltage or some other defect in your drivers. If the problem persists, try replacing the ECU assembly.

Symptom 2. Print has one or more missing dots that resemble "white" lines (this also takes place during a self-test) Assuming that all other operations of the printer are correct, a loss of one or more dot rows suggests that the corresponding print wire(s) will not fire. Unplug the printer and remove the print head from its carriage assembly. *Warning: Hot print heads are a burn hazard; allow plenty of time for the print head to cool before removing it.* Although you have the print head free, check each print wire to be sure that they are free to move without restriction, except for normal return spring tension. Over extended periods of use, a print wire might bend and jam within the head housing. Print wires also can jam from an accumulation of dust and oils that build up during normal printing. Foreign matter can often be wiped away gently with a stiff cotton swap dipped lightly in alcohol or light-duty household oil. You should quickly notice an improvement in the wire's freedom after cleaning. If you encounter bent or broken print wires, your best course is to simply replace the print head. You will find several printer parts suppliers on the companion disk.

When a new print head fails to correct the problem, your next step should be to check continuity across each wire of the print head cable. An open or intermittent cable wire can render any firing solenoid inoperative. Turn off and unplug the printer *before* checking continuity. *Warning: Hot print heads are a burn hazard; allow plenty of time for the print head to cool before removing it.* You might have to disconnect the cable at one end to prevent false readings. Wiggle the cable to stimulate any intermittent connections. Replace any print head cable that appears to be defective.

If everything checks out up to this point, your problem is probably located in a faulty wire driver circuit or a data error from the ECU. Try replacing the ECU board.

Symptom 3. Printer does not print under computer control (operation appears correct in self-test mode) Before you attempt to disassemble the printer, take a moment to check its on-line status. There is almost always an indicator on the control panel that is lit when the printer is selected. If the printer is not selected (on line), then it will not receive information from the computer, even if everything is working correctly.

A printer can be off-line for several reasons. Paper might have run out, in which case you will often have to reselect the printer explicitly after paper is replenished. Even the simplest printers offer a variety of options that are selectable through the keyboard (font style, character pitch, line width, etc.). However, you must often go off-line in order to manipulate those functions, then reselect the printer when done. You might have selected a function incorrectly, or forgotten to reselect the printer after changing modes. Also consider software compatibility. If you are using a canned software package, make sure that its printer driver settings are configured properly for your particular printer. If you are working through Windows, make sure that the proper Windows driver is selected.

Check your communication interface cable next. It might have become loose or unattached at either the printer or computer end. If this is a new or untested cable, make sure that it is wired correctly for your particular interface (that is, serial or parallel). An interface cable that is prone to bending or flexing might have developed a faulty connection, so disconnect the cable at both ends and use your multimeter to check cable continuity. If this is a new, home-made cable assembly, double check its construction against your printer and computer interface diagrams. Try a different cable.

Double check the printer DIP switch settings or set-up configuration. Dip switches are often included in the printer to select certain optional functions such as serial communication format, character sets, default character pitch, or automatic line feed. If you are installing a new printer, or you have changed the switches to alter an operating mode, it might be a faulty or invalid condition. DIP switches also tend to become unreliable after many switch cycles. If you suspect an intermittent dip switch, rock it back and forth several times, then retest the printer. If everything else checks out up to this point, try replacing the ECU board.

Symptom 4. Print head moves back and forth but does not print or prints only intermittently (this also takes place during a self-test) Check your ribbon first. Make sure that it is installed and seated properly between the platen and print head. If the ribbon has dislodged from the head path or is totally exhausted, no ink will be deposited on paper. If the ribbon is in place, make sure that it advances properly as the carriage moves. A ribbon that does not advance properly might be caught or jammed internally, so install a fresh ribbon and retest the printer.

Intermittent connections in the print head or print head cable can lead to highly erratic head operation. A complete cable break can shut down the print head entirely, especially if the break occurs in a common (ground) conductor. Turn off and unplug the printer, then use your multimeter to check continuity across each cable conductor. *Warning: Hot print heads are a burn hazard; allow plenty of time for the print head to cool before removing it.* You might have to disconnect the cable at one end to prevent false readings. Replace any print head cable that appears defective. There also could be an open lead in the print head itself. Try a new print head assembly.

There might be a problem with the print head driver supply voltage(s). Use your multimeter to check each output from the power supply. If you find that one or more power supply voltage(s) are low or erratic, you can attempt to troubleshoot the supply, or replace the supply outright. If the power supply is integrated on the ECU, try replacing the ECU outright.

The paper transport

Although individual paper handling mechanisms will vary slightly from manufacturer to manufacturer, dot-matrix printers use two distinct types: friction feed and tractor feed. Each of these systems operates in a different manner, and suffers from its own unique set of problems.

Friction feed

As its name suggests, a *friction-feed* paper transport uses friction to push paper through the printer as shown in Fig. 21-9. Paper is threaded into the printer along a metal feed guide. The guide ensures that paper is maneuvered properly between the *platen* and *pressure roller(s)*, then up in front of the print head assembly. A set of small, free-rolling *bail rollers* press gently against the paper to help keep it flat around the platen.

In order to allow the free passage of paper during threading, a lever is often included to separate pressure rollers from the platen (not shown in Fig. 21-9). After paper is positioned as desired, the lever can be released to reapply pressure. From then on, paper can only be moved by hand-turning the platen, or the printer's actual operation.

A typical drive system for a friction feed paper transport is shown in Fig. 21-10. High-energy square-wave pulses provided by the ECU's motor drive circuits feed a stepping motor. Depending on the quantity of pulses and their sequence, the motor can be made to step clockwise or counterclockwise by any amount. The stepping motor provides force to a *drive train* of gears. The drive gear (or *primary gear*) operates a *secondary gear* attached to the platen. Gear assemblies are usually used, but pulley systems can sometimes be found. In some designs, a stepping motor is

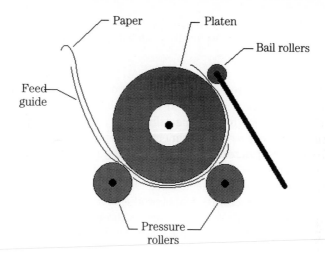

21-9 Diagram of a typical friction-feed paper transport.

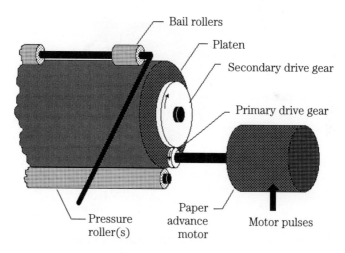

21-10 A typical friction-feed drive system.

used to operate the platen directly (known as *direct drive*). The drive assembly offers several useful features. First, the use of gears provides a reliable drive train—gears do not stretch or tear with age, and they will not jam or slip as long as they are kept clean and aligned properly. Second, the use of a smaller primary gear provides greater positioning accuracy for the platen.

Suppose you are using a 200-step motor (200 steps per revolution). With an equal gear ratio or direct drive, a single pulse would advance the platen $\frac{1}{200}$ of its circumference. With a 1:5 gear ratio (the secondary gear diameter is five times larger than the primary gear diameter), it would take five rotations of the primary gear to cause just one rotation of the secondary gear. If it takes 200 steps to rotate the primary once, it will take [200 × 5] 1000 steps to cause one complete platen rotation, so each motor step now advances the platen ⅟₁₀₀₀ of its circumference. This type of arrangement adds a lot of accuracy for high-resolution printing such as graphic images.

Tractor feed

Tractor feed does not rely on friction to transport paper. Instead, a set of sprocket wheels are mechanically linked to the platen drive train. Pegs on each sprocket wheel mesh perfectly with specially made paper. This type of paper (also called *continuous-feed* or *fan-fold* paper) has holes perforated along both sides. Paper is threaded into the printer along a metal feed guide. There is very little resistance from its contact rollers, so paper can easily be fed through and secured into its sprocket wheels. Most sprocket wheels can slide left or right to accommodate a selection of paper widths or tractor feed label products. Bail rollers are included to help keep paper flat against the platen. Once paper is threaded as shown in Fig. 21-11, it can only be advanced by hand-turning the platen knob, or in actual printer operation.

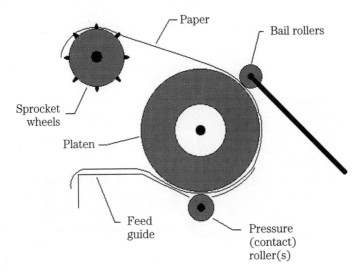

21-11 Diagram of a typical tractor-feed paper transport.

A typical drive system for a tractor-feed paper transport is shown in Fig. 21-12. As with a friction feed system, electrical pulses from the ECU's motor driver circuits operate a stepping motor. Depending on the quantity of pulses and their sequence, a motor can be made to rotate clockwise or counterclockwise by any amount. Force developed by the motor is used to operate the drive train. The platen also might be driven directly. For the system shown, a drive gear operates a secondary gear attached to the platen roller. The ratio of primary to secondary gears offers the same advantages as it does for friction feed systems. An additional drive train of gears or pulleys links the platen and sprocket wheel assemblies.

Troubleshooting a paper transport

Symptom 1. The paper advance does not function, or functions only intermittently (all other functions check properly) When a paper advance fails to

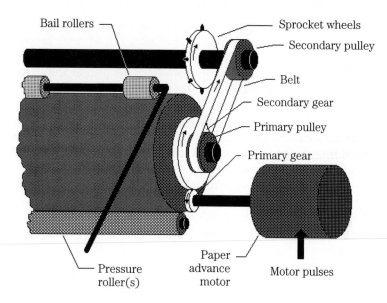

Bail rollers — Sprocket wheels
— Secondary pulley
— Belt
— Secondary gear
— Primary pulley
— Primary gear

Pressure roller(s)

Paper advance motor

Motor pulses

21-12 A typical tractor-feed drive system.

work at all, begin by observing the paper feed drive train assembly. Check any pulleys or gears to ensure that all parts are meshed evenly and are able to move freely. You can watch this by turning the platen knob located outside of the printer. Remove any foreign objects or obstructions that might be jamming the drive train. Never try to force a drive train that does not turn freely! Realign any parts that appear to be slipping or misaligned. Replace any damaged mechanical parts or assemblies.

Turn off all printer power and examine the electrical connections for your paper advance motor. Make sure that all connectors are installed and seated properly. If you suspect a faulty wiring connection, turn off printer power and use your multimeter to measure continuity across any suspicious wires. It might be necessary to disconnect the cable from at least one end to prevent false continuity readings. Replace any faulty wiring.

If everything checks properly up to this point, either the motor or ECU has failed. With printer power still off and the motor disconnected from the ECU, use your multimeter to measure the continuity of each motor winding. This is not difficult, but you will need to check the schematic of your particular printer for specific pin numbers and resistance measurements. A working motor winding exhibits between 4 to 40 Ω. If you read a short circuit (about 0 Ω), or an open circuit (substantial or infinite resistance), the paper advance motor is probably defective and should be replaced. If you cannot determine the location of each motor winding, try replacing the paper advance motor.

If the motor checks out (or a new motor fails to resolve the problem), a fault has likely developed in the ECU. One or more of the motor drive circuits has failed, or the motor voltage output from the power supply has failed. Replace the ECU outright.

Symptom 2. Paper slips or walks around the platen in friction-feed operation Friction feed paper transports are only designed to work with certain types of paper—brands within a certain range of thickness and weight. Very fine (light bond) paper or very heavy (card stock) paper will probably not advance properly. Check the specifications for your particular printer to find its optimum paper type. If you find that you are using an unusual type of paper, try the printer using standard 20-pound bond paper such as photocopier paper.

Keep in mind that friction-feed was intended for single-sheet operation. Some small amount of walking is natural, but feeding extremely long lengths of paper might result in noticeable walking. It is possible to use continuous-feed paper in a friction-feed transport, but you should expect to see a certain amount of walking eventually—try to stay with single sheets.

If the problem persists, take careful note of each roller condition. An even, consistent paper feed depends on firm roller pressure applied evenly across its entire length. Rollers that are very dirty, or old and dry, might no longer be applying force evenly. Clean and rejuvenate your rollers with a good-quality rubber cleaning compound such as Kleen-a-Platen, which is available from almost any comprehensive office supply store. *Caution: Rubber cleaning compounds can be dangerous, and might not be compatible with all types of synthetic roller materials—read instructions on the chemical container carefully, and follow all safety and ventilation instructions.*

Old rollers also might be out of alignment. Mechanical wear on shafts and bushings (or bearings) can allow some rollers to float around in the printer. Carefully examine the condition of each roller shaft. Use the paper loading lever to separate pressure rollers from the platen, then wiggle each shaft by hand. Ideally, each shaft should be fixed firmly within its assembly, so you should feel little or no slack. If you feel or see a roller move within its assembly, replace its bushings, bearing, or shaft. Newer mechanical assemblies make it easier to simply replace the entire transport outright. Some pressure roller assemblies can be adjusted slightly to alter their contact force. If your particular printer uses nonadjustable pressure rollers, there is little more to be done (other than replace the mechanical assembly). If you can adjust roller force (using spring tension or a screw adjustment), do so only as a last resort—and only then in small increments. Careless adjustment can easily worsen the problem.

Check your paper path for any debris or obstructions that might be catching part of the paper. A crumpled corner of paper jammed in the paper path or caught in the feed guide can easily interfere with subsequent sheets. Adhesive label fragments are even more troublesome. Remove all obstructions being careful not to mark any of the rollers. A straightened paper clip can often get into spaces that your fingers and tools will not. Use your needle-nose pliers to put a small hook in the wire's end for grabbing and pulling the obstruction. *Do not disassemble the rollers unless absolutely necessary.*

Symptom 3. Paper wrinkles or tears through the printer in tractor-feed operation Tractor feed paper transport systems are remarkably reliable. As long as the paper advance drive is working, it is very rare to encounter wrinkling problems using the tractor mechanism. Many printer families (especially DMPs) offer a selection of paper feed paths (i.e., friction-feed, tractor-feed pull, and tractor-feed push). A mechanical lever switches between tractor and friction feed modes. If paper suddenly seems to wrinkle or tear along its perforations during printing, the first thing to check should be the paper feed selector lever.

If your printer's paper feed mode is set correctly, check the paper path for any debris or obstructions that might be catching the paper. Fragments of torn paper or adhesive labels caught in the feed guide can easily jam the paper path. Carefully remove all obstructions that you might find. Use extreme caution to prevent damage to your rollers or feed guide. Do not disassemble the paper transport unless it is absolutely necessary.

The carriage transport

Impact printers use *serial* print heads. Fully formed text and graphics are formed by passing a print head left and right across a page surface. As the head moves, it places a series of vertical dots that create the image. In this way, a complete line of text can be generated in a single pass (letter quality text or graphics might require additional passes). As you might imagine, the process of moving a serial print head becomes a serious concern. It must move at the proper time, at the proper speed, and over the proper distance to within several thousandths of an inch on every pass.

Belt drive

The task of moving a serial print head is handled by the *carriage transport*. A print head is mounted to a platform or holder (the *carriage*) as shown in Fig. 21-13. Most serial printers use some type of belt drive. A stepping motor (often in conjunction with a gear train) drives a primary pulley that is connected to a secondary pulley by a drive linkage. A drive linkage might be a wire, belt, or chain, depending on the weight of the print head and its desired left-right speed (or *slew*). At one point, the drive linkage is connected at the carriage, which rides along one or more low-friction

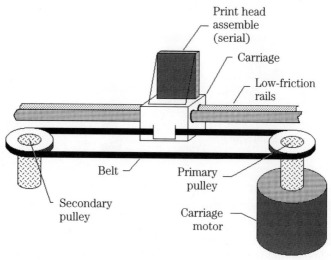

21-13 A typical belt-drive carriage transport.

rails. Rails keep the carriage rigidly parallel to the platen at all points. When the stepping motor turns counterclockwise, the carriage assembly slides left, and vice versa.

Positioning precision for a belt drive is determined by the stepping motor's resolution and the pulley diameter. This holds true for a direct drive mechanism. If the primary pulley works through a gear train, that gear ratio also must be included. As an example, suppose a stepping motor directly drives a pulley 1 inch in diameter. The circumference of the primary pulley would be $[\pi \times d]$ [3.14 × 1] 3.14 inches, so one complete motor revolution (thus one complete pulley revolution) would cause the linkage to travel 3.14 inches. If the stepping motor works at 200 steps per revolution, each step would turn the pulley $\frac{1}{200}$ of a revolution, or [3.14/200] 0.0157 inches of linear travel.

Suppose the pulley was only 0.5 inch in diameter. Its circumference would only be $[\pi \times d]$ [3.14 × 0.5] 1.57 inches, so a single motor rotation would only move the carriage 1.57 inch. At 200 steps per revolution, each step would drive the carriage [1.57/200] 0.0079 inches. Smaller pulleys (or motors with more steps per revolution) can achieve finer positioning, but at the cost of more steps to traverse the platen width.

Screw drive

Sometimes, a pulley system is replaced by a lead-screw type of assembly such as the one in Fig. 21-14. The print head and stepping motor remain unchanged, but the carriage and drive train are modified. A stepping motor now drives a gear train that operates a long, coarsely threaded lead screw. This lead screw is threaded into the carriage to become one of its rails. The second rail remains a simple, low-friction shaft that provides stability and support for the carriage (and print head). When the stepping motor turns, it rotates the lead screw (often through a gear train). Clockwise rotation of the lead screw pushes the carriage left, and counterclockwise rotation pulls the carriage right.

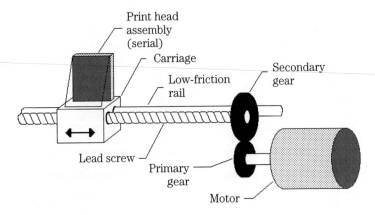

21-14 A typical screw-drive carriage transport

Positioning precision is a bit more complicated for a screw drive. For the sake of simplicity, suppose that there is an equal gear ratio, so one motor revolution will result in one lead screw rotation. In this case, positioning precision is determined by the spacing (or *pitch*) of each lead screw thread, as well as stepping motor resolution. If your lead screw has a pitch of 1 (1 thread per 1 inch of screw length), one motor revolution will move the carriage 1". At 200 steps per revolution, each motor step will turn the lead screw $\frac{1}{200}$ of a turn that results in [1/200] 0.005 inch of carriage travel.

If your lead screw has a pitch of 10 (or 10 threads over 1 inch of screw length), 1 thread covers $\frac{1}{10}$ inch in length. With 200 steps per revolution, one motor step would still turn the lead screw $\frac{1}{200}$ of a turn, but because a thread now occupies $\frac{1}{10}$ inch, the carriage would only turn [0.1/200] 0.0005 inch. The motor would now have to rotate 10 times to achieve a full inch of travel. In practice, lead screws are almost never this fine, but it demonstrates the effects of screw pitch on positioning.

Troubleshooting a carriage transport

Symptom 1. The carriage advance does not function or functions only intermittently (all other functions check properly) During printer initialization, the carriage is taken to its home position. Because the printer has no way of knowing where its carriage is when it is first turned on, finding the carriage home gives the ECU physical evidence of an actual carriage position. Under normal circumstances, the ECU will initialize the carriage to the left side of the printer. A mechanical or optical home sensor will inform the ECU when home is reached. At that point, the exact carriage position is known for certain. As the carriage moves, pulses generated from an optical position encoder confirm that the carriage is in motion.

When the carriage fails to move (or moves only intermittently), suspect a serious mechanical problem. Watch your carriage advance motor and drive train assembly while the printer initializes. A slipping belt or misaligned gear might have to be tightened or replaced. Make sure the primary pulley is attached securely to its drive shaft. Also examine the drive linkage to be sure that it is properly attached to the carriage. Replace any parts that are broken or excessively worn. Remove any obstructions or foreign objects that might interfere with the drive train.

If you see that the carriage advance motor does not turn, turn off and unplug the printer, then check all electrical connections to the motor. Make sure that all connectors are installed properly and firmly seated. Use your multimeter to check continuity across any suspicious wiring. When checking continuity, it might be necessary to disconnect the wire or cable at one end to prevent false readings. Replace any faulty wiring.

If everything checks properly up to this point, either the motor or ECU has failed. With printer power still off and the motor disconnected from the ECU, use your multimeter to measure the continuity of each motor winding. This is not difficult, but you will need to check the schematic of your particular printer for specific pin numbers and resistance measurements. A working motor winding exhibits between 4 to 40 Ω. If you read a short circuit (about 0 Ω), or an open circuit (substantial or infinite resistance), the paper advance motor is probably defective and should be replaced. If you cannot determine the location of each motor winding, try replacing the paper advance motor.

If the motor checks out (or a new motor fails to resolve the problem), a fault has likely developed in the ECU. One or more of the motor drive circuits has failed, or the motor voltage output from the power supply has failed. Replace the ECU outright.

Symptom 2. The carriage operates, but it does not always position properly   Improper carriage positioning can take many forms—character spacing might be erratic, or the carriage might sometimes ram into the left or right side frames. Faulty mechanics are often at the heart of carriage problems. Turn off and unplug the printer, then inspect the carriage drive train very carefully. Pay particular attention to the drive linkage to be sure that it is reasonably tight. One or both pulleys might be loose. Inspect any drive gears between the motor and primary pulley for signs of slipping or broken gear teeth. Replace any parts that appear broken or excessively worn.

An optical encoder provides pulses to the ECU as a carriage moves. The pulses allow the printer to position its carriage. Erratic or inconsistent positioning might be the fault of the encoder. Try replacing the encoder. If the problem persists, there is probably a logic fault in the ECU. Replace the ECU outright.

The ribbon transport

All forms of printing require some sort of media. It is the *media* that becomes a permanent page image. There are various media for different technologies—impact printing requires ink from a fabric ribbon, thermal printing requires heat-sensitive chemicals already in the paper, ink jet printing uses a reservoir of liquid ink, and EP printing takes a supply of toner powder. Media is consumed by the printer during normal operation, so it must be fresh and available at all times. Ribbons must be advanced during the printing process in order to keep fresh media available to the print head. This often complex task is handled by a *ribbon transport* mechanism. Transports for packed ribbon cartridges are often unidirectional—ribbon is advanced in one direction only until it wears out. A typical fabric ribbon will survive several complete passes before wearing out.

Most ribbon transports are driven from carriage motion—either directly from the carriage motor, or from a gear on the carriage itself. An intricate transmission of contact rollers and gears serves to keep the ribbon advancing in the same direction regardless of carriage direction. Ribbon transport mechanisms vary greatly between printers, but you can easily recognize a ribbon transport mechanism from the long spindle that inserts into a ribbon cartridge. In some printer designs, the ribbon cartridge is a small container that snaps into place on the carriage itself. In other systems, a long ribbon cartridge is typically driven from a mechanism on either side of the printer.

Troubleshooting a ribbon transport

Symptom 1. Print is light or nonexistent (all other functions appear correct)   Before you actually begin to troubleshoot a ribbon transport, examine the ribbon cartridge as the printer operates. If the ribbon advances, inspect the ribbon itself—it might simply be exhausted. Replace the ribbon cartridge and retest the printer. A ribbon cartridge that does not advance might be kinked or jammed within its cartridge. Install a fresh ribbon and retest. If normal operation returns, discard the defective ribbon cartridge.

If a fresh ribbon does not correct your problem, examine the ribbon transport mechanics. Turn off and unplug the printer, then remove the ribbon cartridge. *Warning: Hot print heads are a burn hazard—allow plenty of time for the print head to cool before removing it.* You will observe a long sprocket gear that inserts into the ribbon cartridge. Grouped just below the sprocket gear, you will find a series of other small gears and friction rollers that make up the ribbon transport. The mechanism can be assembled on the carriage or on the printer frame.

Although it is *never* desirable to operate a printer without its ribbon, it is usually safe to do for limited periods of time as long as paper is available to absorb print wire impact. Refer to your owner's manual for any specific warnings or cautions. You might have to perform some minor disassembly to observe the entire ribbon transport. While the printer is running, watch the ribbon transport mechanism for any parts that might be loose, sticking, or jammed together. Dust and debris might have accumulated to jam the mechanism. Use a clean cotton swab to wipe away any foreign matter. If the mechanism is severely worn, it should be replaced entirely.

22

CHAPTER

Drive-adapter reference

Hard drives are one of the most fundamental and important elements of a PC. The computers we know today would be very different without the fast performance, high reliability, and huge capacity that hard drives have come to offer over the last decade. Without large, fast hard drives, much of the complex software so common on current systems (namely Windows and its applications) would simply be impossible. However, the hard drive must be interfaced to a computer. A hard drive interface generally consists of two parts: (1) the actual hardware that physically connects the drive and computer, and (2) the firmware (BIOS) that manages the data transfer. As a result, it is the *interface* (or *adapter*) that defines the way data is stored on a drive—not the drive itself. Although newer drive adapters are commonly being fabricated on new-generation PC motherboards, adapters are traditionally implemented in the form of expansion boards (Fig. 22-1). This chapter examines the history, specification, and configuration of three major drive adapters; ST506, ESDI, and IDE. SCSI interfaces are detailed in Chapter 48.

ST506/412

The ST506 interface dates back to 1980 where it was developed by Shugart Associates (now Seagate Technologies) to support their ST-506 5Mb hard drive. It is largely regarded to be the ancestor of all modern hard drive interfaces. The serial interface works at 5Mbits/s using MFM encoding just like floppy drives. In 1981, Seagate revised the 506 interface to support the ST-412 10Mb hard drive; thus, the interface was dubbed ST506/412. Later versions of ST506/412 use RLL encoding instead of MFM at 17 sectors per track (512 bytes per sector). This new encoding, combined with a buffered seek feature, achieved 7.5Mbits/sec. IBM chose the ST-412 drive as the original hard drive for the PC/XT, so competing drive makers embraced the ST506/412 interface as a de-facto standard. As drive technology pushed beyond 10Mb, the interface remained the same. As a result, any hard drive compatible with the interface became known as an "ST506/412" drive.

22-1 A selection of drive adapter boards. Copyright © 1995 Future Domain Corporation. Reprinted with permission.

ST506/412 features and architecture

ST506/412 drives are "dumb" devices; like floppy drives, ST506/412 drives must be told explicitly what to do and when to do it. This necessitated a complex and demanding controller residing on a plug-in expansion board. The host computer addressed the controller board through the main computer buses and sent instructions to the controller's on-board registers. The advantage to this kind of architecture is simple modularity. A larger drive can easily be plugged into the original controller, or a defective controller can be quickly replaced.

The only real issue with an ST506/412 interface is the level of BIOS compatibility provided by the host PC. You see, as drives proliferated, each sported a series of *parameters* (heads, cylinders, sectors, and so on) that you can see today simply by looking at the system CMOS setup. Although it was a simple matter to plug the new drive into an existing controller, the controller needed to be aware of the drive's particular parameters in order to ensure that the controller operated the drive properly. When used in XT systems, the BIOS ROM on the controller contained a table of drive parameters; only drives that were listed in the table could be used with the controller. When used in AT systems, it is the motherboard BIOS that contains the hard drive parameters. CMOS setup allowed you to select the proper drive type whose parameters matched those in the table. As you might imagine, drives not listed in the table could not be used, so drive tables evolved along with the BIOS. To accommodate unusual or advanced drive types that might be newer than the BIOS, setup programs in the late 1980s began providing *user-definable* drive types. All current BIOS supports user-definable drive types.

A typical ST506/412 layout is shown in Fig. 22-2. The physical interface for an ST506 drive consists of three cables: a 4-pin power cable, a 34-pin control cable, and a 20-pin data cable. The *power cable* is a standard, keyed mate-n-lock con-

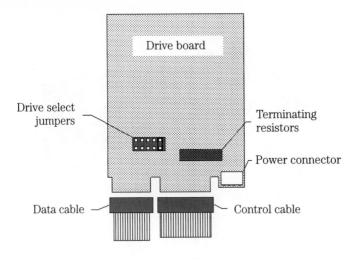

22-2 Connector layout for an ST506/412 drive.

nector that provides +5 Vdc, +12 Vdc, and ground to the drive. The *control cable* is responsible for carrying explicit operating signals to the drive such as Drive Select, Step, Head Select, and so on. The *data cable* supports differential Read and Write lines. Both digital cables are flat or twisted-pair ribbon cable. It is interesting to note that there is a set of *terminating resistors* mounted to the drive. Although terminating resistors are usually discussed only in relation to SCSI interfaces, the resistors are equally vital for proper signal characteristics in an ST506/412 system. In most cases, terminating resistors can be removed, or disabled through a jumper. As described elsewhere in this chapter, proper termination is important when more than one drive is attached to the controller. Although there might be many jumpers on the drive, a set of drive select jumpers are usually located between the data and control cables. Drive select jumpers allow the drive to be set as Drive 0 or Drive 1.

The 34-pin control cable uses 17 single-ended signals as indicated in Table 22-1. Single-ended signals are easy to measure with test instruments, and are quite reliable over short distances. You might notice that almost all signals are active-low. There are four –Head Select inputs (pins 14, 18, 4, and 2 respectively) that select one of up to 16 R/W heads for reading or writing. The –Write Gate input (pin 6) is logic 0 during write operations and logic 1 during read operations. A –Seek Complete output (pin 8) tells the controller when the heads have been moved the desired step distance and settled into their destination track. –Track 0 (pin 10) is an output informing the controller when the heads move from track 1 to track 0.

Table 22-1. Pinout for an ST506/412 control cable

Pin	Name	Pin	Name
1	Ground	2	–Head Select 8
3	Ground	4	–Head Select 4

Table 22-1. Continued

Pin	Name	Pin	Name
5	Ground	6	–Write Gate
7	Ground	8	–Seek Complete
9	Ground	10	–Track 0
11	Ground	12	–Write Fault
13	Ground	14	–Head Select 1
15	Ground	16	not connected
17	Ground	18	–Head Select 2
19	Ground	20	–Index
21	Ground	22	–Ready
23	Ground	24	–Step
25	Ground	26	–Drive Select 1
27	Ground	28	–Drive Select 2
29	Ground	30	–Drive Select 3
31	Ground	32	–Drive Select 4
33	Ground	34	–Direction In

A –Write Fault (pin 12) output tells the controller if an error has occurred during the write operation. There are a number of write faults including: (1) write current in a head without the –Write Gate signal true, (2) no write current in the head with –Write Gate true and the drive selected, (3) –Write Gate true when heads are off the desired track, or dc power to the drive is outside acceptable limits. Writing will be inhibited while the –Write Fault line is true. An –Index output (pin 20) provides a brief active-low pulse whenever a track's index data mark has just passed under the R/W heads. An index pulse appears every 16.6 ms for a disk spinning at 3600 revolutions per minute (once per revolution).

The –Ready output (pin 22) tells the controller when drive speed and dc power are acceptable, and the –Track 0 signal is true; the drive is considered ready for operation. A pulse on the –Step input (pin 24) causes the head stepping motor to move one track position. The direction in which the heads actually step will depend on the –Direction In input condition (pin 34). Finally, there are four –Drive Select inputs (pins 26, 28, 30, and 32) used to identify which drive must be accessed.

Although the data cable carries 20 conductors, there are really only three meaningful signals as shown in Table 22-2. Four reserved lines (pins 3, 5, 9, and 10) are not used at all. The –Drive Selected output (pin 1) acknowledges to the controller when its drive address matches the drive address specified on the control cable's –Drive Select lines. Differential Write Data lines (pins 13 and 14) transmit flux reversals (as opposed to real digital information; 1s and 0s) to the drive from the controller. Differential Read Data signals (pins 17 and 18) send serial flux reversals from the disk back to the controller where the reversals are translated back into digital information.

Table 22-2. Pinout for an ST506/412 data cable

Pin	Name	Pin	Name
1	Drive Selected	2	Ground
3	reserved	4	Ground
5	reserved	6	Ground
7	to control cable pin 15	8	Ground
9	reserved	10	reserved
11	Ground	12	Ground
13	+Write Data	14	−Write Data
15	Ground	16	Ground
17	+Read Data	18	−Read Data
19	Ground	20	Ground

Cabling the ST506/412 interface

ST506/412 interfaces are intended to support up to two drives with the same controller board. You should understand how cable configurations, terminating resistors, and drive jumpers are related. The basic drive system uses a single drive and controller, along with a control cable with one card edge connector (the red or blue wire represents pin 1). It is a simple matter to attach the drive and controller. You should set the only drive as drive 0, and keep the termination resistors in place on the drive.

Many ST506/412 cable assemblies were produced with two drive connectors ganged on the same cable as shown in Fig. 22-3. The end-most card edge connector is always for the first drive, but the drive jumper settings vary. If the cable has no twist, the first drive should be jumpered as drive 0, and the termination resistors should be left in place. When a second drive is added to that untwisted cable, it should be jumpered as drive 1, and its termination resistors should be removed. When the control cable has a twist, things get a bit stickier. The end-most card edge

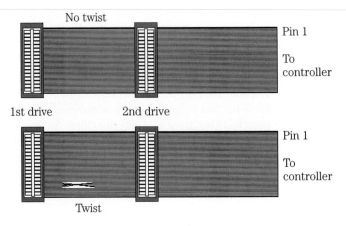

22-3 Control cabling for an ST506/412 drive.

connector is still for the first (or only) drive, but the drive should be jumpered as drive 1, and its termination resistors should be left in place. If a second drive is added to the twisted cable, it also should be jumpered as drive 1, and its termination resistors should be removed. The twist reverses the select pins for the first drive. Be very careful that you do not inadvertently use a floppy drive cable; the twist is in a different place.

Low-level formatting an ST506/412 drive

Preparing a drive for service is typically a three-step process that includes: (1) low-level formatting, (2) DOS partitioning, and (3) DOS formatting. Formatting is used to organize data on a drive, and each subsequent step refines that organization. When an ST506/412 drive is manufactured, its platters contain absolutely blank media. As a result, an operating system has no idea where to store or locate information. *Low-level formatting* lays down the individual tracks and sectors across the entire drive; this builds a basic foundation for data storage. All ST506/412 drives require low-level formatting before using the drive for the first time, or when a serious sector or track failure causes data loss. Low-level formatting is accomplished through the use of a BIOS routine that can be invoked by a DEBUG command such as:

```
C:\> debug ;start DEBUG
- g=c800:5 ;run the LL formatter for the drive
controller in use
```

The 5 indicates the type of drive controller being used. Western Digital, DTC, and Seagate controllers work with a 5 suffix, but Adaptec controllers often use a CCC suffix, and SMS-OMTI controllers use a 6. If your system BIOS does not provide an LL formatter, it might include a routine in the DOS subdirectory. You also can use a commercial LL formatter such as *DrivePro* by MicroHouse.

Low-level formatting accomplishes several specific functions. First, it checks for and maps out any defects detected on the drive during manufacture. This is done by placing invalid checksum values in the header of each defective sector. During later formatting steps, DOS will be unable to use the defective sectors as well. LL formatting also sets the drive's *interleave* factor. Because ST506/412 drives were fast compared to the original circuitry reading the data, the drive had to be delayed by staggering the sector assignments. This forced the drive to rotate several times to read each sector in the track. ST506/412 drives in XT systems often used an interleave of 3:1. In AT systems, this was often set to 2:1. Check the following guidelines before performing a low-level format:

- Back up a used drive first. Low-level formatting is a destructive and unrecoverable procedure, so any data that might have been recorded on the drive will be destroyed. Of course, if the drive were new, there would be nothing to back up. Because you will not encounter "new" ST506/412 drives, it is wise to back up whatever you can before committing to an LL format.
- Format at a running temperature. Let the system warm up for about 30 minutes before attempting an LL format. Because the LL format places tracks and sectors at precise physical locations, the drive should be at a stable running temperature so that the mechanical positioning elements

have undergone full expansion due to heat. The expansion is only microscopic, but when you realize that the data and positioning is microscopic, formatting a cold drive might cause unusual data errors or positioning problems after the drive warms up.

- Format in the final position. Mount the drive as it will be used before attempting an LL format. If the drive is formatted in one orientation, then mounted in another, the effects of gravity might throw positioning off enough to cause an unusual number of data errors.

Partitioning and high-level formatting

Placing a *partition* on a hard drive allocates that area for use by a particular operating system, and allows one partition to boot to that operating system. MS-DOS provides the FDISK utility for assigning partitions to a drive. In most cases, one physical hard drive can be partitioned into four logical drives (or volumes). However, the size of each partition is limited by the DOS version being used. Version 2.0 was limited to a single partition of only 16Mb. Versions 2.1 to 3.2x were limited to a single partition size of 32Mb. Version 3.3 allowed multiple 32Mb partitions. Version 4.xx allowed up to 512Mb partitions. Versions 5.xx and 6.xx allow up to 528Mb partitions. In all cases, no drive can have over 1024 cylinders in the drive parameters. Remember to set the boot partition as *active*.

Once a drive is partitioned, it must be *high-level formatted* by the operating system. This configures the file allocation tables and directory structures to be used by the drive. High-level formatting must be repeated for every logical volume that has been partitioned.

The fate of ST506/412

For its day, the ST506/412 interface proved to be a reliable design—its use of BIOS and flexible parameters also set the stage for future modular drive systems. Unfortunately, the ST506/412 was a slow interface, and PC systems quickly outpaced the drive. The nature of the interface also limited the drives to no more than 60Mb or so. Additional developments in encoding schemes and drive mechanics demanded a much more efficient interface. By 1984, the ST506/412 interface was considered obsolete, and by 1986, virtually no new ST506/412-type drives were being produced. However, you might still encounter these drives in older hand-me-down systems.

ESDI

The *ESDI* (enhanced small device interface) came into being early in 1983 in an effort to replace the already-obsolete ST506/412. Maxtor Corporation (along with a number of other drive and controller manufacturers) led the effort to develop a real drive standard that would extend the speed and capacity of the ST506/412 interface. Originally dubbed the Enhanced Small Disk Interface, it was merged with the Enhanced Small Tape Interface in October of 1983 to form ESDI. By 1985, a version of ESDI was released that was suitable for optical disks. In 1987, tape support was dropped from the ESDI standard. Today, ESDI exists as an interface standard approved by the *ISO* (International Standards Organization).

ESDI drives make extensive use of RLL encoding with 34 sectors per track and a direct 1:1 interleave factor. The ESDI scheme employs data separator/encoder circuitry on the drive itself where ST506/412 drives placed the circuitry on a controller card. With data separator/encoder circuitry already on the drive, an ESDI drive need only send straight binary over its data lines (1s and 0s) rather than flux transitions. This approach gives ESDI the potential for serial data rates up to 24 Mbits/s, although most transfer takes place at 10Mbits/sec. Another improvement to ESDI is the use of *buffered seeks* that allows the drive (not the controller) to manage head step movement. The ESDI drive need only receive a single step command from its controller that could refer to single or multiple track steps. The capacity and performance advantages provided by ESDI systems made them the preferred drive architecture in high-end PCs into the late 1980s when SCSI and IDE architectures came into common use.

ESDI features and architecture

As with ST506/412 drives, ESDI drives are dumb devices; the controller must tell the drive explicitly what to do and when to do it. As a consequence, ESDI controllers are equally complicated devices that reside on a plug-in expansion board. The host computer addressed the controller board through the main computer buses and sent instructions to the controller's on-board registers. Like its older cousin, ST506/412, ESDI architecture benefits from this kind of simple modularity. A larger drive can easily be plugged into the original controller, or a defective controller can be quickly replaced. In addition, EDSI controllers are virtually register-compatible with ST506/412 controllers, so software written for one type of drive will almost always work on the other. ESDI drives also rely on BIOS drive parameter tables in order to configure the system for the particular drive. Where a specific drive type is not available, a user-definable drive type can often be employed to ensure ESDI drive support.

The layout for an ESDI drive is *identical* to the ST506/412 drive shown in Fig. 22-2. The physical interface for an ESDI drive consists of three cables: a 4-pin power cable, a 34-pin control cable, and a 20-pin data cable. The *power cable* is a standard, keyed mate-n-lock connector that provides +5 Vdc, +12 Vdc, and ground to the drive. The *control cable* is responsible for carrying explicit operating signals to the drive such as Drive Select, Attention, Head Select, and so on. The *data cable* supports differential Read and Write lines, along with a series of other signals. Both digital cables are flat or twisted-pair ribbon cable. It is interesting to note that there is a set of *terminating resistors* mounted to the drive. Although terminating resistors are usually discussed only in relation to SCSI interfaces, the resistors are equally vital for proper signal characteristics in an ESDI system. In most cases, terminating resistors can be removed, or disabled through a jumper. As described elsewhere in this chapter, proper termination is important when more than one drive is attached to the controller. Although there might be many jumpers on the drive, a set of drive select jumpers are usually located between the data and control cables. Drive select jumpers allow the drive to be set as Drive 0 or Drive 1.

The pinouts for ESDI cables are shown in Table 22-3. As you look over the pinout labels, you might notice that virtually all of the signals are active-low logic (denoted by the dash next to their names). Physically, the cable layout is identical to the ST506 approach. The 34-pin control cable uses single-ended signaling, and some of the ESDI signals are the same as those used for ST506. There are four –Head Select lines (pins 2, 4, 14, and 18) that select one of up to 16 R/W heads on the drive for reading or writing. The –Write Gate signal (pin 6) enables the selected head for writing. A –Config/Status Data line (pin 8) responds to the controller's request for information by sending 16 or more serial condition bits back to the controller. A –Transfer Request input (pin 24) indicates that the host system wants to begin a data transfer, and the –Transfer Acknowledge output (pin 10) sends a handshaking signal to the controller when a data transfer is permitted to begin. The –Attention output (pin 12) is sent by the drive when the controller must read drive status—usually due to a fault.

Table 22-3. Pinout for an ESDI control cable

Pin	Name	Pin	Name
1	Ground	2	–Head Select 3
3	Ground	4	–Head Select 2
5	Ground	6	–Write Gate
7	Ground	8	–Config/Status Data
9	Ground	10	–Transfer Acknowledge
11	Ground	12	–Attention
13	Ground	14	–Head Select 0
15	Ground	16	–Sector/Address Mark Found
17	Ground	18	–Head Select 1
19	Ground	20	–Index
21	Ground	22	–Ready
23	Ground	24	–Transfer Request
25	Ground	26	–Drive Select 0
27	Ground	28	–Drive Select 1
29	Ground	30	–Drive Select 2
31	Ground	32	–Read Gate
33	Ground	34	–Command Data

The –Sector/Address Mark Found line (pin 16) outputs a pulse to the controller whenever a sector address data passes under a head. An –Index signal (pin 20) produces a pulse every 16.6 ms corresponding to a track's index mark data. The drive –Ready line (pin 22) outputs a signal to the controller when the drive is at operating speed and is ready to accept commands. A –Read Gate signal (pin 32) enables the selected R/W head for a read operation. Commands and data can be sent from controller to drive using the 16-bit serial line called –Command Data (pin 34). Finally, three –Drive Select lines (pins 26, 28, and 30 respectively) form a binary value corresponding to the drive number that the computer wishes to access.

The 20-pin data cable uses a mix of differential and single-ended signals as shown in Table 22-4. A –Drive Selected output (pin 1) tells the controller that the selected drive is responding to commands. The –Sector/Address Mark Found (pin 2) is essentially the same signal used in the 34-pin cable, but is available at all times. When the ESDI drive has finished its last function, it outputs a –Command Complete signal (pin 3) to tell the host that a new command can be accepted. An –Address Mark Enable signal (AME, pin 4) causes the drive to search for the next address mark. The AME also can be used to enable writing address marks and sync data fields to the disk during the format process. The +Write Clock and –Write Clock (pins 7 and 8) are used for synchronizing write data. The +Read/Reference Clock and –Read/Reference Clock (pins 10 and 11) are used for synchronizing read data, and for determining the drive's appropriate data transfer rate. Write data is carried to the drive over the +Write Data and –Write Data lines (pins 13 and 14), and read data is carried to the controller by the +Read Data and –Read Data lines (pins 17 and 18). Finally, an –Index signal (pin 20) generates a pulse signal each time the platters rotate. This signal serves the same purpose as the index signal in the 34-pin cable, but it is available at all times.

Table 22-4. Pinout for an ESDI data cable

Pin	Name	Pin	Name
1	–Drive Selected	2	–Sector/Address Mark Found
3	–Command Complete	4	–Address Mark Enable
5	Reserved for Step Mode	6	Ground
7	+Write Clock	8	–Write Clock
9	Cartridge Changed	10	+Read/Reference Clock
11	–Read/Reference Clock	12	Ground
13	+Write Data	14	–Write Data
15	Ground	16	Ground
17	+Read Data	18	–Read Data
19	Ground	20	–Index

Cabling the ESDI drive system

ESDI systems are cabled almost identically to ST506/412 interfaces; they are intended to support up to two drives with the same controller board. You should understand how cable configurations, terminating resistors, and drive jumpers are related. The basic drive system uses a single drive and controller, along with a control cable with one card edge connector (the red or blue wire represents pin 1). It is a simple matter to attach the drive and controller. You should set the only drive as drive 0, and keep the termination resistors in place on the drive.

Many ESDI cable assemblies were produced with two drive connectors ganged on the same cable as shown in Fig. 22-3. The end-most card edge connector is always for the first drive, but the drive jumper settings vary. If the cable has no twist, the first drive should be jumpered as drive 0, and the termination resistors should be left in place. When a second drive is added to that untwisted cable, it should be jumpered as drive 1, and its termination resistors should be removed. When the control cable has a twist, things get a bit stickier. The end-most card edge connector is still for the first (or only) drive, but the drive should be jumpered as drive 1, and its termination resistors should be left in place. If a second drive is added to the twisted cable, it also should be jumpered as drive 1, but its termination resistors should be removed. The twist reverses the select pins for the first drive. Be very careful that you do not inadvertently use a floppy drive cable; the twist is in a different place.

Low-level formatting an ESDI drive

Preparing a drive for service is typically a three-step process that includes: (1) low-level formatting, (2) DOS partitioning, and (3) DOS formatting. Formatting is used to organize data on a drive, and each subsequent step refines that organization. When an ESDI drive is manufactured, its platters contain absolutely blank media. As a result, an operating system has no idea where to store or locate information. *Low-level formatting* lays down the individual tracks and sectors across the entire drive; this builds a basic foundation for data storage. All ESDI drives require low-level formatting before using the drive for the first time, or when a serious sector or track failure causes data loss. Low-level formatting is accomplished through the use of a BIOS routine that can be invoked by a DEBUG command such as:

```
C:\> debug ;start DEBUG
- g=c800:5 ;run the LL formatter for the drive
controller in use
```

The 5 indicates the type of drive controller being used. Western Digital. DTC, and Seagate controllers work with a "5" suffix, but Adaptec controllers often use a "CCC" suffix, and SMS-OMTI controllers use a 6. If your system BIOS does not provide an LL formatter, it might include a routine in the DOS subdirectory. You also can use a commercial LL formatter such as *DrivePro* by MicroHouse.

Low-level formatting accomplishes several specific functions. First, it checks for and maps out any defects detected on the drive during manufacture. This is done by placing invalid checksum values in the header of each defective sector. During later formatting steps, DOS will be unable to use the defective sectors as well. LL formatting also sets the drive's *interleave* factor. Because ESDI drives are later devices, the controller circuitry is typically fast enough to keep pace with the drive, so there is no need to delay the drive. ESDI is not supported in XT systems, but in AT systems, interleave is almost always set to 1:1.

ESDI low-level formatting also handles two advanced drive features: sector sparing and skewing. *Sector sparing* is a technique of "hiding" one sector per track. This reduces the overall number of sectors, but any bad sector elsewhere in the track is transferred to the hidden sector; this leaves all good sectors in the track. For example, suppose sector 18 of a 36-sector track is bad. Sparing relocates sector 18 to sector 36, and moves sectors 19 to 36 down by one sector. In effect, 35 good sectors will be available, and the bad sector will be hidden. *Sector skewing* is an optimization technique that offsets the first sector of each track. This masks the delay in moving to adjacent tracks—otherwise, the drive might have to make an extra rotation to locate the first sector of a new track. The faster a drive spins, the greater skew value that is required. The outer tracks (which move faster) also use a greater amount of skew. Check the following guidelines before performing a low-level format:

- Back up a used drive first. Low-level formatting is a destructive and unrecoverable procedure, so any data that might have been recorded on the drive will be destroyed. Of course, if the drive were new, there would be nothing to back up. Because you will not encounter new ESDI drives, it is wise to back up whatever you can before committing to an LL format.
- Format at a running temperature. Let the system warm up for about 30 minutes before attempting an LL format. Remember that the LL format places tracks and sectors at precise physical locations, the drive should be at a stable running temperature so that the mechanical positioning elements have undergone full expansion due to heat. The expansion is only microscopic, but when you realize that the data and positioning is microscopic, formatting a cold drive might cause unusual data errors or positioning problems after the drive warms up.
- Format in the final position. Mount the drive as it will be used before attempting an LL format. If the drive is formatted in one orientation, then mounted in another, the effects of gravity might throw positioning off enough to cause an unusual number of data errors.

Partitioning and high-level formatting

Placing a *partition* on a hard drive allocates that area for use by a particular operating system, and allows one partition to boot to that operating system. MS-DOS provides the FDISK utility for assigning partitions to a drive. In most cases, one physical hard drive can be partitioned into four logical drives (or volumes). However, the size of each partition is limited by the DOS version being used. Version 2.0 was limited to a single partition of only 16Mb. Versions 2.1 to 3.2x were limited to a single partition size of 32Mb. Version 3.3 allowed multiple 32Mb partitions. Version 4.xx allowed up to 512Mb partitions. Versions 5.xx and 6.xx allow up to 528Mb partitions. In all cases, no drive can have over 1024 cylinders in the drive parameters. Remember to set the boot partition as *active*.

Once a drive is partitioned, it must be *high-level formatted* by the operating system. This configures the file allocation tables and directory structures to be used by the drive. High-level formatting must be repeated for every logical volume that has been partitioned.

The fate of ESDI

ESDI was envisioned and implemented as a high-performance version of ST506/412. Not only does ESDI offer much faster performance, it provides very high storage capacity (as much as a 1Gb). These advantages made ESDI the drive architecture of choice for network servers and other high-end systems—many of which are still in service today. Unfortunately, the full potential of ESDI was never realized, and SCSI systems have moved in to fill the high-end gap. The chances are good that you will encounter ESDI systems at one time or another, but it might be difficult (or impossible) to obtain replacement parts.

IDE

The *IDE* (integrated drive electronics) interface was developed in 1988 in response to an industry push to create a standard software interface for SCSI peripherals. The industry consortium, known as the *CMAC* (Common Access Method Committee) attempted to originate an *ATA* (AT attachment) interface that could be incorporated into low-cost AT-compatible motherboards. The CAM committee completed its specification that was later approved by ANSI. The term ATA Interface generally refers to the controller interface, and IDE refers to the drive. Today, IDE can refer to either the drive or controller.

IDE features and architecture

IDE drives are typically *intelligent*; that is, almost all functions relegated to a controller board in older drives are now integrated onto the drive itself. Data is transferred through a single cable attached to a *paddle board* (a simple controller board that is often little more than a buffer) attached to the system's expansion bus. Exterior circuitry is so limited that multiple IDE ports can easily be added to new motherboards. IDE drives are fast, offering short seek times and data transfer rates exceeding 10 Mbits/s. IDE also supports reasonably large drives such as 528Mb devices, although enhanced IDE (EIDE) devices are evolving to handle up to several gigabytes. Although IDE lacks the flexibility and expandability of SCSI, IDE is relatively inexpensive to implement; thus, it is often the choice for simple, inexpensive, midrange PCs that are not expected to expand much. The use of an IDE interface has extended beyond just hard drives to include such devices as CD-ROMs and tape drives, but the popularity of those applications is not very high at this point.

A great deal of discussions have concentrated on IDE intelligence. The *intelligence* of an IDE system is determined by the capabilities of the on-board controller. For the purposes of this book, intelligent IDE drives are capable of the following functions. First, intelligent IDE drives support *drive translation*—the feature that allows CMOS drive parameters to be entered in any combination of cylinders, heads, and sectors that add up to equal or less than the true number of sectors. This is particularly handy when the actual number of cylinders exceeds 1024. Nonintelligent IDE drives were limited to physical mode where CMOS parameters were entered to match physical parameters. Intelligent drives also support a number of enhanced commands that are an optional part of the ATA specification.

An advancement of intelligent IDE technology is *zoned recording* that allows a variable number of sectors per track. This allows an overall increase in the number of sectors, and the drive's overall capacity. However, BIOS can only deal with a fixed number of sectors per track, so the zoned IDE drive must always run in translation mode. When running IDE drives in translation mode, you cannot alter interleave or sector skew factors. You also cannot change factory defect information.

A typical IDE layout is shown in Fig. 22-4. The physical interface for a standard IDE drive consists of two cables: a 4-pin power cable and a 40-pin data/control cable (IBM uses either a 44-pin or 72-pin cable). The *power cable* is a standard, keyed mate-n-lock connector that provides +5 Vdc, +12 Vdc, and ground to the drive. The *signal cable* is responsible for carrying data and control signals between the drive

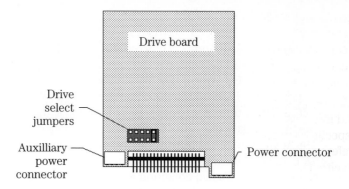

22-4 Connector layout for an IDE drive.

and paddle board. Where other drive designs rely on terminating resistors to establish reliable signal characteristics, IDE drives do not use discrete terminating resistors. A set of drive select jumpers allows the drive to be set as Drive 0 or Drive 1.

The signal cable for an IDE AT-style drive is typically a 40-pin insulation displacement connector (IDC) cable as shown in Table 22-5. Unlike ST506/412 or ESDI interfaces, IDE uses both the even and odd-numbered wires as signal-carrying lines. Also note that most of the signal labels have dashes beside their names. The dash indicates that the particular signal is *active low*; that is, the signal is *true* in the logic 0 state instead of being true in the logic 1 state. All signal lines on the IDE interface are fully TTL-compatible where a logic 0 is 0.0 to +0.8 Vdc, and a logic 1 is +2.0 to Vcc.

Table 22-5. Pinout for an IDE signal cable

Pin	Name	Pin	Name
1	Reset	2	Ground
3	DD7	4	DD8
5	DD6	6	DD9
7	DD5	8	DD10
9	DD4	10	DD11
11	DD3	12	DD12
13	DD2	14	DD13
15	DD1	16	DD14
17	DD0	18	DD15
19	Ground	20	Key (slot only)
21	DMARQ	22	Ground
23	–I/O Write Data (–DIOW)	24	Ground
25	–I/O Read Data (–DIOR)	26	Ground
27	–I/O Channel Ready (–IORDY)	28	unused
29	–DMA Acknowledge (–DMACK)	30	Ground
31	Interrupt Request (INTRQ)	32	–Host 16-bit I/O (–IOCS16)
33	DA1	34	–Passed Diagnostics (–PDIAG)
35	DA0	36	DA2
37	–Host Chip Sel 0 (–CS1FX)	38	–Host Chip Sel 1 (–CS3FX)
39	–Drive Active (–DASP)	40	Ground

Data points and registers in the hard drive are addressed using the Drive Address Bus lines DA0 to DA2 (pins 35, 33, and 36 respectively) in conjunction with the –Chip Select Drive inputs –CS1FX and –CS3FX (pins 37 and 38). When a true signal is sent along the –Drive I/O Read (–DIOR, pin 25) line, the drive executes a read cycle, and a true on the –Drive I/O Write (–DIOW, pin 23) line initiates a write cycle. The IDE interface provides TTL-level input and output signals. Where older interfaces were serial, the IDE interface provides 16 bidirectional data lines (DD0 to DD15, pins 3 to 18) to carry data bits into or out of the drive. Once a data transfer is completed, a –DMA Acknowledge (–DMACK, pin 29) signal is provided to the drive from the hard disk controller IC. Finally, a true signal on the drive's Reset line (pin 1) will restore the drive to its original condition at power on. A Reset is sent when the computer is first powered on or rebooted.

The IDE physical interface also provides a number of outputs back to the motherboard. A Direct Memory Access Request (DMARQ, pin 21) is used to initiate the transfer of data to or from the drive. The direction of data transfer is dependent on the condition of the -DIOR and –DIOW inputs. A –DMACK signal is generated in response when the DMARQ line is asserted (made true). –IORDY (pin 27) is an –I/O Channel Ready signal that keeps a system's attention if the drive is not quite ready to respond to a data transfer request. A drive Interrupt Request (INTRQ, pin 31) is asserted by a drive when there is a drive interrupt pending (i.e., the drive is about to transfer information to or from the motherboard). The –Drive Active line (DASP, pin 39) becomes logic 0 when there is any hard drive activity occurring. A –Passed Diagnostic (PDIAG, pin 34) line provides the results of any diagnostic command or reset action. When PDIAG is logic 0, the system knows that the drive is ready to use. Finally, the 16-bit –I/O Control line (IOCS16, pin 32) tells the motherboard that the drive is ready to send or receive data. Notice that there are several return (ground) lines (pins 2, 19, 22, 24, 26, 30, and 40), and a key pin (20) that is removed from the male connector.

An older XT variation of the IDE signal cable is outlined in Table 22-6. The first thing you should notice about this setup is that there are much fewer signal lines. Even though the same 40-pin cable is used, all of the even numbered pins are ground lines. There are only 8 data signals (D0 to D7). The signals on each odd numbered pin are rearranged a bit, but are identical to those listed for the full AT implementation. The only real exception is the Address Enable (AEN, pin 21) signal that is asserted during a DMA cycle to disable the processing of I/O port addresses.

Table 22-6. Pinout for an IDE XT-type signal cable

Pin	Name	Pin	Name
1	Reset	2	Ground
3	DD7	4	Ground
5	DD6	6	Ground
7	DD5	8	Ground
9	DD4	10	Ground
11	DD3	12	Ground
13	DD2	14	Ground

Table 22-6. Continued

Pin	Name	Pin	Name
15	DD1	16	Ground
17	DD0	18	Ground
19	Ground	20	Key (slot only)
21	Address Enable (AEN)	22	Ground
23	–I/O Write Data (–DIOW)	24	Ground
25	–I/O Read Data (–DIOR)	26	Ground
27	–DMA Acknowledge (–DMACK)	28	Ground
29	DMA Request (DRQ)	30	Ground
31	Interrupt Request (INTRQ)	32	Ground
33	DA1	34	Ground
35	DA0	36	Ground
37	–Host Chip Sel 0 (–CS1FX)	38	Ground
39	unused	40	Ground

Cabling the IDE interface

The ATA IDE interface is intended to support two drives on the same cable in a daisy-chained fashion. A typical IDE controller cable is shown in Fig. 22-5. Although tradition dictates that drive 0 be attached to the end connector (as the *master* drive) and a second drive be attached to the middle connector (as a *slave* drive), it is important to note that IDE supports either drive in either location. For the purposes of IDE, you need only set the proper drive jumpers to select a drive as a master or slave. The 40-pin ribbon cable (IBM uses 44-pin or 72-pin cables) should not exceed 61 centimeters (24 inches) long. Because IDE drives rely on *distributed termination* as a means of signal conditioning, it is not necessary to install or remove terminating resistors.

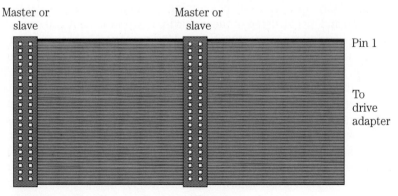

22-5 Data and control cabling for an IDE drive.

However, you might encounter problems when running two IDE drives together. Older IDE drives did not adhere to the CAMC ATA IDE specification. When trying to run older drives together (especially drives from different manufacturers), they might not respond to their master/slave relationship properly, and conflicts will result; in many cases, such problems will disable both drives. When planning a dual-IDE installation, try to use newer drives that are both from the same manufacturer.

Low-level formatting an IDE drive

The question of whether or not to low-level format an IDE drive continues to be a thorn in the side of all technicians. Drive manufacturers claim that low-level formatting might destroy the drive's servo information recorded at the factory. Diagnostic manufacturers claim that their products are smart enough to recognize critical areas of an IDE drive, and perform a safe low-level format. Even today, there is no single consensus on IDE low-level formatting. But there are some guidelines that you can follow.

First, you cannot low-level format an IDE drive using the BIOS formatter at C800h the same way you do with ST506/412 or ESDI drives. Although the heart of an IDE controller is an extension of the basic Western Digital ST506/412 controller architecture, ATA specifications allow for additional commands that are needed to step over servo tracks. However, the fact remains that IDE drives CAN be low-level formatted; after all, the manufacturers do it. Ultimately, you will need to obtain a low-level formatter routine directly from the drive manufacturer. Seagate, Western Digital, Maxtor, and other drive makers offer LL format and spare sector defect management software for their respective drives. In some cases, the LL formatter routine is included on a setup diskette included with many new drives. In the case of Conner drives, you will need a piece of hardware that connects directly to the drive's diagnostic port. TCE makes a Conner hardware formatter. You might also be able to obtain an LL formatter from the manufacturer's technical support department, from their BBS, or from their CompuServe forum.

Some third-party software manufacturers have developed flexible products that recognize the particular drive and use manufacturer-specific commands to achieve proper low-level formatting and defect mapping. Ontrack's *Disk Manager* is perhaps the best-known and most trusted of these third-party products. If you cannot obtain an LL formatter from the manufacturer, *Disk Manager* is probably your best second choice. Keep in mind that no LL format software works with every controller.

Of course, there are limitations to low-level formatting. IDE drives must be running in their *physical mode* instead of translation mode for an LL format to take place. *Zoned* IDE drives are even more limited because only the defect map can be updated, and new defective sectors can be spared. Sector headers are almost never rewritten except to mark bad sectors. Now that you know you can LL format an IDE drive, the question is should you? Note that you should not have to low-level format a new IDE drive when installing it for the first time. *For a technician, LL formatting should be reserved as an emergency measure for drives that have lost track or sector organization data because of defects or age.* Remember that low-level formatting is a destructive and unrecoverable process, so make sure to back up as much of the drive as possible before attempting the procedure.

BIOS support of IDE

Unlike SCSI controllers that use an expansion ROM to provide supplemental BIOS, the firmware needed to provide IDE support is written into the main system BIOS. Although systems manufactured in the last few years (after 1990) are fully compatible with ATA IDE drives, adding an IDE drive to an older PC often resulted in problems. After the broad introduction of IDE, it was discovered that IDE drive operations placed different timing demands on the PC that frequently caused disk errors such as data corruption and failure to boot. BIOS makers quickly found a solution to this timing problem that was incorporated into BIOS that appeared after early 1990. If you encounter a PC with pre-1990 BIOS, you should consider upgrading it before adding an IDE drive, or if the current IDE drive is exhibiting problems.

The growth of EIDE

Although IDE offers some compelling advantages, there are three major limitations that are already becoming noticeable. First, it does not provide very fast data transfer; about as fast as ESDI. Second, drive capacities are limited to about 528Mb, and an IDE interface only supports two drives (almost always hard drives). *Enhanced IDE* (EIDE) is another step in IDE evolution that is attempting to address these limitations. EIDE interfaces promise to support up to four devices (hard drives as well as CD-ROM drives and tape drives that have traditionally relied on proprietary interfaces). EIDE increases the 528Mb capacity limit to 8.4Gb! The data transfer rate for EIDE approaches 13Mbytes/sec as opposed to IDE's 2 or 3 Mbytes/s. The physical interface used for EIDE works with the same 40-pin approach now used with the IDE/AT architecture. To enjoy the benefits of EIDE, you will need an EIDE drive and controller board. However, EIDE is backwardly compatible with current IDE drives.

Controller notes

Because IDE/EIDE drives place the majority of the interface on the drive itself, the adapter board that actually plugs into the expansion slot is virtually fool-proof. You will almost never have to set the system resources on an IDE adapter board. On the other hand, most IDE errors are the result of drive problems rather than adapter problems.

23
CHAPTER

Floppy drives

The ability to interchange programs and data between various compatible computers is a fundamental requirement of almost every computer system. It is just this
kind of file exchange compatibility that helped rocket IBM PC/XTs into everyday use
and spur the personal computer industry into the early 1980s. A standardized operating system, file structure, and recording media also breathed life into the fledgling
software industry. With the floppy disk, software developers could finally distribute
programs and data to a mass-market of compatible computer users. The mechanism
that allowed this quantum leap in compatibility is the *floppy disk drive* (Fig. 23-1).

23-1
An NEC FD1138H floppy
drive.

An *FDD* (floppy disk drive) is one of the least expensive and most reliable forms
of mass-storage ever used in computer systems. Virtually every one of the millions of
personal computers sold each year incorporates at least one floppy drive. Most notebook and laptop computers also offer a single floppy drive. Not only are FDDs useful
for transferring files and data between various systems, but the advantage of removable media—the floppy disk itself—makes floppy drives an almost intuitive backup
system. Although floppy drives have evolved through a number of iterations from

20.32 to 13.34 cm (centimeters) (8 to 5¼ inches) and to 8.89 cm (3½ inches), their basic components and operating principles have changed very little.

Magnetic storage concepts

Magnetic storage media has been attractive to computer designs for many years—long before the personal computer had established itself in homes and offices. This popularity is primarily due to the fact that magnetic media is *nonvolatile*. Unlike system RAM, no electrical energy is needed to maintain the information once it is stored. Although electrical energy is used to read and write magnetic data, magnetic fields do not change on their own, so data remains intact until "other forces" act upon it (such as another floppy drive). It is this smooth, straightforward transition from electricity to magnetism and back again that has made magnetic storage such a natural choice. To understand how a floppy drive works and why it fails, you should have an understanding of magnetic storage. This part of the chapter shows you the basic storage concepts used for floppy drives.

Media

For the purposes of this book, *media* is the physical material that actually holds recorded information. In a floppy disk, the media is a small mylar disk coated on both sides with a precisely formulated magnetic material often referred to as the *oxide* layer. Every disk manufacturer uses their own particular formula for magnetic coatings, but most coatings are based on a naturally magnetic element (such as iron, nickel, or cobalt) that has been alloyed with nonmagnetic materials or rare earth. This magnetic material is then compounded with plastic, bonding chemicals, and lubricant to form the actual disk media.

The fascinating aspect of these magnetic layers is that each and every particle media acts as a microscopic magnet. Each magnetic particle can be aligned in one orientation or another under the influence of an external magnetic field. If you have ever magnetized a screwdriver's steel shaft by running a permanent magnet along its length, you have already seen this magnetizing process in action. For a floppy disk, microscopic points along the disk's surfaces are magnetized in one alignment or another by the precise forces applied by *R/W* (read/write) heads. The shifting of alignment polarities would indicate a logic 1, and no change in polarity would indicate a logic 0 (there is more about data recording and organization in this chapter).

In analog recording (such as audio tapes), the magnetic field generated by read/write heads varies in direct proportion to the signal being recorded. Such linear variations in field strength cause varying amounts of magnetic particles to align as the media moves. On the other hand, digital recordings such as floppy disks save binary 1s and 0s by applying an overwhelming amount of field strength. Very strong magnetic fields *saturate* the media—that is, so much field strength is applied that any further increase in field strength will not cause a better alignment of magnetic particles at that point on the media. The advantage to operating in saturation is that 1s and 0s are remarkably resistant to the degrading effects of noise that can sometimes appear in analog magnetic recordings.

Although the orientation of magnetic particles on a disk's media can be reversed by using an external magnetic field, particles tend to resist the reversal of polarity. *Coercitivity* is the strength with which magnetic particles resist change. Higher coercitivity material has a greater resistance to change, so a stronger external field will be needed to cause changes. High coercitivity is generally considered to be desirable (up to a point) because signals stand out much better against background noise and signals will resist natural degradation because of age, temperature, and random magnetic influences. As you might expect, a highly coercive media requires a more powerful field to record new information.

Another advantage of increased coercitivity is greater information density for media. The greater strength of each media particle allows more bits to be packed into less area. The move from 13.34-cm (5¼ inches) to 8.89-cm (3½ inches) floppy disks was possible due largely to a superior (more coercitive) magnetic layer. This coercitivity principle also holds true for hard drives. In order to pack more information onto ever-smaller platters, the media must be more coercive. Coercitivity is a common magnetic measurement with units in oersteds (pronounced *or-steds*). The coercitivity of a typical floppy disk can range anywhere from 300 to 750 oersteds. By comparison, hard drive and magneto-optical (MO) drive media usually offer coercitivities up to 6000 oersteds or higher.

The central premise of magnetic storage is that it is *static* (once recorded, information is retained without any electrical energy). Such stored information is presumed to last forever, but in actual practice, magnetic information begins to degrade as soon as it is recorded. A good magnetic media will reliably remember (or retain) the alignment of its particles over a long period of time. The ability of a media to retain its magnetic information is known as *retentivity*. Even the finest, best-formulated floppy disks degrade eventually (although it could take many years before an actual data error materializes).

Ultimately, the ideal answer to media degradation is to refresh (or write over) the data and sector ID information. Data is rewritten normally each time a file is saved, but sector IDs are only written once when the disk is formatted. If a sector ID should fail, you will see the dreaded "Sector Not Found" disk error and any data stored in the sector cannot be accessed. This failure mode also occurs in hard drives. There is little that can be done to ensure the integrity of floppy disks other than maintaining one or more backups on freshly formatted disks. However, some commercial software is available for restoring disk data (especially hard drives).

Magnetic recording principles

The first step in understanding digital recording is to see how binary data is stored on a disk. Binary 1s and 0s are not represented by discrete polarities of magnetic field orientations as you might have thought. Instead, binary digits are represented by the presence or absence of flux *transitions* as shown in Fig. 23-2. By detecting the change from one polarity to another instead of simply detecting a discrete polarity itself, maximum sensitivity can be achieved with very simple circuitry.

In its simplest form, a logic 1 is indicated by the presence of a *flux reversal* within a fixed time frame, and a logic 0 is indicated by the absence of a flux reversal. Most floppy drive systems insert artificial flux reversals between consecutive 0s to

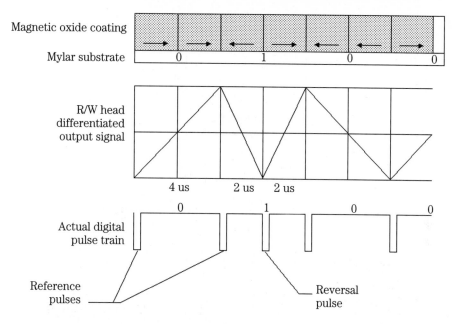

Magnetic oxide coating

Mylar substrate

R/W head
differentiated
output signal

4 us   2 us   2 us

Actual digital
pulse train

Reference
pulses

Reversal
pulse

23-2 Flux transitions in floppy disks.

prevent reversals from occurring at great intervals. You can see some example magnetic states recorded on the media of Fig. 23-2. Notice that the direction of reversal does not matter at all—it is the reversal event that defines a 1 or 0. For example, the first 0 uses left-to-right orientation, and the second 0 uses a right-to-left orientation, but both can represent 0s.

The second trace in Fig. 23-2 represents an amplified output signal from a typical read/write head. Notice that the analog signal peaks wherever there is a flux transition—long slopes indicate a 0, and short slopes indicate a 1. When such peaks are encountered, peak detection circuits in the floppy drive cause marking pulses in the ultimate data signal. Each bit is usually encoded in about 4 μs.

Often, the most confusing aspect to flux transitions is the artificial reversals. Why reverse the polarities for consecutive 0s? Artificial reversals are added to guarantee synchronization in the floppy disk circuitry. Remember that data read or written to a floppy disk is serial, and without any clock signal, such serial data is *asynchronous* of the drive's circuitry. Regular flux reversals (even if added artificially) create reference pulses that help to synchronize the drive and data without use of clocks or other timing signals. This approach is loosely referred to as the *modified frequency modulation* (MFM) recording technique.

The ability of floppy disks to store information depends upon being able to write new magnetic field polarities on top of old or existing orientations. A drive also must be able to sense the existing polarities on a disk during read operations. The mechanism responsible for translating electrical signals into magnetic signals (and vice versa) is the read/write head (R/W head). In principle, a head is little more than a coil of very fine wire wrapped around a soft, highly permeable core material as shown in Fig. 23-3.

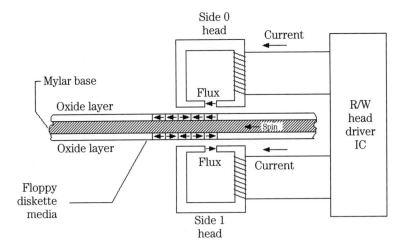

23-3 Floppy drive recording principles.

When the head is energized with current flow from a driver IC, a path of magnetic flux is established in the head core. The direction (or orientation) of flux depends on the direction of energizing current. To reverse a head's magnetic orientation, the direction of energizing current must be reversed. The small head size and low current levels needed to energize a head allow very high-frequency flux reversals. As magnetic flux is generated in a head, the resulting, tightly focused magnetic field aligns the floppy disk's particles at that point. In general practice, the current signal magnetizes an almost microscopic area on the media. R/W heads actually contact the media while a disk is inserted into a drive.

During a read operation, the heads are left unenergized while the disk spins. Just as varying current produces magnetism in a head, the reverse is also true—varying magnetic influences cause currents to be developed in the head(s). As the spinning media moves across an R/W head, a current is produced in the head coil. The direction of induced current depends on the polarity of each flux orientation. Induced current is proportional to the flux density (how closely each flux transition is placed) and the velocity of the media across each head. In other words, signal strength depends on the rate of change of flux versus time.

Data and disk organization

Another important aspect of drive troubleshooting is to understand how data is arranged on the disk. You cannot place data just anywhere—the drive would have no idea where to look for the data later on, or even if the data is valid. In order for a disk to be of use, information must be sorted and organized into known, standard locations. Standardized organization ensures that a disk written by one drive will be readable by another drive in a different machine. Table 23-1 compares the major specifications of today's popular drive types.

Table 23-1. Comparison of floppy disk drive specifications

Spec.	5.25" (360Kb)	5.25" (1.2Mb)	3.5" (720Kb)	3.5" (1.44Mb)	3.5" (2.88Mb)
Bytes per sector	512	512	512	512	512
Sectors per track	9	15	9	18	36
Tracks per side	40	80	80	80	80
Sectors per cluster	2	1	2	1	2
FAT length (sectors)	2	7	3	9	9
Number of FATs	2	2	2	2	2
Root dir. length	7 sectors	14 sectors	7 sectors	14 sectors	15 sectors
Max. root entries	112	224	112	224	240
Total sectors on disk	708	2371	1426	2847	5726
Media base	Ferrite	Ferrite	Cobalt	Cobalt	Cobalt
Coercitivity (oersteds)	300	300	600	600	720
Media descriptor byte	FDh	F9h	F9h	F0h	F0h
Encoding format	MFM or FM	MFM or FM	MFM	MFM	MFM
Data rate (KB/sec)	250 or 125	500 or 250	500	500	500

It is important to note that a floppy disk is a two-dimensional entity possessing both height and width (depth is irrelevant here). This two-dimensional characteristic allows disk information to be recorded in concentric circles that creates a random-access type of media. *Random-access* means that it is possible to move around the disk almost instantly to obtain a desired piece of information. This is a much faster and more convenient approach than a sequential recording medium such as magnetic tape.

Floppy disk organization is not terribly complicated, but there are several important concepts that you must be familiar with. The disk itself is rotated in one direction (usually clockwise) under read/write heads that are perpendicular (at right angles) to the disk's plane. The path of the disk beneath a head describes a circle. As a head steps in and out along a disk's radius, each step describes a circle with a different circumference—rather like lanes on a roadway. Each of these concentric "lanes" is known as a *track*. A typical 8.89-cm disk offers 160 tracks—80 tracks on each side of the media. Tracks have a finite width that is defined largely by the drive size, head size, and media. When an R/W head jumps from track to track, it must jump precisely the correct distance to position itself in the middle of another track. If positioning is not correct, the head might encounter data signals from two adjacent tracks. Faulty positioning almost invariably results in disk errors. Also notice that the circumference of each track drops as the head moves toward the disk's center. With less space and a constant rate of spin, data is densest on the innermost tracks (79 or 159 depending on the disk side) and least dense on the outermost tracks (0 or 80). A track also is known as a *cylinder*.

Every cylinder is divided into smaller units called *sectors*. There are 18 sectors on every track of an 8.89-cm disk. Sectors serve two purposes. First, a sector stores

512 bytes of data. With 18 sectors per track and 160 tracks per disk, an 8.89-cm disk holds 2880 sectors [18 × 160]. At 512 bytes per sector, a formatted disk can handle about [2880 × 512] 1,474,560 bytes of data. In actual practice, this amount is often slightly less to allow for boot sector and file allocation information. Sectors are referenced in groups called *clusters* or *allocation units*. Although hard drives can group 16 or more sectors into a cluster, floppy drives only use one or two sectors in a cluster.

Second, and perhaps more important, a sector provides housekeeping data that identifies the sector, the track, and error checking results from *CRC* (cyclical redundancy check) calculations. The location of each sector and housekeeping information is set down during the *format* process. Once formatted, only the sector data and CRC results are updated when a disk is written. Sector ID and synchronization data is never rewritten unless the disk is reformatted. This extra information means that each sector actually holds more than 512 bytes, but you only have access to the 512 data bytes in a sector during normal disk read/write operations. If sector ID data is accidentally overwritten or corrupted, the user-data in the afflicted sector becomes unreadable.

The format process also writes a bit of other important information to the disk. The boot record is the first sector on a disk (sector 0). It contains several key parameters that describe the characteristics of the disk. If the disk is bootable, the boot sector also will run the files (IO.SYS and MSDOS.SYS) that load DOS. In addition to the boot record, a *file allocation table* (FAT) is placed on track 00. The FAT acts as a table of contents for the disk. As files are added and erased, the FAT is updated to reflect the contents of each cluster. As you might imagine, a working FAT is critical to the proper operation of a disk. If the FAT is accidentally overwritten or corrupted, the entire disk can become useless. Without a viable FAT, the computer has no other way to determine what files are available or where they are spread throughout the disk. The very first byte in a FAT is the *media descriptor* byte that allows the drive to recognize the type of disk that is inserted.

Media problems

Magnetic media has come a long way in the last decade or so. Today's high-quality magnetic materials, combined with the benefits of precise, high-volume production equipment, produces disks that are exceptionally reliable over normal long-term use in a floppy disk drive. However, floppy disks are removable items. The care they receive in physical handling and the storage environment where they are kept will greatly impact a disk's life span.

The most troubling and insidious problem plaguing floppy disk media is the accidental influence of magnetic fields. Any magnetized item in close proximity to a floppy disk poses a potential threat. Permanent magnets such as refrigerator magnets or magnetic paper clips are prime sources of stray fields. Electromagnetic sources like telephone ringers, monitor or TV degaussing coils, and all types of motors will corrupt data if the media is close enough. The best policy is to keep all floppy disks in a dedicated container placed well away from stray magnetic fields.

Disks and magnetic media also are subject to a wide variety of physical damage. Substrates and media are manufactured to very tight tolerances, so anything at all that alters the precise surface features of a floppy disk can cause problems. The introduction of hair, dirt, or dust through the disk's head access aperture, wild temperature variations, fingerprints on the media, or any substantial impact or flexing of the media can cause temporary loss of contact between media and head. When loss of contact occurs, data is lost and a number of disk errors can occur. Head wear and the accumulation of worn oxides also affects head contact. Once again, storing disks in a dedicated container located well out of harm's way is often the best means of protection.

Drive construction

At the core of a floppy drive (Fig. 23-4) is a frame assembly (15). It is the single, main structure for mounting the drive's mechanisms and electronics. Frames are typically made from die-cast aluminum to provide a strong, rigid foundation for the drive. The front bezel (18) attaches to the frame to provide a clean, cosmetic appearance, and to offer a fixed slot for disk insertion or removal. For 8.89-cm drives, bezels often include a small colored lens, a disk ejection button hole, and a flap to cover the disk slot when the drive is empty. A spindle motor assembly (17) uses an outer-rotor dc motor fabricated onto a small PC board. The motor's shaft is inserted into that large hole in the frame. A disk's metal drive hub automatically interlocks to the spindle. For 13.34-cm disks, the center hole is clamped between two halves of a spindle assembly. The halves clamp the disk when the drive lever is locked down. Figure 23-5 shows the spindle motor assembly from the underside of the drive. The *disk activity LED* (20) illuminates through the bezel's colored lens whenever spindle motor activity is in progress.

Just behind the spindle motor is the drive's control electronics (16). It contains the circuitry needed to operate the drive's motors, R/W heads, and sensors. A standardized interface is used to connect the drive to a floppy drive controller. Figure 23-6 shows you a close-up view of a drive's control board (note the optoisolator just below U1). The read/write head assembly (7) (also sometimes called a *head carriage assembly*), holds a set of two R/W heads. Head 0 is the lower head (underside of the disk), and head 1 is on top. A head stepping motor (12) is added to ensure even and consistent movement between tracks. A threaded rod at the motor end is what actually moves the heads. A mechanical damper (5) helps to smooth the disk's travel into or out of the 8.89-cm drive. Figure 23-7 shows a close-up view of the R/W heads and stepping motor.

When a disk is inserted through the bezel, the disk is restrained by a diskette clamp assembly (2). To eject the disk, you would press the ejector button (19) that pushes a slider mechanism (3). When the ejector button is fully depressed, the disk will disengage from the spindle and pop out of the drive. For 13.34-cm drives, the disk is released whenever the drive door is opened. Your particular drive might contain other miscellaneous components. Finally, the entire upper portion of a drive can be covered by a metal shield (1).

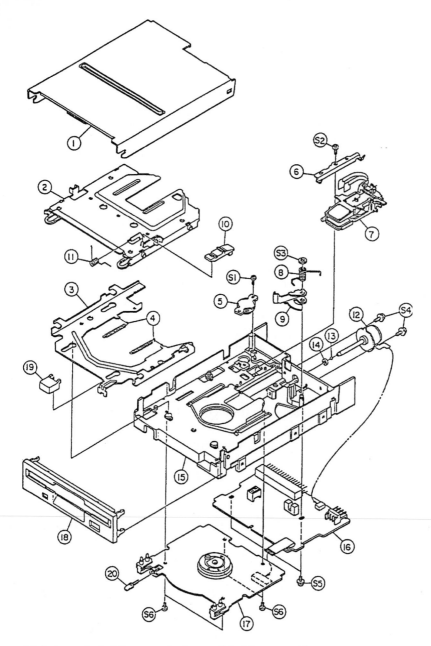

23-4 An exploded diagram of a floppy disk drive assembly. Teac America, Inc.

Drive electronics

Proper drive operation depends on the intimate cooperation between magnetic media, electromechanical devices, and dedicated electronics. Floppy drive electronics is responsible for two major tasks: controlling the drive's physical operations, and

Fixing screws

PCBA spindle motor servo

Connector J5 (CN61)

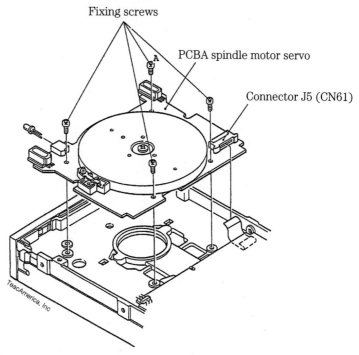

23-5 Underside view of a floppy drive spindle motor assembly.

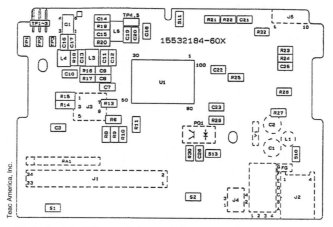

23-6 A typical floppy drive main logic/interface board.

managing the flow of data in or out of the drive. These tasks are not nearly as simple as they sound, but the sleek, low-profile drives in today's computer systems are a far cry from the clunky, full-height drives found in early systems. Older drives needed a large number of ICs spanning several boards that had to be fitted to the chassis. However, the drive in your computer right now is probably implemented with only a

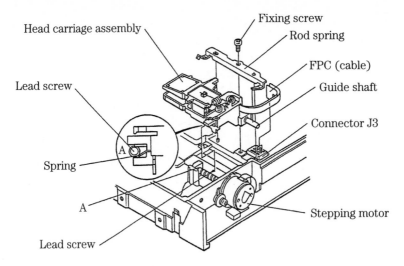

23-7 Detailed view of an R/W head and stepping motor arrangement. Teac America, Inc.

few highly integrated ICs that are neatly surface-mounted on two small, opposing PC boards. This part of the chapter discusses the drive's operating circuits. A complete block diagram for a Teac 8.89-cm (3½-inch) floppy drive is shown in Fig. 23-8. The figure is shown with a floppy disk inserted.

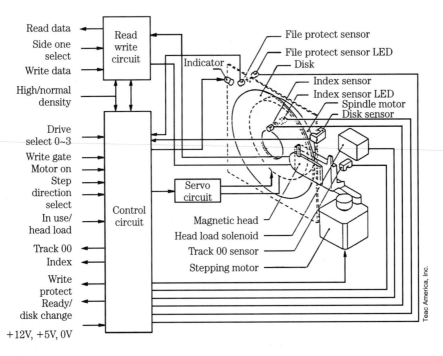

23-8 Block diagram of a floppy drive.

Write-protect sensors are used to detect the position of a disk's file-protect tab. For 8.89-cm disks, the write protect notch must be covered to allow both read and write operations. If the notch is open, the disk can only be read. Optoisolators are commonly used as write protect sensors because an open notch will easily allow light through, and a closed notch will cut off the light path.

Before the drive is allowed to operate at all, a disk must be inserted properly and interlocked with the spindle. A disk-in-place sensor detects the presence or absence of a disk. Like the write protect sensor, disk sensors are often mechanical switches that are activated by disk contact. If drive access is attempted without a disk in place, the sensor causes the drive's logic to induce a DOS "Disk Not Ready" error code. It is not unusual to find an optoisolator acting as a disk-in-place sensor.

The electronics of an 8.89-cm drive must be able to differentiate whether the disk contains normal (double) density or high-density media. A high-density sensor looks for the hole that is found near the top of all high-density disk bodies. A mechanical switch is typically used to detect the high-density hole, but a separate LED/detector pair also might be used. When the hole is absent (a double-density disk), the switch is activated upon disk insertion. If the hole is present (a high-density disk), the switch is not actuated. All switch conditions are translated into logic signals used by the drive electronics.

Before disk data can be read or written, the system must read the disk's boot sector information and FAT. Although programs and data can be broken up and scattered all over a disk, however, the FAT must always be located at a known location so that the drive knows where to look for it. The FAT is always located on track 00—the first track of disk side 0. A track 00 sensor provides a logic signal when the heads are positioned over track 00. Each time a read or write is ordered, the head assembly is stepped to track 00. Although a drive remembers how many steps should be needed to position the heads precisely over track 00, an optoisolator or switch senses the head carriage assembly position. At track 00, the head carriage should interrupt the optoisolator or actuate the switch. If the drive supposedly steps to track 00 and there is no sensor signal to confirm the position (or the signal occurs before the drive has finished stepping), the drive assumes that a head positioning error has occurred. Head step counts and sensor outputs virtually always agree unless the sensor has failed or the drive has been physically damaged.

Spindle speed is a critically important drive parameter. Once the disk has reached its running velocity (300 or 360 rpm), the drive MUST maintain that velocity for the duration of the disk access process. Unfortunately, simply telling the spindle motor to move is no guarantee that the motor is turning—a sensor is required to measure the motor's speed. This is the index sensor. Signals from an index sensor are fed back to the drive electronics that adjusts spindle speed in order to maintain a constant rotation. Most drives use optoisolators as index sensors that detect the motion of small slots cut in a template or the spindle rotor itself. When a disk is spinning, the output from an index sensor is a fast logic pulse sent along to the drive electronics. Keep in mind that some index sensors are magnetic. A magnetic sensor typically operates by detecting the proximity of small slots in a template or the spindle rotor, but the pulse output is essentially identical to that of the optoisolator.

Physical interface

The drive must receive control and data signals from the computer, and deliver status and data signals back to the computer as required. The series of connections between a floppy disk PC board and the floppy disk controller circuit is known as the *physical interface*. The advantage to using a standard interface is that various drives made by different manufacturers can be mixed and matched by computer designers. A floppy drive working in one computer will operate properly in another computer regardless of the manufacturer as long as the same physical interface scheme is being used.

Floppy drives use a physical interface that includes two cables: a power cable and a signal cable. Both cable pinouts are shown in Fig. 23-9. The classical power connector is a 4-pin "mate-n-lock" connector, although many low-profile drives used in mobile computers (laptops or notebooks) might use much smaller connector designs. Floppy drives require two voltage levels: +5.0 Vdc for logic, and +12.0 Vdc for motors. The return (ground) for each supply also is provided at the connector. The signal connector is typically a 34-pin *IDC* (insulation displacement connector) cable. Notice that all odd-numbered pins are ground lines, and the even-numbered pins carry active signals. Logic signals are all TTL-level signals.

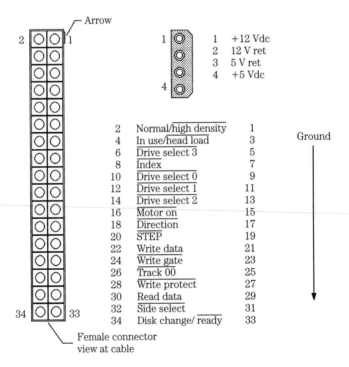

23-9 Diagram of a standard floppy-drive interface.

In a system with more than one floppy drive, the particular destination drive must be selected before any read or write is attempted. A drive is selected using the appropriate Drive Select line (Drive Select 0 to 3) on pins 10, 12, 14, and 6 respectively. For notebook or sub-notebook systems where only one floppy drive is used, only Drive Select 0 is used—the remaining select inputs might simply be disconnected. The spindle motor servo circuit is controlled through the Motor ON signal (pin 16). When pin 16 is logic 0, the spindle motor should *spin up* (approach a stable operating speed). The media must be spinning at the proper rate before reading or writing can take place.

To move the R/W heads, the host computer must specify the number of steps a head carriage assembly must move, and the direction in which steps must occur. A Direction Select signal (pin 18) tells the coil driver circuit whether the heads should be moved inward (toward the spindle) or outward (away from the spindle). The Step signal (pin 20) provides the pulse sequence that actually steps the head motor in the desired direction. The combination of Step and Direction Select controls can position the R/W heads over the disk very precisely. The Side Select control pin (pin 32) determines whether head 0 or head 1 is active for reading or writing—only one side of the disk can be manipulated at a time.

There are two signals needed to write data to a disk. The Write Gate signal (pin 24) is logic 0 when writing is to occur, and logic 1 when writing is inhibited (or reading). After the Write Gate is asserted, data can be written to the disk over the Write Data line (pin 22). When reading, the data that is extracted from the disk is delivered from the Read Data line (pin 30).

Each of the drive's sensor conditions are sent over the physical interface. The Track 00 signal (pin 26) is logic 0 whenever the head carriage assembly is positioned over track 00. The Write Protect line (pin 28) is logic 0 whenever the disk's write protect notch is in place. Writing is inhibited whenever the Write Protect signal is asserted. The Index signal (pin 8) supplies a chain of pulses from the index sensor. Media type is indicated by the Normal/High-Density sensor (pin 2). The status of the disk-in-place sensor is indicated over the Disk Change Ready line (pin 34).

Troubleshooting floppy-disk systems

This section of the chapter is concerned with drive problems that cannot be corrected with cleaning or mechanical adjustments. To perform some of the following tests, you should have a known-good diskette that has been properly formatted. The disk might contain files, but be certain that any such files are backed up properly on a hard drive or another floppy disk—if you can't afford to lose the files on a disk, don't use the disk.

Repair versus replace

As with so many other PC assemblies, the price of floppy drives has dropped tremendously over the last few years. Now that the price of a standard 8.89-cm drive is roughly that of two hours of labor, most technicians ask whether it is better to simply replace a floppy drive outright rather than attempt a repair. Ultimately, the decision should depend on volume. Clearly, it makes little sense for anyone to invest valuable time in repairing a single drive. When there are a large number of drives to be repaired, however, an enterprising technician who chooses to deal in floppy drive service can effectively provide rebuilt or refurbished drives to their customers.

Preliminary testing

Proper testing is essential for any type of drive repair. Most drive alignment packages such as *DriveProbe* by Accurite Technologies or *AlignIt* by Landmark Research measure and display a drive's parameters (Fig. 23-10). When floppy drive trouble occurs, running a diagnostic can help determine whether the drive mechanics or electronics are at fault. Although you can swap a drive symptomatically, thorough testing is an inexpensive means to verify your suspicions before spending money to replace subassemblies.

```
AUTOMATIC Drive Test                            'Esc'- For Previous Menu
```

Test	Track	Head 0 Data	Head 1 Data	Test Limits	Results	
Speed	NA	300 RPM / 199.7 mS		300 ± 6 RPM	Pass	NA
Eccentricity	44	100 uI	NA	0 ± 300 uI	Pass	NA
Radial	0	96% 50 uI	100% 0 uI	60 - 100 %	Pass	Pass
Radial	40	93% -100 uI	90% -150 uI	60 - 100 %	Pass	Pass
Radial	79	96% 50 uI	90% -150 uI	60 - 100 %	Pass	Pass
Azimuth	76	6 Min	4 Min	0 ± 30 Min	Pass	Pass
Index	0	414 uS	407 uS	400 ± 600 uS	Pass	Pass
Index	79	397 uS	380 uS	400 ± 600 uS	Pass	Pass
Hysteresis	40	100 uI	NA	0 ± 250 uI	Pass	NA

```
    uI = Micro-inches       uS = Microsecond      mS = Millisecond
    Min = Minutes           NA = Not Applicable   NT = Not Tested

Note: Radial is expressed as LOBE RATIO and OFFSET from track center line.
          Auto Test Completed  'Esc' For Previous Menu
```

23-10 A DriveProbe screen display for automatic drive testing.

Symptom 1. The floppy drive is completely dead (the disk does not even initialize when inserted) Check that the drive is configured properly in the system's CMOS setup. Begin troubleshooting by inspecting the diskette itself. When a 3½-inch disk is inserted into a drive, a mechanism should pull the disk's metal shroud away and briefly rotate the spindle motor to ensure positive engagement. Make sure that the disk is properly inserted into the floppy drive assembly. If the diskette does not enter and seat just right within the drive, disk access will be impossible. Try several different diskettes to ensure that the test diskette is not defective. It might be necessary to partially disassemble the computer to access the drive and allow you to see the overall assembly. Free or adjust any jammed assemblies or linkages to correct disk insertion. If you cannot get diskettes to insert properly, change the floppy drive.

If the diskette inserts properly but fails to initialize, carefully inspect the drive's power and signal cabling. Loose connectors or faulty cable wiring can easily disable a floppy drive. Also check that the floppy drive controller board is inserted properly. If connectors are secure, use your multimeter to measure dc voltages at the power connector. Place your meter's ground lead on pin 2 and measure +12 Vdc at pin 1. Ground your meter on pin 3 and measure +5 Vdc at pin 4. If either or both of these voltages is low or missing, try a different power cable or troubleshoot your computer power supply.

Most floppy drive cables offer a "twisted end" with a second drive connector; this allows the cable to support two floppy drives (A: and B:). If the drive remains dead, try switching the cable connector and reconfiguring the cable as the opposing drive. If the drive works then, the cable is probably faulty and should be replaced. If the drive remains dead, either the drive or drive controller is defective. Try another drive. If another drive fails to work, try another drive controller board.

Symptom 2. The floppy drive rotates a disk, but will not seek to the desired track DOS might report this type of problem as a "Seek Error" and is generally the result of a jammed or defective stepping motor assembly. Begin by removing all power, then open the computer and removing the floppy drive. Carefully inspect the head positioning assembly to be certain that there are no broken parts or obstructions that could jam the read/write heads. You might wish to examine the mechanical system with a disk inserted to be certain that the trouble is not a disk alignment problem that might be interfering with head movement. Gently remove any obstructions that you might find. Be careful not to accidentally misalign any linkages or mechanical components in the process of clearing an obstruction.

Once confident that the drive's mechanics are intact and appropriate power is available, you must determine whether the trouble is in your floppy drive or floppy drive controller. Try a different floppy drive signal cable (there might be a break in the STEP line). Use your logic probe to measure the STEP signal in the physical interface (pin 20). When drive access is requested, you should find a pulse signal as the floppy controller attempts to position the R/W heads. If STEP pulses are missing, the floppy drive controller board is probably defective and should be replaced. If you do not have a logic probe, or you cannot locate the STEP signal, replace the drive assembly. If another drive does not correct the problem, replace the floppy drive controller board.

Symptom 3. The floppy drive heads seek properly, but the spindle does not turn This symptom suggests that the spindle motor is inhibited or defective, but all other functions are working properly. Remove all power from the computer. Disassemble the system enough to remove the floppy drive. Carefully inspect the spindle motor, drive belt (if used), and spindle assembly. Make certain that there are no broken parts or obstructions that could jam the spindle. If there is a belt between the motor and spindle, make sure the belt is reasonably tight—it should not slip. You also should examine the floppy drive with a diskette inserted to be certain that the disk's insertion or alignment is not causing the problem. You can double-check your observations using several different diskettes. Gently remove any obstruction(s) that you might find. Be careful not to cause any accidental damage in the process of clearing an obstruction. Do NOT add any lubricating agents to the assembly, but gently vacuum or wipe away any significant accumulations of dust or dirt.

Once you are confident that the floppy drive is mechanically sound and appropriate power is available, you must determine whether the trouble is in the floppy drive or the floppy drive controller board. Try a different floppy drive signal cable (there might be a break in the MOTOR ON line). Use your logic probe to measure the MOTOR ON signal in the physical interface (pin 16). When drive access is requested, the MOTOR ON signal should become true (in most cases an active low). If the MOTOR ON signal is missing, the floppy drive controller board is probably defective and should be replaced. If the MOTOR ON signal is present, the floppy drive is probably defective and should be replaced. If you do not have a logic probe (or cannot locate the MOTOR ON signal), try a new drive first. If a new drive does not resolve the problem, replace the floppy controller board.

Symptom 4. The floppy drive will not read from/write to the diskette All other operations appear normal. DOS will typically report this kind of problem as a *Disk Read* or *Disk Write* error. Begin by trying to read or write a file from a known-good, properly formatted diskette. A faulty diskette can generate some very perplexing read/write problems. If a known-good diskette does not resolve the problem, try cleaning the read/write heads. *Do not run the drive with a head cleaning disk inserted for more than 30 seconds at a time, or you risk damaging the heads with excessive friction.*

When a fresh diskette and clean R/W heads do not correct the problem, you must determine whether the trouble exists in the floppy drive or the floppy controller board. Try a new floppy signal cable. If another cable does not work, use your logic probe to measure the READ DATA signal (pin 30). When the disk is idle, the READ DATA line should read as a constant logic 1 or logic 0. During a read cycle, you should measure a pulse signal as data moves from the drive to the floppy controller board. If no pulse signal appears on the READ DATA line during a read cycle, the drive is probably defective and should be replaced. If READ DATA signals are available from the drive, the floppy controller board is probably defective. If you do not have a logic probe (or cannot locate the READ DATA signal), try a new drive first. If the problem persists, try a new floppy drive controller.

When you cannot write data to the floppy drive, use your logic probe to measure the WRITE GATE and WRITE DATA lines (pins 24 and 22 respectively). During a write cycle, the WRITE GATE should be logic 0 and you should read a pulse signal as data flows from the floppy controller IC to the drive. If the WRITE GATE remains logic 1 or there is no pulse on the WRITE DATA line, replace the defective floppy controller board. When the two WRITE signals appear as expected, replace the entire drive outright.

Symptom 5. The drive is able to write to a write-protected disk Before concluding that there is a drive problem, remove and examine the disk itself to ensure that it is actually write protected. If the disk is not write protected, write protect it appropriately and try the disk again. If the disk is already protected, replace the defective floppy drive assembly. In the unlikely event that the problem should persist, try a new floppy signal cable (the WRITE PROTECT line might be broken). If problems continue, replace the floppy controller board.

Symptom 6. The drive can only recognize either high or double-density media, but not both DOS typically reports an error such as "Bad Media Type," and is almost always the result of a fault in the drive's media-type sensor. Try another floppy drive. If problems should continue, try a new floppy signal cable (the MEDIA TYPE signal line might be broken).

Symptom 7. Double-density (720K) 8.89-cm disks are not working properly when formatted as high-density 1.44Mb disks There has been a long-standing belief that 720K disks can be made to serve as 1.44Mb disks by manually punching a media type hole in the disk to correspond to the hole found in 1.44Mb diskettes. It is the presence of this hole that defines an 8.89-cm diskette as high density. Although some brands of diskettes support this sleight-of-hand better than other brands, the fact remains that double-density media is formulated and applied a bit differently than high-density media. During use, the turbocharged double-density diskettes degrade much faster than normal high-density diskettes; this leads to random data loss and premature diskette failure. As a rule of thumb, do not waste your time trying to fool the drive. The few cents per disk that you might save is certainly not worth the frustration of chronic diskette problems.

Symptom 8. DOS reports an error such as "cannot Read From Drive A:" even though a diskette is fully inserted in the drive, and the drive LED indicates that access is being attempted First, make sure that the disk is really inserted properly and completely in the drive. Also make sure that the disk is working and properly formatted. You might wish to try several disks to be sure that the error is not media related. If the problem persists, the disk-in-place sensor in the drive might be defective. Try a new floppy drive assembly. In the unlikely event that a new drive does not correct the problem, try a new floppy drive signal cable and floppy drive controller board (in that order) to resolve the failure.

Symptom 9. When a new diskette is inserted in the drive, a directory from a previous diskette appears You might have to reset the system in order to get the new diskette to be recognized. This is the classic "phantom directory" problem. *If you suspect a phantom directory, do not initiate any writing to the diskette—its FAT table and directories could be overwritten rendering the disk's contents inaccessible without careful data recovery procedures.* When a diskette is read for the first time, its FAT table and directory from the diskette is cached into a small amount of system RAM. The advantage to this kind of system is that the disk's FAT and directory need only to be read once—subsequent diskette access speed is improved. If the disk's contents are changed, the FAT and directories will be reread as needed to refresh the cache.

When the diskette is ejected from the drive (either by opening the lever of a 5¼-inch drive or pressing the ejection button of a 3½-inch drive), a Change Line (also called a *Disk Change*) signal is sent to the drive controller. This signal causes the drive controller to flush the prior information from the cache and refresh the cache with the new disk's FAT and directories when the next diskette read is performed.

If the disk change signal is not sent when a diskette is removed, the cache will never be refreshed to reflect the next diskette. If you check the directory, you will see the old directory listing (even though the drive light might appear for just a moment). As far as the computer is concerned, the original diskette is still installed. If information is written to the newly installed diskette, the disk will place data according to the old FAT and directory structure. This might overwrite existing files on the new diskette. Some or all of the old FAT and directory table also will be written to the newly installed diskette, so other files on the new diskette might become inaccessible. As you might imagine, this is a potentially disastrous problem (especially if the disk you just inserted contains valuable data). Fortunately, this is a fault that is reasonably easy to spot (because the files you know were on the disk are not shown there now). As long as you check the disk contents before you write to it, you can be fairly certain that the drive is functioning properly.

Dealing with a phantom directory problem is a reasonably straightforward process. In the short term, you or your customer can avoid phantom directories by pressing CTRL & Break or CTRL & C just after a new diskette is inserted. These key combinations force DOS to erase the existing cache, so the new disk's FAT and directories will be read to the cache on the next disk read cycle. Check the disk to make sure that the new FAT and directory is loaded by performing a directory of the diskette. This trick will at least keep your customer running until they can get their system to you for repair.

The long-term fix is a bit more involved. First, you should inspect the floppy drive carefully once the system is on your workbench. Pin 34 of this signal cable carries the Disk Change signal from drive to controller. However, many drive brands must be set to send this signal by selecting a jumper or DIP switch on the drive. If this problem manifests itself when you install a new drive, check for the correct setting of the disk change jumper. Make sure that the new drive is installed correctly.

If the disk change jumper is set correctly (or the drive had been working properly until recently), check to make sure that the 34-pin cable is installed properly and completely. Try removing and reseating the cable. Check cable continuity across the cable at pin 34. If continuity is questionable, try replacing the cable. If the cable checks out properly, the drive's disk change sensor is probably dirty or defective. Try cleaning the sensor by blowing out any dust or debris with clean compressed air, or replace the floppy disk drive entirely.

If the problem persists (even with a new floppy drive), the fault is probably in the drive controller. For drive controllers located on expansion boards, replace the drive controller board. For drive controllers integrated onto the motherboard, the drive controller IC should be replaced, but it might be easier to replace the motherboard outright.

Symptom 10. Your 8.89-cm high-density floppy disk cannot format high-density diskettes (but can read and write to them just fine) This is a problem that plagues older computers (i286 and i386 systems) where after-market high-density drives were added. The problem is a lack of BIOS support for high-density formatting; the system is just too old. In this case, you will need the DOS utility DRIVER.SYS added to your CONFIG.SYS file. A typical command line might appear such as:

```
DEVICE = DRIVER.SYS /D:1
```

By using DRIVER.SYS, you are fooling the system into thinking that there is another drive available (although it is your same physical drive), but the new logical drive will be capable of proper formatting. Refer to your DOS documentation for specific switch settings. As an alternative to using the DRIVER.SYS utility, it also is possible to provide full 8.89-cm drive support by installing a new BIOS (especially if your current BIOS is dated 1989 or older).

24
CHAPTER

Floptical drives

The *floptical* drive (Fig. 24-1) represents one of the first serious attempts to marry magnetic recording principles with optical technology in order to achieve an order of magnitude improvement in recording density. By merging both magnetic recording media and optical tracking techniques (thus the term *floptical*), more than 20Mb of data can be stored on a specially designed 8.89-cm (3½-inch) floptical diskette. Because the recording media is still magnetic, floptical drives are backwardly compatible with both high- and double-density 8.89-cm floppy disks. Large recording densities are possible when the floptical disk is used. Drives, diskettes, and controller boards are all available from several sources, but Iomega Corporation is one of the premier providers of floptical products. This part of the chapter shows the major technologies and operations of a floptical drive.

Iomega Corporation

24-1
An Iomega external floptical drive.

Floptical technology

Data that can be stored on a disk is dependent on two key factors: the distance between the head and media, and the ability to position the heads precisely. Because floppy drive read/write heads actually come into contact with the disk media, a floppy drive should (theoretically) be able to store more data per unit area than any hard drive. The problem with floppy drives is that once an R/W head carriage leaves track 00, there is no feedback to determine where the heads actually are—the drive just steps the heads and hopes that they wind up in the proper place. Such dumb positioning has limited floppy drives for years. If head positioning could be continuously checked and adjusted, much higher data densities could be achieved than the 135 tracks per inch currently available on ordinary 8.89-cm floppy disks.

Floptical technology makes a number of improvements to the disk and the drive. The most pronounced changes are in the floptical disk media itself. In principle, the media is still a plastic disk coated with a fine, high-quality magnetic layer (usually barium ferrite, BaFe, for floptical disks), but the floptical disk is segregated into far more tracks than its conventional cousins achieving 1245 tracks per inch. The tracks are separated by a series of concentric grooves that are physically stamped (or laser etched) onto the media. Each track is about 20 microns apart. These physical tracks are used to aid in R/W head positioning. The elevated areas between each groove are called *lands*. Lands provide a more reflective surface than the grooves.

Tracking

Precision tracking is accomplished through the use of an *EO* (electro-optical) head assembly similar to the one shown in Fig. 24-2. As with the optical devices of CD-ROM drives, floptical tracking and positioning are exceptionally delicate and unforgiving if misaligned. This particular type of tracking assembly is referred to as *holographic tracking* because the laser beam directs a computer-generated pattern (the *hologram*) onto the floptical disk surface. Such a projection renders a pattern that covers several contiguous tracks simultaneously, so holographic tracking is typically more stable and responsive than simple optical-servo tracking that deals with only one track. The tracking patterns are compared in Fig. 24-3.

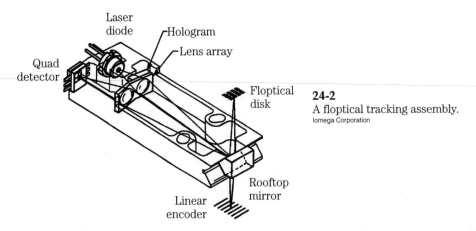

24-2
A floptical tracking assembly.
Iomega Corporation

The solid-state laser is used to project a grating pattern (hologram) through a series of focusing lenses, through a beam splitting prism (called the *mirror*), and out of the device in two simultaneous directions. The holographic pattern is projected onto the disk, as well as a separate linear encoder. The linear encoder serves as a backup positioning mechanism; ordinary 8.89-cm *DD* (double density) and *HD*

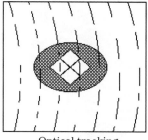

Optical tracking

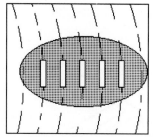

Holographic tracking

24-3 Floptical tracking patterns.

(high density) floppy disks do not have tracking grooves, so the linear encoder provides artificial tracking information when ordinary disks are used. This is what allows ordinary floppy disks to operate reliably in floptical drives. Reflections from either the floptical disk media or the linear encoder (as appropriate) are sent back through the rooftop mirror to a multi-element photodetector (called the *quad detector*). The detector's output is used by the drive's electronics package to continually adjust head position.

Reading and writing

Head tracking and positioning is handled by an optical detection system, but floptical drives utilize magnetic R/W heads that operate using precisely the same principles as ordinary floppy drives. However, floptical head assemblies employ a second, ultrafine head gap to accommodate the tight track dimensions of a floptical diskette. When the drive detects a standard DD or HD floppy diskette, the standard head gaps are used. If the drive detects a floptical (also called a *VHD* or very high density) disk, the ultrafine head gaps are used. Standard diskettes are encoded using MFM, while VHD diskettes are encoded using the 1,7 RLL technique.

Floptical construction

Now that you have seen some concepts and background of floptical drives, you can begin to study their construction. An exploded view of an Iomega floptical drive is shown in Fig. 24-4. As you might see, its assembly is very similar to that of ordinary 8.89-cm floppy drives. The most striking additions to a floptical design are the EO tracking assembly and linear R/W head assembly. Now look at the drive piece by piece.

As with other drive systems, the *chassis* (or frame) is the foundation for the entire drive. Made of cast aluminum or steel, the chassis provides the rigidity and strength to support the other drive components. A molded plastic *bezel* mounts to the chassis and provides the drive's cosmetic appearance, as well as a consistent guide for inserting or removing disks. An eject button and translucent disk-in-use LED cover complete the bezel. A side rail bolts to each side of the chassis that allows the drive to slide in and out of any half-height drive bay.

The disks are inserted, clamped, and ejected through a subassembly known as a *load/unload mechanism* that is virtually identical to the mechanisms used in other

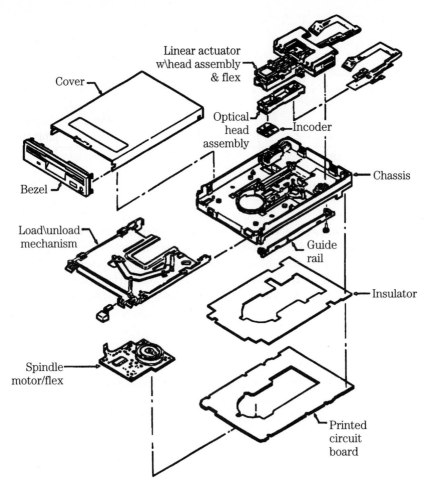

Cover

Linear actuator
w\head assembly
& flex

Optical
head
assembly

Incoder

Chassis

Bezel

Load\unload
mechanism

Guide
rail

Spindle
motor/flex

Insulator

Printed
circuit
board

24-4 An exploded diagram of an Iomega floptical drive. Iomega Corporation

8.89 cm floppy drives. It is advisable to keep the load/unload mechanism together as a subassembly whenever possible; attempt disassembly *only* if you are experiencing problems with disk insertion or removal as you will see in the section on floptical troubleshooting. The large hole in the chassis center accommodates the spindle motor and its associated driver circuit. Note that the spindle motor mounts into the chassis after the drive's main PC board is installed. The drive is controlled through the circuitry contained on a single main printed circuit board. You will see more about floptical drive electronics in the next part of this chapter. A nonconductive insulator is added between the main PC board and chassis to prevent any possibility of a short circuit occurring against the base chassis.

There are three main assemblies located above the chassis besides the load/unload mechanism. An encoder is little more than a piece of glass engraved with an array of microfine lines. The encoder provides tracking signals to the optical assembly whenever ordinary HD and DD floppy disks are being used. *Do not alter or adjust the encoder unless it is absolutely necessary.* Throwing the encoder out of alignment can render the drive inoperative for HD and DD diskettes. Also be very careful not to foul or damage the encoder's surface; each microfine tracking line must be plainly visible to the optical assembly. In spite of its small size, the encoder is a remarkably important component.

The optical head assembly used for tracking floptical, HD, and DD diskettes is attached to the linear actuator/head assembly, and positioned over the encoder. You learned about the operation of this optical tracking mechanism in this chapter. When a floptical disk is inserted, the optical head tracks across the disk using the track grooves placed on the floptical disk. When conventional HD and DD disks are inserted, the optical head tracks the encoder instead.

Disks are inserted and clamped between upper and lower magnetic read/write heads. The heads actually transfer information to and from the disk. Floptical heads use two head gaps: a large gap for working with conventional disks, and a miniature gap for working with very high density (VHD) floptical disks. Read/write heads are mounted on a carriage that is free to slide radially along the disk. Head movement is accomplished using a *linear actuator* (instead of a stepping motor as in ordinary floppy drives). The linear actuator (sometimes called a *linear stepping motor*) provides extremely smooth incremental movement that is so important for fine stepping. Heads and actuator are provided as a single mechanism. A metal cover helps to protect the subassemblies in the drive.

Floptical electronics

The floptical drive electronics package performs several vital functions. First, the electronics is responsible for managing the physical interface between the drive and controller board. Floptical drives typically use a SCSI interface (although proprietary interfaces are often found). The electronics also operates the drive mechanisms (spindle, linear actuator, optical tracking device, and so on), and performs all the conversions and processing of data to and from the disk. Figure 24-5 shows the mounting arrangement for the drive electronics.

The functional block diagram for a floptical drive is shown in Fig. 24-6. Note that a SCSI interface is shown. A SCSI bus connects the drive to its host controller. A single, highly integrated ASIC manages the interface and provides a master drive control function. This master control IC interconnects with the spindle motor, PC board, a RAM buffer used for a cache, a CPU that performs much of the drive's on-board processing, and the read/write electronics that operates the magnetic R/W heads. As you might suspect, most of the drive's physical control resides here.

All CPUs need instructions in order to operate, and the floptical's CPU is no exception. A *firmware* IC supplies the program and data needed for the on-board CPU to operate the digital servo tracking system. A diagnostic port is also available that allows the drive to be connected to a factory test system for in-depth, precise factory diagnostics. Factory diagnostics are vitally important when aligning and adjusting optical tracking after a repair. The actual optical tracking head and the read/write heads are mounted over the media in the carriage assembly.

The digital servo system is responsible for controlling carriage movement over a diskette. Tracking signals from the optical head are amplified by the digital servo and converted into digital signals. A digital signal processor (DSP, a very specialized type

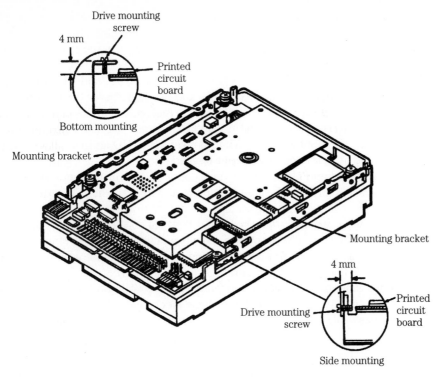

24-5 Electronics mounted on the floptical drive. Iomega Corporation

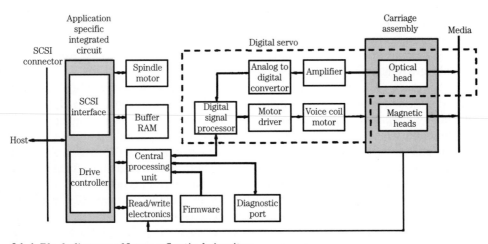

24-6 Block diagram of Iomega floptical circuitry. Iomega Corporation

of CPU) processes those signals under direction of the CPU. When a track must be changed or adjusted, the DSP outputs an appropriate signal to a motor driver that causes the linear motor to move the carriage. New tracking signals are then interpreted and corrected as needed. It is this precise, closed-loop approach to tracking that makes the high recording densities of hard drives and optical drives possible.

Floptical interfaces

The floptical drive is merely another computer peripheral, and it is rather useless by itself. The drive must connect to a computer (referred to as a *host*) in order to serve any useful function. Because the floptical disk drive is operated by the host system, there must be some means of carrying data and control signals into and out of the drive. As with other types of drives, signal exchange is accomplished over the *physical interface*. There are a myriad of possible signal interface schemes, but manufacturers prefer to utilize a standard interface such as SCSI. A standard interface allows a drive built by any manufacturer to run properly on the same computer. There are, however, a small number of manufacturers that choose to implement a custom (proprietary) interface scheme. A host controller board interfaces the floptical drive's signals to the computer's main buses. Interfaces usually fall into two categories: SCSI and proprietary.

SCSI

The *small computer system interface* (SCSI or "scuzzy") is a system-level device interface that can service a wide range of peripheral devices (printers, CD-ROMs, hard drives, tape drives, and so on). A SCSI host controller board would be required in your computer to interface a 50-pin SCSI signal cable to your system's main buses. A single host controller board can support up to 8 SCSI devices simultaneously. The advantages of SCSI are flexibility and performance. Data can be transferred very quickly, and multiple devices can share the same bus system. Because the SCSI interface is discussed in detail in Chapter 48, it is not discussed further here.

Proprietary interface

The SCSI drive interface is not ideally suited to floptical drive systems. The tremendous speed and performance potential of the SCSI technique is often wasted on floppy drive systems—SCSI is simply too fast. No floppy drive made can possibly hope to utilize a SCSI bus to its full potential. In order to achieve reasonable performance for a floptical system, manufacturers can provide host controllers that handle the optimum data transfer rate (usually about 1.6 Mbits/s for VHD, 1.2 Mbits/s for HD, and 0.6 Mbits/s for DD). SCSI interfaces can handle more than 10 Mbits/s. Proprietary controllers are often available as options, so the drive can operate with a native SCSI drive controller, or can operate with a proprietary controller board.

Proprietary interfaces are usually bundled systems—the manufacturer provides any cables and connectors necessary to set up and use their system. In most cases, the manufacturer also supplies the driver software that controls the drive. You will have to refer to a schematic or detailed block diagram for your proprietary drive system to learn the name and function of each signal pin. The proprietary controller board translates the interface cable signals into signals needed by the computer's main buses.

Troubleshooting floptical drives

On the surface, floptical drive troubleshooting is surprisingly similar to ordinary floppy drive troubleshooting—many of the key components perform virtually identical functions, although this chapter has shown you some of the unique features found in floptical drives. It is important to remind you here that the optical tracking system used in floptical drives is extremely delicate and unforgiving. Factory-precise alignments are needed to achieve accurate and reliable operation. As a result, any disassembly represents somewhat of a calculated risk because replacement or adjustment of optical components can throw the drive so far out of alignment that it might be unusable. As a general rule, do not attempt to align or repair a floptical drive. Faulty drives should be replaced outright.

Symptom 1. The floptical drive is completely dead The disk does not even initialize when inserted. Begin troubleshooting by inspecting the diskette itself. When a disk is inserted into a drive, a mechanism should pull the disk's metal shroud away and briefly rotate the spindle motor to ensure positive engagement. Make sure that the disk is properly inserted into the floptical drive assembly. If the diskette does not enter and seat just right within the drive, disk access will be impossible. Try several different diskettes to ensure that test diskette is not defective. It might be necessary to partially disassemble the computer to access the drive and allow you to see the overall assembly. Free or adjust any jammed assemblies or linkages to correct disk insertion. If you cannot get diskettes to insert properly, replace the drive.

If the disk inserts properly but fails to initialize, carefully inspect the drive's power and physical interface cabling. Loose connectors or faulty cable wiring can easily disable any drive. Use your multimeter to measure dc voltages at the power connector. Place your meter's ground lead on pin 2 and measure +12 Vdc at pin 1. Ground your meter on pin 3 and measure +5 Vdc at pin 4. If either of both of these voltages is low or missing, troubleshoot or replace your computer power supply. If power checks correctly, try a new signal cable between the drive and controller.

At this point, the trouble is either a fault in the drive's disk-in-place sensor or the interface board. Try replacing the floptical drive first (because that is the likeliest place for problems to develop, especially if the floptical drive is using a SCSI interface). If problems persist (and the interface is proprietary) try a new adapter board.

Symptom 2. The floptical drive rotates a disk, but will not seek to the desired track This type of symptom generally suggests that the head positioning linear motor is inhibited or defective, but all other floptical drive functions are working properly. Begin by disassembling your computer and removing the floptical drive. Carefully inspect the head positioning assembly to be certain that there are no broken parts or obstructions that could jam the head carriage. You might wish to examine the mechanical system with a disk inserted to be certain that the trouble is not a disk alignment problem that might be interfering with head movement. Gently remove any obstructions that you might find. Be extremely careful not to misalign any optical assemblies or mechanical components in the process of clearing an obstruction.

Check the voltages being delivered to the drive. A +12-Vdc source is usually needed to drive the linear motor. Place your meter's ground lead on pin 2 and measure +12 Vdc at pin 1. If voltage is low or absent (chances are other drives in the PC are also malfunctioning), troubleshoot or replace the system power supply. If voltage levels are normal, replace the drive outright.

Symptom 3. The floptical drive heads seek properly, but the spindle does not turn This symptom suggests that the spindle motor is inhibited or defective, but all other functions are working properly. Remove all power from the computer.

Disassemble the system enough to remove the floptical drive. Carefully inspect the spindle motor and spindle assembly. Make certain that there are no broken parts or obstructions that could jam the spindle. You should also examine the drive with a disk inserted to be certain that the disk's insertion or alignment is not causing the problem. You can double-check your observations using several different diskettes. Gently remove any obstruction(s) that you might find. Be careful not to cause any accidental damage to the optical tracking head in the process of clearing an obstruction. If problems persist, replace the drive outright.

Check the voltages being delivered to the drive. A +12-Vdc source is usually needed to drive the spindle motor. Place your meter's ground lead on pin 2 and measure +12 Vdc at pin 1. If voltage is low or absent (chances are other drives in the PC are also malfunctioning), troubleshoot or replace the system power supply. If voltage levels are normal, replace the drive outright.

Symptom 4. The floptical drive encounters trouble reading or writing to the disk All other operations appear normal. This type of problem can manifest itself in several ways, but your computer's operating system will usually inform you when a disk read or write error has occurred. Begin by trying a known-good, properly formatted disk in the drive. A faulty diskette can generate some very perplexing read/write problems. If a known-good diskette does not resolve the problem, try cleaning the read/write heads according to manufacturer's suggestions. *Do not run the drive with a head cleaning disk inserted for more than 30 seconds at a time (or you risk damaging the heads with excessive friction).* If R/W problems continue, there is either a fault in the R/W head assembly, or in the drive's internal circuitry. In either case, try replacing the floptical drive.

Symptom 5. The drive is able to write to a write-protected disk Before concluding that there is a drive problem, remove and examine the disk itself to ensure that it is actually write protected. If the disk is not write protected, write protect it appropriately and try the disk again. If the disk is already protected, there is probably a fault in the drive's write-protect sensor. Check and clean the write-protect sensor. If problems persist, replace the drive outright.

Symptom 6. The drive will not read or write ordinary HD or DD disks properly An intricate part of floptical drive operation is optical tracking. When floptical disks are being used, the drive tracks the minute grooves pressed into the disk. When standard HD or DD floppy disks are used, however, there are no physical marks for the drive to track, so the drive uses an encoder located just below the optical tracking head to provide tracking signals. If the drive works properly with floptical disks but NOT with standard disks, encoder tracking might be interrupted.

Check *but do not adjust* the small glass encoder located below the optical tracking head. Any accumulation of dust or debris on the encoder can interfere with tracking signals. Use a photography-grade lens brush and *gently* whisk away any accumulation on the encoder. You might also wish to brush any dust or dirt from the optical tracking head aperture pointing at the encoder. Any optical interference can interrupt the light path and result in tracking or R/W problems. Use extreme care when working around the drive's optics. If that fails to restore operation, replace the drive.

Symptom 7. When a new diskette is inserted in the drive, a directory from a previous diskette appears You might have to reset the system in order to get the new diskette to be recognized. This is the classic "phantom directory" problem. *If you suspect a phantom directory, do not initiate any writing to the diskette; its FAT table and directories could be overwritten rendering the disk's contents inaccessible without careful data recovery procedures.* When a diskette is read for the first time, its FAT table and directory from the diskette is cached into a small amount of system RAM. The advantage to this kind of system is that the disk's FAT and directory need only to be read once; subsequent diskette access speed is improved. If the disk's contents are changed, the FAT and directories will be reread as needed to refresh the cache. When the diskette is ejected from the drive (either by opening the lever of a 5¼-inch drive or pressing the ejection button of a 3½-inch drive), a *Change Line* (also called a *Disk Change*) signal is sent to the drive controller. This signal causes the drive controller to flush the prior information from the cache and refresh the cache with the new disk's FAT and directories when the next diskette read is performed.

If the disk change signal is not sent when a diskette is removed, the cache will never be refreshed to reflect the next diskette. If you check the directory, you will see the old directory listing (even though the drive light might appear for just a moment). As far as the computer is concerned, the original diskette is still installed. If information is written to the newly installed diskette, the disk will place data according to the old FAT and directory structure. This might overwrite existing files on the new diskette. Some or all of the old FAT and directory table will also be written to the newly installed diskette, so other files on the new diskette might become inaccessible. As you might imagine, this is a potentially disastrous problem (especially if the disk you just inserted contains valuable data). Fortunately, this is a fault that is reasonably easy to spot (because the files you know were on the disk are not shown there now). As long as you check the disk contents before you write to it, you can be fairly certain that the drive is functioning properly.

Dealing with a phantom directory problem is a reasonably straightforward process. In the short term, you or your customer can avoid phantom directories by pressing CTRL & Break or CTRL & C just after a new diskette is inserted. These key combinations force DOS to erase the existing cache, so the new disk's FAT and directories will be read to the cache on the next disk read cycle. Check the disk to make sure that the new FAT and directory is loaded by performing a directory of the diskette. This trick will at least keep your customer running until they can get their system to you for repair. Once the system is on your bench, replace the floptical drive outright.

25
CHAPTER

Hard drives

There is little doubt that the *hard-disk drive* (or HDD) has become one of the most important elements of a PC. Just consider some of the profound advances that have taken place over the last 15 years. Storage capacities for hard drives have doubled roughly every 24 to 36 months—the 10Mb full-height drives available early in 1982 have been replaced by 1Gb half-height drives (full-height drives can now manage up to 3Gb). *Seek times*, once over 85 ms for a 10Mb drive in 1982, have fallen to only 8–10 ms for current drives. *Data transfer rates*, only 102K/s for a 10Mb drive in 1982, have skyrocketed to over 10Mb/s. Prices for hard drives have dropped from about $150.00/Mb to well under $1.00/Mb. With such startling advances, it is easy to see why we have come to look upon hard drive technology as a measure of PC power.

Not only is a hard drive vital for local storage, but the drive's performance is a gating factor in the system's overall performance. Indeed, much of the software that we have come to rely on would be impossible without the speed and capacity of current hard drives (Fig. 25-1). Today, large hard drives are standard equipment in desktop computers, and available in virtually every notebook and subnotebook computer now in production. This chapter presents the technology and principles of hard-disk drives, and provides you with an array of solutions for drive testing and troubleshooting.

25-1
An NEC D3756 hard drive. NEC
Technologies, Inc.

Drive concepts

The first step in understanding hard drives is to learn the basic concepts involved. Many of the terms covered for floppy drives also apply to hard drives, but the additional performance requirements and operating demands placed on hard drives have resulted in a proliferation of important new ideas. In principle, a hard-disk drive is very similar to a floppy drive. A magnetic recording media is applied to a disk substrate material (such as aluminum or ceramic), which is then spun at a high rate of speed. Magnetic read/write heads in close proximity to the media can step rapidly across the spinning media to detect or create flux transitions as required (Fig. 25-2). When you look closely, however, you can see that there are some major physical differences between floppy and hard drives.

Maxtor Corporation

25-2. A Maxtor hard drive.

Platters and media

Where floppy disks use magnetic material applied over a thin, flexible substrate of mylar or some other plastic, hard drives use rugged, solid substrates called *platters*. You can clearly view the platters of a hard drive in Fig. 25-2. A platter is typically made of aluminum because aluminum is a light material, it is easy to machine to desired tolerances, and holds its shape under the high centrifugal forces that occur at high rotation rates. Because a major advantage of a hard drive is speed, platters are rotated at about 3600 rpm—ten times the rate of floppy drives. Newer, high-performance drives rotate their platters over 5000 rpm. Platters also are made from other materials such as glass and ceramic. Both materials are appealing because of their low thermal coefficient, inherent flatness, and the ability to withstand high rotating forces. A hard drive generally uses two or more platters.

Hard drives must be capable of tremendous recording densities, well over 10,000 *BPI* (bits per inch). To achieve such substantial recording densities, platter media is far superior to the oxide media used for floppy disks. First, the media must possess a high coercivity so that each flux transition is well defined and easily discernible from every other flux transition. Coercitivity of hard drive media typically exceeds 1400 oersteds (compared with 600 oersteds for floppy media). Second, the media must be extremely flat across the entire platter surface to within just a few micro inches. Hard drive R/W heads do not actually contact their platters, but ride within a few micro inches over the platter surfaces. A surface defect of only a few micro inches can collide with a head and destroy it. Such a *head crash* is often a catastrophic defect that requires hard drive replacement. Floppy drive heads do contact the media, so minor surface defects are not a major concern.

Air flow and head flight

R/W heads in a hard-disk drive must travel extremely close to the surface of each platter, but can never actually contact the media while the drive is running. The heads could be mechanically fixed, but fixed-altitude flight does not allow for shock or natural vibration that is always present in a drive assembly. Instead, R/W heads are made to float within micro inches of a platter surface by suspending the heads on a layer of moving air. Figure 25-3 illustrates the typical air flow in a hard drive. Disk (platter) rotation creates a slight cushion that elevates the heads. You also might notice that some air is channeled through a fine filter that helps to remove any particles from within the drive's enclosure.

Air flow path

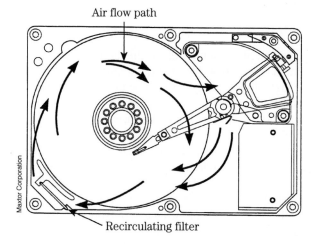

Maxtor Corporation

Recirculating filter

25-3
Air flow patterns in a hard drive.

It is important to note that all hard drives seal their platter assemblies into an air-tight chamber. The reason for such a seal is to prevent contamination from dust, dirt, spills, or strands of hair. Contamination that lands on a platter surface can easily result in a head crash. A head crash can damage the head, the media, or both. Any physical damage can result in an unusable drive. Consider the comparison shown in Fig. 25-4. During normal operation, a hard drive's R/W head flies above the media at a distance of only about 2 microns (micro-inches). It follows then that any variation in surface flatness due to platter defects or contaminants can have catastrophic effects on head height. Even an average particle of smoke is at least ten times wider than the flying height. With such proportions, you can understand why it is critically important that the platter compartment remain sealed at all times. The platter compartment can only be opened in a *cleanroom* environment. A cleanroom is a small, enclosed room where the air is filtered to remove any contaminants larger than 3 microns.

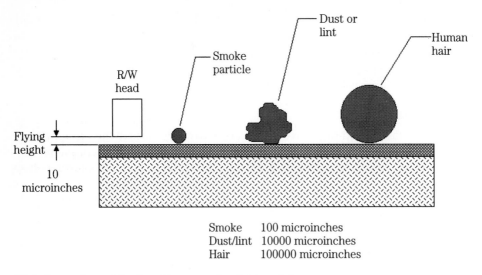

Smoke   100 microinches
Dust/lint 10000 microinches
Hair   100000 microinches

25-4 Comparison of foreign objects on a hard drive platter.

Areal density

It is desirable to pack as much information as possible in the media of hard drive platters. The *areal density* of a media describes this maximum amount of capacity in terms of megabytes per square inch. Today's hard drives used in typical computers use media supporting 100 to 200 megabytes per square inch. As you might imagine, physically smaller platters must hold media with a higher areal density to offer storage capacities similar to larger drives.

There are several major factors that affect areal density. First, the actual size of magnetic particles in the media places an upper barrier on areal density; smaller particles allow higher areal densities. Larger coercitivity of the media and smaller R/W heads with tighter magnetization fields allow higher areal densities. Finally, head height (the altitude of an R/W head over the platter surface) controls density. The closer an R/W head passes to its media, the higher areal densities can be. As heads fly farther away, magnetic fields spread out resulting in lower densities. Surface smoothness is then a major limiting factor in areal density because smoother surfaces allow R/W heads to fly closer to the media.

Latency

As fast as a hard drive is, it does not work instantaneously. There is a finite period of delay between the moment that a read or write command is initiated over the drive's physical interface, and the moment that desired information is available (or placed). This delay is known as *latency*. More specifically, latency refers to the time it takes for needed bytes to pass under an R/W head. If the head has not quite reached the desired location yet, latency can be quite short. If the head has just missed the desired location, the head must wait almost a full rotation before the needed bits are available again, so latency can be rather long. In general, a disk drive is specified with *average latency*, which (statistically) is time for the spindle to make half of a full rotation. For a disk rotating at 3600 rpm (or 60 rotations per second), a full rotation is completed in [1/60] 16.7 ms. Average latency would then be [16.7/2] 8.3 ms. Disks spinning at 5400 rpm offer an average latency of 5.5 ms, and so on. As a rule, the faster a disk spins, the lower latency will be. Ultimately, disk speed is limited by centrifugal forces acting on the platters.

Tracks, cylinders, and sectors

As with floppy drives, you cannot simply place data anywhere on a hard drive platter—the drive would have no idea where to look for data, or if the data is even valid. The information on each platter must be sorted and organized into a series of known, standard locations. Each platter side can be considered as a two-dimensional field possessing height and width. With this sort of geometry, data is recorded in sets of concentric circles running from the disk spindle to the platter edge. A drive can move its R/W heads over the spinning media to locate needed data or programs in a matter of milliseconds. Every concentric circle on a platter is known as a *track*. A platter generally contains 312 to 2048 tracks. Figure 25-5 shows data organization on a simple platter assembly. Note that only one side of the three platters is shown. Although each surface of a platter is a two-dimensional area, the number of platter surfaces involved in a hard drive (four, six, eight, or more) bring a third dimension into play. Because each track is located directly over the same tracks on subsequent platters, each track in a platter assembly can be visualized as a cylinder that passes through every platter. The number of *cylinders* is equal to the number of tracks on one side of a platter.

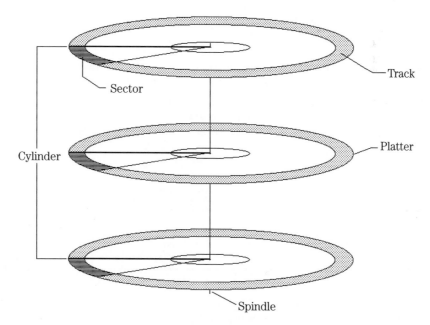

25-5 Data organization on a hard drive.

Once an R/W head finishes reading one track, the head must be stepped to another (usually adjacent) track. This stepping process, no matter how rapid, does require some finite amount of time. When the head tries to step directly from the end of one track to the beginning of another, the head will arrive too late to catch the new track's index pulse(s), so the drive will have to wait almost an entire rotation to synchronize with the track index pulse. By offsetting the start points of each track as in Fig. 25-6, head travel time can be compensated for. This *cylinder skewing* technique is intended to improve hard drive performance by reducing the disk time lost during normal head steps. A head should be able to identify and read the desired information from a track within one disk rotation.

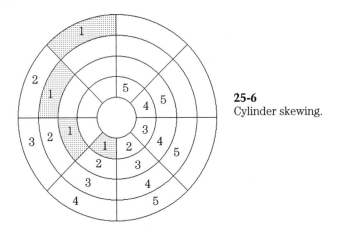

25-6
Cylinder skewing.

Tracks are broken down even further into small segments called *sectors*. As with DOS floppy disks, a sector holds 512 bytes of data, along with error checking and housekeeping data that identifies the sector, track, and results calculated by *CRC* (cyclical redundancy checking). The location and ID information for each sector is developed when the drive is formatted. After formatting, only sector data and CRC bytes are updated during writing. If sector ID information is accidentally overwritten or corrupted, the data recorded in the afflicted sector becomes unreadable.

Figure 25-7 shows the layout for a typical sector on a Maxtor SCSI drive. As you can see, there is much more than just 512 bytes of data. The start of every sector is marked with a pulse. The pulse signaling the first sector of a track is called the *index*

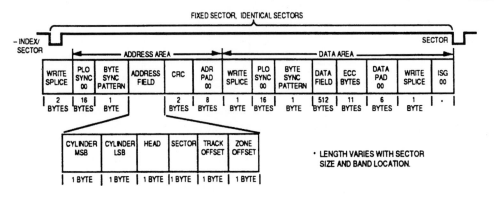

25-7 A typical hard drive sector layout. Maxtor Corporation

pulse. There are two portions to every sector: an address area and data area. The *address area* is used to identify the sector. This is critically important because the drive must be able to identify precisely which cylinder, head, and sector is about to be read or written. This location information is recorded in the address field, and is followed by two bytes of cyclical redundancy check (CRC) data. When a drive identifies a location, it generates a CRC code that it compares to the CRC code recorded on the disk. If the two CRC codes match, the address is assumed to be valid, and disk operation can continue. Otherwise, an error has occurred and the entire sector is considered invalid. This failure usually precipitates a catastrophic DOS error message.

After a number of bytes are encountered for drive timing and synchronization, up to 512 bytes can be read or written to the data field. The data is processed to derive eleven bytes of ECC error checking code using Reed Solomon encoding. If data is being read, the derived ECC is compared to the recorded ECC. When the codes match, data is assumed to be valid and drive operation continues. Otherwise, a data read error is assumed. During writing, the old ECC data is replaced with the new ECC data derived for the current data. It is interesting to note that only the data and ECC fields of a sector are written after formatting. All other sector data remains untouched until the drive is reformatted. If a retentivity problem should eventually allow one or more bits to become corrupt in the address area, the sector will fail. In total, an average sector actually has 583 bytes.

Sectors and clusters

Although the sector is the smallest area of storage on a drive, it is smaller than DOS is capable of working with. When a drive is formatted with DOS, sectors are grouped into *clusters*. The drive's file allocation table (FAT) deals with clusters. There can be up to 64 sectors in a cluster (depending on the size of the drive). Clusters make file housekeeping chores easier for DOS, but will easily waste space if the file being saved is much smaller than the cluster size. Suppose an ordinary cluster is 16 sectors. One cluster would then offer (16×512) 8192 bytes. If a file being saved is only 3K, at least 5K of the cluster is wasted because DOS can only assign one file to any one cluster. If the file is larger than one cluster, DOS will simply store the file in multiple clusters wherever the clusters are available. It's a system that works, but is not terribly efficient.

Sector sparing

Not all sectors on a hard drive are usable. When a drive is formatted, bad sectors must be removed from normal use. The sparing process works to ensure that each track has access to the appropriate number of working sectors. When sparing is performed in-line (as a drive is being formatted), faulty sectors cause all subsequent sectors to be shifted up one sector. In-line sparing is not widely used. *Field defect sparing* (after the format process is complete) assigns (remaps) faulty sectors to other working sectors located in spare disk tracks that are reserved for that purpose.

The only place where faulty sectors are absolutely not permitted is on track 00. Track 00 is used to hold a hard drive's partition and FAT information. If a drive cannot read or write to track 00, the entire drive is rendered unusable. If a sector in track 00 should fail during operation, reformatting the drive to lock out the bad sector will not necessarily recover the drive's operation. Track 00 failures usually necessitate reformatting the drive from scratch or replacing it entirely.

Landing zone

The R/W heads of a hard drive fly within micro inches of their respective platter surfaces—held aloft with air currents produced by the spinning platters. When the drive is turned off, however, the platters slow to a halt. During this *spindown* period, air flow falls rapidly, and heads can literally "crash" into their platter surfaces. Whenever a head touches a platter surface, data can be irretrievably destroyed. Even during normal operation, a sudden shock or bump can cause one or more heads to skid across their surfaces. Although a drive can usually be reformatted after a head crash (faulty sectors spared out), all current data and programs would have to be reloaded from a backup.

In order to avoid head crash during normal spindown, a cylinder is reserved (either the innermost or outermost cylinder) as a *landing zone*. No data is stored on the landing zone, so any surface problems caused by head landings are harmless. Most drives used in small computers automatically move the head assembly over the landing zone before spindown, then gently lock the heads into place until power is restored. Locking helps to ensure that random shocks and vibrations do not shake the heads onto adjacent data-carrying tracks and cause damage while power is off.

Interleave

The *interleave* of a hard drive refers to the order in which sectors are numbered on a platter. Interleave was a critical factor in older desktop computer systems where the core logic (CPU and memory) was relatively slow compared to drive performance. It was necessary to create artificial delays in the drive to allow core logic to catch up. Delays were accomplished by physically separating the sectors (numbering contiguous sectors out of order). This ordering forced the drive to read a sector, then skip one or more sectors (one, two, three, or more) to reach the next subsequent sector. The drive would have to make several rotations before all sectors on a track could be read. The ratio of a sector's length versus the distance between two subsequent sectors is known as the *interleave factor*. For example, if a drive reads a sector and skips a sector to reach the next sequential sector, interleave factor would be 1:3, and so on. The greater the interleave, the more rotations that would be needed to read all the sectors on a track, and the slower the drive would be. To achieve highest disk performance, interleave should be eliminated.

Because core logic today is so much faster than even the fastest hard drive, the issue of interleave is largely irrelevant. Drives no longer interleave their sectors, so all sectors are in sequential order around the track, and the interleave factor is 1:1. All data on a track can be read in one disk rotation (minus latency). An interleave factor of 1:1 yields optimal drive performance.

Write precompensation

As you have already seen, a hard drive spins its platter(s) at a constant rate. This is known as *CAV* (constant angular velocity). Although constant rotation requires only a very simple motor circuit, extra demands are placed on the media. Tracks closer to the spindle are physically shorter than tracks toward the platter's outer edge. Shorter tracks result in shorter sectors. For inner sectors to hold the same amount of data as outer sectors, data must be packed more densely on the inner sectors—each magnetic flux reversal is actually smaller. Unfortunately, smaller flux reversals produce weaker magnetic fields in the R/W heads during reading.

If the inner sectors are written with a stronger magnetic field, flux transitions stored in the media will be stronger. When the inner sectors are then read, a clearer, more well-defined signal will result. The use of increased writing current to compensate for diminished disk response is known as *write precompensation*. The track where write precompensation is expected to begin is specified in the drive's parameter table in CMOS system setup. Write precompensation filled an important role in early drives that used older, oxide-based media. Today's thin-film media and very small drive geometries result in low signal differences across the platter area, so write precompensation (although still specified) is rarely meaningful anymore.

Data transfer rate

Information must be transferred back and forth between the computer's core logic and the drive mechanism. The *data transfer rate* specifies just how fast bits can be sent between a host system and drive. Data transfer rate is generally specified either in megahertz (MHz) or megabytes per second (Mbyte/s). Remember that the Mbyte/s rate should be ⅛ of the MHz rate. The rate of data transfer is a specification that depends on a variety of system conditions: the class and speed of the CPU, core logic overhead (or bus utilization), the physical interface architecture in use, and the design of the hard drive itself.

Today, the major limiting factor of data transfer rate is the physical interface because core logic and hard drives are capable of exceptionally fast operation. Drives using the IDE interface can transfer data up to 4 Mb/s over an 8 bit data bus, and up to 5 Mb/s, while the newer SCSI-2 interface runs up to 10 Mb/s.

Encoding

Binary information must be translated into flux transitions (or *encoded*) for storage on magnetic media. Not only must data be stored, but it is desirable to manipulate data in order to fit more information into limited media space. Floppy drives make use of FM and MFM encoding schemes to encode data. Both FM and MFM encoding cause a 1:1 relationship between the bit being recorded and the flux transition recorded on the disk (1 bit = 1 flux transition). Such a relationship is straightforward, but is certainly not the most efficient way to encode data. Many hard drives today make use of the *Run Length Limited* (RLL) encoding scheme.

Run Length Limited encoding is intended to represent each byte of data as a unique series of 16 flux transitions. Because there are 65,536 possible 16-bit codes (2^{16}), engineers have chosen 256 of those 16-bit combinations to represent each possible byte. Each combination is chosen so that it records easily on the available media. The objective is to choose codes that space digital 1s farther apart—this makes it easier for control circuitry to read and write. Each 16-bit code is actually placed on the media in a much denser fashion than floppy drives. As a result, there are twice as many bits to represent a byte, but the bits are placed many times closer together, resulting in an actual space savings.

Consider the 2,7 RLL scheme. Bytes are converted into 16-bit words where each logic 1 is separated by 2 to 7 logic 0s (thus the term 2,7 RLL). Table 25-1 illustrates some example conversions. Notice that logic 1s never have less than two 0s between them. As a result, there are ⅔ fewer flux transitions per bit (on average). There are twice as many bits, but only ⅓ the number of flux changes. Encoding with 2,7 RLL offers more than 50% more storage capacity than MFM encoding, as well as a 50% increase in the data transfer rate (twice the number of bits being read in the same period of time). Keep in mind that packing so much data requires media with a high coercitivity (usually 600 oersteds or more).

Table 25-1.
An example of 2,7 RLL encoding

Binary data	2,7 RLL interpretation
11	1000
10	0100
011	001000
010	100100
0011	00001000
0010	00100100
000	000100

An advanced version of Run Length Limited encoding is 3,9 RLL. Bytes also are translated into 16-bit patterns, but each binary 1 is separated by 3 to 9 logic 0s. The 3,9 RLL scheme can pack 50% more data on a drive than 2,7 RLL (100% more than MFM encoding), and an even higher data transfer rate. Note that the R/W circuitry required to operate a 3,9 RLL drive must be faster and offer a wider bandwidth than other encoding schemes. Unfortunately, 3,9 RLL is not widely used because data reliability begins to suffer at that level of encoding.

Disk caching

Ideally, a mass-storage device should respond instantaneously; data should be available the moment it is requested. Unfortunately, the instant access and transfer of data is virtually impossible with today's magnetic (and optical) storage technologies. The inescapable laws of physics govern the limitations of mechanical systems such as spindles and head stepping, and mechanical delays will always be present (to some extent) in drive systems.

The problem now facing computer designers is that mechanical drive systems (as fast and precise as they are) are still far slower than the computer circuitry handling the information. In the world of personal computers, a millisecond is a very long time. For DOS-based systems, you often must wait for disk access to be completed before DOS allows another operation to begin. Such delays can be quite irritating when the drive is accessing huge programs and data files typical of current software packages. Designers have developed a technique called *drive caching* to increase the apparent speed of drive systems.

Caching basically allocates a small amount of solid-state memory that acts as an interim storage area (or *buffer*). A cache is typically loaded with information that is anticipated to be required by the system. When a disk read is initiated, the cache is checked for desired information. If the desired information is actually in the cache (a *cache hit*), that information is transferred from the cache buffer to the core logic at electronic rates; no disk access occurs, and very fast data transfer is achieved. If the desired information is not in the cache (a *cache miss*), the data is taken from the hard disk at normal drive speeds with no improvement in performance. A variety of complex software algorithms are used to predict what disk information to load and save in a cache. Some cache can be implemented in the drive itself, while drive caching programs (such as SmartDrive under DOS or Windows) allocate a portion of system RAM for the disk cache.

Although the majority of caches are intended to buffer read operations, some caches also buffer write operations. A write cache accepts the data to be saved from core logic, then returns system control while the drive works separately to save the information. Keep in mind that a cache does not accelerate the drive itself. A cache merely helps to move your system along so that you need not wait for drive delays.

Drive construction

Now that you have a background in major hard drive concepts and operations, it is time to take a drive apart and show you how all the key pieces fit together. Although it is somewhat rare that you should ever need to disassemble a hard drive, the understanding of each part and its placement will help you to appreciate drive testing and the various hard drive failure modes. An exploded diagram for a Quantum hard drive is shown in Fig. 25-8. There are six areas that this book concentrates on: the frame, platters, R/W heads, head actuators, spindle motor, and electronics package. Look at each area.

Frame

The mechanical frame (called a chassis or base casting assembly) is remarkably important to the successful operation of a hard drive. It affects a drive's structural, thermal, and electrical integrity. A frame must be rigid, and provide a steady platform for mounting the working components. Larger drives typically use a chassis of cast aluminum, but the small drive in your notebook or pen computer might use a plastic frame. The particular frame material really depends on the *form factor* (dimensions) of your drive.

Platters

As you probably read in this chapter, *platters* (part of the *disk stack assembly*) are relatively heavy-duty disks of aluminum, glass, or ceramic. Platters are then coated on both sides with a layer of magnetic material (the actual media) and coated with a protective layer. Finished and polished platters are then stacked and coupled

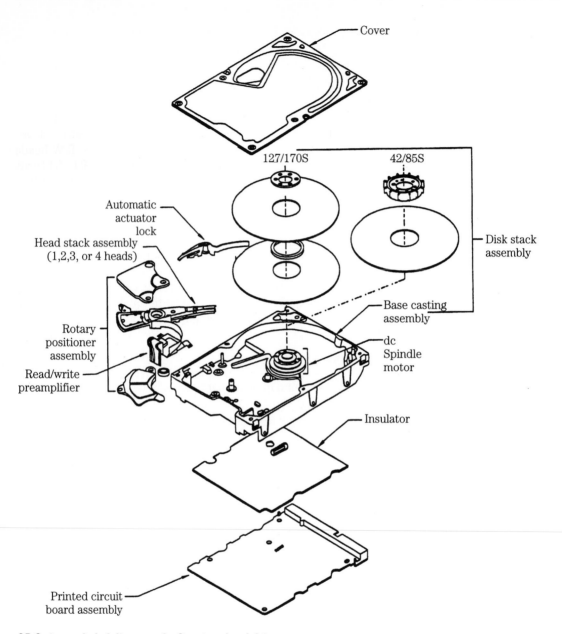

Cover

127/170S

42/85S

Automatic
actuator
lock

Head stack assembly
(1,2,3, or 4 heads)

Disk stack
assembly

Base casting
assembly

Rotary
positioner
assembly

dc
Spindle
motor

Read/write
preamplifier

Insulator

Printed circuit
board assembly

25-8 An exploded diagram of a Quantum hard drive. Quantum Corporation

to the spindle motor (some drives might only use one platter). Before the platter
stack is fixed to the chassis, the R/W heads (part of the head stack assembly) are fitted in between each disk. There is usually one head per platter side, so a drive with
two platters should have three or four heads. During drive operation, the spindle motor spins the platter stack at 3600 rpm or higher.

Read/write heads

As with floppy drives, read/write (R/W) heads form the interface between a drive's electronic circuitry and magnetic media. During writing, a head translates electronic signals into magnetic flux transitions that saturate points on the media where those transitions take place. A read operation works roughly in reverse. Flux transitions along the disk induce electrical signals in the head that are amplified, filtered, and translated into corresponding logic signals. It is up to the drive's electronics to determine whether a head is reading or writing. Early hard drive R/W heads generally resembled floppy drive heads—soft iron cores with a coil of 8 to 34 turns of fine copper wire. Such heads were physically large and relatively heavy that limited the number of tracks available on a platter surface, and presented more inertia to be overcome by the head positioning system.

Hard-drive designs rapidly abandoned classical "wound coil" heads in favor of thin-film R/W heads. Thin-film heads are fabricated in much the same way as ICs or platter media using photochemical processes. The result is a very flat, sensitive, small, and durable R/W head, but even thin-film heads use an air gap and 8 to 34 turns of copper wire. Small size and light weight allow for smaller track widths (more than 1000 tracks per platter side) and faster head travel time. The inherent flatness of thin-film heads helps to reduce flying height to only 5 microns or so.

The most recent advances in hard drive R/W heads use *MR* (magneto-resistive) technology. The resistance of a conductor changes slightly when exposed to an external magnetic field. By passing a known current through the head, the MR head acts as a sensor to detect magnetic alignments. MR heads are two or three times more sensitive than thin-film heads. Unfortunately, MR heads are only good for reading; thin-film heads are still needed for writing. MR heads also are very expensive.

In assemblies, the heads themselves are attached to long metal arms that are moved by the head actuator motor as shown in Fig. 25-9. Read/write preamp ICs are typically mounted on a small PC board that is attached to the head/actuator assembly. The entire subassembly is sealed in the platter compartment, and is generally in-

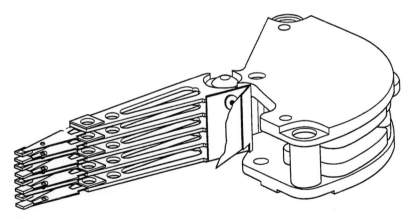

25-9 Close-up view of a head/actuator assembly. Maxtor Corporation

accessible unless opened in a cleanroom environment. The compartment is sealed with a metal lid/gasket configuration.

Head actuators

Unlike floppy motors that step their R/W heads in and out, hard drives swing the heads along a slight arc to achieve radial travel from edge to spindle. Many hard drives use voice coil motors (also called rotary coil motors or servos) to actuate head movement. Voice coil motors work using the same principle as analog meter movements; a permanent magnet is enclosed within two opposing coils. As current flows through the coils, a magnetic field is produced that opposes the permanent magnet. Head arms are attached to the rotating magnet, so the force of opposition causes a deflection that is directly proportional to the amount of driving current. Greater current signals result in greater opposition and greater deflection. Cylinders are selected by incrementing the servo signal and maintaining the signal at the desired level. Voice coil motors are very small and light assemblies that are well suited to fast access times and small hard drive assemblies.

The greatest challenge to head movement is to keep the heads centered on the desired track. Otherwise, aerodynamic disturbances, thermal effects in the platters, and variations in voice coil driver signals can cause head positioning error. Head position must be constantly checked and adjusted in real time to ensure that desired tracks are followed exactly. The process of track following is called servoing the heads. Information is required to compare the head's expected position to their actual position; any resulting difference can then be corrected by adjusting the voice coil signal. Servo information is located somewhere on the platters using a variety of techniques.

Dedicated servo information is recorded on a reserved platter side. For example, a two-platter drive using dedicated servo tracking can use three sides for data, but use a fourth surface exclusively for track locating information. Since all heads are positioned along the same track (a cylinder), a single surface can provide data that is needed to correct all heads simultaneously. Embedded servo information, however, is encoded as short bursts of data placed between every sector. All surfaces then can hold data and provide tracking information. The servo system uses the phase shift of pulses between adjacent tracks to determine whether heads are centered on the desired track, or drifting to one side or another. For the purposes of this book, you are not concerned with the particular tracking techniques; only that tracking information must be provided to keep the heads in proper alignment.

Spindle motor

One of the major factors that contribute to hard drive performance is the speed at which the media passes under the R/W heads. Media is passed under the R/W heads by spinning the platter(s) at a high rate of speed (at least 3600 rpm). The spindle motor is responsible for spinning the platter(s). A spindle motor is typically a brushless, low-profile dc motor (similar in principle to the spindle motors used in floppy disk drives).

An index sensor provides a feedback pulse signal that detects the spindle as it rotates. The drive's control electronics uses the index signal to regulate spindle speed as precisely as possible. Today's drives typically use magnetic sensors that detect iron tabs on the spindle shaft, or optoisolators that monitor holes or tabs rotating along the spindle. The spindle motor and index sensor also are sealed in the platter compartment.

Older hard drives used a rubber or cork pad to slow the spindle to a stop after drive power is removed, but newer drives use a technique called *dynamic braking*. When power is applied to a spindle motor, a magnetic field is developed in the motor coils. When power is removed, the magnetic energy stored in the coils is released as a reverse voltage pulse. Dynamic braking channels the energy of that reverse voltage to stop the drive faster and more reliably than physical braking.

Drive electronics

Hard drives are controlled by a suite of remarkably sophisticated circuitry. The drive electronics board mounted below the chassis contains all of the circuitry necessary to communicate control and data signals with the particular physical interface, maneuver the R/W heads, read or write as required, and spin the platter(s). Each of these functions must be accomplished to high levels of precision. In spite of the demands and complexity involved in drive electronics, the entire circuit can be fabricated on a single PC board.

A practical hard disk is shown in the block diagram of Fig. 25-10. You should understand the purpose of each part. The heart of this drive is a microcontroller (μC). A μC is basically a customized version of a microprocessor that can process program

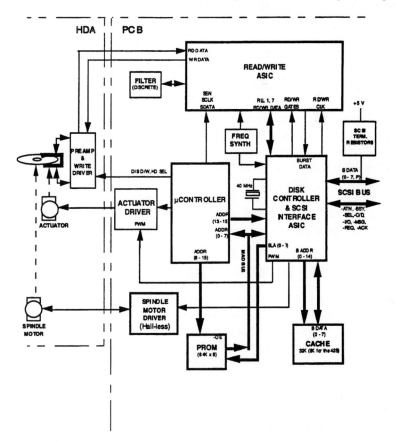

25-10 Block diagram of a high-performance Quantum drive system.
Quantum Corporation

instructions as well as provide a selection of specialized control signals that are not available from ordinary microprocessors. A μC can be considered an application-specific IC (ASIC). The program that operates this drive is stored in a small, programmable read-only memory (PROM). The microcontroller provides enable signals to the voice-coil driver IC, read/write preamplifier IC, read/write ASIC, and disk controller/interface ASIC. A controller/interface ASIC works in conjunction with the μC by managing data and control signals on the physical interface. For the drive shown, the ASIC is designed to support a SCSI interface, but variations of this model can use interface ASICs that support IDE interfaces (you can see physical interfaces in Chapter 22).

The primary activity of the controller/interface ASIC is to coordinate the flow of data into or out of the drive. The controller determines read or write operations, handles clock synchronization, and organizes data flow to the read/write ASIC. The controller also manages the local cache memory (located on the drive itself). Commands received over the physical interface are passed on to the μC for processing and response. The frequency synthesizer helps to synchronize the controller and read/write ASIC. Finally, the disk controller ASIC is responsible for selecting the head position and controlling the spindle and motor driver.

The read/write ASIC is another major IC on the drive's PC board. An R/W ASIC accepts data from the controller IC and translates data into serial signals that are sent to the write driver for writing. The R/W ASIC also receives signals amplified by the read preamp, and translates serial signals into parallel digital information available to the controller ASIC. A discrete filter affects the way in which analog signals are handled. R/W heads are connected directly to the read preamplifier/write driver IC that is little more than a bidirectional amplifier IC.

The actuator driver accepts a logic enable signal from the μC and a proportional logic signal from the controller ASIC. The actuator driver then produces an analog output current that positions the R/W heads by driving a voice coil motor. The spindle motor driver is turned on and off by a logic enable signal from the controller ASIC. Once the spindle motor driver is enabled, it will self-regulate its own speed using feedback from an index sensor. All components within the dotted area marked HDA are located within the sealed platter compartment while other components in the area marked PCB are located on the drive PC board. Most of the drive's intelligence is contained in the μC, controller ASIC, and R/W ASIC.

Concepts of formatting

You can imagine a disk drive as being a big file cabinet. When the drive is first installed, the "file cabinet" is completely empty—there are no dividers or folders or labels of any kind to organize information. In order to make the drive useful, it must be formatted and partitioned. There are basically three steps to the format process: a low-level format, partitioning, and a high-level format. Each of these steps are critically important.

Low-level formatting

The low-level format is perhaps the most important step (and is responsible for most of a drive's long-term problems). While the low-level format of early drives divided each track into a fixed number of sectors, later drives (such as IDE and SCSI) use a technique called zoned recording that writes a variable number of sectors per track. This allows later drives to optimize drive space by placing more sectors on outer tracks and fewer sectors on inner tracks. Sector header and trailer information is written (refer to Fig. 25-7) along with dummy data. Inter-sector and inter-track gaps also are created. As you might imagine, the low-level format forms the foundation of a hard drive's organization. Since this information is only written once, age and wear can allow sector information to eventually fail. When this happens, the failed sector(s) are unreadable.

This problem is compounded by the fact that most current drive makers low-level format their drives at the factory; those routines are rarely made available to technicians and end users. If you determine that an IDE or SCSI drive must be reformatted, make it a point to contact the drive manufacturer and obtain a proper low-level format utility written expressly for that particular drive model. Even leading professional utilities such as DrivePro strongly urge against low-level formats for IDE drives. If you attempt to invoke low-level formatting with a DOS DEBUG sequence or software utility, one of four things can happen:

- The drive will ignore the low-level formatter entirely
- The drive will accept the formatter, but only erase areas containing data (and fail to rewrite sector ID information)
- The drive will accept the formatter and erase vital servo information and other sector information (thus, the drive will be rendered completely unusable)
- The drive will accept the formatter and perform a correct low-level format. *Caution: A low-level format will completely destroy all data on a drive.* Back up as much of the drive as possible before attempting a low-level format.

Partitioning

Hard drives are designed to work with a variety of file systems offered by major operating systems besides DOS. After low-level formatting is complete, the drive must be partitioned before a file system or boot information is written to the drive. Also, partitioning allows a large physical drive to be divided up into several smaller logical drives. There are several file systems in service today, but DOS continues to use the *FAT* (file allocation table) system. The main criticism of the FAT is that sectors are grouped and assigned as clusters; it is a wasteful use of drive space (especially for large drives where up to 64 sectors can be in a cluster). One of the newly created partitions will be assigned as the boot partition, and an *MBS* (master boot sector) containing a special boot program and partition table will be written to the first sector. The MBS is often referred to as the *MBR* (master boot record). FDISK is the DOS utility used for partitioning.

High-level formatting

Even after partitioning, an operating system cannot store files on a drive. A series of data structures must be written to the drive. A *VBS* (volume boot sector), two copies of the file allocation table (FAT), and a root directory are written to each logical partition. High-level formatting also checks and locks out bad sectors so that they will not be used during normal operation. FORMAT is the DOS utility used for high-level formatting. It is interesting to note that the FORMAT utility will perform both low-level and high-level formatting for a floppy disk, but not for a hard drive.

Drive testing and troubleshooting

Hard-disk drives present some perplexing challenges for computer technicians and everyday users alike. The problem with hard drives is that they are inaccessible devices. Unless you have the cleanroom environment to open the sealed drive platters, it is pointless to try replacing failed drive mechanics. Even if you could open a drive safely, the advances in hard drive technology have been so fast and furious that no spare parts market has ever developed. Drive manufacturers themselves rarely bother to repair faulty drives, or invest in specialized drive testing equipment. As a technician, the course for hard drive repair is to replace faulty drives with new (usually better) devices.

Fortunately, not all hard drive problems are necessarily fatal. True, you can lose some programs and data (frequent backups will minimize your losses), but many drive problems are recoverable without resorting to drive replacement. Instead of focusing on repairing a hard drive's electronics or mechanics, today's repair tactics focus on repairing a drive's data. By reconstructing or relocating faulty drive information, it is possible to recover from a wide variety of common drive problems. You will need an assortment of software tools to deal with hard drive problems.

The boot disk

The vast majority of PCs in service today initialize (or boot) from an operating system typically contained on the hard drive. Thus, you do not need a floppy disk to start the system. When a hard drive problem arises, however, normal system initialization is interrupted. When this happens, the PC will not load its operating system (a situation known to rattle the nerves of even the most mild-mannered people). Without an operating system, you can't even start a DOS-based diagnostic. The first line of defense against a hard drive failure is to prepare one or more boot disks containing the operating system files, along with some native DOS utilities.

You will need a floppy disk formatted and configured with system files so that you can boot the computer to DOS from the floppy drive. Refer to your DOS manual for creating a bootable (system) floppy disk. In addition to DOS system files, your bootable disk also should contain six utilities; CHKDSK.EXE (SCANDISK.EXE for DOS 6.2 or later), FDISK.EXE, FORMAT.COM, RECOVER.EXE, SYS.COM, and UNFORMAT.COM (note that all six files are available in DOS 5.0 and higher). You also can add other utilities to the floppy, but these six are most important for our purposes (they also are free with DOS). It is highly recommended that you prepare several of these bootable disks in advance before you encounter drive problems. You cannot be able to access the necessary files to create a bootable disk after a problem arises, but you can make the disk on another compatible machine if necessary.

The CHKDSK.EXE (or SCANDISK.EXE) program checks the directory and FAT, and reports current disk and memory status on your monitor. Any logical errors will be reported and bad sectors will be marked, but CHKDSK.EXE will not locate physical disk errors. FDISK.EXE performs a low-level configuration of your hard drive's logical partition(s) prior to formatting. Do NOT attempt to use low-level formatting on IDE or SCSI (system-level), because low-level formatting can ruin servo information encoded on drive platters. The FORMAT.COM file formats the drive to accept DOS files within the drive partition area specified by FDISK.EXE. Use extreme caution when using FORMAT utilities. Formatting a disk can destroy the original data contained there. The drive should be repartitioned (if appropriate) and reformatted ONLY if data is unrecoverable and the drive cannot be made operable by any other means. Once the drive is reformatted, use SYS.COM to copy system files to the hard drive so it will become bootable. The RECOVER.EXE program can be used to recover readable text or data files from a defective drive. No .EXE or .COM files can be recovered. The UNFORMAT.COM program can be used to restore a drive that had been corrupted or inadvertently formatted. If you are using DOS 6.1 or later, add DEFRAG.EXE to your DOS arsenal. As with all DOS utilities, refer to your DOS reference manual for specific information on using each function.

Hard-disk power tools

Although programs like CHKDSK.EXE can provide basic failure information and correct a few very simple problems, most DOS utilities are simply not powerful or user-friendly enough to tackle serious drive corruption or data damage. However, there is a growing collection of powerful, third-party software being introduced to the marketplace that do have the sophistication to locate (and often correct) hard drive data problems. While most general-purpose PC diagnostics can detect a drive's parameters and test its performance very accurately, but when it comes specifically to drive diagnostics, there are three DOS packages that deserve consideration in your toolbox; DrivePro by MicroHouse, SpinRite by Gibson Research, and PC Tools for DOS by Central Point Software. You can find detailed reviews of these packages in Chapter 6, so they will not be repeated here, but all three packages can be run from a floppy disk (or provide utilities that can be run from floppies).

The value of backups

There are few problems more serious than hard drive failures. The loss of a hard drive often represents a tragedy of epic proportions—most drives contain valuable data that took weeks (sometimes months or even years) to develop. If that data were suddenly inaccessible or unrecoverable, not only would the time and effort that went into it have been wasted, but the time to recreate the data from scratch also would be a loss. This is not an exaggeration. More than one business has gone under because of lax backup procedures. As a technician, the very best advice you can give a client is to keep regular backups. Ultimately, all hard drives will fail. When this happens, a stack of diskettes or a few meters of tape can be all that stands between a quick drive swap, and bankruptcy.

Troubleshooting

Now that you have an idea of what tools are available, you can take a look at some problems and software solutions. The key concept here is that a hard drive problem does not necessarily mean a hard drive failure. While the failure of a sector, cluster, or track can leave a vital file or database unusable, it does not automatically indicate physical head or platter damage; that is why software tools have been so successful. Even if one or more sectors ARE physically damaged, there are tens of thousands of sectors on a hard drive. One of the only times a drive is truly irreparable is when physical media damage occurs on track 00, but software tools help you to identify the scope of the problem. Always refer to the User's Manual(s) for your software tools for more information.

Symptom 1. The computer will not boot to DOS from the hard drive Every system disk (whether a floppy or hard disk) must contain DOS files in order to initialize and execute the disk operating system. If a hard drive fails to boot, one or more DOS files are probably corrupt, the partition table or boot sector (not related to the DOS boot) can be corrupt, or there can be an actual failure in the drive.

Begin your repair by booting the computer from a floppy drive using a bootable disk, and check your system CMOS setup. Just about all computers save their configuration parameters in a small section of battery backed-up CMOS RAM in the *RTC* (real-time clock). Part of the setup information includes descriptions of each installed drive type. If the small lithium backup battery supporting your configuration memory should fail, the setup information can be lost. As a result, your system can forget how it should be set up and not recognize the installed hard drive. If you find that your system's configuration has been lost, replace the CMOS RAM backup battery, re-enter and resave the necessary setup information, and try rebooting the computer from its hard disk. You will probably have to disassemble at least some small part of your computer to install a new battery.

Here is a trick to help you with setup information; check your system's setup parameters before a problem arises, and copy the setup information into your system's DOS or User's Manual. You also could take a PrintScreen of the setup display to print a hard copy of the parameters. That way, you need only refer to your written notes when it is time to reload or modify a missing or corrupt setup parameter.

At this point, you must attempt to make some kind of determination whether the fault is due to hardware or data. Faulty hardware can be replaced, and some faulty data can be corrected. Use a diagnostic such as DrivePro and select the Drive Boot Fixer. The Drive Boot Fixer provides a selection of tools that you can use to back up and reconstruct areas of the drive required for booting. An alternative is DISKFIX included with PC Tools. Here's the test: if the boot files are accessible to the diagnostic, the drive hardware is probably working properly. After all, you can't read files from the disk unless the disk is working. This generally rules out a hardware failure, so you can go on to backup and attempt to reconstruct the boot files. *Remember to always back up boot files first before you attempt to change them.*

By successfully reconstructing the files needed to boot the disk, you stand a good chance of recovering the vital data on that disk, which is really the main objective of drive repairs in the first place. Once files are recovered and backed up, you can repartition and reformat the drive at your leisure and restore the contents from your backup. If you cannot restore the disk, you can still repartition and reformat the drive (which should restore it to operation), but its data will be lost forever. Once again, a good backup is the best protection there is against drive problems.

Now, if you are unable to access the drive's boot files from your diagnostic, then you can suspect a problem with the drive or its controller. Leave the software functions and run the drive hardware diagnostic. If a controller problem is indicated, replace the drive controller board. If the controller checks out, but the drive fails to respond, consider replacing the drive. Before replacing a drive, shut down and unplug the PC. Remove the PC enclosure and check the signal cable between the drive and controller. Make sure that the cable is installed correctly and completely. If the cable is old or appears frayed, try a new signal cable. Also make sure that the power connector is inserted into the drive properly. Re-apply power and reboot the system. You can check voltages on the system with a multimeter, or by using a diagnostic expansion board such as PC PowerCheck by Data Depot. If voltages appear low or absent, you can troubleshoot or replace the power supply. If problems persist, replace the drive. If the data contained on the drive is crucial (and there is no backup), you might be able to use a data recovery firm to off-load as much of the drive's data as possible.

Symptom 2. One or more subdirectories appear lost or damaged Both the root directory of a drive and its FAT contain references to subdirectories. If data in either the root directory or file allocation table is corrupt, one or more subdirectories can be inaccessible by the drive. All other subdirectories, however, are probably working just fine. The computer is probably able to load and save files normally in all other working directories.

Use a data repair utility such as DISKFIX (included with PC Tools). DISKFIX is often used for disk boot problems, but also can be employed when files or entire directories are missing or inaccessible, but have not been deleted. DISKFIX performs a myriad of tests to assess the damage to a drive, then reports those findings and walks you through available solutions (the PC Tools manual covers DISKFIX operations in detail).

If you do not have DISKFIX available, try SCANDISK available with DOS 6.2 and later. While SCANDISK is far less powerful than DISKFIX, it can be able to recover the directory error(s). If you do not even have SCANDISK, you can often fall back to RECOVER included with MS-DOS 2.0 and later. RECOVER will move through each file in a directory and attempt to recover each file that will be copied into the root directory. Caution is needed using RECOVER because the recovered files can easily fill the root directory.

Symptom 3. There are errors during drive reads or writes Magnetic information does not last forever. The ID information written into each disk sector is only written during the format process. Even though data can be rewritten to a sector regularly, its ID information is not. If ID data should fail, the drive can be unable to find an allocated sector for reading or writing, and a DOS disk error results. The entire cluster can be left unusable. This kind of failure can occur sporadically over time, especially if the drive has been used for very long periods of time. Usually only one or two files are affected.

The repair objective is to check the bad sector(s) and transfer as much data as possible to working sectors. Use your drive utility (such as DISKFIX from PC Tools or SCANDISK with MS-DOS) to examine the drive. Sectors that are physically faulty will be marked as bad and never used again. Any sector data that is readable is recovered and placed in known-good sectors. If the error occurred in an .EXE or .COM file, the file is generally corrupt and must be replaced by copying an original or duplicate file from a source or backup disk. When sectors fail, recovery utilities such as SpinRite from Gibson Research can help to recover as many bits as possible. In some cases, entire sectors can be recovered.

Symptom 4. The hard drive was formatted accidentally Every now and then, you or your customer can attempt to format a floppy disk and forget to include the particular drive specification. The high-level format does not actually destroy data, but rather it clears the file names and locations kept in the root directory and FAT. This prevents DOS from finding those files. PC Tools provides an UNFORMAT utility that can reconstruct root directory and FAT data from the information contained in a MIRROR file. If MIRROR has not been run, UNFORMAT can often recover the majority of the drive's contents anyway. When dealing with an accidentally formatted drive, it is vital to not run MIRROR or save new files to the drive before running UNFORMAT; any activity that can alter the drive's contents can make recovery difficult.

Unfortunately, MIRROR and similar recovery tools can have adverse effects on drives that use compression such as Stacker or DoubleSpace, so not all systems will make use of MIRROR. Without such directory tracking utilities, it is not always possible to recover all formatted areas. Ultimately, unformatting is an imperfect process, and it will have varying degrees of success from machine to machine, but recovery tools are constantly improving in their sophistication and reliability.

Symptom 5. A file has been deleted accidentally This particular symptom is more of an inconvenience than an actual problem. Mistyping or forgetting to add a drive specification can accidentally erase files from places you did not intend to erase. DOS 5.0 and PC Tools both offer an UNDELETE program that can restore the deleted file. Undeleting can be very helpful when you accidentally delete a file that took a long time to create, and there is no backup for. Like unformat tools, the success of UNDELETE will depend on the condition of the file (and the drive in general), so not all files will be completely recoverable. Remember that it is vital to avoid writing to the disk before an undelete has been performed.

Symptom 6. The hard drive's root directory is damaged A faulty root directory can cripple the entire disk, rendering all subdirectories inaccessible. A bad FAT or directory tree can sometimes be corrected by booting the computer from a bootable floppy disk and running a fix utility from your software toolkit. In many cases, fix utilities such as PC Tools' DISKFIX can reconstruct damaged FATs or directories and allow you to regain access to at least most of your drive. If you have been running MIRROR to track disk information, DISKFIX should be able to recover a faulty root directory very reliably. Tools such as DrivePro from MicroHouse provide a utility that backs up all of the drive's boot files to a diskette. If you have a recent copy of that key data, you also might be able to restore the FATs and root directory that way. If third-party drive tools are unavailable, you can use SCANDISK (included with DOS 6.2 and later). If your disk utilities are unable to correct or patch the problem, you will have little choice but to reformat the drive and reload it from a recent backup.

Symptom 7. Hard drive performance appears to be slowing down over time As you can recall, hard drives require a relatively long time to search a drive (on the order of milliseconds). Ideally, all information necessary for a file will be stored in contiguous sectors and tracks, and the drive can access the maximum amount of information in the shortest possible time. Unfortunately, as files are updated and saved, they become scattered in noncontiguous sectors and tracks throughout the drive. File fragmentation demands much more seek and access time from a drive. The solution is to unfragment the drive using a software utility.

Boot your computer from a bootable floppy disk, then run an unfragment utility in your software toolkit (such as PC Tools' COMPRESS utility or DEFRAG included with new versions of MS-DOS). As a general rule, there should be no terminate-and-stay-resident (TSR) programs running when a drive is unfragmented. Also, files are rearranged and moved from one place to another on the drive during the unfragment process, so any files that can have been deleted can be totally unrecoverable after unfragmenting the drive. When the drive is defragmented, reboot the PC. You should now notice an improvement in performance.

Symptom 8. In an AT system, the drive light stays on continuously A continuous LED indication is not necessarily a problem as long as the drive seems to be operating properly. Refer to the documentation for your controller board; there can be a jumper available to switch the LED display between a latched mode (the LED is always on) and an activity mode (the LED is only on during drive access). If such a jumper exists on your drive, set the jumper to the activity mode. If the drive does not operate, power down the computer and check the signal cable(s) between the drive and controller board. One end of a signal cable is probably inserted upside down. Re-install the signal cable(s) correctly and retest the system.

Symptom 9. You see a "No Fixed Disk Present" error message displayed on the monitor This kind of problem can occur during installation, or at any point in the PC's working life. If you are installing/upgrading a drive system (or installing a new board in the system), there can be an I/O address or IRQ conflict with other boards in the system—a common difficulty. Because it is very difficult to know the address and IRQ layout of each board in your system, your best strategy is to remove the drive controller and install an IRQ/DMA check card such as The Discovery Card by AllMicro. The Discovery Card will indicate the IRQs and DMA channels in use in the system. You can use this data to select unused IRQ and DMA channels on the drive controller. Re-install the corrected controller board. If the drive now responds, the conflict has probably been cleared.

Refer to your system's setup routine and ensure that the correct drive type and drive parameters are entered in the CMOS setup screen. One or more faulty parameters can disable the drive. You may have to check the drive's parameters (cylinders, heads, sectors, landing zone, and write precompensation) against parameter data from the drive manufacturer. If you cannot find a prefabricated drive type with the appropriate parameters, you can usually enter the proper parameters manually as a Custom drive type. If CMOS RAM has failed, replace the backup battery and re-enter each setting. Be sure to write down each setting (or take a PrintScreen of the display) and tape the notes inside the PC cover.

Check for any loose power and signal cables. In a multidrive system, make sure that any drive jumpers or DIP switches for each drive are configured properly for multidrive operation (master/slave settings). If any IDE or SCSI terminator resistors are needed, make sure that the terminators are installed in the correct locations. If problems persist, the drive cannot be low-level formatted properly. You can try low-level formatting the drive again. If the drive is an IDE type, do not try low-level formatting.

Symptom 10. Your system fails to recognize the presence of the drive
Your computer can flag this as a hard-disk error or hard-disk controller failure during system initialization. Begin your inspection by checking the drive's signal cable orientation. When installing or upgrading a drive, be sure that the red lead of the ribbon cable (pin 1) is oriented toward connector pin 1 at both ends. If the cable is reversed at either side, the controller board will not recognize the presence of a drive. Double-check any jumpers used to configure the drive or drive controller board. Drive configuration jumper settings are even more critical when there is more than one hard drive in the system. Each drive must have unique identifying settings, otherwise, a communication conflict will occur that can temporarily disable all the drives.

If the drive still fails to operate after installation or upgrade, there can be an address or IRQ conflict with other boards in the system—a common difficulty. Because it is very difficult to know the address and IRQ layout of each board in your system, your best strategy is to remove the drive controller and install an IRQ/DMA check card such as The Discovery Card by AllMicro. The Discovery Card will indicate the IRQs and DMA channels in use in the system. You can use this data to select unused IRQ and DMA channels on the drive controller. Re-install the corrected controller board. If the drive now responds, the conflict has probably been cleared.

Next, be sure the drive actually spins up when power is turned on. You should be able to hear this, but some hard drives are extremely quiet. If the drive fails to spin up, check the power supplied through the 4-pin mate-n-lock connector. You also can use the PC PowerCheck board by Data Depot to check the power levels being generated by the supply. If one or more supply voltages is low or absent, the drive will certainly not function. Troubleshoot or replace the power supply.

Double-check the controller board to be sure that it is compatible with the drive you are using (not a problem with IDE drives). While instances of incompatibility between drives and controllers that share the same signal interface are rare, it can happen under some unusual circumstances. Keep in mind that not all SCSI devices are compatible with every host controller. One test of controller incompatibility for ST506/412 and ESDI drives is the system speed test; older PC expansion boards expected the ISA bus to operate at about 8 MHz, but today's powerful systems operate so fast that the controller board cannot keep up. If your computer is in a high-speed (or turbo) mode, take the system out of the turbo mode and retry the drive. If the drive operates when a lower bus speed is used, a more sophisticated controller should probably be used.

Refer to your system's setup routine and ensure that the correct drive type and drive parameters are entered in the CMOS setup screen. One or more faulty parameters can disable the drive. You may have to check the drive's parameters (cylinders, heads, sectors, landing zone, and write precompensation) against parameter data from the drive manufacturer. If you cannot find a prefabricated drive type with the appropriate parameters, you can usually enter the proper parameters manually as a Custom drive type.

Symptom 11. Your IDE drive spins up when power is applied, then rapidly spins down again The drive is not communicating properly with its host system. Check the communication cable between the drive and controller; it should be installed completely at both ends, and it should not be frayed or torn. Try a new signal cable between the drive and its controller board. Next, check the drive settings recorded in the CMOS setup and be sure that they are appropriate. If a new cable and CMOS settings fail to restore the drive, there can be an incompatibility between the drive and your system's BIOS. To confirm this, try the drive and controller board on another system using a newer BIOS, or a BIOS from a different manufacturer. If the problem disappears on another machine, you may need to upgrade the BIOS ROM(s) on the original system.

Symptom 12. You see a "Sector not found" error message displayed on the monitor This problem usually occurs after the drive has been in operation for quite some time, and is typically the result of a media failure. Fortunately, a bad sector will only affect one file. Try a disk fix utility such as SpinRite from Gibson Research. SpinRite will attempt to recover as much of the sector's data as possible before marking the sector bad to prohibit future use. In some cases, the entire sector can be recovered. If the bad sector cannot be recovered completely, you should restore the file from a backup. Incomplete executable files (.EXE and .COM files) will not run properly (if at all). If a utility such as SpinRite is not available, an MS-DOS utility like SCANDISK or CHKDSK will at least evaluate and map out the faulty sector; you will almost certainly have to restore the affected file.

Symptom 13. You see a "1780 or 1781 ERROR" displayed on the monitor The classic 1780 error code indicates a Hard Disk 0 Failure, while the 1781 error code marks a Hard Disk 1 Failure. The term failure is used to suggest that a hardware fault has occurred. In a new installation or upgrade, make sure that the controller is compatible with the drive. When this fault occurs in an established system, your best course is try a diagnostic such as DrivePro by MicroHouse. Try accessing the drive's boot files. If the boot files can be read, the hardware is likely working fine and the trouble is with the boot files. You can then use DrivePro to back up and attempt to reconstruct the boot files. If the boot files cannot be read, you can use DrivePro's diagnostic capabilities (or other diagnostics) to check the drive controller and drive. If you do not have a diagnostic available, check the drive signal cable. If the cable is intact, replace the hard drive. If the problem should persist, try replacing the drive controller board.

Symptom 14. You see a "1790 or 1791 ERROR" displayed on the monitor The classic 1790 error code indicates a Hard Disk 0 Error, while the 1791 error code marks a Hard Disk 1 Error. The term error is used to suggest that a logical or operational fault has occurred (instead of a hardware failure). In many cases, this error is generated when a drive is brand new and needs to be low-level formatted, partitioned, and DOS formatted. Since 1790-type errors are logical in nature, a signal interruption can be occurring between the drive and controller. If the drive has already been prepared by a dealer, try a new signal cable between the controller and drive. Try a diagnostic such as DrivePro by MicroHouse to access the drive's boot files. If the boot files can be read, the hardware is likely working fine and the trouble is with the boot files. You can then use DrivePro to back up and attempt to reconstruct the boot files. If the boot files cannot be read, you can use DrivePro's diagnostic capabilities (or other diagnostics) to check the drive controller and drive. In many cases, the drive controller has failed and should be replaced. If problems persist, replace the drive.

Symptom 15. You see a "1701 ERROR" displayed on the monitor The 1701 error code indicates a hard drive POST error—the drive did not pass its POST test. Check the drive setup data entered in the system CMOS. Also check that the drive's signal and power cables are connected properly. If you are installing a hard drive in an older PC/XT system, you should perform a low-level format on the drive (if appropriate). Try a diagnostic such as DrivePro to check the drive and controller board.

Symptom 16. The system reports random data, seek, or format errors Random errors rarely indicate a permanent problem, but identifying the problem source can be a time-consuming task. Start by checking the drive power using a board such as the PC PowerCheck from Data Depot. Marginal power supply levels (especially in fully loaded systems) can result in strange, random faults. If power is low or unstable, troubleshoot or upgrade the power supply.

Electrical noise in the system also can interfere with normal drive operation. Try rerouting the signal cable away from the power supply and other expansion boards. You also can try placing expansion boards in other slots that are farther away from the drive signal cable. Electrical noise also can affect the drive controller board. Install the controller board away from the power supply, and try to keep it away from the video adapter board. There can be a problem with your system speed. Although most ISA bus systems are designed to run at 8 MHz, some new machines run so fast that communication between the system and drive adapter is marginal. Try taking the PC out of its turbo mode. If the problem disappears, replace the drive controller board with a newer, faster board.

There can be a marginal area on the drive. Back up as much of the hard drive as possible and use a third-party hard drive utility such as PC Tools DISKFIX to perform a thorough scan of the hard drive media. If DISKFIX is not available, try SCANDISK with MS-DOS 6.2 and later. Use such tools to spare out any media errors.

Try the drive and controller in another system. If the drive and controller work in another system, there is probably excessive noise or grounding problems in the original system. Reinstall the drive and controller in the original system and remove all extra expansion boards (except the video adapter). If the problem goes away, replace one board at a time and retest the system until the problem returns. The last board you inserted when the problem returned is probably the culprit. If the problem persists, there can be a ground problem on the motherboard. Try replacing the motherboard.

Symptom 17. You see a "Bad or Missing Command Interpreter" error message This is a typical error that appears when a drive is formatted in one DOS version but loaded with another. Compatibility problems occur when you mix DOS versions. Make sure that the drive is formatted with the DOS version you intend to use, and that the /S option is used with FORMAT in order to transfer the proper system files to the boot device. If this is a new problem on an existing system, you should strongly suspect the presence of a computer virus. Use a clean virus checking disk to examine your hard drive and eliminate the virus if possible (once checking is complete, discard the antivirus work disk). You may need to recopy COMMAND.COM to the hard drive. If you need to reformat the drive again, back up as much of the drive as possible before proceeding.

Symptom 18. You see an "Error reading drive C:" error message Read errors in a hard drive typically indicate problems with the disk media, but it is always worthwhile to check the drive's signal and power cables first to ensure that each is secure. If faulty cabling is not the problem, use some good antivirus software and scan the drive for a computer virus. Remove any infected files. If a computer virus is detected, you also should check every floppy disk that you have available since any disks used in an infected system also can be infected (and can re-infect the hard drive or other PCs). Use a third-party utility such as DISKFIX with PC Tools to scan the hard drive for defects. If defects are detected, try mapping out such defects as dictated by the particular utilities. This also can be a factor if the drive's orientation has changed (you remount the drive vertically where before it was horizontal). If problems persist, try replacing the hard drive.

Symptom 19. You see a "Track 0 not found" error message Begin by checking the interconnecting cables between the drive and controller. Try a new cable. Also check to be sure that you are using DOS 3.3 or later (if you do upgrade, move to MS-DOS 6.22 or later). If cabling and DOS versions are right, the problem is likely on the drive itself. A fault on track 00 can disable the entire drive since track 00 contains the drive's file allocation table (FAT). Use DrivePro from MicroHouse to back up and attempt to reconstruct the drive's boot files. If you cannot access the boot files, the drive is probably damaged and must be replaced. Otherwise, reconstruction can probably restore drive operation.

Symptom 20. Software diagnostics indicate an average access time that is longer than specified for the drive The average access time is the average amount of time needed for a drive to reach the track and sector where a needed file begins. Verify the specifications for your particular drive. Keep in mind that different software packages measure access time differently. Make sure that the diagnostic subtracts system overhead processing from the access time calculation. Try one or two other diagnostics to confirm the measurement. If different software tools confirm the measurement, test several identical drives. If all drives measure the same way and work properly, check with the drive manufacturer for a technical explanation. If only the suspect drive measures incorrectly, consider replacing the drive or at least warn the user to perform a full drive backup as soon as possible.

Symptom 21. Software diagnostics indicate a slower data transfer rate than specified Verify the specifications for your particular drive and controller. Keep in mind that different software packages measure access time differently. Try several different software diagnostics to confirm the measurements. If the drive is an IDE type, make sure that the original user did not perform a low-level format; this can remove head and cylinder skewing optimization and result in a degradation of data transfer. If no low-level formatting was performed, the drive can be failing. Try replacing the drive or at least warn the user to perform a full drive backup as soon as possible.

Symptom 22. Your low-level format operation is taking too long, or it hangs up the system *Note: This procedure does not apply to IDE or SCSI drives.* You probably see a large number of format errors such as code 20 or 80. You also can see Unsuccessful Format error messages. Start your investigation by checking the drive parameters used in the low-level format command string, as well as the drive parameters shown in the CMOS system setup. One or more incorrect parameters can prevent a successful format. If you are working with an older PC/XT that does not use a CMOS setup, check that the system's dynamic configuration is correct.

If the system setup and drive parameters are all in order, you should suspect a communications fault between the drive and controller. Replace the signal cable(s) between the drive and controller and try the system again. Make sure that your cable(s) are inserted into their proper receptacles in the correct orientation. Finally, you need to make sure that the performance of your drive and controller are suitable with your system. For example, an older expansion board in a new system may not be able to keep pace with the system. Try taking the PC out of its turbo mode. If the problem disappears, you may want to use a later drive controller.

Symptom 23: You are unable to access the low-level format window from the DEBUG address *Note: This procedure does not apply to IDE or SCSI drives.* Some systems will not low-level format a drive while its parameters are entered in the CMOS setup, so enter your CMOS setup menu and remove the drive type entries. Make sure to write down the entries first so you can restore them again later. If that fails to clear the problem, return to the CMOS setup again and restore the drive parameters.

Refer to the documentation for the drive controller board and check that the controller's on-board BIOS ROM is enabled. If the controller's BIOS is partially or fully disabled, the DEBUG command cannot be interpreted properly. Also check the base address of the controller against the address used in your DEBUG command. If you are referring DEBUG to the wrong address, the controller will not respond and allow the low-level format to initiate. You will need the documentation for your drive controller to check address settings.

There can be a hardware conflict between the drive controller and one or more other expansion boards in your system (although most conflicts will manifest themselves in a more substantial fault). Remove one board at a time from your system and recheck the system after each board is removed. If DEBUG access is granted after a board is removed, that board is probably experiencing a peculiar conflict with the drive controller. As an alternative, you can remove the drive controller board and install an IRQ/DMA checking board such as The Discovery Card from AllMicro. Compare the IRQ and DMA channels in use against the drive controller. If the drive controller uses resources that overlap resources already in use, try changing the drive controller's settings to correct the trouble.

If you still cannot initiate a low-level format through DEBUG, contact the controller manufacturer. The manufacturer may have specialized low-level formatting software designed for use with your particular controller card. Finally, check your original DEBUG command against one of the following commands. Try using one of the following commands to initiate the DEBUG low-level format menu:

G=C800:5 or
G=CC00:5 or
G=C800:CCC or
G=C800:6 or
G=D800:5 or
G=DC00:5

Symptom 24: The low-level format process regularly hangs up on a specific Head/Cylinder/Sector *Note: This procedure does not apply to IDE or SCSI drives. Not all portions of a manufactured drive are usable.* These are called *hard errors* and the low-level format procedure must recognize and avoid these hard errors. Some low-level format procedures require you to enter these hard errors manually. If you forget to enter a hard error (or enter the wrong location) the format process will stop when the hard error is encountered. Try low-level formatting the drive again, but make sure to enter the proper hard error locations. Also check the CMOS setup parameters to be sure the drive type is correct. Even if the hard error table is entered properly, incorrect drive parameters can cause the drive to look for its errors in the wrong places.

Symptom 25. The FDISK procedure hangs up or fails to create or save partition record for the drive(s) Begin by checking the drive parameters entered into your system's CMOS setup. If the drive parameters are incorrect, FDISK may not be able to produce the proper partition. If you are using an IDE drive and the drive parameters seem correct, you may wish to contact the drive manufacturer and see if there is another appropriate translation geometry (entries for tracks, sectors, cylinders, and so on) that you can use for the drive parameters. When using the FDISK utility, try a different partition size. For large drives, try breaking the drive into two or more smaller partitions.

If you are still encountering FDISK trouble, try a different DOS version or a non-MS-DOS partitioning utility such as DrivePro from MicroHouse. Also try running a surface scan utility such as DISKFIX in PC Tools to check for physical defects at the beginning of the drive. Physical damage to the boot sector, file allocation tables, or the partition table can render the drive useless. It must be replaced unless a tool like DrivePro can reconstruct the boot data. There is a slight possibility that the signal cable(s) can be intermittent or defective. If problems persist, try replacing the signal cable(s).

Symptom 26. You see a "Hard Disk Controller Failure" or a large number of defects in last logical partition Immediately check the hard drive parameters listed in the CMOS setup. Make sure that the parameters used do not define a drive larger than the one actually installed. If a larger drive is specified, the system will try to format areas that don't exist, creating a significant number of errors. Try using the correct drive parameters. Otherwise, the drive controller is likely defective and should be replaced.

Symptom 27. The high-level (DOS) format process takes too long If you are using MS-DOS, check the version in use. MS-DOS version 4.x tries to recover hard errors that can consume quite a bit of extra time. You will probably see a number of "Attempting to recover allocation units" messages. Your best course is to upgrade the MS-DOS version to 6.2 or higher. Later versions of DOS abandon hard error retries, so formatting should take place much faster.

Symptom 28. The drive does not format to full capacity Check the drive parameters used in the system CMOS setup. If the parameters specify a drive that is smaller than it actually is, some portion of the drive will not be used. Also, DOS has a 1024-cylinder limitation. If the drive has more than 1024 cylinders, see if there is an alternate translation geometry that can be used. If not, third-party or manufacturer-specific partitioning software may have to be used. Confirm that the drive parameters reported by FDISK match those of the drive. Check that the drive controller is appropriate for the drive interface being used. Check the DOS version being used. Older DOS versions had a limit of 32Mb per partition. If older DOS is in use, upgrade to MS-DOS 6.2 or later. Some drive controllers use disk space to handle drive defect management. Check the controller manual to see if drive space is being allocated for defect management.

Symptom 29. You do not get full capacity from a large-capacity drive when using partitioning software Chances are very good that you have entered the wrong drive parameters in the system CMOS. Make sure that the correct parameters are entered. Also check to see if there are other translation geometries that can be entered instead, especially for IDE drives. Test those alternate geometries to see if you can coax more space from the drive.

Symptom 30. You see "Disk Boot Failure," "non system disk," or "No ROM Basic - SYSTEM HALTED" error messages Check the drive for computer viruses. Remove any viruses or infected files as required. Make sure that the necessary system files have been transferred to the hard drive (format the hard drive as a system disk). When using FDISK to partition a drive, make sure that the created DOS partition is made active. Check the drive parameters entered in the system CMOS. If any of the drive parameters is incorrect, enter the proper parameters. If the system will not save those parameters, try replacing the CMOS backup battery. Make sure that the floppy drive door is opened. Check to see that all cables are connected properly. If problems continue, try a utility such as DrivePro by MicroHouse to back up and reconstruct the drive's vital boot files.

Symptom 31. The hard drive in a PC is suffering frequent breakdowns (between 6 and 12 months) Typical hard drives offer MTBF rates in excess of 30,000 hours. Even at 10 hours/day, the drive should work for 3000 days (a bit over 8 years). When drives tend to fail within a few months, there are some factors to consider. First, how are the drives being used? If the drive is being worked hard by CAD or database applications, the wear and tear can be crashing the drive prematurely. Consider upgrading the PC to reduce the load on the drives (more memory, caching, and so on). If the drive is heavily fragmented, try running a defragment utility regularly to keep files in order—this will help reduce the physical wear as files are saved and read.

Power is another serious factor in drive operation. Power that is dirty (containing spikes, surges, and sags) can easily play havoc with drive life. Try the PC on another clean line; make sure that inductive or other heavy-load machines (welders, coffee pots, and so on) are not using the circuit. If reliability improves, consider a *UPS* (uninterruptable power supply) to protect the PC.

Finally, consider the PC's environment. Constant, low-level vibrations, such as those in an industrial environment, can kill a drive. Smoke (even cigarette smoke), high humidity, very low humidity, and caustic vapors can ruin drives. Make sure the system is used in a stable office-type environment.

Symptom 32. A hard drive controller is replaced, but during initialization, the system displays error messages such as "Hard Disk Failure" or "Not a recognized drive type" The PC also can lock up. Some drive controllers are unusually picky about the system they are installed in. Controllers can be incompatible in some systems. Check with the controller manufacturer and see if there have been any reports of incompatibilities with your PC. If so, try a different drive controller board. Newer boards are less likely to suffer from compatibility problems, but there are still exceptions.

26
CHAPTER

Ink-jet printers

The concept of forming characters and graphics through the use of dot arrays took on a new life with the introduction of ink-jet technology. Ink-jet printers (Fig. 26-1) offer many of the advantages that impact printers had so long tried to achieve. Primarily, ink-jet printing is quiet. It also is capable of printing high-resolution graphics, as well as color operation, two feats that impact printers never truly mastered. Finally, the power required to operate ink-jet heads is far less than impact printers. Low power results in smaller power supplies, so ink-jet printers are often small, efficient devices that are ideal for mobile printing jobs. The quiet, low-cost, high-quality

26-1
An HP DeskJet 310 and DeskWriter 310.

Hewlett-Packard Company

printing afforded with ink-jet printers is quickly displacing the older impact printers in homes and offices. This chapter is intended to illustrate the major assemblies of a typical ink-jet printer, and show you a selection of troubleshooting procedures.

A typical ink-jet printer is composed of four main areas as illustrated in the block diagram of Fig. 26-2: (1) the print head, (2) the paper transport, (3) the carriage transport, and (4) the *ECU* (electronic control unit). This chapter touches on each of these subassemblies. As with impact printers, data sent from a host computer is interpreted by the printer's main logic (the ECU) and converted to a series of vertical dot patterns. Motor commands start the carriage (and print head) moving across the platen. Simultaneously, printer circuits will send each dot pattern to the print head in series. Each dot pattern fires the corresponding nozzles to leave a permanent mark on the page. This also is called *serial* or *moving-head* operation.

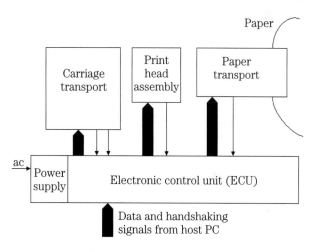

26-2 Block diagram of an ink-jet printer.

The print head

Ink-jet print heads all have one characteristic in common—they *never* touch the page. Where impact printing relies on contact to deliver dots on a page surface, ink-jet printing is a *noncontact* print technology. Ink is literally spray-painted onto the page. The mechanics that control this spraying process make up the ink-jet print head. There are three classical techniques used in an ink-jet print head: continuous flow, piezoelectric pump, and bubble pump. Because continuous flow printing is typically used for high-volume, low-quality industrial marking, it is not covered in this book.

Drop on demand

Generally speaking, a series of fine nozzles (each about ⅛ the diameter of a human hair) are arranged in vertical sets of 9, 12, 24, or more on the face of the print head. Nozzles themselves are little more than microscopic holes drilled into a metal face plate. As you might expect, nozzles are open to the air, but ink's surface tension prevents it from spilling out uncontrollably. Ink reaches each nozzle through a set of open channels, and is gravity-fed from a small ink reservoir that is built into the head (for disposable print heads) or located external to the head in a replaceable ink cartridge (for nondisposable print heads).

Each ink channel is connected to a series of electrical contacts used to operate the ink pumps built into each channel. It is these ink pumps that break up ink in the channels and form individual droplets that are ejected onto the page. There are two types of ink pumps: *piezoelectric* and *thermal* (or *bubble*). Pumps are fired independently by the printer's ECU. The control circuitry that interprets data and translates it into dot patterns is remarkably similar to other printers. Print color is determined by ink color, but multi-color cartridges are available—each with its own set of nozzles and electrical contacts.

Piezoelectric pumps

In a piezoelectric pump, a ring of piezoelectric ceramic material is built into an ink channel as in Fig. 26-3. When a high-energy electrical pulse is applied across the ceramic ring, its piezoelectric quality causes it to constrict the channel. This causes a sudden displacement of volume that pushes out a single droplet of ink. After the electrical driver pulse passes, ceramic returns to its original shape, and more ink is drawn into the channel to make up the expelled droplet.

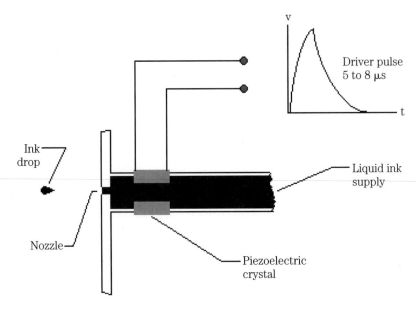

26-3 Diagram of a piezo-pump print head.

Piezoelectric ceramic requires short pulses (in the 5- to 10-μs range) at high energy levels. Pulse amplitudes can be anywhere from 70 to 200 V, depending on the particular design of the channel and the type of ceramic used. One pump is required per channel, and can fire at rates approaching 5 kHz (5000 dots per second); this is one droplet every 200 μs.

Bubble pumps

Bubble pumps (used in thermal ink-jet or bubble jet printers) also are widely used to generate ink droplets. As shown in Fig. 26-4, nozzles and channel construction are very similar to piezoelectric heads, but ceramic rings are replaced by ring heaters. An electrical driver pulse fires a ring heater. In turn, this heats ink in the immediate vicinity. As ink heats, a bubble forms and expands in the channel. When the bubble finally bursts, it ejects an ink droplet, and more ink is drawn in to fill the void. Heated ink droplets also dry faster on paper.

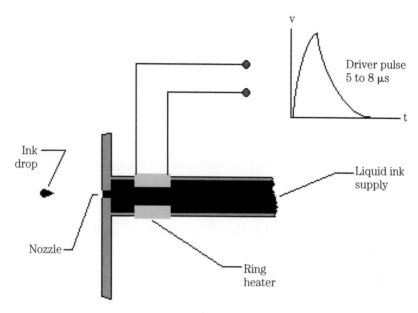

26-4 Diagram of a bubble-pump print head.

Although bubble pumps are fast-working devices, they are limited to firing rates of 1000 dots per second. Ring heaters (like dot heaters) require a finite amount of time to cool after firing. If there is not enough cooling time, ink might actually dry out and clog inside the channel. However, bubble pumps do not require nearly as much energy to operate. Twenty-four- to 50-V pulses are typical.

Ink considerations

The kind of ink used in drop-on-demand printers is typically an indelible, solvent-based chemical that is resistant to drying in air. As a result, most ink-jet heads can be left unattended for prolonged periods of time (often several days to several weeks) without fear of nozzle clogs because of drying. Most ink-jet printers also have a type of ink cap in the printer's carriage home position that wipes each nozzle whenever the head reaches its home position, and covers them whenever the printer is turned off.

Sooner or later, solvent will evaporate into the air. Evaporation begins to increase the ink viscosity inside each channel; it becomes thicker. In early stages, this can cause ink to sputter or travel off course to the page. In advanced stages, solvent might evaporate entirely, or enough to allow ink to dry and harden in the channel. This is a *clog*. The afflicted nozzle(s) might still fire electrically, but no ink will flow until the clog is cleared. The ink-jet head will have to be cleaned or replaced. Clogs also might be dislodged through normal use. Once any viscous ink is forced out through normal use, proper operation will return automatically. In today's ink-jet printers, clogs are rare because the head is kept well-covered when not in use.

Paper considerations

When ink droplets leave a nozzle, they are still in a liquid form. Once a droplet reaches paper, it must dry almost immediately so that the finished page can be handled. This is not always easy to accomplish if you are using the wrong paper type. Paper must accept ink into its fibers just the right way to dry it quickly, yet leave droplets on the surface for a crisp image. If paper absorbs ink too readily, the dried image might appear light or faint, lacking contrast. If paper does not absorb ink quickly enough, ink might remain a liquid that can run with other colors, or smear and smudge when touched. Ordinary xerography-grade paper is actually too porous for ink-jet printers; ink runs and saturates the paper, causing it to bend and buckle. To guarantee just the right drying characteristics, use a specially made ink-jet paper impregnated with clay or solvent-absorbing chemicals that cause ink to dry quickly while leaving a clear, dark image. Ink-jet paper is a bit more expensive than ordinary paper, but the results are often worth it. The best way to determine the compatibility between paper and ink is to test the printer in actual operation. Either ink or paper might have to be changed to optimize the printer's performance.

Advantages and disadvantages of ink-jet printing

Ink-jet dot matrix technology offers a method of noncontact printing that can mark a wide variety of surfaces and paper types. Printing speeds rival any impact printer, yet operation is very quiet. Nozzles and ink channels are incredibly small, so dot resolution can be extremely high, often at 300 DPI. Ink-jet heads have no mechanical parts, so they enjoy high reliability throughout their working life. Because many commercial print heads are disposable after 200 pages or so, reliability should not be a problem. Ink-jet printing has made low-cost color printing available at a reasonable quality level. Because ink-jet heads require little energy to function, the entire printer assembly can be made much smaller and lighter; ideal for use with mobile computers.

Unfortunately, ink-jet heads are sealed devices. If one ink pump fails, the entire head must be replaced. The ink itself can be a frustrating problem. Ruptured print heads or leaking cartridges can spill thick, indelible ink everywhere. Fabrics and other porous materials are particularly susceptible to permanent stains; even your skin can be stained. Cleaning and purging procedures can be very messy, which is largely responsible for the tremendous popularity of disposable heads/reservoirs. Ink-jet printers in graphics mode are typically slow devices. An output of several pages per minute is considered speedy. The need for specialized paper continues to be a problem, although the formulation of new inks and broad availability of ink-jet paper is keeping costs down.

Troubleshooting ink-jet heads

Unlike impact heads that are not convenient to replace, the cartridge design of most ink-jet heads makes troubleshooting very simple—print problems can typically be resolved by replacing the print head, or by replacing the ECU—there is very little else that can precipitate a print problem. Print head problems are typically indicated by faint print, or print that is visually distorted. The following symptoms illustrate this in more detail.

Symptom 1. The print quality is poor (dots appear faded or indistinct)
Unlike impact printers, the quality and type of paper used in an ink-jet system will profoundly impact the print quality. Start by checking your paper supply. Make sure that the paper is well-suited for use in an ink-jet printer. Porous papers such as ordinary xerography-grade paper tend to absorb ink quickly and run the ink through its fibers—the result is typically a dull, faded appearance. This also can happen if the paper has an unusual or chemically coated surface.

If the paper is correct, suspect the print head next. In many cases, light or poorly formed dots can occur as the disposable print cartridge nears exhaustion. The print head also might be dirty; accumulations of dust or debris can eventually block the print head nozzles. Although a typical ink-jet printer routinely cleans a print head, an old or worn cleaning surface might no longer provide sufficient cleaning. If the cleaning pad is worn or missing, it should be replaced. If the problem persists, try a new print head (typically a single head/reservoir assembly that can be replaced in a matter of seconds).

If problems continue, there is probably a fault in the printer's driver circuitry. If signals are not strong enough to fire the head's piezo or bubble pumps correctly, print will easily be distorted. Review the Hewlett-Packard DeskJet assembly of Fig. 26-5. You will notice that there are three main boards in the printer: the *logic board*

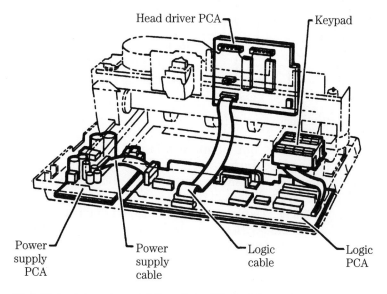

Head driver PCA — Keypad

Power supply PCA — Power supply cable — Logic cable — Logic PCA

26-5 Major internal assemblies of the HP DeskJet series printer. Hewlett-Packard Company

(ECU), the driver board and the power supply. Chances are that one or more elements in the head driver circuit or power supply has become defective. Before replacing anything, check the power supply outputs. If any of the outputs are low or missing, replace the power supply. If all power outputs are correct, the fault is probably in the driver board, so try a new driver board. In some ink-jet printer designs, the power supply, driver circuits, and main logic are all assembled on the same PC board. In that case, simply replace the entire ECU outright. Figure 26-6 illustrates the various functions performed by the main logic and driver boards.

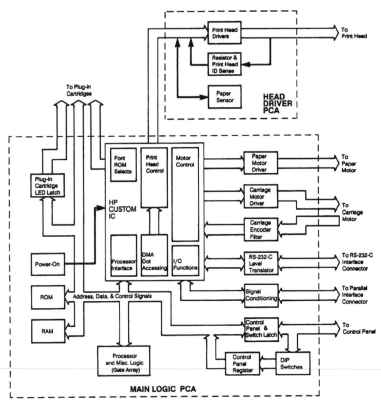

26-6 Block diagram of an HP DeskJet ECU. Hewlett-Packard Company

Symptom 2. Print has one or more missing dots that resemble white lines (this also takes place during a self-test) It seems as if one or more of the print head's nozzles will not fire. Always start by suspecting the print head; if a nozzle has jammed from accumulations of dust or debris, it can shut down the nozzle. Make sure that the print head is clean. Normally, ink-jet printers wipe the print head every certain number of passes. However, you can remove the cartridge and wipe it with a clean lint-free swab. Also wipe the electrical contacts to ensure a good connection. Replace the cartridge and try the printer again. If the problem persists, try another print head. If a new print head does not resolve the problem, your fault lies almost certainly with the print head driver board. If a driver circuit fails, the corresponding nozzle will not fire. Try another drive board.

Symptom 3. Printer does not print under computer control (operation appears correct in self-test mode) Before you attempt to disassemble the printer, take a moment to check its on-line status. There is almost always an indicator on the control panel that is lit when the printer is selected. If the printer is not selected (online), then it will not receive information from the computer, even if everything is working correctly.

A printer can be off-line for several reasons. Paper might have run out, in which case you will often have to reselect the printer explicitly after paper is replenished. Even the simplest printers offer a variety of options that are selectable through the keyboard (font style, character pitch, line width, etc.). However, you must often go off line in order to manipulate those functions, then reselect the printer when done. You might have selected a function incorrectly, or forgotten to reselect the printer after changing modes. Also consider software compatibility. If you are using a "canned" software package, make sure that its printer driver settings are configured properly for your particular printer. If you are working through Windows, make sure that the proper Windows driver is selected.

Check your communication interface cable next. It might have become loose or unattached at either the printer or computer end. If this is a new or untested cable, make sure that it is wired correctly for your particular interface (serial or parallel). An interface cable that is prone to bending or flexing might have developed a faulty connection, so disconnect the cable at both ends and use your multimeter to check cable continuity. If this is a new, home-made cable assembly, double-check its construction against your printer and computer interface diagrams. Try a different cable.

Double-check the printer's dip switch settings or setup configuration. Dip switches are often included in the printer to select certain optional functions such as serial communication format, character sets, default character pitch, or automatic line feed. If you are installing a new printer, or you have changed the switches to alter an operating mode, it might be a faulty or invalid condition. Dip switches also tend to become unreliable after many switch cycles. If you suspect an intermittent dip switch, rock it back and forth several times, then retest the printer. If everything else checks out up to this point, try replacing the ECU board.

Symptom 4. Print head moves back and forth but does not print; or prints only intermittently (this also takes place during a self-test) When the printer carriage moves, but print is absent (or intermittent) check your print head first. The ink-jet head might simply be out of ink. Try a new ink-jet head with a fresh ink supply. If problems continue, check the ribbon cable between the driver circuit and print head. Intermittent connections in the print head or print head cable can lead to highly erratic head operation. A complete cable break can shut down the print head entirely, especially if the break occurs in a common (ground) conductor. Turn off and unplug the printer, then use your multimeter to check continuity across each cable conductor. You might have to disconnect the cable at one end to prevent false readings. Replace any print head cable that appears defective.

There might be a problem with the print head driver supply voltage(s). Use your multimeter to check each output from the power supply. If you find that one or more power supply voltage(s) are low or erratic, you can attempt to troubleshoot the supply, or replace the supply outright. When power supply outputs measure correctly, the fault is probably located in the print head driver board. Replace the driver board. Keep in mind that when the power supply, driver circuits, and main logic are integrated on the same board, the entire ECU will have to be replaced.

The paper transport

Although individual paper handling mechanisms will vary slightly from manufacturer to manufacturer, ink-jet printers use two distinct types: friction feed and tractor feed. Each of these systems operates in a different manner, and suffers from its own unique set of problems.

Friction feed

As its name suggests, a *friction feed* paper transport uses friction to push paper through the printer. Paper is threaded into the printer along a metal feed guide. The guide ensures that paper is maneuvered properly between the *platen* and *pressure roller(s)*, then up in front of the print head assembly. A set of small, free-rolling *bail rollers* press gently against the paper to help keep it flat around the platen. In order to allow the free passage of paper during threading, a lever is often included to separate pressure rollers from the platen. After paper is positioned as desired, the lever can be released to re-apply pressure. From then on, paper can only be moved by hand-turning the platen, or the printer's actual operation.

A drive system for the DeskJet friction-feed paper transport is shown in Fig. 26-7. High-energy square-wave pulses provided by the ECU's motor drive circuits feed a stepping motor. Depending on the quantity of pulses and their sequence, the motor can be made to step clockwise or counterclockwise by any amount. The stepping motor provides force to a *drive train* of gears. The drive gear (or *primary gear*) operates a *secondary gear* attached to the platen. Gear assemblies are usually used, but pulley systems can sometimes be found. In some designs, a stepping motor is used to operate the platen directly (known as *direct drive*). The drive assembly offers several useful features. First, the use of gears provides a reliable drive train;

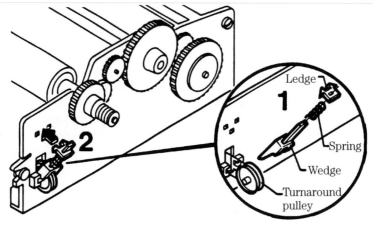

26-7 Basic mechanics of the HP DeskJet paper transport. Hewlett-Packard Company

gears do not stretch or tear with age, and they will not jam or slip as long as they are kept clean and aligned properly. Second, the use of a smaller primary gear provides greater positioning accuracy for the platen.

Tractor feed

Tractor feed does not rely on friction to transport paper. Instead, a set of sprocket wheels are mechanically linked to the platen drive train. Pegs on each sprocket wheel mesh perfectly with specially made paper. This type of paper (also called *continuous-feed* or *fan-fold* paper) has holes perforated along both sides. Paper is threaded into the printer along a metal feed guide. There is very little resistance from its contact rollers, so paper can easily be fed through and secured into its sprocket wheels. Most sprocket wheels can slide left or right to accommodate a selection of paper widths or tractor feed label products. Bail rollers are included to help keep paper flat against the platen. Once paper is threaded, it can only be advanced by hand turning the platen knob, or in actual printer operation. Although older ink-jet printers used tractor-feed transports, virtually all ink-jet printers now use a friction-feed transport that is optimized for stacked single sheets of paper.

Troubleshooting a paper transport

Symptom 1. The paper advance does not function, or functions only intermittently (all other functions check properly) When a paper advance fails to work at all, begin by observing the paper feed drive train assembly. Check any pulleys or gears to ensure that all parts are meshed evenly and are able to move freely. You can watch this by turning the platen knob located outside of the printer. If there is no manual platen, you can run a form feed. Remove any foreign objects or obstructions that might be jamming the drive train. Never try to force a drive train that does not turn freely! Realign any parts that appear to be slipping or misaligned. Replace any damaged mechanical parts or assemblies.

Turn off all printer power and examine the electrical connections for your paper advance motor. Make sure that all connectors are installed and seated properly. If you suspect a faulty wiring connection, turn off printer power and use your multimeter to measure continuity across any suspicious wires. It might be necessary to disconnect the cable from at least one end to prevent false continuity readings. Replace any faulty wiring.

If everything checks properly up to this point, either the motor or ECU has failed. With printer power still off and the motor disconnected from the ECU, use your multimeter to measure the continuity of each motor winding. This is not difficult, but you will need to check the schematic of your particular printer for specific pin numbers and resistance measurements. A working motor winding exhibits between 4 to 40 Ω. If you read a short circuit (about 0 Ω), or an open circuit (substantial or infinite resistance), the paper advance motor is probably defective and should be replaced. If you cannot determine the location of each motor winding, try replacing the paper advance motor.

If the motor checks out (or a new motor fails to resolve the problem), a fault has likely developed in the ECU. One or more of the motor drive circuits has failed, or the motor voltage output from the power supply has failed. Replace the ECU outright.

Symptom 2. Paper slips or walks around the platen in friction-feed operation   Friction feed paper transports are only designed to work with certain types of paper; brands within a certain range of thickness and weight. Very fine (light bond) paper or very heavy (card stock) paper will probably not advance properly. Smooth-coated papers also will probably not work well. Check the specifications for your particular printer to find its optimum paper type. If you find that you are using an unusual type of paper, try the printer using ink-jet paper.

Keep in mind that friction-feed was intended for single-sheet operation. Some small amount of walking is natural, but feeding extremely long lengths of paper might result in noticeable walking. It is possible to use continuous-feed paper in a friction-feed transport, but you should expect to see a certain amount of walking eventually; if you have the option, try to stay with single sheets.

If the problem persists, take careful note of each roller condition. An even, consistent paper feed depends on firm roller pressure applied evenly across its entire length. Rollers that are very dirty, or old and dry, might no longer be applying force evenly. Clean and rejuvenate your rollers with a good-quality rubber cleaning compound such as *Kleen-a-Platen* available from almost any comprehensive office supply store. *Caution: Rubber cleaning compounds can be dangerous, and might not be compatible with all types of synthetic roller materials; read instructions on the chemical container carefully, and follow all safety and ventilation instructions.*

Old rollers also might be out of alignment. Mechanical wear on shafts and bushings (or bearings) can allow some rollers to float around in the printer. Carefully examine the condition of each roller shaft. Ideally, each shaft should be fixed firmly within its assembly, so you should feel little or no "slack." If you feel or see a roller move within its assembly, replace its bushings, bearing, or shaft. Newer mechanical assemblies make it easier to simply replace the entire transport outright. Some pressure roller assemblies can be adjusted slightly to alter their contact force. If your particular printer uses nonadjustable pressure rollers, there is little more to be done (other than replace the mechanical assembly). If you can adjust roller force (using spring tension or a screw adjustment), do so only as a last resort—and only then in small increments. Careless adjustment can easily worsen the problem.

Check your paper path for any debris or obstructions that might be catching part of the paper. A crumpled corner of paper jammed in the paper path or caught in the feed guide can easily interfere with subsequent sheets. Adhesive label fragments are even more troublesome. Remove all obstructions being careful not to mark any of the rollers. A straightened paper clip can often get into spaces that your fingers and tools will not. Use your needle-nose pliers to put a small hook in the wire's end for grabbing and pulling the obstruction. *Do not disassemble the roller assemblies unless absolutely necessary.*

The carriage transport

Ink-jet printers use *serial* print heads—fully formed text and graphics are formed by passing a print head left and right across a page surface. As the head moves, it places a series of vertical dots that creates the image. In this way, a complete line of text can be generated in a single pass (letter quality text or graphics might require additional passes). As you might imagine, the process of moving a serial print head becomes a serious concern. It must move at the proper time, at the proper speed, and over the proper distance to within several thousandths of an inch on every pass. The high-resolution graphics available from ink-jet printers require even greater positioning precision.

Belt drive

The task of moving a serial print head is handled by the *carriage transport*. A print head is mounted to a platform or holder (the *carriage assembly*) as shown in Fig. 26-8. Most serial printers use some type of belt drive. A *carriage motor* (often a stepping motor used in conjunction with a gear train) drives a primary pulley that is connected to a secondary pulley by a drive linkage. A drive linkage might be a wire, belt, or chain, depending on the weight of the print head and its desired left-right speed (or *slew*). At one point, the drive linkage is connected at the carriage, which rides along one or more low-friction rails (or *carriage rod*). Rails keep the carriage rigidly parallel to the platen at all points. When the stepping motor turns counterclockwise, the carriage assembly slides left, and vice versa.

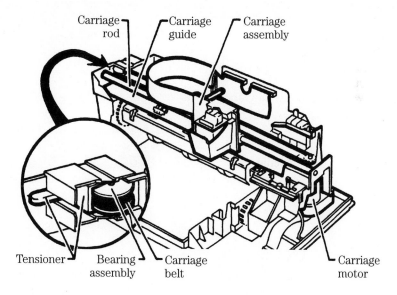

Carriage rod   Carriage guide   Carriage assembly

Tensioner   Bearing assembly   Carriage belt   Carriage motor

26-8 Carriage assembly of the HP DeskJet printer. Hewlett-Packard Company

Positioning precision for a belt drive is determined by the stepping motor's resolution and the pulley diameter. This holds true for a direct drive mechanism. If the primary pulley works through a gear train, that gear ratio also must be included. As an example, suppose a stepping motor directly drives a pulley 1 inch in diameter. The circumference of the primary pulley would be $[\pi \times d]$ $[3.14 \times 1]$ 3.14 inches, so one complete motor revolution (thus one complete pulley revolution) would cause the linkage to travel 3.14 inches. If the stepping motor works at 200 steps per revolution, each step would turn the pulley $\frac{1}{200}$ of a revolution, or [3.14/200] 0.0157 inch of linear travel.

Suppose the pulley was only 0.5 inch in diameter. Its circumference would only be [$\pi \times d$] [3.14 × 0.5] 1.57 inches, so a single motor rotation would only move the carriage 1.57 inches. At 200 steps per revolution, each step would drive the carriage [1.57/200] 0.0079 inch. Smaller pulleys (or motors with more steps per revolution) can achieve finer positioning; but at the cost of more steps to traverse the platen width.

Troubleshooting a carriage transport

Symptom 1. The carriage advance does not function or functions only intermittently (all other functions check properly) During printer initialization, the carriage is taken to its home position. Because the printer has no way of knowing where its carriage is when it is first turned on, finding the carriage home gives the ECU physical evidence of an actual carriage position. Under normal circumstances, the ECU will initialize the carriage to the left side of the printer, although inverted printers such as Hewlett-Packard's DeskJet (Fig. 26-9) initialize the print head at the

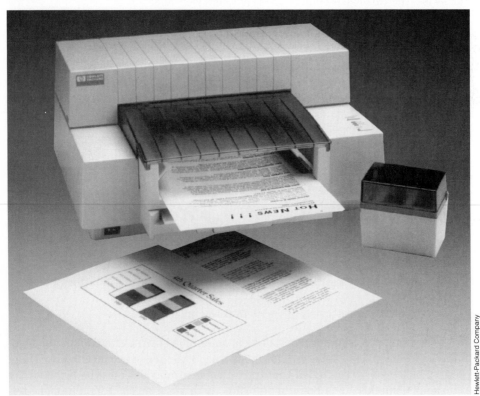

Hewlett-Packard Company

26-9 An HP DeskJet 500C printer.

right. A mechanical or optical home sensor will inform the ECU when home is reached. At that point, the exact carriage position is known for certain. As the carriage moves, pulses generated from an optical position encoder confirm that the carriage is in motion.

When the carriage fails to move (or moves only intermittently), suspect a serious mechanical problem. Watch your carriage advance motor and drive train assembly while the printer initializes. A slipping belt or misaligned gear might have to be tightened or replaced. Make sure the primary pulley is attached securely to its drive shaft. Also examine the drive linkage to be sure that it is properly attached to the carriage. Replace any parts that are broken or excessively worn. Remove any obstructions or foreign objects that might interfere with the drive train.

If you see that the carriage advance motor does not turn, turn off and unplug the printer, then check all electrical connections to the motor. Make sure that all connectors are installed properly and firmly seated. Use your multimeter to check continuity across any suspicious wiring. When checking continuity, it might be necessary to disconnect the wire or cable at one end to prevent false readings. Replace any faulty wiring.

If everything checks properly up to this point, either the motor or ECU has failed. With printer power still off and the motor disconnected from the ECU, use your multimeter to measure the continuity of each motor winding. This is not difficult, but you will need to check the schematic of your particular printer for specific pin numbers and resistance measurements. A working motor winding exhibits between 4 to 40 Ω. If you read a short circuit (about 0 Ω), or an open circuit (substantial or infinite resistance), the paper advance motor is probably defective and should be replaced. If you cannot determine the location of each motor winding, try replacing the paper advance motor.

If the motor checks out (or a new motor fails to resolve the problem), a fault has likely developed in the ECU. One or more of the motor drive circuits has failed, or the motor voltage output from the power supply has failed. Replace the ECU outright.

Symptom 2. The carriage operates, but it does not always position properly Improper carriage positioning can take many forms—character spacing might be erratic, or the carriage might sometimes ram into the left or right side frames. Faulty mechanics are often at the heart of carriage problems. Turn off and unplug the printer, then inspect the carriage drive train very carefully. Pay particular attention to the drive linkage to be sure that it is reasonably tight (Fig. 26-10). One or both pulleys might be loose. Inspect any drive gears between the motor and primary pulley for signs of slipping or broken gear teeth. Replace any parts that appear broken or excessively worn.

An optical encoder provides pulses to the ECU as a carriage moves. The pulses allow the printer to position its carriage. Erratic or inconsistent positioning might be the fault of the encoder. Try replacing the encoder. If the problem persists, there is probably a logic fault in the ECU. Replace the ECU outright.

26-10
Attaching a carriage transport
belt. Hewlett-Packard Company

27
CHAPTER

I/O and support ICs

The concept of miniaturization is hardly a new one. Each transition in the electronics industry (vacuum tube to transistor, from transistor to IC, and from IC to microprocessor) brought with it startling reductions in physical size and increasing speed and functionality. It is no surprise that PC manufacturers have followed this trend. Consider the original IBM PC/AT. Its motherboard was implemented with over 200 ICs. Most of the ICs were basic gates used as interconnecting (or *glue*) logic. Yet, take a look at any i486-based motherboard—you would be hard-pressed to find more than 20 ICs. This continuing evolution of more functions with fewer components has been made possible through the use of *ASICs* (application-specific ICs) as shown in Fig. 27-1.

27-1
Future Domain SCSI interface ICs. Copyright © 1995 Future Domain Corporation. Reprinted with permission.

There is another powerful advantage to ASICs, besides simply a reduction in size; it is *optimization*. When a circuit is designed, the performance of the circuit is limited by the performance of each part; the chain is only as strong as its weakest link. The basic logic gates used in early PCs worked correctly, but few had the characteristics to handle the speeds that PCs would soon be reaching. On the other hand, by designing various functions onto an IC (creating a custom IC from the ground up), each function can be highly optimized for such characteristics as speed or data throughput. When the functions being developed are too complex for one IC to handle alone, a set of ASICs can be designed. This set of highly optimized, special-purpose ICs is referred to as a *chipset*. Most current motherboards now make extensive use of chipsets.

Understanding chipset functions

The first thing you must realize about chipsets is that no two are created equal. Although many chipsets are similar, each chipset performs a slightly different set of functions. Chipsets compete by trying to provide more features with better performance than other sets. However, to really understand chipsets, a technician should have a basic understanding of how functions are divided, and know the importance of each function. This will help you to better understand the results generated by PC diagnostic packages.

Buffers and bus controllers

The classic *buffer* is basically little more than an amplifier designed to take weak or heavily loaded logic signals and restore the signal's integrity before passing it on to another area of the PC. Although it would be a simple matter to combine both buffers on the same IC, they are generally kept separate to reduce the IC's pin count and simplify the motherboard's signal layouts. Another interesting characteristic of buffers is that many are designed to work with multiple buses, which allows much more convenient signal routing and connection between other motherboard components, as well as a bus dedicated to the I/O slots.

When the signals on an expansion bus are extremely similar or identical to the signals being passed around the motherboard, an expansion board can plug directly into a system without any complex signal manipulation. But, when the signals on an expansion bus do not match the signals on a motherboard, an interface must be created in order to manage the expansion bus; this is the task of a bus controller. Because the design of every motherboard is a bit different, you will find that some systems include ISA bus controllers and others do not. More specialized buses (such as EISA, VL, and PCI) typically include a bus controller IC to accomplish this motherboard/bus signal translation. Even SCSI buses are being implemented on motherboards using single-chip bus controllers such as the Future Domain 36C70 SCSI-2 IC.

Peripheral controllers

Interrupts and DMA channels are vital to the proper operation of any PC. Classic i286 and i386 systems used a *PIC* (programmable interrupt controller) to manage interrupts, and a DMA controller to handle DMA channels. In many of today's systems, the interrupt and DMA control are brought together in a single peripheral controller IC. Peripheral controllers typically interact with such elements as the keyboard controller, real-time clock, mouse, and bus slots. DMA and interrupt controller problems can often be traced to a fault in the peripheral controller IC. Newer peripheral controllers also include at least one serial port, one parallel port, one bus mouse port, and also might provide a floppy and IDE adapter—all on the same IC!

System controllers

There are a myriad of routine operations that must be performed regularly on the motherboard. Such activities include timing and clock signal generation, system ready or reset synchronization, wait-state control, math coprocessor control, and error processing logic. To implement these functions on a classical motherboard often required fairly large numbers of ICs, many of which served as glue logic that tied the various functions together. Current motherboards have largely replaced that proliferation of discrete logic with a single system controller IC.

The system controller integrates much of the motherboard's timing, control, and synchronization activities. For example, the system controller provides multiple clock signals (24 MHz and 14.318 MHz). It also distributes clock and control signals to the CPU, math coprocessor, and bus slots, as well as exchanges control data with other key controllers in the system. Some system controllers integrate DMA and memory refresh control circuitry, along with a limited amount of interrupt handling. As you might suspect, the system controller IC is one of the most variable elements of a chipset.

Memory controllers

PC memory is a remarkably sensitive and fragile area. In order to achieve such fast memory access and low-power operation, the *DRAM* (dynamic random-access memory (DRAM) used in virtually all PCs must be *refreshed* every few milliseconds; otherwise, its contents will be irretrievably lost. The memory controller IC is largely designed to automate the refresh process with a minimum of intervention from the CPU or system controller. Of course, refresh is initiated at regular intervals as determined by the real-time clock. The peripheral or system controller can then signal the memory controller that a refresh cycle is needed. Simultaneously, the rest of the system must be halted for the few microseconds that a refresh cycle is in progress.

Clocks and timers

A CPU requires precise, high-frequency timing signals in order to synchronize its operation. In many cases, such timing is provided by the system controller IC, but there are many chipsets that place the clock generator and timing functions on a separate *clock/timer* IC. A separate signal generator might seem excessive, but a separate signal source is less likely to cause random interference with other sections of the system controller. Keep in mind that this is not the *RTC* (real-time clock). The RTC is typically combined with CMOS configuration RAM on a single IC, and supported by a lithium backup battery.

Power management

Mobile computers have become a substantial part of the PC market. As more users become mobile, PC makers are constantly devising new ways to reduce power consumption and preserve battery life. One of the more compelling arguments in mobile PC design is power management; by turning off the elements of a mobile computer that are not being used, battery life can be extended, sometimes dramatically. The power-management IC was developed to track the use of such high-demand components as display backlights, hard drives, and even the CPU. When those items are idle for some predetermined period of time, the power management IC will shut it down until it is needed again. Power management varies in its sophistication, but all power management devices are trying to achieve the same overall goal.

Video controllers

Even the most sophisticated PC needs some kind of display. The video adapter circuit is responsible for taking video data from system bus and storing that data in local memory (video RAM), then converting that data into characters or pixel patterns that are sent on to a monitor for display. At the heart of any video adapter circuit is the video controller IC. In most cases, video controllers are assumed to be off the motherboard (on an expansion card), although many of the newer motherboards being produced today do offer on-board video support.

Video controllers have become a hotly contested part of the modern PC. Graphics-intensive programs (under both DOS and Windows) require a tremendous amount of data to be transferred to the video controller, so much, in fact, that the classic ISA bus is easily overloaded. New bus designs such as PCI and VL have eased the information bottleneck, but the competition between video chipset manufacturers is more intense than ever. Each new video chipset promises higher video modes with ever-faster performance.

Drive controllers

No PC is useful without access to mass-storage devices. Floppy drives, hard drives, CD-ROM drives, and tape drives have all become essential subassemblies of a modern computer. Each type of drive requires a drive adapter card to handle the processing of signals and data between the drive and system buses. At the core of any drive adapter is the drive controller IC. The drive controller helps to synchronize and manage data and control signals at the drive. In most cases, drive controllers are assumed to be off the motherboard (on an expansion card or on the drive itself). Today, many motherboards offer direct connections, but only for SCSI or IDE drives, where the drive controllers are on the drives, and any adapter circuitry is merely a buffer to synchronize data transfer.

As drives continue to improve in capacity and performance, drive controller circuitry plays an increasingly important role. Unlike video controllers, however, drive controllers are typically proprietary to the particular drive manufacturer. For example, a Quantum hard drive will often use Quantum controller ICs. This is because drive mechanics and electronics must be very carefully matched to ensure optimum performance. This trend will probably become even more acute as drives continue to advance.

The major chipsets

Now that you have an understanding of the major chipset categories, it is time to identify a variety of chips in each major set (Fig. 27-2). Table 27-1 presents a break-

27-2
A Chips and Technologies
chipset. Copyright © Chips and Technologies, Inc. 1995. Reprinted with permission of copyright owner. All rights reserved.

down of the IC numbers and functions of various chipsets. Keep in mind that these listings are constantly changing and growing as manufacturers add new devices to their product lines, so use the following information as a guide rather than an absolute index.

Table 27-1. A breakdown of various PC chipsets

ACC 82010 Chipset (i286/i386 systems motherboard chipset)

IC	Function
ACC2000	Integrated Peripheral Controller
ACC2100	System Controller
ACC2210	Data Bus Buffer
ACC2220	Address Bus Buffer

ACC 82020 Chipset (i286/i386 systems motherboard chipset)

IC	Function
ACC2000	Integrated Peripheral Controller
ACC2120	Enhanced System Controller
ACC2210	Data Bus Buffer
ACC2220	Address Bus Buffer
ACC2300	Page Interleaved Memory Controller
ACC2500	System Controller
ACC2030	Single-Chip i286 System Controller
ACC2035	Single-Chip i386SX System Controller

Chips & Technologies CS8230 Chipset (CHIPset i286 motherboard chipset)

IC	Function
82C201	System Controller
82C202	RAM/ROM Decoder and I/O Controller
82C203	High-Address Bus Buffer
82C204	Low-Address Bus Buffer
82C205	Data Bus Buffer and Parity Generator

Table 27-1. Continued

Chips & Technologies CS8221
Chipset **(NEAT i286 motherboard chipset)**

IC	Function
82C211	System Controller and Extended CMOS RAM Control Logic
82C212	I/O and Memory Decode Logic
82C215	Parity Logic and Bus Buffers
82C206	Integrated Peripheral Controller

Chips & Technologies CS8233
Chipset **(PEAK i386 motherboard chipset)**

IC	Function
82C311	CPU, Cache, DRAM Controller
82C316	Peripheral Controller
82C315	Bus Controller
82C452	Super VGA Controller
82C601	Single-Chip Peripheral Controller
82C765	Single-Chip Floppy Disk Controller

Chips & Technologies CB8291/CB8295
Chipset **(ELEAT i286/i386 motherboard chipsets)**

IC	Function
82C235	SCAT System Controller
82C450	1Mb DRAM VGA Graphics Controller
82C451	Integrated VGA Graphics Controller
82C710	Universal Peripheral Controller
82C711	Universal Peripheral Controller II

Chips & Technologies CS8230/CS8231
Chipset **(i386DX motherboard chipsets)**

IC	Function
82C206	Integrated Peripheral Controller
82C301	Bus Controller
82C302	Page/Interleave Memory Controller
82C303	High-Address Bus Buffer
82C304	Low-Address Bus Buffer
82C305	Data Bus Buffers
82C306	Control Buffer
82C307	Cache/DRAM Controller

Chips & Technologies CS8238
Chipset **(i386DX motherboard chipset for MCA bus systems)**

IC	Function
82C226	System Peripheral Controller
82C233	DMA Controller
82C321	CPU/MicroChannel Controller
82C322	Page Interleave/EMS Controller
82C325	Data Bus Buffer

Table 27-1. Continued

Chips & Technologies CS8281
Chipset (NEATsx i386SX motherboard chipset)

IC	Function
82C206	Integrated Peripherals Controller
82C215	Data and Address Buffer
82C811	CPU and Bus Controller
82C812	Page Interleave/EMS Controller

Chips & Technologies CS8285
Chipset (PEAKset/SX i386SX motherboard chipset)

IC	Function
82C235	System Controller
82C835	Cache Controller

Chips & Technologies CS82310 Chipset
(PEAKset i386DX/i486SX/i486DX motherboard chipset)

IC	Function
82C351	CPU/Cache/DRAM Controller
82C355	Data Buffer
82C356	Integrated Peripheral Controller

Chips & Technologies CHIPS 280 Chipset
PS/2 Model 80 i386DX motherboard chipset for MCA bus)

IC	Function
82C226	Page Interleave/EMS Controller
82C233	DMA Controller
82C321	CPU/MicroChannel Controller
82C322	Page Interleave/EMS Controller
82C325	Data Bus Buffer and Controller
82C450	1MB DRAM VGA Graphics Controller
82C607	Multi-function Controller

ETEQ Microsystems 82C390SX
Chipset (Panda i386DX motherboard chipset)

IC	Function
82C390SX	CPU, Cache, and DRAM Controller

ETEQ Microsystems 82C4901/82C4902
Chipset (Bengal i386DX motherboard chipset)

IC	Function
82C4901	CPU, Cache, and DRAM Controller
82C4902	Data Bugger and MCP Interface Controller

ETEQ Microsystems ET2000 Chipset
i386DX/i486SX/i486DX motherboard chipset for EISA bus)

IC	Function
ET2001	EISA Bus Controller
ET2002	EISA Data Buffer

Table 27-1. Continued

ETEQ Microsystems ET2000 Chipset
i386DX/i486SX/i486DX motherboard chipset for EISA bus)

IC	Function
ET2003	EISA Integrated Peripheral Controller
ET2004	EISA Cache/Memory Controller

ITEQ Microsystems ET6000 Chipset
(Cheetah i486SX motherboard chipset)

IC	Function
ET6000	System Controller

Faraday FE3600B Chipset (motherboard chipset)

IC	Function
FE3001	System Controller
FE3010	Peripheral Controller
FE3021	Address Bus and Memory Control Logic
FE3031	Parity and Data Bus Controller

Intel 82350/DT EISA Chipset
(i386DX/i486SX/i486DX chipset for EISA bus)

IC	Function
82077	Floppy Disk Controller
82352	EISA Bus Buffer
82353	Advanced Data Path
82357	Integrated Peripheral Controller
82358	EISA Bus Controller
82359	DRAM Controller

OPTI Chipset (i286/i386 motherboard chipset)

IC	Function
82C381	System and Cache Memory Controller
82C382	Direct Mapped Page Interleaved Memory Controller

OPTI 386WB Chipset (i386DX motherboard chipset)

IC	Function
82C206	Integrated Peripheral Controller
82C391	System Controller
82C392	Data Bus Controller

OPTI 486SXWB Chipset (i486SX motherboard chipset)

IC	Function
82C206	Integrated Peripheral Controller
82C392	Data Bus Controller
83C493	System Controller

Table 27-1. Continued

OPTI 386/486WB Chipset
(i386DX/i486SX/i486DX motherboard chipset for EISA bus)

IC	Function
82C681	EISA Bus Controller
82C682	Memory/Cache Controller
82C686	Integrated Peripheral Controller
82C687	Data Bus Controller

Suntec Chipset (i286 motherboard chipset)

IC	Function
ST62C201	System Bus Controller
ST62C202	Memory Controller
ST62C008	Integrated Peripheral Controller
ST62C010	Address Bus Controller
ST62BC001	System Controller
ST62BC002	High Address Controller
ST62BC003	Low Address Controller
ST62BC004	Data Buffer
ST62C005	I/O Control, DMA Page Register
ST62C006	Integrated Peripheral Controller

Suntec Chipset (i286/i386SX motherboard chipset)

IC	Function
GS62C101	System, Data Bus, Timer, and Interrupt Controller
GS62C102	Memory, DMA, and I/O Controller

Symphony Labs HAYDN AT Chipset
(i386SX/i386DX/i486SX/i486SLC/i486DX motherboard chipset)

IC	Function
SL82C362	Bus Controller
SL82C461	System Controller
SL82C465	Cache Controller

Symphony Labs Mozart Chipset
(i386SX/DX/i486SX/SLC/DX motherboard chipset for EISA bus)

IC	Function
SL82C471	CPU, Cache, and DRAM Controller
SL82C472	EISA Bus Controller
SL82C473	EISA DMA Controller

Western Digital Chipset (motherboard chipset)

IC	Function
75C10	Single-Chip 286 AT Controller
75C20	Floppy Drive, Hard Drive, and Real-Time Clock
Controller	

Table 27-1. Continued

Western Digital Chipset (motherboard chipset)

IC	Function
75C30	Serial and Parallel Port Controller
76C10	High-Speed Single i286 System Controller
WD6000	System, Interrupt, and Timer Controller
WD6010	DMA, Reset, and Parity Controller
WD6020	Address and Data Bus Controller
WD6036	DRAM/Cache Memory Controller

VIA Chipset (FLEXSET motherboard chipset)

IC	Function
SL9011	System Controller
SL9020	Data Bus Controller
SL9023	Address Controller
SL9030	Integrated Peripheral Controller
SL9090	Universal Clock IC
SL9095	Power Management IC
SL9151	i286 Page Interleave Memory Controller
SL9152	i286 System and Memory Controller
SL9250	i386SX Page Mode Memory Controller
SL9251	i386SX Page Interleave Memory Controller
SL9252	i386SX System and Memory Controller
SL9350	i386DX Page Mode Memory Controller
SL9351	i386DX Page Mode Memory Controller
SL9352	i386DX System and Memory Controller

VLSI Technology Chipset (TOPCAT i286/i386SX motherboard chipset)

IC	Function
VL82C331	ISA Bus Controller
VL82C320	System Controller
VL82C106	Multi-function Controller

VLSI Technology Chipset (TOPCAT i386DX motherboard chipset)

IC	Function
VL82C106	Multi-function Controller
VL82C311	ISA Bus Controller
VL82C322	Data Buffer
VL82C330	System Controller

VLSI Technology Chipset (VL82CPCAT-16/20 motherboard chipset)

IC	Function
VL82C100	Peripheral Controller
VL82C201	System Controller
VL82C202	Memory Controller
VL82C203	Address Buffer
VL82C204	Data Buffer

Table 27-1. Continued

Zilog Chipset **(motherboard chipset)**

IC	Function
P90	System, Interrupt, DMA, Clock, and Refresh Controller
P91	Memory Controller
P92	Address and Data Bus Controllers

Zymos Chipset **(motherboard chipset)**

IC	Function
POACH/XTB	Single-Chip XT Controller
POACH1	System Clock, Bus Controller, Interrupt Controller, and RTC
POACH2	DMA, Timer, Refresh, and I/O Controller
POACH4	Single-Chip XT Controller
POACH6	High-Speed i386DX/i486 System Controller
POACH7	System Clock, Bus Controller, Interrupt Controller, and RTC
POACH8	DMA, Timer, Refresh, and I/O Controller

Chipset troubleshooting

It is important for you to understand the role played by chipsets. By knowing the manufacturer and model of the motherboard chipset in use, you can use the error messages provided by your diagnostics to isolate the defect to a particular IC. For example, suppose the system being serviced includes a motherboard with a Chips & Technologies CS8230 chipset (a user's manual will typically tell you this). If your diagnostic tools then indicate a DMA problem, you can see from Table 27-1 that the DMA function is likely in the 82C201 system controller IC. You can then replace the IC if possible. Otherwise, you can replace the entire motherboard. On the other hand, if your motherboard incorporated a Chips & Technologies CS8238 chipset and your diagnostics reported a DMA problem, you would suspect the 82C233 DMA controller IC. Although a diagnostic cannot tell you which IC has failed, a diagnostic can reveal which function has failed by knowing which IC performs which function, you can at least be sure that a new board would correct the fault. This can take a great deal of expensive guesswork out of PC repair.

28
CHAPTER

I/O POST codes

The *POST* (power-on self-test) procedure is embedded into the BIOS of every PC. During initialization, the POST performs a self-diagnostic routine designed to check key areas of the PC for major faults. When an error is detected early in the test cycle, you will probably hear a series of beep codes as described in Chapter 15. However, BIOS makers soon realized that most beep code sequences are not terribly specific, and a beep code can often represent any one of a number of possible failures. In order to make more specific information available, POST procedures are designed to output a single hexadecimal byte to I/O port 80h prior to each step in the initialization. If the PC should fail at any point during start-up, the code at port 80h represents the test that was not successfully completed. By knowing the full sequence of I/O POST codes generated by a BIOS, a technician can quickly determine the test step that failed and thus pinpoint the fault with great accuracy. This chapter presents the I/O POST sequences for popular PC BIOS versions.

The POST board

Although virtually all current PC BIOS versions make use of port 80h, the port itself is merely a repository for that information. In order for you to read the contents of port 80h, you will need a POST board (such as the Micro2000 *Post-Probe* shown in Fig. 28-1) that should be installed in an open slot prior to troubleshooting, and then removed once troubleshooting is completed. Remember to turn the PC off before installing or removing a POST card. Essentially, the design of a POST board is quite simple. It reads the byte at the POST I/O port, and displays the hexadecimal code in the two seven-segment displays. However, many POST boards today provide a technician with a much more powerful troubleshooting tool. As an example, the Post-Probe supplies a series of LEDs that checks for main voltages (+12 Vdc, –12 Vdc, +5 Vdc, and –5 Vdc), and the presence of key signals on the expansion bus (address latch, I/O read, I/O write, memory read, memory write, system clock, and so on). Even an on-board logic probe attachment is provided.

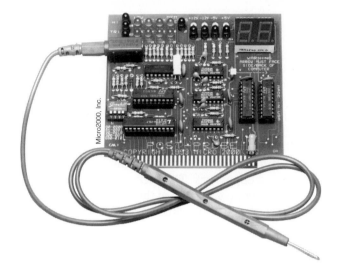

Micro2000, Inc.

28-1
The PostProbe from
Micro2000.

I/O ports

Although most traditional ISA-based PCs make use of port 80h, not all PCs follow this rule. The Compaq PC outputs codes to port 84h, and PS/2 models 25 and 30 send codes to port 90h. PS/2 model 20-286 sends codes to port 190h. Even most EISA-based PCs use port 80h, but Compaq PCs continue to use port 84h. EISA machines with Award BIOS use port 300h. Systems with an *MCS* (micro channel bus architecture) use port 680h. Take note that some PS/2 models, Olivetti, early AT&T, some NCR, and a few AT clones will send POST codes to a printer port at 3BCh, 278h, or 378h. The current generation of POST boards typically provides a DIP switch or jumper array for selecting the active port location. Before choosing a POST board, make sure that it can read the proper port address for your system.

Another issue to keep in mind is that not all PCs produce POST codes. The original IBM PC, the AMI XT, and some systems using HP, DTK, and ERSO BIOS do not send out POST codes during initialization. If you are testing such a system, you will be unable to see hexadecimal codes using the POST card (but power and signal indicators should still work).

Interpreting the LEDs

Before discussing the various POST codes in detail, you should have an understanding of the many discrete signal LEDs that accompany current POST boards. These individual signals can be a great asset when interpreted in conjunction with the POST code. Keep in mind that each POST card will offer a different selection of LEDs, so your own POST card might not have all of the indicators shown here.

- *Power LEDs* The PC will not work correctly (if at all) if one or more power supply voltages is low or absent. Typical POST cards provide four LEDs that light when +5 Vdc, +12 Vdc, –5 Vdc, and –12 Vdc are available. If any of those LEDs are dim or out, there might be a problem with the power supply or its connection to the motherboard. If problems occur after upgrading the system, the power supply might be overloaded. In any case, power LEDs help you to identify power problems quickly and effectively.

- *ALE* The *address latch enable* signal is generated by the CPU, and is used by virtually all devices in the PC that must capture address signals (such as BIOS). When this LED is on, address generation by the CPU is probably working file. If this LED is out, there is a problem manipulating addresses in the system. You should then suspect the CPU, DMA controller, Bus Buffer/Controller, or Clock Generator/System Controller IC. This can be very helpful for technicians who choose to troubleshoot to the component level.

- *I/OW* An I/O write LED will generally light whenever BIOS attempts to write data to an I/O device such as a floppy disk. The BIOS will then attempt to read what was written to confirm that portion of the system is working as expected. If the I/OW LED stays out, you should suspect a fault in either the BIOS or the system's DMA controller IC.

- *I/OR* I/O read LED will generally light whenever BIOS attempts to read data back from an I/O device after data has been written. If this LED remains out, you should suspect a fault in either the BIOS or the system's DMA controller IC.

- *MR/W* During POST, the BIOS will attempt to write various data patterns into memory, then read those patterns back to verify memory integrity. The memory R/W LED will light during both the read and write operations (it will flicker a bit). If the MW/R LED does not light, there is likely to be a problem with the BIOS, DMA controller, memory controller, or system controller IC.

- *Reset* When the system is first turned on, the reset line will be asserted. This keeps the CPU neutralized until the "Power Good" signal is received from the power supply. At this point, the reset line should be released, and the Reset LED should go out; the initialization process will begin. The reset line should not light again unless the PC reset button is pressed. If the Reset LED stays lit, it could indicate a problem with the Power Good signal at the supply or motherboard. The reset line also might be shorted—in which case you might have to replace the motherboard.

- *CLK* The *clock* LED(s) light to indicate the presence of synchronizing signals generated by the PC's clock generator IC. If these signals are not being generated, the CPU simply will not function. If the clock indicator(s) do not light, you should suspect a fault in the system time base crystal or the clock generator IC. Keep in mind that micro-channel systems do not supply clock signals to the bus.

- *OSC* The oscillator LEDs indicate the presence of a 14.138-MHz signal. XT systems used this signal for all internal timing, but AT systems only use the oscillator as a color burst signal for the video adapter. If the oscillator indicator(s) do not light, you should suspect a fault in the color burst crystal or the clock generating circuitry.

Reading the hexadecimal display

POST boards represent their hexadecimal codes on two seven-segment LEDs (which you can see clearly in Fig. 28-1). However, seven-segment displays were not designed to handle letters. As a result, a bit of caution is needed when reading a POST code; otherwise, it is possible to mistake letters for numbers. Figure 28-2 illustrates all 16 hexadecimal characters as they are presented on a typical seven-segment LED.

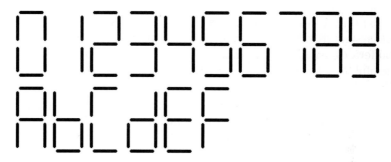

28-2 Hexadecimal characters displayed on seven-segment LEDs.

Interpreting the POST codes

POST codes are a function of the system BIOS. As the PC initializes, BIOS instructions cause the PC to place certain codes at a relatively standard I/O address. By inserting a POST board in the system, you can read each code as it is generated. If the initialization process halts or hangs up for any reason, it becomes a fairly simple matter to identify the faulty area. This part of the chapter explains some realities of POST codes, and provides you with a comprehensive cross-reference of codes for several popular BIOS versions.

When working with POST codes, it is important to understand that not all codes are the direct result of a test. Many codes simply indicate that a CPU is attempting to initialize various areas of the PC. These types of codes are known as checkpoints that simply show that certain initialization steps are being completed. Just because you see a hexadecimal code does not necessarily mean that anything has been tested.

Also remember that few listings of BIOS codes are actually complete. With the exception of publicly available code lists (for the IBM PC, XT, and AT), most BIOS manufacturers have been unwilling to release the full context of their POST codes. As a result, POST code indexes such as those in this book are often compilations of data extracted from a number of different sources. If you encounter a POST code that is not covered in this book, your best course is usually to contact the BIOS manufacturer directly for specific details (and let Dynamic Learning Systems know so we can get it into the next update for this book).

Another area of confusion can arise when the POST process starts and ends. This can sometimes confuse a novice technician. When a system is first started with a POST board installed, the POST display is typically blank; this is normal for the initial moments after PC power is applied. After that, codes should begin flashing across the seven-segment LEDs. If the LEDs remain blank, you can assume that no data is reaching the card. In that event, make sure that your system produces POST codes, and see that the board's I/O address is set properly. After the POST is complete, a system will attempt to boot an operating system. Ordinarily, the last code on the display is 00h or FFh, so don't worry if either of these codes remains on the seven-segment display. In some cases (depending on the BIOS), some other code might be left in the display. If the system appears to be booting, you rarely need to worry about this. Also keep in mind that not all tests are performed in numerical order. You will find that the code sequences in many of the following tables are a bit mixed—look over each table carefully.

ACER

The ACER BIOS is derived from the Award BIOS 3.03. Although the actual BIOS procedure is very similar, the codes (shown in Table 28-1) are somewhat different. The ACER BIOS sends POST codes to port 80h.

Table 28-1. POST codes for ACER BIOS

Hex code	Description
04	POST Start
08	Shutdown Condition 0
0C	Testing the BIOS ROM checksum
10	Testing the CMOS RAM shutdown byte
14	Testing the DMA controller
18	Initializing the system timer
1C	Testing the memory refresh system
1E	Determining the memory type
20	Testing the low 128KB of memory
24	Testing the 8042 keyboard controller IC
28	Testing the CPU descriptor instruction
2C	Testing the 8259 interrupt controller IC
30	Setting up a temporary interrupt
34	Configure the BIOS interrupt vectors and routines
38	Testing the CMOS RAM
3C	Determining the memory size
40	Shutdown Condition 1
44	Initializing the video BIOS ROM
45	Setting up and testing RAM
46	Testing cache memory and controller
48	Testing memory
4C	Shutdown Condition 3
50	Shutdown Condition 2
54	Shutdown Condition 7
58	Shutdown Condition 6
5C	Testing the keyboard and auxiliary I/O
60	Setting up BIOS interrupt routines
64	Testing the real-time clock
68	Testing the diskette
6C	Testing the hard drive

Table 28-1. Continued

Hex code	Description
70	Testing the parallel port
74	Testing the serial port
78	Setting the time of day
7C	Detect and invoke any optional ROMs
80	Checking for the math coprocessor
84	Initializing the keyboard
88	Initializing the system (step 1)
8C	Initializing the system (step 2)
90	Boot the operating system
94	Shutcown Condition 5
98	Shutdown Condition A
9C	Shutdown Condition B

AMI family

American Megatrends Inc. produces some of the most popular and widely-used BIOS products in today's PCs. Traditionally, AMI BIOS will only produce beep codes in the event of a catastrophic failure. Also, AMI BIOS generates POST codes when many tests pass (not just when a test fails). Table 28-2 provides a listing of POST codes for AMI BIOS prior to April of 1990. After 1990, AMI upgraded their BIOS to accommodate the general inclusion of IDE drives in PCs, and better support the system demands made by Windows. Table 28-3 covers the post-1990 AMI BIOS. One of the later BIOS versions produced by AMI is their BIOS version 2.2x that is outlined in Table 28-4. Other late-version AMI BIOS products include the AMI Plus BIOS shown in Table 28-5, the AMI Color BIOS in Table 28-6, and the AMI EZ-Flex BIOS in Table 28-7.

Table 28-2. POST codes for AMI BIOS (prior to April 1990)

Hex code	Description
01	NMI is disabled and the i286 register test is about to start
02	i286 register test has passed
03	ROM BIOS checksum test (32Kb from F8000h) passed OK
04	8259 PIC has initialized OK
05	CMOS interrupt disabled
06	Video system disabled and the system timer checks OK
07	8253/4 programmable interval timer test OK
08	Delta counter channel 2 OK
09	Delta counter channel 1 OK
0A	Delta counter channel 0 OK
0B	Parity status cleared
0C	The refresh and system timer check OK
0D	Refresh check OK
0E	Refresh period checks OK

Table 28-2. Continued

Hex code	Description
10	Ready to start 64Kb base memory test
11	Address line test OK
12	64Kb base memory test OK
13	System interrupt vectors initialized
14	8042 keyboard controller checks OK
15	CMOS read/write test OK
16	CMOS checksum and battery OK
17	Monochrome video mode OK
18	CGA color mode set OK
19	Attempting to pass control to video ROM at C0000h
1A	Returned from video ROM
1B	Display memory R/W test OK
1C	Display memory R/W alternative test OK
1D	Video retrace test OK
1E	Global equipment byte set for proper video operation
1F	Ready to initialize video system
20	Video test OK
21	Video display OK
22	The power-on message is displayed
30	Ready to start the virtual mode memory test
31	Virtual memory mode test started
32	CPU has switched to virtual mode
33	Testing the memory address lines
34	Testing the memory address lines
35	Lower 1MB of RAM found
36	Memory size computation checks OK
37	Memory test in progress
38	Memory below 1Mb is initialized
39	Memory above 1Mb is initialized
3A	Memory size is displayed
3B	Ready to test the lower 1Mb of RAM
3C	Memory test of lower 1Mb OK
3D	Memory test above 1Mb OK
3E	Ready to shutdown for real-mode testing
3F	Shutdown OK - now in real-mode
40	Ready to disable gate A20
41	A20 line disabled successfully
42	Ready to start DMA controller test
4E	Address line test OK
4F	System still in real mode
50	DMA page register test OK
51	Starting DMA controller 1 register test
52	DMA controller 1 test passed, starting DMA controller 2 register test
53	DMA controller 2 test passed
54	Ready to test latch on DMA controller 1 and 2

Table 28-2. Continued

Hex code	Description
55	DMA controller 1 and 2 latch test OK
56	DMA controller 1 and 2 configured OK
57	8259 PIC initialized OK
58	8259 PIC mask register check OK
59	Master 8259 PIC mask register OK
5A	Ready to check timer interrupts
5B	Timer interrupt check OK
5C	Ready to test keyboard interrupt
5D	ERROR detected in timer or keyboard interrupt
5E	8259 PIC controller error
5F	8259 PIC controller OK
70	Start of keyboard test
71	Keyboard controller OK
72	Keyboard test OK
73	Keyboard global initialization OK
74	Floppy setup ready to start
75	Floppy controller setup OK
76	Hard disk setup ready to start
77	Hard disk controller setup OK
79	Ready to initialize timer data
7A	Verifying CMOS battery power
7B	CMOS battery verified OK
7D	Analyzing CMOS RAM size
7E	CMOS memory size updated
7F	Send control to adapter ROM
80	Enable the SETUP Routine if <Delete> is pressed
81	Return from adapter ROM
82	Printer data initialization is OK
83	RS-232 data initialization is OK
84	80×87 check and test OK
85	Display any soft-error message
86	Give control to ROM at E0000h
87	Return from system ROM
00	Call the INT19 boot loader

Table 28-3. POST codes for AMI BIOS (April 1990)

Hex code	Description
01	NMI is disabled and the i286 register test is about to start
02	i286 register test has passed
03	ROM BIOS checksum test (32Kb from F8000h) passed OK
04	Passed keyboard controller test with and without mouse
05	Chipset initialized . . . DMA and interrupt controller disabled
06	Video system disabled and the system timer checks OK

Table 28-3. Continued

Hex code	Description
07	8254 programmable interval timer initialized
08	Delta counter channel 2 initialization complete
09	Delta counter channel 1 initialization complete
0A	Delta counter channel 0 initialization complete
0B	Refresh started
0C	System timer started
0D	Refresh check OK
10	Ready to start 64Kb base memory test
11	Address line test OK
12	64KB base memory test OK
15	ISA BIOS interrupt vectors initialized
17	Monochrome video mode OK
18	CGA color mode set OK
19	Attempting to pass control to video ROM at C0000h
1A	Returned from video ROM
1B	Shadow RAM enabled
1C	Display memory R/W test OK
1D	Alternative display memory R/W test OK
1E	Global equipment byte set for proper video operation
1F	Ready to initialize video system
20	Finished setting video mode
21	ROM type 27256 verified
22	The power-on message is displayed
30	Ready to start the virtual mode memory test
31	Virtual memory mode test started
32	CPU has switched to virtual mode
33	Testing the memory address lines
34	Testing the memory address lines
35	Lower 1Mb of RAM found
36	Memory size computation checks OK
37	Memory test in progress
38	Memory below 1Mb is initialized
39	Memory above 1Mb is initialized
3A	Memory size is displayed
3B	Ready to test the lower 1Mb of RAM
3C	Memory test of lower 1Mb OK
3D	Memory test above 1Mb OK
3E	Ready to shutdown for real-mode testing
3F	Shutdown OK - now in real-mode
40	Cache memory now on . . . Ready to disable gate A20
41	A20 line disabled successfully
42	i486 internal cache turned on
43	Ready to start DMA controller test
50	DMA page register test OK
51	Starting DMA controller 1 register test

Table 28-3. Continued

Hex code	Description
52	DMA controller 1 test passed, starting DMA controller 2 register test
53	DMA controller 2 test passed
54	Ready to test latch on DMA controller 1 and 2
55	DMA controller 1 and 2 latch test OK
56	DMA controller 1 and 2 configured OK
57	8259 PIC initialized OK
70	Start of keyboard test
71	Keyboard controller OK
72	Keyboard test OK . . . Starting mouse interface test
73	Keyboard and mouse global initialization OK
74	Display SETUP prompt . . . Floppy setup ready to start
75	Floppy controller setup OK
76	Hard disk setup ready to start
77	Hard disk controller setup OK
79	Ready to initialize timer data
7A	Timer data area initialized
7B	CMOS battery verified OK
7D	Analyzing CMOS RAM size
7E	CMOS memory size updated
7F	Enable SETUP routine if <Delete> is pressed
80	Send control to adapter ROM at C800h to DE00h
81	Return from adapter ROM
82	Printer data initialization is OK
83	RS-232 data initialization is OK
84	80×87 check and test OK
85	Display any soft-error message
86	Give control to ROM at E0000h
A0	Program the cache SRAM
A1	Check for external cache
A2	Initialize EISA adapter card slots
A3	Test extended NMI in EISA system
00	Call the INT19 boot loader

Table 28-4.
POST codes for AMI BIOS version 2.2x

Hex code	Description
00	Flag test (the CPU is being tested)
03	Register test
06	System hardware initialization
09	Test BIOS ROM checksum
0C	Page register test
0F	8254 timer test
12	Memory refresh initialization

Table 28-4. Continued

Hex code	Description
15	8237 DMA controller test
18	8237 DMA controller initialization
1B	8259 PIC initialization
1E	8259 PIC test
21	Memory refresh test
24	Base 64Kb address test
27	Base 64Kb memory test
2A	8742 keyboard test
2D	MC146818 CMOS IC test
30	Start the protected-mode test
33	Start the memory sizing test
36	First protected-mode test passed
39	First protected-mode test failed
3C	CPU speed calculation
3F	Reading the 8742 hardware switches
42	Initializing the interrupt vector area
45	Verifying the CMOS configuration
48	Testing and initializing the video system
4B	Testing unexpected interrupts
4E	Starting second protected-mode test
51	Verifying the LDT instruction
54	Verifying the TR instruction
57	Verifying the LSL instruction
5A	Verifying the LAR instruction
5D	Verifying the VERR instruction
60	Address line A20 test
63	Testing unexpected exceptions
66	Starting the third protected-mode test
69	Address line test
6A	Scan DDNIL bits for null pattern
6C	System memory test
6F	Shadow memory test
72	Extended memory test
75	Verify the memory configuration
78	Display configuration error messages
7B	Copy system BIOS to shadow memory
7E	8254 clock test
81	MC46818 real-time clock test
84	Keyboard test
87	Determining the keyboard type
8A	Stuck key test
8D	Initializing hardware interrupt vectors
90	Testing the math coprocessor
93	Finding available COM ports
96	Finding available LPT ports

Table 28-4. Continued

Hex code	Description
99	Initializing the BIOS data area
9C	Fixed/Floppy disk controller test
9F	Floppy disk test
A2	Fixed disk test
A5	Check for external ROMs
A8	System key lock test
AE	F1 error message test
AF	System boot initialization
B1	Call Int 19 boot loader

Table 28-5. POST codes for AMI PLUS BIOS

Hex code	Description
01	NMI disabled
02	CPU register test complete
03	ROM checksum tests OK
04	8259 PIC initialization OK
05	CMOS interrupt disabled
06	System timer (PIT) OK
07	PIC channel 0 test OK
08	Delta count channel (DMA) 2 test OK
09	Delta count channel (DMA) 1 test OK
0A	Delta count channel (DMA) 0 test OK
0B	Parity status cleared (DMA/PIT)
0C	Refresh and system time check OK (DMA/PIT)
0D	Refresh link toggling OK (DMA/PIT)
0E	Refresh period on/off 50% OK (RAM IC or address line)
10	Ready to start 64K base memory test
11	Address line test OK
12	64K base memory test OK
13	Interrupt vectors initialized
14	8042 keyboard controller test
15	CMOS read/write test OK
16	CMOS checksum and battery test
17	Monochrome mode set OK (6845 IC)
18	CGA mode set OK (6845 IC)
19	Checking video ROM
1A	Optional video ROM checks OK
1B	Display memory R/W test OK
1C	Alternate display memory checks OK
1D	Video retrace check OK
1E	Global byte set for video OK (video adapter)
1F	Mode set for mono/color OK (video adapter)
20	Video test OK

Table 28-5. Continued

Hex code	Description
21	Video display OK
22	Power-on message display OK
30	Ready for virtual mode memory test
31	Starting virtual mode memory test
32	CPU now in virtual mode
33	Memory address line test
34	Memory address line test
35	Memory below 1Mb calculated
36	Memory size computation OK
37	Memory test in progress
38	Memory initialization below 1Mb complete
39	Memory initialization above 1Mb complete
3A	Display memory size
3B	Ready to start memory below 1Mb
3C	Memory test below 1Mb OK
3D	Memory test above 1Mb OK
3E	Ready to switch to real-mode
3F	Shutdown successful
40	Ready to disable A20 gate (8042 IC)
41	A20 gate disabled (8042 IC)
42	Ready to test DMA controller (8237 DMA IC)
4E	Address line test OK
4F	CPU now in real-mode
50	DMA page register test OK
51	DMA unit 1 base register OK
52	DMA unit 1 channel OK
53	DMA unit 2 base register OK
54	DMA unit 2 channel OK
55	Latch test for both DMA units OK
56	DMA units 1 and 2 initialized OK
57	8259 PIC initialization complete
58	8259 PIC mask register OK
59	Master 8259 PIC mask register OK
5A	Check timer and keyboard interrupt
5B	PIT timer interrupt OK
5C	Ready to test keyboard interrupt
5D	ERROR . . . timer/keyboard interrupt
5E	8259 PIC error
5F	8259 PIC test OK
70	Start the keyboard test
71	Keyboard test OK
72	Keyboard test OK
73	Keyboard global data initialized (8042 IC)
74	Ready to start floppy controller setup
75	Floppy controller setup OK

Table 28-5. Continued

Hex code	Description
76	Ready to start hard drive controller setup
77	Hard drive controller setup OK
79	Ready to initialize timer data
7A	Verifying CMOS battery power
7B	CMOS battery verification complete
7D	Analyze test results for memory
7E	CMOS memory size update OK
7F	Check for optional ROM at C0000h
80	Keyboard checked for SETUP keystroke
81	Optional ROM control OK
82	Printer ports initialized OK
83	Serial ports initialized OK
84	80×87 test OK
85	Ready to display any soft errors
86	Send control to system ROM E0000h
87	System ROM E0000h check complete
00	Call Int. 19 boot loader

Table 28-6. POST codes for AMI Color BIOS

Hex code	Description
01	CPU flag test
02	Power-on delay
03	Chipset initialization
04	Hard/soft reset
05	ROM enable
06	ROM BIOS checksum
07	8042 KBC test
08	8042 KBC test
09	8042 KBC test
0A	8042 KBC test
0B	8042 protected-mode test
0C	8042 KBC test
0D	8042 KBC test
0E	CMOS checksum test
0F	CMOS initialization
10	CMOS/RTC status OK
11	DMA/PIC disable
12	DMA/PIC initialization
13	Chipset and memory initialization
14	8254 PIT test
15	PIT channel 2 test
16	PIT channel 1 test
17	PIT channel 0 test

Table 28-6. Continued

Hex code	Description
18	Memory refresh test (PIT IC)
19	Memory refresh test (PIT IC)
1A	Check 15-µs refresh (PIT IC)
1B	Check 30-µs refresh (PIT IC)
20	Base 64Kb memory test
21	Base 64Kb memory parity test
22	Memory read/write test
23	BIOS vector table initialization
24	BIOS vector table initialization
25	Check of 8042 KBC
26	Global data for KBC set
27	Video mode test
28	Monochrome mode test
29	CGA mode test
2A	Parity enable test
2B	Check for optional ROMs in the system
2C	Check video ROM
2D	Reinitialize the main chipset
2E	Test video memory
2F	Test video memory
30	Test video adapter
31	Test alternate video memory
32	Test alternate video adapter
33	Video mode test
34	Video mode set
35	Initialize the BIOS ROM data area
36	Power-on message display
37	Power-on message display
38	Read cursor position
39	Display cursor reference
3A	Display SETUP start message
40	Start protected-mode test
41	Build descriptor tables
42	CPU enters protected-mode
43	Protected-mode interrupt enable
44	Check descriptor tables
45	Check memory size
46	Memory read/write test
47	Base 640Kb memory test
48	Check 640Kb memory size
49	Check extended memory size
4A	Verify CMOS extended memory
4B	Check for soft/hard reset
4C	Clear extended memory locations
4D	Update CMOS memory size
4E	Display base RAM size

Table 28-6. Continued

Hex code	Description
4F	Perform memory test on base 640Kb
50	Update CMOS RAM size
51	Perform extended memory test
52	Resize extended memory
53	Return CPU to real-mode
54	Restore CPU registers for real-mode
55	Disable the A20 gate
56	Recheck the BIOS vectors
57	BIOS vector check complete
58	Display the SETUP start message
59	Perform DMA and PIT test
60	Perform DMA page register test
61	Perform DMA #1 test
62	Perform DMA #2 test
63	Check BIOS data area
64	BIOS data area checked
65	Initialize DMA ICs
66	Perform 8259 PIC initialization
67	Perform keyboard test
80	Keyboard reset
81	Perform stuck key and batch test (keyboard)
82	Run 8042 KBC test
83	Perform lock key check
84	Compare memory size with CMOS
85	Perform password/soft-error check
86	Run CMOS equipment check
87	CMOS setup test
88	Reinitialize the main chipset
89	Display the power-on message
8A	Display the wait and mouse check
8B	Attempt to shadow any option ROMs
8C	Initialize XCMOS settings
8D	Rest hard/floppy disks
8E	Compare floppy setup to CMOS
8F	Initialize the floppy disk controller
90	Compare hard disk setup to CMOS
91	Initialize the hard disk controller
92	Check the BIOS data table
93	BIOS data table check complete
94	Set memory size
95	Verify the display memory
96	Clear all interrupts
97	Check any optional ROMs
98	Clear all interrupts
99	Setup timer data
9A	Locate and check serial ports

Table 28-6. Continued

Hex code	Description
9B	Clear all interrupts
9C	Perform the math coprocessor test
9D	Clear all interrupts
9E	Perform an extended keyboard check
9F	Set the NumLock on the keyboard
A0	Keyboard reset
A1	Cache memory test
A2	Display any soft errors
A3	Set typematic rate
A4	Set memory wait states
A5	Clear the display
A6	Enable parity and NMI
A7	Clear all interrupts
A8	Turn over system control to the ROM at E0000
A9	Clear all interrupts
AA	Display configuration
00	Call Int. 19 boot loader

Table 28-7. POST codes for AMI EZ-Flex BIOS

Hex code	Description
01	NMI disabled . . . starting CPU flag test
02	Power-on delay
03	Chipset initialization
04	Check keyboard for hard/soft reset
05	ROM enable
06	ROM BIOS checksum
07	8042 KBC test
08	8042 KBC test
09	8042 KBC test
0A	8042 KBC test
0B	8042 protected-mode test
0C	8042 KBC test
0D	Test CMOS RAM shutdown register
0E	CMOS checksum test
0F	CMOS initialization
10	CMOS/RTC status OK
11	DMA/PIC disable
12	Disable video display
13	Chipset and memory initialization
14	8254 PIT test
15	PIT channel 2 test
16	PIT channel 1 test

Table 28-7. Continued

Hex code	Description
17	PIT channel 0 test
18	Memory refresh test (PIT IC)
19	Memory refresh test (PIT IC)
1A	Check 15-µs refresh (PIT IC)
1B	Test 64Kb base memory
20	Test address lines
21	Base 64Kb memory parity test
22	Memory read/write test
23	Perform any setups needed prior to vector table initialization
24	BIOS vector table initialization in lower 1KN of system RAM
25	Check of 8042 KBC
26	Global data for KBC set
27	Perform any setups needed after vector table initialization
28	Monochrome mode test
29	CGA mode test
2A	Parity enable test
2B	Check for optional ROMs in the system
2C	Check video ROM
2D	Determine if EGA/VGA is installed
2E	Test video memory (EGA/VGA not installed)
2F	Test video memory
30	Test video adapter
31	Test alternate video memory
32	Test alternate video adapter
33	Video mode test
34	Video mode set
35	Initialize the BIOS ROM data area
36	Set cursor for power-on message display
37	Display power-on message
38	Read cursor position
39	Display cursor reference
3A	Display SETUP start message
40	Start protected-mode test
41	Build descriptor tables
42	CPU enters protected-mode
43	Protected-mode interrupt enable
44	Check descriptor tables
45	Check memory size
46	Memory read/write test
47	Base 640Kb memory test
48	Find amount of memory below 1Mb
49	Find amount of memory above 1Mb
4A	Check ROM BIOS data area
4B	Clear memory below 1Mb for soft reset
4C	Clear memory above 1Mb for soft reset

Table 28-7. Continued

Hex code	Description
4D	Update CMOS memory size
4E	Display base 64Kb memory test
4F	Perform memory test on base 640Kb
50	Update RAM size for shadow operation
51	Perform extended memory test
52	Ready to return to real-mode
53	Return CPU to real-mode
54	Restore CPU registers for real-mode
55	Disable the A20 gate
56	Recheck the BIOS data area
57	BIOS data area check complete
58	Display the SETUP start message
59	Perform DMA page register test
60	Verify display memory
61	Perform DMA #1 test
62	Perform DMA #2 test
63	Check BIOS data area
64	BIOS data area checked
65	Initialize DMA ICs
66	Perform 8259 PIC initialization
67	Perform keyboard test
80	Keyboard reset
81	Perform stuck key and batch test (keyboard)
82	Run 8042 KBC test
83	Perform lock key check
84	Compare memory size with CMOS
85	Perform password/soft-error check
86	Run CMOS equipment check
87	Run CMOS setup if selected
88	Reinitialize the main chipset after setup
89	Display the power-on message
8A	Display the wait and mouse check
8B	Attempt to shadow any option ROMs
8C	Initialize system per CMOS settings
8D	Rest hard/floppy disks
8E	Compare floppy setup to CMOS
8F	Initialize the floppy disk controller
90	Compare hard disk setup to CMOS
91	Initialize the hard disk controller
92	Check the BIOS data table
93	BIOS data table check complete
94	Set memory size
95	Verify the display memory
96	Clear all interrupts
97	Check any optional ROMs

Table 28-7. Continued

Hex code	Description
98	Clear all interrupts
99	Setup timer data
9A	Locate and check serial ports
9B	Clear all interrupts
9C	Perform the math coprocessor test
9D	Clear all interrupts
9E	Perform an extended keyboard check
9F	Set the NumLock on the keyboard
A0	Keyboard reset
A1	Cache memory test
A2	Display any soft errors
A3	Set typematic rate
A4	Set memory wait states
A5	Clear the display
A6	Enable parity and NMI
A7	Clear all interrupts
A8	Turn over system control to the ROM at E0000
A9	Clear all interrupts
AA	Display configuration
00	Call Int. 19 boot loader

Arche Legacy

The Arche Technologies Legacy BIOS is a close cousin of AMI products, although there are a significant number of different POST codes near the end of the diagnostic process. If the POST code is displayed, the corresponding test did not execute properly. All codes are written to port 80h. Table 28-8 lists the known POST codes for the Arche Legacy BIOS.

Table 28-8. POST codes for Arche Legacy BIOS

Hex code	Description
01	Disable the NMI and test CPU registers
02	Verify the BIOS ROM checksum (32Kb at F8000h)
03	Initialize the KBC and CMOS RAM
04	Disable the DMA and PIC . . . test the CMOS RAM interrupt
05	Reset the video controller
06	Test the 8254 PIT
07	Test delta count timer channel 2
08	Test delta count timer channel 1
09	Test delta count timer channel 0
0A	Test parity circuit and turn on refresh
0B	Enable parity check and test system timer
0C	Test refresh trace link toggle

Table 28-8. Continued

Hex code	Description
0D	Test refresh timing synchronization
10	Disable cache and shadow memory . . . test the 64Kb base memory
11	Perform 64Kb memory R/W test
12	Initialize interrupt vector table in lower 1Kb of RAM
14	Test CMOS RAM shutdown register . . . disable DMA and interrupt controllers
15	Test CMOS RAM battery and checksum
16	Test for floppy drive based on CMOS setup . . . initialize monochrome video
17	Initialize CGA video
18	Clear the parity status (if any)
19	Test for EGA/VGA video BIOS at C0000h and pass control
1A	Return from video ROM
1B	Test primary video adapter . . . test video memory
1C	Test secondary video adapter . . . test video memory
1D	Compare CMOS settings to video adapter
1E	Set video mode according to CMOS settings
20	Display CMOS RAM R/W errors and halt
21	Set cursor and call Int. 10 to display status message
22	Display power-on message
23	Read new cursor position
24	Display AMI copyright message at the bottom of the screen
25	Test shadow RAM
F0	Shadow RAM test failed
30	Ready to enter protected-mode
31	Enter protected-mode (A20 gate) and enable timer interrupt (IRQ0)
32	Get memory size above 1Mb
33	Get memory size below 640Kb
34	Test memory above 1Mb
35	Test memory below 1Mb
37	Clear memory below 1Mb
38	Clear memory above 1Mb
39	Use CMOS shutdown byte and return to real-mode
3A	Test 64Kb R/W
3B	Test RAM below 1Mb and show the area being tested
3C	Test RAM above 1Mb and show the area being tested
3D	RAM test completed OK
3E	Ready to return to real-mode
3F	Back in real-mode
40	Disable A20 gate
41	Check for AMI copyright message in ROM
42	Display the AMI copyright message if found
43	Test cache memory
4E	Process shutdown 1
4F	Restore interrupt vectors and data in BIOS RAM area
50	Test DMA controller
51	Initialize DMA controller

Table 28-8. Continued

Hex code	Description
52	Test the DMA controller with patterns
54	Test DMA controller latches
55	Initialize and enable DMA controllers 1 and 2
56	Initialize 8259 PICs
57	Test 8259 PICs and set up interrupt mask registers
61	Check DDNIL status bit and display message
70	Perform keyboard basic assurance test
71	Program keyboard to AT type
72	Disable keyboard and initialize keyboard circular buffer
73	Display message and initialize floppy controller and drive
74	Attempt to access the floppy drive
75	If CMOS RAM good, check and initialize hard disk controller and drive
76	Attempt to access the hard disk drive
77	Shuffle any internal error codes
79	Check CMOS RAM battery and checksum . . . clear parity status
7A	Compare size of base/extended memory to CMOS info
7C	Display AMI copyright
7D	Set AT memory expansion bit
7E	Verify the ROM contains an AMI copyright
7F	Clear the <Del> message from the display . . . check if <Del> was pressed
80	Locate option ROM at C800h to DE00h and pass control to any found
81	Return from option ROM and initialize timer and data area
82	Setup parallel and serial ports
83	Test for math coprocessor
84	Check if keyboard locked
85	Display any soft error messages
86	Test for option ROM at E0000h
A0	Error found in 256Kb or 1Mb RAM IC in lower 640Kb
A1	Base 64Kb random access and data pattern test
A9	Initialize on-board VGA controller
B0	Error in 256Kb RAM IC in lower 640Kb
B1	Base 64Kb random access and data pattern test
E0	Return to real-mode and initialize base 64Kb RAM
E1	Initialize 640Kb RAM
EF	Configuration memory error—can't find memory
F0	Test shadow RAM from 04000h
00	Call the Int. 19 boot loader

AST

With the exception of two major i286-based machines that use a Phoenix-based BIOS, most AST systems are fitted with an Award-based BIOS version. All codes are written to port 80h and port 1080h. An interesting characteristic of the AST BIOS is that errors below 20h will be accompanied by a corresponding long-short beep sequence. For example, the code 13h will issue one long beep and three short beeps. Errors below 20h will invariably halt the system, and errors of 20h and higher will not halt the system. Table 28-9 lists the AST POST codes.

Table 28-9. POST codes for AST BIOS

Hex code	Description
01	Test CPU registers
02	Test the 8042 KBC buffer
03	Test the 8042 KBC reset
04	Verify presence of keyboard and check communication
05	Read keyboard input port
06	Initialize system board support chipset
09	Test BIOS ROM checksum
0D	Test 8254 PIT registers
0E	Test ASIC registers
0F	Test CMOS RAM shutdown byte
10	Test DMA controller 0 registers
11	Test DMA controller 1 registers
12	Test DMA page registers (EGA/VGA vertical retrace failed)
13	EGA/VGA RAM test failed
14	Test memory refresh toggle (EGA/VGA CRT registers failed)
15	Test base 64Kb memory
16	Set interrupt vectors in base memory
17	Initialize video
18	Test display memory
20	EISA bus board power on
30	Test PIC #1 mask register
31	Test PIC #2 mask register
32	Test PICs for stuck interrupts
33	Test for stuck NMI
34	Test for stuck DDINIL status
40	Test CMOS RAM backup battery
41	Calculate and verify CMOS checksum
42	Setup CMOS RAM options
50	Test the protected-mode
51	Test protected-mode exceptions
60	Calculate RAM size
61	Test RAM
62	Test shadow RAM
63	Test cache memory
64	Copy system BIOS to shadow RAM
65	Copy video BIOS to shadow RAM
66	Test 8254 PIT channel 2
67	Initialize memory

Award family

The Award family makes up a broad range of products that cover XT and AT systems. For the most part, Award products use standard IBM beep codes, and post codes are written to ports 80h and 300h. Table 28-10 outlines the Award XT BIOS. A later XT BIOS (version 3.1) is covered in Table 28-11. Tables 28-12, 28-13, and 28-14 follow the Award POST codes for three versions of AT BIOS (3.0, 3.1, and 3.3 respectively). Table 28-15 provides a listing of codes for an AT/EISA version of BIOS (4.0), and Table 28-16 presents the codes for an Award EISA BIOS.

Table 28-10. POST codes for Award XT BIOS

Hex code	Description
03	Test CPU flag registers
06	Test CPU registers
09	System chipset initialization
0C	Test BIOS checksum
0F	DMA page register initialization
12	Test DMA address and count registers
15	DMA initialization
18	8253 PIT test
1B	8253 PIT initialization
1E	Start RAM refresh
21	Test base 64Kb RAM
24	Setup interrupt vectors and stack
27	Initialize the 8259 PIC
2A	Test PIT interrupt mask register
2D	Test PIC hot interrupt test
30	Run V40 DMA test if present
33	Initialize the system clock
36	Run the keyboard test
39	Setup interrupt vector table
3C	Read system configuration switches
3F	Run video test
42	Locate and initialize serial ports
45	Locate and initialize parallel ports
48	Locate game port
4B	Display copyright message
4E	Calculation of CPU speed
54	Test of system memory
55	Test floppy drive
57	Finish system initialization before boot
5A	Call Int. 19 boot loader

Table 28-11. POST codes for Award XT BIOS version 3.1

Hex code	Description
01	Test CPU flag registers
02	Determine type of POST and check keyboard buffer
06	Initialize the PIT, PIC, DMA, and 6845
07	Check processor registers
09	ROM checksum
0A	Initialize the video system
15	Test the first 64Kb RAM
16	Setup interrupt tables
17	Setup video system
18	Test video memory
19	Test 8259 PIC mask bits channel 1
1A	Test 8259 PIC mask bits channel 2
1E	Check memory size
1F	Test base memory above 64Kb
20	Test stuck interrupts
21	Test stuck NMI
22	Initialize the floppy drive controller
2C	Locate and initialize COM ports
2D	Locate and initialize LPT ports
2F	Initialize the math coprocessor
31	Locate and initialize option ROMs
FF	Call the Int. 19 boot loader

Table 28-12. POST codes for Award AT BIOS version 3.0

Hex code	Description
01	Test CPU flag registers
02	Power-up check . . . initialize motherboard chipset
03	Clear the 8042 KBC
04	Reset the 8042 KBC
05	Test the keyboard
06	Disable video system, parity, and DMA controller
07	Test CPU registers
08	Initialize CMOS/RTC IC
09	Perform BIOS ROM checksum
0A	Initialize the video interface
0B	Test the 8254 timer channel 0
0C	Test the 8254 timer channel 1
0D	Test the 8254 timer channel 2
0E	Test CMOS RAM shutdown byte
0F	Test extended CMOS RAM (if present)
10	Test the 8237 DMA controller channel 0
11	Test the 8237 DMA controller channel 1
12	Test the 8237 DMA controller page registers

Table 28-12. Continued

Hex code	Description
13	Test the 8741 KBC interface
14	Test the memory refresh and toggle circuits
15	Test the first 64Kb of system memory
16	Set up the interrupt vector tables in low memory
17	Set up video I/O operations
18	Test MDA/CGA video memory unless an EGA/VGA adapter is found
19	Test the 8259 PIC mask bits channel 1
1A	Test the 8259 PIC mask bits channel 2
1B	Test the CMOS RAM battery level
1C	Test the CMOS RAM checksum
1D	Set system memory size from CMOS information
1E	Check base memory size 64Kb at a time
1F	Test base memory from 64Kb to 640Kb
20	Test stuck interrupt lines
21	Test for stuck NMI
22	Test the 8259 PIC
23	Test the protected mode and A20 gate
24	Check the size of extended memory above 1Mb
25	Test all base and extended memory found up to 16Mb
26	Test protected mode exceptions
27	Initialize shadow RAM and move system BIOS (and video BIOS) into shadow RAM
28	Detect and initialize 8242 or 8248 IC
2A	Initialize the keyboard
2B	Detect and initialize the floppy drive
2C	Detect and initialize serial ports
2D	Detect and initialize parallel ports
2E	Detect and initialize the hard drive
2F	Detect and initialize the math coprocessor
31	Detect and initialize any adapter ROMs
BD	Initialize the cache controller if present
CA	Initialize cache memory
CC	Shutdown the NMI handler
EE	Test for unexpected processor exception
FF	Call the Int. 19 boot loader

Table 28-13. POST codes for Award AT BIOS version 3.1

Hex code	Description
01	Test CPU flag registers
02	Power-up check . . . initialize motherboard chipset
03	Clear the 8042 KBC
04	Reset the 8042 KBC

Table 28-13. Continued

Hex code	Description
05	Test the keyboard
06	Disable video system, parity, and DMA controller
07	Test CPU registers
08	Initialize CMOS/RTC IC
09	Perform BIOS ROM checksum
0A	Initialize the video interface
0B	Test the 8254 timer channel 0
0C	Test the 8254 timer channel 1
0D	Test the 8254 timer channel 2
0E	Test CMOS RAM shutdown byte
0F	Test extended CMOS RAM (if present)
10	Test the 8237 DMA controller channel 0
11	Test the 8237 DMA controller channel 1
12	Test the 8237 DMA controller page registers
13	Test the 8741 KBC interface
14	Test the memory refresh and toggle circuits
15	Test the first 64Kb of system memory
16	Set up the interrupt vector tables in low memory
17	Set up video I/O operations
18	Test MDA/CGA video memory unless an EGA/VGA adapter is found
19	Test the 8259 PIC mask bits channel 1
1A	Test the 8259 PIC mask bits channel 2
1B	Test the CMOS RAM battery level
1C	Test the CMOS RAM checksum
1D	Set system memory size from CMOS information
1E	Check base memory size 64Kb at a time
1F	Test base memory
20	Test stuck interrupt lines
21	Test for stuck NMI
22	Test the 8259 PIC
23	Test the protected mode and A20 gate
24	Check the size of extended memory above 1Mb
25	Test all base and extended memory found up to 16Mb
26	Test protected mode exceptions
27	Initialize shadow RAM and move system BIOS (and video BIOS) into shadow RAM
28	Detect and initialize 8242 or 8248 IC
2A	Initialize the keyboard
2B	Detect and initialize the floppy drive
2C	Detect and initialize serial ports
2D	Detect and initialize parallel ports
2E	Detect and initialize the hard drive
2F	Detect and initialize the math coprocessor
31	Detect and initialize any adapter ROMs at C8000h to EFFFFh (and F0000h to F7FFFh)

Table 28-13. Continued

Hex code	Description
39	Initialize the cache controller if present
3B	Initialize cache memory
CA	Detect and initialize alternate cache controller
CC	Shutdown the NMI handler
EE	Test for unexpected processor exception
FF	Call the Int. 19 boot loader

Table 28-14. POST codes for Award AT BIOS version 3.3

Hex code	Description
01	Test 8042 KBC
02	Test 8042 KBC
03	Test 8042 KBC
04	Test 8042 KBC
05	Test 8042 KBC
06	Initialize any system chipsets
07	Test the CPU flags
08	Calculate the CMOS checksum
09	Initialize the 8254 PIT
0A	Test the 8254 PIT
0B	Test the DMA controller
0C	Initialize the 8259 PIC
0D	Test the 8259 PIC
0E	Test ROM BIOS checksum
0F	Test extended CMOS
10	Test the 8259 PIT IC
11	Test the 8259 PIT IC
12	Test the 8259 PIT IC
13	Test the 8259 PIT IC
14	Test the 8259 PIT IC
15	Test the first 64Kb of RAM
16	Initialize the BIOS interrupt vector tables
17	Initialize the video system
18	Check video memory
19	Test 8259 PIC 1 mask
1A	Test 8259 PIC 2 mask
1B	Check CMOS battery level
1C	Verify the CMOS checksum
1D	Verify the CMOS/RTC IC
1E	Check memory size
1F	Verify memory in the system
20	Initialize DMA ICs
21	Initialize PIC ICs
22	Initialize PIT ICs

Table 28-14. Continued

Hex code	Description
24	Check extended memory size
25	Test all extended memory detected
26	Enter the protected mode
27	Initialize the shadow RAM and cache controller
28	Test shadow RAM and the cache controller
2A	Initialize the keyboard
2B	Initialize the floppy drive controller
2C	Check and initialize serial ports
2D	Check and initialize parallel ports
2E	Initialize the hard drive controller
2F	Initialize the math coprocessor
31	Check for any option ROMs in the system
FF	Call the Int. 19 boot loader

Table 28-15. POST codes for Award AT/EISA BIOS version 4.0

Hex code	Description
01	Test the CPU flags
02	Test the CPU registers
03	Check the BIOS ROM checksum
04	Test the CMOS battery level
05	Initialize all system chipsets
06	Test the memory refresh toggle
07	Set up low memory
08	Set up interrupt vector table
09	Test CMOS RAM checksum
0A	Initialize the keyboard
0B	Initialize the video controller
0C	Test video memory
0D	Initialize any specialized chipsets
0F	Test DMA controller 0
10	Test DMA controller 1
11	Test DMA page registers
14	Test 8254 timer
15	Verify 8259 PIC channel 1
16	Verify 8259 PIC channel 2
17	Test for stuck interrupts
18	Test 8259 functions
19	Test for stuck NMI
1F	Initialize EISA mode (for EISA systems)
20	Initialize and enable EISA slot 0
21–2F	Initialize and enable EISA slots 1 to 15
30	Check base memory size
31	Check extended memory size

Table 28-15. Continued

Hex code	Description
32	Test any EISA memory found during slot initialization
3C	Enter protected-mode
3D	Detect and initialize mouse
3E	Initialize the cache controller
3F	Enable and test shadow RAM
41	Initialize floppy disk drive controller
42	Initialize hard disk drive controller
43	Detect and initialize serial ports
44	Detect and initialize parallel ports
45	Detect and initialize math coprocessor
46	Display SETUP message
47	Set speed for boot
4E	Display any soft errors
4F	Ask for password (if feature is enabled)
50	Check all CMOS RAM values and clear the display
51	Enable parity, NMI, and cache memory
52	Initialize any option ROMs present from C8000h to EFFFFh or F7FFFh
53	Initialize time value at address 40 of BIOS RAM area
55	Initialize DDNIL counter to NULL
63	Call Int. 19 for boot loader

Table 28-16. POST codes for Award EISA BIOS

Hex code	Description
01	Test the CPU flags
02	Test the CPU registers
03	Initialize the DMA controller, PIC, and PIT
04	Initialize memory refresh
05	Initialize the keyboard
06	Test BIOS ROM checksum
07	Check CMOS battery level
08	Test lower 256Kb of RAM
09	Test cache memory
0A	Configure the BIOS interrupt table
0B	Test the CMOS RAM checksum
0C	Initialize the keyboard
0D	Initialize the video adapter
0E	Test video memory
0F	Test DMA controller 0
10	Test DMA controller 1
11	Test page registers
14	Test the 8254 PIT IC
15	Verify 8259 PIC channel 1
16	Verify 8259 PIC channel 2

Table 28-16. Continued

Hex code	Description
17	Test for stuck interrupts
18	Test 8259 functions
19	Test for stuck NMI
1F	Check extended CMOS RAM (if available)
20	Initialize and enable EISA slot 0
21–2F	Initialize and enable EISA slots 1 to 15
30	Check memory size below 256Kb
31	Check memory size above 256Kb
32	Test any EISA memory found during slot initialization
3C	Enter protected-mode
3D	Detect and initialize mouse
3E	Initialize the cache controller
3F	Enable and test shadow RAM
41	Initialize floppy disk drive controller
42	Initialize hard disk drive controller
43	Detect and initialize serial ports
45	Detect and initialize math coprocessor
47	Set speed for boot
4E	Display any soft errors
4F	Ask for password (if feature is enabled)
50	Check all CMOS RAM values and clear the display
51	Enable parity, NMI, and cache memory
52	Initialize any option ROMs present from C8000h to EFFFFh or F7FFFh
53	Initialize time value at address 40 of BIOS RAM area
63	Call Int. 19 for boot loader
B0	NMI still in protected-mode (protected-mode failed)
B1	Disable NMI
BF	Initialize any system-specific chipsets
C0	Cache memory on/off
C1	Check memory size
C2	Test base 256Kb RAM
C3	Test DRAM Page Select
C4	Check video modes
C5	Test shadow RAM
C6	Configure cache memory
C8	Check system speed switch
C9	Test shadow RAM
CA	Initialize OEM chipset
FF	Call Int. 19 boot loader

Chips & Technologies

Chips & Technologies produces a single version of their BIOS that supports their NEAT, PEAK, 8291, and ELEAT chipsets. The BIOS covers both AT and PS/2 compatible systems. Although codes are passed to port 80h, some of the codes also are padded to the video system as decimal codes. Table 28-17 shows the C&T POST codes.

Table 28-17. POST codes for Chips & Technologies BIOS

Hex code	Description
01	CPU flag test failed
02	CPU register test failed
03	BIOS ROM checksum test failed
04	DMA controller test failed
05	System timer IC failed
06	Base 64K address line test failure
07	Base 64K memory test failure
08	Interrupt controller test failed
09	Hot interrupt occurred
0A	System timer interrupt test failed
0B	CPU won't leave protected-mode
0C	DMA page register test failed
0D	Memory refresh fault
0E	Keyboard controller not responding
0F	CPU could not enter protected-mode
10	KBC protected-mode test failed
11	KBC protected-mode test failed
12	KBC protected-mode test failed
13	KBC protected-mode test failed
14	KBC protected-mode test failed
15	KBC protected-mode test failed
16	KBC A20 gate failed
17	Exception or unexpected exception test failed
18	Shutdown during memory size check
19	BIOS ROM checksum error
1A	BMS checksum error (BIOS, shadow memory or memory controller fault)
50	Initialize system chipsets
51	Initialize system timer IC
52	Initialize DMA controller
53	Initialize the 8259 PIC
54	Initialize system chipsets
56	Entering protected-mode
57	Check memory ICs
58	Configure memory interleave
59	Exit protected-mode
5A	Determine system board memory size
5B	Relocate shadow RAM
5C	Configure possible EMS
5D	Set up wait state configuration
5E	Retest base 64Kb
5F	Test shadow RAM

Table 28-17. Continued

Hex code	Description
60	Test CMOS RAM
61	Test the video controller
63	Protected-mode interrupt test
64	Test the A20 line
65	Test the memory address lines
66	Base 64Kb memory test
67	Run extended memory test
68	Run system timer interrupt test
69	RTC clock test
6A	Keyboard test
6B	Identify and test math coprocessor
6C	Locate and initialize serial ports
6D	Locate and initialize parallel ports
6F	Initialize floppy disk controller
70	Initialize hard disk controller
71	Check for key lock
72	Mouse test
90	System RAM setup
91	Calculate CPU speed
92	Check system configuration against CMOS data
93	BIOS initialized
94	Power-on diagnostic bootstrap (call Int. 19)
95	Reset ICs
96	Setup cache controller
97	VGA power-on diagnostics

Compaq family

Compaq has largely gone their own way in the development of POST codes. The immediate difference for technicians is that POST codes are sent to port 84h rather than port 80h. Also, port 85h is used to indicate the category of the error (00=system BIOS, 01=error after boot, and 05=video POST). Only a very few beep codes are produced by Compaq BIOS (refer to Chapter 15). Table 28-18 illustrates the extensive array of general Compaq POST codes. Tables 28-19, 28-20, and 28-21 list the POST codes for Compaq i286, i386, and i486 Deskpro systems respectively. The POST codes for Compaq's video BIOS are listed in Table 28-22.

Table 28-18. POST codes for general Compaq BIOS

Hex code	Description
00	Initialize and test CPU flags
01	Check manufacturing jumper
02	8042 KBC test
03	No response from 8042 KBC

Table 28-18. Continued

Hex code	Description
04	Look for ROM at E000h
05	Look for ROM at C800h
06	Normal CMOS reset code
08	Initialize the PIT and math coprocessor
09	Jump indexed by CMOS reset code (KBC)
0A	Vector 40:67 reset function (KBC)
0B	Vector 40:67 with E01 function (KBC)
0C	Boot reset function
0D	Test 8254 PIT counter 0
0E	Test 8254 PIT counter 2
0F	Warm boot
10	PPI disabled, test 8254 PIT 0 and 1
11	Initialize video controller
12	Clear display and turn video on
13	Set test time 0
14	Disable RTC interrupts
15	Check battery power levels
16	Battery has lost power
17	Clear CMOS diagnostics
18	Test base memory (first 128K)
19	Initialize base memory
1A	Initialize video adapter
1B	Check BIOS ROM checksum
1C	Check CMOS checksum
1D	Test DMA controller page registers
1E	Test the keyboard controller
1F	Test the protected-mode
20	Test real and extended memory
21	Initialize the time of day
22	Initialize the math coprocessor
23	Test the keyboard and KBC
24	Reset the A20 line and set default CPU speed
25	Test the floppy disk controller
26	Test the fixed disk controller
27	Initialize all printer ports
28	Search for optional ROMs
29	Test system configuration against CMOS setup
2A	Clear the screen
2B	Check for invalid time and date
2C	Search for optional ROMs
2D	Test PIT 2
2F	Write to diagnostic byte
30	Clear the first 128K of RAM
31	Load interrupt vectors 70-77
32	Load interrupt vectors 00-1F

Table 28-18. Continued

Hex code	Description
33	Initialize MEMSIZE and RESETWD
34	Verify CMOS checksum
35	CMOS checksum is not valid
36	Check CMOS battery power
37	Check for game adapters
38	Initialize all serial ports
39	Initialize all parallel ports
3A	Initialize Port and Comm timeouts
3B	Flush the keyboard buffer
40	Save the RESETWD value
41	Check RAM refresh
42	Start write of 128K RAM
43	Rest parity checks
44	Start verify of 128K RAM test
45	Check for parity errors
46	NO RAM errors
47	RAM error detected
50	Check for dual frequency in CMOS
51	Check CMOS video configuration
52	Search for video ROM
53	Send control to video option ROM
54	Initialize the first video adapter
55	Initialize the secondary video adapter
56	No display adapters installed
57	Initialize primary video mode
58	Start of video test
59	Check for the presence of a video adapter
5A	Check video registers
5B	Start screen memory test
5C	Stop video test and clear memory
5D	Error detected on adapter
5E	Test the next detected adapter
5F	All found adapters successfully tested
60	Start of memory tests
61	Enter the protected-mode
62	Find memory size
63	Get CMOS size
64	Start test of real memory
65	Start test of extended memory
66	Save memory size in CMOS
67	128Kb option installed
68	Ready to return to real-mode
69	Successful return to real mode
6A	Protected-mode error during test
6B	Display error message

Table 28-18. Continued

Hex code	Description
6C	End of memory test
6D	Initialize Kb OK string
6E	Determine memory size to test
6F	Start of MEMTEST
70	Display XXXXXKB OK
71	Test each RAM segment
72	High order address test
73	Exit MEMTEST
74	Parity error on the bus
75	Start protected-mode test
76	Ready to enter protected-mode
77	Test software exceptions
78	Prepare to return to real-mode
79	Successful return to real-mode
7A	Back in real-mode (error has been detected)
7B	Exit protected-mode testing
7C	High order address test failure
7D	Start cache controller test
7E	Configuring cache memory
7F	Copy system ROM to shadow RAM
80	Start of 8042 KBC test
81	Run 8042 KBC self-test
82	KBC check result received
83	ERROR returned
84	8042 checks OK
86	Start 8042 test and reset the keyboard
87	Got acknowledge and read the result
88	Got the result and checking it
89	Testing for stuck keys
8A	Key seems to be stuck
8B	Test keyboard interface
8C	Got the result and checking it
8D	End of KBC test—no errors detected
90	Start of CMOS test
91	CMOS checks OK
92	Error in CMOS R/W test
93	Start of DMA controller test
94	DMA page registers test OK
95	DMA controller tests OK
96	8237 DMA initialization is OK
97	Start of RAM test
A0	Start of Diskette tests
A1	FDC reset active
A2	FDC reset inactive
A3	FDC motor on

Table 28-18. Continued

Hex code	Description
A4	FDC time out error
A5	FDC failed reset
A6	FDC passed reset
A8	Determine drive type
A9	Start seek operation
AA	Waiting for FDC seek status
AF	Diskette tests complete
B0	Start of hard drive tests
B1	Controller board not found
B2	Controller test failed
B3	Testing drive 1
B4	Testing drive 2
B5	Drive error
B6	Drive failed
B7	No hard disks detected
B8	Hard drive tests complete
B9	Attempt to boot diskette
BA	Attempt to boot hard drive
BB	Boot attempt has failed
BC	Jump to boot record
BD	Drive error . . . retry boot
BE	Testing Weitek coprocessor
D0	Starting clear memory routine
D1	Ready to switch to protected-mode
D2	Ready to clear extended memory
D3	Ready to return to real-mode
D4	Successful return to real-mode
D5	Clearing base memory
DD	KBC self-test failed
E0	Ready to shadow E000h ROM
E1	Finished shadowing ROM at E000h
E2	Ready to shadow EGA/VGA ROM
E3	Finished shadowing video ROM

**Table 28-19. POST codes
for Compaq i286 Deskpro BIOS**

Hex code	Description
01	Test the CPU
02	Test the math coprocessor
03	Testing 8237 DMA controller
04	Testing 8259 PIC
05	Testing KBC port 61h
06	Testing 8042 KBC

Table 28-19. Continued

Hex code	Description
07	CMOS test
08	CMOS test
09	CMOS test
10	Testing 8254 PIT
11	Testing 8254 PIT refresh detect
12	System speed test
14	Speaker test
21	Memory R/W test
24	Memory address test
25	Memory walking I/O test
31	Keyboard short test
32	Keyboard long test
33	Keyboard LED test
35	Keyboard lock test
41	Printer test failed
42	Testing printer port
43	Testing printer port
48	Parallel port failure
51	Video controller test
52	Video controller test
53	Video attribute test
54	Video character set test
55	Video 80×25 mode test
56	Video 80×25 mode test
57	Video 40×25 mode test
60	Floppy disk ID test
61	Floppy disk format test
62	Floppy disk read test
63	Floppy disk R/W compare test
64	Floppy disk random seek test
65	Floppy disk media ID test
66	Floppy disk speed test
67	Floppy disk wrap test
68	Floppy disk write protect test
69	Floppy disk reset controller test

Table 28-20. POST codes for Compaq i386 Deskpro BIOS

Hex code	Description
01	I/O ROM checksum error
02	System memory board failure
12	System option error
13	Time and date not set (not expected from CMOS)
14	Memory size error (not what was expected from CMOS settings)

Table 28-20. Continued

Hex code	Description
21	System memory error
23	Memory address line error
25	Memory test error
26	Keyboard error
33	Keyboard controller error
34	Keyboard or KBC error
41	Parallel port error
42	Monochrome video adapter failure
51	Display adapter failure
61	Floppy disk controller error
62	Floppy disk boot error
65	Floppy drive error
67	Floppy disk controller failed
6A	Floppy port address conflict
6B	Floppy port address conflict
72	Math coprocessor detected

Table 28-21. POST codes for Compaq i486 Deskpro BIOS

Hex code	Description
01	CPU test failed
02	Math coprocessor test failed
03	Testing 8237 DMA page registers
04	Testing 8259 PIC
05	8042 KBC port 61 error
06	8042 KBC self-test error
07	CMOS RAM test failed
08	CMOS interrupt test failed
09	CMOS clock load data test failed
10	8254 PIT test failed
11	8254 PIT refresh detect test failed
12	System speed test mode too slow
13	Protected-mode test failed
14	Speaker test failed
16	Cache memory configuration failed
19	Testing installed devices
21	Memory configuration test failed
22	BIOS ROM checksum failed
23	Memory R/W test failed
24	Memory address line test failed
25	Walking I/O test failed
26	Memory increment pattern test failed
31	Keyboard short test
32	Keyboard long test

Table 28-21. Continued

Hex code	Description
33	Keyboard LED test
34	Keyboard typematic test failed
41	Printer test failed or not connected (parallel port circuits)
42	Printer data register failed (parallel port circuits)
43	Printer pattern test (parallel port circuits)
48	Printer not connected (parallel port circuits)
51	Video controller test failed
52	Video memory test failed
53	Video attribute test failed
54	Video character set test failed
55	Video 80×25 mode test failed
56	Video 80×25 mode test failed
57	Video 40×25 mode test failed
58	Video 320×200 mode color set 1 test
59	Video 320×200 mode color set 1 test
60	Floppy disk ID drive types test failed
61	Floppy disk format failed
62	Floppy disk read test failed
63	Floppy disk write, read, seek test failed
65	Floppy disk ID media failed
66	Floppy disk speed test failed
67	Floppy disk wrap test failed
68	Floppy disk write protect failed
69	Floppy disk reset controller test failed
82	Video memory test failed
84	Video adapter test failed

Table 28-22.
POST codes for Compaq Video BIOS

Hex code	Description
00	Entry into video ROM
01	Test alternate adapters
02	Perform vertical sync tests
03	Perform horizontal sync tests
04	Perform static system tests
05	Perform bug tests
06	Perform configuration tests
07	Perform alternate ROM tests
08	Run color gun off tests
09	Run color gun on tests
0A	Test video memory
0B	Check that adapter board present
10	ERROR . . . Illegal configuration

Table 28-22. Continued

Hex code	Description
20	ERROR . . . no vertical sync present
21	ERROR . . . vertical sync out of range
30	ERROR . . . no horizontal sync present
40	ERROR . . . color register failure
50	ERROR . . . slot type conflict error
51	ERROR . . . video memory conflict error
52	ERROR . . . ROM conflict error
60	ERROR . . . red DAC stuck low
61	ERROR . . . green DAC stuck low
62	ERROR . . . blue DAC stuck low
63	ERROR . . . DAC stuck high
64	ERROR . . . red DAC fault
65	ERROR . . . green DAC fault
66	ERROR . . . blue DAC fault
70	ERROR . . . bad alternate ROM version
80	ERROR . . . color gun stuck on
90	ERROR . . . color gun stuck off
A0	ERROR . . . video memory failure
F0	ERROR . . . equipment failure
00	Video POST complete

Dell

The Dell systems use a close OEM derivative of Phoenix BIOS. As a result, the Dell beep codes are virtually identical to the Phoenix beep codes (refer to Chapter 15). Table 28-23 lists the Dell POST codes.

Table 28-23. POST codes for Dell BIOS

Hex code	Description
01	CPU register test in progress
02	CMOS R/W test failed
03	BIOS ROM checksum bad
04	8254 PIT test failed
05	DMA controller initialization failed
06	DMA page register test failed
08	RAM refresh verification failed
09	Starting first 64Kb RAM test
0A	First 64Kb RAM IC or data line bad
0B	First 64Kb RAM odd/even logic bad
0C	First 64Kb address line bad
0D	First 64Kb parity error

Table 28-23. Continued

Hex code	Description
10	Bit 0 bad in first 64Kb
11	Bit 1 bad in first 64Kb
12	Bit 2 bad in first 64Kb
13	Bit 3 bad in first 64Kb
14	Bit 4 bad in first 64Kb
15	Bit 5 bad in first 64Kb
16	Bit 6 bad in first 64Kb
17	Bit 7 bad in first 64Kb
18	Bit 8 bad in first 64Kb
19	Bit 9 bad in first 64Kb
1A	Bit 10 bad in first 64Kb
1B	Bit 11 bad in first 64Kb
1C	Bit 12 bad in first 64Kb
1D	Bit 13 bad in first 64Kb
1E	Bit 14 bad in first 64Kb
1F	Bit 15 bad in first 64Kb
20	Slave DMA register bad
21	Master DMA register bad
22	Master interrupt mask register bad
23	Slave interrupt mask register bad
25	Loading interrupt vectors
27	Keyboard controller test failed
28	CMOS RAM battery bad
29	CMOS configuration validation in progress
2B	Video memory test failed
2C	Video initialization failed
2D	Video retrace failure
2E	Searching for a video ROM
30	Switching to video ROM
31	Monochrome operation OK
32	Color (CGA) operation OK
33	Color operation OK
34	Timer tick interrupt in progress (or bad)
35	CMOS shutdown test in progress (or bad)
36	Gate A20 bad
37	Unexpected interrupt in protected mode
38	RAM test in progress or high address line is bad
3A	Interval timer channel 2 bad
3B	Time of day test bad
3C	Serial port test bad
3D	Parallel port test bad
3E	Math coprocessor test bad
3F	Cache memory test bad

DTK

The DTK BIOS (evolved from ERSO BIOS) does not issue many post codes, but Table 28-24 provides a listing of the codes that are available.

Table 28-24. POST codes for DTK BIOS

Hex code	Description
01	Testing the CPU
03	Initialize the 8258 interrupt controller
05	Initialize the video board
0D	Initialize the DMA controller
0E	Initialize the DMA page register
12	Test the 8042 keyboard controller
16	Test the DMA controller and timer
22	Testing DRAM refresh circuitry
25	Base 64Kb memory test
30	Set up system stack
33	Read system configuration through KBC
37	Test keyboard clock and data line
40	Determine video type
44	Locating and testing MDA and CGA video
48	Initialize video 80×25 mode
4D	Display DTK BIOS copyright message
4F	Check serial and parallel ports
50	Check floppy disk controller
55	Check shadow RAM
58	Display total memory and switch to real-mode
5A	Successful switch back to real-mode
60	Check hard disk drive controller
62	Initialize floppy drive
65	Initialize hard drive
67	Initialize the drives
6A	Disable gate A20 and test math coprocessor
70	Set system date and time
77	Call Int. 19 boot loader

Eurosoft/Mylex family

The general-purpose Eurosoft/Mylex BIOS was developed by both of those companies to serve on the Mylex EISA motherboard, but can be found in a few other systems. The Eurosoft/Mylex BIOS generates both beep codes and POST codes at port 80h, but the conventional Eurosoft BIOS only issues POST codes. Table 28-25 lists the POST codes for the Eurosoft/Mylex BIOS, and the Eurosoft version 4.71 BIOS POST codes are listed in Table 28-26.

Table 28-25. POST codes for Eurosoft/Mylex BIOS

Hex code	Description
01	CPU test failed
02	DMA page register test failed
03	Keyboard controller test failed
04	BIOS ROM checksum error
05	Keyboard command test failed
06	CMOS RAM test failed
07	RAM refresh test failed
08	First 64Kb memory test failed
09	DMA controller test failed
0A	Initialize DMA controller
0B	Interrupt test failed
0C	Checking RAM size
0D	Initializing video system
0E	Video BIOS checksum failed
10	Search for monochrome video adapter
11	Search for color video adapter
12	Word splitter and byte shift test failed (KBC)
13	Keyboard test failed
14	RAM test failed
15	System timer test failed
16	Initialize keyboard controller output port
17	Keyboard interrupt test failed
18	Initialize keyboard
19	Real-time-clock test failed
1A	Math coprocessor test failed
1B	Reset floppy and hard drive controllers
1C	Initialize the floppy drive
1D	Initialize the hard drive
1E	Locate adapter ROMs from C800h to DFFFh
1F	Locate and initialize serial and parallel ports
20	Initialize time-of-day in RTC
21	Locate adapter ROMs from E000h to EFFFh
22	Search for boot device
23	Boot from floppy disk
24	Boot from hard disk
25	Gate A20 enable/disable failure
26	Parity error
30	DDNIL bit scan failure
FF	Fatal error . . . .system halted

Table 28-26. POST codes for Eurosoft 4.71 BIOS

Pass	Fail	Description
03	04	DMA page register test
05	06	Keyboard test
07	08	Keyboard self-test
09	0A	8042 KBC checking links
0B	—	RATMOD/DIAG link
0C	0D	Keyboard port 60h test
0E	0F	Keyboard parameter test
10	11	Keyboard command byte
12	13	Keyboard command byte return
14	15	RAM refresh toggle test
16	17	RAM bit test
18	19	RAM parity test
1A	1B	CMOS RAM test
1C	1D	CMOS RAM battery test
1E	1F	CMOS RAM checksum test
—	20	CMOS RAM battery fault bit set
21	22	Master DMA controller 1 test
21	23	Slave DMA controller 2 test
24	—	Protected-mode entered successfully
25	—	RAM test completed
26	27	BIOS RAM checksum test
28	—	Exiting protected-mode
29	2A	Keyboard power-up reply received test
2B	2C	Keyboard disable command test
—	2D	Checking for video system
—	2E	POST errors have been reported
—	2F	About to halt
30	—	Protected-mode entered safely
31	—	RAM test complete
32	33	Master interrupt controller test
34	35	Slave interrupt controller test
36	37	Chipset initialization
38	39	Shadowing system BIOS
3A	3B	Shadowing video BIOS

Faraday A-Tease

The Faraday BIOS is a rarely used BIOS that is owned by Western Digital. Table 28-27 lists the POST codes generated by Faraday A-Tease.

Table 28-27. POST codes for Faraday A-Tease BIOS

Hex code	Description
01	CPU test failed
02	BIOS ROM checksum test failed
03	CMOS shutdown byte failed

Table 28-27. Continued

Hex code	Description
04	Testing DMA page register
05	Testing system timer (PIT)
06	Testing system refresh
07	Testing 8042 keyboard controller
08	Testing lower 128Kb or RAM
09	Testing video controller
0A	Testing RAM 128Kb to 640Kb
0B	Testing DMA controller #1
0C	Testing DMA controller #2
0D	Testing interrupt controller #1
0E	Testing interrupt controller #2
0F	Testing control port
10	Testing parity
11	Testing CMOS RAM checksum
12	Testing for manufacturing mode jumper
13	Configure interrupt vectors
14	Testing the keyboard
15	Configuring parallel ports
16	Configuring serial ports
17	Configuring lower 640Kb RAM
18	Configuring RAM above 1Mb
19	Configuring keyboard
1A	Configuring floppy drive
1B	Configuring hard disk drive
1C	Configuring game port adapter
1D	Testing and initializing math coprocessor
1E	Checking CMOS real-time clock
1F	Calculate and verify CMOS RAM checksum
21	Initialize PROM drivers
22	Test parallel port loopback
23	Test serial port loopback
24	Test CMOS RTC
25	Test the CMOS shutdown
26	Test memory over 1MB
80	ERROR . . . divide overflow
81	ERROR . . . single step fault
82	ERROR . . . NMI stuck or error
83	ERROR . . . breakpoint fault
84	ERROR . . . Int. 0 detect fault
85	ERROR . . . bound error
86	ERROR . . . invalid opcode (BIOS or CPU fault)
87	ERROR . . . processor extension not available
88	ERROR . . . double exception error
89	ERROR . . . processor extended segment error
8A	ERROR . . . invalid task state segment
8B	ERROR . . . needed segment not present
8C	ERROR . . . stack segment not present

Table 28-27. Continued

Hex code	Description
8D	ERROR . . . general protection error
8E	ERROR . . . general protection error
8F	ERROR . . . general protection error
90	ERROR . . . processor extension error
91-FF	ERROR . . . spurious interrupts
F3	ERROR . . . CPU protected-mode fault
F9	ERROR . . . virtual block move error

IBM family

The IBM POST codes represent the classic codes used by the original IBM PC products. Table 28-28 lists the POST codes for an IBM PC/XT. It is important to note that IBM XT POST codes are sent to port 60h. Your POST board might not be able to check this location. However, there are only about five codes generated by the IBM XT. The codes for an IBM PC/AT are listed in Table 28-29. Finally, the POST codes for an IBM PS/2 are listed in Table 28-30.

**Table 28-28.
POST codes for IBM XT BIOS**

Hex code	Description
00 or FF	CPU register test failed
01	BIOS ROM checksum failed
02	System timer 1 failed
03	8237 DMA register R/W failed
04	Base 32Kb RAM failed

Table 28-29. POST codes for IBM AT BIOS

Hex code	Description
01	CPU flag and register test
02	BIOS ROM checksum test
03	CMOS shutdown byte test
04	8254 PIT test—bits on
05	8254 PIT test—bits on
06	8237 DMA initialize registers test 0
07	8237 DMA initialize registers test 1
08	DMA page register test
09	Memory refresh test
0A	Soft reset test
0B	Reset 8042 KBC
0C	KBC reset OK
0D	Initialize the 8042 KBC

Table 28-29. Continued

Hex code	Description
0E	Test memory
0F	Get I/P buffer switch settings
DD	RAM error
11	Initialize protected-mode
12	Test protected-mode registers
13	Initialize 8259 PIC #2
14	Setup temporary interrupt vectors
15	Establish BIOS interrupt vectors
16	Verify CMOS checksum and battery OK
17	Set the defective CMOS battery flag
18	Ensure CMOS set
19	Set return address byte in CMOS
1A	Set temporary stack
1B	Test segment address 01-0000 (second 64Kb)
1C	Decide if 512Kb or 640Kb installed
1D	Test segment address 10-0000 (over 640Kb)
1E	Set expansion memory as contained in CMOS
1F	Test address lines 19–23
20	Ready to return from protected mode
21	Successful return from protected mode
22	Test video controller
23	Check for EGA/VGA BIOS
24	Test 8259 PIC R/W mask register
25	Test interrupt mask registers
26	Check for hot (unexpected) interrupts
05	Display 101 error (system board error)
27	Check the POST logic (system board error)
28	Check unexpected NMI interrupts (system board error)
29	Test timer 2 (system board error)
2A	Test 8254 timer
2B	System board error
2C	System board error
2D	Check 8042 KBC for last command
2F	Go to next area during a warm boot
30	Set shutdown return 2
31	Switch to protected-mode
33	Test next block of 64Kb
34	Switch back to real-mode
F0	Set data segment
F1	Test interrupts
F2	Test exception interrupts
F3	Verify protected-mode instructions
F4	Verify protected-mode instructions
F5	Verify protected-mode instructions
F6	Verify protected-mode instructions

Table 28-29. Continued

Hex code	Description
F7	Verify protected-mode instructions
F8	Verify protected-mode instructions
F9	Verify protected-mode instructions
FA	Verify protected-mode instructions
34	Test keyboard
35	Test keyboard type
36	Check for "AA" scan code
38	Check for stuck key
39	8042 KBC error
3A	Initialize the 8042
3B	Check for expansion ROM in 2Kb blocks
40	Enable hardware interrupts
41	Check system code at segment E0000h
42	Exit to system code
43	Call boot loader
3C	Check for initial program load
3D	Initialize floppy for drive type
3E	Initialize hard drive
81	Build descriptor table
82	Switch to virtual mode
90–B6	Memory and bootstrap tests
32	Test address lines 0–15
44	Attempt to boot from fixed disk
45	Unable to boot . . . go to BASIC

Table 28-30. POST codes for IBM PS/2 BIOS

Hex code	Description
00	CPU flag test
01	32-bit CPU register test
02	Test BIOS ROM checksum
03	Test system enable
04	Test system POS register
05	Test adapter setup port
06	Test RTC/CMOS RAM shutdown byte
07	Test extended CMOS RAM
08	Test DMA and page register channels
09	Initialize DMA command and mode registers
0A	Test memory refresh toggle
0B	Test keyboard controller buffers
0C	Keyboard controller self-test
0D	Continue keyboard controller self-test
0E	Keyboard self-test error

Table 28-30. Continued

Hex code	Description
0F	Set-up system memory configuration
10	Test first 512Kb RAM
11	Halt system if memory test occurs
12	Test protected-mode instructions
13	Initialize interrupt controller 1
14	Initialize interrupt controller 2
15	Initialize 120 interrupt vectors
16	Initialize 16 interrupt vectors
17	Check CMOS/RTC battery
18	Check CMOS/RTC checksum
19	CMOS/RTC battery bad
1A	Skip memory test in protected-mode
1B	Prepare for CMOS shutdown
1C	Set up stack pointer to end of first 64Kb
1D	Calculate low memory size in protected-mode
1E	Save the memory size detected
1F	Set up system memory split address
20	Check for extended memory beyond 64Mb
21	Test memory address bus lines
22	Clear parity error and channel lock
23	Initialize interrupt 0
24	Check CMOS RAM validity
25	Write keyboard controller command byte
40	Check valid CMOS RAM and video system
41	Display error code 160
42	Test registers in both interrupt controllers
43	Test interrupt controller registers
44	Test interrupt mask registers
45	Test NMI
46	NMI error has been detected
47	Test system timer 0
48	Check stuck speaker clock
49	Test system timer 0 count
4A	Test system timer 2 count
4B	Check if timer interrupt occurred
4C	Test timer 0 for improper operation (too fast or too slow)
4D	Verify timer interrupt 0
4E	Check 8042 keyboard controller
4F	Check for soft reset
50	Prepare for shutdown
51	Start protected-mode test
52	Test memory in 64Kb increments
53	Check if memory test done
54	Return to real-mode
55	Test for regular or manufacturing mode

Table 28-30. Continued

Hex code	Description
56	Disable the keyboard
57	Check for keyboard self-test
58	Keyboard test passed
59	Test the keyboard controller
5A	Configure the mouse
5B	Disable the mouse
5C	Initialize interrupt vectors
5D	Initialize interrupt vectors
5E	Initialize interrupt vectors
60	Save DDNIL status
61	Reset floppy drive
62	Test floppy drive
63	Turn floppy drive motor off
64	Set up serial ports
65	Enable real-time clock interrupt
66	Configure floppy drives
67	Configure hard drives
68	Enable system CPU arbitration
69	Scan for adapter ROMs
6A	Verify serial and parallel ports
6B	Set up equipment byte
6C	Set up configuration
6D	Set keyboard typematic rate
6E	Call Int. 19 boot loader

Landmark family

Landmark Research International does not offer BIOS commercially, but includes a custom BIOS as part of their KickStart series of diagnostic cards. The POST codes generated by the JumpStart ROMs are sent to port 80h and port 280h. The diagnostics in Landmark's SuperSoft BIOS product acts as a replacement for system ROMs. Tables 28-31 and 28-32 present the XT and AT JumpStart ROM POST codes, and Table 28-33 illustrates the SuperSoft BIOS POST codes.

Table 28-31. POST codes for Landmark JumpStart XT BIOS

Hex code	Description
01	Jump to reset area in BIOS ROM
02	Initialize DMA page register
03	Initialize DMA refresh register
04	Clear all RAM
05	Perform RAM test on 1st 64Kb
06	Clear first 64Kb
07	Initialize BIOS stack to 0FC0h

Table 28-31. Continued

Hex code	Description
08	Set the equipment flag based on XT switches
09	Initialize default interrupt vectors
0A	Initialize the 8255 if it exists
0B	Initialize the 8259 PIT and enable interrupts
0C	Setup adapters and peripherals
0D	Setup video system
0E	Initialize the video system
0F	Initialize the equipment
10	Initialize memory configuration
11	Setup system timer function
12	Initialize system timer
13	Setup time of day function
14	Initialize time of day from RTC data
15	Setup and initialize "print screen" function
16	Setup and initialize cassette interface if available
17	Setup and initialize bootstrap function
18	Setup and initialize keyboard function
19	Enable speaker
1A	Setup system timer
1B	Enable the RTC
1C	Setup timer 2
1D	Determine memory size
1E	Read first and last word of segment
1F	Compare first and last words
20	Report found memory size to display
21	Perform BIOS ROM checksum test
22	Perform complete RAM testing on cold boot
23	Move system stack to bottom of memory and save pointer
24	Reset parity after RAM sizing
25	Enable timer and keyboard interrupts
26	Setup the serial and parallel ports
27	Setup the game port
28	Setup the floppy disk controller
29	Scan for optional ROMs in 2Kb chunks from C8000h
2A	Call the boot loader

Table 28-32. POST codes for Landmark JumpStart AT BIOS

Hex code	Description
03	Sound one short beep
04	Initialize the bell tone
05	Enable CMOS RAM
06	Reset video controller
07	Disable parity checking

Table 28-32. Continued

Hex code	Description
08	Start memory refresh
09	Clear the reset flag in RAM
0A	Test DMA page registers
10	Use CMOS to determine if a soft reset has occurred
11	Check BIOS ROM checksum
12	Test system timer A
13	Test DMA channel 0
14	Test DMA channel 1
15	Test memory refresh
16	Flush 8042 KBC input buffer
17	Reset the 8042
18	Get keyboard type
19	Initialize the keyboard
1A	Clear any existing parity
1B	Enable on-board parity
1C	Test base 64Kb memory
1D	Test base 64Kb parity
1E	Initialize POST stack
20	Check keyboard type
65	Set video speed
21	Test protected-mode CPU registers
22	Initialize 8259 PIC
23	Initialize all interrupts
24	Test all interrupts
25	Perform DRAM checksum
26	Adjust configuration based on hardware found and CMOS settings
27	Check for presence of manufacturing switch
28	Initialize video controller
2A	Test video memory
2B	Test video sync
2C	Check for auxiliary video controller
2D	Change video configuration
2F	Initialize the video system
30	Change video interrupt
31	Display any POST messages
32	Test memory and calculate size
33	Adjust memory configuration
34	Enable I/O parity
35	Test 8259 PIC
36	Perform byte swap test
37	Test NMI
38	Perform timer test
39	Initialize system timer A
3A	Protected mode memory test
3B	Test keyboard

Table 28-32. Continued

Hex code	Description
3C	Test keyboard interrupt
3D	Enable A20
3E	Reset hard disk controller
3F	Setup floppy disk controller
40	Test floppy drive system
41	Setup keyboard
42	Enable interrupt timer
43	Check for dual floppy disk/hard drive controller
44	Locate floppy drive A
45	Locate floppy drive B
46	Reset hard disk controller
47	Enable slave DMA
48	Locate any external ROMs
49	Initialize the parallel port(s)
4A	Initialize the serial port(s)
4B	Initialize the math coprocessor
4C	Read CMOS RAM status
4D	Check CMOS configuration against detected hardware
4E	Initialize timer ticks
4F	Enable IRQ9
50	Enable on-board parity
51	Run any add-on ROMs
52	Enable keyboard interrupt
53	Reset the parallel port
60	Check for any errors
61	Sound one short beep
62	Print sign-on message
64	Call Int. 19 boot loader

Table 28-33. POST codes for Landmark SuperSoft AT BIOS

Hex code	Description
11	CPU register or logic error
12	ROMPOST A checksum error
13	ROMPOST B checksum error
14	8253 timer channel 0
15	8253 timer channel 1
16	8253 timer channel 2
17	8237 DMA controller 1 error
18	8237 DMA controller 2 error
19	DMA page register error
1A	8042 KBC parity error

Table 28-33. Continued

Hex code	Description
21	Scan 16Kb critical RAM error
22	Memory refresh error
23	CPU protected-mode error
24	8259 interrupt controller 1 error
25	8259 interrupt controller 2 error
26	Unexpected interrupt detected
27	Interrupt 0 (system timer) error
28	CMOS RTC error
29	NMI error
2A	Locate and test math coprocessor
31	Keyboard controller error
32	Stuck key detected or CMOS RAM error
33	Floppy controller error
34	Floppy disk read error
35	MDA video memory error
36	Color video memory error
37	EGA/VGA RAM error
38	BIOS ROM checksum error
41	Memory error
42	Refresh fault
43–45	Display problem
59	No monitor detected

Microroid Research

The Microid Research BIOS (Mr. BIOS 1.0A) is listed in Table 28-34. Note that all codes are delivered to port 80h.

Table 28-34. POST codes for Microid Research BIOS

Hex code	Description
01	Chipset problem
02	Disable NMI and DMA
03	Check BIOS ROM checksum
04	Test DMA page register
05	Keyboard controller test
06	Initialize the RTC, 8237, 8254, and 8259
07	Check memory refresh
08	DMA master test
09	OEM-specific test
0A	Test memory bank 0

Table 28-34. Continued

Hex code	Description
0B	Test PIC units
0C	Test PIC controllers
0D	Initialize PIT channel 0
0E	Initialize PIT channel 2
0F	Test CMOS RAM battery
10	Check video ROM
11	Test RTC
12	Test keyboard controller
13	OEM-specific test
14	Run memory test
15	Keyboard controller
16	OEM-specific test
17	Test keyboard controller
18	Run memory test
19	Execute OEM memory test
1A	Update RTC contents
1B	Initialize serial ports
1C	Initialize parallel ports
1D	Test math coprocessor
1E	Test floppy disk
1F	Test hard disk
20	Validate CMOS contents
21	Check keyboard lock
22	Set number lock on keyboard
23	OEM-specific test
29	Test adapter ROMs
2F	Call Int. 19 boot loader

NCR family

The National Cash Register (NCR) Corporation—now a subsidiary of AT&T—has been providing motherboards for AT&T PCs. Older motherboards used an OEM version of an AMI design (with POST codes matching per-1990 AMI codes). NCR-designed AT and MCA motherboards round out the selection. You should note that NCR XT systems send POST codes to LPT1 at port 378h or 3BCh, and the AT systems provide POST codes to port 80h and LPT1. Micro channel systems supply POST codes to port 680h and LPT1. Before testing an NCR system, make sure that your POST card can read the proper port. Table 28-35 lists the codes for an NCR PC6 (XT-compatible), Table 28-36 outlines the codes for NCR AT-compatible systems (3302, 3304, and 3728). The PC916 AT system codes are shown in Table 28-37.

Table 28-35.
POST codes for NCR PC6 (XT) BIOS

Hex code	Description
AA	8088 CPU failure
B1	2764 EPROM checksum failure
B2	8237 DMA controller failure
B3	8253 PIT failure
B4	RAM failure
B5	8259 PIC failure
B6	RAM parity error
BB	All tests passed, ready to boot

Table 28-36. POST codes for NCR AT BIOS

Hex code	Description
01	Test the CPU registers
02	Test system support I/O
03	Test BIOS ROM checksum
04	Test DMA page registers
05	Test timer channel 1
06	Test timer channel 2
07	Test RAM refresh logic
08	Test base 64Kb
09	Test 8/16 bit bus conversion
0A	Test interrupt controller 1
0B	Test interrupt controller 2
0C	Test I/O controller
0D	Test CMOS RAM R/W operation
0E	Test battery power
0F	Test CMOS RAM checksum
10	Test CPU protected-mode
11	Test video configuration
12	Test primary video controller
13	Test secondary video controller
20	Display results of tests to this point
21	Test DMA controller 1
22	Test DMA controller 2
23	Test system timer channel 0
24	Initialize interrupt controllers
25	Test interrupts
26	Test interrupts
30	Check base 640Kb memory
31	Check extended memory size
32	Test higher 8 address lines
33	Test base memory
34	Test extended memory

Table 28-36. Continued

Hex code	Description
40	Test keyboard
41	Test keyboard
42	Test keyboard
43	Test keyboard
44	Test A20 gate
50	Set up hardware interrupt vectors
51	Enable interrupt timer channel 0
52	Check BIOS ROM
60	Test floppy disk controller and drive
61	Test hard drive controller
62	Initialize floppy drives
63	Initialize hard drives
70	Test real-time clock
71	Set time-of-day in RTC
72	Check parallel interface port(s)
73	Check serial interface port(s)
74	Check for any option ROMs
75	Check math coprocessors
76	Enable keyboard and RTC interrupts
F0	System not configured properly (or hardware defect)
F1	Scan and execute any option ROMs
F2	Call Int. 19 boot loader

Table 28-37. POST codes for NCR PC916 BIOS

Hex code	Description
01	Test CPU registers
03	Test BIOS ROM checksum
04	Test DMA page registers
05	Test timer channel 1
06	Test timer channel 2
0C	Test 8042 keyboard controller
14	Test disabling speed stretch at port 69h
15	Start refresh timer 1
16	Enable speed stretch at port 69h
17	Clear write protect bit
1B	Test 64Kb shadow RAM
18	Write and test interrupt descriptor table
19	Verify RAM
02	Verify port 61h
07	Test refresh logic
08	Test base 64Kb RAM
09	Test 8/16 bit bus conversion logic
0A	Test interrupt mask register A

Table 28-37. Continued

Hex code	Description
0B	Test interrupt mask register B
1A	Check 8042 keyboard controller
0D	Test CMOS RAM shutdown byte
0E	Test CMOS RAM battery power
0F	Test CMOS RAM checksum
10	Test CPU protected-mode
11	Test video configuration
12	Initialize and test primary video controller
13	Primary video error
20	Display results of tests to this point
21	Test DMA controller 1
22	Test DMA controller 2
23	Test timer 1 counter 0 840-nS clock timer
27	Test timer 2 counter 0 for NMI
28	Test timer 2 counter 1
24	Initialize both interrupt controllers
25	Check for unexpected interrupts
26	Wait for interrupt
30	Check base 640Kb memory
31	Check extended memory size
32	Test higher 8 address lines
33	Test base memory
34	Test extended memory (up to 256Mb)
35	Test RAM in segment E000h
40	Test keyboard enable/disable
41	Test keyboard reset command
42	Test keyboard
43	Test keyboard
F4	Display speed setting
45	Initialize the mouse and enable IRQ1
44	Test address overrun capability
50	Set up hardware interrupt vectors
51	Enable IRQ0 interval interrupt from timer 0
60	Test for floppy and hard disk controllers and drives
61	Test disk controller
62	Initialize floppy drives
63	Initialize hard drives
74	Check and execute option ROMs from C8000h to DFFFFh
70	Test RTC
71	Set interval timer
72	Configure and test parallel interface
73	Configure and test serial interface
75	Test math coprocessor if installed
76	Enable keyboard and RTC
F0	Display any logged errors
F6	Test base memory

Table 28-37. Continued

Hex code	Description
F7	Run comprehensive base memory test
F3	Go to setup if F1 was pressed
F4	Display speed setting
F5	Initialize counter 2 for speed testing
F1	Test system code at E0000h and copy video ROM to shadow memory
F2	Call Int. 19 boot loader
F6	Test base memory
F7	Test extended memory

Olivetti family

Olivetti has created a wide selection of BIOS versions to support its PCs since the early 1980s. Most Olivetti BIOS versions provide POST codes to a parallel port (278h or 378h). The Olivetti 1076/AT&T 6312WGS sends the POST codes shown in Table 28-38. The M24 (imported as an AT&T 6300) was Olivetti's first true PC clone, and its POST codes are shown in Table 28-39. A more recent BIOS is the Olivetti EISA BIOS 2.01, and its codes are presented in Table 28-40. Finally, Table 28-41 covers the POST codes for an Olivetti PS/2 BIOS.

Table 28-38.
POST codes for Olivetti 1076/AT&T BIOS

Pass	Fail	Description
41	7F	CPU flag and register test
42	7E	Check and verify CMOS shutdown code
43	7D	BIOS ROM checksum test
44	7C	Test the 8253 timer
45	7B	Start memory refresh
46	7A	Test the 8041 keyboard controller
47	79	Test the first 8Kb of RAM
48	78	Test protected-mode operation
49	77	Test CMOS RAM shutdown byte
4A	76	Test protected-mode operation
4B	75	Test RAM from 8Kb to 640Kb
4C	74	Test all RAM above 1Mb
4D	73	Test NMI
4E	72	Test RAM parity system
50	71	Test 8259 PIC 1
51	6F	Test 8259 PIC 2
52	6E	Test DMA page register
53	6D	Test the 8237 DMA controller 1
54	6C	Test the 8237 DMA controller 2
55	6B	Test PIO port 61h
56	6A	Test the keyboard controller
57	69	Test the CMOS clock/calendar IC

Table 28-38. Continued

Pass	Fail	Description
59	68	Test the CPU protected-mode
5A	66	Test CMOS RAM battery
5B	65	Test CMOS RAM
5C	64	Verify CMOS RAM checksum
5D	63	Test parallel port configuration
5E	62	Test serial port configuration
5F	61	Test memory configuration below 640Kb
60	60	Test memory configuration above 1Mb
61	5F	Detect and test math coprocessor
62	5E	Test configuration of game port adapter
62	5D	Test key lock switch
63	5D	Test hard drive configuration
64	5C	Configure floppy drives
66	5B	Test option ROMs
—	—	Call Int. 19 boot loader

Table 28-39. POST codes for Olivetti M20 BIOS

Note: M20 codes are displayed on the monitor and sent to printer port

Hex code	Description
triangle	Test CPU registers and instructions
triangle	Test system RAM
4 vertical lines	Test CPU call and trap instructions
diamond	Initialize screen and printer drivers
EC0	8255 parallel interface IC test failed
EC1	6845 CRT controller IC test failed
EC2	1797 floppy disk controller chip failed
EC3	8253 timer IC failed
EC4	8251 keyboard interface failed
EC5	8251 keyboard test failed
EC6	8259 PIC IC test failed
EK0	Keyboard did not respond
EK1	Keyboard responds, but self-test failed
ED1	Disk drive 1 test failed
ED0	Disk drive 0 test failed
EI0	Nonvectored interrupt error
EI1	Vectored interrupt error

Table 28-40.
POST codes for Olivetti M24/AT&T BIOS

Hex code	Description
40	CPU flags and register test failed
41	BIOS ROM checksum test failed

Table 28-40. Continued

Hex code	Description
42	Disable 8253 timer channel 1
43	8237 DMA controller test failed
44	8259 PIC test failed
45	Install the real interrupt vectors
48	Send beep and initialize all basic hardware

Table 28-41. POST codes for Olivetti PS/2 BIOS

Hex code	Description
01	Test CPU
02	Check CMOS shutdown byte
03	Initialize the PIC
04	Test refresh
05	Test CMOS/RTC periodic interrupt
06	Test timer ratio
07	Test first 64Kb of RAM
08	Test 8042 keyboard controller
09	Test NMI
0A	Test 8254 PIT
0B	Test port 94h
0C	Test port 103h
0D	Test port 102h
0E	Test port 96h
0F	Test port 107h
10	Blank the display
11	Check the keyboard
12	Test CMOS RAM battery
13	Verify CMOS RAM checksum
14	Verify extended CMOS RAM checksum
15	Initialize system board and adapter
16	Initialize and test RAM
17	Test protected-mode registers
18	Test CMOS RAM shutdown byte
19	Test CMOS protected-mode
1A	Initiate video adapter ROM scan
1B	Test BIOS ROM checksum
1C	Test PIC #1
1D	Test PIC #2
1E	Initialize interrupt vectors
1F	Test CMOS RAM
20	Test extended CMOS RAM
21	Test CMOS real-time clock
22	Test clock calendar
23	Dummy checkpoint
24	Test watchdog timer

Table 28-41. Continued

Hex code	Description
25	Test 64KB to 640Kb RAM
26	Configure lower 640Kb RAM
27	Test extended memory
28	Initialize extended BIOS data segment and log POST errors
29	Configure memory above 1Mb
2A	Dummy checkpoint
2B	Test RAM parity
2C	Test DMA page registers
2D	Test DMA controller registers
2E	Test DMA transfer count register
2F	Initialize DMA controller
30	Test PIO 61
31	Test the keyboard
32	Initialize keyboard typematic rate and delay
33	Test auxiliary device
34	Test advanced protected-mode
35	Configure parallel ports
36	Configure 8250 serial ports
37	Test and configure math coprocessor
38	Test and configure game port adapter
39	Configure and initialize hard disk
3A	Floppy disk configuration
3B	Initialize ROM drivers
3C	Display total memory and hard drives
3D	Final initialization
3E	Detect and initialize parallel ports
3F	Initialize hard drive and controller
40	Initialize math coprocessor
42	Initiate adapter ROM scan
CC	Unexpected processor exception occurred
DD	Save DDNIL status
EE	NMI handler shutdown
FF	Call Int. 19 boot loader

Phillips

Designed by Phillips Home Electronics in Canada, Phillips motherboards make use of a proprietary BIOS that sends POST codes to port 80h. An interesting aspect of Phillips BIOS is that the beep codes use the binary-coded decimal representations of the POST code (where a 1 causes a long beep, and a 0 causes a short beep). As an example, a POST code of 17 has a BCD equivalent of (1 0111). This means that the corresponding beep code is (long, short, long, long, long). Table 28-42 shows the codes for a Phillips BIOS.

Table 28-42. POST codes for Phillips BIOS

Hex code	Description
0A	DMA page register R/W bad
10	CMOS RAM R/W error
11	System BIOS ROM checksum error
12	Timer A error
13	DMA controller A error
14	DMA controller B error
15	Memory refresh error
16	Keyboard controller error
17	Keyboard controller error
19	Keyboard controller error
1C	Base 64Kb RAM error
1D	Base 64Kb RAM parity error
1F	LSI sync missing
21	PVAM register error
25	System options error
2B	Video sync error
2C	Video BIOS ROM error
2D	Monochrome/color configuration error
2E	No video memory detected
35	Interrupt controller error
36	Byte swapper error
37	NMI error
38	Timer interrupt fault
39	LSI timer halted
3A	Main memory test error
3B	Keyboard error
3C	Keyboard interrupt error
3D	DDNIL scan halted and cache disabled
40	Diskette error
48	Adapter card error
4C	CMOS battery/checksum error
4D	System options error
52	Keyboard controller error
6A	Failure shadowing BIOS ROM
70	Memory size configuration error

Phoenix family

Phoenix Technologies Ltd. created one of the first IBM BIOS clones, and now has a very large share of the BIOS market. Part of their great appeal is that Phoenix makes their BIOS available to the OEM market—allowing BIOS to be optimized by other PC makers. The classic Phoenix XT BIOS produces only a few POST codes (shown in

Table 28-43). On the other hand, the Phoenix AT BIOS listed in Table 28-44 (for ISA/EISA/MCA systems) offers a proliferation of POST codes (as well as beep codes).

Table 28-43. POST codes for
Phoenix Technologies XT 2.52 BIOS

Hex code	Description
01	Test 8253 system timer
02	First 64Kb RAM failure
03	First 1Kb parity check failed
04	Initialize the 8259 PIC IC
05	Second 1Kb RAM (BIOS data area) failed
—	Initialize the display

Table 28-44. POST codes for
Phoenix Technologies ISA/EISA/MCA BIOS

Hex code	Description
01	CPU register test
02	CMOS R/W test
03	Testing BIOS ROM checksum
04	Testing 8253 PIT IC
05	Initializing the 8237 DMA controller
06	Testing the 8237 DMA page register
08	RAM refresh circuit test
09	Test first 64Kb of RAM
0A	Test first 64Kb RAM data lines
0B	Test first 64Kb RAM parity
0C	Test first 64Kb RAM address lines
0D	Parity failure detected for first 64Kb RAM
10-1F	Data bit (0-15) bad in first 64Kb RAM
20	Slave DMA register faulty
21	Master DMA register faulty
22	Master PIC register faulty
23	Slave PIC register faulty
25	Initializing interrupt vectors
27	Keyboard controller test
28	Testing CMOS checksum and battery power
29	Validate CMOS contents
2B	Video initialization faulty
2C	Video retrace test failed
2D	Search for video ROM
2E	Test video ROM
30	Video system checks OK
31	Monochrome video mode detected
32	Color (40 column) mode detected
33	Color (80 column) mode detected

Table 28-44. Continued

Hex code	Description
34	Timer tick interrupt test
35	CMOS shutdown byte test
36	Gate A20 failure (8042 KBC)
37	Unexpected interrupt
38	Extended RAM test
3A	Interval timer channel 2
3B	Test time-of-day clock
3C	Locate and test serial ports
3D	Locate and test parallel ports
3E	Locate and test math coprocessor
41	System board select bad
42	Extended CMOS RAM bad

Quadtel family

The Quadtel Corporation provides BIOS versions for XT and AT systems. The POST codes for a Quadtel 16K XT BIOS are listed in Table 28-45. Table 28-46 illustrates the POST codes for a Quadtel AT 3.0 BIOS.

Table 28-45. POST codes for Quadtel XT BIOS

Hex code	Description
03	Test CPU flags
06	Test CPU registers
09	Initialize any system-specific chipsets
0C	Test BIOS ROM checksum
0F	Initialize 8237 DMA page registers
12	Test 8237 DMA address and count registers
15	Initialize 8237 DMA
18	Test 8253 system timer IC (PIT)
1B	Initialize the 8253 PIT
1E	Start memory refresh test
21	Test the base 64Kb RAM
24	Set up interrupt vectors
27	Initialize 8259 PIC
2A	Test interrupt mask register
2D	Test for unexpected interrupt
30	Test V40 DMA if present
31	Test for DDNIL bits
33	Verify system clock interrupt
36	Test the keyboard
39	Set up interrupt table
3C	Read system configuration switches
3F	Test and initialize video

Table 28-45. Continued

Hex code	Description
42	Locate and test COM ports
45	Locate and test LPT ports
48	Locate and test game adapter port
4B	Display BIOS copyright message on screen
4E	Calculate CPU speed
54	Test system memory
55	Test floppy drive
57	Initialize system before boot
5A	Call Int. 19 boot loader

Table 28-46.
POST codes for Quadtel AT 3.00 BIOS

Hex code	Description
02	Test CPU flags
04	Test CPU registers
06	Perform system hardware initialization
08	Initialize specific chipset registers
0A	Test BIOS ROM checksum
0C	Test 8237 DMA page registers
0E	Test 8254 PIT
10	Initialize the 8254 PIT
12	Test 8237 DMA controller
14	Initialize 8237 DMA controller
16	Initialize 8259 PIC
18	Test and set the 8259 PIC
1A	Test memory refresh
1C	Test base 64Kb memory
1E	Test base 64Kb memory
20	Test base 64Kb memory
22	Test keyboard and keyboard controller
24	Test CMOS checksum and battery
26	Start first protected-mode test
28	Check memory size
2A	Autosize memory
2C	Set memory IC interleave
2E	Exit first protected-mode test
30	Unexpected shutdown
32	System board memory size
34	Relocate shadow RAM if available
36	Configure extended memory
38	Configure wait states
3A	Retest 64Kb base RAM

Table 28-46. Continued

Hex code	Description
3C	Calculate CPU speed
3E	Get configuration from 8042 KBC
40	Configure CPU speed
42	Initialize interrupt vectors
44	Verify video configuration
46	Initialize the video system
48	Test unexpected interrupts
4A	Start second protected-mode test
4B	Verify protected-mode instruction
4D	Verify protected-mode instruction
50	Verify protected-mode instruction
52	Verify protected-mode instruction
54	Verify protected-mode instruction
56	Unexpected exception
58	Test address line A20
5A	Test keyboard
5C	Determine AT or XT keyboard
5E	Start third protected-mode test
60	Test base memory
62	Test base memory address
64	Test shadow memory
66	Test extended memory
68	Test extended memory addresses
6A	Determine memory size
6C	Display error messages
6E	Copy BIOS to shadow memory
70	Test 8254 PIT
73	Test RTC
74	Test keyboard for stuck keys
76	Initialize system hardware
78	Locate and test the math coprocessor
7A	Determine COM ports
7C	Determine LPT ports
7E	Initialize the BIOS data area
80	Check for a floppy/ hard drive controller
82	Test floppy disk
84	Test fixed disk
86	Check for option ROMs
88	Check for keyboard lock
8A	Wait for <F1> key pressed
8C	Final system initialization
8E	Call Int. 19 boot loader

Tandon family

Tandon has been producing PC clones for many years. Their Type A BIOS (in Table 28-47) dates back to 1988, and their Type B BIOS (in Table 28-48) was introduced in 1992. Tandon also introduced a BIOS to support i486 EISA systems that is listed in Table 28-49. All Tandon BIOS versions send codes to port 80h.

Table 28-47.
POST codes for Tandon Type A BIOS

Hex code	Description
01	Test CPU flags and registers
02	Test BIOS ROM checksum
03	Test CMOS RAM battery
04	Test 8254 timer
05	8254 timer test failed
06	Test RAM refresh
07	Test first 16Kb RAM
08	Initialize interrupt vectors
09	Test 8259 PIC
0A	Configure temporary interrupt vectors
0B	Initialize interrupt vector table 1
0C	Initialize interrupt vector table 2
0D	Initialize fixed disk vector
0E	Interrupt vector test failed
0F	Clear keyboard controller
10	Keyboard controller test failed
11	Run keyboard controller self-test
12	Initialize equipment check data area
13	Check and initialize math coprocessor
14	Test CMOS RAM contents
15	Test and configure parallel ports
16	Test and configure serial ports
17	Call Int. 19 boot loader

Table 28-48. POST codes for Tandon Type B BIOS

Hex code	Description
01	Cold boot initialization started
06	Initialize any specialized chipsets
07	Warm reboot starts here
08	Keyboard initialization passed
09	Keyboard self-test finished
0A	Test CMOS RAM battery
0B	Cave CMOS RAM battery level in CMOS diagnostic register
0C	Finished saving CMOS battery condition
0D	Test 8254 PIT and disable RAM parity check
0E	8254 PIT test failed

Table 28-48. Continued

Hex code	Description
0F	Initialize 8254 PIT channels and start memory refresh test
10	Refresh test failed
11	Test base 64Kb RAM
12	Base 64Kb RAM test failed
13	Base 64Kb RAM test passed
14	Perform R/W test of CMOS RAM
15	CMOS RAM R/W test complete
16	Calculating CPU speed
18	Test and initialize 8259 PICs
1A	8259 PIC initialization complete
1B	Spurious interrupt detected
1C	Spurious interrupt did not occur
1D	ERROR . . . timer 0 interrupt failed
1E	8259 PIC tests passed
20	Set up interrupt vectors 02 to 1F
21	Set up interrupt vectors 70 to 77
22	Clear interrupt vectors 41 to 46
23	Read 8042 self-test result
24	Test for proper 8042 KBC self-test
25	ERROR . . . KBC self-test failed
26	8042 KBC self-test passed
27	Confirm DMA working
28	Initialize video system
29	Set video with cursor off
2A	Video parameters are initialized
2B	Enable NMI and I/O channel check
2C	Run RAM test to check RAM size
2D	RAM sizing complete
2E	Reset keyboard controller
2F	Initialize the CMOS RTC
30	Initialize floppy drive controller
31	Initialize hard disk controller
32	Disk controller has been initialized
33	Perform equipment check and initialize math coprocessor
34	Initialize serial and parallel ports
35	Test CMOS RAM battery level
36	Check for keystroke
37	Enable 8254 PIT channel 0
38	Configure cache memory
39	Enable keyboard interface and interrupts
3A	Setup finished . . . clear display
3B	Test the floppy and hard disk drives
3C	Scan and run any option BIOS ROMs between C800h and E000h
3D	Disable gate A20
3E	Gate A20 is disabled
3F	Call Int. 19 boot loader

Table 28-49. POST codes for Tandon i486 EISA BIOS

Hex code	Description
01	Disable cache and EISA NMIs, enable BIOS ROM
05	Initialize address decoder and 640Kb RAM
06	Clear CMOS RAM shutdown flag
07	Test 8042 KBC
08	Run 8042 KBC self-test
AA	8042 KBC self-test result
09	Test BIOS ROM checksum
0A	Read CMOS registers 3 times
0B	Bad CMOS RAM battery
0C	Send command to port 61 to disable speaker
0D	Test 8254 PIT
0E	8254 PIT is faulty
0F	Enable and test memory refresh
10	Memory refresh failed
11	Check and clear first 64Kb of RAM
12	First 64Kb RAM failed
13	First 64Kb memory test passed
14	Test CMOS RAM
15	Shadow BIOS and set system speed high
16	Check CMOS shutdown flag
17	Reset was cold boot
18	Prepare 8259 PICs
19	8259 PIC initialization failed
1A	Test 8259 PIC
1B	Check for spurious interrupts
1C	Check system timer IC
1D	PIT failure
1E	Initialize interrupt vectors
1F	Initialize interrupt vectors 00 to 6F
20	Set vectors for interrupt 02-1F
21	Set interrupt vectors for 70-77
22	Clear interrupt vectors for 41 and 46
23	Read 8042 self-test results from DMA page register
24	Test for proper 8042 self-test result
25	8042 self-test failed
26	Initialize the 8042 keyboard controller
27	Check shutdown flag
28	Install video ROM and initialize video
29	Install video ROM, set for mono/color operation, and initialize video
2A	Check for bad CMOS RAM
2B	Check shutdown flag
2C	Test memory for proper size
2D	Display any error messages
2E	Initialize 8042 KBC
2F	Initialize time-of-day in the RTC

Table 28-49. Continued

Hex code	Description
30	Test for and initialize floppy disk controller
31	Enable C&T IDE interface and test for hard drive
32	Test and initialize 8259 DMA registers
33	Test and initialize math coprocessor
34	Test and initialize parallel and serial ports
35	Check CMOS RAM
36	Check for keyboard lock
37	Enable system clock tick, keyboard, and interrupt controller interrupts
38	Initialize RAM variables
39	Enter CMOS SETUP mode if proper keystroke pressed
3A	Clear display
3B	Initialize floppy and fixed disk drives
3C	Scan and run option ROMs
3D	Clear CMOS shutdown flag and turn off gate A20
3E	Set interrupt vectors
3F	Call Int. 19 boot loader

Zenith Orion

Although a few Zenith systems use Phoenix BIOS, the majority of Zenith systems use proprietary BIOS products. POST codes for the Zenith Orion 4.1E BIOS are shown in Table 28-50.

Table 28-50. POST codes for Zenith Orion 4.1E BIOS

Hex code	Description
02	Enter protected-mode
03	Perform main board initialization
F0	Start basic hardware initialization
F1	Clear CMOS status locations
F2	Starting CLIO initialization
F3	Initialize SYSCFG register
F4	DXPI initialization for boot block
F5	Turning cache off
F6	Configure CPU socket
F7	Checking for math coprocessor
F8	82C206 default initialization
F9	Chipset default initialization
FF	End of machine-specific boot block
04	Check the flash ROM checksum
05	Flash ROM OK
06	Reset or power up
07	CLIO default initialization
08	SYSCFG registers initialized

Table 28-50. Continued

Hex code	Description
09	CMOS RAM initialization
10	SCP initialized
11	DRAM autosize detection complete
12	Parity checking enabled
18	Video ROM test at C0000h
19	Internal video ROM checked
1A	Returning to real-mode
1B	Internal video hardware enabled
1D	CPU clock frequency detected
1E	BIOS data area cleared
20	Reset
21	Continue after setting memory size
22	Continue after memory test
23	Continue after memory error
24	Continue with boot loader request
25	Jump to user code
26	Continue after protected-mode passed
27	Continue after protected-mode failed
28	Continue after extended protected-mode test
29	Continue after block move
2A	Jump to user code
30	Exit from protected-mode
31	Test/reset passed
32	Check the ROM checksum
33	Clear the video screen
34	Check system DRAM configuration
35	Check CMOS contents
36	Turn off the UMB RAM
37	Test parity generation
38	Initialize system variables
39	Check for power errors
3A	Initialize SCP mode
3B	Test CMOS diagnostic power reset
3C	Test CPU reset
3D	Save CPU ID
3E	Initialize the video system
3F	Initialize the DMA controllers
40	System speed error detected
41	Test EEPROM checksum
42	Configure parallel ports, floppy disks, and hard disks
43	Test extended video BIOS
44	Turn cache off
45	Test extended RAM
46	Test base RAM
47	Determine the amount of memory in the system

Table 28-50. Continued

Hex code	Description
48	Set warm boot flag
49	Clear 16Kb of base RAM
4A	Install BIOS interrupt vector
4B	Test system timer
4C	Initialize interrupt
4D	Enable default hardware initialization
4E	Determine global I/O configuration
4F	Initialize video
50	Initialize WD90C30 scratchpad
51	Check for errors before boot
53	Test system and initialize
55	Initialize the keyboard processor
56	Initialize the PS/2 mouse
57	Configure CLIO for mouse
58	Configure CLIO for LAN
59	Configure CLIO for SCSI
5A	Configure CLIO for WAM
5B	Wait for user to enter password
5C	Initialize and enable system clock
5D	Test and initialize the floppy drive
5E	Check for Z150-type disk
5F	Initialize hard drive sub-system
60	Set default I/O device parameters
61	Get LAN ID from LAN
62	Install option ROM(s) at C8000h
63	Install option ROM(s) at E0000h
64	Initialize the SCSI interface
65	Run with A20 line off
66	Turn off the SCP
67	Set machine speed based on CMOS contents
68	Turn on cache
69	Calibrate 1-ms constants
6A	Enable NMI
6C	Clear warm boot flag
6D	Check for errors before boot
6E	Call Int. 19 boot loader

POST troubleshooting strategy

Generally speaking, a POST board is one of the best all-around PC hardware troubleshooting tools available. They are quick and easy to use, compatible across ISA, EISA, and MCA platforms, and even the simplest POST board can provide you with a remarkable insight into a system's operation. The trouble with POST boards is that every BIOS, although testing virtually the same functions, uses varying codes that are often cryptic and poorly documented (this chapter takes great pains to provide you with fairly comprehensive index of POST codes). Armed with the proper code list, a POST board can often pinpoint a fault to the exact IC. If not to the exact IC, then certainly to the major subassembly.

Symptom 1. The power and cooling fan(s) are on, but nothing else happens You should first suspect that incoming ac power is very low, or that the power connector between the supply and motherboard has become loose or disconnected. Start by using a multimeter to check ac power available at the wall outlet. *Use extreme caution to protect yourself from accidental electrocution.* If the ac level is unusually low, try the PC in an outlet with an adequate voltage level. If the ac level is acceptable, check the power connector at the motherboard. Observe the power LEDs on the POST board. If one or more power LEDs is dim or absent, there might be a fault in the power supply. Troubleshoot or replace the supply.

Symptom 2. After power-up, you hear the fan change pitch noticeably (there also might be a chirping sound coming from the supply) First, be aware that some PCs use a variable-speed fan to optimize cooling. If you hear the fan pitch vary, you should make sure that this is abnormal for your particular system before pursuing a repair. If varying fan pitch is not correct for your system, the ac power level reaching the PC is probably low and allowing the power supply to drop out of regulation. Use a multimeter and check the ac level at the wall outlet. *Use extreme caution to protect yourself from accidental electrocution.* If the ac level is too low or unsteady, try the PC in a functional ac outlet. If ac levels measure correctly, check the power LEDs on your POST board. If one or more LEDs is dim or out (or if the supply is producing a chirping sound), the supply is probably defective. Troubleshoot or repair the power supply.

Symptom 3. You see one or more POST board power LEDs off, very dim, or flickering Before suspecting a problem with the supply, try the POST board in a different socket; the expansion bus connector at that location might be bad. If the symptom persists (and the PC is behaving strangely), check the power connector between the supply and motherboard. If the connector is intact, the supply might be defective. Troubleshoot or replace the power supply.

Symptom 4. The reset LED remains on (the POST display will probably remain blank) In most PC designs, the CPU is held in the reset state until a power good signal is received from the power supply. This typically requires no more than a few milliseconds. If the reset LED remains on longer than that, it might be held up by a problem with the "power good" signal. Use a logic probe (or probe that comes with the POST board) to check the "power good" signal. If the signal changes state as expected, the reset line might be shorted somewhere on the motherboard; try replacing the motherboard. If the signal does not change as expected, there might be a problem in the power supply. Try replacing the power supply.

Symptom 5. One or more activity LEDs is out (the POST display will probably remain blank) Most POST boards provide a selection of LEDs that are used to indicate signal activity on major bus lines. If one or more of these LEDs is out, there is probably a motherboard fault in the corresponding circuit.

- *ALE* The clock generator, CPU, DMA controller, or bus controller might have failed. Try replacing the motherboard.

- *OSC* The clock generator IC or time-base crystal might have failed. Replace those components, or replace the motherboard.
- *CLK* Check for excessive ripple in the ac source. Try a clean ac source. There also might be a problem with the clock generator or time-base crystal. Replace those components or replace the motherboard.
- *I/OR, I/OW* Check for excessive ripple or inadequate ground in the system power lines. Try a new power supply if necessary. There also might be a fault in the DMA controller, CPU, PIT, or PIC devices. Try another motherboard.
- *MR/W* There might be a fault in the DMA controller, bus controller, BIOS ROM, PIT, or PIC devices. Try another motherboard.

Symptom 6. You hear a beep code pattern from the system speaker, but no POST codes are displayed Any beep pattern other than a single short beep indicates a serious system problem; however, there might be several reasons why the POST board is not displaying POST codes. First, make sure that the BIOS for your system actually generates POST codes—most do, but a few do not. Also be sure that your POST board is set to read the proper I/O address that the codes are being written to. Many systems send codes to port 80h, but other ports such as 1080h, 680h, and 378h might be used. Configure the POST board to use the proper address. If problems persist, the BIOS itself might be defective. Try a different BIOS, or refer to Chapter 15 to troubleshoot the beep code.

Symptom 7. The POST display stops at some code (the system probably hangs up) The CPU and clock systems are probably working to fetch instructions from BIOS, but POST has detected a fault in the system. Use the table for your appropriate manufacturer in this chapter, and find the POST code's meaning. If the code refers to a fault on the motherboard, you can either attempt to replace the defective component, or replace the motherboard outright. If the code refers to an expansion device such as a drive or video adapter, take steps to replace the defective device.

Symptom 8. A POST or beep code indicates a video problem (there is no monitor display) Chances are that the system was unable to detect video ROM instructions or locate video memory. As a result, no display is available. Try a new video adapter board in the system. If the video adapter is located on the motherboard, try a new motherboard, or disable the motherboard video (usually with a jumper) and install an expansion video adapter.

Symptom 9. A POST or beep code indicates a drive or controller problem Chances are that the video system is working. If possible, load the CMOS setup program and make sure that the drive selections entered are accurate for your system. An incorrect set of entries can disable your drives. Make sure that the drive being used is properly formatted and partitioned for your system. If the problem persists, either the drive or drive controller has failed. Start by trying an alternative drive controller. If the problem remains, try a new drive.

ISA/EISA bus operations

When it was first introduced, the IBM PC was no gem. It was a slow, clunky contraption with virtually no system resources (memory, interrupts, DMA channels, and so on). Yet, the IBM PC ushered in the personal computer era that you know today. Certainly, it was not speed or efficiency that brought IBM systems to the forefront of technology. Instead, it was a revolutionary (and rather risky) concept called *open architecture*. Rather than designing a computer and being the sole developer of proprietary add-on devices (as so many other computer manufacturers were at the time), IBM chose to incorporate only the essential processing elements on the motherboard, and leave many of the other functions to expansion boards that could be plugged into standard bus connectors.

By publishing the specifications of this "standard" expansion bus and making it available to the industry as a whole, any company was then able to develop IBM-compatible adapters and add-ons. Those adapters also would work on "clone" PCs that used the same expansion bus. As a result, the PC became a processing platform for some of the most creative video, drive, and communication devices ever devised. As you might suspect, the key to an *open architecture* is the bus connector itself. By understanding the location and purpose of each bus signal, you can follow the operations and limitations of the bus. This chapter is intended to provide you with background information on the two classical bus architectures used in modern PCs—ISA and EISA.

Industry-standard architecture

The venerable *ISA* (industry-standard architecture) shown in Fig. 29-1 is the first open-system bus architecture used for personal computers; any manufacturer was welcome to use the architecture for a small licensing fee. Because there were no restrictions placed on the use of ISA buses (also referred to simply as *PC buses*), they were duplicated in every IBM-compatible clone that followed. Not only did the use of a standard bus pave the way for thousands of manufacturers to produce com-

A1   8-bit (XT) bus   A31

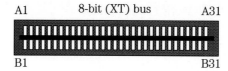

B1   B31

A1   16-bit (AT) bus   A31   C1   C18

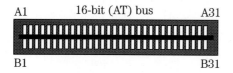 

B1   B31   D1   D18

29-1 Diagram of 8-bit and 16-bit ISA slots.

patible PCs and expansion devices, but it also allowed the use of standardized operating systems and applications software. Both an 8-bit and 16-bit version of the ISA bus are available, although current motherboards have essentially abandoned the 8-bit XT version in favor of the faster, more flexible 16-bit AT version.

8-bit ISA

Use of the 8-bit XT bus started in 1982. The 8-bit ISA bus consists of a single card edge connector with 62 contacts. The bus provides eight data lines and twenty address lines that allow the board to reside within the XT's 1Mb of conventional memory. The bus also supports connections for six interrupts (IRQ2–IRQ7) and three DMA channels. The XT bus runs at the system speed of 4.77 MHz. Although the bus itself is relatively simple, IBM failed to publish specific timing relationships for data, address, and control signals. This ambiguity left early manufacturers to find the proper timing relationships by trial and error.

Although each connector on the bus is supposed to work the same way, early PCs designed with eight expansion slots required any card inserted in the eighth slot (the slot closest to the power supply) to provide a special card-selected signal on pin B8. Timing requirements for the eighth slot also are tighter. Contrary to popular belief, the eighth slot has nothing to do with the IBM expansion chassis. The demands of slot 8 were to support a keyboard/timer adapter board for IBM's special configuration called the 3270PC. Most XT clones did not adhere to this "eighth-slot" peculiarity.

Knowing the XT signals

Table 29-1 shows the pinout for an XT bus configuration. The *Oscillator* pin provides the 14.3-MHz system oscillator signal to the expansion bus, and the Clock pin supplies the 4.77-MHz system clock signal. When the PC needs to be reset, the RESET DRV pin drives the whole system into a reset state. The twenty address pins (0 to 19) connect an expansion board to the system's address bus; when address signals are valid, the Address Latch Enable (ALE) signal indicates that the address can now be decoded. The eight data lines (0 to 7) connect the board to the system's data bus.

Table 29-1. ISA 8-bit (XT) bus pinout

Signal	Pin	Pin	Signal
Ground	B1	A1	–I/O Channel Check
Reset	B2	A2	Data Bit 7
+5 Vdc	B3	A3	Data Bit 6
IRQ 2	B4	A4	Data Bit 5
–5 Vdc	B5	A5	Data Bit 4
DRQ 2	B6	A6	Data Bit 3
–12 Vdc	B7	A7	Data Bit 2
–Card Selected	B8	A8	Data Bit 1
+12 Vdc	B9	A9	Data Bit 0
Ground	B10	A10	I/O Channel Ready
–SMEMW	B11	A11	AEN
–SMEMR	B12	A12	Address Bit 19
–I/O W	B13	A13	Address Bit 18
–I/O R	B14	A14	Address Bit 17
–DACK 3	B15	A15	Address Bit 16
DRQ 3	B16	A16	Address Bit 15
–DACK 1	B17	A17	Address Bit 14
DRQ 1	B18	A18	Address Bit 13
–REFRESH	B19	A19	Address Bit 12
Clock (4.77 MHz)	B20	A20	Address Bit 11
IRQ 7	B21	A21	Address Bit 10
IRQ 6	B22	A22	Address Bit 9
IRQ 5	B23	A23	Address Bit 8
IRQ 4	B24	A24	Address Bit 7
IRQ 3	B25	A25	Address Bit 6
–DACK 2	B26	A26	Address Bit 5
T/C	B27	A27	Address Bit 4
BALE	B28	A28	Address Bit 3
+5 Vdc	B29	A29	Address Bit 2
Oscillator (14.3 MHz)	B30	A30	Address Bit 1
Ground	B31	A31	Address Bit 0

The –I/O Channel Check (–IOCHCK) line flags the motherboard when errors occur on the expansion board. Note that the minus sign (–) preceding the signal indicates that the signal uses active-low logic. The I/O Channel Ready is active when an addressed expansion board is ready. If this pin is logic 0, the CPU will extend the bus cycle by inserting wait states. The six hardware interrupts (IRQ2 to IRQ7) are used by the expansion board to demand the CPU's attention. Interrupts 0 and 1 are not available to the bus because they handle the highest priorities of the timer chip and keyboard. The –I/O Read (–I/O R) and –I/O Write (–I/O W) lines indicate that the CPU or DMA controller want to transfer data to or from the data bus. The –Memory Read (–MEMR) and –Memory Write (–MEMW) signals tells the expansion board that the CPU or DMA controller is going to read or write data to main memory.

The XT bus supplies three DMA Requests (DRQ1 to DRQ3) so that an expansion board can transfer data to or from memory. DMA requests must be held until the corresponding –DMA Acknowledge (–DACK1 to –DACK3) signals become true. If the Address Enable (AEN) signal is true, the DMA controller is controlling the bus for a data transfer. Finally, the Terminal Count (T/C) signal provides a pulse when the DMA transfer is completed.

16-bit ISA

The limitations of the 8-bit ISA bus were soon obvious. With a floppy drive and hard drive taking up two of the six available interrupts, COM 3 and COM 4 taking up another two interrupts (IRQ 3 and IRQ 4), and an LPT port taking up IRQ 7, competition for the remaining interrupt was fierce. Of the three DMA channels available, the floppy and hard drives take two, so only one DMA channel remains available. Only 1Mb of address space is addressable, and 8 data bits form a serious bottleneck for data transfers. It would have been a simple matter to start from scratch and design an entirely new bus, but that would have obsoleted the entire installed base of XT owners.

The next logical step in bus evolution came in 1984/1985 with the introduction of the 80286 in IBM's PC/AT. System resources were added to the bus while still allowing XT boards to function in the expanded bus. The result became what you know today as the 16-bit AT bus. Instead of a different bus connector, the original 62-pin connector was left intact, and an extra 36-pin connector was added as shown in Table 29-2 designated "C" and "D." An extra eight data bits are added to bring the total data bus to 16 bits. Five interrupts and four DMA channels are included. Four more address lines also are provided, in addition to several more control signals. Clock speed is increased on the AT bus to 8.33 MHz. It is important to note that although XT boards should theoretically work with an AT bus, not all older XT expansion boards will work on the AT bus.

Table 29-2. ISA 16-bit (AT) bus pinout

Signal	Pin	Pin	Signal
Ground	B1	A1	–I/O Channel Check
Reset	B2	A2	Data Bit 7
+5 Vdc	B3	A3	Data Bit 6
IRQ 9	B4	A4	Data Bit 5
–5 Vdc	B5	A5	Data Bit 4
DRQ 2	B6	A6	Data Bit 3
–12 Vdc	B7	A7	Data Bit 2
–0 WAIT	B8	A8	Data Bit 1
+12 Vdc	B9	A9	Data Bit 0
Ground	B10	A10	–I/O Channel Ready
–SMEMW	B11	A11	AEN
–SMEMR	B12	A12	Address Bit 19
–I/O W	B13	A13	Address Bit 18
–I/O R	B14	A14	Address Bit 17

Table 29-2. Continued

Signal	Pin	Pin	Signal
–DACK 3	B15	A15	Address Bit 16
DRQ 3	B16	A16	Address Bit 15
–DACK 1	B17	A17	Address Bit 14
DRQ 1	B18	A18	Address Bit 13
–REFRESH	B19	A19	Address Bit 12
Clock (8.33 MHz)	B20	A20	Address Bit 11
IRQ 7	B21	A21	Address Bit 10
IRQ 6	B22	A22	Address Bit 9
IRQ 5	B23	A23	Address Bit 8
IRQ 4	B24	A24	Address Bit 7
IRQ 3	B25	A25	Address Bit 6
–DACK 2	B26	A26	Address Bit 5
T/C	B27	A27	Address Bit 4
BALE	B28	A28	Address Bit 3
+5 Vdc	B29	A29	Address Bit 2
Oscillator (14.3 MHz)	B30	A30	Address Bit 1
Ground	B31	A31	Address Bit 0
Key	Key	Key	Key
–MEM CS16	D1	C1	–SBHE
–I/O CS16	D2	C2	Address Bit 23
IRQ 10	D3	C3	Address Bit 22
IRQ 11	D4	C4	Address Bit 21
IRQ 12	D5	C5	Address Bit 20
IRQ 15	D6	C6	Address Bit 19
IRQ 14	D7	C7	Address Bit 18
–DACK 0	D8	C8	Address Bit 17
DRQ 0	D9	C9	–MEM R
–DACK 5	D10	C10	–MEM W
DRQ 5	D11	C11	Data Bit 8
–DACK 6	D12	C12	Data Bit 9
DRQ 6	D13	C13	Data Bit 10
–DACK 7	D14	C14	Data Bit 11
DRQ 7	D15	C15	Data Bit 12
+5 Vdc	D16	C16	Data Bit 13
–MASTER	D17	C17	Data Bit 14
Ground	D18	C18	Data Bit 15

Knowing the AT signals

The –System Bus High Enable (–SBHE) is active when the upper eight data bits are being used. If the upper eight bits are not being used (i.e., an XT board in the AT slot), –SBHE will be inactive. If the expansion board requires 16-bit access to memory locations, it must return an active –MEM CS16 signal. If the expansion board requires 16-bit access to an I/O location, it must make the –I/O CS16 signal active. The –Memory Read

(–MEMR) and –Memory Write (–MEMW) signals provided by an expansion board tell the CPU or DMA controller that memory access is needed up to 16Mb. The –SMEMR and –SMEMW signals only indicate memory access for the first 1Mb. The –MASTER signal can be used by expansion boards that are able to take control of the bus through use of a DMA channel. It is interesting to note that small, highly integrated AT systems are available for embedded systems and dedicated applications.

Potential problems mixing 8-bit and 16-bit ISA boards

ISA 16-bit architecture that was developed on the foundation of IBM's original 8-bit XT bus. By extending the original XT bus rather than redesigning an expansion bus from scratch, IBM was able to develop their AT, which would accommodate new, more sophisticated 16-bit expansion boards while still being backwardly compatible with the installed base of 8-bit boards. For the most part, this strategy worked quite well; the ISA bus remains a prominent feature of today's PCs. However, there is a potential problem with the ISA bus when inserting an 8-bit and 16-bit adapter that both use ROM residing in the same memory vicinity. Such a problem generally results in trouble with the 8-bit board.

To understand where this problem arises from, you should be familiar with the ISA bus pinout as shown in Table 29-2. There is an initial 62 pin connector (A1 through A31 and B1 through B31), followed by the extended 36-pin connector (C1 through C18 and D1 through D18). Notice that Address Bits 17, 18, and 19 are repeated on pins C8, C7, and C6. When a 16-bit board is inserted in the system, those repeated address lines indicate that a memory access is about to occur somewhere within 128K of the address signals on A17, A18, and A19 (the lower 17 address lines—A0 to A16—specify exactly where in that 128K range the access will take place). If a 16-bit expansion board has memory (such as a Video BIOS ROM or hard drive controller ROM) within the 128K range about to be accessed, it responds to the system using the –MEM CS16 or –I/O CS16 lines that its memory is ready for access in 16-bit transfers. If the system receives no response from either of these lines, data is transferred in 8-bit sections.

The problem here is that 8-bit boards also might have memory within that 128K range, but because they cannot detect the three extra address lines, the board cannot respond to the system. If a 16-bit board tells the system to proceed with a 16-bit data transfer, but there also is an 8-bit board in that same address range, the 8-bit board will be forced to receive 16-bit data transfers. As you might expect, this is quite impossible for an 8-bit board, so the 8-bit board will appear to malfunction. Because most expansion boards reserve their ROM addresses for the 128K block between 768K to 896K (C0000h to DBFFFh, sometimes called the *ROM Reserve*), this is where most problems reside.

It is important for you to understand that this problem does not refer to a hardware conflict. The ROM locations of the 8-bit and 16-bit boards can certainly *not* overlap at any point. As you might realize, however, it is possible to have several different ROMs contained within the same 128K of system memory. If one such ROM is on a 16-bit board and one is on an 8-bit board, the 8-bit board will likely malfunction due to the way in which 16-bit boards handle ISA bus operation. Correcting such a problem is generally a matter of replacing the 8-bit board with a 16-bit version. It also might be possible to disable the 8-bit ROM using an on-board jumper, then use the motherboard BIOS ROM instead.

Extended industry-standard architecture

The *Extended ISA* (or EISA) bus (Fig. 29-2) is a 32-bit bus developed in 1988/89 to address the continuing need for greater speed and performance from expansion peripherals caused by the use of 80386 and 80486 CPUs. It also did not make sense to leave the entire 32-bit bus market to IBM's MCA bus. Even though the bus works at 8.33 MHz, the 32-bit data path doubles data throughput between motherboard and expansion board. Unlike the MCA bus, however, EISA ensures backward compatibility with existing ISA peripherals and PC software. The EISA bus is designed to be fully compatible with ISA boards as shown in the pinout of Table 29-3. The EISA bus switches automatically between 16-bit ISA and 32-bit EISA operation using a second row of card edge connectors and the –EX32 and –EX16 lines. Thus, EISA boards have access to all of the signals available to ISA boards, as well as the second row of EISA signals.

16-bit ISA/32-bit EISA bus

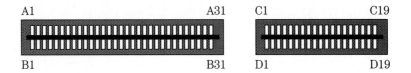

29-2 Diagram of a 32-bit EISA slot.

Table 29-3. EISA 16/32-bit bus pinout

32 bit	16 bit	Pin	Pin	16 bit	32 bit
Ground	Ground	B1	A1	–I/O Channel Check	–CMD
+5 Vdc	Reset	B2	A2	Data Bit 7	–START
+5 Vdc	+5 Vdc	B3	A3	Data Bit 6	EXRDY
Reserved	IRQ 9	B4	A4	Data Bit 5	–EX32
Reserved	–5 Vdc	B5	A5	Data Bit 4	Ground
Key	DRQ 2	B6	A6	Data Bit 3	Key
Reserved	–12 Vdc	B7	A7	Data Bit 2	–EX16
Reserved	–0 WAIT	B8	A8	Data Bit 1	–SLBURST
+12 Vdc	+12 Vdc	B9	A9	Data Bit 0	–MSBURST
M –I/O	Ground	B10	A10	–I/O Channel Ready	W –R
–LOCK	–SMEMW	B11	A11	AEN	Ground
Reserved	–SMEMR	B12	A12	Address Bit 19	Reserved
Ground	–I/O W	B13	A13	Address Bit 18	Reserved
Reserved	–I/O R	B14	A14	Address Bit 17	Reserved
–BE3	–DACK 3	B15	A15	Address Bit 16	Ground
Key	DRQ 3	B16	A16	Address Bit 15	Key

Table 29-3. Continued

32 bit	16 bit	Pin	Pin	16 bit	32 bit
–BE2	–DACK 1	B17	A17	Address Bit 14	–BE1
–BE0	DRQ 1	B18	A18	Address Bit 13	–Addr. 31
Ground	–REFRESH	B19	A19	Address Bit 12	Ground
+5 Vdc	Clock (8.33 MHz)	B20	A20	Address Bit 11	–Addr. 30
–Addr. 29	IRQ 7	B21	A21	Address Bit 10	–Addr. 28
Ground	IRQ 6	B22	A22	Address Bit 9	–Addr. 27
–Addr. 26	IRQ 5	B23	A23	Address Bit 8	–Addr. 25
–Addr. 24	IRQ 4	B24	A24	Address Bit 7	Ground
Key	IRQ 3	B25	A25	Address Bit 6	Key
Addr. 16	–DACK 2	B26	A26	Address Bit 5	Addr. 15
Addr. 14	T/C	B27	A27	Address Bit 4	Addr. 13
+5 Vdc	BALE	B28	A28	Address Bit 3	Addr. 12
+5 Vdc	+5 Vdc	B29	A29	Address Bit 2	Addr. 11
Ground	Osc. (14.3 MHz)	B30	A30	Address Bit 1	Ground
Addr. 10	Ground	B31	A31	Address Bit 0	Addr. 9
Key	Key	Key	Key	Key	Key
Addr. 8	–MEM CS16	D1	C1	–SBHE	Addr. 7
Addr. 6	–I/O CS16	D2	C2	Address Bit 23	Ground
Addr. 5	IRQ 10	D3	C3	Address Bit 22	Addr. 4
+5 Vdc	IRQ 11	D4	C4	Address Bit 21	Addr. 3
Addr. 2	IRQ 12	D5	C5	Address Bit 20	Ground
Key	IRQ 15	D6	C6	Address Bit 19	Key
Data 16	IRQ 14	D7	C7	Address Bit 18	Data 17
Data 18	–DACK 0	D8	C8	Address Bit 17	Data 19
Ground	DRQ 0	D9	C9	–MEM R	Data 20
Data 21	–DACK 5	D10	C10	–MEM W	Data 22
Data 23	DRQ 5	D11	C11	Data Bit 8	Ground
Data 24	–DACK 6	D12	C12	Data Bit 9	Data 25
Ground	DRQ 6	D13	C13	Data Bit 10	Data 26
Data 27	–DACK 7	D14	C14	Data Bit 11	Data 28
Key	DRQ 7	D15	C15	Data Bit 12	Key
Data 29	+5 Vdc	D16	C16	Data Bit 13	Ground
+5 Vdc	–MASTER	D17	C17	Data Bit 14	Data 30
+5 Vdc	Ground	D18	C18	Data Bit 15	Data 31
–MAKx	—	D19	C19	—	–MREQx

As with the MCA bus, EISA supports arbitration for bus mastering and automatic board configuration that simplifies the installation of new boards. The EISA bus can access fifteen interrupt levels and seven DMA channels. To maintain backward compatibility with ISA expansion boards, however, there is no direct bus support for video or audio as there is with the MCA bus. Because the EISA bus clock runs at the same 8.33-MHz rate as ISA, the potential data throughput of an EISA board is roughly twice that of ISA boards. EISA systems are used as network servers, workstations, and high-end PCs. Although EISA systems have proliferated farther than MCA systems, EISA remains a high-end standard—never really filtering down to low-cost consumer systems.

Knowing the EISA signals

The EISA bus uses 30 address lines (Addr. 2 to Addr. 31). The lower two address lines (A0 and A1) are decoded by the Byte Enable lines (–BE0 to –BE3). Data bits 0 to 15 are taken from the ISA portion of the bus, but the upper 16 data lines are provided by (Data 16 to Data 31). The Memory/–I/O (M/–I/O) signal determines whether a memory or I/O bus cycle is being performed, and the Write/–Read (W/–R) line defines whether the access is for reading or writing. When an EISA device is allowed to complete a bus cycle, the EISA Ready (EXRDY) line is used to insert wait states. When the motherboard is providing exclusive access to an EISA board, the –Locked Cycle (–LOCK) signal is true. If an EISA board can run in 32-bit mode, the –EISA 32-bit Device (–EX32) signal is true, but if the board can only run in 16-bit mode, the –EISA 16-bit Device (–EX16) signal is true.

The –Master Burst (–MSBURST) signal is activated by the EISA bus master that informs the EISA bus controller that a burst transfer cycle will commence, thus doubling the bus transfer rate. When an external device must send a data burst, it activates the –Slave Burst (–SLBURST) line. An external device requests control of the EISA bus using the –Master Request (–MREQ) line. If the bus arbitrator decides that the requester can control the bus, a –Master Acknowledge (–MACK) signal is sent to the requesting device. A –Command (–CMD) signal is sent to synchronize the EISA bus cycle with the system clock, and the –Start (–START) signal helps to coordinate the system clock with the beginning of an EISA bus cycle. Finally, the Bus Clock (BCLK) is provided at 8.33 MHz.

General bus troubleshooting

In most cases, you will not be troubleshooting a bus; after all, the bus is little more than a passive connector. However, the major signals that exist on an ISA or EISA bus can provide you with important clues about the system's operation. The most effective bus troubleshooting tool available to you is a POST board (such as the ones covered in Chapter 28). Many POST boards are equipped with a number of LEDs that display power status, along with important timing and control signals. If one or more of those LEDs is missing, a fault has likely occurred somewhere on the motherboard. Refer to Chapter 28 for detailed POST board instructions.

Another point to consider is that bus connectors are mechanical devices. As a result, they do not last forever. If you or your customer are in the habit of removing and inserting boards frequently, it is likely that the metal fingers providing contact will wear and result in unreliable connections. Similarly, inserting a board improperly (or with excessive force) can break the connector. In extreme cases, even the motherboard can be damaged. The first rule of board replacement is: always try removing and reinserting the suspect board. It is common for oxides to develop on board and slot contacts that might eventually degrade signal quality. By removing the board and re-inserting it, you can wipe off any oxides or dust and possibly improve the connections.

The second rule of board replacement is: always try a board in another expansion slot before replacing it. This way, a faulty bus slot can be ruled out before suffering the expense of a new board. If a bus slot proves defective, there is little that a technician can do except:

1. Block the slot and inform the customer that it is damaged and should not be used.
2. Replace the damaged bus slot connector (a tedious and time-consuming task) and pass the labor expense on to the customer.
3. Replace the motherboard outright (also a rather expensive option).

30
CHAPTER

Joysticks and gameports

Few peripheral devices have come to represent PC entertainment like the *joystick* (Fig. 30-1). Although it is one of the simplest peripherals for a PC, the joystick allows a user to bring an element of hand-eye coordination to interactive programs that would simply be impossible with a keyboard or mouse. The joystick interfaces to the host PC through a board called the *gameport adapter* (or simply the gameport). This chapter features the joystick and gameport, then covers a selection of service issues.

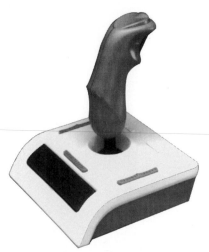

30-1
A Suncom Flightmax joystick. Dan
Zemaitis, Marketing Manager, Suncom Technologies, 6400
W. Gross Point Rd., Niles, IL 60714

Understanding the gameport system

The typical gameport uses a relatively simple interface to the PC. Only the lower 8 data bits are used (which explains why so many gameports still use the older XT-card style rather than switching to a newer AT-card type). Also, only the lower 10 address bits are needed. Because the gameport is an I/O device, the card uses I/OR and

I/OR control signals. On virtually all PCs, port 201h is reserved for the gameport. Figure 30-2 shows a typical gameport system.

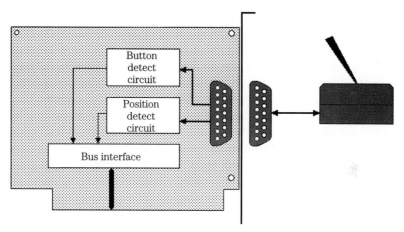

30-2 Simplified diagram of a gameport system.

Inside the joystick

Each analog joystick is assembled with two separate potentiometers (typically 100 kΩ) arranged perpendicularly to one another; one potentiometer represents the X axis, and the other potentiometer represents the Y axis. Both potentiometers are linked together mechanically and attached to a movable stick. As the stick is moved left or right, one potentiometer is moved. As the stick moves up or down, the other potentiometer is moved. Of course, the stick can be moved in both the X and Y axes simultaneously, with the proportions of resistance reflecting the stick's position. You can see the wiring scheme for a standard 15-pin dual joystick port in Fig. 30-3.

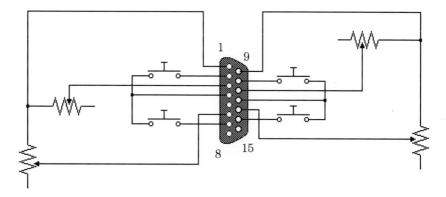

30-3 Wiring diagram for a dual joystick port.

Detecting the stick's X and Y position is not an intuitively obvious process. Ultimately, the analog value of each potentiometer must be converted to a digital value that is read by the application software. This is an important wrinkle because the gameport does not generate an interrupt, it is up to the particular application to interrogate the joystick port regularly. You might imagine that such a conversion would use an *ADC* (analog-to-digital converter). However, an ADC provides much greater resolution than is needed, and its conversions require a relatively long time. Current gameport conversion circuits use a multivibrator element.

Ultimately, the resistance of each potentiometer is determined indirectly by measuring amount of time required for a charged capacitor to discharge through the particular potentiometer. If a certain axis is at 0°, the multivibrator's internal capacitor will discharge in about 24.2 µs, and at 100 kΩ, the multivibrator's capacitor will discharge in about 1124 µs. Because this is a relatively linear relationship, the discharge time can easily be equated to potentiometer position (an actual routine to accomplish this requires only about 16 lines of assembler code). The multivibrator technique also simplifies the circuitry needed on the gameport adapter; it is really the application that is doing the work.

A joystick also has one or two buttons. As shown in Fig. 30-3, the buttons are typically open, and their closed state can be detected by reading the byte at 201h. Because the gameport is capable of supporting two joysticks simultaneously (each with two buttons), the upper four bits of 201h indicate the on/off status of the buttons.

Joystick calibration

Unfortunately, the values of time versus resistance discussed in the previous sections are not the same for every system. Variations in joystick potentiometers, gameport adapter circuits, and computer speed will all affect the relationship of time versus resistance value. This is why each application program that uses a joystick comes with a calibration routine. Calibration allows the application to measure values for center and corner positions. With this data as a base, the application can extrapolate all other joystick positions.

Joystick drift

The term *drift* (or *rolling*) indicates a loss of control by the joystick. There are several possible reasons for this. As a technician, you should understand the reasons why drift occurs, and how to correct such problems. First, drift might be the result of a system conflict. Because the gameport does not generate an interrupt, conflicts rarely result in system crashes or lockups, but another device feeding data to port 201h can easily upset joystick operation. If you have sound boards or multiport I/O boards in your system equipped with gameports, be sure to disable any unused ports (check with the user instructions for individual boards to disable extra game ports).

Another possible cause of drift is because of heat. Once PCs are started up, it is natural for the power used by most components to be dissipated as heat. Unfortunately, heating tends to change the value of components. For logic circuits, this is typically not a problem, but for analog circuits, the consequences can be much more pronounced. As heat changes the values of a multivibrator circuit, timing (and thus positional values) will shift. As the circuit warms up, an error creeps into the joystick. Well-designed gameport adapters will use high-quality, low-drift components that minimize the effects of heat-related drift. It is interesting to note that the joystick itself is rarely the cause of drift. If you can compensate for drift by recalibrating the joystick, try a better-quality gameport adapter board.

Finally, the quality of calibration is only as good as the calibration routine itself. A poor or inaccurate routine will tend to calibrate the joystick incorrectly. Try another application. If another application can calibrate and use the joystick properly, you should suspect a bug in the particular application. Try contacting the application manufacturer to find if there is a patch or fix available.

Cleaning joysticks

Ordinarily, the typical joystick should not require routine cleaning or maintenance. Most joysticks use reasonably reliable potentiometers that should last for the life of the joystick. The two major enemies of a joystick are wear and dust. Wear occurs during normal use as potentiometer sliders move across the resistive surface—it can't be avoided. Over time, wear will affect the contact resistance values of both potentiometers. Uneven wear will result in uneven performance. When this becomes noticeable, it is time to buy a new joystick.

Dust presents another problem. The open aperture at the top of a joystick is an invitation for dust and other debris. Because dust is conductive, it can adversely affect potentiometer values and interfere with slider contacts. If the joystick seems to produce a jumpy or nonlinear response to the application, it might be worth trying to clean the joystick rather than scrapping it. Turn off the computer and disconnect the joystick. Open the joystick that is usually held together by two screws in the bottom housing. Remove the bottom housing and locate the two potentiometers. Most potentiometers have small openings somewhere around their circumference. Dust out the joystick area with compressed air, and spray a small quantity of good-quality electrical contact cleaner into each potentiometer. Move the potentiometer through its complete range of motion a few times, and allow several minutes for the cleaner to dry. Reassemble the housing and try the joystick again. If problems persist, replace the joystick.

Troubleshooting joysticks and gameports

The unique advantage to troubleshooting this area of a PC is that there is surprisingly little to actually go wrong. In virtually all cases, problems reside in either the joystick, the gameport adapter, or the application software. The following are some of the more perplexing joystick system problems.

Symptom 1. The joystick does not respond Make sure that the joystick is plugged into the gameport correctly. When the gameport has more than one connector, be sure that the joystick is plugged into the correct connector. Refer to the application and see that it is configured to run from the joystick (if mouse or keyboard control is selected, the joystick will not function). Now that many new joysticks are appearing with supplemental functions (hat switches, throttle controls, and so on), make sure that the application is written to take advantage of the particular joystick. If problems persist, make sure that the gameport is set for the proper

I/O address (most are fixed at 210h, but check the user documentation to be sure). Try a known-good joystick with the gameport. If a known-good joystick works, the original joystick is defective and should be replaced. If another joystick is not the problem, try a different gameport board.

Symptom 2. Joystick performance is erratic or choppy   Start by checking the joystick to be sure that it is connected properly. Try another joystick. When a new joystick works properly, the original joystick is probably damaged and should be replaced. If a new joystick fails to solve the problem, the gameport board might be too slow for the system. Remember that many gameports still use XT board types. An older board design might not be able to process joystick signals fast enough to provide adequate signaling to the system. Not only should you try another gameport adapter, but you should use a *speed adjusting* gameport.

Symptom 3. The joystick is sending incorrect information to the system; the joystick appears to be drifting   First, check the application to be sure that the joystick is calibrated correctly. If you cannot calibrate the joystick, the application might not support the joystick properly; try another application. Make sure that there are no other active devices in the system (such as other gameports) using I/O port 201h. If this happens, data produced on those other boards will adversely affect the gameport you are using. If all unused gameports are disabled, check the active gameport. Poor-quality gameports can drift. Try a newer, low-drift gameport board.

31
CHAPTER

Keyboards

Keyboards (Fig. 31-1) are the classic input device. By manipulating a matrix of individual electrical switches, commands and instructions can be entered into the computer one character at a time. If you've used computers or typewriters to any extent, you already have an excellent grasp of keyboard handling. However, keyboards are not without their share of drawbacks and limitations. Although today's keyboard switches are not mechanically complex, there are a number of important moving parts. When you multiply this number of moving parts times the 80 to 100-plus keys on a typical keyboard, you are faced with a substantial number of moving parts. A jam or failure in any one of these many mechanical parts results in a keyboard problem. Most keyboard failures are hardly catastrophic, but they can certainly be inconvenient. This chapter gives you the information needed to understand and repair computer keyboards.

Cherry Electrical Products

31-1 A Cherry G83-3000 keyboard.

Keyboard construction

To understand a keyboard, you must first understand the kinds of switches that are used. In general, there are two types of switches that you should be concerned with: *mechanical switches* and *membrane switches*. Both switches are used extensively throughout the computer industry, but any single keyboard will use only one type of switch.

A mechanical key switch is shown in Fig. 31-2. Two tempered bronze contacts are separated by a plastic actuator bar. The bar is pushed up by a spring in the switch base. When the key cap is depressed, the actuator bar slides down. This action compresses the spring and allows the gold-plated contacts to touch. Because gold is a soft metal and an excellent conductor, a good, low-resistance electrical contact is developed. When the key cap is released, the compressed spring expands and drives the plastic actuator bar between the contacts once again. The entire stroke of travel on a mechanical switch is little more than 3.56 mm (0.140 inch), but an electrical contact (a *make* condition) can be established in as little as 1.78 mm (0.070 inch). Mechanical switches are typically quite rugged; many are rated for 100 million cycles or more.

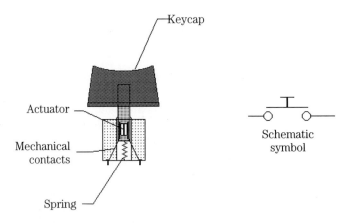

31-2 Drawing of a mechanical switch assembly.

A diagram of a *membrane* key switch is illustrated in Fig. 31-3. A plastic actuator rests on top of a soft rubber boot. Inside the rubber boot is coated with a conductive silver-carbon compound. Beneath the rubber boot are two open PC board contacts. When the key cap is pressed, the plastic actuator collapses the rubber boot. Collapse forces the conductive material across both PC board contacts to complete the switch. When the key cap is released, the compressed rubber boot breaks its contact on the PC board and returns to its original shape. The full travel stroke of a membrane key switch is about 3.56 mm (0.140 inch), roughly the same as a mechanical switch. An electrical contact is established in about 2.29 mm (0.090 inch). Membrane switches are not quite as durable as mechanical switches. Most switches are rated for 20 million cycles or less.

Regardless of which key type is used, the finished assembly appears much like the Cherry keyboard shown in Fig. 31-4. The keyboard contains a matrix of keys, and possibly a number of keyboard control ICs on its small PC board. There also will be one or more connectors on the PC board to connect the keyboard assembly to the motherboard. As you might imagine, keyboard assemblies tend to be very modular

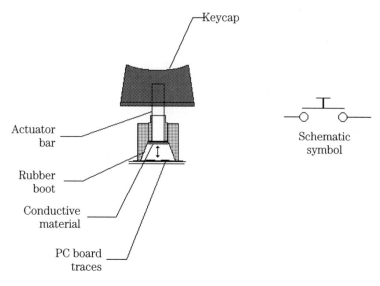

Keycap

Actuator bar

Rubber boot

Conductive material

PC board traces

Schematic symbol

31-3 Drawing of a membrane switch assembly.

Cherry Electrical Products

31-4 A Cherry ML keyswitch assembly.

and self-contained. It is usually a simple matter to access and repair or replace a computer keyboard.

The next step in understanding a keyboard is to learn about the key matrix. Keys are not interpreted individually; that is, each switch is not wired directly to the motherboard. Instead, keys are arranged in a matrix of rows and columns shown in Fig. 31-5. When a key is pressed, a unique row (top to bottom) and column (left to right) signal is generated to represent the corresponding key. The great advantage of a matrix approach is that a huge array of keys can be identified using only a few row and column signals. Wiring from the keyboard is vastly simplified. An 84-key keyboard can be identified using only 12 column signals and 8 row signals.

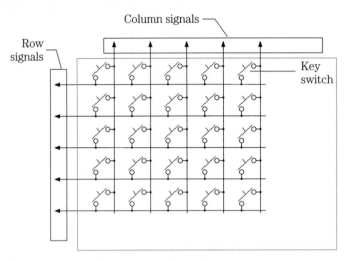

31-5 Simplified diagram of a keyboard matrix.

Key codes

When a key is pressed, the row and column signals that are generated are interpreted by a keyboard interface IC (typically located on the keyboard assembly itself). The keyboard interface converts the row and column signals into a single-byte code (called a *key code* or *scan code*). Two unique scan codes are produced during a key stroke cycle. When the key is pressed, a make code byte is sent along to the system. When the key is released, a break code byte is generated. Both codes are transmitted to the host computer in a serial fashion. For example, a make code of 1Eh is sent when the "A" key is pressed. A 9Eh code is sent when the A key is subsequently released. By using two individual codes, the computer can determine when a key is held down, or when keys are held in combinations. Just about every key on a keyboard is *typematic*, that is, it will repeat automatically if it is held down for more than 500 ms or so. Typematic settings can usually be adjusted in the CMOS advanced settings for your system.

Most computers today are prepared for multinational operation. To accommodate the special characters and punctuation used in various different countries, KBCs can be configured to provide scan codes for different languages. Table 31-1 shows the make and break codes for conventional keyboards used in the United States.

Table 31-1. Standard scan codes for United States keyboards

Key	Make code	Break code	Key	Make code	Break code
A	1E	9E	B	30	B0
C	2E	AE	D	20	A0
E	12	92	F	21	A1
G	22	A2	H	23	A3
I	17	97	J	24	A4
K	25	A5	L	26	A6
M	32	B2	N	31	B1

Table 31-1. Continued

Key	Make code	Break code	Key	Make code	Break code
O	18	98	P	19	99
Q	10	90	R	13	93
S	1F	9F	T	14	94
U	16	96	V	2F	AF
W	11	91	X	2D	AD
Y	15	95	Z	2C	AC
0 /)	0B	8B	1 / !	02	82
2 / @	03	83	3 / #	04	84
4 / $	05	85	5 / %	06	86
6 / ^	07	87	7 / &	08	88
8 / *	09	89	9 / (	0A	8A
. / >	29	A9	- / _	0C	8C
= / +	0D	8D	[	1A	9A
]	1B	9B	; / :	27	A7
' / "	28	A8	, / <	33	B3
/ / ?	35	B5	L Sh	2A	AA
L Ctrl	1D	9D	L Alt	38	B8
R Sh	36	B6	R Alt	E0 38	E0 B8
R Ctrl	E0 1D	E0 9D	Caps	3A	BA
BK SP	0E	8E	Tab	0F	8F
Space	39	B9	Enter	1C	9C
ESC	01	81	F1	3B	BB
F2	3C	BC	F3	3D	BD
F4	3E	BE	F5	3F	BF
F6	40	C0	F7	41	C1
F8	42	C2	F9	43	C3
F10	44	C4	F11	57	D7
F12	58	D8	Up Ar	E0 48	E0 C8
Dn Ar	E0 50	E0 D0	Lt Ar	E0 4B	E0 CB
Rt Ar	E0 4D	E0 CD	Ins	E0 52	E0 D2
Home	E0 47	E0 C7	Pg Up	E0 49	E0 C9
Del	E0 53	E0 D3	End	E0 4F	E0 CF
Pg Dn	E0 51	E0 D1	ScrLk	46	C6

* All MAKE and BREAK codes are given in hexadecimal (hex) values.

* Alphabetic characters represent both upper- and lowercase.

Keyboard interface

Once a key is pressed and the keyboard interface converts the key matrix signals into a suitable scan code, that code must be transmitted to the keyboard controller (KBC) on the host computer motherboard. Once key data reaches the keyboard controller, it is converted to parallel data by the KBC, which in turn generates an interrupt that forces the system to handle the key. The actual transfer of scan codes between the keyboard and PC is accomplished serially using one of the interfaces shown in Fig. 31-6.

IBM PC/XT/AT configuration

6 pin mini-DIN connector

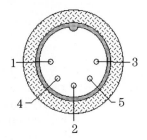
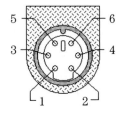

1	KBCLOCK	1	KBDATA
2	KBDATA	2	nc
3	nc	3	Ground
4	Ground	4	+5 Vdc (or +3.0 or +3.3 Vdc)
5	+5 Vdc (or +3.0 or +3.3 Vdc)	5	KBCLOCK
		6	nc

31-6 Keyboard interface connectors.

Note that there are really three important signals in a keyboard interface: the keyboard clock (KBCLOCK), the keyboard data (KBDATA), and the signal ground. Unlike most serial communication that is asynchronous, the transfer of data from keyboard to controller is accomplished synchronously. Data bits are returned in sync with the clock signals. As you might expect, the signal ground provides a common reference for the keyboard and system. The keyboard is powered by +5 Vdc which is also provided through the keyboard interface. It also is important for you to note that most XT-style systems are designed with a unidirectional data path (from keyboard to system). AT-style keyboard interfaces are bidirectional. This feature allows AT keyboards to be controlled and programmed from the PC.

Keyboard cleaning and maintenance

Keyboards are perhaps the most abused part of any computer, yet they are often ignored until serious problems develop. With some regular cleaning and maintenance, however, a keyboard can easily last for the lifetime of a computer. This part of the chapter shows you some practical techniques for keyboard service.

Correcting problem keyboards

Virtually all computer keyboards are open to the air. Over time, everyday dust, pet hair, air vapor, cigar/cigarette smoke, and debris from hands and ordinary use will settle into the keyboard. Eventually, accumulations of this foreign matter will cause keys to stick, or will prevent keys from making proper contact (a key does not work every time it is pressed). In either case, keyboard problems will develop. Fortunately, correcting a finicky keyboard is a relatively straightforward process.

First, start by removing the key caps of the offending keys. *Be sure to note where each key is placed before starting your disassembly, especially if the key-*

board is a DVORAK-type or unusual ergonomic design. To remove a key cap, bend an ordinary paper clip into the shape of a narrow letter U, and bend in small tabs at the tip of the U shape. Slip the small tabs under the key cap and pull up gently. Do not struggle with the key cap. If a cap will not come off, remove one or more adjacent caps. If there is a substantial accumulation of foreign matter in the keyboard, you should consider removing all of the key caps for a thorough cleaning, but this requires more time. *Don't* remove the space bar unless it is absolutely necessary, because the space bar is often much more difficult to replace than ordinary keys.

Flip the keyboard upside down and rap gently on the case. This will loosen and dislodge any larger, heavier foreign matter, and allow it to fall out of the keyboard. A soft-bristled brush will help loosen the debris. Return the keyboard to an upright position. Use a can of compressed air (available from almost any electronics or photography store) to blow out the remainder of foreign matter. Because this tends to blow dust and debris in all directions, you might wish to use the compressed air outside or in an area away from your workbench. A medium or firm-bristled brush will help loosen any stubborn debris.

Now that the keyboard is cleaned out, squirt a small amount of good-quality electronics-grade contact cleaner (also available from almost any electronics store) into each key contact, and work the key to distribute the cleaner evenly. Allow a few minutes for the contact cleaner to dry completely, and test the keyboard again before reinstalling the key caps. If the problems persist, the keyboard might be damaged, or the individual key(s) might simply be worn out. In such an event, replace the keyboard outright.

Vacuum cleaners and keyboards

There is an ongoing debate as to the safety of vacuum cleaners with computer equipment. The problem is static discharge. Many vacuum cleaners—especially small, inexpensive models—use cheap plastic and synthetic fabrics in their construction. When a fast air flow passes over those materials, a static charge is developed (just like combing your hair with a plastic comb). If the charged vacuum touches the keyboard, a static discharge might have enough potential to damage the keyboard controller IC, or even travel back into the motherboard for more serious damage.

If you do choose to use a vacuum for keyboard cleaning, take these two steps to prevent damage. First, make sure that the computer is powered down and disconnect the keyboard from the computer before starting service. If a static discharge does occur, the most that would be damaged is the keyboard itself. Second, use a vacuum cleaner that is made for electronics work and certified as static safe. Third, try working on an antistatic mat (such as the mat in Fig. 31-7) that is properly grounded. This will tend to bleed-off static charges before they can enter the keyboard or PC.

Replacing the spacebar

Of all the keys on the keyboard, replacing the spacebar is probably the most difficult. The spacebar is kept even by a metal wire that is inserted into slots on each

Curtis, a division of Rolodex, Secaucus, NJ 07094

31-7
A Curtis antistatic
keyboard mat.

leg of the bar. However, you have to get the wire into the slots without depressing the wire. If you push the wire down, you compress the wire and installation becomes impossible. As a general rule, do not remove the spacebar unless absolutely necessary. If you must remove the spacebar, remove several surrounding key caps also. This will let you get some tools under the spacebar wire later on. Once the spacebar is reinserted, you can easily replace any of the other key caps.

Preventing the problems

Keyboard problems do not happen suddenly (unless the keyboard is dropped or physically abused). The accumulation of dust and debris is a slow process that can take months, sometimes years, to produce serious, repetitive keyboard problems. By following a regimen of regular cleaning, you can stop problems before they manifest themselves in your keyboard. In normal office environments, keyboards should be cleaned once every four months. Keyboards in home environments should be cleaned every two months. Keyboards in harsh or industrial environments should be cleaned even more frequently.

Turn your keyboard upside-down and use a soft-bristled brush to clean between the keys. This prevents debris that might already be on the keys from entering the keyboard. Next, run the long, thin nozzle of your compressed air can between the key spaces to blow out any accumulations of dust. Because compressed air will tend to blow dust in all directions, you might consider *blowing down* the keyboard outside, or in an area away from your workbench. Instead of compressed air, you might use a static-safe vacuum cleaner to remove dust and debris.

Dealing with large objects

Staples and paper clips pose a clear and present danger to keyboards. Although the odds of a staple or paper clip finding its way into a keyboard are generally slight, foreign objects can jam the key, or short it out. If the keyboard is moved, the object can wind up in the keyboard's circuitry where serious damage can occur. When a foreign object falls into the keyboard, *do not move the keyboard*. Locate the object and find the nearest key. Use a paper clip bent in a letter U shape with the ends of the U angled inward to remove the nearest key cap. Use a pair of nonconductive tweezers or needle-nose pliers to remove the object. Replace the key cap.

Dealing with spills

Accidental spills are probably the most serious and dangerous keyboard problem. Coffee, soda, and even tap water is highly conductive (even corrosive). Your keyboard will almost certainly short circuit. Immediately shut down your computer (you might be able to exit your application using a mouse) and disconnect the keyboard. The popular tactic is to simply let the liquid dry. The problem is that most liquids contain minerals and materials that are corrosive to metals—your keyboard will never be the same unless the offending liquid is removed before it dries.

Disassemble the keyboard's main housings and remove the keyboard printed circuit assembly. As quickly as you can after the incident, rinse the assembly thoroughly in clean, room-temperature, demineralized water (available from any pharmacy for contact lens cleaning). You can clean the plastic housings separately. *Do not use tap water.* Let the assembly drip dry in air. *Do not attempt to accelerate the drying process with a hair dryer or other such heat source.* The demineralized water should dry clean without mineral deposits or any sticky, conductive residue. Once the assembly is dry, you might wish to squirt a small amount of good-quality, electronics-grade contact cleaner into each key switch to ensure no residue on the contacts.

Assuming that the keyboard's circuitry was not damaged by the initial spill, you should be able to reassemble the keyboard and continue using it without problems. If the keyboard behaves erratically, or not at all, replace the keyboard outright.

Keyboard troubleshooting

Although their appearance might seem daunting at first glance, keyboard systems are not terribly difficult to troubleshoot. This ease is primarily due to the keyboard's modularity; if all else fails, it's a simple matter to replace a keyboard outright. The keyboard's great weakness, however, is its vulnerability to the elements. Spills, dust, and any other foreign matter that finds its way between the key caps can easily ruin a keyboard. The keyboard's PC board also is a likely candidate to be damaged by impacts or other physical abuse. The following procedures address many of the most troublesome keyboard problems.

Symptom 1. During initialization, you see an error message indicating that there is no keyboard connected Check your keyboard cable and see that it is inserted properly and completely into the PC connector. Remember that you will have to reboot your system to clear this error message. Try another compatible keyboard. If a new keyboard assembly works properly, there is probably a wiring fault in the original keyboard. Given the very low price of new keyboards, it is usually most economical to simply replace a defective keyboard.

If a known-good keyboard fails to function, try the original keyboard on a known-good PC to verify that the keyboard itself is indeed operational. If so, your trouble now lies in the PC. Check the wiring between the PC keyboard connector and the motherboard. Check the connector pins to make sure that none of them have been bent or pushed in (resulting in a bad connection). You also might want to check the soldering connections where the keyboard connector attaches to the motherboard. Repeated removals and insertions of the keyboard might have fatigued the solder joints. Reheat any defective solder joints. If the keyboard connector is intact, it is likely that the *KBC* (keyboard controller IC) has failed. Try booting the PC with a POST board installed (as discussed in Chapter 28). A KBC failure will usually be indicated by the system stopping on the appropriate POST code. You can attempt to replace the KBC, or replace the motherboard outright. If a POST board indicates a fault other than a KBC (such as the programmable interrupt controller that manages the KBC's interrupt), you can attempt to replace that component, or simply exchange the motherboard anyway.

Symptom 2. During initialization, you see an error message indicating that the keyboard lock is on In many cases, the detection of a locked keyboard will halt system initialization. Make sure that the keyboard lock switch is set completely to the unlocked position. If the switch is unlocked, but the system detects it as locked, the switch might be defective. Turn off and unplug the system, then use a multimeter to measure continuity across the lock switch (you might need to disconnect the lock switch cable from the motherboard). In one position, the switch should measure as an open circuit. In the opposing position, the switch should measure as a short circuit. If this is not the case, the lock switch is probably bad and should be replaced. If the switch measures properly, there is probably a logic fault on the motherboard (perhaps the keyboard controller). Your best course is to try another motherboard.

Symptom 3. The keyboard is completely dead—no keys appear to function at all All other computer operations are normal. This symptom assumes that your computer initializes and boots to its DOS prompt or other operating system as expected, but the keyboard does not respond when touched. Keyboard status LEDs might or might not be working properly. Your first step in such a situation is to try a known-good keyboard in the system. Note that you should reboot the system when a keyboard is replaced. If a known-good keyboard works, the fault is probably on the keyboard interface IC. You can attempt to replace this IC if you wish, but it is often most economical to simply replace the keyboard outright.

If another keyboard fails to correct the problem, use a multimeter and check the +5-Vdc supply at the keyboard connector (refer to Fig. 31-6). If the +5-Vdc signal is missing, the female connector might be broken. Check the connector's soldering junctions on the motherboard. Reheat any connectors that appear fatigued or intermittent. If problems continue, replace the motherboard.

Symptom 4. The keyboard is acting erratically. One or more keys appear to work intermittently, or are inoperative The computer operates normally and most keys work just fine, but there seems to be one or more keys that do not respond when pressed. Extra force or repeated strikes might be needed to operate the key. This type of problem can usually range from a minor nuisance to a major headache. Chances are that your key contacts are dirty. Sooner or later, dust and debris works into all key switches. Electrical contacts eventually become coated and fail to make contact reliably. This symptom is typical of older keyboards, or keyboards that have been in service for prolonged periods of time. In many cases, you need only vacuum the keyboard and clean the suspect contacts with a good-quality electronic contact cleaner.

Begin by disconnecting the keyboard. Use a static-safe, fine-tipped vacuum to remove any accumulations of dust or debris that might have accumulated on the keyboard PC board. You might wish to vacuum your keyboard regularly as preventive maintenance. Once the keyboard is clean, *gently* remove the plastic key cap from the offending key(s). The use of a keycap removal tool is highly recommended, but you also might use a modified set of blunt-ended tweezers with their flat ends (just the tips) bent inward. Grasp the key cap and pull up evenly. You can expect the cap to slide off with little resistance. Do not rip the key cap off; you stand a good chance of marring the cap and causing permanent key switch damage.

Use a can of good-quality electronics-grade contact cleaner and spray a little bit of cleaner into the switch assembly. When spraying, attach the long narrow tube to the spray nozzle; this directs cleaner into the switch. Work the switch in and out to distribute the cleaner. Repeat once or twice to clean the switch thoroughly. Allow residual cleaner to dry thoroughly before retesting the keyboard. *Never use harsh cleaners or solvents.* Industrial-strength chemicals can easily ruin plastic components and housings. Re-apply power and re-test the system. If the suspect key(s) respond normally again, install the removed key caps and return the system to service. As a preventive measure, you might wish to go through the process of cleaning every key.

Membrane keys must be cleaned somewhat differently from mechanical keys. It is necessary for you to remove the rubber or plastic boot to clean the PC board contacts. Depending on the design of your particular membrane switch, this might not be an easy task. If you are able to see the contact boot, use a pick or tweezers to gently lift the boot. Spray a bit of cleaner under the boot, then work the key to distribute the cleaner. If the boot is confined within the individual key, you might have to remove the suspect key before applying cleaner.

If cleaning does not work, your next step should be to disassemble the keyboard and replace the defective key switch(es). Observe the board closely for cracks or fractures. Many key switch designs still utilize through-hole technology, but you should exercise extreme care when desoldering and resoldering. Extra care helps prevent accidental damage to the PC keyboard. You also have the more economical option of replacing the entire keyboard assembly outright.

Symptom 5. The keyboard is acting erratically. One or more keys might be stuck or repeating Suspect a shorted or jammed key. Short circuits can be caused by conductive foreign objects (such as staples or paper clips) falling into the keyboard and landing across PC board contacts. Remove all power and disassemble the keyboard housing assembly. Once the keyboard is exposed, shake out the foreign object or remove it with a pair of long needle-nose pliers or sharp tweezers.

Accumulations of dirt or debris can work into the key actuator shaft and restrict its movement. Apply good-quality electronics-grade cleaners to the key, and work the key in and out to distribute cleaner evenly. If the key returns to normal, you might reassemble the computer and return it to service. Keys that remain jammed should be replaced. If you cannot clear the jammed key, simply replace the entire keyboard assembly outright. If you elect to replace the keyboard assembly, retain the old assembly for parts—key caps, good switches, and cable assemblies can be scavenged for use in future repairs.

Symptom 6. You see "KBC Error" (or similar message) displayed during system startup When your small computer initializes, either from a warm or cold start, it executes a comprehensive self-test routine that checks the key ICs in the system (the CPU, memory, drive controllers, and so on). As part of this power-on self-test (POST) routine, the computer looks for the KBCLK signal, along with a series of test scan codes generated by the KB controller IC (you can see the keyboard LEDs flash as the controller sequences through its codes). If either the keyboard clock or keyboard data signals are missing, the POST knows that either the keyboard is disconnected, or the keyboard controller has failed. If you are using a POST board, it will probably be displaying a code corresponding to a KBC error. Unless you have the tools and inclination to replace a KBC controller IC, your best course is simply to replace the motherboard outright.

32
CHAPTER

Laser/LED printers

EP (electrophotographic) printers are fundamentally different from traditional moving-carriage printers (such as ink jet or dot-matrix). Those conventional printers develop dots as a one-step process moving a discrete print head across a page surface. EP printers (Fig. 32-1) are not nearly as simple. EP images are formed by a complex and delicate interaction of light, static electricity, chemistry, pressure, and heat; all guided by a sophisticated *ECE* (electronic control unit). This chapter details the background of EP technology, and provides you with a series of image formation troubleshooting procedures.

Hewlett-Packard Company

32-1 The HP LaserJet 4MP.

Understanding electrophotographic operation

Electrophotographic printing is accomplished through a process rather than a print head. The collection of components that performs the EP printing process is called an *IFS* (image formation system). An IFS is made up of eight distinctive areas: a photosensitive drum (#14), cleaning blade, erasure lamp (#3), primary corona (#4), writing mechanism (#5 and 6), toner, transfer corona (#13), and fusing rollers (#18 and 19). Each of these parts, as shown in Fig. 32-2, play an important role in the proper operation of an IFS.

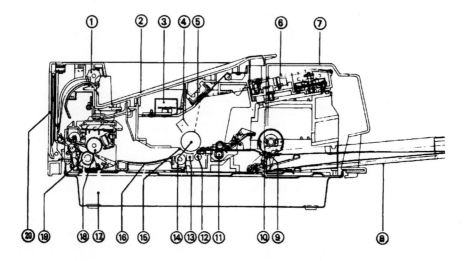

1. Delivery Assembly	11. Registration Rollers
2. Face-Down Tray	12. Transfer Corona Roller
3. Erase Lamp Assembly	13. Transfer Corona Assembly
4. Primary Corona	14. Photosensitive EP Drum
5. Beam-to-Drum Mirror	15. EP Drum Protective Shield
6. Laser/Scanning Assembly	16. Feed Guide Assembly
7. Main Body Covers	17. Lower Main Body
8. Paper Tray	18. Upper Fusing Roller
9. Separation Pad	19. Lower Pressure Roller
10. Feed Roller Assembly	20. Face-Up Output Tray (Closed)

32-2 Cross-section of an HP LaserJet-type printer. Hewlett-Packard Company

A *photosensitive drum* is generally considered to be the heart of any IFS. An extruded aluminum cylinder is coated with a nontoxic organic compound that exhibits photo-conductive properties. That is, the coating will conduct electricity when exposed to light. The aluminum base cylinder is connected to ground of the high-voltage power supply. It is the drum that actually receives an image from a writing mechanism, develops the image with toner, then transfers the developed image to paper. Although you might think that this constitutes a print head because it delivers an image to paper, the image is not yet permanent—other operations must be performed by the IFS. Complete image development is a six-step process that involves all eight IFS components: cleaning, charging, writing, developing, transfer, and fusing. To really understand the IFS, you should know each of these steps in detail.

Cleaning

Before a new printing cycle can begin, the photosensitive drum must be physically cleaned and electrically erased. Cleaning might sound like a rather unimportant step, but not even the best drum will transfer every microscopic granule of toner to a page every time. A rubber cleaning blade is applied across the entire length of the drum to gently scrape away any residual toner that might remain from a previous image. If residual toner were not cleaned, it could adhere to subsequent pages and appear as random black speckles. Toner that is removed from the drum is deposited into a debris cavity as shown in Fig. 32-3. Keep in mind that cleaning *must* be accomplished without scratching or nicking the drum. Any damage to the drum's photosensitive surface would become a permanent mark that appears on every subsequent page. Some EP printer designs actually return scrap toner back to the supply for reuse. This kind of recycling technique can extend the life of your *EP* (electrophotographic) cartridge and eliminate the need for a large debris cavity.

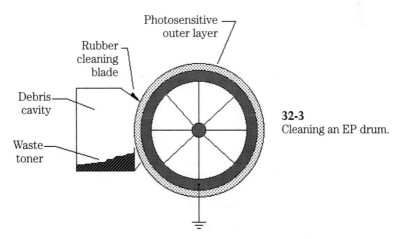

32-3
Cleaning an EP drum.

Images are written to a drum's surface as horizontal rows of electrical charges that correspond to the image being printed. A dot of light causes a relatively positive charge at that point. This corresponds to a visual dot in the completed image. Absence of light allows a relatively negative charge to remain and no dots are generated. The charges caused by light must be removed before any new images can be written, otherwise images would overwrite and superimpose on one another. A series of erase lamps are placed in close proximity to the drum's surface. Their light is filtered to allow only effective wavelengths to pass. Erase light bleeds away any charges along the drum. Charges are carried to ground through the aluminum cylinder as shown in Fig. 32-4. After erasure, the drum's surface is completely neutral; it contains no charges at all.

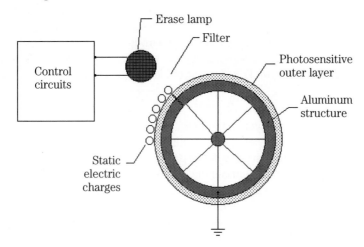

32-4 Erasing all charges from an EP drum.

Charging

A neutral drum surface is no longer receptive to light from the writing mechanism. New images cannot be written until the drum is charged again. In order to charge (or *condition*) the drum, a uniform electrical charge must be applied evenly across its entire surface. Surface charging is accomplished by applying a tremendous negative voltage (often more than –6000 V) to a solid wire called a *primary corona* located close to the drum. Because the drum and high-voltage power supply share the same ground, an electrical field is established between the corona wire and drum as in Fig. 32-5.

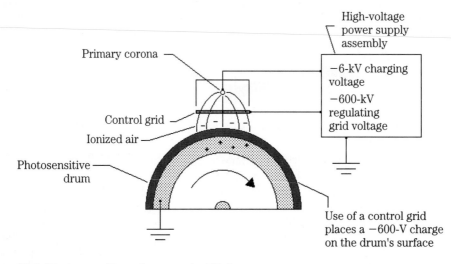

32-5 Placing a uniform charge on the EP drum.

For low voltages, the air gap between a corona wire and drum would act as an insulator. With thousands of volts of potential, however, the insulating strength of air breaks down and an electric *corona* forms. A corona ionizes any air molecules surrounding the wire, so negative charges migrate to the drum's surface. The trouble with ionized gas is that it exhibits a very low resistance to current flow. Once a corona is established, there is essentially a short-circuit between the wire and drum. This is not good for a high-voltage power supply. A *primary grid* (part of the primary corona assembly) is added between the wire and drum. By applying a negative voltage to the grid, charging voltage and current to the drum can be carefully regulated. This regulating grid voltage (often -600 to -1000 V) sets the charge level actually applied to the drum that is typically equal to the regulating voltage (-600 to -1000 V). The drum is now ready to receive a new image.

Writing

In order to form a latent image on a drum surface, the uniform charge that has conditioned the drum must be discharged in the precise points where images are to be produced. Images are written using light. Any points on the drum exposed to light will discharge to a very low level (about -100 V), and any areas left unexposed retain their conditioning charge (-600 to -1000 V). The device that produces and directs light to the drum surface is called a *writing mechanism*. Because images are formed as a series of individual dots, a larger number of dots per area will allow finer resolution (and higher quality) of the image.

For example, suppose a writing mechanism can place 300 dots per inch along a single horizontal line on the drum, and the drum can rotate in increments of $\frac{1}{300}$ of an inch. This means your printer can develop images with a resolution of 300×300 dots per inch (DPI). Current EP printers are reaching 600×600 DPI. Lasers have been traditionally used as writing mechanisms (thus the name *laser printer*), and are still used in many EP printer designs, but new printers are replacing lasers with bars of microscopic light-emitting diodes (LEDs) to direct light as needed. Once an image has been written to a drum, that image must be developed.

Developing

Images written to the drum by laser or LED are initially invisible, merely an array of electrostatic charges on the drum's surface. There are low charges where the light strikes, and high charges where the light skips. The latent image must be developed into a visible one before it can be transferred to paper. *Toner* is used for this purpose. Toner itself is an extremely fine powder of plastic resin and organic compounds bonded to iron particles. Individual granules can be seen under extreme magnification of a microscope.

Toner is applied using a toner cylinder (or developer roller) as shown in Fig. 32-6. A toner cylinder is basically a long metal sleeve containing a permanent magnet. It is mounted inside the toner supply trough. When the cylinder turns, iron in the toner attracts it to the cylinder. Once attracted, toner acquires a negative static charge provided by the high-voltage power supply. This static charge level falls between the photosensitive drum's exposed and unexposed charge levels (anywhere from -200

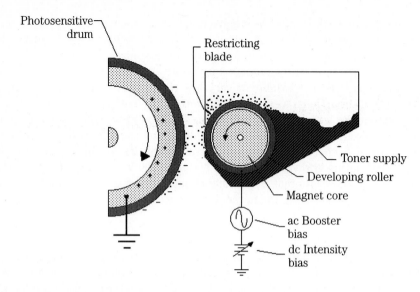

Photosensitive drum

Restricting blade

Toner supply

Developing roller

Magnet core

ac Booster bias

dc Intensity bias

32-6 Developing the latent drum image with toner.

to –500 V depending in the intensity control setting). A restricting blade limits toner on the cylinder to just a single layer.

Charged toner on the cylinder now rotates into close proximity with the exposed drum. Any points on the drum that are not exposed will have a strong negative charge. This repels toner that remains on the toner cylinder and is returned to the supply. Any points on the drum that are exposed now have a much lower charge than the toner particles. This attracts toner from the cylinder to corresponding points on the drum. Toner "fills-in" the latent image to form a visible (or developed) image.

Notice that an ac booster bias (more than 1500 Vpp) is added in series to the dc intensity bias. Alternating current causes strong fluctuations in the toner's charge level. As the ac signal goes positive, the intensity level increases to help toner particles overcome attraction of the cylinder's permanent magnet. As the ac signal goes negative, intensity levels decrease to pull back any toner particles that might have falsely jumped to unexposed areas. This technique greatly improves print density and image contrast. The developed image can now be applied to paper.

Transfer

At this point, the developed toner image on the drum must be transferred onto paper. Because toner is now attracted to the drum, it must be pried away by applying an even larger attractive charge to the page. A transfer corona wire charges the page as shown in Fig. 32-7. The theory behind the operation of a transfer corona is exactly the same as that for a primary corona, except that the potential is now positive. This places a powerful positive charge onto paper that attracts the negatively charged toner particles. Remember that this is not a perfect process; not all toner is transferred to paper. This is why a cleaning process is needed.

Caution is needed here. Because the negatively charged drum and positively charged paper tend to attract each other, it is possible that paper could wrap around

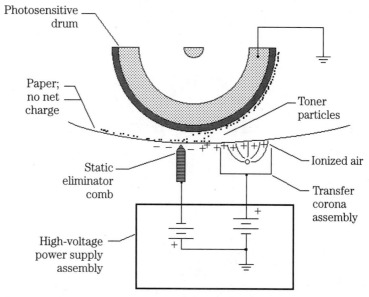

32-7 Transferring the developed image to paper.

the drum. Even though the small-diameter drum and natural stiffness of paper tend to prevent wrapping, a static charge eliminator (or *static-eliminator comb*) is included to counteract positive charges and remove the attractive force between paper and drum immediately after toner is transferred. Paper now has no net charge. The drum can be cleaned and prepared for a new image.

Fusing

Once the toner image has reached paper, it is only held to the page by gravity and weak electrostatic attraction; toner is still in its powder form. Toner must be fixed permanently (or *fused*) to the page before it can be handled. Fusing is accomplished with a heat and pressure assembly like the one shown in Fig. 32-8. A high-intensity quartz lamp heats a nonstick roller to about 180°C. Pressure is applied with a pliable rubber roller. When a developed page is passed between these two rollers, heat from the top roller melts the toner, and pressure from the bottom roller squeezes molten toner into the paper fibers where it cools and adheres permanently. The finished page is then fed to an output tray. Note that both rollers are referred to as fusing rollers, even though only the heated top roller actually fuses. To prevent toner particles from sticking to a fusing roller, it is coated with a nonstick material such as Teflon. A cleaning pad is added to wipe away any toner that may yet adhere. The pad also applies a thin coating of silicon oil to prevent further sticking.

Fusing temperature must be carefully controlled. Often a thermistor is used to regulate current through the quartz lamp in order to maintain a constant temperature. A snap-action thermal switch also is included as a safety interlock in the event that lamp temperature should rise out of control. If temperature is not controlled carefully, a failure could result in printer damage, or even a fire hazard.

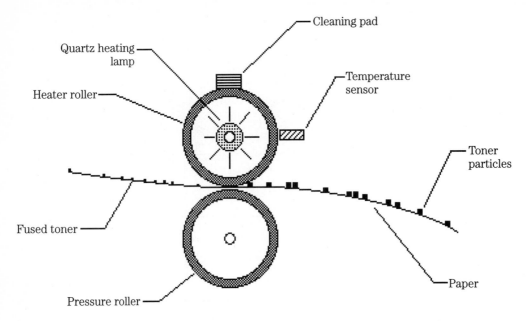

32-8 Fusing the toner image to the page.

Understanding writing mechanisms

After charging, the photosensitive drum contains a uniform electrostatic charge across its surface. In order to form a latent image, the drum must be discharged at any points that comprise the image. Light is used to discharge the drum as needed. Such a *writing mechanism* is shown in Fig. 32-9. Images are scanned onto the drum one horizontal line at a time. A single pass across the drum is called a *trace* or *scan line*. Light is directed to any points along the scan line where dots are required. When a scan line is completed, the drum increments in preparation for another scan line. It is up to the printer's control circuits to break down an image into individual scan lines, then direct the writing mechanism accordingly.

Lasers

Lasers have been around since the early 1960s, and since have developed to the point where they can be manufactured in a great variety of shapes, sizes, and power output. To understand why lasers make such a useful writing mechanism, you must understand the difference between laser light and ordinary white light. Ordinary white light is actually not white. The light you see is composed of many different wavelengths, each traveling in their own directions. When these various wavelengths combine, they do so virtually at random. This makes everyday light very difficult to direct and almost impossible to control as a fine beam. As an example, take a flashlight and direct it at a far wall. You will see just how much white light can scatter and disperse over a relatively small distance.

The nature of laser light, however, is much different. A laser beam contains only one major wavelength of light (it is *monochromatic*). Each ray travels in the same

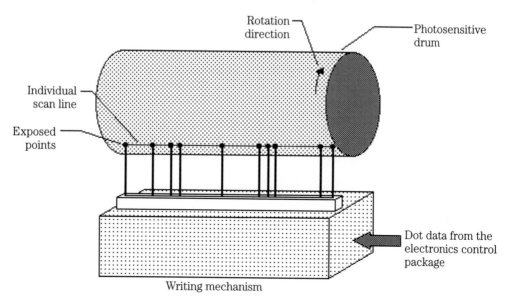

32-9 Simplified diagram of a generic writing mechanism.

direction and combines in an additive fashion (known as *coherence*). These characteristics make laser light easy to direct at a target as a hair-thin beam, with almost no scatter (or *divergence*). Older EP printers used helium-neon (HeNe) gas lasers, but strong semiconductor laser diodes have essentially replaced gas lasers in just about all laser printing applications.

Laser diodes appear very similar to ordinary light-emitting diodes. When the appropriate amount of voltage and current is applied to a laser diode, photons of light will be liberated that have the characteristics of laser light (coherent, monochromatic, and low divergence). A small lens window (or *laser aperture*) allows light to escape, and helps to focus the beam. Laser diodes are not very efficient devices; a great deal of power is required to generate a much smaller amount of light power, but this trade-off is usually worthwhile for the small size, light weight, and high reliability of a semiconductor laser.

Generating a laser beam is only the beginning. The beam must be modulated (turned on and off) while being swept across the drum's surface. Beam modulation can be accomplished by turning the laser on and off as needed (usually done with semiconductor laser diodes) as shown in Fig. 32-10, or by interrupting a continuous beam with an electro-optical switch (typically used with gas lasers that are difficult to switch on and off rapidly). Mirrors are used to alter the direction of the laser beam, and lenses are used to focus the beam and maintain a low divergence at all points along the beam path. Figure 32-10 is just one illustration of a laser writing mechanism, but it shows some of the complexity that is involved. The weight of glass lenses, mirrors, and their shock mountings have kept EP laser printers bulky and expensive.

Alignment has always been an unavoidable problem in complex optical systems such as Fig. 32-10. Consider what might happen to the beam if any optical compo-

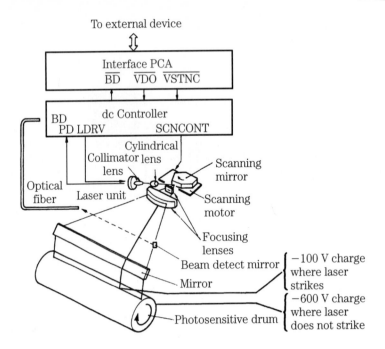

To external device

Interface PCA
$\overline{BD}$ $\overline{VDO}$ $\overline{VSTNC}$

dc Controller
BD
PD LDRV   SCNCONT

Cylindrical
Collimator lens
lens

Optical
fiber   Laser unit

Scanning
mirror

Scanning
motor

Focusing
lenses

Beam detect mirror

Mirror

Photosensitive drum

−100 V charge
where laser
strikes

−600 V charge
where laser
does not strike

32-10 A LaserJet-type laser scanning assembly. Hewlett-Packard Company

nent should become damaged or fall out of alignment; focus and direction problems could render a drum image unintelligible. Realignment of optical systems is virtually impossible without special alignment tools, and is beyond the scope of this book. Finally, printing speed is limited by the speed of moving parts, and the rate at which the laser beam can be modulated and moved.

LEDs

Fortunately, a laser printer's photosensitive drum is receptive to light from many different sources. Even light from light-emitting diodes (LEDs) can expose the drum. By fabricating a series of microscopic LEDs into a single scan line, an LED can be provided for every possible dot in a scan line. For example, the ROHM JE3008SS02 is an LED print bar containing 2560 microscopic LEDs over 8.53 inches. This equates to 300 dots per inch. Each LED is just 50×65 micro-meters (μm) and they are spaced 84.6 μm apart. The operation of an LED print bar is remarkably straightforward. An entire series of data bits corresponding to each possible dot in a horizontal line is shifted into internal digital circuitry within the print bar. Dots that will be visible are represented by a logic 1, and dots that are not visible will remain at logic 0. For a device such as the JE3008SS02, 2560 bits must be entered for each scan line.

You can probably see the advantages of an LED print bar system over a laser approach. There are no moving parts involved in light delivery; no mirror motor to jam or wear out. The printer can operate at much higher speeds because it does not have to overcome the dynamic limitations of moving parts. There is only one focusing lens between the print bar and drum. This greatly simplifies the optics assembly, and removes substantial weight and bulk from the printer. An LED system overcomes almost all alignment problems, so a defective assembly can be replaced or aligned quickly and easily.

The electrophotographic cartridge

Electrostatic printers mandate the use of extremely tight manufacturing tolerances to ensure precise, consistent operation. A defect of even a few thousandths of an inch could cause unacceptable image formation. Even the effects of normal mechanical wear can have an adverse effect on print quality. Many key IFS components would have to be replaced every 5000 to 10,000 pages to maintain acceptable performance. Clearly it would be undesirable to send your printer away for a complete (and time-consuming) overhaul every 10,000 pages.

In order to ease manufacturing difficulties and provide fast, affordable maintenance to every EP printer user, critical components of the IFS, as well as a supply of toner, are assembled into a replaceable electrophotographic (or EP) cartridge. As Fig. 32-11 shows, a typical EP cartridge contains the toner roller, toner supply, debris cavity, primary corona (and primary grid), photosensitive drum, and cleaning blade assembly. All necessary electrical connectors and drive gears are included. By assembling sensitive components into a single replaceable cartridge, printer reliabil-

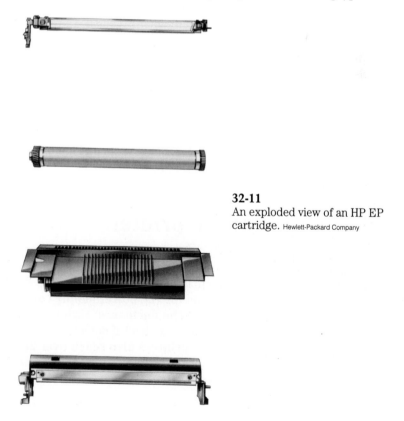

32-11
An exploded view of an HP EP
cartridge. Hewlett-Packard Company

ity is substantially improved by preventing problems before they ever become noticeable. The cost of an EP cartridge is low enough to consider it a disposable part.

A typical EP cartridge is capable of producing 200 to 5000 printed pages. The exact number varies depending upon just how much toner is available, and which critical parts are placed in the cartridge. Highly integrated EP cartridges will last longer than simple toner cartridges. Because toner is comprised partially of organic materials, it has a limited useful life (often 6 months after the cartridge is removed from its sealed container).

Protecting an EP cartridge

As you might imagine, the precision components in an EP cartridge are sensitive and delicate. The photosensitive drum and toner supply are particularly sensitive to light and environmental conditions, so it is important to follow several handling and storage guidelines.

First, the photosensitive drum is coated with an organic material that is extremely sensitive to light. Although a metal shroud covers the drum when the cartridge is exposed, light can still penetrate the shroud and cause exposure (also known as *fogging*). Deactivating the printer for a time will often eliminate mild fogging. *Do not defeat the shroud in the open light unless absolutely necessary, and then only for short periods.* This action will certainly fog the drum. A seriously fogged cartridge might have to be placed in a dark area for several days. *Never* expose the drum to direct sunlight; direct sunlight can permanently damage the drum's coating.

Next, avoid extremes of temperature and humidity. Temperatures exceeding 40°C can permanently damage an EP cartridge. Extreme humidity is just about as dangerous. Do not allow the cartridge to become exposed to ammonia vapors or other organic solvent vapors; they break down the drum's coating VERY quickly. Finally, keep a cartridge secure and level. Never allow it to be dropped or abused in any way.

Finally, as the toner supply diminishes, it might be necessary to redistribute remaining toner so that it reaches the toner roller. Because toner is available along the entire cartridge, it must be redistributed by rocking the cartridge back and forth along its long axis. If you tip a cartridge upright, remaining toner will fall to one end and cause uneven distribution.

Troubleshooting an EP printer

Now that you have an understanding of EP technology, the following sections of the chapter will present a series of printer problems and solutions. Before you begin troubleshooting, however, a word of caution is in order. **Shock warning: Be sure to unplug the printer and allow ample time for the power supply (or supplies) to discharge before attempting to open the enclosure**. High-voltage supplies are especially dangerous, and can result in a nasty shock if not allowed to discharge. **Burn warning: Fusing assemblies in EP printers also reach over 200°F during normal operation. Even when opening the EP printer for routine maintenance, allow ample time for the fuser to cool (at least 10 minutes) before reaching inside.**

System start-up problems

EP printers perform a self-test on start-up to ensure that the ECU is active and responding normally. The self-test also checks communication between the printer and host computer. After the self-test is passed, the fusing assembly must reach upwards of 180°C within 90 seconds. When a self-test and warm-up occur normally, the printer is generally ready to operate as long as paper and toner are detected. Unfortunately, printer start-ups are not always so smooth. This part of the chapter details the symptoms and solutions for the most perplexing start-up problems.

Symptom 1. Nothing happens when power is turned on You should hear the printer respond as soon as power is turned on. You should see a power indicator on the control panel (alphanumeric displays will typically read "self-test"). You also should hear and feel the printer's cooling fan(s) in operation. If the printer remains dead, there is probably trouble with the ac power. Check the ac line cord for proper connection with the printer and wall outlet. Try the printer in a known-good ac outlet. Also check the printer's main ac fuse. When the ac and fuse check properly, there is probably a problem with the printer's power supply.

If the printer's fan(s) and power indicator operate, you can be confident that the printer is receiving power. If the control panel remains blank, there might be a problem with the dc power supply or ECU. You might troubleshoot or replace the dc power supply at your discretion. When the power supply checks properly, the trouble is likely somewhere in the ECU or control panel assembly itself. Remove power from the printer and check the control panel cable. If there are no indicators at all on the control panel, replace the control panel cable. If problems remain, try replacing the ECU. When only one or a few indicators appear on the control panel, try replacing the control panel cable. If problems remain, replace the control panel.

Symptom 2. Your printer never leaves its warm-up mode. There is a continuous WARMING UP status code or message The initial self-test usually takes no more than 10 seconds from the time power is first applied. The fusing roller assembly then must warm up to a working temperature, and is typically acceptable within 90 seconds from a cold start. At that point, the printer will establish communication with the host computer and stand by to accept data, so its WARMING UP code should change to an ON-LINE or READY code.

When the printer fails to go on line, it is generally the result of a faulty communication interface, or a control panel problem. Turn the printer off, disconnect its communication cable, and restore power. If the printer finally becomes ready without its communication cable, check the cable itself and its connection between the computer and printer. The cable might be faulty, or you might have plugged a parallel printer into the computer's serial port (or vice versa). There also might be a faulty interface in your host computer or printer. Try a known-good printer with the computer to ensure that the computer port is working correctly.

If the printer still fails to become ready with the communication cable disconnected, unplug the printer and check that the control panel cables or interconnecting wiring are attached properly. Try reseating or replacing the control panel cable. Check the control panel to see that it is operating correctly. Try replacing the control panel. If problems persist, replace the ECU, which usually contains the control panel interface circuitry. Depending on the complexity of your particular printer, the interface/formatter might be a separate printed circuit plugged into the main logic board, or its functions might be incorporated right into the main logic board itself.

Symptom 3. You see a CHECKSUM ERROR message indicating a fault has been detected in the ECU program ROM During a self-test, the ECU will test its program ROM to see that it is working properly. This is typically a checksum test of ROM contents. If the calculated checksum does not match with the checksum recorded on ROM, an error is generated. A checksum error usually indicates a failure of the ECU's ROM device. Try powering down the printer. Wait several minutes, then restore power. If the problem persists, try replacing the printer's ROM IC(s) if possible. Otherwise, replace the ECU or its interface/formatter module.

Symptom 4. You see an error indicating communication problems between the printer and computer The printer and computer are not communicating properly. This symptom is typical in serial communication setups when baud rates or serial transfer protocols do not match exactly. Check your serial communication cable first. Make sure that the cable is installed properly. Also make sure that it is the correct type and is wired properly for your printer. Keep in mind that pins 2 and 3 on the printer cable might need to be reversed for proper operation. If the pins must be reversed, use a *null modem* (available from almost any consumer electronics store) on the printer end of the cable. Also be aware of the cable length. Serial communication cables are typically limited to 15 meters (50 feet), and Centronics (parallel) cables are limited to 3 meters (10 feet). Try a shorter cable if necessary.

There are five communication parameters that must match between the host computer and printer: start bits, stop bits, data bits, parity type, and baud rate. If any one of these parameters do not match, communication will not take place. At the printer end, there are usually DIP switch settings or control panel key sequences that define each parameter (you might need to refer to the user's manual for the printer to determine how each parameter is set). At the computer end, you can usually set communication parameters directly through the application software that is doing the printing. Change parameters if necessary to set both printer and computer to the same parameters. Reboot the printer and computer.

Check that both the printer and computer are using the same serial flow control. Flow control is important because the host computer often must wait for the printer to catch up. XON/XOFF (software) and DTR/DSR (hardware) flow control are typically used. Adjust the printer or computer so that both use the same transfer flow control. Reboot the printer and computer. If the printer still fails to operate (and you are certain that the computer is communicating properly), the communications port is probably defective. Try replacing the ECU or interface module.

Laser delivery problems

Once the photosensitive drum obtains a uniform electrical charge from the primary corona, a latent image is written to the drum surface. Writing is accomplished by discharging desired points along the drum surface with directed light. The classic method of writing is to scan a laser beam across the drum surface as shown in Fig. 32-12. This is where the term *laser print* comes from. The laser beam originates at

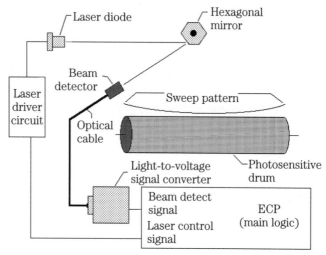

32-12 Scanning a laser beam across a drum surface.

a single stationary point in the printer, and is directed at a hexagonal mirror that is rotated at high speed. As a mirror rotates, the laser beam is directed (or scanned) through a compensating lens and across the drum's surface. By turning the laser beam on and off corresponding to the presence or absence of dots along any one scan line, the desired bit-image is written one line at a time. Typical laser printers can turn the laser on or off 300 times in any inch of scan line. When a scan line is completed, the drum rotates $\frac{1}{300}$ of an inch, and the next scan line begins. This is what determines the printer's overall resolution (300 × 300 DPI in this case).

Symptom 1. You see a BEAM DETECTION error At the beginning of every scan line, the laser beam strikes an optical beam sensor. This registers the start of a new scan line and ensures that the data composing the new scan line is synchronized with the beam. In most cases, the beam sensor is the only feedback that synchronizes the scan line and tells the laser printer that its laser is working. From time to time, unexpected variations in mirror rotation speed, age of the laser source, or the eventual buildup of dust or debris on laser optics might cause the beam to miss its sensor. When this occurs, the printer will register an error; the scan line will probably be missing on the printed page, but the error is usually recoverable.

If you find that the printer is registering random and occasional beam detection errors, check the printer's optics. Printers with long service lifetimes might have accumulated enough dust or debris on the optics or beam sensor face to reduce beam power just enough to produce intermittent problems. Use a can of photography-grade compressed air and gently try blowing the dust away. If contamination refuses to clear, use lint-free, photography-grade wipes lightly dampened with high-quality, photography-grade lens cleaners to wipe the lenses. *Remember to be very gentle— take your time and let the wipe do the work.* If you knock optics out of alignment, it will be virtually impossible to realign them again without factory service. If you scratch the lens, it will be permanently damaged. You would have to have the lens replaced and realigned.

If the optics look good, the laser source might be failing. Older laser printers use a small, gas-filled helium-neon laser to produce the beam. Over time, the helium-neon gas will escape and laser power will fall off. In that case, the laser will have to be replaced and realigned (which requires factory service). Most current laser printers use solid-state laser diodes as the laser source. The semiconductor laser is combined with some switching and control circuitry and incorporated into a laser assembly along with the scanning mirror and scanner motor. This is called the *LS* (laser/scanning assembly). Because the L/S assembly is completely prefabricated and designed as a replaceable component, it can be replaced outright with little risk of alignment problems.

Use extreme caution whenever working with laser beams. Although the beam is invisible to the human eye and contains only a few milliwatts (mW) of power, looking directly at the beam (or reflections of the beam from other objects) can cause eye injury. Refer to warnings listed on the laser/scanning assembly for specific instructions.

Symptom 2. You see a BEAM LOST error Although intermittent beam loss might result in a recoverable beam detection error, a prolonged loss of the laser beam (more than two seconds) will result in a more severe printer fault. There are many possible causes of laser loss. Start by checking each voltage at the dc power supply. Most supplies mark their output levels, so you can check each output with a multimeter. If any dc level is low or absent, you can troubleshoot or replace the supply. Check all connectors between the laser/scanning assembly and the printer to be sure that each is seated properly. Pay particular attention to the fiberoptic cable running from the L/S assembly to the ECU. This is the cable that carries laser light to the detector. If this cable is loose, damaged, or disconnected, little or no laser signal will be delivered to the ECU.

There is a mechanical interlock (a shutter) that blocks the laser aperture whenever the printer's case is opened. If the mechanical interlock becomes stuck or damaged, no laser beam will be available. Check the mechanical interlock carefully. You might have to remove the laser/scanning assembly in order to check the interlock. If the interlock is damaged, it will have to be replaced.

In most cases, the solid-state laser diode in the laser/scanning assembly has failed, or the scanning mirror motor had stopped working. In either case, replace the L/S assembly outright, and make sure to reattach each cable properly and completely.

Symptom 3. You see a SCAN BUFFER error Remember that the laser beam must be turned on and off as the beam is scanned across the drum surface. Each dot across the image corresponds to the presence or absence of a bit in memory (called the *laser buffer*). As the laser sweeps across the drum, contents of the laser buffer are used to turn the laser on and off. If there is a problem with laser buffer memory, an error message will be generated. In many cases, this is an intermittent fault that occurs randomly. Simply power down the printer, allow several minutes for it to clear, and reboot the printer again. If the problem persists, replace the ECU.

Fusing assembly problems

Once a toner image has been transferred from the drum to the page, toner must be permanently fixed (or fused) to the paper's fiber. This is accomplished using heat and pressure produced by a fusing assembly as shown in Fig. 32-13. In its simplest form, a fusing assembly is composed of five major parts: a heating roller, a pressure roller, a quartz heating lamp, a cleaning pad, and a temperature sensor. Although there is certainly other hardware in the assembly, these are the parts that are actually doing the work.

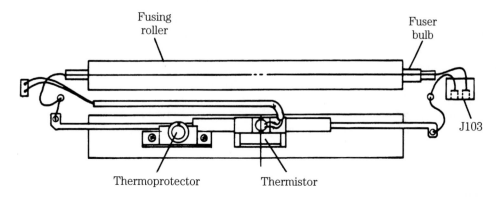

Fusing roller

Fuser bulb

J103

Thermoprotector   Thermistor

32-13 A protected fusing assembly. Hewlett-Packard Company

Paper passes between the two rollers. The bottom roller simply provides pressure against the top roller. The top roller is heated from the inside by a long, thin quartz lamp powered by your printer's ac supply. Although the top roller is made with a material that prevents toner from sticking, some toner particles will inevitably stick. If those particles are not cleaned away, they could stick on later parts of the page and cause problems. A cleaning pad is included in the fusing assembly to wipe off any toner particles on the heating roller. Many manufacturers provide an easily replaceable cleaning pad that can be changed when a new toner cartridge is installed. Finally, a temperature sensor (usually a thermistor) is included with the assembly in order to regulate the heat being applied to the page.

Symptom 1. You see a SERVICE error indicating a fusing malfunction Fusing is integral to the successful operation of any EP printer. Toner that is not fused successfully remains a powder or crust that can flake or rub off onto your hands or other pages. Main logic interprets the temperature signal developed by the thermistor and modulates ac power to the quartz lamp. Three conditions will generate a fusing malfunction error: (1) fusing roller temperature falls below about 140°C, (2) fusing roller temperature climbs above 230°C, or (3) fusing roller temperature does not reach 165°C in 90 seconds after the printer is powered up. Your particular printer might utilize slightly different temperature and timing parameters. When such an error occurs, your first action should be to power down the printer and reboot. Note that a fusing error will often remain with a printer for 10 minutes or so after it is powered down, so be sure to allow plenty of time for the system to cool before rebooting after a fusing error.

If the error persists, power down the printer and examine the installation of your fusing assembly. Check to see that all wiring and connectors are tight and seated properly. An ac power supply is often equipped with a fuse or circuit breaker that protects the printer. If this fuse or circuit breaker is open, replace your fuse or reset your circuit breaker, then retest the printer. Remember to clear the error, or allow enough time for the error to clear by itself. If the fuse or breaker trips again during retest, you have a serious short circuit in your fusing assembly or ac power supply. You can attempt to isolate the short circuit, or simply replace your suspected assemblies. Replace the ac power supply first; then the fusing assembly.

Unplug the printer and check your temperature sensor thermistor by measuring its resistance with a multimeter. At room temperature, the thermistor should read about 1 kΩ (depending on the particular thermistor). If the printer has been at running temperature, thermistor resistance might be much lower. If the thermistor appears open or shorted, replace it with an exact replacement part and retest the printer.

A thermal switch (sometimes called a *thermoprotector*) is added in series with the fusing lamp. If a thermistor or main logic failure should allow temperature to climb out of control, the thermal switch will open and break the circuit once it senses temperatures over its preset threshold. This protects the printer from severe damage and possibly a fire hazard. Unplug the printer, disconnect the thermal switch from the fusing lamp circuit, and measure its continuity with a multimeter. The switch should normally be closed. If you find an open switch, it should be replaced. Check the quartz lamp next by measuring continuity across the bulb itself. If you read an open circuit, replace the quartz lamp (or the entire fusing assembly). Be sure to secure any disconnected wires. If the printer still does not reach its desired temperature, or continuously opens the thermal switch, there is probably a fault in the ECU. Try replacing the ECU.

Image-formation problems

There are many variables at work in the formation of an electrophotographic image, so even though the printer might be operating within safe limits where no error messages are generated, the printed image might not be formed properly. Although print quality is always a subjective decision, there are certain physical characteristics in EP printing that signal trouble in image formation. It is virtually impossible to define every possible image formation problem, but this part of the chapter illustrates a broad range of basic symptoms that can tell you where to look for trouble.

Symptom 1. Pages are completely blacked out, and might appear blotched with an undefined border (Fig. 32-14) Unplug the printer, remove the EP cartridge, and examine its primary corona wire. A primary corona applies an even charge across a drum surface. This charge readily repels toner, except at those points exposed to light by the writing mechanism that attract toner. A failure in the primary corona will prevent charge development on the drum. As a result, the entire drum surface will tend to attract toner (even if your writing mechanism works perfectly). This creates a totally black image. If you find a broken or fouled corona wire, clean the wire or replace the EP cartridge.

If your blacked-out page shows print with sharp, clearly defined borders, your writing mechanism might be running out of control. LEDs in a solid-state print bar or laser beam might be shorted in an on condition, or receiving erroneous data bits from its control circuitry (all logic 1s). In this case, the primary corona is working

32-14
Page is blacked out.

just fine, but a writing mechanism that is always on will effectively expose the entire drum and discharge whatever charge was applied by the primary corona. The net result of attracting toner would be the same, but whatever image is formed would probably appear crisper, more deliberate. Your best course here is to simply replace the ECU. If the problem persists, try another writing mechanism.

Symptom 2. Print is very faint (Fig. 32-15) Before attempting anything else, try adjusting the printer's contrast control. If that fails to help, unplug the printer, remove the EP cartridge, and try redistributing toner in the cartridge. Your user's manual probably offers preferred instructions for redistributing toner. Remember that toner is largely organic, as such it has only a limited shelf and useful life. If redistribution temporarily or partially improves the image, or if the EP cartridge has been in service for more than six months, replace the EP cartridge. If you are using a paper with a moisture content, finish, or conductivity that is not acceptable, image formation might not take place properly.

32-15
Print is very faint.

Check your transfer corona. It is the transfer corona that applies a charge to paper that pulls toner off the drum. A weak transfer corona might not apply enough charge to attract all the toner in a drum image. This can result in very faint images. *Unplug the printer, allow ample time for the high-voltage power supply to discharge completely, then inspect all wiring and connections at the transfer corona.* If the monofilament line encircling the transfer corona is damaged, replace the transfer corona assembly, or attempt to rethread the monofilament line. If faint images persist, repair or replace the high-voltage power supply assembly. Finally, check the drum ground contacts to be sure that they are secure. Dirty or damaged ground contacts will not readily allow exposed drum areas to discharge. As a result, very little toner will be attracted and only faint images will result.

Symptom 3. Print appears speckled (Fig. 32-16) Your first step should be to power down the printer and check the cleaning pad on the fusing roller. A pad that is old or well-worn will not wipe the roller properly and should be replaced. Replace the cleaning pad if necessary and retest the printer. If the cleaning pad checks out, speckled print is probably the result of a fault in your primary corona grid. A grid is essentially a fine wire mesh between the primary corona and drum surface. A constant voltage applied across the grid serves to regulate the charge applied to the drum to establish a more consistent charge distribution. Grid failure will allow much higher charge levels to be applied unevenly. This results in dark splotches in the print. Because the primary grid assembly is part of the EP cartridge, replace the EP cartridge and retest the printer. If speckled print persists, repair or replace the high-voltage power supply assembly.

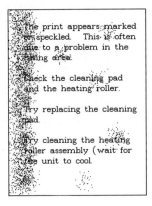

32-16
Print appears speckled or dirty.

Symptom 4. There are one or more vertical white streaks in the print (Fig. 32-17) Begin by checking your toner level. Toner might be distributed unevenly along the cartridge's length. Unplug the printer, remove the EP cartridge, and

32-17
One or more white streaks in the print.

redistribute the toner. Follow your manufacturer's recommendations when handling the EP cartridge. If this improves your print quality (at least temporarily), you know that the EP cartridge must be replaced soon.

Next, examine your transfer corona for areas of blockage or extreme contamination. Such faults would prevent the transfer corona from generating an even charge along its length; corrosion acts as an insulator that reduces the corona's electric field. Uncharged page areas will not attract toner from the drum, so those page areas will remain white. Clean the transfer corona very carefully with a clean cotton swab. If your printer comes with a corona cleaning tool, use that instead. When cleaning, be sure to avoid the monofilament line wrapped around the transfer corona assembly. If the line breaks, it will have to be rewrapped, or the entire transfer corona assembly will have to be replaced.

Check the optics for any accumulation of dust or debris that could block out sections of light. Because EP drums are only scanned as fine horizontal lines, it would take little more than a fragment of debris to block light through a focusing lens. Gently blow off any dust or debris with a can of high-quality, photography-grade compressed air available from any photography store. For stains or stubborn debris, clean the afflicted lens gently with high-quality, lint-free wipes and lens cleaner from any photography store. *Be very careful not to dislodge the lens from its mounting. Never blow on a lens or mirror yourself—breath vapor and particles can condense and dry on a lens to cause even more problems in the future.*

Symptom 5. Right-hand text appears missing or distorted (Fig. 32-18) In many cases, this is simply a manifestation of low toner in your EP cartridge. If any area of the development roller receives insufficient toner, it will result in very light or missing image areas. Unplug the printer, remove the EP cartridge, and redistribute the toner. Follow your manufacturer's recommendations for toner redistribution. If you see an improvement in image quality (at least temporarily), replace the EP cartridge.

32-18
Right-most text appears missing or distorted.

Examine the mountings that support your writing mechanism. The mechanism, along with its associated optics, is usually mounted to a removable cover. Make sure that the writing mechanism (laser or LED) is mounted correctly, and that its cover is closed completely. If the writing mechanism is not mounted correctly, scan lines might not be delivered to the proper drum locations. Try replacing the writing mechanism. If you are using a laser writing mechanism, pay special attention to the installation and alignment of the laser/scanning assembly. If the assembly is not installed with the correct alignment, the scanning beam might start or stop at different points along the drum. An end portion of the image might be distorted or missing. Reseat or replace any incorrectly positioned laser/scanning assembly. If you are working with an older laser printer, check the alignment of the scanning mirror.

Symptom 6. You consistently encounter faulty image registration (Fig. 32-19) Paper sheets are drawn into the printer by a pickup roller, and held by a set of registration rollers until a drum image is ready to be transferred to paper. Under normal circumstances, the leading edge of paper will be matched (or *registered*) precisely with the beginning of a drum image. Poor paper quality, mechanical wear, and paper path obstructions can all contribute to registration problems.

```
There is faulty image
registration in the printed
image.   The paper may be
of the wrong weight,  finish,
or moisture content.   Try
new paper in the printer.

If the problem persists,
check the registration
assembly for damage or
wear.   Try replacing the
registration assembly
```

32-19
The image does not register properly.

Begin by inspecting your paper and paper tray assembly. Unusual or specialized paper might not work properly in your paper transport system (this also can lead to PAPER JAM errors). Check the paper specifications for your printer listed in your user's manual. If you find that the paper is nonstandard, try about 50 sheets of standard-bond xerographic paper and retest the printer. Because paper is fed from a central paper tray, any obstructions or damage to the tray can adversely affect page registration (or even cause paper jams). Examine your tray carefully. Correct any damage or restrictions that you might find, or replace the entire tray outright.

If registration is still incorrect, it usually suggests mechanical wear in your paper feed assembly. Check the pickup roller assembly first. Look for signs of excessive roller wear. Remove your printer housings to expose the paper transport system. You will have to defeat any housing interlock switches, and perhaps the EP cartridge sensitivity switches. Perform a self-test and watch paper as it moves through the printer. The paper pickup roller should grab a page and move it about 3 inches or more into the printer before registration rollers activate. If the pickup roller clutch solenoid turns on, but the pickup roller fails to turn immediately, your pickup assembly is worn out. The recommended procedure is to simply replace the pickup assembly, but you might be able to adjust the pickup roller or clutch tension to somewhat improve printer performance.

Another common problem is wear in the registration roller assembly. If this set of rollers does not grab the waiting page and pull it through evenly at the proper time, misregistration also can occur. As you initiate a printer self-test, watch the action of your registration rollers. They should engage immediately after the pickup roller stops turning. If the registration clutch solenoid activates, but paper does not move immediately, your registration roller assembly is worn out. The recommended procedure is to simply replace the registration assembly, but you might be able to adjust torsion spring tensions to somewhat improve printer performance.

Pay particular attention to the components in your drive train assembly. Dirty or damaged gears can jam or slip. This leads to erratic paper movement and faulty registration. Clean your drive train gears with a clean, soft cloth. Use a cotton swab to clean gear teeth and tight spaces. Remove any objects or debris that might block the drive train, and replace any gears that are damaged.

Symptom 7. You encounter horizontal black lines spaced randomly through the print (Fig. 32-20) Remember that black areas are ultimately the result of light striking the drum. If your printer uses a laser writing mechanism, a defective or improperly seated beam detector could send false scan timing signals to the main logic. The laser would make its scan line while main logic waits to send its data. At the beginning of each scan cycle, the laser beam strikes a detector. The detector carries laser light through an optical fiber to a circuit that converts light into an electronic logic signal that is compatible with main logic. Main logic interprets this beam detect signal and knows the scanner mirror is properly aligned to begin a new scan. Main logic then modulates the laser beam on and off corresponding to the presence or absence of dots in the scan line.

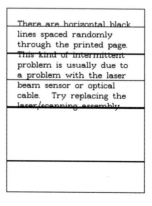

32-20
One or more horizontal black lines appear in the print.

Positioning and alignment is crucial here. If the beam detector is misaligned or loose, the printer's motor vibrations might cause the detector to occasionally miss the beam. Main logic responds to this by activating the laser full-time in an effort to synchronize itself again. Reseat or replace the beam detector and optical fiber. A loose or misaligned laser/scanning assembly also can cause this type of problem. Vibrations in the mirror might occasionally deflect the beam around the detector. Realign, reseat, or replace the laser/scanning assembly.

Symptom 8. Print is just slightly faint Print that is only slightly faint does not necessarily suggest a serious problem. There are a series of fairly simple checks that can narrow down the problem. Check the print contrast control dial. Turn the dial to a lower setting to increase contrast (or whatever darker setting there is for your particular printer). If the contrast control has little or no effect, your high-voltage power supply is probably failing. Replace your high-voltage power supply.

Check your paper supply. Unusual or specially-coated paper might cause fused toner images to appear faint. If you are unsure about the paper currently in the printer, insert a good-quality, standard-weight xerographic paper and test the printer again. Next, check your toner level. Unplug the printer, remove the EP cartridge, and redistribute toner. Follow all manufacturer's recommendations when it comes to redistributing toner. The toner supply might just be slightly low at the developing roller.

Unplug your printer and examine the EP cartridge sensitivity switch settings. These microswitches are actuated by molded tabs attached to your EP cartridge. This tab configuration represents the relative sensitivity of the drum. Main logic uses this code to set the power level of its writing mechanism to ensure optimum print quality. These switches also tell main logic whether an EP cartridge is installed at all. If one of these tabs is broken, or if a switch has failed, the drum might not be receiving enough light energy to achieve proper contrast. Try a different EP cartridge.

Over time, natural dust particles in the air will be attracted to the transfer corona and accumulate there. This eventually causes a layer of debris to form on the wire. This type of accumulation cuts down on transfer corona effectiveness, which places less of a charge on paper. Less toner is pulled from the drum, so the resulting image appears fainter. Unplug the printer, allow ample time for the high-voltage power supply to discharge, then gently clean the transfer corona with a clean cotton swab or corona cleaning tool. Be very careful NOT to break the monofilament line wrapped about the transfer corona assembly. If this line does break, the transfer corona assembly will have to be rewrapped or replaced.

Symptom 9. Print has a rough or suede appearance (Fig. 32-21) In almost all cases, "suede" print is the result of a serious failure in the main logic system (ECU). The writing mechanism is being allowed to turn on and off randomly during its scanning cycles. This type of symptom is dominant in laser printers where a faulty laser driver can allow the beam to act erratically. Your best course is usually to replace the ECU outright. If problems persist, replace the laser/scanner assembly.

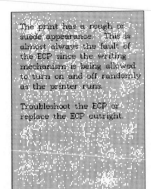

32-21
Print appears rough or suede.

Symptom 10. Print appears smeared or fused improperly (Fig. 32-22) Temperature and pressure are two key variables of the EP printing process. Toner

The print appears smeared or fused improperly.

The fusing assembly is probably defective. Try replacing the fusing assembly.

32-22
Print appears smudged or fused improperly.

must be melted and bonded to a page in order to fix an image permanently. If fusing temperature or roller pressure is too low during the fusing operation, toner might remain in its powder form. Resulting images can be smeared or smudged with a touch.

Perform a simple fusing check by running a number of continuous self-tests (the printer does not have to be disassembled for this). After about ten printouts, place the first and last printout on a firm surface and rub both surfaces with your fingertips. No smearing should occur. If your fusing level varies between pages (one page might smear, and another might not), clean the thermistor temperature sensor and repeat this test. *Remember to let the printer cool for 10 minutes or so before working on the fusing assembly.* If fusing performance does not improve, replace the fusing assembly and cleaning pads. If problems continue, replace the ECU.

Static teeth just beyond your transfer corona are used to discharge the paper once toner has been attracted away from the drum. This helps paper to clear the drum without being attracted to it. An even charge is needed to discharge paper evenly, otherwise, some portions of the page might retain a local charge. As paper moves toward the fusing assembly, remaining charge forces might shift some toner resulting in an image that does not smear to the touch, but has a smeared or pulled appearance. Examine the static discharge comb once the printer is unplugged and discharged. If any of its teeth are bent or missing, replace the comb.

A cleaning pad rubs against the fusing roller to wipe away any accumulations of toner particles or dust. If this pad is worn out or missing, contamination of the fusing roller can be transferred to the page, resulting in smeared print. Check your cleaning pad in the fusing assembly. Worn out or missing pads should be replaced immediately.

Inspect your drive train for any gears that show signs of damage or excessive wear. Slipping gears could allow the EP drum and paper to move at different speeds. This can easily cause portions of an image to appear smudged; such areas would appear bolder or darker than other portions of the image. Replace any gears that you find to be defective. If you do not find any defective drive train components, try replacing the EP cartridge. Finally, a foreign object in the paper path can rub against a toner powder image and smudge it before fusing. Check the paper path and remove any debris or paper fragments that might be interfering with the image.

Symptom 11. Printed images appear to be distorted (Fig. 32-23) Distortion is at best a vague term when applied to printed images, but for the purpose of this

Image distortion is shown
by characters which
appear too large or small
in the vertical direction

Scanning distortion is
typically the result of
a laser/scanning
assembly problem

32-23
The image appears distorted.

symptom, you might see one of two types of distortion: image size distortion, and scanning distortion.

Image size distortion is indicated when characters appear too large or too small in the vertical direction. Large (or stretched) characters suggest that some portion of the pickup or registration assemblies is failing, or that there is some obstruction in the paper path causing excessive drag on the paper. Characters that are too small (or squashed) suggest a main motor problem; it might be moving the drum too fast.

Examine your pickup and registration assemblies for signs of unusual wear and replace any rollers or other mechanics that appear worn or damaged. Also inspect your EP cartridge. If the cartridge is very new or very old, it might be worth trying a replacement cartridge. If characters appear compressed, check your main motor and motor drive signals. Finally, look for any debris or obstructions that might interfere with drive train operation. Remove any obstructions immediately.

Scanning distortion (found in laser printers) is indicated by wavy, irregularly-shaped characters. This wavy distortion also can be seen in the page's margins. In most cases, a marginal scanning motor causes minor variations in scanning speed (the motor speeds up and slows down erratically). For example, consecutive horizontal scan lines will not appear parallel. If all connectors and interconnecting wiring to the laser/scanning assembly appear correct, simply replace the laser/scanning assembly outright. If you are working on an older laser printer, you can probably replace the mirror scanner assembly as a separate unit.

Symptom 12. Print shows regular or repetitive defects (Fig. 32-24) Repetitive defects are problems that occur at regular intervals along a page (as opposed to random defects) and are most often the result of roller problems. Rollers have fixed circumferences, so as paper moves through the printer, any one point on a roller might reach a page several times. For example, if a drum has a circumference (not a diameter) of 3 inches, any one point on the drum will reach a standard 8.5-x-11 inch page up to three times. If the drum is damaged or marked at that point, those imperfections will repeat regularly in the finished image.

Many repetitive defects take place in the EP cartridge that contains the photosensitive drum and developing roller. A typical drum has a circumference of about 3.75 inches. Defects that occur at that interval can often be attributed to a drum defect. A developing roller has a circumference of about 2 inches, so problems that re-

Repetitive defects occur
when rollers in the printer
are damaged or fouled
with debris or toner

The best solution is to
determine the problem
location, then clean the
offending roller or replace
the roller outright.

32-24
Regular or repetitive defects.

peat every 2 inches are usually associated with the developing roller. In either case, replace the EP cartridge and retest the printer.

A fusing roller has a circumference of about 3 inches. Image marks or defects at that interval suggest a dirty or damaged fusion roller. *Unplug the printer, allow at least 10 minutes for the fusion assembly to cool, then gently clean the fusion rollers.* If you find that the fusion rollers are physically damaged or are unable to clean them effectively, replace the fusing roller assembly. Any roller that is fouled with debris or toner particles can contribute to a repeating pattern of defects. Make sure to examine each of your rollers carefully. Clean or replace any roller that you find to be causing marks.

Symptom 13. The page appears completely black except for horizontal white stripes (Fig. 32-25) This symptom indicates an intermittent loss of the laser beam either in the laser/scanning assembly itself or in the fiberoptic detector cable. If the printer cannot detect the laser beam, the laser will fire full-duty as the printer tries to re-establish synchronization. This will expose the drum and result in black print. The white lines indicate that synchronization is briefly restored. Your first action should be to check the fiberoptic cable between the laser/scanning assembly and the ECU. If the cable appears to be connected properly, it should be replaced. Note that you also might see a BEAM DETECTION error with this type of problem. If the problem persists, the trouble is probably due to a defect in the laser/scanner assembly. Try replacing the laser/scanner assembly outright.

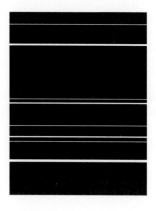

32-25
The page is black except for random white stripes.

Symptom 14. The image appears skewed (Fig. 32-26) Image skew is usually the result of a problem in the paper path; something is happening as paper travels through the printer. Start by checking the paper tray. Make sure that the right type and weight of paper is installed properly in the tray (the tray might be overfilled). Remove and reseat the paper tray to be sure that it is inserted evenly and completely. Try switching trays with another compatible printer.

> The image seems to be skewed at one or more points along the page.
>
> This is usually the result of some sort of physical obstruction in the paper handling path.
>
> Check the paper path and clear any obstructions that you may find.

32-26
Image appears skewed at one or more points.

If the paper and tray both appear intact, unplug the printer and open the outer covers. Inspect the paper pickup roller for signs of unusual or uneven wear. If the pickup roller is uneven, paper will walk (or skew) before it reaches the registration rollers. When you find a worn or damaged paper pickup roller, you might be able to adjust the roller's tension mechanism to compensate, but you are usually best advised to simply replace the paper pickup assembly.

If the paper pickup assembly looks good, check the registration roller assembly next. Registration rollers hold the page in place until the latent drum image is positioned properly for the page. As with the paper pickup, a worn or damaged registration assembly will allow the page to skip or walk as it is being passed through the printer. Note that the registration assembly uses torsion springs to ensure even pressure across the rollers. A missing or defective spring can result in uneven pressure. If you find uneven pressure, you can readjust the torsion springs, but your best course (especially for older printers) is to replace the registration roller assembly outright.

If the problem persists, there is probably an obstruction somewhere in the paper path. You will need to examine the paper path very carefully in order to look for obstructions. Stuck labels and paper fragments are typical causes. Gently clear any obstructions that you find; be very careful not to damage any rollers or mechanisms in the process of clearing an obstruction.

Symptom 15. The image is sized improperly The EP printer's control circuitry sizes an image based on the paper in the tray. Start by checking the software application to be sure that the image is set to the proper size initially. Printers use a series of microswitches that are actuated by a specially shaped tab attached to each tray, and each tray uses a differently shaped tab to actuate these tray-detect switches in a unique sequence. Make sure that each tray is fitted with the proper tab for the tray being used. If the tray is fitted with the proper tab, there might be a problem with the printer's tray-detect microswitches. Either the switches or ECU might be at fault.

Symptom 16. There are vertical black streaks in the image (Fig. 32-27)
This symptom is indicated by one or more dark vertical lines. Each line might be a different width, but the width of each line will remain constant throughout the length of the page. In most cases, you will find that the primary corona is dirty. Any gunk or debris that accumulates on the primary corona will prevent an even charge distribution. Fortunately, this problem can be rectified simply by cleaning the primary corona wire. Use care when cleaning the primary corona. If it breaks, the EP cartridge will have to be replaced. If the primary corona is clean but the problem persists, there might be a manufacturing problem with the EP cartridge itself. Nicks or manufacturing defects around the development roller can allow much more toner in proximity of the drum. Try a new EP cartridge. For LED printers, there might be a problem with the scan line buffer memory. A scan line buffer holds the individual pixels that will ultimately appear in the line. If a new EP cartridge does not solve the problem, try replacing the ECU in order to exchange the scan line memory.

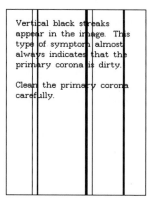

32-27
One or more vertical black stripes appear in the image.

33
CHAPTER

LCD assemblies

Traditional computer monitors have been based on the CRT. Although CRTs have evolved to meet the demands of improved resolution and color depth, they are still limited by their unwieldy size, weight, and heavy power consumption—certainly undesirable factors for mobile computing. Flat-panel displays (based on *liquid crystal* technology) offer the small size, light weight, reasonably low power consumption, and general ruggedness that are ideal for notebook, palmtop, and pen systems. Concerns about the environment and monitor emissions have even pushed flat-panel displays into use as desktop monitors. Given the growing importance of mobile computers, liquid crystal displays (or LCDs) will become even more important in the coming years. This chapter will show you the technology behind LCDs, and present a series of display troubleshooting procedures.

Flat-panel display characteristics

Before jumping right into detailed discussions of flat-panel display technologies, it would be helpful for you to have a clear understanding of an LCD's major characteristics. This part of the chapter also presents a set of cautions to ensure safe display handling. Even if you are already familiar with flat-panel specifications, take a moment to review their handling precautions.

Pixel organization

As with CRT-based displays, the images formed on a flat-panel display are not solid images. Instead, images are formed as an array of individual picture elements (*pixels*). Pixels are arranged into a matrix of columns (top-to-bottom) and rows (left-to-right) as shown in Fig. 33-1. Each pixel corresponds to a location in video RAM (not core memory that holds programs and data). As data is written into video RAM, pixels in the array will turn on and off. The on/off patterns that appear in the array form letters and graphics.

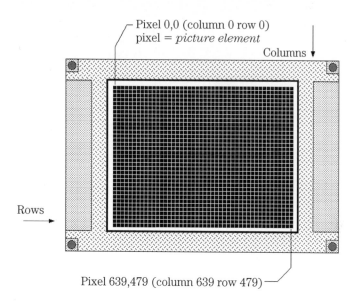

33-1 Flat-panel display organization.

The resolution of a flat-panel display is little more than the number of pixels that can be displayed. More pixels allow the display to present finer, higher-quality images. As an example, many notebook computer displays are capable of showing 307,200 dots arranged in a standard VGA array of 640 columns by 480 rows [640 × 480 = 307,200], and older laptop and notebook displays are capable of only 128,000 pixels arranged as 640 columns by 200 rows (or less).

Aspect ratio

The *aspect ratio* is basically the squareness of each pixel, and indirectly, the squareness of the display. For example, a display with perfectly square pixels has an aspect ratio of 1:1. A rectangle box 100 pixels wide and 100 pixels high would appear as an even square. However, pixel aspect ratios are not always 1:1. Typical pixels are somewhat higher than they are wide. For a display with 320 × 200 resolution, a pixel width of 0.34 mm and height of 0.48 mm (1:1.41) is not uncommon. Higher resolution displays use smaller dots to fit more pixels into roughly the same viewing area. As a result, smaller pixels tend to approach 1:1 aspect ratios. Keep in mind that aspect ratio might not be shown as an individual display specification. Figure 33-2 shows the concept of aspect ratio.

Viewing angle

Every display has a particular *viewing angle*. It is the angle through which a display can be viewed clearly as shown in Fig. 33-3. Viewing angle is rarely a concern for bright, crisp displays such as CRTs and gas plasma flat-panels. Such displays generate light, so they can be seen up to a very wide angle (usually up to 70° from center). For liquid crystal displays, however, the viewing angle is a critical specification.

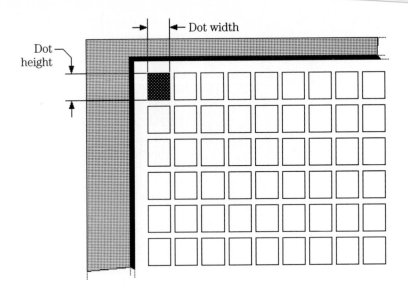

$$Aspect\ ratio = \frac{Dot\ width}{Dot\ height}$$

33-2 LCD aspect ratio.

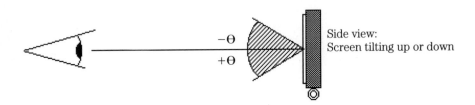

Side view:
Screen tilting up or down

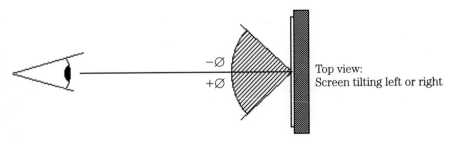

Top view:
Screen tilting left or right

33-3 LCD viewing angle.

LCDs do not generate their own light, so the display contrast tends to degrade quickly as you leave a direct line of sight.

Position yourself or your small computer so that you look directly at the display (a perpendicular orientation). Tilt the screen up and away from you. Do you see how the contrast and brightness of the display decreases as you tilt the screen? The angle the display is at when the picture just becomes indiscernible is the negative vertical limit ($-\theta$). Return the screen to a direct line of sight, then slowly tilt the screen down toward you. Once again, you will see the display degrade. The angle the display is at when the display becomes indiscernible is the positive vertical limit ($+\theta$). Ideally, both vertical limits should be the same. Return the display to a direct line of sight, then repeat this test in the horizontal orientation. Swing the display left or right until the image becomes indiscernible. These are the negative and positive horizontal limits respectively ($-\phi$) and ($+\phi$). Ideally, both horizontal limits should be the same. Generally, the larger a viewing angle is, the easier the display is to look at.

Contrast

The *contrast* of an image is loosely defined as the difference in luminous intensity between pixels that are fully ON and pixels that are fully OFF. The greater this difference is, the higher the contrast is, and the image appears sharper. Many graphic flat-panel LCDs offer contrast ranging from a low of four to nine and higher. For the purposes of this book, contrast is a unit-less number. Because luminous intensity is strongly dependent on a display's particular viewing angle, a reference angle is typically added to the contrast specification—usually a straight-on view.

Remember that contrast is a comparison of black versus white. It is desirable (especially with monochrome displays) to simulate 16, 32, 64, or more gray levels that are somewhere between black and white. Any gray level other than pure black provides a lower contrast versus white; do not confuse gray scale levels with poor contrast.

Response time

The *response time* of a display is the time required for a display pixel to reach its ON or OFF condition after the pixel has been addressed by the corresponding driver circuitry. Such on/off transitions do not occur instantaneously. Depending on the vintage and quality of the display, pixel response times can vary anywhere from 40 to 200 ms. Active-matrix LCDs typically offer the shortest response times, while older passive-matrix LCDs provide the slowest performance. You can read much more about the various display types and techniques in this chapter.

Handling precautions

Next to magnetic hard drives, flat-panel displays are some of the most sophisticated and delicate assemblies in the computer industry. Although most displays can easily withstand the rigors of everyday use, there are serious physical, environmental, and handling precautions that you should be aware of before attempting any sort of repair.

You must be extremely careful with all liquid crystal assemblies. Liquid crystal material is sandwiched between two layers of fragile glass. The glass can easily be fractured by abuse or careless handling. If a fracture should occur and liquid crystal material happens to leak out, use rubber gloves and wipe up the spill with soap and water. Immediately wash off any LC material that comes in contact with your skin. *Do not, under any circumstances, ingest or inhale LC material.* Avoid applying pressure to the surface of a liquid crystal display. You risk scratching the delicate polarizer layer covering the display's face. If the polarizer is scratched or damaged in any way, it will have to be replaced. Excessive pressure or bending forces can fracture the delicate connections within the display.

You can use very gentle pressure to clean the face of a display. Lightly wet a soft (lint-free), clean cloth with fresh isopropyl alcohol or ethyl alcohol, then *gently* wipe away the stain(s). You might prefer to use photography-grade lens wipes instead of a cloth. Never use water or harsh solvents to clean a display. Water drops can accumulate as condensation, and high-humidity environments can corrode a display's electrodes. When a display assembly is removed from a system, keep the assembly in an antistatic bag in a dry, room-temperature environment. Never store a display assembly in a cold vehicle, room, or other cold environment. Liquid crystal material coagulates (becomes firm) at low temperatures (below 0°C or 32°F). Exposure to low temperatures can cause black or white bubbles to form in the material.

Flat-panel display circuitry is very susceptible to damage from electrostatic discharge (ESD). Make certain to use antistatic bags or boxes to hold the display. Use an antistatic wrist strap to remove any charges from your body before handling a display. Use a grounded soldering iron and tools. Work (if possible) on an antistatic workbench mat. Try to avoid working in cool, dry environments where static charges can accumulate easily. If you use a vacuum cleaner around your display, make sure that the vacuum is static safe.

Basic LCD technology

Liquid crystal is an unusual organic material that has been known by science for many years. Although it is liquid in form and appearance, LC exhibits a crystalline molecular structure that resembles a solid. If you were to look at a sample of LC material under a microscope, you would see a vast array of rod-shaped molecules. In its normal state, LC is virtually clear; light would pass right through a container of LC. When LC material is assembled into a flat panel, the molecules have a tendency to twist.

Quite by accident, it was discovered that a voltage applied across a volume of liquid crystal forces the molecules between the active electrodes to straighten. When the voltage is removed, the straightened LC molecules return to their normal twisted orientation. It would have been a simple matter to have dismissed the liquid crystal effect as little more than a scientific curiosity, but further experiments revealed an interesting phenomenon when light polarizing materials (or *polarizers*) are placed on both sides of the liquid crystal layer; areas of the LC material that are excited by an external voltage became dark and visible. When voltage was removed, the area became clear and invisible again. A *polarizer* is a thin film that allows light to pass in only one orientation. By using electrodes with different patterns, various images can be formed. The earliest developments in commercial liquid crystal displays were simply referred to as *twisted nematic* (TN) displays. A basic LCD assembly is shown in Fig. 33-4. Notice that an array of transparent electrodes are printed and sealed on the inside of each glass layer.

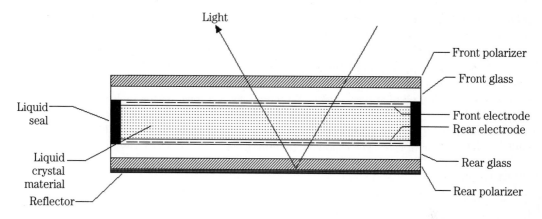

33-4 Side view of a basic LCD assembly.

There are four major varieties of liquid crystal assemblies that you should be familiar with: *TN* (twisted nematic), *STN* (super twisted nematic), *NTN* or *NSTN* (neutralized super twisted nematic), and *FTN* or *FSTN* (film-compensated super twisted nematic). Each of these variations handles light somewhat differently, and offers unique display characteristics that a technician should be familiar with.

TN LCDs

The twisted nematic (TN) display is shown in Fig. 33-5. Light can originate from many different sources and strike the front polarizer, but the vertically oriented polarizer only allows light waves in the vertical orientation to pass through into the LC cell. As vertically oriented light waves enter the LC assembly, its orientation twists 90° following the molecular twist in the LC material. As light leaves the LC cell, its

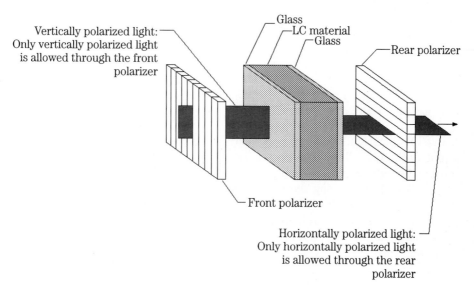

33-5 Operation of a TN LCD.

orientation is now horizontal. Because the rear polarizer is aligned horizontally, light passes through and the LC display appears transparent.

When a pixel is activated, the LC material being energized straightens its alignment; twist will become 0°, and light will not change its polarization in the LC cell. Vertically polarized light is blocked by the horizontally oriented rear polarizer. This makes the activated pixel appear dark. TN technology is appealing for its low cost, simple construction, and good response time, but it is limited by poor viewing angle and low contrast in high-resolution displays. Today, TN displays have been largely replaced by any one of the three following technologies.

STN LCDs

A *super twisted nematic* (STN) approach is shown in Fig. 33-6. Initially, the STN approach appears identical to the TN technique, but there are two major differences. First, a super twisted LC material is used that provides more than 200° of twist instead of only 90° with the TN formulation. The rear polarizer angle also must be changed to match the twist of the LC material. For example, if the LC material has a twist of 220°, the rear polarizer must be aligned to that same orientation.

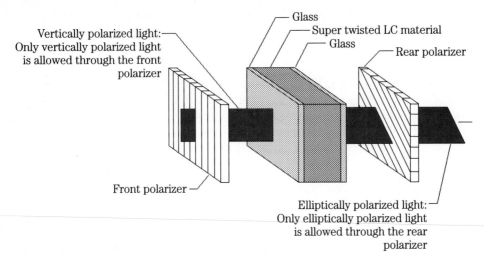

33-6 Operation of an STN LCD.

In STN operation, the vertically oriented light passing through the front polarizer enters the LC cell. As light passes through the LC cell, its orientation changes following the formulation's particular twist. The twist might be as little as 200°, or as much as 270°. Light leaving the LC cell should then pass through the customized rear polarizer and make the display appear transparent. If a pixel is activated, the LC material at that point will straighten completely. Light no longer twists to match the rear polarizer, so the pixel appears dark. STN displays offer much better contrast and viewing angle than TN versions because of the additional twist. STN technology also performs very well at high resolutions (up to 1024 × 800 pixels). However, STN displays cost more than regular TN displays, and the response time to activate each pixel is somewhat slow because of the extra twist.

NTN LCDs

The *neutralized super twisted nematic* (NTN or NSTN) display is shown in Fig. 33-7. Light is vertically oriented by the front polarizer before being admitted to the first LC cell. Light entering the first LC cell is twisted more than 270°. A second LC cell (known as a *compensator cell*) adds extra twist to light polarization resulting in a horizontally oriented light output. Light that passes through the second LC cell also passes through the rear polarizer and results in a clear (transparent) display. Keep in mind that only the first LC cell offers active pixels. The compensator cell only adds twist.

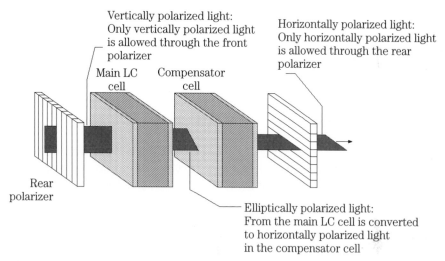

33-7 Operation of an NSTN LCD.

When a pixel is activated in the first LC cell, the LC molecules align so light at that point is not twisted. The untwisted light is not twisted enough by the compensator cell, so that point is blocked by the rear polarizer and appears dark. Light passing through an idle pixel is twisted, then twisted again by the compensator cell. With this additional twist, light passes through the rear polarizer and the deactivated points appear transparent. NTN displays produce some of the finest, high-contrast, high-viewing-angle images available, but NTN displays also are much heavier, thicker, and costlier than other types of displays. It also is difficult to backlight such a configuration of LC cells. For most small-computer applications, FTN displays are preferred over NTN models.

FTN LCDs

Figure 33-8 shows the basic structure of a *film-compensated super twist nematic* (FTN or FSTN) display. As you might see, the FTN display is very similar to the NTN display shown in Fig. 33-7. However, an FTN display uses a layer of optically compensated film instead of a second LC cell to achieve horizontal light polarization. Vertically oriented light passes through the front polarizer, than is twisted more than 200° by the LC cell. When light emerges from the LC cell, it passes

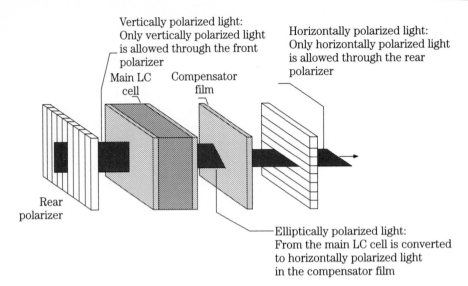

Vertically polarized light:
Only vertically polarized light is allowed through the front polarizer

Horizontally polarized light:
Only horizontally polarized light is allowed through the rear polarizer

Main LC cell

Compensator film

Rear polarizer

Elliptically polarized light:
From the main LC cell is converted to horizontally polarized light in the compensator film

33-8 Operation of an FSTN LCD.

through a compensator film. Assuming that light is oriented properly from the LC cell, the compensator layer changes light polarization to a horizontal orientation. Light then passes through the horizontal polarizer causing a clear (transparent) display.

When a pixel is activated, the LC material at that point straightens and light polarization does not occur. As unaltered light passes through the compensation film, it does not twist enough to pass through the rear polarizer, so the pixel appears dark. FTN LCDs are much lighter, thinner, and less expensive than their NTN counterparts. The FTN display does not have nearly as much optical loss as NTN versions, so FTN displays are easy to backlight. The only major disadvantage to an FTN display is that its contrast and viewing angle are slightly reduced because of the compensating film.

Viewing modes

It is important for you to realize that light plays a critical role in the formation of liquid crystal images. The path that light takes through the LC assembly and your eye can have a serious impact on the display's image quality, as well as the display's utility in various environments. There are three classical viewing "modes" that you should understand: reflective LCD, transflective LCD, and transmissive LCD. Figure 33-9 shows the action of each mode.

In the *reflective* viewing mode, only available light is used to illuminate the display. A metallized reflector is mounted behind the display's rear polarizer. Light from the outside environment that penetrates the LC assembly is reflected back to your eye resulting in a clear (transparent) image. Light that is blocked due to an activated pixel appears dark. Reflective displays work best when used in an outdoor or well-lit environment. If light is blocked from the display, the image will virtually disappear. However, because no backlighting is used, the display consumes very little power.

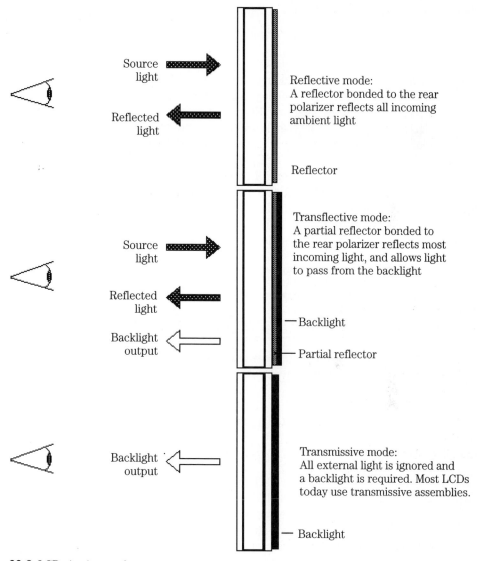

Source
light

Reflected
light

Reflective mode:
A reflector bonded to the rear
polarizer reflects all incoming
ambient light

Reflector

Source
light

Reflected
light

Backlight
output

Transflective mode:
A partial reflector bonded to
the rear polarizer reflects most
incoming light, and allows light
to pass from the backlight

Backlight

Partial reflector

Backlight
output

Transmissive mode:
All external light is ignored and
a backlight is required. Most LCDs
today use transmissive assemblies.

Backlight

33-9 LCD viewing modes.

The *transflective* viewing mode uses a partial reflector behind the LC cell's rear
polarizer. This partial reflector will reflect light provided by the outside environment, and pass any illumination provided from behind the assembly (the backlight).
Transflective operation allows the display to be operated in direct light with the
backlight turned off. The backlight can then be activated in low-light conditions.

A *transmissive* LCD uses a transparent rear polarizer with no reflector at all.
Light entering the LCD assembly from the outside environment is not reflected back
to your eye. Instead, a backlight is required to make the image visible. When pixels
are off, backlight illumination passes directly through the display to your eye resulting in clear (transparent) pixels. Activated pixels block the backlight and result in

dark points. The backlight can be overpowered by bright light or sunlight, so the transmissive display can appear pale or washed out when used outdoors.

Backlighting

Backlighting is the process of adding a known light source to a liquid crystal display in order to improve the display's visibility in low-light situations. Mobile computers use one of two approaches to backlighting: EL panels or *CCFTs* (cold-cathode fluorescent tubes). *EL* (electroluminescent) panels are thin, lightweight, and produce a very even light output across their surface area. EL panels are available in several colors, but white is preferred for computer displays. The EL panel is usually mounted directly behind the display's rear polarizer (or transflector if used) as shown in Fig. 33-10. EL panels are reasonably rugged and reliable, but they require a substantial ac excitation voltage in order to operate. An ac inverter supply is used to convert low-voltage dc into a high-voltage ac level of 100 Vac or more. A disadvantage to EL panels is their relatively short working life (2000 to 3000 hours) before a serious loss of backlight intensity occurs.

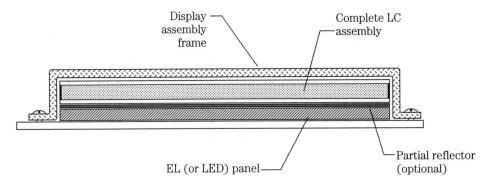

33-10 A typical backlight assembly.

Cold-cathode fluorescent tubes (CCFTs) offer an inexpensive source of very bright white light that consumes reasonably little power. CCFTs also enjoy a long life (10,000 to 15,000 hours) without serious degradation. Such characteristics have made CCFTs very popular in a great many notebook and pen-computer displays. As Fig. 33-11 shows, there are two common methods of mounting CCFTs: edgelighting and backlighting.

As you might imagine, edgelighting is favored in thin or low-profile displays. A layer of translucent material referred to as the diffuser distributes the lamp's light evenly behind the LC cell. To create an even brighter display, a second CCFT can be added on the opposite edge of the diffuser. If a smaller, thicker display assembly is preferred, one or two CCFTs can be mounted in a cavity directly behind the LC cell. A diffuser is still used to spread light evenly behind the LC cell. CCFTs need a high-voltage ac source in order to operate, so an inverter supply is employed to provide the high voltages that most CCFTs need.

Passive and active matrix operation

Now that you understand what liquid crystal displays are and how they are constructed, you must understand how each pixel in a display is controlled (or *ad-*

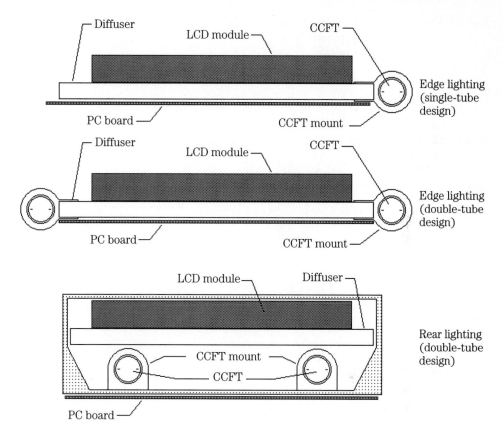

33-11 Basic backlighting techniques.

dressed). There are two classical methods of LCD addressing: passive addressing and active addressing. You will probably encounter both types of addressing at one time or another.

A *passive-matrix* LCD is shown in Fig. 33-12. Each layer of glass in an LC cell contains transparent electrodes deposited on the inside of the glass sheet. The upper (or front) glass contains column electrodes, and the lower (or rear) glass is printed with row electrodes. When both sheets of glass are fitted together as shown, a matrix is formed. Every point where a row electrode and a column electrode intersect is a potential pixel. To light a pixel, the appropriate row and column electrodes must be energized. Wherever an energized row and column intersect, a visible pixel will appear. In order to excite a pixel, a voltage potential must be applied across the LC material. For the example of Fig. 33-12, if a voltage is applied to column 638 and row 1 is connected to ground, pixel (638,1) should appear.

A small transistor is used to switch power to each electrode. These driver transistors are operated by digital control signals generated in a matrix control IC that is usually located on the LCD panel itself. When a row electrode is selected, multiple column electrodes can be addressed along that row. In this way, a complete display can be developed an entire row at a time instead of a pixel at a time. The passive-matrix display is updated continually by scanning rows in sequence and activating each

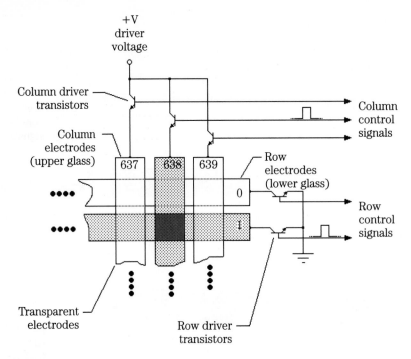

33-12 Configuration of a passive-matrix LCD.

column necessary to display all of the pixels in the selected row. Most displays can update row data several times per second.

Although passive-matrix displays are simple and straightforward to design and build, the inherent need to scan the display slows down its overall operation. It is difficult to display computer animation or fast graphics on many passive monochrome displays. Even a mouse cursor might disappear while moving around a passive-matrix LCD.

To overcome the limitations of classical passive LCDs, the *active-matrix* display was developed. As shown in Fig. 33-13, each pixel is handled directly by a dedicated electrode instead of using common row and column electrodes. Individual electrodes are driven by their own transistors, so there is one transistor driver for every pixel in a monochrome display. Driver transistors are deposited onto the rear glass substrate (foundation) in much the same way that integrated circuits are fabricated. For a display with 640-x-480 resolution, a total of [640 × 480] 307,200 thin film transistors (TFTs) must be fabricated onto the rear glass. A single, huge, common electrode is deposited onto the front glass. To excite the desired pixel, it is only necessary to activate the corresponding driver transistor. The ICs that manage operation of the driver transistor array are generally included in the display panel.

When a driver transistor is fired, a potential is applied to the corresponding electrode. This potential establishes an electric field between the electrode and the common electrode on the front panel. For the example of Fig. 33-13, you will see that the pixel in row 2 and column 0 is activated simply by applying a control signal to its

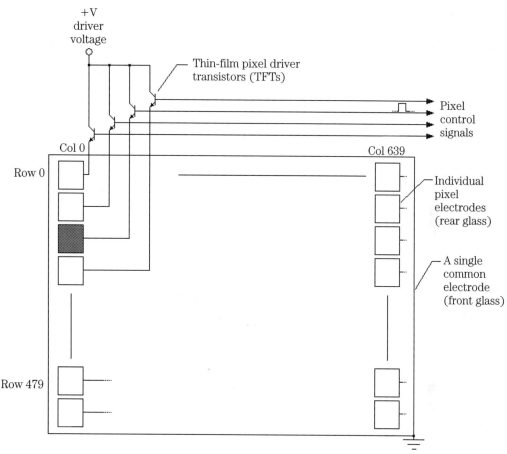

33-13 Configuration of an active-matrix LCD (AMLCD).

driver transistor. Because each pixel in an active-matrix LCD can be addressed individually, there is no need to continually update the display as with passive displays. Active-matrix addressing is much faster than passive matrix addressing. As a result, active-matrix displays offer impressive response time with extremely good contrast. Unfortunately, active-matrix LCDs also are some of the most expensive parts of your laptop or notebook computer.

Color LCD technology

The desire for high-quality flat-panel color displays continues to be somewhat of a quest for display designers. Although two very effective color LCD techniques are well-established, both types of color displays offer their own particular drawbacks. Passive-matrix FSTN and active-matrix TFT color displays are the two dominant color LCD technologies available. This section of the chapter describes today's color technologies.

Passive-matrix color

Passive-matrix color LCD technology is based on the operation of film-compensated super twisted nematic (FSTN or FTN) LCDs. FSTN principles are presented in this chapter. The most striking difference between color and monochrome LCDs is that the color LCD uses three times as many electrodes as the monochrome display. This is necessary because three primary colors (red, green, and blue) are needed to form the color of each dot that your eye perceives. As shown in Fig. 33-14, each colored dot is made up of three tiny pixels.

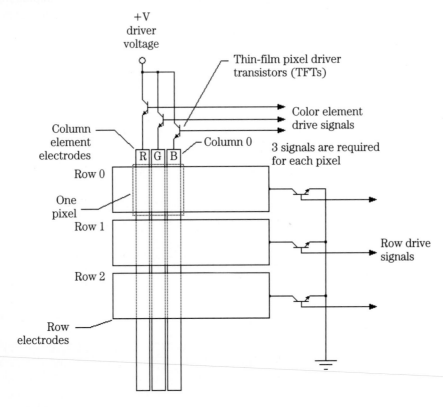

33-14 Configuration of a passive-matrix color LCD.

Pixels do not actually generate the colors that you see. It is the white light passing through each pixel that is filtered to form the intended color. The front glass is coated with color filter material in front of each "red," "green," and "blue" dot. For example, if the dot at row 0 column 0 is supposed to be red, the green and blue dots turn on at that point to block white light through all but the "red" filter. White light travels through the red filter on the front glass where it emerges as red. When the red, green, and blue dots are all on, ALL light is blocked and the pixel appears black. If all three dots are off, all light passes through and the pixel appears white. By controlling the three dot elements at each pixel, up to eight colors can be produced (including black and white). Intermediate color shades can be produced using color hatching schemes between adjacent dots.

The red, green, and blue (RGB) column electrodes for each pixel are deposited onto the front glass, while a single row electrode for each dot is fabricated onto the rear glass. As you might imagine, tripling the number of column electrodes complicates the manufacture of passive color displays. Not only is electrode deposition more difficult because electrodes are close together, but three times the number of column driver transistors and IC driver signals are needed. Like monochrome LCDs, the color display is updated by scanning each row sequentially, then manipulating the RGB elements for each column. Typical color LCD data can be updated several times per second.

FSTN color displays suffer from many of the disadvantages inherent in monochrome passive matrix displays. First, response time is slow (about 250 ms). This means that no matter how fast data is delivered to the display, the image you see will only change about four times per second. Such slow update times make passive displays poor choices for fast graphic operations or animation. Their contrast ratio is a poor 7:1 that generally results in washed out or hazy displays. Viewing angles for color passive-matrix LCDs also are poor at around 45°. Your clearest view of the display will be to look at it straight on. Constant advances in materials and fabrication techniques are improving the speed and quality of passive color displays.

Active-matrix color

Active-matrix color LCD technology takes the contents of monochrome active panels one step further by using three electrodes for every dot. Each electrode is completely independent and is driven by its own thin-film transistor (TFT). The three elements control the "red," "green," and "blue" light source for each pixel that your eye perceives. Figure 33-15 shows the structure of a TFT active matrix color LCD. Every electrode driver transistor and all interconnecting wiring is fabricated onto the rear glass plate. With three transistors per dot, a 640 column × 480 row color display requires [640 × 480 × 3] 921,600 individual transistors. Essentially, the rear plate of a TFT color display is one large 25.4-cm (10 inches) diagonal integrated circuit. The front glass plate is fabricated with a single, large common electrode that every screen element can reference to.

As with passive-matrix displays, the LC material used in active-matrix displays does not actually generate color. The individual elements simply turn white light on or off. White light that is permitted through an element is filtered by colored material applied to corresponding locations on the front glass. When the red, green, and blue elements are all off, white light shines through the three elements, and the pixel appears white. If the red, green, and blue elements are all on, all light is blocked, and the pixel appears black. The ability to closely control contrast in individual dots allows active-matrix color LCDs to produce 512 individual hues of color; 256 colors is standard.

Active-matrix color displays do away with many of the limitations found in passive-matrix displays. Response time is very fast; on the order of 20 ms or better. Such fast response times allow the screen image to change up to 30 times per second. This

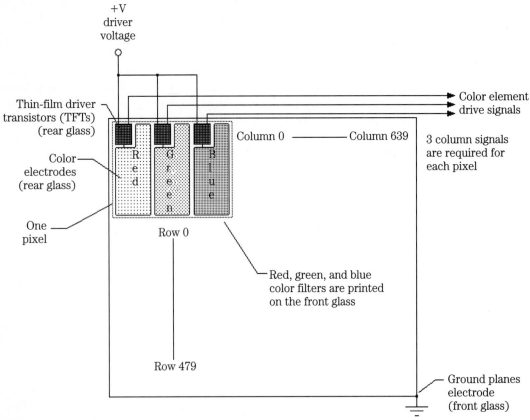

33-15 Configuration of an active-matrix color LCD.

provides excellent performance for graphics or animation applications. The control afforded by active-matrix screens provides a brilliant contrast ratio of 60:1 with a comfortable viewing angle of 80° or so. Color active-matrix displays will most likely reflect the state-of-the-art in small-computer technology for quite some time.

Dual-scan color

Cost has been a major constraint for active-matrix displays. The addition of an active-matrix color display can raise the cost of a notebook or subnotebook computer by up to $1000 (US). Designers have sought to improve the speed of flat-panel displays without incurring the cost of active-matrix technology. The dual-scan technique is a recent improvement for passive-matrix displays. Instead of scanning the entire display in one pass, the display area is broken up into upper and lower halves. Each half of the display is scanned independently. This allows any one row in the display to be updated at least twice as fast. Passive-matrix performance is improved without a substantial increase in display complexity or cost. The disadvantage to dual-scan displays is that a faint horizontal bar becomes visible along the center of the display (where the upper and lower scanning areas meet). Some users might find this objectionable.

Troubleshooting flat-panel displays

There are seven major parts of an LCD system as shown in Fig. 33-16:

- A microprocessor
- A system controller (if used)
- Video memory (VRAM)
- A backlight voltage source
- A highly integrated display controller IC
- A contrast control
- The flat-panel display assembly itself

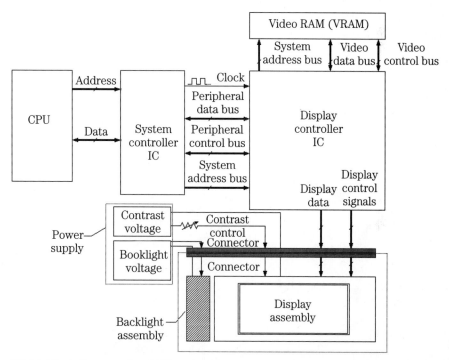

33-16 Block diagram of an LCD system.

The microprocessor is the heart of all small computers. A microprocessor is responsible for executing the instructions contained in BIOS or core memory (RAM). As the CPU executes its program(s), it directs the operations of a system controller IC. A system controller is a sophisticated ASIC that is used to handle the majority of small computer's overhead operations. Although it is not mandatory that a computer utilize a system controller, a single controller IC can effectively replace dozens of discrete logic ICs.

The display controller IC is addressed by the system controller over the common system address bus. This is the "video adapter" for small computers. Once the display controller is addressed, the system controller writes display information and commands over a secondary (or peripheral) data bus. A clock and miscellaneous control signals manage the flow of data into the display controller. Display data is interpreted and stored in video RAM (VRAM). Each pixel in the physical display can be traced back to a specific logical location (address) in VRAM. As new data is written to the display controller, VRAM addresses are updated to reflect any new information. During an update, the display controller reads through the contents of VRAM and sends the data along to the flat-panel display. There are two other signals required by an LCD assembly: contrast voltage and backlight input voltage.

A complete flat-panel display assembly is shown in Fig. 33-17. The plastic outer housings (marked K1 and K22) form the cosmetic shell of the display panel. An LC cell with its driver ICs and transistors (marked E6) is mounted to the front housing. A number of insulators can be added to protect the LC cell from accidental short circuits. Note that the front polarizer layer is built into the LC cell. A rear polarizer (marked K15) is placed directly behind the LC cell, followed by the translucent backlight diffuser panel (marked K16). The backlight mechanism is a long, thin CCFT (marked K13) located along the bottom of the diffuser. Several spacers/brackets are used to secure the diffuser panel and tie the entire assembly together. Finally, a rear housing is snapped into place to cover the display. A cable (marked K19) connects the display assembly to the motherboard.

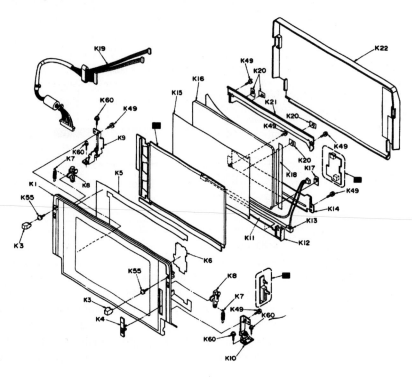

33-17 An exploded diagram of a Tandy 1500HD display system. Tandy Corporation

Symptoms

In spite of the complexity found in most LCDs, they are remarkably modular devices. The flat-panel display contains all of the driver circuitry needed to turn each pixel or dot element on and off. The backlight assembly produces the light that makes each dot visible. The display controller, VRAM, system controller, and other circuitry needed to convert raw data into video signals is typically contained on the mobile computer's motherboard. The LCD panel and motherboard are interconnected by a cable (usually a ribbon cable). Chances are very good that regardless of the particular symptoms that you see, the error can be tracked to one of these three areas.

Symptom 1. A portion of the display drops out or flickers intermittently
For example, the entire top 25% of the display cuts out or displays garbage, while the remainder of the display continues working fine. More or less of the display might be defective, but the problem typically extends all the way across the image. This problem also tends to be intermittent; flexing the flat-panel slightly or tilting the panel toward or away from you might stop the problem. Generally speaking, an intermittent connection has developed in either the flat-panel driver circuitry (on the rear of the display itself), or the display cable that connects the LCD and motherboard. Unfortunately, because the problem is intermittent, it might be extremely difficult to pinpoint.

Open the housing covering the LCD and check the interconnecting signal cable. Make sure that the cable is inserted into the LCD completely. You also might take a peek and see that the cable is inserted properly at the motherboard connector as well. Gently prod and flex the signal cable. If the intermittent appears, you might have a faulty signal cable. Try a new signal cable. If the cable appears steady, the problem is likely in the flat-panel assembly. In that event, the best course is to replace the LCD assembly outright; it would be virtually impossible to fix intermittent circuitry on the back of an LCD; the assembly is simply too delicate. Given the expense of most LCDs, you might want to check the price and availability of a new display panel, and contact your customer for their approval prior to actually ordering a new display.

There might be another option when it comes to repairing faulty LCDs. Although the procedure is too involved for the purposes of this book, there are some companies that specialize in LCD panel repairs specifically (such as Man & Machine, Inc. listed at the end of this chapter). You might be able to send the LCD out for repair or exchange for a much lower price than purchasing one new.

Symptom 2. After the backlight times out, you notice that the display appears rather dim after the backlight kicks in again After several minutes, display contrast improves, and the image looks fine. This is not necessarily a problem. The "even-ness" of a backlight source is somewhat dependent on heat that is produced as a CCFT warms a diffuser. Contrast adjustments are typically optimized for a warm backlight. If the backlight shuts off to conserve battery power, the CCFT and diffuser cool. Once mouse or keyboard activity start the backlight again, contrast might appear dull for several minutes as the backlight warms up again. Also check the contrast control to be sure that it is set at an optimum level after the backlight assembly is warm.

If it takes a relatively long time to restore contrast, or contrast is chronically dull, it might indicate that the CCFT or EL element is failing; both enjoy only limited working lives. If the mobile PC is over several years old, or has logged an unusually large number of working hours, it is probably time to change the backlight element.

Symptom 3. One or more pixels is defective. The defective pixel might be black (opaque), white (clear), or fixed at some color Before beginning any repair procedure, turn off your computer and initialize it from a cold start. A cold start ensures that your pixels are not being locked up due to any possible software glitch. If the questionable pixels disappear, there might be a bug in your application software—not in your hardware.

Run a diagnostic and test video memory thoroughly. If an error in VRAM is detected, one or more VRAM address locations might be defective, resulting in faulty video data being provided to the display. It is unusual for a problem in VRAM to manifest itself in this way, but you should be prepared for this possibility. If you do not have the proper tools or inclination to replace defective surface-mount ICs, you might prefer to replace the entire motherboard.

Faulty pixels are a symptom that commonly occurs with active-matrix display panels. Because each screen dot is driven by either one or three individual driver transistors, the loss of one or more drivers will ruin a pixel. For monochrome displays, the single driver transistor might be open (pixel will not turn on) or shorted (pixel will not turn off). For color displays, damage to a driver transistor might cause a certain color to appear and remain fixed on the screen as long as the computer is running. Unfortunately, there is no way to repair a failed screen driver transistor. Active-matrix flat-panel circuitry is fabricated much the same way as any integrated circuit, so when any part of the IC fails, the entire IC must be replaced. Your best course is simply to replace the suspect LCD assembly. An outside LCD repair organization might be able to repair or exchange the LCD for less than it would cost to purchase a new one. It is important for you to remember that active-matrix LCD manufacturers might allow up to 10 bad pixels in a new assembly, so replacing the LCD might still leave you with a few bad pixels.

Symptom 4. There is poor visibility in the LCD. The image is easily washed out in direct or ambient light The vast majority of current mobile computer LCDs operate in the *transmissive* mode; the light that your eyes see is generated from a backlight system. As a result, the strength and quality of the backlight directly affects the display visibility. If the computer is older and has accumulated a great deal of running time, the EL backlight panel or CCFT(s) might be worn out or failing. The high-voltage power supply that is operating the backlight also might be faulty. Check your LCD's contrast control. Contrast adjusts the amount of driver voltage that is used to light the CCFT or EL panel. Less driver voltage means less light. This results in less contrast.

Disassemble your flat-panel assembly to expose the backlight unit (either an EL panel or a CCFT assembly) as well as the inverter power supply. GENTLY brush away any dust or debris that might have accumulated on the EL panel, CCFT(s), or diffuser. If the light source has been badly fouled by dust, retry the system with the cleaned light source. Use your multimeter to measure the ac output voltage from your inverter power supply. A working inverter should output 150 to 200 Vac for an EL panel, or 200 to 1000 Vac for CCFTs. *Remember to be extremely cautious when measuring high voltages.* If your inverter output is low or nonexistent, troubleshoot or replace your faulty backlight power supply. If the inverter's output voltage appears normal, replace the failing CCFT(s) or EL panel assembly.

Symptom 5. The display is completely dark. There is no apparent display activity This symptom assumes that your computer has plenty of power and attempts to boot up with all normal disk activity. You simply have no display. If there are no active LEDs to indicate power or disk activity, there might be a more serious problem with your system. Begin by removing all power from your system. Remove the outer housings of your computer and inspect all connectors and wiring between the motherboard and display. Tighten any loose connectors and reattach any loose or broken wiring. Defective connections can easily disable your display.

Check to see if the backlight illuminates. If there is no backlight, you will not see the display. Chances are that the backlight inverter power supply has failed. Measure the inverter output with your multimeter. Depending on the type of backlight being used, you might see anywhere from 200 to 1000 Vac. *Remember to use extreme caution when measuring high voltages.* If this voltage is absent, the inverter is probably defective and should be replaced. If this voltage is present, the CCFT or EL panel are probably defective and should be replaced.

If the backlight fires, but there is no display, the fault is likely in the display control circuit. If your mobile PC has a connector for an external analog monitor, attach one and see if a display is being generated. If an external monitor works, check the display cable leading from the motherboard to the LCD. Try a new cable. Run a diagnostic to check the video controller IC. If the video controller checks bad, it should be replaced (you might have to replace the entire motherboard). If the video controller checks OK, the LCD assembly might be defective. Try a new LCD.

Symptom 6. The display appears erratic. It displays disassociated characters and garbage This is another symptom that assumes your mobile computer has plenty of power and attempts to boot up with normal disk activity. Your display is simply acting erratically. If no power indicators or disk activity LEDs are lit, there might be a much more serious problem in your system. Remove all power from your system and remove the outer housings to expose the motherboard and display assembly. Inspect all cables and connectors between the motherboard and display assembly. Tighten any loose connectors and secure any loose or broken wiring. Defective connectors or wiring can easily interfere with normal display operation. You also might wish to check the voltage levels powering your display.

Run a diagnostic and inspect the video system. Chances are that the video controller or VRAM has failed. If either part of the video system is identified as faulty, you should replace the motherboard outright. If your diagnostic(s) report the video system to be working properly, check or replace the video cable between the motherboard and LCD. Signal interruptions can easily interfere with the LCD. If another cable does not correct the problem, try a new LCD assembly.

34
CHAPTER

MCA bus operations

With the introduction and widespread use of 32-bit microprocessors such as the Intel 80386 and 80486, the 16-bit ISA bus faced a serious data throughput bottleneck. Passing a 32-bit word across the expansion bus in two 16-bit halves presented a serious waste of valuable processing time. Not only was data and CPU speed an issue, but video and audio systems in PCs also had been improving and demanding an increasing share of bus bandwidth. By early 1987, IBM concluded that it was time to lay the ISA bus to rest, and unleash an entirely new bus structure that it dubbed the *MCA* (MicroChannel Architecture). IBM incorporated the MCA bus into their PS/2 series of personal computers, and also in their System/6000 workstations. This chapter shows you the layout and operations of the MCA bus.

MCA bus configuration and signals

All things considered, the MCA bus was a revolutionary—and superior—design. One of the most substantial advantages is a reduction in electrical noise because of a radical rearrangement of bus signals. Unlike the ISA or EISA bus (which had only a few ground lines), the MCA bus provides an electrical ground every fourth pin. Superior grounding and the corresponding reduction in electrical interference also meant that the MCA bus can operate at higher frequencies than XT or AT buses (10 MHz as opposed to the ISA/EISA 8.33 MHz). The MCA bus also offers extended performance in data and addressing. You already know that an MCA bus can work with up to 32 bits of data. However, the bus also has an increased number of address lines (32 instead of 24). This increases the amount of directly addressable memory from 16 Mb to 4 Gb.

The MCA also brings sound and video to the bus. A single analog audio channel is added to the 8-bit bus segment. The audio channel can handle voice and music, and is intended to be almost as good as FM radio (roughly about 50 Hz to 10 kHz). Because the audio channel is available to all expansion devices, the signal can be exchanged and processed among each device independently. A VGA video extension also is provided with the MCA bus. This allows expansion video boards to be installed and work in concert with the VGA circuitry already existing on the MCA motherboard. An 8-bit video data bus and all necessary synchronization signals are available to an expansion board. Typically, only one video extension connector is included on an MCA motherboard.

Still more advances include such features as matched memory cycles, burst and streaming data modes, data multiplexing, and bus mastering. A *matched memory cycle* is supported with a small expansion connector. When a device is capable of sustaining matched memory transfers, the typical memory transfer cycle of 250 ns is increased 25% to only 187 ns. The *burst* data transfer mode allows data to be transferred in blocks without the intervention of a CPU (unlike ordinary data transfers that require multiple CPU cycles for each transfer). The *streaming* data transfer mode allows even faster transfers during bus-mastering operation. Using a *data multiplexing* technique, the MCA bus can accomplish 64-bit data transfers by multiplexing the upper 32 data bits on the 32 idle address lines. Finally, the MCA bus supports *bus mastering*, a technique that allows other devices besides the main CPU to take control of the system buses to accomplish their respective tasks.

Although MCA offers many tangible enhancements over the ISA bus, computer users refused to abandon their hardware and software investment in order to scramble for limited MCA-compatible peripherals to fill their needs. As a result, the MCA bus has never become the new standard that IBM hoped it would be. Still, there are many MCA systems in the field today.

MCA layout

The layout for an MCA bus slot is shown in Fig. 34-1. Note that there are up to four segments to the bus connector: an 8-bit portion, a 16-bit portion, a 32-bit portion, and a video extension. There also is an auxiliary video extension connector that is usually available on only one slot. The first thing you should realize about the MCA bus is that it is physically much smaller than an ISA or EISA bus; as a result, it is totally incompatible with ISA or EISA expansion products.

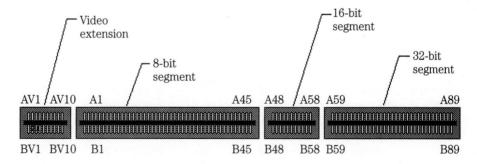

34-1 The various elements of an MCA bus.

The pinout for a 16-bit MCA slot is shown in Table 34-1. This is the primary type of MCA connector that combines video and audio signals in the expansion bus. The connection itself can be divided into three sections: the video section (pins xV00 to xV10), the 8-bit section (pins 1 through 45), and the 16-bit section (pins 48 to 58). Power, ground, and interrupt lines are easy to spot, but most other signals are new. The signal pinout for a 32-bit MCA slot is shown in Table 34-2. The 32-bit bus replaces the video section with a smaller matched memory control section (pins xM4 to xM1), but 8-bit and 16-bit sections remain the same. The 32-bit MCA slot also includes a 32-bit section (pins 59 to 89).

Table 34-1. MCA 16-bit bus pinout

Signal	Pin	Pin	Signal
ESYNC	BV10	AV10	VSYNC
Ground	BV9	AV9	HSYNC
P5	BV8	AV8	BLANK
P4	BV7	AV7	Ground
P3	BV6	AV6	P6
Ground	BV5	AV5	EDCLK
P2	BV4	AV4	DCLK
P1	BV3	AV3	Ground
P0	BV2	AV2	P7
Ground	BV1	AV1	EVIDEO
Key	Key	Key	Key
AUDIO Ground	B1	A1	– CD Setup
AUDIO	B2	A2	MADE 24
Ground	B3	A3	Ground
Oscillator (14.3 MHz)	B4	A4	Address Bit 11
Ground	B5	A5	Address Bit 10
Address Bit 23	B6	A6	Address Bit 9
Address Bit 22	B7	A7	+5 Vdc
Address Bit 21	B8	A8	Address Bit 8
Ground	B9	A9	Address Bit 7
Address Bit 20	B10	A10	Address Bit 6
Address Bit 19	B11	A11	+5 Vdc
Address Bit 18	B12	A12	Address Bit 5
Ground	B13	A13	Address Bit 4
Address Bit 17	B14	A14	Address Bit 3
Address Bit 16	B15	A15	+5 Vdc
Address Bit 15	B16	A16	Address Bit 2
Ground	B17	A17	Address Bit 1
Address Bit 14	B18	A18	Address Bit 0
Address Bit 13	B19	A19	+12 Vdc
Address Bit 12	B20	A20	–ADL
Ground	B21	A21	–PREEMPT
–IRQ 9	B22	A22	–BURST
–IRQ 3	B23	A23	–12 Vdc
–IRQ 4	B24	A24	ARB 00
Ground	B25	A25	ARB 01
–IRQ 5	B26	A26	ARB 02
–IRQ 6	B27	A27	–12 Vdc

Table 34-1. Continued

Signal	Pin	Pin	Signal
–IRQ 7	B28	A28	ARB 03
Ground	B29	A29	ARB/ –GNT
Reserved	B30	A30	–TC
Reserved	B31	A31	+5 Vdc
–CHCK	B32	A32	–SO
Ground	B33	A33	–S1
–CMD	B34	A34	M/ –I/O
CHRDYRTN	B35	A35	+12 Vdc
–CD SFDBK	B36	A36	CD CHRDY
Ground	B37	A37	Data Bit 0
Data Bit 1	B38	A38	Data Bit 2
Data Bit 3	B39	A39	+5 Vdc
Data Bit 4	B40	A40	Data Bit 5
Ground	B41	A41	Data Bit 6
CHRESET	B42	A42	Data Bit 7
Reserved	B43	A43	Ground
Reserved	B44	A44	–DS 16 RTN
Ground	B45	A45	–REFRESH
Key	Key	Key	Key
Key	Key	Key	Key
Data Bit 8	B48	A48	+5 Vdc
Data Bit 9	B49	A49	Data Bit 10
Ground	B50	A50	Data Bit 11
Data Bit 12	B51	A51	Data Bit 13
Data Bit 14	B52	A52	+12 Vdc
Data Bit 15	B53	A53	Reserved
Ground	B54	A54	–SBHE
–IRQ 10	B55	A55	–CD DS 16
–IRQ 11	B56	A56	+5 Vdc
–IRQ 12	B57	A57	–IRQ 14
Ground	B58	A58	–IRQ 15
Reserved	B59	A59	Reserved
Reserved	B60	A60	Reserved

Table 34-2. MCA 32-bit bus pinout

Signal	Pin	Pin	Signal
Ground	BM4	AM4	Reserved
Reserved	BM3	AM3	–MMC CMD
–MMCR	BM2	AM2	Ground
Reserved	BM1	AM1	–MMC
AUDIO Ground	B1	A1	–CD Setup
AUDIO	B2	A2	MADE 24
Ground	B3	A3	Ground

Table 34-2. Continued

Signal	Pin	Pin	Signal
Oscillator (14.3 MHz)	B4	A4	Address Bit 11
Ground	B5	A5	Address Bit 10
Address Bit 23	B6	A6	Address Bit 9
Address Bit 22	B7	A7	+5 Vdc
Address Bit 21	B8	A8	Address Bit 8
Ground	B9	A9	Address Bit 7
Address Bit 20	B10	A10	Address Bit 6
Address Bit 19	B11	A11	+5 Vdc
Address Bit 18	B12	A12	Address Bit 5
Ground	B13	A13	Address Bit 4
Address Bit 17	B14	A14	Address Bit 3
Address Bit 16	B15	A15	+5 Vdc
Address Bit 15	B16	A16	Address Bit 2
Ground	B17	A17	Address Bit 1
Address Bit 14	B18	A18	Address Bit 0
Address Bit 13	B19	A19	+12 Vdc
Address Bit 12	B20	A20	−ADL
Ground	B21	A21	−PREEMPT
−IRQ 9	B22	A22	−BURST
−IRQ 3	B23	A23	−12 Vdc
−IRQ 4	B24	A24	ARB 00
Ground	B25	A25	ARB 01
−IRQ 5	B26	A26	ARB 02
−IRQ 6	B27	A27	−12 Vdc
−IRQ 7	B28	A28	ARB 03
Ground	B29	A29	ARB/ −GNT
Reserved	B30	A30	−TC
Reserved	B31	A31	+5 Vdc
−CHCK	B32	A32	−SO
Ground	B33	A33	−S1
−CMD	B34	A34	M/ −I/O
CHRDYRTN	B35	A35	+12 Vdc
−CD SFDBK	B36	A36	CD CHRDY
Ground	B37	A37	Data Bit 0
Data Bit 1	B38	A38	Data Bit 2
Data Bit 3	B39	A39	+5 Vdc
Data Bit 4	B40	A40	Data Bit 5
Ground	B41	A41	Data Bit 6
CHRESET	B42	A42	Data Bit 7
Reserved	B43	A43	Ground
Reserved	B44	A44	−DS 16 RTN
Ground	B45	A45	−REFRESH
Key	Key	Key	Key
Key	Key	Key	Key
Data Bit 8	B48	A48	+5 Vdc
Data Bit 9	B49	A49	Data Bit 10

Table 34-2. Continued

Signal	Pin	Pin	Signal
Ground	B50	A50	Data Bit 11
Data Bit 12	B51	A51	Data Bit 13
Data Bit 14	B52	A52	+12 Vdc
Data Bit 15	B53	A53	Reserved
Ground	B54	A54	–SBHE
–IRQ 10	B55	A55	–CD DS 16
–IRQ 11	B56	A56	+5 Vdc
–IRQ 12	B57	A57	–IRQ 14
Ground	B58	A58	–IRQ 15
Reserved	B59	A59	Reserved
Reserved	B60	A60	Reserved
Reserved	B61	A61	Ground
Reserved	B62	A62	Reserved
Ground	B63	A63	Reserved
Data Bit 16	B64	A64	Reserved
Data Bit 17	B65	A65	+12 Vdc
Data Bit 18	B66	A66	Data Bit 19
Ground	B67	A67	Data Bit 20
Data Bit 22	B68	A68	Data Bit 21
Data Bit 23	B69	A69	+5 Vdc
Reserved	B70	A70	Data Bit 24
Ground	B71	A71	Data Bit 25
Data Bit 27	B72	A72	Data Bit 26
Data Bit 28	B73	A73	+5 Vdc
Data Bit 29	B74	A74	Data Bit 30
Ground	B75	A75	Data Bit 31
–BE 0	B76	A76	Reserved
–BE 1	B77	A77	+12 Vdc
–BE 2	B78	A78	–BE 3
Ground	B79	A79	–DC 32 RTN
TR 32	B80	A80	–CD DS 32
Address Bit 24	B81	A81	+5 Vdc
Address Bit 25	B82	A82	Address Bit 26
Ground	B83	A83	Address Bit 27
Address Bit 29	B84	A84	Address Bit 28
Address Bit 30	B85	A85	+5 Vdc
Address Bit 31	B86	A86	Reserved
Ground	B87	A87	Reserved
Reserved	B88	A88	Reserved
Reserved	B89	A89	Ground

Knowing the MCA signals

Enable Synchronization (ESYNC) controls VGA signals (VSYNC, HSYNC, and BLANK) on the motherboard. When ESYNC is true, the Vertical Synchronization

(VSYNC) pulses, Horizontal Synchronization (HSYNC), and Blanking (BLANK) signals control the display. An independent 8-bit video data bus (P0 to P7) supports 256 colors on the VGA display. VGA timing signals are controlled by the Enable Data Clock (EDCLK) and Data Clock (DCLK) signals. The Enable Video (EVIDEO) signal switches control of the palette bus allowing an external video adapter to provide signals on P0 to P7. Audio (AUDIO) and Audio Signal Ground (Audio GROUND) allow the expansion board to send tone signals to the motherboard speaker.

There are 32 address bits (Address Bit 0 to Address Bit 31), 11 interrupts, and 32 data bits (Data Bit 0 to Data Bit 31). The –Address Latch (–ADL) signal is true when a valid address exists on the address lines. A –Channel Check (–CHCK) signal flags the motherboard when an error is detected on the expansion board. When data on the data bus is valid, the –Command (–CMD) is true. The Channel Ready Return (CHRDYRTN) signal is sent to the motherboard when the addressed expansion board I/O channel is ready. A Channel Reset (CHRESET) signal can be used to reset all expansion boards. The –Card Setup (–CDSETUP) instructs an addressed board to perform a setup. The Memory Address Enable 24 (MADE24) line activates address line 24. The Channel Ready (CHRDY) line that the board addressed is idle after completing its access. When –Burst (–BURST) is true, the system bus will execute a burst cycle.

The –Data Size 16 Return (–DS16RTN) and –Data Size 32 Return (–DS32RTN) tell the motherboard whether the board is running at a 16 or 32-bit bus width. The System Byte High Enable (SBHE) signal is true when the upper 16 data bits are being used, but the Card Data Size 16 (CDDS16) signal is true when only 16 data bits are being used. If all 32 bits of data are being transferred, the –Card Data Size 32 (–CDDS32) signal is true. When the main memory is being refreshed, the –Refresh (–REF) line is true. This allows any dynamic memory on expansion boards to be refreshed as well. The Memory/–I/O (M/–I/O) signal defines whether the expansion board is accessing a memory or I/O location. Signals –S0 and –S1 carry the status of a MicroChannel bus.

The –Preempt (–PREEMPT) signal is true when a bus arbitration cycle begins. The Arbitration signals ARB00 to ARB03 indicate (in BCD) which of the 16 possible bus masters has won arbitration. The Arbitration/–Grant (ARB/–GNT) is high when the bus is in arbitration, and low when bus control has been granted. When a DMA transfer has finished, the Terminal Count (TC) signal is true. –Byte Enable signals 0 to 3 (–BE0 to –BE3) indicate which four bytes of a 32-bit data bus are transferring data. When an external bus master is a 32-bit device, the Translate 32 (TR32) line is true. The –MMCR, –MMCCMD, and –MMC lines are matched memory control signals.

General bus troubleshooting

In most cases, you will not be troubleshooting a bus; after all, the bus is little more than a passive connector. However, the major signals that exist on an MCA bus can provide you with important clues about the system's operation. The most effective bus troubleshooting tool available to you is a POST board (such as the ones discussed in Chapter 28). Many POST boards are equipped with a number of LEDs that display power status, along with important timing and control signals. If one or more of those LEDs is missing, a fault has likely occurred somewhere on the motherboard. Refer to Chapter 28 for detailed POST board instructions. Although most POST boards are designed for ISA bus work, Micro2000 provides an MCA adapter for their POST-Probe.

Another point to consider is that bus connectors are mechanical devices; as a result, they do not last forever. If you or your customer are in the habit of removing and inserting boards frequently, it is likely that the metal fingers providing contact will wear and result in unreliable connections. Similarly, inserting a board improperly (or with excessive force) can break the connector. In extreme cases, even the motherboard can be damaged. The first rule of board replacement is: *always try removing and reinserting the suspect board*. It is not uncommon for oxides to develop on board and slot contacts that might eventually degrade signal quality. By removing the board and reinserting it, you can wipe off any oxides or dust and possibly improve the connections.

The second rule of board replacement is: *always try a board in another expansion slot before replacing it*. This way, a faulty bus slot can be ruled out before suffering the expense of a new board. If a bus slot proves defective, there is little that a technician can do except:

1. Block the slot and inform the customer that it is damaged and should not be used.
2. Replace the damaged bus slot connector (a tedious and time-consuming task) and pass the labor expense on to the customer.
3. Replace the motherboard outright (also a rather expensive option).

35
CHAPTER

Memory troubleshooting

Solid-state memory faults constitute a large percentage of computer problems. When you consider that memory ICs must contain the program instructions and data needed for execution by a microprocessor, the loss of even one bit can have catastrophic effects for the system. This chapter introduces you to some of the most important memory concepts, shows you a selection of IC configurations, and presents a series of practical troubleshooting techniques that can help you track down and correct memory problems.

Understanding memory basics

Before you jump right into memory troubleshooting, you should take some time to understand the concepts behind memory device organization and operation. Memory devices have evolved along with microprocessors over the last decade or so. Such intense evolution has resulted in an amazingly diverse selection of devices that are tailored to optimize almost any computer system. In spite of such diversity, however, the elementary concepts and operations of solid-state memory are virtually universal. Experienced technicians can feel free to skip the next few sections, but novices might find the following information to be helpful.

The storage cell

Memory ICs store programs and data as a huge series of binary digits (1s and 0s) where a 1 represents the presence of a signal voltage, and a 0 represents the absence of a signal voltage. Because each bit represents a voltage level, the voltage must be stored in an electronic circuit. Each circuit is known as a *storage cell*. The contents of storage cells can be copied to a bus or other waiting device (known as *reading*). Some storage cells can be set to new values by copying data from external bus signals (called *writing*). The exact structure and construction of a storage cell depends on the characteristics of the particular memory device. By combining storage cells into arrays as shown in Fig. 35-1, memory circuits can be created to hold many

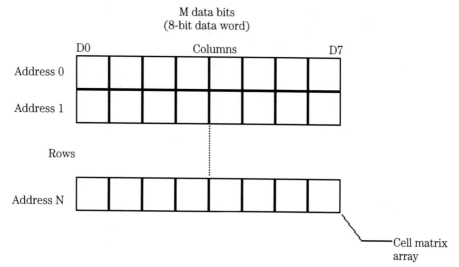

35-1 Simplified diagram of a memory array.

millions of bits. There are typically six broad types of storage cells in use today: SRAM, DRAM, ROM, PROM, EPROM, and EEPROM.

SRAM

SRAM (static RAM) stores bits in cells that act rather like electronic switches. SRAM cells turn electricity on (logic 1) or off (logic 0) to reflect the cell's state. In practice, an SRAM cell is usually a flip-flop circuit that is preset (logic 1) or reset (logic 0) when written. The flip-flop stores the condition of the bit until it is altered by a subsequent write operation (or until power is removed). Once data is stored in an SRAM cell, it will be retained indefinitely without any further interaction by the computer. Unfortunately, SRAM cells are physically large and consume a relatively large amount of power in active use. Today's SRAM ICs are generally limited to 262,144 (256K) bits.

DRAM

DRAM (dynamic RAM) uses an approach that stores bits in the form of electrical charges on incredibly small solid-state capacitors. A single MOS transistor is included with each capacitor to act as a switch or control element. The presence or absence of a charge defines whether the bit is a logic 1 or logic 0. By making each storage capacitor very small, charges can be added or withdrawn from a capacitor in only a few nanoseconds. Because each storage cell is extremely small and uses almost no current, storage density is exceptionally high, and power dissipation is very low. The system memory found in virtually all PCs is DRAM.

Unfortunately, DRAMs are not nearly as simple to operate as SRAM devices. The electrical charges used to represent each bit condition only have a limited life span of a few milliseconds or so. After a few milliseconds, charge levels are irretrievably lost and memory is corrupted. To preserve the charge conditions in a DRAM, each cell must be periodically *refreshed*. It is this need for regular, active maintenance that earned these devices the term *dynamic*. Refresh operation is covered in this chapter.

ROM

Mask ROM (conventional ROM) cells are nothing more than the absence (logic 1) or presence (logic 0) of a physical electrical connection. The precise pattern of 1s and 0s is specified by the purchaser and fabricated onto the ROM during its manufacturing process. Once a mask ROM IC is created, its contents can never be changed. Because no active circuitry is needed to store 1s and 0s, ROM ICs offer some of the highest storage densities available. ROM devices also are available in a number of other programmable versions (PROM, EPROM, and EEPROM). As with all types of ROM devices, mask ROM cannot lose its contents when computer power is turned off. The BIOS ROM used in many PCs are mask-type (although there is a growing trend toward PROM devices).

PROM

Because of the time delays and expense of having ROMs manufactured, it is usually much faster and less expensive for PC BIOS makers to program their own ROMs, at least until the code is proven and thoroughly debugged. *PROM* (programmable read-only memory) ICs work very much like mask ROMs in that logic levels are established by the presence of simple electrical connections. However, PROMs are manufactured with all possible connections in place (all logic 0s). A piece of equipment called a *PROM Programmer* reads the program to be loaded from the computer and steps through each address. Each bit that must be a logic 1 is zapped with a high-voltage pulse that destroys that connection to form a logic 1. This zapping process is called *burning* the PROM. Once a PROM is programmed, its contents cannot be cleared or rewritten.

EPROM

Naturally, it is desirable to recycle memory devices as much as possible instead of throwing them away over as much as a single bit error. *EPROM*s (erasable PROMS) are used to provide thousands of erase-rewrite cycles in a useful lifetime. EPROM bits are not stored as physical connections, but as electrical charges deposited onto the IC's substrate. Microscopic transistors detect the presence or absence of charge as a logic 1 or logic 0 respectively. Once a charge is deposited, it remains in place almost permanently (unlike DRAM devices whose charges last only a few milliseconds).

To erase an EPROM, the semiconductor die holding the electrical charges must be excited by short-wavelength ultraviolet (UV) light. UV allows the charges to dissipate and return each EPROM storage cell to a blank condition. You can recognize EPROMs by the quartz or plastic window in the IC body. Note that sunlight and fluorescent light contain wavelengths that will erase EPROM data, so it is always a good policy to keep the erasure window covered with a piece of black tape or a label sticker.

EEPROM

Removing an IC from a circuit in order to erase and reprogram it can be a very inconvenient (and potentially damaging) task. An *Electrically Erasable PROM*

(EEPROM or *flash memory*) is a modified version of EPROM technology whose contents can be erased using electrical pulses instead of ultraviolet light. This approach allows blocks of addresses (not necessarily the entire device) to be erased and rewritten while the IC is still in the circuit, yet the IC retains its information without power. A large number of PC manufacturers are using flash memory instead of conventional ROM devices. This allows BIOS upgrades to be programmed right on the motherboard without even removing the BIOS IC.

Memory operations

It takes much more than just a few storage cells to make a working memory IC. Most memory ICs can be broken down into four major segments: the storage array, the address buffer and decoding circuits, the data bus buffer circuits, and the control circuits. Each of these elements is very important to all memory operation. Figure 35-2 illustrates these areas in a typical memory IC.

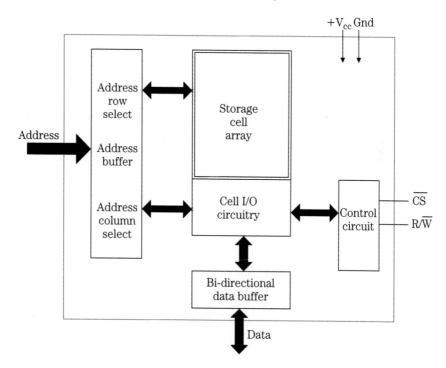

35-2 Diagram of a typical memory IC.

Storage array

Storage cells must be organized into a two-dimensional *array* (or matrix) made up of rows and columns. This memory array is where information is actually stored. Depending on the type of cells used, there can be millions of cells in the array. However, additional circuitry is needed to select which cells in the array are active, manage the data at those cells, and control the flow of data into or out of the IC.

Address circuits

Address signals select the active cells. Once valid address signals are applied to the IC, address decoding circuitry enables the proper cells. Each address can select 1, 2, 4, 8, or 16 cells depending on the array's configuration and its address decoding circuitry. It is important for you to note that memory ICs are defined by their address/data organization. For example, an IC can hold 16 kilobits, but that does not tell you how the IC is organized. That 16-kilobit IC can be organized as 16K × 1 bit (16,384 address locations with 1 bit at every location), or 4K × 4 bits (4096 addresses with 4 bits per address), 2K × 8 bits (2048 addresses with 8 bits per address), and so on, but each of these organizations would still be 16-kilobit ICs.

Control and data circuits

Once the desired cells are active, control signals determine how the IC responds to data. There are two common control signals: –Chip Select (–CS) and –Write Enable (–WE) or Read/–Write (R/–W). When the chip select is logic 1, the IC is disabled, so it will not interact with the data bus at all regardless of what address is applied. In the disabled state, the IC's data lines are neither logic 1 nor logic 0, but a high-impedance state that effectively disconnects the IC from the data bus. The chip select signal is handy for controlling multiple memory ICs that share the same bus.

When the chip select is logic 0, the IC is enabled. Data signals at the selected address will leave (or enter) the memory array normally. The read/write signal defines the direction of data flow. When the read/write signal is logic 1, data at the selected address will leave the IC through a data buffer; the IC is read. If the read/write signal is logic 0 (and the storage array uses RAM cells) data entering the IC is buffered and stored in the cells selected by the address signals; the IC is written. Address decoding, data buffering, and IC control must work together to operate the storage array.

Access time

In an ideal memory device, selected data would be instantly available at the IC's data lines. In the real world, however, there is always some finite amount of time delay between the point at which an address input is valid, and the point at which selected data becomes valid at the data lines. This time delay is known as *access time*. Even though memory IC access time is on the order of nanoseconds, it can have a profound impact on the overall performance of your computer. Table 35-1 illustrates typical access times for DRAM, cache, and tag memory versus CPU speed. Memory devices that are not fast enough to keep pace with the microprocessor can seriously impair performance and necessitate the use of *wait states* (explained in this chapter). SRAM components typically offer the lowest access times, and EPROM and EEPROM devices usually offer the highest access times.

**Table 35-1. Typical memory
speed parameters**

CPU speed	DRAM	Cache	Tag
8 MHz	120 ns	35 ns	35 ns
10 MHz	120 ns	35 ns	30 ns
12 MHz	120 ns	35 ns	30 ns

Table 35-1. Continued

CPU speed	DRAM	Cache	Tag
16 MHz	100 ns	30 ns	30 ns
20 MHz	100 ns	30 ns	25 ns
25 MHz	80 ns	25 ns	25 ns
33 MHz	80 ns	25 ns	20 ns
40 MHz	80 ns	20 ns	20 ns
50 MHz	70 ns	20 ns	15 ns
66 MHz	70 ns	20 ns	15 ns

As you might recognize from this discussion, it is very important that each memory device used in a PC provide an access time at least as fast as the slowest rate. For example, the DRAM used in a 33-MHz PC should have an access time of 80 ns or faster. Using faster memory (70 ns) should work without a problem. However, there should be no devices slower than 80 ns (100 ns). If slower devices are used, chronic memory errors will result. Although it is technically possible to mix memory speeds (so long as none is too slow), it is advisable to keep memory speeds as close as possible. If problems continue, make sure that the memory is all from the same manufacturer.

Wait states

The importance of memory performance became evident in the early 1980s during the introduction of 286-class machines (IBM ATs). Memory ICs of the day were unable to keep pace with the 80286, which led to serious system performance problems. Designers overcame this problem by "slowing down" the microprocessor during memory access. This is done by adding *wait states*. A wait state causes the microprocessor to suspend its activities for one or more clock cycles, thus allowing slower memory to catch up. The number of wait states depends on memory speed related to microprocessor speed. Larger disparities require more wait states, and vice versa. Wait states are still used in some low-end computers today, but they are a much more significant factor in older computers.

Refresh operation

The electrical charges placed in each DRAM storage cell must be replenished (or *refreshed*) periodically every few milliseconds. Without refresh, DRAM data will be lost. In principle, refresh requires that each storage cell be read and rewritten to the memory array. This is typically accomplished by reading and rewriting an entire row of the array at one time. Each row of bits is sequentially read into a sense/refresh amplifier (part of the DRAM IC) that basically recharges the appropriate storage capacitors, then rewrites each row bit to the array. In actual operation, a row of bits is automatically refreshed whenever an array row is selected. Thus, the entire memory array can be refreshed by reading each row in the array every few milliseconds.

The key to refresh is in the way DRAMs are addressed. Unlike other memory ICs that supply all address signals to the IC simultaneously, a DRAM is addressed in a two-step sequence. The overall address is separated into a row (low) address and a column (high) address. Row address bits are placed on the DRAM address bus first, and the Row Address Select (RAS) line is pulsed logic 0 to multiplex the bits into the IC's address decoding circuitry. The low portion of the address activates an entire array row and causes each bit in the row to be sensed and refreshed. Logic 0s remain logic 0s, and logic 1s are recharged to their full value.

Column address bits are then placed on the DRAM address bus, and the column address select (CAS) is pulsed to logic 0. The column portion of the address selects the appropriate bits within the chosen row. If a read operation is taking place, the selected bits pass through the data buffer to the data bus. During a write operation, the read/write line must be logic 0, and valid data must be available to the IC before CAS is strobed. New data bits are then placed in their corresponding locations in the memory array.

Even if the IC is not being accessed for reading or writing, the memory array must still be refreshed to ensure data integrity. Fortunately, refresh can be accomplished by interrupting the microprocessor to run a refresh routine that simply steps through every row address in sequence (column addresses need not be selected for simple refresh). This row-only (or RAS only) refresh technique speeds the refresh process. Although refreshing DRAM every few milliseconds might seem like a constant aggravation, the computer can execute quite a few instructions before being interrupted for refresh. There are several other refresh techniques that can be used in DRAM systems, but they are not covered in this edition.

Enhanced memory concepts

Memory speed is intimately related to your computer system's performance. Microprocessors regularly access system memory for instructions and data. If memory is not fast enough to keep up with the CPU, the wait states that must be added slow down the system and waste the potential power offered by today's new CPUs. A large portion of computer design has been directed toward improving memory performance. In some cases, memory technology has been modified and tweaked to supply enhanced performance in certain operating modes. In other cases, ordinary memory ICs are used in optimized circuit arrangements. The following few sections introduce you to some of the memory enhancement techniques that might be used in your computer.

Page-mode RAM

One of the main objectives of memory is to keep wait states at zero. No wait states result in faster system performance. Page-mode RAM uses elements of both static and dynamic memory to reduce wait states. Page-mode RAM divides its total memory array onto subsections (called *pages*) of about two kilobytes each. When data is repeatedly addressed from within the same page, memory can be accessed without wait states. When memory access must take place from a different page, wait states are added until the new page is accessed. The most efficient operation is achieved when page-to-page access is kept to a minimum. Using page-mode RAM can improve overall memory performance by up to 60%.

Banked memory

Another method of improving system memory performance is to bank (or *interleave*) the system RAM. Interleaved memory is similar to page-mode RAM because system performance is improved when sequential (contiguous) memory locations are read, but ordinary system RAM ICs can be used instead of specialized page-mode RAM, and bank sizes can be on the order of megabytes.

System RAM is divided into 2 or 4 banks (or more). Sequential bits are held on alternate banks (byte 1 is in bank 1, byte 2 is in bank 2, byte 3 is in bank 1, byte 4 is in bank 2, and so on) so the CPU steps from bank to bank. While the microprocessor is reading one bank, the alternate bank is cycling so that no waiting is required when the CPU reads again; thus, wait states can be eliminated as long as the next bits to be read are in an alternate bank. If data must be accessed out of order, wait states are inserted automatically until a new alternating sequence is running. Banked memory can improve system performance by up to 75% while still using standard memory ICs.

Video memory

The image you see on a computer's display is actually held in a small area of memory called *VRAM* (video RAM). Video RAM acts as a frame buffer where a bit, byte, or several bytes are used to represent each element (or *pixel*) of the picture (depending on the screen mode). The display controller reads through video memory about 30 to 60 times each second and re-creates (or *retraces*) the image specified in memory. The computer writes to VRAM in order to update the image being displayed.

However, ordinary memory ICs cannot be read and written simultaneously. The time delay incurred waiting for reading to finish before writing can begin is very perplexing. Many high-end video adapters now use specialized VRAM ICs with two data paths, one input path and one output path. By using two independent data paths, the same memory location CAN be read and written simultaneously. A CPU can write updated image information to video memory at its own pace. The video controller can sequentially read image data independently.

Cache and tag memory

Unfortunately, even the fastest DRAM is still hard-pressed to keep pace with the current generation of fast CPUs. *Caching* is a memory speed enhancement technique used with today's highest-performance systems. A cache places a (relatively) small amount of very fast memory (typically SRAM) between the CPU and the bulk of system memory as shown in Fig. 35-3. By keeping fast cache memory filled with data that the CPU needs, data can be accessed without wait states; performance is improved. There are generally three elements to a cache system: tag RAM, cache logic, and cache RAM.

It is important to know if a copy of needed information is in the cache or not. When information is copied into the cache, the system memory address where that data is stored is kept in *tag RAM* along with status bits needed by the cache logic. Each cache entry is referred to as a *tab*. Thus, tag RAM acts as the cache librarian.

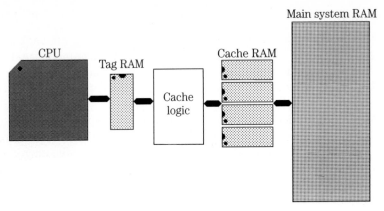

35-3 Major cache system components.

Cache controller logic keeps track of the microprocessor's memory access and tries to keep the cache filled with data that the CPU is most likely to need next. The cache memory itself is typically an amount of fast, expensive SRAM. A *cache hit* occurs when the needed data is indeed in the cache; the data is accessed without wait states and system performance is enhanced. If needed data is not in the cache, a *cache miss* occurs and data is accessed from system memory at normal speeds (including wait states). The cache is then refilled if necessary and the hit-or-miss access continues.

There are generally two ways of implementing a cache system: internal or external. Internal cache is part of the CPU; all of the elements of a cache system are fabricated right into the microprocessor itself. For example, Intel's Pentium microprocessor contains two internal 8K caches (one for instructions, and the other for data). External cache is built onto the motherboard. Although external cache is a bit slower byte-for-byte when compared with an internal cache, the size and expandability of an external cache often provides superior performance overall.

The size of a cache is the biggest overall performance factor. Most practical caches contain 8K to 256K. Of course, larger or smaller caches can be used, but small caches mean more cache misses (and lower overall system performance). Large caches certainly mean more cache hits, but the cost and physical size of additional memory becomes impractical. The microprocessor uses one of three methods to determine whether needed data is in the cache: direct-mapped, full-associative, and set-associative. However, this chapter does not detail these particular methods.

Shadow memory

ROM devices (whether the BIOS ROM on your motherboard, or a ROM IC on an expansion board) are frustratingly slow with access times often exceeding several hundred nanoseconds. ROM access then requires a large number of wait states that slow down the system's performance. This problem is compounded because the routines stored in BIOS (especially the video BIOS ROM on the video board) are some of the most frequently accessed areas in your computer.

Beginning with the 80386-class computers, some designs employed a memory technique called *shadowing*. ROM contents are loaded into an area of fast RAM during system initialization, then the computer maps the fast RAM into memory locations used by the ROM devices. Whenever ROM routines must be accessed during run-time, information is taken from the shadow ROM instead of the actual ROM IC. The ROM performance can be effectively improved by at least 300%.

Shadow memory also is useful for ROM devices that do not use the full available data bus width. For example, a 16-bit computer system might hold an expansion board containing an 8-bit ROM IC. The system would have to access the ROM not once but twice to extract a single 16-bit word. If the computer is a 32-bit machine, that 8-bit ROM would have to be addressed four times to make a complete 32-bit word. Imagine the hideous system delays that can be encountered. Loading the ROM to shadow memory in advance virtually eliminates such delays. Shadowing can usually be turned on or off through the system's setup routines.

PC memory organization

When the original PC/XT was designed, it used the Intel 8086 microprocessor. The 8086 could only work with 1Mb of RAM, so DOS was designed to work within 1Mb as well (technicians refer to this as *real-mode addressing*). When Intel's 80286 microprocessor appeared in the PC/AT, the i286 could work with 16Mb of RAM, but the 1Mb limit remained to ensure backward compatibility with DOS and 8086 systems. Working with RAM above the 1Mb limit required the microprocessor to change its operating mode (known as *protected-mode addressing*). Every Intel CPU to follow (the i386, i486, and Pentium) also kept this shortcoming for the sake of backward compatibility.

Conventional and upper memory

Out of the original 1Mb of real-mode memory space, the lower 640K was allocated as the user memory area as shown in Fig. 35-4. This is where programs and data are loaded and executed under DOS. In time, this area became known as the *conventional memory* area. You might wonder why the PC would only set aside 640K for applications if 1Mb is readily accessible. The answer is that there is much more than applications that have to be handled within the first 1Mb. BIOS instructions, DOS itself, TSRs and device drivers, video memory, and expansion ROMs (for disk drives, video adapters, and so on) all need a part of the available space.

To ensure that video memory and expansion ROMs would always have plenty of room, PC designers allocated the upper portion of 1Mb (about 384K from 640K to 1024K) exclusively for such support purposes. This became known as the *upper memory area* (or UMA). The first 640K (*conventional memory*) was left over to load BIOS data, DOS, TSRs and device drivers, and any applications and files. Until the release of MS-DOS 5.0, it was virtually impossible to access upper memory. But the inclusion of DOS memory managers allows TSRs, device drivers, and often DOS itself to be loaded into unused areas of upper memory, thus freeing conventional memory for larger, more demanding DOS applications. Table 35-2 provides a detailed breakdown of a PC memory map. You can see how each address is utilized.

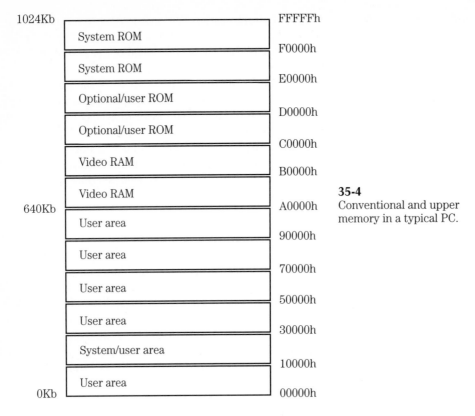

35-4
Conventional and upper memory in a typical PC.

Table 35-2. Real-mode memory map of a typical PC

Address Range (h)	Description
00000-003FF	**Interrupt Vector Table (256 double words):**
00000	INT 00H Divide by Zero interrupt handler
00004	INT 01H Single Step interrupt handler
00008	INT 02H Non-Maskable Interrupt (memory parity or I/O error)
0000C	INT 03H Breakpoint
00010	INT 04H Arithmetic Overflow interrupt handler
00014	INT 05H Print Screen
00018	INT 06H Reserved
0001C	INT 07H Reserved
00020	INT 08H Timer Interrupt Routine (18.21590 /sec) IRQ0
00024	INT 09H Keyboard Service Routine IRQ1
00028	INT 0AH VGA Retrace (and AT Slave Interrupts) IRQ2
0002C	INT 0BH Serial Device 2 Service Routine IRQ3
00030	INT 0CH Serial Device 1 Service Routine IRQ4
00034	INT 0DH Hard Disk Interrupt Routine IRQ5
00038	INT 0EH Diskette Interrupt Routine IRQ6
0003C	INT 0FH Parallel Port Service Routine IRQ7
00040	INT 10H Video Services

Table 35-2. Continued

Address Range (h)	Description
00044	INT 11H Equipment Check
00048	INT 12H Memory Size Check
0004C	INT 13H Diskette and Hard Disk I/O
00050	INT 14H RS-232 Service Call
00054	INT 15H System Services Calls
00058	INT 16H Keyboard Call
0005C	INT 17H Printer I/O Call
00060	INT 18H Basic ROM Entry (startup)
00064	INT 19H Boot Loader: Implement System (IPL) from disk
00068	INT 1AH Time of Day Call
0006C	INT 1BH Keyboard Break Address
00070	INT 1CH User Timer Interrupt
00074	INT 1DH Monitor ROM—or 6845 Video Initialization
00078	INT 1EH Disk Control Table Pointer
0007C	INT 1FH Alphanumeric Character Pattern Table Pointer
00080	INT 20H DOS Terminate Program
00084	INT 21H Microsoft DOS Function Calls
00088	INT 22H DOS Terminate Address (not a callable function)
0008C	INT 23H DOS Ctrl-break Exit Address (not a callable function)
00090	INT 24H DOS Fatal Error Exit Address (not a callable function)
00094	INT 25H DOS Absolute Disk Read
00098	INT 26H DOS Absolute Disk Write
0009C	INT 27H Terminate and Stay Resident (control passes to COMMAND.COM)
000A0	INT 28H Idle Loop, spooler waiting; issued by DOS when waiting
000A4	INT 29H CON Device Raw Output Handler
000A8	INT 2AH 3.x Network Communications
000AC	INT 2BH-2DH Reserved for DOS
000B8	INT 2EH Execute DOS Command (undocumented)
000BC	INT 2FH Print Spool Control (Multiplex Interrupt)
000C0	INT 30H-31H Internal Use
000C8	INT 32H Reserved for DOS
000CC	INT 33H Microsoft Mouse Driver Calls
000D0	INT 34H-3EH Reserved for DOS
000FC	INT 3FH Used by LINK to manage overlay segments
00100	INT 40H Fixed disk/Floppy Disk Handler
00104	INT 41H ROM pointer; Fixed Disk Parameters
00108	INT 42H EGA: Video Vector Screen BIOS Entry
0010C	INT 43H EGA: Initialization Parameters
00100	INT 44H EGA: Graphics Character Patterns
00114	INT 45H Reserved
00118	INT 46H AT: Pointer to Second Fixed Disk Parameters
0011C	INT 47H Reserved
00120	INT 48H PCjr Cordless Keyboard Xlat Routine
00124	INT 49H PCjr Non-Keyboard Scan Code Xlat Table

Table 35-2. Continued

Address Range (h)	Description	
00128	INT 4AH AT, PS/2 User Alarm Routine	
0012C	INT 4BH-4FH Reserved	
00140	INT 50H Periodic Alarm Interrupt from Timer	
00144	INT 51H-59H Reserved	
00168	INT 5AH Cluster Adapter BIOS-entry Address	
0016C	INT 5BH Cluster Boot	
00170	INT 5CH NETBIOS Entry Point	
00174	INT 5DH-5FH Reserved	
00180	INT 60H-66H Reserved for user program interrupts	
0019C	INT 67H EMM: Expanded Memory Manager Routines	
001A0	INT 68H-6BH Unused	
001B0	INT 6CH System Resume Vector	
001B4	INT 6DH-6FH Unused	
001C0	INT 70H Real Time Clock	IRQ8
001C4	INT 71H LAN Adapter	IRQ9
001C8	INT 72H Reserved	IRQ10
001CC	INT 73H Reserved	IRQ11
001D0	INT 74H Mouse Interrupt	IRQ12
001D4	INT 75H 80287 NMI Error	IRQ13
001D8	INT 76H Fixed disk controller	IRQ14
001DC	INT 77H Reserved	IRQ15
001E0	INT 78H-7FH Unused	
00200	INT 80H-85H Reserved for BASIC	
00218	INT 86H AT: NetBIOS relocated INT 18H	
0021C	INT 87H-F0H Reserved for BASIC Interpreter	
003C4	INT F1H-FFH Reserved for User Program Interrupts	
003FF	Used for power-on and initial boot stack	

00400-004FF	**BIOS Data Area:**	
00400	COM1: to COM4: port addresses	
00408	LPT1: to LPT3: port addresses	
0040E	LPT4: address except PS/2 Reserved	
00410	Equipment flag	
	bits: 15-14 number of LPTs attached	
	13 internal modem (CVT) or reserved	
	12 joystick	
	11-9 number of COMs	
	8 unused (jr: DMS chip present)	
	7-6 number of disk drives	
	5 $1 = 80 \times 25$ $0 = 40 \times 25$ screen	
	4 1 = color 0 = monochrome	
	3-2 00 = 64K chips; 11 = 256K chips (PC,XT,AT)	
	1 math coprocessor installed	
	0 IPL disk installed	
00412	Init Flag; Reserved (CVT self-test status)	

Table 35-2. Continued

Address Range (h)	Description
00413	Memory size in K bytes
00415	Reserved
00416	Reserved
00417	Keyboard monitor flag bytes 0 and 1:

bit:

	Byte 0	Byte 1
7	ins lock	ins pressed
6	caps lock	caps pressed
5	num lock	num lock pressed
4	scroll lock	scroll pressed
3	alt pressed	pause locked
2	crtl pressed	sysreq pressed
1	<shift press	<alt pressed
0	>shift press	>alt pressed

Address Range (h)	Description
00419	Alternate keypad entry
0041A	Keyboard buffer head pointer
0041C	Keyboard buffer tail pointer
0041E	Keyboard buffer
0043E	Drive recalibration status

bit:

7	Interrupt flag
6-4	reserved
3	recalibrate drive 3
2	recalibrate drive 2
1	recalibrate drive 1
0	recalibrate drive 0

0043F — Motor Status

bit:

7	Currently reading or writing	
6	reserved	
5-4	00 drive	0 selected
	01 drive	1 selected
	10 drive	2 selected
	11 drive	3 selected
3-0	Drive 3-0 Motor On status	

Address Range (h)	Description
00440	Motor Control time-out counter
00441	Diskette Status Return Code

- 00H - No error
- 01H - Invalid diskette drive parameter
- 02H - Address Mark not found
- 03H - Write-protect error
- 04H - Requested   Sector not found
- 05H - reserved
- 06H - Diskette Change Line active
- 07H - reserved
- 08H - DMA overrun on operation
- 09H - Attempt to DMA across a 64K boundary
- 0AH - reserved
- 0BH - reserved

Table 35-2. Continued

Address Range (h)	Description

0CH - Media Type not found

0DH - reserved

0EH - reserved

0FH - reserved

10H - CRC error on diskette read

20H - General Controller failure

40H - Seek operation failed

80H - Diskette drive not ready

| 00442 | Diskette Drive Controller Status Bytes (NEC) |
| 00449 | CRT_MODE |

bit:	7	text 80 × 25 mono on mono card
	6	graphics 640 × 200 mono on color card
	5	graphics 320 × 200 mono on color card
	4	graphics 320 × 200 on color card
	3	text 80 × 25 color
	2	text 80 × 25 mono on color
	1	text 40 × 25 color
	0	text 40 × 25 mono on color card

0044A	CRT_COLS Number of columns (80)
0044C	CRT_LEN Length of Regen Buffer in bytes
0044E	CRT_START Starting Address in Regen Buffer
00450	Cursor Position on each of eight pages
00460	CURSOR_MODE top-bottom line of cursor (Cursor Type)
00462	ACTIVE_PAGE index
00463	ADDR_6845 Base Address for 6845 Display Chip

3B4H for monochrome

3D4H for color

| 00465 | CRT_MODE_SETting for 3x8 Register |

3B8H for MDA

3D8H for CGA

00466	CRT_PALLETTE Setting Register (3D9H) on Color Card
00467	Temporary storage for SS:SP during shutdown
0046B	Flag to indicate interrupt
0046C	Timer counter (Timer Low, Timer High words)
00470	Timer overflow (24 hour roll over flag byte)
00471	Break key state (bit 7 = 1 if break key pressed)
00472	Reset flag word:

1234 bypass memory test

4321 preserve memory

5678 system suspend

9ABC manufacturing test

ABCD system POST loop (CVT)

| 00474 | Hard Disk status or Reserved for ESDI Adapter/A |

00H - No error

Table 35-2. Continued

Address Range (h)	Description
	01H - Invalid Function Request
	02H - Address Mark not found
	03H - Write Protect error
	04H - Requested Sector not found
	05H - Reset Failed
	06H - Reserved
	07H - Drive Parameter Activity Failed
	08H - DMA overrun on operation
	09H - Data boundary error
	0AH - Bad Sector Flag detected
	0BH - Bad Track detected
	0CH - Reserved
	0DH - Invalid number of sectors on format
	0EH - Control Data Address Mark detected
	0FH - DMA Arbitration Level out of range
	10H - Uncorrectable ECC or CRC error
	20H - General Controller failure
	40H - Seek operation failed
	80H - Time out
	AAH - Drive not ready
	BBH - Undefined error occurred
	CCH - Write fault on selected drive
	E0H - Status error/Error Register 0
	FFH - Sense operation failed
00475	Number of hard disk drives
00476	Fixed Disk Drive Control byte (PC XT)
00477	Fixed Disk Drive Controller Port (PC XT)
00478	LPT1: to LPT4: timeout byte values (PS/2 has no LPT4:)
0047C	COM1: to COM4: timeout byte values
00480	Keyboard buffer start pointer (word)
00482	Keyboard buffer end pointer (word)
00484	ROWS Video Character Rows - 1
00485	POINTS Height of character matrix-bytes per character
00487	INFO byte:

bit:

7	Video mode number (of INT 10H funct.0)	
6-5	Size of video RAM	00-64K
		10-192K
		01-128K
		11-256K
4	reserved	
3	(1) video subsystem is inactive	
2	reserved	
1	(1) video subsystem on monochrome	
0	(1) alphanumeric cursor emulation enabled	

Table 35-2. Continued

Address Range (h)	Description		
00488	INFO_3 byte:		
	bit:	7	Input FEAT1 (bit 6 of ISR0) (Input Status Reg.)
		6	Input FEAT1 (bit 5 of ISR0)
		5	Input FEAT0 (bit 6 of ISR0)
		4	Input FEAT0 (bit 5 of ISR0)
		3	EGA Config. switch 4 (1 = off)
		2	EGA Config. switch 3
		1	EGA Config. switch 2
		0	EGA Config. switch 1
00489	Flags		
	bit:	7	bit 4 Alphanumeric scanlines:
			00 350 line mode
			01 400
			10 200
			11 reserved
		6	(1) display switching enabled
		5	reserved
		3	(1) default palett loading is disabled
		2	(1) using monochrome monitor
		1	(1) gray scale is enabled
		0	(1) VGA is active
0048A	DCC Display Combination Code table index (VGA)		
0048B	Media Control		
	bit:	7-6	Last diskette drive data rate selected
			00 - 500Kb per second
			01 - 300Kb per second
			10 - 250Kb per second
			11 - reserved
		5-4	Last diskette drive step rate selected
		3-0	reserved
0048C	Hard Disk Status Register		
0048D	Hard Disk Error Register		
0048E	Hard Disk Interrupt Control Flag		
0048F	Combination Hard Disk/Floppy Card (bit 0 = 1)		
00490	Drive 0 media state byte		
00491	Drive 1 media state byte		
00492	Drive 2 media state byte		
00493	Drive 3 media state byte		
	bit:	7-6	Diskette drive date rate
			00 - 500Kb per second
			01 - 300Kb per second
			10 - 250Kb per second
			11 - reserved
		5	Double stepping required

Table 35-2. Continued

Address Range (h)	Description

	4	Media established
	3	Reserved
	2-0	Drive/Media State

000 - 360Kb diskette/360Kb drive not established

001 - 360Kb diskette/1.2Mb drive not established

010 - 1.2Mb diskette/1.2Mb drive not established

011 - 360Kb diskette/360Kb drive established

100 - 360Kb diskette/1.2Mb drive established

101 - 1.2Mb diskette/1.2Mb drive established

110 - Reserved

111 - None of the above

00494	Drive 0 track currently selected
00495	Drive 1 track currently selected
00496	Keyboard mode state and type flags

bit:	7	Read ID in progress
	6	Last character was first ID character
	5	Force Num Lock if read ID and KBX
	4	101/102 keyboard installed
	3	right Alt key pressed
	2	Right Ctrl key pressed
	1	Last code was E0 hidden code
	0	Last code was E1 hidden code

| 00497 | Keyboard LED flags |

bit:	7	Keyboard transmit error flag
	6	Mode indicator update
	5	Cancel receive flag
	4	Acknowledgment received
	3	= 0 reserved
	2-0	Keyboard LED state bits

00498	Offset address to user wait complete flag
0049A	Segment to user wait complete flag
0049C	User wait count, microseconds low word
0049E	User wait count, microseconds high word
004A0	Wait active flag

| bit: | 7 | wait-time elapse and post flag |
| | 6-1 | reserved |

004A1	LANA DMA channel flags
004A2	LANA 0 status
004A3	LANA 1 status
004A4	Saved hardfile interrupt vector

Table 35-2. Continued

Address Range (h)	Description
004A8	BIOS Video Save Table and overrides
004AC	Reserved
004B4	Keyboard NMI control flags (CVT)
004B5	Keyboard break pending flags (CVT)
004B9	Port 60 single byte queue (CVT)
004BA	Scan code of last key (CVT)
004BB	Pointer to NMI buffer head (CVT)
004BC	Pointer to NMI buffer tail (CVT)
004BD	NMI scan code buffer (CVT)
004CE	Day counter (CVT and after)
004D0	Reserved
004F0	Application program communication area
00500-005FF	**DOS Data Area:**
00500	Print screen status flag
	1 = printer active
	0FFH = printer fault
00501	Reserved for BASIC and POST work area
00504	Single-drive mode status byte
	0 = drive A
	1 = drive B
00505	Reserved POST work area
00510	Reserved for BASIC
0050F	BASIC Shell
	Flag = 2 if current shell
00510	BASIC segment address storage set with DEF SEG
00512	BASIC int 1Ch clock interrupt vector
00516	BASIC int 23h ctrl-break interrupt vector
0051A	BASIC int 24h disk error interrupt vector
0051B	BASIC dynamic storage
00520	DOS dynamic storage
00522	Used by DOS for diskette initialization
00530	Used by MODE command
00534	Reserved for DOS data
00600	Reserved for DOS
00700	I/O drivers from xIO.SYS
00847-0FFFF	xIO.SYS IRET for interrupts 1, 3, and 0FH during POST
	MS-DOS kernel from xDOS.SYS: Interrupt handlers and routines
	MS-DOS disk buffer cache, FCBs and installable device drivers
	MCB (Memory control block, 16 bytes, paragraph aligned)
	Start of Transient Program
10000-9FFFF	**User Data Area (programs and data)**
A0000-AFFFF	Start of EGA and VGA graphics display RAM Modes 0Dh and above

Table 35-2. Continued

Address Range (h)	Description
B0000-B3FFF	Start of MDA and Hercules graphics display RAM
B4000-B7FFF	Reserved for Graphics display RAM
B8000-BBFFF	Start of CGA Color graphics display RAM
BC000-BFFFF	Reserved for Graphics display RAM
C0000-C3FFF	EGA BIOS ROM
C4000-C5FFF	Video adapter ROM space
C6000-C63FF	256 bytes of PGA communication area
C6400-C7FFF	Last 7Kb of video adapter ROM space
C8000-CBFFF	16K of hard disk BIOS adapter ROM space
CC000-CFFFF	
D0000-D7FFF	32K cluster adapter BIOS ROM
D8000-DBFFF	
DC000-DFFFF	Last 16Kb of adapter ROM space
E0000-EFFFF	64K expansion ROM space (AT, PS/2)
F0000-F3FFF	System Monitor ROM
F4000-F7FFF	System Expansion ROMs
F8000-FBFFF	
FC000-FEFFF	BIOS ROM, BASIC, and simple BIOS
FF000-FFFEF	System ROM
FFFF0-FFFF3	Hardware boot far jump vector

High memory

There has been a great deal of confusion expressed about high memory. Generally, *high memory* has come to mean any memory beyond 1Mb. Although this is a harmless simplification, it is not entirely correct. There is a peculiar anomaly that occurs with CPUs designed to use extended memory; they can access one segment (64K) of extended memory beyond the real-mode area (1048K to 1114K). This capability arises because of the address line layout on late model CPUs. As a result, the real-mode operation can access roughly 64K above the 1Mb limit.

Like upper DOS memory, this found 64K is not contiguous with the normal 640K DOS memory range, so DOS cannot use this high memory to load a DOS application, but device drivers and TSRs can be placed in high memory. MS-DOS versions 5.0 and later are intentionally designed so that its 40+ kilobytes of code can be easily moved into this high memory area (or HMA). With DOS loaded into high memory, an extra 40K (DOS 5.0) or so will be available within the 640K DOS range. Keep in mind that both HIMEM.SYS and EMM386.EXE must be loaded before anything can be used in high memory.

Extended and expanded memory

Today's CPUs are designed to access a great deal of potential memory space above the 1Mb mark, as much as 4Gb of RAM (though many current PCs are designed to hold up to 32Mb of RAM). However, the problem of a 1Mb limit still exists.

PCs must use memory management software that allows DOS to reach out beyond 1Mb. There are two broad types of memory beyond 1Mb: extended and expanded. The physical RAM that is installed beyond 1Mb can be used as either extended or expanded memory depending on what memory management software is being used.

Extended memory (XMS) is a simple and straightforward technique that just tacks memory onto the first 1Mb. This results in memory addresses that are larger than FFFFFh (which is hexadecimal notation for 1024K). Windows is designed to work with addresses larger than FFFFFh, so XMS is well suited for Windows. On the other hand, DOS and DOS applications are not written to work with addresses larger than FFFFFh. As a result, XMS is virtually useless for DOS. An extended memory manager (such as HIMEM.SYS) must be loaded to give your PC access to extended memory.

Expanded memory (EMS) is a bit more complicated than extended memory. Unlike extended memory that can be accessed directly (by protected-mode software such as Windows), EMS is divided into small segments called *pages*. Each page is typically 16K long. Each page can contain program code or data, but none of it can be executed from EMS directly. When the program running within the 640K limit needs code or data held in EMS, the expanded memory manager maps the required page(s) into a reserved area of conventional memory called a *page frame*. The application can then execute the information contained in the page frame. Using EMS, a real-mode program can cheat the 1Mb limit. EMM386.EXE is an extended memory manager that allows XMS to simulate EMS.

Memory packaging

Another important aspect of memory troubleshooting is recognizing the packaging that contains memory ICs. Although memory circuits are all fabricated onto minute pieces of silicon wafer, each "chip" is hermetically sealed into a leaded container that allows the device to be handled and integrated into larger circuit assemblies. You will encounter several major classes of IC packaging: DIPs, SIPs, ZIPs, and SIMMs. The package style used in a computer generally depends on the vintage of the system, so you should be familiar with each package type as shown in Fig. 35-5.

DIPs

*DIP*s (dual in-line packages) are the oldest solid-state memory device package. They have been used for the original IBM PC, XT, and 286 AT classes of computer. DIPs are easy to handle, and can be inserted into IC sockets with very little skill. Many early computers provided empty expansion sockets on the motherboard to allow the addition of memory ICs (which were very expensive commodities at that time). If you have ever worked on older computers, you have probably seen the long rows of empty IC sockets in a central location on the motherboard, or on third-party memory expansion cards.

Inserting a DIP is a simple matter of straightening its pins (DIP pins usually have a slight outward bend that is marginally wider than the socket), aligning pin 1 in the proper orientation, and gently pushing the IC into its socket without bending any of its pins in the process. If a pin is bent by accident, the IC is probably ruined. Remov-

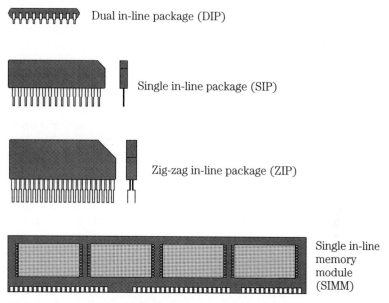

35-5 A comparison of typical memory IC packages.

ing a DIP can easily be accomplished by pulling the IC evenly out of its socket with an inexpensive DIP removal tool. You also can use a regular screwdriver blade to *gently* pry the IC up and out of its socket. Pry just a bit on alternating ends of the IC to keep the pins from bending. If you pry only one end of the IC out of its socket, the pins remaining in the socket will bend. Excessively bent leads will ruin the IC.

SIPs and ZIPs

DIPs are certainly not the only type of memory package. As memory density increased and computer sizes decreased, other packaging techniques were used for memory ICs. The *SIP* (single in-line package) placed all of its pins along one edge of a vertically-oriented container. The *ZIP* (zig-zag in-line package) also places its pins along one side of a vertically oriented container, but ZIPs overcome the pin spacing limitations of a SIP by staggering its pins in a zig-zag pattern. A ZIP can handle many more pins than a similarly sized SIP, so ZIPs were used more often for high-density memory in the later AT clones and early 386-class PCs.

Like any DIP, SIPs and ZIPs are through-hole components that can either be hard soldered into place during motherboard (or expansion module) assembly, or inserted into preexisting sockets during your upgrade. Unfortunately, SIPs and ZIPs never gained tremendous popularity because their single-edge design did not remain in sockets very well. Thermal heating and cooling tended to rock the ICs right out of their sockets.

SIMMs

Another reason for the demise of DIPs, SIPs, and ZIPs was the introduction and broad adoption of surface-mount ICs. It was no longer possible for users to expand memory by simply plugging in ICs because surface-mount ICs cannot be plugged in (except for PLCCs and PGAs, but they are not popular memory packages at this time). Surface-mount memory ICs are fabricated onto small printed circuit modules. These memory modules could then be plugged into corresponding receptacles on the motherboard. The *SIMM* (single in-line memory module) remains a popular approach for later 386-class and almost all 486-class computers. SIMMs also make it cost effective to create bulk modules—memory can be expanded by megabytes at a time instead of kilobytes. There are no pins to bend or break, and the module assembly can easily be clipped into place by plastic retainers. SIMMs are vertically oriented, so they take up the absolute minimum real estate on the motherboard.

SIMMs are relatively easy items to install or remove. You need only be concerned with aligning the SIMM correctly and making sure it is evenly and completely inserted into its socket. No special tools are needed. Removing a SIMM is equally easy. You need only unclip the module and pull it out of its socket, but be careful not to accidentally snap or crack the module by squeezing it. *Always wear an antistatic wrist strap and antistatic packaging when handling SIMMs.*

Troubleshooting memory

Now that you have an understanding of basic memory concepts and packaging, it is time to cover memory troubleshooting. Ultimately, the objective of memory troubleshooting is to locate the defective memory module (or IC in older computers) and replace it. The trick is to locate the defective item. Every computer performs a check of its memory components when the computer is first activated, and continues to check the integrity of memory contents on an ongoing basis. If a memory problem exists or develops during operation, the computer will almost always be able to identify the problem's location. It is then a matter of replacing the IC or module that resides in that location.

The problem commonly encountered in memory troubleshooting is that the translation from a hexadecimal address (shown in an error message) to an actual IC or SIMM is hardly straightforward. Every computer is designed a bit differently and uses memory components of varying configurations. Even SIMMs are built a bit differently for every system model. Unless you have a memory map comparing address ranges with IC or SIMM slots for your particular machine, you will have to troubleshoot memory on a trial-and-error basis. Isolation by substitution is the most common approach to memory repair.

Memory test equipment

If you are working in a repair-shop environment, or plan to be testing a substantial number of memory devices, you should consider acquiring some specialized test equipment. A memory tester, such as the SIMCHECK from Innoventions, Inc. (Fig. 35-6), is a modular microprocessor-based system that can perform a thorough, comprehensive test of various SIMMs and indicate the specific IC that has failed (if any). The system can be configured to work with specific SIMMs by installing an appropriate adapter module like the one shown in Fig. 35-7. Intelligent testers work auto-

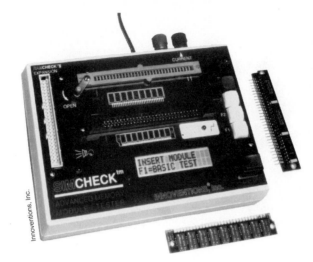

35-6
The SIMCHECK main unit.

35-7
The SIMCHECK PS/2 adapter.

matically, and show the progress and results of their examinations on a multiline LCD; guesswork is totally eliminated from memory testing.

Single ICs such as DIPs, SIPs, ZIPs, and PLCC/SOJ ICs can be tested using plug-in modules such as the ones shown in Figs. 35-8 and 35-9. The static RAM checker shown in Fig. 35-10 is another test bed for checking high-performance static RAM components in a DIP package. Both Innoventions test devices work together to provide a full-featured test system. Specialized tools can be an added expense, but no more so than an oscilloscope or other piece of useful test equipment. The return on your investment is less time wasted in the repair, and fewer parts to replace.

Memory problems and CMOS setup

The variables that define how your system is configured are typically held in roughly 64 bytes of RAM managed by the computer's CMOS/RTC IC. The RTC/CMOS IC requires very little power (micro amperes) in order to maintain its contents. One or more small lithium cells can typically back up your RTC's setup information for

35-8
The SIMCHECK RAM bank
adapter.

35-9 The SIMCHECK ZIP adapter.

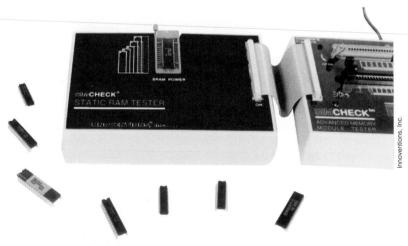

35-10 The SIMCHECK Static RAM unit.

several years. Part of the CMOS setup includes entries for the amount of conventional and expansion memory available in the system. The system reads the amount of memory that should be available from CMOS memory and compares that amount to the memory that it actually finds during POST testing. When a memory error is indicated, your first step should be to check the variables in your CMOS setup. If the backup battery should fail, the memory amounts listed in CMOS memory will probably not match the actual amount of installed memory, and a POST error will occur. Try entering the proper amount of memory and warm booting the computer. If the error goes away, try replacing the backup battery. If the error remains (or the CMOS setup contents are correct), suspect a fault in one or more memory ICs.

Troubleshooting classic XT memory

It seems only fitting to start an examination of memory problems with a brief overview of the original IBM PC/XT computer. In the "good old days" of personal computing when there were only one or two commercial computers in the market, there were few memory arrangements. POST could be written very specifically, and errors could be correlated directly to memory IC location. The POST routine in an XT's BIOS ROM is designed to identify the exact bank and bit where a memory error is detected, and display that information on the computer's monitor.

IBM PC/XT computers classify a memory (RAM) failure as error code 201. In actual operation, a RAM error would appear as XXYY 201, where XX is the bank, and YY is the bit where the fault is detected. As a result, it was often a simple matter to locate and replace a defective RAM IC. An XT is built with four RAM banks, each with nine bits (parity plus eight bits). Table 35-3 shows some bank and bit error codes for XT-class computers. As an example, suppose an XT system displayed 0002 201. This would indicate a memory failure in bank 0 at data bit D1. You need only replace the DIP memory IC residing at that location.

Table 35-3. Index of IBM PC/XT memory error codes

XXYY 201: Memory Failure

XX	Bank	YY	Bit
00	0	00	parity bit
04	1	01	D0
08	2	02	D1
0C	3	04	D2
		08	D3
		10	D4
		20	D5
		40	D6
		80	D7

Symptom 1. You see 1055 201 or 2055 201 displayed on the monitor Both of these error codes indicate an problem with the system's DIP switch settings. Re-

member that XTs do not use CMOS RAM to contain a system setup configuration, so DIP switches are used to tell the system how much memory should be present. If memory is added or removed, the appropriate switches in switch bank 2 (bits 1 to 8) and switch bank 1 (bits 3 and 4) must be set properly. Turn off the computer, check your switch settings and reboot the computer.

Symptom 2. You see a "PARITY CHECK 1" error displayed on the monitor This error typically suggests a power supply problem—RAM ICs are not receiving the proper voltage levels, so their contents are being lost or corrupted. When this happens, parity errors will be produced. Remove all power from the computer and repair or replace the power supply.

Symptom 3. You see an XXYY 201 error message displayed on the monitor This is a general RAM failure format for XT computers indicating the bank and bit where the fault is located. XX is the faulty bank, and YY is the faulty bit. See Table 35-3 to decipher the specific bank and bit in an XT. For example, an error code of 0004 201 indicates a memory fault in bank 0 (00) and bit D2 (04). Replace the defective IC, or bank of ICs.

Symptom 4. You see a "PARITY ERROR 1" message displayed on the monitor Multiple addresses or multiple data bits are detected as faulty in the XT. In some cases, one or more ICs might be loose or inserted incorrectly in their sockets. Remove power from the system and reseat all RAM ICs. If all RAM ICs are inserted correctly, rotate a new DRAM IC through each occupied IC location until the defective IC is located.

Troubleshooting classic AT memory

Like the XT, IBM's PC/AT was the leader of the 80286 generation. Because there was only one model (at the time), ATs also use some specific error messages to pinpoint memory (RAM or ROM) problems on the motherboard, as well as in its standard 128K and multiple 512K memory expansion devices. The 200 series error codes represent system memory errors. ATs present memory failures as AAXXXX YYYY 20x. The ten-digit code can be broken down to indicate the specific system bank and IC number, although the particular bit failure is not indicated. The first two digits (AA) represent the defective bank, and the last four digits (YYYY) show the defective IC number. It is then a matter or finding and replacing the faulty IC. Table 35-4 shows a set of error codes for early AT-class computers. For example, suppose an IBM PC/AT displayed the error message 05xxxxxx 0001 201 (we don't care about the x's). That message would place the error in IC 0 of bank 1 on the AT's system memory.

**Table 35-4. Index of IBM PC/AT
memory error codes**

AAXXXXYYYY 20x: Memory Failure

AA	Board	Bank
00 01 02 03	Motherboard	0
04 05 06 07	Motherboard	1
08 09	128Kb memory expansion	n/a
10 11 12 13	1st 512Kb memory adapter	0

Table 35-4. Continued

AAXXXXYYYY 20x: Memory Failure

AA	Board	Bank
14 15 16 17	1st 512Kb memory adapter	1
18 19 1A 1B	2nd 512Kb memory adapter	0
1C 1D 1E 1F	2nd 512Kb memory adapter	1
20 21 22 23	3rd 512Kb memory adapter	0
24 25 26 27	3rd 512Kb memory adapter	1
28 29 2A 2B	4th 512Kb memory adapter	0
2C 2D 2E 2F	4th 512Kb memory adapter	1
30 31 32 33	5th 512Kb memory adapter	0
34 35 36 37	5th 512Kb memory adapter	1

YYYY	Failed IC
0000	parity IC
0001	0
0002	1
0004	2
0008	3
0010	4
0020	5
0040	6
0080	7
0100	8
0200	9
0400	10
0800	11
1000	12
2000	13
4000	14
8000	15

Symptom 1. You see the number 164 displayed on the monitor This is a memory size error—the amount of memory found during the POST does not match the amount of memory listed in the AT's CMOS setup. Run the AT CMOS system setup routine. Make sure that the listed memory amount matches the actual memory amount. If memory has been added or removed from the system, you will have to adjust the figure in the CMOS setup to reflect that change. If CMOS setup parameters do not remain in the system after power is removed, try replacing the battery or CMOS/RTC IC.

Symptom 2. You see an "INCORRECT MEMORY SIZE" message displayed on the monitor This message can be displayed if the CMOS system setup is incorrect, or if there is an actual memory failure that is not caught with a numerical 200-series code. Check your CMOS system setup as described in Symptom 1 and correct the setup if necessary. If the error persists, there is probably a failure in some portion of RAM.

Without a numerical code, it can be difficult to find the exact problem location, so adopt a divide-and-conquer strategy. Remove all expansion memory from the system, alter the CMOS setup to reflect base memory (system board) only, and retest the system. If the problem disappears, the fault is in some portion of expansion memory. If the problem still persists, you know the trouble is likely in your base (system board) memory. Take a known-good RAM IC and swap RAM ICs until you locate the defective device.

If you successfully isolate the problem to a memory expansion board, you can adopt the same strategy for the board(s). Return one board at a time to the system (and update the CMOS setup to keep track of available memory). When the error message reappears, you will have found the defective board. Use a known-good RAM IC and begin a systematic swapping process until you have found the defective IC.

Symptom 3. You see a "ROM ERROR" message displayed on your monitor To guarantee the integrity of system ROM, a checksum error test is performed as part of the POST. If this error occurs, one or more ROM locations might be faulty. Your only alternative here is to replace the system BIOS ROM(s) and retest the system.

Symptom 4. You see a "PARITY CHECK" error or numerical 200-series error displayed on your monitor The system has identified a specific bit level or address line fault in at least one memory device. With a numerical error, you can find the bank and IC that has failed. It is then a simple matter of replacing the defective IC and retesting the system. Use Table 35-4 to locate the bank and IC in an AT system.

A PARITY CHECK error, however, is not so specific as to the fault location. Start by checking the outputs from your power supply. If one or more outputs are low or absent, troubleshoot or replace the power supply assembly. If the supply measures properly, you will have to adopt a divide-and-conquer strategy as outlined in Symptom 2 to isolate the general failure area, then find the defective IC through trial and error.

Troubleshooting contemporary memory errors

Since the introduction of i286-class computers, the competition among motherboard manufacturers, as well as the rapid advances in memory technology, has resulted in a tremendous amount of diversity in the design and layout of memory systems. Although the basic concepts of memory operation remain unchanged, every one of the hundreds of computer models manufactured today use slightly different memory arrangements. Today's PCs also hold much more RAM than XT and early AT systems.

As a consequence of this trend, specific numerical (bank and bit) error codes have long since been rendered impractical in newer systems where megabytes can be stored in just a few ICs. Today's i386 and i486 computers use a series of generic error codes. The address of a fault is always presented, but there is no attempt made to correlate the fault's address to a physical IC. Fortunately, today's memory systems are so small and modular that trial-and-error isolation can often be performed rapidly. Let's look at some typical errors.

Symptom 1. You see an "XXXX OPTIONAL ROM BAD CHECKSUM = YYYY" error message on your monitor Part of the POST sequence checks for the presence of any other ROMs in the system. When another ROM is located, a checksum test is performed to check its integrity. This error message indicates that the external ROM (such as a SCSI adapter or Video BIOS) has checked bad, or its address conflicts with another device in the system. In either case, initialization cannot continue.

If you have just installed a new peripheral device when this error occurs, try changing the device's I/O address jumpers to resolve the conflict. If the problem remains, remove the peripheral board—the fault should disappear. Try the board on another PC. If the problem continues on another PC, the adapter (or its ROM) might be defective. If this error has occurred spontaneously, remove one peripheral board at a time and retest the system until you isolate the faulty board, then replace the faulty board (or just replace its ROM if possible).

Symptom 2. You might see any one of the following general RAM errors
a. Memory address line failure at XXXX, read YYYY, expecting ZZZZ
b. Memory data line failure at XXXX, read YYYY, expecting ZZZZ
c. Memory high address failure at XXXX, read YYYY, expecting ZZZZ
d. Memory logic failure at XXXX, read YYYY, expecting ZZZZ
e. Memory odd/even logic failure at XXXX, read YYYY, expecting ZZZZ
f. Memory parity failure at XXXX, read YYYY, expecting ZZZZ
g. Memory read/write failure at XXXX, read YYYY, expecting ZZZZ

Each of the errors shown are general RAM error messages indicating a problem in base or extended/expanded RAM. The code XXXX is the failure segment address—an offset address might be included. The word YYYY is what was read back from the address, and ZZZZ is the word that was expected. The difference between these read and expected words is what precipitated the error. In general, these errors indicate that at least one base RAM IC or at least one SIMM has failed. A trial-and-error approach is usually the least expensive route in finding the problem. First, reseat each SIMM and retest the system to be sure that each SIMM is inserted and secured properly. Rotate a known-good SIMM through each occupied SIMM socket in sequence. If the error disappears when the known-good SIMM is in a slot, the old SIMM that had been displaced is probably faulty. You can go on to use specialized SIMM troubleshooting equipment to identify the defective IC, but such equipment is rather expensive unless you intend to repair a large volume of SIMMs to the IC level.

If the problem remains unchanged even though every SIMM has been checked, the error is probably in the motherboard RAM or RAM support circuitry. Run a thorough system diagnostic if possible, and check for failures in other areas of the motherboard that affect memory (such as the interrupt controller, cache controller, DMA controller, or memory management chips. If the problem prohibits a software diagnostic, use a POST board and try identifying any hexadecimal error code. If a support IC is identified, you can replace the defective IC, or replace the motherboard outright. If RAM continues to be the problem, try replacing the motherboard RAM (or replace the entire motherboard), and retest the system.

Symptom 3. You see a "CACHE MEMORY FAILURE—DISABLING CACHE" error displayed on your monitor The cache system has failed. The tag RAM, cache logic, or cache memory on your motherboard is defective. Your best course is to replace the cache RAM IC(s). If the problem persists, try replacing the cache logic or tag RAM (or replace the entire motherboard). You will probably need a schematic diagram or a detailed block diagram of your system in order to locate the cache memory IC(s).

Symptom 4. You see a "DECREASING AVAILABLE MEMORY" message displayed on your monitor   This is basically a confirmation message that indicates a failure has been detected in extended/expanded memory, and that all memory after the failure has been disabled to allow the system to continue operating (although at a substantially reduced level). Your first step should be to reseat each SIMM and ensure that they are properly inserted and secured. Next, take a known-good SIMM and step through each occupied SIMM slot until the problem disappears—the SIMM that had been removed is the faulty SIMM. Remember that you might have to alter the system's CMOS setup parameters as you move memory around the machine (an incorrect setup can cause problems during system initialization).

Symptom 5. You see a "MEMORY PARITY INTERRUPT AT ADDRESS XXXX" message displayed on your monitor   The system has detected a parity bit error in at least one memory location. Your first step should be to reseat each SIMM to ensure that they are properly inserted and secured. Next, take a known-good SIMM and step through each occupied SIMM slot until the problem disappears—the SIMM that had been removed is the faulty SIMM. If you cannot detect a faulty SIMM, the error is probably in RAM located on the system motherboard. Since there are usually few memory ICs on the motherboard, you can replace the RAM ICs or replace the entire motherboard at your discretion.

Troubleshooting beep codes

Remember that error messages will only be displayed *after* your computer's video system has been loaded and initialized. Any errors that might occur to your memory system before the video system is active will not be displayed. To get around this limitation, POST designers have used a series of sequential tone patterns (called *beep codes*) that notify you of the particular error condition. The specific pattern of beeps indicates the problem. When you encounter beep codes during a system's initialization, refer to Chapter 15 for a comprehensive set of code tables.

36
CHAPTER

Mice and trackballs

As software packages evolved beyond simple menus and began to make use of the powerful graphics systems coming into popular use during the mid-1980s (EGA and VGA graphics), ever-larger amounts of information were presented in the display. Simple, multilayered text menus were aggressively replaced with striking *GUIs* (graphic user interfaces). System options and selections were soon represented with symbols (buttons or icons) instead of text. Using a keyboard to maneuver through such visual software soon became a cumbersome (if not impossible) chore.

Peripheral designers responded to this situation by developing a family of *pointing devices* (Fig. 36-1). Pointing devices use a combination of hardware and software to produce and control a graphical screen *cursor*. A software device driver generates the cursor and reports its position. As the pointing device is moved around, signals are interpreted by the device driver that moves the cursor in a like manner. By positioning the cursor over a graphic symbol and activating one, two, or three of the buttons on the pointing device, it is now possible to select (click or double click) and manipulate options in the application program instead of using a keyboard.

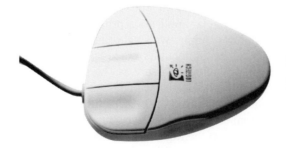

36-1
A Logitech MouseMan. Copyright © 1995
Logitech, Inc.

There are three factors needed to make pointing devices work: the physical signal-generating hardware itself, a software driver (the device driver), and the application program must be written to make use of the device driver. If any of these three items are missing, the pointing device will not work. This chapter looks at the technology, maintenance, and troubleshooting of two popular pointing devices: the mouse and the trackball.

The mouse

Although the development of computer pointing devices (Fig. 36-2) has been ongoing since the early 1970s, the first commercial pointing device for IBM-compatible systems was widely introduced in the early 1980s. The device was small enough to be held under your palm and your fingertips rested on its button(s). A small, thin cord connects the device to its host computer. The device's small size, long tail-like cord, and quick scurrying movements immediately earned it the label of *mouse*.

36-2
A Logitech trackball for notebook/subnotebook applications. Copyright © 1995 Logitech, Inc.

Every mouse needs at least one button. By pressing the button, you indicate that a selection is being made at the current cursor location. Many mouse-compatible software packages only make use of a single mouse button even to this day. A two-button mouse is more popular (reflecting the endurance of Microsoft's mouse design) because a second button can add more flexibility to the mouse. For example, one button can work to select an item, and the second button can be used to deselect that item again. A few mouse designs use three buttons, but the third button is rarely supported by application programs.

The first mouse gesture is called *clicking*, which is little more than a single momentary press of the left mouse button (on a two-button mouse). Clicking is the primary means of making a selection in the particular application program. The second common gesture is *double-clicking*, which is simply two single clicks in immediate succession. A double click also represents selection, but its exact use depends upon the application program. The third type of mouse gesture is the *drag*, where a graphical item can literally be moved around the display. Dragging is almost always accomplished by pressing the left mouse button over the desired item, then (without releasing the button) moving the item to its new location. When the item is in place, releasing the left mouse button will drop the item in that location.

It is interesting to note that pen gestures are interpreted by the computer's operating system, but mouse movements and button conditions are handled by the actual application program (such as a word processor or game). Thus, the same mouse gestures can be made to represent different actions depending on which program is executing.

Mouse construction

A mouse is a relatively straightforward device consisting of four major parts: the plastic housing, the mouse ball, the electronics PC board, and the signal cable. Figure 36-3 shows a typical mouse assembly. The housing assembly will vary a little depending on the manufacturer and vintage of your particular mouse, but the overall scheme is almost always identical. The *mouse ball* is a hard rubber ball situated up inside the mouse body just below a small PC board. When the mouse is positioned on a desktop, the ball contacts two actuators that register the mouse ball's movement in the X (left-to-right) and Y (up-to-down) directions. Both sensors generate a series of pulses that represent movement in both axes. Pulses equate to mouse movement; more pulses mean more movement. The pulses from both axes are amplified by the PC board and sent back to the computer along with information on the condition of each mouse button. Figure 36-4 shows a Suncom Crystal mouse that allows you to see the internal mouse construction.

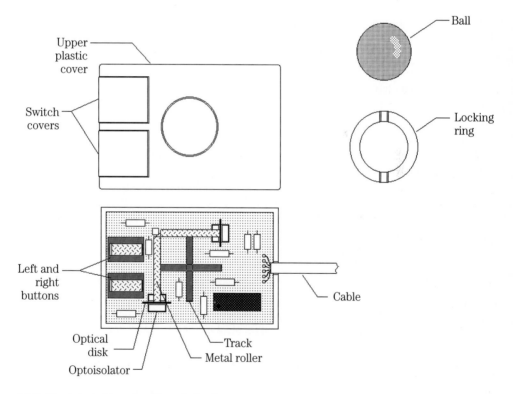

36-3 The internal construction of a basic mouse.

The mouse device driver already running in your computer (most systems load the mouse's device driver such as Microsoft's MOUSE.COM during computer initialization) interprets these pulses and translates them into X and Y screen locations where the mouse cursor is positioned. As the mouse moves left and right or up and down, pulses are added or subtracted from the cursor's X and Y screen coordinates by the device

36-4
The Crystal mouse from Suncom
Technologies. Dan Zemaitis, Marketing Manager, Suncom Technologies, 6400 W. Gross Point Rd.,
Niles, IL 60714

driver. The application program can then call for the X and Y coordinates, as well as button states. The key to a working mouse is its sensor devices. Sensors (or actuators) must be responsive enough to detect minute shifts in mouse position and generate pulses accordingly, yet be reliable enough to withstand wear, abuse, and environmental effects. There are two general types of sensors: mechanical and opto-mechanical.

Mechanical sensors

The greatest challenge in mouse design (and the largest cause of failures) is the reliable and repeatable conversion of mouse movement into serial electrical pulses. Early mouse versions used purely mechanical sensors to encode mouse ball movements. As the mouse ball turned against a roller (or shaft), copper contacts on the shaft would sweep across contacts on the mouse PC board—much like commutating rings and brushes on a dc motor. Each time a roller contact touches a corresponding contact in the mouse, an electrical pulse is generated. Because a mouse must typically generate hundreds of pulses for every linear inch of mouse movement, there are several sets of contacts for each axis.

It is important to note that mouse pulses can be positive or negative depending on the relative direction of the mouse in an axis. For example, moving the mouse right might produce positive pulses, and moving the mouse left might produce negative pulses. Similarly, moving the mouse down along its Y axis might produce positive pulses, and moving the mouse up might produce negative pulses. All pulses are then interpreted and tracked by the host computer.

Although mechanical sensors are simple, straightforward, and very inexpensive to produce, there are some significant problems that can plague the mechanical mouse. Mechanical mouse designs are not terribly reliable. The metal-on-metal contact sets used to generate pulses are prone to wear and breakage. Dust, dirt, hair, and any other foreign matter carried into the mouse by the ball also can interfere with contacts. Any contact interference prevents pulses from being generated. This condition results in an intermittent skip or stall of the cursor while you move the mouse. Fortunately, it is often a simple matter to disassemble and clean the contacts.

Opto-mechanical sensors

The next generation of mouse designs replaced the mechanical contacts with an *optoisolator* arrangement as illustrated in Fig. 36-5. A hard rubber mouse ball still

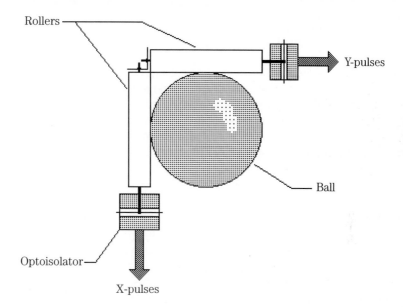

Rollers

Y-pulses

Ball

Optoisolator

X-pulses

36-5 Sensor layout for an opto-mechanical mouse or trackball.

rests against two perpendicularly opposed metal actuator rollers, but instead of each roller driving an array of contacts, the rollers rotate slotted wheels that are inserted into optoisolators. An optoisolator shines LED light across an air gap where it is detected by a photodiode or phototransistor. When a roller (and slotted wheel) spins, the light path between LED and detector is alternated. This causes the detector output signal to oscillate, thus, pulses are generated. The pulse frequency is dependent upon mouse speed. As with the mechanical mouse, the *opto-mechanical* mouse produces both positive and negative serial pulses depending on the direction of mouse movement.

The opto-mechanical mouse is a great improvement over the plain mechanical approach. By eliminating mechanical contacts, wear and tear on the mouse is significantly reduced, resulting in much longer life and higher reliability. However, the mouse is still subject to the interference of foreign matter that invariably finds its way into the mouse housing. Regular cleaning and internal dusting can prevent or correct instances of cursor skip or stall. Most mouse models in production today use opto-mechanical sensors.

The trackball

The *trackball* is basically an inverted mouse. Instead of using your hand to move a mouse body around on a desk surface, a trackball remains stationary. Your hand or fingertips move the ball itself that is mounted through the top of the device. The advantage to a trackball is that it does not move. As a result, trackballs can be incorporated into desktop keyboards, or added to your work area with a minimum of required space. Such characteristics have made trackballs extremely popular with laptop and notebook computers. Some small computers even incorporate trackballs directly.

In spite of their advantages, however, a trackball is not quite as easy to use as a mouse. The successful use of a mouse is largely a matter of hand-eye coordination; a flick of the wrist and a click or two can maneuver you through a program at an impressive rate. Because you can move the mouse and manipulate its buttons simultaneously, dragging is a very intuitive gesture. Trackballs are usually turned with only your thumb. This positions the rest of your hand such that you can only reach one trackball button. That is a fine arrangement as long as you are only clicking a single button, but you often have to move your hand around completely to get to the second button (or you must at least let go of the ball). Dragging also is typically a cumbersome effort. Even a clumsy trackball is better than none at all, so you should be as familiar with trackballs as with a mouse.

Trackball construction

Virtually all trackballs use the same opto-mechanical sensor technology that is used with mice. Instead of the mouse PC board resting over the ball, a trackball sits on top of a PC board. The hard rubber ball sits at the intersection of a set of small plastic rails (or *tracks*), thus, the term *trackball*. This positions the ball between two perpendicularly oriented metal rollers. Each roller drives a slotted wheel that, in turn, runs between the LED and detector of an optoisolator. As the ball and rollers are made to turn, the slotted wheels cause the respective optoisolator's light path to alternate and generate signal pulses. Pulse frequency is dependent on the relative movements of each roller. Pulses are read and interpreted just like a mouse.

During initialization, your small computer must load a short piece of software (called a *device driver*) designed to read the proper port, interpret any signals generated by the trackball, and make switch and roller information available to whatever program calls for it. Any mouse-compatible program is then capable of accessing trackball data and responding just like a mouse. Because the technologies and construction techniques of mice and trackballs are virtually identical, the remainder of this chapter treats a mouse and trackball as interchangeable devices.

Cleaning a pointing device

Pointing devices are perhaps the simplest peripheral available for your small computer. Although they are reasonably forgiving to wear and tear, trackballs and mice can easily be fouled by dust and debris or foreign matter introduced from the ball. Contamination of this sort is almost never damaging, but it can cause some maddening problems when using the pointing device. A regimen of routine cleaning will help to prevent contamination problems. Turn your small computer off before performing any cleaning procedures.

You will need to gather some cleaning materials before performing your maintenance. Make sure to have some clean cotton swabs and a small quantity of isopropyl alcohol on hand, along with a glass of warm water and mild detergent. You also might like to include a canister of compressed air available from any electronics store (the air does not have to be photography grade). Remove the ball by turning the retaining ring to the open position. The ring can then be removed, and the ball will fall out easily. Refer to the user's manual accompanying your pointing device for a specific explanation of disassembly. For a mouse, the retainer ring and mouse ball would be removed from the underside of the device. For a trackball, the ring and ball would be removed from the top of the device.

Once the retaining ring is off, remove the ball and set both items aside. Use your canister of compressed air and blow out any accumulation of dust or debris that might have settled into the housing. Dampen a cotton swab with fresh isopropyl alcohol and wipe each roller very carefully. Gently scrub away any accumulation of gunk that might be deposited. Set the pointing device aside. Wash the ball thoroughly in warm soapy water. You also can use an ammonia/water mix. Dry the ball completely using a lint-free cloth or paper towel. be sure to remove any hair or debris that remains on the ball. Once everything is clean and dry, reinsert the ball and secure it with the retaining ring. Return the pointing device to service. *Warning: do not use harsh solvents, wood alcohol or chemicals inside the device, or on the ball.* Chemicals can easily melt the plastic and result in permanent damage to the pointing device. You can assemble the materials for mouse cleaning yourself, but you can easily find prefabricated packages such as the Curtis mouse cleaning kit shown in Fig. 36-6.

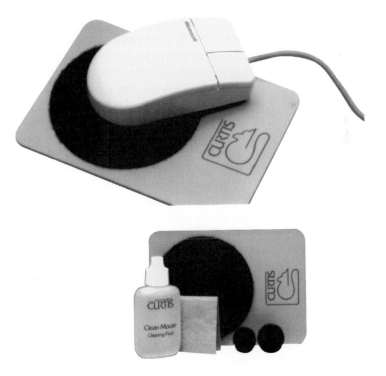

36-6 A Curtis mouse cleaning kit. Curtis, a division of Rolodex, Secaucus, NJ 07094

Troubleshooting a pointing device

The weakest link in a pointing system is the peripheral pointing device itself. Few peripheral devices are subjected to the wear and general abuse seen by trackballs or mice. They are dropped, yanked, and moved constantly from place to place.

Damage to the device PC board, cabling, and connector is extremely common due to abuse. Accumulations of dust and debris can easily work into the housing and create havoc with the rubber ball, tracks, and rollers. This part of the chapter guides you through some simple troubleshooting techniques for your trackball and mouse.

Symptom 1. The trackball cursor appears, but it only moves erratically as the ball moves (if at all) This symptom might occur in either the horizontal or vertical axis. This symptom suggests that there is an intermittent condition occurring somewhere in the pointing device. You should not have to disassemble your computer at all during this procedure. Start your investigation by powering down the computer. Check the device's cable connector at the computer. Make sure the connector is tight and inserted properly. If you are in the habit of continually plugging and unplugging the trackball, excessive wear can develop in the connector pins over time. If the connector does not seem to fit tightly in the computer, try a new pointing device.

A more likely problem is that the device's rollers are not turning, or turning only intermittently. In most cases, roller stall is caused by a dirty or damaged ball, or an accumulation of dirt blocking one or both sensors. Clean the ball and blow out any dust or debris that might have settled into the trackball housing. Refer to the preceding section on cleaning and attempt to clean the device thoroughly. *Never use harsh solvents or chemicals to clean the housings or ball.*

If you have the mouse connected to a standard serial communication port (a COM port), you should check that there are no other devices using the same interrupt (IRQ). For example, COM1 and COM3 use the same IRQ, and COM2 and COM4 share another IRQ. If you have a mouse on COM1 and a modem on COM3, there will almost invariably be a hardware conflict. If possible, switch the mouse (or conflicting device) to another port and try the system again.

If there is no hardware conflict, and cleaning does not correct an intermittent condition, remove the device's upper housing to expose the PC board, and use your multimeter to check continuity across each wire in the connecting cable. Because you probably will not know which connector pins correspond to which wires at the sensor PC board, place one meter probe on a device's wire and ring out each connector pin until you find continuity. Make a wiring chart as you go. Each time you find a wire path, wiggle the cable to stimulate any possible intermittent wiring. Repair any intermittent wiring if possible. If you cannot find continuity or repair faulty wiring, simply replace the pointing device.

Symptom 2. One or both buttons function erratically (if at all) Buttons are prone to problems from dust accumulation and general contact corrosion. Your first step should be to power down your computer and disconnect the pointing device. Remove the ball and upper housing to expose the PC board and switches. Spray a small amount of electronics-grade contact cleaner into each switch, then work each switch to circulate the cleaner.

If cleaning does not improve intermittent switch contacts, you might wish to check continuity across the connecting cable. With the ball and housing cover removed, use your multimeter to check continuity across each wire in the connecting cable. Because you probably do not know which connector pins correspond to which wires at the device, place one meter lead on a device wire and ring out each connector pin until you find continuity. Once you find continuity, wiggle the cable to stimulate any possible intermittent wiring. Repair any intermittent wiring if you can, or simply replace the pointing device.

Symptom 3. The screen cursor appears on the display, but it does not move If the cursor appears, the device driver has loaded correctly and the application program is communicating with the driver. Your first step should be to suspect the serial connection. If there is no serial connection, however, there will be no pulses to modify the cursor's position. If you find a bad connection, power down your small computer before reattaching the device's serial connector, then restore power and allow the system to reinitialize.

If the device is attached correctly to its proper serial port, the problem probably exists in the pointing device's wiring. Remove the ball and upper housing to expose the PC board, then use your multimeter to check continuity across each wire in the connecting cable. Because you probably do not know which connector pins correspond to which wires in the device, place one meter lead on a device wire and ring out each connector pin until you find continuity. Once you find continuity, wiggle the cable to stimulate any possible intermittent wiring. Repair any intermittent or open wiring if you can, or simply replace the pointing device.

Symptom 4. The mouse or trackball device driver fails to load The device driver is a short program that allows an application program to access information from a pointing device. Most computer users prefer to load their device drivers during system initialization by invoking the drivers in the CONFIG.SYS or AUTOEXEC .BAT files. Most drivers are written to check for the presence of their respective device first; if the expected device does not respond, the driver will not be loaded into memory. Other drivers load blindly regardless of whether the expected device is present or not.

If the device driver fails to load during initialization, your pointing device might not have been detected. Power down your computer and check the connection of your pointing device. Ensure the device is securely plugged into the proper serial port (or other mouse port). If the device is missing or incorrectly inserted, install or resecure the pointing device and allow the system to reinitialize. If you see a "File Not Found" error message displayed at the point your device driver was supposed to load, the driver might have been accidentally erased, might be corrupted, or might be located in a subdirectory where the CONFIG.SYS or AUTOEXEC.BAT files are not looking. Try re-installing a valid copy of your mouse device driver and ensure that the driver is located where your calling batch file can access it. Reboot your system.

Most well-designed application programs check for the presence of a pointing device through the device driver during initial program execution. If the application program aborts or fails to execute because of a "No Mouse Found" or "No Mouse Driver" error, return to the previous paragraphs and recheck the device and driver installation.

Symptom 5. When installing a new mouse and driver, you see a "General Protection Fault" when trying to use the mouse with one or more applications under Windows First, this is probably not a hardware fault (although it would be helpful to check any mouse driver command-line switches in CONFIG.SYS or AUTOEXEC.BAT). It is more likely that the new mouse driver is conflicting with one or more applications. Try several different applications; most will probably work just fine. Check with the mouse manufacturer to see if there are any other reported problems, and find if any patches are planned. If you have an older version of the mouse driver available, try replacing that one. An older driver might not work as well as a newer one, but it might not suffer from this kind of compatibility problem. If there are no older drivers available, and no patches that you can use, you might be forced to change the mouse and mouse driver to something completely different in order to eliminate the conflict.

37
CHAPTER

Modems and fax cards

Long before computers ever became personal, the mainframe and mini computers of the 1960s and 1970s needed to communicate over large geographic distances that could sometimes stretch across town, and sometimes around the world. Designers faced the problem of wiring the computers together—stringing a cable across even a few miles represents a serious logistical challenge. Instead of installing a network of new cabling, computer designers realized that they already had a sophisticated, world-wide wiring system in place; the *public switched telephone network* (PSTN). By enabling one computer to call another and exchange data, computers could communicate over telephone lines.

Of course, computers cannot work directly on your telephone line. The digital information processed by computers must be translated (or *modulated*) into audible sounds that are carried across telephone lines to a remote location. Sound signals returning over the telephone lines must be converted back into digital information (or *demodulated*) for the computer. This continuous process of modulation and demodulation between a computer and telephone line is performed by a device called a *mo*dulator/*dem*odulator or *modem* (Fig. 37-1). As the number of personal com-

37-1 The Multi-Tech 28.8K MultiModem II. Multi-Tech Systems, Inc.

puters has grown into the millions, the demand for faster and more reliable modem communication has resulted in impressive speed and performance. Today's modems have also enabled entirely new developments such as fax machines and bulletin board systems. This chapter is intended to explain the operations, standards, and connections of today's modems, as well as provide you with a compendium of modem symptoms and solutions.

Understanding modem construction and operation

To understand how a modem works and how to react when things go wrong, you should be familiar with the typical sections of a modem circuit. Although most modems today can be fabricated with only a few ASICs and discrete parts, virtually all computer communication systems contain the same essential parts. First, data must be translated from parallel into serial form and back again. Serial data being transmitted must be converted into an audio signal, then placed on an ordinary telephone circuit. Audio signals received from the telephone line must be separated from transmitted signals, then converted back into serial data. All of these activities must take place under the direction of a controller circuit. Finally, a modem uses nonvolatile RAM (NVRAM) to maintain a lengthy list of setup parameters. For the purposes of this book, there are two types of modems: internal and external.

The internal modem

The internal modem is fabricated as a stand-alone board that plugs directly into the PC expansion bus. You can see each major modem function detailed in the block diagram of Fig. 37-2. The internal modem contains its own universal asynchronous receiver/transmitter (UART). As you will see in Chapter 49, it is the UART that is responsible for manipulating data into and out of serial form. A UART forms the foundation of a serial port, and this can represent a serious hardware conflict for your PC; when installing an internal modem, be sure that the IRQ line and I/O address chosen for the UART serial port does not conflict with other serial ports already in the system. It might be necessary to disable conflicting ports.

Before being transmitted over telephone lines, serial data must be converted into audio signals. This process is carried out by a modulator circuit. The modulated audio is then coupled to the telephone line using a circuit very similar to that used by ordinary telephones to couple voice. Audio signals are made available to a single RJ11-type (telephone line) connector at the rear of the modem. Many modems provide a second RJ11 jack for a telephone; this allows you to check the line and make calls while the modem is idle. Signals received from the telephone line must be translated back into serial data. The telephone interface separates received signals and passes them to the demodulator. After demodulation, the resulting serial data is passed to the UART, which in turn converts the serial bits into parallel words that are placed on the system's data bus.

Besides combining and separating modulated audio data, the telephone interface generates the *DTMF* (dual-tone multifrequency) dialing signals needed to reach a remote modem—much the same way as a touch-tone telephone. When a re-

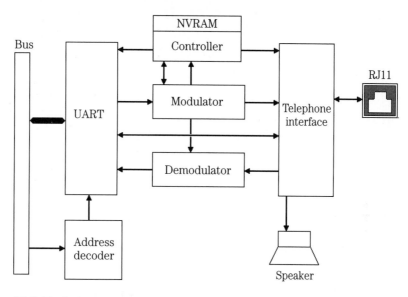

37-2 Block diagram of an internal modem.

mote modem dials in, the telephone interface detects the incoming ring, and alerts the UART to begin negotiating a connection. Finally, the telephone interface drives a small speaker. During the first stages of modem operation, the speaker is often used to hear dial tone, dialing signals, and audio negotiation between the two modems. Once a connection is established, the speaker is usually disabled.

A controller circuit manages the overall operation of the modem, but in a more general sense, it switches the modem between its control and data operating modes. The controller accepts commands from the modulator that allows modem characteristics and operating parameters to be changed. In the event of power loss or reset conditions, default modem parameters can be loaded from NVRAM. Permanent changes to modem parameters are stored in NVRAM.

The external modem

The external modem provides virtually all the essential functions offered by an internal modem. As you can see by the block diagram of Fig. 37-3, many of the external functions are identical to those of an internal modem. The major difference between modems is that the external modem does not include a built-in UART to provide a serial port. Instead, the external modem relies on a serial port already configured in the PC. A 9-pin or 25-pin serial cable connects the PC serial port to the modem as shown in Chapter 49. This often makes external modem setup faster and easier than internal modems, because you need not worry about interrupt lines and I/O address settings; hardware conflicts are rare with external modems.

The other practical differences in an external modem is the way it is powered. Where internal modems are powered from the expansion bus, external modems must be powered from a small ac adapter. In locations where ac outlets are scarce, this might be a problem. On the other hand, external modems provide a series of signal status LEDs. The LEDs allow you to easily check the state of serial communications.

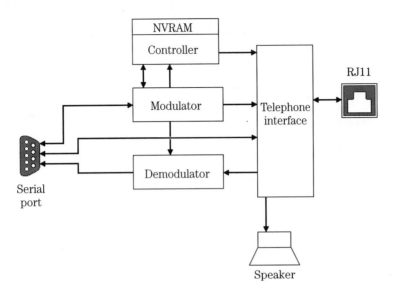

37-3 Block diagram of an external modem.

Modem commands

Modems used to be dumb devices. It was almost impossible for them to do things like answer the ringing telephone line, dial a number, set speaker volume, and so on. Hayes Microcomputer Products developed a product called a Smartmodem that accepted high-level commands in the form of ASCII text strings. This was dubbed the *Hayes AT command set*, and has been the de facto standard for modem commands ever since. As a consequence, virtually every modem that is *Hayes-compatible* is capable of using the AT command set. Ultimately, the AT commands go a long way to simplify the interface between a modem and communication software. Table 37-1 provides a general index of the AT commands; this can be particularly helpful when trying to interpret command strings.

Table 37-1. The standard AT command set and S-registers

Command	Description
On-line control commands	
AT	A standard prefix that informs the modem a command is coming
A/	Repeat the previous command (this does not have to be prefixed by an AT)
+++	Switch modem from data mode to command mode
O0	Switch modem from command mode to data mode
Dialing and answering commands	
A	Answer the telephone manually
D	Dial the phone (usually used with a dial modifier code)
H0	Hang up the telephone immediately
H1	Pick up the telephone immediately
Dialing modifiers (used with the D command)	
P	Pulse dial (simulate a rotary telephone)

Table 37-1. Continued

Command	Description
R	Originate the call and switch to answer mode (useful for originate-only modems)
T	Tone dial (simulate a touch-tone telephone)
W	Wait for a second dial tone (useful for dialing out of a PBX or other telco system)
,	Pause 2 seconds while dialing
!	Flash the switch hook (simulate tapping the hook switch)
/	Pause ⅛ second while dialing
@	Wait for 5 seconds of silence before continuing (often requires 30 to 60 seconds)
;	Return modem to command mode after dialing
Controlling the modem speaker	
L0	Set very low speaker volume
L1	Set low speaker volume
L2	Set medium speaker volume
L3	Set high speaker volume
M0	Shut off the speaker
M1	Disable speaker when connection is established
M2	Turn on speaker
Controlling result codes	
C0	Return an error response
C1	Use normal transmit carrier switching
Q0	Go ahead and send result codes
Q1	Do not send result codes
V0	Select numeric result codes
V1	Select text result codes
Controlling S-register settings	
Sn?	Display the stored value at register "n"
Sn=m	Load the value of "m" into register "n"
General modem commands	
B0	Use ITU protocols
B1	Use Bell protocols
E0	Disable the command echo
E1	Enable the command echo
F0	Select half-duplex operation
F1	Select full-duplex operation
H0	Force modem hang-up
H1	Force modem off hook
N0	Make connections at speed specified in S37
N1	Make connection at any available speed
X0	Do not wait for dial tone before dialing and do not report busy signals
X1	Do not wait for dial tone before dialing and do not report busy signals (extra result codes)
X2	Wait for a dial tone before dialing, but do not report busy signals
X3	Do not wait for a dial tone before dialing, but report busy signals
X4	Wait for a dial tone before dialing, and report busy signals

Table 37-1. Continued

Command	Description
Y0	Disable the long space disconnect
Y1	Enable the long space disconnect
Z	Reset the modem to its power up defaults

Ampersand commands

Command	Description
&C0	Always assert the DCD signal
&C1	Only assert DCD while connected to a remote modem
&D0	Ignore the state of the DTR signal
&D1	Switch from data mode to command mode when DTR switches from on to off
&D2	Hang up and switch from data mode to command mode when DTR switches off
&D3	Reset the modem when DTR switches from on to off
&F	Restore the factory default settings
&J0	System uses RJ11 telephone jack
&J1	System uses RJ12 or RJ13 telephone jack
&K0	Disable flow control
&K3	Enable RTS/CTS flow control
&K4	Enable XON/XOFF flow control
&K5	Enable transparent XON/XOFF control
&L0	Using a dial-up telephone line
&L1	Selects a leased telephone line
&Q0	Use asynchronous operation in the direct mode
&Q1	Synchronous mode 1
&Q2	Synchronous mode 2
&Q3	Synchronous mode 3
&Q5	Modem negotiates error correcting protocol
&Q6	Asynchronous operation in normal mode
&R0	Assert CTS only when RTS is asserted
&R1	Always assert CTS signal
&S0	Always assert DSR signal
&S1	Assert DSR only when in on-line mode
&W	Save current configuration settings in NVRAM
&Z	Reset the modem and recall settings from NVRAM

S-register assignments

Command	Description
S0	Number of rings to wait before answering a call
S1	Check signal quality
S2	Escape code character (ASCII 43)
S3	Carriage return character (ASCII 13)
S4	Line feed character (ASCII 10)
S5	Backspace character (ASCII 8)
S6	Number of seconds to wait for dial tone before dialing
S7	Number of seconds to wait for carrier connection before hanging up
S8	Pause time represented by comma
S9	Length of time a carrier must be present before modem will recognize carrier
S10	Delay between carrier loss
S11	Duration of time between each touch tone signal when dialing
S12	Escape code guard time

Virtually all AT command strings start with the prefix AT (Attention). For example, the command string ATZE1Q0V1 contains five separate commands: attention (AT), reset the modem to its power-up defaults (Z), enable the command echo to send command characters back to the sender (E1), send command result codes back to the PC (Q0), and select text result codes that causes words to be used as result codes. Although this might seem like a mouthful, a typical modem can accept command strings up to 40 characters long. The term *result codes* are the messages that the modem generates when a command string is processed. Either numbers (default) or words (using the V1 command) can be returned. When a command is processed correctly, a result code OK is produced, or CONNECT when a successful connection is established.

Many attributes of the Hayes-compatible modem are programmable. To accommodate this feature, each parameter must be held in a series of memory locations (called *S-registers*). Each S-register is described in Table 37-1. For example, the default escape sequence for the AT command set is a series of three plusses: +++. You could change this character by writing a new ASCII character to S2. For the most part, default S-register values are fine for most work, but you can often optimize the modem's operation by experimenting with the register values. Because S-register contents must be maintained after power is removed from the modem, the registers are stored in *NVRAM* (nonvolatile RAM).

Modem modes

The modem is always in one of two primary modes: the command mode or the data mode. When first switched on (or reset), the modem starts up in command mode. In this mode, the controller circuit (sometimes called a *command processor*) is constantly checking to see if you have typed a valid AT command. When the modem receives a valid command, it executes that command for you. While your modem is in the command mode, you can instruct it to answer the telephone, change an S-register value, hang up or dial the telephone, and perform any number of other command functions.

The other mode is the data mode. In the data mode, your modem is transmitting all of the data it receives from your computer or terminal along the telephone line to the remote modem. Your modem is constantly checking the state of the Data Carrier Detect (DCD) and DTR (Data Terminal Ready) signals (depending on the system configuration). It is also watching the local data stream for a command mode escape sequence. The default escape sequence the AT command set is +++. When the proper escape sequence or a change in the state of the DCD or DTR signal occurs, the modem returns to a command mode where it waits for the next AT command.

Modem negotiation

Now that you have seen the essential elements of a modem and learned about modem signaling, you can use that background to form a picture of how the modem works in actual practice. You see, modem communication is not an event; it is a process whose success depends not only on your modem, but on the modem and PC you are trying to communicate with. This part of the chapter is intended to familiarize you with a typical operating session for an external modem.

Communication begins when you instruct the communication software to establish a connection. Control signals sent to the selected serial port cause the UART to assert the Data Terminal Ready (DTR) signal. This tells the attached modem that the PC is turned on and ready to transmit. The modem responds by asserting the Data Set Ready (DSR) line. The serial port receives this signal and tells the software that the modem is ready—both DTR and DSR must be present for communication to take place.

The communication software then sends an AT initialization string to the COM port (which forwards the string to the modem). In the command mode, the controller circuit interprets the initialization string that tells the modem to go off hook (get dial tone), then dial the telephone number of the destination modem. Dialing might take place in pulse (rotary) or tone mode depending on the initialization string. The modem transmits an acknowledgment back to the COM port; this is often displayed right on the communication software window. The line at the destination end begins to ring. If configured properly, and running communication software of its own, the remote modem will pick up the ringing line and a complete wiring path will be established between the two modems.

When the destination modem picks up the line, your local modem sends out a standard tone (a carrier tone) that lets the remote modem know it's being called by another modem. If the remote modem recognizes the carrier, it sends out an even higher-pitched tone. You can often hear these tones when your modem is equipped with a speaker. Once your modem recognizes the remote modem, it sends a Carrier Detect (CD) signal to the serial port. These mutual carriers will be modulated to exchange data.

OK, both modems know they are talking to other modems, but now there has to be a mutual agreement on how they'll exchange data. They must agree on transmission speed, the proper size of a data packet, the signaling bits on each end of the data packet, whether or not parity will be used, and if the modems will operate in half or full duplex mode—both modems must settle on these parameters or the data exchanged between them will make no sense. This process is known as *negotiation*. Assuming that the negotiation process is successful, both modems can now exchange data.

When the communication software attempts to send data, it tells the serial port to assert the Request to Send (RTS) signal. This checks to see if your modem is free to receive data. If the PC is busy doing something else (such as disk access), it will disable the RTS signal until it is ready to resume sending. When the modem is ready for data, it will return a Clear to Send (CTS) signal to the serial port. The PC can then begin sending data to the modem, and receiving data returned from the remote end. If the modem gets backed up with work, it will drop the CTS line until it is ready to resume communication. Because a standard system of tones is used, both modems can exchange data simultaneously. Data can now be exchanged between the two systems simultaneously.

When the time comes to terminate the connection, the communication software will send another AT command string to the serial port that causes it to break the connection. If the connection is broken by the remote modem, the local modem will drop the Carrier Detect line. The communication software will interpret this as a Dropped Carrier condition. That is basically all the phases involved in modem communication.

Reading the lights

One of the appealing attributes of external modems is the series of lights that typically adorns the front face. By observing each light and the sequence in which they light, you can often follow the progress of a communication or quickly discern the cause of a communication failure. The following markings are typical of many modems, but keep in mind that your particular modem might use fewer indicators (or be marked differently).

- *HS (High Speed)* When this indicator is lit, the modem is operating at its very highest transfer rate.
- *AA (Auto Answer)* When lit, your modem will answer any incoming calls automatically. This feature is vital for unattended systems such as bulletin boards.
- *CD (Carrier Detect)* This lights whenever the modem detects a carrier signal. This means it has successfully connected to a remote computer. This LED will go out when either one of the modems drops the line.
- *OH (Off Hook)* This LED lights anytime the modem takes control of the telephone line; it is equivalent to taking the telephone off hook.
- *RD (Receive Data)* Also marked Rx. This LED flickers as data is received by the modem from a remote modem.
- *SD (Send Data)* Also marked Tx. This LED flickers as data is sent from your modem to the remote modem.
- *TR (Terminal Ready)* This light illuminates when the modem detects a DTR signal from the communication software.
- *MR (Modem Ready)* A simple power-on light that indicates the modem is turned on and ready to operate.

Understanding signal modulation

Once the modem accepts a bipolar signal from an RS-232 port, the carrier signal being generated on the telephone line must be modulated to reflect the logic levels being transmitted. Several different means of signal modulation have been developed through the years to improve the efficiency of data transfers. This section gives you a brief explanation of each scheme. As you would expect, both modems must be capable of the same modulation scheme.

Bps versus baud rate

In the early days of modem communication, each audio signal transition represented a single bit. Each audio signal is known as a *baud*, and the *baud rate* naturally equaled the transmission rate in bps (or bits-per-second). Unlike those early modems, newer modem schemes can encode 2, 3, 4, or more bits into every audio signal transition (or baud). This means that modem throughput now equals 2×, 3×, or 4× the baud rate being carried across the telephone line.

For example, a modem operating at 2400 baud (2400 audio signal transitions per second) can carry 4800 bps if two bits are encoded onto every baud. The same 2400-baud modem could also carry 9600 bps if four bits are encoded onto every baud. Today, the modem's baud rate rarely matches the modem's throughput in bps unless a very old signaling standard is being used. If the modem were operating at 4800 baud and used 3-bit encoding, the modem would be handling 14,400 bps (14.4 Kbps), and so on. The concept of *encoding* is different from *data compression* because encoding transfers all original data bits from system to system, while data compression replaces repeating sequences of bits with much shorter bit sequences (known as *symbols* or *tokens*). You will see much more about encoding schemes and data compression in this chapter.

Modulation schemes

To discuss modulation, you must first understand a sinusoidal waveform. There are basically three physical characteristics to any waveform: amplitude, frequency, and phase. Each of these characteristics can be adjusted to represent a bit. *Amplitude* is simply the magnitude of the wave (usually measured in volts peak-to-peak or volts rms). Amplitude represents how far above and below the zero axis that waveform travels. *Frequency* indicates the number of times that a single wave will repeat over any period of time (measured as cycles per second, hertz, or Hz). An 1800-Hz signal repeats 1800 times per second. The signal also has a time reference known as *phase*. Phase is measured in degrees where 90° is the time to travel 25% of a wave, 180° is the time to travel 50% of the wave, 270° is the time to travel 75% of a wave, and so on. Because phase can take on any one of four states (degrees), phase shifts can be made to represent two bits simultaneously. Data between modems is modulated by altering the amplitude, frequency, and phase of a carrier signal.

FSK (frequency shift keying) is very similar to frequency modulation (FM) where only the frequency of a carrier is changed, and is one of the oldest modulation schemes still in service. FSK sends a logic 1 as one particular frequency (usually 1750 Hz), and a logic 0 is sent as another discrete frequency (often 1080 Hz). Frequencies are typically sent at 300 baud and each baud can carry one bit, so FSK can send 300 bps. This early technique resulted in the classic baud = bps confusion that is still prevalent today.

PSK (phase shift keying) is a close cousin of FSK, but the phase timing of a carrier wave is altered while the carrier's frequency stays the same. By altering the carrier's phase, a logic 1 or 0 is represented. Because phase can be shifted in several precise increments (0, 90, 180, or 270°), PSK can encode 1, 2, 3, or more bits per baud. For example, a 1200-baud modem using PSK can transmit 2400 bps over an 1800-Hz carrier. PSK can also be used in conjunction with FSK to encode even more bits per baud.

QAM (quadrature amplitude modulation) uses both phase and amplitude modulation to encode up to six bits onto every baud, although four bits are usually reserved for data. Not only can four phase states represent two bits, but four levels of amplitude can represent another two bits. Most QAM modems use a 1700-Hz or 1800-Hz carrier and a base rate of 2400 baud, so they carry up to 9600 bps.

TCQAM or *TCM* (trellis coded quadrature amplitude modulation) also uses an 1800-Hz carrier at a 2400-baud base rate, but uses the full 6-bit encoding capability of QAM to handle 14,400 bps. Most newer modems using TCM offer high speed and excellent echo cancellation circuitry. TCM is currently the most popular modulation scheme for high-performance modems because data can be checked on the fly with much better reliability than using a parity bit.

Signaling standards

Now that you have covered serial concepts and modulation techniques, you can see how modulation is used in conjunction with the many communications standards (or *protocols*) that have appeared. This part of the chapter details each of the major standards for modems, data compression, and error correction that are now in force today. In addition to simply transferring data, however, current modem standards embrace two other facets of data communication: data compression and error correction.

Most data sent between modems contains some amount of repetitive or redundant information. If the redundant information is located and replaced by a small token during transmission, the data is compressed. A token could be passed much faster than the redundant data, and the receiving modem accurately recreates the original data based on the token. *Data compression* has become an important technique that allows modems to increase their data throughput without increasing the baud rate or bps. Data compression can occur only when the two communicating modems support the same compression protocol. If modems support more than one type of compression, the communicating modems will use the most powerful technique common to both.

Modem *error correction* is the ability of some modems to detect data errors that might have occurred in transit between modems, then automatically resend the faulty data until a correct copy is received. As with modulation standards, both modems must be using the same error correction standard in order to operate together. However, there are few error correction standards, and most modem manufacturers adhere closely to the few that are available.

Bell standards

The Bell System largely dictated North American telecommunications standards before it was broken up into AT&T and seven regional operating companies in 1984. Before that time, two major standards were developed that set the stage for future modem development.

- BELL103 was the first widely accepted modem standard using simple FSK modulation at 300 baud. This is the only standard where the data rate matches the baud rate. It is interesting to note that many modems today still support BELL103 as a lowest common denominator when all other modulation techniques fail.
- BELL212A represents a second widely accepted modem standard in North America using PSK modulation at 600 baud to transmit 1200 bps. Many European countries ignored BELL212A in favor of the similar (but not entirely identical) European standard called V.22.

ITU (CCITT) standards

After the Bell System breakup, AT&T no longer wielded enough clout to dictate standards in North America, and certainly not to the international community that had developed serious computing interest. It is at this time that the ITU (International Telecommunications Union, formally the CCITT) gained prominence and acceptance in the U.S. All U.S. modems have been built to ITU standards ever since. ITU specifications are characterized by the symbol V (V.17). The term V simply means standard (rather like the RS in RS-232). The subsequent number simply denotes the particular standard. Some standards also add the term bis that means the second version of a particular standard. You might also soon see the term terbo that is the third version of a standard. The following list provides a comprehensive look at ITU standards. This index might aid you in understanding the broad specifications that are required to fully characterize the computer communications environment.

- V.1 is a very early standard that defines binary 0/1 bits as space/mark line conditions and voltage levels.
- V.2 limits the power levels (in decibels or dB) of modems used on phone lines.
- V.4 describes the sequence of bits within a character as transmitted (the data frame).
- V.5 describes the standard synchronous signaling rates for dialup lines.
- V.6 describes the standard synchronous signaling rates for leased lines.
- V.7 provides a list of modem terms in English, Spanish, French.
- V.10 describes unbalanced high-speed electrical interface characteristics (RS-423)
- V.11 describes balanced high-speed electrical characteristics (RS-422)
- V.13 explains simulated carrier control (with a full-duplex modem used as half-duplex modem).
- V.14 explains the procedure for asynchronous to synchronous conversion.
- V.15 describes the requirements and designs for telephone acoustic couplers. This is largely unused today because most telephone equipment is modular and can be plugged into telephone adapters directly rather than loosely attached to the telephone handset.
- V.17 describes an application-specific modulation scheme for Group 3 fax that provides 2-wire half-duplex trellis-coded transmission at 7200, 9600, 12,000, and 14,400 bps. In spite of the low number, this is a fairly recent standard.
- V.19 describes early DTMF modems using low-speed parallel transmission. This standard is largely obsolete.
- V.20 explains modems with parallel data transmission. This standard is largely obsolete.
- V.21 provides the specifications for 300-bps FSK serial modems (based upon BELL103).
- V.22 provides the specifications for 1200-bps (600 baud) PSK modems (based upon BELL212A).
- V.22bis describes 2400-bps modems operating at 600 baud using QAM.
- V.23 describes the operation of a rather unusual type of FM modem working at 1200/75 bps. That is, the host transmits at 1200 bps and receives at 75 bps. The remote modem transmits at 75 bps and receives at 1200 bps. V.23 is used in Europe to support some videotext applications.

- V.24 is known as EIA RS-232 in the U.S. V.24 defines *only* the functions of the serial port circuits. EIA-232-E (the current version of the standard) also defines electrical characteristics and connectors.
- V.25 defines automatic answering equipment and parallel automatic dialing. It also defines the answer tone that modems send.
- V.25bis defines serial automatic calling and answering that is the ITU (CCITT) equivalent of AT commands. This is the current ITU standard for modem control by computers via serial interface. The Hayes AT command set is used primarily in the U.S.
- V.26 defines a 2400-bps PSK full-duplex modem operating at 1200 baud.
- V.26bis defines a 2400-bps PSK half-duplex modem operating at 1200 baud.
- V.26terbo defines a 2400-/1200-bps switchable PSK full-duplex modem operating at 1200 baud.
- V.27 defines a 4800-bps PSK modem operating at 1600 baud.
- V.27bis defines a more advanced 4800-/2400-bps switchable PSK modem operating at 1600/1200 baud.
- V.27terbo defines a 4800-/2400-bps switchable PSK modem commonly used in half-duplex mode at 1600/1200 baud to handle Group 3 fax rather than computer modems.
- V.28 defines the electrical characteristics and connections for V.24 (RS-232). Where the RS-232 specification defines all necessary parameters, the ITU (CCITT) breaks the specifications down into two separate documents.
- V.29 defines a 9600-/7200-/4800-bps switchable PSK/QAM modem operating at 2400 baud. This type of modem is often used to implement Group 3 fax rather than computer modems.
- V.32 defines the first of the truly modern modems as a 9600-/4800-bps switchable QAM full-duplex modem operating at 2400 baud. This standard also incorporates trellis coding and echo cancellation to produce a stable, reliable, high-speed modem.
- V.32bis is a fairly new standard extending the V.32 specification to define a 4800-/7200-/9600-/12,000-/14,400-bps switchable TCQAM full-duplex modem operating at 2400 baud. Trellis coding, automatic transfer rate negotiation, and echo cancellation make this type of modem one of the most popular and least expensive for everyday PC communication.
- V.32terbo continues to extend the V.32 specification by using advanced techniques to implement a 14,400-/16,800-/19,200-bps switchable TCQAM full-duplex modem operating at 2400 baud. Unlike V.32bis, V.32terbo is not widely used because of the rather high cost of components.
- V.32fast is the informal name of a standard that the ITU (CCITT) has not yet completed. When finished, a V.32fast modem will likely replace V.32bis with speeds up to 28,800 bps. It is anticipated that this will be the last analog protocol—eventually giving way to all-digital protocols as local telephone services become entirely digital. V.32fast will probably be renamed V.34 on completion and acceptance.
- V.33 defines a specialized 14,400-bps TCQAM full-duplex modem operating at 2400 baud.

- V.36 defines a specialized 48,000-bps group modem that is rarely (if ever) used commercially. This type of modem uses several conventional telephone lines.
- V.37 defines a specialized 72,000-bps group modem that combines several telephone channels.
- V.42 is the only ITU error-correcting procedure for modems using V.22, V.22bis, V.26ter, V.32, and V.32bis protocols. The standard is also defined as a Link Access Procedure for Modems (LAPM) protocol. ITU V.42 is considered very efficient, and is about 20% faster than MNP4. If a V.42 connection cannot be established between modems, V.42 automatically provides fallback to the MNP4 error correction standard.
- V.42bis uses a Lempel-Ziv-based data compression scheme for use in conjunction with V.42 LAPM (error correction). V.42bis is a data-compression standard for high-speed modems that can compress data by as much as 4:1 (depending on the type of file you send). Thus, a 9600-baud modem can transmit data at up to 38,400 bps using V.42bis. A 14.4-kbps modem can transmit up to a startling 57,600 bps.
- V.50 sets standard telephony limits for modem transmission quality.
- V.51 outlines required maintenance of international data circuits.
- V.52 describes apparatus for measuring data transmission distortion and error rates.
- V.53 outlines impairment limits for data circuits.
- V.54 describes loop test devices for modem testing.
- V.55 describes impulse noise measuring equipment for line testing.
- V.56 outlines the comparative testing of modems.
- V.57 describes comprehensive test equipment for high-speed data transmission.
- V.100 describes the interconnection techniques between *PDNs* (public data networks) and *PSTNs* (public switched telephone networks).

MNP standards

The *MNP* (microcom networking protocol) is a complete hierarchy of standards developed during the mid 1980s that are designed to work with other modem technologies for error correction and data compression. Although most ITU standards refer to modem data transfer, MNP standards concentrate on providing error correction and data compression when your modem is communicating with another modem that supports MNP. For example, MNP class 4 is specified by ITU V.42 as a backup error control scheme for LAPM in the event that V.24 cannot be invoked. Out of nine recognized MNP levels, your modem probably supports the first five. Each MNP class has all the features of the previous class plus its own.

- *MNP class 1 (block mode)* An old data transfer mode that sends data in only one direction at a time—about 70% as fast as data transmissions using no error correction. This level is now virtually obsolete.
- *MNP class 2 (stream mode)* An older data transfer mode that sends data in both directions at the same time—about 84% as fast as data transmissions using no error correction.
- *MNP class 3* The sending modem strips start and stop bits from data block before sending it, while the receiving modem adds start and stop bits before

passing the data to the receiving computer. About 8 percent faster than data transmissions using no error correction. The increased throughput is realized only if modems on both ends of the connection are operating in a split speed (or locked COM port) fashion; that is, the rate of data transfer from computer to modem is higher than the data transfer rate from modem to modem. Also, data is being transferred in big blocks (1K) or continuously (using the Zmodem file transfer protocol).

- *MNP class 4* A protocol (with limited data compression) that checks telephone connection quality and uses a transfer technique called *Adaptive Packet Assembly*; on a noise-free line, the modem sends larger blocks of data. If the line is noisy, the modem sends smaller blocks of data (less data will have to be re-sent). This means more successful transmissions on the first try. About 20% faster than data transmissions using no error correction at all, so most current modems are MNP4 compatible.

- *MNP class 5* Classic MNP data compression. MNP5 provides data compression by detecting redundant data and recoding it to fewer bits thus increasing effective data throughput. A receiving modem decompresses the data before passing it to the receiving computer. MNP5 can speed data transmissions up to 2× over using no data compression or error correction (depending on the kind of data transmitted). In effect, MNP5 gives a 2400-bps modem and effective data throughput of as much as 4800 bps, and a 9600-bps system as much as 19,200 bps.

- *MNP class 6* Uses Universal Link Negotiation to let modems get maximum performance out of a line. Modems start at low speeds, then move to higher speeds until the best speed is found. MNP6 also provides *Statistical Duplexing* to help half-duplex modems simulate full-duplex modems.

- *MNP class 7* Offers a much more powerful data compression process (Huffman encoding) than MNP5. MNP7 modems can increase the data throughput by as much as 3× in some cases. Although more efficient than MNP5, not all modems are designed to handle the MNP7 protocol. Also, MNP7 is faster than MNP5, but MNP7 is still generally considered slower than the ITU's V.42bis.

- *MNP class 9* Reduces the data overhead (the housekeeping bits) encountered with each data packet. MNP9 also improves error correction performance because only the data that was in error has to be re-sent instead of re-sending the entire data packet.

- *MNP class 10* Uses a set of protocols known as Adverse Channel Enhancements to help modems overcome poor telephone connections by adjusting data packet size and transmission speed until the most reliable transmission is established. This is a more powerful version of MNP4.

File-transfer protocols

Even with powerful data transfer, compression, and correction protocols, the way in which data is packaged and exchanged is still largely undefined by ITU and MNP standards. You see, a typical modem has no way of knowing the difference between a keyboard stroke or data being downloaded from a hard drive; the modem does not understand a file. Instead, it only works with bytes, bits, timing, and tones. As a consequence, the modem relies on communications software to manage file characteristics such as filename, file size, and content. The software routines that bundle and organize data between modems are called *file-transfer protocols*. Errors that occur during file transfer are automatically detected and corrected by file transfer protocols. If a block of data is received incorrectly, the receiving system sends a message to the sending system and requests the retransmission. This process is automatic, and essentially transparent to the computer users (except perhaps for a display in the communication software's file transfer status window). The following are some of the more common transfer protocols:

- *ASCII* This protocol is designed to work with ASCII text files only. Notice that you do not have to use this protocol when transferring text files. The ASCII protocol is useful for uploading a text file when you are composing e-mail on line.

- *Xmodem* This is one of the most widely used file transfer protocols. Introduced in 1977 by Ward Christensen, this protocol is slow, but reliable. The original Xmodem protocol used 128-byte packets and a simple checksum method of error detection. A later enhancement, Xmodem-CRC, uses a more secure Cyclic Redundancy Check (CRC) method for error detection. Xmodem protocols always attempt to use CRC first. If the sender does not acknowledge the requests for CRC, the receiver shifts to the checksum mode and continues its request for transmission. Mismatching the two variants of Xmodem during file transfers is usually the reason for transfer problems, although many communication systems can now detect the differences automatically.

- *Xmodem-1K* The Xmodem-1K protocol is essentially Xmodem CRC with 1K (1024-byte) packets. On some systems and bulletin boards, it might also be referred to as Ymodem. Some communication software programs (most notably Procomm Plus 1.x) also list Xmodem-1K as Ymodem. Procomm Plus 2.0 no longer refers to Xmodem-1K as Ymodem.

- *Ymodem* A Ymodem protocol is little more than a version of Xmodem-1K that allows multiple batch file transfer (sending/receiving several files one after another unattended). On some systems it is listed as Ymodem Batch (and is sometimes called true Ymodem). Ymodem offers a faster transmission rate than Xmodem, and better data security through a refined CRC checksum method.

- *Ymodem-g* The Ymodem-g protocol is a variant of basic Ymodem. It is designed to be used with modems that support error correction. This protocol does not provide software error correction or recovery itself, but expects the modem to provide the service. It is a streaming protocol that sends and receives 1K packets in a continuous stream until instructed to stop. It does not wait for positive acknowledgment after each block is sent, but rather sends blocks in rapid succession. If any block is unsuccessfully transferred, the entire transfer is canceled.

- *Zmodem* This is generally the best protocol to use if the electronic service you are calling supports it. Zmodem has two significant features: it is extremely efficient, and it provides automatic crash recovery. Like Ymodem-g, Zmodem does not wait for positive acknowledgment after each block is sent, but rather sends blocks in rapid succession. If a Zmodem transfer crashes (is canceled or interrupted for any reason), the transfer can be resurrected later and the previously transferred information need not be re-sent. Zmodem can detect excessive line noise and automatically drop to a shorter, more reliable data packet size when necessary. Data integrity and accuracy is assured by the use of reliable 16-bit CRC (cyclic redundancy check) methods rather than less reliable CRC checking of Ymodem and Xmodem.

- *Kermit* The Kermit protocol was developed at Columbia University. It was designed to facilitate the exchange of data among very different types of computers (mainly minicomputers and mainframes). You probably will not need to use Kermit unless you are calling a minicomputer or mainframe at an educational institution.
- *Sealink* The Sealink protocol is a variant of Xmodem. It was developed to overcome the transmission delays caused by satellite relays or packet-switching networks.

Testing a newly installed modem

Okay, the new modem is installed, the communication software is loaded, the telephone line is connected . . . and nothing happens. This is an all-too-common theme for today's technicians and computer users. Although the actual failure rate among ordinary modems is quite small, it turns out that modems (and serial ports as you can see in Chapter 49) are some of the difficult and time-consuming devices to set up and configure. As a consequence, proper setup initially can simplify troubleshooting significantly. When a new modem fails to work properly, there are a number of conditions to explore:

- *Incorrect hardware resources* An internal modem must be set with a unique IRQ line and I/O port. If the assigned resources are also used by another serial device in the system (such as a mouse), the modem, the conflicting device (or perhaps both) will not function properly. Remove the modem and use a diagnostic to check available resources. Reconfigure the internal modem to clear the conflict. External modems make use of existing COM ports.
- *Defective telecommunication resources* All modems need access to a telephone line in order to establish connections with other modems. If the telephone jack is defective or hooked up improperly, the modem might work fine, but no connection is possible. Remove the telephone line cord from the modem and try the line cord on an ordinary telephone. When you lift the receiver, you should draw dial tone. Try dialing a local number; if the line rings, chances are good that the telephone line is working. Check the RJ11 jack on the modem. One or more bent connector pins can break the line even though the line cord is inserted properly.
- *Improper cabling* An external modem must be connected to the PC serial port with a cable. Traditional serial cables were 25-pin assemblies. Later,

9-pin serial connectors and cables became common; out of those 9 wires, only three are really vital. As a result, quite a few cable assemblies might be incorrect or otherwise specialized. Make sure that the serial cable between the PC and modem is a straight-through type cable. Also check that both ends of the cable are intact (installed evenly, no bent pins, and so on). Try a new cable if necessary.

- *Improper power* External modems must receive power from batteries, or from an ac eliminator. Make sure that any batteries are fresh and installed completely. If an ac adapter is used, see that it is connected to the modem properly.

- *Incorrect software settings* Both internal and external modems must be initialized with an AT ASCII command string before a connection is established. If these settings are absent or incorrect, the modem will not respond as expected (if at all). Check the communication software and make sure that the AT command strings are appropriate for the modem being used; different modems often require slightly different command strings.

- *Suspect the modem itself* Modems are typically quite reliable in everyday use. If there are jumpers or DIP switches on the modem, check that each setting is placed correctly. Perhaps their most vulnerable point is the telephone interface that is particularly susceptible to high-voltage spikes that might enter through the telephone line. If all else fails, try another modem.

Checking the command processor

The command processor is the controller that manages the modem's operation in the command mode. It is the command processor that interprets AT command strings. When the new modem installation fails to behave as it should, you should first check the modem command processor using the following procedure. Before going too far with this, make sure you have the modem's user guide on hand (if possible). When the command processor checks out, but the modem refuses to work under normal communication software operations, the software might be refusing to save settings such as COM port selection, speed, and character format.

1. Make sure the modem is installed properly and connected to the desired PC serial port. Of course, if the modem is internal, you will only need to worry about IRQ and I/O port settings.

2. Start the communication software and select a direct connection to establish a path from your keyboard to the modem. You will probably see a dialog box appear with a blinking cursor. If the modem is working and installed properly, you should now be able to send commands directly to the modem.

3. Type the command AT and then press the <ENTER> key. The modem should return an OK result code. When an OK is returned, chances are that the modem is working correctly. If you see double characters being displayed, try the command ATE0 to disable the command mode echo. If you do not see an OK, try issuing an ATE1 command to enable the command mode echo. If there is still no response, commands are not reaching the modem, or the modem is defective. Check the connections

between the modem and serial port. If the modem is internal, check that it is installed correctly and that all jumpers are placed properly.

4. Try resetting the modem with the ATZ command and the <ENTER> key. This should reset the modem. If the modem now responds with OK, you might have to adjust the initialization command string in the communication software.

5. Try factory default settings by typing the command AT&F than pressing the <ENTER> key. This should restore the factory default values for each S-register. You might also try the command AT&Q0 and <ENTER> to deliberately place the modem into asynchronous mode. You should see OK responses to each attempt that indicate the modem is responding as expected; it might be necessary to update the modem's initialization command string. If the modem still does not respond, the communication software might be incompatible, or the modem is defective.

Checking the dialer and telephone line

After you are confident that the modem's command processor is responding properly, you can also check the telephone interface by attempting a call; this also can verify an active telephone line. When the telephone interface checks out, but the modem refuses to work under normal communication software operations, the software might be refusing to save settings such as COM port selection, speed, and character format.

1. Make sure the modem is installed properly and connected to the desired PC serial port. Of course, if the modem is internal, you will only need to worry about IRQ and I/O port settings.

2. Start the communication software and select a direct connection to establish a path from your keyboard to the modem. You will probably see a dialog box appear with a blinking cursor. If the modem is working and installed properly, you should now be able to send commands directly to the modem.

3. Dial a number by using the DT (dial using tones) command followed by the full number being called. For example, ATDT15083667683 followed by the <ENTER> key. If your local telephone line only supports rotary dialing, use the modifier R after the D. If calling from a PBX, be sure to dial 9 or other outside-access codes. Listen for a dial tone, followed by the tone dialing beeps. You should also hear the destination phone ringing. When these occur, they ensure that your telephone interface dials correctly, and the local phone line is responding properly.

4. If there is no dial tone, check the phone line by dialing with an ordinary phone. Note that some PBX systems must be modified to produce at least 48 Vdc for the modem to work. If there is no dial tone, but the modem attempts to dial, the telephone interface is not grabbing the telephone line correctly (the dialer is working). If the modem draws dial tone, but no digits are generated, the dialer might be defective. In either case, try another.

Modem settings

Modem settings are critically important to inter-modem communication. The number of data bits, use of parity, number of stop bits, and data transfer speed must be set precisely the same way on both modems. Otherwise, the valid data leaving one modem will be interpreted as complete junk at the receiving end. Normally, this should not happen when modems are set to auto-answer; negotiation should allow both modems to settle at the same parameters. The time that incompatible settings really become a factor is when negotiation is unsuccessful, or when communication is being established manually. A typical example is an avid BBS user with communication software set to eight data bits, no parity bit, and one stop bit trying to use a network that runs at seven data bits, even parity, and two stop bits. The aspect that stands out with incompatible settings is that virtually nothing is intelligible, and the connection is typically lost.

Line noise

Where faulty settings can load the display with trash, even a properly established connection can lose integrity periodically. Remember that serial communication is made possible by an international network of switched telephone wiring. Each time you dial the same number, you typically get a different set of wiring. Faulty wiring at any point along the network, electrical storms, wet or snowy weather, and other natural or man-made disasters can interrupt the network momentarily, or cut communication entirely. Most of the time, brief interruptions can result in small patches of garbled text. This type of behavior is most prominent in real-time on-line sessions (such as typing in an e-mail message). When uploading or downloading files, file transfer protocols can usually catch such anomalies and correct errors or request new data packets to overcome the errors. When you have trouble moving files or notice a high level of junk on line, try calling back; when a new telephone line is established, the connection might be better.

Transmit and receive levels

Other factors that affect both leased and dial-up telephone lines are the transmit and receive levels. These settings determine the signal levels used by the modem in each direction. Some Hayes-compatible modems permit these levels to be adjusted. The range and availability of these adjustments is in large part controlled by the local telephone system. For example, the recommended settings and ranges are different for modems sold in the UK than for those sold in the U.S. See the documentation accompanying the modem to determine whether this capability is supported.

System-processor limitations

Some multitasking operating systems can occasionally lose small amounts of data if the computer is heavily loaded and cannot allocate processing time to the communications task frequently enough. In this case, the data is corrupted by the host computer itself. This could also cause incomplete data transmission to the remote system. Host processor capabilities should be a concern when developing software for data communications when the line speed is greater than 9600 bps and the modem-to-DTE connection is 19,200 bps or higher (for example, when data compression is used). The modem will provide exact transmission of the data it receives, but if the host PC cannot keep up with the modem because of other tasks or speed restrictions, precautions should be taken when writing software or when adding modems with extra high speed capabilities. One way to avoid the problem of data loss caused by the host PC is the use of an upgraded serial port such as a Hayes Enhanced Serial Port card or a newer modem with a 16550 UART. Such advanced modems are powerful enough to take some of the load off of the PC processor. When processor time is stretched to the limit, try shutting down any unnecessary applications to reduce load on the system.

Call waiting

The call waiting feature now available on most dial-up lines momentarily interrupts a call. This interruption causes a click that informs voice call users that another call is coming through. Although this technique is dynamite for voice communication, it is also quite effective at interrupting a modem's carrier signal and can cause some modems to drop the connection. One way around this is to set S-register S10 to a higher value so the modem tolerates a fairly long loss of carrier signal. Data loss might still occur, but the connection will not drop. Of course, the remote modem must be similarly configured. When originating the call, a special prefix can be issued as part of the dialing string to disable call waiting for the duration of the call. The exact procedure varies from area to area, so contact your local telephone system for details.

Automatic timeout

Some Hayes-compatible modems offer an automatic timeout feature. Automatic timeout prevents an inactive connection from being maintained. This watchdog feature prevents undesired long-distance charges for a connection that was maintained for too long. This inactivity delay can be set or disabled with S-register S30.

System lock up

There are situations where host systems do lock up, but in many cases it is simply that one or the other of the computers has been *flowed off*; that is, the character that stops data transfer has been inadvertently sent. This can happen during error-control connections if the wrong kind of local flow control has been selected. In addition, the problem could be the result of incompatible EIA 232-D/ITU V.24 signaling. When systems seem to cease transmitting or receiving without warning, but do not disconnect, perform a thorough examination of flow control.

Modem troubleshooting

As you can see from the previous discussions in this chapter, many of the problems that you will encounter with modem/fax boards are related to their physical and software configuration. The host PC also plays an important role in the modem's overall performance and reliability. Modems themselves are rarely at fault, although they are hardly invulnerable. This part of the chapter presents you with an index of potential troubleshooting problems and solutions. When you determine that the modem itself is at fault, you should replace the modem outright. When replacing the modem, remember that the initialization and operating strings often vary slightly between modem manufacturers; be sure to alter any AT command strings in the communication software to accommodate the new modem.

Symptom 1. The modem appears to be functioning properly, but you cannot see what you are typing There are two types of duplex, full and half. Half-duplex systems simply transmit to and receive from each other. Full-duplex systems do that, plus they receive what they transmit, echoing the data back to the sender. Because half-duplex systems do not echo, what is being sent is typically not shown on the screen. Most terminal programs have an option to enable LOCAL ECHO so that what is transmitted is also displayed. You can often enable the modem's local echo by typing the ATE1 command during a direct connection, or add the E1 entry to the modem's initialization string. When local echo is not an option, switching to full duplex will often do the same thing. Customer complaints that they can't see what they are typing are solved by turning on local echo, or switching to full duplex.

Symptom 2. The modem appears to be functioning properly, but you see double characters print while typing By their nature, full-duplex modem connections produce an echo. If local echo is enabled in addition, you'll see not only what you are transmitting but also that character being echoed, creating a double display; when you hit A, you'll see AA. Customer complaints of double letters are solved by turning off local echo by entering the ATE0 command during direct connection, or adding the E0 command to the modem's initialization string.

Symptom 3. The modem will not answer at the customer's site, but it works fine in the shop Since deregulation of the original Bell Telephone company, customers have been allowed to attach devices to phone lines with the proviso that they notify the phone company of the device FCC registration and ringer equivalence numbers. Although few customers make it a point of informing their local telephone company how many phones and gadgets are connected to the telephone line, there is a good reason for having it; you see, the amount of ringing voltage supplied to a site is fixed. If you load down the line beyond its maximum rating, not enough voltage will be available to ring all of the bells. The ringer equivalence is the amount of load that the device will place on the line. Modems have to be able to detect a ring signal before they know to pick up. If the ringing signal is too weak, the modem will not detect it properly and initiate an answer sequence.

Have the customer remove some other equipment from their phone lines and see if the problem disappears. With today's fax machines, modems, multiple extension phones and answering machines all plugged into the same line, it would be easy to overload the ringing voltage. The customer should also take a listing of the registration numbers and ringer equivalence numbers on ALL devices connected to phone lines and notify the local phone company of them. The phone company can then boost the ringer voltage to compensate for the added loads.

As a precaution, make sure that your customer is starting the communication software properly before attempting to receive a modem call; the modem will not pick up a ringing line unless the proper software is running, and the modem is in an auto-answer mode.

Symptom 4. Your modem is receiving or transmitting garbage, or is having great difficulty displaying anything at all Serial communication is totally dependent on the data frame settings and transfer rate of the receiver and the transmitter being an exact match. The baud rate, word bits, stop bits and parity must all match exactly or errors will show up. These errors can show as either no data or as incorrect data (garbage) on screen. You'll see this one crop up a lot when customers switch from calling a local BBS to CompuServe. Local BBSs are usually set for eight-bit words, no parity and one stop bit. CompuServe, on the other hand, uses seven-bit words, even parity and 2 stop bits. The terminal software must be reconfigured to match the settings of each service being called. Most programs allow for these differences by letting you specify a configuration for each entry in the dialing directory.

Baud rate mismatches most often result in what looks like a dead modem; often, nothing is displayed on either end. Modems will automatically negotiate a common baud rate to connect at without regard to the terminal settings. The modems will normally connect at the highest baud rate available to the *slowest* modem, so if a 14,400-bps modem connects to a 2400-bps modem, both will set themselves to 2400 bps. If the software on the higher speed modem is still set for the higher speed, you'll typically get large amounts of garbage, or nothing at all.

If the problem is a result of being connected to a service such as a BBS, call the SYSOP and find out the settings. You can also let the modem tell you what transfer rate it connects at. Before dialing, set a direct connection and send the command ATQ0V1 to the modem. This tells the modem to send result codes in plain English. When connected, you'll see a message similar to CONNECT 2400. The number is the bps rate and you can reconfigure your software accordingly. Working out the word, stop and parity bits might be a process of trial and error, but almost all BBS installations use 8 data bits, no parity, and 1 stop bit. If you are forced to attempt trial and error, target one item to get right at a time. First get the baud rates to match. Next get word bits settled down and then go for parity and stop bits. If you make more than one change you'll never know which change made the difference. It might seem slower, but your overall service time will be cut.

Symptom 5. The modem is connected and turned on, but there is no response from the modem The communication software configuration must match the port settings of the modem. Check that any modem parameters are entered and saved properly. Establish a direct connection with the modem and enter the ATZ command. This will reset the modem. The modem should respond OK or 0. If that doesn't work, change to COM2 and try again, then COM3 and COM4. If none of the combinations work, check the DIP switches or jumpers on the modem for the correct configuration.

Symptom 6. The modem will not pick up the phone line The modem is not able to initiate a call or answer an incoming call. Most modems today come with two RJ11 telephone line connectors for the phone lines: one labeled LINE (where the outside line enters the modem) and the other labeled PHONE (where an extension telephone can be plugged in). Check that the outgoing telephone line is plugged into the LINE jack. Leave the PHONE connector disconnected while the modem is in use.

Test the modem manually by establishing a direct connection and typing a dial command such as ATDT15083667683 (the number for TechNet BBS). When you enter this command string, the modem should go off hook, draw dial tone, and dial the numbers. If this happens as expected, you can be reasonably sure that the modem is working properly, and the communication software is at fault. Check the modem initialization strings, or try a new communication package. If the modem does not respond during a direct connection, check that the modem is installed and configured properly. You might need to try a new modem.

Symptom 7. The modem appears to work fine, but prints garbage whenever it's supposed to show IBM text graphics such as boxes or ANSI graphics The communication software is probably set for 7-bit words. The IBM text graphic character set starts at ASCII 128 and has to have the eighth bit. Adjust the communication software configuration to handle 8-bit words. You might also be using an unusual ASCII character set during the connection; try setting the character set emulation to ANSI BBS or TTY.

Symptom 8. You frequently see strange character groups like [0m appearing in the text These are *ANSI* (American National Standards Institute) control codes attempting to control your display. Popular among BBS software, ANSI codes can be used to set colors, clear the screen, move the cursor, and so on. DOS provides an ANSI screen driver called ANSI.SYS that can be loaded into the CONFIG.SYS when the computer is rebooted. Most of today's terminal software will offer a setting for this as well. If you are able to select character set emulation in your communication software, try setting to ANSI BBS.

Symptom 9. The modem makes audible clicking noises when hooked to phone line There is probably a short in the phone line. The clicking is the noise of the modem trying to pick up when it sees the short and hang up when the short clears. Try replacing the line cord going from the modem to the telephone wall jack; line cords don't last very long under constant use and abuse. If problems continue, try using a different telephone line; the physical wiring might be defective between the wall jack and telephone pole. Contact your local telephone company if you suspect this to be the case. Next, try establishing a direct connection to the modem and enter an AT&F command that will restore the modem's factory default settings. If that clears the problem, the modem's initialized state might not be fully compatible with the current telephone line characteristics. Check each modem setting carefully and adjust parameters to try and settle its operation down. If factory default settings do not help and the telephone line seems reliable, there might be a problem with the modem's telephone interface circuit; try replacing the modem.

Symptom 10. The modem is having difficulty connecting to another modem The modem is powered and connected properly. It dials the desired number and you can hear the modems negotiating, but they never quite seem to make a connection. This is a classic software configuration problem. You might often see a NO CARRIER message associated with this problem. Check each parameter in your communication software, especially the modem's AT initialization string. Make sure that each entry in the string is appropriate for your modem. If the string appears to be correct, try disabling the modem's MNP5 protocol. You will have to refer to the modem's manual to find the exact command, but many modems use AT\N0. If your modem is using MNP5 and the destination modem does not support it, the negotiation can hang up. If problems persist, try lowering the modem's data transfer rate. Although most modems can set the proper transfer rate automatically, some modems that do not support it might also cause the negotiation to freeze.

Another problem might be that your modem is not configured to wait long enough for carrier from the remote modem. You can adjust this delay by entering a larger number for S-register S7. Start the communication software, establish a direct connection, and type ATS7? followed by the <ENTER> key. This will return the current value of register S7. You can then use the command ATS7=10 to enter a larger delay (in this case, 10 seconds). That should give the destination modem more time to respond. If all else fails, try a modem from a different manufacturer.

Symptom 11. The modem starts dialing before it draws dialtone As a result one or more of the numbers are lost during dialing making it difficult to establish a connection. Chances are that the modem is working just fine, but the modem does not wait long enough for dial tone to be present once it goes off hook. The solution is to increase the time delay before the modem starts dialing. This can be done by changing the value in S-register S6. To find the current value, start the communication software and establish a direct connection, then type ATS6? followed by the <ENTER> key. This queries the S-register. You can then enter a new value such as ATS6=10 to provide a 10-second delay.

Symptom 12. The modem has trouble sending or receiving when the system's power-saving features are turned on This type of problem is most prevalent with PCMCIA modems running on a notebook PC. The power conservation features found on many notebook systems often interfere with the modem's operation; proper modem operation typically relies on full processing speed that is often scaled back when power conservation is turned on. Ultimately, the most effective resolution to this problem is simply to turn the power conservation features off while you use the modem (you can reset the power features later).

Symptom 13. You see an error message reading something like Already on line or Carrier already established These types of errors often arise when you start a communications package while the modem is already on-line. You might also find this problem when the Carrier Detect (CD) signal is set to always on (using a command string such as AT&C0). To make sure that the CD signal is on only when the modem makes a connection, use a command string such as AT&C1&D2&W. The &W suffix loads the settings into nonvolatile RAM. If this problem arises when you hang up the connection without signing off the modem, you will have to reboot the system to clear CD—AT&F and ATZ will not clear the signal.

Symptom 14. The modem refuses to answer the incoming line First, make sure to set the communication software to answer the calling modem or set the modem to auto-answer mode (set S-register S0 to 1 or more). On external modems, you will see the AA LED lit when the auto-answer mode is active. Problems can also occur if your external modem does not recognize the DTR signal generated by the host PC. The command AT&D controls how the modem responds to the computer's DTR signal. An external modem turns on the TR light when it is set to see the DTR signal. If the TR light is out, the modem will not answer (regardless of whether the auto-answer mode is enabled or not). Use the AT&D0 command if your serial port does not support the DTR signal, or if your modem cable does not connect to it. Otherwise, you should use the AT&D2 command.

Symptom 15. The modem switches into the command mode intermittently When this problem develops, you might have to tweak the DTR arrangement. To correct this fault, try changing the modem's DTR setting using the command AT&D2&W.

38
CHAPTER

Monitor troubleshooting

From their humble beginnings as basic monochrome text displays, the monitor (Fig. 38-1) has grown to provide real-time photo-realistic images of unprecedented quality and color. Monitors have allowed stunning graphics and information-filled illustrations to replace the generic command line user interface of just a few years ago. Monitors have become a virtual window into the modern computer. With many millions of computers now in service, the economical maintenance and repair of computer monitors represents a serious challenge to technicians and hobbyists alike. Fortunately, the basic principles and operations of a computer monitor have changed very little since the days of terminal displays. This chapter explains the basic concepts behind today's computer monitors, and provides a cross-section of troubleshooting procedures.

Tandy Corporation

38-1
A Tandy PC with a VGM-450 monitor.

Monitor specifications and characteristics

Although PCs are defined by a set of fairly well-understood specifications such as RAM size, hard drive space, and clock speed, monitor specifications describe a

626

whole series of physical properties that PCs never deal with. With this in mind, perhaps the best introduction to monitor troubleshooting is to discuss each specification in detail and show you how each specification and characteristic affects a monitor's performance.

CRT

The cathode ray tube (or CRT) is essentially a large vacuum tube. One end of the CRT is formed as a long, narrow neck, and the other end is a broad, almost-flat surface. A phosphor coating is applied inside the CRT along the front face. The neck end of the CRT contains an element (called the *cathode*) that is energized and heated to very high temperatures (much like an incandescent lamp). At high temperatures, the cathode liberates electrons. When a very high positive voltage potential is applied at the front face of the CRT, electrons liberated by the cathode (which are negatively charged) are accelerated toward the front face. When the electrons strike the phosphor on the front face, light is produced. By directing the stream of electrons across the front face, a visible image is produced. Of course, there are other elements needed to control and direct the electron stream, but this is CRT operation in a nutshell. CRT face size (or screen size) is generally measured as a diagonal dimension; that is, a 43.2-cm (17 inches) CRT is 43.2 cm (17 inches) between opposing corners. Larger CRTs are more expensive, but produce larger images that are usually easier on the eyes.

Pixels and resolution

The picture element (or *pixel*) is the very smallest point that can be controlled on a CRT. For monochrome displays, a pixel can simply be turned on or off. For a color display, a pixel can assume any of a number of different colors. Pixels are combined in the form of an array (rows and columns). It is the size of that pixel array that defines the display *resolution*. Thus, resolution is the total number of pixels in width by the total number of pixels in height. For example, a typical EGA resolution is 640 pixels wide by 350 pixels high, and a typical VGA resolution is 640 pixels wide by 480 pixels high. Typical Super VGA (SVGA) resolution is 800 pixels wide by 600 pixels high. Resolution is important for computer monitors because higher resolutions allow finer image detail.

Triads and dot pitch

Although monochrome CRTs use a single, uniform phosphor coating (usually white, amber, or green), color CRTs use three color phosphors (red, green, and blue) arranged as triangles (or *triads*). Figure 38-2 illustrates a series of color phosphor triads. On a color monitor, each triad represents one pixel (even though there are three dots in the pixel). By using the electron streams from three electron guns—one gun for red, one for blue, and another for green—to excite each dot, a broad spectrum of colors can be produced. The three dots are placed so close together that they appear as a single point to the unaided eye.

The quality of a color image is related to just how close each of the three dots are to one another. The closer together they are, the purer the image appears. As the dots are spaced farther apart, the image quality degrades because the eye can begin

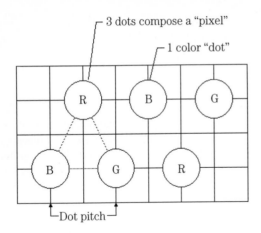

3 dots compose a "pixel"

1 color "dot"

R   B   G

B   G   R

Dot pitch

38-2
Arranging color phosphors in a triad.

to discern the individual dots in each pixel. This results in lines that no longer appear straight and colors are no longer pure. *Dot pitch* is a measure of the distance between any two phosphor dots on the display. Displays with a dot pitch of 0.31 mm or less generally provide adequate image quality.

Shadow and slot masks

The *shadow mask* is a thin sheet of perforated metal that is placed in the color CRT just behind the phosphor coating. Electron beams from each of the three electron guns are focused to converge at each hole in the mask, not at the phosphor screen (Fig. 38-3). The microscopic holes act as apertures that let the electron beams through only to their corresponding color phosphors. In this way, any stray electrons are masked, and color is kept pure. Some CRT designs substitute a shadow mask with a slot mask (or aperture grille) that is made up of vertical wires behind the phosphor screen. Dot pitch for CRTs with slot masks is defined as the distance between each slot. Not all CRT designs use a mask. Monochrome CRTs do not need a shadow mask at all because the entire phosphor surface is the same color.

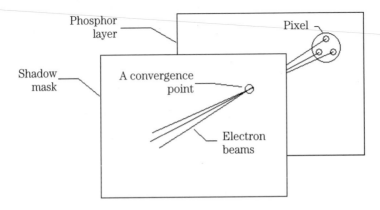

Phosphor layer

Pixel

Shadow mask

A convergence point

Electron beams

*Sizes and distances are NOT shown to scale.

38-3 The importance of convergence in a color monitor.

Convergence

Remember that three electron guns are used in a color monitor—each gun excites a particular color phosphor. All three electron beams are tracking around the screen simultaneously, and the beams converge at holes in the shadow mask. This *convergence* of electron beams is closely related to color purity in the screen image. Ideally, the three beams converge perfectly at all points on the display and the resulting color is perfectly pure throughout (pure white). If one or more beams do not converge properly, the image color will not be pure. In most cases, poor convergence will result in colored shadows. For example, you might see a red, green, or blue shadow when looking at a white line. Serious convergence problems can result in a blurred or distorted image. Monitor specifications usually list typical convergence error as *misconvergence* at both the display center and the overall display area. Typical center misconvergence runs approximately 0.45 mm, and overall display area misconvergence is about 0.65 mm. Larger numbers result in poorer convergence.

Pincushion and barrel distortion

The front face of most CRTs is slightly convex (bulging outward). Images are perfectly square. When a square image is projected onto a curved surface, distortion results. Ideally, a monitor's raster circuits will compensate for this screen shape so that the image appears square when viewed at normal distances. In actual practice, however, the image is rarely square. The sides of the image (top-to-bottom) and (left-to-right) might be bent slightly inward or slightly outward. Figure 38-4 illustrates an exaggerated view of these effects. *Pincushioning* occurs when sides are bent inward making the image's border appear concave. *Barreling* occurs when the sides are bent outward making the image's border appear convex. In most cases, these distortions should be just barely noticeable (no more than 2.0 or 3.0 mm). Keep in mind that many technicians refer to barrel distortion as pincushioning as well.

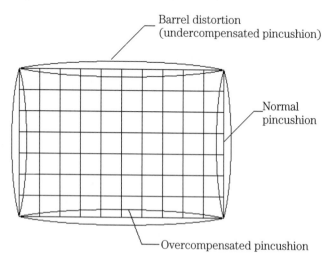

38-4 The effects of pincushion and barrel distortion.

Horizontal scanning, vertical scanning, raster, and retrace

To understand what scanning is, you must first understand how a monitor's image is formed. A monitor's image is generated one horizontal line of pixels at a time starting from the upper left corner of the display (Fig. 38-5). As the beams travel across the line, each pixel is excited based on the video data contained in the corresponding location of video RAM on the video adapter board. When a line is complete, the beam turns off (known as *horizontal blanking*). The beam is then directed horizontally (and slightly vertically) to the beginning of the next subsequent line. A new horizontal line can then be drawn. This process continues until all horizontal lines are drawn and the beam is in the lower right corner of the display. When the image is complete, the beam turns off (called *vertical blanking*) and is redirected to the upper left corner of the display to start all over again.

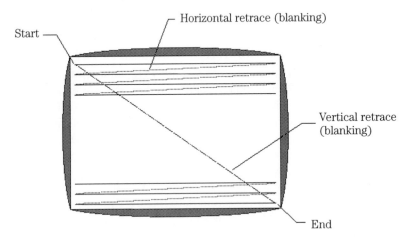

38-5 Forming a screen image on a CRT.

The rate at which horizontal lines are drawn is known as the *horizontal scanning rate* (sometimes called *horizontal sync*). The rate at which a complete "page" of horizontal lines is generated is known as the *vertical scanning rate* (or vertical sync). Both the horizontal and vertical blanking times are known as *retrace times* because the deactivated beams are retracing their path before starting a new trace. A typical horizontal retrace time is 5 μs, and the typical vertical retrace time is 700 μs. This continuous horizontal and vertical scanning action is known as raster.

We can easily apply numbers to scanning rates to give you an even better idea of their relationship. A typical VGA monitor with a resolution of 640-x-480 pixels uses a horizontal scanning rate of 31.5 kHz. This means that 31,500 lines can be drawn in one second, or a single line of 640 pixels can be drawn in 31.7 μs. Because there are 480 horizontal lines to be drawn in one page, a complete page can be drawn in (480 × 31.7 μs) 15.2 ms. If a single page can be drawn in 15.2 ms, the screen can be refreshed 65.7 times per second (65.7 Hz); this is roughly the vertical rate that will be set for VGA operation at 640-x-480 resolution. In actual practice, the vertical scanning rate will be set to a whole number such as 60 Hz, which leaves a lot of spare time for blanking and synchronization. It was discovered early in TV design that vertical scanning rates under 60 Hz resulted in perceivable flicker that causes eye strain and fatigue. You can start to see now that horizontal scanning rates are not chosen arbitrarily. The objective is to select a horizontal frequency that will cover a page's worth of horizontal pixel lines for any given resolution at about 60 times per second.

Interlacing

Images are "painted" onto a display one horizontal row at a time, but the sequence in which those lines are drawn can be *noninterlaced* or *interlaced*. As you see in Fig. 38-6, a noninterlaced monitor draws all of the lines that compose an image in one pass. This is preferable because a noninterlaced image is easier on your eyes—the entire image is refreshed at the vertical scanning frequency—so a 60-Hz vertical scanning rate will update the entire image 60 times in one second. An interlaced display draws an image as two passes. Once the first pass is complete, a second pass fills in the rest of the image. The effective image refresh rate is only half the stated vertical scanning rate. The typical 1024-x-768 SVGA monitor offers a vertical scanning rate of 87 Hz, but because the monitor is interlaced, effective refresh is only 43.5 Hz; screen flicker is much more noticeable.

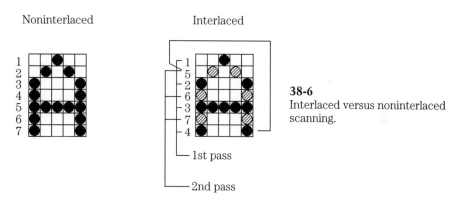

38-6
Interlaced versus noninterlaced scanning.

Bandwidth

In the very simplest terms, the *bandwidth* of a monitor is the absolute maximum rate at which pixels can be sent to the monitor. Typical VGA displays offer a bandwidth of 30 MHz. That is, the monitor could generate up to 30 million pixels per second on the display. Consider that each scan line of a VGA display uses 640 pixels and the horizontal scan rate of 31.45 kHz allows 31,450 scan lines per second to be written. At that rate, the monitor is processing (640 pixels/scan line × 31,450 scan lines/second) 20,128,000 pixels/second, well within the monitor's 30-MHz bandwidth. The very newest color monitors offer bandwidths of 135 MHz. Such high-resolution 1280-x-1024 monitors with scanning rates of 79 kHz would need to process at least (1280 pixels/scan line × 79,000 scan lines/second) 101,120,000 pixels/second (101.12 MHz), so enhanced bandwidth is truly a necessity for high resolutions.

Swim, jitter, and drift

The electron beam(s) that form an image are directed around a display using variable magnetic fields generated by separate vertical and horizontal deflection coils mounted around the CRT's neck. The analog signals that drive each deflection coil are produced by horizontal and vertical deflection circuitry. Ideally, deflection circuitry should steer the electron beam(s) precisely the same way in each pass. This would result in an absolutely rock-solid image on the display. In the real world, however, there are minute variations in the placement of images over any given period of time. *Jitter* is a term used to measure such variation over a 15-second period. *Swim* (sometimes called *wave*) is a measure of position variation over a 30-second period. *Drift* is a measure of position variation over a one-minute period. Note that all three terms represent essentially the same problem over different amounts of time. Swim, jitter, and drift can be expressed as fractions of a pixel or as physical measurements such as millimeters.

Video signal

This specification lists signal levels and characteristics of the analog video input channel(s). In most cases, a video signal in the 0.7-Vpp (peak to peak) range is used. Circuitry inside the monitor amplifies and manipulates these relatively small signals. A related specification is input impedance that is often at 75 Ω. Older monitors using digital (on-off) video signals typically operate up to 1.5 V.

Synchronization and polarity

After a line is drawn on the display, the electron beams are turned off (blanked) and repositioned to start the next horizontal line. However, no data is contained in the retrace line. In order for the new line to be in sync with the data for that line, a synchronization pulse is sent from the video adapter to the monitor. There is a separate pulse for horizontal synchronization and vertical synchronization. In most current monitors, synchronization signals are edge triggered TTL (transistor-transistor logic) signals. *Polarity* refers to the edge that triggers the synchronization. A falling trigger (marked "–" or "positive/negative") indicates that synchronization takes place at the high-to-low transition of the sync signal. A leading trigger (marked "+" or "negative/positive") indicates that synchronization takes place on the low-to-high transition of the sync signal.

The color circuits

In order to have a full understanding of color monitors, it is best to start with a block diagram. The block diagram for a VGA monitor is shown in Fig. 38-7. Three complete video drive circuits are needed (one for each primary color—red, green, and blue). Although early color monitors used logic levels to represent video signals, current monitors use analog signals that allow the intensity of each color to be varied. The CRT is designed to provide three electron beams that are directed at corresponding color phosphors. By varying the intensity of each electron beam, virtually any color can be produced. For all practical purposes, the color monitor can be considered in three subsections: the video drive circuits, the vertical drive circuit, and the horizontal drive circuit (including the high-voltage system).

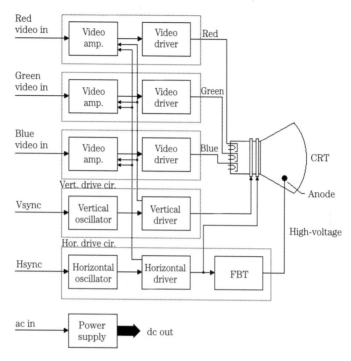

38-7 Block diagram of a color (VGA) monitor.

Video drive circuits

The schematic diagram for a typical RGB (Red, Green, and Blue) drive circuit is shown in Fig. 38-8. This schematic is actually part of a Tandy VGM220 analog color monitor. You will see that there are three separate video drive circuits. Components with a 5xx designation (for example, IC501) are part of the red video drive circuit. The 6xx designation (for example, Q602) shows a part in the green video drive circuit. A 7xx marking (for example, C704) indicates a component in the blue video drive circuit. Other components marked with 8xx designations (for example, Q803) are included to operate the CRT control grid. Follow through with the operation of one of these video circuits.

The red analog signal is filtered by the small array of F501. The ferrite beads on either side of the small filter capacitor serve to reduce noise that might otherwise interfere with the weak analog signal. The video signal is amplified by transistor Q501. Potentiometer VR501 adjusts the signal gain (the amount of amplification applied to the video signal). Collector signals are then passed to the differential amplifier circuit in IC501. Once again, noise is a major concern in color signals, and differential amplifiers help to improve signal strength while eliminating noise. The resulting video signal is applied to a *push-pull* amplifier circuit consisting of Q503 and Q504, then fed to a subsequent push-pull amplifier pair of Q505 and Q506. Potentiometer VR502 controls the amount of dc bias used to generate the final output signal. The

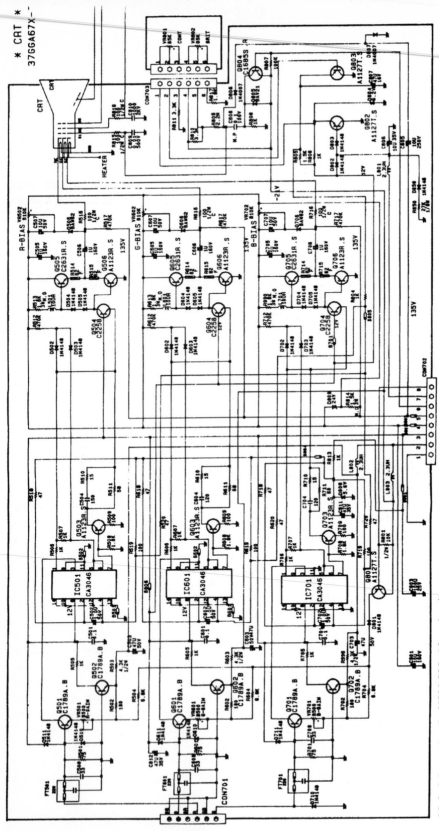

38-8 Schematic of a VGM-220 video circuit. Tandy Corporation

output from this final amplifier stage is coupled directly to the corresponding CRT video control grid. The remaining two drive circuits both work the same way.

Problems with the video circuits in color monitors rarely disable the image entirely. Even if one video drive circuit should fail, there are still two others to drive the CRT. Of course, the loss of one primary color will severely distort the image colors, but the image should still be visible. You can tell when one of the video drive circuits fails; the faulty circuit will either saturate the display with that color or cut that color out completely. For example, if the red video drive circuit should fail, the resulting screen image will either be saturated with red, or red will be absent (leaving a greenish-blue or cyan image).

Vertical drive circuit

The vertical drive circuit is designed to operate the monitor's vertical deflection yoke (dubbed V-DY). To give you a broad perspective of vertical drive operation and its inter-relation to other important monitor circuits, Fig. 38-9 illustrates the vertical drive, horizontal drive, high-voltage, and power supply circuits all combined together in the same schematic. This schematic is essentially the main PC board for the Tandy VGM220 monitor. Components marked with 4xx numbers (for example, IC401) are part of the vertical drive system.

The vertical sync pulses enter the monitor at connector CH202 (the line marked V). A simple exclusive-OR gate (IC201) is used to condition the sync pulses and select the video mode being used. Because the polarity of horizontal and vertical sync pulses will be different for each video mode, IC201 detects those polarities and causes the digitally controlled analog switch (IC401) to select one of three vertical size (V-SIZE) control sets that is connected to the vertical sawtooth oscillator (IC402). This mode-switching circuit allows the monitor to auto-size the display.

The vertical sync pulse fires the vertical sawtooth oscillator on pin 2 of IC402. The frequency of the vertical sweep is set to 60 Hz, but can be optimized by adjusting the vertical frequency control (V-FREQ) VR404. It is highly recommended that you do *not* attempt to adjust the vertical frequency unless you have an oscilloscope available. Vertical linearity (V-LIN) is adjusted through potentiometer VR405. Vertical centering (V-CENTER) is controlled through VR406. Linearity and centering adjustments should only be made while displaying an appropriate test pattern. It is interesting to note that there are no discrete power amplifiers needed to drive the vertical deflection yoke—IC402 pin 6 drives the deflection yoke directly through an internal power amplifier.

The pincushion circuit forms a link between the vertical and horizontal deflection systems through the pincushion transformer (T304). Transistors Q401 and Q402 form a compensator circuit that slightly modulates horizontal deflection. This prevents distortion in the image when projecting a flat, two-dimensional image onto a curved surface (the CRT). Potentiometer VR407 provides the pincushion control (PCC). As with other alignments, you should not attempt to adjust the pincushion unless an appropriate test pattern is displayed.

Problems that develop in the vertical amplifier will invariably affect the appearance of the CRT image. A catastrophic fault in the vertical oscillator or amplifier will

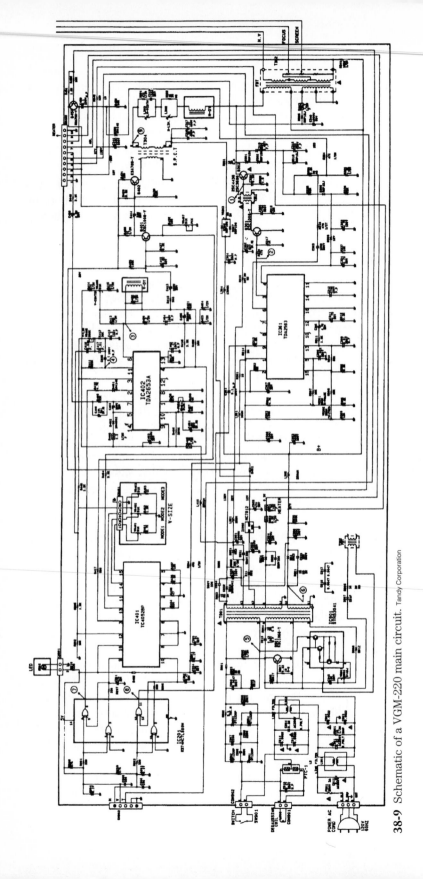

38-9 Schematic of a VGM-220 main circuit. Tandy Corporation

leave a narrow horizontal line in the display. The likeliest cause is the vertical drive IC (IC402) because that component handles both sawtooth generation and amplification. If only the upper or lower half of an image disappears, only one part of the vertical amplifier in IC402 might have failed. However, any fault on the PC board that interrupts the vertical sawtooth will disable vertical deflection entirely. When the vertical deflection is marginal (too expanded or too compressed), suspect a fault in IC402, but its related components also might be breaking down. An image that is over-expanded will usually appear folded over with a whitish haze along the bottom. It also might be interesting to note that vertical drive problems do not affect display colors.

Horizontal drive circuit

The horizontal drive circuit is responsible for operating the horizontal deflection yoke (H-DY). It is this circuit that sweeps the electron beams left and right across the display. To understand how the horizontal drive works, you should again refer to the schematic of Fig. 38-9. All components marked 3xx numbers (for example, IC301) relate to the horizontal drive circuit. Horizontal sync signals enter the monitor at connector CH202 (the line marked H) and are conditioned by the exclusive-OR gates of IC201. Conditioned sync pulses fire the horizontal oscillator (IC301). Horizontal frequency should be locked at 31.5 kHz, but potentiometer VR302 can be used to optimize the frequency. Do not attempt to adjust horizontal frequency unless you have an oscilloscope available. Horizontal phase can be adjusted with VR301. You should avoid altering any alignments until a suitable test pattern is displayed as discussed in chapter 68.

IC301 is a highly integrated device that is designed to provide precision horizontal square wave pulses to the driver transistors Q301 and Q302. IC301 pin 3 provides the horizontal pulses to Q301. Transistor Q301 switches on and off causing current pulses in the horizontal output transformer (T303). Current pulses produced by the secondary winding of T303 fire the horizontal output transistor (Q302). Output from the HOT drives the horizontal deflection yoke (H-DY). The deflection circuit includes two adjustable coils to control horizontal linearity (H-LIN; L302) and horizontal width (H-WIDTH; L303). You also will notice that the collector signal from Q302 is directly connected to the flyback transformer (FBT). Operation of the high-voltage system is covered in the next section.

Problems in the horizontal drive circuit can take several forms. One common manifestation is the loss of horizontal sweep leaving a vertical line in the center of the display. This is generally due to a fault in the horizontal oscillator (IC301) rather than the horizontal driver transistors. The second common symptom is a loss of image (including raster), and is almost always the result of a failure in the HOT (or high-voltage circuit). Because the HOT also operates the flyback transformer, a loss of horizontal output will disrupt high-voltage generation; the image will disappear.

The flyback circuit

The presence of a large positive potential on the CRT's anode is needed in order to accelerate an electron beam across the distance between the cathode and CRT phosphor. Electrons must strike the phosphor hard enough to liberate visible light. Under normal circumstances, this requires a potential of 15,000 to 30,000 V. Larger CRTs need higher voltages because there is a greater physical distance to overcome. Monitors generate high-voltage through the flyback circuit.

The heart of the high-voltage circuit is the flyback transformer (FBT) as shown in Fig. 38-9. The FBT's primary winding is directly coupled to the horizontal output transistor (Q302). Another primary winding is used to compensate the high-voltage level for changes in brightness and contrast. Flyback voltage is generated during the *horizontal retrace* (the time between the end of one scan line and the beginning of another) when the sudden drop in deflection signal causes a strong voltage spike on the FBT secondary windings. You will notice that the FBT in Fig. 38-9 provides one multitapped secondary winding. The top-most tap from the FBT secondary provides high voltage to the CRT anode. A high-voltage rectifier diode added to the FBT assembly forms a half-wave rectifier; only positive voltages reach the CRT anode. The effective capacitance of the CRT anode will act to filter the high-voltage spikes into dc. You can read the high-voltage level with a high-voltage probe. The CRT needs additional voltages in order to function. The lower tap from the FBT secondary supplies voltage to the focus and screen grid adjustments. These adjustments, in turn, drive the CRT directly.

Trouble in the high-voltage circuit can render the monitor inoperative. Typically, a high-voltage fault manifests itself as a loss of image and raster. In many cases where the HOT and deflection signals prove to be intact, the flyback transformer has probably failed causing a loss of output in one or more of the three FBT secondary windings. The troubleshooting procedures in the next section of this chapter will cover high-voltage symptoms and solutions in more detail.

Construction

Before jumping right into troubleshooting, it would be helpful to understand how the circuits shown in Fig. 38-9 are assembled. A wiring diagram for the Tandy VGM220 is shown in Fig. 38-10. There are two PC boards: the video drive PC board, and the main PC board. The main PC board contains the raster circuits, power supply, and high-voltage circuitry. The video drive PC board contains red, green, and blue video circuits. Video signals, focus grid voltage, screen grid voltage, and brightness and contrast controls connect to the video drive board. The video PC board plugs in to the CRT at its neck (although the diagram of Fig. 38-10 might not show this clearly). A power switch, power LED, and CRT degaussing coil plug into the main PC board. There also are connections at the main PC board for the ac line cord and video sync signals.

Troubleshooting the color monitor

Any discussion of monitor troubleshooting must start with a reminder of the dangers involved. Computer monitors use very high voltages for proper operation. **Potentially lethal shock hazards exist within the monitor assembly—both from ordinary ac line voltage, as well as from the CRT anode voltage developed by**

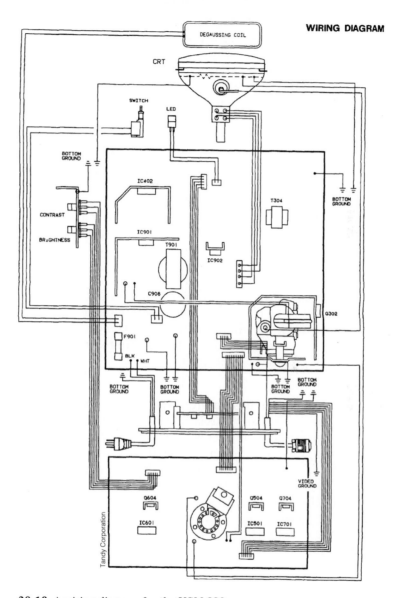

WIRING DIAGRAM

38-10 A wiring diagram for the VGM-220.

**the flyback transformer. Be extremely cautious whenever a monitor's outer
housings are removed**. If you are uncomfortable with the idea of working around
high voltages, defer your troubleshooting to an experienced technician.

Wrapping it up

When you finally get your monitor working again and are ready to reassemble it,
be very careful to see that all wiring and connectors are routed properly. No wires

should be pinched or lodged between the chassis or other metal parts (especially sharp edges). After the wiring is secure, make sure that any insulators, shielding, or protective enclosures are installed. This is even more important for larger monitors with supplemental X-ray shielding. Replace all plastic enclosures and secure them with their full complement of screws.

Post-repair testing and alignment

Regardless of the problem with your monitor or how you go about repairing it, a check of the monitor's alignment is always worthwhile before returning the unit to service. Your first procedure after a repair is complete should be to ensure that the high-voltage level does not exceed the maximum specified value. Excessive high voltage can liberate X radiation from the CRT. Over prolonged exposure, X rays can present a serious biohazard. The high-voltage value is usually marked on the specification plate glued to the outer housing, or recorded on a sticker placed somewhere inside the housing. If you cannot find the high-voltage level, refer to service data from the monitor's manufacturer. Once high voltage is correct, you can proceed with other alignment tests. Refer to Chapter 68 for testing and alignment procedures. When testing (and realignment) is complete, it is wise to let the monitor run for 24 hours or so (called a *burn-in test*) before returning it to service. Running the monitor for a prolonged period helps ensure that the original problem has indeed been resolved. This is a form of quality control. If the problem resurfaces, there might be another more serious problem elsewhere in the monitor.

Symptoms

Symptom 1. The image is saturated with red, or appears greenish-blue (cyan) If there are any user color controls available from the front or rear housings, make sure those controls have not been accidentally adjusted. If color controls are set properly (or not available externally), the red video drive circuit has probably failed. Refer to the example circuit of Fig. 38-8. Use your oscilloscope to trace the video signal from its initial input to the final output. If there is no red video signal at the amplifier input (for example, the base of Q501), check the connection between the monitor and the video adapter board. If the connection is intact, try a known-good monitor. If the problem persists on a known-good monitor, replace the video adapter board. As you trace the video signal, you can compare the signal to characteristics at the corresponding points in the green or blue video circuits. The point at which the signal disappears is probably the point of failure, and the offending component should be replaced. If you do not have the tools or inclination to perform component-level troubleshooting, try replacing the video drive PC board entirely.

If the video signal measures properly all the way to the CRT (or a new video drive PC board does not correct the problem), suspect a fault in the CRT itself; the corresponding cathode or video control grid might have failed. If you have access to a CRT tester/rejuvenator, test the CRT. If the CRT measures bad (and cannot be recovered through any available rejuvenation procedure), it should be replaced. Keep in mind that a color CRT is usually the most expensive component in the monitor. As with any CRT replacement, you should carefully consider the economics of the repair versus buying a new or rebuilt monitor.

Symptom 2. The image is saturated with blue, or appears yellow If there are any user color controls available from the front or rear housings, make sure those controls have not been accidentally adjusted. If color controls are set properly (or not available externally), the blue video drive circuit has probably failed. Refer to the example circuit of Fig. 38-8. Use your oscilloscope to trace the video signal from its initial input to the final output. If there is no blue video signal at the amplifier input (for example, the base of Q701), check the connection between the monitor and the video adapter board. If the connection is intact, try a known-good monitor. If the problem persists on a known-good monitor, replace the video adapter board. As you trace the video signal, you can compare the signal to characteristics at the corresponding points in the green or red video circuits. The point at which the signal disappears is probably the point of failure, and the offending component should be replaced. If you do not have the tools or inclination to perform component-level troubleshooting, try replacing the video drive PC board entirely.

If the video signal measures properly all the way to the CRT (or a new video drive PC board does not correct the problem), suspect a fault in the CRT itself; the corresponding cathode or video control grid might have failed. If you have access to a CRT tester/rejuvenator, test the CRT. If the CRT measures bad (and cannot be recovered through any available rejuvenation procedure), it should be replaced. Keep in mind that a color CRT is usually the most expensive component in the monitor. As with any CRT replacement, you should carefully consider the economics of the repair versus buying a new or rebuilt monitor.

Symptom 3. The image is saturated with green, or appears bluish-red (magenta) If there are any user color controls available from the front or rear housings, make sure those controls have not been accidentally adjusted. If color controls are set properly (or not available externally), the green video drive circuit has probably failed. Refer to the example circuit of Fig. 38-8. Use your oscilloscope to trace the video signal from its initial input to the final output. If there is no green video signal at the amplifier input (the base of Q601), check the connection between the monitor and the video adapter board. If the connection is intact, try a known-good monitor. If the problem persists on a known-good monitor, replace the video adapter board. As you trace the video signal, you can compare the signal to characteristics at the corresponding points in the red or blue video circuits. The point at which the signal disappears is probably the point of failure, and the offending component should be replaced. If you do not have the tools or inclination to perform component-level troubleshooting, try replacing the video drive PC board entirely.

If the video signal measures properly all the way to the CRT (or a new video drive PC board does not correct the problem), suspect a fault in the CRT itself; the corresponding cathode or video control grid might have failed. If you have access to a CRT tester/rejuvenator, test the CRT. If the CRT measures bad (and cannot be recovered through any available rejuvenation procedure), it should be replaced. Keep in mind that a color CRT is usually the most expensive component in the monitor. As with any CRT replacement, you should carefully consider the economics of the repair versus buying a new or rebuilt monitor.

Symptom 4. Raster is present, but there is no image When the monitor is properly connected to a PC, a series of text information should appear as the PC initializes. We can use this as our baseline image. Isolate the monitor by trying a known-good monitor on your host PC. If the known-good monitor works, you prove that the PC and video adapter are working properly. Reconnect the suspect monitor to the PC and turn up the brightness (and contrast if necessary). You should see a faint white haze covering the display. This is the raster generated by the normal sweep of an electron beam. Remember that the PC *must* be on and running. Without the horizontal and vertical retrace signals provided by the video adapter, there will be no raster.

For a color image to fail completely, all three video drive circuits will have to be disabled. You should check all connectors between the video adapter board and the monitor's main PC board. A loose or severed wire can interrupt the voltage(s) powering the board. You also should check each output from your power supply. A low or missing voltage can disable your video circuits as effectively as a loose connector. If you find a faulty supply output, you can attempt to troubleshoot the supply, or you can replace the power supply outright. For monitors that incorporate the power supply onto the main PC board, the entire main PC board would have to be replaced.

If supply voltage levels and connections are intact, use an oscilloscope to trace the video signals through their respective amplifier circuits. Chances are that you will see all three video signals fail at the same location of each circuit. This is usually due to a problem in common parts of the video circuits. In the example video drive board of Fig. 38-8, such common circuitry involves the components marked with 8xx numbers (for example, Q801). If you do not have the tools or inclination to perform such component-level troubleshooting, replace the video drive PC board.

You also should suspect a problem with the raster blanking circuits. During horizontal and vertical retrace periods, video signals are cut off. If visible raster lines appear in your image, check the blanking signals. If you are unable to check the blanking signals, try replacing the video drive PC board. If a new video drive board fails to correct the problem, replace the main PC board.

If you should find that all three video signals check correctly all the way to the CRT (or replacing the video drive circuit does not restore the image), you should suspect a major fault in the CRT itself; there is little else that can fail. If you have a CRT tester/rejuvenator available, you should test the CRT thoroughly for shorted grids or a weak cathode. If the problem cannot be rectified through rejuvenation (or you do not have access to a CRT tester, try replacing the CRT. Keep in mind, however, that a CRT is usually the most expensive part of the monochrome monitor. If each step up to now has not restored your image, you should weigh the economics of replacing the CRT versus scrapping it in favor of a new or rebuilt unit.

Symptom 5. A single horizontal line appears in the middle of the display The horizontal sweep is working properly, but there is no vertical deflection. A fault has almost certainly developed in the vertical drive circuit (refer to Fig. 38-9). Use your oscilloscope to check the sawtooth wave being generated by the vertical oscillator/amplifier IC (pin 6 of IC402). If the sawtooth wave is missing, the fault is almost certainly in the IC. For the circuit of Fig. 38-9, try replacing IC402. If the sawtooth wave is available on IC402 pin 6, you should suspect a defect in the horizontal deflection yoke itself, or one of its related components. If you are not able to check signals to the component level, simply replace the monitor's main PC board.

Symptom 6. Only the upper or lower half of an image appears In most cases, there is a problem in the vertical amplifier. For the example circuit of Fig. 38-9, the trouble is likely located in the vertical oscillator/amplifier (IC402). Use your oscilloscope to check the sawtooth waveform leaving IC402 pin 6. If the sawtooth is distorted, replace IC402. If the sawtooth signal reads properly, check for other faulty components in the vertical deflection yoke circuit. If you do not have the tools or inclination to check and replace devices at the component level, replace the monitor's main PC board. When the image is restored, be sure to check vertical linearity as described in Chapter 68.

Symptom 7. A single vertical line appears along the middle of the display The vertical sweep is working properly, but there is no horizontal deflection. However, in order to even see the display at normal brightness, there must be high voltage present in the monitor; the horizontal drive circuit must be working (refer to Fig. 38-9). The fault probably lies in the horizontal deflection yoke. Check the yoke and all wiring connected to it. It might be necessary to replace the horizontal deflection yoke, or the entire yoke assembly.

If horizontal deflection is lost as well as substantial screen brightness, there might be a marginal fault in the horizontal drive circuit. If there is a problem with the horizontal oscillator pulses, the switching characteristics of the horizontal amplifier will change. In turn, this affects high-voltage development and horizontal deflection. Use your oscilloscope to check the square wave generated by the horizontal oscillator IC301 pin 3 as shown in Fig. 38-9. You should see a square wave. If the square wave is distorted, replace the oscillator IC (IC301). If the horizontal pulse is correct, check the horizontal switching transistors (Q301 and Q302). Replace any transistor that appears defective. If the collector signal at the HOT is low or distorted, there might be a short circuit in the flyback transformer primary winding. Try replacing the FBT. If you do not have the tools or inclination to check components to the component level (or the problem persists), replace the monitor's main PC board. When the repair is complete, check the horizontal linearity and size as described in Chapter 68.

Symptom 8. There is no image and no raster When the monitor is properly connected to a PC, a series of text information should appear as the PC initializes. We can use this as our baseline image. Isolate the monitor by trying a known-good monitor on your host PC. If the known-good monitor works, you prove that the PC and video adapter are working properly. Reconnect the suspect monitor to the PC and turn up the brightness (and contrast if necessary). Start by checking for the presence of horizontal and vertical synchronization pulses. If pulses are absent, no raster will be generated. If sync pulses are present, there is likely a problem somewhere in the horizontal drive or high-voltage circuits.

Always suspect a power supply problem, so check every output from the supply (especially the 20-Vdc and 135-Vdc outputs as shown in Fig. 38-9). A low or absent supply voltage will disable the horizontal deflection and high-voltage circuits. If one or more supply outputs are low or absent, you can troubleshoot the power supply circuit, or replace the power supply outright (when the power circuit is combined on the monitor's main PC board, the entire main PC board would have to be replaced).

If the supply outputs read correctly, suspect your horizontal drive circuit. Use your oscilloscope to check the horizontal oscillator output at the base of Q301 as shown in Fig. 38-9. You should see a square wave. If the square wave is low, distorted, or absent, replace the horizontal oscillator IC (IC301). If a regular pulse is present, the horizontal oscillator is working. Because Q301 is intended to act as a switch, you also should find a pulse at the collector of Q301. If the pulse output is severely distorted or absent, Q301 is probably damaged (remove Q301 and test it). If Q301 reads as faulty, it should be replaced. If Q301 reads good, check the horizontal coupling transformer (T303) for shorted or open windings. Try replacing T303 (there is little else that can go wrong in this part of the circuit).

Check the HOT (Q302) next by removing it from the circuit and testing it. If Q302 reads faulty, it should be replaced with an exact replacement part. If Q302 reads good, the fault probably lies in the flyback transformer. Try replacing the FBT. If you do not have the tools or inclination to perform these component-level checks, simply replace the monitor's main PC board outright.

In the event that these steps fail to restore the image, the CRT has probably failed. If you have access to a CRT tester/rejuvenator as discussed in Chapter 3, you can test the CRT. When the CRT measures as bad (and cannot be restored through rejuvenation), it should be replaced. If you do not have a CRT test instrument, you can simply replace the CRT. Keep in mind, however, that a CRT is usually the most expensive part of a color monitor. If each step up to now has not restored your image, you should weigh the economics of replacing the CRT versus scrapping it in favor of a new or rebuilt unit. If you choose to replace the CRT, you should perform a full set of alignments as described in Chapter 5.

Symptom 9. The image is too compressed or too expanded. A whitish haze might appear along the bottom of the image Start by checking your vertical size control to be sure that it was not adjusted accidentally. Because vertical size is a function of the vertical sawtooth oscillator, you should suspect the vertical oscillator circuit. A sawtooth signal that is too large will result in an over-expanded image, and a signal that is too small will appear to compress the image. Use your oscilloscope to check the vertical sawtooth signal. For the vertical drive circuit of Fig. 38-9, you should find a sawtooth signal on IC402 pin 6. If the signal is incorrect, try replacing IC402. You also might wish to check the PC board for any cracks or faulty soldering connections around the vertical oscillator circuit. If the problem persists, or you do not have the tools or inclination to perform component-level troubleshooting, simply replace the monitor's main PC board outright.

Symptom 10. The displayed characters appear to be distorted The term *distortion* can be interpreted in many different ways. For our purposes, we will simply say that the image (usually text) is difficult to read. Before even opening your toolbox, check the monitor's location. The presence of stray magnetic fields in close proximity to the monitor can cause bizarre forms of distortion. Try moving the monitor to another location. Remove any electromagnetic or magnetic objects (such as motors or refrigerator magnets) from the area. If the problem persists, it is likely that the monitor is at fault.

If only certain areas of the display appear affected (or affected worse than other areas), the trouble is probably due to poor linearity (either horizontal, vertical, or both). If raster speed varies across the display, the pixels in some areas of the image might appear too close together, and the pixels in other areas of the image might appear too far apart. You can check and correct horizontal and vertical linearity using a test pattern such as the one described in Chapter 68. If alignment fails to correct poor linearity, your best course is often simply to replace the monitor's main PC board. If the image is difficult to read because it is out of focus, you should check the focus alignment. If you cannot achieve a sharp focus using controls either on the front panel of the monitor or on the flyback transformer assembly, there is probably a fault in the flyback transformer. Try replacing the FBT. If the problem persists, your best course is often simply to replace the monitor's main PC board.

Symptom 11. The display appears wavy There are visible waves appearing along the edges of the display as the image sways back and forth. This is almost always the result of a power supply problem—one or more outputs is failing. Use your multimeter and check each supply output. If you find a low or absent output, you can proceed to troubleshoot the supply, or you can simply replace the supply outright. If the power supply is integrated onto the main PC board, you will have to replace the entire main PC board.

Symptom 12. The display is too bright or too dim Before opening the monitor, be sure to check the brightness and contrast controls. If the controls had been accidentally adjusted, set contrast to maximum, and adjust the brightness level until a clear, crisp display is produced. When front panel controls fail to provide the proper display (but focus seems steady), suspect a fault in the monitor's power supply. Refer to the example schematic of Fig. 38-9. If the 135-Vdc supply is too low or too high, brightness levels controlling the CRT screen grid will shift. If you find one or more incorrect outputs from the power supply, you can troubleshoot the supply or replace the supply outright. For those monitors that incorporate the power supply on the main PC board, the entire main PC board will have to be replaced.

Symptom 13. You see visible raster scan lines in the display The very first thing you should do is check the front panel brightness and contrast controls. If contrast is set too low and/or brightness is set too high, raster will be visible on top of the image. This will tend to make the image appear a bit fuzzy. If the front panel controls cannot eliminate visible raster from the image, chances are that you have a problem with the power supply. Use your multimeter and check each output from the supply. If one or more outputs appear too high (or too low), you can troubleshoot the supply or replace the supply outright. If the supply is integrated with the monitor's main PC board, the entire PC board will have to be replaced.

If the power supply is intact, you should suspect a problem with the raster blanking circuits. During horizontal and vertical retrace periods, video signals are cut off. If visible raster lines appear in your image, check the blanking signals. If you are unable to check the blanking signals, try replacing the video drive PC board. If a new video drive board fails to correct the problem, replace the main PC board.

39
CHAPTER

Motherboards

The *motherboard* is the heart of any personal computer (Fig. 39-1). It is the motherboard that handles system resources (such as IRQ lines, DMA channels, and I/O locations) as well as core components such as the CPU, math coprocessor, and all system memory (including DRAM, BIOS ROM, and CMOS RAM). Indeed, most of a PC's capabilities are defined by motherboard components. This chapter is intended to provide a guided tour of contemporary motherboards, and show you how to translate error information into motherboard repairs.

39-1 A Hauppauge i386DX motherboard.

Active, passive, and modular

Before going any further, you should understand the difference between a motherboard and a backplane. For the purposes of this book, a *motherboard* is a printed circuit board containing most of the processing components required by the computer. PC purists often refer to a motherboard as an *active backplane*. The term *active* is used because there are ICs running on the board. The advantage of a motherboard is its simplicity—the motherboard virtually is the PC. Unfortunately, the motherboard has disadvantages. Namely, it is difficult to upgrade. Aside from plugging in an OverDrive CPU or adding RAM, the only real way to upgrade a motherboard is to replace it outright with a newer one. For example, the only way to add PCI bus slots to an all-ISA motherboard is to replace the motherboard with one containing PCI slots.

On the other hand, a *backplane* (also referred to as a *passive backplane*) is little more than a board containing interconnecting slots—there are no ICs on the backplane (except perhaps some power supply regulating circuitry). The CPU, DRAM, BIOS ROM, and other central processing components are fabricated onto a board that simply plugs into one of the backplane slots. Other boards (video board, drive controller, sound board, and so on) just plug into adjacent slots. The PS/2 was one of the first PCs to use a backplane design. Backplane systems are easy to troubleshoot, unlike traditional motherboards that require the entire system to be disassembled, a processor board can be removed and replaced as easily as any other board. It also is a simple matter to upgrade the PC by installing a new processor board. The great limitation to backplanes is the bus. Where traditional motherboards can optimize a system with different buses, the backplane is limited to a single bus style (usually ISA or MCA). High-performance bus architectures like VL or PCI are not available.

In an effort to provide a motherboard that is more upgradeable and serviceable, manufacturers are beginning to develop modular motherboards. The modular motherboard places the CPU, math coprocessor, and key support ICs on a replaceable card that plugs into a motherboard that holds BIOS ROM, CMOS RAM, DRAM, other system controllers, and bus interfaces. The modular approach allows a motherboard to be upgraded far more than a traditional motherboard without having to replace it outright. The replacement processing card is then much cheaper than a new motherboard.

Contrary to popular belief, expansion bus connectors are not needed to make a motherboard. You can see this in any laptop or notebook computer motherboard (Fig. 39-2). The devices that traditionally demanded expansion slots (video and drive controllers) are easily fabricated directly onto the motherboard. Even the motherboards used in contemporary desktop and tower PCs now integrate video and drive controller circuits. If upgrades are needed in the future, the motherboard-based circuits can be disabled with jumpers, and replacement subsystems are plugged into expansion slots.

Understanding the motherboard

Before you can troubleshoot a motherboard effectively, it is important that you know your way around and be able to identify at least most of the available components. Although each motherboard is designed differently, this is not nearly as difficult as it might sound. This part of the chapter familiarizes you with the functions of a typical motherboard such as the AMI motherboard shown in Fig. 39-3. Table 39-1 is intended to help you match IC numbers and functions; this can aid in your troubleshooting.

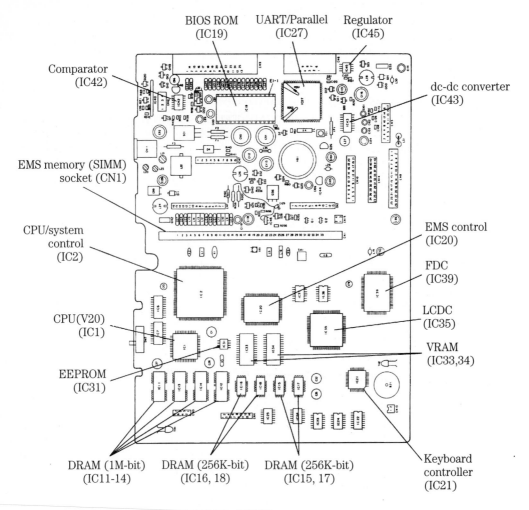

39-2 Motherboard assembly for the Tandy 1500HD. Tandy Corporation

- *CPU (central processing unit)* A programmable logic device that performs all of the instruction, logic, and mathematical processing in the PC. This is the single most important IC in the computer. A CPU fault is usually detected by the BIOS POST, but a complete CPU failure can disable the entire PC.
- *MCP (the math coprocessor)* A programmable logic device (closely related to the CPU) that is tailored to handling floating-point math operations. Math-intensive application software that is written to take advantage of the MCP can realize substantial improvements in performance.
- *BIOS (basic input/output system)* The code used to initialize the PC and perform low-level motherboard operations. Traditionally, BIOS has been stored on DIP ICs that could be easily removed and replaced as needed. Such ICs started with a 27 prefix, then two or three digits indicating the number of kilobits (divide by eight for kilobytes). For example, the 2764 is a

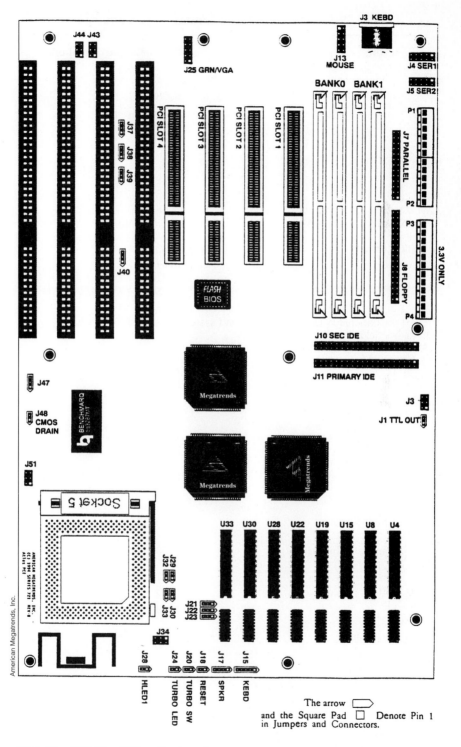

39-3 The AMI Atlas PCI motherboard.

Table 39-1 Motherboard IC functions vs. part numbers

Function	Typical motherboard part numbers
CPU	8086
	8088
	80286
	80386
	80486
	Pentium
MCP	8087
	80287
	80387*
	80487*

(DX versions of the i386 and i486 and all Pentium have internal MCPs)

BIOS ROM**	2732
	2764
	27218
	27256
	27512

**Conventional ICs shown. Many newer systems use Flash BIOS which allows field-reprogrammability.

CMOS/RTC	MC146818
	Dallas 1287
	Dallas 1387
Clock Generator	82284
Programmable Interval Timer (PIT)	8253 (XT)
	8254 (AT)
Direct Memory Access Controller (DMAC)	8237
DMA Page Registers	74LS612
Programmable Interrupt Controller (PIC)	8259
Keyboard Controller (KBC)	8042
	8742
Bus Controller	82288
Universal Asynchronous Receiver/Transmitter (UART)	8250
	8250A
	8250B
	16450
	16550
	16550B

ROM providing 8KB of storage. If Flash BIOS is used (as in Fig. 39-3) you will find the BIOS ROM in a PLCC holder.

- *CMOS/RTC* This is a dual-function IC that maintains system setup variables in 64 bytes of CMOS RAM. It also supplies a *real-time clock* that keeps track of the date, day, and time. Traditional PCs used the Motorola MC146818, but many other variations have come into use. You can often locate the CMOS/RTC IC by its large, rectangular shape. It also will be located near the system backup battery.
- *Clocks* Proper synchronization and signaling of the motherboard requires the use of precision oscillating ICs. There are typically two clock ICs—one for the 14.318-MHz OSC signal on the ISA bus, and one driving the CPU clock (and other processing ICs). The CPU clock IC accepts the *Power Good* signal from the power supply, and generates the system-wide reset signal. The OSC clock IC also produces a 1.19-MHz signal for a PIT.
- *PIT (programmable interval timer)* The interval timer provides three channels for the AT. Channel 0 is set to produce an interrupt every 54.94 ms (the RTC time base). Channel 1 is programmed to produce an interrupt every 15.12 µs to signal the start of a memory refresh cycle that must be performed at least once every few milliseconds. Channel 2 is a noncritical timer that serves to support speaker signals.
- *DMAC (direct-memory access controllers)* DMA is critical to the operation of an XT or AT system. Normally, the CPU must handle each byte of data transferred in the system. It is not a bad system, but it's slow when large volumes of data must be transferred. DMA allows data transfer without the intervention of the CPU. A single DMA controller provides four channels (an AT uses two DMACs to provide eight channels). Table 39-2 shows AT DMA assignments.

Table 39-2. At DMA assignments

DMA	Function	Bus slot required
DMAC #1		
0	unused	Yes (16 bit)
1	unused	Yes (8 bit)
2	Floppy Disk Controller Board	Yes (8 bit)
3	unused	Yes (8 bit)
DMAC#2		
4	First DMA Controller IC	No (motherboard)
5	unused	Yes (16 bit)
6	unused	Yes (16 bit)
7	unused	Yes (16 bit)

- *DMA page registers* These are relatively simple buffers that point to the 64K area (page) where DMA transfers will take place from (or to). Early PCs used one page register, but i386 and later systems often use two. Remember that it is common for newer systems to indicate a fault in the second page register because the page registers are usually integrated into chipsets.

- *PIC (the programmable interrupt controller)* The PIC recognizes and prioritizes hardware interrupts, then passes the interrupt signal to the CPU along with a vector that points to the location of the interrupt handler routine. The XT used one PIC that supplied eight channels, but ATs use two PICs for sixteen channels (IRQ 0-15). Table 39-3 shows AT IRQ assignments.

Table 39-3. AT interrupt assignments

IRQ	Function	Bus slot required
PIC #1		
0	System Timer IC	No (motherboard)
1	Keyboard Controller IC	No (motherboard)
2	Second IRQ Controller IC	No (motherboard)
3	Serial Port 2 (COM2)	Yes (8 bit)
4	Serial Port 1 (COM1)	Yes (8 bit)
5	Parallel Port 2 (LPT2)	Yes (8 bit)
6	Floppy Disk Controller Board	Yes (8 bit)
7	Parallel Port 1 (LPT1)	Yes (8 bit)
PIC #2		
8	Real-Time Clock (RTC)	No (motherboard)
9	unused (redirected to IRQ 2)	Yes (8 bit)
10	unused	Yes (16 bit)
11	unused	Yes (16 bit)
12	Motherboard Mouse Port	Yes (16 bit)
13	Math Co-processor	No (motherboard)
14	Hard Disk Controller Board	Yes (16 bit)
15	unused	Yes (16 bit)

- *KBC (the keyboard controller)* The KBC is a very specialized single-chip microcontroller (including its own small amount of BIOS) designed as an interface between the system and the AT serial keyboard. On system initialization, the POST will cause a KBC self-test. If the self-test passes, the system can proceed to test the keyboard. Another vital part of the keyboard controller is that it handles the A20 Gate. The A20 Gate handles access to extended/expanded memory (protected-mode addressing). If the KBC fails, the system will be unable to work in the protected mode.
- *Gate A20* This is the simple gate that controls address line A20, and thus controls protected-mode operation by accessing memory over 1Mb. The A20 Gate is operated from the KBC.
- *Bus controller* This device accepts control and timing signals from the system, and generates the I/O and memory read and write signals needed to transfer data among system components on the motherboard, as well as the

expansion bus. The bus controller also manages the translation of 16-bit words into 8-bit words for single-byte data transfers, and back again.

- *UART (universal asynchronous receiver/transmitter)* These are the key components in serial communication ports. They translate parallel data into framed serial data for transmission, and reverses the process to convert framed serial data back into parallel data during reception. Current systems use 16550A UARTS. When a serial port error is reported, the UART has probably failed. UARTs incorporated on the motherboard are typically provided with jumpers that will set the port I/O address, IRQ line, and allow you to disable the UART in favor of expansion board communication devices.
- *DRAM* General storage and main system memory is provided by *dynamic RAM*. Modern DRAM ICs can hold a great deal of data, but it must be refreshed every few milliseconds, otherwise, the data will be lost. A key purpose if the DMAC and PIC is to manage refresh. Some DRAM is fabricated on the motherboard, but much more DRAM can be added in the form of SIMMs.
- *Cache* Cache has become an important element of PC performance improvement. By loading data and instructions into fast static RAM in advance of the CPU's need, memory wait states can be eliminated. Many systems are equipped with 128K to 256K of external cache, but some systems can have up to 512K of cache. To boost performance even further, newer CPUs are designed with a small amount of internal cache. If external cache fails, you might be able to circumvent the error by disabling the cache through the CMOS setup. If internal cache fails, the CPU would have to be replaced.

The role of chipsets

A word about PC chipsets. In the drive to make motherboards smaller and less expensive, many of the individual ICs referred to have been combined into chipsets— a set of related ASICs that supply the bulk of motherboard functions. When inspecting a motherboard, you will need to know which IC in the chipset performs what functions (refer to Chapter 27 for a discussion of chipsets). It is the use of chipsets that has allowed advanced features to be incorporated on the motherboard.

- *Video controller* A video controller IC allows a VGA port to be built into the motherboard (you can find the 15-pin video connector at the rear of the motherboard). This eliminates the need for a separate video board. If video needs to be upgraded, however, the video controller can often be disabled through a jumper that would then allow an expansion video board (usually SVGA) to be installed.
- *IDE port(s)* The advantage of an IDE drive is that most of the drive's intelligence is located directly on the drive itself rather than on the drive controller board as in ST-506 and ESDI drives. As a result, the IDE drive typically only needs a bus interface IC to connect the drive and the PC. In many cases, the IDE interface IC can be fabricated right on the

motherboard. If you look at Fig. 39-3, you will see two IDE connectors (one for a primary drive, and one for a secondary drive). If you install an expansion board with an IDE interface, you will need to disable the interface, or disable the IDE ports on the motherboard.

- *Floppy port* Although floppy disk drives have the same interface requirements that they have had for a decade, IC fabrication techniques allow an entire floppy controller to be integrated into a single IC and included on the motherboard. You can see the floppy drive connector in Fig. 39-3. Because the ordinary floppy signal cable can connect two drives, the one port will support up to two floppy drives.

Troubleshooting a motherboard

Because motherboards contain the majority of system processing components, it is likely that you will encounter a faulty motherboard sooner or later. The BIOS POST is written to test each sub-section of the motherboard each time the PC is powered up, so most problems are detected well before you ever see the DOS prompt. Errors are reported in a myriad of ways. Beep codes (Chapter 15) provide audible indications of fatal errors that occur before the video system is initialized. I/O POST codes (Chapter 28) shows you how to use a POST board to extract and interpret hexadecimal error codes. IBM POST diagnostic codes (Chapter 44) offer a comprehensive index of visual codes and their meanings. Regardless of the indication, this book is designed to ensure that you have plenty of diagnostic reference material. For subtle problems that might escape the POST, software diagnostics (Chapter 6) can often isolate the fault.

Repair versus replace

This is the perennial troubleshooting dilemma. The problem with motherboard repair is not so much the availability of replacement parts (although that can be a challenge) as it is the use of surface-mount soldering (SMT). You see, a surface-mounted IC cannot be desoldered with conventional tools. To successfully desolder a surface-mounted IC, you need to heat each of the IC's pins (often in excess of 100) simultaneously, then lift the IC off the board. It is then a simple matter to clean up any residual solder. Unfortunately, specialized surface-mount soldering equipment is required to do this. The equipment is readily available commercially, so it is easy to buy—but you can invest $1000 to $2000 to equip your work bench properly.

As you can imagine, the repair versus replace decision is an economic one. It makes little sense for the part-time PC enthusiast to make such a substantial investment to exchange a defective IC (which are usually under $30). It is generally better to replace the motherboard outright, which is only a fraction of the cost of such SMT equipment. On the other hand, professionals who intend to pursue PC repair as a living are well served with surface-mount equipment. The customer's cost for labor, the part(s), and markup is typically much less than purchasing a new motherboard (especially the high-end boards such as i486/66 and Pentium motherboards).

Begin with the basics

Because motherboard troubleshooting does represent a significant expense, you should be sure to start any motherboard repair by inspecting the following points in the PC. *Remember to turn all power off before performing these inspections.*

- *Check all connectors* Loose connectors can happen easily when the PC is serviced or upgraded, and you accidentally forget to replace every cable. Start with the power connector, and inspect each cable and connector attached to the motherboard. Frayed cables should be replaced. Loose or detached cables should be reattached.
- *Check all socket-mounted ICs* Many ICs in the computer (especially the CPU) get hot during normal operation. It is not unheard of for the repetitive expansion and contraction encountered with everyday use to eventually "rock" an IC out of its socket. The CPU, math coprocessor, BIOS ROM, and often the CMOS/RTC module are socket mounted, so check them carefully.
- *Check power levels* Low or erratic ac power levels can cause problems in the PC. Use a multimeter and check ac at the wall outlet. Be very careful whenever dealing with ac. Take all precautions to protect yourself from injury. If the ac is low or is heavily loaded by motors, coffee pots, or other highly inductive loads, try the PC in another outlet running from a different circuit. If ac checks properly, use your multimeter (or a measurement tool such as PC Power Check from Data Depot) to check the power supply outputs. If one or more outputs is low or absent, you should repair or replace the supply (refer to Chapter 46).
- *Check the motherboard for foreign objects* A screw, paper clip, or free strand of wire can cause a short circuit that might disable the motherboard.
- *Check that all motherboard DIP switches and jumpers are correct* For example, if the motherboard provides a video port, and you have a video board plugged into the expansion bus, the motherboard video circuit will have to be disabled through a switch or jumper—otherwise, a conflict can result that might interfere with motherboard operation. You will need the user manual for the PC in order to identify and check each jumper or switch.
- *Check for intermittent connections and accidental grounding* Inspect each of the motherboard's mounting screws, and see that they are not touching nearby printed traces. Also check the space under the motherboard and see that there is nothing that might be grounding the motherboard and chassis. As an experiment, you might try loosening the motherboard mounting screws. If the fault goes away, the motherboard might be suffering from an intermittent connection. When all screws are tight, the board is bent just enough to let the intermittent connection appear. Unfortunately, intermittent connections are almost impossible to find.

Symptoms

Symptom 1. A motherboard failure is reported, but goes away when the PC's outer cover is removed There is likely an intermittent connection on the motherboard. When the housing is secured, the PC chassis warps just slightly; this might be enough to precipitate an intermittent contact. When the housing is removed, the chassis relaxes and hides the intermittent connection. Replace the outer cover and gently retighten each screw with the system running. Chances are that you will find one screw that triggers the problem. You can leave that screw out, but it is advisable to replace the motherboard as a long-term fix.

Symptom 2. The POST or your software diagnostic reports a CPU fault This error is a fatal error, and chances are that system initialization has halted. CPU problems are generally reported when one or more CPU registers do not respond as expected, or has trouble switching to the protected mode. In either case, the CPU is probably at fault. Fortunately, the CPU is socket mounted, and should be very straightforward to replace. Be sure to remove all power to the PC, and make careful use of static controls when replacing a CPU. Mark the questionable CPU with indelible ink *before* replacing it.

ZIF (zero-insertion force) sockets are easiest, because the IC will be released simply by lifting the metal lever at the socket's side. Slide out the original CPU and insert a new one. Secure the metal lever, and try the PC again. However, most CPUs are mounted in *PGA* (pin grid array) sockets, and a specialized PGA removal tool is strongly suggested for proper removal. You also should be able to use a small, regular screwdriver to gently pry up each of the four sides of the CPU, but be very careful to avoid cracking the IC, the socket, or the motherboard—never use excessive force. When the IC is free, install the new CPU with close attention to pin alignment, then gently press the new CPU into place.

A word about heatsinks. Most i486 and later CPUs are equipped with a metal heatsink assembly. It is vital to the proper operation of your system that the heatsink be reinstalled correctly—otherwise, the new CPU will eventually overheat and lock up or fail. Be sure to use good-quality thermal compound to ensure proper heat transfer to the heatsink (remember that a sound mechanical connection does not guarantee a good thermal connection).

Symptom 3. The POST or your software diagnostic reports a problem with the math coprocessor MCP problems are generally reported when one or more MPC registers do not respond as expected. Fortunately, MCP faults are not always fatal. It is often possible to remove the MCP and disable the MCP availability through system SETUP. Of course, programs that depend on the MCP will no longer run, but at least the system can be used until a new one is installed. The MCP is socket mounted, and should be very straightforward to replace. Be sure to remove all power to the PC, and make careful use of static controls when replacing an MPC. Mark the questionable MPC with indelible ink *before* replacing it. MCPs that are integrated into the CPU (i386DX, i486DX, and Pentiums) are a bit more expensive, but are no more difficult to exchange. Refer to Symptom 2 for notes on sockets and heatsinks.

Symptom 4. The POST or your software diagnostic reports a BIOS ROM checksum error The integrity of your system BIOS ROM is verified after the CPU is tested. This is necessary to ensure that there are no unwanted instructions or data that might easily crash the system during POST or normal operation. A checksum is performed on the ROM contents, and that value is compared with the value stored in the ROM itself. If the two values are equal, the ROM is considered good and initialization continues—otherwise, the BIOS is considered defective and should be replaced. Chapter 15 provides an index of major BIOS manufacturers.

Traditionally, BIOS ROM is implemented as one or two ICs that are plugged into DIP sockets. They can be removed easily with the blade of a regular screwdriver, as long as you pry the IC up slowly and gently (be sure to pry the IC evenly from both ends). When installing new DIP ICs, you might have to straighten their pins against the surface of a table, or use a DIP pin straightening tool. Ultimately, the IC pins will fit nicely into each receptacle in the DIP socket. You can then ease the IC evenly down into the socket. Alignment is critical to ensure that all pins are inserted. If not, one or more pins might be bent under the IC and ruin the new ROM. Also, be sure to insert the new IC(s) in the proper orientation. If they are accidentally installed backward, they might be damaged.

Newer BIOS ICs use flash EEPROM technology that allows the device to be erased and reprogrammed in the field without having to replace the entire BIOS ROM IC. When a flash BIOS fails its checksum test, it also has probably failed. Because flash BIOS devices are often fabricated as PLCC ICs, it is a bit easier to replace them, but you will need a PLCC removal tool to take the original IC out of its socket—there simply is not enough room for a screwdriver.

Symptom 5. The POST or software diagnostic reports a timer (PIT) failure, an RTC update problem, or a refresh failure The PIT is often an 8254 or compatible device. Ultimately, one or more of the its three channels might have failed, and the PIT should be replaced. It is important to realize that many modern motherboards incorporate the PIT functions into a system controller or other chipset IC (refer to Chapter 27 for a listing of chipsets and functions). Because the PIT is typically surface mounted, you can attempt to replace the device, or replace the motherboard entirely.

Symptom 6. The POST or software diagnostic reports an interrupt controller (PIC) failure The PIC is often an 8259 or compatible device, and there are two PICs on the typical AT motherboard (PIC#1 handles IRQ0 through IRQ7, and PIC#2 handles IRQ8 through IRQ15). Of the two, PIC#1 is more important because the lower interrupts have a higher priority, and the lowest channels handle critical low-level functions such as the system timer and keyboard interface. Generally, a diagnostic will reveal which of the two PICs have failed. Make sure that there are no interrupt conflicts between two or more system devices. You can then replace the defective PIC. In many current systems, both PICs are integrated into a system controller or chipset IC. You can replace the defective IC if you have the appropriate surface-mount equipment available, or replace the motherboard entirely.

Symptom 7. The POST or software diagnostic reports a DMA controller (DMAC) failure The DMAC is often an 8237 or compatible device, and there are two DMACs on the typical AT motherboard (DMAC#1 handles channel 0 through channel 3, and DMAC#2 handles channel 4 through channel 7). Of the two, DMAC#1 is more important because channel 2 runs the floppy disk controller. Generally, a diagnostic will reveal which of the two DMACs have failed. Make sure that there are no DMA conflicts between two or more system devices. You can then replace the defective DMAC. In many current systems, both DMACs are integrated into a system controller or chipset IC. You can replace the defective IC if you have the appropriate surface-mount equipment available, or replace the motherboard entirely.

Symptom 8. The POST or software diagnostic reports a KBC fault The keyboard controller is often either an 8042 or an 8742. Because the KBC is a micro-controller in its own right, diagnostics can usually detect a KBC fault with great accuracy. The KBC might either be a socket-mounted PLCC device, or (in rare cases) a surface-mounted IC. Remember remove all power and mark the old KBC before you remove it from the PC. You will probably need a PLCC removal tool to take out the old KBC.

Symptom 9. A keyboard error is reported, but a new keyboard has no effect The keyboard fuse on the motherboard might have failed. Many motherboard designs incorporate a small fuse (called a *pico-fuse*) in the +5-Vdc line that drives the keyboard. If this fuse fails, the keyboard will be dead. Use your multimeter and measure the +5-Vdc line at the keyboard connector. If this reads 0 Vdc, locate the keyboard fuse on the motherboard and replace it (you might have to trace the line back to the fuse that looks almost exactly like a resistor).

Symptom 10. The POST or shareware diagnostic reports a CMOS or RTC fault With either error, it is the same device that is usually at fault. The CMOS RAM and RTC are generally fabricated onto the same device. RTC problems indicate that the real-time clock portion of the IC has failed, or is not being updated. CMOS RAM failure can be due to a dead backup battery, or a failure of the IC itself. When dealing with a CMOS or SETUP problem, try the following protocol. First, try a new backup battery and reload the CMOS SETUP variables. If a new battery does not resolve the problem, the CMOS/RTC IC should be replaced. Often, the CMOS/RTC IC is surface-mounted, and will have to be replaced (or the motherboard will have to be replaced). However, there is a growing trend toward making the IC socket-mounted and including the battery into a single replaceable module (such as the Dallas Semiconductor devices). Modules are typically replaceable DIP devices.

Symptom 11. The POST or software diagnostic reports a fault in the first 64K of RAM The first RAM page is important because it holds the BIOS data area and interrupt vectors; the system will not work without it. When a RAM error is indicated, your only real recourse is to replace the motherboard RAM. If the diagnostic indicates which bit has failed, and you can correlate the bit to a specific IC, you can replace the defective IC (typically surface-mounted). Otherwise, you will need to locate and replace all of the motherboard RAM, or replace the motherboard entirely.

Symptom 12. The math coprocessor does not work properly when installed on a motherboard when external caching is enabled Some non-Intel math coprocessors work in areas that must be noncached. For example, a Cyrix EMC87 MCP with an AMI Mark IV i386 motherboard has been known to cause problems. When MCP problems arise (especially during upgrades), try disabling the external cache through CMOS SETUP. As another alternative, try a different math coprocessor.

40
CHAPTER

Parallel (Centronics) port troubleshooting

Even after more than a decade of intense computer development, the *parallel port* (also called the *printer port*) remains the fastest and most reliable printer connection technique in the computer industry. By sending an entire byte of data from computer to printer simultaneously, and managing the flow of data with discrete handshaking signals, the circuitry required to bundle and decode data and control signals (such as that needed by serial ports) is virtually eliminated. The longevity of parallel ports has been due largely to the their simplicity and good overall performance. However, today's parallel ports are not invulnerable to failure. Cable problems, static discharge damage, and spontaneous IC faults can easily disable printer communication. Additional parallel port problems can arise from new, complex software and high-performance hardware devices such as parallel-to-SCSI adapters, parallel port tape drives, and parallel port audio modules—each seeking to take advantage of a parallel port as a system-level bus. This chapter explains the pinout and operation of conventional parallel ports, and present a series of troubleshooting procedures intended to help you isolate and correct port problems.

Understanding the parallel port

The parallel port interface is one of the simplest and most straightforward circuits that you will encounter in a PC. Figure 40-1 illustrates a typical bidirectional port. A parallel port is composed of three separate registers; the data register, the status register, and the control register. Address bits A0 to A9 are decoded to determine which of the three registers are active. The use of –I/OR (I/O Read) and –I/OW (I/O Write) lines determine whether signals on the data bus (D0 to D7) are being read from or written to the respective register. When the port is ready to accept another character, handshaking line conditions will trigger an interrupt to request a new character.

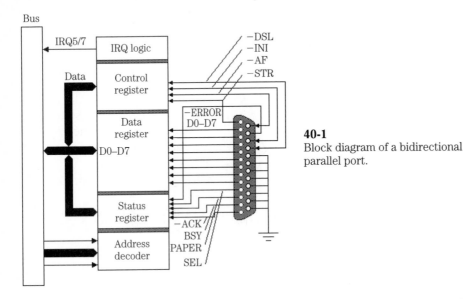

40-1
Block diagram of a bidirectional parallel port.

The heart of a parallel port is the *data register*. In older PCs, the data register could only be written to (which renders the port unidirectional). But virtually all PCs since the release of i386 systems provide data registers that can be read and written (which makes the port bidirectional). To access a printer, the system CPU simply loads the port data register with the value to be passed. The bidirectional control register manages the behavior of the port, and affects the conditions under which new characters are requested from the CPU. For example, the control register is typically set up to generate an interrupt whenever the printer is ready to accept another character (IRQ7 for LPT1, and IRQ5 for LPT2). Finally, the *status register* is read to determine the printer's status (extracted from the logic conditions of several printer handshaking lines). All that remains is the port connector, which is a female 25-pin subminiature D-type connector.

Addresses and interrupts

As you saw, the conventional parallel port in a PC is implemented through a series of three registers; one register simply buffers the eight data bits while the other two registers handle the port's handshaking lines. Although older BIOS versions only supported two or three parallel ports, today's PCs use BIOS written to support up to four complete parallel ports (designated LPT1, LPT2, LPT3, and LPT4). The base addresses allocated for each port are 0378h (LPT1), 0278h (LPT2), 03BCh (LPT3), and 02BCh (LPT4). The base address of each port corresponds to the data register. The status register of a respective port is accessed from the base address with an offset of 01h (0379h, 0279h, 03BDh, and 02BDh), and the control register is accessed with an offset of 02h (037Ah, 027Ah, 03BEh, and 02BEh).

During initialization, ports are checked in the following order; 03BCh, 0378h, 0278h, and 02BCh, and LPT designations are assigned depending on what ports are found , so keep in mind that LPT addresses might be exchanged depending on your particular system. The specific I/O addresses for each port are kept in the BIOS data area of RAM starting at 0408h (see Table 35-2). As you might expect, only one set of LPT port can be assigned to a base address. If more than one parallel port is assigned to the same address, system problems will almost certainly occur.

The use of interrupts gets a bit complicated. There are basically two modes of requesting new characters for the printer; polling and interrupt-driven. Polling is the most popular method where BIOS polls (or checks) the respective port's status register to see if it is ready to accept another character; no interrupts are generated. An interrupt-driven interface is much more efficient, but can bog down other important operations during printing.

For technicians who work on older machines, keep in mind that address 03BCh was originally reserved for a parallel port located on the IBM *MDA* (monochrome display adapter). If you are servicing an older system with no video support on the motherboard, the address 03BCh might be reserved in the event you (for some reason) want to install an IBM MDA card. For newer systems with video support located on the motherboard, address 03BCh might be the first parallel port address.

Always begin your service examination by checking the number of parallel ports in your system. Parallel ports are so simple and easy to add to various expansion cards, you can exceed the limit of four parallel ports without even knowing it. If more than four ports are active, the conflicts that result can crash the system so you will have to remove or disable the extra ports.

Parallel port signals

IBM and compatible PCs implement a parallel port as a 25-pin subminiature D-type female connector similar to the one shown in Fig. 40-2. The parallel connection at the printer uses a 36-pin Centronics-type connector (Amphenol type 57-30360). The exact reasoning for this rather specialized connector is not clear because 11 pins of the Centronics connector will remain unused. There are three types of signals to be concerned with in parallel connections; data lines, control (or *handshaking*) lines, and ground lines. Table 40-1 identifies the name and description of each pin.

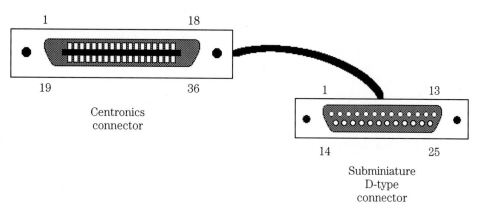

40-2 A typical parallel cable assembly.

The following section describes each signal. Keep in mind that the pin numbers shown refer to the 25-pin interface at the PC. Also remember that all signals on the parallel port are compatible with TTL signal levels.

Table 40-1. Pinouts for a Centronics-type cable

Computer end	Printer end	Designation		Description
1	1	–STR	–Strobe	(send character)
2	2	D0	Data Bit 0	
3	3	D1	Data Bit 1	
4	4	D2	Data Bit 2	
5	5	D3	Data Bit 3	
6	6	D4	Data Bit 4	
7	7	D5	Data Bit 5	
8	8	D6	Data Bit 6	
9	9	D7	Data Bit 7	
10	10	–ACK	–Acknowledge	(character received)
11	11	BSY	Busy	(processing character)
12	12	PAPER	Paper Out	(out of paper)
13	13	SEL	Select	(printer is on/off line)
14	14	–AF	–Auto Feed	(line feed manual/automatic)
15	32	–ERROR	–Error	(printer error)
16	31	–INI	–Initialize	(reset the printer)
17	36	–DSL	–Device Select	(master printer control)
18–25	19–30, 33	Ground	Common electrical ground	
n/a	16	0 V	Open	
n/a	17	Frame	Frame electrical ground	
n/a	18	+5 Vdc	Remote voltage source	
n/a	34, 35	n/a	Unused	

Data lines

The data lines are the actual data-carrying conductors that carry information from the parallel port to (or from) the printer (or other peripheral). There are eight data lines (D0 to D7) located on pins 2 through 9. To reduce the effects of signal noise on parallel cables, each data line is given a corresponding data ground line (pins 18 to 25). Ground lines also provide a common electrical reference between the computer and peripheral. The remainder of a parallel port is devoted to handshaking.

Initialize and Select

To ensure that the printer starts in a known initialized state, an –Initialize signal (–INI on pin 16) sent from the computer is used to reset a printer to the state it powered up in. Initializing the peripheral has the same effect as turning it off, then turning it on again. The –Initialize line is active-low, so the printer must apply a logic 0 to trigger an initialization.

The Select line (SEL on pin 13) tells the waiting computer that the peripheral is on line and ready to receive data. Select is an active-high logic signal, so a logic 1 indicates that a device is on line and ready, while a logic 0 indicates that the printer is not ready to receive data. The computer will not send data when the select line is logic 0. You can usually determine the select line's general condition from the printer's front panel "on-line" light.

Strobe, Busy, and Acknowledge

Once a computer has placed eight valid bits on the parallel data lines, the peripheral must be told that the data is ready. A –Strobe signal (–STR on pin 1) is applied to the peripheral from the computer just after data is valid. The brief –Strobe signal causes the peripheral to accept the byte and store it in the printer's internal buffer for processing.

Under ideal circumstances, parallel printer ports can achieve data rates of up to 500,000 characters per second. With such a tremendous throughput, the printer needs some method of coordinating data transfer. The computer must wait between characters until the printer is ready to resume accepting new characters. Printers use the Busy signal (BSY on pin 11) to delay the computer until the printer is ready. Peripherals drive the Busy line to logic 1 anytime a –Strobe signal is received. The Busy signal remains logic 1 for as long as it takes the peripheral to prepare for the next byte. It is important to note that a Busy signal can delay the computer indefinitely if a serious peripheral error has occurred (i.e., paper exhausted or ribbon jammed).

When the peripheral has received a byte and dealt with it, the peripheral must then request another character from the waiting computer. The printer drops the Busy line and initiates a brief –Acknowledge pulse (–ACK on pin 10). –Acknowledge signals are always active-low logic signals, and a typical acknowledge pulse lasts about 8 s. It is this interaction of data, –Strobe, Busy, and –Acknowledge signals that handles the bulk of data transfer in a parallel port.

Auto Feed

Some printers make the assumption that a carriage return signal (or <CR>) will automatically advance the paper to the next line, while other printers simply return the carriage to the beginning of the existing line without advancing the paper. Many printers make this feature selectable through the use of a DIP switch in the printer, but an –Auto Feed signal (–AF on pin 14) from the computer can control that feature. A TTL logic 0 from the computer causes the printer to feed one line of paper automatically when a carriage return command is detected. A *TT* (transistor-transistor logic) logic 1 from the computer allows only a carriage return (paper would have to be fed manually). Most computer parallel ports keep this line at logic 0.

Device Select

The –Device Select line (–DSL on pin 17) allows the computer to bring the peripheral on- and off-line remotely. Many parallel ports leave this signal as a logic 0 so that peripherals will automatically accept data. A logic 1 on this line would inhibit printer operation.

Error

The –Error signal (–ERROR on pin 15) generated by a printer (or other peripheral) tells the computer that trouble has occurred, but is not specific about the exact problem. A variety of problems can cause an error; it depends on your particular peripheral and what it is capable of detecting. The error line uses active-low logic, so it is normally logic 1 until an error has occurred. An –Error signal can typically indicate an "Out of Paper", "Printer Offline", or "General Printer Fault" error condition.

Port operation

This part of the chapter describes a standard sequence of events in a parallel port. The parallel data transfer begins by placing the printer on line. Strobe and –Acknowledge must be TTL logic 1, and Busy must be logic 0. In this state, the peripheral can now accept a byte of data. When printing is attempted, the CPU polls the desired LPT port and checks its status register. If the post is ready, a byte is written to the data register, and passed to the peripheral.

Data must be valid for at least 0.5 s before the computer initiates a logic 0 –Strobe. The printer responds by returning a logic 1 Busy signal that changes the port's status. Subsequent polling of the status register will indicate that the port is unavailable. The –Strobe pulse must last at least 1.0 s. Data must be held valid at least 0.5 s after the –Strobe pulse passes. This timing ensures that the peripheral has enough time to receive the data. Because Busy is now logic 1, communication stops until the data byte has been processed. Processing can take 1 ms if the printer's buffer is not full. If the printer's buffer is full, communication can be halted for a second or more. After the data byte has been processed, Busy is dropped to logic 0 and the printer sends a 5.0 s logic 0 –Acknowledge pulse to request another data byte from the waiting computer. Once the –Acknowledge line returns to a TTL logic 1 condition, the interface is ready to begin a new transfer. The status register then indicates the port is ready, and when the port is next polled, a new byte can be written. Figure 40-3 shows this relationship; one complete cycle can take a bit over 1 ms.

Troubleshooting the parallel port

Although the typical parallel port is a rather simple I/O device, it presents some special challenges for the technician. Older PCs provided their parallel ports in the form of 8-bit expansion boards. When a port failed, it was a simple matter to replace the board outright. Today, however, virtually all PCs provide at least one parallel port directly on the motherboard, usually integrated into a component of the main chipset. When a problem is detected with a motherboard parallel port, a technician often has three choices:

- Replace the chipset IC that supports the parallel port(s). This requires access to surface-mount soldering tools and replacement ICs, and can be quite economical in volume.
- Replace the motherboard outright. This is a simple tactic that requires little overhead equipment, but can be rather expensive.

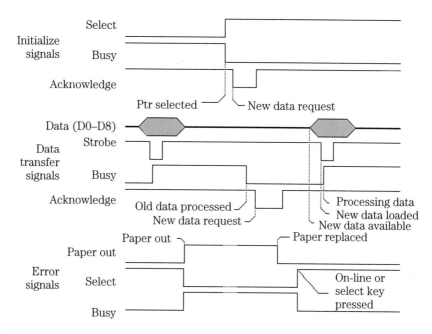

40-3 Typical parallel port timing diagram.

- Set the motherboard jumpers (if possible) to disable the defective parallel port, and install an expansion board to take the place of the defective port. This assumes there is an available expansion slot.

Virtually all commercial diagnostics are capable of locating any installed parallel ports, and testing the ports thoroughly through a loopback plug. Now that you have reviewed the layout, signals, and operation of a typical parallel port, you can take a clear look at port troubleshooting procedures:

Symptom 1. You hear a beep code or see a POST error indicating a parallel port error The system initialization might or might not halt depending on how the BIOS is written. Low-level initialization problems generally indicate trouble in the computer's hardware. If the computer's beep code sequence is indistinct, you could try rebooting the computer with a POST analyzer card installed. The BIOS POST code displayed on the card could be matched to a specific error explanation in the POST card's documentation. Once you have clearly identified the error as a parallel port fault, you can proceed with troubleshooting.

Begin with the system as a whole and remove any expansion boards that have parallel ports available. Retest the computer after removing each board. If the error disappears after removing a particular card, then that card is likely at fault. You can simply replace the card with a new one, or attempt to repair the card to the component level. If there is only one parallel port in the system, it is most likely built into the motherboard.

For older systems, the fault is probably in one or more of the discrete I/O ICs or latches directing the port's operation. You will need to refer to the schematic(s) for your particular system motherboard to determine exact signal flows and component locations. Newer system motherboards enjoy a far lower component count, so all parallel port circuitry is usually integrated onto the same application-specific IC (ASIC). A schematic would still be valuable to determine signal paths, but you could probably trace the parallel port connector directly to its controlling IC. Replace any defective components, or replace the motherboard outright.

Symptom 2. You see a 9xx parallel adapter displayed on your XT or early AT system BIOS has not located any parallel circuit defects on initialization, but has been unable to map LPT labels to the appropriate hardware-level ports. As in Symptom 1, the 9xx series error codes usually indicate a hardware fault in the computer. Follow the procedures in Symptom 1 to isolate and resolve the problem.

Symptom 3. The computer initializes properly, but the peripheral (printer) does not work. Your applications software might indicate a "printer timeout" or "general printer" error Before you even open your tool kit, you must determine whether the trouble lies in your computer or your peripheral. When your printer stops working, run a self-test to ensure the device is at least operational. Check all cables and connectors (perhaps try a different cable). If the peripheral offers multiple interfaces such as serial and parallel, make sure the parallel interface is activated in the peripheral. Also be sure to check the software package being used (word processor, painting package, system diagnostic, and so on) to operate the printer. Ensure that the software is configured properly to use the appropriate LPT port, and that any necessary printer driver is selected. If no software is available, you can try printing from the DOS command line using the <shift> and <print screen> keys. This key sequence will dump the screen contents to a printer.

Disconnect the printer at the computer and install a parallel loopback plug. Run a diagnostic to inspect each available parallel port. Take note of any port(s) that register as defective. Locate the corresponding parallel port. If the port is installed as an expansion board, replace the defective expansion board. If the port is on the motherboard, you can replace the defective port controller IC, install an alternate expansion board, or replace the motherboard outright.

Symptom 4. The peripheral (printer) will not go on line Before data can be transferred across a parallel port, proper handshaking conditions must exist; the Busy (pin 11) and Paper Out (pin 12) lines must be TTL logic 0, and the Select (pin 13) and –Error (pin 15) lines must be TTL logic 1. All four signals are outputs from the peripheral. You can examine these levels with an ordinary logic probe. If any of these signals is incorrect, the peripheral will not be on line. First, try a new communication cable. An old or worn cable might have developed a fault in one or more connections. Next, try the computer with a different peripheral. If a new peripheral *does* come on line, the error exists in the original peripheral's parallel port circuitry.

If a different peripheral does not operate properly, there is a problem with the computer's parallel port. Examine and alter the computer configuration to ensure that there is no conflict between multiple parallel ports. Disconnect the printer at the computer and install a parallel loopback plug. Run a diagnostic to inspect each available parallel port. Take note of any port(s) that register as defective. Locate the corresponding parallel port. If the port is installed as an expansion board, replace the defective expansion board. If the port is on the motherboard, you can replace the defective port controller IC, install an alternate expansion board, or replace the motherboard outright.

Symptom 5. Data is randomly lost or garbled Your first step should be to check the communication cable. Make sure the cable is intact and properly secured at both ends. The cable should also be less than 2 meters (about 6') long. Very long cables can allow crosstalk to generate erroneous signals. If the cable checks properly, either the port or peripheral is at fault. Start by suspecting the parallel port. Disconnect the printer at the computer and install a parallel loopback plug. Run a diagnostic to inspect each available parallel port. Take note of any port(s) that register as defective. Locate the corresponding parallel port. If the port is installed as an expansion board, replace the defective expansion board. If the port is on the motherboard, you can replace the defective port controller IC, install an alternate expansion board, or replace the motherboard outright.

If you cannot test the computer's parallel port directly, test the port indirectly by trying the peripheral on another known-good computer. If the peripheral works properly on another computer, the trouble is probably in the original computer's parallel port circuitry. Replace any defective circuitry or replace the motherboard. If the peripheral remains defective on another computer, the peripheral itself is probably faulty.

Symptom 6. You see a continuous "paper out" error even though paper is available and the printer's paper sensor works properly Plenty of paper is installed in the printer, and you have already checked the paper sensor. Try another printer. If another printer works, the problem is in your original printer and not in the parallel port. Use a logic probe and check the Paper Out signal at the computer. Try removing and re-inserting paper while the printer is running. You should see the Paper Out signal vary between a TTL logic 0 (paper available) and a TTL logic 1 (paper missing). If the signal remains TTL logic 1 regardless of paper availability, the printer's sensor or communication circuits are probably defective. If the Paper Out signal correctly follows the paper availability, the trouble is probably in your computer's communication circuitry.

When you suspect that the problem is in the parallel port, disconnect the printer at the computer and install a parallel loopback plug. Run a diagnostic to inspect each available parallel port. Take note of any port(s) that register as defective. Locate the corresponding parallel port. If the port is installed as an expansion board, replace the defective expansion board. If the port is on the motherboard, you can replace the defective port controller IC, install an alternate expansion board, or replace the motherboard outright.

41
CHAPTER

PCI bus operations

By the late 1980s, the proliferation of 32-bit CPUs and graphics-intensive operating systems made it painfully obvious that the 8.33-MHz ISA bus was no longer satisfactory. The PC industry began to develop alternative architectures for improved performance. Two architectures are now prominent; VL and PCI. Although the VL bus seems ideal, there are some serious limitations that must be overcome. Perhaps most important is the VL bus dependence on CPU speed. Fast computers must use wait states with the VL bus, and only supports one or two slots maximum. Another problem is that the VL standard is voluntary, and not all manufacturers adhere to VESA specifications completely. In mid-1992, Intel Corporation and a comprehensive consortium of manufacturers introduced the Peripheral Component Interconnect (PCI) bus. Where the VL bus was designed specifically to enhance PC video systems, the 188-pin PCI bus looks to the future of CPUs (and PCs in general) by providing a bus architecture that also supports peripherals such as hard drives, networks, and so on. This chapter shows you the layout and operations of the PCI bus.

PCI bus configuration and signals

The PCI architecture is capable of transferring data at 132Mb/s, a great improvement over the 5Mb/s transfer rate of the standard ISA bus. Another key advantage of the PCI bus is that it will have automatic configuration capabilities for switchless/jumperless peripherals. Autoconfiguration (the heart of "plug-and-play") will take care of all addresses, Interrupt request, and DMA used by a PCI peripheral.

The PCI bus supports linear bursts, which is a method of transferring data that ensures the bus is continually filled with data. The peripheral devices expect to receive data from the system main memory in a linear address order, this means that large amounts of data is read from or written to a single address, which is then incremented for the next byte in the stream. The linear burst is one of the unique aspects of the PCI bus because it will perform both burst reads and burst writes. In short, it will transfer data on the bus every clock cycle; this doubles the PCI throughput compared to buses without linear burst capabilities.

The devices designed to support PCI have low access latency, reducing the time required for a peripheral to be granted control of the bus after requesting access. For example, an Ethernet controller card connected to a LAN has large data files from the network coming into its buffer. Waiting for access to the bus, the Ethernet is unable to transfer the data to the CPU quickly enough to avoid a buffer overflow, forcing it to temporarily store the file's contents in extra RAM. Because PCI-compliant devices support faster access times, the Ethernet card can promptly send data to the CPU.

The PCI bus supports *bus mastering*, which allows one of a number of intelligent peripherals to take control of the bus in order to accelerate a high-throughput, high-priority task. PCI architecture also supports *concurrency*, a technique that ensures the microprocessor operates simultaneously with these masters, instead of waiting for them. As one example, concurrency allows the CPU to perform floating-point calculations on a spreadsheet while an Ethernet card and the LAN have control of the bus. Finally, PCI was developed as a dual-voltage architecture. Normally, the bus is a +5-Vdc system like other buses. However, the bus also can operate in a +3.3-Vdc (low-voltage) mode.

PCI layout

The layout for a PCI bus slot is shown in Fig. 41-1. Note that there are two major segments to the +5-Vdc version connector. A +3.3-Vdc version connector adds a key in the 12/13 positions to prevent accidental insertion of a +5-Vdc PCI board into a +3.3-Vdc slot. Similarly, the +5-Vdc slot is keyed in the 50/51 position to prevent placing a +3.3-Vdc board into a +5-Vdc slot. The pinout for a PCI bus is shown in Table 41-1.

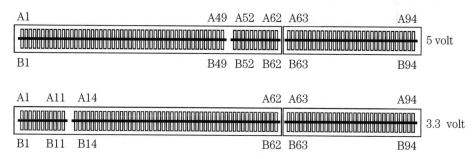

41-1 5-V and 3.3-V PCI expansion bus diagrams.

Table 41-1. PCI bus pinout—5 volt and 3.3 volt (Rev. 2.0)

5 volt	3.3 volt	Pin	Pin	3.3 volt	5 volt
–12 Vdc	–12 Vdc	B1	A1	–TRST	–TRST
TCK	TCK	B2	A2	+12 Vdc	+12 Vdc
Ground	Ground	B3	A3	TMS	TMS
TDO	TDO	B4	A4	TDI	TDI
+5 Vdc	+5 Vdc	B5	A5	+5 Vdc	+5 Vdc
+5 Vdc	+5 Vdc	B6	A6	–INTA	–INTA
–INTB	–INTB	B7	A7	–INTC	–INTC
–INTD	–INTD	B8	A8	+5 Vdc	+5 Vdc

Table 41-1. Continued

5 volt	3.3 volt	Pin	Pin	3.3 volt	5 volt
–PRSNT1	–PRSNT1	B9	A9	Reserved	Reserved
Reserved	Reserved	B10	A10	+3.3 Vdc (I/O)	+5 Vdc
–PRSNT2	–PRSNT2	B11	A11	Reserved	Reserved
Ground	Key	B12	A12	Key	Ground
Ground	Key	B13	A13	Key	Ground
Reserved	Reserved	B14	A14	Reserved	Reserved
Ground	Ground	B15	A15	–RST	–RST
Clock	Clock	B16	A16	+3.3 Vdc	+5 Vdc
Ground	Ground	B17	A17	–GNT	–GNT
–REQ	–REQ	B18	A18	Ground	Ground
+5 Vdc	+3.3 Vdc	B19	A19	Reserved	Reserved
Adr/Dat 31	Adr/Dat 31	B20	A20	Adr/Dat 30	Adr/Dat 30
Adr/Dat 29	Adr/Dat 29	B21	A21	+3.3 Vdc	+5 Vdc
Ground	Ground	B22	A22	Adr/Dat 28	Adr/Dat 28
Adr/Dat 27	Adr/Dat 27	B23	A23	Adr/Dat 26	Adr/Dat 26
Adr/Dat 25	Adr/Dat 25	B24	A24	Ground	Ground
+5 Vdc	+3.3 Vdc	B25	A25	Adr/Dat 24	Adr/Dat 24
C/–BE3	C/–BE3	B26	A26	IDSEL	IDSEL
Adr/Dat 23	Adr/Dat 23	B27	A27	+3.3 Vdc	+5 Vdc
Ground	Ground	B28	A28	Adr/Dat 22	Adr/Dat 22
Adr/Dat 21	Adr/Dat 21	B29	A29	Adr/Dat 20	Adr/Dat 20
Adr/Dat 19	Adr/Dat 19	B30	A30	Ground	Ground
+5 Vdc	+3.3 Vdc	B31	A31	Adr/Dat 18	Adr/Dat 18
Adr/Dat 17	Adr/Dat 17	B32	A32	Adr/Dat 16	Adr/Dat 16
C/–BE2	C/–BE2	B33	A33	+3.3 Vdc	+5 Vdc
Ground	Ground	B34	A34	–FRAME	–FRAME
–IRDY	–IRDY	B35	A35	Ground	Ground
+5 Vdc	+3.3 Vdc	B36	A36	–TRDY	–TRDY
–DEVSEL	–DEVSEL	B37	A37	Ground	Ground
Ground	Ground	B38	A38	–STOP	–STOP
–LOCK	–LOCK	B39	A39	+3.3 Vdc	+5 Vdc
–PERR	–PERR	B40	A40	SDONE	SDONE
+5 Vdc	+3.3 Vdc	B41	A41	–SBO	–SBO
–SERR	–SERR	B42	A42	Ground	Ground
+5 Vdc	+3.3 Vdc	B43	A43	PAR	PAR
C/–BE1	C/–BE1	B44	A44	Adr/Dat 15	Adr/Dat 15
Adr/Dat 14	Adr/Dat 14	B45	A45	+3.3 Vdc	+5 Vdc
Ground	Ground	B46	A46	Adr/Dat 13	Adr/Dat 13
Adr/Dat 12	Adr/Dat 12	B47	A47	Adr/Dat 11	Adr/Dat 11
Adr/Dat 10	Adr/Dat 10	B48	A48	Ground	Ground
Ground	Ground	B49	A49	Adr/Dat 9	Adr/Dat 9
Key	Ground	B50	A50	Ground	Key
Key	Ground	B51	A51	Ground	Key
Adr/Dat 8	Adr/Dat 8	B52	A52	C/–BE0	C/–BE0
Adr/Dat 7	Adr/Dat 7	B53	A53	+3.3 Vdc	+5 Vdc

Table 41-1. Continued

5 volt	3.3 volt	Pin	Pin	3.3 volt	5 volt
+5 Vdc	+3.3 Vdc	B54	A54	Adr/Dat 6	Adr/Dat 6
Adr/Dat 5	Adr/Dat 5	B55	A55	Adr/Dat 4	Adr/Dat 4
Adr/Dat 3	Adr/Dat 3	B56	A56	Ground	Ground
Ground	Ground	B57	A57	Adr/Dat 2	Adr/Dat 2
Adr/Dat 1	Adr/Dat 1	B58	A58	Adr/Dat 0	Adr/Dat 0
+5 Vdc	+3.3 Vdc	B59	A59	+3.3 Vdc	+5 Vdc
−ACK64	−ACK64	B60	A60	−REQ64	−REQ64
+5 Vdc	+5 Vdc	B61	A61	+5 Vdc	+5 Vdc
+5 Vdc	+5 Vdc	B62	A62	+5 Vdc	+5 Vdc
Key	Key	Key	Key	Key	Key
Key	Key	Key	Key	Key	Key
Reserved	Reserved	B63	A63	Ground	Ground
Ground	Ground	B64	A64	C/−BE7	C/−BE7
C/−BE6	C/−BE6	B65	A65	C/−BE5	C/−BE5
C/−BE4	C/−BE4	B66	A66	+3.3 Vdc	+5 Vdc
Ground	Ground	B67	A67	PAR64	PAR64
Adr/Dat 63	Adr/Dat 63	B68	A68	Adr/Dat 62	Adr/Dat 62
Adr/Dat 61	Adr/Dat 61	B69	A69	Ground	Ground
+5 Vdc	+3.3 Vdc	B70	A70	Adr/Dat 60	Adr/Dat 60
Adr/Dat 59	Adr/Dat 59	B71	A71	Adr/Dat 58	Adr/Dat 58
Adr/Dat 57	Adr/Dat 57	B72	A72	Ground	Ground
Ground	Ground	B73	A73	Adr/Dat 56	Adr/Dat 56
Adr/Dat 55	Adr/Dat 55	B74	A74	Adr/Dat 54	Adr/Dat 54
Adr/Dat 53	Adr/Dat 53	B75	A75	+3.3 Vdc	+5 Vdc
Ground	Ground	B76	A76	Adr/Dat 52	Adr/Dat 52
Adr/Dat 51	Adr/Dat 51	B77	A77	Adr/Dat 50	Adr/Dat 50
Adr/Dat 49	Adr/Dat 49	B78	A78	Ground	Ground
+5 Vdc	+3.3 Vdc	B79	A79	Adr/Dat 48	Adr/Dat 48
Adr/Dat 47	Adr/Dat 47	B80	A80	Adr/Dat 46	Adr/Dat 46
Adr/Dat 45	Adr/Dat 45	B81	A81	Ground	Ground
Ground	Ground	B82	A82	Adr/Dat 44	Adr/Dat 44
Adr/Dat 43	Adr/Dat 43	B83	A83	Adr/Dat 42	Adr/Dat 42
Adr/Dat 41	Adr/Dat 41	B84	A84	+3.3 Vdc	+5 Vdc
Ground	Ground	B85	A85	Adr/Dat 40	Adr/Dat 40
Adr/Dat 39	Adr/Dat 39	B86	A86	Adr/Dat 38	Adr/Dat 38
Adr/Dat 37	Adr/Dat 37	B87	A87	Ground	Ground
+5 Vdc	+3.3 Vdc	B88	A88	Adr/Dat 36	Adr/Dat 36
Adr/Dat 35	Adr/Dat 35	B89	A89	Adr/Dat 34	Adr/Dat 34
Adr/Dat 33	Adr/Dat 33	B90	A90	Ground	Ground
Ground	Ground	B91	A91	Adr/Dat 32	Adr/Dat 32
Reserved	Reserved	B92	A92	Reserved	Reserved
Reserved	Reserved	B93	A93	Ground	Ground
Ground	Ground	B94	A94	Reserved	Reserved

Knowing the PCI signals

To reduce the number of pins needed in the PCI bus, data and address lines are multiplexed together (Adr./Dat 0 to Adr./Dat 63). It also is interesting to note from the table that PCI is the first bus standard designed to support a low-voltage (+3.3 Vdc) logic implementation. On inspection, you will see that +5-Vdc and +3.3-Vdc implementations of the PCI bus place their physical key slots in different places so that the two implementations are not interchangeable. The Clock (CLOCK) signal provides timing for the PCI bus only, and can be adjusted from dc (0Hz) to 33 MHz. Asserting the –Reset (–RST) signal will reset all PCI devices. Because the 64-bit data path uses eight bytes, the Command/–Byte Enable signals (C/–BE0 to C/–BE7) define which bytes are transferred. Parity across the Address/Data and Byte Enable lines is represented with a Parity (PAR) or 64-Bit Parity (PAR64) signal. Bus mastering is initiated by the –Request (–REQ) line and granted after approval using the –Grant (–GNT) line.

When a valid PCI bus cycle is in progress, the –Frame (–FRAME) signal is true. If the PCI bus cycle is in its final phase, –Frame will be released. The –Target Ready (–TRDY) line is true when an addressed device is able to complete the data phase of its bus cycle. An –Initiator Ready (–IRDY) signal indicates that valid data is present on the bus (or the bus is ready to accept data). The –FRAME, –TARGET READY, and –INITIATOR READY signals are all used together. A –Stop (–STOP) signal is asserted by a target asking a master to halt the current data transfer. The ID Select (IDSEL) signal is used as a chip select signal during board configuration read and write cycles. The –Device Select (–DEVSEL) line is both an input and an output. As an input, –DEVSEL indicates if a device has assumed control of the current bus transfer. As an output, –DEVSEL shows that a device has identified itself as the target for the current bus transfer.

There are four interrupt lines (–INTA to –INTD). When the full 64-bit data mode is being used, an expansion device will initiate a –64-Bit Bus Request (-REQ 64) and await a-64-Bit Bus Acknowledge (–ACK64) signal from the bus controller. The –Bus Lock (–LOCK) signal is an interface control used to ensure use of the bus by a selected expansion device. Error reporting is performed by –Primary Error (–PERR) and –Secondary Error (–SERR) lines. Cache memory and JTAG support also are provided on the PCI bus.

General bus troubleshooting

In most cases, you will not be troubleshooting a bus; after all, the bus is little more than a passive connector. However, the major signals that exist on a PCI bus can provide you with important clues about the system's operation. The most effective bus troubleshooting tool available to you is a POST board (such as the ones discussed in Chapter 28). Many POST boards are equipped with a number of LEDs that display power status, along with important timing and control signals. If one or more of those LEDs is missing, a fault has likely occurred somewhere on the motherboard. Keep in mind that the vast majority of POST boards are designed for the ISA bus. You can plug a POST board (with a built-in logic probe capable of 33 MHz operation) into an ISA connector, then use the logic probe to test key signals. Because the signals on a PCI bus are quite different than those on an ISA bus, try the following signals:

- *Voltage* Use your multimeter and check each voltage level on the PCI bus. You should be able to find -12 Vdc and $+5$ Vdc regardless of whether the bus is standard or low-voltage. For a low-voltage bus, you also should be able to find a $+3.3$-Vdc supply. If any of these supply levels are low or absent, troubleshoot or replace the power supply.
- *CLOCK (pin B16)* The Clock signal provides timing signals for the expansion device. It can be adjusted between dc (0 Hz) and 33 MHz. If this signal is absent, the expansion board will probably not run. Check the clock generating circuitry on the motherboard, or replace the motherboard outright.
- *RST (pin B18)* The Reset line can be used to reinitialize the PCI expansion device. This line should not be active for more than a few moments after power is applied or after a warm reset is initiated.

Another point to consider is that bus connectors are mechanical devices. As a result, they do not last forever. If you or your customer are in the habit of removing and inserting boards frequently, it is likely that the metal fingers providing contact will wear and result in unreliable connections. Similarly, inserting a board improperly (or with excessive force) can break the connector. In extreme cases, even the motherboard can be damaged. The first rule of board replacement is: always try removing and reinserting the suspect board. It is not uncommon for oxides to develop on board and slot contacts that might eventually degrade signal quality. By removing the board and re-inserting it, you can wipe off any oxides or dust and possibly improve the connections.

The second rule of board replacement is: always try a board in another expansion slot before replacing it. This way, a faulty bus slot can be ruled out before suffering the expense of a new board. Keep in mind that many current PCI motherboards have only one or two PCI slots; the remainder are ISA slots. If a bus slot proves defective, there is little that a technician can do except:

1. Block the slot and inform the customer that it is damaged and should not be used.
2. Replace the damaged bus slot connector (a tedious and time-consuming task) and pass the labor expense on to the customer.
3. Replace the motherboard outright (also a rather expensive option).

42
CHAPTER

PCMCIA cards and peripherals

Although desktop computers have always provided a standardized interface—the expansion bus—mobile computers have traditionally lacked all the most basic upgrade potential. By the late 1980s, it was clear that a standard would be needed to allow rapid and convenient upgrades for mobile computers. Neil Chandra of Poquet Computer (now part of Fujitsu) took a vision originally conceived to provide memory for the hand-held Poquet computer, and brought together industry leaders to forge a standard. In 1989, Chandra's brainchild, the *PCMCIA* (Personal Computer Memory Card International Association), was formed as a standards body and trade association. The objective of the PCMCIA is to provide universal, nonproprietary expansion capability for mobile computer systems (Fig. 42-1). More than 475 organizations are affiliated with the PCMCIA, which also works very closely with other major standards organizations such as the *JEIDA* (Japan Electronics Industry Development Association), the *EIA* (Electronics Industries Association), the *JEDEC* (Joint Electron Device Engineering Council), and the *ISO)* (International Standards Organization). This chapter explains the inner workings of a PCMCIA interface and cards that use it. You also will learn a selection of troubleshooting procedures intended to help you overcome many of the problems attributed to the PCMCIA interface.

Understanding the PC Card

Ultimately, the universal expansion standard envisioned by the PCMCIA has taken the form of a card (called a *PC Card*), which is roughly the length and width of a credit card (Fig. 42-2). This basic shape has remained virtually unchanged because the initial release of PCMCIA standards (version 1.0) in September 1990. The original specification (reflecting the original Poquet vision) defined an interface that was intended exclusively for memory cards such as DRAM, flash EEPROM, and ROM. However, a memory-only interface did not even come close to fulfilling the promise of universal expansion capability; there is much more to PCs than memory.

42-1
A Future Domain PCMCIA SCSI adapter.

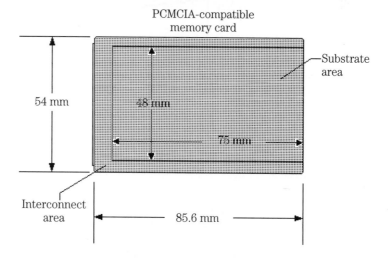

PCMCIA-compatible
memory card

54 mm

48 mm

75 mm

Substrate
area

Interconnect
area

85.6 mm

42-2 Basic PC Card dimensions.

PCMCIA release 2.0 followed a year later in September 1991. Version 2.0 took the quantum leap that version 1.0 ignored and incorporated I/O capability and software support into the PC Card. It was this addition of I/O capability that PC Card technology finally began to attract serious attention from mobile computer manufacturers. PC Card makers could now move past memory products and offer a wealth of other expansion products such as LAN cards, fax/modems, and disk drives. Release 2.1 followed in July of 1993 that specifies software support and BIOS card and socket services.

Making it work

Of course, integrating a PC Card into a computer is not as easy as just attaching a connector to the PC buses. A selection of system hardware and software is needed as illustrated in Fig. 42-3. This multilayered approach is typical of most PC peripherals; if you've ever installed a CD-ROM drive before, this type of diagram probably looks very familiar.

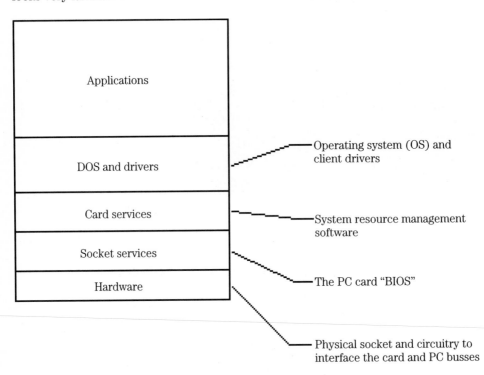

42-3 Simplified PC Card architecture.

At the foundation of PC Card architecture is the hardware layer. This represents the physical card itself, its connectors, and the circuitry needed to interface the card to the PC buses. In most cases, PC Card support can be added to a computer with one or two *VLSI* (very large scale integration) ICs and a bit of glue logic. You can see this hardware implemented for a desktop or tower PC in the QuaTech card drive shown in Fig. 42-4.

The next layer above hardware is called the *Socket Services* layer. Socket Services act as a supplement for system BIOS by providing the low-level routines needed to access the card hardware. It is important to note that Socket Services

42-4 A Quatech PCMCIA adapter for the PC. Quatech

software is always implemented as firmware; either in the system BIOS itself (often in new BIOS versions) or on an expansion ROM included on the adapter board. Socket Services are used by the computer to identify how many sockets are in the system, and whether cards are inserted or removed while system power is applied.

The *Card Services* layer forms the interface between the operating system and Socket Services. When Socket Services detects the presence of a card, Card Services allocates and manages the system resources (interrupts, DMA channels, and addressing) needed by the card(s). When a card is removed, Card services will free those system resources again. It is this unique ability to find, use, and then free system resources that gives PC Cards their powerful I/O capability and plug-and-play flexibility. Because Card Services software is universal across hardware platforms, it can be loaded either as a DOS device driver, or can be part of the operating system, such as IBM's DOS 6.1 and OS/2 2.1.

Unfortunately, not all notebook and subnotebook systems use Socket and Card Services; this is a major reason for PCMCIA compatibility problems. Some PCMCIA cards come with software device drivers that attempt to communicate directly with the system hardware. These cards were developed prior to the release of the PCMCIA Card Services standard, and such cards will only work on certain hardware platforms. Also, not all notebooks provide PCMCIA Socket Services. Some vendors provide proprietary BIOS firmware that supports a specific, limited set of PCMCIA cards. Just recently, some vendors have begun bundling PCMCIA 2.01 compatible card and socket services with their systems.

Above Card Services, you see the familiar DOS and application layers. Specialized (client) device drivers that might be needed for particular cards (such as an ATA card driver or flash file driver) are considered as part of the DOS layer.

Card types

CMCIA standards also define the physical dimensions that a PC Card is limited to. There are three types of cards: Type I, Type II, and Type III. Although the length and width of each card remains the same, the thickness of their *substrate area* can vary (as shown in Fig. 42-5) to accommodate different applications. The classic Type

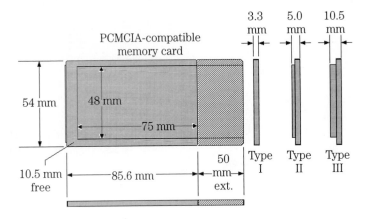

42-5 Comparison of PC card thicknesses.

I card is only 3.3 mm thick. Although this is too thin for mechanical assemblies, it is ideal for most types of memory enhancements. Type II cards run 5.0 mm thick, which make them ideal for larger memory enhancements and most I/O cards. Note in Fig. 42-5 that the edges and connector area (the *interconnect area*) of the card remain at 3.3 mm. The Type III card is a full 10.5 mm thick, which is large enough to accommodate the components for a complete hard drive or radio communication device. Like Type II cards, the interconnect area remains 3.3 mm. This 3.3-mm rail height permits thinner cards to be inserted into thicker slots (but not vice versa).

Inside the card

You can develop a tremendous respect for PC Cards by understanding the fragile and compact assemblies that are inside it. Consider the Maxtor MobileMax Lite shown in Fig. 42-6. The drive contains a single platter, upper and lower R/W heads, a voice coil servo motor to position the heads, a spindle motor to spin the platters, and the circuitry required to handle all drive functions and interfacing. As you might imagine, each element of the PC Card must be kept extremely thin; still, it is sometimes difficult to believe that the assembly actually fits into a shell only 0.5 cm thick

42-6
Internal view of a Maxtor
MobileMax Lite PCMCIA hard
drive. Maxtor Corporation

(Type II). Another important consideration in memory card design is the control and suppression of electrostatic discharge (ESD). Static electricity must be prevented from reaching the card's PC board where IC damage can occur. Once a card is inserted into a system, a *discharge tab* at the physical interface connector carries away any accumulation of charges to system ground. Until a card is inserted, a card protects its circuitry from damage using the Faraday cage principle; the same principle used by antistatic bags to protect their contents. The shell of most PCMCIA cards is either constructed of a metal (such as stainless steel) or some sort of metalized plastic. Both shell halves are bonded together by a small spring. Any charge introduced to the card is quickly dispersed over the entire shell surface instead of being allowed to enter the card.

Hot insertion and removal

One of the great disadvantages to most expansion devices is that computer power must be completely off before the device can be installed or removed. Not only is this necessary to prevent accidental damage from improper insertion, but the traditional BIOS and DOS only allocate system resources when the system is first initialized; they were not designed to accommodate allocating system resources on-the-fly. PCMCIA take a major step toward this type of dynamic resource allocation with the support of hot swapping. *Hot swapping* (or *hot insertion and removal*) refers to the ability to insert and remove cards while the PC power is still on without any degradation or damage to the system or card. Ideally, software applications can recognize the card's function and adjust accordingly.

Although PCMCIA supports hot swapping, very few operating systems or application programs are currently PCMCIA aware. That is, they do not recognize when cards have been inserted or removed. Therefore, users of any computer with PCM-CIA slots should close any open application programs before inserting or removing a PCMCIA card. Otherwise, the application might not initialize a card that has been inserted, and might lock up when a card is removed.

Understanding attribute memory

One of the greatest challenges facing PCMCIA cards is cross-compatibility; the ability to use various card species from diverse manufacturers in the same card slot. There are quite a few card sizes and types currently in production, and many more card models will be available by the time you read this book. How does the computer know when you have replaced your 2-Mb SRAM card with a 20-Mb Flash card, or a 100-Mb PCMCIA hard drive? You should understand that a computer capable of accepting PCMCIA cards must be able to detect and adjust to the diverse attributes of each card it might encounter, even though each card can use the same physical interface.

The best analogy to this are hard drives that are available in a staggering array of capacities, heads, cylinders, sectors, and so on, but all those drives can use the same physical interface. A computer interacts properly with a hard drive because you enter the drive's key parameters in the computer's CMOS setup routine. The same basic problem exists for PCMCIA cards. However, memory cards are intended to be transient items; inserted and removed at will. Imagine the inconvenience of having to re-enter a card's key parameters each time a new card is inserted. Even a single typing error can be disastrous for some cards and their contents.

The PCMCIA has supported a standard for memory card services that defines the software interface for accessing cards (PCMCIA 2.1). The interface can either be a device driver loaded when the computer boots, or designed directly into BIOS ROM or the operating system. In order for this driver system to work, each card must be able to identify itself to the computer. The complete characteristic and ID data for a memory card is held in the *attribute memory* area of each individual card.

Attribute memory contains a surprising amount of information—it must, considering the huge number of potential differences in card layout and features. Attribute memory tells the computer how much storage a card contains, the particular device type (memory, disk, I/O, and so on), the card's data format, speed capabilities, and many other variables.

The contents of attribute memory is typically setup information that falls into one of four categories of PCMCIA's Card Identification System (CIS)—otherwise known as the card's *meta-format*. Those four layers are: the *basic compatibility layer* indicating how the card's storage is organized, the *data-recording format layer* specifying how blocks of card information are to be stored, the *data-organization layer* defining the card's operating system format (DOS, Microsoft's Flash-File system, PCMCIA's XIP, and so on), and any *specific standards* needed to support an operating system.

Connections

The standard PC Card is connected to a PC through a 68-pin header arranged in two rows of 34 pins as shown in Fig. 42-7. If you look at the header pins closely, you will notice that several of the pins are longer than the others; these are ground pins. By making them longer, a card will be attached to ground first when inserted. Figure 42-8 shows how a PC Card interfaces to its mating connector. When the card is removed, ground will still be attached after the power pins have been disconnected. Good grounding helps to ensure the card's reliability, and permit hot insertion and removal. When you look at the assignment of each pin in

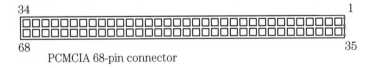

34   1

68   35
         PCMCIA 68-pin connector

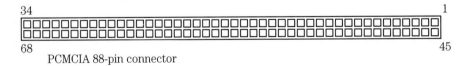

34   1

68   45
         PCMCIA 88-pin connector

42-7 PCMCIA header diagrams.

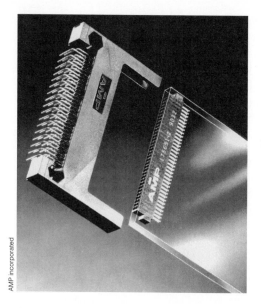

42-8
Typical PCMCIA connector
products.

AMP incorporated

Table 42-1, you will see that there are basically four types of signals at the PCM-CIA interface: data pins, address pins, power (and ground), and control signals. It is this healthy mix of signals that make it possible to support many of the PC Card applications that are available today.

Table 42-1. The PCMCIA 68-pin pinout

Pin	Label	Pin	Label	Pin	Label	Pin	Label
1	Ground	20	A15	39	D13	58	reset
2	D3	21	A12	40	D14	59	wait
3	D4	22	A7	41	D15	60	reserved
4	D5	23	A6	42	-Card En 2	61	-Register Select
5	D6	24	A5	43	Refresh	62	-Batt Detect 2
6	D7	25	A4	44	reserved	63	-Batt Detect 1
7	-Card En 1	26	A3	45	reserved	64	D8
8	A10	27	A2	46	A17	65	D9
9	-Output En	28	A1	47	A18	66	D10
10	A11	29	A0	48	A19	67	-Card Detect 2
11	A9	30	D0	49	A20	68	Ground
12	A8	31	D1	50	A21		
13	A13	32	D2	51	+Vcc		
14	A14	33	-Write Protect	52	Prog Voltage 2		
15	-Write/Program	34	Ground	53	A22		
16	-Ready/Busy	35	Ground	54	A23		
17	+Vcc	36	-Card Detect 1	55	A24		
18	Prog Voltage 1	37	D11	56	A25		
19	A16	38	D12	57	reserved		

Although the 68-pin header reigns supreme in the PC Card arena, there also is an 88-pin variation shown in Fig. 42-7. This 88-pin interface traces its roots back to the earliest implementations of PC Cards as memory expansion devices. As you look over the pin assignments in Table 42-2, you might notice that there are 34 data lines and a series or row (RAS) and column (CAS) refresh signal lines that made the 88-pin interface ideal for large volume dynamic RAM (DRAM) cards. However, there are almost no I/O signals such as those in the 68-pin interface. Without I/O signals, the 88-pin PC Card is rarely found in new mobile computers, and is never used for I/O devices.

Table 42-2. The PCMCIA 88-pin pinout

Pin	Label	Pin	Label	Pin	Label	Pin	Label
1	Ground	23	-CAS0	45	Ground	67	Ground
2	D0	24	-CAS1	46	D18	68	CAS3
3	D1	25	+Vcc	47	D19	69	RAS3
4	D2	26	-RAS2	48	D20	70	-Write Enable
5	D3	27	+Vcc	49	D21	71	PD1
6	D4	28	PD2	50	D22	72	PD3
7	D5	29	PD4	51	D23	73	Ground
8	D6	30	PD6	52	D24	74	PD5
9	+Vcc	31	nc	53	D25	75	PD7
10	D7	32	nc	54	D26	76	PD8
11	+Vcc	33	D17	55	nc	77	nc
12	D8	34	D9	56	Ground	78	nc
13	A0	35	+Vcc	57	A1	79	D35
14	A2	36	D10	58	A3	80	D27
15	+Vcc	37	+Vcc	59	A5	81	D28
16	A4	38	D11	60	A7	82	D29
17	+Vcc	39	D12	61	A9	83	D30
18	A6	40	D13	62	A11	84	D31
19	A8	41	D14	63	Ground	85	D32
20	A10	42	D15	64	A13	86	D33
21	A12	43	D16	65	-RAS1	87	D34
22	-RAS0	44	Ground	66	-CAS2	88	Ground

Understanding PC card applications

Now that PC Cards are being developed according to release 2.1, they offer a series of compelling advantages for mobile computer users:

- The I/O support offered by PCMCIA specifications allows virtually any product to be incorporated into a PC Card. Modems, network adapters, video capture modules, audio cards, and hard drives are just some of the devices that PCMCIA standards now embrace.
- PC Cards can be made to operate in a *dual-voltage* mode (either 5.0 volts or 3.3 volts) depending on the design of the mobile PC. Low-voltage compatibility saves power and extends battery life.

- The programs and applications stored on PC Cards can now be executed in place rather than having to load the card's contents into main memory. This *XIP* (execute-in-place) technology reduces the demand for large amounts of on-board RAM.
- The *Socket Services* software defined by release 2.1 describes a BIOS-level interface that allows applications to access the card's hardware. The device drivers written to operate specific PC Cards will run on any PC that supports Socket Services.
- The *Card Services* software automatically allocates system resources (memory and IRQs) once a PC Card is inserted into a system (referred to as dynamic resource allocation). Information (called *tuple information*) contained in the *CIS* (Card Information Structure) of a card describes the characteristics and abilities of that card. In turn, the host system can automatically configure the card for proper operation. This type of operation is the earliest implementation of a plug-and-play architecture.

PC Card problems

Like all new PC technologies, however, there are some disappointing problems with the early implementations of PCMCIA. Before you decide to buy that next PC Card-compatible system, you should understand some of the factors that have contributed to PCMCIA's poor showing. When the PCMCIA issued release 1.0 in 1990, Socket and Card services did not exist; card makers had to supply their own specific drivers that had to be tested on each specific computer. If the host computer were updated or upgraded, the cards that worked on the older systems would probably not work on the newer ones. This resulted in perplexing compatibility problems.

Socket and Card services were added in 1991 with PCMCIA release 2.0, but the release also brought I/O devices into the PC Card picture. Although this made PCM-CIA much more versatile, I/O brought in a host of new problems. Although all I/O cards are supposed to be treated as a generic device, an operating system does not see all devices the same way. For example, an operating system does not treat a hard drive and a modem the same way, but card makers did not take that into account, so compatibility between systems is still an issue. Also, most operating systems are designed to work with resources that are present when a system is booted, so although you might be able to insert and remove cards safely, the operating system can rarely adjust the system resources properly. As a result, many cards have to be installed before the system boots.

Today, most PCMCIA cards work in most systems, and can be inserted and removed without rebooting the computer, but there are no guarantees. The situation has gotten much better over the last year or so, but beware of older PCMCIA systems.

Today's cards

PCMCIA cards have come a long way since the early memory cards of 1990. Virtually any device that can be implemented on an expansion card can be fabricated as a PC Card. As a technician, you should understand the range of devices that you might encounter when servicing notebook and subnotebook systems.

- *Memory cards* Memory expansion devices continue to be popular PC Card devices, not so much for added system memory, but to run prefabricated applications directly off the card.
- *Modem cards* PCMCIA modems (such as Fig. 42-9) are rapidly replacing proprietary modems as internal communication devices. PCMCIA modems are easily matching the speed and performance of stand-alone modems, and are even being equipped with cellular connections for true mobile operation.

42-9
A Toshiba Noteworthy cellular-ready modem. Toshiba America Information Systems, Inc. Computer Systems Division

- *LAN cards* Local area networks are becoming more popular as businesses integrate their operations and add connections to such resources as the Internet. LAN cards allow mobile computers to play a constructive role on networks using topologies such as Ethernet, Token Ring, and 3270 Emulation.
- *Digital video cards* The soaring popularity of multimedia applications has dramatically increased the demand for video and still-frame capture products. PCMCIA technology allows video and audio capture capability in PC Card products (such as Fig. 42-10) for high-quality multimedia on the road.

42-10
A Toshiba Noteworthy portable digital video card. Toshiba America Information Systems, Inc. Computer Systems Division

- *Hard-drive cards* Until the advent of PCMCIA, it was virtually impossible to add a second hard drive to a portable PC. Fortunately, the use of PCMCIA combined with the stunning advances in hard-drive technology allow substantial hard drive capacities in a Type III form factor.
- *Audio cards* Games and music composition software demands high-quality sound reproduction. PCMCIA audio cards provide SoundBlaster-compatible sound to external speakers. The trend toward mobile multimedia is integrating sound systems and speakers right into the mobile PC, but stand-alone sound cards are available.
- *SCSI adapter cards* The Small Computer System Interface (SCSI) is a system-level interface scheme that allows a multitude of devices (CD-ROM, scanners, tape drives, and so on) to be connected to a system. A PCMCIA SCSI adapter card opens a whole new level of compatibility for a mobile computer.
- *Floppy drive cards* The recent trend among subnotebook and palmtop computers has been to forego the floppy drive in favor of a PCMCIA slot. However, PCMCIA floppy disk adapters such as the Accurite Technologies PassportCard bring a standard floppy drive to any mobile PC that lacks an internal floppy drive.

Troubleshooting PCMCIA interface problems

The PCMCIA represents an interface—not a particular card. As a consequence, PCMCIA troubleshooting is rather like solving problems with any other type of bus interface (SCSI, ISA, VL, and so on). The objective is not to repair a PC Card, but rather to isolate a functional problem to the card, the interface itself, or some portion of the system's configuration. When you determine a PC Card to be defective, your best course is to replace the card outright.

Symptom 1. The SRAM or flash card loses its memory when powered down or removed from the system Because flash cards make use of advanced EEPROMs you might wonder why batteries would be incorporated. Some flash cards use a small amount of SRAM to speed the transfer of data to or from the card. Batteries would be needed to back up the SRAM only. If your memory card does not appear to hold its memory, you should start your investigation by removing the memory card and testing its batteries. Make sure the card's batteries are inserted properly. Use your multimeter to check the battery voltage(s). Replace any memory card batteries that appear marginal or low. You should expect a two to five year backup life from your memory card batteries depending on the amount of card memory; more memory results in shorter battery life. All battery contacts should be clean and bright, and contacts should make firm connections with the battery terminals.

Try a known-good working memory card in your system. You can verify a new or known-good memory card on another computer with a compatible card slot. If another card works properly, your original memory card is probably defective and should be replaced. It is not recommended for you to open or attempt to troubleshoot a memory card without comprehensive experience in surface-mount device repair and high-quality surface-mount desoldering equipment.

Symptom 2. You are unable to access the card for reading. You might not be able to write to the card either Begin troubleshooting by checking memory card compatibility (programmed OTPROM cards and Mask ROM cards cannot be written to). If a memory card is not compatible with the interface used by your small-computer, the interface might not access the card. For example, a PCMCIA-compatible 68-pin card will probably not work in a 68-pin card slot that is not 100% PCMCIA compatible. Try a known-good compatible card in the suspect card slot. Also check your CONFIG.SYS or AUTOEXEC.BAT files to be sure that any required device drivers have been installed during system initialization. If you are having difficulty writing to an SRAM or flash card, take a moment and inspect the card's write protect switch. A switch left in the protected position prevents new information from being written to the card. Move the switch to the unprotected position and try the memory card again.

If you are having difficulty writing to EEPROM or Flash EEPROM cards, check your programming voltages (V_{pp1} and V_{pp2}). Without high-voltage pulses, new data cannot be written to such cards. Measure V_{pp1} and V_{pp2} with your oscilloscope with the card removed from your system (it might be necessary to ground the card detect lines (CD1 and CD2) to fool the host system into believing that a card is actually installed. You will probably have to disassemble your small computer housing to gain easy access to the motherboard's card connector. If one or both programming pulses are missing during a write operation, check your power supply output(s). When high-voltage supplies are missing, troubleshoot your computer's power supply. If programming voltage(s) are present, there might be a defect in the card controller IC or board, or any discrete switching circuitry designed to produce the programming pulses. Try replacing the card controller (or motherboard).

The memory card can be inserted incorrectly. Two card detect signals are needed from a PCMCIA-compatible card to ensure proper insertion. If the card is not inserted properly, the host system will inhibit all card activities. Remove the card and reinsert it completely. Make sure the card is straight, even, and fully inserted. Try accessing the card again.

If trouble remains, remove the card and inspect the connector on the card AND inside the computer. Check for any contacts that might be loose, bent, or broken. It might be necessary to disassemble the mobile computer in order to inspect its connector, but a clear view with a small flashlight will tell you all you need to know. Connections in the computer that are damaged or extremely worn should be replaced with a new connector assembly. When a memory card connector is worn or damaged, the memory card should be replaced.

If your results are still inconclusive, try a known-good memory card in the system. Keep in mind that the new card must be fully compatible with the original one. Make sure that there are no valuable or irreplaceable files on the known-good card before you try it in a suspect system. If a known-good card works properly, then the old memory card is probably damaged and should be replaced. If a known-good card also does not work, the original card is probably working properly. Your final step is to disassemble your small-computer and replace the memory card controller or motherboard. A defective controller can prevent all data and control signals from reaching the card.

Symptom 3. You see an error message indicating that a PCMCIA card will not install or is not recognized Chances are that one or more device drivers in the system are interfering with the offending PCMCIA card. Load your CONFIG.SYS file into an ordinary text editor and systematically edit out any other PCMCIA drivers. Try re-initializing the system after each change. Once you locate the offending driver, try reconfiguring the driver such that it will not interfere (maybe a new driver or patch is available).

Symptom 4. Even though a desired card is installed, an error message or warning is displayed asking you to insert the card The PCMCIA card might not be installed properly. Try removing the card, then re-insert it carefully. The card socket might not be enabled, so the application might not be able to see it. Make sure that the card socket is enabled. For most systems (such as the Canon NoteJet 486, which ships with the PCMCIA socket turned off), the solution is to get into the BIOS setup for the computer, and to enable the PCMCIA socket. Check the documentation for your system to find out how to get into the BIOS setup. Sometimes this feature is located in the advanced settings or in the power-management area of the BIOS settings. After you have changed the settings, save the changes and restart your system. In more advanced systems (such as the Compaq Concerto), you can turn the PCMCIA socket off and on with the computer's setup utility under Windows. After changing the settings, save the changes and restart your system.

Another possibility might be that the application program interacting with the PCMCIA slot is addressing the wrong interrupt line for insertion or removal. Check for any card socket diagnostics and determine which interrupt(s) the application is trying to use for Card Status Change. Check the device driver for the card and add an explicit command line switch to specify the desired interrupt. If an interrupt is already specified, make sure that this is the correct one.

Symptom 5. You encounter a number of card service errors or other problems when antivirus programs are used Such errors include "Card Services Allocation Error," "Error: configuration file not found," "Error: Could Not Open Configuration File," or "Error using Card Services." Under some circumstances, an antivirus program can interfere with PCMCIA card services. The Norton antivirus program NAV&.SYS is known to cause this sort of problem if it is loaded before the card services software. There are typically three ways around this type of problem. First, rearrange the order of drivers called in your CONFIG.SYS file so that NAV&.SYS comes after the card services software. Second, use NAV_.SYS instead of NAV&.SYS. Although NAV_.SYS requires more space than NAV&.SYS, but it is better at co-existing with other memory-resident programs. Third, remove NAV&.SYS and use NAVTSR instead. If you are using antivirus programs, try remarking them out of CONFIG.SYS or AUTOEXEC.BAT.

Symptom 6. There are no pop-up displays when a PC Card is inserted or removed Normally, when a card is installed or removed, a dialog box will appear indicating the card that has been inserted or removed. However, there are three reasons why this might happen. First, the DOS pop-up function is disabled under DOS (but still works under Windows). Check the card services software and make sure that the proper command line switches are set to enable the DOS pop-up. Second, there might be an *UMA* (upper memory area) conflict. Many card managers require 10K or more of UMA. If there is no free UMA, the card manager cannot read the card's attribute memory to install the card. Make sure that there is plenty of UMA space available for the card services software, and check that it loads properly. Third, the PCMCIA card might not be supported by the card services software; the two might not be fully compatible. Try a different card, or update the card services software.

Symptom 7. The application locks up when a PC Card is inserted or removed Not all applications are fully PCMCIA-aware; that is, they do not recognize card insertion and removal properly. If your application crashes or locks up when a card is inserted or removed, chances are that the application is not written to handle hot insertion or removal with the card services software being used. Try inserting the card before starting the application, or close the application before removing it.

43
CHAPTER

Pen systems

The most remarkable difference between a pen-based computer and other mobile computers is the method of input. Where laptop, notebook, and palmtop computers utilize keyboards or mice as their primary input devices, pen-computers (Fig. 43-1) use a hand-held *stylus* to write against a sensitive surface. Many pen computers (especially the larger, more powerful models) do offer support for an external keyboard, but the pen is intended to supply the primary input. However, the differences go beyond hardware. The operating system (OS) used with pen computers provides the software routines that allow applications to interact with the pen and display, and to interpret the various pen gestures available for selecting or modifying desired items on the display. The two popular operating systems in use today are *Windows for Pen Computing* (also called *PenWindows*) by Microsoft, and *PenPoint* by GO Corporation. This chapter is intended to explain the essential principles of pen input, and present a series of service procedures that can be used to correct pen problems.

43-1.
A pen computer from GRID Systems.
Copyright © 1995 Logitech, Inc.

Understanding pen digitizers

The key to any pen computer is the pen system itself, which is referred to as the *digitizer*. A digitizer converts the analog position of a pen on the display into a set of horizontal (X) and vertical (Y) coordinate data. The operating system interprets those coordinates and will either activate pixels on the display that echo the pen's position (called the *ink*), or respond to a *gesture* according to the rules of an operating system. To interpret cursive (handwritten) characters or gestures drawn with a stylus, the operating system compares the size, direction, and sequence of each stroke against information contained in a database. When a match occurs, the computer responds accordingly. For instance, the pen computer might interpret a cross-out pen motion as a delete command, or as an upper- or lowercase x. This chapter covers three major digitizer technologies: resistive, capacitive, and electromagnetic.

Resistive digitizers

Resistive digitizers are the simplest and least expensive type of digitizer. They are applied in most low-end pen-computer systems. You might encounter two varieties of resistive digitizer: single-layer digitizers and double-layer digitizers. The diagram for a single-layer resistive digitizer is shown in Fig. 43-2. A layer of conductive transparent film is applied over a protective glass cover. The film and glass are then mounted in position over a liquid crystal display module. Notice how the film's four corners are attached to voltage sources switched by the overlay controller IC. In the idle state, all four corners of the film are held at +5 Vdc (low-voltage systems can use +3.0 or +3.3 Vdc).

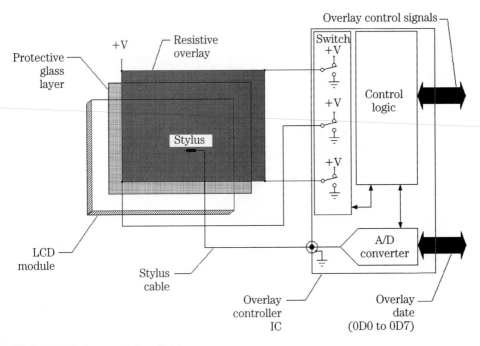

43-2 A single-layer resistive digitizer.

X and Y coordinates are read in sequence. The overlay controller IC sets up to measure the Y coordinate by switching controls B and C to the ground position. This configuration keeps the top two corners of the conductive overlay at +V, and places the two lower corners at ground. Because the overlay film has a known resistance (per square area), linear voltage gradients are set up from top to bottom. When a stylus is applied against the conductive overlay, the stylus cable carries a voltage to an analog-to-digital (A/D) converter. As the stylus nears the overlay top, its terminal voltage nears +V. As the stylus nears the overlay bottom, its terminal voltage approaches 0 V (ground). The A/D converter translates the analog stylus voltage into an 8-, 12-, or 16-bit data word. An 8-bit A/D converter allows the overlay to resolve 256 (2^8) distinct positions in the vertical (Y) direction, and a 12-bit A/D converter lets the overlay resolve 4096 (2^{12}) Y locations. As you might see, more bits used in a conversion allow the computer to resolve finer pen positions.

Once the Y coordinate is generated, the overlay controller sets up to measure the horizontal (X) coordinate by switching control C to +V and switching controls A and B to ground. This configuration raises the two left corners of the conductive overlay to +V, and places the two right corners at 0 V (ground). Linear voltage gradients then develop from left to right. Assuming the stylus has not been moved since the Y coordinate was just taken, its output voltage now represents the X location. As the stylus nears the left of the overlay, its output voltage to the A/D converter approaches +V. As the stylus nears the right side of the overlay, its voltage nears 0 V.

Double-layer resistive digitizers are a bit more involved as shown in Fig. 43-3. The upper conductive layer and controller IC are virtually identical to the compo-

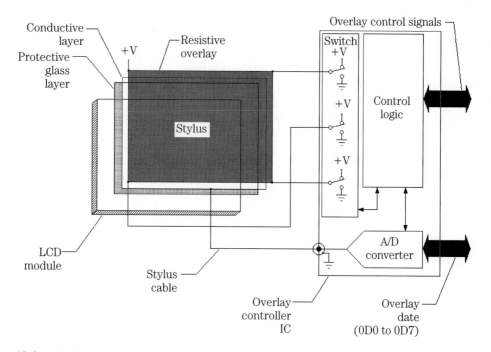

43-3 A dual-layer resistive digitizer.

nents shown already, but the transparent conductive film is laminated to a substrate of clear, flexible polyester. The lower conductive layer is highly conductive—virtually zero resistance. The lower layer is bonded to a sheet of protective glass. Upper and lower conductive layers are separated by a series of carefully placed flexible spacers. When a stylus pushes the two layers into contact, it is the lower conductive layer (not the stylus) that conducts the analog position voltage to the A/D converter. Because no cabled stylus is needed, almost any pointing device will suffice. You could even use your finger as the stylus. The basic methodology of determining X and Y coordinates is very much the same for two-layer digitizers as for single-layer digitizers.

Resistive digitizers are not without their drawbacks. First, the glass and conductive film(s) placed over the LCD take away from the display's visibility. A single-layer digitizer can reduce optical transmission by 15%. Two layers can reduce a display's optical transmission by 30% or more. Such substantial reductions in visibility can make LCDs unacceptably dark. Additional backlighting can be used to counter the optical reduction, but only at the cost of shorter battery life or heavier systems. Also, resistive digitizers only measure position, not contact pressure. Intuitive pen-based systems should ideally leave darker ink when the stylus is under strong pressure, and should leave lighter ink when a light touch is used. Because a resistive digitizer simply makes contact (or not), there is little interest in resistive digitizers for *pen-cnn tric* (character recognition-oriented) pen systems. Finally, resistive material tends to drift with temperature, humidity, and wear. Drift can cause inaccuracies that carry over into the digitizer's output.

Capacitive digitizers

A *capacitive digitizer* (also called an *electrostatic digitizer*) uses a single protective layer of glass with a layer of conductive film bonded underneath as shown in Fig. 43-4. The digitizer controller IC generates a low-power, high-frequency signal that is conducted down the tether wire to the stylus tip. As the stylus nears the glass, the conductive layer bonded underneath the glass picks up this signal and generates a voltage at that point. This overlay voltage is proportional to stylus proximity. The closer the stylus is to the glass, the larger the signal will be on the conductive layer, and vice versa. By comparing signal amplitudes from top to bottom and left to right, the digitizer controller IC can extrapolate the stylus' X and Y coordinates, as well as its proximity to the glass. Because the pattern of capacitive coupling changes as stylus orientation changes, the digitizer controller IC also can detect stylus tilt and accent the ink feedback to show that tilt.

Capacitive digitizers are an improvement over resistive digitizers because the capacitive approach allows the pen computer to sense pen proximity as well as X and Y position. The front glass used in capacitive digitizers makes the overlay virtually immune to wear. On the down side, the overlay must be positioned in front of the LCD that can reduce the display's visible output by up to 15%. The stylus also must be cabled to the system by a wire.

Electromagnetic digitizers

An electromagnetic digitizer (or *RF digitizer*) is generally considered to be the top-of-the-line digitizer technique for pen computers. A thin glass sheet is placed over the top of a standard LCD and backlight assembly as shown in Fig. 43-5. The

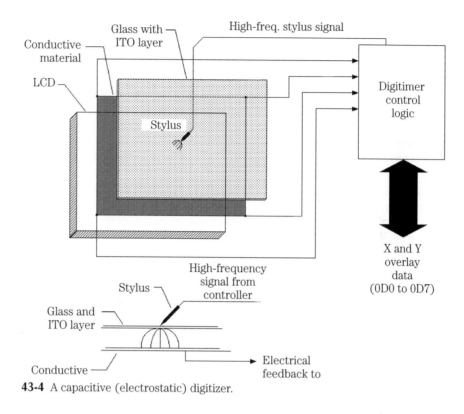

43-4 A capacitive (electrostatic) digitizer.

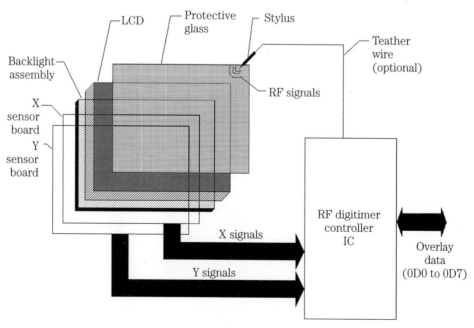

43-5 An electromagnetic (RF) digitizer.

glass provides a wear-resistant writing surface for a stylus. Glass also is treated with an antireflective coating on its bottom surface (LCD-side), and the upper surface is gently etched with mild acid to provide paper-like friction for writing utensils. An RF stylus is designed to produce a very low-power, high-frequency RF signal. The transmitter circuit can be entirely self-contained in a free stylus, or contained in the computer and wired to the stylus through a tether cable (depending on the designer's particular preference). The PenMan RF digitizer manufactured by Logitech Incorporated is an OEM product intended for use in new, high-end pen-computer designs.

The central element in an RF digitizer is the sensor PC board. Signals generated by the stylus must be detected and converted to X and Y coordinates. The stylus transmitter itself is usually powered by one or more batteries, but the very low transmission power allows hundreds of operating hours. Sensor PC boards are five-layer boards fabricated as multilayer PC boards. Four board layers are dedicated to signal detection, and one layer serves as the ground plane. A ground plane is needed to prevent stylus signals from causing interference with motherboard circuitry.

Each board layer is etched with sensing coils—two layers sense in the X direction, and two layers sense in the Y orientation. The actual patterns and physical layout of these copper trace loops are patented because they define the performance characteristics of the digitizer module. Whenever pen transmissions are detected, the digitizer is activated, and it scans across the active digitizing area to determine pen position. The stylus also transmits serial pulses that indicate its switch positions and battery level(s). The 3D sensing structure developed in an RF digitizer also can detect pen proximity and tilt (usually up to 45° from perpendicular).

Sensor PC boards must be mounted within 13 mm (0.5 inch) below the writing surface. Because the digitizer PC board is the last part of the display section (below the LCD and backlight), you can count on a very dense, precise assembly. It is critically important that you exercise caution when disassembling and reassembling the digitizer. Be certain to maintain all mounting positions and clearances. Erroneous reassembly can easily upset the digitizer's operation. The digitizer can detect the pen transmitter up to 25 mm (1.0 inch) above the writing surface.

Electromagnetic shielding and the placement of metals also are important concerns in RF digitizer systems. Make sure to replace any and all ground planes or shields before testing a reassembled digitizer. Not only is it necessary to replace shields around and behind the digitizer, it is not allowed to add any metal within the digitizer assembly. Metals between the writing surface and sensor PC board will interfere with the pen signal and cause erroneous operation. Even the step-up transformer used in a CCFT backlight power supply must be shielded to prevent unwanted electromagnetic signals from causing faulty operation. Now that you have a basic understanding of the major pen digitizer techniques, you should learn a few details about stylus/panel interaction.

A pen environment

The pen environment is almost entirely software dependent. It is the computer's operating system that provides the driver programs and routines for writing and working with the pen. Experienced Windows or PenPoint programmers also can write application programs that recognize and utilize the pen. Of course, a pen computer will usually run software that does not use the pen. Such programs are known as pen-oblivious applications. To make the program useful, however, input will have to be provided from elsewhere (such as an external keyboard or mouse). The next level of software is capable of checking for and using a pen if one is available, but will run with external input if a pen is not available—much the same way that many DOS programs check for the presence of a mouse and use it if available. These programs are pen enhanced. The highest level of pen software supports all pen functions and gestures, as well as the capture and recognition of written input. Such pen dependent applications are called *pen-centric programs.*

Just how a pen's movements are interpreted depend on how the program divides the screen graphically. For example, handwriting can only be entered into certain, predefined areas of the display, and gestures can only be interpreted outside of those handwriting areas—how else would the computer be able to tell the difference between the two? To understand why this is important, you should see a bit more about the two major pen input modes: gestures and glyphs.

Gestures

For anyone who has never worked with pen computers before, the change from keyboards to pens requires somewhat of a mental jump. Instead of interacting with the computer by entering text or individual keystrokes, or using a mouse to click and drag items around the screen, pen systems rely on a series of movements (called *gestures*). A gesture is a type of motion, or sequence of subsequent motions, that the computer's operating system recognizes and uses. Gestures can be used for two general purposes: editing and navigation. Editing gestures affect information. For example, an X motion made through a word can delete that word, and drawing a line under a word or sentence can select the text for character enhancement (i.e. italic, bold, and so on). Navigation gestures are used primarily to interact with the pen operating system. As an example, tapping on a menu choice might cause a new option bar to be displayed, but tapping and holding a screen item can allow you to move an item around the screen—rather like the click and drag of a mouse or trackball. Figure 43-6 shows the suite of pen gestures for both PenWindows and PenPoint.

The variations in gestures between operating systems might prove to be a source of some confusion, so you should always make it a point to be aware of your computer's operating system before beginning a repair. Remember, just because a gesture does not work does NOT indicate a fault in the computer—you might be performing the gesture incorrectly. Even though pen computers and their operating systems strive to be intuitive, there are definite limits to their tolerance in accepting gestures.

Glyphs

The process of acquiring a handwritten image, translating the image into individual characters or commands, and sending the translated image to an actual application program (such as a word processor) is an unbelievably involved and complex software process that is well beyond the scope of this book. However, you should have some understanding of the basic steps involved. The algorithms used to evaluate handwritten input are improving constantly.

	Pen Windows			PenPoint
•	Choose insertion point.		•	Tap or select.
—	Select characters.		◉	Press and hold.
↑↓	Extends selection.		•◉	Tap and hold.
ℐ	Deletes current selection.		|	Flick (four direction).
⇌	Deletes words or objects.		✕	Cross out.
↘	Backspace/delete.		＝	Scratch out.
⌐	Insert space.		○	Circle.
⌐↑	Insert line.		✓	Check.
⌐	Insert tab.		∧	Caret.
✓	Places checked word in dialog box.		[ ]	Brackets.
⫽	Cuts selection and places it on clipboard.		ℐ	Pigtail.
∝	Copies selection and places it on clipboard.		L	Down-right.
∧	Pastes contents on clipboard.			
୪	Reverses previous action.			

43-6 Comparison of typical pen gestures.

The first step is to provide a known, rectangular area of the display where handwriting can be entered. In the PenWindows environment, this is usually accomplished by opening a small working window. Whenever pen contact is registered within the handwriting window, the master pen device driver software tracks the pen's motion. As it tracks, the device driver calls a display driver program that echos the pen's path; this is the "ink" that you see on the display. The pen driver then stores the X and Y coordinates at the beginning and end of each pen stroke. Every alphanumeric character is composed of one or more unique strokes.

A recognition program organizes each set of strokes into an item called a *glyph*. Glyphs are then matched against a set of prototype glyphs, and every possible corresponding character for a glyph is recorded as a symbol graph. The symbol graph is passed along to another program that adds extra information about the glyph (i.e., text in a word processor, numbers in a spread sheet, and so on) and a customized dictionary evaluates the enhanced symbol graph and determines the likeliest translation that is finally passed to the actual application program utilizing the handwriting feature. The processing overhead required to handle handwriting recognition is quite demanding, so it is not yet possible to recognize written characters in real-time; there will be delays between the writing and the result. This discussion is certainly not comprehensive, but perhaps you will have an appreciation for pen software, and how important it is for hardware and software to work together.

Troubleshooting pen systems

The great advantage to pen systems is modularity. There are really only four components in a digitizer: the overlay, the stylus, the overlay controller, and the bus interface ASIC. When trouble occurs in the pen system, your problem is almost always located in at least one of these four operating areas. For resistive digitizers, most of the wear and tear in a pen digitizer takes place in the stylus and overlay, so you will probably find that most problems occur there. Other digitizer technologies, however, have virtually no wear between the pen and glass writing surface. Typical problems with electrostatic and RF digitizers involve the stylus and its cable (if a cable is used). The following symptoms will give you some additional insight.

Symptom 1. The stylus seems to operate intermittently as it moves along the overlay When you slide a stylus across the overlay, some portions of the stroke might not be visible as ink feedback on the LCD. In other cases, entire strokes might be missing while other strokes are fully visible. Fortunately, the ink that does appear shows up in the right places. This problem can be maddening, especially when attempting to write cursive characters. Resistive digitizers are extremely sensitive to stylus contact. Be certain to hold the stylus gently but firmly in contact. A careless touch might allow bad contact between the overlay and stylus.

Such a symptom is almost always the result of a faulty stylus cable. Remove your stylus from its input jack, open the stylus body and jack (if possible), and use your multimeter to check the continuity along each cable wire. Once your multimeter is connected, wiggle the cable to stimulate any intermittent wiring. If your stylus cable is hard wired into the computer, you should remove the pen computer's outer housing to expose the cable wiring. Should you encounter a faulty stylus, repair or replace the defective wiring, or replace the stylus altogether.

If your stylus checks out properly (or is not cabled to begin with), suspect a fault with your resistive overlay. Both single-layer and double-layer resistive digitizers are extremely prone to wear. As the stylus wears out, overlay resistance and surface features might become irregular. Your stylus might not make proper contact at all points of a worn surface. Try replacing the resistive overlay. Some small-computer manufacturers sell overlay assemblies as component parts. Use *extreme* caution when replacing an overlay to avoid accidental damage to the LCD or backlight assemblies. Take careful notes and pay close attention to maintain proper assembly dimensions.

For RF digitizers such as Logitech's PenMan, the multilayer PC board is very rarely at fault because writing takes place against a sheet of thin, tempered glass. Intermittent writing performance with an RF digitizer is usually the result of a faulty stylus transmitter. Check or replace the stylus batteries and try the system again. If the problem persists, try a new stylus.

Symptom 2. The stylus or overlay does not appear to respond at all. Other pen-computer functions seem normal The external keyboard adapter (if available) appears to work properly. Before you check anything else, make sure that the stylus is properly plugged into the pen computer. Also make sure that the stylus tip is in good contact with the overlay. Good contact is critical for resistive digitizers. A careless touch might allow bad contact between an overlay and stylus—especially when the overlay is worn. For RF digitizers, you should suspect the stylus transmitter first. Check the batteries or cabling to your stylus. Replace the batteries if necessary and try the system again. Otherwise, try a new stylus.

An open stylus wire can easily disable your pen input. Remove your stylus from its input jack, open the stylus body and jack (if possible), and use your multimeter to measure continuity along each cable wire. Once your multimeter is connected, wiggle the cable to stimulate any possible intermittent wiring. Repair or replace any faulty wiring, or replace the defective stylus outright. If your stylus cable is hard wired into the computer, you should remove the pen-computer's housing to expose the cable wires.

If the digitizer still does not function, you should suspect your overlay or overlay controller IC. Disassemble your pen computer to expose the motherboard, and check any cabling between the overlay and motherboard. Try replacing the overlay controller IC. If you lack the tools or inclination to perform surface-mount work, try replacing the entire motherboard. If the problem persists, try another overlay assembly.

Symptom 3. Ink appears on the LCD as the stylus moves, but ink is not exactly under the stylus This symptom is much more of a nuisance than an actual defect in resistive digitizers. You might assume that the stylus is working adequately. The trouble is most likely in the resistive overlay material itself. Resistance is a characteristic that is extremely dependent on temperature and humidity. Variations in an overlay's temperature or humidity can introduce small analog voltage errors when a stylus passes over the resistive surface. The net result is a small shift in the visual feedback that appears on the LCD.

There is little you can do with temperature or humidity problems except to keep the pen computer in a stable, consistent room environment. If the overlay is damp for any reason, be certain to dry its surface *very* carefully.

Problems also can occur when the overlay is extremely worn. As resistive material becomes thinner, its resistance at the thinner areas becomes greater. Worn areas can upset the overall resistance of the overlay and result in erroneous voltage signals at the stylus. Again, such errors are digitized and appear somewhere in the display. Your best course of action with a worn resistive overlay is simply to replace it entirely. Use *extreme* caution when replacing an overlay to avoid accidental damage to the LCD or backlight, and to maintain all dimensional tolerances in the assembly.

Symptom 4. The pen computer locks up or suffers other strange problems once the RF digitizer has been repaired or replaced This kind of a follow-up problem is not unusual for pen computers using RF digitizers. The RF sensor PC board located behind the backlight must be re-installed *exactly* as it was removed. No metal objects can be added or removed. Make sure that any and all shielding is installed properly. Missing or damaged shields can allow stray RF signals to reach the motherboard and cause peculiar EMI problems that result in system crashes and intermittent bad data. It only takes one bad bit to crash a computer. Also inspect the way in which the display and digitizer arrangement has been reassembled. Missing spacers or loose screws can change the physical spacing of the display components and also result in system problems.

It is important that no metal objects be added to the display/digitizer assembly as well. Metal acts as a shield that can interfere with RF signals. The presence of unwanted metal might cause trouble in pen tracking and system operation. Remove any metal that might have been added to the system or digitizer. As a general rule, it is worthwhile to keep thorough notes when working on a display/digitizer system. Notes help to ensure that you reassemble the small-computer exactly as it should be.

Symptom 5. As you write, no "ink" appears on the display, but the characters are recognized and translated properly This is almost invariably a problem with the Windows video driver. When the pen operating system is installed—especially as an extension such as *Microsoft Pen Extensions for Windows*—the video driver will be required to produce the "ink". Unfortunately, not all video drivers interact so smoothly with pen-enhanced or pen-centric applications, and an "ink" trail is not left under the pen. Although hardly damaging, it can be a significant nuisance. Try a video driver designed to deal with pen operations. In actual practice, this might be difficult because many pen-compatible video drivers do not provide extended color depths or resolutions that many Windows users have come to expect.

Symptom 6. The DOS device driver(s) will not load as the system initializes This is typical of external, stand-alone tablets, and is often indicated by an error code or message when the PC initializes. First, make sure that the tablet is turned on (if necessary) and receiving power. Next, check that the tablet is connected properly to its serial port, and that the COM number and IRQ number correspond to any command line settings used to execute the driver. For example, suppose the tablet driver is being started in your CONFIG.SYS file and its command line says that the driver should be installed for COM1 using IRQ3. If the tablet is plugged into COM2, the driver will probably not be able to load.

Symptom 7. The stylus buttons do not work correctly in your software Button assignments for a stand-alone pen tablet are typically made in the tablet device driver's command line (in CONFIG.SYS or AUTOEXEC.BAT). Check the command line against your pen tablet's documentation and make sure that any button assignments are correct. Check your particular application as well to see if there are any options that control button functions. If your application allows you to select a pointing device, you can usually keep the *Microsoft Mouse* selection.

Symptom 8. The pen tablet does not work in Windows This problem often surfaces with stand-alone pen tablets. If the tablet works with DOS applications (or its diagnostic), the problem is likely due to a Windows driver conflict. Check the device driver used in Windows Setup and make sure that the appropriate driver is selected to support the tablet. Many tablets give you the option of using the tablet as the sole pointing device, or using both the tablet and mouse together. The driver used with the tablet will depend on whether the tablet is used alone or with a mouse.

Symptom 9. Windows locks up or the tablet fails to respond This type of problem might show up intermittently and is generally related to the cursor speed that is set through the Windows control panel. When the tablet is set to work in relative mode and the cursor speed is set to fast, older PCs might not be able to respond to button clicks or pen movement fast enough under some circumstances. This condition almost always results in a fault that can crash Windows or its application. The easiest way to correct this type of problem is to reduce the cursor sensitivity to a low level (50% or so) when working in the relative mode. Most pen tablets designed to work with Windows provide a Windows utility that allows you to adjust the tablet parameters.

Symptom 10. The cursor is too sensitive or not sensitive enough to pen movement When operating a stand-alone tablet in the "relative" mode, you might need to reduce the cursor sensitivity parameter. When working in the absolute mode, you can adjust sensitivity by altering the size of the cursor's active area. Most stand-alone pen tablets designed to work in Windows provide a Windows adjustment utility that allows you to adjust the tablet parameters such as sensitivity and active area.

Symptom 11. The cursor seems to jitter or leave spikes when drawing

This type of problem is usually related to the serial port being used with the stand-alone pen tablet. Older serial ports using the 8250 or 8250A UARTs have a subtle bug that the Windows environment tends to find. The older serial port does not support current tablets as well as current serial ports. Running Windows in the standard mode can sometimes improve the situation, but the very best solution is to replace the older UART (or entire serial port) with a current version.

44
CHAPTER

POST diagnostic codes

IBM has taken an unusually thorough approach to diagnosing and reporting system errors. IBM has developed an *Advanced Diagnostics* program that can be purchased directly from IBM (but is available on many PS/2 reference disks). When the diagnostic is run, it will test and report on every possible subsystem—new or old—that might be in the PC. Unfortunately, IBM has never really done a very good job of documenting their vast array of codes. This chapter is intended as a source of reference to assist you in interpreting these codes, and to help you select some repair alternatives.

Reading the codes

Diagnostic codes are split into two sections: the test code, and the fault code. The test code is simply the number that corresponds to the particular test being run. The fault code is a two-digit decimal number that corresponds to the specific type of error that is identified. A fault code of 00 indicates that no problem was found. For example, the message 100 means that the motherboard was tested (01), and that no errors were detected (00), thus 0100, or just 100. If a fault code appears other than 00, a problem has been detected that a technician will have to address. System initialization might or might not continue depending on the location and severity of the error. Table 44-1 provides a relatively comprehensive list of diagnostic codes for XT, AT, PS/2 systems.

Table 44-1. IBM Diagnostic codes

SYSTEM BOARD (01xx)

101	Interrupt failure (unexpected interrupt)
102	BIOS ROM checksum error (PC, XT); timer error (AT, MCA)
103	BASIC ROM checksum error (PC, XT); timer interrupt error (AT, MCA)
104	Interrupt controller error (PC, XT); protected mode error (AT, MCA)
105	Timer failure (PC, XT); keyboard controller failure (MCA)
106	System board converting logic test failure
107	System board adapter card or math coprocessor fault; Hot NMI test failed (MCA)

Table 44-1. Continued

SYSTEM BOARD (01xx)

108	System board timer bus failure
109	DMA test memory select failure
110	PS/2 system board memory problem (ISA); system board parity check error (MCA)
111	PS/2 adapter memory problem (ISA); memory adapter parity check error (MCA)
112	PS/2 watchdog time-out error
113	PS/2 DMA arbitration time-out error
114	PS/2 external ROM checksum error
115	Cache parity error, BIOS ROM checksum error, or DMA error.
116	System board port R/W error
118	System board L2 cache error
119	2.88MB floppy drive installed but not supported by floppy disk controller.
120	CPU self-test error
121	Unexpected hardware interrupt occurred
131	Cassette wrap test (PC)
132	DMA extended registers error
133	DMA verify logic error
134	DMA arbitration logic error
151	Battery, real-time clock, or CMOS RAM failure
152	Real-time clock or CMOS RAM failure
160	PS/2 system board ID not recognized
161	CMOS chip lost power - battery dead
162	CMOS checksum or CRC error
163	CMOS error - time & date not set (the clock not updating)
164	Memory size error - CMOS data does not match system memory found
165	PS/2 adapter ID mismatch
166	PS/2 adapter time-out card busy
167	PS/2 system clock not updating
168	Math co-processor error in the CMOS configuration
169	System board and processor card configuration mismatch
170	ASCII setup conflict error
171	Rolling bit test failure on CMOS shutdown byte
172	Rolling bit test failure on NVRAM diagnostic byte
173	Bad CMOS/NVRAM checksum
174	Bad system configuration
175	Bad EEPROM CRC
177	Bad password CRC
178	Bad EEPROM
179	NVRAM error log full
180X	Sub address data error in slot
181	Unsupported configuration
182	Password switch is not in the writing position
183	System halted - password required
184	Bad power-on password
185	Bad startup sequence
186	Password protection hardware error

Table 44-1. Continued

SYSTEM BOARD (01xx)

187	Serial number error
188	Bad EEPROM checksum
189	Too many incorrect password attempts
191	Cache controller test failure (82385)
194	System board memory error
199	User-indicated device list not correct

SYSTEM MEMORY (02xx)

201	Memory error (physical location will likely be displayed)
202	Memory address line 0-15 error
203	Memory address line 16-23 error; line 16-31 error (MCA)
204	Memory remapped to compensate for error (PS/2)
205	Error in first 128K (PS/2 ISA) of RAM
207	BIOS ROM failure
210	System board memory parity error
211	Error in first 64K of RAM (MCA)
212	Watchdog timer error
213	DMA bus arbitration time-out
215	Memory address error; 64K on daughter/SIP 2 failed (70)
216	Memory address error; 64K on daughter/SIP 1 failed (70)
221	ROM to RAM copy (shadowing) failed (MCA)
225	Wrong speed memory on system board (MCA)
230	Memory on motherboard and adapter board overlaps
231	Noncontiguous adapter memory installed
235	Stuck data line on memory module
241	Memory module 2 failed
251	Memory module 3 failed

KEYBOARD (03xx)

301	Keyboard did not respond correctly (stuck key detected)
302	Keyboard locked (AT, models 25, 30)
303	Keyboard/system board interface error - keyboard controller fault
304	Keyboard or system unit error (keyboard clock stuck high)
305	Keyboard fuse failed on system board (PS/2 50, 60, 80) or +5V error (PS/2 70)
306	Unsupported keyboard attached
341	Keyboard error
342	Keyboard cable error
343	Enhancement card or cable error
365	Keyboard failure
366	Interface cable failure
367	Enhancement card or cable failure

MONOCHROME DISPLAY ADAPTER (04xx)

401	Memory, horizontal sync frequency, or vertical sync test failure
408	User-indicated display attribute failure
416	User-indicated character set failure
424	User-indicated 80 × 25 mode failure
432	MDA card parallel port test failure

Table 44-1. Continued

COLOR GRAPHICS ADAPTER (05xx)

501	Memory, horizontal sync frequency, or vertical sync test failure
503	CGA adapter controller failure
508	User-indicated display attribute failure
516	User-indicated character set failure
524	User-indicated 80 × 25 mode failure
532	User-indicated 40 × 25 mode failure
540	User-indicated 320 × 200 graphics mode failure
548	User-indicated 640 × 200 graphics mode failure
556	Light pen test failed
564	User-indicated screen paging test failed

FLOPPY DRIVES AND ADAPTERS (06xx)

601	General diskette or adapter test failure
602	Diskette boot sector is not valid
603	Diskette size error
604	Media sense error
605	Diskette drive locked
606	Diskette verify test failure
607	Write protect error
608	Drive command error
610	Diskette initialization failure
611	Drive time-out error
612	NEC drive controller IC error
613	Floppy system DMA error
614	Floppy system DMA boundary overrun error
615	Drive index timing error
616	Drive speed error
621	Drive seek error
622	Drive CRC error
623	Sector not found error
624	Disk address mark error
625	NEC drive controller IC seek error
626	Diskette data compare error
627	Diskette change line error
628	Diskette removed from drive
630	Drive A: index stuck high
631	Drive A: index stuck low
632	Drive A: track 0 stuck off
633	Drive A: track 0 stuck on
640	Drive B: index stuck high
641	Drive B: index stuck low
642	Drive B: track 0 stuck off
643	Drive B: track 0 stuck on
645	No index pulse
646	Drive track 00 detection failed
647	No transitions on Read Data line

Table 44-1. Continued

FLOPPY DRIVES AND ADAPTERS (06xx)

648	Format test failed
649	Incorrect media type in drive
650	Drive speed incorrect
651	Format failure
652	Verify failure
653	Read failure
654	Write failure
655	Drive controller error
656	Drive mechanism failure
657	Write protect stuck in "protected" state
658	Change line stuck in "changed" state
659	Write protect stuck in "unprotected" state
660	Change line stuck in "unchanged" state

MATH CO-PROCESSOR (07xx)

701	MCP presence or initialization error
702	Exception errors test failure
703	Rounding test failure
704	Arithmetic test 1 failure
705	Arithmetic test 2 failure
706	Arithmetic test 3 (80387 only)
707	Combination test failure
708	Integer load/store test failure
709	Equivalent expressions errors
710	Exception (interrupt) errors
711	Save state errors
712	Protected mode test failure
713	Voltage/temperature sensitivity test failure

PARALLEL PRINTER ADAPTER (09xx)

901	Data register latch error
902	Control register latch error
903	Register address decode error
904	Address decode error
910	Status line wrap connector error
911	Status line bit 8 wrap error
912	Status line bit 7 wrap error
913	Status line bit 6 wrap error
914	Status line bit 5 wrap error
915	Status line bit 4 wrap error
916	Printer adapter interrupt wrap error
917	Unexpected printer adapter interrupt
92x	Feature register error

ALTERNATE PRINTER ADAPTER (10xx)

1001	Data register latch error
1002	Control register latch error
1003	Register address decode error

Table 44-1. Continued

ALTERNATE PRINTER ADAPTER (10xx)

1004	Address decode error
1010	Status line wrap connector error
1011	Status line bit 8 wrap error
1012	Status line bit 7 wrap error
1013	Status line bit 6 wrap error
1014	Status line bit 5 wrap error
1015	Status line bit 4 wrap error
1016	Printer adapter interrupt wrap error
1017	Unexpected printer adapter interrupt
102x	Feature register error

COMMUNICATION DEVICES (11xx)

1101	16450/16550 UART error
1102	Card-selected feedback error
1103	Port 102h register test failure
1106	Serial option cannot be shut down
1107	Communications cable or system board error
1108	IRQ 3 error
1109	IRQ 4 error
1110	16450/16550 chip register failure
1111	UART control line internal wrap test failure
1112	UART control line external wrap test failure
1113	UART transmit error
1114	UART receive error
1115	UART transmit & receive data unequal - receive error
1116	UART interrupt function error
1117	UART baud rate test failure
1118	UART interrupt-driven receive external data wrap test error
1119	UART FIFO buffer failure
1120	UART interrupt enable register failure: all bits cannot be set
1121	UART interrupt enable register failure: all bits cannot be reset
1122	Interrupt pending - stuck on
1123	Interrupt ID register - stuck on
1124	Modem control register failure: all bits cannot be set
1125	Modem control register failure: all bits cannot be reset
1126	Modem status register failure: all bits cannot be set
1127	Modem status register failure: all bits cannot be reset
1128	Interrupt ID error
1129	Cannot force overrun error
1130	No modem status interrupt
1131	Invalid interrupt pending
1132	No data ready
1133	No data available at interrupt
1134	No transmit holding at interrupt
1135	No interrupts
1136	No received line status interrupt

Table 44-1. Continued

COMMUNICATION DEVICES (11xx)

1137	No receive data available
1138	Transmit holding register not empty
1139	No modem status interrupt
1140	Transmit holding register not empty
1141	No interrupts
1142	No IRQ4 interrupt
1143	No IRQ3 interrupt
1144	No data transferred
1145	Maximum baud rate error
1146	Minimum baud rate error
1148	Time-out error
1149	Invalid data returned
1150	Modem status register error
1151	No DSR and delta DSR
1152	No DSR
1153	No delta DSR
1154	Modem status register not clear
1155	No CTS and delta CTS
1156	No CTS
1157	No delta CTS

ALTERNATE COMMUNICATIONS DEVICES (12xx)

1201	16450/16550 UART error
1202	Card-selected feedback error
1203	Port 102h register test failure
1206	Serial option cannot be shut down
1207	Communications cable or system board error
1208	IRQ 3 error
1209	IRQ 4 error
1210	16450/16550 chip register failure
1211	UART control line internal wrap test failure
1212	UART control line external wrap test failure
1213	UART transmit error
1214	UART receive error
1215	UART transmit & receive data unequal - receive error
1216	UART interrupt function error
1217	UART baud rate test failure
1218	UART interrupt-driven receive external data wrap test error
1219	UART FIFO buffer failure
1220	UART interrupt enable register failure: all bits cannot be set
1221	UART interrupt enable register failure: all bits cannot be reset
1222	Interrupt pending - stuck on
1223	Interrupt ID register - stuck on
1224	Modem control register failure: all bits cannot be set
1225	Modem control register failure: all bits cannot be reset
1226	Modem status register failure: all bits cannot be set

Table 44-1. Continued

ALTERNATE COMMUNICATIONS DEVICES (12xx)

1227	Modem status register failure: all bits cannot be reset
1228	Interrupt ID error
1229	Cannot force overrun error
1230	No modem status interrupt
1231	Invalid interrupt pending
1232	No data ready
1233	No data available at interrupt
1234	No transmit holding at interrupt
1235	No interrupts
1236	No received line status interrupt
1237	No receive data available
1238	Transmit holding register not empty
1239	No modem status interrupt
1240	Transmit holding register not empty
1241	No interrupts
1242	No IRQ4 interrupt
1243	No IRQ3 interrupt
1244	No data transferred
1245	Maximum baud rate error
1246	Minimum baud rate error
1248	Time-out error
1249	Invalid data returned
1250	Modem status register error
1251	No DSR and delta DSR
1252	No DSR
1253	No delta DSR
1254	Modem status register not clear
1255	No CTS and delta CTS
1256	No CTS
1257	No delta CTS

GAME PORT ADAPTERS (13xx)

1301	Game port adapter test failure
1302	Joystick test failure

MATRIX PRINTERS (14xx)

1401	Printer test failure
1402	Printer not ready, not on-line, or out of paper
1403	Printer "no paper" error
1404	Matrix printer test failure; system board time-out
1405	Parallel adapter failure
1406	Printer presence test failed

SDLC COMMUNICATIONS ADAPTER (15xx)

1501	SDLC adapter test failure
1510	8255 port B failure
1511	8255 port A failure
1512	8255 port C failure

Table 44-1. Continued

SDLC COMMUNICATIONS ADAPTER (15xx)

1513	8253 timer #1 did not reach terminal count
1514	8253 timer #1 output stuck on
1515	8253 timer #0 did not reach terminal count
1516	8253 timer #0 output stuck on
1517	8253 timer #2 did not reach terminal count
1518	8253 timer #2 output stuck on
1519	8273 port B error
1520	8273 port A error
1521	8273 command/read time-out error
1522	Interrupt level 4 error
1523	Ring indicator stuck on
1524	Receive clock stuck on
1525	Transmit clock stuck on
1526	Test Indicate stuck on
1527	Ring Indicate not on
1528	Receive clock not on
1529	Transmit clock not on
1530	Test Indicate not on
1531	Data Set Ready not on
1532	Carrier Detect not on
1533	Clear-To-Send not on
1534	Data Set Ready stuck on
1535	Carrier Detect stuck on
1536	Clear-To-Send stuck on
1537	Interrupt level 3 failure
1538	Receive interrupt results error
1539	Wrap data compare error
1540	DMA channel 1 transmit error
1541	DMA channel 1 receive error
1542	8273 error-checking or status-reporting error
1547	Stray interrupt level 4 error
1548	Stray interrupt level 3 error
1549	Interrupt presentation sequence time-out

DSEA UNITS (16xx)

1604	DSEA or Twinaxial network adapter
1608	DSEA or Twinaxial network adapter
1624 through 1658	DSEA system error
1662	DSEA interrupt level error
1664	DSEA system error
1668	DSEA interrupt level error
1669	DSEA diagnostics error
1674	DSEA diagnostics error
1684	DSEA device address error
1688	DSEA device address error

Table 44-1. Continued

HARD DRIVES AND ADAPTERS (17xx)

1701	Fixed disk or adapter general error
1702	Drive and controller time-out error
1703	Drive seek error
1704	Drive controller failed
1705	Drive sector not found error
1706	Write fault error
1707	Drive track 00 error
1708	Head select error
1709	Bad ECC returned
1710	Sector buffer overrun
1711	Bad address mark
1712	Internal controller diagnostics failure
1713	Data compare error
1714	Drive not ready
1715	Track 00 indicator failure
1716	Diagnostics cylinder errors
1717	Surface read errors
1718	Hard drive type error
1720	Bad diagnostics cylinder
1726	Data compare error
1730	Drive controller error
1731	Drive controller error
1732	Drive controller error
1733	BIOS undefined error return
1735	Bad command error
1736	Data corrected error
1737	Bad drive track error
1738	Bad sector error
1739	Bad initialization error
1740	Bad sense error
1750	Drive verify error
1751	Drive read error
1752	Drive write error
1753	Drive random read test failure
1754	Drive seek test failure
1755	Drive controller failure
1756	Controller ECC test failure
1757	Controller head select failure
1780	Drive seek failure (Drive 0)
1781	Drive seek failure (Drive 1)
1782	Hard disk controller failure
1790	Diagnostic cylinder read error (Drive 0)
1791	Diagnostic cylinder read error (Drive 1)

I/O EXPANSION UNIT (18xx)

1801	Expansion Unit POST error

Table 44-1. Continued

I/O EXPANSION UNIT (18xx)

1810	Enable/disable failure
1811	Extender card wrap test failure while disabled
1812	High-order address lines failure while disabled
1813	Wait state failure while disabled
1814	Enable/disable could not be set on
1815	Wait state failure while enabled
1816	Extender card wrap test failure while enabled
1817	High-order address lines failure while enabled
1818	Disable not functioning
1819	Wait request switch not set correctly
1820	Receiver card wrap test failed
1821	Receiver high-order address lines failure

BI-SYNCHRONOUS COMMUNICATIONS ADAPTERS (20xx)

2001	BSC adapter test failure
2010	8255 port A failure
2011	8255 port B failure
2012	8255 port C failure
2013	8253 timer #1 did not reach terminal count
2014	8253 timer #1 output stuck on
2015	8253 timer #2 did not reach terminal count
2016	8253 timer #2 output stuck on
2017	8251 Data-Set-Ready failed to come on
2018	8251 Clear-To-Send not sensed
2019	8251 Data-Set-Ready stuck on
2020	8251 Clear-To-Send stuck on
2021	8251 hardware reset failure
2022	8251 software reset command failure
2023	8251 software error-reset command failure
2024	8251 Transmit-Ready did not come on
2025	8251 Receive-Ready did not come on
2026	8251 could not force overrun error status
2027	Interrupt failure - no timer interrupt
2028	Interrupt failure - replace card or planar board
2029	Interrupt failure - replace card only
2030	Interrupt failure - replace card or planar board
2031	Interrupt failure - replace card only
2033	Ring Indicate signal stuck on
2034	Receive clock stuck on
2035	Transmit clock stuck on
2036	Test Indicate stuck on
2037	Ring Indicate not on
2038	Receive clock not on
2039	Transmit clock not on
2040	Test Indicate not on
2041	Data-Set-Ready stuck on

Table 44-1. Continued

BI-SYNCHRONOUS COMMUNICATIONS ADAPTERS (20xx)

2042	Carrier Detect not on
2043	Clear-To-Send not on
2044	Data-Set-Ready stuck on
2045	Carrier Detect stuck on
2046	Clear-To-Send stuck on
2047	Unexpected transmit interrupt
2048	Unexpected receive interrupt
2049	Transmit data did not equal receive data
2050	8251 detected overrun error
2051	Lost Data-Set-Ready signal during data wrap
2052	Receive time-out during data wrap

ALTERNATE BI-SYNCHRONOUS COMMUNICATIONS ADAPTERS (21xx)

2101	BSC adapter test failure
2110	8255 port A failure
2111	8255 port B failure
2112	8255 port C failure
2113	8253 timer #1 did not reach terminal count
2114	8253 timer #1 output stuck on
2115	8253 timer #2 did not reach terminal count
2116	8253 timer #2 output stuck on
2117	8251 Data-Set-Ready failed to come on
2118	8251 Clear-To-Send not sensed
2119	8251 Data-Set-Ready stuck on
2120	8251 Clear-To-Send stuck on
2121	8251 hardware reset failure
2122	8251 software reset command failure
2123	8251 software error-reset command failure
2124	8251 Transmit-Ready did not come on
2125	8251 Receive-Ready did not come on
2126	8251 could not force overrun error status
2127	Interrupt failure - no timer interrupt
2128	Interrupt failure - replace card or planar board
2129	Interrupt failure - replace card only
2130	Interrupt failure - replace card or planar board
2131	Interrupt failure - replace card only
2133	Ring Indicate signal stuck on
2134	Receive clock stuck on
2135	Transmit clock stuck on
2136	Test Indicate stuck on
2137	Ring Indicate not on
2138	Receive clock not on
2139	Transmit clock not on
2140	Test Indicate not on
2141	Data-Set-Ready stuck on
2142	Carrier Detect not on

Table 44-1. Continued

ALTERNATE BI-SYNCHRONOUS COMMUNICATIONS ADAPTERS (21xx)

2143	Clear-To-Send not on
2144	Data-Set-Ready stuck on
2145	Carrier Detect stuck on
2146	Clear-To-Send stuck on
2147	Unexpected transmit interrupt
2148	Unexpected receive interrupt
2149	Transmit data did not equal receive data
2150	8251 detected overrun error
2151	Lost Data-Set-Ready signal during data wrap
2152	Receive time-out during data wrap

CLUSTER ADAPTERS (22xx)

22xx	A cluster adapter error has been encountered - replace the cluster adapter

PLASMA MONITOR ADAPTER (23xx)

23xx	A plasma display fault has been detected - replace the plasma monitor assembly

ENHANCED GRAPHICS ADAPTER (24xx)

2401	Video adapter test failure
2402	Video display (monitor) error
2408	User-indicated display attribute test failed
2409	Video display (monitor) error
2410	Video adapter error
2416	User-indicated character set test failed
2424	User-indicated 80×25 mode failure
2432	User-indicated 40×25 mode failure
2440	User-indicated 320×200 graphics mode failure
2448	User-indicated 640×200 graphics mode failure
2456	User-indicated light pen test failure
2464	User-indicated screen paging test failure

ALTERNATE ENHANCED GRAPHICS ADAPTER (25xx)

2501	Video adapter test failure
2502	Video display (monitor) error
2508	User-indicated display attribute test failed
2509	Video display (monitor) error
2510	Video adapter error
2516	User-indicated character set test failed
2524	User-indicated 80×25 mode failure
2532	User-indicated 40×25 mode failure
2540	User-indicated 320×200 graphics mode failure
2548	User-indicated 640×200 graphics mode failure
2556	User-indicated light pen test failure
2564	User-indicated screen paging test failure

PC/370-M ADAPTER (26xx)

2601 through 2672	370-M (memory) adapter error
2673 through 2680	370-P (processor) adapter error

Table 44-1. Continued

PC/370-M ADAPTER (26xx)

2681	370-M (memory) adapter error
2682 through 2697	370-P (processor) adapter error
2698	XT or AT/370 diagnostic diskette error

PC3277 EMULATION ADAPTER (27xx)

2701	3277-EM adapter error
2702	3277-EM adapter error
2703	3277-EM adapter error

3278/3279 EMULATION ADAPTER (28xx)

28xx	An emulation adapter fault has been detected - replace the adapter

COLOR/GRAPHICS PRINTERS (29xx)

29xx	A general fault has been detected with the printer or its printer port - replace the printer or adapter port

PRIMARY PC NETWORK ADAPTER (30xx)

3001	Network adapter test failure
3002	ROM checksum test failure
3003	Unit ID PROM test failure
3004	RAM test failure
3005	Host Interface Controller (HIC) test failure
3006	+/-12Vdc test failure
3007	Digital loopback test failure
3008	Host-detected HIC failure
3009	Sync signal failure & no-go bit
3010	HIC test OK & no-go bit
3011	Go bit OK but no command 41
3012	Card not present
3013	Digital failure - fall-through
3015	Analog failure
3041	Hot carrier - on other card
3042	Hot carrier - on this card

SECONDARY PC NETWORK ADAPTER (31xx)

3101	Network adapter test failure
3102	ROM checksum test failure
3103	Unit ID PROM test failure
3104	RAM test failure
3105	Host Interface Controller (HIC) test failure
3106	+/-12Vdc test failure
3107	Digital loopback test failure
3108	Host-detected HIC failure
3109	Sync signal failure & no-go bit
3110	HIC test OK & no-go bit
3111	Go bit OK but no command 41
3112	Card not present
3113	Digital failure - fall-through
3115	Analog failure
3141	Hot carrier - on other card
3142	Hot carrier - on this card

Table 44-1. Continued

3270 PC/AT DISPLAY (32xx)

32xx	A fault has been detected in the display system - replace the display system

COMPACT PRINTER ERRORS (33xx)

33xx	A fault has been detected in the printer or printer adapter - replace the printer or adapter

ENHANCED DSEA UNITS (35xx)

3504	Adapter connected to twinaxial cable during off-line test
3508	Workstation address error
3509	Diagnostic program failure; retry on new diskette
3540	Workstation address invalid
3588	Adapter address switch error
3599	Diagnostic program failure; retry on new diskette

IEEE 488 (GPIB) ADAPTER (36xx)

3601	Adapter test failure
3602	Write error at Serial Poll Mode Register (SPMR)
3603	Adapter addressing problems
3610	Adapter cannot be programmed to listen
3611	Adapter cannot be programmed to talk
3612	Adapter control error
3613	Adapter cannot switch to standby mode
3614	Adapter cannot take control asynchronously
3615	Adapter cannot take control asynchronously
3616	Adapter cannot pass control
3617	Adapter cannot be addressed to listen
3618	Adapter cannot be un-addressed to listen
3619	Adapter cannot be addressed to talk
3620	Adapter cannot be un-addressed to talk
3621	Adapter cannot be addressed to listen with extended addressing
3622	Adapter cannot be un-addressed to listen with extended addressing
3623	Adapter cannot be addressed to talk with extended addressing
3624	Adapter cannot be un-addressed to talk with extended addressing
3625	Adapter cannot write to self
3626	Adapter error - cannot generate handshake signal
3627	Adapter error - cannot detect Device Clear (DCL) message
3628	Adapter error - cannot detect Selected Device Clear (SDC) message
3629	Adapter error - cannot detect end of transfer with EOI signal
3630	Adapter error - cannot detect end of transmission with EOI signal
3631	Adapter cannot detect END with 0-bit EOS
3632	Adapter cannot detect END with 7-bit EOS
3633	Adapter cannot detect Group Execute Trigger (GET)
3634	Mode 3 addressing not functioning
3635	Adapter cannot recognize undefined command
3636	Adapter error - cannot detect REM, REMC, LOK, or LOKC signals
3637	Adapter error - cannot clear REM or LOK signals
3638	Adapter cannot detect Service Request (SRQ)
3639	Adapter cannot conduct serial poll
3640	Adapter cannot conduct parallel poll
3650	Adapter error - cannot DMA to 7210

Table 44-1. Continued

IEEE 488 (GPIB) ADAPTER (36xx)

3651	Data error on DMA to 7210
3652	Adapter error - cannot DMA from 7210
3653	Data error on DMA from 7210
3658	Uninvoked interrupt received
3659	Adapter cannot interrupt on ADSC signal
3660	Adapter cannot interrupt on ADSC signal
3661	Adapter cannot interrupt on CO
3662	Adapter cannot interrupt on DO
3663	Adapter cannot interrupt on DI
3664	Adapter cannot interrupt on ERR
3665	Adapter cannot interrupt on DEC
3666	Adapter cannot interrupt on END
3667	Adapter cannot interrupt on DET
3668	Adapter cannot interrupt on APT
3669	Adapter cannot interrupt on CPT
3670	Adapter cannot interrupt on REMC
3671	Adapter cannot interrupt on LOKC
3672	Adapter cannot interrupt on SRQI
3673	Adapter cannot interrupt on terminal count on DMA to 7210
3674	Adapter cannot interrupt on terminal count on DMA from 7210
3675	Spurious DMA terminal count interrupt
3697	Illegal DMA configuration setting detected
3698	Illegal interrupt level configuration setting detected

SYSTEM BOARD SCSI CONTROLLER (37xx)

37xx	The system board SCSI controller has failed - replace the motherboard

DATA ACQUISITION ADAPTER (38xx)

3801	Adapter test failure
3810	Timer read test failure
3811	Timer interrupt test failure
3812	Binary input 13 test failure
3813	Binary input 13 test failure
3814	Binary output 14 - interrupt request test failure
3815	Binary output 0, count-in test failure
3816	Binary input strobe (STB), count-out test failure
3817	Binary output 0, Clear-To-Send (CTS) test failure
3818	Binary output 1, binary input 0 test failure
3819	Binary output 2, binary input 1 test failure
3820	Binary output 3, binary input 2 test failure
3821	Binary output 4, binary input 3 test failure
3822	Binary output 5, binary input 4 test failure
3823	Binary output 6, binary input 5 test failure
3824	Binary output 7, binary input 6 test failure
3825	Binary output 8, binary input 7 test failure
3826	Binary output 9, binary input 8 test failure
3827	Binary output 10, binary input 9 test failure

Table 44-1. Continued

DATA ACQUISITION ADAPTER (38xx)

3828	Binary output 11, binary input 10 test failure
3829	Binary output 12, binary input 11 test failure
3830	Binary output 13, binary input 12 test failure
3831	Binary output 15, analog input CE test failure
3832	Binary output Strobe (STB), binary output GATE test failure
3833	Binary input Clear-To-Send (CTS), binary input HOLD test failure
3834	Analog input Command Output (CO), binary input 15 test failure
3835	Counter interrupt test failure
3836	Counter read test failure
3837	Analog output 0 ranges test failure
3838	Analog output 1 ranges test failure
3839	Analog input 0 values test failure
3840	Analog input 1 values test failure
3841	Analog input 2 values test failure
3842	Analog input 3 values test failure
3843	Analog input interrupt test failure
3844	Analog input 23 address or value test failure

PROFESSIONAL GRAPHICS ADAPTER (PGA) (39xx)

3901	PGA test failure
3902	ROM1 self-test failure
3903	ROM2 self-test failure
3904	RAM self-test failure
3905	Cold start cycle power error
3906	Data error in communications RAM
3907	Address error in communications RAM
3908	Bad data detected while read/write to 6845 register
3909	Bad data detected in lower E0h bytes while read/writing 6845 registers
3910	Display bank output latch error
3911	Basic clock error
3912	Command control error
3913	Vertical sync scanner error
3914	Horizontal sync scanner error
3915	Intech error
3916	Lookup Table (LUT) address error
3917	LUT "red" RAM chip error
3918	LUT "green" RAM chip error
3919	LUT "blue" RAM chip error
3920	LUT data latch error
3921	Horizontal display error
3922	Vertical display error
3923	Light pen error
3924	Unexpected error
3925	Emulator addressing error
3926	Emulator data latch error
3927 through 3930	Emulator RAM error

Table 44-1. Continued

PROFESSIONAL GRAPHICS ADAPTER (PGA) (39xx)

3931	Emulator Horizontal/Vertical display problem
3932	Emulator cursor position error
3933	Emulator attribute display problem
3934	Emulator cursor display error
3935	Fundamental emulation RAM problem
3936	Emulation character set problem
3937	Emulation graphics display error
3938	Emulation character display problem
3939	Emulation bank select error
3940	Display RAM U2 error
3941	Display RAM U4 error
3942	Display RAM U6 error
3943	Display RAM U8 error
3944	Display RAM U10 error
3945	Display RAM U1 error
3946	Display RAM U3 error
3947	Display RAM U5 error
3948	Display RAM U7 error
3949	Display RAM U9 error
3950	Display RAM U12 error
3951	Display RAM U14 error
3952	Display RAM U16 error
3953	Display RAM U18 error
3954	Display RAM U20 error
3955	Display RAM U11 error
3956	Display RAM U13 error
3957	Display RAM U15 error
3958	Display RAM U17 error
3959	Display RAM U19 error
3960	Display RAM U22 error
3961	Display RAM U24 error
3962	Display RAM U26 error
3963	Display RAM U28 error
3964	Display RAM U30 error
3965	Display RAM U21 error
3966	Display RAM U23 error
3967	Display RAM U25 error
3968	Display RAM U27 error
3969	Display RAM U29 error
3970	Display RAM U32 error
3971	Display RAM U34 error
3972	Display RAM U36 error
3973	Display RAM U38 error
3974	Display RAM U40 error
3975	Display RAM U31 error
3976	Display RAM U33 error

Table 44-1. Continued

PROFESSIONAL GRAPHICS ADAPTER (PGA) (39xx)

3977	Display RAM U35 error
3978	Display RAM U37 error
3979	Display RAM U39 error
3980	Graphics controller RAM timing error
3981	Graphics controller read/write latch error
3982	Shift register bus output latch error
3983	Addressing error (vertical column of memory; U2 at top)
3984	Addressing error (vertical column of memory; U4 at top)
3985	Addressing error (vertical column of memory; U6 at top)
3986	Addressing error (vertical column of memory; U8 at top)
3987	Addressing error (vertical column of memory; U10 at top)
3988 through 3991	Horizontal bank latch errors
3992	RAG/CAG graphics controller error
3993	Multiple write modes, nibble mask errors
3994	Row nibble (display RAM) error
3995	Graphics controller addressing error

5278 Display Attachment Unit and 5279 Display (44xx)

44xx	A fault has been detected with the display system - replace the display system

IEEE 488 (GPIB) Interface Adapter (45xx)

45xx	A fault has been detected with the GPIB - replace the adapter

ARTIC Multiport/2 Interface Adapter (46xx)

4611	ARTIC adapter error
4612 or 4613	Memory module error
4630	ARTIC adapter error
4640 or 4641	Memory module error
4650	ARTIC interface cable error

Internal Modem (48xx)

48xx	The internal modem has failed - replace the internal modem

Alternate Internal Modem (49xx)

49xx	The alternate internal modem has failed - replace the alternate internal modem

PC CONVERTIBLE LCD (50xx)

5001	LCD buffer failure
5002	LCD font buffer failure
5003	LCD controller failure
5004	User-indicated PEL/drive test failed
5008	User-indicated display attribute test failed
5016	User-indicated character set test failed
5020	User-indicated alternate character set test failure
5024	User-indicated 80 × 25 mode test failure
5032	User-indicated 40 × 25 mode test failure
5040	User-indicated 320 × 200 graphics test failure
5048	User-indicated 640 × 200 graphics test failure
5064	User-indicated paging test failure

Table 44-1. Continued

PC CONVERTIBLE PORTABLE PRINTER (51xx)

5101	Portable printer interface failure
5102	Portable printer busy error
5103	Portable printer paper or ribbon error
5104	Portable printer time-out
5105	User-indicated print pattern test error

FINANCIAL COMMUNICATION SYSTEM (56xx)

56xx	A fault has been detected in the financial communication system - replace the financial communication system

PHOENIX BIOS/CHIPSET SPECIFIC ERROR CODES (70xx)

7000	Chipset CMOS failure
7001	Shadow RAM failure (ROM not shadowed to RAM)
7002	Chipset CMOS configuration data error

VOICE COMMUNICATIONS ADAPTER (VCA) (71xx)

7101	Adapter test failure
7102	Instruction or external data memory error
7103	PC to VCA interrupt error
7104	Internal data memory error
7105	DMA error
7106	Internal registers error
7107	Interactive shared memory error
7108	VCA to PC interrupt error
7109	DC wrap error
7111	External analog wrap & tone output error
7114	Telephone attachment test failure

3.5" FLOPPY DISK DRIVE (73xx)

7301	Diskette drive/adapter test failure
7306	Diskette change line error
7307	Write-protected diskette
7308	Drive command error
7310	Diskette initialization failure - track 00 error
7311	Drive time-out error
7312	NEC drive controller IC error
7313	DMA error
7314	DMA boundary overrun error
7315	Drive index timing error
7316	Drive speed error
7321	Drive seek error
7322	Drive CRC check error
7323	Sector not found error
7324	Address mark error
7325	NEC controller IC seek error

8514/A DISPLAY ADAPTER (74xx)

7426	8514 display error
7440 through 7475	8514/A memory module error

Table 44-1. Continued

4216 PAGE PRINTER ADAPTER (76xx)

7601	Adapter test failure
7602	Adapter card error
7603	Printer error
7604	Printer cable error

PS/2 SPEECH ADAPTER (84xx)

84xx	A fault has been detected in the speech adapter - replace the speech adapter

2MB XMA MEMORY ADAPTER (85xx)

85xx	A fault has been detected in the memory adapter - replace the memory adapter

PS/2 POINTING DEVICE (86xx)

8601	Pointing device; mouse time-out error
8602	Pointing device; mouse interface error
8603	System board; mouse interrupt failure
8604	Pointing device or system board error
8611	System bus error
8612	TrackPoint II error
8613	System bus or TrackPoint II error

MIDI INTERFACE (89xx)

89xx	A fault has been detected in the MIDI adapter - replace the MIDI adapter

3363 WORM OPTICAL DRIVE/ADAPTERS (91xx)

91xx	A fault has been detected in the drive or adapter - replace the adapter and the drive

SCSI ADAPTER (W/32-BIT CACHE) (96xx)

96xx	A fault has been detected in the SCSI adapter - replace the adapter board

MULTIPROTOCOL ADAPTERS (100xx)

10001	Presence test failure
10002	Card selected feedback error
10003	Port 102h register rest failure
10004	Port 103h register rest failure
10006	Serial option cannot be disabled
10007	Cable error
10008	IRQ3 error
10009	IRQ4 error
10010	UART register failure
10011	Internal wrap test of UART control line failed
10012	External wrap test of UART control line failed
10013	UART transmit error
10014	UART receive error
10015	UART receive error - data not equal to transmit data
10016	UART interrupt error
10017	UART baud rate test failure
10018	UART receive external wrap test failure
10019	UART FIFO buffer failure
10026	8255 Port A error
10027	8255 Port B error
10028	8255 Port C error

Table 44-1. Continued

MULTIPROTOCOL ADAPTERS (100xx)

10029	8254 timer 0 error
10030	8254 timer 1 error
10031	8254 timer 2 error
10032	Bi-sync Data Set Ready (DSR) response error
10033	Bi-sync Clear-To-Send (CTS) error
10034	8251 hardware reset test failed
10035	8251 function generator
10036	8251 status error
10037	Bi-sync timer interrupt error
10038	Bi-sync transmit interrupt error
10039	Bi-sync receive interrupt error
10040	Stray IRQ3 error
10041	Stray IRQ4 error
10042	Bi-sync external wrap error
10044	Bi-sync data wrap error
10045	Bi-sync line status error
10046	Bi-sync time-out error during wrap test
10050	8273 command acceptance or time-out error
10051	8273 Port A error
10052	8273 Port B error
10053	SDLC modem status logic error
10054	SDLC timer IRQ4 error
10055	SDLC IRQ4 error
10056	SDLC external wrap error
10057	SDLC interrupt results error
10058	SDLC data wrap error
10059	SDLC transmit interrupt error
10060	SDLC receive interrupt error
10061	DMA channel 1 transmit error
10062	DMA channel 1 receive error
10063	8273 status detect failure
10064	8273 error detect failure

INTERNAL 300/1200BPS MODEM (101xx)

10101	Presence test failure
10102	Card-selected feedback error
10103	Port 102h register test error
10106	Serial option cannot be disabled
10108	IRQ3 error
10109	IRQ4 error
10110	UART chip register failure
10111	UART control line internal wrap test failure
10113	UART transmit error
10114	UART receive error
10115	UART error - transmit & receive data not equal
10116	UART interrupt function error
10117	UART baud rate test failure

Table 44-1. Continued

INTERNAL 300/1200BPS MODEM (101xx)

10118	UART interrupt driven receive external data wrap test failure
10125	Modem reset result code error
10126	Modem general result code error
10127	Modem S registers write/read error
10128	Modem echo on/off error
10129	Modem enable/disable result codes error
10130	Modem enable number/word result codes error
10133	Connect results for 300 baud not received
10134	Connect results for 1200 baud not received
10135	Modem fails local analog loopback 300 baud test
10136	Modem fails local analog loopback 1200 baud test
10137	Modem does not respond to escape/reset sequence
10138	S register 13 shows incorrect parity or number of data bits
10139	S register 15 shows incorrect bit rate

ESDI or MCA IDE DRIVE/ADAPTERS (104xx)

10450	Write/read test failed
10451	Read verify test failed
10452	Seek test failed
10453	Wrong drive type indicated
10454	Controller failed sector buffer test
10455	Controller failed - invalid
10456	Controller diagnostic command failure
10461	Drive format error
10462	Controller head select error
10463	Drive write/read sector error
10464	Drive primary defect map unreadable
10465	Controller ECC 8-bit error
10466	Controller ECC 9-bit error
10467	Drive soft seek error
10468	Drive hard seek error
10469	Drive soft seek error count exceeded
10470	Controller attachment diagnostic error
10471	Controller wrap mode interface error
10472	Controller wrap mode drive select error
10473	Error during ESDI read verify test
10480	Seek failure on drive 0
10481	Seek failure on drive 1
10482	Controller transfer acknowledge error
10483	Controller reset error
10484	Controller head select 3 selected bad
10485	Controller head select 2 selected bad
10486	Controller head select 1 selected bad
10487	Controller head select 0 selected bad
10488	Read gate command error
10489	Read gate command error
10490	Diagnostic read error on drive 0

Table 44-1. Continued

ESDI or MCA IDE DRIVE/ADAPTERS (104xx)

10491	Diagnostic read error on drive 1
10492	Drive 1 controller error
10493	Drive 1 reset error
10499	Controller failure

5.25" EXTERNAL DISK DRIVE/ADAPTER (107xx)

107xx	A fault has been detected in the drive or adapter - replace the adapter and drive

SCSI ADAPTER (16-BIT W/O CACHE) (112xx)

112xx	A fault has been detected in the SCSI adapter - replace the SCSI adapter

SYSTEM BOARD SCSI ADAPTER (113xx)

113xx	A fault has been detected in the SCSI adapter - replace the motherboard

CPU BOARD (129xx)

12901	Processor test failed
12902	CPU board cache test failed
12904	Second level (L2) cache failure
12905	Cache enable/disable errors
12907	Cache fatal error
12908	Cache POST program error
12912	Hardware failure
12913	MCA bus time-out
12914	Software failure
12915	CPU board error
12916	CPU board error
12917	CPU board error
12918	CPU board error
12919	CPU board error
12940	CPU board error
12950	CPU board error
12990	CPU serial number mismatch

P70/P75 PLASMA DISPLAY/ADAPTER (149xx)

14901	Plasma display adapter failure
14902	Plasma display adapter failure
14922	Plasma display failure
14932	External display device failure

XGA DISPLAY ADAPTER (152xx)

152xx	A fault has been detected in the XGA adapter - replace the adapter

120MB INTERNAL TAPE DRIVE (164xx)

164xx	A fault has been detected in the tape drive - replace the tape drive

6157 STREAMING TAPE DRIVE (165xx)

16520	Streaming tape drive failure
16540	Tape attachment adapter failure

PRIMARY TOKEN RING NETWORK ADAPTERS (166xx)

166xx	A fault has been detected with the network adapter - replace the network adapter

Table 44-1. Continued

SECONDARY TOKEN RING NETWORK ADAPTERS (167xx)

167xx	A fault has been detected with the network adapter - replace the network adapter

PS/2 WIZARD ADAPTER (180xx)

18001	Interrupt controller failure
18002	Incorrect timer count
18003	Timer interrupt failure
18004	Sync check interrupt failure
18005	Parity check interrupt failure
18006	Access error interrupt failure
18012	Bad checksum
18013	MCA bus interface error
18021	Wizard memory compare or parity error
18022	Wizard memory address line error
18023	Dynamic RAM controller failure
18029	Wizard memory byte enable error
18031	Wizard memory expansion module compare or parity error
18032	Wizard memory expansion module address line error
18039	Wizard memory expansion module byte enable error

DBCS JAPANESE DISPLAY ADAPTER (185xx)

185xx	A fault has been detected in the display adapter - replace the adapter

80286 MEMORY EXPANSION OPTION MODULE (194xx)

194xx	A fault has been detected in the memory module - replace the memory module

IMAGE ADAPTER (200xx)

200xx	A fault has been detected in the image adapter - replace the image adapter

UNKNOWN SCSI DEVICES (208xx)

208xx	A fault has been detected in an unknown SCSI device - systematically isolate and replace the defective SCSI device

SCSI REMOVABLE DISK (209xx)

209xx	A fault has been detected in the SCSI removable disk - replace the removable disk

SCSI FIXED DISK (210xx)

210xx	A fault has been detected in the SCSI fixed disk - replace the fixed disk

Troubleshooting with diagnostic codes

Now that you have an idea of the diagnostic areas that are covered and error codes you can expect to see, you should have an understanding of how to deal with those errors when they occur. Generally speaking, a PC can be divided down into a motherboard, expansion boards, drives, and a power supply; each area can be considered as a replaceable module. When an error code is generated, you can match the code to its description in Table 44-1. The rule of thumb here is that you should replace the failed module. For example, if a video adapter fails, it should be replaced.

If a motherboard fails, it should be replaced, if a hard drive fails, it should be replaced, and so on. The following notes will explain some of the finer points.

Motherboard notes

The motherboard manages virtually all of the PC's processing resources (DMAs, IRQs, memory, and so on). As a consequence, the motherboard is perhaps the most expensive module to replace. Before electing to replace the motherboard, be certain that the faulty component(s) cannot be swapped out. For example, the CPU, BIOS ROM, math coprocessor, expansion memory (SIMMs), RTC/CMOS IC, and CMOS backup battery are almost always socket mounted. In fact, when you purchase a new motherboard, it typically comes without those socket-mounted elements. If an error message indicates that the CPU has failed, try another CPU. If the math coprocessor appears defective, try a new MCP. Of course, if the defective element is hard-soldered to the motherboard, you should probably go ahead and order another motherboard, then simply transfer any of the socket-mounted devices from the old motherboard.

Memory notes

Memory plays a vital role in every PC; the CPU is useless unless there is memory to hold data and program instructions. Because even one bad bit can cause an error that might crash a system, memory is perhaps the most thoroughly tested area of a computer. From a troubleshooting standpoint, memory can often be divided into two areas, the memory located on the motherboard, and the memory added in the form of SIMMs. When a failure occurs in a SIMM, it is a simple matter to locate and replace the SIMM. If the fault is on the motherboard, you are often faced with the prospect of replacing the defective RAM IC(s), or (more frequently) replacing the entire motherboard.

Keyboard notes

Not only is the keyboard the most popular and reliable input device for the PC, the keyboard controller IC also is in control of the A20 Gate that allows the CPU to enter its protected mode. Although in the protected mode, a CPU can address memory above 1Mb. When a problem is detected in the keyboard assembly itself, it is usually a quick and easy process to replace the keyboard assembly. When a problem is located outside of the keyboard itself (or a protected-mode fault is found), the keyboard controller IC on the motherboard has probably failed. On some motherboards, the keyboard controller is mounted in an IC socket, and can be replaced easily. Where the keyboard controller is hard-soldered to the motherboard, it will probably be easiest to simply replace the motherboard outright.

Video notes

As you look over the error codes in Table 44-1, you might notice that there are sections dedicated to older video standards such as MDA and CGA. If you encounter a system with older video adapters that prove to be defective, it will be extremely difficult (if not impossible) to locate new replacement boards. As a result, you should expect to replace an older video board with one of the newer video adapters such as VGA or SVGA that offer backward compatibility to the older standards. Unfortunately, older video used TTL monitors, where VGA and SVGA adapters are designed for analog monitors. Keep in mind that it might be necessary to upgrade your customer's monitor as well as their video adapter.

Serial/parallel notes

Diagnostics typically attempt to test any serial or parallel ports that can be identified. In the early days of PCs, serial and parallel ports were typically added as expansion boards. When such add-on ports fail, it is a simple matter to replace the defective board. With most of today's systems, however, at least one serial and parallel port are integrated right on the motherboard. When these built-in ports check bad, there is often little that can be done other then replace the motherboard outright. Also, if an error code indicates a fault outside of the port circuit (the modem or printer), always try a new cable between the port and peripheral first. If a new cable does not correct the problem, try replacing the suspect peripheral. Also keep in mind that some test procedures require you to attach a loop-back plug (rather than connect a live peripheral).

Drive notes

Diagnostics typically check the complete suite of floppy drives, hard drives, and even CD-ROM drives. However, you must realize that a drive system includes not only the drive itself, but its controller board. When a drive problem is indicated, you should automatically inspect the signal and power cables at the drive. A loose power connector or frayed signal cable can easily disable the drive. If in doubt, try a new signal cable (much less expensive than replacing a drive).

Of course, if a new cable fails to correct the fault, you must decide whether the drive or controller has failed. Often, the diagnostic error code will pinpoint the fault to either the drive or controller circuit for you. If the drive has failed, replace the drive. If the controller has failed, things can get a bit more complicated. If the controller is implemented as an expansion board, it is easy enough to replace, but make sure that the new controller has any jumpers and DIP switches set similarly to the defective controller. If the controller is incorporated on the motherboard, you might find yourself replacing the entire motherboard.

45
CHAPTER

Linear power supplies

All electronic devices require the appropriate amount of voltage and current in order to function properly. Unfortunately, the ac supply provided from any ordinary wall outlet cannot power a PC or its peripherals directly. Instead, the ac has to be converted and manipulated to achieve the necessary levels; this is the task of a power supply. For the purposes of this book, we have broken power supplies down into three classes: linear supplies, switching supplies, and high-voltage supplies. Linear power supplies are rarely used in PCs and major peripherals such as printers and monitors. Such equipment demands the efficiency provided by switching supplies covered in Chapter 46. However, you will frequently encounter linear supplies in ac adapters (battery eliminators) used to power mobile computers and minor peripherals such as external tape drives or CD-ROM drives. This chapter illustrates the operation and troubleshooting approaches for a linear power supply.

Understanding linear supplies

The first step toward troubleshooting a linear power supply is to understand its operation. The term *linear* means line or straight. As shown in block diagram of Fig. 45-1, a linear supply essentially operates in a straight line from ac input to dc output(s). It is important for you to realize that the exact component parts and supply

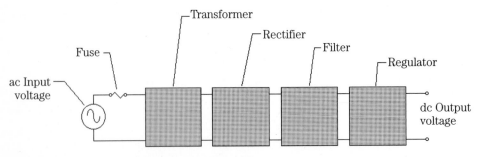

45-1 Block diagram of a linear power supply.

specifications will vary greatly from supply to supply, but ALL linear supplies contain the same basic subsections: a transformer, a rectifier, a filter, and a regulator.

Transformers

A *transformer* constitutes the vast majority of a power supply's weight and overall size. Transformers use the principles of *magnetic coupling* to alter the ac input voltage and current levels. The transformer's output (secondary) is not directly connected to its input. Instead, the output signal is generated by magnetism induced by fluctuations of the ac at the transformer's primary (input). By altering the proportion of primary vs. secondary windings, it is possible to convert an ac input signal into a higher (step-up) or lower (step-down) level. Current also is stepped—but in a proportion *opposite* to that of voltage. For example, it is often desirable to transform 120-Vac line voltage into one or more lower levels of ac voltage (27 Vac or 18 Vac). Such transformation requires a *step-down* transformer. By stepping the line voltage down, current is stepped up by the same factor. Suppose a 10:1 step-down transformer reduces 120 Vac to 12 Vac. An input current of 100 mA (0.10 A) would be multiplied to 1000 mA (1.00 A).

Rectifiers

The secondary (output) voltage from a transformer is still in ac form. Alternating current and voltage must be converted into dc before powering electronic circuits. The process of converting ac into dc is known as *rectification*. To achieve rectification, only one polarity of the ac signal is allowed to reach the rectifier's output. Even though the rectifier's output can vary greatly, the output's polarity will remain either positive or negative. This fluctuating dc is called *pulsating dc*. Diodes are ideal for use as rectifiers because they allow current to flow in only one direction. You might encounter any of three classical rectifier circuits: half-wave, full-wave, and bridge.

A *half-wave* rectifier is shown in Fig. 45-2. It is the simplest and most straightforward type of rectifier because only one diode is required. As secondary voltage from the transformer exceeds the diode's turn-on voltage (about 0.6 V), the diode begins to conduct current. This condition generates an output that mimics the positive half of the ac signal. If the diode were reversed, the output polarity also would be reversed. The disadvantage with half-wave rectifiers is that they are very inefficient. Only half of the ac wave is handled; the other half is basically ignored and wasted. The resulting gap between pulses causes a lower average output voltage and a higher amount of ac noise contained in the final dc output. Half-wave rectifiers are rarely used in commercial linear supplies.

Full-wave rectifiers such as the one shown in Fig. 45-3 offer substantial advantages over the half-wave design. By using two diodes in the configuration shown, both polarities of the ac secondary voltage can be rectified into pulsating dc. Because a diode is at each terminal of the secondary signal, polarities at each diode are opposite. When the ac signal is positive, the upper diode conducts and the lower diode is cutoff. When the ac signal is negative, the upper diode is cutoff and the lower diode conducts. This means that there is always *one* diode conducting, so there are no gaps in the pulsating dc signal. The only disadvantage to full-wave rec-

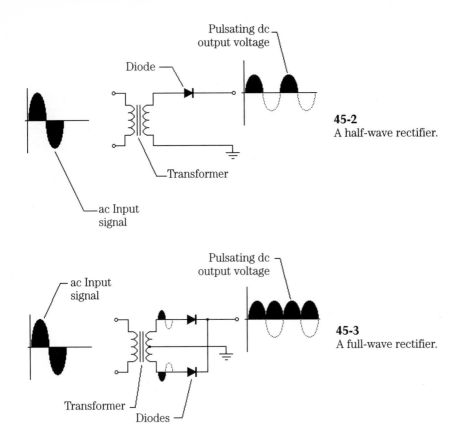

45-2
A half-wave rectifier.

45-3
A full-wave rectifier.

tifiers is that a center-tapped transformer is needed. Tapped transformers are often heavier and bulkier than nontapped transformers.

Diode bridge rectifiers use four diodes in a bridge configuration to provide full-wave rectification without the hassle of a center-tapped transformer. Fig. 45-4 illustrates a typical bridge rectifier. Two diodes provide forward current paths for rectification, and the other two diodes supply isolation to ground. When ac voltage is positive, diode D1 conducts and D4 provides isolation. When ac voltage is negative, diode D2 conducts while D3 provides isolation. Bridge rectifiers are by far the most popular type of rectifier circuit.

Filters

By strict technical definition, pulsating dc is dc because its polarity remains constant (even if its magnitude changes periodically). Unfortunately, pulsating dc is still unsuitable for any type of electronic power source. Voltage magnitude must be constant over time in order to operate electronic devices properly. Pulsating dc is converted into smoothed dc through the use of a filter as illustrated in Fig. 45-5. Electrolytic capacitors typically serve as the filter elements because they act as voltage storage devices. When pulsating dc is applied to a capacitive filter, the capacitor charges and voltage across the capacitor increases. Ultimately, the capacitor's charge reaches the peak value of pulsating dc. When a dc pulse falls off back toward zero,

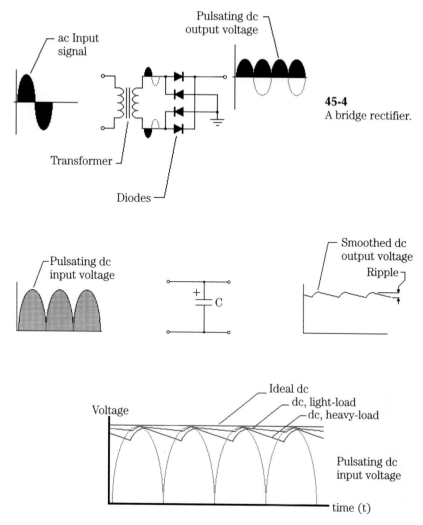

45-4
A bridge rectifier.

45-5 The effect of capacitive filtering.

the capacitor continues to supply current to the load. This action tends to hold up the output voltage over time; dc is filtered.

However, filtering is not a perfect process. As current is drained away from a filter by the load, voltage across the filter decreases. Filter voltage continues to drop until a new pulse of dc from the rectifier recharges the filter for another cycle. This action of repetitive charging and discharging results in regular fluctuations in the filter output. These fluctuations are called *ripple*, and it is an undesirable noise component of a smoothed dc output.

The diagram of Fig. 45-5 also shows a sample plot of voltage versus time for a typical filter circuit. The ideal dc output would be a steady line indicating a constant dc output at all points in time. In reality, there will always be some amount of filter ripple. Just how much ripple is present will depend on the load being supplied. For a light load (a circuit drawing little current), discharge is less between pulses, so the magnitude of ripple is lower. A large load (a circuit drawing substantial current), requires greater amounts of current, so discharge is deeper between pulses. This results in greater magnitudes of ripple. The relationship of dc pulses is shown for reference.

Beware of shock hazards from power supply filters. Large electrolytic capacitors tend to accumulate substantial amounts of charge, and hold that charge for a long time. If your fingers or hands touch the leads of a charged capacitor, it might discharge through you. Although a capacitor shock is rarely dangerous, it can be very uncomfortable, and perhaps result in a mild burn. Before working on a power supply, be certain that the capacitor is discharged completely by placing a large-value resistor across the capacitor as shown in Fig. 45-6. This bleeder resistor slowly drains off any charge remaining on the filter once the power supply is turned off. *Never attempt to discharge a capacitor by shorting its leads with a screwdriver blade or wire.* The sudden release of energy can actually weld a wire or screwdriver directly to the capacitor leads, as well as damage the capacitor internally.

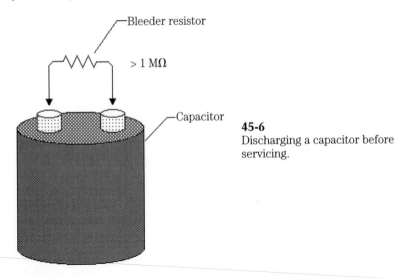

45-6
Discharging a capacitor before servicing.

Regulators

A transformer, rectifier, and filter are essential in every power supply. These parts combined will successfully convert ac into dc that is capable of driving many electrical and electronic loads. However, such unregulated power supplies have two major disadvantages: ripple is always present on the supply's output, and the output level varies with the load. Although this might not pose a problem for robust devices such as motors and solenoids, even the most forgiving ICs can perform erratically if they are operated with unregulated dc. Ideal dc should be ripple-free and constant regardless of load. A *regulator* is needed to fix dc from a filter's output.

Linear regulation is just as the name implies—current flows from the regulator's input to output as shown in Fig. 45-7. When voltage is applied to the regulator's input, internal circuitry within the regulator manipulates input voltage to provide a steady, consistent output voltage. The output will remain steady under a wide range of input conditions as long as the input voltage is above the desired output voltage

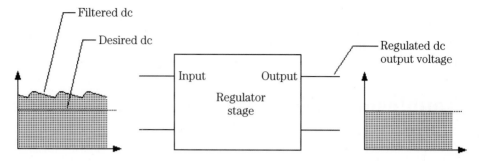

Filtered dc

Desired dc

Input   Output

Regulator
stage

Regulated dc
output voltage

45-7 The action of a typical regulator.

(often by 3 V or more). If input voltage falls to or below the desired output voltage, the regulator falls out of regulation. In such a case, the regulator's output signal tends to follow the input signal, including ripple.

A linear regulator works by "throwing away" the extra energy provided by a filter; whatever is left over is the desired output. Energy is discarded in the form of heat. This explains why so many regulators are attached to large metal heatsinks. Although linear regulation is a simple and reliable method of operation, it also is very inefficient. Typical linear power supplies are only up to 50% efficient. This means that for every 10 watts of power provided to the supply, only 5 watts is provided to the load. Most of this waste occurs in the regulation process itself.

Regulator circuits are typically fabricated as integrated circuits as shown in Fig. 45-8. Additional performance features such as automatic current limiting and over-temperature shutdown circuitry can be included to improve the regulator's reliabil-

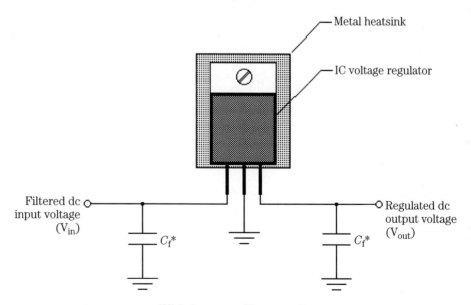

Metal heatsink

IC voltage regulator

Filtered dc
input voltage
(V_{in})

C_f*

Regulated dc
output voltage
(V_{out})

C_f*

*High-frequency filter capacitors

45-8 Schematic fragment of an IC voltage regulator.

ity. Input voltage must exceed the desired output by several volts, but IC regulators are simple to use. One additional consideration for IC regulators is the use of small-value capacitors at the IC's input and output. Small capacitors (0.01 F to 0.1 F) filter high-frequency noise or signals that could interfere with the regulator's operation.

Troubleshooting linear power supplies

Under most circumstances, linear power supplies are reasonably simple and straightforward to troubleshoot. You can usually make use of your multimeter or oscilloscope to trace voltage through the supply. The point at which your expected voltage disappears is probably the point of failure. Keep in mind that many of the following procedures must be performed on powered circuitry. *Take every precaution to protect yourself and your equipment before beginning your repair.* The use of an isolation transformer to provide ac is highly recommended.

Start your repair by removing all power from the supply. Disassemble the power supply enough to expose the power supply circuit. In some cases, you will find the power supply on a stand-alone PC board. In other cases, the power supply circuit will be incorporated into another PC board. Be certain to insulate any loose assemblies or circuits to prevent accidental short circuits or physical damage. For the following procedures, refer to the example linear power supply shown in Fig. 45-9.

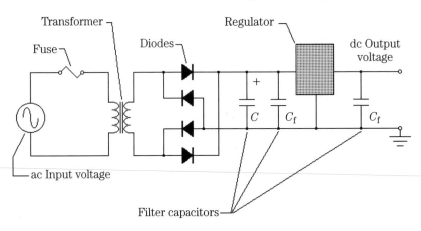

45-9 Schematic diagram of a linear power supply.

Symptom 1. The device (external tape drive, CD-ROM drive, and so on) is dead—there is no activity in the device, and drivers or application software does not recognize the device When the device is completely inoperative, you should immediately suspect a fault in one or more of the power supply outputs. Begin by checking the ac line voltage into the power supply. Use your multimeter to measure ac voltage at your power supply's plug. If you are using an isolation transformer, you should check the transformer's ac output to your supply. You should normally read 105 to 130 Vac (210 to 240 Vac in Europe). More or less line voltage can cause the supply to malfunction. *Use extreme caution whenever measuring ac line voltage levels.*

Check the device's power switch to be sure that it is in the ON position. This might sound silly, but it really *is* a common oversight. All power supplies contain some sort of fusing, so unplug the power supply and inspect the main line fuse. If the fuse is externally mounted, it is usually accessible from the device's outer housing. If there is no external fuse, you must disassemble the device to check the fuse(s) that would be located either in the power supply circuit itself, or in the device. You can test a fuse by removing it from the circuit and measuring its continuity with a multimeter. A working fuse should register as a complete short circuit (zero ohms). If you read infinite resistance, the fuse is defective and should be replaced. Replace defective fuses *only* with fuses of equal size and current rating.

While the device is unplugged, check all connectors and wiring to be sure that everything is intact. A loose connector or wire can easily disable the supply. If your supply has failed after being dropped or abused, consider the possibility of printed circuit board damage. Faulty soldering at the factory (or on your test bench) also can cause PC board problems. The power PC board might be cracked, one or more component leads might have pulled away from their solder pads, or a trace (or traces) might have broken from impact stress. Inspect the PC board(s) carefully for signs of damage.

Apply power to the device again, and use your multimeter to measure the dc output(s) from the supply. Each output is generally well marked, so you should have no trouble determining what the output should be. When an output is low or zero, disconnect the power supply from its load (if possible) and measure its output(s) again. If you find the same measurements with the load disconnected, the trouble is probably in your supply. If the output returns to its rated value, the supply is probably being shorted by the load circuit(s). Check the device for damage or short circuits that might be pulling down the supply output(s).

If there are no obvious failures up to this point, you can try replacing the power supply outright. If the supply is fabricated on its own PC board, you need only replace the power supply assembly. If the supply is incorporated on a larger PC board, you would have to replace the entire PC board. You also might choose to troubleshoot the supply circuit to the component level. For the purposes of this discussion, you should follow the procedure with Fig. 45-9. In linear supply troubleshooting, it is often best to start your tracing at the supply output and work backward through the supply toward the ac input.

Measure dc voltage at the regulator's output and input. Regulator output should equal the final supply output measured earlier. If the regulator's input voltage is several volts higher than the expected output and the actual output is low or nonexistent, your regulator is probably defective. Try replacing the regulator. If the regulator's input voltage is low or absent, examine the filter network. Assuming the PC board is intact, the filter voltage should roughly equal the regulator's input voltage. Remove all power from the supply, discharge the filter capacitor(s) with a high-value resistor (100 kΩ or larger), and check each capacitor. Replace any faulty filter capacitors. If the filter circuit checks properly, check the junction of each rectifier diode. An open rectifier diode can disable the supply. Replace any faulty rectifier diodes.

Should your rectifier diodes check properly, reapply power to the supply and measure ac voltage across the transformer's secondary (output) winding. The expected output is typically marked on the windings. Also check the ac voltage across the transformer's primary coil. You should find about 120 Vac across the primary (or about 220 Vac in Europe). If there is no voltage across the primary, there will be no signal across the secondary. This suggests a faulty fuse or circuit breaker, or some other circuit interruption in the primary transformer circuit. When primary voltage is normal and secondary voltage is low or absent, suspect a failure in the transformer. Finally, if ac is available to the supply, but you cannot find the point where ac or dc disappears, you can simply replace the power supply outright.

Symptom 2. The device operates only intermittently. You might see the power indicator LED blink on and off An intermittent problem has likely developed in the power supply. Begin by checking the ac input voltage into the power supply. *Use extreme caution whenever measuring ac line voltage.* Use your multimeter to measure ac voltage at your power supply's plug. If you are using an isolation transformer as recommended, you should check the transformer's ac output to your supply. You should normally read 105 to 130 Vac (210 to 240 Vac in Europe). More or less line voltage can cause the supply to malfunction. Use a multimeter and measure each power supply output before and after an intermittent failure. If any of the supply outputs quit during an intermittent fault, the problem is likely in the power supply. If each of the supply outputs remain steady during an intermittent fault, the supply is likely working properly and the problem is likely elsewhere (such as in the device itself).

When the power supply is suspect, consider the possibility of a PC board failure, especially if the supply (or device) has only recently been dropped or severely abused. Faulty soldering at the factory (or on your test bench) also can cause PC board problems. The PC board might be cracked, one or more component leads might have pulled away from their solder pads, or a trace (or traces) might have broken from the stress of impact. Inspect the power supply PC board assembly carefully and repair any damage that you might find. If the board damage is very extensive or you are unable to find any damage, you should probably replace the power supply outright because intermittent problems are difficult to track down unless they are obvious.

In addition to physical intermittents, you also should check the supply for thermal intermittent problems. Thermal problems typically occur in semiconductor devices such as transistors or ICs, so your supply's regulator(s) are likely candidates. A thermal failure is usually indicated when the supply works once turned on, then cuts out after some period of operation. The supply can then remain disabled until it is turned off, or can cut in and out while running. Often, a thermally defective regulator can operate when cool (room temperature), but as it runs and dissipates power, its internal temperature climbs. When temperature climbs enough, the device might stop working. If you remove power from the supply and let it cool again, the supply can resume operation.

If you detect any hot components in your intermittent supply, you might suspect a thermal intermittent problem. Spray the suspect part(s) with electronics-grade refrigerant available from almost any electronics store. Leave power applied to the part and spray in short, very controlled bursts. Many short bursts are cleaner and more effective than one long burst. If the supply stabilizes or stops cutting out, you have probably identified the faulty part. Replace any thermally intermittent components, or replace the entire power supply at your discretion.

46
CHAPTER

Switching power supplies

As you saw in the previous chapter, power supplies play a vital role in the operation of PCs and their peripherals—a supply converts commercial ac into various levels of dc that can be used by electronic and electromechanical devices. For the purposes of this book, power supplies are put into three classes: linear supplies, switching supplies, and high-voltage supplies. Although linear power supplies are popular because of their simplicity, they are inefficient. As a result, linear supplies are typically relegated to low-end applications such as ac adapters and battery eliminators. On the other hand, *switching* power supplies are well entrenched in PC applications. Virtually all PC and peripheral designs incorporate a switching supply. This chapter shows the operation and troubleshooting approaches for a switching power supply.

Understanding switching supplies

The great disadvantage to linear power supplies is their tremendous waste. At least half of all power provided to a linear supply is literally thrown away as heat; most of this waste occurs in a regulator. Ideally, if there was just enough energy supplied to the regulator to achieve a stable output voltage, regulator waste could be reduced almost entirely.

Concepts of switching regulation

Instead of throwing away extra input energy, a *switching* power supply creates a feedback loop. Feedback senses the output voltage provided to a load, then switches the ac primary (or secondary) voltage on or off as needed to maintain steady levels at the output. In effect, a switching power supply is constantly turning on and off in order to keep the output signals steady. A block diagram of a typical switching power supply is shown in Fig. 46-1. There are a variety of configurations that are possible, but Fig. 46-1 shows one classic design.

Raw ac line voltage entering the supply is immediately converted to pulsating dc, then filtered to provide a primary dc voltage. Notice that unlike a linear supply,

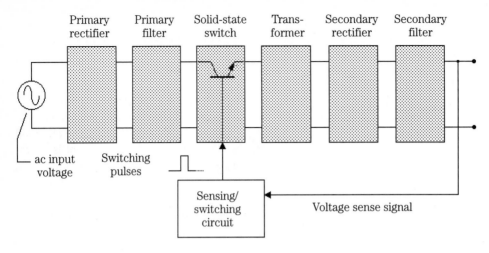

46-1 Block diagram of a switching power supply.

ac is not transformed before rectification, so primary dc can easily reach levels exceeding 170 V. Remember that ac is 120 V rms. Because capacitors charge to the peak voltage (*peak = RMS* × 1.414), dc levels can be higher than your ac voltmeter readings. *Also keep in mind that high-voltage pulsating dc can be as dangerous as ac line voltage, and should be treated with extreme caution.*

On start-up, the switching transistor is turned on and off at a high frequency (usually 20 kHz to 40 kHz), and a long duty cycle. The switching transistor acts as a "chopper" that breaks up this primary dc to form *chopped dc* that can now be used as the primary signal for a step-down transformer. The duty cycle of chopped dc will affect the ac voltage level generated on the transformer's secondary. A long duty cycle means a larger output voltage (for heavy loads) and a short duty cycle means lower output voltage (for light loads). *Duty cycle* itself refers to the amount of time that a signal is on compared to its overall cycle. The duty cycle is continuously ad-

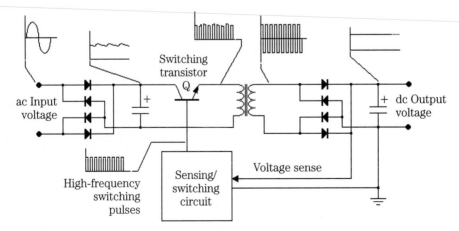

46-2 Simplified schematic of a switching power supply.

justed by the sensing/switching circuit. You can use an oscilloscope to view switching and chopped dc signals. Figure 46-2 shows a more practical representation for a switching supply.

Alternating current produced on the transformer's secondary winding (typically a step-down transformer) is not a pure sine wave, but it alternates regularly enough to be treated as ac by the remainder of the supply. Secondary voltage is re-rectified and refiltered to form a secondary dc voltage that is actually applied to the load. Output voltage is sensed by the sensing/switching circuit that constantly adjusts the chopped dc duty cycle. As the load increases on the secondary circuit (more current is drawn by the load), output voltage tends to drop. This is perfectly normal, and the same thing happens in every unregulated supply. However, a sensing circuit detects this voltage drop and increases the switching duty cycle. In turn, the duty cycle for chopped dc increases, which increases the voltage produced by the secondary winding. Output voltage climbs back up again to its desired value; output voltage is regulated.

The reverse will happen as load decreases on the secondary circuit (less current is drawn by the load). A smaller load will tend to make output voltage climb. Again, the same actions happen in an unregulated supply. The sensing/switching circuit detects this increase in voltage and reduces the switching duty cycle. As a result, the duty cycle for chopped dc decreases, and transformer secondary voltage decreases. The output voltage drops back to its desired value and it remains regulated.

Consider the advantages of a switching power circuit. Current is only drawn in the primary circuit when its switching transistor is on, so very little power is wasted in the primary circuit. The secondary circuit will supply just enough power to keep load voltage constant (regulated), but very little power is wasted by the secondary rectifier, filter, or switching circuit. Switching power supplies can reach efficiencies higher than 85% (35% more efficient than most comparable linear supplies). More efficiency means less heat is generated by the supply, so components can be smaller and packaged more tightly.

Unfortunately, there are several disadvantages to switching supplies that you must be aware of. First, switching supplies tend to act as radio transmitters. Their 20-kHz to 40-kHz operating frequencies can wreak havoc on radio and television reception, not to mention the circuitry within the PC or peripheral itself. This is why you will see most switching supplies somehow covered or shielded in a metal casing. It is critically important that you replace any shielding removed during your repair. Strong *EMI* (electromagnetic interference) can easily disturb the operation of a logic circuit.

Second, the output voltage will always contain some amount of high-frequency ripple. In many applications, this is not enough noise to present interference to the load. In fact, most of the noise is filtered out in a carefully designed supply. Finally, a switching supply often contains more components, and is more difficult to troubleshoot than a linear supply. This is often outweighed by the smaller, lighter packaging of switching supplies.

Today, sensing and switching functions can be fabricated right onto an integrated circuit. IC-based switching circuits allow simple, inexpensive circuits to be built as shown in Fig. 46-3. Notice how similar this looks versus a linear supply. Alternating-current line voltage is transformed (usually stepped down), then it is rectified and filtered before reaching a switch regulating IC. The IC chops dc voltage at

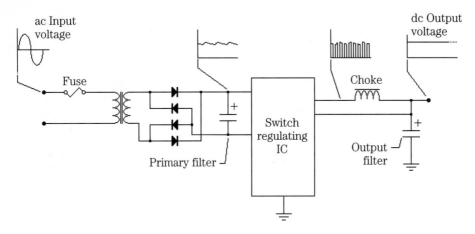

46-3 Simplified schematic of an IC-based switching power supply.

a duty cycle that will provide adequate power to the load. Chopped dc from the switching regulator is filtered by the combination of choke and output filter capacitor to reform a steady dc signal at the output. The output voltage is sampled back at the IC that constantly adjusts the chopped dc duty cycle.

Troubleshooting switching power supplies

Troubleshooting a switching power supply can be a complex and time-consuming task. Although the operation of rectifier and filter sections are reasonably straightforward, sensing/switching circuits can be complex oscillators that are difficult to follow without a schematic. Subassembly replacement of dc switching supplies is quite common. For the purposes of this troubleshooting discussion, consider the IC-based switching supply of Fig. 46-4.

The STK7554 is a switching regulator IC manufactured as a 16-pin SIP (single in-line package). It offers a dual output of 24 Vdc and 5 Vdc. Notice that both output waveforms from the STK7554 are 38-V square waves, but it is the *duty cycle* of those square waves that sets the desired output levels. The square wave's amplitude simply provides energy to the filter circuits. Filters made from coils (or "chokes") and high-value polarized capacitors smooth the square-wave input (actually a form of pulsating dc) into a steady source of dc. There will be some small amount of high-frequency ripple on each dc output. Smaller, nonpolarized capacitors on each output act to filter out high-frequency components of the dc output. Finally, note the resistor-capacitor-diode combinations on each output. These form a surge and flyback protector that prevents energy stored in the choke from re-entering the IC and damaging it. Refer to Fig. 46-4 for the following symptoms.

Symptom 1. The PC or peripheral is completely dead—no power indicators are lit As with linear supplies, check the ac line voltage entering the PC before beginning any major repair work. Use your multimeter to measure the ac line voltage available at the wall outlet powering your computer or peripheral. Use extreme caution whenever measuring ac line voltage levels. Normally, you should read between

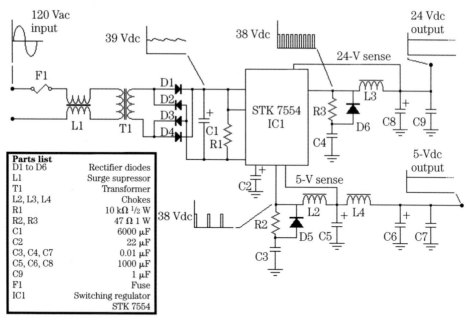

46-4 A complete IC-based switching power supply.

105 and 130 Vac to ensure proper supply operation. If you find either very high or low ac voltage, try the device in an outlet that provides the correct amount of ac voltage. Unusual line voltage levels might damage your power supply, so proceed cautiously.

If ac line voltage is normal, suspect the main power fuse in the supply. Most power fuses are accessible from the rear of the computer near the ac line cord, but some fuses might only be accessible by disassembling the device and opening the supply. Unplug the device and remove the fuse from its holder. You should find the fusible link intact, but use your multimeter to measure continuity across the fuse. A good fuse should measure as a short circuit (0 Ω), but a failed fuse will measure as an open circuit (infinity). Replace any failed fuse and retest the PC. If the fuse continually fails, there is a serious defect elsewhere within the power supply or other computer/peripheral circuits. If your supply has an ac selector switch that sets the supply for 120-Vac or 240-Vac operation, be sure that switch is in the proper position for your region of the world (an improperly set ac switch can disable the entire system).

Unplug the computer and disassemble it enough to expose the power supply clearly. Restore power to the PC and measure each dc output with your multimeter or oscilloscope (you can usually find a power connector at the motherboard or other main board). Make sure that any power cables are securely attached. If each output measures correctly, then your trouble lies outside of the supply—a key circuit has failed elsewhere in the device. You can try a POST board or diagnostic to trace the specific problem further. A low output voltage suggests a problem within the supply itself. Check each connector and all interconnecting wiring leading to or from the supply. Remember that many switching supplies *must* be attached to a load for proper switching to occur. If the load circuit is disconnected from its supply, the voltage signal could shutdown or oscillate wildly.

When supply outputs continue to measure incorrectly with all connectors and wiring intact, chances are that your problem is inside the supply. With a linear supply, you begin testing at the output, then work back toward the ac input. For a switching supply, you should begin testing at the ac input, then work toward the defective output.

Measure the primary ac voltage applied across the transformer (T1). Use extreme caution when measuring high-voltage ac. You should read approximately 120 Vac for Fig. 46-4. If voltage has been interrupted in that primary circuit, you will read 0 Vac. Check the primary circuit for any fault that might interrupt power. Measure secondary ac voltage supplying the rectifier stage. It should read higher than the highest output voltage that you expect. For the example of Fig. 46-4, the highest expected dc output is 24 V, so ac secondary voltage should be several volts higher than this. The example shows this as 28 Vac. If primary voltage reads correctly and secondary voltage does not, you might have an open circuit in the primary or secondary transformer winding; try replacing the transformer.

Next, check the preswitched dc voltage supplying the switching IC. Use your multimeter or oscilloscope to measure this dc level. You should read approximately the peak value of whatever secondary ac voltage you just measured. For Fig. 46-4, a secondary voltage of 28 Vac should yield a dc voltage of about [28 Vac rms × 1.414] 39 Vdc. If this voltage is low or nonexistent, unplug ac from the supply and check each rectifier diode, then inspect the filter capacitor.

Use your oscilloscope to measure each chopped dc output signal. You should find a high-frequency square wave at each output (20 kHz to 40 kHz) with an amplitude approximately equal to the preswitched dc level (38 to 39 volts in this case). Set your oscilloscope to a time base of 5 or 10 S/DIV and start your VOLTS/DIV setting at 10 VOLTS/DIV. Once you have established a clear trace, adjust the time base and vertical sensitivity to optimize the display.

If you do not read a chopped dc output from the switching IC, either the IC is defective, or one (or more) of the polarized output filter capacitors might be shorted. Unplug the PC and inspect each questionable filter capacitor. Replace any capacitors that appear shorted. As a general rule, filter capacitors tend to fail more readily in switching supplies than in linear supplies because of high-frequency electrical stress, and the smaller physical size of most switching supply components. If all filter capacitors check out correctly, replace the switching IC. Use care when desoldering the old regulator. Install an IC socket (if possible) to prevent repeat soldering work, then just plug in the new IC. If you do not have the tools to perform the work outlined above (or the problem persists), replace the power supply outright.

Symptom 2. Supply operation is intermittent—device operation cuts in and out with the supply Begin by inspecting the ac line voltage into your printer. Be sure that the ac line cord is secured properly at the wall outlet and printer. Make sure that the power fuse is installed securely. If the PC/peripheral comes on at all, the fuse *must* be intact. Unplug the device and expose your power supply. Inspect every connector or interconnecting wire leading into or out of the supply. A loose or improperly installed connector can play havoc with the system's operation. Pay particular attention to any output connections. In almost all cases, a switching power supply must be connected to its load circuit in order to operate. Without a load, the supply might cut out or oscillate wildly.

In many cases, intermittent operation might be the result of a PC board problem. PC board problems are often the result of physical abuse or impact, but they also can be caused by accidental damage during a repair. Lead pull-through occurs when a wire or component lead is pulled away from its solder joint, usually through its hole in the PC board. This type of defect can easily be repaired by reinserting the pulled lead and properly resoldering the defective joint. Trace breaks are hairline fractures between a solder pad and its printed trace. Such breaks can usually render a circuit inoperative, and they are almost impossible to spot without a careful visual inspection. Board cracks can sever any number of printed traces, but they are often very easy to spot. The best method for repairing trace breaks and board cracks is to solder jumper wires across the damage between two adjacent solder pads. You also might simply replace the power supply outright.

Some forms of intermittent failures are time or temperature related. If your system works just fine when first turned on, but fails only after a period of use, then spontaneously returns to operation later on (or after it has been off for a while), you might be faced with a thermally intermittent component—a component might work when cool, but fail later on after reaching or exceeding its working temperature. After a system quits under such circumstances, check for any unusually hot components. *Never touch an operating circuit with your fingers—injury is almost certain.* Instead, smell around the circuit for any trace of burning semiconductor or unusually heated air. If you detect an overheated component, spray it with a liquid refrigerant. Spray in short bursts for the best cooling. If normal operation returns, then you have isolated the defective component. Replace any components that behave intermittently. If operation does not return, test any other unusually warm components. If problems persist, replace the entire power supply outright.

47
CHAPTER

High-voltage power supplies

Although linear and switching power supplies provide the conventional dc voltage levels needed for PC and peripheral operation, they are not well suited for high-voltage applications. In order to power specialized devices such as CRTs and LCD backlights, the ordinary power supply is supplemented by high-voltage supply circuits which can turn relatively low voltages into high voltages that range anywhere from several hundred volts to tens of thousands of volts, depending on the particular need. This chapter illustrates the operation and troubleshooting approaches to two important high-voltage circuits; the backlight supply, and the CRT flyback supply.

Backlight power supplies

Today's notebook and subnotebook LCDs are almost always based on a *transmissive* light design; that is, the light you see from the display is generated entirely from behind the LCD by a *backlight* assembly. Whatever light emanates from the display is interpreted as being transparent (or colored). Light that is absorbed by energized liquid crystal material appears opaque. In order to run a CCFT (cold cathode fluorescent tube) or EL (electroluminescent) backlight, a source of several hundred volts is needed (often 200 V or more). Because the battery pack in a mobile computer is certainly not capable of sourcing that much voltage, it must be created on-the-fly. If you remove the front housing from an LCD panel, you can locate the backlight supply right next to the LCD as shown in Figure 47-1.

Inverter principles

The key to a backlight power supply is the principle of *inversion*, converting ("chopping") dc into an ac signal. A simple inverter circuit is shown in the illustration of Figure 47-2. dc from the battery pack is fed to an oscillator. The oscillator chops the dc into low-voltage pulsating dc. In turn, the pulsating dc is applied across a small,

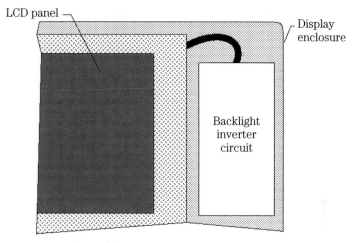

47-1 Locating the LCD backlight inverter.

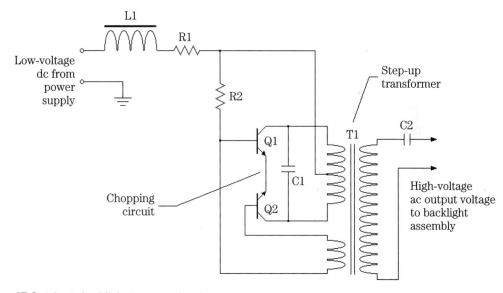

47-2 A basic backlight inverter circuit.

high-ratio step-up transformer which multiplies the pulsating dc into a rough ac signal. This high-voltage ac signal can then be used to run a *CCFT* (cold-cathode fluorescent tube) or *EL* (electroluminescent) backlight. As you might notice, the conversion of dc into ac is virtually opposite of the process used in linear power supplies (thus the term *inverter*) where ac is transformed into dc. If dc is required from the inverter rather than ac, there will be a subsequent rectifier and filter after the transformer output.

Troubleshooting backlight supplies

Backlight problems usually manifest themselves in the LCD itself. Without proper backlighting, the contrast and brightness of a display will be extremely poor.

The display might appear clearly in strong daylight, but disappear in low light or darkness. When backlight problems occur, you should investigate your inverter supply as well as the particular mechanism (CCFT or EL panel) producing the light.

Symptom 1. The backlight appears inoperative The LCD might seem washed out or invisible in low light. Remember that virtually all notebook and sub-notebook computers are designed to shut down the backlight after some period of inactivity regardless of whether the system is being powered by battery or line voltage. Backlights such as CCFTs and EL panels do not last forever, so disabling the backlight not only saves power during battery operation, but saves the backlight itself. If the backlight cuts out suddenly, it might simply have timed out. Try pressing a key or moving a mouse to restore backlight power. You can usually select the backlight timeout period through the system setup software.

Disassemble the display portion of your display to expose the inverter board (typically located behind or next to the LCD). Apply power to the system, then use your multimeter to measure the inverter's dc input voltage. Input voltage usually runs anywhere from 6 to 32 Vdc, depending on your particular system and backlight type. In any case, you would expect to measure a strong, steady dc voltage. If input voltage is low or absent, there might be a faulty connection to the system motherboard.

Next, use your multimeter to measure the inverter's ac output voltage. Fluorescent tubes and electroluminescent panels typically require 200 to 600 Vac for starting and running illumination. *Warning: the insulation of ordinary test leads might break down measuring voltages over 600 V. If you will be measuring voltages over 500 or 600 V, be sure to use better-insulated test probes.* If output voltage is low or absent, the inverter circuit is probably defective. You might simply replace the inverter circuit outright, or attempt to troubleshoot the inverter to the component level. If output voltage measures an acceptable level, your inverter board is probably working correctly. The trouble might exist in the light source itself. For example, a CCFT might have failed, or an EL panel might be damaged. Try replacing the suspect light source.

If you elect to try troubleshooting the inverter board itself, you might see from Fig. 47-2 that there is little to fail. Remove all power from the computer and check the oscillator transistors. A faulty transistor can stop your inverter from oscillating, so no ac voltage will be produced. Replace any defective transistors. Beyond faulty transistors, inspect any electrolytic capacitors on the inverter board. A shorted or open tantalum or aluminum electrolytic capacitor might prevent the oscillator from functioning. The transformer might also fail, but they are often specialized components that are difficult to find replacements for. If you are unable to locate any obvious component failures, go ahead and replace the inverter board.

CRT flyback supplies

High-voltage is perhaps the most critical (and dangerous) aspect of any computer monitor. A CRT requires an extremely high potential to accelerate an electron beam from the cathode to its phosphor-coated face (easily a distance of 12 to 14 inches or more). To accomplish this feat of physics, a positive voltage of 15,000 to 30,000 Vdc is applied to the CRT's face through a connection known as the *anode*. It is easy to identify the anode connection—it is underneath the thick red rubber cap on the upper right corner of the CRT (with the neck toward you). Fortunately, the high-voltage system is relatively easy to understand.

A typical high-voltage system is shown in the schematic fragment of Fig. 47-3. As you probably see, there is really only one critical part—the flyback transformer (or FBT) marked T302. The horizontal output transistor (Q302) generate high-current pulses that control the horizontal deflection yoke (H-DY). Horizontal output signals are also fed to the FBT which boosts the signal to its final high-voltage level. The lower primary winding is connected back to the video circuit and acts as an "error amplifier." This allows the high-voltage level to vary as contrast and brightness are adjusted. The FBT assembly produces three outputs. The high-voltage output is connected directly to the CRT anode through a well-insulated, high-voltage cable. A

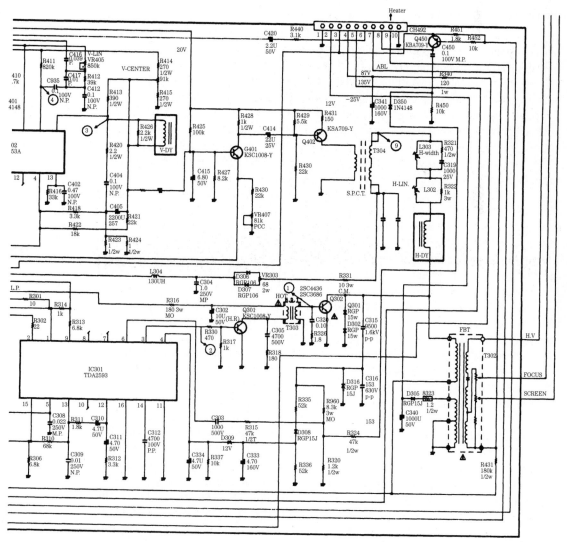

47-3 High-voltage schematic fragment from a Tandy VGM-220 monitor. Tandy Corporation

supplemental output of several hundred volts feeds a small voltage divider network consisting of two potentiometers and a fixed resistor. The top potentiometer controls the higher voltages and is used to drive the CRT's focus electrode(s). The second potentiometer drives the CRT's screen electrode(s).

The voltages generated by an FBT are all *pulsating dc* signals. Because all transformers work with ac rather than dc, there is always a question of how dc is produced by an ac device. The answer is in the small diode located between the top and middle coils of the FBT secondary. This diode forms a half-wave rectifier built right into the FBT. Pulsating high-voltage is smoothed by the characteristic capacitance of the CRT. The pulsating focus and screen voltages are smoothed by filtering components located on the video board attached to the CRT.

Troubleshooting flyback supplies

The loss of high-voltage can manifest itself in several ways depending on exactly where the fault occurs, but in virtually all cases, the screen image and raster will be disturbed or disappear completely. Whenever a screen image disappears, you should first suspect a fault in the conventional power supply. By measuring each available output with a multimeter, you can often determine whether the problem is inside or outside of the power supply. When one or more conventional power output levels appear low or absent, concentrate your troubleshooting on the conventional supply. When all outputs appear normal, the problem is likely in the high-voltage system. Refer to Fig. 47-3.

Symptom 1. Anode high-voltage measures very low; there is no raster and no picture, or there is a vertical line against the raster The power LED appears steadily lit, and all conventional power supply outputs measure correctly. Make sure that the display contrast and brightness controls are set to acceptable levels. Also check that the video signal cable from the video adapter is connected properly. Use your oscilloscope and measure the horizontal pulse at the collector of the horizontal output transistor (Q302). If the pulse is present, the fault is likely in the flyback transformer assembly. Try replacing the FBT. Keep in mind that the FBT is a critical part and must be replaced with an identical part. If the problem persists, suspect the CRT. Use a CRT analyzer/rejuvenator (if possible) to check the CRT. If the CRT checks bad or the equipment is not available, try replacing the CRT. Note that the CRT is often the most expensive part of a monitor. Before replacing the CRT, you should carefully weigh the cost of another CRT against the cost of another monitor.

If the horizontal pulse is missing from the collector, use your oscilloscope to check the input at the base of Q302. You should find approximately a 5-V pulse. If the pulse is present, Q302 has failed and should be replaced with an exact replacement part. If the pulse is missing from the base, check the collector of the horizontal switching transistor (Q301). If the pulse is present at the collector of Q301 but missing from the base of Q302, the fault is likely in the horizontal output transformer (T303). Try replacing T303. If you find the pulse signal missing from the collector of Q301, check for the pulse at the base of Q301. If the pulse is present, Q301 is defective and should be replaced. If the pulse is still missing from the base of Q301, the problem is likely in the horizontal output controller. Try replacing the horizontal controller IC. If you are unable to trace the circuit or locate the defect, you can simply replace the main monitor PC board.

<h1>48</h1>

SCSI system troubleshooting

Many contemporary PC interfaces require a plug-in expansion board that provides the circuitry needed for the computer to communicate with the device (such as a CD-ROM controller or floppy drive controller). There are two drawbacks to these interfaces: (1) they will only control one specific type of device, and (2) the peripheral device must rely on the computer itself to direct all their operations. Although this has been a tried-and-true approach for many years, it reduces the amount of time that a computer has to perform its primary task—processing data.

The *SCSI* (small computer system interface, affectionately pronounced "scuzzy") was developed to provide a PC with a *system-level* interface. Such an interface effectively buffers the PC from SCSI peripherals. SCSI has enjoyed a growing popularity in computer designs since it became an ANSI standard in 1986. You have probably seen the term used many times in conjunction with new products, but there is very little literature available regarding the use and troubleshooting of SCSI systems. This chapter examines the inner workings of the SCSI interface, and shows you how to deal with installation and troubleshooting problems.

Understanding SCSI concepts

Ideally, peripherals should be independent of the microprocessor's operation. The computer should only have to send commands and data to the peripheral, and wait for the peripheral to respond. Printers work this way. The parallel and serial ports are actually device-level interfaces. The computer is unconcerned with what device is attached to the port. In other words, you can take a printer built 12 years ago and connect it to a new Pentium-based system; the printer will work just fine because only data and commands are being sent across the interface. Essentially, this is the concept behind SCSI. Computers and peripherals can be designed, developed, and integrated and you don't need to worry about hardware compatibility; such compatibility is established by the SCSI interface.

A bit of history

SCSI originally evolved from IBM 360 mainframe computers, so it has existed in one form or another for many years. Shugart Associates (now known as Seagate Technologies) scaled down this overpowered system-level interface to serve as an intelligent hard disk drive interface. Shugart Associates called their development the *SASI* (Shugart Associates Systems Interface or *sassy*). When ANSI began discussions on a standard in 1982, the SASI interface was expanded to include a large number of possible peripherals that were not even on the drawing board yet. Tape drives, optical disk drives, printers, scanners, and communication devices were considered in the early SCSI standard. Since 1986, SCSI has been upgraded to recognize such design advances as caching, command queuing, device self-testing, an extended 32-bit data bus, and up to 10 MHz of transfer speed. The second major iteration (SCSI-2, approved by ANSI in 1992) is now the standard commonly used in computer designs.

Device independence

From a practical standpoint, SCSI is a *bus*, an organization of physical wires and terminations where each wire has its own name and purpose. SCSI also consists of a *command set*, a limited set of instructions that allow the computer and peripheral to communicate over the physical bus. The SCSI bus is used in systems that want to achieve device independence. For example, all hard disk drives look alike to the SCSI interface (except for their total capacity), all optical drives look alike, all printers look alike, and so on. For any particular type of SCSI device, you should be able to replace an existing device with another device without any system modifications, and new SCSI devices can often be added to the bus with no hardware changes at all. Because the intelligence of SCSI resides in the peripheral device itself and NOT in the computer, the computer is able to use a small set of standard commands to accomplish data transfer back and forth to the peripheral. Now that you understand a bit about the history and purpose of the SCSI interface, the following sections explain some of the important terms and concepts you'll need to know.

Initiators and targets

There are basically two types of devices on the SCSI bus: initiators and targets. An *initiator* starts communication when something has to be done, and a *target* responds to the initiator's commands. The important thing for you to understand here is that this master-slave relationship is not a one-way arrangement; an initiator might become a target at some points in the data transfer cycle, and the target might become the initiator at other points. You will see more about this role duality later in this chapter. A SCSI bus can support up to eight devices simultaneously, but there MUST be at least one initiator and one target in the system. A SCSI *host adapter* (the expansion card installed in one of the computer's expansion slots) is typically the initiator, and all other devices (hard drives or CD-ROMs) are usually targets, but that is not necessarily the only possible case.

Many kinds of computer peripherals are candidates for the SCSI bus. Each peripheral offers unique characteristics and applications, but each also requires different methods of control. By adding SCSI intelligence to these devices, they can all be made to share the same bus together. The SCSI nomenclature groups similar devices together into specific device types. The original SCSI standard defines six devices:

- Random-access devices (hard drives)
- Sequential access (tape drives)
- Printers
- Processors
- WORM (write-once, read-many) drives
- Read-only random access devices.

The SCSI-2 interface adds five more devices to the specification:

- CD-ROM
- Scanners
- Magneto-optical drives
- Media changer (jukebox)
- Communication devices.

Synchronous and asynchronous

As a system-level interface, SCSI requires an operating *handshaking protocol* that organizes the transfer of data from a sending point to a requesting point. There are typically three handshaking protocols for SCSI: asynchronous, synchronous, and fast synchronous. The *asynchronous* protocol works rather like a parallel port. Each byte must be requested and acknowledged before the next byte can be sent. Asynchronous operation generally results in very reliable (but slower) performance. *Synchronous* and *fast synchronous* operation both ignore the request/acknowledge handshake for data transfer only. This allows slightly faster operation than an asynchronous protocol, but a certain fixed amount of time delay (sometimes called an *offset*) must be allowed for request and acknowledge effects. The fast synchronous protocol uses slightly shorter signals, resulting in even faster speed.

An important point to remember is that SCSI systems can typically use any of these three protocols as desired. The actual protocol that is used must be mutually agreed to by the initiator and the target through their communications. SCSI systems normally initialize in an asynchronous protocol.

Disconnect and reconnect

In a number of instances, it would be desirable to allow a target to operate offline while the initiator is occupied elsewhere. Tape rewind time is just one example. An important feature of SCSI is the ability to *disconnect* two communicating devices, then *reconnect* them later. Disconnect and reconnect operations allow several different operations to occur simultaneously in the system and is the reason why SCSI is so desirable in a multitasking environment. It is up to the initiator to grant a disconnect privilege to a target.

Single-ended and differential

The signal wiring used in a SCSI bus has a definite impact on bus performance. There are two generally used wiring techniques for SCSI: single-ended and differential. Both wiring schemes have advantages and disadvantages.

The single-ended wiring technique is just as the name implies—a single wire carries the particular signal from initiator to target. Each signal requires only one wire. Terminating resistors at each end of the cable help to maintain acceptable signal levels. A common ground (return) provides the reference for all single-ended signals. Unfortunately, single-ended circuitry is not very noise resistant, so single-ended cabling is generally limited to about 6 meters at data transfer speeds of 5 MHz or less. In spite of the disadvantages, single-ended operation is simple and popular.

The differential wiring approach uses two wires for each signal (instead of one wire referenced to a common ground). A differential signal offers excellent noise resistance because it does not rely on a common ground. This allows much longer cables (up to 25 meters) and higher-speed operation (10 MHz). An array of pull-up resistors at each end of the cable help to ensure signal integrity. The problem with differential wiring is that it is more complicated than single-ended interfaces.

SCSI variations

Since ANSI approved the original SCSI standard in 1986, there have been a number of modifications and advancements that you should be familiar with. Unfortunately, SCSI-1 suffered from serious compatibility problems. Many commands and features were optional, and were implemented differently by different manufacturers; not all devices, drivers, and adapters were compatible. This resulted in a fragmentation of the SCSI market that hampered the widespread acceptance of SCSI on the PC platform.

The development of SCSI-2 promised to provide the standard implementation of a Common Command Set (CCS) that SCSI-1 lacked, as well as support for a broader array of devices (like CD-ROMs). SCSI-2 also set down the foundation for variations such as fast SCSI and wide SCSI. Fast SCSI improves data transfers by boosting the throughput from 5Mb/sec to 10Mb/sec. Wide SCSI offers a 16-bit data path instead of an 8-bit path that also boosts data throughput to 10Mb/sec. When fast and wide variations are combined, the SCSI system can handle data at 20Mb/sec.

Terminators

When high-frequency signals are transmitted over adjacent wires, signals tend to degrade and interfere with one another over the length of the cable. This is a very natural and relatively well-understood phenomenon. In the PC, signal integrity is enhanced by using powered resistors at each end of the data cable to pull up active signals. Most high-frequency signal cables in the PC are already terminated by pull-up resistors at drives and controller cards. The small resistor array is known as a terminator. Because there is a distinct limit to the number of devices that can be added to a floppy drive or IDE cable, designers have never made a big deal about termination; they just added the resistors and that was it. With SCSI, however, up to eight devices can be added to the bus cable. The SCSI cable also must be terminated, but the location of terminating resistors depends on which devices are added to the bus, and where they are placed. As a result, termination is a much more vital element of SCSI setup and troubleshooting. As you will see later in this chapter, poor or incorrect termination can cause intermittent signal problems. Later on you will see how to determine the proper placement of terminating resistors.

Termination is typically either active or passive. Basically, passive termination is simply plugging a resistor pack into a SCSI device. Passive resistors are powered by the TERMPWR line. Passive termination is simple and effective over short distances (up to about 1 meter) and usually works just fine for the cable lengths inside a PC, but can be a drawback over longer distances. Active terminators provide their own regulated power sources that makes them most effective for longer cables (such as those found in external SCSI devices like page scanners) or Wide SCSI systems. A variation on active termination is forced perfect termination (or FPT). FPT includes diode clamps that prevent signal overshoot and undershoot. This makes FPT effective for long SCSI cable lengths.

SCSI IDs

A SCSI bus will support up to 8 devices. This means each device on the bus must have its own unique ID number (0 to 7). If two devices use the same ID, there will be a conflict. IDs are typically set on the SCSI adapter and each SCSI device using jumpers or DIP switches. Typically, the SCSI adapter is set for ID 7, the primary SCSI hard drive is set to ID 0, and a second SCSI hard drive is ID 1. Other devices can usually be placed anywhere from ID 2 to ID 6.

Bus configurations

Most of the SCSI implementations currently available use single-ended cabling that supports an 8-bit data bus (known as an *A-cable*). An A-cable is a 50-pin assembly outlined in Table 48-1. There are three major sections to the 50-pin single-ended SCSI cable: ground wires, data signals, and control signals. You will notice that at least half of the single-ended interface carries ground lines. There are eight data lines (D0 to D7) and a data parity bit (DPAR). Note that parity is always odd. There are four terminator power lines (TERMPWR) and nine control signal wires.

Control/Data (driven by target) allows the target device to select whether it will be returning a command or data to the initiator.

–I/O Input/Output (driven by target) allows the target device to determine whether it will be receiving or sending information along the data bus.

–MSG Message (driven by target) allows the target device to send coded status or error messages back to the initiator during the message portion of the SCSI bus cycle.

–REQ Request (driven by target) a data strobe signal that allows a potential target device to obtain data on the bus.

–ACK Acknowledge (driven by initiator) is a data strobe signal sent in response to the target's REQ signal that informs the target device that it has gained use of the bus.

–BSY Busy (driven by initiator or target) allows a device to inform the bus that the device is currently busy.

–SEL Select (driven by initiator or target) is a signal used by an initiator in order to select a target device.

–ATN Attention (driven by initiator) is a signal produced by the initiator that informs the target that the initiator has a message ready. The target should switch to the message phase.

–RST Reset (driven by initiator or target) is a strobe signal that triggers a bus-wide reset of all devices. Usually, only one device produces a Reset signal.

Table 48-1. Pinout of a standard single-ended A-cable

Signal	Pin	Pin	Signal
Ground	1	2	Data 0
Ground	3	4	Data 1
Ground	5	6	Data 2
Ground	7	8	Data 3
Ground	9	10	Data 4
Ground	11	12	Data 5
Ground	13	14	Data 6
Ground	15	16	Data 7
Ground	17	18	Data Parity
Ground	19	20	Ground
Ground	21	22	Ground
reserved	23	24	reserved
open	25	26	TERMPWR
reserved	27	28	reserved
Ground	29	30	Ground
Ground	31	32	–ATN (–Attention)
Ground	33	34	Ground
Ground	35	36	–BSY (–Busy)
Ground	37	38	–ACK (–Acknowledge)
Ground	39	40	–RST (–Reset)
Ground	41	42	–MSG (–Message)
Ground	43	44	–SEL (–Select)
Ground	45	46	–C/D (–Control/Data)
Ground	47	48	–REQ (–Request)
Ground	49	50	–I/O (–Input/Output)

The differential SCSI interface replaces most of the ground wires with +signal leads. For example, pin 2 represents +D0, and pin 27 is –D0. These + and – signal pairs are the differential signals. Note that there are still a few ground wires, but the grounds are not related to differential signals as they are to single-ended signals. Just about all of the data and control signals in the differential interface serve an identical purpose in the single-ended interface, but you will notice that the signal locations have been rearranged as shown in Table 48-2. There is one additional differential signal—the DIFFSENS (differential sense) line that provides an active high enable for differential drivers. Remember that plugging a differential cable into a single-ended interface (or vice versa) can damage the device, the SCSI adapter, or both.

Table 48-2. Pinout
of a standard differential A-cable

Signal	Pin	Pin	Signal
Ground	1	2	Ground
+Data 0	3	4	−Data 0
+Data 1	5	6	−Data 1
+Data 2	7	8	−Data 2
+Data 3	9	10	−Data 3
+Data 4	11	12	−Data 4
+Data 5	13	14	−Data 5
+Data 6	15	16	−Data 6
+Data 7	17	18	−Data 7
+Data Parity	19	20	−Data Parity
DIFFSENS	21	22	Ground
reserved	23	24	reserved
TERMPWR	25	26	TERMPWR
reserved	27	28	reserved
+ATN	29	30	−ATN (Attention)
Ground	31	32	Ground
+BSY	33	34	−BSY (Busy)
+ACK	35	36	−ACK (Acknowledge)
+RST	37	38	−RST (Reset)
+MSG	39	40	−MSG (Message)
+SEL	41	42	−SEL (Select)
+C/D	43	44	−C/D (Control/Data)
+REQ	45	46	−REQ (Request)
+I/O	47	48	−/O (Input/Output)
Ground	49	50	Ground

As you might imagine, wide SCSI implementations will not work with A-cables. A 16-bit cable is needed. Early implementations of wide SCSI used a second cable to provide the extra signal lines, but was quickly abandoned for a single cable assembly (called a *P-cable*). The single-ended P-cable is shown in Table 48-3. Although many of the signals might look familiar, you will notice that there are 68 pins instead of 50, primarily to support the 8 additional data lines (D8 to D15). Control lines are identical to those in the A-cable. Table 48-4 shows the pinout for a differential 68 pin P-cable.

Table 48-3. Pinout
of a standard single-ended P-cable

Signal	Pin	Pin	Signal
Ground	1	35	Data 12
Ground	2	36	Data 13
Ground	3	37	Data 14
Ground	4	38	Data 15
Ground	5	39	Data Parity 1

Table 48-3. Continued

Signal	Pin	Pin	Signal
Ground	6	40	Data 0
Ground	7	41	Data 1
Ground	8	42	Data 2
Ground	9	43	Data 3
Ground	10	44	Data 4
Ground	11	45	Data 5
Ground	12	46	Data 6
Ground	13	47	Data 7
Ground	14	48	Data Parity 0
Ground	15	49	Ground
Ground	16	50	Ground
TERMPWR	17	51	TERMPWR
TERMPWR	18	52	TERMPWR
reserved	19	53	reserved
Ground	20	54	Ground
Ground	21	55	−ATN (-Attention)
Ground	22	56	Ground
Ground	23	57	−BSY (−Busy)
Ground	24	58	−ACK (−Acknowledge)
Ground	25	59	−RST (−Reset)
Ground	26	60	−MSG (−Message)
Ground	27	61	−SEL (−Select)
Ground	28	62	-C/D (−Control/Data)
Ground	29	63	−REQ (−Request)
Ground	30	64	−I/O (−Input/Output)
Ground	31	65	Data 8
Ground	32	66	Data 9
Ground	33	67	Data 10
Ground	34	68	Data 11

Table 48-4. Pinout of a standard differential P-cable

Signal	Pin	Pin	Signal
+Data 12	1	35	−Data 12
+Data 13	2	36	−Data 13
+Data 14	3	37	−Data 14
+Data 15	4	38	−Data 15
+Data Parity 1	5	39	−Data Parity 1
Ground	6	40	Ground
+Data 0	7	41	−Data 0
+Data 1	8	42	−Data 1
+Data 2	9	43	−Data 2
+Data 3	10	44	−Data 3
+Data 4	11	45	−Data 4

Table 48-4. Continued

Signal	Pin	Pin	Signal
+Data 5	12	46	−Data 5
+Data 6	13	47	−Data 6
+Data 7	14	48	−Data 7
+Data Parity 0	15	49	−Data Parity 0
DIFFSENS	16	50	Ground
TERMPWR	17	51	TERMPWR
TERMPWR	18	52	TERMPWR
reserved	19	53	reserved
+ATN	20	54	−ATN (Attention)
Ground	21	55	Ground
+BSY	22	56	+BSY (Busy)
+ACK	23	57	−ACK (Acknowledge)
+RST	24	58	−RST (Reset)
+MSG	25	59	−MSG (Message)
+SEL	26	60	−SEL (Select)
+C/D	27	61	−C/D (Control/Data)
+REQ	28	62	−REQ (Request)
+I/O	29	63	−I/O (Input/Output)
Ground	30	64	Ground
+Data 8	31	65	−Data 8
+Data 9	32	66	−Data 9
+Data 10	33	67	−Data 10
+Data 11	34	68	−Data 11

Understanding SCSI bus operation

Now that you have learned about SCSI bus concepts and structure, you can see how the interface behaves during normal operation. Because bus wires are common to every device attached to the bus, a device must obtain permission from all other devices before it can take control of the bus. This attempt to access the bus is called the *arbitration phase*. Once a device (such as the SCSI controller) has won the bus arbitration, it must then make contact with the device to be communicated with. This device selection is known as the *selection phase*. When this contact is established, data transfer can take place. This part of the article will detail negotiation and information transfer over the SCSI bus.

Negotiation

Devices must negotiate to access and use a SCSI bus. Negotiation begins when the bus is free (BSY and SEL lines are idle). A device begins arbitration by activating the BSY line and its own data ID line (data bit D0 to D7 depending on the device). If more than one device tries to control the bus simultaneously, the device with the higher ID line wins. The winning device (an initiator) attempts to acquire a target device by asserting the SEL line and the data ID line (data bit D0 to D7) of the desired device. The BSY line is then released by the initiator, and the desired target device asserts the BSY line to confirm it has been selected. The initiator then releases the SEL and data bus lines. Information transfer can now take place.

Information

The selected target controls the data being transferred, and the direction of transfer. Information transfer lasts until the target device releases the BSY line, thus returning the bus to the idle state. If a piece of information will take a long time to prepare for, the target can end the connection by issuing a disconnect message. It will try to re-establish the connection later with a new arbitration and selection procedure.

During information transfer, the initiator tells its target how to act on a command, and establishes the mode of data transfer during the message-out phase. A specific SCSI command follows the message during the command phase. After a command is sent, data transfer takes place during the data-in and/or data-out phases. The target relinquishes control to the initiator during the command phase. For example, the command itself might ask that more information be transferred. The target then tells the initiator whether the command was successfully completed or not by returning status information during a status phase. Finally, the command is finished when the target sends a progress report to the initiator during the message-in phase. Consider this simple SCSI communication example:

1. Bus Free Phase (system is idle)
2. Arbitration Phase (a device takes control of the bus)
3. Select Phase (the desired device is selected)
4. Message-Out Phase (target sets up data transfer)
5. Command Phase (send command)
6. Data-In Phase (exchange data)
7. Status Phase (indicate the results of the exchange)
8. Message-In Phase (indicate exchange is complete)
9. Bus Free Phase (system is idle)

Upgrading a PC for SCSI

Whether you are considering adding SCSI to your own computer, or planning an upgrade for a customer, there are four essential elements that you must consider: the SCSI peripheral, the SCSI host adapter, the SCSI cable assembly, and the SCSI software driver(s). If any one of these four elements is missing or ill planned, your installation is going to run into problems.

SCSI peripherals

The first item to consider is the SCSI peripheral itself. You first need to know what type of device is needed (such as a SCSI hard drive or CD-ROM). The peripheral should be compatible with SCSI-2 architecture. Although SCSI-3 is a newer architecture, it is a serial standard and might take some years before finding a home in everyday PCs. The peripheral also should have a wide range of available SCSI ID settings. SCSI typically handles eight IDs (0 to 7) and the peripheral should have the flexibility to run on any ID. If only a few IDs are available, you might be limited when it comes time to add other SCSI devices. Peripherals should support SCSI parity.

SCSI devices are available in both internal and external versions. If you consider an internal peripheral, make sure that there is adequate drive space in the PC to accommodate the new peripheral. Either there is a drive bay available, or an existing device can be removed to make room. If the peripheral is to be an external device (such as a printer or scanner), there should be two SCSI connectors on the device to allow for daisy-chaining additional devices later. All SCSI peripherals will require device drivers. Make sure that the device driver is compatible with the same standard protocol used by the adapter (ASPI, CAM, or LADDR). This is a serious consideration because peripherals using incompatible device driver standards will not work properly. Finally, try to choose SCSI peripherals that offer built-in cable termination.

SCSI host adapter

The next item to be considered is the SCSI adapter that fits in the PC expansion bus. Make sure to choose an adapter that is compatible with the PC bus in use (ISA, EISA, MCA, PCI, and so on). Bus-mastering (MCA), 32-bit (EISA), and PCI adapters will provide superior performance if your system will support them. Like the peripheral itself, the adapter also should be designed to support the SCSI-2 standard. Although most adapters are assigned a SCSI ID of 7, the adapter should be flexible enough to work with any ID from 0 to 7. The host adapter also will require a device driver. Make sure that the host device driver uses the same standard as the peripheral(s) (ASPI, CAM, or LADDR). It is important to note here that the driver standard has nothing to do with the choice of SCSI, SCSI-2, or SCSI-3. It is only important that the peripherals and the adapter use the same driver standard.

SCSI Cables and terminators

Check that you select the proper cabling for the SCSI level you are using. Although SCSI cabling should now be relatively standardized, some older cables might use slight modifications for particular peripherals. Be certain that you know of any specialized cabling requirements when choosing peripherals. Try to avoid specialized cabling if at all possible, but if you must use specialized cabling, you should determine what impact the cabling will have on any other SCSI peripherals that can be installed (or can be installed later). Use good-quality SCSI cables specifically intended for the SCSI level you are using (probably SCSI-2), and keep the cables short to minimize signal degradation.

SCSI cables must be terminated at the beginning (host adapter) and end (after the last device) of the SCSI chain. Try to choose internal peripherals that have built-in terminators. Also try to select a host adapter and peripherals that use the same type of terminator resistor network. SCSI-2 systems use active terminator networks. You will see much more about cabling and termination a bit later in this article.

SCSI drivers

Device drivers provide the instructions that allow the SCSI host adapter to communicate with the PC, as well as the peripherals in the SCSI chain (or the SCSI bus). The host adapter itself will require a device driver, as will every peripheral that is added. For example, a SCSI system with one CD-ROM will need a driver for the host adapter and a driver for the CD-ROM. Make sure that driver standards (ASPI, CAM, or LADDR) are the SAME for the host adapter and peripherals. The only exception to the device driver requirement (at this time) is the SCSI hard drive that can be supported by the SCSI adapter's BIOS ROM.

Drivers are added by including them in your PC's CONFIG.SYS and AU-TOEXEC.BAT files. One issue to keep in mind when adding device drivers is that drivers use conventional memory (unless you successfully load the drivers into high memory). The more drivers that are added, the more memory that will be consumed. It is possible that a large number of device drivers might prevent certain memory-demanding DOS applications from running. To keep as much conventional memory (the first 640K in RAM) free as possible, use the DOS *devicehigh* and *loadhigh* features to load the drivers into upper memory (from 640K to 1Mb in RAM).

Tips for a smooth upgrade

SCSI upgrades are not terribly difficult to perform properly, but the subtle considerations and inconsistencies that have always been a part of SCSI implementations can result in confusion and serious delays for you and your customer. The following tips should help to ease your upgrades. First, only add one device at a time. By adding one device at a time and testing the system after each installation, it becomes much easier to determine the point where problems occur. Suppose what happens when you add an adapter, hard drive, and CD-ROM? If the system fails to function, you will have to isolate and check each item to locate the fault. On the other hand, by adding the adapter and testing it, then adding the hard drive and testing it, then adding the CD-ROM and testing it, installation troubleshooting becomes a much simpler matter (although it might take a bit more time overall).

One of the most difficult aspects of troubleshooting is determining what the configuration of a system is. This is especially important during an upgrade because you must know the interrupts (IRQs), DMA channel(s), and I/O ranges used by other expansion devices in the PC. Any overlap in the use of these system resources will eventually result in a hardware conflict. When you install a SCSI host adapter, make it a point to record its IRQ, DMA, and I/O settings along with the SCSI ID settings of all devices that are installed. Because it will be difficult to determine resource settings on sight, try a software diagnostic, or a hardware resource too, such as The Discovery Card by AllMicro. Tape the record to the inside of the PC's cover. Next time the PC returns for service or upgrade, you'll have the information right at your fingertips.

Using the correct terminators and cables can have a profound effect on the performance of your SCSI installation. Good-quality cables and terminators provide electrical characteristics that support good signal transfer. This results in good data reliability between the host controller and peripherals. If cable quality is substandard or terminator networks are not correct for the SCSI level being used, the cable's electrical characteristics and data transfer will be degraded.

Configure and install the SCSI adapter

The SCSI adapter is an expansion board—much like any other expansion board in your PC. You will need to configure the adapter before installing it. Most SCSI adapters need four system resources: an IRQ, a DMA channel, an I/O range, and ROM addresses. Settings are typically made by changing jumper placement. The user's manual for your particular adapter will outline precisely what selections are available, and how to change each one. When choosing system resources, be very careful to avoid conflicts with other adapters in your system. Although manufacturers try to avoid conflicts by presetting the adapter to rarely used settings, you should check for possible conflicts anyway.

You also can set the adapter's SCSI ID and the SCSI parity. In almost all circumstances, the adapter will use a SCSI ID of 7. Parity is a means of error checking the data passed along a SCSI data path. The problem with parity is that all installed SCSI devices must support it, or parity should be disabled. If you select only peripheral devices that support SCSI parity, you can enable it on the adapter. Record the settings on paper and tape the paper inside the PC's cover. Insert the adapter into an available expansion slot and secure the board properly.

Configure and install the SCSI peripheral

It should not be difficult to configure a SCSI peripheral. You are concerned with setting the SCSI ID and SCSI parity. The ID (also called Target ID or Target SCSI ID) can range from 0 to 7. Because the adapter is almost always set at 7, only 0-6 remain. However, SCSI hard drives for AT-compatible machines should be issued IDs of 0 or 1. As a general rule, do not use ID 0 or ID 1 for any devices but hard drives. If you intend to boot your PC from the SCSI hard disk, assign it an ID of 0. PS/2 machines place the bootable hard drive on SCSI ID 6. When assigning IDs in systems with more than one SCSI peripheral, be careful not to use duplicate IDs. Each device must have its own unique ID number.

If the device supports SCSI parity, the setting should be enabled. Keep in mind that to use SCSI parity, all SCSI devices in the system must support it. If even one device does not support it, parity must be disabled system-wide. When another device already in the system relies on SCSI parity (such as a CD-ROM drive), disabling parity to accommodate a new device can render an existing device inoperative. You might need to change your selection of peripheral to one that supports SCSI parity.

Depending on the SCSI device being installed, you also might need to set a Start On Command jumper. Drives draw a serious amount of power during startup. If a large number of devices are trying to draw power, the power supply can be overloaded. A Start On Command option (if available on your peripheral) will keep the device idle until a start command is sent from the SCSI adapter. This way, multiple SCSI devices can be started in a staggered fashion to spread out the power load. For external SCSI devices, situate the device close to the computer. SCSI cables tend to be kept short. If the peripheral is an internal device, you should now mount it in an available drive bay.

Cabling and termination

Once the host adapter and peripheral are configured and installed, you must connect them with a cable. Internal devices are typically connected with a 50-pin *IDC* (insulation displacement connector) ribbon cable (an A-cable). By placing multiple connectors along the length of cable, daisy chaining can be achieved with a single connector on each internal device. External devices typically connect to an external 50-pin connector on the rear of the SCSI adapter, and each device offers two connectors that allow daisy chaining to additional devices. Most commercial adapter and drive kits are packed with an appropriate cable.

The cable(s) must be terminated. There are internal and external SCSI cable terminators, along with SCSI devices that have terminating resistor networks already built in. The concept of termination is reasonably simple—achieve the desired signal cable characteristics by loading each end of the SCSI "chain" with resistors. If the chain is not terminated properly, signals will not be carried reliably (which invariably results in system errors). The trouble usually arises in determining where the ends are. A number of examples will help to clarify how to determine the chain ends.

For a single SCSI drive and adapter as shown in Fig. 48-1, the ends are easy to see. One end should be terminated at the host adapter (which usually has terminating resistors built in). The other end should be terminated at the SCSI hard drive (which also usually has terminating resistors built in). In this type of situation, you need only connect the cable between both devices.

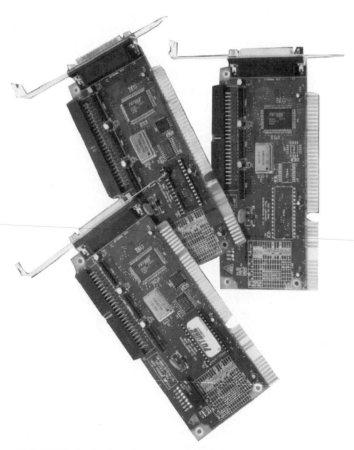

48-1 SCSI adapter boards. Copyright © 1995 Future Domain Corporation. Reprinted with permission.

When a second SCSI peripheral is added as shown in Fig. 48-2 or a second and third (Fig. 48-3), termination becomes a bit more complex. Suppose a CD-ROM is added with a SCSI ID of 6. The terminator on the existing SCSI hard drive is no longer appropriate; it should be removed, and the termination should be on the CD-ROM, which is now the last device in the SCSI chain. In most cases, a terminator network can be deactivated by flipping a DIP switch or changing a jumper on the peripheral itself. If the terminator cannot be shut off, it can almost always be removed by gently easing the resistor network out of its holder using needle-nose pliers. If you remove a terminator, place it in an envelope and tape it to the inside of the PC enclosure. If it is simply impossible to remove the existing terminator on the hard drive, place the CD-ROM between the adapter and hard drive and remove the CD-ROM's terminator (rearrange the chain).

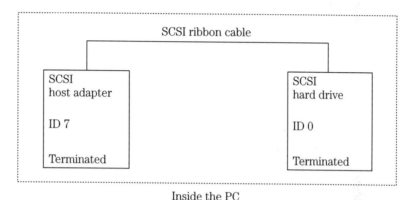

48-2 Terminating an internal SCSI adapter and hard drive.

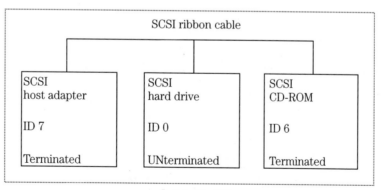

48-3 Terminating an internal SCSI adapter, HDD, and CD-ROM.

What happens if an external device is used (such as a scanner) as in Fig. 48-4? An external cable connects the adapter to the scanner. Because the scanner (ID 6) and adapter (ID 7) are the only two points in the chain, both are terminated. Most

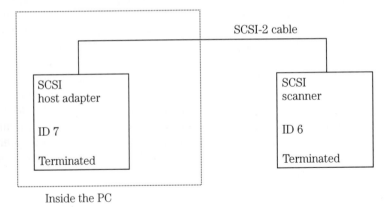

48-4 Terminating an external SCSI device.

external devices designed for SCSI-2 compatibility allow the active terminator built into the peripheral to be switched off if necessary.

Suppose both an internal and an external SCSI device are being used as shown in Fig. 48-5. The SCSI host adapter (ID 7) is no longer at an end of the chain, so its terminator should be switched off or removed. It is the internal hard drive (ID 0) and external scanner (ID 6) that now form the ends, so both devices should be terminated. Because both peripherals should ideally support internal termination, nothing needs to be done except to confirm that the terminators are in place and switched on.

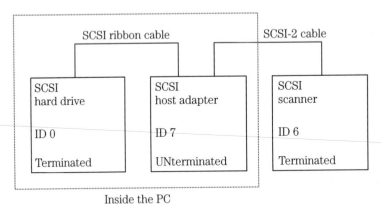

48-5 Terminating mixed internal and external SCSI devices.

SCSI driver software

Hardware configuration and installation is only one part of the SCSI installation. Software needs to be in order to allow the hardware to interact with your system. The problem with SCSI drivers is that prior to 1991, various drivers were rarely compatible. For example, an adapter and hard drive might have worked fine, but adding a CD-ROM would create havoc because the CD-ROM driver was not compatible with the hard drive or the host adapter driver (or both). After 1991, a set of universal driver standards appeared that created a buffer between the operating system and hardware that isolated each particular driver from one another. Drivers can now be written for each peripheral without worry of incompatibility so long as the drivers are written to be compatible with the standard.

There are now three competing SCSI standards: *ASPI* (advanced SCSI programming interface), *CAM* (common access method), and *LADDR* (layered device driver architecture). ASPI is the most popular of the three standards. The idea for compatibility is to select a host adapter and peripherals that support the same standard. For example, if you select a host adapter that uses an ASPI driver, each of the peripherals that you choose also must use ASPI drivers. If you upgrade the host adapter later, you also upgrade the host's ASPI driver—full compatibility should be maintained.

The actual installation process varies little from other software installations. The driver files for your adapter and peripheral(s) are copied to a subdirectory on the hard drive, then the CONFIG.SYS and AUTOEXEC.BAT files are updated to load the appropriate drivers on system startup. If your particular system commits too much conventional memory to drivers, you can manually optimize your startup files later to load as many drivers as possible into upper memory.

Troubleshooting the SCSI system

As far as the bus is concerned, there is very little that can go wrong—wires and connectors do not fail spontaneously. However, it never hurts to examine the wiring, connectors, and terminator network(s) to ensure that the physical connections are intact (especially after installing or configuring new devices). The most likely areas of trouble are in the installation, setup, and operation of the devices residing on the bus.

Isolating trouble spots

Assuming that your SCSI devices have been installed correctly, problem scenarios can occur during normal operation. The first indication of a problem usually comes in the form of an error message from your operating system or application program. For example, your SCSI hard drive might not be responding, or the host PC might not be able to identify the SCSI host controller board, and so on.

The advantage to SCSI architecture is that it is reasonably easy to determine problem locations using intuitive deduction. Consider a typical SCSI system with one initiator (a host controller) and one target (a hard drive). If the hard drive fails to function, the trouble is either in the host controller or the drive itself. When you see drive access being attempted, but an error is generated, the trouble is probably in the drive. If no drive access is attempted before an error is generated, the error is likely in the host controller. As another example, consider a setup with one initiator and two or more targets (i.e., a hard drive and CD-ROM). If both the hard drive and CD-ROM become inoperative, the problem is likely in the host controller card because the host adapter controls both targets. If only one of the devices becomes inoperative (and the other device works just fine) the trouble is likely in the particular device itself.

Of course, these are only common isolation methods, and their effectiveness will depend on the sophistication of the particular system you are working with. There is always some amount of uncertainty in the intuitive approach because it is not quantitative. You can suspect where the trouble is coming from, but you cannot prove it. Given the great expense of many SCSI peripherals, it is often unwise to purchase replacement parts based solely on intuitive techniques. To prove the problem's source, you can track communication along the SCSI bus using a specialized SCSI tester. If you perform extensive SCSI testing, you might wish to invest in an SCSI bus tester such as Ancot's DSC-216 portable SCSI bus analyzer. An analyzer can let you track the communication process along the SCSI bus, as well as provide bus speed calculations and command profiling. Once you have located the problem device, you can deal with that device specifically through replacement or repair.

However, specialized test equipment carries a significant price tag—a worthy investment if you have the service volume to justify it, but hardly a reasonable outlay for the casual PC hobbyist. Fortunately, a growing number of contemporary diagnostic software packages are being upgraded with SCSI test capabilities. For example, the *PC Technician* software by Windsor Technologies can test a limited number of SCSI adapters (such as Western Digital, Adaptec, and NCR) and associated peripherals. SCSIDiag by AMI is a diagnostic specifically designed for SCSI system testing.

The reason for this lack of broad diagnostic software support is simple; SCSI is not supported by the PC motherboard BIOS (IDE is supported). As a result, the diagnostic must be written to handle specific SCSI controllers. The issue to keep in mind when selecting a diagnostic for SCSI testing is that the software MUST be compatible with the SCSI adapter in your system; just because a diagnostic says "SCSI-compatible" does not necessarily make it so for the PC setup you are faced with. As an alternative to commercial diagnostics, you might be able to find small controller diagnostics right on the software disks that accompany the SCSI adapter. You would run the test routine after installation to see that the controller is working, but you also can use it in a pinch for as-needed troubleshooting for that particular controller. Check with the manufacturer's BBS or CompuServe forum to find up-to-date test routines for various controllers.

Installation troubleshooting tips

No matter how many precautions you take, you cannot always prevent problems from striking during a SCSI installation. Fortunately, if you are installing devices one-by-one as suggested, you will have far fewer problem areas to check. Your first diagnostic for a SCSI installation should be the adapter's SCSI BIOS initialization message. If you see no initialization message when the system powers up, the problem is likely with the adapter itself. Either it is not installed properly or it is defective. Make sure that the adapter is set to the desired ID (usually 7). Try a new or alternate SCSI adapter. If the adapter provides its initialization message as expected, the problem is probably related to driver installation. Check the installation and any command line switches for each device driver. When installing a SCSI hard drive, you must ensure that any previous hard drive references are mapped out of the CMOS setup. If pre-existing drive references are not removed, there will likely be a conflict.

Be aware that faulty SCSI ID settings can result in system problems such as ghost disks—disks that the system says are there but that cannot be read from or written to. Some peripherals also might not work properly with the ID that has been assigned. If you have problems interacting with an installed device, try the device with a different ID, and make sure that there are no two devices using the same ID. Don't be surprised to find that certain types of cables don't work properly with SCSI installations. Make sure that everything is terminated correctly. Also be sure that any external SCSI devices are powered up (if possible) before the PC is initialized. If problems persist, try different cables.

System troubleshooting

Even the best-planned SCSI installations go wrong from time to time, and SCSI systems already in the field will not run forever. Sooner or later, you will have to deal with a SCSI problem. This part of the chapter is intended to show you a variety of symptoms and solutions for many of the problems that you will likely encounter.

Symptom 1. After initial SCSI installation, the system will not boot from the floppy drive You might or might not see an error code corresponding to this problem. Suspect the SCSI host adapter first. There might be an internal fault with the adapter that is interfering with system operation. Check that all of the adapter's settings are correct and that all jumpers are intact. If the adapter is equipped with any diagnostic LEDs, check for any problem indications. When adapter problems are indicated, replace the adapter board. If a SCSI hard drive has been installed and the drive light is always on, the SCSI signal cable has probably been reversed between the drive and adapter. Make sure to install the drive cable properly.

Check for the SCSI adapter BIOS message generated when the system starts. If the message does not appear, check for the presence of a ROM address conflict between the SCSI adapter and ROMs on other expansion boards. Try a new address setting for the SCSI adapter. If there is a BIOS wait state jumper on the adapter, try changing its setting. If you see an error message indicating that the SCSI host adapter was not found at a particular address, check the I/O setting for the adapter.

Symptom 2. The system will not boot from the SCSI hard drive Start by checking the system's CMOS setup. When SCSI drives are installed in a PC, the corresponding hard drive reference in the CMOS setup must be changed to none. If previous hard drive references have not been mapped out, do so now and save the CMOS setup. If the problem persists, check that the SCSI boot drive is set to ID 0. You will need to refer to the user manual for your particular drive to find how the ID is set.

Next, check the SCSI parity to be sure that it is selected consistently among all SCSI devices. Remember that ALL SCSI devices must have SCSI parity enabled or disabled. If even one device in the chain does not support parity, it must be disabled on all devices. Check the SCSI cabling to be sure that all cables are installed and terminated properly. Finally, be sure that the hard drive has been partitioned and formatted properly. If not, boot from a floppy disk and prepare the hard drive as required.

Symptom 3. The SCSI drive fails to respond with an alternate HDD as the boot drive Technically, you should be able to use a SCSI drive as a nonboot drive (drive D:) while using an IDE drive as the boot device. If the SCSI drive fails to respond in this kind of arrangement, check the CMOS setting to be sure that drive 1 (the SCSI drive) is mapped out (or set to none). Save the CMOS setup. If the problem persists, Check that the SCSI drive is set to SCSI ID 1 (the non-boot ID).

Next, make sure that the SCSI parity is enabled or disabled consistently throughout the SCSI installation. If the SCSI parity is enabled for some devices and disabled for others, the SCSI system might function erratically. Finally, check that the SCSI cabling is installed and terminated properly. Faulty cables or termination can easily interrupt a SCSI system. If the problem persists, try another hard drive.

Symptom 4. The SCSI drive fails to respond with another SCSI drive as the boot drive This is a dual-drive system using two SCSI drives. Check the CMOS setup and make sure that both drive entries in the setup are set to none. Save the CMOS setup. The boot drive should be set to SCSI ID 0, and the supplemental drive should be set to SCSI ID 1. You will probably have to refer to the manual for the drives to determine how to select a SCSI ID. The hard drives should have a DOS partition and format. If not, create the partitions and format the drives as required.

Check to be sure that SCSI parity is enabled or disabled consistently throughout the SCSI system. If some devices use parity and other devices do not, the SCSI system might not function properly. Make sure that all SCSI cables are installed and terminated properly. If the problem persists, try systematically exchanging each hard drive.

Symptom 5. The system works erratically. The PC hangs or the SCSI adapter cannot find the drive(s) Such intermittent operation can be the result of several different SCSI factors. Before taking any action, be sure that the application software you were running when the fault occurred did not cause the problem. Unstable or buggy software can seriously interfere with system operation. Try different applications and see if the system still hangs up. Check each SCSI device and make sure that parity is enabled or disabled consistently throughout the SCSI system. If parity is enabled in some devices and disabled in others, erratic operation can result. Make sure that no two SCSI devices are using the same ID. Cabling problems are another common source of erratic behavior. Make sure that all SCSI cables are attached correctly and completely. Also check that the cabling is properly terminated.

Next, suspect that there might be a resource conflict between the SCSI host adapter and another board in the system. Check each expansion board in the system to be sure that nothing is using the same IRQ, DMA, or I/O address as the host adapter. If you find a conflict, you should alter the most recently installed adapter board. If problems persist, try a new drive adapter board.

Symptom 6. You see an 096xxxx error code This is a diagnostic error code that indicates a problem in a 32-bit SCSI adapter board. Check the board to be sure that it is installed correctly and completely. The board should not be shorted against any other board or cable. Try disabling one SCSI device at a time. If normal operation returns, the last device to be removed is responsible for the problem (you might need to disable drivers and reconfigure termination when isolating problems in this fashion). If the problem persists, re-install all devices and try a new adapter board.

Symptom 7. You see a 112xxxx error code This diagnostic error code indicates a problem in a 16-bit SCSI adapter board. Check the board to be sure that it is installed correctly and completely. The board should not be shorted against any other board or cable. Try disabling one SCSI device at a time. If normal operation returns, the last device to be removed is responsible for the problem (you might need to disable drivers and reconfigure termination when isolating problems in this fashion). Try a new adapter board.

Symptom 8. You see a 113xxxx error code This is a diagnostic code that indicates a problem in a system (motherboard) SCSI adapter configuration. If there is a SCSI BIOS ROM installed on the motherboard, be sure that it is up-to-date and installed correctly and completely. If problems persist, try replacing the motherboard's SCSI controller IC, or replace the system board.

Symptom 9. You see a 210xxxx error code There is a fault in a SCSI hard disk. Check that the power and signal cables to the disk are connected properly. Make sure the SCSI cable is correctly terminated. Try a new SCSI hard disk.

Symptom 10. A SCSI device refuses to function with the SCSI adapter even though both the adapter and device check properly This is often a classic case of basic incompatibility between the device and host adapter. Even though SCSI-2 helps to streamline compatibility between devices and controllers, there are still situations when the two just don't work together. Check the literature included with the finicky device and see if there are any notices of compatibility problems with the controller you are using. If there are warnings, there also might be alternative jumper or DIP switch settings to compensate for the problem and allow you to use the device after all. A call to technical support at the device's manufacturer might help shed light on any recently discovered bugs or fixes. If problems remain, try using a similar device from a different manufacturer (try a Connor tape drive instead of a Mountain tape drive).

Symptom 11. You see a "No SCSI Controller Present" error message Immediately suspect that the controller is defective or installed improperly. Check the host adapter installation (including IRQ, DMA, and I/O settings), and see that the proper suite of device drivers have been installed correctly. If the system still refuses to recognize the controller, try installing it in a different PC. If the controller also fails in a different PC, the controller is probably bad and should be replaced. However, if the controller works in a different PC, your original PC might not support all the functions under the interrupt 15h call required to configure SCSI adapters (such as an AMI SCSI host adapter). Consider upgrading the PC BIOS ROM to a new version, especially if the BIOS is older. There also might be an upgraded SCSI BIOS to compensate for this problem.

49
CHAPTER

Serial (RS-232)
port troubleshooting

Although the parallel port is slowly gaining acceptance as a peripheral communication port, early PCs used the parallel port almost exclusively for local printers. As more and more peripherals became available for the PC, alternative methods of communication were required that were ill-suited for parallel connections at the time. The Electronics Industry Association (EIA) developed a standard for serial communication. Instead of sending eight bits at a time over a set of data lines, only two data lines were used—one to transmit data, and one to receive data. The EIA denoted its serial standard as RS-232 (or simply the *serial port*). A serial port offers several distinct advantages over early parallel ports. First, the serial port was designed to be bidirectional right from the start. This made serial the preferred method for interactive devices such as modems, mice, and so on. Second, the serial port used fewer lines than the parallel port. Where a printer cable is generally limited to two meters, a serial cable can easily exceed 60 meters, and opened the way for basic local networking. This chapter shows you the essential concepts of serial communication and port operation, then guides you through a series of troubleshooting procedures.

Understanding
asynchronous communication

The serial port is not terribly difficult to grasp, but its operation is a bit more involved than that of a parallel port. In order to appreciate the operations and signals of a typical serial port, there are a variety of concepts that you should be familiar with. When a parallel port strobes a printer, the printer "knows" that all 8 bits of data are available and valid. However, a serial port must take 8 data bits, and send them one at a time over a single data line. As you might imagine, this presents some serious challenges for the receiving device that must determine where the data stream starts and ends—hardly a simple task. It is certainly possible to send a synchronizing clock signal along with the data wire. The receiving device could easily use the clock to detect each data bit. This technique is known as *synchronous* serial communication. It is reliable, but rarely used in PCs, so it will not be discussed further.

Instead of using a discrete clock signal to accompany the data, it is possible to eliminate the clock by embedding synchronization information along with the data bits. Thus, when a data stream reaches a receiving device, it can strip away the synchronization bits, leaving the original data. As a result, serial communication is not constrained by a clock. This is *asynchronous* communication—a popular and inexpensive serial technique. The remainder of this chapter deals with asynchronous communication.

The data frame

Asynchronous communication requires that data bits be combined with synchronization bits before transmission. Synchronization bits provide three important pieces of information to the receiving device; where the data starts, where the data ends, and if the data is correct. These bits, combined with the data byte, form the *data frame* as is shown in Fig. 49-1. The first thing you should notice about serial data is that it is bipolar; that is, there are both positive and negative voltages. Contrary to what you might guess, a +voltage represents a logical 0 (called a *space*), and a –voltage represents a logical 1 (called a *mark*). The next thing you should note is that the serial signal line is normally idle in the logic 0 (space) state.

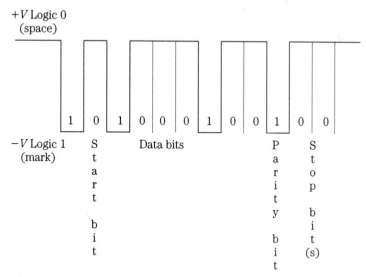

49-1 A typical data frame.

The first element of all asynchronous data frames is a single *start bit* that is always a logic 1 (mark). When the receiver detects a logic 1, it "knows" the data frame has started. The next 5 to 8 bits are always the *data bits*. The exact number of bits (usually 8) can be set by the communication software. After data, a single error-checking bit (called a *parity bit*) can be included if desired. Parity is calculated at the sending device and sent with the word. Parity also is calculated at the receiving device and checked against the received parity bit. If the two match, the data is assumed to be correct. If the two do not match, an error is flagged. There are five classes of parity:

- *none* No parity bit is added to the word. This is typical for much of today's serial communication.
- *even* If the number of 1s in the data word is odd, parity is set to 1 to make the number of 1s even.
- *odd* If the number of 1s in the data word is even, parity is set to 1 to make the number of 1s odd.
- *mark* Parity is always set to 1.
- *space* Parity is always set to 0.

A note about parity. Many communication connections today abandon the use of parity in favor of the more reliable and sophisticated *CRC* (cyclical redundancy check). A CRC has the same effect as a parity check, but instead of checking one byte at a time, an entire block of data is checked. The last part of the data frame is the stop bit(s). Typically only one bit is used, but two can be used. Stop bits are always logic 0 (space). After the receiving device detects the stop bit(s), the line remains idle in the space condition awaiting the next subsequent start bit. Framing is usually denoted as data/parity/stop. For example, the connection to TechNet BBS uses 8/N/1 framing (8 data bits/no parity bit/1 stop bit).

Signal levels

Where the parallel port uses TTL-compatible logic signals in its communication, a serial port uses bipolar signaling (both positive and negative voltages). The advantage of bipolar signaling is that it supports very long cabling with minimum noise. A logic 0 (*space*) condition is represented by a positive voltage between +3 Vdc to +15 Vdc. A logic 1 (*mark*) condition is represented by a negative voltage between −3 Vdc to −15 Vdc. On the average, you can expect to see serial ports using ±5 Vdc or ±12 Vdc because those voltages are already produced by the PC power supply.

Baud versus bps

Another key concept of asynchronous communication is the concept of rate. Because data is traveling across a serial link versus time, the rate at which that data passes becomes an important variable. Although rate is not a literal part of the data frame, it is every bit as important. Simply stated, data rates are measured in *bps* (bits per second). This is a simple and intuitive measurement. If the serial port is delivering 2400 bits in one second, it is working at 2400 bps. At that rate, the average bit is ($\frac{1}{2400}$ bps) 417 μs. When you are dealing with a serial port, you are dealing with bps.

Traditionally, when the bits from a serial port are processed through a modem, a modem will modulate the data through a series of phase, frequency, or amplitude transitions. A transition is referred to as a *baud* (named for French mathematician J.M.E. Baudot). Older modems designed to operate with signal rates of 2400 bps or less could modulate the telephone line at the bit rate, thus baud would be the same as bps. However, this is a faulty comparison. Because later modems were restricted by the limited bandwidth of a telephone line, modems had to encode more than one bit in every transition. As a result, the effective bps of a modern modem usually exceeds its baud rate by several times. For example, a modem that can encode four bits in every transition can work at 2400 baud, yet be sending the equivalent of 9600 bps. See the difference? As modems evolved to encompass data compression standards, effective bps has been increased even more (yet the modem still only works at a relatively low baud rate). When you are dealing with modems, you are usually talking about baud rates.

There's another catch you need to be aware of. Because baud refers to ANY transition (Baudot never said a word about modems), it is technically valid to measure a serial port speed in baud, although it can be terribly confusing. For example, today's serial port circuits can sustain data rates of 115,200 bps. Now, because every bit from the serial port is treated as a transition, it becomes just as correct to say 115,200 baud. The thing to remember here is that most modems don't operate over 2400 baud. The telephone line just cannot handle faster signal rates. So if you see high baud rates quoted in books or specifications, it probably refers to the performance of the serial port, and not the modem.

Understanding the serial port

A serial port must be capable of several important operations. It must convert parallel data from the PC system bus into a sequence of serial bits, add the appropriate framing bits (which can be changed for different serial connections), then provide each of those bits to the data line at the proper rate. The serial port also must work in reverse, accepting serial data at a known rate, stripping off the framing bits, converting the serial data bits back into bus form, and checking blocks of data for accuracy. The heart of the serial port is a single IC—the *UART* (universal asynchronous receiver/transmitter). A simplified block diagram for a serial port is shown in Fig. 49-2.

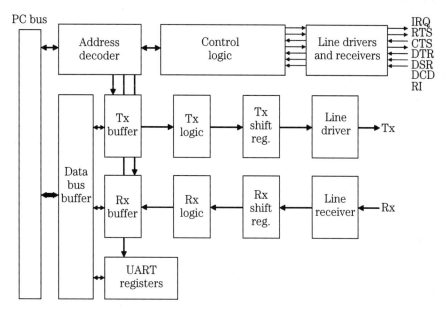

49-2 Block diagram of a UART.

The UART connects directly to the PC bus architecture, either added to the motherboard, or incorporated on an expansion board. A UART IC contains all of the internal circuitry necessary to process, transmit, and receive data between the serial line and the PC bus. Because the UART is programmable, its configuration (framing format and baud rate) can be set through DOS or Windows communication software. All data output, data input, and handshaking signals needed by the serial port are generated within the UART itself. It is interesting to note that the UART is powered by +5 Vdc only—just like any other ASIC in the system. This means data and hand-shaking signals entering and leaving the UART are all TTL-compatible. Transmitted data is converted to bipolar signals through a line driver IC. Bipolar data that appears on the receive line is converted back to TTL levels through a line receiver IC. All that remains is the port connector itself. The original serial port design used a 25-pin male subminiature D-type connector, but newer ports have abandoned the extra hand-shaking signals to accommodate a 9-pin male subminiature D-type connector.

Addresses and interrupts

The UART is controlled through a series of important registers that allow the se-rial port characteristics to be programmed, and channel transmitted and received data as required. Older BIOS versions supported only two serial (or COM) ports, but newer BIOS releases support four COM ports (designated COM1, COM2, COM3, and COM4). MicroChannel bus systems can support up to eight COM ports (COM1 through COM8). The typical base addresses for the COM ports are shown in Table 49-1. When a new COM port is installed in the system, it must be assigned to a valid base address. During actual operation, communication software deals with each port register individually. Table 49-2 lists the standard base address offsets for UART reg-isters. Note that with no offset, both transmit and receive registers are available.

Table 49-1. Typical serial port addresses and IRQ assignments

Bus architecture	Port	Address	IRQ
All Systems	COM1	03F8h	IRQ4
All Systems	COM2	02F8h	IRQ3
ISA*	COM3	03E8h	IRQ4
ISA	COM4	02E8h	IRQ3
ISA	COM3	03E0h	IRQ4
ISA	COM4	02E0h	IRQ3
ISA	COM3	0338h	IRQ4
ISA	COM4	0238h	IRQ3
MCA	COM3	3220h	IRQ3
MCA	COM4	3228h	IRQ3
MCA	COM5	4220h	IRQ3
MCA	COM6	4228h	IRQ3
MCA	COM7	5220h	IRQ3
MCA	COM8	5228h	IRQ3

* Systems with DOS 3.3 and later

Table 49-2. Typical
UART register address offsets

Register	Offset
Receive register	00h
Transmit register	00h
Interrupt enable register	01h
Interrupt ID register	02h
Data frame register	03h
UART control register	04h
Serialization status register	05h
UART status register	06h
General-purpose register	07h

During system initialization, COM ports are checked in the following order; 03F8h, 02F8h, 03E8h, 02E8h, 03E0h, 02E0h, 0338h, and 0238h (MicroChannel systems use a different order), and COM designations are assigned depending on what ports are actually found, so keep in mind that the COM addresses can be exchanged depending on your particular system. In virtually all cases, COM1 is available at 03F8h. The specific I/O addresses for each COM port are kept in the BIOS data area of RAM starting at 0400h (see Table 35-2). As you might expect, only one COM port can be assigned to a base address. If more than one COM port is assigned to the same base address, system problems will almost certainly occur.

The use of interrupts in conjunction with COM ports can easily be confusing. Unlike parallel ports that can be polled by BIOS, a serial port demands the use of interrupts. Because early PCs allocated space for two COM ports, only two IRQ lines were reserved (IRQ4 for COM1 and IRQ3 for COM2). Unfortunately, when PC BIOS expanded its support for additional COM ports, there were no extra IRQ lines available to assign. Thus, COM ports had to "share" interrupts. For example, COM1 and COM3 must share IRQ4, and COM2 and COM4 must share IRQ3. The problem is that no two devices can use the same IRQ at the same time, otherwise a system conflict will result. Ultimately, though a typical PC can use four COM ports, only two of the four can be used at any one time (COM1 & COM2, COM3 & COM4, COM1 & COM4, or COM2 & COM3). Further, the assignment of COM port address and IRQ lines must match. Although COM3 and COM4 can be polled by BIOS, the speed and asynchronous nature of contemporary data transmission make polling very unreliable for serial ports.

Always begin a service examination by checking the number of serial ports in your system. Serial ports are so simple and easy to add to various expansion cards, that you might exceed the maximum number of ports, or allow two ports to conflict without even realizing it. Be sure to remove or disable any unused or conflicting COM ports by removing the offending port, or disabling it through jumpers or DIP switches.

DTE versus DCE

As you work with serial ports and peripherals, you will often see the acronyms *DTE* and *DCE* used very frequently. DTE stands for data terminal equipment, which is typically the computer containing the serial port. The modem, serial printer, or other serial peripheral is referred to as the data carrier equipment (or DCE). The distinction becomes important because the data and handshaking signals are swapped at the DCE end. For example, the Tx pin (usually on pin 3 of a 9-pin DTE) cannot connect directly to the same pin on the DCE; it must route to the Rx pin instead. The DCE connector makes those swaps, so pin 3 of the DCE would be the Rx pin, and a straight-through cable can be used without difficulty.

However, suppose that two DTEs had to be connected. Because both devices carry the same signals on the same pins, a straight-through cable would cause confusion (the Tx line would connect to the Tx line on the other device, Rx would connect to Rx, and so on). As you can imagine, two DTEs cannot be connected with a straight-through cable. Of course, a specialized cable can be built that contains the proper wire swaps, but an easier alternative is simply to use a *null modem* that plugs into one end of the straight-through cable. The null modem is little more than a jumper box that contains all of the proper swaps. This allows two DTEs to work as if one were a DTE and one were a DCE.

Serial port signals

IBM and compatible PCs implement a serial port as either a 25-pin or 9-pin subminiature D-type connector similar to the ones shown in Fig. 49-3. Both ends of the serial cable are identical. There are three type of signals to be concerned with in a serial connection; data lines, control (or handshaking) lines, and ground lines. Table 49-3 identifies the name and description of each conductor for both 25-pin and 9-pin serial connections. Keep in mind that all data and control signals on the serial port are bipolar.

49-3
Serial port connectors.

25-pin M   9-pin M

Table 49-3. Serial port connector pinouts (at the PC end)

25-pin connector	9-pin connector	Signal	Direction
1	n/a	Protective Ground	n/a
2	3	Tx Transmit Data	Output
3	2	Rx Receive Data	Input
4	7	RTS Request to Send	Output
5	8	CTS Clear to Send	Input
6	6	DSR Data Set Ready	Input
7	5	Signal Ground	n/a
8	1	DCD Data Carrier Detect	Input
9	n/a	+Transmit Current Loop	Output
11	n/a	−Transmit Current Loop	Output
18	n/a	+Receive Current Loop	Input
20	4	DTR Data Terminal Ready	Output

Table 49-3. Continued

25-pin connector	9-pin connector	Signal	Direction
22	9	RI Ring Indicator	Input
23	n/a	DSRD Data Signal Rate Indicator	I/O
25	n/a	–Receive Current Loop	Input

Tx and Rx

These are simply the data lines into and out of the port. Tx is the Transmit line that outputs serial data from the PC, and Rx is the Receive line that accepts serial data from the serial peripheral.

RTS and CTS

The RTS (Request to Send) signal is generated by the DTE. When asserted, it tells the DCE (the modem) to expect to receive data. However, the DTE can't just dump data to DCE. The DCE must be ready to receive the data, so after the RTS line is asserted, the DTE waits for the CTS (Clear to Send) signal back from the DCE. Once the DTE receives a valid CTS signal, it can begin transferring data. This RTS/CTS handshake forms the basis for data flow control.

DTR and DSR

When the DTE is turned on or initialized and ready to begin serial operation, the DTR (Data Terminal Ready) line is asserted. This tells the DCE (modem) that the DTE (computer) is ready to establish a connection. When the DCE has initialized and is ready for a connection, it will assert the DSR (Data Set Ready) line back to the DTE. Once the DTE is ready and recognizes the DSR signal, a connection is established. This DTR/DSR handshake is established only once when the DTE and DCE devices are first initialized, and must remain active throughout the connection. If either the DTR or DSR signal should fall, the communication channel will be interrupted (and the RTS/CTS handshake will no longer have any effect).

DCD

The DCD (Data Carrier Detect) signal is particularly useful with modems. It is produced by the DCE when a carrier is detected from a remote target, and the DCE is ready to establish a communications pathway. The DCD signal is then sent back to the DTE. Once the DCD line is asserted, it will remain so as long as a connection is established.

RI

The RI (Ring Indicator) signal is asserted by the DCE, and also is particularly useful with modems. It is produced by the DCE when a telephone ring is detected. This becomes a vital signal if it is necessary for a remote user to call in and access your computer (a BBS configuration).

Troubleshooting the serial port

Although the typical serial port is a rather simple I/O device, it presents some special challenges for the technician. Older PCs provided their serial ports in the form of 8-bit expansion boards. When a port failed, it was a simple matter to replace the board outright. Today, however, virtually all PCs provide at least one serial port directly on the motherboard—usually integrated into a component of the main chipset. When a problem is detected with a motherboard serial port, a technician often has three choices:

- Replace the UART (responsible for virtually all serial port failures) on the motherboard. This requires access to surface-mount soldering tools and replacement ICs, and can be quite economical in volume.
- Replace the motherboard outright. This is a simple tactic that requires little overhead equipment, but can be rather expensive.
- Set the motherboard jumpers (if possible) to disable the defective serial port, and install an expansion board to take the place of the defective port. This assumes there is an available expansion slot.

Virtually all commercial diagnostics are capable of locating any installed serial ports, and testing the ports thoroughly through a loopback plug. Now that you have reviewed the layout, signals, and operation of a typical serial port, you can take a clear look at port troubleshooting procedures.

Serial port conflicts

Hardware and software conflicts with a system's serial ports are some of the most recurring and perplexing problems in PC troubleshooting. Although PC purists are pleased with the fact that current DOS and BIOS supports four COM ports, they cannot overcome the fact that there are still only two interrupts available to run the ports from. Technicians trying to upgrade a PC often encounter problems adding I/O adapters because many current PCs already provide two COM ports right out of the factory. If a PC offers only one COM port (COM1) and another serial port is placed in the system (by accident or on purpose), be aware that you must choose a port and IRQ that does not conflict with the existing port (COM 2 or COM4). If the PC already provides two COM ports (COM1 and COM2), adding a third COM port to the system will cause a hardware conflict. You can rectify the conflict by disabling the new COM port, or by disabling one of the two existing COM ports, and jumpering the new COM port to those settings.

Serial device drivers also can be a source of problems for COM ports. Incorrectly written mouse drivers, printer drivers, or third-party interrupt handlers can leave a port inoperative or erratic. If problems develop after a new driver is installed, disable the driver's reference in CONFIG.SYS. TSRs (often loaded in AUTOEXEC.BAT) can cause problems as well. If problems develop after a new TSR is installed, disable the offending TSR and try the system again. Remember that drivers and TSRs can easily be disabled by adding the REM statement before the command line in CONFIG.SYS or AUTOEXEC.BAT. If the communication trouble is under Windows, strongly suspect the Windows communication package.

Match the settings

It's bad enough that you can only (practically) use two COM ports, but you also have to make sure that the port addresses and IRQ assignments match as shown in Table 49-1. For example, suppose that there is no COM1 at 03F8h, but there is a COM port at 02F8h. During system initialization, BIOS locates each available port and assigns a COM designation, so because there is no port at 03F8h, the port at 02F8h (normally COM2) is the first port detected, and assigned as COM1. However, DOS and BIOS expect COM1 to use IRQ4, but the port at 02F8h uses IRQ3. If you attempt to use BASIC or DOS for COM1, the standard interrupt handlers will not work. You would have to use communication software that talks to the port directly (and thus avoids using DOS interrupt handlers) and can be assigned with the address and IRQ setting of your choosing. As an alternative, you can switch the COM port to 03F8h and set the interrupt to IRQ4—that should restore normal COM1 operation through DOS.

Frame it right

The data frame and rate play very important roles in serial communication. The sending and receiving ends of the serial link must be set to the same configuration. If not of the same configuration, the received data will be interpreted as garbage. If you encounter such troubles, be sure to check the settings for data bits, parity bit, stop bits, and baud rate. Change the data frame at either end of the serial link such that all devices are running with the same parameters.

Symptoms

Symptom 1. You hear a beep code or see a POST error indicating a serial port fault The system initialization might or might not halt depending on how the BIOS is written. Low-level initialization problems generally indicate trouble in the computer's hardware. If the computer's beep code sequence is indistinct, you could try rebooting the computer with a POST analyzer card installed. The BIOS POST code displayed on the card could be matched to a specific error explanation in the POST card's documentation. Once you have clearly identified the error as a serial port fault, you can proceed with troubleshooting.

Start with the system as a whole and remove any expansion boards that have serial ports available. Retest the computer after removing each board. If the error disappears after removing a particular card, then that card is likely at fault. You can simply replace the card with a new one, or attempt to repair the card to the component level. If there is only one serial port in the system, it is most likely built into the motherboard. Again, you can replace the defective UART, replace the motherboard, or disable the defective motherboard port.

Symptom 2. You see an 11xx or 12xx serial adapter error displayed on your system A hardware fault has been detected in one of the COM ports. The 11xx errors typically indicate a fault in COM1, and 12xx errors suggest a problem with COM2, COM3, or COM4. In most cases, the fault is in the UART. You have the option whether to replace the UART IC, replace the motherboard, or disable the defective COM port and replace it with an expansion board.

Symptom 3. The computer initializes properly, but the peripheral does not work. Your applications software might indicate that no device is connected Before you even open your tool kit, you must determine whether the trouble lies in your computer or your peripheral. When your modem or printer stops working, run a self-test to ensure the device is at least operational. Check all cables and connectors (perhaps try a different cable). Also be sure to check the software package being used to operate the serial port. Ensure that the software is configured properly to use the appropriate COM port, and that any necessary drivers are selected.

Disconnect the peripheral at the computer and install a serial loopback plug. Run a diagnostic to inspect each available serial port. Take note of any port(s) that register as defective. Locate the corresponding serial port. If the port is installed as an expansion board, replace the defective expansion board. If the port is on the motherboard, you can replace the defective UART IC, install an alternate expansion board, or replace the motherboard outright.

Symptom 4. Data is randomly lost or garbled Your first step should be to check the communication cable. Make sure the cable is intact and properly secured at both ends. Try a different cable. If the cable checks properly, either the port or peripheral is at fault. Start by suspecting the serial port. Make sure that the DTE and DCE are both set to use the same data frame and data rate. Incorrect settings can easily garble data. If problems persist, disconnect the printer at the computer and install a serial loopback plug. Run a diagnostic to inspect each available serial port. Take note of any port(s) that register as defective. Locate the corresponding serial port(s). If the port is installed as an expansion board, replace the defective expansion board. If the port is on the motherboard, you can replace the defective port controller IC, install an alternate expansion board, or replace the motherboard outright.

If you cannot test the computer's serial port directly, test the port indirectly by trying the peripheral on another known-good computer. If the peripheral works properly on another computer, the trouble is probably in the original computer's serial port circuitry. Replace any defective circuitry or replace the motherboard. If the peripheral remains defective on another computer, the peripheral (printer or modem) is probably faulty.

50
CHAPTER

Sound boards

Sound is an area of the PC that has been largely overlooked in early systems. Aside from a simple, oscillator-driven speaker, the early PCs were mute. Driven largely by the demand for better PC games, designers developed a stand-alone sound board that could read sound data recorded in separate files, then reconstruct those files into basic sound, music, and speech. Because from the beginning of the decade, those early sound boards have blossomed into an array of powerful, high-fidelity sound products capable of duplicating voice, orchestral soundtracks, and real-life sounds with uncanny realism (Fig. 50-1). Not only have sound products helped the game industry to mature, but they have been instrumental in the development of *multimedia* technology—the integration of sound and picture. This chapter is intended to explain the essential ideas and operations of a contemporary sound board, and show you how to isolate a defective sound board when problems arise.

50-1 A Logitech SoundMan Wave sound board. Copyright © 1995 Logitech Corporation

Understanding sound boards

Before you attempt to troubleshoot a problem with a sound board, you should have an understanding of how the board works, and what it must accomplish. This type of background helps you when recommending a sound board to a customer, or choosing a compatible card as a replacement. If you already have a strong background in digital sound concepts and software, feel free to skip directly to the troubleshooting portion of this chapter.

The recording process

All sound starts as pressure variations traveling through the air. Sound can come from almost anywhere—a barking dog, a laughing child, a fire engine's siren, a person speaking—you get the idea. The process of recording sound to a hard drive requires sound to be carried through several manipulations (as shown in Fig. 50-2). First, sound must be translated from pressure variations in the air to analog electrical signals. This is accomplished by a microphone. These analog signals are amplified by the sound card, then digitized (converted to a series of representative digital words each taken at a fixed time interval). The resulting stream of data is processed and organized through the use of software, which places the data (as well as any overhead or housekeeping data) into a standard file format. The file is saved to the drive of choice, typically a hard drive.

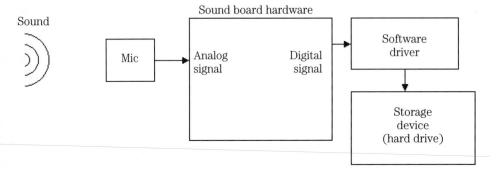

50-2 The sound board recording process.

The playback process

Simply speaking, the playback process is virtually the reverse of recording (Fig. 50-3). A software application opens a sound file on the hard drive, then passes the digital data back to the sound card. Data is translated back into equivalent analog levels. Ideally, the reconstructed shape of the analog signal closely mimics the original digitized signal. The analog signal is amplified, then passed to a speaker. If the sound was recorded in stereo, the data is divided into two channels that are separately converted back to analog signals, amplified, and sent to their corresponding speakers. Speakers convert the analog signal back into traveling pressure waves that you can hear.

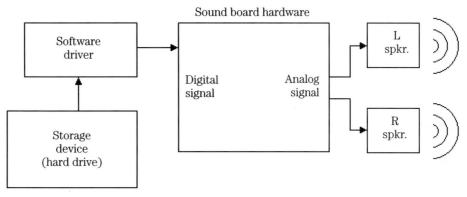

Sound board hardware

50-3 The sound board playback process.

The concept of sampling

To appreciate the intricacies of a sound card's operation, you must understand the concept of *digitization*, otherwise known as *sampling*. In principle, sampling is a very straightforward concept: an analog signal is measured periodically, and its voltage at each point in time is converted to a digital number. The device that performs this conversion is known as an *analog-to-digital converter* (ADC). It sounds simple enough in principle, but there are some important wrinkles.

The problem with sampling is that a digitizer circuit has to capture enough points of an analog waveform to reproduce it faithfully. The example in Fig. 50-4 shows the importance of sampling rate. Waveforms A and B represent the same original signal. Waveform A is sampled at a relatively slow rate; only a few samples are taken. The problem comes when the signal is reconstructed with a *digital-to-analog converter* (DAC). As you see, there are not enough sample points to reconstruct

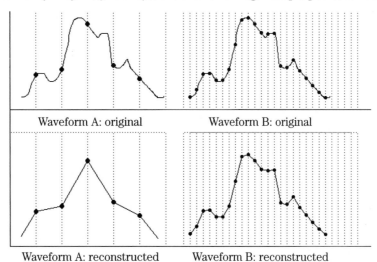

Waveform A: original   Waveform B: original

Waveform A: reconstructed   Waveform B: reconstructed

50-4 The concept of sampling rate.

the original signal. As a result, some of the information in the original signal is lost. This is a form of distortion known as *aliasing*. Waveform B is the same signal, but it is sampled at a much higher rate. When that data is reconstructed, the resulting signal is a much more faithful reproduction of the original.

As a rule, a signal should be sampled at least twice as fast as the highest frequency in the signal; this is known as Nyquist's Sampling Theorem. The lowest standard sampling rate used with today's sound boards is 11 kHz, which allows fair reproduction of normal speech and vocalization (up to about 5.5 kHz). However, most low-end sound boards can digitize signals up to 22 kHz. Unfortunately, the human range of hearing is about 22 kHz. To capture sounds reasonably well throughout the entire range of hearing, you would need a sampling rate of 44 kHz; this is often known as *CD-quality* sampling because it is the same rate used to record audio on CDs. The disadvantage to high sampling rates is disk space (and sound file size). Each sample is a piece of data, so the more samples taken each second, the larger and faster a file grows.

Data bits versus sound quality

Not only does the number of samples affect sound quality, but also the precision (or number of bits) of each sample. Suppose that each sample is converted to a 4-bit number. That means each point can be represented by a number from 0 to 15—not much precision there. If eight bits are used for each sample, 256 discrete levels can be supported. But the most popular configuration is 16-bit conversion that allows a sample to be represented by one of 65,536 levels. At that level of resolution, samples will form a very close replica of the original signal. Virtually all of today's sound boards are 16-bit.

The role of MIDI

Although the major part of a sound card is geared toward handling the recording and playback of sound files, the *musical instrument digital interface* (MIDI) port has become an inexpensive and popular addition to many sound card designs. MIDI is a standard protocol that is defined by hardware, software, and electrical interconnections. At the core of a MIDI interface is a *synthesizer* IC. Unlike a sound file, which basically contains the digital equivalent of an analog waveform, a MIDI file is a set of instructions for playing notes. Each note is sent to the synthesizer, along with duration, pitch, and timing specifications. The synthesizer can be made to replicate a variety of musical instruments such as a piano, guitar, harmonica, or flute. The high-end sound boards are capable of synthesizing a small orchestra. Because most synthesizers can process several channels simultaneously, the MIDI standard supports playing a number of "instruments" (or *voices*) at the same time. Thus, very high-quality music can be produced on a PC. The two most common synthesizer types are FM and Wavetable.

Figure 50-5 shows the kinds of things MIDI is capable of. Prerecorded MIDI files can be read from a storage device like a hard drive file, or from CD-ROM. The MIDI data is passed through to the sound board's synthesizer that reproduces the sound, and out to the amplified speakers. If you plan on composing music yourself, you can interface a MIDI instrument to the sound board's MIDI port. Using MIDI sequencer software, the notes played on the instrument will be heard through the speaker, as well as recorded to the MIDI file on the hard drive. Note that you do not need a MIDI instrument to play back a MIDI file, but you need an instrument and sequencer soft-

Sound board hardware

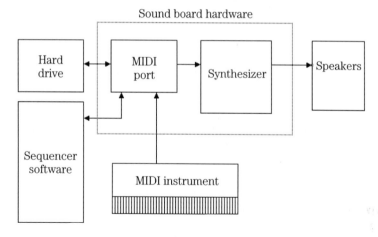

50-5 The path of MIDI signals through the PC.

ware to create a MIDI file. Also, because MIDI is not sound (but rather sound "blueprints"), the same MIDI composition entered on a keyboard can be played back as a harp, or a guitar, or a flute.

Inside a sound board

Now that you are aware of the major functions a sound board must perform, you can see those functions in the context of a complete board. Figure 50-6 shows a simplified block diagram of a sound board. It is important to note that your own particular sound board might differ somewhat, but all contemporary boards should contain these subsections.

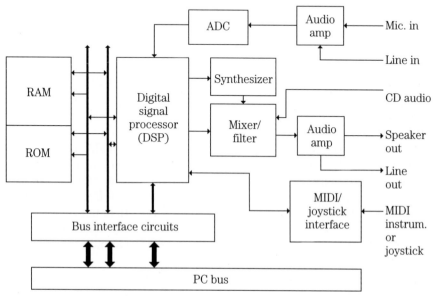

50-6 Simplified block diagram of a sound board.

The core element of a sound board is the *DSP* (digital signal processor). A DSP is a variation of a microprocessor that is specially designed to manipulate large volumes of digital data. Like all processor components, the DSP requires memory. A ROM contains all of the instructions needed to operate the DSP and direct the board's major operations. A small quality of RAM serves two purposes: it provides a "scratch pad" area for the DSP's calculations, and serves as a buffer for data traveling to or from the PC bus.

Signals entering the sound board are passed through an amplifier stage and provided to an A/D converter. When recording takes place, the DSP runs the A/D converter and accepts the resulting conversions for processing and storage. Signals delivered by a microphone are typically quite faint, so they are amplified significantly. Signals delivered to the line input are often much stronger (such as the output from a CD player or stereo preamp), so it receives less amplification.

For signals leaving the sound board, the first (and often most important) stop is the mixer. It is the mixer that combines CD-audio, DSP sound output, and synthesizer output into a single analog channel. Because most sound boards now operate in a stereo mode, there will usually be two mixer channels and amplifier stages. The audio amplifier stage(s) boost the analogs signal for delivery to stereo speakers. If the sound will be driving a stereo system, a line output provides a separate output. Amplifier output can be adjusted by a single master volume control located on the rear of the board.

Finally, a MIDI controller is provided to accommodate the interface of a MIDI instrument to the sound board. In many cases, the interface can be connected with a jumper to switch the controller to serve as a joystick port. That way, the sound board can support a single joystick if MIDI instrument will not be used. MIDI information processed by the DSP will be output to the on-board synthesizer.

Knowing the benchmarks

An important aspect of sound boards is their audio benchmarks. Unlike logic and processing circuitry that is measured in terms of millions of operations per second, the benchmarks that define a sound card are very much analog. If you are an audiophile, many of the following terms might already be familiar. If most of your experience has been with logic systems, however, these concepts will appear very different than many of the other discussions in this book.

Decibels

No discussion of sound concepts is complete without an understanding of the *dB* (decibel). Decibels are used because they are logarithmic—human hearing is not a linear response. If you increase the power of your stereo output from 4 W to 16 W, the sound is not 4 times louder, in fact, it is only twice as loud. If you increase the power from 4 W to 64 W, the sound is only three times as loud. In human terms, amplitude perception is measured logarithmically. As a result, very small decibel values actually relate to substantial amounts of power. The accepted formula for decibels is:

$$\text{gain (in dB)} = 10 \log_{10} \frac{P_{\text{out}}}{P_{\text{in}}}$$

Don't worry if this formula looks intimidating; you will not need to use it, but consider what happens when output power is greater than input power. Suppose a 1 mW is applied to a circuit, and a 2-mW signal leaves, the circuit provides a gain of +3 dB. Suppose the situation was reversed where a 2 mW signal were applied to the circuit, and a 1-mW signal left it. The circuit would then have a gain of –3 dB. Negative gain is called *attenuation*. As you see, a small dB number represents a large change in signal levels.

Frequency response

Expressed simply, the *frequency response* of a sound board is the range of frequencies that the board will handle uniformly. Examine the sample graph of Fig. 50-7. Ideally, a sound board should be able to produce the same amount of power (0 dB) across the entire working frequency range (usually 20 Hz to 20 kHz). This would show up as a flat line across the graph. In actual practice, however, this is not practical, and there will invariably be a *rolloff* of signal strength at both ends of the operating range. A good-quality sound board will demonstrate sharp, steep rolloffs. As the rolloffs get longer and more shallow at high and low frequencies, the board has difficulty producing sound power at those frequencies. The result is that bass and treble ranges might sound weak, and this affects the sound's overall fidelity. By looking at a frequency response curve, you can anticipate the frequency ranges where a sound board might sound weak.

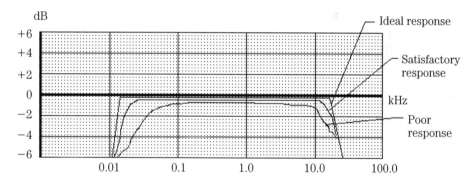

50-7 A sample sound board frequency-response curve.

Signal-to-noise ratio

The *SNR* (signal-to-noise ratio) of a sound board is basically the ratio of maximum undistorted signal power to the accompanying electronic noise being generated by the board (primarily hum and hiss) expressed in decibels. Ideally, this will be a very large dB number that would indicate that the output signal is so much stronger than the noise signal, that for all intents and purposes, the noise is imperceptible. In actual practice, a good-quality sound board will enjoy an SNR of 85 dB or higher, but these are difficult to find. For most current sound boards with SNR levels below 75 dB, there might be audible hum and hiss present during silent periods, as well as a certain amount of sound grit underlying sound and music reproduction. Some very inexpensive sound boards are on the market with SNR levels as low as 41 dB.

You also might find the SNR value expressed as an A-weighted decibel number. The reason for this is that human hearing is not equal at all frequencies, so we cannot hear all noise equally. The process of A-weighting emphasizes the noise levels at frequencies we are most sensitive to. Resulting SNR values are often several dB higher (better) than nonweighted SNR values. Be careful here, a sound board with a low SNR might use the A-weighted value in the specification sheet. If this is the case, subtract about 3 or 4 dB for the actual SNR figure.

Total harmonic distortion

Sound and music are rich in harmonics (overtones) that are basically integer multiples of an original frequency (although at much lower levels). As a consequence, harmonics are a valuable attribute of sound. The number and amplitude of harmonics provide the sound characteristics that allow you to distinguish between a guitar, flute, piano, or any other musical instrument played at the same note. Without harmonics, every instrument would just produce flat tones, and every instrument would sound exactly the same.

However, when sound is produced in an electronic circuit, other unwanted harmonics are generated that can alter the sound of the music being produced (thus the term harmonic *distortion*). The *total harmonic distortion* (THD) of a sound board is the root-mean squared (rms) sum of all unwanted harmonic frequencies produced, expressed as a percentage of the total undistorted output signal level. In many cases, the RMS value of noise is added to THD (expressed as THD+N). The lower this percentage is, the better. THD+N values over 0.1% can often be heard, and suggest a less than adequate sound board design.

Intermodulation distortion

This figure is related to harmonics. When two or more tones are generated together, amplifiers create harmonics, as well as tone combinations. For example, if a 1 kHz and 60 Hz tone are mixed together, *intermodulation harmonics* will be generated (940 Hz, 880 Hz, 1060 Hz, 1120 Hz, and so on). It is this intermodulation that gives sound a harsh overtone. Because intermodulation is not related to sound quality, it is a form of distortion that should be kept to a very low level. Like THD, intermodulation distortion (IMD) is the RMS sum of all unwanted harmonic frequencies expressed as a percentage of the total undistorted output signal level. IMD should be under 0.1% on a well-designed board.

Sensitivity

Although it does not directly affect the fidelity of sound reproduction, sensitivity can be an important specification. *Sensitivity* is basically the amplitude of an input signal that will produce the maximum undistorted signal at the output(s) with volume at maximum.

Gain

By itself, sensitivity is hard to apply to a sound board, but if you consider the board's output power versus its input signal power and express the ratio as a decibel, you would have the *gain* of the sound board. Many sound boards offer a potential gain of up to 6 dB. However, it is important to note that not all sound boards provide positive gain. Some boards actually attenuate the signal even with the volume at maximum. In practical terms, this usually forces you to keep the volume control at maximum.

Troubleshooting a sound board

Traditionally, sound boards use many of the same chipsets and basic components, but because each board is designed a bit differently, it is very difficult for commercial diagnostic products to identify failed IC functions. For the most part, commercial and shareware diagnostics can only identify whether a brand-compatible board is responding or not. As a result, this chapter takes the subassembly replacement approach. When a sound board is judged to be defective, it should be replaced outright. This part of the chapter reviews the problems and solutions for sound boards under both DOS and Windows.

Update the drivers

Unlike most other expansion devices that are driven by system or supplemental BIOS, sound boards make use of small device drivers to set up their operations. These drivers are generally included in CONFIG.SYS and AUTOEXEC.BAT, and are called when the system is first initialized. Most sound board drivers are only used to initialize and set up the board, so they do not remain resident; this is good because it reduces the load on conventional and upper memory. However, these initialization routines vary from board to board. For example, the files installed for a Creative Labs Sound Blaster will not support a Turtle Beach MultiSound board. When you elect to replace a sound board, you also must disable any current sound board drivers, and include any new supporting driver files. The process is not difficult. Just follow the installation instructions for the board, but the software consideration does add another wrinkle to the replacement process.

Symptoms

Symptom 1. A noticeable buzz or hum is produced in one or both speakers Low-cost speakers use unshielded cables. Unfortunately, strong signals from ac cords and other signal-carrying conductors can easily induce interference in the speaker wires. Try rerouting speaker cables clear of other cables in the system. If problems persist, try using higher-quality speakers with shielded cables and enclosures. In most cases, that should resolve everyday noise problems. If the noise continues regardless of what you do, there might be a fault in the sound board amplifier. Try moving the sound board to another bus slot away from other boards or the power supply. If that does not resolve the problem, try a new sound board.

Symptom 2 No sound is produced by the speaker(s) The lack of sound from a sound board can be caused by any one of a wide range of potential problems. If the sound board works with some applications, but not with others, it is likely that the problem is caused by an improperly installed or configured application. See that the offending application is set up properly (and make sure it is even capable of using the sound card). Also check that the proper sound driver files (if any) are loaded into CONFIG.SYS and AUTOEXEC.BAT as required. In many cases, there are one or two sound-related environment variables that are set in AUTOEXEC.BAT. Make sure that your startup files are configured properly.

Check your speakers next. See that they are turned on and set to a normal volume level. The speakers should be receiving adequate power, and should be plugged properly into the correct output jack. If speakers have been plugged into the wrong jack, no sound will be produced. If the cable is broken or questionable, try a new set of speakers. Also see that the master volume control on the sound board is turned up most (or all) of the way.

If problems continue, there might be a resource conflict between the sound board and another device in the system. Examine the IRQ, DMA, and I/O settings of each device in the system. Make sure that no two devices are using the same resources. You might like to use the PC Configuration Form at the end of this book to record your settings. If problems persist, and no conflict is present, try another sound board.

Symptom 3. CD audio will not play through the sound card This problem can occur under both DOS and Windows. First, make sure that the sound board is actually capable of playing CD-audio (older boards might not be compatible). If the sound card is playing sound files, but is not playing CD-audio, there are several things for you to check. First, open the PC and make sure that the CD-audio cable (a thin, four-wire cable) is attached from the CD-ROM drive to the sound board. If this cable is broken, disconnected, or absent, CD-audio will not be passed to the sound board. If the cable is intact, make sure that the CD-audio player is configured properly for the sound board you are using, and check the startup files to see that any drivers and environment variable needed by CONFIG.SYS and AUTOEXEC.BAT are available. If the CD-audio fails to play under Windows, make sure that a MCI (multimedia control interface) CD Audio driver is included in the Drivers dialog box under your Windows Control Panel.

Symptom 4. You see an error message indicating "No interrupt vector available" The DOS interrupt vectors used by the sound board's setup drivers (usually INT 80h to BFh) are being used by one or more other drivers in the system. As a consequence, there is a software conflict. Try disabling other drivers in the system one at a time until you see the conflict disappear. Once you have isolated the offending driver(s), you can leave them disabled, or (if possible) alter their command line settings so that they no longer conflict with the sound board's software.

Symptom 5. There is no MIDI output Make sure that the file you are trying to play is a valid MIDI file (usually with a .MID extension). In most cases, you will find that the *MIDI Mapper* under Windows is not set up properly for the sound board. Load the Windows *MIDI Mapper* applet from the *Control Panel*, and set it properly to accommodate your sound board.

Symptom 6. Sound play is jerky Choppy or jerky sound playback is typically the result of a hard drive problem; more specifically, the drive cannot read the sound file to a buffer fast enough. In most cases, the reason for this slow drive performance is excessive disk fragmentation. Under DOS, the sound file(s) might be highly fragmented. Under Windows, the permanent or temporary swap files might be highly fragmented. In either case, use a reliable DOS defragmenter such as *PC Tools* or Norton Utilities (leave Windows before defragmenting the disk), and defragment the disk thoroughly.

Symptom 7. You see an error message indicating "Out of environment space" The system is out of environment space. You will need to increase the system's environment space by adding the following line to your CONFIG.SYS file:

```
shell=c:\command.com /E:512 /P
```

This command line sets the environment space to 512 bytes. If you still encounter the error message, change the E entry to 1024.

Symptom 8. Regular "clicks," "stutters," or "hiccups" occur during the playback of speech In virtually all cases, the system CPU is simply not fast enough to permit buffering without dropping sound data. Systems with i286 and slower i386 CPUs typically suffer with this kind of problem. This is often compounded by insufficient memory (especially under Windows) that automatically resorts to virtual memory. Because virtual memory is delivered by the hard drive, and the hard drive is much slower than RAM anyway, the hard drive simply can't provide data fast enough. Unfortunately, there is little to be done in this kind of situation (aside from adding RAM, upgrading the CPU, or changing the motherboard). If it is possible to shut off various sound features (music, voice, effects, and so on), try shutting down any extra sound features that you can live without.

Symptom 9. The joystick is not working, or not working properly on all systems This problem only applies to sound boards with a multifunction MIDI/joystick port being used in the joystick mode. Chances are that the joystick is conflicting with another joystick port in the system. Disable the original joystick port or the new joystick port. Only one joystick port (game adapter) can be active at any one time in the system. Because joystick performance is dependent on CPU speed, the CPU might actually be too fast for the joystick port. Disable the joystick port, or try slowing the CPU down.

Symptom 10. You install a sound board and everything works properly, but now the printer does not seem to work There is an interrupt conflict between the sound board, and an IRQ line used by the printer. Although parallel printers are often polled, they also can be driven by an IRQ line (IRQ5 or IRQ7). If the sound board is using either one of these interrupts, try changing to an alternative IRQ line. When changing an IRQ line, be sure to reflect the changes in any sound board files called by CONFIG.SYS or AUTOEXEC.BAT.

51
CHAPTER

Tape drives

Floppy disks have long been a favorite backup media. Cheap, light, and fast, a floppy disk is an excellent choice for copying individual files such as word processor documents or CAD drawings, but floppy disks are notoriously limited in their storage capacity. Extensive backup operations can require a handful of floppies. Backing up an entire hard drive can require boxes of floppy disks and a cumbersome, time-consuming swap and copy procedure. As a popular alternative, tape-drive systems (Fig. 51-1) are capable of storing hundreds of megabytes on a single tape cartridge. This chapter explains the construction and operation of typical tape drives, and offers some maintenance and troubleshooting procedures that can help you resolve tape drive problems.

51-1 Mountain Network FileSafe systems. Copyright © 1995 Mountain Network Solutions, Inc.

Understanding tape media

Magnetic tape is the oldest form of magnetic mass storage. Tape systems served as the primary mass-storage technique for older mainframes (obsoleting the aging punched card and punched paper tape environment of the day). Tape systems proved to be inexpensive and reliable, so much so that even the original IBM PC was outfitted with a drive port for cassette tape storage. With the development of floppy and hard drives, tape systems became obsolete as a primary storage method, but retain a valuable role as backup systems.

Although the size, shape, and standards used for tape packaging and recording has advanced, the tape itself is virtually unchanged in principle from the very first incarnation. Figure 51-2 shows a tape cartridge used in an Iomega tape backup system. A tape is a long, slender length of polyester substrate which is much more flexible than the mylar substrate used in floppy disks. Polyester also sustains a bit of stretch to help the tape negotiate the high tensions and sharp turns encountered in today's tape cartridge assemblies. As with all other magnetic storage media, the substrate is coated with a layer of magnetic material that is actually magnetized to retain digital information. Many different coatings have been tried through the years, but tapes still use coatings of conventional magnetic oxides similar to older floppy disk coatings. More exotic coatings such as metal films and pure metal particles suspended in a binder material also have been used.

Drive roller

Write protect

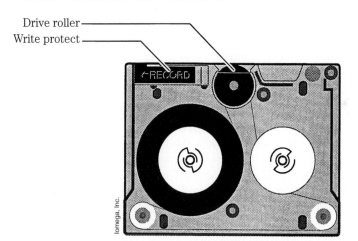

51-2
A typical minicartridge.

Unlike floppy disks and hard drive platters that are random-access media, tapes represent a *sequential* type of storage media; that is, a tape drive stores its data sequentially along the length of its media. Where floppy and hard disks store bits along a two-dimensional plane that read/write heads can access in a matter of milliseconds, tapes must be searched bit-by-bit from beginning to end in order to locate a desired file. A tape search can take minutes—far too long for use as primary storage. There are four major approaches to tape packaging: reels, cassettes, quarter-inch cartridges, and helical scan cartridges. Due to the age and extreme expense of reel-to-reel tape storage systems, reel-to-reel (or *open reel*) tape will not be covered in this book.

Cassette tapes

The audio cassette as we know it today was originally developed and patented by the Philips Corporation as a way of overcoming the disadvantages of open reel audio tape. Philips had created a self-contained tape module that was small, compact, relatively rugged and reliable, and offered a reasonably high fidelity that appealed to the consumer market. As personal computers entered the marketplace, the conventional audio cassette and cassette tape player were pressed into service as a simple, inexpensive storage system. Even the original IBM PC provided a cassette interface port. However, the slow speed and access techniques required for cassette tapes soon led to the introduction and widespread adoption of inexpensive 13.34-cm (5¼-inch) floppy disk drives. Cassette tape drives as primary storage systems disappeared from personal computers virtually overnight.

However, Teac Corporation has re-introduced the compact cassette as a refined, data-only digital cassette (called a *D/CAS*). Teac's high-speed cassette transport mechanism uses the D/CAS to provide tape backup storage with performance levels equal to the better cartridge systems. Teac D/CAS tapes are intentionally incompatible with conventional audio cassettes. Although dimensions between audio and digital cassettes are very similar, digital cassettes use a single large notch on the cassette that allows a D/CAS to fit in the drive, but prohibits audio cassettes from being used. The notch also prohibits the D/CAS from being inserted into the drive upside down. An auto-reverse mechanism allows both sides of the tape to be used. A typical Teac D/CAS system stores 160Mb on a tape, but new models can handle up to 600Mb. Teac plans to increase that limit even further in the next few years. You can see more of Teac's D/CAS drive system in this chapter.

Quarter-inch cartridge

The concept of the quarter-inch tape cartridge (*QIC*) is identical to the compact cassette tape: a plastic shell contains two spools that hold a length of tape. Enclosing the tape supply in a prefabricated shell eliminates the need for handling open reel tape, or threading the tape through the labyrinth of a mechanical handling system. The original QIC was introduced by 3M in the early 1970s as a recording medium for telecommunication system programming and high-volume data acquisition.

Although QIC and cassette tapes might appear similar by outward appearances, the means used to drive both tapes is radically different. Cassette tapes are driven using a capstan drive system where the tape is pulled by a take-up reel as it winds across a R/W head. A QIC (Fig. 51-3) uses a small belt that loops around and contacts both the supply and take-up spools, as well as a rubber drive wheel. The capstan in a QIC system contacts the drive wheel (but not the tape), so only the belt's contact friction is used to drive the tape. Drive forces are spread evenly over a long length of tape, so the tape can be moved faster and sustain more direction reversals than a cassette, so tape reliability and working life are greatly improved. Because the components needed to handle the tape are already contained in the QIC shell, the drive mechanism is simple because only a motor and R/W head is required.

With the introduction of personal computers and the subsequent discard of audio cassettes as mass-storage devices, the quarter-inch cartridges emerged as the premier tape mechanism, but early QIC systems were riddled with incompatibilities; each manufacturer had their own ideas about how QIC systems should work. A number of tape drive companies met in the early 1980s to decide on a set of standards for the new QIC devices. In 1982, this group of industrial manufacturers formed an organization called the QIC Committee. The QIC Committee is responsible for developing standards for all aspects of tape drive construction and application.

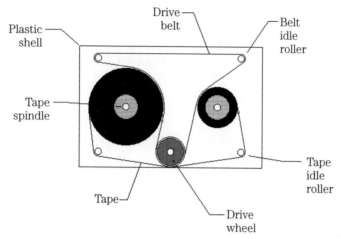

51-3 A typical QIC tape.

QIC details

A classic QIC can be identified by its general dimensions. The cartridge is 15.24 cm (6 inches) wide, 10.16 cm (4 inches) long, and 1.59 cm (⅝ inches) deep, somewhat smaller than a VHS video cassette. Although dimensions have not changed significantly through the years, there have been several iterations of standard quarter-inch cartridges. The earliest type of QIC tape was the DC300 cartridge produced by 3M Company, named for the 91.44 meter (300 feet) of tape that it contained. However, the DC300 cartridge proved limited, so the tape length was increased to 181.88 meter (600 feet) and renamed as the DC600 cartridge (although the designation was later changed to DC6000). For our purposes, all current QIC drives will be using DC6000 cartridges. Storage capacities for the DC6000 cartridge vary from 60Mb at the low end, to 2.1Gb at the high end.

Minicartridge details

The major drawback to standard QICs is their overall large size; they do not fit well into today's small drive bays, so most QIC systems are external desktop devices. To address the need for smaller-sized QIC systems, the QIC Committee created the *minicartridge*: an 8.26 cm (3.25 inches) × 6.35 cm (2.5 inches) × 1.59 cm (⅝ inch) assembly holding about 62.48 m (205 feet) of quarter-inch tape. Minicartridges use a DC2000 designation where the last three digits in the number reflect the cartridge's capacity. For example, a DC2080 minicartridge is designated to hold 80Mb, and so on. Any time you see a tape or tape drive associated with a DC2000 designation, you know you must use a minicartridge.

QIC drive standards

Of course, it takes much more than a blank tape to make a tape drive. The drive mechanism itself actually defines how the tape is formatted, and how much data it can ultimately hold. Since the early 1980s, there have been a proliferation of drive standards to keep pace with the continuing push for ever-greater storage capacity. Table 51-1 shows the tape and drive standards for PCs. QIC-02 was the first real tape drive standard, but its 15Mb capacity was limited. As a result, its success was short lived as it was pushed aside by the 60Mb capacity of QIC-24. PC tape drives broke the 100Mb mark with a QIC-120 drive, and moved to a capacity of 250Mb with QIC-150. Drive standards developed after QIC-150 used designations that matched the capacity. For example, the QIC-525 drive provides 525Mb of storage on a DC6000 cartridge. Today, DC6000 cartridges are providing 2.1Gb of storage using QIC-2100 drives. Future QIC drives are looking toward 35Gb of storage.

51-1. Comparison of QIC tapes and drives

Tape Designation	W	L	H	Length
DC300	15.24mm	10.16mm	1.59mm	91.44mm
DC6000	15.24mm	10.16mm	1.59mm	181.88mm
DC2000	8.26mm	6.35mm	1.59mm	62.48mm

Drive Standard	Tape	Capacity	Tracks
QIC-02	DC300	15MB	9
QIC-24	DC6000	60MB	9
QIC-40	DC2000	40MB	20
QIC-80	DC2000	80MB*	32
QIC-100	DC2000	40MB	12/24
QIC-120	DC6000	125MB	9
QIC-150	DC6000	250MB	18
QIC-500	QIC-143	500MB	—
QIC-525	DC6000	525MB	18
QIC-1000	DC6000	1.0GB	30
QIC-1350	DC6000	1.35MB	30
QIC-2100	DC6000	2.1GB	30

* with longer tapes and compression, storage can approach 250MB or higher

Drive standards also have been developed for minicartridges by the QIC Committee as shown in Table 51-1. QIC-40 was a simple, inexpensive tape backup standard that used an ordinary floppy drive interface controller to store up to 40Mb. Another interesting aspect of the QIC-40 specification is that the standard also covers data formatting. Sectors and tracks are allocated for files in much the same way that floppy or hard drive space is allocated. Any bad sectors also are listed to prohibit data storage in defective media areas. As with floppy disks, QIC-40 tapes must be formatted prior to their use. The enduring advantage to QIC-40 formatting is that the tape can be randomly accessed like a floppy disk (although MUCH more slowly) without having to search the entire tape to find a file. Files also can be appended because the QIC-40 drive can find free space on the formatted tape.

Today, QIC-40 tape systems are inexpensive and easy to use, but QIC-80 has become a very popular minicartridge tape standard. QIC-80 extends the QIC-40 approach by placing 32 tracks across the tape and increasing the data density, which effectively increases storage capacity to 80Mb (formatted). By using extended-length tapes and data compression, a QIC-80 drive can store up to 250Mb or more.

Although QIC-80 systems can read but not write older QIC-40 systems, QIC-80 drives also are compatible with conventional floppy drive controllers.

The QIC-100 standard is actually older than the QIC-80 standard, and can only support capacities of 40Mb. The advantage of QIC-100 was its performance because it used specialized interface hardware for high data transfer rates. QIC-100 stores data on 12 or 24 tracks recorded in a serpentine (back and forth) fashion. For practical purposes, you might never encounter tape drives using a QIC-100 system or its 86 Byte successor, the QIC-128 standard.

New standards for QIC minicartridges are always being developed. The QIC-500M standard is intended to eventually replace QIC-80 systems. A QIC-500M drive should be able to pack 500Mb on a minicartridge without using any data compression at all. The QIC-500M standard also is intended to be compatible with QIC-40 and QIC-80 systems, and connect to your computer using a conventional floppy drive interface.

Helical scan tapes

The rate at which data is transferred in tape systems has long been an issue. Transfer rates of 250 or 500 kilobits per second (floppy-drive rates) can seem extraordinarily slow when there are hundreds of megabytes (even gigabytes) to move onto a tape. Because the conventional tape systems you have seen so far move tape across stationary heads, data transfer rates are ultimately limited by the tape speed, and a tape can only be moved just so fast. Data transfer also is affected by the drive electronics, but even new encoding techniques are of limited utility. Tape drive designers realized that the head and tape can be moved together to increase the relative speed between the two, while allowing the tape transport mechanism itself to continue operating at a normal speed.

It was discovered that a set of R/W heads mounted on a cylindrical drum could be spun across a length of moving tape wrapped about 90° around the drum's circumference as shown in Fig. 51-4. The drum itself would be offset (or cantered) at a slight angle relative to the tape's path of travel. During normal operation, the spinning drum describes a *helical* path (thus the term *helical scan*) across the tape as shown in Fig. 51-5. Such a helical pattern allows more information to be written to the tape faster than conventional stationary head systems. There are currently two major helical recording systems: 4-mm digital audio tape (DAT) and 8-mm tape (8 mm). DAT heads are cantered about 6°, and 8-mm tape heads use a 5° tilt. DAT

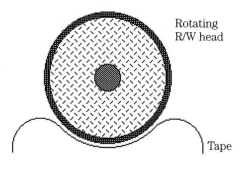

Rotating
R/W head

51-4
Helical scan tape configuration.

Tape

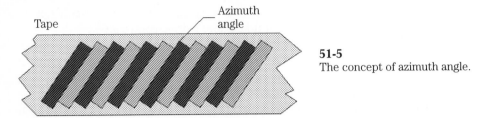

51-5
The concept of azimuth angle.

heads spin at 2000 rpm, and lay down 1869 tracks (traces) in every linear inch (2.54 cm) of tape. Each trace is only 4 mm wide.

Data can be packed very tightly on DAT tapes because each trace (or scan line) is recorded at a unique *azimuth angle*. Each head in the drum is skewed slightly from the perpendicular such that the data on adjacent traces is oriented very differently. During playback, a head responds well to signals written in the same orientation, but it responds poorly to signals written in the other orientation, so blank space between each signal is not required. Another advantage to helical scan is data integrity. By adding two more heads to the rotating drum (total of four heads), data can be read immediately after writing. Any errors that are detected can be corrected by repeating the data on subsequent traces until data is valid. Physically, helical scan tape is about 4mm wide and wound into a plastic cartridge roughly the size of a credit card. A DAT usually packs 1.3 to 2.0Gb of data in up to 90 meters of 1450-oersted tape.

Probably the greatest disadvantage to helical scan tape systems is the additional mechanical complexity required to wrap the tape around a spinning drum. Where cassettes, QICs, and minicartridges allow only a single point of contact with a stationary R/W head, helical scan tapes must be pulled out and away from its shell and wrapped the rotating drum as shown in Fig. 51-6. Note the series of rollers and guides that are needed to properly position and tension the tape.

Eight-mm tape is twice as wide as DAT media in a 9.53 cm (3.75 inch) × 6.35 cm (2.5 inch) × 1.27 cm (0.5 inch) cassette that appears rather like a VHS cassette. Using file-compression techniques, 8-mm systems can store up to 10Gb on a single cassette. The exorbitantly high cost of 8-mm tape backup systems are well beyond the means of most hobbyists and enthusiasts—even some small companies. This book does not deal with 8-mm systems any further.

Tape drive construction

Now that you have an understanding of basic tape styles and drive standards, this part of the chapter shows you how tape drives are physically assembled. Figure 51-7 shows an exploded diagram for a Teac D/CAS tape drive mechanism. Although the construction of most fixed-head tape drives is not incredibly complex, it is rather involved and delicate. Helical scan tape drives, however, can offer significant technical challenges because of the added heads and tape-handling mechanisms. For the purposes of this book, only fixed-head tape drives will be discussed.

Mechanical construction

At the core of the mechanical assembly is the drive chassis (1), also called the transport subassembly. This chassis forms the foundation for all other drive compo-

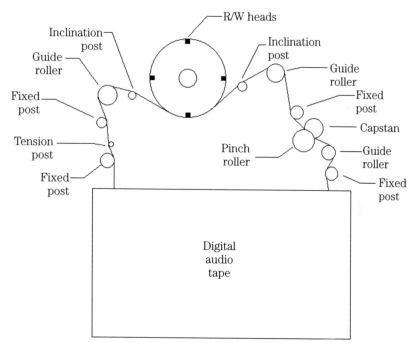

51-6 Example of a helical scan tape path.

nents including two PC boards. The chassis is built with four assemblies already in place (two loading base assemblies, a lever base assembly, and a loading arm assembly). These mechanical assemblies are responsible for loading and ejecting the tape. When you encounter difficulties with tape loading or unloading, you should suspect a problem in one or more of these mechanical areas. The chassis mechanics also are responsible for allowing tapes to be inserted on one side only (Side A). If the tape is inserted with side B up, the mechanics will not allow the tape to seat in the drive. A front bezel/door assembly (28) and an eject button (29) give the drive its cosmetic appearance once the completed drive is mounted in its drive bay.

A D/CAS tape is transported through the drive using two reel motors: a forward reel motor (9), and a reverse reel motor (10). These are both dc motors that are driven by control circuitry on the drive control PC board (26). Ideally, these reel motors should turn at a constant rate of speed, but tape speed tends to vary as tape is unwound from one spool and wound onto another. To keep tape velocity constant, the tape contacts an encoder roller (15) that drives an encoder assembly (12). Data generated by the encoder is used to regulate reel motor speed, much the same way that an index sensor is used to regulate spindle speed in a floppy or hard drive. Tension on the encoder roller is maintained and adjusted by tweaking the encoder spring (13) and pin spring (14) with a screw.

D/CAS tape is separated into individual tracks along the tape's width. The read/write head assembly (22) is actually composed of five separate magnetic heads: two read heads, two write heads, and an erase head. During a write operation, the erase head erases any previous data that might have existed on the tape, the write head(s) then lay down new flux transitions, and the read head(s) immediately

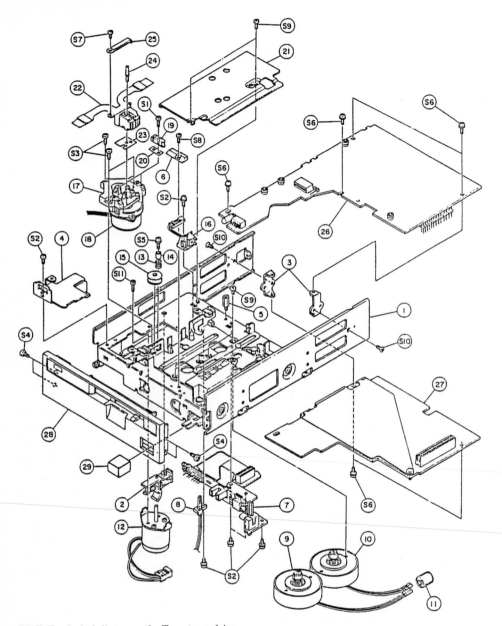

51-7 Exploded diagram of a Teac tape drive. Teac America, Inc.

reread the written data to ensure its integrity. During a read operation, the erase and write heads are idle, and only the read(s) respond. The head assembly is held in place with a head mounting screw (24). A clamp (25) holds the head's flat cable.

The head assembly is mounted to a head seek assembly (17) through an electrical isolation sheet (23). A head seek unit raises or lowers the head to the desired track as the tape moves past. A stepping motor (18) drives the head seek assembly using a lead screw. As the stepping motor turns in one direction, the force of rotation is translated to linear motion by the lead screw; the head moves in a fashion similar to head stepping in a floppy drive. There also are several tape guides (6 and 19). The remainder of mechanical parts are generally brackets and screws. Always make it a point to note the locations of all screws and brackets during disassembly.

Electronic circuitry

The electronics involved in the Teac D/CAS drive also are called out in the exploded view of Fig. 51-7. There are two printed circuit boards: the drive control PC board (26) and the drive interface PC board (27). The drive control board contains all the circuitry necessary for operating the drive's physical devices such as the R/W head(s), the reel motors, the stepping motor, reading the encoder, and reading the other drive sensor elements. A drive interface board contains the high-level processing circuitry needed to communicate with a host computer, and operate the drive control board.

There are three discrete sensors in the drive (not counting the encoder): a cassette load sensor (7), a file protect sensor (7), an LED hole sensor (8), and a sensor guide pair (16). Notice that cassette and file sensors are both held on the same sub PC board. The cassette load sensor is an optoisolator that produces a logic 0 when a tape is absent, and a logic 1 when a tape is present (similar to the disk-in-place sensor of a floppy drive). A file protect sensor produces a logic 0 when the tape is protected (writing is inhibited), and a logic 1 when writing is allowed (similar to a floppy drive's write protect sensor). All sensors are important parts of the drive and its ability to interact with the outside world.

Figure 51-8 presents these major electronic sections as a block diagram. The left portion of the diagram shows you how a D/CAS tape will interact with the R/W head and system sensors. When the cassette is inserted properly, it will engage into the forward and reverse reel motors. A properly inserted tape also asserts the cassette load sensor. The signal being generated by a file protect sensor depends on whether the cassette's write protect notch is exposed or covered. The beginning of tape (BOT) and end of tape (EOT) contain a short series of holes. An LED source is placed on one side of the tape, and a sensor is placed on the other side. When EOT and BOT holes are encountered, a pulse signal is returned to drive control circuitry. During reading or writing, a R/W head assembly is engaged to contact the tape. The encoder wheel also contacts the tape. Resulting encoder signals are used by drive control circuits to regulate tape speed by adjusting reel speed. The head is mounted to its track seeking stepping motor that also is operated by drive control circuits.

The tape drive control PC board handles the drive's physical operations and processes all sensor readings. Analog head signals are processed through a read circuit where they are converted into logic signals and sent along to the R/W head control circuit on the drive's interface control PC board. Write signals leave the R/W control circuit in logic form and are sent to the write/erase circuit on the drive control PC board. Logic write signals are converted to analog signals and sent to the R/W head. During writing, the write/erase circuit also actuates the erase head to clear any previous data before new data is written. The drive control board is managed by the

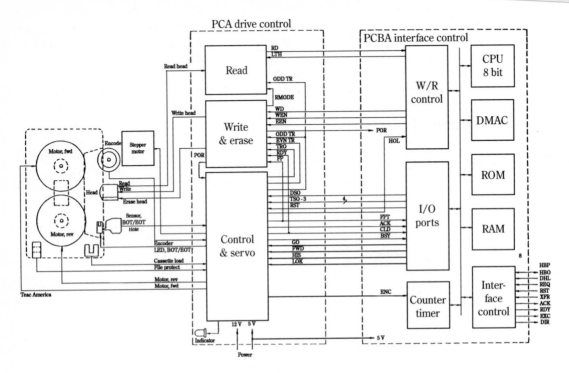

51-8 Block diagram of a Teac tape drive. Teac America, Inc.

control/servo circuit that communicates with I/O ports on the drive interface board. The control/servo circuit also lights an LED on the drive's front panel when any drive activity takes place.

The tape drive interface control PC board is a microprocessor-driven system that handles high-level drive operations. A CPU is responsible for processing system instructions provided by an on-board ROM, as well as any variables or data information held in RAM. The CPU handles the physical interface through the interface control circuit, and directs the drive's control board utilizing I/O circuits. Data flowing into or out of the drive is processed through a write/read control circuit. System synchronization is maintained by reading the counter/timer circuit being driven by the control/servo circuit. The particular layout and control structure of your particular tape drive might vary quite a bit from the Teac system illustrated here, but all major operating areas should be present to one extent or another. You also might encounter several functions integrated into a single high-density ASIC, so you should regard Fig. 51-8 as more of a conceptual guideline than an absolute rule.

Drive cleaning

As with floppy disk drives, tape drives bring magnetic media directly into contact with magnetic R/W heads. Over time and use, magnetic oxides from the tape rub off onto the head surface. Oxides (combined with dust particles and smoke contamination) accumulate and act as a wedge that forces the tape away from the head surface. Even if you never have cause to actually disassemble your tape drive, you should make it a point to perform routine cleaning. Regular cleaning improves the working life of your recording media and can significantly reduce the occurrence of data errors.

In general, the objective of cleaning is remarkably simple: remove any buildup of foreign material that might have accumulated on the R/W head. The most common cleaning method uses a prepackaged cleaning cartridge. The cartridge contains a length of slightly abrasive cleaning material. When cleaning tape is run through the drive, any foreign matter on the head is rubbed away. The cleaning tape can often be used for several cleanings before being discarded. Some cleaning tapes can be run dry, and others might have to be dampened with an alcohol-based cleaning solution. The advantage to a cleaning cartridge is simplicity; the procedure is quick and you never have to disassemble the drive. Because QIC tape moves much more slowly across a head than floppy media does, you need not worry about damaging the R/W head because of friction. DAT heads *do* move across the tape quickly, however, so you must be cautious about cleaning times. You will likely have better results over the long term using dry cleaning cartridges that are impregnated with a lubricating agent to reduce friction.

You also can clean R/W heads manually that can be convenient during a repair when the drive is already opened. Start by vacuuming away any debris that might be in the drive. Use a small, hand-held vacuum to reach tight spots. Heads can be cleaned with a fresh, lint-free swab dipped lightly in a head cleaning solution. If no head cleaning solution is available, use fresh ethyl or isopropyl alcohol. Rub the head gently but firmly to remove any debris. You might wish to use several swabs to ensure a thorough cleaning. Allow the head to dry completely before running a tape.

It is very important for you to remember that these are only general guidelines. Refer to the user's manual or reference manual for your particular drive to find the cleaning recommendations, procedures, and cautions listed by the manufacturer. Every drive has slightly different cleaning and preventive maintenance procedures. Some drives also might require periodic lubrication.

Tape drive troubleshooting

Tape drive systems (especially DAT systems) are some of the most complex and expensive mass-storage devices. The motors, sensors, and mechanisms in a typical tape drive are all prone to eventual failure. Even the natural wear that occurs in mechanical systems has an impact on drive performance and data error rates. This part of the chapter is intended to provide some general service guidelines and basic troubleshooting procedures. Bear in mind that tape drives (especially DAT drives) contain a substantial amount of mechanical and electromechanical components. Given the nature of mechanical parts, many of your problems will be mechanically oriented.

Symptom 1. The tape drive does not work at all Begin your repair by checking for obvious setup and configuration errors. First, make sure that power is available to the drive (a power indicator will usually be lit on the drive). An internal tape drive is usually powered from the host computer, so be sure that the internal 4-pin power connector is correctly attached. External drives are almost always powered from a separate ac adapter or power supply, but a few proprietary drives can be powered through their interface cables. Check the output of any external ac adapter or power supply. If the ac adapter output is low or nonexistent, replace the ac adapter.

Check that the interface cable between drive and tape controller card is connected properly. Also check that your backup software is running and properly configured to your particular drive. If you are troubleshooting a new, unproven installation, inspect the tape controller board address, interrupt, and DMA settings as necessary; configuration conflicts can lock up a software package or render a drive inoperative. Check the tape itself to be sure it is inserted properly and completely.

If power, interface cables, and software setup check properly, your trouble is likely in your drive or host controller. Ideally, your next step would be to isolate further by substitution. Try a known-good tape drive and/or controller card in your system. For most of us, however, tape drives are few and far between, so simply plugging in a compatible system from a friend or colleague is not nearly as likely as it would be with floppy or even hard drives.

If your tape drive is being controlled by an ordinary floppy drive controller board, turn system power off and try disconnecting your tape drive and plugging in a floppy drive. When power is restored, you might have to disable any TSRs installed (to manage the tape drive) and change the CMOS system setup such that the floppy drive will be recognized. If your test floppy drive works properly, you can be confident that the controller board works properly. The problem is then likely in your tape drive, or there is still a problem in your tape system setup. If you cannot get the test floppy drive to work, the floppy controller board might be defective, so try a new controller board. If a new controller board supports the test floppy drive, return the floppy drive to its original port, re-install the tape drive, restore the system setup for the tape drive, and try the tape drive again.

As an alternative to hardware swapping, many drives are now shipped with a simple diagnostic routine on the installation disk. Try a diagnostic if it is available. If a diagnostic recognizes the controller but not the drive, the drive is either defective, or is connected or set up incorrectly. You might see an error message such as "No tape drive found." If the diagnostic does not recognize the controller, at all, the controller is defective, or the controller is configured improperly. A typical error message might be something like "No tape controller found."

Symptom 2. The tape does not read or write, but the tape and head seem to move properly You will probably find read/write errors indicated by your backup software. Start your repair by inspecting the tape cartridge itself. The cartridge should be inserted completely and properly into the drive, and sit firmly over the reel as shown in Fig. 51-9. If the current tape is inserted properly, try loading from another tape. Old tapes might have degraded to a point where data can no longer be read or written reliably. If an alternate tape works properly, discard and replace the old tape. If problems persist, try cleaning the tape drive's R/W heads. Excessive buildups of dust or residual oxides can easily interfere with normal tape recording/playback operations. If you still encounter R/W trouble, the R/W heads or their associated circuitry has probably failed. Try replacing the tape drive.

Symptom 3. The R/W head does not step from track to track The remainder of the drive appears to work properly. This problem also might result in tape read

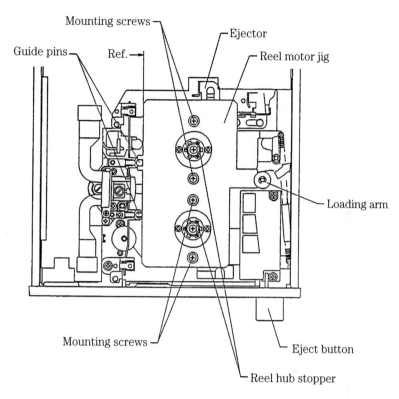

51-9 Carriage view of a Teac tape drive. Teac America, Inc.

or write errors. The head assembly must step across very small tracks laid out along the width of the tape. Depending on the vintage of tape and drive you are faced with, the tape might have 9 to 30 tracks. When the tape reaches its end, the head is positioned to another track, tape direction reverses, and reading or writing continues. There are two physical elements responsible for positioning a R/W head: a head stepping motor and a mechanism called the head seek assembly. A defect or jam in either one of these components can prevent the head from moving. You can see the stepping motor in the underside view of Fig. 51-10.

Check the LED/sensor pair that detect the EOT/BOT holes. If the LED transmitter or phototransistor receiver is defective, the drive will not know when to switch tracks. Remove the tape and place your multimeter across the receiving sensor. As you alternately pass and interrupt the light path from transmitter to receiver, you should see the logic output from the detector sensor switch from logic 1 to logic 0 (or vice versa). If the sensor does not work, replace the LED and phototransistor, and try the sensor pair again. If the sensor pair still malfunctions, replace the drive's control PC board, or replace the entire drive. If problems persist, the drive's control circuitry has probably failed. Try replacing the drive.

Symptom 4. The tape does not move, or its speed does not remain constant When a tape is set into motion for reading or writing, it is vitally important that tape speed remain constant. Tape speed is a function of the reel motors and the

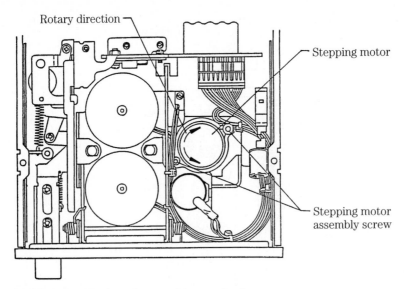

Rotary direction

Stepping motor

Stepping motor
assembly screw

51-10 Underside view of a tape drive mechanism. Teac America, Inc.

encoder that produces speed feedback signals. Begin by removing the tape and check for any accumulation of dust and debris that might be interfering with drive operation. Carefully clear away any obstruction that you might find.

If the tape does not move at all, check the dc motor signal across the reel motor(s) with your multimeter. When activated, there should be about +12 Vdc across the appropriate motor (forward or reverse motor depending on the tape's initial direction). If no excitation voltage is present, there is probably a fault in the drive's control PC board. Try replacing the drive control PC board, or replace the entire drive. If drive voltage is present but the tape does not turn, replace both reel motors as in Fig. 51-11 or replace the drive.

If the reel motors turn as expected but their speed is not constant, the problem might be in the encoder. Tape is normally kept in contact with a rubber encoder roller. As a tape moves, the encoder roller turns and spins the encoder. Pulse signals from the encoder are used by the drive control PC board to regulate reel motor speed. Check the encoder roller. Tighten the encoder roller if it is loose or worn. A heavily worn encoder roller should be replaced. Make sure one roller turn results in one encoder turn; the roller must not slip on the encoder shaft. Place your logic probe on the encoder output and check for pulses as the tape moves. If there are no pulses, replace the defective encoder or replace the drive. If pulses are present, replace the drive's control PC board, or replace the entire drive.

Symptom 5. There are problems in loading or ejecting the tape Most of the mechanisms for loading or unloading a tape are incorporated directly into the drive chassis itself as you saw in Fig. 51-7. Physical abuse and the accumulation of dust and debris can eventually cause problems in your tape handling mechanisms. Before you disassemble your drive, however, check your tape very carefully. Old tapes can jam or wear out, and some tapes (such as Teac's digital cassette) can only be inserted into the drive in one orientation. Try a fresh tape and make sure that the tape is inserted properly into the drive.

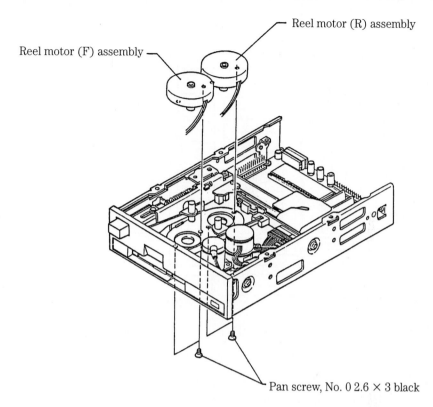

Reel motor (R) assembly

Reel motor (F) assembly

Pan screw, No. 0 2.6 × 3 black

51-11 A Teac tape drive with drive motors removed. Teac America, Inc.

If the tape continues to load or unload with resistance, expose the drive's mechanical assemblies and inspect all levers and linkages (Fig. 51-12) for any signs of obstruction or damage. Gently clear away any obstructions that you might find. You might wish to use a fresh, dry cotton swab to wipe away any accumulations of debris. *Do not add any lubricant to the load/unload mechanism unless there was lubricant there to begin with, then use only the same type of lubricant.* Replace any components that show signs of unusual wear.

Use extreme caution when working with tape assemblies. Mechanical systems are very precisely designed, so make careful notes and assembly diagrams during disassembly. An improperly reassembled mechanical system might damage the tape, or hold the tape in an improper position resulting in read/write or motor speed errors. If you cannot rectify the problem, replace the drive outright.

Symptom 6. The drive writes to write protected tapes When a tape is write protected, the drive should not be able to write to that protected tape. Your first step should be to remove and inspect the tape itself. Check to make sure that the write protect lever is in the *protect* position. If the protect lever is not in the right place, the tape is vulnerable to writing. If the tape protect lever is set properly, expose the drive mechanism and place your voltmeter across the sensor's output. Alternately, interrupt and free the optoisolator beam by hand and watch the sensor's output on your multimeter. If the output switches logic levels as you actuate the sensor manually, the trouble is probably in your drive's control PC board. Replace the drive con-

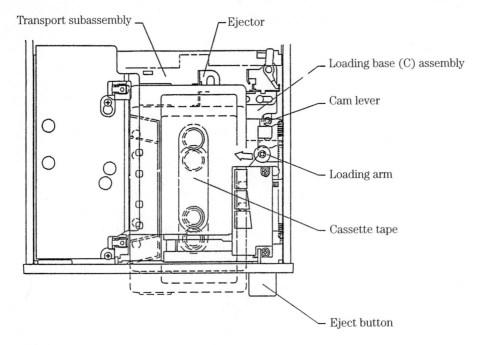

Transport subassembly

Ejector

Loading base (C) assembly

Cam lever

Loading arm

Cassette tape

Eject button

51-12 Close-up view of a carriage load/unload mechanism. Teac America, Inc.

trol PC board, or replace the entire drive. If the output does not shift logic levels as expected, the sensor might be defective. Replace the write protect sensor and repeat your test. If the sensor remains inoperative, replace the drive control PC board or replace the entire drive.

Symptom 7. The drive does not recognize the beginning or end of the tape A tape drive must know when the end or beginning of a tape has been reached. The majority of tapes use a series of small holes at each end of the tape. An optoisolator provides a pulse signal to the drive control PC board when holes pass by. Begin by removing the tape and checking for the presence of end holes. The wrong type of tape (such as a tape without holes) can cause problems for the drive. If the wrong type of tape is being used, retry the system using the correct type of tape.

Focus next on the BOT/EOT sensor that is an optoisolator located across the tape path (an LED on one side and a detector on the other). Remove the tape, expose the system, and place your multimeter across the detector's output. Alternately interrupt and free the light path by hand and watch the detector's output on your multimeter. If the output switches logic levels as expected, the trouble is probably in your drive's control PC board. Replace the drive control PC board, or replace the entire drive. If the output does not shift as expected, replace the LED source and detector elements together and retest the sensor pair. If the sensor remains inoperative, replace the drive control PC board or replace the entire drive.

Symptom 8. A software program using a hardware copy protection device on the parallel port locks up This symptom is typical of parallel port tape drives. The backup software attempts to communicate with the tape drive, but it winds up communicating with the copy protection device instead. You can either switch the tape to a free parallel port, or remove the copy protection device.

Symptom 9. The backup software indicates "Too many bad sectors" on the tape You also might see an error such as "Error correction failed." This type of error generally indicates that more than 5% of the sectors on a tape are unreadable. In many cases, this is caused by dirty R/W heads. Try cleaning the R/W head assembly. If problems continue, try a new tape cartridge. If problems persist, check the drive's power and signal cables and make sure that they are installed properly and completely.

Symptom 10. The tape backup software produces a "Tape drive error XX" where "XX" is a specific fault type The fault type will depend on the particular drive and tape backup software you are using, so refer to the user manual for exact code meanings. The following codes are for the Colorado Tape Backup Software:

- *0Ah—Broken or dirty tape* Clean the R/W heads carefully, and replace the tape (if broken).
- *0Bh—Gain error* Reformat the tape before attempting a backup.
- *1Ah—Power-on reset occurred* Check the drive's power and signal connections and try again.
- *1Bh—Software reset occurred* Shut down any application that might be conflicting with the tape backup software.
- *04h—Drive motor jammed* Remove the tape and make sure that there is nothing (including the tape) blocking the motor(s). Insert a new tape and try the system again.

52
CHAPTER

Video adapters and accelerators

The monitor itself is merely an output device (a peripheral) that translates synchronized analog or TTL video signals into a visual image. Of course, a monitor alone is not good for very much—except perhaps as a conversation piece or a room heater. The next logical question is: where does the video signal come from? All video signals displayed on a monitor are produced by a *video adapter* circuit (Fig. 52-1). The term *adapter* is used because the PC is adapted to the particular monitor through this circuit. In most cases, the video adapter is an expansion board that plugs into the PC's available bus slots. The video adapter converts raw data from the PC into image data that is stored in the adapter's *video memory*. The exact amount of memory available depends on the particular adapter and the video modes that the adapter is designed to support. Simple adapters offer as little as 256K, and the latest

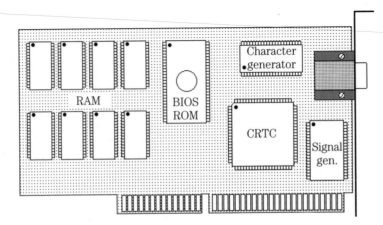

52-1 A typical video adapter board.

adapters provide 2Mb or more. The video adapter then translates the contents of video memory into corresponding video signals that drive a monitor.

The actual operations of a video adapter are certainly more involved than described, but you can begin to appreciate the critical role that the video adapter plays in a PC. If a video adapter fails, the monitor will display gibberish (or nothing at all). To complicate matters even further, many current software applications require small device drivers (called *video drivers*). A video driver is a rather small program that allows an application to access a video adapter's high-resolution or high-color video modes (usually for SVGA operation) with little or no interaction from the system BIOS. During troubleshooting, it will be necessary for you to isolate display problems to either the monitor, the video adapter, or driver software before a solution can be found. This chapter explains the operation and troubleshooting of typical video adapters.

Understanding conventional video adapters

The conventional frame buffer is the oldest and most well-established type of video adapter. The term *frame buffer* refers to the adapter's operation—image data is loaded and stored in video memory one frame at a time. Frame buffer architecture (as shown in Fig. 52-2) has changed very little since PCs first started displaying text and graphics. The heart of the frame-buffer video adapter is the highly integrated display controller IC (sometimes called a *CRTC* or cathode ray tube controller). The CRTC generates control signals and supervises adapter operation. It is the CRTC

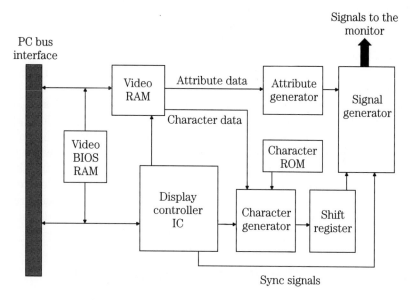

52-2 Block diagram of a frame buffer video adapter.

that reads *video RAM* (or VRAM) contents and passes those contents along for further processing. Many new video boards use specially designed IC groups (called *chipsets*) that are intended to work together. Chipsets provide fast, efficient video performance while minimizing the amount of circuitry needed on a video adapter.

Text versus graphics

Video RAM also plays a vital role because it is RAM that holds the image data to be displayed. The video adapter can operate in two modes: text and graphic. In the text mode, ASCII characters are stored in video RAM. A character ROM, character generator, and shift register produce the pixel patterns that form ASCII screen characters. The character ROM holds a pixel pattern for every possible ASCII character (including letters, numbers, and punctuation). The character generator converts ROM data into a sequence of pixel bits and transfers them to a shift register. The shift register produces a bit stream. At the same time, an attribute decoder determines whether the defined ASCII character is to be displayed as blinking, inverted, high-intensity, standard text, or a text color (for color monitors). The signal generator is responsible for turning the ASCII serial bit stream from the shift register into the video and synchronization signals that actually drive the monitor. The signal generator can produce either analog or TTL video signals.

In the graphic mode, video RAM locations already contain the color/gray scale information for each screen pixel rather than ASCII characters, so the character ROM and character generating circuitry used in text mode is bypassed. For example, monochrome graphics use a single bit per pixel, 16-color graphics use 4 bits per pixel, 256-color graphics use 8 bits per pixel, and so on. Pixel data taken from VRAM by the CRTC is passed through the character generator without any changes. Data is then sent directly to the shift register and on to the signal generator. It is the signal generator that produces analog or TTL video signals along with sync signals as dictated by the CRTC.

ROM BIOS (video BIOS)

There is one part of the classical video adapter that has not been mentioned yet—the video BIOS. The display controller requires substantial instruction changes when it is switched from text mode to any one of its available graphics modes. Because the instructions required to reconfigure and direct the CRTC depend on its particular design (and the video board design in general), it is impossible to rely on the software application or the PC's BIOS to provide the required software. As a result, all video adapters from EGA on use local BIOS ROM to hold the firmware needed by the particular display controller. Current PC architecture allocates about 128K of space from C0000h to DFFFFh within upper memory. This space is reserved for devices with expansion ROMs such as hard drive controllers and video adapters. Motherboard BIOS works in conjunction with the video BIOS.

Reviewing video-display hardware

The early days of PC development left users with a simple choice between monochrome or color graphics (all video adapters support text modes). In the years that followed, however, the proliferation of video adapters have brought an array of video modes and standards that you should be familiar with before upgrading a PC or attempting to troubleshoot a video system. This part of the chapter explains each of the video standards that have been developed in the last 15 years and shows you the video modes that each standard offers.

MDA (Monochrome Display Adapter—1981)

The Monochrome Display Adapter is the oldest video adapter available for the PC. Text is available in 80 column × 25 row format using 9 × 14-pixel characters as shown in Table 52-1. Being a text-only system, MDA offered no graphics capability, but it achieved popularity because of its relatively low cost, good text display quality, and integrated printer port. Figure 52-3 shows the video connector pinout for an MDA board. The 9-pin monitor connection uses four active TTL signals: intensity, video, horizontal, and vertical. Video and intensity signals provide the on/off and high/low intensity information for each pixel. The horizontal and vertical signals control the monitor's synchronization. MDA boards have long been obsolete and the probability of your encountering one is remote at best.

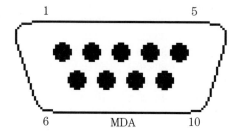

1. Ground
2. Ground
3. n/a
4. n/a
5. n/a
6. (+) Intensity
7. (+) vdeo
8. (+) Horizontal sync
9. (−) Vertical sync

52-3 Pinout of an MDA video connector.

Table 52-1. Comparison of video modes and standards

Standard	Resolution(s)	Colors	Mode	Text Format	Vert. Scan	Horiz. Scan
MDA	n/a	n/a	Text	80×25	50 Hz	18.432 kHz
CGA	320×200	16	Text	40×25	60 Hz	15.750 kHz
	640×200	16	Text	80×25	60 Hz	15.750 kHz
	160×200	16	Graphics	n/a	60Hz	15.750 kHz
	320×200	4	Graphics	40×25	60 Hz	15.750 kHz
	640×200	2	Graphics	80×25	60 Hz	15.750 kHz
EGA	320×350	16	Text	40×25	60 Hz	21.850 kHz
	640×350	16	Text	80×25	60 Hz	21.850 kHz
	720×350	4	Text	80×25	50 Hz	18.432 kHz
	320×200	16	Graphics	40×25	60 Hz	15.750 kHz
	620×200	16	Graphics	80×25	60 Hz	15.750 kHz
	640×350	4	Graphics	80×25	50 Hz	18.432 kHz
	640×350	16	Graphics	80×25	60 Hz	21.850 kHz
PGA	320×200	16	Text	40×25	60 Hz	15.750 kHz
	640×200	16	Text	80×25	60 Hz	15.750 kHz

Table 52-1. Continued

Standard	Resolution(s)	Colors	Mode	Text Format	Vert. Scan	Horiz. Scan
	320×200	4	Graphics	40×25	60 Hz	15.750 kHz
	640×200	2	Graphics	80×25	60 Hz	15.750 kHz
	640×480	256	Graphics	n/a	60 Hz	30.480 kHz
MCGA	320×400	16	Text	40×25	70 Hz	31.500 kHz
	640×400	16	Text	80×25	70 Hz	31.500 kHz
	320×200	4	Graphics	40×25	70 Hz	31.500 kHz
	640×200	2	Graphics	80×25	70 Hz	31.500 kHz
	640×480	2	Graphics	80×30	60 Hz	31.500 kHz
	320×200	256	Graphics	40×25	70 Hz	31.500 kHz
VGA	360×400	16	Text	40×25	70 Hz	31.500 kHz
	720×400	16	Text	80×25	70 Hz	31.500 kHz
	320×200	4	Graphics	40×25	70 Hz	31.500 kHz
	640×200	2	Graphics	80×25	70 Hz	31.500 kHz
	720×400	16	Text	80×25	70 Hz	31.500 kHz
	320×200	16	Graphics	40×25	70 Hz	31.500 kHz
	640×200	16	Graphics	80×25	70 Hz	31.500 kHz
	640×350	4	Graphics	80×25	70 Hz	31.500 kHz
	640×350	16	Graphics	80×25	70 Hz	31.500 kHz
	640×480	2	Graphics	80×30	60 Hz	31.500 kHz
	640×480	16	Graphics	80×30	60 Hz	31.500 kHz
	320×200	256	Graphics	40×25	70 Hz	31.500 kHz
8514	1024×768	256	Graphics	85×38	43.48 Hz	35.520 kHz
	640×480	256	Graphics	80×34	60 Hz	31.500 kHz
	1024×768	256	Graphics	146×51	43.48 Hz	35.520 kHz
XGA	360×400	16	Text	40×25	70 Hz	31.500 kHz
	720×400	16	Text	80×25	70 Hz	31.500 kHz
	320×200	4	Graphics	40×25	70 Hz	31.500 kHz
	640×200	2	Graphics	80×25	70 Hz	31.500 kHz
	720×400	16	Text	80×25	70 Hz	31.500 kHz
	320×200	16	Graphics	40×25	70 Hz	31.500 kHz
	640×200	16	Graphics	80×25	70 Hz	31.500 kHz
	640×350	4	Graphics	80×25	70 Hz	31.500 kHz
	640×350	16	Graphics	80×25	70 Hz	31.500 kHz
	640×480	2	Graphics	80×30	60 Hz	31.500 kHz
	640×480	16	Graphics	80×30	60 Hz	31.500 kHz
	320×200	256	Graphics	40×25	70 Hz	31.500 kHz
	1056×400	16	Text	132×25	70 Hz	31.500 kHz
	1056×400	16	Text	132×43	70 Hz	31.500 kHz
	1056×400	16	Text	132×56	70 Hz	31.500 kHz
	1056×400	16	Text	132×60	70 Hz	31.500 kHz
	1024×768	256	Graphics	85×38	43.48 Hz	35.520 kHz
	640×480	65536	Graphics	80×34	60 Hz	31.500 kHz
	1024×768	256	Graphics	128×54	43.48 Hz	35.520 kHz
	1024×768	256	Graphics	146×51	43.48 Hz	35.520 kHz

CGA (Color Graphics Adapter—1981)

The Color Graphics Adapter was the first to offer color text and graphics modes for the PC. A 160-x-200 low-resolution mode offered 16 colors, but such low resolution received very little attention. A 320-x-200 medium-resolution graphics mode allowed finer graphic detail, but with only 4 colors. The highest resolution mode provided 640×200 at 2 colors (usually black and one other color). The relationship between resolution and colors is important because a CGA frame requires 16K of video RAM. 640-x-200 resolution results in 128,000 pixels. With 8 bits able to represent 8 pixels, (128,000/8) 16,000 bytes are adequate. A resolution of 320×200 results in 64,000 pixels, but with 2 bits needed to represent 1 pixel (4 pixels/byte), (64,000/4) 16,000 bytes are still enough. You can see that video RAM is directly related to video capacity. Because there is typically much more video RAM available than is needed for an image, video boards support multiple video *pages*. Figure 52-4 shows the pinout for a typical CGA video connector. As with the earlier MDA design, CGA video signals reserve pins 1 and 2 as ground lines, and the horizontal sync signal is produced on pin 8 and the vertical sync signal is produced on pin 9. CGA is strictly a digital display system with TTL signals used on the Red (3), Green (4), Blue (5), and Intensity (6) lines.

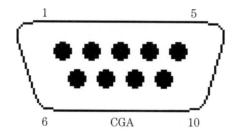

1. Ground
2. Ground
3. Red
4. Green
5. Blue
6. Intensity
7. n/a
8. Horizontal sync
9. Vertical sync

52-4 Pinout of a CGA video connector.

EGA (Enhanced Graphics Adapter—1984)

It was not long before the limitations of CGA became painfully apparent. The demand for higher resolutions and color depths drove designers to introduce the next generation of video adapter known as the *Enhanced Graphics Adapter*. One of the unique appeals of EGA was its backward compatibility; an EGA board would emulate CGA and MDA modes on the proper monitor, as well as its native resolutions and color depths when using an EGA monitor. EGA is known for its 320-x-200-x-16, 640-x-200-x-16, and 640-x-350-x-16 video modes. More memory is needed for EGA and 128K is common for EGA boards (although many boards could be expanded to 256K).

The EGA connector pinout is shown in Fig. 52-5. TTL signals are used to provide Primary Red (3), Primary Green (4), and Primary Blue (5) color signals. By adding a set of secondary color signals (or color intensity signals) such as Red Intensity (2), Green Intensity (6), and Blue Intensity (7), the total of six color control signals allow the EGA to produce up to 64 possible colors. Although 64 colors are possible, only 16 of those colors are available in the palette at any one time. Pin 8 carries the horizontal sync signal, pin 9 carries the vertical sync signal, and pin 1 remains ground.

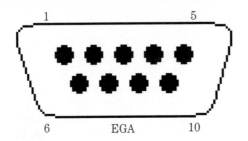

1. Ground
2. Red intensity
3. Primary red
4. Primary green
5. Primary blue
6. Green intensity
7. Blue intensity
8. Horizontal sync
9. Vertical sync

52-5 Pinout of an EGA video connector.

PGA (Professional Graphics Adapter—1984)

The Professional Graphics Adapter was introduced in 1984. This system offered a then-revolutionary display capability of 640 × 480 × 256. Three-dimensional rotation and graphic clipping was included as a hardware function, and the adapter could update the display at 60 frames per second. The PGA was incredibly expensive and beyond reach of all but the most serious business user. In actual operation, a PGA system required two or three expansion boards, so it also represented a serious commitment of limited system space. Ultimately, PGA failed to capture any significant market acceptance. It is unlikely that you will ever encounter a PGA board—most that ever saw service in PCs have since been upgraded.

MCGA (Multicolor Graphics Array—1987)

The Multicolor Graphics Array had originally been integrated into the motherboard of IBM's PS/2-25 and PS/2-30. As Table 52-1 shows, MCGA supports all of the CGA video modes, and also offers several new video modes including a 320-x-200-x-256 mode that has become a preferred mode for game software. MCGA was one of the first graphic systems to use analog color signals rather than TTL signals. Analog signals were necessary to allow MCGA to produce its 256 colors using only three primary color lines.

IBM also took the opportunity to use a new, high-density 15-pin connector as shown in Fig. 52-6. One of the striking differences between the analog connector and

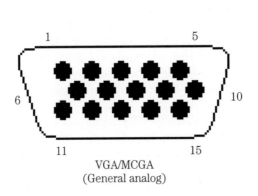

1. Red
2. Green
3. Blue
4. Ground
5. Ground
6. Red ground
7. Green grpund
8. Blue ground
9. n/a
10. Ground
11. Ground
12. n/a
13. Horizontal sync
14. Vertical sync
15. n/a

52-6 Pinout of a VGA/MCGA/SVGA video connector.

older TTL connectors is the use of individual ground lines for each color. Careful grounding is vital because any signal noise on the analog lines will result in color anomalies. If you inspect a video cable closely, you will find that one or both ends are terminated with a square metal box that actually contains a noise filter. It is important to realize that although the MCGA could *emulate* CGA modes, older TTL monitors were no longer compatible.

Although there were a number of notable technical improvements that went into the PS/2 design, none of them could ensure broad acceptance. However, the MCGA ushered in a new age of analog display technology, and virtually all subsequent video adapters now use the 15-pin analog format shown in Fig. 52-6. Although MCGA adapters also are (technically) obsolete, the standard lives on in MCGA's cousin, VGA.

VGA (Video Graphics Array—1987)

The video graphics array was introduced along with MCGA and implemented in other members of the PS/2 line. The line between MCGA and VGA has always been a bit fuzzy because both were introduced simultaneously (both using the same 15-pin video connector), and VGA can handle every mode that MCGA could. For all practical purposes, you can say that MCGA is a subset of VGA.

VGA provides the familiar 640-x-480-x-16 screen mode that has become the baseline for Microsoft Windows displays. The use of analog color signals allow VGA systems to produce a palette of 16 colors from 262,144 possible colors. As you see in Table 52-1, VGA also provides backward compatibility for all older screen modes. Although the PS/2 line has been discontinued, the flexibility and backward compatibility of VGA proved so successful that VGA adapters were soon developed for the PC. For a time, VGA support was considered to be standard equipment for all new PCs sold today, but SVGA boards are rapidly replacing VGA systems, and most SVGA adapters offer full VGA support.

8514 (1987)

The 8514/A video adapter is a high-resolution system also developed for the PS/2. In addition to full support for MDA, CGA, EGA, and VGA modes, the 8514/A can display 256 colors at 640-x-480 and 1024-x-768 (interlaced) resolutions. Unfortunately, the 8514/A was a standard ahead of its time. The lack of available software and the demise of the PS/2 line doomed the 8514/A to extinction before it could become an accepted standard. Today, the XGA is rapidly becoming the PC standard for high-resolution/high-color display systems.

SVGA (Super Video Graphics Array)

Ever since VGA became the de facto standard for PC graphics, there has been a strong demand from PC users to move beyond the 640-x-480-x-16 limit imposed by conventional VGA to provide higher resolutions and color depths. As a result, a new generation of extended or super VGA (SVGA) adapters have moved into the PC market. Unlike VGA that adhered to strict hardware configurations, there is no generally accepted standard on which to develop an SVGA board (this is why there is no SVGA reference in Table 52-1). Each manufacturer makes an SVGA board that supports a variety of different—and not necessarily compatible—video modes. For example, one manufacturer might produce an SVGA board capable of $1024 \times 768 \times 65{,}536$, and another manufacturer might produce a board that only reaches $640 \times 480 \times 16M$ (more than 16 million colors).

This mixing and matching of resolutions and color depths has resulted in a very fractured market; no two SVGA boards are necessarily capable of the same things. This proliferation of video hardware also makes it impossible for applications software to take advantage of super video modes without supplemental software called *video drivers*. Video drivers are device drivers (loaded before an application program is started) that allow the particular program to work with the SVGA board hardware. Video drivers are typically developed by the board manufacturer and shipped on a floppy disk with the board. Windows takes particular advantage of video drivers because the Windows interface allows ALL Windows applications to use the same graphics system rather than having to write a driver for every application as DOS drivers must be. Using an incorrect, obsolete, or corrupted video driver can be a serious source of problems for SVGA installations. The one common attribute of SVGA boards is that most offer full support for conventional VGA (which requires no video drivers). There are only a handful of SVGA board manufacturers that abandon conventional VGA support.

Today, most SVGA boards offer terrific video performance, a wide selection of modes, and prices that rival high-end VGA adapters. If it were not for the lack of standardization in SVGA adapters, VGA would likely be considered obsolete already. *VESA* (Video Electronics Standards Association) has started the push for SVGA standards by proposing the VESA BIOS Extension—a universal video driver. The extension would provide a uniform set of functions that allow application programs to detect a card's capabilities and use the optimum adapter configuration regardless of how the particular board's hardware is designed. Many of the quality SVGA boards in production today support the VESA BIOS Extensions, and it is worthwhile to recommend boards that support VESA SVGA. Some SVGA boards even incorporate the extensions into the video BIOS ROM that saves the RAM space that would otherwise be needed by a video driver.

XGA (1990)

The XGA and XGA/2 are 32-bit high-performance video adapters developed by IBM to support microchannel based PCs. XGA design with microchannel architecture allows the adapter to take control of the system for rapid data transfers. The XGA standards are shown in Table 52-1. You see that MDA, CGA, EGA, and VGA modes are all supported for backward compatibility. In addition, several color depths are available at 1024-x-768 resolution, and a photo-realistic 65,536 colors are available at 640-x-480 resolution. To improve performance even further, fast video RAM and a graphics coprocessor are added to the XGA design. For the time being, XGA is limited to high-performance applications in microchannel systems. The migration to ISA-based PCs has been slow because the ISA bus is limited to 16 bits and does not support *bus-mastering* as microchannel buses do. For PCs, SVGA adapters will likely provide extended screen modes as they continue to grow in sophistication as graphics accelerators.

Understanding graphics accelerators

When screen resolutions approach 640 × 480 and beyond, the data needed to form a single screen image can be substantial. Consider a single 640-x-480-x-256 image. There are (640 × 480) 307,200 pixels. Because there are 256 colors, 8 bits are needed to define the color for each pixel. This means 307,200 bytes are needed for every frame. When the frame must be updated 10 times per second, (307,200 × 10) 3,072,000 bytes per second (3.072Mb/s) must be moved across the ISA bus. If a 65,536 color mode is being used, two bytes are needed for each pixel, so (307,200 × 2) 614,400 bytes are needed for a frame. At 10 frames per second, (614,400 × 10) 6,144,000 bytes per second (6.144Mb/s) must be moved across the bus; this is just for video information and does not consider the needs of system overhead operations such as memory refresh, keyboard and mouse handling, drive access, and other data-intensive system operations. When such volumes of information must be moved across an ISA bus limited at 8.33 MHz, you can see how a serious data transfer bottleneck develops. This results in painfully slow screen refreshes, especially under Windows, which requires frequent refreshes.

Video designers seek to overcome the limitations of conventional video adapters by incorporating processing power onto the video board itself rather than relying on the system CPU for graphic processing. By off loading work from the system CPU and assigning the graphics processing to local processing components, graphics performance can be improved by a factor of three or more. There are several means of acceleration depending on the sophistication of the board (Fig. 52-7). Fixed-function acceleration relieves load on the system CPU by providing adapter support for a limited number of specific functions such as BitBlt or line draws. Fixed-function accelerators were an improvement over frame-buffers, but do not offer the performance of more sophisticated accelerators. A graphics accelerator uses an application-specific IC (ASIC) that intercepts graphics tasks and processes them without the intervention of the system CPU. Graphics accelerators are perhaps the most cost-effective type of accelerator. Graphics coprocessors are the most sophisticated type of accelerator. The coprocessor acts as a CPU that is dedicated to handling image data. Current

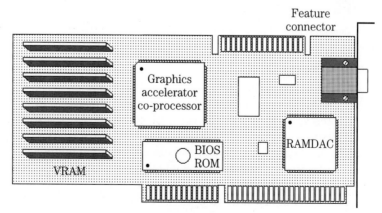

52-7 A typical video accelerator board.

graphics coprocessors such as the TMS34010 and TMS34020 represent the *TIGA* (Texas Instruments Graphical Architecture) that is broadly used for high-end accelerators. Unfortunately, not all graphics coprocessors provide increased performance to warrant the higher cost.

Figure 52-8 shows the block diagram for a typical graphics accelerator. The core of the accelerator is the graphics IC (or chipset). The graphics IC connects directly with the PC expansion bus. Graphics commands and data are translated into pixel data that is stored in video RAM. High-performance video memory offers a second data bus that is routed directly to the board's RAMDAC (random access memory video-to-analog converter). The graphics IC directs RAMDAC operation and ensures that VRAM data is available. The RAMDAC then translates video data into red, green, and blue analog signals along with horizontal and vertical synchronization signals. Output signals generated by the RAMDAC drive the monitor. This architecture might appear simple, but that is due to the extremely high level of integration of ICs and chipsets being used.

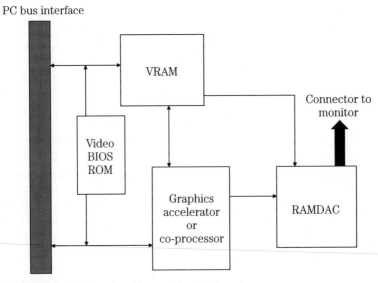

52-8 Block diagram of a video accelerator board.

Video speed factors

There is no one element that defines the performance of an accelerator board. Overall performance is actually a combination of five major factors: (1) the video accelerator IC, (2) the video RAM, (3) the video BIOS/drivers, (4) the RAMDAC, and (5) the bus architecture. By understanding how each of these factors relate to performance, you can make the best recommendations for system upgrades or replacement boards. The companion software available for this book provides a utility that checks the specifications of your particular video adapter.

Of course, the video accelerator IC itself (or the graphics chipset being used) is at the core of the accelerator board. The type of IC (fixed-function, graphics accelerator, or graphics coprocessor) loosely defines the board's capabilities. All other factors being equal, a board with a graphics accelerator will certainly perform better than a fixed-function accelerator. Companies like ATI Technologies, Advance Logic, Chips & Technologies, Headland Technology, Matrox Electronic Systems, and Primus Technology develop many of the accelerator ICs in use today. Many of the ICs provide a 32-bit data bus (even newer designs are providing a 64-bit data bus), and they sustain very high data rates, but a data bottleneck across a 16-bit expansion bus can seriously degrade the IC's capability. This means you should match the recommended board to the particular system; a state-of-the-art graphics accelerator will not necessarily make your old i286 shine.

Video adapters rely on RAM to hold image data, and accelerators are no exception. Although the current amount of video RAM typically varies from 512K to 2Mb (some accelerator boards offer 4Mb), the amount of RAM is not so important to a video accelerator as the RAM's speed. Faster memory is able to read and write image data faster, so adapter performance is improved. The introduction of specialized video RAM (VRAM—memory devices with two separate data buses that can be read from and written to simultaneously—is reputed to be superior to conventional dynamic RAM (DRAM) such as the kind used for ordinary PC memory. Recent advances in DRAM speed have narrowed that gap while still remaining very economical. At this point, adapters with fast DRAM are just about as fast as adapters with specialized video RAM for video modes up to $1024 \times 768 \times 256$. For higher modes and color depths found on high-end accelerators, specialized video RAM is still the way to go for optimum performance.

Software is often considered as an after-thought to adapter design, yet it plays a surprisingly important role in an accelerator performance. Even the finest accelerator board can bog down when run with careless, loosely written code. There are two classes of software that you must be concerned with: video BIOS and drivers. The video BIOS is *firmware* (software that is permanently recorded on a memory device such as a ROM). Video BIOS holds the programming that allows the accelerator to interact with DOS applications software. VESA BIOS extensions are now being used as part of the video BIOS for many accelerators as well as conventional frame-buffer adapters. By adding VESA BIOS extensions to video BIOS, it eliminates the need to load another device driver.

However, there are compelling advantages to video drivers. Windows works quite well with drivers (and ignores video BIOS entirely). Unlike BIOS ROMs that can never change once programmed, a video driver can change very quickly as bugs are corrected and enhancements are made. The driver can be downloaded from a manufacturer's BBS or their forum on CompuServe (or other on-line information service) and installed on your system in a matter of minutes without ever having to disassemble the PC. It also is possible for you to use third-party video drivers. Hardware manufacturers are not always adept at writing efficient software. A third-party driver developed by an organization that specializes in software might actually let your accelerator perform better than the original driver shipped from the manufacturer.

Just about every analog video system in service today is modeled after the 15-pin VGA scheme that uses three separate analog signals to represent the three primary colors. The color for each pixel must be broken down into component red, green, and blue levels, and those levels must be converted into analog equivalents. The conversion from digital values to analog levels is handled by a digital-to-analog converter (or DAC). Each conversion also requires a certain amount of time. Faster DACs are needed to support faster horizontal refresh rates. Remember that each video adapter uses a *palette* that is a subset of the colors that can possibly be produced. Even though a monitor might be able to produce 262,144 colors, a VGA board can only produce 256 of those colors in any 256 color mode. Older video boards stored the palette entries in registers, but the large-palette video modes now available (64K colors through 16 million colors) require the use of RAM. Boards that incorporate a RAMDAC (Random Access Memory Digital-to-Analog Converter) are preferred because memory integrated with DACs tends to be much faster than accessing discrete RAM elsewhere on the board.

Finally, graphic data must be transferred between the PC motherboard and the adapter as you saw early in this section. Such transfer takes place across the PC's expansion bus. If data can be transferred between the PC and adapter at a faster rate, video performance should improve. Consequently, the choice of bus architecture has a significant impact on video performance. Video accelerators are available to support three bus architectures: ISA, VL, and PCI.

The venerable *ISA* (Industry Standard Architecture) has remained virtually unchanged since its introduction with the PC/AT in the early 1980s. The ISA continues to be a mature interface standard for most IBM-compatible expansion devices. The sheer volume of ISA systems currently in service guarantees to keep the ISA on desktops for at least another 10 years. However, ISA's 16-bit data bus width, its lack of advanced features such as interrupt sharing or bus mastering, and its relatively slow 8.33 MHz operating speed form a serious bottleneck to the incredible volume of video data demanded by Windows and many DOS applications. ISA works, but it is no longer the interface of choice to achieve optimum video performance. When recommending an accelerator product, look to the newer buses for best results.

The Video Standards Electronics Association (VESA) has invested a great deal of time and effort to develop a standard bus interface that has been optimized for video operation. In essence, this new video bus is local to the system CPU that allows faster access without the 8.33-MHz limitation imposed by ISA. The actual bus speed is limited by the system clock speed. The VESA Local bus (VL bus) has achieved a remarkable level of industry acceptance and success in boosting video performance, especially when used with a high-quality graphics accelerator board. However, the 32-bit VL bus is generally limited to video systems. Other peripherals such as IDE hard drive controllers have been built for the VL bus, but it is far too early to predict their acceptance. As a result, current VL-compatible PCs typically offer only one or two VL expansion slots—the other expansion slots are ISA. Just about every accelerator product on the market today is available in a VL bus implementation. VL accelerators are a safe, inexpensive choice for current systems.

Intel's *PCI* (peripheral component interconnect) bus is one of the newest and most exciting bus architectures to reach the PC. The PCI bus runs at 33 MHz and offers a full 64-bit data bus that can take advantage of new 64-bit CPUs such as Intel's Pentium. Although the PCI bus also hopes to overcome the speed and functional limitations of ISA, the PCI architecture is intended to support all types of PC peripherals (not just video boards). Current PCI video boards are relatively expensive and appear to be delivering performance that is roughly equivalent to VL adapters, but as 64-bit CPUs and motherboards become common, it is likely that PCI boards will easily outperform 32-bit VL boards while their prices drop sharply. At the time of this writing, no other PCI-compatible peripherals are known to be in mass production other than video adapters.

Troubleshooting video adapters

A PC video system consists of four parts: the host PC itself, the video adapter, the monitor, and the software (video BIOS and drivers). To deal with a failure in the video system, you must be able to isolate the problem to one of these four areas. When isolating the problem, your best tool is a working (or *testbed*) PC. With another PC, you can systematically exchange hardware to verify each element of the video system.

Isolating the problem area

The first step is to verify the monitor by testing it on a known-good working PC. Keep in mind that the monitor must be compatible with the video adapter on which it is being tested. If the monitor works on another PC, the fault lies in one of the three remaining areas. If the monitor fails on a known-good machine, try the known-good monitor on the questionable machine. If the known-good monitor then works on your questionable machine, you can be certain that the fault lies in your monitor, and you can refer to the appropriate chapter here for detailed troubleshooting if you wish. If the monitor checks out, suspect the video adapter. Follow the same process to check the video adapter. Try the suspect video adapter on a known-good PC. If the problem follows the video adapter, you can replace the video adapter. If the suspect video adapter works in a known-good system, the adapter is probably good. Replace the adapter in the suspect machine, but try another expansion slot and make sure that the monitor cable is attached securely.

If both the monitor and the video adapter work in a known-good PC, but the video problem persists in the original machine, suspect a problem with the PC motherboard. Try the working video adapter in another expansion slot. Either the expansion slot is faulty, or a fault has occurred on the motherboard. Run some PC diagnostics if you have some available. Diagnostics can help to pinpoint motherboard problems. You might then choose to troubleshoot the motherboard further or replace the motherboard outright at your discretion.

When the video system appears to work properly during system initialization but fails with a particular application (or in Windows), strongly suspect a problem with the selected video driver. Because almost all video adapters support VGA at the hardware level, set your application (or change the Windows setup) to run in standard VGA mode. If the display functions properly at that point, you can be confident that the problem is driver related. Check with the manufacturer to see that you have the latest video driver available. Reload the driver from its original disk (or a new disk) or select a new driver. If the problem persists in VGA mode, the trouble might be in the video adapter.

Symptoms and solutions

Symptom 1. The computer is on, but there is no display (the PC seems to initialize properly) If you hear a series of beeps during system initialization, refer to Chapter 15 to determine the error. Make sure that the monitor is turned on and plugged into the video adapter properly. Also check that the monitor's brightness and contrast controls are turned up enough (it sounds silly, but it really does happen). Try the monitor on a known-good PC. If the monitor works properly, suspect the video adapter. Power down the PC and make sure the video adapter is seated properly in its expansion slot. If any of the board contacts are dirty or corroded, clean the contacts by rubbing them with an eraser. You also can use any electronics-grade contact cleaner. You might want to try the video board in another expansion slot.

Chances are that the video adapter has at least one hardware jumper or DIP switch setting. Contact the manufacturer or refer to the owner's manual for the board and check that any jumpers or DIP switch settings on the board are configured properly. If this is a new installation, check the adapter board settings against the configuration of other expansion boards in the system. When the hardware settings of one board overlap the settings of another, a hardware conflict can result. When you suspect a conflict, adjust the settings of the video adapter (or another newly installed device) to eliminate the conflict. There also might be a memory conflict. Some video adapters make unusual demands of upper system memory (the area between 640K and 1Mb). It is possible that an EXCLUDE switch must be added to the EMM386.EXE entry in a CONFIG.SYS file. Check with the adapter's instruction manual to see if there are any memory configuration changes or optimizations that are required.

Symptom 2. There is no display, and you hear a series of beeps when the PC initializes The video adapter failed to initialize during the system's POST. Because the video adapter is not responding, it is impossible to display information. That is why a series of beeps are used. Bear in mind that the actual beep sequence can vary from system to system depending on the type of BIOS being used. You can probably find the beep code for your BIOS in Chapter 15. In actual practice, there might be several reasons why the video adapter fails. Power down the PC and check that the video adapter is installed properly and securely in an expansion slot. Make sure that the video adapter is not touching any exposed wiring or any other expansion board.

Isolate the video adapter by trying another adapter in the system. If the display works properly with another adapter installed, check the original adapter to see that all settings and jumpers are correct. If the problem persists, the original adapter is probably defective and should be replaced. If a new adapter fails to resolve the problem, there might be a fault elsewhere on the motherboard. Install a POST board in the PC and allow the system to initialize as shown in Chapter 28. Each step of the initialization procedure corresponds to a two-digit hexadecimal code shown on the POST card indicators. The last code to be displayed is the point at which the failure occurred. POST cards are handy for checking the motherboard when a low-level fault has occurred. If a motherboard fault is detected, you can troubleshoot the motherboard or replace it outright at your discretion.

Symptom 3. You see large blank bands at the top and bottom of the display in some screen modes, but not in others Multifrequency and multimode monitors sometimes behave this way. This is not necessarily a defect, but it can cause some confusion unless you understand what is going on. When screen resolution changes, the overall number of pixels being displayed also changes. Ideally, a multifrequency monitor should detect the mode change and adjust the vertical screen size to compensate (a feature called auto-sizing). However, not all multifrequency monitors have this feature. When video modes change, you are left to adjust the vertical size manually. Of course, if there is information missing from the display, there can be a serious problem with VRAM or the adapter's graphics controller IC. In this event, try another video adapter board.

Symptom 4. The display image rolls Vertical synchronization is not keeping the image steady (horizontal sync also can be affected). This problem is typical of a monitor that cannot display a particular screen mode. Mode incompatibility is most common with fixed-frequency monitors, but also can appear in multifrequency monitors that are being pushed beyond their specifications. The best course of action here is to simply reconfigure your software to use a compatible video mode. If that is an unsatisfactory solution, you will have to upgrade to a monitor that will support the desired video mode.

If the monitor and video board are compatible, there is a synchronization problem. Try the monitor on a known-good PC. If the monitor also fails on a known-good PC, try the known-good monitor on original PC. If the known-good monitor works on the suspect PC, the sync circuits in your original monitor have almost certainly failed. If the suspect monitor works on a known-good PC, the trouble is likely in the original video adapter. Try replacing the video adapter.

Symptom 5. An error message appears on system startup indicating an invalid system configuration The system CMOS backup battery has probably failed. This is typically a symptom that occurs in older systems. If you enter your system setup (either through a BIOS routine or through a disk-based setup utility) and examine each entry, you will probably find that all entries have returned to a default setting, including the video system setting. Your best course is to replace the CMOS backup battery and enter each configuration setting again (hopefully you have recorded each setting on paper already, or saved the CMOS contents to floppy disk using a CMOS backup utility). Once new settings are entered and saved, the system should operate properly. If the CMOS still will not retain system configuration information, the CMOS RAM itself is probably defective. Use a software diagnostic to check the RTC/CMOS IC (and the rest of the motherboard) thoroughly. If a motherboard fault is detected, you can troubleshoot the motherboard or replace it outright at your discretion.

Symptom 6. Garbage appears on the screen or the system hangs up There are a variety of reasons why the display can be distorted. One potential problem is a monitor mismatch. Check the video adapter jumpers and DIP switch settings and be sure that the video board will support the type of monitor you are using. It is possible that the video mode being used is not supported by your monitor (the display also can roll as described in Symptom 4). Try reconfiguring your application software to use a compatible video mode. The problem should disappear. If that is an unsatisfactory solution, you will have to upgrade to a monitor that will support the desired video mode.

Some older multifrequency monitors are unable to switch video modes without being turned off, then turned on again. When such monitors experience a change in video mode, they will respond by displaying a distorted image until the monitor is reset. If you have an older monitor, try turning it off, wait several minutes, then turn it on again.

Conflicts between device drivers and terminate-and-stay-resident (TSR) programs will upset the display, and are particularly effective at crashing the computer. The most effective way to check for conflicts is to create a backup copy of your system startup files CONFIG.SYS and AUTOEXEC.BAT. From the root directory (or directory that contains your startup files), type:

```
copy autoexec.bat autoexec.xyz
copy config.sys config.xyz
```

The extensions *xyz* suggest that you use any three letters, but avoid using *bak* because many ASCII text editors create backup file with this extension.

Now that you have backup files, go ahead and use an ASCII text editor (such as the text editor included with DOS) to REM-out each driver or TSR command line. Reboot the computer. If the problem disappears, use the ASCII text editor to re-enable one REMed-out command at a time. Reboot and check the system after each command line is re-enabled. When the problem occurs again, the last command you re-enabled is the cause of the conflict. Check that command line carefully. There might be command line switches that you can add to the startup file that will load the driver or TSR without causing a conflict. Otherwise, you would be wise to leave the offending command line REMed-out. If you encounter serious trouble in editing the startup files, you can simply recopy the backup files to the working file names and start again.

Video drivers also play a big part in Windows. If your display problems are occurring in Windows, make sure that you have loaded the proper video driver, and that the driver is compatible with the video board being used. If problems persist in Windows, load the standard generic VGA driver. The generic VGA driver should function properly with virtually every video board and VGA (or SVGA) monitor available. If the problem disappears when using the generic driver setup, the original driver is incorrect, corrupt, or obsolete. Contact the driver manufacturer to obtain a copy of the latest driver version. If the problem persists, the video adapter board might be defective or incompatible with Windows. Try another video adapter.

Symptom 7. When returning to Windows from a DOS application, the Windows screen "splits" from top-to-bottom This is a DOS problem that is seen under Windows that indicates an obsolete or corrupted video driver (for example, using a Windows 3.0 video driver under Windows 3.1). Chances are that the video adapter is running just fine. Make sure that the proper DOS grabber file is installed and specified in the SYSTEM.INI file. Check with the video board manufacturer to obtain the latest assortment of drivers and grabber files. Try re-installing the drivers from their master disk. If you do not have current drivers available, try switching to the generic VGA driver.

Symptom 8. The system hangs up during initialization, some characters might be missing from the display, or the screen colors might be incorrect These are classic symptoms of a hardware conflict between the video adapter and one or more cards in the system, or an area of memory. Some video boards use an area of upper memory that is larger than the classical video area. For example, the Impact SVGA board imposes itself on the entire address range between A0000h and DFFFFh. In this kind of situation, any other device using an address in this range will conflict with the video board. A conflict can occur when the video board is first installed, or the board might work fine until another device is added or modified.

Resolving a hardware conflict basically means that something has to give—one of the conflicting elements (IRQ lines, DMA channels, or I/O addresses) must be adjusted to use unique system resources. As a technician, it rarely matters which of the conflicting devices you change, but remember that system startup files, device drivers, and application settings also might have to change to reflect newly-selected resources. You also might be able to resolve some memory conflicts by adding the EXCLUDE switch to EMM386.EXE. The video adapter manual will indicate when an EXCLUDE switch is necessary.

Symptom 9. Your system is generating DMA errors with a VGA board in the system, and video BIOS shadowing disabled This is a fairly rare symptom that develops only on some older i486 systems, and is usually caused by an 8-bit VGA board in a system equipped with a slower version of the i486 CPU (in the 25-MHz range). The 8-bit access takes so long that some DMA requests are ignored; thus an error is generated. If you find such a problem, try enabling video ROM shadowing through the CMOS setup to allow faster access to video instructions. Also, you might try a newer revision of the i486 CPU.

Symptom 10. The system hangs up using a 16-bit VGA board, and one or more 8-bit controllers This is typically a problem that arises when 8-bit and 16-bit ISA boards are used in the same system. Because of the way that an ISA bus separates the 8-bit and 16-bit segments, accessing an 8-bit board when there are 16-bit boards in the system can cause the CPU to (falsely) determine that it is accessing a 16-bit board. When this occurs, the system will almost invariably crash. Try removing any 8-bit boards from the system. If the crashes cease, you have probably nailed down the error. Unfortunately, the only real correction is to either remove the 8-bit board(s), or reconfigure the board(s) to use a higher area of memory.

Symptom 11. You have trouble sizing or positioning the display, or you see error messages such as "Mode Not Supported" or "Insufficient Memory" These kinds of errors can occur in newer or high-end video boards if the board is not set up properly for the monitor it is being used with. Most new video boards include an installation routine that records the monitor's maximum specifications such as resolution (and refresh frequencies), horizontal scanning frequencies, and vertical scanning frequencies. If such data is entered incorrectly (or the monitor is changed) certain screen modes might no longer work properly. Check the video adapter's installation parameters and correct its setup if necessary.

53
CHAPTER

Video-capture boards

Of all the expansion devices that have become available for PCs over the last decade, the *video-capture board* (Figure 53-1) is probably the most exciting. The ability to record sound and video on a PC has been an important element in the push toward desktop multimedia PCs. The captured data can then be edited, enhanced, and incorporated into any manner of computerized presentation. Such potential makes the video-capture board ideal for applications ranging from real estate to business to medicine. The technology of video capture is improving constantly, and costs are falling quickly. It is only a matter of time before a video-capture board reaches your workbench. This chapter introduces you to basic video recorder concepts, and shows you how to deal with a wide range of problems that accompany the hardware and *Video for Windows* software.

53-1 An Intel Smart Video Recorder board.

Understanding the video-capture board

The first step in dealing with video-capture problems is to understand the processes that make the board work in the first place. Figure 53-2 shows a multifunction video board that doubles as a capture board, a VGA video adapter, and a video output system (to drive things such as a TV monitor or VCR). The capture board plugs right into any available ISA slot. Keep in mind that this is only one type of video-capture product.

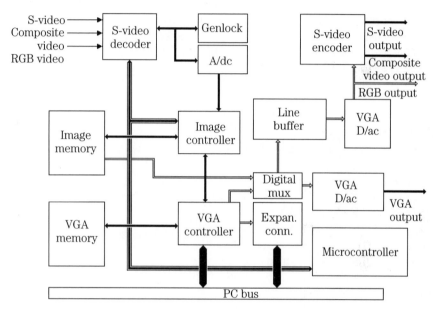

53-2 Block diagram of an integrated video capture/VGA board.

How a capture board works

The heart of the board is a microcontroller that directly operates the video decoder and image controller ICs. Video signals entering the decoder are converted to analog RGB (red, green, and blue) data. The *genlock* circuit is a high-frequency clock source that is phase-locked to the horizontal sync signal of the video source. The ADC (analog-to-digital converter) circuits use the genlock signal as a basis for digitizing the video (not all video capture products offer a genlock feature). The image controller (which can be set to operate in 15-bit, 16-bit, and 24-bit color modes) directs the transfer of digitized image data into image memory. Image memory can then be read from a second data bus directly to a digital multiplexer. The multiplexer selects data from either the image memory or the VGA controller to be passed on to the *VGA DAC* (digital-to-analog converter) where data is converted into analog form to drive the monitor. Thus, you can see the digitized video image on the monitor while it is being recorded.

The capture board also contains a standard VGA subsystem that provides a VGA video adapter for the PC on the same board. The VGA controller IC manages the video adapter operations, and stores graphic information in the VGA memory. The VGA controller can be addressed directly from the expansion bus. When the capture circuit is idle, the VGA controller passes data from the VGA memory on to the data multiplexer where it is converted to analog RGB monitor signals.

The capture board in Fig. 53-2 offers an added bonus—a video drive subsystem. Video data is passed through a line buffer. The line buffer converts data to NTSC data rates, then passes the data on to a stand-alone VGA DAC. The analog RGB signals are sent to an output port, as well as processed through an S-video encoder that provides an independent video source. This is ideal for observing the VGA image on a TV, or recording it to a VCR. Figure 53-3 shows you the typical connector arrangement for such a multifunction capture board. As a technician, you should realize that only a few video-capture boards provide built-in VGA adapter support or an independent video output.

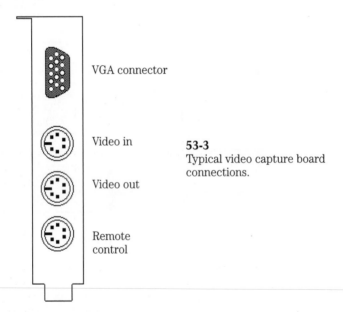

VGA connector

Video in

Video out

Remote control

53-3
Typical video capture board connections.

The capture environment

Now that you have some insight into how a video-capture board works, you can understand how the video capture process works in the PC as a whole. Figure 53-4 shows you a road map of audio and video data through the PC. As with all capture systems, the process begins with a video source. In today's PCs, the source can be any S-video device such as a camcorder, VCR, or laser disk player. Video signals are sent to the capture board while sound is sent to the PC sound board.

The video-capture board digitizes the video signal. Some boards, such as Intel's *SVR* (Smart Video Recorder), will process and compress the video data on-the-fly (also known as hardware-based compression). Data is then stored in system RAM. The digitized sound also is placed in system RAM. Under software tools like Microsoft Video for Windows, sound and video data are synchronized together, then stored on the hard drive in a standard format such as Audio-Video Interleave (or

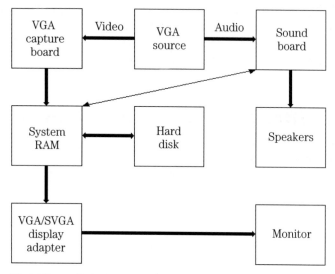

53-4 The audio/video capture and playback map.

AVI). While data is being moved to the hard drive, additional data compression techniques (or software-based compression) can be applied to reduce the overall resulting file size.

During the playback process, files are read from the hard drive, and expanded (if necessary with software decompression techniques) into system RAM. Sound and video data are separated. Video data is sent to the display adapter, and on to the monitor. Sound data is sent to the sound board where it is processed and passed to the speakers. Thus, sound and video can be repeated as required, or used in conjunction with other computer packages.

The role of a CODEC

Video capture produces a tremendous amount of data. Just consider a single 320-×-200 frame that is made up of 64,000 pixels (320 × 200). If you are using a color depth of 65536 colors, each pixel would need 16 bits (two bytes) or 128K per frame. If you are trying to capture 10 complete frames per second, more than 1.28Mb per second will have to be channeled into system RAM. As you might imagine, it would not take more than a few seconds to use up all the available RAM in a PC. However, much of the video data captured in each frame is repetitive; it can be compressed before storing data in RAM or on the hard drive, then decompressed during playback. As a result, the actual data stored in the system can be much less than it would be otherwise.

The *CODEC* (compressor/decompressor) is responsible for reducing this data load. A well-designed CODEC can reduce data without measurably reducing the quality of an image. CODEC functions can be implemented in hardware as a digital signal processor, or in software as a driver. Today, there are four major CODEC techniques: Cinepack, Indeo, Video 1, and RLE. Cinepack is perhaps the best codec, offering very good compression for fast action sequences (where data changes rapidly) with little loss of image quality. However, Cinepack compression is a very slow process, certainly not appropriate for on-the-fly compression. Indeo is much faster than Cinepack, but is not well-suited for quickly-changing data such as that found in fast action sequences. Video 1 and RLE are generally used only for slow animation or palletized video.

Troubleshooting video-capture boards

Like most other expansion boards, video-capture products generally make use of highly-integrated, proprietary ICs. As a result, it can be extremely difficult to troubleshoot the capture board to the component level. Fortunately, there are a large number of capture problems that can be tracked to installation, setup, and operational errors. When the use of diagnostics allow problems to be isolated to the capture board itself, it is a simple matter to replace the capture board outright.

Effects of hardware conflicts in video capture

Hardware conflicts are much more prevalent in today's systems than in systems only a few years ago. Sound boards, CD-ROM interfaces, modems, and video-capture boards all contribute to the congestion that fills up a system and demands its available resources. Most devices require an interrupt (IRQ), one or more I/O address settings, and possibly some small amount of buffer memory. Unfortunately, those resources are scarce in most PCs, and you must be aware of what resources are available and what is being used before adding new devices to your system. When configuring a system from scratch, it is a simple matter to make a written record of each device setting. But with so many new upgrade options, keeping a written list up-to-date can be a difficult effort. As a technician servicing and upgrading customer's systems, you will rarely have the luxury to perform such a thorough analysis. Your most effective course is to use a diagnostic tool such as Microsoft's MSD, or a hardware tool like the Discovery Card by AllMicro to quickly check your system and report on the resources being used.

All CPUs operate linearly; that is, they only tackle one task at a time. When a device such as the keyboard needs the CPU to perform important work that cannot wait for free CPU time, an interrupt signal is generated that forces the CPU to put aside whatever it was doing and respond to the interrupt immediately. When the device requesting the interrupt has been taken care of, the CPU can return to whatever it was doing until the next interrupt comes along. The problem is that only one device can use any one interrupt. If two or more devices try to use the same interrupt at the same time, one of those conflicting devices will not operate properly. In mild cases, this might appear simply as system hesitation. In serious cases, IRQ conflicts can crash your system. When you find that more than one device is using an interrupt, you must place one of those conflicting devices on an unused IRQ. IRQs can usually be changed by altering a jumper or DIP switch on the expansion board. You can recognize the effects of IRQ conflicts between a video capture board and other devices in your system from the following symptoms.

- Video frames are dropped during video capture or playback.
- The video capture or playback process is slow or jumpy.
- The system hesitates or hangs up (crashes) completely.

- The display or data file generated during capture is corrupt.
- Audio is not captured or played back properly (if at all).

An I/O address works a bit differently. Most devices require one or more addresses to exchange data and instructions with the system's data bus. This I/O address works in conjunction with an IRQ, although an IRQ can be changed without changing the I/O address. All devices must use a unique I/O address. Otherwise, one device might try writing data while another device tries to read data, and the operation of both devices will be affected. I/O conflicts also might result in system crashes. Like IRQs, it is important that each device be assigned to its own unique I/O address. If more than one address is needed, there can be no overlap of addresses at all. When more than one device attempts to use the same address(es), you must move one of the devices to an unused area. I/O settings can usually be changed by altering hardware jumpers or DIP switch settings on the expansion board. You can recognize the effects of I/O conflicts between a video capture board and other devices in your system from the following symptoms.

- The video capture board installation program or device driver refuses to recognize or initialize the capture board.
- Microsoft Video for Windows can't initialize the capture device.
- The video-capture board works erratically or fails to respond.

Installation symptoms

Symptom 1. There are problems installing the S-Video cable Most video-capture boards are designed to accept composite audio/video signals from either a single RCA connector or an S-Video connector. Unfortunately, the S-Video connector is not keyed to prevent incorrect insertion. This generally means that signals will not reach the capture board. It is possible to install the S-Video cable rotated 90 degrees from where it should be. Make sure that the arrow on the cable matches the marking on the capture board.

Symptom 2. Even though a valid video source is available, you see vertical multicolored lines appearing in the capture application window This is a problem particular to capture boards when the board is loose or installed improperly, or the signal cabling is not secure. Check the capture board to see that it is fully inserted in the expansion slot. If there are any modules or subboards attached to the capture board, see that they are secure and inserted properly. Also check connectors and cables to be sure that they are all installed correctly.

Symptom 3. Even though a valid video source is available, you see nothing but black in the capture application window There are several possible reasons for this symptom. First, check the video signal being fed to the capture board. If there is no signal, the Video for Windows VIDCAP window will be dark. You can test the video signal by disconnecting the video cable from the capture board and connecting it to a stand-alone monitor such as a TV set. Damaged or defective video cables and connectors should be replaced. If you are using a camcorder as the video source, make sure that the camera is turned on, the lens cover is off, and that you have selected the correct video source (composite or S-Video). Also check that the board is inserted in the system properly and completely. Any modules should be attached securely to the main expansion board.

Finally, there might be an IRQ conflict between your video-capture board and another device in your system. If you attempt to capture a video file while the VID-CAP monitor is dark and receive an error such as "Wave input device not responding", there is almost certainly an IRQ problem. Run a diagnostic such as Microsoft's MSD (or use a hardware tool such as AllMicro's Discovery Card) to identify unused IRQs, then set the video-capture board to use an available IRQ. In some cases, you must run an installation routine for the capture board when changing settings. If problems persist, the capture board might have failed.

Symptom 4. During installation, you see the error message "Unable to locate an available interrupt" This type of symptom occurs with an IRQ conflict, or when a device driver or TSR interferes with the installation. Make sure that the capture board DIP switches are set to an available IRQ (9, 10, 11, or 12). You might have to use a diagnostic (such as Microsoft's MSD or the Discovery Card by AllMicro) to locate available interrupts. Try booting the system from a clean DOS disk to prevent any TSRs or device drivers from interfering with installation.

Unfortunately, if there is a conflict during installation, there also will probably be conflicts during actual use. So, if you suspect a TSR or device driver conflict, you will have to disable TSRs and device drivers one-by-one until the conflict disappears, then work with the offending TSR or device driver configuration to eliminate the conflict.

Symptom 5. When starting the capture utility, you see the error message "Unable to initialize a capture device" This is an error message produced by the Video for Windows VIDCAP utility when the capture board cannot be located. For most capture boards, there is probably an IRQ conflict with one or more devices in the system, which can occur easily when new devices are added to the system after the capture board has been installed. Use a diagnostic (such as Microsoft's MSD or the Discovery Card by AllMicro) to locate unused IRQs. If new equipment has been added, change the new equipment to relieve the conflict. If the error manifested itself when the capture board was installed, change the board's IRQ to an available setting.

If interrupts check out properly, make sure the capture board is inserted properly and completely into the motherboard. If there are any modules or subboards attached to the capture board, see that they are inserted and secured properly. You also might have installed the capture software in the wrong order. Some boards require that DOS software be installed first, then Windows software drivers must be installed. If this process is reversed, the capture board's Windows drivers might not install properly. Try reinstalling the capture software. If software is correct, try another capture board.

Video capture symptoms

Symptom 1. Colors appear washed out or bleeding This can occur while viewing the video image before capture, or during the actual playback of an image file. If the problem is manifesting itself before capture, begin by checking the signal quality from your video source such as a VCR or video camera. A loose or damaged cable, or poor-quality video source can result in signal degradation at the video-capture board.

If the video signal and connections are intact (and the signal looks good on a monitor such as a TV set), the problem might be in the Windows video driver being used. Better color depth in the video driver will result in better color quality in the video capture. If you are using a 256-color video driver, suggest an upgrade to a 32K, 64K, or 16M color driver. You might have to contact the manufacturer of the particular video board to obtain an advanced video driver for Windows 3.1.

Symptom 2. The video signal appears to be weak or washed out even though the video signal source is acceptable This is typical when a composite video signal output is being sent to the video-capture board as well as to a stand-alone monitor through a Y-connector. Composite output signals are usually power balanced for one connection only. When the load on a composite output is not balanced properly, the video signal at your capture board will not contain enough power. Try connecting the video signal directly to the video-capture board.

Symptom 3. Up to 50% of small frames are being dropped (large frames appear to capture properly) This symptom might occur in systems using fast 32-bit SCSI adapter boards, and is almost always due to the effects of double buffering in the SMARTDRV.EXE utility. If possible, try to disable SMARTDRV in CONFIG.SYS. If SMARTDRV cannot be disabled, try capturing video at a larger frame size (320 × 240) *before* capturing at a small frame size. This lets SMARTDRV adjust to the data needs of the larger frame size, so subsequent captures at a smaller frame size should work correctly until the system is rebooted.

Symptom 4. When capturing video, the corresponding screen image appears broken-up or jerky If the image being previewed on the screen prior to capture looks smooth and the captured video looks smooth when played back, you should suspect that the customer's hardware platform is not quite fast enough to update the screen while capturing. This is not necessarily a problem because Video for Windows is designed to sacrifice screen updates for the sake of smooth captures. If you need a smooth display during capture, start by relieving any unnecessary processing loads from the system.

- Close other Windows applications running in the background.
- Close any DOS applications running through Windows.
- Make sure the Windows disk cache is set to at least 2Mb (4Mb if possible)
- Set audio capture specifications to 8-bit, mono, 11-kHz sample frequency for the lowest audio processing overhead.

Your customer might need to optimize their system to the following specifications. If the captured image plays back poorly or has dropped frames, refer to one of the other symptoms in this section.

- System Bus—EISA bus and Local Bus systems that can use 32-bit EISA bus or Local Bus add-in boards.
- Processor—486D × /50 or 486D × 2/66
- Video Card—EISA or VESA Local Bus accelerated video cards that speed up Windows performance
- Video Drivers—640 × 480, 24-bit display drivers
- Hard-Drive Controller—EISA or VESA Local bus SCSI hard drive controllers
- Hard Drive—SCSI hard drives with fast access speeds and data rates
- RAM—16Mb

Symptom 5. The video-capture board is working, but captures are occurring very slowly In most cases, very slow recording performance is caused as the result of an IRQ conflict between the capture board and another device on the system. Evaluate the components in your system or run a diagnostic (such as Microsoft's MSD) to locate and identify any unused interrupts in your system. If you are faced with a jumper-only capture board, set the jumper(s) to use a free valid IRQ. If your capture board requires a software setup, run its setup utility and choose another valid interrupt (9, 10, 11, or 15).

Symptom 6. You find that you cannot use the Super Compressor option in Video for Windows This is not an actual user problem. The Super Compressor is an off-line compression utility that compresses and stores video files captured at 320 × 240, 15 frames per second (fps) at the same data rate as CD-ROM (150K/s). Video for Windows version 1.0 does not support the Super Compressor function when used with Indeo 3.0 device drivers. Only the Quick Compressor in the VIDEDIT utility is available. Later versions of Video for Windows will likely make use of this function.

Symptom 7. The color video being captured is shown as black and white There are two possible causes for this. First, the Video for Windows VIDCAP utility is set to receive a Composite video source, but the video signal is being fed to the capture board through its S-Video cable. Check the configuration settings in VIDCAP's Options. Make sure that the correct input type (Composite or S-Video) is selected in VIDCAP.

Another possible source of problems is a bad connection. Check that the video signal is indeed color, and that a good cable is securely attached to the capture board. Try a different video source. Next, check that the capture board is inserted properly and completely in the expansion slot. If there are any modules or subboards attached to the capture board, see that they are secured correctly. If problems persist, try another capture board.

Symptom 8. The video image shown in the VIDCAP capture window appears torn or bent at the top This symptom is typical of signals being supplied by VCRs (or camcorders used as VCRs), and is almost always the result of a weak video synchronization signal from the signal source. The problem can often be rectified by using a different (stronger) signal source (i.e. another camcorder or VCR). If you are using a VCR signal source, make sure that the Video for Windows VCR box is checked.

Use the S-Video signal source if possible because S-Video signals are less prone to noise and losses than composite signals. Also make sure that the video cable feeding your capture board is not lying parallel to power cables because the power cable can induce unwanted noise into the video signal. Try placing the video-capture board in another expansion slot as far as possible from the system power supply and other expansion boards because electrical signals generated by other boards might cause interference with the video data. As a sanity check, make sure that any modules or subboards for the video capture device are attached properly.

Video playback symptoms

Symptom 1. The video playback is choppy or contains dropped frames This is typically not related to the video-capture board. For most video-capture systems, playback speed and quality is very dependent on machine speed. Faster machines with higher-performance equipment will play back video files better than slower, simpler systems. Make sure that your customer's system is equipped with at least the minimum amount of hardware to ensure a proper playback. If playback performance still seems choppy, your customer might have to upgrade their hardware platform. If a platform upgrade is out of the question, try reducing the system load during capture and playback. For example, close all unused Windows and DOS applications, close any unused data files, and select a larger virtual memory size.

This also is a symptom that appears frequently in EISA systems, even on fast EISA systems up to 50 MHz. In many cases, the afflicted EISA system CMOS was not reconfigured properly after adding memory. An EISA configuration diskette might have to be run in order to cache new memory even though the new memory might be recognized correctly. Try booting the EISA system from its configuration disk and adjust the system from there.

Symptom 2. You see an initial flash of color when playing back video files Chances are that your customer is trying to play video files using the *VIDEDIT* or *VIDCAP* utilities in Video for Windows. This is a known problem with these utilities, and Microsoft is working to resolve the problem. Unfortunately, there is little that you can do other than suggest that they play back video clips using the Windows Media Player or *Media Browser*. Future versions of Video for Windows should correct this problem.

Symptom 3. There is no sound heard during playback Not all video capture products capture sound at the same time video is captured. If no sound was captured (intentionally), no sound will be heard when the video clip is played back through Video for Windows. Some capture boards (such as Intel's Smart Video Recorder) do capture sound and video simultaneously as long as audio is made available on the composite or S-Video signal cables, and the Audio box is checked in the Video Capture options dialog. Also check the Audio Setup and Audio Level settings in Video for Windows before proceeding.

If all is well with Video for Windows, check to make sure that sound was provided to the SVR during capture. If sound was recorded, you should check the configuration of your sound board. The sound board should contain appropriate hardware settings (such as I/O, IRQ, and DMA). The proper Windows device driver for the sound board also must be installed, and the driver must be loaded with other Windows drivers. A missing Windows sound driver will inhibit sound. If the system is configured properly and sound is available, but no sound is recorded, the capture board might be defective—try another capture board. If sound is being captured by the sound card, the sound card might be defective.

Symptom 4. There are sound gaps, and the image appears choppy during playback This is a symptom that is particular to capture boards (such as the Smart Video Recorder) that integrates audio and video into a single AVI capture file. The integrated file prevents audio and video from slipping out of sync. However, playing capture files requires substantial processing power. If a system is not fast enough, sound can hiccup and the video can be choppy. Unfortunately, this kind of playback problem is not a fault or defect; it is a limitation of slower PC systems.

First, remove any Windows or DOS applications running in the background so that Windows can concentrate on Video for Windows. If playback does not improve enough, try running the playback in a smaller window. For example, try playing back in a 160-x-120 window instead of a 320-x-240 window. Smaller windows require less processing overhead for each frame. Beyond that, the hardware platform might need to be upgraded.

Symptom 5. The video looks grainy (or otherwise poor quality) when playing back or recording This is a symptom that can occur across all video capture devices. Image quality is closely related to the color depth of your Windows video driver. Many Windows installations use the default 16-color VGA video driver supplied with the Windows operating system. Sixteen colors are almost never adequate to define a video image, so the image will look washed out or grainy. You must install a 256-color (or higher) video driver written for the video board in your system. Contact the video board manufacturer for their latest Windows 3.1 drivers. Most manufacturers will send a driver for free, or place the driver on a BBS or on-line service for free download.

54
CHAPTER

Virus symptoms and countermeasures

Although most of the software products in the marketplace today are useful, constructive, and beneficial, there also is other software that serves a darker purpose—the computer "virus." Such rogue software is designed to load and run without the user's knowledge, often hiding in normal programs. Viruses also execute their functions without prompting users for permission, they do not warn of potential dangers to the system, and they do not produce error messages when problems are encountered. Essentially, a computer virus is a fragment of executable code that runs secretly, and is capable of cloning itself in other programs.

Technically, there is nothing in this definition to indicate that a virus is necessarily destructive—that's a twist added by the virus programmers themselves. But legitimate software does not need to run secretly, hide itself in other programs, or duplicate itself without a user's knowledge or permission. So the very nature of a computer virus makes it an ideal vehicle for spreading computer chaos. This chapter is intended to explain the nature and operations of computer viruses, show you how they spread and manifest themselves, and explain some procedures you can take to protect yourself and your customer from their effects.

Understanding virulent software

The term *virus* is used to describe virtually any type of destructive software. Although this is a good, general term, it also is a misnomer. A *virus* is actually only one of many destructive software types. There are at least nine types of recognized rogue software, and most are considered every bit as deadly as a virus. Each type of software has a different mode of operation. As a technician, you should understand how these software types operate.

Software bugs

Simply speaking, a *software bug* is an error in program coding or logic that results in faulty or unexpected operation. Bugs are rarely intentional, but the vast majority of serious system-crippling bugs are caught during the developer's alpha and beta testing processes. In order for serious bugs to get through into a finished product (the kinds of bugs that can cause serious memory errors or damage hard drive files), the developer would have to do little (if any) testing on various PC platforms. Serious bugs are typically not intended as malicious, but they suggest a dangerous lack of concern on the part of the software developer. There are two clues that suggest the presence of software bugs: first, it is only a single program (usually the one you just installed or started using) that causes the problem, and the problem will not be detected by any antivirus tool (the application will be reported as clean). Software containing serious bugs is often referred to as "bug ware."

Trojan horses

The *Trojan horse* is largely considered to be the grandparent of today's virulent software. Basically, the Trojan horse is a destructive computer program concealed in the guise of a useful, run-of-the-mill program such as a word processor or graphics program. Well-developed user shells or seemingly normal operations trick the user into believing that the program is harmless—until the virulent code is triggered—then the program's true nature is revealed. The Trojan horse tactic is the most popular means of introducing viruses by distributing seemingly harmless software that actually contains virulent code. Fortunately, most virulent code can be detected by scanning new software before it is executed for the first time. To prevent the spread of Trojan horses, be suspicious of unwanted or unsolicited software arriving through the mail. Also beware of software that sounds too good to be true (a TSR that will increase Windows performance by 100X, get SVGA graphics on an EGA video adapter, etc.)

Software chameleons

Just as a chameleon hides itself by mimicking its background, *software chameleons* mask virulent code with an image of a legitimate application. Of course, the mask is just a facade, like a demonstration program or a simulation. What makes a chameleon different is that it almost never causes system damage. Instead, it generally makes a modification to a program. In one classic case, a chameleon was introduced to a large multiuser platform. When the user typed in their name and password, it was recorded to a secret file. The chameleon's author later accessed the system, entered their own code, and downloaded the accumulated list. Thus, the author now had access to various user data for their own illegal purposes. In another case, a chameleon was planted into a banking program that diverted a few tenths of a cent (round-offs) off of every transaction into a secret account. Ultimately, the chameleon's author had hundreds of thousands of dollars in the secret account.

Software bombs

The *software bomb* is just what the name implies. When the infected program is launched, the virulent "bomb" code executes almost immediately and does its damage. As a consequence, software bombs typically contain no bells or whistles; they also make little effort to cloak themselves, and almost no effort to replicate. As a consequence, the software bomb is easy to develop. Its somewhat clumsy nature also make them fairly easy to spot with antivirus tools.

Logic bombs

Where the software bomb is used for immediate and indiscriminate destruction, a *logic bomb* is set to go off when a particular logical condition is met. For example, the logic bomb might detonate (erase files, calculate subsequent payroll records incorrectly, reformat the disk, or so on) if payroll records indicate that the bomb's author is fired or laid off, or their payroll statements do not appear for over four weeks. A logic bomb can be triggered by virtually any system condition. However, the bomb approach is fairly easy to spot with antivirus techniques.

Time bombs

Instead of triggering a bomb immediately or through system status conditions, a *time bomb* uses time or repetition conditionals. For example, a time bomb can be set to detonate after some number of program runs, on a particular day (April 1st or Friday 13th), or at a certain time (for example, midnight). This kind of bomb architecture is relatively easy to spot with antivirus tools.

Replicators

The purpose of a *replicator* (also called a *rabbit*) is to drain system resources. It accomplishes this function by cloning copies of itself. Each clone copy is launched by the parent that created it. Before long, the multitude of copies on disk and in memory soak up so many resources that the system can no longer function. In effect, the system is crippled until the copies are removed and the replicating virus is eliminated. This type of behavior is particularly effective at shutting down large, multiuser systems or networks. Because the virulent code is self-replicating, it is easy to spot with antivirus tools.

Worms

Unlike most other types of virulent code, the *worm* travels through a network computer system. The worm travels from computer to computer, usually without doing any real damage. Worms rarely replicate except in cases where it is absolutely necessary to continue traveling through the system, and delete all traces of their presence. A worm is another typical network presence used to seek out and selectively alter or destroy a limited number of files or programs. For example, a worm can be used to enter a network and alter or erase passwords. Because worms can be tailored for specific jobs, they are often difficult to spot unless the worm is known.

Viruses

The most recognized and dynamic of the rogue software is the virus. A virus modifies other programs to include executable virulent code—in some cases, the virulent code mutates and changes as it is copied. Expertly engineered viruses do not change the infected file date, time stamps, file size, its attributes, or its checksums. As a result, viruses can be extremely difficult to detect and even harder to erase, and the task becomes even more difficult as viruses become increasingly powerful and sophisticated. Given their predilection toward stealth and replication, viruses tend to linger in systems to spread themselves between hard drives and floppy disks, disrupt data, cause system errors, and generally degrade system performance. Eventually, most viruses will self-destruct, taking the hard drive files with it.

Types of viruses

As you might have suspected, all virulent code is not created equal. Viruses are as varied as legitimate application software—each technique provides the virus author with an array of advantages and disadvantages. Some viral techniques are preferred because they are more difficult to detect and remove, but require extra resources to develop. Other viral techniques are easier to develop, but lack the stealth and sophistication that more powerful viruses demand. Still other viral techniques stand a better chance of infecting multiple systems. This part of the chapter explains the major infection modes used by modern viruses.

Command-processor infection

DOS relies on a series of hidden files (IO.SYS and MSDOS.SYS). The files are hidden, they cannot be directly executed, and they are not easily deleted, renamed, or copied. Thus, it is necessary to have a command processor that allows the user to interact with the operating system. For DOS, the command processor is COMMAND.COM. When you see the command line prompt (i.e., A:\> or C:\>), you know that COMMAND.COM is loaded and active. When you enter a command line, the processor *parses* (interprets) the command and attempts to determine a proper response.

By placing a virus in the command processor (infecting the COMMAND.COM), the virus has access to a large number of DOS facilities, especially user interface and disk access. Consider the DIR command used to produce a disk directory. An infected COMMAND.COM can allow its virus to search for and infect other files before running the actual directory function (thus the virus is concealed). The function might take a bit longer to execute, but most users barely notice. If you insert a floppy disk in drive A: and take a directory, you risk infecting files on the floppy disk. By making a bootable floppy disk, that disk will likely contain an infected COMMAND.COM file as well. Because viruses are active once a program is started, and COMMAND.COM is started every time DOS is loaded, command processor infections are serious and spread viruses very quickly.

Boot-sector infection

Every PC ever made requires a bootable disk that has access to DOS. When the PC boots (starts up), the computer automatically attempts to load the operating system files from the boot disk. Startup files are typically kept in the disk *boot sector* (sometimes referred to as the *master boot record*). If a virus is able to infiltrate the boot sector and interfere with the loading process, it can very effectively cripple the entire computer. Viruses that infect the boot sector but do not shut the boot disk down are often capable of remaining resident in memory, even during a warm boot. When bootable floppy disks are used during the warm boot, boot sector viruses can easily infect the bootable floppy.

Because boot sector viruses are loaded along with the DOS kernel and command processor, they are typically active before a user ever has a chance to launch an antivirus application. With access to all of DOS's resources, the boot sector virus can alter directory listings to show an expected file date, size, and attributes when in fact such files have been infected—a tactic that can render some antivirus packages useless.

Executable-file infection

Unlike command processor or boot sector infections that target a limited number of low-level operating system files, many viral strains today simply focus on the infection of any executable file (.EXE or .COM files). Because COMMAND.COM is executable, it also can be infected by these general-purpose viruses, but not as deeply or cleverly as viruses specially designed for that purpose. Often, general file infections are loaded into memory once an infected application is started. Afterward, the virus can easily spread to other executable files anytime other executable files are listed (open file, save file, and so on). This type of infection tends to proliferate very quickly within the infected PC. Because disks are often shared between various computers, general infections also stand a good chance of infecting multiple machines, creating an epidemic. The problem with such proliferation is that you must locate and disinfect every copy of the virus (on common floppies as well) to remove it. If you miss a copy and run that infected application later, the whole cycle can start all over again.

Multipurpose infections are a more potent form of general-purpose virus that combines two or more virus techniques. For example, a multipurpose virus can infiltrate a system's boot sector, then move on to the command processor, then spawn parasitic viruses that infect ordinary executable files. Because the virus finds its way into so many areas of the PC, it is very difficult to remove completely. If the virus changes or morphs as it works, it might be virtually impossible to spot with antivirus tools. As a consequence, multipurpose infections are particularly pernicious.

File-specific infection

The file-specific infection is generally a type of worm specifically designed to seek out and corrupt specific files or types of files. Often, the file-specific infection is created and introduced by someone with a score to settle, perhaps an ex-employee or competitor. Because an outright search for the desired file(s) would take some time (and almost certainly be noticed), the file-specific infection latches onto a variety of files throughout the system, spreading its search capability without attracting attention. When the desired files are located, the virus either erases them outright, or corrupts them over time resulting in application or data corruption. Another advantage of infecting multiple files is that the damaged file(s) will invariably be reloaded, so the virus is able to hang around in the system to continue harassing the target file(s).

Memory-resident infection

Where many viruses are loaded and active only while the infected file is running, the memory-resident infection remains active in memory throughout the entire computing session. The advantage to memory-resident viruses is that, like ordinary TSRs, the virus can continue infecting other files and corrupting data throughout the system regardless of which application is running.

Protecting the PC

Even with the most comprehensive, accurate, aggressive, up-to-the-minute antivirus package available, antivirus tools alone will not always protect a PC from the ravages of a virus or other rogue software. Trying a suspicious piece of software without testing it first, forgetting to virus scan the system regularly, and even intentional sabotage can render an antivirus tool useless. Before trouble strikes, you can take some pro-active steps to prevent the spread of viruses, and ease your recovery should a virus actually strike.

- *Check for viruses regularly* You would be surprised how many people buy antivirus products only to use them sporadically or leave them sitting unused until it is too late. Remember that antivirus tools are always behind viruses. You need to use your antivirus tools consistently and aggressively in order to catch viruses before they do their damage. If you are regularly trying new shareware or commercial products, you should be sure to check for viruses religiously. Also check for viruses if you routinely swap disks between home and work PCs or a variety of different computers.
- *Back up your data* This rule might sound like a cliché, but frequent, complete backups are one of the most foolproof and reliable means of protecting your vital data. No virus can destroy the backup. Even though the backup might contain a virus, it is better to restore an infected backup (then clean it immediately) than forego the backup entirely. The problem with backups is frequency—how often should it be done? That really depends on how often you use your system. Businesses with active, rapidly changing databases should backup their data at least daily. Casual home users who use only a few utilities infrequently would probably receive little benefit from frequent backups. Most small offices and home offices would be well-served to backup every month or so. If new applications or data files are changed dramatically in the mean time, the backup can be updated as needed. The yardstick is simple enough. Ask the question: If my hard drive were erased now, would I be able to restore it and move on? When the answer to that question is no, it's time to back up the system. If the contents of your system changes frequently, it might make sense to keep several generations of backup. That way, if Thursday's backup doesn't have the files you need, maybe Monday's will.

- *Keep your original disks write-protected* Although write protection is not foolproof, it can prevent an infected system from spreading its infection to the diskettes and thereby proliferating to other systems. This can be doubly important for original program distribution disks.
- *Keep an eye out for mysterious or hidden files* Although most modern drive utilities have no trouble revealing hidden files, some virulent code might indeed be saved with hidden file attributes. Also check batch files before running them to be sure that there are no destructive commands (such as FORMAT C:).
- *Beware of famous dates* Time bombs often trigger on holidays such as Christmas, New Years, July 4th, or other famous holidays or dates. The day before a special day, set the system clock to the day after. For example, on July 3rd, set the system calendar to July 5th. After the holiday has passed, you can easily reset the clock to the correct date.
- *Keep a bootable diskette on hand* Before trouble strikes, invest about five minutes and make yourself a clean bootable floppy disk. The disk also should have a copy of FORMAT, FDISK, DEBUG, PKUNZIP (or your favorite decompression utility), and any other DOS utilities that you need during startup. Be sure to write-protect the floppy disk and keep it in a safe place.

Recognizing an infection

As any doctor will tell you, the first step toward recovery is diagnosis—recognizing the subtle (and not so subtle) signs of viral activity can give you an edge in stopping the activities of a virus, and save you a substantial amount of time in needless hardware troubleshooting. The following part of this chapter illustrates some of the more important signs of virus activity.

- *You see a warning generated by a virus scanner* Your antivirus package has detected a virus either in memory, or in one or more executable files. Once the antivirus package has completed its infection report, go ahead and attempt to disinfect as many files as possible. Many of today's viruses cannot be removed without damaging the executable file, so be prepared to restore the infected files from a backup. After the system is cleaned (and damaged files restored), go ahead and check for viruses again. Repeat this procedure until the entire system is clear.
- *You see some sort of bizarre message ("legalize marijuana" or "your computer is stoned")* Unfortunately, when a virus reveals itself in this way, it has probably already done its damage to your system. Launch your antivirus software as soon as possible and remove any occurrences of the virus. Be prepared to restore damaged executable files and corrupted data files.
- *You notice that your machine is acting strangely for no apparent reason* This problem might happen on holidays and other important days of the year. Applications might freeze, crash, or produce unusual DOS error messages without warning. You might notice excessive or random disk

access where there was none before. The system might behave unusually slowly; files and programs might take a long time to load. Familiar applications might not respond to the keyboard or mouse properly. Leave the application as soon as possible and run your antivirus tools.

- *The computer starts to boot, but freezes before displaying a DOS prompt* Chances are that you've got a command processor infection. Boot the system from a clean, write-protected floppy disk, then try switching to the infected hard drive. If you cannot access the hard drive, it might be defective, or the virus might have affected the drive's partition table. Run an antivirus package to check the system and eliminate any virulent code. When the system is clean, try a drive maintenance package such as DrivePro from MicroHouse to check and rebuild any corrupted boot sector/partition table data.

- *Programs and data files become erased or corrupted without warning* This problem is a classic sign of a virus at work. It is highly unlikely that the random loss of a single file is caused by a hardware defect. DOS drive access works in terms of clusters, and most files require several clusters. If a cluster, or a sector within that cluster, were to fail, the file would still appear in the directory. Run your antivirus package and check for viruses in memory as well as on disk.

- *You see a DOS error message indicating a problem with the file allocation table or the partition table* Although this might indeed be the result of a hard drive fault, you should make it a point to boot the system from a write-protected floppy disk and check for viruses. If the system checks clear, go ahead and try a package like Drive Pro by MicroHouse to check and reconstruct the damaged boot areas.

- *Programs access more than one disk drive where they did not before* It is exceptionally rare for a program to try accessing more than one drive unless it is explicitly instructed to do so by you. For example, if you save your new word processing document to drive C:, there will be no reason for the program to access drive A:. This kind of behavior suggests that a virus is attempting to slip its operations into normal disk access activities. Leave your application and run a virus checker.

- *The number of bad disk sectors increases steadily* It is not uncommon for viruses to create bad disk sectors and hide within them to escape detection. Because DOS is designed to step over bad sectors, some antivirus programs will not detect viruses using that tactic, leaving you to back up as much of the drive as possible and perform a new low-level format of the drive. Before resorting to that tactic, however, try an antivirus package.

- *The amount of available system RAM suddenly or steadily decreases* DOS provides the MEM function that allows you to peek at conventional, upper, extended, and expanded memory. If you find that certain programs no longer have enough memory to run, consider the possibility of a memory-resident virus or replicator of some sort. Try your antivirus package. If you have a memory-resident antivirus product available, try loading that on the system for a while.

- *Memory maps (such as the DOS MEM function) reveal strange TSRs not loaded by CONFIG.SYS or AUTOEXEC.BAT* You can use the MEM function to reveal any drivers or TSRs loaded in the system. If you see a strange or unexpected TSR, you might be faced with a memory-resident virus. Run your antivirus package. If you have a memory-resident antivirus product available, try loading that on the system for a while.
- *File names, extensions, attributes, or date codes are changed unexpectedly* This sign is another sign of viral activity that is usually attributable to older virulent code that lacked the sophistication to hide its own actions. A reliable antivirus program should be able to deal with any viruses effectively.
- *Unknown files mysteriously appear* This is a tough call for technicians new to a system, but as a computer user, you are generally pretty aware when a new data file is created on your own system (i.e. a new word processor document or a new spreadsheet). However, when unknown executable files are created, a virus might be at work. Newly created files might be hidden, so use a directory tool that displays hidden files (such as PC Tools). Try your antivirus software to locate and eliminate potential viruses.

Dealing with an infection

Even with the best antivirus tools, regular testing, and consistent backups, systems can still be susceptible to the ravages of computer viruses. When dealing with viruses, you must understand what can and cannot be infected. Programs can be infected—that's all. Programs are any file that has an extension of: .EXE, .COM, .BAT, .SYS, .BIN, .DRV, .OVL, and of course the two hidden system files that make up the DOS kernel. Data files certainly can be corrupted, damaged, or completely destroyed, but they cannot be infected. For example, if you recover a Lotus spreadsheet (a .WK1 file), it cannot contain a virus. It is not impossible to infect programs inside an archive (such as .ZIP, .ARC, .ARJ, .LZH, or .ZOO), but it is extremely unlikely because a virus does not want you to know it's there, but the programs might have been contaminated before being placed in the archive. When you suspect the presence of a virus in the system, the following procedures can help you optimize the damage control.

1. Boot from a clean, write-protected floppy disk. One of the most fundamental rules of virus defense is that a virus is harmless until it is launched by the boot sector, command processor, or application. If you can prevent the virus from loading in the first place, you stand a good chance of running an antivirus tool successfully. Make sure that the boot disk is prepared on a virus-free PC. The disk also should contain a copy of your antivirus package (most are designed to run from a floppy disk). Do not attempt to launch applications from the questionable hard drive until it has been checked and cleaned.
2. Use your antivirus tools. If the system booted properly from your write-protected floppy disk, the virus(es) in your system should now be

neutralized. Start the antivirus tool contained on your floppy disk and run a comprehensive test of all system files. Also make it a point to check the boot sector and command processor. If your current tool does not support boot sector or command processor testing, you should consider using a second tool that does. When viruses are detected (chances are that more than one file will be infected), attempt to remove as many instances as possible. With luck, you can remove viruses without damaging the infected file, but this is often not possible with today's viruses. When a file cannot be cleaned, it should be erased. Be sure to log each erased file and directory path so that you can replace only those files rather than restore entire sub-directories.

3. Start a quarantine for your computer. Because many viruses propagate by infecting floppy disks, any disks that have been in your computer should be assumed to have the virus on them. By assuming the worst case situation, you are possibly saving many others from getting and spreading the virus even further. Gather up as many disks as you can find and check each for viruses. Also, do not share disks between other systems until your system has run for a while and proven itself to be virus free.

4. Restore the backups. It is very likely that you had to destroy one or more executable files. Systematically reload any files that were erased during the cleaning process. In most cases, you can restore the damaged files from their original, write-protected installation disks. A tape backup is another popular backup source. Try to avoid re-installing the entire application unless there is no other alternative.

5. Recheck the backup. After the deleted files have been destroyed, it is vitally important to restart your antivirus tool and check the suspect disk again. It is not uncommon for recent backups to be contaminated as well. Verify that the drive is still virus free. If you locate new viruses introduced in the restored files, remove the viruses again and restore the files from original, write-protected floppy disks.

6. Minimize the collateral damage. Immediately notify anybody to whom you have given any software, bootable disks, or even read their disks on your computer. If you have uploaded any programs to a BBS, notify the SysOp of that system immediately.

Understanding antivirus tools

As the awareness of computer viruses grew through the last decade, so did the proliferation of antivirus tools designed to combat the threat. However, you should understand that every antivirus tool is created as a response to viruses that have already penetrated the PC environment. As a result, antivirus products are forever playing catch-up with ever-more sophisticated virus programmers. No antivirus product is 100% effective in all forms of detection. The one rule to remember with all antivirus tools is that they become outdated very quickly. As a technician, you must make it a point to keep your antivirus tools current. In the perpetual virus arms race, you should seriously consider updating any product over six months old. This part of the chapter examines the major antivirus tactics, and explains the limitations of each approach.

Vaccines

Vaccines are the earliest form of virus protection that appended small programs and checksums to various executable files. When the modified program is run, the antivirus vaccine calculates the program's checksum and compares it to the appended checksum. If the two checksums match, control is returned to the executable file and it runs normally. When the comparison fails because of file damage or the presence of a virus, a warning is generated and corrective action can be taken. There are a number of serious drawbacks to the vaccine technique that you should be familiar with.

The vaccine (or *antigen* as it was called) is little more than a virus itself. Although it does not reproduce without permission or harm files, many users felt uncomfortable inoculating their files intentionally.

When there are a large number of executable files, the increased disk space needed for each appended vaccine can become significant.

Device drivers, overlay files, packed .EXE files, and executable data files cannot be vaccinated.

False alarms are typical, especially for self-modifying programs like Borland's SideKick that force users to remove vaccine protection.

In some cases, the modifications to an executable file in order to vaccinate it can cause unpredictable program operation. Some programs simply do not work with vaccine-based viral defense.

The virus-type behavior of vaccines often cause false alarms with other nonvaccine antivirus programs.

Because vaccine techniques are the same for every file, it is a simple matter for a virus to bypass the vaccine's loading checksum test, so vaccines provided limited viral protection.

File comparisons

File comparison is a plain and simple technique that utilized byte-by-byte comparisons between known-good files and potentially infected files. Any variation between the two signaled the possibility of a virus. File comparison techniques were initially embraced because they were easy to develop and quick to document, so they were an inexpensive option for antivirus developers. However, file comparison presents some serious disadvantages in the marketplace.

The most critical problem is the need for known-good files to be added to the disk (in addition to the normal operating files). Even for large drives, this is a hideous waste of valuable disk space.

File comparison antivirus tools often lack the typical resources that are considered to be standard equipment for virus management (i.e. activity logs, data encryption, comprehensive warnings indicating which virus is at work, system lockouts, and wild card file searches).

It is a simple matter for viruses to search a disk looking for multiple copies of a file, and infect both copies, rendering the file comparison technique useless.

Antidotes

Software antidotes (sometimes called disinfectors or eradicators) are a close cousin to vaccines, where the antidote surgically removes the virus. But antidotes are designed specifically to deal with a limited set of viral strains within a small group of program types. Often, an antidote is designed to check and remove a particular virus. For example, the media scare surrounding the Michaelangelo virus some years back resulted in a number of related antidote products developed specifically to check for and eradicate the virus. Such limited operation presents several serious limitations.

The limited nature of antidotes makes them unsuited for general, system-wide use. Viruses not specifically addressed by the antidote remain totally untouched.

Because viruses are constantly changing, antidotes must continuously be updated and expanded, otherwise the antidotes quickly become useless. The constant expense of regular updates is often too much for the average computer user.

Antidotes often destroy program files while trying to remove virulent code, and are reputed to suffer frequent false alarms that cause the antidote to alter good files in an attempt to remove a virus that is not there. Effectively, this destroys good files as well.

Each executable file has its own particular characteristics and internal structure. As a result, it is virtually impossible for any one infection antidote to remove a virus from every possible file type.

Generally, it is safer and more reliable to recover an infected file by overwriting it with an uninfected copy rather than trust an antidote to surgically remove the virus.

Signature scanners

Currently, the virus scanner is the most widely accepted type of antivirus tool. Scanning basically checks each executable file against a fixed set of virus *signatures*, telltale fragments of code that indicate the presence of particular viruses. When the virulent code is identified, it can be removed fairly accurately, but many executable files are still destroyed. The technique is fast and flexible, viruses can be identified very accurately, and there are few instances of false alarms or incompatibilities that older techniques suffer from. However, there are still limitations to virus scanning.

Scanners rely on a fixed set of signatures; if a signature is not in the database, it is not checked. Signature databases are easy to update, but the updates can often be costly. Because viruses are constantly changing, signature databases become outdated quickly.

Virus scanners cannot detect signatures that change or mutate as the infection propagates through the system. As a result, scanners are largely ineffective against stealth or polymorphic viruses.

Memory-resident utilities

One breed of antivirus tool can be loaded into memory where it will remain resident (TSR) and provide last-minute protection against viral infiltration of disk commands and viral activity. Unfortunately, this class of antivirus tool suffers from a set of very serious problems.

As a TSR, the program must remain in memory. This consumes valuable memory (often significant amounts of memory) that are needed by other applications. It is not uncommon to eventually disable TSRs to free extra memory for large applications.

False alarms are commonplace with antivirus TSRs that mistake disk caching or normal system activity with virus activity. Even communication functions such as e-mail downloads are often interrupted as virus attacks.

Many systems respond poorly to TSRs. When you consider that TSR technology is intended to coerce DOS to perform multitasking—a feature it was not intended to do—it is no wonder that TSR development is not standardized. As a consequence, TSRs are often quite troublesome. When used with combinations of other device drivers and TSRs, antiviral TSRs can present a serious problem.

Viruses can circumvent antivirus TSRs by accessing PC hardware directly (such as direct access of disk controllers).

Disk mappers

The disk mapping technique is similar to the file comparison process. A mapper maintains a single data file that contains a coded snapshot of the protected disk. Each time a mapper is run, it notifies you about any variations between the protected disk files and the key map. Ideally, these variations will alert you to the possibility of a virus. Many later disk-mapping schemes allow users to specify exactly which files (or file types) must be monitored. However, this is not enough to overcome some inherent problems.

Creating a key map of the disk can require a substantial amount of space. The space demand increases along with the number of files that must be mapped.

For most professional users, the state of a PC is changing constantly as files are created, modified, and deleted. This demands regular maintenance of the key map. Such maintenance is often cumbersome and time consuming because disk mappers are typically complex systems to use.

Disk mappers are typically tied into the boot process to ensure regular key map checks and updates. This results in longer (sometimes much longer) boot times.

Disk mappers are not immune to infiltration and damage by viruses. Some viruses seek out and destroy key map files.

Troubleshooting antivirus tools

Symptom 1. You cannot run more than one antivirus product at a time
This is not an uncommon problem, and occurs most frequently when memory-resident virus protectors conflict with file-based antivirus tools. When you run more than one antivirus program, there is always the risk of strange results and false alarms. For example, some antivirus programs store their virus signature strings unprotected in memory. Running incompatible or conflicting antivirus tools might detect other signature strings or memory-resident activity as a virus. Run only one antivirus program at a time.

Symptom 2. Your antivirus tool does not function, or causes other drivers to malfunction Some terminate-and-stay-resident (TSR) software might conflict with some antivirus programs, especially memory-resident antivirus programs. When problems occur, try booting the system from a clean bootable disk so that there are no other drivers or TSRs in the system aside from the antivirus tool.

Symptom 3. You notice that your antivirus tool is slowing disk access dramatically, or it locks up under Windows Normally, many antivirus tools (especially memory-resident tools) will slow disk access a bit. When there is a tremendous reduction in disk performance, or the tool freezes during operation, it might be that the disk cache being used conflicts with the antivirus product. Try increasing the number of buffers in the CONFIG.SYS file. If problems continue, try disabling the disk caching software while running the antivirus product.

Symptom 4. The antivirus tool is reporting false alarms It is not uncommon for antivirus products to report false alarms. This happens most often due to conflicts with other memory-resident software running in the system. Try running the software from a clean boot disk. The nature of antiviral detection techniques also plays a role in reporting false errors. For example, file comparison is a typical technique, but files can be changed for many reasons other than a virus, so false alarms are a strong possibility. Other techniques also have flaws that might result in false alarms.

Symptom 5. You are unable to remove the memory-resident antivirus tool There is probably another TSR running in the system that is conflicting with the antivirus tool. You might have to reboot the system in order to clear the antivirus tool. In the future, try loading the antivirus tool last—after all other drivers and TSRs are loaded.

<h1>55</h1>

VL bus operations

The demands of data transfer across the expansion bus have continued to evolve faster than the throughput of classic ISA/EISA bus architectures allow. The volumes of data required by graphic user interfaces (such as Microsoft's Windows) present serious challenges to conventional video adapter and memory design. Early in 1992, the *VESA* (Video Electronics Standards Association) proposed a new local bus standard (called the *Video Local* [VL] bus) intended to improve the performance of graphics and video sub-systems. In general terms, a 'local bus' is a pathway that allows peripherals to access the system's main memory quickly. For the VL bus, such improved access means higher data throughput and performance for video information at the speed of the CPU itself. By using a stand-alone bus for video, ISA or EISA buses can be implemented for backward system compatibility—that is, users can upgrade to a new motherboard and graphics card, but all other peripherals and software remain compatible.

VL bus configuration and signals

Of course, the path to a standard local bus was not an easy one. In 1991 and 1992, a few chip set suppliers and manufacturers implemented nonstandard high-performance I/O buses. For example, some OPTi chip sets were designed to support an OPTi local bus. Unfortunately, the OPTi local bus was supported by only a small handful of manufacturers, and because the OPTi approach was specific to their chip sets, few (if any) I/O cards were ever actually developed for these buses and few manufacturers provided them. Thus, OPTi and other proprietary buses met the same fate as all other nonstandardized approaches in the PC industry—they disappeared. However, the failure of proprietary local bus designs did not prevent industry acceptance of a standard VL bus design developed by VESA in late 1992. By placing the VL extension connectors in-line with standard ISA connectors, the VL board also can serve as an ISA board only with far higher data throughput.

The essential advantage of a VL bus is direct access to the CPU's main buses. This allows a VL device to rapidly transfer the large quantities of data that are vital for high-performance video under Windows. Further, there is no limit on the clock speed of a VL bus; with such close interaction between the bus and CPU, the bus speed is linked to that of the CPU. As a result, faster CPU speed will result in faster bus speed. Unfortunately, this is where the advantages end.

Although virtually direct connection to the CPU might seem like a real asset, there also are some serious drawbacks that you should understand. Processor dependence can ultimately become a disadvantage for the VL bus. Because higher processor speed results in higher bus capacitance, VL signals can lose reliability at high CPU clock frequencies. Further, the processor signals were intended to attach to only a few chips (like the RAM controller) and have very precise timing rules. In fact, each type of Intel i486 chip (i486SX, i486DX, and i486DX/2) has slightly different timing requirements. When additional capacitance loads are added by adding multiple connectors and multiple local-bus chips, all sorts of undesirable things can happen. The two most likely problems are: (1) data glitches caused by slowed processor bus signals, and (2) out-of-spec timing for different I/O cards with different loading characteristics.

Although the VL specification does not list an upper frequency limit, the potential load problems discussed dictate a practical limit. With a clock speed of 33 MHz, a VL motherboard should be able to support two VL devices reliably. At 40 MHz, only one VL device should be used. Above 40 MHz, the chances of unreliable operation with even one VL device become substantial. If you find yourself working on a fast VL system with random system errors, see if the problem goes away when the VL device(s) are removed (and replaced with ISA equivalents if necessary).

Another problem is the lack of *concurrency*. For a PCI bus, the CPU can continue operating when a PCI device takes control of the system buses. VL architecture also allows for bus mastering operation, but when a VL device takes control of the bus, the CPU must be stopped. Although this is technically not a defect, it clearly limits the performance of high-end devices (SCSI controllers) that might attempt to use a VL architecture. Finally, there are several other disadvantages to the VL bus. It is a +5-Vdc architecture (where PCI can support +3.3 Vdc). Unlike PCI, there is no *auto-configuration* capability in the VL bus (jumpers and DIP switches are required).

VL bus layout

The VL bus uses a 116-pin card edge connector with small contacts (similar in appearance to MicroChannel contacts) as shown in Fig. 55-1. The current VL bus release (2.0) offers a 32-bit data path with a maximum data throughput of about 130MB/s, and the full 64-bit implementation provides a 64-bit data path (Data 0 to Data 63) with a maximum rated data throughput of about 260MB/s. The pinout for a VL bus is shown in Table 55-1. One of the most interesting things to note about the VL bus is that it is an extension to the standard ISA/EISA bus. The two right connectors are 16-bit ISA bus connectors. It is the two left connectors that provide the VL compatibility. The long VL connector portion provides the 32-bit VL support, and the left-most connector handles 64-bit support.

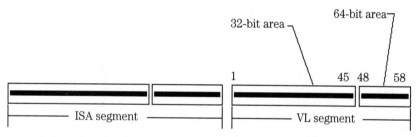

55-1 A simplified drawing of the VL bus.

Table 55-1. VL-bus pinout (Rev. 2.0)

64 bit	32 bit	Pin	Pin	32 bit	64 bit
———	Data 00	A01	B01	Data 01	———
———	Data 02	A02	B02	Data 03	———
———	Data 04	A03	B03	Ground	———
———	Data 06	A04	B04	Data 05	———
———	Data 08	A05	B05	Data 07	———
———	Ground	A06	B06	Data 09	———
———	Data 10	A07	B07	Data 11	———
———	Data 12	A08	B08	Data 13	———
———	+ Vcc	A09	B09	Data 15	———
———	Data 14	A10	B10	Ground	———
———	Data 16	A11	B11	Data 17	———
———	Data 18	A12	B12	+ Vcc	———
———	Data 20	A13	B13	Data 19	———
———	Ground	A14	B14	Data 21	———
———	Data 22	A15	B15	Data 23	———
———	Data 24	A16	B16	Data 25	———
———	Data 26	A17	B17	Ground	———
———	Data 28	A18	B18	Data 27	———
———	Data 30	A19	B19	Data 29	———
———	+ Vcc	A20	B20	Data 31	———
Data 63	Address 31	A21	B21	Address 30	Data 62
———	Ground	A22	B22	Address 28	Data 60
Data 61	Address 29	A23	B23	Address 26	Data 58
Data 59	Address 27	A24	B24	Ground	———
Data 57	Address 25	A25	B25	Address 24	Data 56
Data 55	Address 23	A26	B26	Address 22	Data 54
Data 53	Address 21	A27	B27	+ Vcc	———
Data 51	Address 19	A28	B28	Address 20	Data 52
———	Ground	A29	B29	Address 18	Data 50
Data 49	Address 17	A30	B30	Address 16	Data 48
Data 47	Address 15	A31	B31	Address 14	Data 46
———	+ Vcc	A32	B32	Address 12	Data 44
Data 45	Address 13	A33	B33	Address 10	Data 42
Data 43	Address 11	A34	B34	Address 8	Data 40

Table 55-1. Continued

64 bit	32 bit	Pin	Pin	32 bit	64 bit
Data 41	Address 9	A35	B35	Ground	——
Data 39	Address 7	A36	B36	Address 6	Data 38
Data 37	Address 5	A37	B37	Address 4	Data 36
——	Ground	A38	B38	–WBAK	——
Data 35	Address 3	A39	B39	–BE 0	–BE 4
Data 34	Address 2	A40	B40	+ Vcc	——
–LBS64	n/c	A41	B41	–BE 1	–BE 5
——	–RESET	A42	B42	–BE 2	–BE 6
——	D/ –C	A43	B43	Ground	——
——	M /–I/O	A44	B44	–BE 3	–BE 7
——	W/ –R	A45	B45	–ADS	——
Key	Key	Key	Key	Key	Key
Key	Key	Key	Key	Key	Key
——	–RDYRTN	A48	B48	–LRDY	——
——	Ground	A49	B49	–LDEV	——
——	IRQ 9	A50	B50	–LREQ	——
——	–BRDY	A51	B51	Ground	——
——	–BLAST	A52	B52	–LGNT	——
Data 32	ID 0	A53	B53	+ Vcc	——
Data 33	ID 1	A54	B54	ID 2	——
——	Ground	A55	B55	ID 3	——
——	LCLK	A56	B56	ID 4	–ACK64
——	+ Vcc	A57	B57	n/c	——
——	–BS16	A58	B58	–LEADS	——

Knowing the VL signals

The Data/ –Command (D/ –C) signal tells whether information on the bus is data or a command. Clock signals from the CPU are provided through the Local Bus Clock (LCLK) line. Memory/–I/O (M/ –I/O) distinguishes between memory and I/O access, and the Write/-Read (W/-R) signal differentiates between read or write operations. Because the VL bus is 64-bits wide, the –Byte Enable lines (–BE0 to –BE7) indicate which 8 bit portions of the 64-bit bus are being transferred. A –Reset signal (–RESET) will initialize the VL device. The –Ready Return (–RDYRTN) line indicates that the VL bus is free for access. Data bus width is determined by the –Local Bus Size 16 (–LBS16) or –Local Bus Size 64 (–LBS64) signals. If a 64-bit bus width is used, the –Acknowledge 64-Bit (–ACK64) signal is true.

Accessing the VL bus is a process of arbitration, much like the arbitration that takes place on an MCA or EISA bus. Each VL device is defined by its own ID number (ID0 to ID4). The –Local Bus Ready (–LRDY), –Local Bus Device (–LDEV), –Local Bus Request (–LREQ), and –Local Bus Grant (–LGNT) lines are used to negotiate for control of the VL bus. In most cases, there is only one VL device on the bus, but arbitration must be performed to ensure proper access to memory.

General bus troubleshooting

In most cases, you will not be troubleshooting a bus. After all, the bus is little more than a passive connector. However, the major signals that exist on a VL bus can provide you with important clues about the system's operation. The most effective bus troubleshooting tool available to you is a POST board (such as the ones discussed in Chapter 28). Many POST boards are equipped with a number of LEDs that display power status, along with important timing and control signals. If one or more of those LEDs is missing, a fault has likely occurred somewhere on the motherboard. Keep in mind that the vast majority of POST boards are designed for the ISA bus. You can plug a POST board (with a built-in logic probe capable of 33-MHz operation) into an ISA connector (which will check the ISA portion of the VL connector arrangement), then use the logic probe to test key signals on the VL extension. Because the signals on a VL extension are quite different than those on an ISA bus, try the following signals:

- *Voltage* Use your multimeter and check each voltage level on the VL bus. You should be able to find +5 Vdc. If any of these supply levels are low or absent, troubleshoot or replace the power supply.
- *LCLK (pin A56)* The Local Bus Clock signal provides timing signals for the expansion device. It will typically be at the processor frequency. If this signal is absent, the expansion board will probably not run. Check the clock generating circuitry on the motherboard, or replace the motherboard outright.
- *–RESET (pin A42)* The Reset line can be used to reinitialize the VL expansion device. This line should not be active for more than a few moments after power is applied, or after a warm reset is initiated.
- *M/–I/O (pin A44)* The Memory/–I/O line indicates whether memory or I/O locations are being accessed. You can expect this signal to flicker or remain dim because it should switch modes very regularly. A problem here usually indicates a problem with the CPU or intervening logic. Try replacing the motherboard.
- *W/–R (pin A45)* The Write/-Read line defines whether data is being read or written across the bus. This signals also should flicker or remain dim because it should switch modes regularly. Problems with this signal usually indicate a problem with the CPU or intervening logic. Try replacing the motherboard.
- *–LRDY (pin B48)* The Local Bus Ready signal tells VL devices that the bus is ready for use. If this signal is frozen at logic 1, the VL device might not be releasing the bus, or a problem with motherboard logic might be disabling the bus. Try removing the VL device or moving it to another slot. If that fails, try replacing the motherboard.

Another point to consider is that bus connectors are mechanical devices. As a result, they do not last forever. If you or your customer are in the habit of removing and inserting boards frequently, it is likely that the metal fingers providing contact will wear and result in unreliable connections. Similarly, inserting a board improperly (or with excessive force) can break the connector. In extreme cases, even the motherboard can be damaged. The first rule of board replacement is: always try removing and reinserting the suspect board. It is not uncommon for oxides to develop on board and slot contacts that might eventually degrade signal quality. By removing the board and reinserting it, you can wipe off any oxides or dust and possibly improve the connections.

The second rule of board replacement is: always try a board in another expansion slot before replacing it. This way, a faulty bus slot can be ruled out before suffering the expense of a new board. Keep in mind that many current VL motherboards have only one or two VL slots; the remainder are ISA slots. If a bus slot proves defective, there is little you can do except:

1. Block the slot and inform the customer that it is damaged and should not be used.
2. Replace the damaged bus slot connector (a tedious and time-consuming task) and pass the labor expense on to the customer.
3. Replace the motherboard outright (also a rather expensive option).

3
SECTION

System maintenance and support

56
CHAPTER

Adding a CD-ROM drive

CD-ROM technology offers two characteristics that make it exceptionally well-suited for multimedia systems (Fig. 56-1). First, CDs can reliably hold more than 600Mb of information, perfect for storage-hungry MIDI or WAV sound files, graphic images, and video files. Second, CD-ROM drives can transfer data to the system at a rate fast enough to support full-motion video. If you do not have a CD-ROM in your PC yet, chances are that you'll be installing one soon. This article shows you the characteristics to look for in CD-ROM drives, and what is required for multimedia operation. You also will learn how to install typical CD-ROM hardware and software, and deal with typical CD-ROM installation problems.

56-1
A Gateway 2000 4DX2-66P
computer system. Gateway 2000, Inc.

CD-ROM characteristics

Before you read about the CD-ROM drive, you must understand the concepts of the CD itself. In terms of technology, the computer CD is not very different from the selection of audio CDs that you've probably got in your living room. A CD is little more than a plastic disk. One surface of the disk (the surface opposite of the silk-screened label) contains digital data encoded in the form of microscopic *pits* and *lands* that are wound in a continuous spiral pattern from disk edge to disk spindle. Each turn of pits and lands is less than 2 microns (2 millionths of a meter) apart. If the spiral data could be unwound and held out straight, it would stretch for almost three miles!

In reality, the data recorded on audio and computer CDs is very similar, both contain digital information, you can even play an audio CD in many computer CD-ROM drives. However, you need a utility to interpret the audio CD information because the audio CD data format is not in a form that is directly usable by the computer such as executable files, image files, or database files. You cannot use computer CDs in audio CD players because audio CD players lack the sophisticated data error correcting circuitry that is so vital in computer data handling. After all, if the audio CD misses a few bits here and there, your ears will never know the difference. If your computer misses so much as a single bit, however, your system might crash, or your vital data might be irretrievably destroyed.

Digital information on your CDs is read by rotating the CD and tracking a reading head along the spiral data path of pits and lands—very similar in form to the way record players used to work. Instead of a diamond stylus, a laser beam is used to detect the pits and lands. Because the laser's light reflects differently off the pits versus the lands, the CD-ROM drive can tell where the pits and lands are by looking at the laser's reflection from the CD surface. The pit-and-land information can then be decoded into individual bits by the drive's internal circuitry.

The extracted binary information then represents executable programs, data or image files, sound files, or video files in some established format that your multimedia application can work with. You can read the contents of a CD-ROM disk in a directory just as you would read the directory of a floppy disk or hard drive; the CD-ROM drive is even assigned a drive letter (D:, E:, or F:) just like other drives in your system. In order to be useful for multimedia applications, your CD-ROM drive must meet two important performance criteria: data transfer rate and seek time.

The *DTR* (data transfer rate) of your CD-ROM drive is the rate at which information from the CD is read into your computer. Original (single-speed) drives provided a DTR of only 150K per second. This worked, but could not transfer enough data to handle full-motion video. Double-speed CD-ROM drives can approach 300K per second while using no more than 40% of your CPU's processing capacity (30% or less is even better). The amount of CPU capacity is important because the CPU also has to run the rest of the computer and continue to execute the current program(s) while the CD's data is being transferred. If the CPU has to give all of its attention to getting data from your CD-ROM, the system will run very sluggishly or hesitantly. For this reason, a computer with a fast CPU such as a 386 is required, and a 486 is preferred.

The *ST* (seek time) of your CD-ROM drive is the amount of time needed to locate the necessary data file or program on the CD. The maximum acceptable time is one second (for single-speed drives), but most inexpensive double-speed CD-ROM drives can accomplish a seek in 0.5 seconds (500 ms or milliseconds). Drives with 300-ms seek times are available. Seek time is important because even the fastest computer must stop and wait for the CD-ROM to locate the needed information before it can be accessed. Half a second sounds fast, but the delays add up, and can become very annoying over long periods of use. The total time needed to access data is the seek time plus the data transfer time. Faster is definitely better here.

Installing CD-ROM hardware

Generally speaking, the installation of a CD-ROM drive involves the drive unit itself, an adapter board, and a connecting cable. Many CD-ROM drives are added to multimedia kits such as the Diamond Multimedia Kit shown in Fig. 56-2. The following information is intended to explain some general guidelines and objectives for you to keep in mind. The precise bolt-by-bolt procedure will certainly vary slightly from computer to computer.

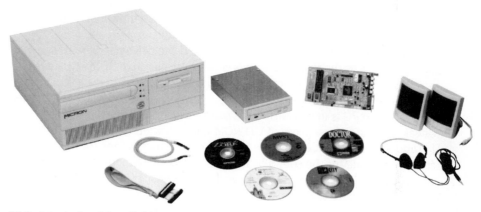

56-2 A typical multimedia kit. Diamond Multimedia Systems, Inc.

Selecting a CD-ROM

As with most "construction" projects, advance planning is important to ensuring a smooth, trouble-free PC upgrade. Most problem upgrades occur because of limitations or incompatibilities between the current PC configuration and the CD-ROM or adapter that passed unnoticed (until it was too late and the PC was in pieces). Try the following guidelines when selecting a new CD-ROM:

- Make sure the CD-ROM drive is compatible with the latest MPC standards for *seek time* and *data transfer rate*. The host PC also should have the minimum requirements for proper MPC operation (see Appendix A). The current standard is MPC-2. If the CD-ROM (or any element of the PC) is not adequate for MPC-2, many of the CD packages available today will not run properly.
- Check the PC's operating system. If the system is using an OS other than DOS or Windows (i.e., Windows NT, UNIX, or OS/2), the drivers needed to operate the CD-ROM will probably be incompatible. Check with the operating system maker in advance to determine the specific driver requirements, and see that the drivers are readily available before purchasing upgrade hardware.

- Check the available drive bays and determine if an internal or external CD-ROM will be needed. If you have two floppy drives, you can always find an extra drive bay by replacing the two drives with a single, dual-drive floppy assembly that fits in one drive bay. Most CD-ROM drives cannot be mounted vertically (especially drives that take caddies). Remember that an external CD-ROM costs more than an internal version, and takes more desk space.
- Check the available PC expansion slots. A CD-ROM with a proprietary interface will need a free slot for the adapter board, as well as a slot for a sound board. If the adapter has a sound board built in, only one slot will be required. If the CD-ROM is designed for SCSI, you will need a SCSI adapter (if not in the system already) and a sound board. Also check that the adapter board's length will not be obstructed by CPU cooling fans or other devices in the system.
- Check the internal power connectors. Internal CD-ROM drives will need a standard 4-pin power cable. If there is no free cable, you will need to add a Y cable and tap into a connector already being used.
- Check the CD-ROM mounting requirements. If the drive needs rails, see that there are rails in the PC, or that rails come with the drive. If the CD-ROM bolts into the drive bay directly, check that the mounting holes will align, and that properly sized screws come with the drive. It sounds trivial now, but just wait until the PC is in pieces and the screws won't fit.
- Check the system resources. A CD-ROM configuration typically needs two I/O addresses, two IRQs, and one or two DMA channels (one for the drive adapter and one for the sound board, even if the two functions are integrated onto the same adapter board). If the host PC is stuffed with other devices, make sure that you have the system resources available before installation. A software utility or a hardware diagnostic board such as The Discovery Card by AllMicro will reveal active IRQs and DMAs.
- Check for conflicts with other devices in the system. For example, if there is already a sound board in the PC, and the CD-ROM adapter provides sound board features, you will have to remove the original sound board, or disable the new sound board circuitry. Use caution when deciding what to disable. Some stand-alone sound boards provide joystick ports and MIDI capabilities that integrated CD-ROM adapters/sound boards do not. Disabling the wrong item can inhibit other features of the PC that are important to the customer.
- Position the sound output carefully. Most commercial speaker assemblies are not shielded against magnetic fields that can interfere with media and PC operations. If you will be using stand-alone powered speakers, be sure to keep the speakers positioned away from the PC or magnetic media.
- Cable lengths can be a problem in tower case installations. Often, the cable between the adapter and CD-ROM is too short. When installing a CD-ROM in any PC larger than a desktop, get a longer data cable.

Installing the drive

As with all new peripheral installations, you must turn off and unplug the computer. This might sound ridiculously obvious, but you would be amazed by the number of inexperienced users who injure themselves or damage their expensive system by leaving the computer power on. You also should make it a point to use static controls (wrist strap and antistatic bags) to prevent damage to the new equipment. Next, you must get into the computer. Remove the top cover to your machine. This procedure will depend on the number and location of housing screws in your particular system.

If your CD-ROM drive is an internal version, you will have to locate an empty drive bay in your computer (Fig. 56-3). Because you will need to access the drive regularly, it should be mounted in an empty bay located either above or below your existing floppy drive(s). If there are no empty flush drive bays available, you might have to free a bay by relocating a nonaccessible drive (such as a hard drive) to a rear bay located deep in your machine. If there is simply no room to be had anywhere, you will have to decide between removing an existing drive or rethinking your approach and exchanging the internal CD-ROM for an external CD-ROM drive. Assuming that you have the space available, you will have to slide the drive into the bay (along existing or newly installed rails) and bolt it into place. If your drive is external, your problem is simplified to just finding space near the computer's cabinet, and plugging the external power adapter between an available power outlet and your drive. Remember that external drives do not receive power from your system.

56-3 Opening an external drive bay.

Installing the adapter

Once the physical drive is installed, you will need to install the drive's adapter card. An adapter card is a small, plug-in expansion board that allows the drive to interface with your computer's main buses; this establishes the drive's physical and electronic connection to your system. Before installation, you might need to configure your adapter board by altering jumper or dip switch settings to select an appropriate I/O address, interrupt request line (IRQ), or direct memory access (DMA) channel. Because all adapter boards are designed and laid out differently, refer to the documentation enclosed with your adapter board for more detailed configuration procedures. When you decide on resource settings for the adapter board, note the IRQ, I/O, and DMA, and driver names on a sheet of paper, and tape the paper to the inside of the computer cover. You also can use the PC Configuration Form in Appendix F.

Typically, adapter card installation involves choosing an available expansion slot in your computer, removing the narrow metal cover plate for that slot, sliding the board gently into the expansion connector until it is seated completely (Fig. 56-4). *Be extremely careful when installing any adapter board! Careless or excessive force could damage the adapter, or even damage your system's motherboard.* Use the screw removed with the metal cover plate to secure the new adapter board into place, and keep the blank metal plate aside for future use.

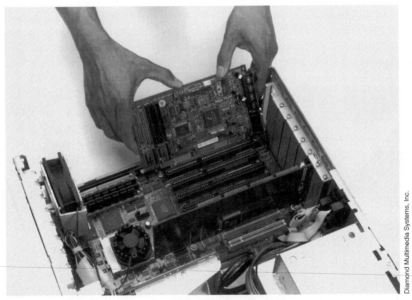

Diamond Multimedia Systems, Inc.

56-4 Inserting a sound board/CD-ROM adapter into an available expansion slot.

SCSI variations

Although many CD-ROM drives make use of proprietary or nonstandard interface schemes, the small computer system interface (SCSI) is rapidly growing in popularity. For practical purposes, SCSI is little more than a bus extending from an SCSI host controller card plugged into your computer's motherboard. The CD-ROM (or other SCSI-compatible device) can plug into this *peripheral bus*. As described in Chapter 48, the advantage of SCSI is that it is a system-level bus. In other words, the intelligence of the bus is placed in each device, not in the host controller. Using this approach, new and more sophisticated devices can be added to a computer system without concern for the host, so no additional hardware would be needed. A common language composed of about a dozen or so commands can be used to move data back and forth to the peripheral. Only a new device driver would need to be written for a new peripheral.

Each device on the SCSI bus requires its own unique ID number so that the host controller can identify the desired peripheral. The original SCSI implementation used an 8-bit data bus, so only up to eight devices can be used. The wide SCSI-2 implementation can be configured to include 16 or 32 data lines, so even more devices could be added. The ID is generally determined by setting a series of dip switches in the peripheral itself. CD-ROMs are part of the SCSI-2 description, and are often assigned a SCSI ID of 6. Connection to the SCSI bus is accomplished using a single 50 conductor cable (wide SCSI uses a 68-pin cable). Note that there are two general implementations for the 50-pin cable: single-ended and differential. The single-ended SCSI cable is used for short distances in relatively low-noise environments, and the differential is suitable for carrying signals over longer distances.

As with conventional adapter installations, the host computer should be turned off and unplugged before being opened to receive the drive. Under no circumstances should you attempt to install host adapters or drive cables while the computer is running. Not only is a serious shock hazard present for your customers, but the hardware will likely be destroyed. The SCSI host adapter board must be installed in an expansion slot on the host system's motherboard (if it has not been done already). Most SCSI host controllers come with their own installation and setup instructions, but there are several common guidelines to remember. First, an address location, interrupt number, and DMA channel will have to be selected for the board. This is typically accomplished by setting one or more jumpers or dip switches. The board should be inserted evenly and completely into its expansion slot, then screwed securely into place by its board bracket.

Carefully unpack the CD-ROM drive from its packing materials and locate the drive's ID selector jumpers or dip switches. The selectors are usually located on the rear of the drive next to the SCSI cable connector. There also might be a *parity* selector as well. Parity is a means of error checking, but it is usually disabled at the factory, because the use of parity is not standard among SCSI devices. If all SCSI devices in the system support parity, it can be enabled for all devices; otherwise, it must be disabled for all devices. The drive's ID might be set to some low number such as 1 (often a factory default). Because low ID numbers have higher priority on the SCSI bus, low numbers are ideal for slower devices such as CD-ROMs. Making the slower device a higher priority prevents faster peripherals from hogging the bus. Keep in mind that bootable SCSI hard drives are assigned an ID of 0, and a second SCSI hard drive is typically set to ID 1. As a result, you should set the CD-ROM between 2 and 6 (start with the lowest available ID in the SCSI chain). You need not worry about such things as address, interrupt, or DMA for the drive, because those are hardware-level concerns assumed by the host controller board.

If the drive is internal, you should mount it into an available drive bay and secure it into place. If the drive is external, locate it in a convenient place near the host computer. Connect the power cable to the drive (but do not apply power yet) and attach any ground straps that might be required. Attach the SCSI bus cable from the host controller board to the drive. If the CD-ROM is the last internal device in the sequence, attach any terminator module to the SCSI bus cable. If the drive is external, you might have to remove the cable's terminator module. Remember that even though this is a SCSI installation, you will need to load device drivers.

Installing the cables

There will be a ribbon cable to connect the drive and adapter card. This is the signal (or data) cable. Gently install the cable, and be very careful to keep the proper pin orientation. Otherwise, you might wind up reversing one end of the signal cable. Signal reversal is rarely damaging to the drive, but it can prevent the drive from working. Many connectors today are keyed to prevent accidental reversal. Keep in mind that only digital information is passed along the data cable. Audio, however, must be passed to the sound board through a small, shielded audio cable. Many multimedia kits supply this audio cable that plugs directly into the sound board, which often doubles as the CD-ROM adapter.

Finally, connect an available power cable from the system into the drive. Most internal CD-ROM drives use the same power cable configuration as hard and floppy drives. You should be able to locate an extra drive power cable (a 4-pin Molex-type connector) and attach it to your drive. Power cables are keyed, so accidentally reversing the power is impossible. If all 4-pin power connectors from your supply are in use with other drives, you can use a Y power cable with an existing power cable to "tap" an extra connector for the CD-ROM drive. If your CD-ROM adapter card offers amplified speaker outputs, you can connect your external speakers at this point. Fig. 56-5 and 56-6 show the cabling between a drive and adapter.

56-5 Connecting cables to the CD-ROM drive.

Diamond Multimedia Systems, Inc.

56-6 Connecting cables to the interface board.

Configuring CD-ROM software

In addition to hardware installation, you will have to install at least two pieces of software before you can make use of the CD-ROM drive. Locate the device driver disk supplied with the CD-ROM drive. Insert the disk in your floppy drive, change to that drive, then start the installation program supplied on the disk (see the disk label for the appropriate setup name). Follow the setup program's instructions to install the required device drivers and perform any additional system configuration as requested.

Typically, the installation diskette will copy two files to your system. MSCDEX. EXE (Microsoft CD Extension) is a required device driver for all CD-ROM installations so that the drive will work with DOS. MSCDEX.EXE assigns the drive letter to the CD-ROM and allows your computer to treat the CD-ROM drive just like any other drive in the system. There also will be at least one device driver (usually a file with a .SYS extension) that is drive-specific, and controls the flow of information between the drive and adapter board.

After the necessary device drivers are installed, the CONFIG.SYS and AU-TOEXEC.BAT files will usually be altered to call the new device drivers automatically during system startup. The device-specific CD-ROM device driver will typically be added to your CONFIG.SYS file, and the MSCDEX.EXE device driver will be added to your AUTOEXEC.BAT file. The exact location and command line switches that are installed with your device drivers will depend on your system itself and the particular CD-ROM being installed. Once installation is complete, you can use the commands:

```
type autoexec.bat
```

or

```
type config.sys
```

to view the new file contents.

After installation is finished, reboot the system so that the new drivers can be loaded and the new system configuration will take hold. You should now have access to your new CD-ROM drive. Install a CD, switch to the drive (D: [Enter]), and type DIR [Enter] to view the CD's file directory.

When using the CD-ROM through Windows, you also will need to install an MCI (Multimedia Control Interface) driver in the Drivers dialog box under the Windows Control Panel. This will allow Windows to play CD audio. After the driver(s) are installed, you will have to exit Windows and restart it in order for the new drivers to take effect. If you will not be playing audio, you can generally omit the driver; the CD-ROM will still be accessible under Windows, but no audio will be available.

Troubleshooting CD-ROM installations

In spite of the best efforts and all of the documentation on hand, there will be occasions where the installation of a new CD-ROM is fraught with problems. Any incorrect or omitted step in hardware or software installation can spell trouble. The following section shows you some of the more common problems that can arise during CD-ROM installation, and gives you the information needed to resolve those problems.

Careful of compression

Stacker and DoubleSpace are very powerful and effective utilities for increasing the effective space on your hard drive. However, adding compression to a system after the CD-ROM is installed might cause some problems for the drive. Fortunately, the problem can be corrected fairly easily. You see, a compressor creates a new logical drive on the existing hard drive. Therefore, a new drive letter will be required. If your original hard drive is C: the compressor will often assign D: as the new drive. If the CD-ROM is already assigned to D:, however, there will be a conflict problem. If you are in the process of installing a compressor and have the chance to enter a new drive letter, use a letter other than the CD-ROM (or any other drive in your system). If the compressor installed with its defaults and absconded with your CD-ROM's drive letter, you can alter the CD-ROM drive letter with the command line switches of the low-level driver and MSCDEX, often with MSCDEX alone. Refer to Chapter 16 for a listing of MSCDEX command line switches. Keep in mind that you also might need to alter the LASTDRIVE setting in your startup files.

Non SCSI installation symptoms

Symptom 1. The computer does not initialize This symptom assumes that you have proper power connected to the computer, and that the power switch is on.

If the system's power light comes on but there is no system activity (or the system begins its memory test and initialization, but freezes or hangs up), there might be a problem with your new CD-ROM adapter board. Turn off all power to the system, open the computer, and check again to see that the adapter board (and all available expansion boards) are inserted properly and completely. Also double-check the board's configuration to be sure that its base I/O address, IRQ line, or DMA channel do not conflict with other devices that might be present in your system. You might have to remove the adapter board to check its configuration settings. Finally, double-check the data cable running between the drive and adapter board. If one end of the cable is reversed, the confused flow of data might be enough to freeze some computer designs—it really depends on your adapter board and computer—but it is always worth a second look.

If you are unable to resolve the problem with the new CD-ROM installed, try disabling the CD-ROM by removing the adapter board and data cable. You may leave the actual CD-ROM drive in its drive bay, but you also should disconnect the drive's power cable. If the system then initializes normally (although you will see errors when the system tries to load the CD-ROM device drivers), you will know the problem lies in your CD-ROM installation. Try a new adapter board.

Symptom 2. The computer fails to recognize the CD-ROM drive The typical causes of this problem relate to the device drivers that must be loaded to support your CD-ROM; one or more device drivers might not be loading properly. If a driver fails to load or loads improperly, the CD-ROM drive will not operate properly (if at all). Check that the Microsoft MSCDEX.EXE device driver is installed in your system, and that it is located in the path called out in your AUTOEXEC.BAT file. If the driver is in a different path, adjust the calling line in AUTOEXEC.BAT. If the driver is not found, copy the driver to the location called out in AUTOEXEC.BAT, or re-install the CD-ROM device driver software from scratch. If you make any changes, be sure to reboot your computer to effect the change.

Next, check that the manufacturer's drive-specific device driver (usually with a .SYS extension) is installed in the system, and that it is located in the path called out in your CONFIG.SYS file. If the driver is in a different path, adjust the calling line in CONFIG.SYS. If the driver is not found, copy the driver to the location called out in CONFIG.SYS, or re-install the CD-ROM device driver software from scratch. If you make any changes, be sure to reboot your computer to effect the change. When dealing with CD-ROM drivers, the command line switches for both drivers MUST match in order to address the drive properly. Check the command line switches for the low-level CD-ROM driver and MSCDEX.

There also might be a problem with your CD-ROM adapter board. Turn off all power to the system, open the computer, and check again to see that the adapter board (and all available expansion boards) are inserted properly and completely. Double-check the board's configuration to be sure that its base I/O address, IRQ line, or DMA channel do not conflict with other devices that might be present in your system. You might have to remove the adapter board to check its configuration settings.

Symptom 3. The CD-ROM drive will not read a CD correctly As a sanity check, make sure that a CD is indeed inserted in the CD-ROM drive in its proper orientation (usually silk-screen side up). Also make sure that the CD in the drive is the right kind of disk. For example, an audio CD cannot be accessed for programs and data files like a computer-compatible CD. Try accessing the disk a number of times before giving up. Try removing and reinserting the disk several times as well—inexpensive drives do not always center the disk very well.

Once you know the disk is appropriate and installed correctly, the problem might be in the adapter board or the data cable. There might be a problem with your new CD-ROM adapter board. Turn off all power to the system, open the computer, and check again to see that the adapter board (and all available expansion boards) are inserted properly and completely. Double-check the data cable running between the drive and adapter board. If the cable is loose, or one end of the cable is reversed, data will not flow properly from drive to adapter. Double-check the board's configuration to be sure that its base address, interrupt line, or DMA channel do not conflict with other devices that might be present in your system. You might have to remove the adapter board to check its configuration settings.

Symptom 4. The drive is recognized, but no audio is produced Remember that a CD-ROM adapter is generally a data-only device; the analog signals produced by CD audio must be routed to a sound board. If the CD-ROM adapter doubles as a sound board, there will likely be an audio amplifier available. To hear the audio, you must connect one or more speakers (and sometimes an amplifier as well) to the audio output plug(s) on the adapter board (often known as the line output). The CD audio, as well as sound files, will be mixed and played through the sound board. Adjust the sound board's volume control to achieve an adequate output. You also could plug in at the drive's headphone jack. Adjust the CD-ROM headphone volume control for an adequate output. If your amplifier/speakers are not producing sound from the line output, try using headphones in the drive's headphone jack. If there is sound from the headphones but none from the adapter board, the adapter board might be faulty, or the cable carrying the audio signal to the adapter board might be disconnected or faulty. If the audio is absent under Windows, check that the necessary Windows MCI driver(s) are installed under the Windows Control Panel.

SCSI installation symptoms

If CD-ROM hardware and software are both installed properly, you should see several boot messages during system initialization. These are some typical messages for an NEC system:

NECCD: NEC CDROM Driver version 2.20a (low-level CD-ROM driver)
SCSI Host Adapter Detected at Address [address]h (SCSI adapter driver)
Device [device ID] Read only optical device (Removable Media)
MSCDEX version 2.20 (DOS MSCDEX driver)
Copyright [copyright date]
Drive [drive letter]:=Drive:NECCD unit [SCSI ID#]

If these messages are displayed during system initialization, you should be able to access the CD-ROM just as you would any floppy or hard drive. Insert a CD-ROM disk into the drive, then switch to the drive by typing the letter of the drive from the DOS prompt (d: <ENTER>). If you type dir <Enter> for a directory, you should see a complete directory listing of the CD-ROM disk. A successful directory listing will suggest that the CD-ROM is installed properly and ready for service. If the CD-ROM does not function properly during an application program, there might be other problems with the disk or drive.

Symptom 1. You see the following message when attempting to list a directory: Not ready reading drive [drive letter] There is a communication problem between the SCSI host controller and the CD-ROM drive caused by an undesirable SCSI address for the CD-ROM or excessive bus speed. Your first step should be to power down the computer and check that the drive is connected properly to the SCSI host controller. Also make sure that the CD-ROM is inserted into the drive with the right side facing up. If problems continue, change the drive's switch settings to select a new SCSI device number. Reboot the computer and try the directory listing again. If the error message persists, you might need to try several different SCSI device ID numbers. If a new SCSI number does not correct the trouble, the bus speed of the computer might be at fault. Bus speed should generally not exceed 8 MHz, so take the computer out of its turbo or high-speed mode and try the directory again.

Symptom 2. You see the following message when attempting to list a directory: CDROM not High Sierra or ISO 9660 format This error code (or if your bundled software's SCSI test program fails to detect a host adapter) suggests a memory conflict in your system—more than one device is attempting to use the same memory address(es). Conflicts are typically caused by expanded memory managers (EMM386, QEMM, 386MAX, and so on). Check your CONFIG.SYS file for the presence of a valid memory manager. You should see a device driver line such as:

```
device=c:\qemm\qemm386.sys
device=c:\dos\emm386.exe
```

Try adding parameters to your memory managers that will exclude the addresses used by your SCSI host adapter. You need to know the active addresses of the SCSI host adapter card from the settings of its configuration switches. Each setting should define a range of addresses (CC00 to CDFF, C800 to C9FF, DC00 to DDFF, D800 to D9FF, and so on). Refer to the documentation for your SCSI host adapter for more information. Once you know the address range of your adapter, add exclusion parameters to your CONFIG.SYS file:

```
[parameters] exclude=aaaa-bbbb
[parameters] x=aaaa-bbbb
```

(where *aaaa* and *bbbb* are hexadecimal addresses). Reboot the computer and try the CD-ROM again. Other possible sources of conflict exist in the use of memory shadowing or disk caching that are enabled through your system CMOS setup program. Access your CMOS setup and set all disk caching, BIOS shadow, Shadow RAM, Video BIOS Shadow, or any shadow options to the DISABLE condition. Reboot the computer and try the CD-ROM again.

Last-ditch sources of conflict can occur in the various computer peripherals (such as your 16-bit video card, modem card, scanner card, and so on). If your SCSI host adapter address range overlaps the address(es) of any other board, your system can encounter problems. Check the address settings of each installed peripheral and move that peripheral's address out of range of the SCSI controller and modify the address (if necessary) in the peripheral's setup or configuration program. As a check, you might wish to simply remove the peripheral to see if the problem goes away. Once you make a change, reboot the computer and try the CD-ROM again.

Symptom 3. You see the following message during initialization: No SCSI host adapter(s) detected Your system cannot find the SCSI host controller board. This can be due to faulty I/O, IRQ, or DMA settings on the host controller itself, or a memory conflict in hardware or software. Begin your investigation by powering down the computer and checking the host controller's resource settings. Use your documentation for the host controller and carefully verify each jumper or dip switch setting. A missing or improperly configured jumper can render the controller inoperative. Reset the controller board if necessary, then reboot the computer.

If the problem persists (or if you cannot find faulty controller settings), you might be encountering trouble because of memory conflicts. Possible sources of conflict exist in the use of memory shadowing or disk caching that are enabled through your system CMOS setup program. Access your CMOS setup and set all disk caching, BIOS shadow, Shadow RAM, Video BIOS Shadow, or any shadow options to the DISABLE condition. Reboot the computer and try the CD-ROM again.

Sources of conflict also can occur in various computer peripherals (your video card, modem card, scanner card, and so on). If your SCSI host adapter address range overlaps the address(es) of any other board, your system can encounter problems. Check the address settings of each installed peripheral and move that peripheral's address out of range of the SCSI controller and modify the address (if necessary) in the peripheral's setup or configuration program. As a check, you might wish to simply remove the peripheral to see if the problem goes away. Once you make a change, reboot the computer and try the CD-ROM again. Finally, if the system simply refuses to acknowledge the SCSI controller, you might wish to try replacing the SCSI host controller.

Symptom 4. You see the following message during initialization: No xxxCD functions in use First, make sure the CD-ROM is powered on before the computer starts to initialize. The CD drive must be available to the SCSI host controller in order for the CD-ROM device driver MSCDEX to be loaded into memory. If the CD-ROM drive is turned on as expected and the MSCDEX driver will not load, check to see that the device driver is listed in the AUTOEXEC.BAT file similarly to:

```
[drive letter]
```

or:

```
[drive letter]
```

in the AUTOEXEC.BAT file. If the problem persists, try moving the calling line to the first line. Reboot the computer and try the drive again.

57
CHAPTER

Adding a floppy drive

Early PCs suffered from a serious problem of compatibility—it was extremely difficult (if not impossible) to transfer files from one type of system to another. Commodore, Apple, Sinclair, and the host of other pre-IBM systems sold in relatively small quantities, and each used different media formats. When the IBM PC first appeared, it also touted a simple cassette interface for storing files. With the introduction of the PC/XT, however, IBM added a new means of storage—the *FDD* (floppy disk drive). Not only was the FDD much faster than the tape cassette, its random-access nature allowed multiple applications and files on the same diskette to be located very quickly.

Even though the floppy drive was overshadowed by hard drives in a matter of just a few years, the FDD remains an important part of even the most powerful contemporary PC. The floppy drive might not look like much today, but it serves three critical functions; the FDD, (1) allows you to load new applications and files on the PC, (2) allows files to be shared or distributed between multiple PCs, and (3), allows you to boot the PC should the hard drive fail. Although the floppy drive design has not been significantly revised in almost 10 years, it remains a popular replacement component, and many systems are upgraded to include a second floppy drive. This chapter outlines the considerations for choosing a new floppy drive, provides instructions for adding a second drive, and offers some troubleshooting guidelines to follow when an upgrade fails.

Choosing a second floppy drive

Unlike many of the various peripherals and drives that are available for a PC, floppy drives are almost universal in their design and features. There is usually nothing to consider because the drives are all the same. However, there are two concerns that remain constant; available space and BIOS compatibility. This part of the chapter looks at those two issues.

Drive space

The trend toward smaller, low-profile enclosures have put a lot of pressure on available drive space. Given that many systems are already fitted with a floppy drive, hard drive, and CD-ROM drive, there is rarely a fourth bay available for a second hard drive. One of the first considerations when contemplating a new floppy drive is space: where will it go? Of course, if you have an available bay, the problem is moot, but if you do not, there are some tricks you can play to free the space. First, hard drives do not have to be mounted in a front drive bay. If there is a rear bay available in the system, it might be possible to relocate the hard drive and free a bay for another floppy drive. If there are no other bays handy (and relocating an existing drive is out of the question), you might be able to use a dual-floppy drive—an assembly that contains both a 5¼- and 3½-inch drive in the same half-height assembly. You can replace the existing floppy drive with the dual-floppy drive.

BIOS compatibility

One of the problems with the PC/AT (i286) and early i386 systems was that their BIOS often did not support formatting the high-density 3½-inch drive. The drive could be read from and written to properly, but the BIOS would only allow diskettes to be formatted to 720K (instead of 1.44Mb). The solution to this incompatibility has been to either upgrade the BIOS (to a version later than 11/85), or use the DOS DRIVER.SYS to explicitly specify the physical drive as a high-density device. If you suspect that DRIVER.SYS is needed to support a 3½-inch high-density floppy drive, open your CONFIG.SYS file and try a command line such as:

```
device=c:\dos\driver.sys /D:1 /F:7
```

This command creates a new logical drive that is actually the physical drive specified by the D switch (0=A:, 1=B:). The F switch determines the type of drive to be created. In this case, a value of 7 indicates a 3½-inch 1.44Mb drive. Check your DOS manual for additional parameters. This problem has been completely eliminated in virtually all subsequent BIOS releases after 11/85, but it can cause some confusion when dealing with older PCs.

Installing the second floppy drive

In most cases, installing a second floppy drive is a three-step process; (1) configure the drive, (2) mount and cable the drive, and (3) configure the new drive in CMOS. Although a floppy drive installation is often a quick and painless procedure—even for a novice—there are a few nuances that you should be aware of. This part of the chapter outlines a typical installation procedure. When followed carefully, this process can typically be completed in 10 minutes.

Preparing the system

At this point, you can prepare the system for its upgrade. A word of caution is in order: *be especially careful of screwdriver blades when working inside the PC.* If you should slip, the blade can easily strike the drive or gouge an expansion board. It pays to be careful and gentle when upgrading an expansion device. *Before you even consider opening the PC cover, turn the system off, and unplug it from the ac receptacle.* This helps to ensure your safety by preventing the PC from being powered accidentally while you are working on it.

Remove the screws holding down the outer cover, and place those screws aside in a safe place. Gently remove the PC's outer cover and set it aside (out of the path of normal floor traffic). You should now be able to look into the PC and observe the open drive bay, the motherboard, and any expansion boards and drives that are installed.

Prepare the drive bay

Now that the outer cover is removed, you should open the desired drive bay. In many cases, this is as simple as just removing the plastic bezel covering an empty bay (the bezel will usually pop right out). If you must relocate an existing drive, things get a bit more complicated. First, decide where the hard drive will be located; often an internal bay is in the rear of the PC. You can then remove the mounting screws, disconnect the power and signal cables from the hard drive, and slide the hard drive out of the bay. Remount the hard drive in the internal bay, and gently secure each screw into place; be careful not to over-tighten the screws. Re-attach the power and signal cables to the hard drive. Pay particular attention when connecting the signal cable. If the cable is installed backward, the hard drive will not function.

The procedure is a bit different when replacing an existing floppy drive with a dual floppy drive. Unbolt the existing drive, then disconnect the power and signal cables. Slide the unneeded drive out of the bay and set it aside carefully. If you have a good-quality antistatic bag available, seal the old drive in the antistatic bag. At this point, you should now have an open drive bay. Take a quick inventory and make sure that you have a floppy signal cable and power connector available; you might need a Y connector in order to tap power from another drive.

Setting the drive jumpers

Before installing the new drive, remove it from any protective packaging and locate any jumpers or DIP switches on the drive. A manual will be important here. It will be necessary to set at least four conditions; the drive select jumper, the disk change jumper, the media sensor jumper, and the terminating resistors.

The Drive Select (or DS) jumper allows the drive to be set as drive 0, 1, 2, or 3. Although most XT and AT type controllers support four floppy drives, each cable supports only two. As a general rule, you will set the drives as A: and B:. However, interpreting the jumper selections is not always intuitive, because different manufacturers mark the jumpers differently. For example, instead of 0, 1, 2, and 3, a drive might be labeled 1, 2, 3, and 4. Other variations include DS0 and DS1, or DS1 and DS2. As a rule of thumb, the lowest number is generally considered to be drive A:, the next highest digit is considered drive B:, and so on. Because just about all floppy drive cables use a twist at the end (as shown in Fig. 57-1), both floppy drives can be set to the second jumper position (drive B:). As a consequence, the twist will automatically swap the endmost drive to A:. If in doubt, and there's a twist in the cable, set the drive select jumper to B:. Now, if there is no twist in the floppy cable (a very rare occurrence) be sure to set the endmost drive to A:, and set the middle drive to B: (because this is a daisy-chain configuration, you could actually reverse this order, but it is not traditional).

Terminating resistors add another wrinkle to the drive setup. As with many other daisy chain cable applications, terminating resistors are used at both ends of the signal cable to establish ideal signal characteristics. Normally, floppy drives come

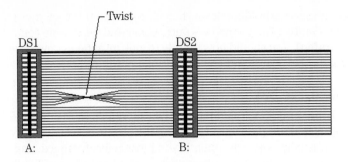

57-1 Diagram of a floppy drive cable.

equipped with terminating resistors installed. Because most systems use a single drive installed at the end of the cable (as drive A:), this is generally a good default. When installing a single drive, be sure that the drive has terminating resistors installed. When installing a second floppy drive as drive A:, be sure it has terminating resistors in place, and check that the second drive (in the middle position) has no terminating resistors. When installing a second floppy drive as drive B:, be sure that the terminating resistors are removed.

The disk change jumper is a vital part of almost all contemporary drives. This signal tells the PC when a disk is removed so that when a new disk is inserted and read, the directory information will be cached in the system. The disk change signal should be enabled on all drives except for 3½-inch 360K drives. Finally the media sensor (on 1.44Mb and 2.88Mb drives) jumper should be enabled wherever possible; the sensor allows the drive to detect whether a 760K, 1.44Mb, or 2.88Mb disk is installed.

Mounting the drive

Now that the floppy drive is configured, slide it gently into the open drive bay. Line up the four mounting holes, and screw the drive in carefully. Be sure not to tighten the drive excessively. Make it a point to use screws of the proper size and length to do the job.

Connecting power and signal cables

Once the drive is installed and mounted securely, connect the power and signal cables as required. The 4-pin power cable is relatively foolproof because of its keyed shape. For the signal cable, however, take care to install the card edge or IDC-type connector in the correct orientation. If the signal cable is installed backward, the drive will not work (the system might not even boot).

Update CMOS settings

When performed correctly, the new floppy drive should now be fully installed. Before you can actually use the drive, you must update the system CMOS entries to accommodate the new drive. Make sure that any tools or extra hardware are removed from the system, re-attach the AC cord to the power supply, then reboot the computer. As the system boots, start the CMOS setup routine and adjust the configuration as needed for your new floppy drive. If you have updated an existing drive, make sure that the drive parameters reflect the new device. If you have added a second drive, enter the appropriate parameters. When the settings are correct, save the system CMOS and reboot the system so that your changes can take effect.

Test the drive

If all has gone well up to now, the system should be fully booted at the DOS prompt (or the Windows Program Manager). Insert a known good disk and switch to the drive. If the installation is correct, you should see the new drive designator under DOS, or as an available option under the Windows File Manager. Try writing and reading a few files from the drive. You also might try formatting a blank diskette in the new drive. If these tests are successful, you can be confident that the new drive is working properly. Be sure to remove any tools or hardware from the system, then re-install the system's outer housings. Do not use excessive pressure to tighten the screws. Try the drive one more time, and return the system to service.

Troubleshooting the floppy installation

As you probably noticed in the last section, floppy drive installations are typically brief and smooth (so long as each available setting is checked properly). However, just because the procedure should be easy does not mean it is always easy. There are some problems that can creep into even the most careful installation. This part of the chapter guides you through several of the more typical problems, and shows you how to deal with each one.

Symptom 1. The new drive does not work, or the system does not recognize the new drive This is a classic problem where the system does not recognize the new drive, and is typically the result of incorrect or overlooked CMOS settings. Reboot the system and start the CMOS setup routine. Check the floppy drive parameters against the actual physical drives in the system, then make sure that the correct data is entered in CMOS. You might have forgotten to save the data initially. Save the new data correctly and try the system again.

If the CMOS data is correct, turn off the power, open the system, and check the power and signal cables at the drive. Loose or incorrectly attached cables can effectively disable the drive. Install each cable carefully and try the system again. If problems continue, the drive might be defective. Try another drive.

Symptom 2. You cannot boot the system from the new floppy drive If the drive is recognized properly and operates as expected, the failure to boot actually might not be a failure; rather, the boot order established in CMOS might not be set to include the new drive. Often, the boot order is A: then C:, or C: then A:. If you installed a new floppy as B:, the system will not attempt to boot because it is not included in the boot order. Restart the CMOS setup routine and adjust the boot order to address your new floppy drive first.

Symptom 3. After the second floppy is installed, there are a lot of signal problems such as read or write errors Chances are that you left the terminating resistors in place on the second (middle) floppy drive, resulting in signal errors. You should have a terminating resistor pack on the drive at the end of the daisy chain cable. Check that the terminating resistors are in place on drive A:, and remove the terminating resistors from the middle drive (B:). Also check that the signal cables are installed securely on both drives. Loose cables can cause signal problems.

58
CHAPTER

Adding memory

Of all the possible upgrades that are available for a PC, the memory upgrade is most popular. The growing movement toward sophisticated, memory-intensive environments (Windows and Win95), forces many users to quickly outgrow the 4Mb to 8Mb that most new systems are sold with. Even DOS-based applications (especially games and multimedia products) demand a startling amount of extended or expanded memory. Extra RAM reduces the demands on Windows swap files. This not only speeds system performance under Windows, but allows more applications to be run simultaneously. This chapter is intended to illustrate the considerations behind a memory upgrade, explain a typical upgrade process, and guide you through the symptoms and solutions of various upgrade problems.

Considering a memory upgrade

Fortunately, memory upgrades are really quite modular (even for older systems). Every motherboard provides plug-in receptacles for additional memory, and there are no cables or signal wiring to worry about as there is with most drives. When performed properly, you can add memory to a PC in as little as 15 minutes. As with all upgrades, however, a successful upgrade depends on proper planning. It is vital that you have the appropriate numbers of correct parts on hand before starting the upgrade process. This part of the chapter outlines the major considerations when preparing an upgrade.

1. Select the memory type. One of the very first considerations when planning a memory upgrade is the type of memory to be installed. Generally speaking, there are two types of memory—chip RAM and SIMMs. Chip RAM are the individual RAM ICs typically found in XT and older AT systems. These are usually DIP-style ICs that are added individually to the motherboard or expansion memory board. *SIMM*s (single in-line memory modules) provide a set of RAM ICs on the same slender plug-in module. SIMMs allow you to install large volumes of memory with a much lower risk of damage due to installation error. Figure 58-1 shows the two most popular types of SIMM: 30 pin and 72 pin.

Improve Technologies, Inc.

58-1
An Improve Technologies
SIMM expander board.

SIMMs offer some special problems because you must determine the exact number of SIMMs required to fill a bank. The classic 30-pin SIMM provides 9 bits (8 data bits and 1 parity bit). If the data bus in your system is 16 bits (i286 and i386SX systems), you will need two SIMMs to handle the 16 bits (plus 2 parity bits). For most i386 and i486 systems, the data bus width is 32-bits; this means you will need four 30-pin SIMMs to fill a 32-bit bank (32 bits plus 4 parity bits). The 72-pin SIMM tries to reduce the number of individual SIMMs by providing 36 bits (32 data bits and 4 parity bits) on a single assembly. Newer i486 and just about all Pentium systems use 72-pin SIMMs.

2. Consider specialized memory. Although many current PC motherboards are designed to accommodate relatively standard RAM ICs and SIMMs, older systems (late-model i286 and many i386 systems) often used customized memory modules designed specifically for a particular system. Early NEC and Compaq computers were notorious for this. When choosing a memory upgrade, make it a point to check the user documentation for the system and ensure that the memory device is compatible. Another common tactic for nonstandard systems is to use unusual memory devices such as single in-line (SIP) or zigzag in-line (ZIP) packages. There are two problems with specialized memory. First, specialized memory might not be available; given the speed with which systems become obsolete, custom expansion devices rarely remain on the shelves. Second, even if custom devices are available, they are likely to be much more expensive than the RAM itself is actually worth.

3. Select the RAM speed. Memory performance is invariably tied to its memory access time (measured in nanoseconds or ns). Ideally, memory must be fast enough to keep pace with the system CPU; otherwise, the CPU must use wait states to artificially delay the system until memory can catch up. For example, an i286 system often used 120-ns to 150-ns RAM, i386 systems favored 70-ns to 100-ns devices, and i486 systems required 60-ns to 80-ns RAM. The motherboard's manufacturer typically determines the working speed range for memory, although some motherboards allow you to set wait

states in order to use slower (less expensive) memory. System documentation will often list a recommended RAM speed. If not, you can usually determine speed by looking at the markings on other memory devices. For example, a part number such as MB81256-10 indicates a 100-ns device (taken from the -10).

4. Select the RAM size. Because there are many forms and configurations of RAM, it is vital that you use the correctly sized memory devices for your upgrade. Chip RAM ICs are typically available in 16K, 64K, 256K, and 1Mb sizes. 30-pin SIMMs are generally available in 1Mb and 4Mb varieties, and 72-pin SIMMs provide 1Mb, 2Mb, 4Mb, 8Mb, and 16Mb capacities. User documentation for the motherboard or the system will provide the specifications for expansion memory devices. If you have no documentation available, record the markings on any SIMMs that are installed; a reputable memory vendor should be able to identify the parts and recommend some suitable replacement options.

5. Consider specialized memory. When PCs exceed 16MHz, memory speed requirements become quite demanding. It is possible to add wait states, but that defeats the advantage of a faster system. There are several advanced architectures used to enhance system performance by increasing the efficiency of memory. When choosing memory, it is important to consider any specialized architectures as well. The three particular architectures that you are likely to encounter are paged memory, interleaved memory, and cache memory.

    Cache memory is by far the most widely used type of memory enhancement for the PC. Even though today's systems demand fast RAM, a wait state is still often needed to support the CPU. By placing a small amount (128K to 512K) of extremely fast RAM (20 ns or less) between the CPU and system RAM, the CPU works directly with the cache, and the cache reads and writes to system RAM. By predicting what the CPU will need and loading those RAM contents into cache in advance, the CPU can read the cache without wait states, resulting in significant system improvements.

    Paged memory is an enhancement technique that divides system RAM into "pages"; each page ranges from 512 bytes to several kilobytes long. Paging circuitry on the motherboard enables memory within the page to be accessed without wait states. If the memory being accessed is outside of the page, one or more wait states can be included until a new page is selected. Paging is popular in late-model i286 and many i386 systems.

    Interleaved memory alternates access between two banks of memory where one bank holds "even" bytes, and the associated bank holds "odd" bytes. That way, the memory access can begin in one bank while memory is being read or written in the opposing bank. When configured properly, interleaving eliminates wait states, while allowing slower memory to be used in the system. A typical clue to interleaved systems is the use of matched memory banks.

6. Consider specialized memory adapters. Although new motherboard designs easily accommodate large quantities of expansion RAM, older motherboards suffered from serious physical limitations that prevented adding RAM over

that amount. When additional RAM must be added to i286 and i386 systems, specialized memory adapters (such as the Improve Technologies Extend It board in Fig. 58-2) can be installed in an available ISA expansion board to provide extra memory capacity. Because of the speed limitations of the ISA bus, such memory rarely provides top performance, but it is often the only practical means of expanding memory above the motherboard's physical limit.

30-pin SIMM

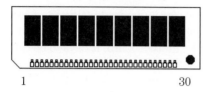

1   30

72-pin SIMM

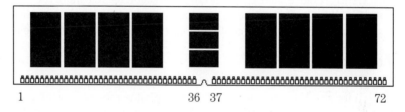

1   36 37   72

58-2 A comparison of typical SIMM configurations.

7. Weigh the cost. Traditionally, RAM is rather expensive (around $50/Mb as opposed to under $1/Mb for hard drives). At that price, the cost of memory can add up quickly. When planning an upgrade, consider whether the cost of the extra RAM is justified for the age and other features of the system; do you really want to spend $200 upgrading an i286 system? Of course, that is a question that only you or your customer can answer, but it is a valid one to ask.

Performing the memory upgrade

Mechanically speaking, the actual addition of memory ICs or SIMMs during a memory upgrade is extremely straightforward. This part of the chapter covers the essential steps and precautions that you will need to remember along the way. Before starting any kind of memory upgrade, run a diagnostic program such as *PC Technician* to check the existing system memory thoroughly before upgrading; this should limit any errors or upgrade problems to only the memory that is added.

Static precautions

As with today's CPUs, memory devices contain an astounding number of individual transistors. To achieve such a dense concentration of components, memory ICs are fabricated with semiconductor technologies that make them *extremely* sensitive to damage from *ESD* (electrostatic discharge). Before you even open the PC or remove the new memory from its containers, make it a point to take the following precautions. First, be sure to use an antistatic wrist strap connected to a proper earth ground. Second, have some antistatic foam on hand to rest the memory if necessary. *Never* leave it on a synthetic or static-prone surface. Third, never handle memory ICs or SIMMs by their metal pins.

Prepare the system

At this point, you can prepare the system for its upgrade. A word of caution: *be especially careful of screwdriver blades when working inside the PC.* If you slip, the blade can easily strike a drive or gouge the motherboard. It pays to be careful and gentle when upgrading a memory device. *Before you even consider opening the PC cover, turn the system off, and unplug it from the ac receptacle.* This helps to ensure your safety by preventing the PC from being powered accidentally while you are working on it.

Remove the screws holding down the outer cover, and place those screws aside in a safe place. Gently remove the PC's outer cover and set it aside (out of the path of normal floor traffic). You should now be able to look into the PC and observe the motherboard. Note the number and location of memory expansion sockets that are available.

Install the devices

Installing a memory device is certainly not difficult, but you should make it a point to watch for several common problems that plague memory installations. First, check the orientation of the memory device before attempting to install it. For example, RAM ICs must be positioned in the DIP socket so that pin 1 on the IC is aligned with pin 1 on the socket as shown in Fig. 58-3. Otherwise, you will install the IC backwards. A backward IC can easily be destroyed; it will at least result in a memory error when the system is powered up again. A similar problem occurs with SIMMs that also can be installed backward. When you observe a SIMM from the front (memory ICs facing you), pin 1 is typically the left-most metal contact. Make sure that pin 1 on the SIMM is aligned with pin 1 on the SIMM socket. This can be a bit tricky because not all SIMM sockets are marked. In that case, insert the new SIMMs in the same orientation as other SIMMs in the system. If there are no other SIMMs, check the user documentation that comes with the PC. When no user data is available, insert the SIMMs so that their metal contacts are inserted against metal contacts in the SIMM socket.

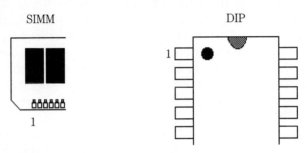

SIMM   DIP

58-3 Checking the proper orientation of memory devices.

Second, when actually inserting the new memory device(s), make sure that they are installed completely. RAM ICs in DIP-style packages should slide into their sockets fully. Be extremely careful that all pins are inserted properly; bent pins will almost certainly ruin the IC. SIMMs are a bit more forgiving because there are no pins to bend or break, but be sure to snap each SIMM into its respective holder; loose or unsecured SIMMs will result in intermittent memory problems.

Finally, it is important to fill banks in order; PCs cannot tolerate gaps in contiguous memory. Start by filling the lowest banks first (bank 0, bank 1, bank 2, and so on). Unfortunately, not all motherboards mark each bank so clearly. Refer to the user documentation for your system to determine which SIMM sockets are related to each bank.

Set the DIP switches

When memory is added to a PC, the system must be made aware of the expansion. Older PCs, used a series of DIP switches that can be enabled as new banks of ICs or SIMMs become available. Other motherboard designs use jumpers instead of DIP switches. Check the user documentation for your particular system, and determine whether there are any DIP switches or jumpers that must be adjusted. Set the switches or jumpers appropriately. Unfortunately, there is really no substitute for user documentation here. If the user documentation is missing, contact the system manufacturer; they might be able to fax you a copy of any switch or jumper settings. You also might be able to reference the settings in the *Encyclopedia of Main Boards* published by MicroHouse.

Set the CMOS

In addition to switches or jumpers on the motherboard, you will have to update the amount of expansion memory available in the system CMOS. At this point, check the PC and remove any tools or extra hardware from the system. Connect the AC cord and start the PC. As the system boots, start the Setup routine (older systems might need to boot from a Setup disk). Find the memory entries and update the extended or expanded entry to reflect the additional RAM. Be sure to save the new CMOS settings, then reboot the computer. If the upgrade has been successful, you should see the system test all of the available memory (including the RAM you just installed) and initialize to the DOS prompt without errors.

Test the system

When the memory installation is complete, run a diagnostic such as *PC Technician* to carefully inspect system RAM. Run repeated tests to ensure that the new memory has no hidden problems that might materialize during actual use. When the system RAM checks properly, replace the outer housing and return the PC to service.

Troubleshooting memory upgrades

Although memory upgrades are among the fastest and easiest procedures for PCs, the variety of memory devices, sizes, configurations, and speeds presents an array of potential problems for a technician. No matter how much planning you put into a memory upgrade, trouble can easily creep into the system. This part of the chapter guides you through some of the more frequently encountered memory problems.

Symptom 1. System freezes or fails to boot One or more memory devices might be installed incorrectly. This can happen when a RAM IC or SIMM is installed backward or incompletely. Open the system and review each new memory device carefully. Be certain that all ICs or SIMMs are oriented properly, and inserted into their respective holders correctly. Check for any bent or broken pins on RAM ICs. Also check for the presence of any stray pins or wiring that might be shorting out against other devices.

Symptom 2. You see an error message indicating that the memory in the system does not match the memory in CMOS This is a classic problem where the amount of memory listed in CMOS does not match the amount of physical memory detected. You might have forgotten to adjust the memory DIP switches or jumpers, or set the switches or jumpers improperly. You also might have neglected to update the CMOS memory configuration, updated the memory entry in CMOS incorrectly, or forgotten to save the new CMOS entry before rebooting the system. Start by checking the physical jumpers or DIP switches; correct any erroneous settings. Check the system CMOS configuration next and be sure that the amount of memory entered actually matches the amount of memory installed. Be certain to save the new CMOS entries before rebooting the PC.

Symptom 3. After a new memory installation, you find that there are an unusual number of memory errors or operating faults Chances are that you have installed the new memory correctly, but the devices are either loose, or mismatched for the system in use. Check the installation of each memory device. Make sure that ICs or SIMMs are inserted in the system completely and securely. Next, check the speed rating of the original memory against the speed rating of the new memory; the new memory should be at least as fast as the original memory; otherwise the new memory will not keep pace with the system (resulting in random, unpredictable errors). If you find a speed mismatch, your ideal solution is to replace the new memory with devices of the proper speed. If this is not practical for logistical or financial reasons, see if you can add one or more wait states to compensate for the slower memory (often accomplished through jumpers or a CMOS setting). This will reduce the system's performance, but should eliminate memory errors due to a speed mismatch. If problems continue, there might be a fault in one or more of the memory devices. Try running a thorough diagnostic to inspect memory performance. Replace any defective devices.

Symptom 4. A memory error is generated at a specific address There is a high probability that one of the new memory devices has failed. It might have been faulty from the factory, or it might have been damaged by static discharge or mishandling during installation. In either case, the device must be isolated and replaced. When the fault appears in an array of SIMMs, use a new SIMM and cycle it through each occupied position. Be sure to shut off and unplug the PC before attempting to exchange a SIMM. Each time you exchange SIMMs, power up the PC again and allow the system to reboot. When the error disappears, the SIMM you removed and replaced is the defective one.

RAM ICs pose a slightly more complicated problem. If the system is old enough to indicate which bank and IC has failed, it is then a simple matter of replacing the designated IC. For most systems, however, error messages do not correlate directly to IC position. When this happens, you will have little choice except to use a new IC and cycle it through each new RAM position (similar to the approach you used for the SIMMs). Be sure to turn the PC power off and disconnect the AC cord before attempting to exchange any ICs. When you do make a swap, be extremely careful to avoid bending or breaking IC pins. Each time you shift an IC, power up the PC and allow it to reboot. When the problem disappears, the IC that you had just removed is the defective one.

59
CHAPTER

Adding a second hard drive

Storage space is one of those resources that you never seem to have enough of. No matter how large the drive is, it always seems that you need to make room for something else. With new drive capacities doubling every 18 to 24 months, and prices continuing to fall, most PCs will be upgraded with a new hard drive sooner or later. As a technician, you should be familiar with installing new hard drives (and be able to troubleshoot those installations). The process of adding a hard drive is not a difficult one, but there are a series of drive settings and compatibility issues that you must be familiar with. This chapter explains the considerations involved in a drive upgrade, shows you the step-by-step procedure involved, and covers a set of important troubleshooting points. Although this chapter mentions ST506/412 and ESDI drives, these are both considered obsolete, and emphasis is given to IDE and SCSI drives.

New drive considerations

Under normal conditions, hard drives are certainly not difficult to install in a PC; an open drive bay and a free expansion slot are all that's required. Unfortunately, there is very little that is normal about the relentless proliferation of today's PCs. The mix of motherboards, BIOS, operating systems, drives, and expansion devices often present problems for a technician. A fast and successful upgrade depends on good planning. This part of the chapter lists the important considerations for a smooth drive upgrade.

1. Choose the architecture. The choice between an ST506/412, ESDI, IDE, and SCSI drive will depend on the vintage of the system you are working on. Because the ST506/412 interface is long obsolete, chances are that you will be unable to locate compatible drives and controllers. When faced with such an old architecture, it is often wisest to replace the old drive system with an IDE interface if possible, but even then, the host system might require a BIOS upgrade. ESDI also is obsolete, but you might yet be able to find replacement drives and controllers for several more years. However, ESDI systems were intended for high-end systems. Today, SCSI interfaces fill that role. If performance is still an important system consideration, upgrade an

ESDI installation to SCSI. By updating the older interfaces, you ensure that replacement drives and controllers will be available into the foreseeable future. Of course, if your system already contains an IDE or SCSI drive system, a new drive is easy enough to obtain.

2. Consider IDE versus EIDE. When you opt for an IDE interface, consider the advantages that Enhanced IDE offers (faster data transfer, large drive capacities, and support for more than two devices). If your customer is looking for optimum IDE performance and upgradeability beyond a second hard drive, EIDE might be a solution. Remember that you will need an EIDE adapter and EIDE drives to take advantage of such improvements, but the 40-pin interface is identical to IDE.

3. Replacing the drive versus adding a drive. In many cases, by the time you're ready to upgrade a drive, the new drive is at least twice as big as the original drive. Often, technicians will back up the original drive and swap it for the new drive. However, this is only advisable when there is no space available to add a second drive, or when you are upgrading the drive system from an older architecture. PC users can make use of as much space as you give them, so plan on installing a second drive wherever possible.

4. Check the resources. Adding a hard drive will demand three system resources: space, power, and cabling. Examine the system and make sure that there is an available drive bay suitable for the drive you plan to add. In most full-size desktop and virtually all tower enclosures, drive space is not a problem. Only in mini (or *baby*) cases will drive space be a limited commodity. If you must free a drive bay, one popular tactic is to replace separate 3½-inch and 5¼-inch floppy drives with a single half-height combination drive. Another problem is power; there has to be a 4-pin power connector available to feed the new drive. If there are no free power cables, you might need to insert a Y cable into an existing power connector to provide the extra cable. Finally, the existing hard drive cabling must support a second drive. SCSI devices are daisy chained, so this is rarely a problem, but IDE and earlier drives require a secondary set of drive connectors in the signal cable(s). Take a look at the signal cable(s). If there are only connectors at either end, you will need to obtain new cabling.

5. Check the power supply capacity. Hard drives are some of the most power-hungry devices in a PC. For systems that are already heavily expanded, adding a hard drive might be enough to load down the power supply and result in system problems. As a general rule, use your multimeter, or a power checking tool such as PC PowerCheck by Data Depot to measure the supply outputs before the new drive is added, then check the supply outputs after the drive is added. If the outputs fall by more than 0.25 Vdc, you might have to consider upgrading the power supply as well.

6. Check the BIOS date before an IDE upgrade. BIOS versions developed prior to the broad release of IDE in 1990 often do not accommodate the unique timing requirements of IDE drives. The result is often a corruption of data or failure of the drive to boot properly. In either case, a BIOS upgrade typically corrects the problem. When upgrading an ST506/412 or ESDI system to IDE, you might have to consider a BIOS upgrade also.

Pros and cons of a second hard drive

Given the ever-increasing demands for storage space, there are very few negative aspects to adding a second hard drive. Drives are getting continuously larger, and their prices are falling regularly. The problem is often in dealing with older architectures. As a technician, you have to balance customer service with the practical availability of parts. One of the adverse side effects of rapid improvement is rapid obsolescence. Let's face it, ST506/412 drives (a common sight 10 years ago) are virtually impossible to come by, and ESDI drives (popular only five years ago) are fading fast. Attempting to acquire and add such older devices to a system is about as practical as finding a new CGA board. As a consequence, it is often best to upgrade an older drive by replacing it outright with a current, readily available architecture. This involves replacing both the drive and adapter. To allow a smooth replacement, you also will need to perform a full system backup, and restore that backup to the new drive.

Performing the upgrade

In most cases, adding or replacing a hard drive in a system is a simple and straightforward procedure. The only real problem areas are in hardware conflicts and drive interoperability. This part of the chapter covers the essential steps and precautions that you will need to remember when installing or adding a hard drive. Although the chances of a system failure during the upgrade are extremely remote, it is always a wise policy to back up any vital files or programs before opening the system. If you will be replacing a drive outright, you must perform a complete backup that will be restored to the new drive later.

Static and handling precautions

Most of the ICs used in today's expansion boards are fabricated with technologies that make them *extremely* sensitive to *ESD* (electrostatic discharge). To ensure the safe handling of drive adapters and other system components during the upgrade, make it a point to take the following precautions. First, use an antistatic wrist strap whenever handling components or tools inside the PC. Cable the wrist strap to another reliable earth ground. Next, always try to handle expansion boards by their edges; avoid touching the individual IC pins or printed wiring. Third, if you will be removing an old drive adapter, have a good-quality antistatic bag on hand to store it in. Under no circumstances should you allow a drive adapter (or any expansion board) to rest on a synthetic or static-prone surface. As for the drive itself, handle it with extreme care. Avoid any impacts or rough handling. Keep the drive in its foam packaging until you are ready to mount it in a drive bay. If you will be removing an old drive, store it in the new drive's packaging.

Prepare the system

At this point, you can prepare the system for its upgrade. *A word of caution: be especially careful of screwdriver blades when working inside the PC.* If you should slip, the blade can easily bang the drive or gouge an expansion board. It pays to be careful and gentle when upgrading a expansion device. *Before you even consider opening the PC cover, turn the system off, and unplug it from the ac receptacle.* This helps to ensure your safety by preventing the PC from being powered accidentally while you are working on it.

Remove the screws holding down the outer cover, and place those screws aside in a safe place. Gently remove the PC's outer cover and set it aside (out of the path of normal floor traffic). You should now be able to look into the PC and observe the motherboard, along with any expansion boards and drives that are installed.

Configuring and refitting the adapter

If you will be adding a second hard drive to an existing system, you should not need to make any changes to the existing drive adapter. However, if you are upgrading the original drive system, you will need to remove the original adapter, then configure and install a new drive adapter. Seal the original drive adapter in an antistatic bag, and set it aside. Open the new adapter and check for the following jumper settings:

- *Interrupt Line* Most current 16-bit hard drive adapters are set to use IRQ 14, but 8-bit adapters used IRQ 5. If there are no jumpers to set a specific interrupt, the adapter probably uses IRQ 14 by default. Make sure that no other devices in the PC use the same IRQ line.
- *DMA Channel* 8-bit drive adapters typically used DMA 3 to facilitate rapid data transfer. However, current 16-bit drive adapters abandon DMA in favor of programmed I/O (PIO). You should not have to worry about DMA settings. On the other hand, floppy drives still use DMA 2 for data transfer. If the new drive adapter provides an on-board floppy drive adapter, there might be a DMA jumper; leave it set to DMA 2.
- *I/O Address* Hard drive adapters traditionally use ports 1F0h to 1F7h, and these are the only ports supported by motherboard BIOS. If you add a second drive controller to your system, it might use any other unused I/O address (often 170h to 177h), but it will have to have its own on-board BIOS (such as a SCSI adapter). It is extremely rare to suffer I/O conflicts with drive adapters, but it is always worth a brief examination of other devices just to be safe. If the adapter provides a floppy drive port, there might be an additional jumper for the floppy drive I/O address.

IDE adapters rely on motherboard BIOS for proper operation, so you will not need to deal with this setting in an IDE architecture. For SCSI adapters that use their own BIOS ROM, you will often be able to select the Upper Memory Area (UMA) where the BIOS resides. Generally speaking, the 64K segments at C000h and D000h are reserved for expansion ROMs, so you must select an area that is not in use by another ROM (such as video BIOS). If another device uses any portion of that memory area, you will encounter a hardware conflict.

Once you are satisfied with the available settings, go ahead and install the adapter into an available expansion slot, then secure the board with a chassis screw.

Configuring and refitting the drive

If you are upgrading the original drive system, you will need to start by removing the old drive. Disconnect the signal and power cables from the drive, then remove the four screws (or two brackets) holding the drive in place. You can then slide the drive out of its bay. Be sure to store the old drive in the new drive's packaging.

When adding a new drive, remove the drive from its packaging and place it onto a padded surface with its jumpers exposed. You will need to set the drive jumpers and check terminating resistors before mounting the new drive.

- *ESDI* The ESDI interface supports two drives (primary and secondary) with the control cabling as shown in Fig. 59-1. When the control cable is straight-through, the endmost connector is attached to drive 0 that has its terminating resistors in place. Your new drive will probably be attached to the middle connector as a secondary drive, so set the drive jumper to drive 1, and remove the terminating resistor. You can now install and cable the drive. If you are assigning the new ESDI drive as the primary drive, you should set it to drive 0 and leave its terminating resistors in place. Change the original drive to drive 1 and remove its terminating resistors. Cable the arrangement with the new drive attached to the endmost connector, and the old drive attached to the middle connector.

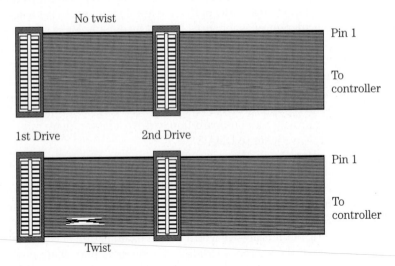

59-1 ESDI control cables (with and without twist).

The arrangement gets a bit more complicated when the ESDI control cable has a twist. Both the original and new drives should be set to drive 1. If the original drive is being left as the primary drive attached to the endmost connector, remove the new drive's terminating resistors and cable the drive to the middle connector. If you wish to reverse the configuration where the original drive would be secondary, both drives would still be jumpered to drive 1, but the new drive would have its terminating resistors left in place, and it would be cabled to the endmost connector. The original drive would have its terminating resistors removed, and would be cabled to the middle connector.

- *IDE* The IDE interface supports a master and slave drive on the same cable as shown in Fig. 59-2. When setting a second IDE drive, you need only set the drive as a slave; you can insert the drive into either of the signal cable's

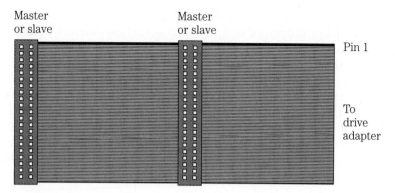

Master
or slave

Master
or slave

Pin 1

To
drive
adapter

59-2 A typical IDE cable.

connectors. You also do not need to set terminating resistors since IDE uses distributed termination for proper signal characteristics. Check to be sure that the original drive is jumpered as a master. Of course, you can reverse this where the original drive is jumpered as a slave, and the new IDE drive is jumpered as the master. The problem with IDE is that not all older drives were suitable as slaves or masters. If you encounter drive problems with your master/slave arrangement, try reversing the master/slave assignments.

• *SCSI* The SCSI bus supports up to 8 devices (including the adapter itself). The jumpers on a SCSI drive are used to set the drive's ID. The first SCSI hard drive is traditionally set to ID0, and the second hard drive is set to ID1. Once the jumper is properly set, you should remove the terminating resistors if the drive is *not* at either end of the SCSI chain. If the drive is at the end of the device chain, leave its terminating resistors in place, and remove the terminating resistors from the device that was formerly at the end. Refer to Chapter 48 for a more detailed discussion of SCSI chain termination. After the drive is configured, it is a simple matter to connect it into the daisy chain.

Mounting and cabling the drive

Now that the drive is configured, it should be mounted into place in an available drive bay. Secure the drive with four screws or a set of brackets as required. Be careful that the drive screw holes line up properly with the chassis holes, and see that the mounting screws are the proper size and thread pitch. Further, do not force the screws into the drive; excessive force can warp the drive case and result in premature failure. It is important that the drive be mounted securely to prevent excessive vibrations from causing undue noise, or a premature drive failure. After the drive is secure, attach the power cable and signal cable(s) as outlined in the previous section. At this point, the physical installation of the drive is essentially complete. You can re-attach the PC's outer housing at this point.

Setting CMOS parameters

Re-attach the ac cable to the system. Make sure that your hands and any tools are clear of the PC, then turn the power on. As the system boots, start the CMOS setup routine. Newer systems incorporate the setup on BIOS, but older systems require the use of a setup floppy disk. Once setup is running, find the hard drive parameter area and enter the proper parameters for the drive you have installed. If you have replaced an existing drive, you will need to correct the current parameters. If you have added a second drive, you will need to set the parameters for that second drive. Proper parameters are typically included with the new drive. If you are installing a SCSI drive system, you should enter "NONE" in the drive entries. You see, SCSI uses its own internal BIOS, so you should tell the motherboard setup that *no* IDE, ST506/412, or ESDI drives are in the system. Once the changes are complete, make a record of the changes, save the new setup, and reboot the PC. If the new drive is the only hard drive in the system, you might need to boot from a formatted floppy disk.

Preparing the new drive

Once the system initializes, let the system run for about 15 to 30 minutes before preparing the drive. SCSI systems typically come with a software installation disk that automatically loads the SCSI drivers needed to run the adapter, and can low-level format the SCSI drive if necessary. However, SCSI drives are pre low-level formatted, so once the system is rebooted again with the SCSI adapter running, you can use FDISK to partition the drive, and FORMAT (use FORMAT /S if the new drive is to serve as the boot device) to prepare the DOS format. At that point you can use the new drive.

IDE systems require no additional device drivers, and are low-level formatted at the factory, so the new drive can be partitioned with FDISK and formatted with FORMAT (use FORMAT /S if the new drive is to serve as the boot device) right away. If there are problems preparing a second IDE drive, there might be an error in the CMOS Setup parameters, or a master/slave conflict with the other IDE drive.

ESDI drives also need no extra device drivers, but they must be low-level formatted first. You can low-level format the new drive by starting DEBUG and typing g=c800:5 or a similar command specified in the drive's documentation. If a formatting program is provided with the drive, use that instead of the DEBUG approach. After the low-level format is done, you can use FDISK to partition the drive, and use FORMAT to handle DOS high-level formatting (if the drive is to be bootable, use FORMAT /S). Your new drive should now be ready to use.

Restoring the data

If you've merely added a second drive to the system, you can skip this section. If you've upgraded an older drive system, however, you will need to restore the files that were backed up before the old drive was removed. Start the restore procedure (typically from a routine on floppy disk), and copy the backed-up filed to the new hard drive. The new drive should now contain exactly the same information as the original drive (except that the new drive will run much faster and offer a lot more space). Test a few of your applications to see that they are working properly.

Troubleshooting the installation

In spite of the best planning and most careful efforts, hard drive installations (especially second hard drives) are hardly immune to problems. Given our strong dependence on hard drive reliability, any errors or erratic behavior can appear particularly troublesome. This part of the chapter is intended to provide you with some guidelines for checking newly installed drives.

Symptom 1. The screen goes blank when the system is powered up This problem is frequently encountered during new drive installation. If the display does not appear immediately after power up (you should initially see a BIOS ROM Copyright notice and the memory test), there is likely to be a hardware conflict between the drive controller board and your system. Make a quick check of the monitor to be sure its power cord or video cable has not worked loose during the hard drive installation process. Power down the computer, remove the new controller board, and check the I/O address, DMA, and IRQ settings on the drive controller board.

However, if the controller board settings check properly, reinstall the drive and controller board, power up the system again, and measure each output from your power supply. If one or more supply outputs becomes low or absent, the supply might be undersized, or there might be a serious short circuit somewhere in the controller or drive. Try a new or similar controller. If the problem persists, try a larger power supply, or remove other expansion boards from the system to reduce loading on the supply.

Symptom 2. Your IDE drive fails to spin up properly after power is applied This problem usually occurs when a new drive or controller board is installed or upgraded. A signal cable between the drive and controller board is probably flipped on one side. Check the signal cable alignments and ensure that both ends of the cable(s) are inserted properly.

Symptom 3. You see a "Drive not ready" error or similar message displayed on the monitor This problem is typically encountered during installations and upgrades. The system is not recognizing your drive. Begin your inspection by checking the signal cable between the controller and drive. One end of the cable might be reversed. Inspect outputs from the power supply next. Power is typically through a 4-pin mate-n-lock connector. The middle two pins are ground. One end provides +5 Vdc and the other end provides +12 Vdc. If one or both of the supply voltages is low or absent, the supply might be undersized for the power load demanded by the system. You could try a larger supply. If power is adequate, make sure that the drive spins up.

Inspect any jumpers or dip switches and make sure the drive is set properly for the type of controller being used. An ESDI drive must be set to drive 0 or drive 1, an IDE drive must be set for master or slave, and a SCSI drive must have a valid, unique ID. If the drive is not configured properly, your system will not recognize the drive. For all drives but IDE, you also should check for the proper positions of terminating resistors. An ESDI drive might be low-level formatted improperly. Check the low-level drive parameters used in low-level formatting. If any of the parameters are incorrect, correct the parameters and try reformatting the drive again.

Symptom 4. You install a drive that has been formatted by a dealer, but it does not operate after installation Start by checking the controller and cable installation. Also check the system CMOS to be sure that the proper parameters are entered for the drive being used. This is especially important when using an IDE drive in translation mode. Find out if the DOS version used to partition and high-level format the drive is compatible with your current system. A hard drive with an incompatible format or partition table will not function in your system. Make sure that you are using the same drive controller board used by the dealer who prepared the drive. Also check that you are using the same type of cables. It might be necessary to repartition the hard drive from scratch to ensure compatibility.

Symptom 5. You see a "No SCSI device found" or some similar error Check the installation of any SCSI adapter software; if you booted from a clean floppy, the SCSI drivers did not load, so the adapter will not be available. If the adapter software is installed and running properly, check that the SCSI cables are attached to each device. No cables should be pinched, scraped, or cut. Next, check the SCSI adapter to see that all jumper or DIP switch settings are made properly; a hardware conflict can easily cause problems with the adapter. If problems persist, try a new SCSI adapter. On the other hand, if the drive shows a series of LED flashes when powered up, it might be the SCSI hard drive that is defective.

Symptom 6. While using FDISK, you see an error such as "Error reading fixed disk" or "No fixed disk present" Double-check the signal cable(s) connected to the drive, and make sure that the drive select jumper is set properly. Try a different signal cable. Also check the drive adapter's installation. Next, try a fresh version of FDISK—the version you are using might be corrupted. If you are using a dual-drive system, try swapping the drive 0/drive 1 (master/slave) relationship. If the problem persists, removing one of the two drives; they might simply be incompatible together. Try a drive from another manufacturer.

Symptom 7. After running FDISK, you receive an error message indicating an "Invalid drive specification" or similar problem FDISK failed to create a proper partition on your hard drive. Try running FDISK again, and be sure to save the partition configurations. Try shutting down the system before attempting a DOS format. Try a fresh version of FDISK; the version you are using might be corrupted. In a dual-drive configuration, try reversing the drive 0/drive 1 (master/slave) relationship; the drives might be incompatible with one another. Try each drive individually. If problems continue on the offending drive when used alone, the drive's partition table can be damaged. Try a new drive.

Symptom 8. You see an error such as "Track 0 bad, disk unusable" This is perhaps the most serious indication of a drive failure. With track 0 damaged, there is no partition or boot sector information available to the drive, so the system cannot use it. Check the CMOS setup to verify the drive parameters. If the drive is an ESDI-type, check the DEBUG command used for low-level formatting, and try the LL format again. For IDE and SCSI drives, the drive is probably defective. If you have an LL format routing for the IDE drive, you might give that a try. Otherwise, replace the defective drive.

Symptom 9. You are unable to access the second physical hard drive This is a classic sign of configuration problems. Check the drive jumper settings and see that the drive 0/drive 1 (master/slave) assignments are correct. Also check that any terminating resistors are inserted or removed as required. Try reversing the drive assignments; the drives might be incompatible together. Try each drive separately. If the offending hard drive fails to work alone, it is probably defective and should be replaced. If both hard drives work individually, the drives are incompatible together; try a new drive from a different manufacturer.

60
CHAPTER

Adding a sound card

Of all the expansion devices developed for the PC, the sound board is probably the fastest-growing and most exciting. Only a few years ago, sound boards were little more than high-end replacements for the PC's internal speaker. But today, the sound board represents a sophisticated piece of audio engineering and digital signal processing that is capable of reproducing human speech and sound files with a startling fidelity. Current sound boards offer many extra features such as rudimentary speech recognition, and sophisticated MIDI ports capable of synthesizing orchestral-quality music. Although the sound board has become a vital element of most modern games, it also has become a staple of business presentations and multimedia displays. Practically speaking, the sound board is standard equipment for today's PCs. You will probably find yourself adding sound boards to older systems (Fig. 60-1), or recommending and replacing the sound boards in current systems to take advantage of

Diamond Multimedia Systems, Inc.

60-1 Inserting a sound board into an available expansion slot.

newer features. This chapter is intended to explain the important points to keep in mind when planning an upgrade, illustrate a typical upgrade procedure, and show you how to deal with upgrade problems.

Considering a sound board upgrade

Choosing a sound board is not always an easy task. There are at least 25 different models to choose from, which cover a wide range of price and performance levels. Although virtually all sound boards exhibit similar basic functions, their noise and distortion levels can be noticeably different, as well as their performance in the bass and treble frequency regions. Sound boards also compete based on added functionality such as a MIDI port, joystick port, CD-ROM adapter, and add-on software utilities. As with all upgrades, advance planning is important for success, and a vendor with liberal return or exchange policies is often your best ally.

1. Check your customer. Selecting an appropriate board is largely driven by your customer's preferences. For example, a customer looking for a basic sound board to support game play is probably looking to spend as little as possible, and will likely be satisfied by a simple, low-cost board. On the other hand, an audiophile who plans to connect a MIDI organ and compose music needs a very wide response, low-noise, low-distortion sound board, and a MIDI port with a large selection of "voices." If you're replacing a sound board, the replacement should have features and performance specifications similar to the original board (unless the customer specifies something different).

2. Consider the PC system resources needed by the board. This consideration is an important one (and often neglected), because sound boards are often the single greatest resource load in a PC. Don't consider anything other than a 16-bit board, so the host PC must have a full ISA slot available. A sound board will require at least one IRQ line, one DMA channel, and one I/O port address (an extra I/O area might be needed for a joystick port). However, many of the current general-purpose sound boards are being built with integrated CD-ROM drive controllers. The drive controller also will require an IRQ line, DMA channel, and I/O port. A MIDI port often requires an additional DMA channel, and as many as five I/O ranges for a base address and advanced synthesizer operation. Thus, one sound board (such as the Creative Labs AWE32) might demand up to two IRQ lines, three DMA channels, and eight I/O port ranges to support all of the board's features.

3. Consider MPC compatibility. Although MPC support is not mandatory for a working sound board, it might complicate operations under Windows, but virtually all sound boards manufactured today are compatible with the *MPC* (multimedia PC) standards supported by Microsoft Corporation and other MPC members. Sound boards that are MPC-compatible will often bear the MPC logo somewhere on the box or manuals. Sound boards made by companies that are not members of the MPC council might carry markings on the box such as "MPC-compliant." You can find MPC specifications in Appendix A.

4. Choose the speakers. No matter how good your sound board is, the output quality that you hear is a function of your speakers (Fig. 60-2). Using a set of cheap, unshielded $20 speakers with a high-end $300 sound board is a serious waste of money and performance. Similarly, feeding the signal from a $70 Sound Blaster into a $200–$300 amplified speaker system will not improve the sound card's output. For best results, match the quality of the speakers with the quality of the board. If the customer does not want to spend extra money on an appropriate speaker setup, they can run the sound card's "line" output to the auxiliary input of a stereo system.

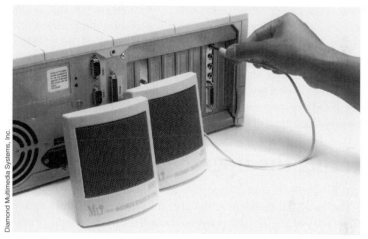

60-2 Connecting speakers to the sound board.

5. Choose the microphone. As with speakers, the sound recordings made by even the best sound board are only as good as the microphone itself. A good-quality, sensitive (–47 dB or better) microphone with a wide frequency response, a low impedance (about 680 Ω), and a high signal-to-noise ratio (60 dB or better) and shielded cabling will yield a better recording than low-end microphones. Once again, match the microphone with the application.

6. Consider the package deals. Sound boards are typically available as stand-alone products, but the explosive growth of multimedia applications has resulted in the trend toward multimedia kits (hardware and software bundles including a CD-ROM, integrated sound board/drive controller, interconnecting cables, and piles of software titles). Such kits are just a bit more expensive than sound cards alone, but provide several upgrade options in the same purchase. The sound board contained in a kit also is a bit lower end. Audiophiles might be disappointed, but it is often satisfactory for casual and business use. General-purpose users who need a CD-ROM drive and sound board might find a multimedia kit to be an unbeatable value.

7. Check the cost and availability. The prices for sound boards are dropping quickly, and older models are rapidly being obsoleted by newer, more powerful designs. As a result, the sound board installed in a system today will

likely not be available in 18 to 24 months. This makes direct replacement of failed sound boards very difficult. On the other hand, it offers the customer an interesting choice: (1) replace the board with a similar model that will probably be much less expensive than the original, or (2) buy a new card for about the same money as the original, and take advantage of new features.

The pros and cons of sound boards

There are very few negative aspects of a sound board; even a low-end sound board is generally better than no sound board at all. However, the playback of sound and voice files requires a substantial amount of data (especially at high sampling rates). All of this data must be moved across the expansion bus that is almost always ISA. The problem is that older systems (usually i286 and many i386 systems) could not process data fast enough to keep up, and still handle all of the system's other processing demands (timers, drives, video, and so on). The net result was invariably problems with the playback such as clicks, pops, hiccups, and outright sound interruptions. Ultimately, sound boards are well-suited for newer i486 and Pentium-based systems with plenty or processing power. But in older systems, sound boards are sometimes a less-than-ideal choice.

Performing the upgrade

Fortunately, adding a sound card to a system is a remarkably straightforward procedure. The only real problem areas are in hardware conflicts and software installation. This part of the chapter covers the essential steps and precautions that you will need to remember when installing a sound card. Although the chances of a system failure during the upgrade are extremely remote, it is always a wise policy to back up any vital files or programs before opening the system.

Static precautions

Most of the ICs used in today's expansion boards are fabricated with technologies that make them *extremely* sensitive to *ESD* (electrostatic discharge). To ensure the safe handling of sound boards and other system components during the upgrade, make it a point to take the following precautions. First, use an antistatic wrist strap whenever handling components or tools inside the PC. Cable the wrist strap to another reliable earth ground. Next, always try to handle expansion boards by their edges; avoid touching the individual IC pins or printed wiring. Third, if you will be removing an old sound board, have a good-quality antistatic bag on hand to store it in. Under no circumstances should you allow a sound board (or any expansion board) to rest on a synthetic or static-prone surface. Finally, excessively dry environments tend to allow substantial buildups of static charges in objects, clothing, and bodies. If it is possible, try to work in an environment with at least 40% humidity.

Prepare the system

At this point, you can prepare the system for its upgrade. A word of caution: *be especially careful of screwdriver blades when working inside the PC*. If you should slip, the blade can easily gouge the motherboard (or an expansion board) and result in broken traces. It pays to be careful and gentle when upgrading a expansion device. *Before you even consider opening the PC cover, turn the system off, and unplug it from the ac receptacle.* This helps to ensure your safety by preventing the PC from being powered accidentally while you are working on it.

Remove the screws holding down the outer cover, and place those screws aside in a safe place. Gently remove the PC's outer cover and set it aside (out of the path of normal floor traffic). You should now be able to look into the PC and observe the motherboard, along with any expansion boards and drives that are installed. If you will be replacing an existing sound board, now is the time for you to label any cables connected to it. Labels need not be fancy; a roll of masking tape and an indelible marker are all that is required.

Removing the old board

If there is no sound board already in the PC, feel free to skip right down and continue with the next step. Otherwise, start by disconnecting any cables that are attached to the current sound board (make sure each cable is labeled). You can then remove the screw that attaches the board to the chassis, then gently ease the board from its expansion slot. Be sure to handle the board by its edges. When the old board is removed, seal it in an antistatic bag and set it aside.

Install the new board

Find an open expansion slot for the new sound board. Virtually all sound boards today are 16-bit devices, so you will need a full ISA slot. Check each jumper on the new sound board and see that none of the IRQ, DMA, or I/O settings conflict with other devices in the system. Use the PC Configuration Form in the Appendix to record the sound board's settings, and tape the form inside the PC enclosure. If problems arise, this list will help isolate conflict problems. Ease the new board into its expansion slot (as in Fig. 60-1), and be careful to avoid flexing the motherboard too much in the process. Once the board is installed properly, secure the board to the PC chassis with the single screw.

Connect the cables

Now that the new sound board is in place, reconnect the cables as required. As a minimum, you will need to connect speakers, but you also might have to connect a CD-audio cable, CD-ROM data cable, microphone, MIDI or joystick cable, and so on. After each of the cables are secured, you can reconnect ac to the computer and reboot the system.

Install the software

Sound boards require the installation of DOS driver software to set up and configure the board each time the PC is initialized. Other sound board-specific software is needed to operate the CD-ROM drive (if the sound board contains a drive controller). Where configuration utilities are loaded, executed, then discarded during initialization, drive controller software typically takes the form of device drivers that stay resident in memory after initialization. If you are installing a CD-ROM also, you will need the DOS extension MSCDEX.EXE.

When installing a new sound board to replace an old board, you will need to replace the software already configured in CONFIG.SYS and AUTOEXEC.BAT. Before installing the new software, open CONFIG.SYS and AUTOEXEC.BAT into a text editor, and place a REM statement before each command line that references the old sound board software; this effectively disables those lines without removing them. Be sure to save each of the changes you make. You can then proceed to install the new sound board's software. Most current installation routines will automatically add the new command line references to CONFIG.SYS and AUTOEXEC.BAT.

Test the sound board

Many different sound boards include a small test routine on the accompanying software disk. You can usually run such a routine directly from the floppy disk, or install it on the hard drive and run it from there. Typically, the test routine will check sound and MIDI (music) operation. If both features work as expected, you can be confident that the speakers are connected, and the sound board is installed properly. If either (or both) features fail to work, re-examine the installation, check that all necessary software was installed correctly, and check for any hardware conflicts between the sound board and other devices in the system.

Install the Windows drivers

To support the sound board in Windows, you will have to see that any needed sound board Windows drivers are loaded under the Control Panel. Add any necessary drivers. If you have a CD-ROM drive and CD-audio cable attached to the sound board, be sure to include the MCI CD-audio driver that allows CD-audio to be played through the sound board. Your sound board installation should now be complete. Be sure to replace the PC housing securely.

Troubleshooting the upgrade

Sound boards are modular devices that are interconnected by relatively few cables. As a result, sound boards are reasonably easy to troubleshoot. The most difficult part of troubleshooting is the inconvenience of removing and re-installing the board to check jumper settings. The following symptoms are intended to help guide you through some of the more difficult installation problems.

Symptom 1. After a new sound board is installed, the system locks up when trying to play sound and/or MIDI files This is typical of a system hardware conflict between the new sound board, and one or more other devices in the PC. Unfortunately, the only real way to resolve this type of problem is to remove the sound board and check its IRQ, DMA, and I/O settings against other boards in the PC; this is often a cumbersome and time-consuming process. As an alternative, try a diagnostic such as *MSD* or one of the shareware diagnostic tools included with this book. If the diagnostic results prove inconclusive, try a hardware diagnostic such as *The Discovery Card* by AllMicro that reveals active IRQ lines and DMA channels. You can compare the active resources against the sound board settings, then adjust any settings that overlap. Also check the sound board software that is called by CON-

FIG.SYS and AUTOEXEC.BAT. If you have replaced an older sound board, make sure that any command line references to the older software have been properly disabled with the REM statement.

Symptom 2. The system does not lock up during use, but there is no sound provided by the board Start with the basics. Make sure that the speakers are turned on and powered properly, then check that the speaker cable is properly plugged into the Speaker Out jack. Speakers inadvertently plugged into the Microphone In jack will not produce any sound. Next, check the sound board's volume control and make sure it is turned up at least 75%.

Check the sound board software that is called by CONFIG.SYS and AUTOEXEC.BAT. See that the sound board software is installed properly. If you have replaced an older sound board, make sure that any command line references to the older software have been properly disabled with the REM statement.

If problems persist, there might yet be a hardware conflict between the sound board and PC. Remove the sound board and check its IRQ, DMA, and I/O settings against other boards in the PC. This is often a cumbersome and time-consuming process. As an alternative, try a diagnostic such as MSD or one of the shareware diagnostic tools included with this book. If the diagnostic results prove inconclusive, try a hardware diagnostic such as *The Discovery Card* by AllMicro that reveals active IRQ lines and DMA channels. You can compare the active resources against the sound board settings, then adjust any settings that overlap. If all else fails, try another sound board.

Symptom 3. The sound board works, but there is no CD-audio under DOS In almost all cases there is no CD-audio cable between the CD-ROM drive and sound board, or the cable is damaged. Check the cable and try a new one.

Symptom 4. The sound board works, but there is no CD-audio under Windows Suspect that the CD-audio cable between the CD-ROM and sound board is absent, disconnected, or damaged. Check the cable and try a new one. If the cable checks properly, the Windows MCI CD-audio driver has probably not been loaded. Open Drivers dialog under the Control Panel and add the necessary drivers.

Symptom 5. There is no sound during Windows events. Windows sounds are selected through the Sounds dialog under the Control Panel If no sounds are assigned, there will be no sounds generated during Windows events. Check the Sounds dialog and make sure the desired sounds are assigned. If the proper sounds are assigned (but there are still no event sounds), check for the presence of sound board drivers in the Drivers dialog.

Symptom 6. The sound board appears to work properly after installation, but now there is not enough conventional memory to run DOS applications This is a typical problem with current systems; the many drivers and TSRs used to support advanced features each demand their own area of memory. Eventually, there will no longer be enough memory for running applications. Use memory optimization techniques to load as many drivers and TSRs as possible into the *UMA* (upper memory area).

61
CHAPTER

Backing up the system

Few events are as frightening or disturbing as losing your data. It really doesn't make much difference how it happens—virus damage, drive failure, sabotage, user error, an improper software installation, or old age are all equally effective at disabling your computer and rendering your data inaccessible. There are a myriad of preventive maintenance tools and data recovery tactics available (as you can see in Chapter 62), but regardless of manufacturer's claims, all of those recovery techniques have limitations, especially when the drive fails outright. The only certain means of protecting your valuable data is to back up your system (Fig. 61-1). This chapter covers some important backup considerations, offers some guidelines for preparing backups, and explains the major limitations and pitfalls of backup strategies.

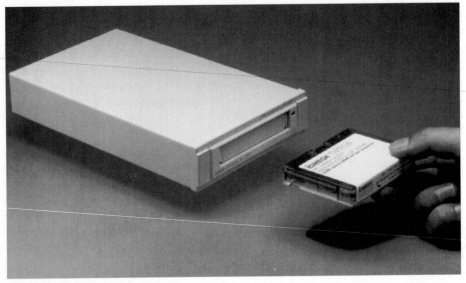

61-1 An Iomega Tape 510 parallel port tape drive.

Backup considerations

Although it is not terribly expensive or difficult to start a backup regimen, it is hardly a trivial concern. Whether protecting your system against data loss or archiving unused applications and data, proper backups depend on understanding the needs of the particular system being backed up. One of the most common misconceptions about backups is that they are used solely for the purposes of protecting data. True, the threat of data loss is a major factor in any backup strategy, but there are other advantages of backups as well.

For example, backups are often used to archive older or unused files. Let's face it, even the largest hard drive will eventually run short of space. Older applications and work files can be off-loaded through a backup and then erased from the hard drive, thus freeing valuable drive space. Backups also play an important role in periodic drive maintenance. As magnetic media ages, the sector and track IDs decay slowly. In extreme cases, the ID data might become irretrievable and result in the loss of an application or its data. By maintaining timely backups, a drive can be low-level formatted (using a formatting program designed for the particular drive) to rewrite sector and track ID information, then reloaded from a most recent backup. The refreshed drive might then continue providing years of trouble-free service. Effective backups also demand a variety of other considerations:

1. Consider the backup frequency. How often should a backup be performed? This is one of the most perplexing questions surrounding tape backups, and the answer is different depending on who you talk to. The most common yardstick is need. If you can't afford to lose what you've got, back it up. Although this might be effective for individual PC owners, it is not quite so simple to evaluate the backup needs of business and professional users. In such cases, need should be based on the value of data contained in the PC, and how often it changes. For example, a graphic design or desktop publishing firm might be suited to backing up every week or two. On the other hand, a busy order-entry system would probably be best served making daily backups.

2. Consider the most effective type of backup. Traditionally, there are three different types of backups; total, selective, and modified. The total backup is just as the name implies—all files and directories on the specified drive are saved to the backup device. Total backups provide the best protection of data and files can be restored selectively, but total backups take the longest to complete. Selective backups allow you to back up only desired files or directories. This is particularly handy for archival purposes, or if the majority of new data on the system is limited to a number of known directories. Selective backups take less time than total backups (depending on the number of files selected). Modified backups copy only the files that were changed since the last backup. This is the fastest but least flexible type of backup. It is often a combination of these strategies that provides the best level of data protection.

3. Consider the hardware and media requirements. There are many means of producing backups. Diskettes, floptical disks, tape (in all its variations), and

optical disks are just a few of the available options. Some years ago, diskettes were often used for backups. Today, however, it would take hundreds of diskettes to perform a total backup of one contemporary hard drive. Diskettes are still used for small groups of files (DTP files, graphics, and data files) that are considered work in progress, but they are hardly useful for serious backup work. On the other side of the scale, *MO* (magneto-optical) devices provide tremendous storage capacity, but their price and sophistication are often best suited for busy networks and high-end workstations. For the individual PC or a small network, tape drives generally provide the best cost/performance tradeoff. A single low-end tape drive can back up 120Mb to 320Mb on one tape; more expensive drives can hold over 2Gb. In most installations, a tape drive will provide more than adequate backup power.

4. Get the media "preformatted." If you've ever had to format a box of diskettes, you know what a cumbersome, time-consuming process it can be. Tapes are even more difficult to deal with. A typical minicartridge can take up to one hour to format. Although this might not be a problem for individual users who back up infrequently, business users might have trouble committing hours of PC time to tape formatting. Use factory-formatted media wherever possible. Even though preformatted media might cost a bit more, the savings in time is often well worth it.

5. Consider where to store the backups. Because backups can serve a number of practical purposes, it is important to plan where the backups will be kept, and who will have access to them. Again, individuals who use their PC for casual applications can probably keep their backup tape in a desk drawer or filing cabinet without a second thought. For businesses and busy professional systems, the problem becomes a bit more complicated. One of the key reasons for backups is disaster recovery, so the backup should be protected from disaster. Often, this means securing backups in a fireproof safe or fireproof file cabinet in another room away from the original system. Sometimes away from the site of business entirely. Another reason for this concern is security; you would not want confidential files falling into the wrong hands. In many companies, backup, restoration, and security are assigned to authorized individuals.

6. Consider compression. Data compression is an excellent means of expanding the capacity of a tape. If your compression software provides the capability of tape compression, use it. There might be a small penalty in reading or writing speed, but the extra capacity is usually worth it.

7. Consider manual versus automatic backups. If you run your system for regular, prolonged periods of time, automatic backups can be configured with a scheduler feature of most backup software. This makes it possible to save desired files at regular times while remaining virtually transparent to the user. Businesses with extensive computer time can usually take advantage of automatic backups. Individuals who use PCs inconsistently are probably best served with manual backups.

Tape rotation tactics

Tape cartridges are the most common medium for backup systems. Although the number of backups you perform per week or per month will depend entirely on the amount of activity on your system or network, backup integrity is limited by the tapes themselves. By using more than one tape as part of your backup regimen, you will not find yourself writing over a current backup (potentially disastrous if the backup process is interrupted). Tape rotation is a tactic that helps to ensure that data is protected and integral at all times.

Two tapes

This is generally considered to be the most rudimentary strategy, ideal for individual or infrequent PC users. There are usually two variations with a two-tape strategy. The most common implementation is simply to make full backups, alternating the tapes each time. For example, tape A is reformatted and used for a backup on March 1, tape B is reformatted and used on April 1, then tape A is reformatted and reused for a complete backup on May 1, and so on. This approach guarantees that you are never overwriting a current backup. An alternative strategy is to create a total backup on tape A, then make modified backups on tape B as needed.

Three tapes

The three-tape cycle is frequently used for small offices or home offices where there are a limited number of files changing from day to day. The process is easy to understand if you look at it over a 1 week period. On Monday, make a complete backup on tape A. Tuesday through Friday, make modified backups on tape B (each modified backup should have its own tape volume). The next week, make a total backup on tape C, and store tape A in a secure location off site. Erase or reformat tape B, then use it for modified backups throughout the week. On Monday of the subsequent week, store tape C off site, and return tape A to be erased or reformatted for a new complete backup. Thus tapes A and C are alternated each week for complete system backups, and tape B remains on-site for daily modified backups.

If you are not using the system enough to justify daily maintenance, try a weekly approach. Use tape A for a total backup on the first of the month, then use tape B for modified backups once a week during the month (or whenever important new files must be protected). The first of the next month, perform a total backup on tape C and store tape A in a secure location off site. Erase tape B and reuse it for modified backups throughout the month. On the first of the third month, move tape C off site, erase tape A and perform a complete backup, then erase tape B and use it for modified backups. This way, tapes A and C are alternated the first of every month rather than the first of every week.

Six tapes

The six-tape rotation is intended for businesses and busy offices where important files are changed and updated daily. Start the week by erasing or reformatting tapes A and F, then creating total backups on both tapes. Store tape F in a secure location off site. Use tapes B, C, D, and E to perform modified backups on Tuesday through Friday. On the subsequent Monday, tapes A and F would be erased and backed up once again. Each day through the week, the tape designated for that particular day would be erased and saved with a modified backup.

Ten tapes

When you need to maintain weekly and monthly off-site archives of on-going work, you can use a ten-tape rotation cycle (which is really just an adjustment to the six-tape cycle). By adding four more tapes to the six-tape cycle, you can create a total backup the first of every week, then store those weekly backups off site. For example, on the first Monday of the month, a total backup is made on tapes A and F (just as in the six-tape rotation) and tape F is stored off site. On Tuesday through Friday, tapes B, C, D, and E hold modified backups of each day. Tape F becomes the archive of week 1. The next week, total backups are made on tapes A and G, and tapes B, C, D, and E provide modified backups. Tape G would be the archive for week 2. The third week, tapes A and H would be the total backups, and tape H would archive the third week. Tapes A and I would hold total backups on the forth week, so tape I would archive the forth week. Finally, tape J would be used as a total backup on the last day of the month. Although this process is overkill for many businesses, it might come in handy for businesses that require longterm archives of their work (for example, government contractors).

Backup limitations

Although backups are usually considered to be a cost-effective form of data archiving and a reliable means of data protection, backups are hardly perfect. There are a whole array of limitations that can adversely affect your backup efforts (or those of your customer). This part of the chapter is designed to illustrate the pitfalls to look out for when planning and executing backups.

Be sure to pay adequate attention to media. Like diskettes, tapes are magnetic media. Unfortunately, magnetic media does not last forever. One of the big problems with frequent backups is that users mistake backup or compare errors as a problem with the drive or backup software, where it is actually the tape that has worn out. As a general rule, plan on replacing your tapes at least once a year. If you are performing frequent backups, plan on replacing your tapes even more frequently. Tape life also depends on tape quality—high-quality tapes last longer than low-quality tapes. It is often more prudent to spend a bit more for a reliable, good-quality tape, than save a little money on a low-cost tape, only to find that the tape wears out much sooner, or loses data when it's needed.

62
CHAPTER

Data-recovery techniques

It is almost ironic that the value of a PC's hardware is often insignificant when considered against the data that PC contains. Recent history is replete with examples of businesses that have suffered terrible financial hardship—even gone out of business—after losing vital files. Although the consequences are not nearly as severe for home offices or casual PC users, hard drive failures are always difficult. This chapter is intended to provide some guidance that will protect the drive from failure, and offer some procedures that will help you recover a drive that has actually failed. It is important for you to remember that it is not always possible to resurrect a dead drive. Even under the best of circumstances, data recovery is more of an art than a science. Circuit and media failures can easily prevent a complete recovery.

Protecting the drive

Sooner or later, your hard drive is going to fail. It is not a question of whether, it is a question of when. Although this might sound gloomy, there is absolutely no reason why a hard drive should not perform perfectly through its entire working life. Just as a person can improve the quality of life by eating right and exercising regularly, drive life can be lengthened by taking some fairly common-sense precautions. This is not exactly data recovery, but any strategies that can reduce down time are sure ways to win a customer's loyalty.

1. Check the power quality. Hard drives tend to be quite sensitive to variations in ac power, especially voltage spikes caused by lightning or inductive equipment sharing the same ac circuit in your home or office. If there is a lot of motorized equipment or high-energy equipment in the same area as the PC, consider having a new ac line installed exclusively for the computer, or consider investing in a *UPS* (uninterruptable power supply).

2. Look for smoke. Cigar and cigarette smoke can be detrimental to a hard drive. Although the air drawn into a hard drive is passed through an extremely fine filter, any smoke particles that do manage to penetrate the

drive housing are much larger than the spacing between a R/W head and platter. A single smoke particle caught between the head and platter can be dragged along the disk resulting in media damage.

3. Mount carefully. In spite of their rigid enclosure, hard drives can be warped just slightly when tightly secured by four screws. In some cases, this effect is just enough to throw out a drive's alignment and cause data problems. If you encounter drive problems after moving or remounting the drive, try loosening one or more of the screws (you need not remove them). Just taking the pressure off will usually eliminate the problem.

4. Handle carefully. If you must remove the drive for any reason (during an upgrade), be very careful to handle the drive gently and rest it on a soft foam surface. You should avoid any impacts or hard surfaces. When re-installing the drive, be certain to use only the correct screws; otherwise, screws that are too long will warp the drive. Worse, excessive force can crack the cast enclosure allowing dust and smoke to enter the drive freely, and precipitate a rapid drive failure.

5. Minimize vibration. Hard drives are very sensitive to physical vibration. Shocks and impacts can cause R/W heads to mark platter surfaces. If the drive is not secured properly, a pattern of regular vibrations might set up in the mechanical assemblies. Although such subtle vibrations will rarely damage the drive outright, they can certainly shorten the drive's working life.

6. Format in the proper environment. Because the drive works in terms of microscopic dimensions, the effects of gravity and thermal expansion play a role in the accuracy of head positioning. Make sure that the drive is at a running temperature (perhaps 15 minutes or more) before formatting it. Also see that the drive is oriented correctly (horizontally or vertically) prior to formatting.

7. Keep the disk defragmented. The DOS file system has the ability to divide a file into clusters (groups of sectors) that can be spread all over the drive. Ideally, clusters should be contiguous along adjacent tracks of the disk, which reduces the amount of seek time required to position R/W heads. As files grow beyond their original cluster size, DOS will assign other (sometimes distant) clusters to hold part of the file. It is this "scattering" of clusters that fragments files. By itself, fragmentation is a normal part of DOS, but excessive fragmentation forces the drive to rush all over the disk. Over time, a large number of fragmented files can cause enough wear to shorten the drive's life. Use a DOS disk defragmenter (such as the DOS DEFRAG utility) regularly to keep the disk file clusters contiguous. PC Tools is a popular package for disk management.

8. Avoid double parking. In the early days of hard drives, designers realized that head impact could damage the media. Drive designers allowed for a landing zone—an unused track where heads could be positioned before power down. With a landing zone, it did not matter if heads contacted the platter because there was no data there to lose. A utility could park the reads over the landing zone. However, most newer drives are designed to be

auto-parking. Before the drive spins down, heads are automatically positioned over the landing zone based on CMOS data. Parking programs are no longer needed, and can even position the heads incorrectly before power down (a common problem with IDE drives that operate in translation mode). Also, many drives are dynamically loaded, so R/W heads are removed from the platters once power is removed. Avoid using parking utilities unless the utility is intended specifically for the drive.

9. Keep the drive backed up. Regular, complete system backups are generally regarded to be the best, most reliable protection against drive failures. No matter what happens to the drive, you can't really lose anything as long as you have a copy of it (Fig. 62-1). In addition to applications and data files, however, you also should make it a point to back up the partition table, auto-configure record, file allocation table, and root directory. DrivePro from MicroHouse can create backup copies of these critical areas. If you have a sound low-level formatter for your drive, you might try backing up the drive completely, performing a fresh low-level format to rewrite track and sector IDs, then repartitioning, reformatting, and restoring the drive.

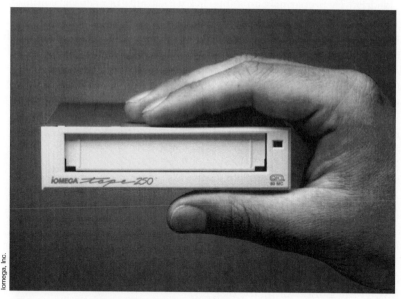

Iomega, Inc.

62-1 An Iomega Tape 250 internal tape drive.

Understanding drive boot problems

Today, virtually all PCs boot from a local hard drive. Why not? The hard drive is much larger and faster than any floppy drive could ever hope to be. Indeed, it is the huge space provided by a contemporary drive that makes today's graphic-oriented operating systems (Windows or OS/2) and their applications possible (imagine loading Windows from a floppy). With this great storage potential, however, has come a sometimes-dangerous reliance on your hard drive. For most users, a single drive holds all of the data and applications that we ever use. When that drive fails, not only does the PC refuse to boot, but it loses access to the entire contents of the drive.

Hard drives fail for a lot of reasons. Power surges, manufacturing defects, viruses or other rogue software, and simple old age are just a few of the factors that can damage a drive. Although mechanical and electronic faults will require drive (or controller) replacement, the effects of age and viruses can sometimes be corrected; this is the nature of data recovery. Where Chapter 25 focuses on irreversible electromechanical damage and replacement, this chapter is concerned with data problems that can often be corrected given the proper software tools. The following sections explain key points in the drive boot process, and illustrate some of the problems that might occur each step of the way.

A maintenance disk

Before starting into a disk recovery, you should have a bootable utility floppy available. Because the hard drive will not boot, it is unlikely that you will be able to access the drive. By preparing a bootable disk with a suite of necessary utilities in advance, you will be able to work with the needed utilities regardless of what is available on the hard drive. Be sure to write-protect the disk before using it in a defective system. Of course, the exact files added to your utility floppies are largely at your discretion, but the following files are usually a minimum:

- *IO.SYS, MSDOS.SYS, and COMMAND.COM* Provided when the floppy disk is formatted and made bootable. If you are using IBM DOS, the files would be IBMBIO.COM and IBMDOS.COM.
- *FORMAT* For performing DOS-level formats of the hard drive
- *SYS* For adding system files to the hard drive
- *FDISK* For partitioning a hard drive
- A low-level formatter suitable for the hard drive in use (a good general-purpose low-level formatter is *DrivePro* from MicroHouse or *PC Technician* from Windsor Technologies).
- *DEBUG* To activate a low-level formatter
- *DEFRAG* Similar DOS defragmenter utility
- *CHKDSK or SCANDSK* To deal with lost clusters and cross-linked files
- *MIRROR and UNFORMAT* To save and restore the hard drive partition
- *RECOVER* For restoring the disk FAT
- *MSAV (or some other antivirus product)* For checking for viruses in the boot sector or command processor.
- *DrivePro from MicroHouse* Offers a very handy feature called Important Info Backup that allows you to save the DOS boot sector, partition table, DOS boot record, file allocation table, and CMOS drive settings. It also offers a Drive Boot Fixer that can often reconstruct damaged boot information. Such tools might not restore a drive fully, but it might make data accessible enough to backup.

Check for viruses

When you finally boot the system from a floppy drive, one of the first tasks you should perform is a thorough virus check using MSAV or some other antivirus tool. A virus in the boot sector or command processor (COMMAND.COM) can easily prevent the drive from booting, so pay particular attention to any anomalies in those two areas.

Hardware check

This is the first phase of all PC initialization. POST checks the drive controller hardware (along with all of the other system hardware) to determine if a hard drive is even available, and if it is responding. If the system does not even attempt to boot from the drive, chances are that you've got a bad drive or controller. An error message displayed on the monitor indicating a drive failure is another symptom of drive trouble. Before attempting to replace hardware, make sure that all cables and connectors are installed completely and correctly. If the error indicates an adapter problem, replace the adapter. If the error indicates a drive problem, try replacing the drive.

Partition table

The partition table also is called the *MBR* (master boot record) that resides on head 0, cylinder 0, sector 1. You see this as an initial flash on the drive LED early in the boot-up process. If BIOS is unable to read the partition table (because of media age or damage to the table itself), the drive will be ignored. You might see this type of problem indicated as an "Invalid drive specification" error. Without a valid partition table, the PC simply does not recognize the hard drive at all.

Use FDISK to test the drive's partition. If FDISK refuses to run at all, there might be a hardware problem. Go back and check the drive and its controller. You might wish to try a self-booting diagnostic such as PC Technician to test the drive hardware more thoroughly. If FDISK runs, choose the Display Partition Status option and examine the drive's partition(s). Check to see if the partition(s) make sense.

If you see a small DOS partition and a large non-DOS partition, this might be correct because current DOS versions are only capable of working with hard drives up to 528Mb, a number of third-party vendors have developed supplemental utilities to allow larger partitions. As a consequence, such configurations use a small DOS partition for booting the system, and a large non-DOS partition, and a device driver that allows DOS to work in the non-DOS partition. Remember, the purpose of using FDISK here is merely to check the available partitions and not to repartition the drive. Don't be hasty and repartition the drive.

The time to really be concerned is when FDISK reports that "No Partitions Are Defined." This means something has destroyed the partition table. Do not use FDISK to re-create a partition table, because this also overwrites the DOS boot record and FAT. Try a rebuilding utility such as *DrivePro* to recreate the damaged partition table. If you are unable to rebuild the partition table, you might have to repartition and reformat the drive after all. If problems continue, the disk media itself might be damaged. In that case, you might have to replace the damaged drive.

Boot record

Next, the PC attempts to read the DOS Boot Record (DBR) located at cylinder 0, sector 1, head 1. If the drive cannot access DBR information, you will probably encounter error messages such as "Non System Disk or Disk Error", or "Disk Boot Failure." It is likely that the DBR has been damaged or erased, so try a rebuilding utility such as DrivePro to reconstruct the DBR.

Hidden files

After the partition table and boot record are read, the hidden system files (DOS kernel) are loaded next. The two hidden files are IO.SYS and MSDOS.SYS (or IBM-BIO.COM and IBMDOS.COM under IBM DOS). In actual operation, there is rarely a problem with these files unless one or both of the files has become corrupt, or the FAT has been damaged. When this occurs, you might receive a boot error message, or the system might simply lock up. For systems using DOS 5.x and later, restoring system files is a simple matter of booting from the floppy disk and typing SYS C: to transfer system files to the hard drive. If SYS fails to restore the hidden files, try the DOS CHKDSK or ScanDisk to examine and repair the drive FAT(s).

Command processor

Once hidden files are loaded and CONFIG.SYS has executed, the system attempts to load the command processor (COMMAND.COM). A frequent problem with COMMAND.COM occurs when someone copies files to a hard disk from a floppy that contains an older version of COMMAND.COM; this overwrites the current COMMAND.COM. When a system tries to boot with the older COMMAND.COM, it will lock up, or you will see a message such as "Bad or Missing Command Interpreter." A popular method of protecting your COMMAND.COM from accidental overwrites is to alter attributes making COMMAND.COM a read-only file using a DOS command such as:

```
attrib +R c:\command.com
```

When you find a faulty version of COMMAND.COM, try copying a correct version to the hard drive, or use SYS C: from the floppy disk to restore the correct system files to the hard drive. When COMMAND.COM is restored, you can try the ATTRIB command shown previously to protect the file. Another possibility is that a bad sector has developed in one of the clusters containing COMMAND.COM. You can use the DOS RECOVER utility on the floppy disk to locate and mark out the bad sectors, then recopy a fresh version of COMMAND.COM to the hard drive.

Recovering FAT and directory damage

Many drives eventually develop file structure problems because of viruses, age, and even through normal everyday operation. DOS provides tools that allow you to check the disk's condition and (to some extent) define and repair problems with the DOS directory structure and *FAT* (file allocation table). The CHKDSK utility is the first DOS disk recovery utility that you should be familiar with.

What CHKDSK does

Although it is rather crude compared to after-market software tools, CHKDSK allows you to perform several important disk operations. First, CHKDSK processes the disk to provide a detailed disk space and available memory report. The disk report is what most users think of when they consider CHKDSK, but its real function is to inspect directories and FATs to see if any discrepancies are found. Keep in mind that CHKDSK does not actually check individual files. CHKDSK also can check files for contiguity. Contiguous files occupy adjacent clusters on a disk, which makes the files much faster to load and save. When files become noncontiguous (fragmented), not only does disk access take longer, but portions of the fragmented file might become lost or disassociated. CHKDSK can identify and recover such lost clusters (also known as *allocation units*).

Running CHKDSK

The generic DOS command line for CHKDSK is:

```
CHKDSK drive:\path filename /F /V
```

The *drive* parameter specifies which logical drive is to be analyzed. By default, the current drive will be examined, but if you boot from the A: drive, you should specify C:\ as the drive and path. If you wish to check specific files for fragmentation (in addition to the full drive analysis), you should include the appropriate entries for the path and filename parameters. The /F switch allows CHKDSK to fix any problems that it finds with directories or FATs. Keep in mind that if the /F switch is removed, CHKDSK is prohibited from writing to the disk, which allows you to run CHKDSK at your discretion without the danger of accidental file corruption. You are advised to always run CHKDSK in this read-only mode until you understand the nature and extent of any problems. The /V switch forces CHKDSK to display the test verbatim that will list all files in a disk's directories and (in some cases) provide details of any errors encountered. *Warning: before initiating CHKDSK, you must exit Windows or DOS shell.* It also is wise to boot the system with an absolute minimum of device drivers and TSRs. As a general rule, CHKDSK should only be run with all other files closed and unchanging.

Understanding the CHKDSK report

By itself, the report (such as the one shown in Table 62-1) is pretty straightforward. The first five lines indicate the overall drive size, how much of that space is consumed by files, and how much space is left. If there were bad sectors on the disk, a sixth report line would be added to show the number of bytes in bad sectors. Keep in mind that a bad sector report poses no danger and does not reflect a faulty drive. Virtually all drives have some bad sectors that are marked in the FAT so that DOS will never attempt to use those bad areas. Most IDE drives are able to map out such elements entirely so that DOS does not even have to deal with such problems; you might not see a bad sector report, but even the best drives have bad sectors.

**Table 62-1. A typical
report generated by CHKDSK**

129652736	bytes total disk space
282624	bytes in 3 hidden files
409600	bytes in 156 directories
126298112	bytes in 3930 user files
2662400	bytes available on disk
2048	bytes in each allocation unit
63307	total allocation units on disk
1300	available allocation units on disk
655360	total bytes memory
517088	bytes free

The next three lines indicate the size of each cluster (or allocation unit), the total number of clusters, and the remaining clusters. For this particular drive, you see that each cluster is 2K. You also see that there are 63307 available allocation units on the disk ($63307 \times 2048 = 129652736$, which is the total disk space shown in line 1). The last two lines indicate the total amount of DOS memory available, and the amount of free DOS memory.

If you were to add a path and filename to the CHKDSK command line, one or more lines would be added to the report indicating the files contiguity. If the file was contiguous, you would see "All specified file(s) are contiguous." If there are one or more noncontiguous file blocks, you would see a report similar to "filename contains xxx noncontiguous blocks" where the filename is the name of the file being tested, and *xxx* corresponds to the number of noncontiguous blocks found. If disk errors are detected, one or more error messages will be produced.

Using CHKDSK

Simply stated, CHKDSK is a directory checker and patcher. CHKDSK compares the drive's directory tree with the FAT to ensure that there is a match between the two. When a discrepancy is detected between the FAT and directory structure, a corresponding error message is generated. As a result of this operation, most problems that CHKDSK reports are software related rather than a drive hardware fault. Four types of errors are reported most commonly: lost allocation units, allocation errors, cross-linked files, and invalid allocation units. Of these four categories, CHKDSK will only help you resolve lost allocation units and cross-linked files.

Recovering lost allocation units

Lost allocation units are generated when a program stops running unexpectedly without saving or deleting temporary files. Over time, lost allocation units can accumulate and take up valuable file space. When lost allocation units are detected, CHKDSK will alert you with an error message such as:

```
10 lost allocation units found in 3 chains.
Convert lost chains to files?
```

If you answer Y, lost allocation units will be converted to files with filenames such as FILE0000.CHK. You can then delete such files to free the recovered space for reuse. It's a great idea to use CHKDSK to recover lost allocation units before running a defragmenter or compression utility such as *DoubleSpace*. *Warning: it is important for you to realize that this is the only type of problem that CHKDSK can actually "fix" effectively*. Any other errors reported by CHKDSK cannot be fixed with CHKDSK. This is why it is so important that CHKDSK be run without the /F switch until you are aware of any particular problems. Allowing CHKDSK to "fix" a disk indiscriminately can do more harm than good.

Freeing cross-linked files

Cross-linked files are generated when two or more files or directories are listed in the FAT as using the same disk space (one or more allocation units are overlapping). When cross-linked files are detected, you will see an error message similar to:

JOHNSON.TXT is cross linked on allocation unit 11234

CHKDSK cannot "fix" a cross-linked file; it has no way to separate the overlap in allocation units. You should copy the file(s) specified in the error message somewhere else on the drive (so it will use different allocation units), then erase the original file(s). Keep in mind that some information in the cross-linked files might be corrupt. You might have to restore any such damaged files from a backup.

Limitations of CHKDSK

There are a number of instances where CHKDSK might not operate properly (if at all). CHKDSK will not process drives—or portions of drives—that have been created using SUBST, ASSIGN, or JOIN commands. CHKDSK also does not work on network drives. SUBST creates a virtual volume, which is little more than a subdirectory under the original volume that uses a different logical drive name. To use CHKDSK in a subdirectory created using SUBST, you must use the TRUENAME function to specify the actual path to the desired files. Note that TRUENAME is only available in DOS 4.0 and later. Suppose you used the SUBST function to create a virtual volume such as:

```
C:\>SUBST E: C:\TESTS\DIAGNOSTICS
```

When you switch to the E: drive, you are actually switching to the C:\TESTS\DIAGNOSTICS subdirectory. If you do not know what the actual subdirectory is, use the TRUENAME function:

```
E:\>TRUENAME E:
```

the system would respond:

```
C:\TESTS\DIAGNOSTICS
```

you can then use the CHKDSK function on the true directory listing:

```
E:\>CHKDSK C:\TESTS\DIAGNOSTICS\*.*
```

To use CHKDSK on an ASSIGNed drive, you must first "unassign" the drive. For example, if you assign a drive such as ASSIGN A=B, you will have to unassign the drive such as ASSIGN A=A. You can then run CHKDSK. After CHKDSK is complete, you can reassign the drive. There is no known way to use CHKDSK on a JOINed drive that is basically a directory tree created by the JOIN command. JOIN adds one disk volume to another disk volume as a subdirectory. Only the portion that is JOINed is skipped; all other portions of the drive are checked. In order to run CHKDSK on a network drive, you must reach the desired PC with the drive to be tested and suspend or disable any sharing of the drive while CHKDSK is executed.

Recovering files with damaged sectors

Even after decades of development, however, magnetic media is not perfect. Any physical defect on the media surface will render the entire file inaccessible. Over time, an aging hard drive will develop bad sectors. Bad sectors might be due to physical damage, or the gradual magnetic decay of sector ID information that is written then the disk is low-level formatted. In either case, a bad sector will ruin a file. This part of the chapter explains how to use the DOS RECOVER function to recover at least some of the damaged file.

Recognizing a damaged file

DOS is quite explicit when a bad sector is located. It will return a "bad sector" or "sector not found" error, or some similar error message indicating a defect in the file. Unfortunately, DOS does not take a proactive role in detecting and mapping out bad sectors. That is usually handled during the formatting process. As a result, files that might have once been running fine can suddenly develop faults. Similarly, unused sectors that fail can lay in wait to wreak havoc with new files.

What RECOVER does

The RECOVER command tells DOS to read the damaged file sector by sector (instead of by cluster) and reconstruct as much of the file as possible. The reconstructed file is placed in the root directory and assigned a filename with an .REC extension. Damaged sectors are removed from the file, and DOS marks the bad sectors automatically so that they cannot be used in the future. Recovered files are named sequentially, starting with FILE0001.REC. A typical example would be:

```
recover c:\mydir\myfile.dat
```

This syntax will scan the myfile.dat file in the mydir directory, then reconstruct as much of it as possible and place the reconstructed file (for example, FILE0001. REC) in the root directory of the c: drive. Other than the drive, path, and filename to be recovered, there are no command line switches associated with the RECOVER command. RECOVER also works on floppy disks with a syntax such as:

```
recover a:\flopfile.dat
```

Perhaps even more important than recovering individual files, the RECOVER command also can recover the contents of entire directories that might be inaccessible. This offers a powerful tool that can allow a technician to access a multitude of files (most or all of which are probably intact) that might otherwise be beyond reach. *A word of caution when recovering directories: recovered files are stored in the root directory of the selected drive.* There are only a limited number of entries supported in a root directory. If you try to recover more files than the root directory can hold, some files will be lost.

Now that you have discovered a faulty file and tried to recover as much of it as you can, you are faced with the awful question of damage control—how to restore the data that has been lost. Remember that RECOVER can help to make a damaged file accessible, but there is no guarantee that the recovered file will be usable at all. As a rule, recovered executable files (.EXE or .COM files) are probably useless. Even if you can start the recovered executable, the lost data will probably hang up the system or cause unpredictable operation. Data files (images, sound, text, pictures, and so on) are a bit more forgiving, but the lost data will likely result in distortion. The most effective means of repairing a damaged file is to replace it with a fresh copy from a backup. As always, a backup is your very best protection from disk problems. If you do not have a backup, you might be able to reconstruct the image or text file, but executable files cannot be saved.

Locking out bad sectors

The next question is: why bother recovering a file that will almost certainly be incomplete? One compelling reason for using RECOVER is the automatic bad sector marking feature; the bad sector will be locked out of use in the future. If a current backup is not available, the RECOVER function might be the only way for you to access your valuable data; better to lose a little bit of a file than the entire file. Third, RECOVER can save the day when there is trouble accessing a directory.

Recovering the MBR and DBR

The partition table (the master boot record or MBR) is the single most important sector on your hard drive. This one sector (512 bytes) contains specifications for up to four logical partitions, but it also provides instructions for starting the operating system (through the DBR). Without a viable MBR, the system will not even recognize the presence of the drive, let alone boot from it. Unfortunately, when the MBR is lost, it is extremely difficult to reconstruct (without losing all the data on the hard drive). The DOS boot record (DBR) is every bit as important because it is this sector that causes the DOS kernel files to load. There are no DOS utilities suited to MBR or DBR recovery. Of course, there is FDISK, but using FDISK destroys all data on the disk. For the purposes of this chapter, you need to access the existing data. You can always repartition and reformat the drive later. Luckily, there are some third-party tactics that might help.

Using MIRROR and UNFORMAT

Prevention is always faster and easier than a cure—the same is true of data recovery. If you are using DOS 5.0 or later, you have access to two DOS utilities that will allow you to back up and restore the MBR: MIRROR.EXE and UNFORMAT.COM. Before the hard drive fails, type:

```
MIRROR /PARTN
```

MIRROR will start and prompt you for a drive. Place a bootable floppy disk in A: (or B:) and let MIRROR copy the partition table to the floppy drive. If you do this regularly (say twice a year), you will have a good emergency backup in the event of drive trouble. When trouble occurs, simply boot from the floppy disk (which should contain UNFORMAT and the partition backup file) then type:

```
UNFORMAT /PARTN
```

UNFORMAT will ask for the location of the backup file (usually named PARTNSAV.FIL). Reference drive A: or B: (whichever drive contains the file) and continue. If the partition information looks appropriate, you can confirm the restoration, then reboot the system from the hard drive. Assuming a faulty MBR was the only problem, the hard drive should now work properly.

Using DrivePro

DrivePro from MicroHouse is one of the handiest commercial drive maintenance programs available. Like the MIRROR/UNFORMAT combination, DrivePro allows you to back up all vital boot information to a floppy before trouble strikes, then restore that data in the event of a problem. If you do not save the boot data in advance, you can use the Drive Boot Fixer function that will attempt to rebuild vital disk areas (specifically the MBR and DBR). There is certainly no guarantee that DrivePro can recover the boot records under all possible circumstances—media damage and drive/controller faults can still render the drive unusable—but it is often successful enough to allow you to recover your data. For technicians who typically do not have access to such backups from the customer, rebuilding is usually the only available tactic to resurrect a drive.

Using FDISK /MBR

You read that FDISK should not be used for data recovery because it made changes that would render your data inaccessible; that is not entirely true. There is an undocumented feature of FDISK that restores the startup code at the beginning of the MBR without touching the partition table itself. When the MBR cannot be rebuilt or restored, it may be possible to use FDISK /MBR and attempt to rebuild part of the MBR. When FDISK is run in this way, it is virtually automatic. You will not even see the FDISK menu; it will simply restore the startup code and return to the DOS prompt. Given the touchy nature of FDISK, you should attempt this undocumented function only as a last resort before scrapping the drive with a new low-level format.

Using rescue professional

So what happens when you need the data on a hard drive, but the partition data is lost and unrecoverable, or you see an error such as "Track 0 bad, disk unusable?" *Rescue Professional* by AllMicro is a self-booting data-recovery tool that is designed to interact directly with drive hardware and recover individual files or entire subdirectories. Unlike other procedures covered in this chapter that attempt to restore some sort of functionality to the drive, *Rescue Professional* makes no attempt to correct lost partition tables or DOS boot records. Its sole job is to operate the hard drive (if physically possible) and recover as many files as it can locate.

63
CHAPTER

Enhancing drive
performance

Hard drives have come to play an important role in PCs; not just as a storage medium, but as an extension to memory (Fig. 63-1). The new generation of graphic-oriented operating systems (Windows, Win95, Windows NT, OS/2, and so on) make use of drive space as virtual memory. This can dramatically extend the amount of apparent memory available in a system. However, the trend toward very large programs, extensive data files, and virtual memory operations have a disadvantage; drives operate much more slowly than system RAM. This is not a trivial difference. RAM is six orders of magnitude (not 6×, but 10^6) faster than a hard drive. As a consequence, hard drive performance has become a limiting factor in today's PCs. Making the hard drive faster and more efficient is now an important part of system optimization. This chapter is intended to help you understand the factors the influence drive performance, and provide a series of guidelines to maximize that performance.

63-1 A Toshiba Noteworthy 105Mb hard-disk drive.

Drive performance factors

In order to improve the performance of a hard drive, you must first understand the factors that influence drive performance in the first place. The two most important factors are time related: the amount of time it takes to locate a file, and the rate at which data can be passed back and forth between the drive and system; every other concern is intimately related to those two criteria.

Seek time

Because read/write heads are mechanical devices, it takes a finite amount of time to move them across a disk platter. The amount of time required to accomplish this move depends on several things: the size of the drive, and the type of mechanism moving the heads. Newer drives are typically quite small, so the distances that must be traversed are short. Smooth and efficient voice-coil actuators are the head drive mechanism of choice, so movement also is enhanced. The combination of these factors have drastically reduced seek time over the last 10 years, but seek time is still a major part of overall drive delays.

Unfortunately, *seek time* is a rather generic term; different manufacturers each measure seek time as a slightly different parameter. The best-case seek time is referred to as *track-to-track seek time* where the R/W heads only need to step in or out to the next adjacent track (or cylinder). This time is typically only a few hundred microseconds. If the best-case seek time is the time required to step between two adjacent tracks, the worst-case seek time is the time needed to step from the outermost track to the innermost track (or vice versa). Few manufacturers actually use this time since it seems so large. Instead, most drive manufacturers use an *average seek time*, which is the time needed to step halfway across the disk surface. Today, most drives offer average seek times between 8 and 15 ms.

File fragmentation

The interaction of operating systems also affects drive performance. When a drive is high-level formatted with an operating system, the drive's space is segregated into sets of adjacent sectors (called *clusters*). The size of a cluster depends on the size of the drive, but today's large (+500Mb) drives usually use 8K to 16K clusters. The cluster approach was designed to simplify file housekeeping—easing file storage tracking requirements while keeping wasted space acceptable. Although the system is less than ideal, it works, and has been in use since DOS was able to support hard drives. The problem with cluster-based file storage is that files are stored wherever clusters are available. Ideally, all of the clusters that compose a file should be contiguous, but that is a rare occurrence in actual practice. As a drive fills and old files are erased, clusters are filled and reclaimed throughout the drive.

Over time, files become scattered across the drive as DOS searches frantically for any available clusters. This scattering behavior is called *file fragmentation*, and it is a natural side effect of DOS. The problem with file fragmentation is that each time the continuity of a file is broken, the R/W heads have to be repositioned before another cluster can be read. If a file uses four clusters, and each cluster is several tracks apart, the heads will have to be repositioned four times to read or write that file. These additional seek times all add together to prolong the loading or saving of a file. In addition to these delays, the extra demands of R/W head positioning can eventually lead to premature drive failure.

Data transfer rate

Once the R/W heads have moved into position (during the seek time), data can flow to or from the drive. The rate at which data can flow is known as the *data transfer rate*. Data transfer is generally given in Mbits/s (megabits per second. If you divide this figure by 8, you will get Mbits/s. Most IDE drives operate at about 10Mbits/s, and some SCSI implementations can approach 20Mbits/s. Transfer rate is a key part of drive delay, because DOS is a single-task operating system, so it must wait for a file to be loaded or saved before any other operations can continue. The faster a file's data can be transferred to or from the drive, the shorter those delays would be.

The drive adapter

Where the process of R/W head seek is a function of the drive's internal construction, data transfer is largely a function of the drive's controller circuitry (or drive adapter). There are three factors influencing the data rate: the width of the data path, the technology of the drive, and the overall construction of the drive adapter circuit itself. The data path width is the number of bits that travel simultaneously between the drive and the PC. Older XT-type controllers used an 8-bit data width. Most traditional ISA-based systems use 16-bit controllers. IDE and SCSI drives typically use 16-bit interfaces. A 16-bit interface can carry twice as much data at any one moment in time than an 8-bit interface. As the adoption of 32-bit expansion ports becomes more commonplace, drives and drive adapters will certainly grow to take full advantage of the data path.

The drive/interface technology relates to the way in which data is encoded to and decoded from the drive. Some of the original drive technologies used MFM and RLL recording techniques. They were effective, but they limited data transfer. As drives became more sophisticated, improved encoding techniques not only helped to increase the drive's density, but supported faster data transfer as well. SCSI and IDE interfaces use some of the most efficient encoding available. Circuit design is a more indirect variable affecting adapter performance. Today's highly integrated controllers are able to process and transfer data far faster than older controller circuits. When combined with other hardware techniques such as drive caching, performance can be fundamentally enhanced at the hardware level. Ultimately, the drive's underlying technology affects data transfer.

Drive interleave

In the early days of PCs, drive data could be delivered at a much higher rate than the interface and system CPU were capable of handling. This presented a problem for early drive designers; how do you slow down a drive spinning at 3200 rpm so that the CPU can keep pace? Drive designers answered this question by introducing the idea of *interleave*. By staggering the order of each sector around a track, the drive is forced to make several complete rotations in order to read all sectors. Although the drive rotates at the same speed, larger amounts of interleave affect the drive's apparent speed; larger interleaves slow the drive (and vice versa). A 3:1 interleave is typical of XT-style MFM drives. The disk has to rotate three times in order to read all 17 sectors. A 2:1 interleave is more efficient, and is often found in older AT MFM and RLL drives. Two complete rotations are needed to read all 17 sectors. The most efficient interleave is 1:1 (effectively no interleave) where all the sectors are in order around the track. An entire track can be read in one rotation. As a general rule, the larger the interleave, the slower the drive.

Hardware drive enhancements

Although shaving a few milliseconds from a drive's performance might seem unnecessary, streamlining the drive hardware can have some substantial advantages, most noticeably a reduction in hesitation when files are loaded or saved. Fewer drive errors and greater overall reliability are other advantages worth considering. This part of the chapter outlines some recommendations for improving drive performance through hardware.

Check the drive connections

The integrity of electrical cables and contacts play a surprisingly vital role in drive performance. It is not unusual for errors to creep into data transferred between the drive and system. In many cases, the error correction techniques used with hard drives will successfully compensate for such problems, but the recovery process demands extra time as the system tries to read or write the erroneous data again. By improving the quality of signal connections, data errors can be reduced, resulting in slightly faster drive performance.

As a general rule, start with the data cable(s) between the drive and its adapter board. *Be sure to remove all power from the PC and disconnect the ac cable from the wall outlet.* Make sure that the cables are installed properly and completely. Loose connectors can easily result in intermittent data problems. It is natural for a layer of oxide to cover the contact metals in each connector. However, oxides act as an insulator, raising the resistance of a connection and increasing the probability of data errors. Try removing each connector (one at a time) and re-insert it carefully; this will help to wipe away any oxides. Also inspect each data cable. There should be no cuts, wear, or abrasions in the cable insulation. If you find a worn or damaged cable, try replacing it. The overall length of data cables also affects signal integrity; longer cables allow for greater data errors. If you find an unusually long cable, try replacing it with a shorter one. For example, you might only have one hard drive in the system, but the data cable can be fitted for a dual-drive installation.

Next, check the drive adapter and make sure that it is installed properly and completely in its expansion slot. Remove the drive adapter and re-insert it in its expansion slot; this will scrape off any buildup of oxidization on the adapters card-edge fingers. If the adapter board seems loose in its expansion slot, try moving the board to a new slot.

Manage the interleave

Most of the contemporary hard drives in service today (IDE and SCSI) use an interleave of 1:1 to allow for the fastest possible transfer of data off the drive platters. If you find yourself low-level formatting a hard drive, be careful to avoid a less efficient interleave factor; even if it is provided as a recommended default. A drive that's working properly at 1:1 will not work any better at a different interleave. For older drives that use a larger interleave, however, it might be possible to reset the interleave when the drive is low-level formatted. Most PCs since 1986 have been fast enough to tolerate a 1:1 interleave given a fairly recent controller. If you encounter an ST506/412 or an ESDI drive system with an interleave of 2:1 or 3:1 (or more), try altering the interleave during a low-level format. Keep in mind that an old drive controller might not tolerate a lower interleave.

Manage the bad sectors

Another function of low-level formatting is to identify and mark bad sectors and tracks to prevent their being used by DOS. If the low-level format utility for your particular drive offers the ability to find bad areas (sometimes called a *surface scan* or *media analysis* option), you can locate and lock out any bad drive areas that might have failed since the drive left the factory. Reducing the number of bad sectors available to DOS will help to prevent file errors.

Upgrade the drive hardware

The points covered are largely issues of drive maintenance. Although they will all contribute to faster and more reliable drive performance, few tactics improve drive performance as much as a new drive system. As seek times fall, transfer rates climb, and reliability continues to improve, a new hard drive and adapter might be an appropriate and timely solution to a slow, old drive. In some cases, a new drive adapter alone might be enough to enhance an existing drive, but because IDE and SCSI drives contain the vast majority of their controlling circuitry right on board the drive itself, you will most likely be replacing the drive and adapter card.

Software drive enhancements

Although hardware upgrades provide some impressive improvements, system software has come to play an important role in drive performance as well. Disk caching and compression techniques are constantly attempting to push the limits of PC processing capabilities. This part of the chapter covers a variety of software tactics to enhance drive operations.

Keep the drive defragmented

As you saw in this chapter, file fragmentation can slow a drive by forcing excessive R/W head positioning. This can cause particular problems for disk-intensive environments such as Windows, especially the Windows swap file. A *defragmenter* is a disk utility that re-arranges files to make each related cluster contiguous. By defragmenting the drive regularly, you can avoid the delays of excessive head positioning, and keep the drive running smoothly.

Make Use of buffers

DOS provides a primitive form of caching through the use of RAM buffers. Buffers are allocated through the BUFFERS command in your CONFIG.SYS file. Each buffer sets aside 528 bytes of RAM; 512 bytes to bold a sector's worth of disk information, and 16 bytes for overhead data. The memory required for each buffer is drawn from conventional memory. So the number of buffers set aside for drive use is often a tradeoff of conventional memory for performance. As a minimum, 20 buffers should be set aside for a hard drive (although 30 to 40 buffers is more common in to-day's systems). Depending on the speed of your system, you should be able to adjust the number of buffers for optimum drive performance. Remember that you must re-boot the system each time a change is made to the CONFIG.SYS file.

Make use of caching

The premise of *disk caching* is fundamentally the same as memory caching; when the disk is read into memory, extra information is read into cache memory as well (known as *read caching*). Because RAM can be read much faster than the disk, the effective disk speed is greatly improved. Another caching technique stores file data in memory until there is an idle moment for the system to copy the file to disk. Once again, the speed of RAM allows the file to appear written almost immediately (known as *write caching*). There are generally two forms of caching used with disk drives: hardware and software.

Hardware caching uses a limited amount of RAM implemented on the hard drive itself under the control of drive BIOS. Software caching uses a utility (such as Smart-Drive) to allocate and manage a portion of system RAM as the disk cache. The advantage of software caching is that many different drives are supported (floppy drives and CD-ROM drives). On the negative side, software caching requires conventional or upper memory for the utility itself, as well as extra RAM for the cache. If you are able to activate caching, it is almost always worthwhile.

Eliminate drive compression

Drive compressors such as DoubleSpace and Stacker have proven to be very effective and reliable tools for extending limited drive capacity. Unfortunately, the translation of data to and from a compressed state requires more time during drive operations; there's no way around it. If you are already faced with a compressed drive, it is possible to uncompress the drive if you need to squeeze out every last element of performance (but it is often more work than it is worth). If you are contemplating adding compression, consider the tradeoff between speed and performance first.

64
CHAPTER

Fans and cooling devices

When electrical power is applied to a circuit, the circuit uses that power to perform work. In the case of a PC, work would be the myriad of processing operations that go on throughout the computer every moment. For computers, as with all machines, the conversion of power into work is not a perfect one—a portion of power is dissipated in the form of heat. Over time, the buildup of heat will cause a PC to fail prematurely. As a result, it is very important that a computer system be properly outfitted to deal with heat.

You might wonder why heat is taken so seriously; after all, the vast majority of ICs and passive components found in a PC dissipate very little heat at all. Unfortunately, it is the few components that do produce heat that cause most problems: drive motors, power supply regulating circuits, and the CPU. When taken together with the lower heat output from other devices, the temperature inside a PC cabinet can easily exceed 80°C. Heat has dramatic effects on materials and semiconductors. Heat accelerates the breakdown of insulating enamel on transformer and motor windings. Excessive heat also causes semiconductor junctions to change characteristics and eventually break down. Thus, proper cooling is vital to a computer's overall reliability. This chapter is intended to illustrate the various methods used to cool a PC, explain the effects that inhibit cooling, and show you how to deal with cooling problems.

Understanding cooling methodologies

In order to understand how various cooling devices work, you must understand some basic principles about heat transfer. First, heat tends to travel from places of more heat to places of less heat. If you don't believe this, apply a hot soldering iron to one end of a wire, and see how long it takes for the other end to get warm. Although this is a tremendous oversimplification, you get the basic idea. There are three general modes of heat transfer: convection, conduction, and radiation.

Convection is the transfer of heat through air currents. A heat source warms nearby air that rises. The warmer rising air is replaced by cooler air that is then heated. Eventually, a circulating airflow develops. This is the basic principle behind all home heating systems. It also is an essential element of PC cooling. You might ask how heating and cooling can be the same thing—well, as heat is transferred to the air, the device providing the heat is cooled. When a CPU heats up, it tends to heat the surrounding air. Unfortunately, such static convection has limited effect in a PC. Static convection does not remove enough heat to cool a very hot device (such as a CPU). Static convection also relies on circulating flows of air that is difficult to establish in the close quarters of a highly obstructed PC. A way to multiply the effect of convection is to force an airflow across the heated device. Fans are used to force air through the PC. This forced convection provides much more effective cooling, and can be directed to specific areas around the PC. Most of the cooling methods covered in this chapter rely on forced convection.

Conduction is the transfer of heat through physical contact. The radiator system in your car works this way. By circulating cooler liquid around a warmer surface, the cooler liquid picks up the surface heat, thus cooling the surface. The liquid, now warmed, is circulated to a chilling assembly that is intended to take away any heat picked up by the liquid, so the liquid is kept cooled. In a car, this is the front radiator that is cooled by the forced air of a large fan. Although conduction is a much more effective means of cooling than convection, conduction can only cool the areas of contact, and convection can cool large areas. Some CPU cooling devices use circulating liquid, but these are rare and expensive. As a consequence, you will rarely find conductive cooling techniques in PCs.

Finally, *radiation* is the transfer of heat through infrared emission. For example, the warmth you feel from sunlight or a sun lamp is caused by the effects of infrared radiation. Because there are no significant infrared emission sources in a PC, radiation will not be discussed further. At this point, you can see how these heat transfer principles are used in a PC environment.

Natural convection

Natural (or static) convection is the cooling technique used in most computer monitors. Take a look at the rear enclosure on your monitor, and notice that there are open slots along the top and bottom of the enclosure. The openings beneath the monitor are for air intake, and the upper slots allow air to escape. These slots provide a free flow of air through the monitor. Yet, this process works without the benefit of a fan. You can easily see how this process works. Let the monitor run for a while, and place your hand over the upper slots; you can feel hot air rising. The warm circuitry inside the running monitor heats the surrounding air that rises up and out. As warm air is displaced, new cooler air is drawn in from the bottom slots. Although monitor circuits will heat up (especially the power supply), none of the components become hot enough to require forced convection.

As you might expect, the success of this method depends on an unobstructed air path. If Fluffy the cat curls up on top of the monitor, the exhaust vents will be blocked. This interrupts the flow of air, and temperatures inside the monitor will increase. Eventually, you might notice the display rolling or shifting position; these are initial warnings that the monitor circuits are overheating. If the blockage continues for an extended period, the monitor might fail prematurely. Besides monitors, dot matrix and ink jet printers typically rely on convection to cool their circuits.

Heatsinks

Another rule of heat transfer is that the effectiveness with which heat is transferred depends on the amount of surface area that is exposed. Check out the radiator in your car, each of those small fins adds a small amount of surface area to the overall radiating surface. This is the principle behind heatsinks (Figs. 64-1 and 64-2). By adding a heatsink to a heated component, you increase the effective surface area that is open to the air. Because more air can flow over a larger surface (through natural or forced convection), the component stays cooler. For components that become inordinately hot during normal operation (such as regulator ICs or CPUs), a heatsink is a very simple and inexpensive way to enhance cooling. Of course, heatsinks are not just for ICs. Take a look at the print head of a dot matrix printer. You'll find a set of cast aluminum fins set right into the head assembly.

64-1 IERC self-adhesive heatsinks. IERC (International Electronic Research Corporation), Burbank, CA

64-2
An IERC CPU fan and heatsink.
IERC (International Electronic Research Corporation),
Burbank, CA

Chassis fans

Although natural convection is fine for cooling monitors and printers, PCs are too cramped and obstructed to establish a consistent airflow. As a result, air must be forced through the system. This is usually accomplished with one or more fans positioned in the rear chassis. By positioning the fans blowing out of the enclosure, cooler air can be vacuumed into the system through strategically located intake slots in the housing. Some systems use a second fan blowing into the enclosure from the front chassis. This kind of push-pull cooling develops a very strong airflow.

Fan cards

Even with good-quality, chassis-mounted fans, some high-performance systems require an extra measure of cooling—especially in the CPU area. A growing trend in PC cooling is the use of a fan card, a standard-sized expansion board with one or two +12-Vdc fans mounted to it. This allows you to place the fan card in the immediate vicinity of a CPU or drive to improve the local airflow. However, there are some limitations to fan cards that you should be aware of. First, many expansion boards are full-size, 16-bit boards, so the chances are very good that at least one side of the fan card will be somewhat obstructed by another expansion board. As long as the fan card is blowing away from the adjacent expansion board, this should not present a problem. If the fan card is blowing toward the adjacent expansion board, a region of turbulent air will be produced that reduces the fan card's overall effectiveness.

Another concern is *EMI* (electomagnetic interference) produced by the fan motors. As inductive devices, fans are notorious for electromagnetic interference. If the fan card is placed in close proximity of a sensitive device such as a drive controller or video capture board, the electrical noise produced by the fans can degrade the other device's performance, or cause operating errors. There also is the possibility that electrical noise from the fans might travel back along the +12-Vdc voltage line and interfere with other devices in the system using +12 Vdc. It is always wise to approach fan cards with a certain amount of suspicion.

CPU fans

CPUs have always run hot, and the reason is readily understandable; a single microscopic transistor dissipates virtually no heat, but the combined heat from over three million transistors crammed into a wafer the size of a fingernail becomes extreme. The surface temperature of a Pentium can easily exceed 100°C. With such a strong concentration of heat, even forced air through a heatsink can leave a CPU running hot. To manage heat in the latest clock tripled CPUs and Pentiums, a CPU fan can be used. Basically, a CPU fan mounts a small, high-speed fan that blows down into a heatsink assembly. The inrushing air cools the heatsink (and the CPU) very effectively.

Unfortunately, there are some disadvantages to the CPU fan. First, the added height of a heatsink/fan combination can obstruct full-length expansion boards. Similarly, if your particular motherboard places the CPU under a low-hanging drive or other chassis obstruction, a CPU fan might not fit. Before using a CPU fan, make sure that you have several cubic inches of available space over the CPU. The CPU fan also requires power. Check that you have a power connector available from the power supply and make sure that the CPU fan assembly comes with a built-in Y connector. Another possible problem involves vibration. Because the fan is now physically coupled to the CPU, there is a bit of debate over what (if any) damage is done to the CPU by fan vibrations over the long term.

Liquid and piezoelectric devices

CPU cooling also can be accomplished through conductive devices. There are a small number of liquid cooling devices available for CPUs, most of which are used in Pentium notebook systems that do not have the space for heatsinks or CPU fans. The drawback to a liquid-cooled system is clear enough—a breach in the cooling loop can deposit liquid onto the motherboard and result in real damage. Extra expense is another consideration.

Piezoelectric devices mount a layer of piezoelectric material over the CPU. As the crystal layer vibrates, a temperature differential develops through it, which actually results in a cooler surface (applied against the CPU). The problem with piezoelectric chillers is their expense, as well as the yet-unclear potential for CPU damage from long-term exposure to vibration.

Cooling problems

Cooling is often the most overlooked and neglected features of a PC. In many off-the-shelf systems, cooling is sufficient. But over time, constant use, environmental factors, and upgrades, the cooling plan might need to be reviewed or revised. As with so many other elements of PC service, successful troubleshooting means knowing where to look. This part of the chapter shows you the factors to consider when evaluating PC cooling and cooling problems.

Fan wear

Fans do not last forever. They are electromechanical devices, and eventually the motor or rotating shaft will wear out and fail. Normally, PC cooling fans are very quiet devices; they have to be, because loud operation in a home or office environment would quickly become maddening. The first sign of fan failure is excessive noise. A persistent buzz or grinding sound immediately points to a fan problem. The fan motor also might be unusually hot. In extreme cases, the fan will hang up and stop altogether (it might start again if you nudge it gently). The best way to deal with a cranky fan is to replace it outright. A new fan must have the same three major characteristics of the original fan: (1) physical mounting dimensions, (2) operating voltage, usually +12 Vdc, and (3) airflow rate.

Bad heatsink contact

In order for a heatsink to be effective, it must have a strong physical connection to the host IC, which ensures that the maximum amount of heat is transferred from the IC to the heatsink. The better that contact is, the more heat is transferred into the heatsink, and the cooler the IC runs. There are a variety of ways to secure a heatsink, but clipping the IC and heatsink together has been easiest and most popular. However, not all heatsink clips are tight, and even a tight clip does not guarantee good contact. Check to see that the heatsink is attached securely, and be sure to add a layer of thermally conductive compound (typically a thick white cream) between the IC and heatsink. Thermal grease fills in any air space between the IC and heatsink, so heat transfer is enhanced. Suspect heatsink problems when the system locks up randomly for no apparent reason, or the CPU suffers chronic failures.

One of the more recent trends in heatsink marketing is the use of stick-on heatsinks—just peel off an adhesive backing and stick the heatsink in place. It sounds terrific in principle, but adhesive is often more of a thermal insulator than a thermal conductor. As a general rule, go with the clip-on heatsinks wherever possible.

CPU vibration failure

CPU fans are generally regarded as one of the most effective CPU cooling devices available, but there is a certain amount of debate over the effect of long-term fan vibration on the CPU. Some manufacturers argue that because the fan is physically attached to the heatsink (and CPU), the fan's vibrations will be carried directly into the CPU that will shorten the CPU's working life. However, there are no studies available to confirm or deny that possibility. As a result, you should rely on your own experience when checking or recommending CPU heatsinks. Normally, it is reasonable to expect that the cooler CPU should run longer and more reliably. So if you find that the CPU fails frequently when fitted with a CPU fan, try a large heatsink instead.

Sunlight

Anyone who has ever been in the sunlight understands how warming it can be. This natural warming can be magnified through glass, so sunlight indoors can feel even warmer. When a PC sits exposed to sunlight for prolonged periods, the metal enclosures tend to pick up much of that heat (and heat the air inside). Although sunlight alone rarely provides enough heating to endanger the system, it can intensify the cooling demands while the system is operating. As a general rule, keep the PC and its peripherals out of direct sunlight for extended periods of time.

Thermal cycling

Turn it off or leave it on? This is the perennial PC question, and one that continues to be a hotbed of debate among technicians. The best way to answer this question is to approach it both theoretically and practically. Theoretically, each time material heats up, it expands. When the material cools down again, it contracts. Thus, every time a PC is turned on, the ICs, solder joints, and wiring tend to expand until the system reaches a stable operating temperature. When the PC is turned off, it gradually cools down, and its components contract until the PC returns to room temperature. Over time, this accordion effect of expansion and contraction (or *thermal cycling*) is known to cause material to fatigue and fracture—an IC breaks down, or a solder joint becomes intermittent. As a consequence of this effect, long-time PC veterans argue that the PC should be left on constantly. This allows the system to achieve a stable temperature, so thermal cycling is eliminated.

From a practical standpoint, however, the view is a bit different. First, the damaging effect of thermal cycling is dependent on the amount of temperature difference. Frankly, today's PCs just don't get that hot (although the CPUs can blaze if not properly cooled). Cooler PCs are affected less by thermal damage. Drive wear also is another nonissue, with current, cool-running designs exhibiting *MTBF*s (mean time between failure) of over 300,000 hours. The other consideration is the rising cost of power, which is wasted by simply leaving the PC on overnight. On the other hand, there is no reason to power down the PC each time you get up for a coffee. Ultimately, the current thinking is to go ahead and turn the PC off overnight, or whenever you must leave the system for more than a few hours.

Excessive devices

Many PCs are eventually upgraded with more RAM, more drives, new CPUs, and so on. Each new device added to the system contributes to its overall heat production. For heavily expanded systems, it might be necessary to augment cooling with a supplemental exhaust fan or inlet fan. The general yardstick for judging the need for extra cooling is to feel the air exhausting from the system. If the air feels comfortable or somewhat warm, chances are that cooling is adequate. If the air feels hot, it's time to add a new fan. True, this is a rather subjective means of measurement, but it is accurate enough for most situations.

Dust

Perhaps the most significant problem of reliable, long-term PC cooling is dust, which is always present in everyday air. For the purposes of this book, dust includes other contaminants such as pet hair and cigarette smoke. Dust has two effects on the PC. First, dust collects on the fan blades and intake vents. This interrupts and limits airflow into and out of the system. Second, dust can collect on a printed circuit board where airflow is limited. The dust acts as a thermal blanket that prevents normal convective cooling. When upgrading or servicing a PC, make it a point to vacuum any accumulations of dust in or around the system.

Alternating-current power problems

Power supplies can be serious sources of heat, especially in the regulator portion of the supply that is designed to maintain a stable voltage output as ac input levels and load demands change. If ac climbs over its nominal value, the regulator must work harder to maintain a constant output; this results in excessive power supply heating. Lagging ac levels result in larger amounts of current being drawn to keep the power output steady; this also causes extra heating. Persistent power supply failures or unusually hot operation might suggest problems with ac (or an overloaded supply).

Blocked vents

Air needs a clear path into and out of the system, which is usually accommodated through vent slots located around the enclosure. If the vent slots are obstructed or blocked, airflow might be interrupted (this is especially detrimental to devices relying on natural convection for cooling). You can see the importance of proper ventilation by reviewing the installation guidelines for almost any piece of consumer electronics. Most guidelines recommend that you leave several inches of free space on each side of the enclosure. Make sure that vent slots are unobstructed, and clear of dust or debris.

Troubleshooting cooling problems

Cooling problems manifest themselves in a variety of ways, usually through intermittent system operation and frequent failures. This part of the chapter is intended to illustrate some of the more perplexing cooling problems that you should be aware of.

Symptom 1. The fan is producing an unusual amount of noise, but it seems to be working properly This can often happen after replacing a fan, and is typically the result of fan vibrations being introduced to the PC chassis. Although this is rarely harmful to the system, it can become quite annoying. Check the way in which the new fan is mounted, and be sure that any damping material is in place. Otherwise, you might try adding small standoffs of foam around each mounting screw to damp vibration. Of course, if the fan is original equipment, it might be wearing out and need to be replaced. Try a new fan.

Symptom 2. The fan has stopped turning First, check to see if the fan has an intermittent-type controller by a small internal thermostat. If so, it might simply be that the fan has stopped normally. You should see it start and stop as required. However, most fans turn continuously, so if the fan has stopped, it might have become disconnected, or it might have failed. Check the fan's power connection. If the problem persists, try a new fan.

Symptom 3. The CPU freezes intermittently This is a classic sign of CPU overheating. Although overheating will not necessarily destroy a CPU immediately, prolonged or repeated overheating can precipitate a permanent failure. Check the heatsink or CPU fan attached to the CPU. *Warning: be sure to let the system cool before touching the heatsink.* If the cooling device is loose, re-attach it securely (be sure to use thermal compound). If the heatsink is secure, but overheating continues, try a more aggressive device such as a CPU fan.

Symptom 4. You are experiencing frequent CPU failures Chronic CPU failures are rare occurrences, and can often be traced to insufficient cooling. If the CPU does not have a heatsink, try adding one. If a heatsink is already attached, try a larger heatsink or CPU fan. However, if a CPU fan is already in use, there might be a vibration problem that shortens the CPU's working life; try downgrading to a regular heatsink.

Symptom 5. You are experiencing frequent drive failures This is typical of the hard drive in an overloaded system. When replacing the hard drive, take careful note of the exhaust heat, and the overall number of devices in the system. If the exhaust is unusually warm, or there are many adjacent drives in the system, try mounting the replacement drive by itself away from other drives; maybe in a rear drive bay. If possible, try mounting the drive vertically. If it is impossible to relocate the offending drive, try adding a supplemental fan, or a fan card, to improve airflow over the drive.

65

CHAPTER

Floppy-drive testing and alignment

Floppy disk drives (Fig. 65-1) are electromechanical devices. Their motors, lead screws, sliders, levers, and linkages are all subject to wear and tear. As a result, a drive can develop problems that are caused by mechanical defects instead of electronic problems. Fortunately, few mechanical problems are fatal to a drive. With the proper tools, you can test a troublesome drive and often correct problems simply through careful cleaning and alignment. This chapter explains the concepts and procedures for floppy drive testing and alignment.

65-1 A Teac FD-235 3½-inch floppy drive. Teac America, Inc.

Recognizing the problems

As a technician, you will need to understand when a floppy drive is showing signs that might be related to alignment errors. In general, you should always respond to a chronic drive error by examining the disk media itself. Slowly spin the disk and observe both sides of the oxide layer. The layer should be smooth and even throughout like the smooth surface of a quiet pond. If you see any marks or scratches on the disk, you should suspect that either the R/W heads are misaligned, or that there is a significant buildup of oxides on the R/W head(s). If you have not already cleaned the R/W heads as part of your regular repair practices, clean them now. If the problem persists, the head assembly is probably severely misaligned, and you should replace the drive or re-align it as you see fit.

Other classic indicators of alignment trouble are reading and writing errors. You see, data is checked when it is read from or written to a drive. When you encounter a drive that has difficulty reading diskettes that were written on another PC (or writes diskettes that other PCs have difficulty reading), the drive's alignment is in serious doubt. Fortunately, alignment software can test the drive and report on its specifications, allowing you to see any unacceptable performance characteristics. If you find that the drive is faulty, you can then decide to replace or re-align the drive at your discretion.

Repair versus replace

Floppy drive alignment continues to be a matter of debate. The cost of a floppy drive alignment package is often as high as the cost of a new drive. When compared with the rising costs of labor and alignment packages, many technicians question the practice of drive alignment when new drives are readily available. True, most casual PC enthusiasts would not choose to align a misbehaving drive. However, testing software has an important place in any toolbox. At the very least, test software can confirm a faulty drive and eliminate the guesswork involved in drive replacement. For enthusiasts and technicians who have a volume of drives to service, alignment tools offer a relatively efficient means of recovering drives that might otherwise be discarded. Ultimately, one of a technician's most vital tools is an open mind; you can repair or replace the drive depending on what makes the most economic sense.

Using the tools

Drive alignment is not a new concept. Technicians have tested and aligned floppy drives for years using oscilloscopes and test disks containing precise, specially recorded data patterns. You might already be familiar with the classical "cat's eye" or "index burst" alignment patterns seen on oscilloscopes. This kind of manual alignment required you to find the right test point on your particular drive's PC board, locate the proper adjustment in the drive assembly, and interpret complex (sometimes rather confusing) oscilloscope displays. Traditionally, manual alignment required a substantial investment in an oscilloscope, test disk, and stand-alone drive exerciser equipment to run a drive outside of the computer.

Although manual drive alignment techniques are still used today, they are being largely replaced by automatic alignment techniques. Software developers have created interactive control programs to operate with their specially recorded data disks. These software tool kits provide all the features necessary to operate a suspect drive through a wide variety of tests while displaying the results numerically or graphically right on a computer monitor (Fig. 65-2). As you make adjustments, you can see real-time results displayed on the monitor. Software-based testing eliminates the need for an oscilloscope and ancillary test equipment. You also do not need to know the specific signal test points for every possible drive. There are three popular tool kits on the market; *AlignIt* by Landmark Research International Corp., *FloppyTune* by Data Depot, Inc., and *DriveProbe* by Accurite Technologies Incorporated. The contact information for each manufacturer is included in the companion disk.

```
AUTOMATIC Drive Test                              'Esc'- For Previous Menu
```

Test	Track	Head 0 Data		Head 1 Data		Test Limits	Results	
Speed	NA	300 RPM	/ 199.7 mS			300 ± 6 RPM	Pass	NA
Eccentricity	44	100 uI		NA		0 ± 300 uI	Pass	NA
Radial	0	96%	50 uI	100%	0 uI	60 - 100 %	Pass	Pass
Radial	40	93%	-100 uI	90%	-150 uI	60 - 100 %	Pass	Pass
Radial	79	96%	50 uI	90%	-150 uI	60 - 100 %	Pass	Pass
Azimuth	76	6 Min		4 Min		0 ± 30 Min	Pass	Pass
Index	0	414 uS		407 uS		400 ± 600 uS	Pass	Pass
Index	79	397 uS		380 uS		400 ± 600 uS	Pass	Pass
Hysteresis	40	100 uI		NA		0 ± 250 uI	Pass	NA

```
     uI = Micro-inches      uS = Microsecond       mS = Millisecond
     Min = Minutes          NA = Not Applicable    NT = Not Tested
Note: Radial is expressed as LOBE RATIO and OFFSET from track center line.
         Auto Test Completed  'Esc' For Previous Menu
```

65-2 The DriveProbe automatic drive test display. Accurite Technologies, Inc.

Advanced tools

Although software tools make up a majority of the typical floppy drive service options, the tools available to serious floppy drive service technicians do not stop at software. With the proper supplemental test hardware (such as the DriveProbe standard or advanced edition from Accurite Technologies). The advanced edition is shown in Fig. 65-3), a PC can be turned into a comprehensive floppy drive test bed that supports all types of standard PC drives, as well as Macintosh drives and many types of floppy-disk duplicator drives.

Aligning the drive

At this point in the chapter, you are ready to start the testing/alignment software and go to work. Before starting your software, however, you should disable any caching software that will cache your floppy drive or drives. Because caching software affects the way in which data is read or written to the floppy disk, caching will adversely affect the measurements produced by the alignment software. To ensure the truest transfer of data to or from the floppy disk, boot the PC from a clean boot disk to disable all TSRs or device drivers in the system. Once the alignment software is started, there are eight major tests to gauge the performance of a floppy drive; clamping, spindle speed, track 00, radial alignment, azimuth alignment, head step, hystere-

Accurite Technologies, Inc.

65-3 DriveProbe: the advanced edition.

sis, and head width. Keep in mind that not all tests have adjustments that can correct the corresponding fault.

Drive cleaning

Floppy drive R/W heads are not terribly complex devices, but they do require precision positioning. Heads must contact the disk media in order to read or write information reliably. As the disk spins, particles from the disk's magnetic coating wear off and form a deposit on the heads. Accumulations of everyday contaminants such as dust and cigarette smoke also contribute to deposits on the heads. Head deposits present several serious problems. First, deposits act as a wedge, forcing heads away from the disk surface resulting in lost data and read/write errors, and generally unreliable and intermittent operation. Deposits tend to be more abrasive than the head itself, so dirty heads can generally reduce a disk's working life. Finally, dirty heads can cause erroneous readings during testing and alignment. Because alignment disks are specially recorded in a very precise fashion, faulty readings will yield erroneous information that can actually cause you to adjust the drive incorrectly. As a general procedure, clean the drive thoroughly before you test or align it.

R/W heads also can be cleaned manually or automatically. The manual method is just as the name implies. Use a high-quality head cleaner on a soft, lint-free, antistatic swab, and scrub both head surfaces by hand. Wet the swab but do not soak it. You might need to repeat the cleaning with fresh swabs to ensure that all residual deposits are removed. Be certain that all computer power is *off* before manual cleaning, and allow a few minutes for the cleaner to dry completely before restoring power. If you do not have head cleaning chemicals on hand, you can use fresh ethyl or isopropyl alcohol. The advantage to manual cleaning is thoroughness; heads can be cleaned very well with no chance of damage due to friction.

Most software tool kits provide a cleaning disk and software option that allows you to clean the disk automatically. With computer power on and the software tool kit loaded and running, insert the cleaning disk and choose the cleaning option from your software menu. Software will then spin the drive for some period of time—10 to 30 seconds should be adequate, but do not exceed 60 seconds of continuous cleaning. Choose high-quality cleaning disks that are impregnated with a lubricant. Avoid bargain off-the-shelf cleaning disks that force you to wet the disk. Wetted cleaning disks are often harsh, and prolonged use can actually damage the heads from excessive friction. Once the drive is clean, it can be tested and aligned.

Clamping

A floppy disk is formatted into individual tracks laid down in concentric circles along the media. Because each track is ideally a perfect circle, it is critical that the disk rotate evenly in a drive. If the disk is not on-center for any reason, it will not spin evenly. If a disk is not clamped evenly, the eccentricity introduced into the spin might be enough to allow heads to read or write data to adjoining tracks. A clamping test should be performed first, after the drive is cleaned, because high eccentricity can adversely affect disk tests. Clamping problems are more pronounced on 13.34-cm (5¼ inch) drives where the soft mylar hub ring is vulnerable to damage from the clamping mechanism.

Start your software tool kit from your computer's hard drive, then insert the alignment disk containing test patterns into the questionable drive. Select a clamping or eccentricity test (Fig. 65-4) and allow the test to run a bit. Typical software tool kits can measure eccentricity in terms of microinches-from-true-center. If clamping is off by more than a few hundred microinches, the spindle or clamping mechanisms should be replaced. You also can simply replace the floppy drive. Try reinserting and retesting the disk several times to confirm your results. Repeated failures confirm a faulty spindle system.

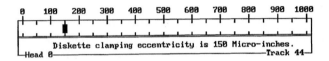

65-4 Screen display from a DriveProbe eccentricity test. Accurite Technologies, Inc.

Spindle speed

Media must be rotated at a fixed rate in order for data to be read or written properly. A drive that is too fast or too slow might be able to read files that it has written at that wrong speed without error, but the disk might not be readable in other drives operating at a normal speed. Files recorded at a normal speed also might not be readable in drives that are too fast or too slow. Such transfer problems between drives is a classic sign of speed trouble (usually signaled as general disk read/write errors). Drive speeds should be accurate to within ±1.5%, so a drive running at 300 rpm should be accurate to ±4.5 rpm (295.5 to 304.5 rpm), and a drive running at 360 rpm should be accurate to within ±5.4 rpm (354.6 rpm to 365.4 rpm).

After cleaning the R/W heads and testing disk eccentricity, select the spindle speed test from your software menu. The display will probably appear much like the one in Fig. 65-5. Today's floppy drives rarely drift out of alignment because rotational speed is regulated by feedback from the spindle's index sensor. The servo circuit is constantly adjusting motor torque to achieve optimal spindle speed. If a self-compensating drive is out of tolerance, excess motor wear, mechanical obstructions, or index sensor failure is indicated. Check and replace the index sensor, or the entire spindle motor assembly. You also can replace the entire floppy drive outright.

MOTOR SPEED Test   'Esc'- For Previous Menu

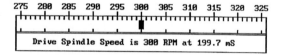

Drive 1 Selected as [3 1/2" 1.4Mb 300 RPM]   Location: Track 0   Head 0

65-5 Screen display from a DriveProbe motor speed test. Accurite Technologies, Inc.

Track 00 test

The first track on any floppy disk is the outermost track of side 0, which is track 00. Track 00 is important because it contains the boot record and file allocation information vital for finding disk files. The particular files saved on a disk can be broken up and spread out all over the disk, but the FAT data must always be in a known location. If the drive cannot find track 00 reliably, the system might not be able to boot from the floppy drive or even use disks. Floppy drives utilize a sensor such as an optoisolator to physically determine when the R/W heads are over the outermost track.

Select the track 00 test from your software menu and allow the test to run. A track 00 test measures the difference between the actual location of track 00 versus the point at which the track 00 sensor indicates that track 00 is reached. The difference should be less than ±1.5 mils (one-thousandths of an inch). A larger error might cause the drive to encounter problems reading or writing to the disk. The easiest and quickest fix is to alter the track 00 sensor position. This adjustment usually involves loosening the sensor and moving it until the monitor display indicates an acceptable reading. Remember that you only need to move the sensor a small fraction, so a patient, steady hand is required. The track 00 sensor is almost always located along the head carriage lead screw. Mark the original position of the sensor with indelible ink so that you can return it to its original position if you get in trouble.

Radial alignment

The alignment of a drive's R/W heads versus the disk is critical to reliable drive operation because alignment directly affects contact between heads and media. If head contact is not precise, data read or written to the disk might be vulnerable. The radial alignment test measures the head's actual position versus the precise center of the outer, middle, and inner tracks (as established by ANSI standards). Ideally, R/W heads should be centered perfectly when positioned over any track, but any differences are measured in microinches. A radial alignment error more than several hundred microinches might suggest a head alignment error.

Select the radial alignment test from your software tool kit and allow the test to run. A typical radial alignment test display is illustrated in Fig. 65-6. If you must perform an adjustment, you can start by loosening the slotted screws that secure the stepping motor, and gently rotate the motor to alter lead screw position. As you make adjustments with the test in progress, watch the display for the middle track. When error is minimized on the inner track, secure the stepping motor carefully to keep the assembly from shifting position. Use extreme caution when adjusting radial head position; you only need to move the head a fraction, so a very steady hand is needed. You

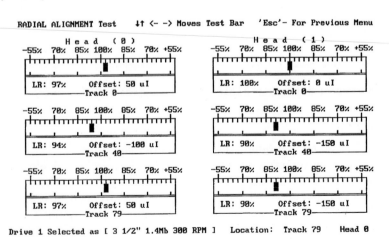

65-6 Screen display from a DriveProbe radial alignment test. Accurite Technologies, Inc.

also should recheck the track 00 sensor to make sure the sensor position is acceptable. If you are unable to effect radial head alignment, the drive should be replaced.

Azimuth alignment

Not only must the heads be centered perfectly along a disk's radius, but the heads also must be perfectly perpendicular to the disk plane. If the head azimuth is off by more than a few minutes (⅙₀ of a degree), data integrity can be compromised and disk interchangeability between drives—especially high-density drives—might become unreliable. When the heads are perfectly perpendicular to the disk (at 90°), the azimuth should be 0 minutes.

Select the azimuth test from your software tool kit and allow the test to run. Figure 65-7 shows an azimuth alignment test display. An azimuth alignment test measures the rotation (or twist) of R/W heads in terms of + or – minutes. A clockwise twist is expressed as a plus (+) number, and a counterclockwise twist is expressed as a negative (–) number. Heads should be perpendicular to within about ±10 minutes. It is important to note that most floppy drives do not allow azimuth adjustments easily. Unless you want to experiment with the adjustment, it is often easiest to replace a severely misaligned drive.

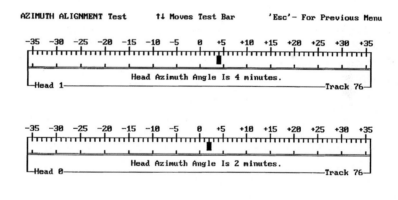

Drive 1 Selected as [3 1/2" 1.4Mb 300 RPM]   Location: Track 76 Head 0

65-7 Screen display from a DriveProbe azimuth alignment test. Accurite Technologies, Inc.

Head step

The head step (or index step) test measures the amount of time between a step pulse from the coil driver circuits and a set of timing mark data recorded on the test disk. In manual oscilloscope adjustments, this would be seen as the index burst. Average index time is typically 200 μs for 13.34-cm (5¼ inch) drives, and 400 μs for 8.89-cm (3½ inch) drives. In automatic testing with your software tool kit, you will see time measurements for both heads on the inner and outer tracks as shown in Fig. 65-8. The actual range of acceptable time depends on your particular drive, but variations of ±100 μs or more is not unusual.

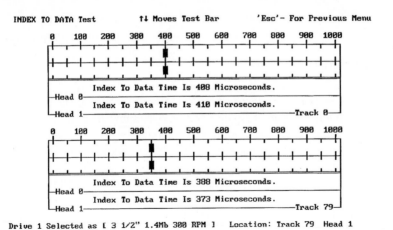

65-8 Screen display from a DriveProbe index-to-data test. Accurite Technologies, Inc.

If the head step timing is off too far, you can adjust timing by moving the index sensor. As with all other drive adjustments, you need only move the sensor a small fraction, so be extremely careful about moving the sensor. A steady hand is very important here. Make sure to secure the sensor when you are done with your timing adjustments.

Hysteresis

It is natural for wear and debris in the mechanical head positioning system to result in some "play." That is, the head will not wind up in the exact same position moving from outside in, as moving from the inside out. Excessive play, however, will make it difficult to find the correct track reliably. Testing is accomplished by starting the heads at a known track, stepping the heads out to track 00, then stepping back to the starting track. Head position is then measured and recorded. The heads are then stepped in to the innermost track, then back to the starting track. Head position is measured and recorded again. Under ideal conditions, the head carriage should wind up in precisely the same place (zero hysteresis), but natural play almost guarantees some minor difference. You can see a typical hysteresis test measurement display in Fig. 65-9. If excessive hysteresis is encountered, the drive should be replaced because it is difficult to determine exactly where the excess play is caused in the drive.

Head width

Another test of a drive's R/W heads is the measurement of their effective width. Effective head widths are 12 or 13 mils for 13.34-cm (5¼ inch) double-density drives, 5 or 6 mils for 13.34-cm high-density drives, and 4 or 5 mils for all 8.89-cm (3½ inch) drives. As you run the head width test with your software tool kit, you will see effective width displayed on the monitor as shown in Fig. 65-10. As R/W heads wear down, their effective width increases. If the effective width is too low, the heads

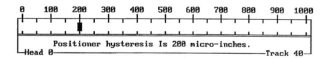

POSITIONER HYSTERESIS Test   'Esc'- For Previous Menu

Positioner hysteresis Is 200 micro-inches.

Drive 1 Selected as [3 1/2" 1.4Mb 300 RPM]   Location: Track 1 Head 0

65-9 Screen display from a DriveProbe hysteresis test. Accurite Technologies, Inc.

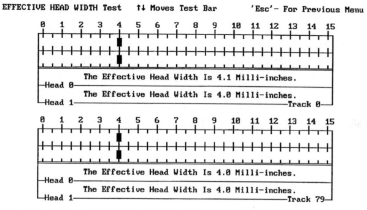

EFFECTIVE HEAD WIDTH Test   ↑↓ Moves Test Bar   'Esc'- For Previous Menu

The Effective Head Width Is 4.1 Milli-inches.
Head 0
The Effective Head Width Is 4.0 Milli-inches.
Head 1   Track 0

The Effective Head Width Is 4.0 Milli-inches.
Head 0
The Effective Head Width Is 4.0 Milli-inches.
Head 1   Track 79

Drive 1 Selected as [3 1/2" 1.4Mb 300 RPM]   Location: Track 79 Head 1

65-10 Screen display from a DriveProbe head-weight test. Accurite Technologies, Inc.

might be contaminated with oxide buildup. When small head widths are detected, try cleaning the drive again to remove any remaining contaminates. If the width reading remains too small (or measures too large), the heads or head carriage might be damaged. You can replace the R/W head assembly, but often the best course is simply to replace the drive outright.

Monitor testing and alignment

When set up and ventilated properly, computer monitors are notoriously rugged devices. The CRT itself enjoys a reasonably long life span. By their very nature, CRTs are remarkably tolerant to physical abuse and can withstand wide variations in power and signal voltages. However, even the best CRT and its associated circuitry suffers eventual degradation with age and use. Monitor operation also can be upset when major subassemblies are replaced such as circuit boards or deflection assemblies. Maintenance and alignment procedures are available to evaluate a monitor's performance and allow you to keep it working within its specifications. This chapter illustrates a comprehensive set of procedures that can be performed to test and adjust the monitor's performance. Keep in mind that this chapter uses test patterns generated with the shareware utility MONITORS, which is available on the companion diskette.

Before you begin

Adjusting a monitor is a serious matter, and should not be undertaken without careful consideration. A myriad of adjustments are found on the main circuit board; any of which can render a screen image unviewable if adjusted improperly. The delicate magnets and deflection assemblies around the CRT's neck can easily be damaged or knocked out of alignment by careless handling. *In short, aligning a monitor can do more harm than good unless you have the patience to understand the purpose of each procedure.* You also need to have a calm, methodical approach. The following points might help to keep you out of trouble.

Testing versus alignment

There is a distinct difference between monitor testing and monitor alignment. *Testing* is a low-level operation. Testing also is unobtrusive, so you can test a monitor at any point in the repair process. By using the companion software with your PC, you can test any monitor that is compatible with your video adapter. Testing is accomplished by displaying a test pattern on the monitor. After observing the condition of the pattern, you can usually deduce the monitor's fault area very quickly. Once the monitor is working (able to display a steady, full-screen image), you also can use test patterns to evaluate the monitor's alignment.

Alignment is a high-level operation—a task that is performed only after the monitor has been completely repaired. Because alignment requires you to make adjustments to the monitor circuits, the monitor circuits must be working properly. After all, alignment does no good if a fault is preventing the monitor from displaying an image in the first place. Proper alignment is important to ensure that the monitor is displaying images as accurately as possible.

Know the warranty

A warranty is a written promise made by a manufacturer that their product will be free of most problems for some period of time. For monitors, typical warranties cover parts and labor for a period of one year from the date of purchase. The CRT itself is often covered up to three years. Before even touching the monitor, you should check to see if the warranty is still in force. Monitors that are still under warranty should be sent back to the manufacturer for repair. This book does not advocate voiding any warranty and the reasoning is very simple: why spend your time and effort to do a job that the manufacturer will do for free? You paid for that warranty when you bought the monitor. Of course, most monitors in need of service are already out of warranty.

There are only three exceptions that might prompt you to ignore a warranty. First, the warranty might already be void if you purchased the monitor used. Manufacturers typically support the warranty only for the original purchaser (the individual that returns the warranty card). Third-party claims are often refused, but it might still be worth a call to the manufacturer's service manager just to be sure. Second, any warranty is only as good as the manufacturer. A manufacturer that goes out of business is not concerned with supporting your monitor, although reputable manufacturers that close their doors will turn over their service operations to an independent repair house. Again, a bit of detective work might be required to find out if the ultimate service provider will honor the unit's warranty. Finally, you might choose to ignore a warranty for organizations with poor or unclear service performance. Call the service provider and ask about the turn-around time and return procedures. If they "don't know" or you can't get a straight answer, chances are that your monitor is going to sit untouched for quite a while.

Getting from here to there

Monitors require special care in moving and handling. A monitor is typically a heavy device (most of the weight being contributed by the CRT and chassis). Back injury is a serious concern. If you must move the monitor between places, remember to lift from the knees and not from the back; it's hard to fix a monitor while you're in traction. When carrying the monitor, keep the CRT screen toward your chest with your arms wrapped carefully around the enclosure to support the weight. Large monitors (17 to 20 inches and bigger) are particularly unwieldy. You are wise to get another person's help when moving such bulky, expensive devices. If the monitor is to be used in-house, keep it on a roll-around cart so that you will not have to carry it.

When transporting a monitor from place to place in an automobile, the monitor should be sealed in a well-cushioned box. If an appropriate box is not to be had, place the monitor on a car seat that is well-cushioned with soft foam or blankets; even an old pillow or two will do. Sit the monitor on its cushioning face down because that will lower the monitor's center of gravity and make it as stable as possible. Use twine or thin rope to secure the monitor so it will not shift in transit.

When shipping the monitor to a distant location, the monitor should be shipped in its original container and packing materials. If the original shipping material has been discarded, purchase a heavy-gauge cardboard box. The box dimensions should be at least 4 to 6 inches larger in every dimension than the monitor. Fill the empty space with plenty of foam padding or bubble-wrap that can be obtained from any full-service stationary store. The box should be sealed and reinforced with heavy-gauge box tape. It does not pay to skimp here; a monitor's weight demands a serious level of protection.

High-voltage cautions

It is important to remind you that a computer monitor uses very high voltages for proper operation. *Potentially lethal shock hazards exist within the monitor assembly—both from ordinary ac line voltage, as well as from the CRT anode voltage developed by the flyback transformer. You must exercise extreme caution whenever the monitor's outer housings are removed.*

The mirror trick

Monitor alignment poses a special problem for technicians; you must watch the adjustment that you are moving while also watching the display to see what effect the adjustment is having. Sure, you could watch the display and reach around the back of the monitor, but given the serious shock hazards that exist with exposed monitor circuitry, that is a very unwise tactic (you would place your personal safety at risk). Monitor technicians use an ordinary mirror placed several feet in front of the CRT. That way, you can watch inside the monitor as you make an adjustment, then glance up to see the display reflected in the mirror. If a suitable mirror is not to be found, ask someone to watch the display for you and relate what is happening. Ultimately, the idea is that you should *never take your eyes off of your hand(s)* while making an adjustment.

Making an adjustment

Monitor adjustments are not difficult to make, but each adjustment should be the result of careful consideration rather than a random, haphazard shot in the dark. The reason for this concern is simple—it is just as easy to make the display worse. Changing adjustments indiscriminately can quickly ruin display quality beyond your ability to correct it. The following three guidelines will help you make the most effective adjustments with the greatest probability of improving image quality.

First, mark your adjustment as shown in Fig. 66-1. Use a narrow-tip indelible marker to make a reference mark along the body of the adjustment. It does not have to be anything fancy. By making a reference mark, you can quickly return the adjustment to the exact place it started. A reference mark can really save the day if you get lost or move the wrong adjustment.

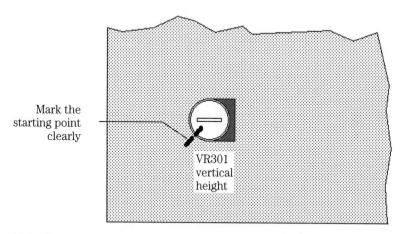

Mark the starting point clearly

VR301 vertical height

66-1 Mark a starting point before starting an adjustment.

Second, concentrate on only *one* adjustment for any one alignment procedure. For example, if you are trying to optimize horizontal linearity, you should only be concerned with the horizontal linearity adjustment. If you do not have documentation that describes the location of each control, check the silk-screen labels on the PC board. If you absolutely cannot locate the needed adjustment point, skip the alignment and move on to the next test. When you do move an adjustment, move it slowly and in very small increments (perhaps ⅛ to ¼ turn). Check the display after each step. If the display fails to improve, return the control to its original location (a snap to do if you've made a reference mark) and try it in the opposite direction.

Finally, avoid using metal tools (such as screwdrivers) to make your adjustments. Some of the controls in a monitor are based on coils with permeable cores. Inserting steel tools to make an adjustment will throw the setting off; the display might look fine with the tool inserted, but degrade when the tool is removed. As a general rule, use plastic tools (such as TV alignment tools) that are available from almost any electronics store.

Tests and procedures

Testing a computer monitor is easy, and can be accomplished through the use of relatively standard test patterns. Once the companion alignment software is started, you can select the test pattern for the specific test you wish to run, Each of the following procedures discusses how to interpret the pattern, and provides a step-by-step procedure for making adjustments. For the purposes of this discussion, you should refer to the sample main board shown in Fig. 66-2. Remember that the PC board(s) used in your particular monitor might be quite different, so examine your own PC board very closely before attempting an adjustment.

High-voltage test and regulation

The high-voltage test is one of the more important tests that you will perform on computer monitors. Excessive high-voltage levels can allow X radiation to escape the CRT. Over long-term exposure, X rays pose a serious biohazard. Your first check should be to use a high-voltage probe. Ground the probe appropriately and insert the metal test tip under the rubber CRT anode cap. You can then read the high-voltage level directly from the probe's meter. *Be certain to refer to any particular operating and safety instructions that accompany your high-voltage probe.* If the high-voltage level is unusually high or unusually low, carefully adjust the level using a high-voltage control (Fig. 66-2 shows VR501 as the high-voltage control) that is usually located near the flyback transformer.

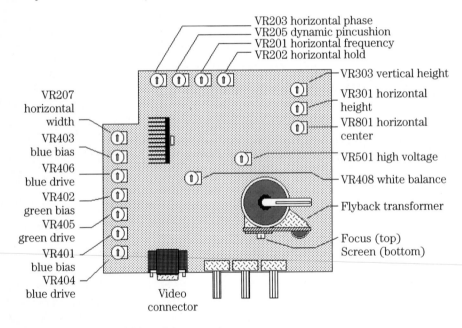

66-2 A typical main PC board for a monitor.

Regulation is the ability of a power supply to provide a constant output as the load's demands change. The high-voltage supply also must provide regulation within specified limits. As the display image changes, high-voltage levels should remain relatively steady. If not, the display image will flinch as height and width changes. Select the High-Voltage Test pattern (Fig. 66-3) from the alignment software main menu. This is a narrow white double boarder with a solid white center. Watch the boarder as the center switches on and off at 2 second intervals. A well-regulated high-voltage system set at the correct level will keep the white border reasonably

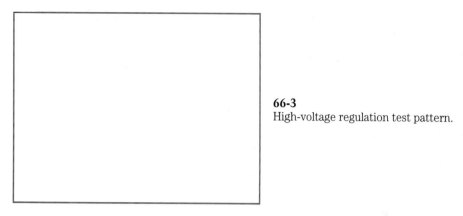

66-3
High-voltage regulation test pattern.

steady; there should be very little variation in image height or width. If the image flinches significantly, the high-voltage system might be damaged or failing.

Screen control

The CRT screen grid provides a form of master control over the electron beam(s) that affects the display's overall brightness. A proper screen grid setting is important so that the brightness and contrast controls work within an appropriate range. Select the Blank Raster test from the alignment software main menu. Adjust the monitor's brightness and contrast controls to their maximum levels; the background raster should be plainly visible.

Locate the screen voltage control. In Fig. 66-2, the screen voltage control is located just below the focus control on the flyback transformer assembly. Slowly adjust the screen voltage control until the background raster is just barely visible. Set the monitor's brightness control to its middle (detent) position. The background raster should now be invisible. Press any key to return to the main menu. You might reduce the monitor's contrast control to achieve a clear image.

Focus

When an electron beam is first generated in a CRT, electrons are not directed very well. A focus electrode in the CRT's neck acts to narrow the electron stream. An improperly focused image is difficult to see, and can lead to excessive eye strain resulting in headaches, fatigue, and so on. The Focus test pattern allows you to check the image clarity and optimize the focus if necessary. Keep in mind that focus is a subjective measurement; it depends on your perception. You would be wise to confer with another person while making focus adjustments because their perception of the display might be different than yours.

Because focus is indirectly related to screen brightness and contrast, you should set the screen controls for an optimum display. An image that is too bright or has poor contrast might adversely affect your perception of focus. Start the companion software if it is not running already. Select the Blank Raster test from the alignment software main menu. Adjust screen brightness to its middle (detent) position, or until the display's background raster disappears (the screen should be perfectly dark).

Press any key to return to the main menu, then select the White Purity test. The display should be filled with a solid white box. Adjust screen contrast to its maximum position, or until a good white image is achieved. Once the display conditions are set properly, press any key to return to the main menu.

Now, select the Focus Test pattern (Fig. 66-4) from the main menu. You will see a screen filled with the letter m. Review the entire screen carefully to determine if the image is out of focus. Again, it is wise to get a second opinion before altering the focus. If the image requires a focus adjustment, gently and slowly alter the focus control. For the sample main board shown in Fig. 66-2, the focus control is located on the flyback transformer assembly. Once you are satisfied with the focus, press any key to return to the main menu.

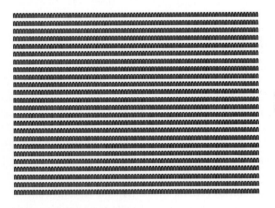

66-4
Screen focus test pattern.

Dynamic pincushion

A computer-generated image is produced in two dimensions; it is essentially flat. Unfortunately, the traditional CRT face is not flat (although some new CRT designs use an extremely flat face). When a flat image is projected onto a curved surface, the image becomes distorted. Typically, the edges of the image bow outward making straight lines appear convex (barrel distortion). Monitor raster circuitry is designed to compensate for this distortion and allows the image to appear flat even though it is being projected onto a slightly curved surface. This is known as the *dynamic pinchushion* circuit (or just the pincushion). However, if the pincushion circuit overcompensates for curvature, the edges of an image will appear to bow inward making straight lines appear concave.

It is a simple matter to check the dynamic pincushion. Select the Convergence Test (crosshatch) pattern from the main menu. A white grid will appear in the display. Inspect the outer boarder of the grid pattern. If the edges of the boarder appear straight and true, the dynamic pincushion is set properly and no further action is needed. If the edges appear to bow outward, the pincushion is undercompensated. If the edges appear to bow inward, the pincushion is overcompensated. In either case, you will need to make a minor adjustment to the dynamic pincushion control. Fig. 66-2 lists VR205 as the dynamic pincushion control, but your monitor probably uses different nomenclature. Before making such an adjustment, you might wish to confer with another individual because their perception of the display might be different from yours. If you cannot locate the dynamic pincushion control, simply move on to the next test.

Horizontal phase

When brightness and contrast are set to their maximum levels, you will see a dim, dark gray rectangle formed around the screen image. This boarder is part of the raster; the overall area of the screen that is hit by the electron beam(s). Ideally, the raster is just slightly larger than the typical image. You are able to control the position of an image within this raster area. This is known as *horizontal phase*. The image should be horizontally centered within the raster area. The term *phase* is used because phase refers to the amount of delay between the time the horizontal scan (raster) starts and the time where pixel data starts. By adjusting this delay, you effectively shift the image left or right in the raster area (which should remain perfectly still).

Select the Phase Test pattern from the alignment software main menu. A phase pattern will appear as shown in Fig. 66-5. Set the monitor's brightness and contrast controls to their maximum values; raster should now be visible around the image. Locate the horizontal phase control. The sample main board shown in Fig. 66-2 indicates VR203 as the horizontal phase control. Carefully adjust the horizontal phase control until the image is approximately centered in the raster. This need not be a precise adjustment, but a bit of raster should be visible all around the image. Return the monitor brightness control to its middle (detent) position, reduce the monitor contrast control if necessary to achieve a crisp, clear image.

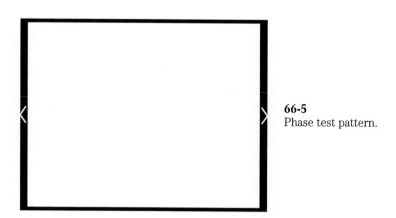

66-5
Phase test pattern.

Horizontal and vertical centering

Now that the image has been centered in the raster, it is time to center the image in the display. Centering ensures that the image is shown evenly so that you can check and adjust linearity later on without the added distortion of an off-center image. Select the Convergence Test (Crosshatch) pattern from the alignment software main menu. If the image appears well centered, no further action is required.

The sample main PC board shown in Fig. 66-2 indicates VR801 as the horizontal centering control. Adjust the centering control so that the image is centered horizontally in the display. Fig. 66-2 also shows VR303 as the vertical centering control. Adjust this centering control so that the image is centered vertically in the display. These need not be precise adjustments. Keep in mind that many monitors make their centering controls user accessible from the front or rear housings (along with brightness and contrast).

Horizontal and vertical size (height and width)

Many monitors are capable of displaying more than one video mode. Unless the monitor offers an auto-sizing feature, however, the image will shift in size (especially vertical height) for each different video mode. Now that you have a focused, centered image, it should be set to the proper width and height. Remember that image size depends on the CRT size, so you will have to check the specifications for your particular monitor. If you do not have specifications available (or they do not specify image dimensions), you can at least approach a properly proportioned image using alignment software.

Select the Convergence Test (crosshatch) pattern from the main menu. This pattern produces a grid, and each square of the grid should be roughly square. If the image is proportioned correctly, no further action is needed. Fig. 66-2 uses VR301 to control vertical height. Slowly adjust vertical height until the grid squares are actually about square. The entire grid will be a rectangle that is wider than it is high. If the overall image is too small, you can adjust the horizontal width (VR207 is shown in Fig. 66-2) to make the grid wider, then adjust the vertical height again to keep the grid squares in a square shape. Of course, if the image is too large, you can reverse this procedure to shrink the image.

If your monitor is a multimode design and able to display images in several different graphics modes, there might be several independent vertical height adjustments; one for each available mode. You will have to check the test mode you have selected against the vertical control to be sure that the vertical height control you are changing is appropriate for the test mode being used. If you are using a 640-x-480 graphics mode, for example, you should be adjusting the vertical height control for the monitor's 640-x-480 mode. If the monitor offers an auto-sizing feature that automatically compensates image size for changes in screen mode, there might not be a vertical height adjustment available on the main PC board.

Horizontal and vertical linearity

The concept of linearity is often a difficult one to grasp because there are so few real-life examples for us to draw from. Linearity is best related to consistency; everything should be the same as everything else. For a computer monitor, there must be both horizontal and vertical linearity for an image to appear properly. An image is formed as a series of horizontally scanned lines. Each line should be scanned at the same speed from start to finish. If horizontal scanning speed fluctuates, vertical lines will appear closer together (or farther apart) than they actually are. Circles will appear compressed (or elongated) in the horizontal direction. Each horizontal line should be spaced exactly the same vertical distance apart. If the spacing between scanned lines should vary, horizontal lines will appear closer together (or farther apart) than they actually are. Circles will appear compressed (or elongated) in the vertical direction. Any nonlinearity will result in distortion to the image.

Before testing, you should understand that the screen mode will have an effect on the test pattern. When screen modes change, the vertical height of the image also will change. This is especially prevalent in multifrequency and multimode monitor designs that can display images in more than one graphics mode. Before testing for linearity, the height and width of the image should be set properly for the selected screen mode as described in the previous procedures. Otherwise, the image might appear compressed or elongated and result in a false diagnosis.

Select the Linearity Test (Lines & Circles Test) from the alignment software main menu. A grid will appear with an array of five circles as shown in Fig. 66-6. Observe the test pattern carefully. The spacing between each horizontal line should be equal. The spacing between each vertical line should be equal. Assuming the vertical height and horizontal width are set properly, each of the five circles should appear round and even. Each grid square should appear square. If the image appears correct, no further action is needed.

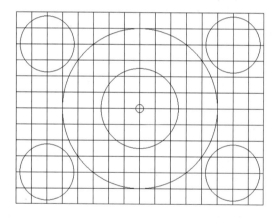

66-6
Linearity test pattern.

If the vertical lines are not spaced evenly apart, there might be a horizontal linearity problem. Find the horizontal linearity adjustment (Fig. 66-2 shows VR202). Be sure to mark the starting point, then slowly adjust the control until the horizontal linearity improves. If there is no improvement in one direction (or linearity worsens), return to the starting point and try the adjustment in the opposite direction. If there is still no improvement (or linearity worsens again), return the control to its starting position and take no further action; there might be a fault in the horizontal drive circuit.

If the horizontal lines are not spaced evenly apart, there might be a vertical linearity problem. Find the vertical linearity adjustment (Fig. 66-2 shows VR201). Mark the starting point, then slowly adjust the control until the vertical linearity improves. If there is no improvement in one direction (or linearity worsens), return to the starting point and try the adjustment in the opposite direction. If there is still no improvement (or linearity worsens again), return the control to its starting position and take no further action; there might be a fault in the vertical drive circuit. Refer to the chapters on monitor troubleshooting for detailed service procedures.

Convergence

Convergence is a concept that relates expressly to color CRTs. A color CRT produces three electron beams, one for each of the primary colors (red, green, and blue). These electron beams strike color phosphors on the CRT face. By adjusting the intensity of each electron beam, any color can be produced, including white. The three electron beams must converge at the shadow mask that is mounted just behind the phosphor layer. The shadow mask maintains color purity by allowing the beams to impinge only where needed (any stray or misdirected electrons are physically blocked). Without the shadow mask, stray electrons could excite adjacent color phosphors and result in strange or unsteady colors. If the beams are not aligned properly, a beam might pass through an adjacent mask aperture and excite an undesired color dot. Proper convergence is important for a quality color display.

It is a simple matter to check convergence. Be certain to allow at least 15 minutes for the monitor to warm up. Select the Convergence Test (Dots) from the alignment software main menu. An array of white dots should appear on the display. Observe the dots carefully. If you can see any shadows of red, green, or blue around the dots, convergence alignment might be necessary. If the dot pattern looks good, then select the Convergence Test (crosshatch) pattern from the main menu. A white grid should appear. Once again, observe the display carefully to locate any primary color shadows that might appear around the white lines. If the crosshatch pattern looks good, no further action is necessary, so press any key to return to the main menu.

When you determine that a convergence alignment is necessary, be sure to select the Convergence Test (crosshatch) from the main menu. Locate the convergence rings located on the CRT's neck just behind the deflection yokes as shown in Fig. 66-7. Using a fine-tip black marker, mark the starting position of each convergence ring relative to the glass CRT neck. This is a vital step because it will allow you to quickly return the rings to their original positions if you run into trouble. Convergence alignment is delicate, so it is easy to make the display *much* worse if you are not very careful. *Also, this alignment must be performed with monitor power applied, so be extremely careful to protect yourself from shock hazards.* The alignment process is not difficult, but requires a bit of practice and patience to become proficient. As the following procedure shows, you will align the red and blue electron beams to make magenta, then you will align the green electron beam over the magenta pattern to make white. Keep in mind that this procedure uses the monitor alignment software (MONITORS) included on the companion disk.

Although the crosshatch pattern is displayed, press the letter M, which will switch the crosshatch pattern to a magenta color. Magenta is a combination of blue and red (by choosing magenta, the green electron beam is effectively shut down, so there is less clutter in the display). Loosen the metal band holding the rings in place. *Do not remove the band.* You also might have to loosen a locking ring before moving the convergence rings. Move the magenta convergence rings together or separately until the blue and red shadows overlap to form a uniform magenta crosshatch pat-

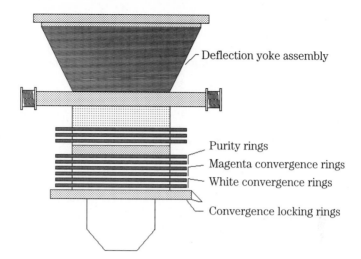

Deflection yoke assembly

Purity rings
Magenta convergence rings
White convergence rings

Convergence locking rings

66-7 A typical convergence ring assembly.

tern. Be sure to move these rings only in small, careful steps. By moving the rings together, you adjust red and blue overlap in the vertical lines. By moving the rings separately, you adjust red and blue overlap in the horizontal lines. If you get into trouble, use the starting marks to return the rings to their original locations and start again.

Once the magenta pattern is aligned, press the letter W, which will switch the crosshatch pattern to its original white color (thus activating the green electron beam). Adjust the white convergence rings until any green shadows overlap the crosshatch to form a uniform white grid as desired. As with the magenta rings, moving the white convergence rings together will adjust green overlap in the vertical lines. Moving the white convergence rings separately will adjust green overlap in the horizontal lines. When the image appears white, carefully secure the locking ring and setup band. Recheck the convergence as you tighten the assembly to be sure nothing has shifted. *Do not over-tighten the setup band*—you stand a good chance of damaging the CRT.

You will probably hear convergence referred to as *static* and *dynamic.* These terms refer to the convergence in different areas of the display. Static refers to the convergence in the center area of the display. Dynamic refers to the convergence around the perimeter of the display. The alignment procedure provided in this section deals with static convergence because this provides a good overall alignment with a minimum of fuss. Dynamic convergence is a more difficult alignment because it requires inserting rubber wedges and tilting deflection yokes, touchy procedures even for a practiced hand. Static convergence should be sufficient for an acceptable display. If there is visible misconvergence around the display perimeter even after a careful static convergence alignment, you will have to obtain a service manual that outlines dynamic convergence techniques for your particular monitor.

Color purity

Another concern is color purity; that is, a solid color should have the same hue across the entire display. If discoloration develops in the display, purity might need to be restored by degaussing (demagnetizing) the monitor. Typically, the discoloration follows a semicircular pattern around one side or corner with several bands of different color distortions (Fig. 66-8); the color banding appears almost like a rainbow. Sometimes the discoloration involves the entire screen, but that is rare.

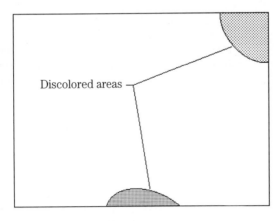

Discolored areas

66-8
Typical locations of color
banding (color distortion).

Such discoloration might be caused by an externally induced magnetic field that has permanently magnetized some material in the monitor. The three CRT electron beams are guided to their appropriate phosphor dots by a magnetic deflection system. The beams converge and pass through a shadow mask near the phosphor surface assuring that the red beam hits the red phosphor, the blue beam hits the blue phosphor, and the green beam hits the green phosphor. If some component within the CRT (frequently it is the shadow mask itself) has become sufficiently magnetized, then the beams receive an undesired deflection, and will not land on the appropriate phosphor (or will land partly on one color and partly on another). The result is an impure color that arcs around the magnetized area.

Location is an important clue to this problem. If the discoloration moves or disappears when the monitor is moved, it is not being caused by a permanent magnetization, but by some magnetic interference in or near the monitor. Placing a highly magnetic or electromagnetic source (such as a strong industrial magnet or power supply) on or near the monitor can cause such discoloration. If the discoloration does not move when the monitor is moved, it might be caused by permanent magnetization in the shadow mask. In that case, degaussing is necessary.

Checking color purity is a straightforward procedure. Select the White Purity test from the main menu. A white box will fill the entire screen. If there are any areas of discoloration, degaussing is probably necessary. Degaussing removes permanent magnetization by introducing an alternating magnetic field that is stronger than the offending permanent magnetization. This field will energize the magnetic domains of the material and induce an alternating magnetic field. Then, if the amplitude of the alternating magnetic field is gradually reduced to zero, the magnetic domains in the material will be left disorganized and scrambled; this effectively demagnetizes the monitor.

The easiest way to degauss a monitor is often to let the monitor do it. All modern color monitors have built-in degaussing coils and circuits. There will be a thick, black coil of wire wrapped in tape or other insulation surrounding the CRT face plate. Usually, it is coiled around the CRT behind its mounting ears. That is the internal degaussing coil. The coil is connected to the ac supply through a thermistor current limiting circuit. The thermistor has a low resistance when cold and a higher resistance when warm (typically a 10:1 ratio). It is in series with the degaussing coil so that when started cold, a large current will flow through the coil and then will decrease to a low value. The internal degaussing coil thus automatically degausses the monitor every time it is turned on. This degaussing takes place while the monitor screen is blank (the video system has not yet initialized) so that the resulting discoloration during auto-degaussing is not visible. Unfortunately, design limitations reduce the magnetic field strength available from internal degaussing coils. That limits the amount of permanent magnetization that can be neutralized by internal degaussing. If a monitor has been strongly magnetized, internal degaussing might not be enough and discoloration eventually results.

Manual degaussing requires a hand-held degaussing coil. You might have to search a bit to find one, but they are available. The basic principle involved in operating a manual degaussing coil is the same as the auto-degaussing assemblies already in place on color monitors; introduce a strong alternating magnetic field, then slowly reduce it's amplitude to zero. Start the companion software (if it is not already running) and select the White Purity test from the main menu. A white rectangle should fill the entire image. Discoloration should be visible. Hold the degaussing coil near the monitor, flip the degaussing coil switch on, and slowly move the coil away from the monitor as smoothly as you can. The image will discolor drastically when the degaussing coil is activated. When the coil is at arms length from the monitor flip the degaussing switch off. You might need to repeat this procedure several times. When the monitor is degaussed properly, the white image should be consistent at all points on the display.

Color drive

Once color convergence and purity are set correctly, you should turn your attention to the color drive levels (also known as White Balance). Select the White Purity test from the alignment software main menu. A white box will fill the entire screen. Set screen contrast to its highest level and reduce brightness to its middle (detent) position. The background raster should disappear. Ideally, all three color signal levels should be equal, and the resulting image should be a pure white, rather like a blank piece of white photocopier paper. However, judging the quality of a display color is largely a subjective evaluation. You will need an oscilloscope to measure the actual voltage level of each color signal in order to set them equally. If you do not have an oscilloscope (or do not have access to one), do not attempt to adjust the color drive settings by eye.

Use your oscilloscope to measure the signal levels being generated by the red, green, and blue video drivers. These are the three color signals that are actually driving the CRT. With the full white pattern being displayed, all three color signals should be equal (probably around 30 volts, although your own monitor might use slightly different signal levels). Even if you are not quite sure what the level should be, all three signals must be set to the same level to ensure a white image. If you do not know what the level should be, find the highest of the three color signals and use that as a reference. Adjust the gain levels of the other two colors until both levels match the reference. Reduce contrast and inspect the image again. It should remain white (and all three signals should be equal). Disconnect your oscilloscope and press any key to return to the main menu.

Cleaning/vacuuming

Once the monitor is checked and aligned, your final step before returning the unit to service should be to inspect the housings and PC boards for accumulations of dust and debris. Look for dust accumulating in the housing vents. A monitor is typically cooled by convection (hot air rises). If these vents become clogged, heat will build up inside the monitor and lead to operational problems and perhaps even cause a premature breakdown. Dust also is conductive. If enough dust builds up within the monitor, the dust might short-circuit two or more components and cause operational problems. Vacuum away any dust or debris that might have accumulated in the outer housing. When you see dust buildup around the monitor PC boards and CRT, turn off and unplug the monitor, then vacuum away any buildups. Carefully re-assemble the monitor's housing(s) and return it to service.

67
CHAPTER

Power protection

Power is one of those attributes of PCs that is often taken for granted (or at least treated as an afterthought). Surges, spikes, and other power anomalies that occur in commercial power systems every day can damage the PC power supply and often affect the drives and motherboard circuitry as well. Even when no serious damage occurs to the system, a loss of power can result in a loss of time and vital data for any office or organization. This chapter is intended to explain the concepts of power protection, and show you the four major types of power protection devices that are available. As a PC technician, this information will allow you to assist your customers in developing an adequate and reliable power protection plan that will suit their needs and budget. Proper power protection improves system reliability and reduces down time.

Understanding power problems

Most people have come to take power for granted. In most cases, people simply plug a device in the nearest available outlet and turn it on assuming that an appropriate amount of voltage and current is available. If the device fails to function as expected, the natural assumption is that the device is at fault. In truth, this is not always the case. Computers and peripherals need certain minimum amounts of current and voltage at the ac line. If either value is too high or too low, the computer might behave erratically (or not work at all).

Commercial power is generated as a sinusoidal (ac) wave similar to the one shown in Fig. 67-1. The amplitude of the wave represents voltage, and the rate at which the wave repeats represents frequency. Voltage and frequency characteristics vary in different regions of the world. Regardless of region, however, the ac signal should be perfectly smooth and regular. In actual practice, ac can suffer from a variety of ills: blackouts, brownouts, surges, and spikes.

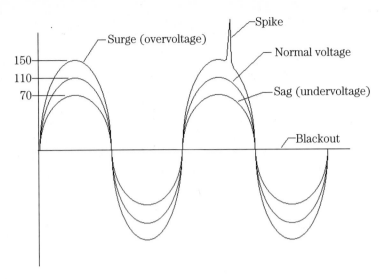

67-1 A comparison of ac sine waves during typical power problems.

Blackouts

A blackout is a complete loss of electrical power where voltage and current drop to a very low value (typically zero). Blackouts are usually caused by a physical interruption in the local power network due to accidental damage by a person or nature. The interruption will usually affect an area that can be as small as a street, or as large as an entire region depending on the point in the power distribution network where damage occurs.

Unless backup power is available, the loss of ac will invariably shut down the computer in a matter of milliseconds. In most cases, simply losing power does not damage a PC; memory is simply lost. For casual home computer users, this is often just an inconvenience. For business users, however, losing power can mean the loss of valuable data, and hours of lost productivity. The best and least expensive means of protection against a rare blackout is to save work regularly; every 30 minutes to an hour. That way, if power should fail, no more than an hour of work could be lost. For remote areas or regions that are subject to frequent power outages, a fast-switching *BPS* (backup power supply) or a reliable *UPS* (uninterruptible power supply) is highly recommended.

Brownouts

Perhaps more dangerous than sudden, complete power losses are *brownouts*, undervoltage conditions (also called *sags*) caused by questionable electrical wiring or excessive electrical load on an ac circuit. High-load items (like air conditioners, coffee pots, fan motors, overhead projectors, photocopiers, and so on) draw so much current that the ac voltage level drops. PC supplies are *regulated*, which means the dc output provided to the computer circuitry will be constant over a range of ac input conditions. However, when ac conditions fall outside of that tolerable range, the supply will fall out of regulation. This condition results in intermittent system operation (the system mysteriously freezes, random memory errors occur, files can be lost on the hard drive, etc.)

Undervoltage conditions also can damage the power supply. Because the PC's power supply responds to low ac voltages by drawing excessive current, serious undervoltage conditions can cause unusual heating that will eventually damage a PC power supply. If your customer complains of unusual system problems such as those described, ask them to try their system on another circuit. Although one circuit might be loaded down, other circuits are probably not. It your customer cannot find a lightly used circuit (or does not have access to one), ask you customer to try disconnecting high-load devices in their area such as air conditioners, fans, and heaters. If the problems disappear, advise your customer to have a new ac circuit installed from the circuit breaker (make it very clear that the new ac circuit should be from another line phase). Urban areas suffer from summer brownouts that affect entire areas. Such regional brownouts are usually due to massive air conditioner load.

It is difficult to overcome brownout conditions because most backup power supplies do not engage until voltage levels drop below brownout levels (usually 85 to 95 Vac). However, an uninterruptible power supply will prevent unpleasant surprises because the computer runs from the UPS normally anyway. Brownouts and blackouts do not interrupt UPS operation.

Surges and spikes

Basically, spikes and surges are the same villain; they just take different forms. *Surges* are small overvoltage conditions (140 Vac or more) that occur over relatively long periods (usually more than one second). In order to regulate power to a desired level, excess energy must be switched (in switching power supplies) or thrown away (in linear power supplies). In either case, excessive voltage creates overheating in the supply, and will eventually destroy it. Some supplies are designed to shut down in the event of voltage or thermal overloads, but you cannot count on this feature in today's proliferation of inexpensive clone PCs.

A *spike* is a large overvoltage condition (perhaps as much as 2500 V) that occurs in the space of milliseconds. Lightning strikes and high-energy switching can cause spikes on the ac line. For example, heavy equipment like drill presses, welders, grinders, and other heavy motorized devices can produce tremendous spikes in operation, or when switched on and off. If your PC is on the same ac circuit as that heavy equipment, the spikes can damage the power supply. Although some supplies are designed with surge suppression components (transformers, capacitors, gas discharge tubes, and *MOV*s [metal oxide varistors]), spikes that pass through surge suppression can damage the supply regulator, or pass through the supply to damage any portions of the motherboard. Also, remember that spikes also can pass along the everyday telephone line and damage your modem.

Protection devices

A well-designed power supply is built to withstand many of the ills found in an ac power line. Unfortunately, the never-ending push to reduce component count and cost in clone systems has meant that compromises have been made in the PC supply.

You cannot count on the presence of effective spike or overvoltage protection in original or replacement supplies. Therefore, you should understand the various options that are available to your customer.

Surge and spike suppressers

Surge suppressers (such as the Best SpikeFree in Fig. 67-2) are simple and relatively inexpensive devices ($20 to $200 US) that are designed to absorb high-voltage transients produced by lightning and high-energy equipment. Protection is accomplished by clamping (or shunting) voltages above a certain level (usually greater than 200 V). MOVs are often included that can respond quickly and clamp voltages as high as 6000 V. However, powerful surges such as direct lightning strikes can blow right through an MOV. Also, MOVs degrade with each spike. Once they have passed a number of surges, they are destroyed and must be replaced. There is no way to know whether the MOV is working or not, so there is no way to really tell if a surge suppresser is actually protecting the system.

67-2 The SpikeFree line from Best Power. Best Power Technology, Inc.

Many protectors show a neon lamp or LED that goes out when the MOV has blown, or the protector is no longer active. Good suppressers also incorporate a circuit breaker rather than a fuse. This represents a good convenience because a circuit breaker can be reset, and many fused units must be disassembled to replace the fuse. If possible, select a surge suppresser approved under UL1449 (or international equivalent). As a rule, remember that surge/spike protectors are the simplest and least expensive power protection devices; they also are the most limited.

Modems and fax boards also are susceptible to damage from spikes present on everyday telephone lines. When recommending protection schemes, do not forget to include telephone line spike protection as well. Several of the Best SpikeFree devices shown in Fig. 67-2 also provide data line protection along with ac line protection.

Line power conditioners

Line conditioners perform all of the functions that a surge suppresser does, but they provide some additional power protection. Where surge suppressers are passive devices, functioning only when a surge is present, line conditioners (such as the Best Citadel line conditioners in Fig. 67-3) use transformers and capacitors for power isolation and high-frequency rf noise filtering. This results in a larger and more expensive, but more effective, power protection scheme. Another advantage of line conditioners is their tolerance to brief brownout conditions. Because transformers and capacitors are energy storage components, those components will continue to provide energy to the power supply during short brownouts (on the order of several milliseconds).

67-3 The Citidel ac line conditioner line from Best Power. Best Power Technology, Inc.

Backup power

Surge suppressers and line conditioners will only take your customers just so far. Those devices can protect a computer from brief power anomalies and keep their systems off your workbench until it is time to upgrade. Sooner or later, though, power will fail. When your customer cannot afford to be in the dark (literally), you should recommend a supplemental power system. A backup power system (BPS) is an off-line power system that provides power to your computer only when main ac power fails. Power is supplied from a series of batteries that are kept charged while ac power is available. When ac fails, the dc battery power is modulated into ac and switched in-line to provide power to the system. Any decent BPS (like the Best Patriot backup supply in Fig. 67-4) can provide power for 15 to 60 minutes depending on the amount of load attached to it, plenty of time to save any work in progress and shut down in an orderly fashion.

The problem with some bargain-priced BPS units is their switching time. It may take several milliseconds to detect the loss of power and actually initiate the

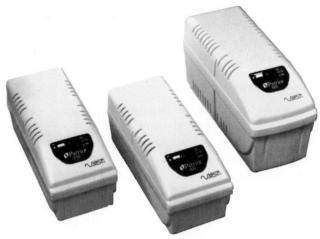

67-4 The Patriot Battery backup line from Best Power. Best Power Technology, Inc.

switchover to battery power. In that few milliseconds, a PC can brownout or re-boot anyway and defeat the point of having backup power in the first place. If a customer is having problems with power switch over, ask them to lighten the load on the BPS. Instead of trying to backup four machines with a BPS, try one or two and experiment a bit. A lighter load might allow the BPS to switch faster and pre-serve the PC's operation. If operation is acceptable with a lighter load, the pre-scription might be more BPS installations. If problems persist, find a better BPS for your customer. A BPS that offers an *FRT* (ferroresonant transformer) is often a good bet because an FRT can provide energy for several milliseconds to smooth the transfer to battery power.

Another problem to remember is that a backup power system might not offer any significant level of power protection. Because battery power is free of ac anomalies, inexpensive BPS designs might omit surge suppression or line conditioning features for the direct ac circuit. If power protection devices are already available, the prob-lem is moot. However, if your customer is not yet using power protection devices, recommend a BPS (such as the Best Patriot) that incorporates surge protection.

Uninterrputible power supplies

The UPS is probably the best all-around form of power protection available. It also is the most expensive. Where a BPS only provides modulated power when ac fails, a UPS is designed to provide modulated dc continuously. The PC runs from bat-tery power all the time. Alternating current keeps the batteries charged, but line ac does not power the PC. As a result, the PC is isolated from even the worst line power anomalies. Like a BPS, a UPS will only provide power for a limited time after ac fails (depending on the attached load), which allows the user to save data and shut down. However, there are no switching problems to contend with. High-end UPS systems, such as the Best Fortress UPS in Fig. 67-5, provide an excellent combination of un-interruptible power, brownout correction, and surge and spike protection.

67-5 The Fortress UPS line from Best Power. Best Power Technology, Inc.

One thing to consider when recommending a UPS is the type of modulation provided by the modulator. Inexpensive UPS devices modulate dc battery power into an ac square wave. This is technically ac, but remember that some PCs and peripherals do not work well with square waves. It is preferable to recommend a UPS with a power *inverter* circuit. The inverter produces a precise sine wave (rather than a square wave) that is compatible with all PCs and peripherals.

Backup, backup, backup

It is a strange fact of today's society that the information contained in computers is often more valuable than the computer system itself. Serious power interruptions can damage a computer, but even more important is that vital data also might be lost from memory or the hard drive. Power protection devices are intended to protect the PC from damage and keep the system operating in the face of poor or absent ac. However, power protection devices are not foolproof. Regular backups of memory and disk files are vital to any protection plan.

Advise your customers to save their work religiously. Saving every 30 to 60 minutes is usually prudent (more often in a busy office environment); it also is free. If your customer does not have a tape backup to support their hard drive files, seriously recommend a tape drive. System backups once a day (even once a week) can preserve vital data in the rare event that a hard drive is damaged by a spike or brownout.

68
CHAPTER

Printer cleaning—dot matrix and ink jet

Although laser printers have received much of the attention (and glamour) in the PC industry, dot matrix printers (DMPs) have served as reliable workhorses in homes and businesses all over the world. Ink jet printers are another type of moving-carriage printer that have enjoyed tremendous improvements in technology over the last few years. Both printer types have proven to be remarkably reliable. As reliable as they are, however, moving-carriage type printers require routine cleaning and maintenance to ensure continuous quality printing. PC enthusiasts will find this chapter useful because regular cleaning will avoid potential service calls. Experienced technicians might be able to enhance the value of their service with printer cleaning specials.

Reviewing the conventional printer

Before you disassemble a printer to clean it, you should know your way around. In most cases, a moving carriage printer is assembled as shown in Fig. 68-1. The printer's power supply converts the high ac line voltage from any wall outlet into one or more levels of dc suitable for operating the printer electronics. All the circuitry required to operate the printer can usually be held on a single PC board. This *electronics control unit* (ECU) is a microprocessor-based system that handles the printer's interface (serial or parallel) to the host computer. The ECU (#25) also directs the mechanical subassemblies of the printer, and reads the status of several sensors. For the purposes of this chapter, you need not be concerned with these electronic assemblies other than to understand their purpose and importance.

A moving-carriage printer works by assembling characters as a series of discrete dots, which allows the printer to create multiple fonts and graphic images. Today's printers often incorporate most of the mechanical components on a single replaceable assembly (#9). The print head is the electromechanical assembly used to generate those dots.

968

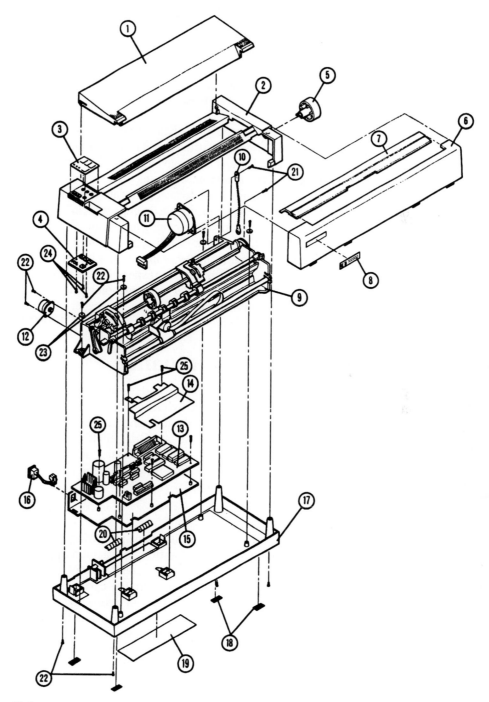

68-1 An exploded view of a carriage-type printer. Hewlett-Packard Company

For a dot-matrix printer, dot signals produced in the ECU drive small solenoids in the print head. Each solenoid contains a moveable print pin. When a solenoid fires, the print pin is pushed out of the head at a high velocity and strikes the paper through an inked ribbon. After the brief firing pulse, the print pin is withdrawn back into the print head leaving a dark dot on your page surface. By firing the solenoids in specific combinations, virtually any character or image can be formed. Typical print heads use 9 or 24 print pins.

For an ink jet printer, dot signals produced in the ECU drive small piezoelectric crystals or heaters in the print head. When fired, the crystal or heater element acts to pump an ink droplet out of the head toward the page surface. After firing, capillary action will draw in more ink from the reservoir. Older ink jet heads provided 12 or 24 nozzles, but newer heads provide many more to accommodate current 300 dpi ink jet resolution. Regardless of whether your printer uses impact or ink jet technologies, the print head will be a focal point in your cleaning and maintenance.

Of course, the print head serves little purpose standing still. It must be moved back and forth across the page surface at regular intervals in order for its dots to form a meaningful image. The *carriage transport assembly* is responsible for moving the print head left and right across the paper surface under the direction of the ECU. Finally, the paper must be advanced through the printer. The paper transport assembly will handle either friction-feed or tractor-feed paper under the direction of the ECU.

Printer cleaning and maintenance

After you have finished removing the outer housings and tested the printer thoroughly, you can begin the cleaning regimen. Start by cleaning the printer's outer case. A paper towel dampened lightly with water can go a long way in cleaning the printer's housing. To remove pesky stains or dirt, try a bit of household detergent on a clean, lint-free cloth or paper towel. Never spray water or cleaner directly onto a printer housing or vent holes, especially if the enclosures are still on the printer, and never use solvents or harsh chemicals for cleaning.

Clean the carriage area

Next, vacuum the carriage transport area—that big, open space where the print head moves back and forth. You should use a small, "static safe" vacuum to prevent accidental damage to the printer's ECU. Clean away any accumulations of dust, dirt, paper fragments, or other debris that might have settled into the carriage area. Although cleaning the carriage area, check for any obstructions or debris that might interfere with normal carriage operation. Gently remove any obstructions without damaging any of the other mechanisms. As simple and unexciting as this housekeeping might sound, most customers genuinely appreciate any extra added care and attention shown to their systems.

Check/tighten the carriage belt

Most print head carriages are carried back and forth by a heavy-duty wire or plastic belt. Check the condition and tension of the carriage transport belt. The belt should be reasonably tight and should not slip if pulled. Press the belt in the center— it should move no more than about 0.635 cm (0.25 inch). If the belt appears loose, you should consider tightening or replacing it. Replace the belt if it appears excessively worn or frayed. Loose drive belts can account for printing misalignment between passes.

Clean the dot-matrix print head

Every time a print pin strikes a page surface, a small amount of paper fibers are liberated into the air. When combined with the oils and inks of the printer ribbon, a sticky kind of gunk can form and work its way into the print pins. This can eventually jam one or more print pins or severely restrict its movement. Your next step should be to clean the print head face, and lubricate the pins (if possible).

Remove the ribbon from the carriage assembly and disengage the print head from its carriage mount (you should not have to remove the print head ribbon cable). Examine the print head's face. You should see all 9 or 24 pins inserted flush with the face. If any pins are not sitting flush, they might be jammed with foreign matter. Use a pair of fine tweezers and gently draw the pin out of the head. *Be very careful to avoid ripping the pin out of the print head here because pins only travel a few millimeters anyway.* Use a fresh, clean, lint-free swab to gently wipe away any accumulation of gunk. You might dampen the swab lightly in fresh ethyl or isopropyl alcohol. Once the pin is freed and sitting flush with the rest of the pins, wipe the front face of the print head to clean away any further accumulation of gunk. When the face is clean, wipe the face with a fresh swab dipped in light household oil. *Do not use heavy machine oils or grease.* Leave only a thin layer of oil on the face. The oil will help to lubricate the other pins once the printer is returned to service. Re-install the print head on its carriage mount and install a fresh ribbon for optimum print quality.

Clean the ink-jet print head

As a general rule, today's disposable ink-jet heads do not require routine manual cleaning. Printers typically provide a parking position for the head that places the nozzles on an *absorber pad*. The pad acts to clean the print head face, and cap the nozzles at the same time, which prevents ink in the nozzles from drying out and clogging. If the absorber pad is removed, or becomes hard and crusted with waste ink, it should be replaced.

If the ink jet-head does clog, it would be a simple matter to just replace the disposable print head with a fresh one. If the head is a fixed type, you might need to purge the print head. Remove the head from the carriage (you should not disconnect the print head cable. Remove the ink cartridge and inject a cleaning solution (usually available from the printer manufacturer) into the ink channel. Gently forcing cleaner through the print head will loosen and eliminate any clogged nozzles (but it makes a phenomenal mess; have rubber gloves and plenty of rags handy). Make sure to prevent cleaner from running down into the mechanics or printer circuits. You might have to repeat the process several times to clear stubborn clogs. Once the clogs are cleared, re-install a fresh ink cartridge and run the print head to circulate fresh ink.

Clean residual ink

When cleaning an ink-jet printer, be sure to check for the buildup of ink on the carriage mechanics such as the carriage guide or ink "spittoon." If the spittoon contains any substantial amount of ink, you should clean out the ink buildup with a clean, dry cotton swab. Ink buildup along the carriage rod can interfere with print head movement and cause faulty dot placement. Wipe off any accumulations with a clean, lint-free cloth moistened with isopropyl alcohol. When cleaning the assembly, be careful not to get alcohol on any of the rollers.

Rejuvenate the rollers

Paper is wrapped around a pliable rubber roller called the *platen*, and the platen is usually placed in contact with one or more other small rollers. A supple, pliable rubber surface is vital for proper paper handling. Old or worn rollers lose their pliability, so paper handling can be affected (especially in printers using friction-feed transport). Check the condition of the platen and other rollers. If the printer has a lot of running time on it, you might wish to rejuvenate the rollers.

Rejuvenation is accomplished by cleaning and coating the rollers with a chemical solvent formulated specifically for rubber rollers such as Solvene from the Stanford Corporation, or Clean-A-Platen from Lee Products Company. Both solvents are readily available from most office supply stores. Follow the use and ventilation instructions for both products carefully. To clean away general stains on a roller, use a clean, lint-free cloth lightly dampened with ordinary water or household detergent. *Never use harsh solvents or chemicals to clean printer rollers.* Once you are finished cleaning or rejuvenating the platen, run several pieces of paper through by hand to help absorb any residual solvent or water.

Warning: with all the new materials being used in printers today, it is not always certain that a rejuvenating solvent will be compatible with the roller material. Before beginning a major cleaning procedure, test the cleaning solvent on a very small area of a roller to ensure that the solvent does not damage the rollers.

Check the print quality

Once you have finished cleaning and maintaining the printer, your final step should be to power up the printer again and run a comprehensive self-test before reinstalling the outer housings. If you are performing these services professionally, leave the self-test results for your customer, along with the invoice and any warranty information regarding your repair.

Lubrication notes

The use of lubricants in computer printers is an arguable issue. Old, heavy printers certainly needed regular lubrication. Virtually all newer printers, however, use light, high-strength mechanisms and low-friction plastic gears and bushings. Designs have become so light and small that lubrication is generally not necessary—the lifetime of the plastic parts exceeds the expectant life of the device. In fact, lubrication added indiscriminately can actually hinder a printer's operation and serve to attract more foreign material in the future. *As a general guideline, lubricants may be added only on metal-to-metal surfaces (a metal carriage mount on metal guide rails) where there was lubrication to begin with.* Make every attempt to use the original type of lubricant, and use lubricant sparingly. If no lubricant was included originally, do not add it—replace the mechanical assembly instead.

69
CHAPTER

Printer cleaning—
laser/LED

The last few years have seen a tremendous improvement in the quality and speed of *EP* (electrophotographic) printers. Falling costs, unsurpassed image reproduction, and intense competition between manufacturers have made laser/LED printers an accepted and indispensable addition to every user's desktop. Although today's EP printers are designed to require only a little routine maintenance, many casual users tend to ignore even simple maintenance until a problem develops. The effects of such neglect can easily be interpreted as an actual defect by users and result in an unneeded service call. This chapter is intended to provide a regular, reliable procedure that service professionals and in-house PC managers can use to spot potential service neglect and maintain typical EP printers.

Reviewing the EP printer

As you probably learned in Chapter 32, an EP printer relies on a delicate balance of chemical and optical properties, as well as intricate mechanical and electronic systems, in order to perform its functions. This can sometimes make troubleshooting difficult because print quality can be adversely affected by such subtle factors as paper humidity, long-term mechanical wear, toner chemistry, and overall laser age. With so many factors influencing printer performance, the first emphasis should be to understand the EP technique. Fig. 69-1 shows a cross-sectional diagram of a typical laser printer's internal assembly.

Image formation begins when image data is sent to the printer. When printing is ready to begin, a sheet of paper (#1) is grabbed by the paper pickup roller (#5) where it is aligned by the registration rollers (#8). The photosensitive drum (#13) turns where it is cleaned and charged by the primary corona (part of the EP cartridge symbol). The writing mechanism then selectively discharges the drum at desired points that represent dark areas of the image, and toner is attracted to the discharged areas (also accomplished within the EP cartridge).

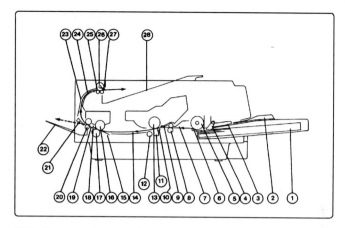

69-1 Cross-sectional view of an EP printer. Hewlett-Packard Company

When the leading edge of the paper is aligned with the leading edge of the image, the registration rollers will start the page through where it will pass in close proximity of the drum. The page is then charged by the transfer corona (#11) that attracts toner away from the drum to the page surface. Immediately after the page has attracted its toner, the static charge on the page is removed. The page now travels to the fusing assembly where a heating roller (#16) and pressure roller (#17) work together to melt toner and force it into the paper fibers. The completed page is then fed out of the printer.

Maintenance precautions

Before you jump right into procedures, it is important that you test all laser printers brought in for service before beginning maintenance. Begin by turning the printer on and running a self-test with standard-weight xerography- grade (photocopier) paper. The self-test printout will show you if there are any distinct maintenance-related problems (or serious faults) that you should be concerned with. This gives you a benchmark to work from, because you can tell how much better (or worse) the printing is after your service. If the self-test is clean and clear, reported problems can almost always be traced to user-related problems (operator error).

After obtaining one or more self-test printouts, you can then turn off and unplug the printer. *Be certain to allow 10 minutes or more before opening the printer to begin service. Remember that the fusing roller assembly can reach several hundred degrees in normal operation, so there is a burn potential around hot rollers.* Also keep in mind that the corona power supply must deliver up to 1000 V, a nasty shock hazard. *Allow plenty of time for the high-voltage power supply to discharge before opening the printer.* Safety hazards do exist in a laser printer if you are not careful.

You also need to understand what toner is. Toner is a combination of plastic, iron, and pigment (usually black) that is ground into a microfine powder. The iron component allows the toner to adhere to the magnetized development roller. The plastic component is melted under heat and pressure that allows it to adhere to the porous surface of paper. Toner can be cleaned by wiping it away with a clean towel moistened with cold water. *Never use hot water to clean up toner or wash toner from clothing.* Hot water will melt the toner and cause it to adhere permanently. *Never use any type of solvent in or around your laser printer, especially ammonia-based cleaners.* Ammonia vapors will damage the photosensitive coating of your drum. You can vacuum spilled or excess toner, but you will need a special vacuum bag to hold the toner. Most ordinary vacuum bags allow toner to pass right through and cause a mess.

Typical cleaning and maintenance

When a printer is brought in for repair and you have run at least one self-test, start your maintenance by performing a regimen of routine cleaning. There are two replaceable components of most laser printers: the toner cartridge, and the development engine containing the drum and primary corona. Upon close inspection, you can probably find where these components are latched into a swinging deck. Release the latches, and swing the toner cartridge and EP engine up and away from you.

Clean the transfer corona

Use a clean, lint-free swab dipped lightly in pure isopropyl alcohol to clean in and around the transfer corona rail. The high voltage along the wire tends to attract dust and debris in the air nearby. Foreign matter tends to collect on the corona wire and can eventually affect the image quality that is transferred to paper. Clean the length of wire gently but firmly. Be *extremely* careful not to break the corona wire. If it breaks, it must be replaced. Also clean inside of the metal track surrounding the corona and be sure that all residue is removed.

Caution: notice the thin monofilament line that is wrapped around the transfer corona case. This prevents the attracted paper from being drawn into the corona case and jamming. You must be extremely careful to avoid breaking the line. If it breaks, the transfer corona will have to be rewrapped or replaced.

Clean the transfer guide

Next, use a lint-free wipe dampened lightly with cold water to clean the transfer guide area that is located just before the transfer corona assembly. The paper passes through this guide to be charged and obtain its image from the drum. Be sure to clean up any paper dust, debris, or residual toner that might be in the area. If it is possible to open the transfer guide lock tray, do so and clean inside the lock tray area. Also wipe the adjoining transfer guide roller. Use caution when cleaning; remember that the assemblies inside a laser printer are delicate and unforgiving. Excessive force and carelessness can easily result in collateral damage to the printer.

Clean the static comb

If you look between the transfer corona and the paper feed guide, you will see a row of metallic teeth that are the antistatic teeth. Once the paper (charged by the transfer corona) receives its latent toner image from the drum, the paper must be discharged. If discharge does not occur, the paper will retain a static charge and each sheet will cling to one another. Worse yet, the charged sheet might jam in the printer paper path. Use a fine brush (such as the brush end of the corona cleaning brush) to sweep away any accumulations of paper dust or debris.

Clean the paper guide

You should clean the paper feed guide next, located between the transfer corona and fusing assembly. Use a lint-free wipe dampened lightly with cold water to wipe away any dust or residual toner in the feed guide area. This is just straightforward cleaning, but be careful not to wipe debris into more critical areas of the printer. Be very careful to avoid using excess water, and dry everything carefully.

Clean the primary corona

Locate the primary corona integrated into the EP assembly that has been swung up and away from the rest of the printer. Like the transfer corona, the primary corona's high-voltage operation tends to attract dust and debris from the nearby air. As debris coats the wire, the corona surface charge becomes uneven and can affect the image quality on the drum. If you have not already found the primary corona cleaning brush (which is usually kept near the paper feed guide), look for it now. Gently ease the felt-tipped brush over the primary corona wire and slide the brush back and forth a few times to clean away any residue that might have accumulated. If you cannot find a brush, use a clean, lint-free swab dipped lightly in fresh isopropyl alcohol. Use caution when cleaning the primary corona. If the wire breaks, the entire EP assembly will have to be replaced.

Clean the separation pawls

Clean the fuser separation pawls next. To find the pawls, open the printer's fuser area located near the paper ejection area. You will see several large plastic pawls (claws) leading to the fusing roller assembly. Use a clean, lint-free wipe dampened lightly with clean water to wipe the leading edge of each pawl. Be careful not to touch the fusing roller assembly.

Replace the cleaning pad

Although the fusing rollers should not retain any toner, long-term use can wear the roller's lubricant and allow spots of toner to remain on the roller. This residual toner can then appear on subsequent sheets of paper as spots or stains. A cleaning pad installed against the heated fusing roller wipes away any residual toner that might adhere during toner fusing, and helps to keep the fusing roller lubricated so that toner will not stick. New cleaning pads are often included with new toner cartridges, so you need not usually replace the cleaning pad unless it is time to replace a toner cartridge.

Replace the ozone filter

During normal operation, the coronas in your printer generate ozone from the high-energy ionization of surrounding air. Because ozone can be an irritant given sufficient exposure time, an ozone filter is often added to laser printers to reduce the amount of ozone gas released into the air. Typical ozone filters should be replaced after about 40,000 to 50,000 pages. Confer with your customer to find if a new ozone filter is warranted. Most ozone filters are readily accessible while the printer is open for standard cleaning.

Redistribute the toner

Swing down the frame with the toner cartridge and EP assembly and relatch it into place. Unlatch and remove the toner cartridge itself and rock it back and forth along its long axis. Although many toner cartridge designs now allow for an agitator to keep toner evenly distributed, heavy or irregular use might allow the toner to become thin in one or more areas. Agitating the toner cartridge ensures that remaining toner will be evenly distributed. This also helps maximize toner cartridge life. Re-install the toner cartridge and secure all outer doors or panels. Cleaning should now be complete.

Close up the printer

Restart the printer and initiate one or more self-tests. Compare the new and old self-tests. Under routine conditions, you should see no substantial difference between the tests. If the original self-test suggested maintenance neglect, you should see a noticeable improvement in the newer self-test.

Spotting maintenance-related problems

It is not uncommon for incidental or infrequent users to overlook or neglect routine maintenance. When maintenance is neglected for too long, a number of problems can occur in the final printed product. This part of the chapter shows you six typical maintenance-related problems.

Vertical fade

The vertical fade (Fig. 69-2) is characterized by one or more faded streaks in the vertical direction. Under most circumstances, the toner level is getting low. Remove the toner cartridge and rock it back and forth to redistribute the toner evenly in its container. Replace the toner cartridge and adjust the print density. Another cause of vertical fade occurs when the transfer corona is fouled because of dust or debris. Uneven charge distribution will allow light streaks to form. Check the transfer corona and clean it with a lint-free swab dipped lightly in fresh isopropyl alcohol. After cleaning the wire, swab out any residue within the corona case. *Be extremely careful not to break the monofilament line wrapped around the corona.* If the corona or wrap is broken, the transfer corona assembly will have to be replaced.

Dropouts

Dropouts generally appear as faded areas that are typically round in shape as shown in Fig. 69-3. The most common source of dropouts is due to problems with the paper itself. Paper with uneven moisture content or moist spots can result in

In vertical fade, faint
or white strips appear
in the vertical direction

This is often caused by
low toner levels or a
fowled transfer corona.

69-2
An example of vertical fade.

Dropouts are often
patches or areas of print
that appear faded or
faint. More often than
not, dropouts are caused
by problems with the
paper itself. Try paper
from a fresh source.

69-3
An example of dropouts.

dropouts. Even poor paper manufacturing can result in paper that produces dropout spots. Try fresh, dry paper from a different source. It also is remotely possible that the transfer corona is slightly dirty. If new paper fails to correct the problem, try cleaning the transfer corona.

Vertical lines

Vertical lines appear as one or more black streaks or smears directly from top to bottom of the page as shown in Fig. 69-4. When vertical lines appear, it usually indicates that one or more areas of the primary corona wire are fouled with accumulations of dust or debris. Clean the primary corona wire. If the dark vertical marks appear smeared, it is possible that the fuser roller cleaning pad might be dirty and need replacement. If you do not have another cleaning pad on hand, you can gently clean the pad by removing it from the fuser assembly and gently brushing away any obvious accumulations of toner. A new cleaning pad should be installed as soon as possible. If a new cleaning pad is available, replace it according to the instructions for the particular printer.

Finally, it is possible that the photosensitive drum has been scratched; this problem is rare but can occur in printers serving a heavy work load. Unfortunately, the drum would have to be replaced, but the drum is typically part of the image forma-

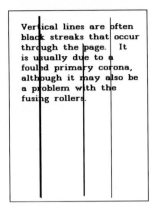

69-4
An example of vertical lines.

tion engine that can easily be replaced as an entire module. Replace the EP cartridge or engine assembly and try the printer again.

Staining

A stain is typically a dark horizontal patch that reoccurs to lesser degrees down the page as shown in Fig. 69-5. In many cases, the transport rollers that handle the paper are dirty. Clean the transport rollers and transport feed guide. It also is possible that the fuser roller cleaning pad might be dirty and need replacement. If you do not have another cleaning pad on hand, you can gently clean the pad by removing it from the fuser assembly and gently brushing away any obvious accumulations of toner. A new cleaning pad should be installed as soon as possible. If a new cleaning pad is available, replace it according to the instructions for the particular printer.

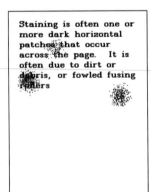

69-5
An example of staining.

Repetitive defects

Repetitive defects occur at regular intervals along the page as shown in Fig. 69-6. It is the spacing of the defects along the page that can really queue you to the actual problem. When the defects are spaced closely together (under 2 inches), there is possibly a problem with your paper transport roller(s). Check and clean

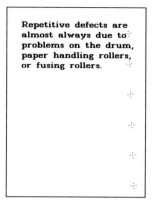

69-6
An example of repetitive
defects.

each roller to remove all debris. If the defects occur at intervals of 2 inches or greater, then there is a defect on either the development roller or the drum. Because both elements are incorporated into the image formation engine (or the EP cartridge), the entire assembly will have to be replaced in either case. Try replacing the EP cartridge.

Badly formed characters

Characters that are badly formed usually appear wavy or unsteady as in the example of Fig. 69-7. This is almost always caused by paper stock that is too slick or slippery; the rollers have a difficult time handling the paper. Try the printer again with standard 20 pound xerography-grade paper. If the problem still occurs on standard paper, the printer's scanner assembly is defective and the printer will require much more extensive bench repair.

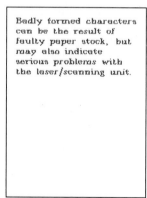

69-7
An example of badly formed
characters.

Spotting user-related problems

Beyond simple neglect, there also are a number of laser printer problems that are caused by oversights or errors in judgment. This section of the chapter shows you some of the typical user-related problems encountered with laser printers.

1. The customer complains of frequent jams. An EP printer is only as good as the medium that is used with it. Paper, envelopes, and labels must be chosen carefully to ensure proper printer operation. Remember that the printer's mechanics are designed to work with media of certain thicknesses, textures, finishes, and weights. Media that are too heavy or flimsy, or have an unusual or chemically treated finish, might not be handled properly by the printer's paper handling mechanism. Refer to the printer's manual to find what is allowable, but standard white 20 pound bond xerography-grade paper should always work properly. Ask your customer to try a different type of medium.

2. The customer complains of unusually light or dark images. Adjust the print density control to achieve an optimum print density. Casual users often forget that they must adjust the print density wheel throughout the life of the toner cartridge. When a new toner cartridge is installed, the print density must be reduced or the resulting image might be too dark. As the toner is consumed, print will become lighter, so print density must be increased. Very light print might indicate that the toner cartridge must be replaced.

3. The customer complains that it runs out of printer memory. The memory in your printer serves as a buffer for data being sent from the host computer. For moving-carriage printers, the buffer need not be very large. For laser printers, however, there must be enough memory to hold complex, high-resolution images (usually on the order of 1 or 2Mb). The entire image must be loaded into the laser printer's buffer before the page is printed. If the image to be printed is too large to fit into existing memory, the printer will register an *out of memory* error. Get your customer to scale down their image or add memory to their printer.

4. Paper holds too much static when ejected—could cause paper jams. The paper itself is often to blame. Try a standard 20-pound xerographic-grade paper with average moisture content. Paper that is too dry would tend to retain static charges. It also is possible that the static eliminator teeth in the printer are not working properly. Try cleaning the static teeth as described in this chapter.

70
CHAPTER

Upgrading a microprocessor

Most people have grown accustomed to the rapid advance of personal computers. That office system that seemed lightning-fast just a few years ago is now at least a generation out of date; it's considered virtually obsolete and probably still under warranty. Systems that are more than five or six years old are barely capable of running the applications we count on today. As you can imagine, few PC users really need (or can afford) state-of-the-art systems. However, given the choice between shelling out thousands of dollars for a new system, and spending a few hundred dollars to upgrade a current system's performance, most prudent PC users would make the upgrade investment if it meant a tangible improvement.

There are many ways to upgrade a PC. This section of the book is dedicated to many such upgrade options, but this chapter deals with the implications and techniques of microprocessor upgrades. This chapter shows you the majority of upgrade options available for PCs, illustrates the precautions and procedures for performing the upgrade, and explains some of the problems you might face in the upgrade process.

Considering the upgrade

CPU upgrades are not difficult; most can be performed in a matter of 15 minutes. Before you order that new CPU, though, you should take a bit of time and do your homework. Remember, the success of any upgrade depends on proper planning. Calling around can get you the best prices and delivery terms, but make sure that you can bring the upgrade CPU back if it does not work.

1. Check the original CPU. If the CPU is hard-soldered into place, a CPU upgrade will be impossible. Only socket-mounted CPUs can be upgraded. For hard-soldered CPUs, you will have to consider a motherboard upgrade. Also note the CPU package style. There are typically three popular package

styles: PLCC, LCC, and PGA. Many upgrades are fabricated for PGA or PLCC insertion. You might need to purchase a special adapter for LCC insertion.

2. Check motherboard compatibility. Not every motherboard is compatible with every CPU upgrade product. Before actually placing an order, it is always worthwhile to determine the motherboard's manufacturer, and check that the new CPU is indeed compatible. If the upgrade manufacturer can't tell you for certain, make sure they have a solid return policy, otherwise call elsewhere.

3. Check the size. Be careful with dimensions. Many older CPUs are mounted close to the motherboard in a low-profile fashion. Most CPU upgrades are small modules that mount into the existing CPU socket; hardly a behemoth, but it might rise high enough to interfere with an expansion board. This is an even more important consideration for low-space systems like laptops and notebooks.

4. Consider the heat. Newer CPUs (especially the i486 family) run faster and much hotter than older CPUs. When planning an upgrade, determine if a CPU heatsink will be needed. If so, see that there is space for the heatsink. Some upgrade packages will include an appropriate heatsink.

5. Consult with your customer. Finally, be candid with your customer. Find out what they expect the upgrade to accomplish for them. The customer that thinks a new CPU will bring their old i286 system on-par with an i486DX/66 is in for a rude awakening. Even a top-of-the-line CPU upgrade will be hindered in a system with slow RAM and old BIOS. In most cases, a CPU upgrade will provide a measure of improvement in overall performance, and allow broader software compatibility, but it will not work miracles.

6. Weigh the cost. Although CPU upgrades have been falling in price, and are considered rather economical in terms of an overall upgrade, the mid-to-high range upgrades can still approach $1000. Given the age of the system being upgraded, the intentions and expectations of the customer, and the plummeting cost of new systems, it might be in your customer's best interest to avoid the upgrade and invest their money elsewhere. Base your opinions on a case-by-case basis.

The pros and cons of CPU upgrades

For the most part, CPU upgrades do provide a measurable improvement in system performance, and can extend the working life of older PCs, but the return is not always worth the investment. On the positive side, CPU upgrades are simple; a plug-in replacement CPU (or CPU module) can be installed in a matter of minutes. Other than ease of installation, CPU upgrades are a mixed bag. Performance improvements range anywhere from 30% to 300% depending on the upgrade. It is important to realize that this improvement is for the *microprocessor*, and *not* for the entire system. Thus, a new CPU will not turbocharge slow RAM, speed up a lackluster hard drive, or provide advanced bus architectures (VL or PCI). Next, CPU upgrades are not cheap; the cost can range from $200 to $900 (or more) depending on the particular product. For that amount of money, it might be almost as much for a whole new motherboard, so weigh your options carefully.

The modular upgrades

All upgrades are not created equal—more specifically, there are upgrades for i286, i386, and i486 systems (Fig. 70-1). Upgrading an i286 or i386 CPU to an i486 CPU is accomplished through the use of an upgrade *module* (a small PC board holding the new CPU and any supporting circuitry). Upgrading an i386 to an i486 generally requires only a single, specially designed IC (such as the Cyrix Cx486DLC or Cyrix Cx486SRx2) that is pin-compatible with the i386, but offers the functions of the i486.

70-1
A Cyrix i386-to-i486 CPU upgrade.

The clock multipliers

The problem with older CPUs is that they were never intended to be upgraded, but systems designed around the i486 CPU envisioned a scenario where system performance could be improved by simply plugging in an improved, pin-compatible microprocessor. The problem is "Where does that new CPU come from?" After all, it's easy to see how an i486 can boost an i286 or i386 system, but once you're using an i486, improvements get a little harder to come by. True, you could go to the Pentium, PowerPC, or Blue Lightning CPU, but none of those advanced CPUs have arrived in upgrade modules yet.

The way to boost i486 performance (as Intel discovered) is to multiply the internal CPU clock. All of the logic inside a CPU is driven by a single master clock delivered to the CPU by a clock generator circuit. The higher the clock frequency, the faster the CPU can carry out its operations. Theoretically, boosting a system's performance is then just a matter of turning up the system clock. Although this is dynamite in theory, there are some real practical problems. First, the components on the motherboard (CPU included) will only work so fast; increasing the clock frequency past a certain point will cause the logic to malfunction. Second, high-frequency signals cause RF (radio frequency) interference. The higher the frequency, the more interference. Once motherboard clocks exceed 33 MHz or so, designers have to take very specialized (and expensive) RF precautions.

The solution is to multiply the motherboard clock at 25 MHz or 33 MHz, and leave the CPU's internal clock alone. For example, this allows the motherboard to run at 25 MHz with almost no modification, but the CPU can run at 50 MHz. For a 33-MHz motherboard, the CPU would run at 66 MHz. This is known as *clock doubling*, and Intel designates this as DX2 (or OverDrive technology). Because the i486 and later CPUs were designed to keep the vast majority of operations right on the CPU itself, clock doubling is very effective. By comparison, clock doubling an i386 would not have been nearly as effective because caching and floating-point operations were performed off chip, and would not have been able to enjoy the benefits of higher CPU frequencies.

Internal clocks can be multiplied by more than two, which has given rise to Intel's DX4 designation. However, the DX4 does *not* mean clock quadrupling; multiplication factors of 2.5 to 3 are more common (clock tripling). The interesting point with clock multiplication is that because surrounding hardware is generally much faster than that of older systems, upgrading an i486 CPU generally results in better performance than upgrading an i386 to an i486. For example, a 66-MHz i486DX2 offers a SPEC benchmark of 37. Simply dropping in a 100-MHz i486DX4 raises the score to 51 (a 39% improvement). As semiconductor technology continues to improve, it is likely that much faster CPUs will be developed.

Performing the upgrade

Mechanically speaking, the actual exchange of components in a CPU upgrade is very straightforward. This part of the chapter covers the essential steps and precautions that you will need to remember along the way. Before starting any kind of CPU upgrade, run a benchmarking program such as *PC Tools System Info* and note the system performance benchmark before upgrading; this gives you something to measure the system against once the upgrade is complete.

Static precautions

Today's CPUs contain over three million individual transistors. To achieve such a dense concentration of components, CPUs are fabricated with semiconductor technologies that make them *extremely* sensitive to damage from *ESD* (electrostatic discharge). Before you even open the PC or the new CPU, make it a point to take the following precautions. First, be sure to use an antistatic wrist strap connected to a proper earth ground. Second, have some antistatic foam on hand to hold the original CPU; *never* leave it on a synthetic or static-prone surface. Third, never handle the CPUs by their metal pins. Instead, handle them by their ceramic housings.

Prepare the system

As with all computer service procedures, *safety* is the primary concern. Start by turning off the PC, then unplug it from the ac outlet. Remove the screws from the outer housing, and remove the housing to expose the motherboard. Keep all of the housing screws together.

Next, locate the original CPU. It is usually the largest socket-mounted IC on the motherboard. It will be marked with numbers such as 80386DX, 80286, and so on. Look for obstructions. Note if the CPU is tucked underneath a drive, or if it is blocked by an expansion board. If the obstruction is an expansion board, try relocating the board to another slot. If the CPU is blocked by a drive or chassis, you will have to disassemble the PC in order to free the obstruction. Keep in mind that the new CPU will probably sit a bit higher than the original CPU, and need a heatsink as well. If there is not enough space to accommodate the extra bulk, *do not* proceed with the upgrade unless you can safely reposition any obstructions.

Remove the original CPU

Now that the CPU is exposed, it must be removed. However, this is not always a simple task depending on the CPU's package style. Start by locating pin 1, which is often at the beveled edge of the IC socket. Note pin 1 carefully because you will need to install the upgraded CPU in the proper orientation. Incorrectly installing the new CPU can easily damage it. PLCC packages are often the most difficult to remove because the IC literally fits into a four-sided receptacle; there is no place to fit a screwdriver under the IC. You will need a PLCC removal tool that inserts into the slots in opposing corners of the PLCC socket, and allows you to gently rock the IC out. There might be a disposable PLCC removal tool already included in the upgrade package.

PGA packages are usually a bit easier to remove. As with the PLCC IC, mark the location of pin 1 carefully. You can remove the PGA IC with a specialized PGA removal tool, or with a regular-blade screwdriver. If you use a screwdriver, gently ease the blade between the IC and socket, and pry the IC up evenly on all four sides instead of prying it up from only one side (which can damage the pins). It pays to be patient here.

LCC packages are perhaps the easiest of all to remove. Mark the location of pin 1 on the motherboard. You can then gently pry out the spring-loaded metal clip holding the IC in place. Once the retaining clip is removed, you should simply be able to lift the IC out. Be careful not to bend or break the retainer clip, because you will need it when reinstalling the CPU upgrade.

When you have finally removed the original CPU, place it into an antistatic bag, or insert it into a layer of antistatic foam for safe handling. *Never* handle the IC's metal pins, or leave it in a synthetic surface where static charges can build up.

Install new CPU

While paying close attention to the proper orientation of pin 1, insert the CPU upgrade into its adapter (if necessary), then insert the upgrade into the motherboard IC socket. Use care to insert the upgrade evenly and completely. If the upgrade is mounted on an LCC adapter, secure the adapter into place with the metal retaining clip.

Deal with the heatsink next. Many upgrades rely on a heatsink to keep the CPU at an acceptable temperature, especially i486 CPUs that tend to run fast and generate a great deal of heat. Chances are good that a heatsink has been included with the upgrade package. Be sure to use the recommended heatsink; it has been fabricated specifically to match the dimensions of the CPU. If there was an original heatsink in place, put it aside with the original CPU. If there was no heatsink included with the upgrade, and you find that the CPU is locking up for no reason at all, try adding a heatsink and thermal compound to the new CPU.

Finish up

Once the new CPU is properly installed, the upgrade should be complete. Before you restore power, though, be sure to reassemble any chassis or expansion devices that might have been removed prior to CPU removal. Once the PC is properly re-assembled, you can reconnect ac and turn the PC on. The system should boot and initialize as usual (probably faster). The final step before returning the PC to service is the installation of an i486 *caching driver* utility. This is needed for i286 and i386 systems to activate the i486 cache. The driver is typically added to the AUTOEXEC.BAT file, but it does not remain resident after the system boots, so there is no memory penalty. To get an idea of the relative performance improvement with your CPU upgrade, run a benchmarking program such as *PC Tools System Info*, and compare the new performance benchmark to the original one.

Troubleshooting the upgrade

Unfortunately, not every microprocessor upgrade goes as smoothly as the instructions say it should. Although the upgrade process is not difficult, there are some problems that can crop up unexpectedly. This part of the chapter outlines some of the most common upgrade problems and solutions.

Symptom 1. The computer powers up, but nothing happens You might have a compatibility problem. Power down the system, take a deep breath and double check the compatibility of the upgrade CPU against the motherboard. If the two are incompatible with one another, you will have to return the upgrade CPU and obtain one that IS compatible. If the two are indeed compatible after all, there might be a problem with the installation.

Check that the new CPU is oriented properly with pin 1. If not, the CPU might be in backward. When this happens, the CPU might be damaged. Try re-installing the CPU in the proper orientation and test the system again. If problems persist, the CPU is probably defective; try another CPU. If the CPU is already in the proper orientation, make sure that the CPU is seated evenly and completely. Bent or broken pins will ruin the CPU; try another CPU. If you notice any pins that are corroded, try cleaning them with a good-quality electrical contact cleaner (allow plenty of time for the cleaner to dry before re-applying power to the system).

Symptom 2. The upgrade is complete, but the performance you are seeing is less than expected First, it is impossible to predict the exact amount of performance improvement for a CPU upgrade in every possible motherboard configuration. Before you suspect a problem, ask yourself if the improvement was reasonable for the particular system. If the performance is off by 5% or 10%, it might simply be the way in which the new CPU is operating in the system. If you want to double-check your expectations, contact the upgrade manufacturer and see what kind of performance they have been getting with similar PCs.

Next, check the caching driver that is usually included with the i486 upgrade. Although upgrades to native i486 systems will not need them, i286 and i386 systems will need to activate the upgrade i486 internal cache using a small driver called during system initialization. See that the caching driver is installed properly, and loading at boot time. Even is it loads properly, other memory managers such as EMM386 .EXE can affect its performance. Make sure that any memory managers load BEFORE the caching driver is executed.

Symptom 3. The system works for a while, but then it mysteriously locks up and requires a cold reboot This can be an issue of clock frequency or heat. Check the clock speed of the motherboard against the frequency of the CPU. If the motherboard's frequency is higher than the CPU's required frequency, the CPU will be *overclocked*, in which case it might work, but freeze at random. For instance, suppose you are installing an i486DX2/50 into a 33-MHz motherboard. The clock doubling circuitry on the CPU will double the 33 to 66 MHz; this is faster than the 50 MHz i486DX2 was designed to operate. It might run for a while in the overclocked state, but it will dissipate excessive heat and eventually lock up. Install a CPU of the proper speed.

If the CPU is matched properly for speed, it should be checked for heat. CPUs that run too hot can lock up. Make sure that any heatsink provided with the upgrade is installed properly (including the use of thermal compound). Try resecuring the heatsink. If there was no heatsink provided with the upgrade, try adding a heatsink.

71
CHAPTER

Upgrading a motherboard

For the great majority of personal computers in the marketplace today, the *mother-board* represents the single, most complex (and expensive) subassembly in the system (Fig. 71-1). The motherboard contains the core processing elements (the CPU, math coprocessor, and RAM), manages the system resources (IRQ lines, DMA channels, and so on), and supports the system's expansion bus architectures (ISA, VL, PCI). More than any other part of the PC, a motherboard defines the capabilities and overall performance of a system.

71-1 A Hauppauge AT33 motherboard.

As a PC ages, however, the motherboard limits the system's upgradeability. True, you can add RAM and upgrade a CPU, and although these tactics can prolong the working life of older systems, they have a limited impact on the overall performance of a motherboard (especially older i286 and early i386 motherboards). As PC technology surges ahead, and the price of advanced motherboards continues to drop, replacing an outdated motherboard outright is becoming an ever more cost-effective upgrade option. This chapter illustrates the most important concerns when planning a motherboard upgrade, walks you through an upgrade process, and shows you how to deal with upgrade problems.

Considering the upgrade

Upgrading a motherboard is not particularly difficult, but it is a time-consuming, detail-oriented process. As a result, advance planning can be a substantial benefit. This part of the chapter covers the important points to keep in mind then planning a motherboard upgrade. As with any upgrade, make it a point to call around and find the best price and delivery terms. Given the added expense of a motherboard, you should find a vendor with a liberal return policy just in case you accidentally obtain an incorrect replacement.

1. Check the features. All motherboards are not created equal, so check the specifications closely before making a choice. BIOS now plays a vital role in such advanced features as Plug and Play, IDE and EIDE support, and virus protection. The move toward PC power conservation (so-called *green* PCs) is resulting in features like drive spindown and monitor blanking. Cache has a great impact on CPU performance. The number and type of I/O slots defines system expandability. If your major interest is enhanced video performance, a motherboard with a single VL bus slot will probably do the trick. If you're looking to position a system for the next few years, a motherboard with several PCI slots might be more appropriate. To get an overall perspective of motherboard performance, check the benchmarks such as MIPS as listed by PowerMeter, or measurements like WinMark or DOSMark from PCLabs.

2. Check the costs. Choose your new motherboard carefully. New products are expensive, and top-of-the-line motherboards will always be pricey, but you can usually find a great deal if you look 6 to 12 months back. For example, a new Pentium motherboard (with the Pentium installed) can easily run over $1300, but a recent i486DX2/66 motherboard (plus CPU) can be had for well under $900. Perhaps even more important, make sure you are aware of any hidden costs with the motherboard. For example, make sure that you know whether or not the new motherboard comes with BIOS, a CPU, and CMOS backup battery. If you plan to be running software that demands a math coprocessor, see that the CPU has an MCP built in (or find how much more that would cost). Also find out how much RAM is on the motherboard, and see if your current RAM is compatible; you might find yourself buying 4Mb to 12Mb of new SIMMs (or more) that will bump up the cost of the upgrade by at least several hundred dollars.

3. Check the dimensions and mounting. You cannot overlook the nuts and bolts involved in a motherboard upgrade. Unfortunately, this is often the most difficult (and neglected) consideration. First, the physical dimensions of the motherboard *must* fit within the space currently available in your PC. A smaller motherboard is generally not a problem, but a larger (or oddly shaped) motherboard will invariably encounter interference from drives and the power supply. The other issue is *mounting holes*. Chances are very good that mounting holes on the new motherboard will not match the original mounting holes. If you can find a perfect match, that's great, but it is unlikely. In many cases, you will have to drill new holes in the PC chassis to accommodate a new motherboard. Although this is not an absolute requirement for desktop PCs, it is for tower enclosures.

4. Check the CPU location. Check the sales literature for the new motherboard and find the location of the new CPU relative to the expansion slots. Because it is assumed that you will be upgrading your system to an i486 or Pentium motherboard, the use of a CPU heatsink will be mandatory. As a result, the CPU/heatsink combination could easily interfere with the installation of one or more expansion boards; this could be a real problem if your current system is heavily loaded. Try to pick a motherboard that places the CPU out of the way of expansion boards.

5. Weigh the cost. Before finally committing to a new motherboard, take a moment to evaluate the other subassemblies found in the PC, and anticipate any other immediate upgrade needs. How old is the hard drive? Do you need a 3½-inch floppy drive or CD-ROM? Will an SVGA board be added? Each of these added extras will boost the ultimate cost of the upgrade that much higher, so it is always worthwhile to compare this adjusted cost against the purchase price of a similar PC available off the shelf. In some cases, it might be in your customer's best interest to simply buy a new PC.

The pros and cons of traditional upgrades

Motherboard upgrades provide a much more sweeping and comprehensive improvement in system performance than changing any one element on the motherboard itself. A new motherboard not only upgrades the CPU, it provides better caching, space for faster RAM, advanced bus slots for added system performance, and superior data handling through the use of current BIOS and streamlined, highly integrated chipsets. Although new motherboards are generally regarded as the best way to rejuvenate an outdated system, however, the motherboards are expensive. If you are upgrading from an i286 or i386 motherboard, you will need a new CPU (and probably new system RAM) in addition to the motherboard. Such upgrades also can consume a fair amount of time (sometimes an hour or more) depending on the amount of mechanical disassembly that is required. The other disadvantage is that of physical incompatibility. If the mounting holes on a new motherboard do not align with the original mounting standoffs, new mounting holes will have to be created (which further lengthens the upgrade time).

The pros and cons of proprietary daughtercard upgrades

The two great drawbacks to motherboard replacement are price and time. Some companies like Compaq addressed these disadvantages by designing a *modular motherboard*—a unit that mounts the CPU, cache, and often the system RAM, on a readily accessible module referred to as a *daughtercard*. The daughtercard can be replaced in a matter of only a few minutes, with no real disassembly required. Because the daughtercard is specifically designed to carry the core processing components, an upgrade can easily yield a 100% to 600% performance improvement. These are compelling advantages, especially when there are a large number of systems that need to be upgraded. The problem with daughtercards is that they are proprietary devices that must be designed to mate with a specific motherboard. As a result, a daughtercard is generally quite expensive, sometimes more than a conventional motherboard. Daughterboard upgrades also prevent new bus architectures from being introduced to the system.

The pros and cons of processor card upgrades

Bus-mastering systems (such as the PS/2) have found another alternative to motherboard upgrades. Instead of taking the time to replace the main motherboard assembly, MicroChannel systems allow a supplemental CPU board (called a *processor card*) to be installed in any available expansion slot. Because the MicroChannel architecture allows bus mastering, the processor card can take over system control from the CPU resident on the motherboard, effectively shutting down the original CPU and providing a CPU enhancement of 200% or more. As with any expansion board, the processor card can be configured and installed in a matter of minutes. On the down side, a processor card is still rather pricey (ranging from $500 up to $1300), and more expensive than a conventional motherboard. Although processor cards are more standardized than daughtercards, they are limited to MCA systems. Processor cards also do not support the introduction of new bus architectures into a system.

Performing the upgrade

Unlike CPU or expansion card upgrades, replacing an entire motherboard is a rather involved process that requires a substantial amount of care to be accomplished successfully. This part of the chapter covers the essential steps and precautions that you will need to remember during the upgrade. Before starting the upgrade, it is a good idea to run a benchmarking program such as *PC Tools System Info* and note the system performance benchmark figure; this gives you something to measure the system against once the upgrade is finished. *You also are strongly urged to perform a complete system backup before proceeding; collateral system damage during an upgrade is a serious possibility.*

Static precautions

Most of the ICs used in today's computers are fabricated with technologies that make them *extremely* sensitive to *ESD* (electrostatic discharge). To ensure the safe handling of motherboards and other system components during the upgrade, make it a point to take the following precautions. First, invest in an antistatic mat that is large enough to cover a majority of your work area. See that the antistatic mat is properly cabled and attached to a reliable earth ground. Under no circumstances should you allow a motherboard to rest on a synthetic or static-prone surface. Second, use an antistatic wrist strap whenever handling components or tools inside the PC. Cable the wrist strap to the antistatic mat, or to another reliable earth ground. Third, always try to handle printed circuit boards by their edges—avoid touching the individual IC pins or printed wiring. Fourth, have a supply of good-quality antistatic bags on hand to hold the system's expansion boards as they are temporarily removed. Finally, excessively dry environments tend to allow substantial buildups of static charges in objects, clothing, and bodies. If it is possible, try to work in an environment with at least 40% humidity.

Save your CMOS

Before starting your upgrade, make it a point to obtain a current record of your CMOS settings. You can do this by taking PrintScreen shots of each CMOS setup page, you can photocopy and fill-in the *CMOS Configuration Form* at the back of this book, or you can use a software utility like CMOS RAM on the companion disk. You should be particularly interested in the hard drive setup information, because you will certainly need to load that data into the new motherboard's CMOS before the system will recognize your boot drive. Once you have the CMOS information, set it aside in a safe place.

Prepare the system

At this point, you can prepare the system for its upgrade. *A word of caution: be especially careful of screwdriver blades when working inside the PC.* If you should slip, the blade can easily gouge the motherboard and result in broken traces. It pays to be careful and gentle when upgrading a motherboard. *Before you even consider opening the PC cover, turn the system off, and unplug it from the ac receptacle.* This helps to ensure your safety by preventing the PC from being powered accidentally while you are working on it.

Remove the screws holding down the outer cover, and place those screws aside in a safe place. Gently remove the PC's outer cover and set it aside (out of the path of normal floor traffic). You should now be able to look into the PC and observe the motherboard, along with any expansion boards and drives that are installed. Now that you are looking at the complete PC, this is the time for you to label things. Clearly marked labels will help you remember the purpose of each cable (power, drives, key lock, speaker, drive light, and so on), and show you where each item went on the original motherboard or on various expansion boards. Don't be afraid to label things. Labels need not be fancy; a roll of masking tape and an indelible marker are all that is required. Remember that you'll have to take this all apart, so anything that will help you remember where things go will be an asset.

Remove the original motherboard

At this point, you should begin clearing the obstructions to the motherboard. Start by removing each expansion board. Place each board into an antistatic bag, and set the bag aside on the antistatic mat. Next, remove any cables that are attached to the motherboard (such as the key lock or speaker cables). If there are drive cables connected to the motherboard, remove them as well. Finally, disconnect the power cables. If there are any drives or chassis assemblies interfering with the motherboard, remove them now, and set them aside carefully.

You should now have an unobstructed view of the motherboard. Locate and remove each of the screws holding the motherboard in place. In many cases, there might be at least six (sometimes eight or more). Once each of the screws have been removed, gently lift out the motherboard and lay it aside onto the antistatic mat (the whole board should fit on the mat). Frankly, the motherboard should lift out without difficulty. If the motherboard does not budge or lift out easily, you might have overlooked a screw or cable. *Do not force the motherboard!* Carefully locate the obstruction and clear it properly.

Machining changes

If you are very fortunate, you might be able to obtain a new motherboard with screw hole locations that are identical to those of the original board. In that case, you can simply drop down to the next step and proceed to install the new motherboard. If not, life gets a bit more complicated. You see, that new motherboard has to be secured to the chassis; this is to ensure a strong platform for adding the expansion boards more than for electrical grounding. Any bending or flexing of the motherboard can result in failures.

The general solution in this case is to mount threaded, nonconductive standoffs to the motherboard, then position the motherboard so that expansion boards would be positioned properly against the rear of the machine. Mark the location of as many standoffs as possible, then drill new holes just big enough to accommodate screws inserted from under the chassis. If you *must* drill new holes, drill slowly and carefully to prevent sending metal shrapnel all over the PC. You can then vacuum any metal particles with a static-safe vacuum. Note that you do not have to place a hole for every standoff, just three or four—enough to hold the motherboard securely in place. Remaining standoffs will simply serve to keep the motherboard rigid.

Install the new motherboard

You can now place the new motherboard into the chassis and secure it into place. Do not use excessive force when tightening the screws; excessive force can cause the motherboard to warp and result in failure. When securing the board, check that there are no metal brackets or standoffs that might touch the new motherboard and cause a short circuit. Once the new motherboard is installed mechanically, you can start reassembling the system.

Refer to the user's guide that accompanies the new motherboard, and check each jumper or DIP switch. This is a particularly important step because many contemporary motherboards provide services right on-board that have traditionally been assigned to expansion boards (such as video adapters and drive controllers). For example, if you used a dual serial port board with your original motherboard, but your new motherboard provides two serial ports, you won't need the dual serial port board. If you need to use that board, you will have to set motherboard jumpers to disable the on-board serial ports. The same thing is true of video adapters. If a VGA port is available on the new motherboard, but you have an SVGA video board on hand, you will have to disable the on-board video port to prevent a hardware conflict. If the new motherboard provides a floppy and IDE controller, you can abandon that drive controller board and plug the drives right into the appropriate connectors on the motherboard. In that case, check the drive control jumpers to be sure they are enabled. Be sure to review each available jumper carefully.

Reassemble the system

Once the motherboard jumpers are set, you can install the CPU, system RAM, and cables. CPU installation should go easily, but be aware that the CPU must be oriented properly in the socket relative to pin 1. Chances are that the CPU will require a heatsink, so be sure to install it securely (along with thermal compound to improve heat transfer between the CPU and heatsink). If you need to install the BIOS IC(s), you might do that next. Be careful to orient each BIOS ROM properly relative to pin 1. If there is more than one BIOS ROM, be sure to install IC1 and IC2 in their proper places. Reversing the BIOS ROM locations should not damage them, but the system will probably not boot. The new motherboard will need a backup battery to support the CMOS/RTC IC. If there is not a battery already on the new motherboard, install a new battery (or reconnect the original battery pack).

Make sure that each SIMM snaps gently into place; if they do not, they might be inserted backward. When inserting cables, note that the red strip on each ribbon cable is pin 1. Make sure that pin 1 on the cable is matched to pin 1 on the corresponding connector. Inserting a ribbon cable backward is rarely damaging, but it might prevent the system from booting. Reconnect the power cables. Finally, install the expansion boards that you will need in the system. Remember that you might not need all of the adapter boards you started with if the motherboard will be taking over particular functions. If you had disassembled any drives or chassis subassemblies before removing the original motherboard, be sure to reassemble any of those items now, and check that their power and signal cabling are secure. Reconnect any ancillary devices such as the mouse, keyboard, and monitor.

Testing the system

At last, you will face the moment of truth. If things have gone well, this procedure should have taken no more than an hour. Once the components and cabling are all secure, it will be time to reconnect the ac line cord and try applying power to the system. Make sure that your hands and any tools are clear of the PC. Turn on the monitor, double-check your power cable installation one more time, then go ahead and hit the power switch.

After a moment or two, you should see a BIOS message appear on the monitor—this is a good sign. When the POST displays its message asking to start the SETUP procedure (usually by pressing the F1 key), go ahead and start it. Review each screen in the SETUP routine, and restore as many CMOS settings as possible (especially the memory amount, floppy drive types, and hard drive configuration). Chances are that there will be several SETUP variables that were not in the original system. Just leave these in their default states for now—you can always optimize them later. Save the CMOS setup and reboot the computer. Your upgraded system should now complete its POST successfully, and boot to DOS as expected. Congratulations, you have completed your motherboard upgrade.

When the system boots as expected, the last step should be to power down the computer and reassemble the outer housing. You can then run your benchmarking program again (such as PC Tools System Info) to determine the new benchmarks for your PC. You can see the relative improvement in performance over that of the original system.

Troubleshooting the upgrade

Unfortunately, motherboard upgrades are frequently fraught with problems. The sheer number of jumpers, DIP switches, cables, and CMOS settings frequently provide problems for the novice. This part of the chapter outlines a series of problems and solutions that typically plague motherboard upgrades.

Symptom 1. The motherboard is installed, but the system won't boot This is a classic sign of installation problems. Start with the basics. Check all of the cables and connectors, especially the power connectors. Also make sure that there are no metal standoffs or brackets shorting the motherboard from underneath. Next, check for any wiring or cables that might be installed backward. Although this will rarely keep a PC from booting, it is possible. Be sure that pin 1 on each cable aligns with pin 1 of each connector. Finally, double check the socket-mounted ICs such as the CPU, BIOS ROM(s), and SIMMs. They should all be aligned properly, and inserted evenly and completely. If you locate an incorrectly installed IC, it might or might not be damaged. Remove it from the motherboard, check it for bent or broken pins, reinsert it correctly, and try the motherboard again. If the IC is damaged, it should be replaced.

Symptom 2. The motherboard starts, but it will not boot from the hard drive or recognize the correct amount of RAM in the system You might see an error message such as "CMOS Error; press F1 to run SETUP." This error generally indicates that the motherboard is working, but the system CMOS contains incorrect information. Either you forgot to enter the new CMOS variables, you forgot to save the settings, or the backup battery is not installed and CMOS contents were lost after the system was powered down. Check the backup battery first. If the battery is a coin cell, see that it is inserted properly and completely into its holder. If the battery is a pack type, check to see that it is plugged into the proper motherboard connector in the right polarity. If the battery is installed correctly, try a new one. Run the SETUP program and check each drive and memory setting. If you entered a drive parameter or RAM amount improperly, correct the settings and save CMOS again. Reboot the PC. If new CMOS settings are lost after the PC is powered down, the backup battery has failed, try a new battery.

Symptom 3. You cannot use one or more drives in the PC Either the drive(s) have been entered improperly in the CMOS setup routine, or the drive(s) are cabled improperly. Start by checking the CMOS setup. Make sure that there are proper references for the floppy drives and hard drives in the system. Fill in any missing information, and reboot the computer. If the CMOS settings are all correct, check the data cables and power cables at each drive; loose power or signal cables can easily disable a drive.

Symptom 4. The system boots and runs, but it locks up unpredictably Check the system CPU for excessive heat. An overheated CPU can lock up without warning. If the CPU is fitted with a heatsink, make sure that the heatsink is securely attached, and that you have used ample amounts of thermal compound to aid heat transfer. If the CPU runs hot and there is no heatsink, try adding one.

Another factor to consider is the possibility of controller conflicts. For example, if there is a video port on the new motherboard, but you also have a video board installed in an expansion slot, you will have to set jumpers to disable the motherboard's video port. The same thing is true for drive controller conflicts, as well as serial or parallel port conflicts. Take another close look at the expansion boards in your system, and make sure that the board functions do not conflict with the functions provided on the motherboard.

Symptom 5. There is system activity, but the video is erratic or absent Check to see that there is no video conflict between the motherboard and a video expansion board. If there is a video port on the motherboard, it probably should be disabled when an expansion video board is used in the system. Also check that the monitor is turned on, and that the video cable is securely connected to the video port. If problems persist, check that the video board is installed correctly, and that if extra memory must be excluded from the upper memory area, that the proper command line switches are included with EMM386 in the CONFIG.SYS file.

72
CHAPTER

Upgrading a power supply

Power is the lifeblood of every PC. Each element of a PC (hard drives, memory SIMMs, video boards, motherboards, and all other components) demands energy from the power supply (Fig. 72-1). Many of today's IBM-compatible clones cut costs by using power supplies that provide enough power to run the basic system but not much else. When you upgrade or refit such a PC, you can often run into system problems such as random lockups, error messages, and strange behavior. This chapter shows you how to recognize potential power problems and upgrade the supply if needed. *Use extreme caution whenever working with power systems.* Alternating current at the wall outlet (and inside the power supply itself) can be very dangerous in the hands of untrained personnel. If you are uncomfortable dealing with the hazards of ac, refer the actual testing and upgrade procedures shown here to more experienced individuals.

72-1
A TurboCool 300AT power supply.

Recognizing potential power problems

As with most PC problems, the key to recognizing power problems is proper diagnosis. Diagnosing a failed power supply is a relatively simple process. First, a supply malfunction will typically prevent a PC from booting—a fairly obvious symptom. A low or absent power output registered on a multimeter or POST board offers a direct indication of the problem. After you identify a failed supply, it becomes a matter of troubleshooting the supply or replacing it outright. Unfortunately, a great many power problems are intermittent. The power supply has not necessarily failed, but it is not able to supply enough power to keep the system running properly. The following chronic problems can often help you navigate this gray area.

- *The computer freezes intermittently* Just because your system locks up does not necessarily mean that you should call the power company. Most computers are prone to freeze due to software application and configuration errors (which are never due to power problems), especially after you install a new application. The time you should be suspicious of power problems is when your system (that has been working fine for some time) suddenly starts freezing for no reason at all. Not just once, but several times a day, and maybe even several times an hour. If the system tends to freeze when it is moved to a new location, power problems also might be to blame.

- *There are random memory errors* As with system lockups, an occasional memory error message does not necessarily indicate a power problem, especially if you have just added a new application or device driver. If you suddenly see a rash of memory errors (or have just finished upgrading the system), it's time to check your power. When memory errors occur after moving the PC to another location, power problems are likely at fault.

- *Data is lost or corrupted on the hard drive* Hard-drive problems can be the result of several factors—everything from a loose data cable to operator error. Check the drive carefully to be sure that it is connected securely. If the drive seems to be having difficulty reading or writing the disk, check power first before attempting to back up the disk or run any disk-based diagnostics. If you attempt to defragment or test the disk with power problems present, subsequent problems can do even more damage. This symptom also suggests that the supply might be overloaded. This might be the case if problems developed after you installed another drive or a power-hungry expansion board into your system. If power checks correctly, you can proceed with disk diagnostics.

- *Trouble communicating with modems or peripherals* You might see a rash of communication errors when trying to use a modem or mouse (you might see other communication driver error messages). Make sure that the peripherals connected to your system are installed and configured properly. Established systems that suddenly have trouble staying on-line or interacting with the printer might be suffering from a power problem.

- *The system suffers from chronic hardware failures* Such a problem is characterized by a fault that seems to reoccur after a few days or a week. For example, you see a memory error, replace the memory, and the fault went away, but the same fault returns a few days later. This type of problem suggests that power spikes (brief high-voltage surges of electricity) are entering the system from the ac line. Many economy power supplies omit even the most rudimentary spike and surge suppression circuitry, so power anomalies often pass through the supply to the motherboard and drives with little (if any) protection at all. In most cases, a power anomaly will crash the system, but does not result in any real damage. In extreme cases, a strong power anomaly can actually damage one or more ICs on the motherboard, expansion board(s), or drive(s).

Dealing with power problems

Now that you have an idea how power problems tend to manifest themselves in the PC, you can take some decisive steps to isolate and rectify the problem. Regardless of what symptoms your particular system might be exhibiting, you should not automatically assume that your system (or power supply) is at fault. Before you even think about opening the PC, you should check the ac line voltage.

Checking the ac

Even the most forgiving power supply needs a stable source of ac in order to function correctly. Industrial devices such as motors and heaters can draw so much power that there is insufficient ac remaining to power the computer. Commercial and domestic appliances such as air conditioners, stoves, coffee makers, and refrigerators also can result in low or unsteady ac levels. Appliances also are notorious for their introduction of voltage spikes that can easily result in circuit damage.

For the most part, it is rather pointless to look for power problems with ordinary test instruments. Multimeters are good for testing overall ac levels, but they are usually too slow to catch rapidly changing power levels such as spikes. Even most surges will go undetected. Oscilloscopes are too expensive for casual 50-/60-Hz measurements, and they rarely save any anomalies that are detected. Once the problem is displayed, it is gone. As a result, you are forced to sit and watch the oscilloscope until a problem occurs. Serious power observations require a dedicated power test instrument with data logging or long-term chart recording capabilities. Such equipment is available, but is far too expensive for ordinary users. Fortunately, there are some trial-and-error steps that can be taken to test the problem.

First, you need to make sure that your ac outlet is providing the right amount of voltage. Use a multimeter and measure the output at your wall outlet. Domestic US voltage levels should be between 110 and 130 Vac. If voltage is too low (or too high), the objective is to find out if there is anything on the line that might be causing the voltage problem. Check to see if there are any high-energy devices on the same circuit (such as coffee makers or air conditioners). If so, try turning those devices off. If the ac at your computer's outlet returns to a normal value, try your system now—that might have been the problem. Eventually, you will need to turn your air conditioner or coffee maker back on, so be sure to shut down your system until you can have a new line installed or find another line for the computer.

If there are no other devices on the line (or the line voltage fails to return to a normal level), your next step should immediately be to find an outlet with the proper voltage level. If an outlet with a proper voltage cannot be found, an electrician should be consulted to install a proper ac line. An electrician also should be able to ensure that the ac line is properly grounded. When the ac line voltage seems correct, suspect the computer supply itself.

Suspect the supply

When the ac input seems correct, you should suspect the computer supply. If the system is suffering from chronic hardware problems, try putting a good-quality surge protector between the ac wall outlet and computer ac cord. It also would be acceptable to try the system on another ac line that might be free of surges or spikes. Open the computer and use a multimeter to check the voltage level at each supply output. You can choose any available 4-pin mate-n-lock connector for this test. You can check against the pinout shown in Table 72-1. The +12-Vdc and +5-Vdc levels should be correct. The power LEDs on a POST board also will give you an approximation of supply output levels.

Table 72-1. Pin assignments for a 4-pin mate-n-lock connector

Pin 1	+12Vdc	Yellow
Pin 2	Ground	Black
Pin 3	Ground	Black
Pin 4	+5Vdc	Red

Other Wire Color Designations

Blue	-12Vdc
Yellow	-5Vdc (older PC designs)
Orange	Power Good signal

If either supply output level is low, the supply might be overloaded by too many devices in the system. If you have just upgraded the system with a new drive or expansion board, try removing or disabling the upgrade and see if dc voltages climb to their normal levels. If they do, the supply is overloaded and should be upgraded as shown in a following section. If levels do not return to normal (or either or both of the voltages are high), the supply might be defective. If you determine the supply to be defective, you might troubleshoot or replace the supply at your discretion.

Upgrading the supply

It is not uncommon for power supplies to become overloaded by upgrades and peripherals. When most consumers go out to buy a PC, the power supply capacity is often the last specification on their minds. It is the more exciting specifications such as CPU speed and hard drive capacity that get all the attention. Few people worry about upgrading a brand new system. As a technical professional, the best advise you can give consumers is very simple: "don't skimp on power." If you buy a new system, get one with a supply capacity that will be big enough to support a few typical upgrades like a video capture board, an additional hard drive, a CD-ROM, an internal modem, and at least double the amount of memory currently fitted into the system. You need not invest in the biggest and best supply (unless you've got a lot of expansion devices from a previous system), but don't trap yourself by getting the smallest (cheapest) one either.

Choosing a supply

When you determine that your supply has failed (or needs to be upgraded), there are two important factors that you need to consider; the power capacity of the new supply, and its physical dimensions. The capacity of a power supply is measured in watts (W). This is the maximum amount of power that can be supplied to a load (the computer) safely. Table 72-2 shows a comparison of power supply ratings for various PCs. Today's PC power supplies range from about 50 W to 300 W. Choosing the proper power rating for an upgraded supply is often a matter of approximation— you can usually calculate a safe upgrade by adding 50 W to the original supply rating. For example, a fair upgrade for an IBM AT supply (usually 192 W) would be the next closest rating to (192 +50) 242 W. The actual supply might be 230 W or 260 W or something in that range, but at least you're in an acceptable range of ratings.

**Table 72-2. Typical
PC power capacities**

IBM PC (original)	63.5W
IBM XT	130W
IBM AT	192W
PS/2 Model 50	94W
PS/2 Model 50Z	94W
PS/2 Model 60	225W
PS/2 Model 70	105W
PS/2 Model 80	225W

Before you finally choose a replacement supply, you will need to consider its physical dimensions. The new supply must be able to fit within the space allotted inside the PC. The new supply must be bolted into place, so its mounting holes should align properly with the holes in the original supply. A new supply also must have connector scheme that is compatible with the motherboard. The 4-pin mate-n-lock connectors are standard, but motherboard power connectors can vary a bit from model to model. Figure 72-2 illustrates a typical motherboard power connector set. Be sure to get a supply with the correct connector configuration for your motherboard. If you cannot find a compatible third-party supply, contact the PC's manufacturer. Some computer enthusiasts might be tempted to splice a power supply into the old motherboard connector. This should be *avoided* at all costs. A new power supply is typically warranted for 90 days to 1 year. Splicing its wiring immediately voids any warranty.

1	1.	Orange	PwrGood
	2.	Red	+5
	3.	Yellow	+12
	4.	Blue	−12
	5.	Black	Gnd
6	6.	Black	Gnd
1	1.	Black	Gnd
	2.	Black	Gnd
	3.	White	−5
	4.	Red	+5
	5.	Red	+5
6	6.	Red	+5

72-2 Motherboard power connectors.

Test the upgrade carefully

When installing a new supply, be sure that it is unplugged and turned off. Before firing up the supply for the first time, remove any optional or noncritical expansion boards until you can verify that the PC is working correctly. You can then power-down the PC again and re-install any additional boards or peripherals, then burn-in the system for at least 48 hours before returning it to service.

73
CHAPTER

Upgrading a system BIOS

As you saw in Chapter 15, the *basic input/output system* (or BIOS) forms an interface between nonstandardized PC hardware produced by a variety of manufacturers and the standard software used as an *operating system* (OS). BIOS is typically implemented on a *read-only memory* (ROM) IC and installed on the motherboard. It is the BIOS that gives an operating system access to disk drives, memory, and other functions that are so transparent in everyday operation. This chapter shows you the reasons for upgrading a BIOS ROM, and gives you the procedures to make the process as painless as possible.

Considering an upgrade

You might wonder why it would even be necessary to bother with an upgrade. Ideally, a BIOS ROM should be viable for the life of a PC. Although this is true in a majority of situations, there are two compelling reasons to undertake a BIOS upgrade. First, a newer BIOS can add support for drives and devices that currently require device drivers or TSRs. Placing support on a BIOS ROM means that there is one less device driver demanding space in your conventional memory. This factor is most important in older systems (i386 and slower i486-based PCs). Second (and maybe even more important), BIOS ROM is fundamentally a piece of software. Like all software, there are sometimes defects or oversights (*bugs*) that cause problems with system operations. This is especially true when the same BIOS is incorporated into a variety of motherboards. Bugs and compatibility problems virtually demand a BIOS upgrade.

Recognizing BIOS problems

Unfortunately, diagnosing a BIOS bug is not a simple task. There are no diagnostics to check BIOS operations. BIOS manufacturers rarely publicize their errors, so there is no centralized index of symptoms that you can refer to that suggest a faulty BIOS or incompatibility. However, BIOS problems tend to fall into several categories that might alert you to the possibility of BIOS trouble. You can then address the symptoms with the BIOS manufacturer directly.

1. There is trouble with Windows (usually regarding drive access or keyboard operations). Some newer versions of BIOS intended to enhance Windows can cause certain motherboard designs to crash or hang up intermittently. When the drives and keyboard check properly (and work just fine under DOS) a BIOS upgrade might be in order. You also might have to replace the keyboard controller IC.

2. There is trouble with *IDE* (integrated drive electronics) support. IDE came to prominence in late 1989 and early 1990. Because of their unique timing requirements, early IDE devices were susceptible to such errors as data corruption, failure to boot, and so on. By Q2 of 1990, most BIOS versions had streamlined their IDE support. When you encounter difficulties installing an IDE drive in an older PC, check the BIOS date. If the date is 1989 or earlier, consider a BIOS upgrade,

3. There is trouble with floppy disk support. Random disk errors might occur when a 720K diskette is used in a 1.44Mb drive, or the 1.44Mb drive might be unable to format 1.44Mb diskettes. Once again, this symptom is seen most frequently on older PCs (1988–1991) when 1.44Mb floppy drives were becoming commonplace in PCs. Floppy drive problems might be coupled to the mouse configuration.

4. There is trouble with network support. In some circumstances, the PC will not work properly when integrated into a Novell Netware system (or other network). This is often due to the inability of older Novell versions to work with PC user-defined drive types. ROM shadowing usually has to be enabled to allow user-defined drive types. Unfortunately, not all motherboard chipsets support ROM shadowing. BIOS versions later than 1990 have generally corrected this problem.

5. There is trouble with one or both serial ports. BIOS problems often manifest themselves as COM port difficulties under DOS or Windows (often when a mouse is installed). If the serial port circuitry checks properly under diagnostics, suspect a BIOS bug. Check with the BIOS manufacturer to find if an upgrade or patch file are available.

Gathering information

The BIOS upgrade process is not terribly difficult, but success depends on obtaining the correct material. To ensure that you order the proper upgrade part, it is important to collect some information about the system. In most cases, the following five specifications should help ensure an accurate upgrade:

- PC make and model
- Motherboard manufacturer and CPU
- Make and version of existing BIOS (shown on the display during initialization)
- Part number of the ROM IC itself (you might have to peel back the ROM label)
- Make, model, and part numbers of main motherboard chipset(s) (if any)

When you consider how closely BIOS is related to PC hardware, you can understand why this information is necessary. Feel free to photocopy the *BIOS Upgrade Form* in the appendix of this book. Upgrades can be purchased from many of the third-party vendors listed on the companion disk. *For your protection, though, place orders only with firms that offer a reasonable return policy (in the event that the new BIOS does not work as expected).*

Performing the upgrade

There are several methods of incorporating a BIOS upgrade into your PC, and in all cases, the proper solution will rely on an understanding of the options available to you. For the purposes of this book, there are four solutions available to a technician: (1) using a BIOS patch, (2) replacing the IC, (3) burning a new EPROM, and (4) re-programming a flash BIOS. The solution you choose will depend on the age of the particular machine.

Patching a faulty function

As distracting and unsettling as a BIOS problem might be, few BIOS problems are fatal. Because device drivers and TSRs can serve to supplement a BIOS, they also can support shortfalls in BIOS operation. By adding a corrective file to CONFIG.SYS or AUTOEXEC.BAT, many BIOS problems can be at least abated without even opening the PC enclosure. As just one example, an AMI BIOS error concerning a problem with COM2 can be corrected by adding the FIFO-OFF.COM file to AUTOEXEC.BAT. Although this will not repair the problem entirely, a corrective routine can at least allow the system to work. To find patches and corrective files for a BIOS, you will need to search the on-line resources for your particular BIOS manufacturer. On-line resources include forums on such services as CompuServe and America On-Line, or go direct to manufacturer's BBSs.

Replacing ICs

Replacing the BIOS IC(s) outright is the classic solution for many PC designs. Traditional ROMs are 28 pin dual in-line (DIP) devices such as those in Fig. 73-1, IBM PC/XT, PC/AT (i286), (i386), and many i486-based motherboards use traditional DIP ROM ICs. Fast i486 and Pentium-based motherboards use a socket-mounted *PLCC* (plastic-leaded chip carrier) IC for BIOS. Although today's PCs and expansion products make extensive use of surface-mount ICs and other components, BIOS devices are the single remaining element still implemented in DIP sockets. PC/XT systems use a single ROM to supply a 32K BIOS, most PC/AT systems use two ROMs to supply a 64K BIOS, and newer i486 and Pentium-based systems incorporate a 128K BIOS on a single ROM. You can obtain updated ROMs from the motherboard's manufacturer, or one of the BIOS vendors listed on the companion disk (in a few cases, you might be able to obtain updates directly from the BIOS manufacturer).

Before proceeding with a BIOS upgrade, remove all power from the PC and disconnect the ac line cord. Remove the outer enclosure and locate the BIOS ROM(s) on the motherboard. Remember to make use of your static controls. Pay particular attention to the orientation (or *keying*) of pin 1. When more than one IC is involved, also note which ROM is "even" and which one is "odd." Remove DIP ICs carefully. You can use a DIP removal tool, or rock the IC gently from its socket using the wide edge

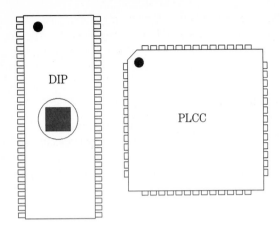

73-1
Two typical BIOS IC types.

of a regular screwdriver. *Be extremely careful when removing DIP ICs—you might have to put them back if things go wrong. Gentle* is definitely better. A specialized tool will be needed to remove PLCC devices.

You should be equally cautious when installing new DIP ICs. If those 28 little pins are not inserted evenly and straight, they will bend and break. PLCCs are a bit more forgiving because there are no leads to bend. Make sure to install ICs completely. Before restoring power, make sure the ICs are inserted in their proper orientation. If the ICs are installed in an orientation opposite from the one intended, you might damage the ROM. If the system fails to initialize, the IC(s) might not be inserted completely, or you might have transposed the "even" and "odd" ROMs. Double-check your work if necessary. Depending on your particular upgrade, you also might find yourself replacing the motherboard's keyboard controller IC.

Reprogramming EPROMS

If you handle a large number of BIOS upgrades, and have access to PC-based EPROM programming equipment, you can program (or *burn*) your ROMs. The term EPROM stands for *erasable programmable read-only memory*, so given the proper BIOS data, you can translate the contents of a BIOS disk file to a physical IC (BIOS "while-u-wait"). EPROM programming equipment is not terribly expensive, and can be obtained from any full-service electronics catalog store, but a good model with PC compatibility can easily run over $500. As you might expect, this kind of workbench BIOS requires a bit of technical skill, and is certainly not a worthwhile endeavor for the occasional PC hobbyist.

However, the ability to burn your own EPROMs does offer some unique advantages for an enterprising technician. Knowledgeable technicians versed in machine language can actually customize the BIOS (adding new hard drive parameters to the hard drive table). You also can create backup copies of older BIOS for systems that might no longer be in production, as well as other BIOS for video or drive systems. Of course, modifying a BIOS can have unforeseen consequences for a system; mistakes and errors will disable or crash the PC. Fortunately, you are not altering the original BIOS ROM, so you can always restore the original IC.

It is a simple matter to back up your BIOS contents to a disk file. All you need is the DOS DEBUG utility. *Remember: altering or duplicating BIOS code might breach the copyright of the BIOS manufacturer.* A BIOS should only be duplicated or modified for the benefit of your individual customers. The typical DEBUG BIOS backup procedure is:

```
C:\> DEBUG ;start the DEBUG utility
- N BIOSBACK.ROM ;name the backup file
- R BX ;alter the CPU's BX register
BX 0000 ;from zero
:1 ;to one (this indicates a 64K file)
- M F000:0 FFFF CS:0 ;move BIOS data in preparation
for recording
- W 0 ;write the file from offset 0
Writing 10000 bytes ;10000h = 64K
- Q ;quit DEBUG
```

This procedure will save the entire 64K data segment from F000:0000h to F000:FFFFh as a disk file. If the BIOS in your particular system is 128K (usually starting at E000:0000h) replace the starting address in the Move command. You also can back up other ROMs to disk, but you must know the starting address and size of the ROM. For example, a ROM that starts at D400:0000h and is 16K long can be backed up with a procedure such as:

```
C:\> DEBUG ;start the DEBUG utility
- N TEST.ROM;choose a name for the file
- R CX ;alter the CPU's CX register (for short
transfers)
CX 0000 ;from zero
:4000 ;to 4000h (16K)
- M D400:0 3FFF CS:0 ;move BIOS data in preparation
of recording
- W 0 ;write the file from offset 0
Writing 04000 bytes ;4000h = 16K
- Q ;quit DEBUG
```

Updating flash BIOS

Flash BIOS represents the newest class of BIOS ROM ICs that are typically found in fast i486 and Pentium-based PCs. A flash BIOS is essentially an *EEPROM* (electrically erasable programmable read-only memory); that is, the IC can be re-programmed right on the motherboard. Rather than worry about providing new BIOS ICs, a BIOS or motherboard manufacturer can provide updated BIOS code as a BBS or on-line file. The name of the file is typically coupled to only a particular motherboard. For example, updating the flash BIOS on an AMI Atlas ISA/PCI Pentium motherboard requires a file named S721P.ROM. If this filename is not used, the BIOS will not be reprogrammed. The AMI Excalibur PCI-II ISA/PCI Pentium motherboard requires the filename S722P.ROM.

An updated BIOS file can be downloaded from the motherboard manufacturer and placed in the root directory of a bootable floppy disk. Power down the PC and set the flash enable jumper to allow reprogramming (this jumper forms a "write protect" for the flash BIOS). The number and location of the enable jumper will vary from mother-board-to-motherboard. Consult your system documentation to find the specific jumper. Also, the system should have its speaker connected because the programming process often generates a series of audio codes. Apply power to the system while holding the Home key for several seconds (your system might use a different key). The mother-board will search for the needed BIOS filename, erase the flash IC, reprogram the flash IC with data from the .ROM file, and reboot the system. When reprogramming is complete, remove the jumper to disable the flash programming feature.

If there is an error at any point in the reprogramming process, you might hear one or more beeps. Table 73-1 outlines the beeps and descriptions for AMI flash BIOS. These are not beep codes as described in Chapter 15, but flash BIOS procedural errors. Keep in mind that the flash BIOS procedures outlined here might vary for your particular system.

Table 73-1. AMI Flash programming beep messages

Beeps	Meaning
None	No error. Successful completion
Continuous single beep	No floppy disk in drive A:
Five beeps	Needed .ROM program not present on floppy disk
Seven beeps	Floppy read error
Six beeps	BIOS file size error
Eight beeps	The expected flash EEPROM is not present
Continuous two beeps	Problem erasing the flash EEPROM
Continuous three beeps	Problem programming the flash EEPROM
Continuous four beeps	BIOS is not able to reset the CPU

The keyboard controller

The keyboard controller is a remarkably important element of the PC. In addition to handling system interaction with the keyboard, the keyboard controller manages the A20 gate. The A20 gate allows modern CPUs to operate in the protected mode and address memory above 1Mb. Some keyboard controllers also serve to select CPU clock speed. Because the keyboard controller contains a small amount of on-board ROM, the controller might become outdated or suffer from software defects just as any other BIOS element. Keyboard controller problems often manifest themselves under Windows or OS/2. As a result, it might be necessary to replace the keyboard controller IC along with BIOS ROM ICs.

A

APPENDIX

MPC standards for the PC

Minimum Requirements	MPC Level 2	MPC Level 3
RAM	4MB	8MB
Microprocessor	25 MHz 486 SX or equivalent	75 MHz Pentium™ or other processor capable of running x86 binaries at a comparable level.
Hard Drive	160 MB	540 MB
CD-ROM Drive	300 KB/second sustained transfer rate, average access time of 400 ms; CD-ROM XA ready; multisession capable.	600 KB/second sustained transfer rate, average access time of 250 ms; CD-ROM XA ready; multisession capable.
Audio	16-bit digital sound, 8 note synthesizer, MIDI playback.	16-bit digital sound, wavetable, MIDI playback; if speakers are included, they must be measured and tested at minimum of 3 watts/channel.
Graphics Performance	Delivery of 1.2 megapixels/second given 40% of CPU bandwidth.	Color space conversion and scaling capability; direct access to frame buffer for video-enabled graphics subsystem with a resolution of 352×240 at 30 fps (or 352×288 at 25 fps) at 15 bits/pixel, unscaled, without cropping.
Video Playback	N/A	MPEG1 (hardware or software) with OM-1 compliance; direct access to frame buffer with a resolution of 352×240 at 30 fps (or 352×288 at 25 fps) at 15 bits/pixel, unscaled, without cropping; all codecs (hardware and/or software) must support a synchronized audio/video stream with a resolution of 352×240 at 30 fps (or 352×288 at 25 fps) at 15 bits/pixel without dropping a frame.
User Input	101-key IBM-style keyboard or keyboard that delivers same functionality; two-button mouse.	101-key IBM-style keyboard or keyboard that delivers same functionality; two-button mouse.
I/O	MIDI, joystick, serial, parallel	MIDI, joystick, serial, parallel
System Software	Windows 3.0 plus Multimedia Extensions or binary compatible.	Windows 3.11 and DOS 6.0 or binary compatible.

B
APPENDIX

Standard ASCII chart (0 to 127)

Character	Decimal	Hex	Character	Decimal	Hex
NUL	0	00h	SOH	1	01h
STX	2	02h	ETX	3	03h
EOT	4	04h	ENQ	5	05h
ACK	6	06h	BEL	7	07h
BS	8	08h	HT	9	09h
LF	10	0Ah	VT	11	0Bh
FF	12	0Ch	CR	13	0Dh
SO	14	0Eh	SI	15	0Fh
DLE	16	10h	DC1	17	11h
DC2	18	12h	DC3	19	13h
DC4	20	14h	NAK	21	15h
SYN	22	16h	ETB	23	17h
CAN	24	18h	EM	25	19h
SUB	26	1Ah	ESC	27	1Bh
FS	28	1Ch	GS	29	1Dh
RS	30	1Eh	US	31	1Fh
SP	32	20h	!	33	21h
"	34	22h	#	35	23h
$	36	24h	%	37	25h
&	38	26h	'	39	27h
(	40	28h	)	41	29h
*	42	2Ah	+	43	2Bh
,	44	2Ch	-	45	2Dh
.	46	2Eh	/	47	2Fh
0	48	30h	1	49	31h
2	50	32h	3	51	33h
4	52	34h	5	53	35h

Character	Decimal	Hex	Character	Decimal	Hex
6	54	36h	7	55	37h
8	56	38h	9	57	39h
:	58	3Ah	;	59	3Bh
<	60	3Ch	=	61	3Dh
>	62	3Eh	?	63	3Fh
@	64	40h	A	65	41h
B	66	42h	C	67	43h
D	68	44h	E	69	45h
F	70	46h	G	71	47h
H	72	48h	I	73	49h
J	74	4Ah	K	75	4Bh
L	76	4Ch	M	77	4Dh
N	78	4Eh	O	79	4Fh
P	80	50h	Q	81	51h
R	82	52h	S	83	53h
T	84	54h	U	85	55h
V	86	56h	W	87	57h
X	88	58h	Y	89	59h
Z	90	5Ah	[	91	5Bh
\	92	5Ch	]	93	5Dh
^	94	5Eh	_	95	5Fh
`	96	60h	a	97	61h
b	98	62h	c	99	63h
d	100	64h	e	101	65h
f	102	66h	g	103	67h
h	104	68h	i	105	69h
j	106	6Ah	k	107	6Bh
l	108	6Ch	m	109	6Dh
n	110	6Eh	o	111	6Fh
p	112	70h	q	113	71h
r	114	72h	s	115	73h
t	116	74h	u	117	75h
v	118	76h	w	119	77h
x	120	78h	y	121	79h
z	122	7Ah	{	123	7Bh
¦	124	7Ch	}	125	7Dh
~	126	7Eh	DEL	127	7Fh

Parts and services vendors

The following list has been compiled from a variety of sources and is believed to be accurate. However, businesses move, change contact numbers, go out of business, merge with other businesses, and so on. If you find an error or omission with this listing, go ahead and let us know! Photocopy the info form at the back of this book, fill it in, and mail or fax it to Dynamic Learning Systems. You can also leave CIS messages for us at 73652,3205. Let us know how we can make this listing even better!

Parts vendors

Computer Component Source, Inc.
P.O. Box 9022
135 Eileen Way
Syosset, NY 11791-9022
Tel: 800-356-1227
Fax: 800-926-2062

Computer Parts Unlimited
5320 Derry Ave.
Suite U
Agoura Hills, CA 91301
Tel: 818-879-1100
Fax: 818-879-1199

DakTech
4900 Ritter Rd.
Mechanicsburg, PA 17055
Tel: 800-325-3238
Fax: 717-795-9420

Fedco Electronics, Inc. (Batteries)
P.O. Box 1403
Fond Du Lac, WI 54936
Tel: 414-922-6490
Fax: 414-922-6750

Laser Impact
10435 Burnet Rd., #114
Austin, TX 78758
Tel: 512-832-9151
Fax: 512-832-9321

NIE International, Inc.
3000 East Chambers
Phoenix, AZ 85040
Tel: 602-470-1500
Fax: 602-470-1540

PC Service Source
1221 Champion Circle
Suite 105
Carrollton, TX 75006
Tel: 214-406-8583
Fax: 214-406-9081

ProAmerica
959 E. Collins
Richardson, TX 75081
Tel: 214-680-9600
Fax: 214-690-8648

TOPS Computer Company, Inc.
461 Boston St., E-2
Topsfield, MA 01983
Tel: 508-887-5915
Fax: 508-887-9216

Service vendors

Advanced Computer Service, Inc.
 (Monitors)
241 South Madison Ave.
Loveland, CO 80537
Tel: 800-227-3504

Dataserv, Inc. (IBM Think Pads)
19011 Lake Dr. East
Minneapolis, MN 55317
Tel: 800-838-4299

Depot America (Printer Service)
1340 Campus Pkwy.
Neptune, NJ 07753
Tel: 800-648-6833

Dot Shop (Print Head Service)
12025 NE Sumner St.
Portland, OR 97220
Tel: 503-256-7585
Fax: 503-256-7588

Diversified Electronic Services
(Monitors, Printers, PCs)
4741 Troudsdale Dr.
Suite 8
Nashville, TN 37220
Tel: 800-737-9920

Electroservice Laboratories (Drives,
 Monitors)
6085 Sikorsky St.
Ventura, CA 93003
Tel: 805-644-2944
Fax: 805-644-5006

Fessenden Technologies (Monitors,
 Hard Drives)
116 North 3rd St.
Ozark, MO 65721
Tel: 417-485-2501
Fax: 417-485-3133

Hong Video Technology, Inc.
 (Monitors)
4467 Park Dr. NW
Suite E
Norcross, GA 30093
Tel: 404-931-0346
Fax: 404-931-4070

Market Point, Inc. (IBM and Lexmark
 Laser/Dot-Matrix Printers)
312 County Line Rd.
Wayne, PA 19087
Tel: 610-687-4900
Fax: 610-687-4901

Peak Technologies (Printer Service)
8990 Old Annapolis Rd.
Columbia, MD 21045-2179
Tel: 800-950-6372

Princeton Computer Support
 (Computers | Laptops | Notebooks)
5 Crescent Ave.
P.O. Box 787
Rockey Hill, NJ 08553
Tel: 609-921-8889
Fax: 609-921-7691

Printech Enterprises, Inc. (HP
  Printers | WYSE Systems | IBM
  PS/2 Motherboards)
1490 Premier Rd.
Suite E
Troy, MI 48084
Tel: 800-346-2618

Raynet Electronics Co. (Monitors |
  Printers)
16810 Barker Springs Rd.
Suite 200
Houston, TX 77084
Tel: 713-578-3802
Fax: 713-578-9127

Valtron Technologies, Inc. (Hard
  Drive Repair)
28309 Crocker Ave.
Valencia, CA 91355
Tel: 800-2-VALTRO

D

Index of PC manufacturers

The following list has been compiled from a variety of sources and is believed to be accurate. However, businesses move, change contact numbers, go out of business, merge with other businesses, and so on. If you find an error or omission in this listing, go ahead and let us know! Photocopy the information form at the back of this book, fill it in, and mail or fax it to Dynamic Learning Systems. You can also leave CIS messages for us at 73652,3205. Let us know how we can make this listing even better!

Aberdeen, Inc.
Unit D
7801 E. Telegraph Road
Montebello, CA 90640
Tel: 800-552-6868

Acer America Corp.
2641 Orchard Pkwy.
San Jose, CA 95134
Tel: 800-733-2237

ACMA Computers, Inc.
47988 Fremont Blvd.
Fremont, CA 94538
Tel: 800-786-6888

Advanced Logic Research, Inc.
9401 Jeronimo
Irvine, CA 92718
Tel: 800-444-4257

Ambra Computer Corp.
3200 Beechleaf Court
Raleigh, NC 27604
Tel: 800-252-6272

American Multisystems
538 Oakmead Pkwy.
Sunnyvale, CA 94086
Tel: 800-888-6615

AST Research
16215 Alton Pkwy
Irvine, CA 92718
Tel: 800-876-4278

Austin Computer Systems
10003 Metric Blvd.
Austin, TX 78758
Tel: 800-752-1577

Axik Computer, Inc.
268 Santa Ana Ct.
Sunnyvale, CA 94086
Tel: 800-234-2945

Blue Star Marketing, Inc.
2312 Central Ave.
Minneapolis, MN 55418
Tel: 800-950-8884

C²Micro Systems, Inc.
47560 Seabridge Dr.
Fremont, CA 94538
Tel: 510-683-8800

CAF Technology, Inc.
1315 Johnson Dr.
City of Industry, CA 91745
Tel: 818-369-3690

Compaq Computer Corp.
M120208
P.O. Box 692000
Houston, TX 77269
Tel: 800-378-8820

Compudyne Products
15167 Business Ave.
Dallas, TX 75244
Tel: 800-266-7872

Comtrade
15314 E. Valley Blvd.
City of Industry, CA 91746
Tel: 800-969-2123

Data Storage Marketing, Inc.
5718 Central Ave.
Boulder, CO 80301
Tel: 800-543-6098

Digital Equipment Corp.
40 Old Bolton Road
Stow, MA 01775
Tel: 800-722-9332

Dell Computer Corp.
9505 Arboretum Blvd.
Austin, TX 78759
Tel: 800-289-3355

Destiny Computers
3480 Investment Blvd.
Hayward, CA 94545
Tel: 800-337-8469

Diamond Technologies, Inc.
1275 S. Lewis St.
Anaheim, CA 92805
Tel: 800-989-7253

Duracom Computer Systems
1425 Greenway Dr.
Irving, TX 75038
Tel: 800-551-9000

Dyna Micro, Inc.
30 W. Montague Expwy.
San Jose, CA 95134
Tel: 800-362-3962

Eltech Research, Inc.
48890 Milmont Dr. #108D
Fremont, CA 94538
Tel: 800-358-8330

Epson Direct
20770 Madrona Ave.
Torrance, CA 90503
Tel: 800-289-3776

Everex Systems, Inc.
901 Page Ave.
Fremont, CA 94538
Tel: 800-952-1556

First Computer Systems, Inc.
Suite 107
6000 Line Oak Parkway
Norcross, GA 30093
Tel: 800-325-1911

FutureTech Systems, Inc.
Six Bridge St.
Hackensack, NJ 07601
Tel: 800-275-4414

Gateway 2000
610 Gateway Dr.
N. Sioux City, SD 57049-2000
Tel: 800-846-2000

Golden Star Technology
17707 Valley View Ave.
Cerritos, CA 90701
Tel: 800-675-2489

Hewlett-Packard Co.
3000 Hanover
Palo Alto, CA 94086
Tel: 800-322-4772

HiQ Systems, Inc.
740 North Mary Ave.
Sunnyvale, CA 94086
Tel: 800-827-5836

Hi-Tech USA
1562 Centre Pointe Dr.
Milpitas, CA 95035
Tel: 800-831-2888

IBM Personal Computer Co.
Route 100
Somers, NY 10589
Tel: 800-772-2227

Insight
1912 W 4th St.
Tempe, AZ 85281
Tel: 800-927-7848

International Instrumentation, Inc.
2282 Townsgate Road
Westlake Village, CA 91361
Tel: 800-543-3475

Mega Computer Systems
10840 Thornmint Road
San Diego, CA 92127
Tel: 800-338-6628

Micro Express
1801 Carnegie Ave.
Santa Ana, CA 92705
Tel: 800-989-9900

Micron Computer, Inc.
915 E. Karcher Road
Nampa, ID 83687
Tel: 800-438-3343

MS Engineering, Inc.
10601 South DeAnza Blvd. #214
Cupertino, CA 95014
Tel: 408-257-4249

National MicroComputers
3855 South 500
W. Salt Lake City, UT 84115
Tel: 800-424-2983

NCR Corp.
1700 S. Patterson Blvd
Dayton, OH 45479
Tel: 800-637-2600

NEC Technologies, Inc.
1414 Massachusetts Ave.
Boxboro, MA 01719
Tel: 800-632-4636

Pactron Integration Computer,
Inc.
9421 Winnetka Ave. Unit L
Chatsworth, CA 91311
Tel: 800-775-8766

Personal Computer Graphics
Corp.
3914 901 Del Amo Blvd.
Torrance, CA 90503
Tel: 800-255-9893

Polywell Computers, Inc.
61C Airport Blvd.
S. San Francisco, CA 94080
Tel: 800-999-1278

Quill Corp.
100 Schelter Road
Lincolnshire, IL 60069
Tel: 708-634-6650

Reason Technology
290 Coon Rapids Blvd.
Minneapolis, MN 55433
Tel: 800-800-4860

Swan Technologies, Inc.
3075 Research Dr.
State College, PA 16801
Tel: 800-382-4924

Sys Technology, Inc.
10655 Humbolt St.
Los Alamitos, CA 90702
Tel: 310-498-6888

Tangent Computer, Inc.
197 Airport Blvd.
Burlingame, CA 94010
Tel: 800-800-5550

TC Computers
1310 Carroll St.
Kenner, LA 70062
Tel: 800-723-8282

Touche Micro Technologies
23824 Andrew Road
Plainfield, IL 60544
Tel: 815-439-9000

Tri-Star Computer Corp.
120 S. Webber Dr.
Chandler, AZ 85226
Tel: 800-678-2799

Unisys Corp.
P.O. Box 500
Blue Bell, PA 19424
Tel: 800-448-1424

Unitek Technology, Inc.
1917 S. Vineyard Ave.
Ontario, CA 91761
Tel: 800-944-5650

Xinetron, Inc.
2302 Walsh Ave.
Santa Clara, CA 95051
Tel: 800-345-4415

ZEOS International, Ltd.
1301 Industrial Blvd.
Minneapolis, MN 55413
Tel: 800-554-7172

E
APPENDIX

The PC Toolbox™ subscriptions and shareware registration

See the ad and order form on the next page.

Tired of fixing your PC "in the dark"?

Now you don't have to! Subscribe to:

The PC Toolbox™

Hints, Tips, and Fixes for Every PC User

A publication of Dynamic Learning Systems, P.O. Box 805, Marlboro, MA 01752
Tel: 508-366-9487 Fax: 508-898-9995 BBS: 508-366-7683 Internet: sbigelow@cerfnet.com

Finally, there is a newsletter that brings computer technology into perspective for PC users and electronics enthusiasts. Each issue of *The PC Toolbox™* is packed with valuable information that you can use to keep your system running better and longer:

♦   Step-by-step PC troubleshooting information that is easy to read and inexpensive to follow. Troubleshooting articles cover all aspects of the PC and its peripherals including monitors, modems, and printers.

♦   Learn how to upgrade and configure your PC with hard drives, video boards, memory, OverDrive™ microprocessors. scanners, and more.

♦   Learn to understand the latest terminology and computer concepts. Shop for new and used systems with confidence.

♦   Improve system performance by optimizing your MS-DOS® and Windows™ operating systems.

♦   Review the latest PC, DOS, and Windows™ books and software *before* you buy them.

♦   Get access to over 1800 PC utilities and diagnostic shareware programs through the Dynamic Learning Systems BBS.

There is no advertising, no product comparisons, and no hype - just practical tips and techniques cover to cover that you can put to work right away. If you use PCs or repair them, try a subscription to *The PC Toolbox™*. If you are not completely satisfied within 90 days, just cancel your subscription and receive a full refund - *no questions asked!* Use the accompanying order form, or contact:

Dynamic Learning Systems, P.O. Box 805, Marlboro, MA 01752.

MS-DOS and Windows are trademarks of Microsoft Corporation. The PC Toolbox is a trademark of Dynamic Learning Systems.
The PC Toolbox logo is Copyright©1995 Corel Corporation. Used under license.

The PC Toolbox™/MONITORS

Use this form when ordering *The PC Toolbox™* or the registered version of **MONITORS**.
You may tear out or photocopy this order form.

YES! Please accept my order as shown below: (check any one)

_____ Send me the registered version of **MONITORS** for **$20** (US)
Massachusetts residents please add $1 sales tax.

Keep the software, but start my 1 year subscription (6 issues) to *The PC Toolbox™* for
_____ **$39** (US). I understand that I have an unconditional 90 day money-back guarantee
with the newsletter.

A special offer for readers of "Troubleshooting, Maintaining, and Repairing
_____ **Personal Computers"!** I'll take the registered version of **MONITORS** *and* the 1 year
subscription to *The PC Toolbox™* (6 issues) for *only* **$49** (US). I understand that the
newsletter has an unconditional 90 day money-back guarantee.

SPECIFY YOUR DISK SIZE: (check any one)

_____ **3.5"** High-Density (1.44MB)   _____ **5.25"** High-Density (1.2MB)

PRINT YOUR MAILING INFORMATION HERE:

Name: Company:

Address:

City, State, Zip:

Country:

Telephone: (   )   Fax: (   )

PLACING YOUR ORDER:

By FAX: Fax this completed order form (24 hrs/day, 7 days/week) to 508-898-9995

By Phone: Phone in your order (Mon-Fri; 9am-4pm EST) to 508-366-9487

___ MasterCard   Card: ___ ___ ___ ___ ___ ___ ___ ___ ___ ___ ___ ___ ___ ___ ___ ___

___ VISA   Exp: ___/___   Sig: _____

Or by Mail: Mail this completed form, along with your check, money order, PO, or credit card info to:
***Dynamic Learning Systems*, P.O. Box 805, Marlboro, MA 01752 USA**

F
APPENDIX

Forms

The forms in this appendix are provided for your convenience and use. You may tear these forms out or photocopy them as required. As the purchaser of this book, you have nonexclusive rights to photocopy the following forms so long as you do so *only* for your own use or use within your own organization. Duplication, copying, or other distribution of these forms for sale or use by others is *strictly prohibited*.

1. *PC Configuration Form* Use this form when installing or configuring the PC and its expansion boards.
2. *System CMOS Sheet* Use this form to record system parameters as shown in the system SETUP screens.
3. *BIOS Upgrade* Use this form when planning a BIOS upgrade for your PC.
4. *Customer Billing* A simple time and material form for beginning technicians.
5. *DLS Info Form* Use this form to report changes, additions, suggestions, questions, and so on to Dynamic Learning Systems.

Ordering more forms

If you find yourself using many of these forms, you can order them in quantity directly from Dynamic Learning Systems. Contact Dynamic Learning Systems for more details or to place an order.

PC Configuration Form

System: _____

Serial #: _____ Mfg. Date: _____

Customer: _____

_____

Phone: _____ Fax: _____

Notes: _____

_____

_____

Power Supply Mfg: _____ Wattage: _____W

Motherboard Mfg: _____ Part: _____

CPU: _____ BIOS: _____

RAM: _____

Board Description	IRQ	DMA	I/O	Misc

System CMOS Setup

System: _____

Serial #: _____ Mfg. Date: _____

BIOS Mfg.: _____ Version: _____

BIOS Date: _____

Notes: _____
_____

Base Memory: _____ KB Ext. Memory: _____ KB

FDD A: _____ FDD B: _____

DRIVE	TYPE	CYL	HEADS	SECTORS	SIZE (MB)
C:					
D:					
E:					
F:					
G:					
H:					
I:					

Typematic Rate Programming: _____ Typematic Rate Delay: _____ mS

Typematic Rate (char/Sec): _____ Setup Message Disp.: _____

Num Lock on Boot: _____ Boot Sequence: _____ CPU Speed: _____

Cache Memory: _____ Password: _____ ISA Buffer: _____

ISA Buf. Addr.: _____ Enhanced ISA Timing: _____

Shadow Memory Size: _____ Shadow Memory Base: _____

IDE DMA Xfer Mode: _____ IDE Multiple Sector Mode: _____

IRQ 9 State: _____ IRQ 10 State: _____ IRQ 11 State: _____

BIOS Upgrade Data

PC Mfg.: _____   PC Model: _____

Motherboard Mrg.: _____   CPU: _____

BIOS Mfg.: _____   BIOS Ver.: _____

BIOS Date: _____   BIOS Part Number: _____

Number of BIOS ICs: _____   Main Chipset: _____

Notes: _____

_____

_____

BIOS Upgrade Data

PC Mfg.: _____   PC Model: _____

Motherboard Mrg.: _____   CPU: _____

BIOS Mfg.: _____   BIOS Ver.: _____

BIOS Date: _____   BIOS Part Number: _____

Number of BIOS ICs: _____   Main Chipset: _____

Notes: _____

_____

_____

Customer Billing Sheet

Customer: _____   Cust#: _____

Address: _____

City, State, Postal Code: _____

Telephone: _____   Fax: _____

System: _____

Serial #: _____

Description of Work: _____

_____

_____

_____

PART NUMBER	DESCRIPTION	QUAN	COST	TOTAL

Notes:		
	SUBTOTAL	
	SALES TAX	
	SHIPPING/MISC.	
	>>> TOTAL	

Stay In Touch With DLS

We want this book to be your #1 PC troubleshooting resource. To do that, we need your comments, criticisms, suggestions, questions, and feedback. It's easy to reach us. You can use this sheet for any communications.

You can reach us by mail:

Dynamic Learning Systems
Attn: Customer Service
P.O. Box 805
Marlboro, MA 01752 USA

You can fax us: 508-898-9995

You can leave e-mail on our BBS: 508-366-7683 (up to 14.4KB - 8 data, no parity, 1 stop)

We're on CompuServe: 73652,3205

We're on the Internet: sbigelow@cerfnet.com

Message:

_____

_____

_____

_____

_____

_____

_____

_____

_____

_____

_____

_____

_____

_____

G
APPENDIX

Using the companion software

Understanding shareware

You've probably heard the terms *public domain*, *freeware*, *shareware*, and others like them. Your favorite *BBS* (bulletin board system) probably has many programs described by one or more of these words. There's a lot of confusion about these terms, but they actually have specific meanings and implications. Once you understand them you will have a much easier time navigating the maze of programs available to you, and understanding what your obligations are, or aren't, with each type of program. Start with some basic definitions.

Public domain has a very specific legal meaning. It means that the creator of a work (in this case, a piece of software) who had legal ownership of that work, has given up ownership and dedicated the work to the public domain. Once something is in the public domain, anyone can use it in any way they choose, and the author has no control over the use and cannot demand payment for it.

If you find a program that the author has explicitly put into the public domain, you are free to use it however you see fit, without paying for the right to use it. But use care. Because of the confusion over the meaning of the words, programs are often described by others as being public domain when in fact they are shareware or free copyrighted software. To be sure a program is public domain, you should look for an explicit statement from the author to that effect.

Copyrighted is the opposite of public domain. A copyrighted program is one where the author has asserted their legal right to control the program's use and distribution by placing the legally required copyright notices in the program and its documentation. The law gives copyright owners broad rights to restrict how their work is distributed, and provides penalties for those who violate these restrictions. Virtually all commercial software is copyrighted. When you find a program that is copyrighted, you *must* use it in accordance with the copyright owner's restrictions on distribution and payment. Usually these are clearly stated in the program documentation and disk package.

Maintaining a copyright does not necessarily imply charging a fee, so it is perfectly possible and legal to have copyrighted programs that are distributed free of charge. Such programs are often referred to as *freeware*, though this term was in fact trademarked by the late Andrew Flugelman and the legality of its use by others could be questioned. In any case, the fact that a program is free does *not* mean that it is in the public domain, though this is a common confusion.

Shareware is copyrighted software that is distributed by authors through bulletin boards, on-line services, disk vendors, and copies passed among friends. It is commercial software that you are allowed to try out *before* you pay for it. Shareware authors use a variety of licensing restrictions on their copyrighted works, but most authors who support their software require you to pay a registration fee, the purchase price of the software, if you continue to use the product after the trial period. Some authors indicate a specific trial period after you must pay this fee; others leave the time period open and rely on you to judge when you have decided to use the program, and therefore should pay for it. Occasionally a shareware author requires registration, but does not require payment—this is called *0$ shareware*.

The shareware system and the continued availability of quality shareware products depend on your willingness to register and pay for the shareware you *use*. The registration fees you pay allow authors to support and continue to develop their products. As a software user, you benefit from this system because you get to try the software and determine whether it meets your needs *before* you pay for it. Authors benefit because they are able to get their products into your hands with little or no expense for advertising and promotion. As a result, it is not unusual to find shareware products that rival retail software in quality and performance, but costs only a fraction of commercial software.

ASP members' shareware meets additional quality standards beyond ordinary shareware. Members' programs must be fully functional (not crippled, demonstration, or out-of-date versions); program documentation must be complete and must clearly state the registration fee and the benefits received when registering; members must provide free mail or telephone support for a minimum of three months after registration; and members must meet other guidelines that help to ensure that you as a user receive good value for your money and are dealt with professionally. The ASP also provides an Ombudsman program to assist in resolving disputes between authors and users.

For more information on the ASP or to contact the ASP Ombudsman, write to:

ASP
545 Grover Road
Muskegon, MI USA 49442-9427
or fax 616-788-2765
CompuServe 70007,3536

You also can contact the Ombudsman on CompuServe via an electronic mail message to 70007,3536.

The ASP Ombudsman

Dynamic Learning Systems is an approved BBS member of *ASP* (Association of Shareware Professionals). The ASP wants to ensure that the shareware principle works for you. If you are unable to resolve a shareware problem with an ASP member by contacting the member directly, the ASP might be able to help. The ASP Ombudsman can help you resolve a problem or dispute with an ASP member, but does not provide technical support for member's products or documentation. Please write to the ASP Ombudsman at the address in the previous paragraph.

The Companion Software

To make your testing and troubleshooting even more effective, we've put together a collection of outstanding shareware utilities. You'll find the software in the rear binding of this book. This part of the appendix gives you some background on each utility. Keep in mind that the utilities are provided in compressed format to save space. Before attempting to use these utilities, you will need to decompress them with PKUNZIP from PKWARE, Inc. If you need a copy of PKUNZIP, you can download it from TechNet BBS.

CTS Serial Port Utilities 2.2 (CTSSPU22.EXE self-extracting)

The CTS *SPU* (Serial Port Utilities) is a collection of DOS software utilities that provide you with control over the serial ports in your computer. Most serial port problems can be resolved by using these utilities. Each of the utilities support all standard and any user-defined serial ports. Version 2 allows each of the utilities to operate as a Windows or OS/2 DOS application.

PortInfo is a comprehensive utility that tests your system to determine everything possible about your serial ports, including interrupt and addressing conflicts. PortInfo provides you with FAILURE and WARNING messages about actual and possible conflicts. An ideal utility for serial port testing and troubleshooting. PortInfo provides details on the following:

- Detects multiple serial ports at the same address (for example, two COM1 ports)
- Serial ports that have failed
- Interrupt conflicts between a mouse and a serial port
- Shared interrupts (2 serial ports, or a serial port and a serial mouse sharing an IRQ)
- Conflicts between COM4 and 8514/A compatible monitors
- Unusual BIOS serial port setups
- Serial ports that cannot generate interrupts
- Helps to determine when interrupts can be shared
- Actual IRQ used by each port and the current IRQ status
- DOS port assignments (COM1–COM4, mouse)

- Detects which ports have modems or FAX modems connected, and (in many cases) if the modem is internal or external
- Detects which FAX classes are supported by the modem(s)
- Port (UART) Identification (8250, 8250A/16450, 16550, 16550A, ESP, HSSP, the T/Port, and some "emulated UARTs"
- FIFO status: If it exists, on / off, else 'None'

John Jerrim
Founder & Chief Technical Officer
Computer Telecommunication Systems, Inc.
3847 Foxwood Road, Suite 1000
Duluth, Georgia 30136-6100 USA
Orders: 1-800-380-2666
HelpLine: 1-404-263-8623
FAX: 1-404-263-0124
CompuServe: 76662,2315
Internet: 76662.2315@compuserve.com

Snooper 3.30 (SNOOP330.ZIP)

This handy and thorough system information utility reports many operating characteristics of your computer. Snooper tells you all about your computer's CPU, MCP, bus, memory, ports, IRQs, DMA, mouse, disks, network, and much more. It can run unattended (for batch files), print its screens to a file or printer, and automatically configure itself for Desqview, color or monochrome video cards, and much more. A great tool for reviewing a system's configuration, or testing recognized devices after an upgrade. Please read Snooper's manual (included on disk) to learn how to use it most effectively.

John Vias
Vias and Associates
PO Box 470805
San Francisco, CA 94147-0805
Orders: 800-332-8234
Voice: 415-921-6262 (international orders, and tech support)
Fax: 415-922-3197
CompuServe: 72260,1601

The Ref 4.3 (THEREF43.ZIP)

THEREF™ is a comprehensive directory of Hard Drives, Floppy Drives, Optical Drives, and Drive Controllers & Host Adapters. It is designed to help the novice and professional alike with integration problems and system setups. This is one of the handiest and most thorough shareware reference products available. Information is provided in two handy formats: *portrait* mode for those who prefer a normal book-type format or do not have a printer with landscape capability and *landscape* mode, for those who prefer a computer-printout type format. For printing, a LaserJet is preferred, but not necessary, and printer setup info is provided. For viewing, LIST™ by Vernon Buerg, will provide an excellent result, and allow text searches for finding specific models.

Robert Falbo
7983 Cedarwood Dr.
Rome, NY 13440-2029

BurnIn 4.5 (BURNIN45.ZIP)

Once you've repaired a system, it's usually a good idea to run it for a while to exercise the new components. BurnIn 4.5 is a system stress tester from OsoSoft designed to run on all PCs. Run BurnIn for 72 hours on all new systems and whenever you upgrade. BurnIn checks the CPU, system memory, disk drives, the video card and monitor, and more. It also can run third-party software as part of test. For simplicity, BurnIn provides command line options, and allows you to save setup configurations.

George Campbell
OsoSoft
1472 Sixth Street
Los Osos, CA 93402
Voice: (805) 528-1759
Fax: (805) 528-3074
OsoSoft BBS: (805) 528-3753 300-14400 bps, 8/N/1
CompuServe ID: 71571,222

Parallel Port 1.4 (PARA14.ZIP)

A handy utility that examines your system's parallel ports and reports the Port Type, I/O address, IRQ level, BIOS name, and an assortment of informative notes and warnings in a compact and easy to read display. Parallel operates by testing each of the standard addresses in your system where parallel ports might be found, then gathers a broad assortment of useful information about the specific port behavior. Parallel tests the ports and then produces a compact display that is convenient and easy to read. The output might be redirected to a file for tech support purposes. Parallel uses very sophisticated techniques for port and IRQ detection and is aware of a broad range of quirky port features.

Parallel is the definitive parallel port tech support tool. Parallel is freeware (subject to a restricted license agreement). It may be used free of charge for any personal, noncommercial purpose.

Jay Lowe
Parallel Technologies, Inc.
10603 170th Ct NE
Redmond, WA 98052
Lab 206-869-1136
Fax 206-869-1133

CompuServe 76640,203
Internet 76640.203@COMPUSERVE.COM

CMOS RAM 2.0 (CMOSRAM2.ZIP)

The configuration of every AT-type computer is stored in a small area of CMOS RAM and backed up with a battery. If the battery should die, the PC's configuration will be lost, often making the hard drive inaccessible until the CMOS data is restored. CMOS RAM is a utility designed to save the contents of CMOS RAM to a disk file (on floppy disk). By adding the CMOS RAM utility to your disaster floppy, you can restore lost CMOS contents in a matter of seconds; this capability makes CMOS RAM a remarkably handy tool for PC users and technicians of all levels.

Thomas Mosteller
Tellerware
1872 Rampart Lane
Lansdale, PA 19446-5051
Fax: (215) 368-5072

Sys Check 2.4 (SYSCHK40.ZIP)

SYSCHK is a professional-quality program that provides comprehensive, highly-detailed information about the devices installed in your system. This makes SYSCHK invaluable for anyone testing or upgrading PCs. The following are some of the items SYSCHK will search for:

- Computer model type including manufacturer if known
- Micro Processor including the Intel Pentium™
- Complete IRQ listing including usage and availability
- Detection of the older 80386 that had a 32-bit multiply bug
- Math coprocessor type
- Microsoft Windows setup information
- Detection of slave 8259 Interrupt controller
- Presence of a real-time clock
- Presence of a ISA, PCI, Micro Channel, or EISA bus
- System BIOS including source, date and size
- A listing of all known BIOS extensions in the system, and the size of those BIOS
- Type of keyboard attached (84 key or 101 key) and keyboard status
- Type of mouse installed, number of buttons, and interrupt used
- Number of parallel ports in system and the base addresses
- Number of serial ports in system, base addresses and parameters of the port including IRQ.
- Type of Serial port UART chip including 16550
- Complete information on any Network connection
- Hard disk size including tracks, heads, sectors and CMOS type
- Hard-disk controller manufacturer

- Hard-disk partition information
- Disk cache info including hits and misses
- Floppy-disk size and parameters
- Video type, chipset, video memory, and BIOS source
- Maximum video resolution and maximum color capability
- Amount of environment space used and available
- Amount of conventional, extended, and expanded memory
- Listing of all resident programs both conventional and UMB including size and location of those programs
- Listing of all non standard device drivers installed
- Throughput speed of system, taking into account CPU speed and wait states
- Video and hard-disk speed
- Listing of all CMOS values

Paul Griffith
Advanced Personal Systems
105 Serra Way, Suite 418
Milpitas, CA. 95035
Tel: (408) 298-3703
Fax: (408) 945-0242

Monitors 1.01 (MONITORS.ZIP)

Whether you are testing or repairing a monitor, you can use MONITORS to check and correct alignment problems in a variety of different screen modes. MONITORS allows you to work with such important parameters as linearly, phase, centering, convergence, and color purity. You also can use MONITORS to test your video adapter to determine its characteristics and available graphics modes. A valuable tool for anyone troubleshooting or working with video systems.

Stephen J. Bigelow
Dynamic Learning Systems
P.O. Box 805
Marlboro, MA 01752 USA
Tel: 508-366-9487
Fax: 508-898-9995
BBS: 508-366-7683
CompuServe: 73652,3205
Internet: sbigelow@cerfnet.com

H
APPENDIX

Using TechNet BBS

A technician today faces a problem of information. With the proliferation of PCs and peripherals expanding every day, keeping pace with the changes can become a real challenge. Sometimes it seems that just when you've got one concept or standard figured out, it's abandoned in favor of a something new. Dynamic Learning Systems is dedicated to helping you stay in touch with the latest PC technical info by offering access to *TechNet* BBS. *TechNet* is set up to provide the very best in shareware, freeware, and public domain diagnostic and business utility software. You can also exchange e-mail with other professionals and PC enthusiasts.

Connecting To TechNet BBS

TechNet BBS operates a single node 24 hours a day, 7 days a week. The resident modem can handle from 300 baud, up to 14.4K using a data configuration of 8 data bits, no parity bit, and only 1 stop bit (set your communication software for 8/N/1). Be sure to adjust the configuration of your modem to accommodate this data frame. New users are allowed on the system up to 30 minutes per day. Professional Subscribers (see Appendix E) have 60 minutes a day with extensive file area access. First-time users are asked to fill out a brief on-line questionnaire to identify their name, choose a password, and provide address/phone number information. When filling out the questionnaire, be sure to be complete in your answers—incomplete questionnaires are automatically erased.

Getting started

TechNet BBS is menu driven from your keyboard. You will find that selecting options and navigating from menu to menu is fast and convenient. Menu entries that are "blued out" are not available to your current level of access. Once a first-time user has logged onto *TechNet* BBS and completed the new user questionnaire, please take a moment to review the *Newsletter* file, as well as the various *Bulletins* that are on the system. These files are updated regularly, and will keep you informed of changes and additions to *TechNet* BBS resources.

Notes on downloading

TechNet BBS is primarily an electronic information service. Shareware, public domain utilities and applications are downloaded by our users for their private use. The BBS is approved by the Association of Shareware Professionals (ASP) and we are fortunate to receive regular mailings of the latest and best shareware available. Most common file transfer protocols are supported, but the Zmodem protocol provides best performance. When signing on for the first time, you can select a default transfer protocol, but you can also elect to choose the protocol on each download session; this is the preferred setting if you are new to downloading or want to try different settings to find the optimum transfer technique.

Notes on uploading

Of course, we also welcome new files and documents from our users, and *TechNet* BBS often receives new files as on-line uploads from our users. However, since each file must be sorted and checked for viruses, you will only be able to upload files to several limited areas. When uploading from *TechNet's FILE* menu, you will be asked to enter the DOS-compatible filename, along with a brief text description of the file. We encourage you to password-protect your file(s). When uploading, you are also encouraged to compress the various file(s) comprising your upload using the PKZIP compression utility from PKWARE.

Security and operations policy

You will see a disclaimer in the initial logon screen. Please make it a point to read and understand the disclaimer *completely* before logging onto *TechNet* BBS. If you do not understand the disclaimer or do not agree to its terms, disconnect from *Tech-Net immediately* without logging on. We are proud of the high-quality reputation *TechNet* BBS has earned. As a professional BBS devoted to technical enthusiasts, technicians, and designers, no profane, pornographic, insulting, degrading, or otherwise unprofessional material is allowed on *TechNet* BBS at any time under any circumstances. Dynamic Learning Systems reserves the right to decide whether or not an upload falls into one or more of the above categories. Continued attempts to upload undesirable material is considered to be an abuse of the system. Repeated abusers will be permanently restricted from system access. As a *TechNet* BBS user, remember to change your password frequently.

When problems occur

Because of drastic variations in telecommunication quality around the world, as well as differences in modem setups and configurations, Dynamic Learning Systems cannot guarantee the integrity of serial communication for any length of time. Serial communication is intrinsically prone to problems such as initial Connect Failures and Dropped Carrier, and any other random occurrence beyond our control that may accidentally disconnect you from the system.

We recommend that if you consistently encounter problems connecting to or dropping off *TechNet* BBS, check your modem's initialization and setup strings in your communications software. Altering an operating parameter can often radically improve the modem's integrity. If new settings do not work, try slowing down the communications speed. Although *TechNet* BBS will work with error-correcting modems up to 14.4K, you might wish to try 2400, 4800, or 9600 baud, which is much less demanding of a typical telephone voice channel.

I
APPENDIX

The DLS Technician's Certificate

The certification of technical knowledge serves several important goals. It gives the person being certified an opportunity to review and tie together the important ideas they have learned. Successful certification also demonstrates proficiency in the subject area to employers and customers. There are many different approaches to education and certification in the PC industry. Most involve off-site testing or training to one extent or another, although many firms provide very good home-study PC courses.

The problem with most educational courses is that they are terribly expensive for the PC enthusiast or entry-level technician. This book has been designed to serve as both a practical reference text, as well as a learning tool. The *DLS Technician's Certificate* allows you to test your understanding of the topics covered here, and provides you with a printed certificate upon successful completion of the final examination.

Why bother with a certificate?

The big complaint about certificates is that they are "just pieces of paper." Frame them, hang them on a wall, dust them off—big deal. Fortunately, there are some very real incentives to shoot for the DLS Technician's Certificate

First, the certificate offers something for everyone—novices have an inexpensive means to build their knowledge. Veteran troubleshooters can use this test to check their knowledge and keep important skills up-to-date. Any professional will tell you that up-to-date skills are a key to employability.

There's also a financial incentive. NRI (a continuing education division of McGraw-Hill) offers a $100 discount on any of their electronics courses for those readers who successfully earn the DLS Technician's Certificate.

What it costs

There is a one-time test processing fee of $25 (U.S.) to offset the administrative cost of grading, printing, and mailing. If you pass the test, you will receive a *Certificate of Completion*. If you should fail the test for any reason, you will be informed of your grade in writing, and a new set of information/answer sheets will be sent to you. You may then take the test again as often as you like at no additional cost.

But I'm no good at tests

Fair enough—that statement happens to a lot of people. There's no reason to feel badly. But before you say "I can't do that" and close this appendix, completing the *DLS Technician's Certificate* exam can be surprisingly painless. Go ahead and give it a try. Just consider some of the following:

- *There is no pressure* Work at your own pace. The questions on the companion disk are intended to reinforce the important ideas of each chapter of the book. Take the exam on your own schedule when you are ready.
- *There are no time limits* You can take as long as you need to finish the exam. Spread it out over a weekend or several weeks as your time permits.
- *You don't have to cram* The exam is open-book. Purists might criticize this as an unfair advantage, but the answers do not come directly from the book. Besides, how many professionals out there know everything there is without having to refer to a book or magazine at one time or another?
- *You can't lose money* Because there is only a one-time fee, you can retake the test as many times as you need to.

Test instructions

Taking the exam is very easy. Just follow the steps outlined below, and you should have no problems at all:

1. Carefully tear out and photocopy the Information Cover Sheet and both pages of the Answer Sheet.
2. Photocopy the information and answer sheets, and use the photocopied pages to complete the test (keep the original pages tucked away).
3. Open the book and start the test at question 1.
4. Fill in your answers by *carefully* circling or blacking in the desired letter using a #2 pencil. Although you can use marker or pen as well, pencil is strongly recommended because it can be erased completely. *Remember that answers with more than one letter circled or blacked out must be marked incorrect.*
5. When you have completed all questions, fill out the Information Cover Sheet. The information must be filled in completely.
6. Send the completed Information Cover Sheet and Answer Sheets with payment to Dynamic Learning Systems.
7. If you are paying by check, mail the forms and check or money order to:

Dynamic Learning Systems
P.O. Box 805
Marlboro, MA 01752

If you are paying by credit card, you can mail the forms or fax them to:508-898-9995.

Your exam will be graded, and you will receive a reply within four weeks. If you have questions or trouble understanding the instructions listed above, contact Customer Service at 508-366-9487. Best of luck!

Making the grade

So, how do you pass? You need a 70% or higher score to pass the exam. With 120 questions, you will need to answer 84 questions correctly. The grade is strictly pass or fail; there will be no letter grade assigned.

Exam questions

1. When two ST506/412 or ESDI drives are connected with a control cable containing a twist, the first drive must be set to:
   A. Drive 0
   B. Drive 1
   C. Drive 2
   D. None of the above
2. When setting up a SCSI installation, the following SCSI IDs are typical for a controller and two drives:
   A. The controller is ID0, the first hard drive is ID1, and a second hard drive is ID2
   B. The controller is ID7, the first hard drive is ID1, and a second hard drive is ID2
   C. The controller is ID7, the first hard drive is ID0, and a second hard drive is ID1
   D. None of the above
3. When configuring a typical sound board equipped with an on-board CD-ROM interface, you should be sure to set the proper jumpers for:
   A. The IRQ, DMA, and I/O of the sound circuit itself
   B. The DMA and I/O of the MIDI circuit
   C. The IRQ, DMA, and I/O of the CD-ROM drive interface
   D. All of the above
4. A new power supply is installed in a PC, but the system fails to initialize. Chances are that...
   A. The new supply is defective
   B. The power connector is not installed properly, or is not providing a PowerGood signal
   C. The power supply is oversized or not sized properly for the system
   D. None of the above

5. When a new floppy disk is inserted in the drive, the directory from a previous diskette appears. You should suspect...
   A. That the media sensor on the drive is defective
   B. That the change line signal on the drive is defective
   C. That the spindle motor on the drive is defective
   D. That the index motor on the drive is defective
6. The main battery in a notebook or subnotebook system does not retain a proper change, you should suspect...
   A. The battery pack is not connected properly
   B. The system's internal charging circuitry is defective
   C. The battery pack is old, worn, or damaged
   D. The wrong battery is being used in the system
7. For no apparent reason, the PC powers up and indicates that the system configuration detected does not match the setup recorded in CMOS. The best probability is that...
   A. The CMOS RAM backup battery has failed
   B. The CMOS/RTC IC has failed
   C. The CMOS setup has been altered incorrectly
   D. The CMOS/RTC IC has been removed
8. You find that the system does not recognize the installed CD-ROM. You should suspect that...
   A. The CD-ROM signal cable is disconnected
   B. There is no CD in the drive
   C. The CD-ROM controller has failed
   D. Either the low-level driver or MSCDEX has failed to load
9. When a single ST506/412 or ESDI drive is connected with a control cable containing no twist, that drive...
   A. Should be set to drive 0, connected to the end connector, and its terminating resistors should be removed
   B. Should be set to drive 1, connected to the middle connector, and its terminating resistors should be installed or left in place
   C. Should be set to drive 0, connected to the middle connector, and its terminating resistors should be left in place
   D. Should be set to drive 0, connected to the end connector, and its terminating resistors should be left in place
10. A system fails to boot. You insert a POST card, and you find that the card stops after code 15h. You also see that the system is using an AMI AT/EISA BIOS (pre-1990). You should...
    A. Replace the IRQ controller IC
    B. Replace the DMA controller IC
    C. Replace the CMOS backup battery
    D. Replace the BIOS ROM IC
11. When selecting a file transfer protocol for use with modems, your best choice for fastest, most efficient file transfer is:
    A. Zmodem
    B. Xmodem

      C. Ymodem

      D. Kermit

12. When an application freezes as a PCMCIA card is inserted or removed, you should...

      A. Assume that the application does not support hot insertion and removal, and only insert or remove the card while the application is shut down

      B. Assume that the card is defective and replace it outright

      C. Assume that the card services software is corrupt or loaded improperly. Reload the card services software or find a patch.

      D. Assume that the application is corrupt or defective. Try reloading the application.

13. The monitor forms an image correctly, but it is saturated with blue. You should suspect the likeliest cause might be...

      A. That the blue output from the video controller has failed

      B. That the blue video amplifier circuit in the monitor has failed

      C. That the blue signal in the monitor cable has shorted

      D. That the blue CRT electron gun has failed

14. Your memory-resident antivirus package fails to function, or generates an unusual number of false alarms. Suspect that...

      A. An undetected virus is at work in your system. Update the antivirus product and resume testing.

      B. The memory-resident package is outdated or obsolete. Update the antivirus product and resume testing.C. The memory-resident package is defective or otherwise corrupted. Try a different antivirus package.

      D. The memory-resident package is conflicting with other device drivers or TSRs. Try booting the PC from a clean floppy disk before running the antivirus package.

15. During system initialization, you see an error message such as "Keyboard controller failure." You should respond to this fault by...

      A. Replacing the keyboard assembly

      B. Replacing the keyboard controller IC

      C. Replacing the motherboard

      D. Replacing the BIOS IC

16. You see that the subnotebook display is acting erratically. As you flex the display gently, you notice that the top quarter of the image drops out or flickers. The remainder of the image appears steady. You should plan on...

      A. Replacing the backlight power inverter

      B. Inspecting the LCD carefully for any loose internal wiring or connections

      C. Replacing the LCD panel outright because it is impossible to repair LCD internal wiring

      D. None of the above

17. You see an error message indicating an "Optional ROM checksum bad" and system initialization halts. You suspect that...

      A. The system BIOS ROM IC has failed on the motherboard. The system ROM should be replaced.

B. A supplemental BIOS ROM IC has failed on an expansion device (a video, SCSI, or network adapter). The adapter (or its ROM alone) should be replaced.

C. There is a problem in system RAM. One or more SIMMs might have failed. The defective RAM devices should be isolated and replaced.

D. The BIOS POST has detected a problem with the CPU. Replace the defective CPU.

18. The mouse responds to your movements, but only hesitantly. The cursor seems "stuck." You suspect that...

A. The mouse is defective. Replace the troublesome pointing device.

B. The mouse driver is corrupt or not installed properly. Try rebooting the system, or try reinstalling the defective mouse driver.

C. The mouse is not connected securely at the computer. Check and reattach the mouse cable.

D. The mouse tracking device is just dirty. Gently clean the mouse ball and rollers with light household detergent and water on a clean rag.

19. You encounter a motherboard fault, but the problem goes away as soon as you remove the top enclosure. You assume that...

A. The motherboard is defective and should be replaced as soon as possible.

B. The top enclosure is short circuiting the motherboard at one or more points.

C. excessive pressure from the enclosure has warped the chassis and motherboard just enough to precipitate a failure.

D. None of the above

20. A fault is detected in the motherboard's integrated parallel port. As a technician, you can...

A. Replace the on-board chip or chipset supporting the parallel port

B. Replace the motherboard outright

C. Disable the motherboard parallel port and install an expansion-card port

D. All of the above

21. You encounter random or unexpected PCMCIA card service errors during normal operation. You should suspect that...

A. The card is defective or is not installed properly

B. The application(s) in use does not support PCMCIA cards properly

C. An antivirus program is interfering with card services software

D. DoubleSpace or Stacker is interfering with card services software

22. When using a pen computer, you notice that the stylus is working intermittently. Chances are that...

A. The stylus cable is intermittent (or batteries are failing).

B. The pen overlay is defective

C. The stylus is defective

D. None of the above

23. Your pen stylus moves across the overlay, but no "ink" is displayed on the LCD, but characters and gestures are interpreted correctly. You should suspect that...

A. The LCD is defective. Replace the LCD assembly.

B. The video driver in use does not support the video functions needed for pen computing. Update the video driver to a more compatible version.

C. The stylus is defective or cabled improperly. Replace the stylus assembly.

D. The pen overlay is defective. Replace the pen overlay.

24. When examining a SCSI setup for the first time and not being familiar with the devices installed, where would you expect the terminating resistors to be:

A. On the controller and hard drive

B. On the controller and SCSI CD-ROM drive

C. On both ends of the SCSI chain regardless of what devices are connected

D. On the controller and page scanner

25. The image displayed on a monitor rolls rapidly and cannot be controlled. In most DOS applications, however, the image is formed correctly. The problem is likely that...

A. The monitor's horizontal sync circuit has failed. Try replacing the main monitor circuit board.B. The video board has failed. Try replacing the video board assembly

C. There is a memory conflict between the video board and another area of memory. Add an Exclude command to the EMM386 line in CONFIG.SYS

D. The monitor is not capable of operating at the horizontal sync rate being produced by the video board. Drop the video mode to a lower resolution.

26. The customer complains the single sheets of paper seem to pull unevenly or walk as they travel through the printer. You should...

A. Take a close look at the paper transport assembly. Clean the rollers or replace the transport assembly.

B. Take a close look at the print head assembly. It is probably obstructing the paper as it moves through the printer.

C. Take a close look at the paper type. Smooth or coated papers can slip when used in a friction feed assembly.

D. Answers A and C are equally correct

27. The images produced by your laser printer look just fine, but when you rub your finger over the printed page, the image smudges. You should suspect...

A. The paper is damp or chemically coated

B. The fuser is defective or set improperly

C. There is an obstruction in the paper path

D. The high-voltage power supply has failed

28. When your modem is receiving or transmitting great deals of garbage, you should suspect...

A. A faulty modem or serial cable

B. A faulty data frame or transfer rate

C. A faulty telephone line or line cord

D. None of the above

29. A customer spills liquid such as coffee or a soft drink into their keyboard, and now the keyboard is acting erratically. You power down the PC, disconnect the keyboard, and...

    A. Install a new keyboard assembly because you know the contaminated keyboard cannot be saved.

    B. Allow the foreign liquid to dry completely before attempting to use the keyboard again.

    C. Rinse the keyboard PC board in fresh, demineralized water, then spray each key with contact cleaner before the foreign liquid dries. If problems continue, replace the keyboard outright.

    D. None of the above

30. The LCD image appears dim or washed out. You should first suspect that...

    A. The LCD panel is defective and should be replaced

    B. The backlight CCFT(s) or EL panel are growing old and should be replaced

    C. The backlight power supply is defective and should be replaced

    D. The backlight diffuser is dirty or misaligned

31. An updated BIOS ROM is installed in the motherboard, but the system now refuses to boot. You should strongly suspect that...

    A. The new BIOS ROM is installed backward or incorrectly

    B. The incorrect ROM IC has been installed

    C. Accidental static discharge has damaged the motherboard

    D. None of the above

32. The text or image data being sent to the printer appears randomly lost or garbled. The very first thing you should check is:

    A. That the printer is on-line and passes its self-test as expected

    B. That the parallel port cable is installed correctly and securely between the PC and printer

    C. That any necessary printer drivers are installed and ready

    D. That the correct Centronics cable is being used

33. During system initialization, the mouse driver fails to install. You should suspect that...

    A. The mouse driver is corrupt

    B. The mouse driver is missing

    C. The hardware interface (bus mouse port or serial port) is defective

    D. The mouse is missing or connected improperly

34. You see a 118 error code. You suspect that...

    A. The system CPU has failed

    B. One or both DMA controllers have failed

    C. The L2 cache memory has failed

    D. The math coprocessor has failed

35. A power supply works intermittently. As you tap it (or around it) you find one or more outputs cutting in and out. To a technician, this kind of behavior suggests...

    A. The supply's output regulator is damaged

    B. The supply's rectifier or transformer are damaged

    C. That the power supply PC board or wiring are damaged

    D. None of the above

36. After a new SCSI adapter is installed in the system, the PC will no longer boot from the floppy drive. You must suspect that...
    A. The SCSI controller is defective and should be replaced
    B. The floppy disk drive has failed and should be replaced
    C. The bootable floppy disk is defective and should be replaced or reformatted
    D. The SCSI hard drive is defective which is generating collateral problems for the FDD

37. A tape drive generates an inordinate number of read/write errors. Before attempting to replace or disassemble the tape drive, you should...
    A. Try cleaning the drive's R/W heads with a cleaning tape or isopropyl alcohol on a swab
    B. Try a known-good working tape in the drive
    C. Carefully inspect the tape drive's signal and power cables
    D. All of the above

38. While under Stacker, an error message indicates that both copies of the FAT are not identical. You should...
    A. Use Stacker's CHECK utility to isolate the defective FAT, then copy the good FAT to the defective FAT.
    B. Use Stacker's CHECK utility to reformat the drive
    C. Use Stacker's CHECK utility to reconstruct the FAT
    D. None of the above

39. The laser printer is producing unusually light print, or there might be light areas in the print. You should suspect...
    A. That the optics directing the laser beam are out of alignment
    B. That the laser itself is damaged or worn out
    C. That the toner cartridge is almost exhausted
    D. That the paper is damp or chemically coated

40. You notice an unusual amount of disk activity in the system, or the system's performance seems unusually slow. You should suspect that...
    A. The hard drive has failed
    B. The hard drive data cable is loose or frayed
    C. The hard drive might be unusually fragmented
    D. A virus might be at work in the system

41. IDE drive interfaces use data/control cables with...
    A. 40 pins
    B. 44 pins
    C. 72 pins
    D. All of the above

42. Your system fails to initialize. You insert a POST card, and the initialization process stops when code 0Ch is displayed. Your system is using a Chips & Technologies BIOS. Chances are...
    A. That the CPU has failed
    B. The DMA page register has failed
    C. The DMA controller has failed
    D. The BIOS ROM has failed

43. The computer seems to power up and initialize properly, but there is no image on the monitor. You should first check that...
    A. The monitor is turned on and plugged into the video adapter properly
    B. The video adapter is working as expected
    C. The correct video driver is installed (under Windows)
    D. The correct amount of memory has been excluded when EMM386 is invoked

44. When preparing to capture a video clip, the image in the preview window appears unusually grainy. First, make sure that...
    A. you are drawing video from a quality source
    B. All of the wiring between the video source and capture board is connected properly
    C. You are using a video adapter and driver with 256 colors or more
    D. The video you are trying to capture illustrates relatively slow action

45. During system initialization, you see an error message indicating a problem with cache memory. Your best course of action is to...
    A. Replace the defective cache memory IC(s)
    B. Replace the entire motherboard
    C. Disable cache memory in order to continue using the system
    D. None of the above

46. A computer virus (or other rogue software) is transmitted most often between PCs by...
    A. Sharing floppy disks that contain infected files
    B. Loading infected software obtained from commercial sources
    C. Loading infected software obtained from shareware sources
    D. Deliberate sabotage

47. A floppy drive reports a general read or write error. Before you attempt to replace the drive, try...
    A. A new, known-good floppy disk
    B. A new floppy signal cable
    C. Cleaning the drive's read/write heads
    D. Realigning the floppy drive

48. A monitor displays a single bright line running horizontally across the CRT. It is most likely that...
    A. The vertical amplifier circuit has failed
    B. The vertical deflection coil has failed
    C. The CRT has failed
    D. None of the above

49. You install a second IDE drive in your system, and now either or both of the drives do not work.
    A. You did not set the second IDE drive as the slave drive
    B. You did not plug the second IDE drive in correctly
    C. You are using two IDE drives made by different manufacturers
    D. All of the above

50. In addition to a hexadecimal display, some POST boards provide a set of signal LEDs. These LEDs are used...

A. To show the state of key bus signals to facilitate bus troubleshooting

B. To show the state of major components on the motherboard

C. To show the status of the POST board itself

D. None of the above

51. After you repair a pen computer, you notice that the system locks up or suffers other strange operational problems. You should suspect that...

A. The stylus is damaged or connected improperly

B. You neglected to replace EMI shielding, or replaced it incorrectly

C. One or more components on the pen computer's main board have been damaged

D. None of the above

52. You install a SCSI adapter and drive as a nonboot drive (an IDE drive acts as the boot device), but the SCSI drive fails to respond. The very first thing you should check when encountering this sort of problem is...

A. That the drive entries and parameters in the CMOS setup are mapped correctly

B. That all of the cabling between the drives and their respective controllers is correct

C. That the SCSI drive is set to its proper ID (0 or 1) and the IDE drive is set to master

D. That the SCSI adapter checks out properly

53. When you encounter an error message such as "Track 0 bad, disk unusable." it's a good bet that...

A. The hard drive is defective

B. There is a hardware conflict between the drive adapter and another device in the system

C. The hard drive is disconnected

D. The hard drive cable is installed backward

54. The display image appears extremely distorted, and the system might lock up. You should suspect that...

A. There is a conflict between the video driver and other driver software operating in the system

B. Memory needed by the video board was not properly excluded in EMM386

C. Both of the above

D. None of the above

55. You are finished installing and configuring a mouse, but the mouse only functions erratically (if at all). You should suspect that...

A. The mouse is defective and should be replaced as soon as possible.

B. There is a hardware conflict between the bus port or serial port, and some other device in the system. Diagnose and correct the hardware conflict.

C. The mouse is not connected properly at the PC. Check the mouse connectors carefully.

D. The mouse driver is corrupt or outdated. Reinstall the mouse driver and reboot the PC.

56. You add a second floppy drive to the system, but the PC does not recognize the new drive. You probably forgot to...
    A. Insert a bootable diskette in the new drive
    B. Remove the terminating resistors from the new drive
    C. Connect the power or signal cables to the new drive
    D. Update the CMOS setup information to reflect the new drive

57. The system begins to boot from the hard drive, but initialization stops before you see the DOS prompt. You should suspect that...
    A. The hard drive is defective and should be replaced
    B. The hard drive has a bad sector which in interfering with COMMAND.COM
    C. You have contracted a command processor virus
    D. None of the above

58. You install additional memory in the PC, but the system freezes or fails to boot. Chances are that...
    A. One or more memory devices is defective
    B. One or more memory devices have been installed backward
    C. One or more memory devices are mismatched or incorrect for your system
    D. None of the above

59. When a new expansion device is added to a system and the system begins to suffer random lockups for no apparent reason, the first fault you should suspect is...
    A. A hardware conflict between the new expansion device and another device in the system
    B. A software conflict between newly added drivers and other system software
    C. A defect in the newly added expansion device
    D. A bug or other defect in newly added software

60. In spite of the number of very good antivirus and data recovery products that are available, the only absolute protection for files and data is...
    A. A regimen of regular, complete system cleaning
    B. A regimen of regular, complete system upgrades or enhancements
    C. Computer insurance to replace stolen, damaged, or failed equipment
    D. A regimen of regular, complete system backups

61. With the drive running under Stacker, you see an error message indicating that the STACVOL file is not mounted. Chances are...
    A. The hard drive has failed and needs to be reformatted
    B. The STACVOL file has been erased and needs to be restored from a backup
    C. The STACVOL header has been corrupted and should be restored from backup headers
    D. The STACVOL header has been infected by a virus

62. During the exchange of text through your modem, you notice anomalous text strings such as "[0m." Chances are that...
    A. You have a faulty telephone line or line cord

    B. You have a faulty modem which should immediately be replaced

    C. You have not selected the correct character emulation in communication software

    D. You have not selected the correct data transfer rate in communication software

63. When capturing video, you find that a large number of video frames are dropped. You can correct this problem by...

    A. Reducing the size of the capture window

    B. Using a faster PC

    C. Stopping any other applications running in the background

    D. All of the above

64. A hard drive's partition table or FAT can often be damaged by...

    A. A computer virus

    B. A worn or failed disk sector ID

    C. A failed or damaged drive

    D. All of the above

65. When attempting to enhance the performance of a hard drive, you can...

    A. Replace the hard drive with a newer, faster unit

    B. Use a good-quality disk caching utility

    C. Remove hard-drive compression if possible

    D. All of the above

66. A narrow white line appears vertically along the images produced by a laser printer. You should check that...

    A. A fragment of paper, dust, or other object is interfering with the laser beam path. You should clean the printer's optics.

    B. The laser/scanner assembly is loose or installed incorrectly. Try replacing the laser/scanner assembly.

    C. The laser printer's power supply has failed. Try replacing the high-voltage supply.

    D. The printer's ECU has failed. Try replacing the ECU.

67. You add memory or change the hard drive in a PC. The next time you start the PC after the upgrade is complete, you should make it a point to...

    A. Check each power supply output to ensure there is no overload

    B. Update the appropriate entries in CMOS

    C. Run a diagnostic to check the upgraded component(s)

    D. None of the above

68. When trouble strikes a directory or FAT, you can often use which utilities to correct the problem...

    A. MIRROR and UNFORMAT

    B. RECOVER and DEBUG

    C. FDISK and FORMAT

    D. CHKDSK and Scan Disk

69. You experience frequent hard drive failures. It is possible that...

    A. There is an excess amount of heat building up in and around the hard drive

    B. There are excessive spikes or surges entering the system power supply

C. The PC is being subjected to an unusual amount of shock or vibration

D. All of the above

70. A new hard drive is installed, but now the screen stays blank when the system is powered up. There is most probably...

    A. A conflict between the drive controller and another device in the system

    B. A defective hard drive

    C. A defective power supply

    D. All of the above

71. The video capture board appears to be working, but captures are unusually slow. This is usually due to...

    A. A fault with the video board itself

    B. A hardware IRQ conflict between the video capture board and another device in the system

    C. A large number of applications running in the background

    D. An old or corrupted video capture CODEC

72. You see a 207 error message. You suspect that...

    A. There is an undefined fault on the motherboard

    B. The system BIOS ROM has failed

    C. There is a fault in the CMOS/RTC IC

    D. There is a fault somewhere in the first 64K of memory

73. You add a second floppy drive to the system, but now you encounter frequent read/write errors. You might have neglected to...

    A. Update the CMOS setup to reflect the second floppy drive

    B. Remove the terminating resistors from the second floppy drive

    C. Set the drive select jumper properly for the second floppy drive

    D. Insert a bootable diskette in the second floppy drive

74. The POST or third-party diagnostic reports a fault with DMAC#1. Your only real course of action is to...

    A. Replace the defective power supply

    B. Replace the 8259 PIC (or replace the entire motherboard)

    C. Replace the 8237 DMAC (or replace the entire motherboard)

    D. Replace the 8254 PIT (or replace the entire motherboard)

75. There is no image displayed on the monitor (although the power LED indicates that power is available). It is possible that...

    A. The monitor's ac power supply has failed

    B. The monitor's high-voltage flyback supply has failed

    C. The monitor's horizontal output circuit has failed

    D. All of the above

76. When the system is initialized, you see an error message such as "Keyboard not connected." You see that a keyboard is indeed connected to the PC, so you first suspect that...

    A. The keyboard assembly is defective

    B. The keyboard connector is defective

    C. The attached keyboard is not appropriate for the system

    D. One or more CMOS settings in the system setup have changed

77. When the modem starts dialing an outgoing number before it successfully draws dialtone, you will have to...
    A. Replace the defective modem
    B. Increase the delay value in the S6 register
    C. Have a new telephone line installed
    D. None of the above

78. The very first step that you should take before attempting to align any floppy drive is:
    A. Remove the drive from its drive bay
    B. Disconnect the signal cable
    C. Disconnect the power cable
    D. Carefully clean the R/W heads and retest the drive

79. You notice multiple defective pixels in an LCD display. The pixels might be black or white, or remain fixed at a particular color. The only method of resolving this problem is to...
    A. Replace the backlight assemblyB. Replace the LCD panel
    C. Replace the backlight power supply
    D. None of the above

80. The customer complains that their stand-alone tablet seems to jitter or leave visible spikes while drawing. You should check that...
    A. The tablet is connected properly at the serial port
    B. The stylus is connected properly
    C. Any necessary tablet drivers are installed properly
    D. The serial port is using a newer UART (such as a 16550A) rather than an old 8250

81. You measure a monitor's anode voltage and find it to be several thousand volts higher than the maximum recommended voltage. You should be concerned that...
    A. Excessive high voltage will allow X radiation to escape from the CRT
    B. Excessive high voltage will present a larger shock hazard.
    C. Excessive high voltage will shorten the working life of the CRT
    D. Excessive high voltage will result in premature failures in the flyback transformer

82. After a new game port board is installed, the joystick does not respond. You should first suspect that...
    A. The game port board is installed in the wrong expansion slot
    B. The joystick is defective
    C. The game port board is defective
    D. The game port board is set to use the wrong I/O address

83. When a PC is powered up, it emits a series of beeps in a 1-1-4 pattern, and the initialization process halts. You find that the PC is using Phoenix BIOS. The fault is likely...
    A. In the CMOS
    B. In the CPU
    C. In the lower 64K of RAM
    D. In the BIOS ROM

84. You are able to read from disks that have been formatted and written to in a particular floppy drive, buy you cannot read such disks reliably in other floppy drives. You should suspect...
    A. The original floppy drive is working properly, and the other drive is defective
    B. The original floppy drive is defective and should be replaced
    C. The original floppy drive is in need of alignment
    D. The diskette itself is defective

85. When you see an error message indicating a memory fault at a particular address. It is usually safe to assume that...
    A. The motherboard's parity generator circuit has failed, and the entire motherboard will have to be replaced.
    B. The motherboard's memory addressing circuits have failed, and the entire motherboard will have to be replaced.
    C. A memory IC or SIMM has failed, and must be isolated and replaced.
    D. A rogue application has precipitated a fault at that address.

86. The power supply seems to work fine when the PC first initializes, but one or more outputs fail after the supply has an opportunity to warm up. As a technician, you should suspect that...
    A. There is a thermal fault in the output regulator or another area of the supply
    B. There is an intermittent connection between two or more supply components
    C. The power supply connector attached to the motherboard is not connected securely
    D. The fault is on the motherboard rather than in the power supply

87. The system will not recognize a SCSI drive which has previously been working in the system. As a technician, you should first check that...
    A. The CMOS entry for the SCSI drive is set to "none"
    B. The drive is connected properly and that the SCSI chain is correctly terminated
    C. The SCSI adapter is operating correctly
    D. Any SCSI drivers are loaded as expected

88. After returning to Windows from a DOS program, the Windows screen "splits" from top to bottom. It's a good bet that...
    A. The Windows driver you are using is incompatible with the video driver
    B. Windows is using an old or corrupted video driver
    C. The video adapter is defective or installed improperly
    D. Windows cannot access the DOS application properly

89. You experience problems loading or ejecting the tape (even new tapes). If you cannot locate and clear the mechanical malfunction, your best course is to...
    A. Try lubricating the tape drive's load/unload mechanism
    B. Try a different type of tape in the drive
    C. Try rebuilding the load/unload mechanism
    D. Try replacing the tape drive outright

90. The POST or third-party diagnostic reports a fault with PIC#1. Your only real course of action is to...
    A. Replace the defective power supply
    B. Replace the 8259 PIC (or replace the entire motherboard)
    C. Replace the 8237 DMAC (or replace the entire motherboard)
    D. Replace the 8254 PIT (or replace the entire motherboard)
91. The video image appearing in the capture preview window appears bent or torn at the top. You recognize this to be caused by...
    A. A fault in the video capture board
    B. Insufficient video memory
    C. Insufficient PC processing power
    D. A weak video signal
92. While running under DoubleSpace, you see an error message indicating that the CVF is damaged. In most cases, this is...
    A. A nonfatal problem that can usually be corrected by running DOS ScanDisk or CHKDSK on the compressed volume
    B. A catastrophic failure of the CVF that cannot be restored. You must reformat the drive and restore the CVF from a backup
    C. A catastrophic failure of the drive itself that cannot be restored. You must replace the defective drive
    D. A nonfatal problem that can usually be corrected by defragmenting the hard drive
93. The hard drive fails to boot, and you might see an error message such as "No boot device present." Before attempting to reformat or replace the drive, you should...
    A. Run a diagnostic to check the drive and controller
    B. Check the power and signal cables attached to the drive
    C. Check the hard drive for viruses
    D. None of the above
94. You see a 604 error message. You interpret this to mean that...
    A. The drive is running at the wrong speed
    B. There is a problem with the floppy disk controller
    C. There is a problem with the diskette's boot sector
    D. An error has occurred in the disk drive's media sensor
95. Which DOS utility can be used to recognize damaged files and lock out bad disk sectors...
    A. DEBUG
    B. RECOVER
    C. CHKDSK
    D. FDISK
96. You add memory to your system, but during initialization, you see an error message that indicates the amount of memory found does not match the amount expected. You should suspect that...
    A. You did not update the CMOS setup after adding the new memory
    B. One or more of the new memory devices are defective

C. One or more of the new memory devices is installed incorrectly

D. One or more of the new memory devices is incorrect for your system

97. As you observe white lines and areas of a monitor's image, you note areas of green and blue "bleeding" out from around the edges. You can be confident that...

    A. The monitor is suffering from convergence problems and should be realigned

    B. The monitor is suffering from a defective CRT which should be replaced

    C. The monitor is suffering from a defective deflection yoke which should be replaced

    D. The video adapter is sending faulty signals to the monitor

98. When you start an antivirus tool on your system, you find that hard disk access is slowed dramatically. It is possible that...

    A. The hard disk is failing or close to failure

    B. Your antivirus tool is conflicting with the disk caching driver

    C. The disk caching driver is not fully compatible with the drive

    D. Your antivirus tool is incompatible with your hard drive

99. There is a SCSI adapter in the system, but you receive an error message indicating that the SCSI controller cannot be found (or is not present). You should suspect...

    A. That the SCSI adapter has failed, or is conflicting with a newly installed device

    B. That one or more SCSI devices has failed and is disrupting the adapter

    C. That one or more SCSI drivers is corrupt or is conflicting with other software

    D. That CMOS setup variables have been changed or erased

100. A low-current, high-voltage inverter circuit is needed to drive an LCD backlight. If the backlight inverter fails...

    A. The LCD will be unable to display colors or shades of gray

    B. The LCD image will be washed out by a flat white screen

    C. The LCD image will still be perfectly visible outdoors, but not visible indoors

    D. The LCD image will appear washed out (or will disappear entirely)

101. The monitor displays an image, but the image is out of focus. The local focus control is working, but it does not restore focus properly. You should suspect the most likely cause of failure is that...

    A. The CRT focus control grid has failed

    B. The focus control voltage regulator circuit has failed

    C. The video amplifier circuits have failed

    D. The horizontal output amplifier has failed

102. Of all the possible power protection tactics available for PCs and other computer equipment, the most fool-proof and reliable is...

    A. A battery backup power supply between the wall ac and the computer equipment

    B. A surge suppresser inserted between the wall ac and the computer equipment

    C. An uninterruptable power supply between the wall ac and the computer equipment

    D. None of the above

103. When the sound coming from a sound board contains a great deal of buzzing and humming noise, you should first...

    A. Update the sound board's drivers or TSRs

    B. Replace the sound board outright

    C. Move the speakers away from nearby sources of interference or replace the speakers

    D. Replace the speakers with a magnetically shielded model

104. Low, unstable, or dirty power provided to a PC can result in...

    A. System lockups or memory corruption

    B. Power supply failures

    C. Hard drive failures of data loss

    D. All of the above

105. You attach a parallel port tape drive to a parallel port fitted with a hardware copy protection device. When the tape backup fails to function or the system locks up, you should suspect...

    A. That the tape drive has failed and should be replaced

    B. That the tape backup software is incompatible with the hardware device

    C. That the parallel port is defective and must be corrected

    D. That the hardware device is interfering with the parallel port and it should be removed

106. You just finished adding a new hard drive to the PC, but now the system acts erratically, especially when drives are accessed. You have eliminated the new drive as a problem, but you should also remember to check:

    A. That the new drive ID or select jumper setting does not conflict with the other hard drive

    B. That the new drive controller is configured and installed properly

    C. That the new drive signal and power cables are connected properly

    D. Each output from the power supply to be sure that it is not being overloaded

107. The print being produced by an ink jet printer is faded or indistinct, perhaps a bit light. You should suspect:

    A. That the ink reservoir is almost exhausted and should be replaced

    B. That the print head nozzles are becoming clogged and should be cleaned

    C. That the type of paper being used is not compatible with ink jet printing

    D. All of the above

108. You notice that the cooling fan is making an unusual amount of noise. You can address this problem by...

    A. Replacing the fan outright

    B. Remounting the fan using foam or pliable washers to dampen the noise

    C. Replacing the power supply or any other chassis assemblies in the immediate vicinity

    D. All of the above

109. There are sound gaps and choppy video when playing back a video file. You can correct this problem by...
    A. Increase processing power with system upgrades of a faster PC
    B. Reduce the size of the playback window
    C. Shutting down any applications that are running in the background
    D. All of the above

110. You see a 1704 error message. This suggests that...
    A. The hard drive is defective
    B. The hard drive controller circuit has failed
    C. Track 00 has failed on the hard drive
    D. One or more sectors on the hard drive have failed

111. You notice areas of the monitor display that are discolored or "banded" with unwanted color. As a technician, you should suspect that...
    A. The monitor's color drive circuits are defective and should be replaced
    B. The CRT itself is defective and should be replaced
    C. The CRT has been magnetized and must be degaussed
    D. None of the above

112. A system using an AST BIOS emits a series of 10 short beeps, then initialization stops. The probability is that...
    A. The master timer IC has failed
    B. The DMA controller 0 has failed
    C. The IRQ controller has failed
    D. The keyboard controller has failed

113. You find that you are having difficulty running a memory-resident antivirus tool. Chances are that...
    A. The antivirus tool is too old or outdated to adequately test the system
    B. The antivirus tool is incompatible with the drive being tested
    C. The antivirus tool is infected itself and should be removed from the system
    D. The antivirus tool is conflicting with one or more TSRs already running in the system

114. In addition to a hexadecimal display, many POST cards provide a series of four LEDs. These four LEDs are typically used...
    A. To display the operating status of the POST card itself
    B. To display warnings about defective drives in the PC
    C. To display a quick-and-dirty indication of power levels in the PC
    D. None of the above

115. The print produced by a dot-matrix printer is suffering from a horizontal white line through the type. You should suspect that...
    A. One of the print wires has jammed or broken
    B. A signal wire in the print head cable has broken
    C. A print head driver circuit has failed
    D. All of the above

116. Your tape backup software produces an error such as "Too many bad sectors." The first thing you should try is to...
    A. Use a known-good working tape in the drive
    B. Clean the tape drive's R/W heads thoroughly

      C. Check the drive's power and signal cables

      D. None of the above

117. The POST and/or third-party diagnostics report a problem with the math coprocessor. In most cases, your only real course of action is to...

      A. Replace the defective math coprocessor (or combined CPU/MCP)

      B. Replace the defective motherboard entirely

      C. Disable the math coprocessor in CMOS or through a jumper

      D. None of the above

118. You have upgraded your system CPU and the PC boots just fine, but now the system runs for a while and freezes. After you shut off the system for a few minutes, it boots again fine. You should...

      A. Replace the defective CPU because it is obviously defective

      B. Make sure the CPU is installed properly and in the correct orientation

      C. Check that a heat sink is attached properly and uses thermal grease

      D. Reload the applications that are running when the system freezes

119. Your customer complains that the performance of their joystick seems inconsistent or erratic. When you have the system on the bench, you suspect that...

      A. The expansion port containing the game port board is defective. Try the game port in another expansion slot.

      B. The joystick is dirty. Try cleaning each of the joystick's switch contacts and potentiometers.

      C. The game port board is defective. Try replacing the game port board.

      D. The game port board is too old and slow for the system. Try a speed-adjusting game port.

120. The print being produced by a dot-matrix printer is extremely light. Even though you replaced the ribbon, print becomes light again after just a few minutes of operation. You should suspect that...

      A. The print head wires are jammed or clogged

      B. The ribbon is exhausted and should be replaced

      C. The ribbon transport assembly is jammed or broken

      D. None of the above

Congratulations. You have completed the examination for the *DLS Technician's Certificate*. Before sending in the exam, be sure to take some time and check your answers, make sure that only *one* answer is marked for each question, and see that your contact information on the cover sheet is correct and complete.

DLS Technician's Certificate

Answer Sheet 1 of 2
Please Circle Only One Letter Corresponding to Each Answer

1	A B C D	23	A B C D	45	A B C D
2	A B C D	24	A B C D	46	A B C D
3	A B C D	25	A B C D	47	A B C D
4	A B C D	26	A B C D	48	A B C D
5	A B C D	27	A B C D	49	A B C D
6	A B C D	28	A B C D	50	A B C D
7	A B C D	29	A B C D	51	A B C D
8	A B C D	30	A B C D	52	A B C D
9	A B C D	31	A B C D	53	A B C D
10	A B C D	32	A B C D	54	A B C D
11	A B C D	33	A B C D	55	A B C D
12	A B C D	34	A B C D	56	A B C D
13	A B C D	35	A B C D	57	A B C D
14	A B C D	36	A B C D	58	A B C D
15	A B C D	37	A B C D	59	A B C D
16	A B C D	38	A B C D	60	A B C D
17	A B C D	39	A B C D	61	A B C D
18	A B C D	40	A B C D	62	A B C D
19	A B C D	41	A B C D	63	A B C D
20	A B C D	42	A B C D	64	A B C D
21	A B C D	43	A B C D	65	A B C D
22	A B C D	44	A B C D	66	A B C D

DLS Technician's Certificate

Answer Sheet 2 of 2
Please Circle Only One Letter Corresponding to Each Answer

67	A B C D	89	A B C D	111	A B C D
68	A B C D	90	A B C D	112	A B C D
69	A B C D	91	A B C D	113	A B C D
70	A B C D	92	A B C D	114	A B C D
71	A B C D	93	A B C D	115	A B C D
72	A B C D	94	A B C D	116	A B C D
73	A B C D	95	A B C D	117	A B C D
74	A B C D	96	A B C D	118	A B C D
75	A B C D	97	A B C D	119	A B C D
76	A B C D	98	A B C D	120	A B C D
77	A B C D	99	A B C D		
78	A B C D	100	A B C D		
79	A B C D	101	A B C D		
80	A B C D	102	A B C D		
81	A B C D	103	A B C D		
82	A B C D	104	A B C D		
83	A B C D	105	A B C D		
84	A B C D	106	A B C D		
85	A B C D	107	A B C D		
86	A B C D	108	A B C D		
87	A B C D	109	A B C D		
88	A B C D	110	A B C D		

End of Exam>

DLS Technician's Certificate

Information Cover Sheet
Please print clearly

Name: _

Address: _

_ _

City: _

State: _ _ Zip or Postal Code: _ _ _ _ _ _ _ _ _ _ _

Country (other than USA): _ _ _ _ _ _ _ _ _ _ _ _ _ _ _ _ _ _

Telephone: _ _ _ _ _ _ _ _ _ _ _ _ _ _ _

Fax: _ _ _ _ _ _ _ _ _ _ _ _ _ _

◆ the above information is required for proper graing, and to receive proper credit from NRI. Tests with incomplete information can not be processed.

Method of Payment
Please Check One

__ Personal or Business *check* for **$25** (US)‡

__ MasterCard *charge* of $25 (US). Card: _ _ _ _ _ _ _ _ _ _ _ _ _ _ _ _ _ _ _

__ VISA *charge* of $25 (US). Exp: _/_/_ Sig: _____

Mail to: **Dynamic Learning Systems, P.O. Box 805, Marlboro, MA 01752 USA**

Fax to: **508-898-9995** (24 hrs/day, 7 days/week)

‡ mail *only* - tests without payment can not be processed.

Index

Illustrations are in **boldface**.

About the author

Stephen J. Bigelow is the founder and president of Dynamic Learning Systems—a technical writing, research, and publishing company specializing in electronic and PC service topics. Bigelow is the author of 10 books for TAB/McGraw-Hill, and almost 100 major articles for mainstream electonics magazines, such as Popular Electronics, Electronics NOW, Circuit Cellar INK, and Electronic Service & Technology. He is also the author and editor and publisher of The PC Toolbox(TM), a premier PC service newsletter for computer enthusiasts and technicians.

DISK WARRANTY

This software is protected by both United States copyright law and international copyright treaty provision. You must treat this software just like a book, except that you may copy it into a computer in order to be used and you may make archival copies of the software for the sole purpose of backing up our software and protecting your investment from loss.

By saying "just like a book," McGraw-Hill means, for example, that this software may be used by any number of people and may be freely moved from one computer location to another, so long as there is no possibility of its being used at one location or on one computer while it also is being used at another. Just as a book cannot be read by two different people in two different places at the same time, neither can the software be used by two different people in two different places at the same time (unless, of course, McGraw-Hill's copyright is being violated).

LIMITED WARRANTY

McGraw-Hill takes great care to provide you with top-quality software, thoroughly checked to prevent virus infections. McGraw-Hill warrants the physical diskette(s) contained herein to be free of defects in materials and workmanship for a period of sixty days from the purchase date. If McGraw-Hill receives written notification within the warranty period of defects in materials or workmanship, and such notification is determined by McGraw-Hill to be correct, McGraw-Hill will replace the defective diskette(s). Send requests to:

McGraw-Hill, Inc.
Customer Services
P.O. Box 545
Blacklick, OH 43004-0545

The entire and exclusive liability and remedy for breach of this Limited Warranty shall be limited to replacement of defective diskette(s) and shall not include or extend to any claim for or right to cover any other damages, including but not limited to, loss of profit, data, or use of the software, or special, incidental, or consequential damages or other similar claims, even if McGraw-Hill has been specifically advised of the possibility of such damages. In no event will McGraw-Hill's liability for any damages to you or any other person ever exceed the lower of suggested list price or actual price paid for the license to use the software, regardless of any form of the claim.

McGRAW-HILL, INC. SPECIFICALLY DISCLAIMS ALL OTHER WARRANTIES, EXPRESS OR IMPLIED, INCLUDING, BUT NOT LIMITED TO, ANY IMPLIED WARRANTY OF MERCHANTABILITY OR FITNESS FOR A PARTICULAR PURPOSE.

Specifically, McGraw-Hill makes no representation or warranty that the software is fit for any particular purpose and any implied warranty of merchantability is limited to the sixty-day duration of the Limited Warranty covering the physical diskette(s) only (and not the software) and is otherwise expressly and specifically disclaimed.

This limited warranty gives you specific legal rights; you may have others which may vary from state to state. Some states do not allow the exclusion of incidental or consequential damages, or the limitation on how long an implied warranty lasts, so some of the above may not apply to you.